OXFORD
BBC GUIDE TO
PRONUNCIATION

OXFORD
BBC GUIDE TO
PRONUNCIATION

Lena Olausson
Catherine Sangster

OXFORD
UNIVERSITY PRESS

OXFORD
UNIVERSITY PRESS

Great Clarendon Street, Oxford OX2 6DP

Oxford University Press is a department of the University of Oxford.
It furthers the University's objective of excellence in research, scholarship,
and education by publishing worldwide in

Oxford New York

Auckland Cape Town Dar es Salaam Hong Kong Karachi
Kuala Lumpur Madrid Melbourne Mexico City Nairobi
New Delhi Shanghai Taipei Toronto

With offices in

Argentina Austria Brazil Chile Czech Republic France Greece
Guatemala Hungary Italy Japan Poland Portugal Singapore
South Korea Switzerland Thailand Turkey Ukraine Vietnam

Oxford is a registered trade mark of Oxford University Press
in the UK and in certain other countries

BBC is a trade mark of the British Broadcasting Corporation
and is used under licence

Published in the United States
by Oxford University Press Inc., New York

British Library Cataloguing in Publication Data
Data available

Library of Congress Cataloging in Publication Data
Data available

ISBN 0-19-280710-2
ISBN 978-0-19-280710-6

Typeset in Miller
by Interactive Sciences Ltd, Gloucester
Printed in Italy by
Legoprint S.p.A.

1 3 5 7 9 10 8 6 4 2

Contents

Preface

The *Oxford BBC Guide to Pronunciation* gives guidance on the pronunciation of names, words, and phrases. Despite its A-Z format it is not so much a dictionary as a collection of particular pronunciations which are tricky, much debated, curious, or exotic. It is intended for students, teachers, actors, journalists, broadcasters, and anyone interested in 'saying things right'. The pronunciations are given in an easy-to-read phonetic respelling and also in the system familiar to users of larger Oxford dictionaries, the alphabet of the International Phonetic Association (IPA). Information panels and notes discuss particular pronunciation issues in more detail. Its compact size means that it can be accommodated on a crowded desk, or even slipped into a bag, and be referred to quickly. The book's main source is the BBC Pronunciation Unit's own database, and the wide range of topics and languages covered reflects the great diversity of the BBC's output.

Since its earliest days the BBC has taken pronunciation very seriously. Lord Reith, the first Director General, set up an Advisory Committee on Spoken English in 1926. This committee included Robert Bridges, the then Poet Laureate, playwright George Bernard Shaw, and phonetician Daniel Jones. Their task was to advise announcers on 'words of doubtful pronunciation'; they also turned their attention to place names in the British Isles and beyond. The committee was disbanded with the outbreak of the Second World War. Since then the provision of pronunciation advice within the BBC has been the responsibility of the full-time staff of the Pronunciation Unit. Like our predecessors we are linguists with specific skills in phonetics and languages, and our remit is broad: to research and advise on the pronunciation of any name, word, or phrase in any language required by anyone in the BBC. It is on our work, and our collection of approximately 200,000 pronunciations, that this book is based.

For this reason we owe particular thanks to all our predecessors in the Unit and the Advisory Committee, on whose shoulders we stand. We are also indebted to the editors of the English pronunciation dictionaries which are always at our elbow as we work, especially John Wells, Clive Upton, Peter Roach, and Jane Setter, and to those of pronunciation dictionaries in other languages, in particular *Duden Aussprachewörterbuch*, *Larousse Dictionnaire de la Prononciation*, and *RAI Dizionario d'Ortografia e di Pronunzia*. Thanks are due to Angus Stevenson, James McCracken, Judy Pearsall, and Gillian Evans at OUP, and to Trish Stableford for proofreading. At the BBC, this book would not have got off the ground without the support of Guy Strickland, Jenny Martin, and Chris Cullen, and would not have stayed in the air without Martha Figueroa-Clark and Nick Marcus.

Lena Olausson
Catherine Sangster

Note on trademarks and proprietary terms

Introduction

About the book

Our job in the BBC Pronunciation Unit is to help broadcasters correctly pronounce anything they may need to say, and this book is a distillation of our advice. Compared to a standard pronunciation dictionary, therefore, its contents are more varied and the balance is shifted away from words towards proper names and other encyclopedic entries. The pronunciations we have chosen include those for famous people, capital cities, rivers and other geographical features, plants and animals, food and drink, scientific terms, drugs and diseases, musical instruments, composers and their works, and characters from literature and myth. We have selected only those words and phrases which we believe a native speaker of English might be unsure how to pronounce, rather than supplying a larger, more exhaustive set of lexical items. Any such selection process will of course be subjective, and our broad scope means that many interesting pronunciations will inevitably be missing from this small book. However, we decided it best to adopt a magpie-like approach, informed by the usual eclecticism of a day's work in the Pronunciation Unit, where we regularly flit from news stories to music to drama to quizzes or science programmes.

For each entry (with the exception of a few family names for which multiple pronunciations are possible) we give just one correct pronunciation. Where more than one pronunciation would be acceptable we do not list all the possible slight variants, but where variant pronunciations are significant or noteworthy they are discussed in a note. The pronunciations must reflect one particular accent, and in most respects this is the standardized accent of British English known as Received Pronunciation. However, our English pronunciations do not reflect any systematic model of RP in terms of features such as *yod coalescence* (ch and j instead of ty and dy in words like *Tuesday* and *seduce*): for this level of detail readers should consult an English pronunciation dictionary such as the *Longman Pronunciation Dictionary*, the *Oxford Dictionary of Pronunciation for Current English*, or the *Cambridge English Pronouncing Dictionary*. This topic is discussed further in the **Respelling** and **IPA** sections of this introduction and also the panel on **BBC English**.

> **Gaddafi, Mu'ammer** (also **Qaddafi**)
> Libyan head of state
> muu-**um**-uhr guh-**dah**-fi /mʊˌʌmə(r)
> gəˈdɑːfi/, Arabic [muˈʌmmə(r)
> qaðˈðæːfi]
> • Established anglicization; see ARABIC
> panel.

Personal names are listed surname-first for ease of location, although pronunciations of full names are given in their natural order. Significant variant spellings are given, as are unusual plural forms. If both a non-standard plural and a regular -*s* plural are possible, this is indicated in a note. A brief definition indicates nationality or language where appropriate, and helps confirm that you are looking at the right entry: this is not a full-scale dictionary-type definition. The pronunciation is given first in respelling, and then in IPA; in some cases native IPA will also be given in square brackets. Cross-references and indications of established anglicizations are given in short (bulleted) notes, and longer notes (between ruled lines) discuss more complex aspects such as variant pronunciations or common mispronunciations.

Abbreviations used:

AM = American English	pl. = plural
BR = British English	sing. = singular

Pronunciation policy

How does the Pronunciation Unit decide what the 'right' pronunciation is? Our work is mostly concerned with foreign pronunciations, and here we consult native speakers as often as possible. The BBC World Service currently broadcasts in over thirty languages, and we work closely with the different language teams. We have a network of contacts outside the BBC, such as embassies, universities, and museums. We also hold a wide range of specialist pronunciation dictionaries and other written material that has been collected since the days of the Advisory Committee on Spoken English.

All our foreign pronunciations are subject to a degree of anglicization. Our general aim is to recommend pronunciations that are as close as possible to the native language in question, but modified slightly so that they still flow naturally in an English broadcast. The level of anglicization has altered over the years as broadcasters and audiences have become more familiar with the sounds of foreign languages and the BBC has served an increasingly global audience. There are also what we call *established anglicizations*, which are foreign names that have accepted English forms, either of both spelling and pronunciation (e.g. *Warsaw* for Polish *Warszawa*), or just of pronunciation (e.g. *Paris*). We always recommend that established anglicizations are used wherever they exist, as using a native pronunciation instead can confuse the listener, or even sound affected. For more on this topic, see the **Anglicization** panel.

Personal names, foreign or English, are researched with the owner of the name whenever possible.

For English place names our aim is to recommend a standardized version of the local pronunciation. However, the Pronunciation Unit has never issued any recommendations in regard to British dialects, so we would certainly not insist that someone with a northern accent use a long ah in *Bath*, even though that is the local pronunciation—and vice versa for *Newcastle*. Where more than one form is used locally it can still be useful to recommend a single pronunciation, for the sake of consistency.

When deciding on recommendations for particular English words we rely heavily on other specialist English pronouncing dictionaries. Sometimes our particular experience can guide us on certain words that always seem to cause controversy. Our advice on words like *kilometre, schedule,* and *controversy* itself, for which more than one pronunciation is listed in the many dictionaries we consult, is that both pronunciations are acceptable and can be defended if we should receive complaints. However, programme makers sometimes find it useful to know if audiences dislike one particular form, and may in certain contexts find it 'safer' to go for the more traditional pronunciation. When providing this context for our users we make it very clear that it is not a judgement of right and wrong on our part, and we do our best to encourage announcers to use whichever form feels natural in their speech.

Our aim is to reflect current spoken language, not, as some people think, to set and uphold a fixed standard for all to emulate. This is no easy task. Language is in constant flux, and it can be tricky to avoid 'holding back the tide' by recommending pronunciations which are too old-fashioned, while at the same time not giving 'new' pronunciations before they have become established. We want to acknowledge language change, not instigate it ourselves.

Panels

Panels discussing pronunciation of specific languages, as well as some other topics, are dispersed throughout the book. We have included panels on Accents, Anglicization, Arabic, BBC English, Clicks, Czech, Dutch, French, Gaelic, German, Greek, Italian, Japanese, Latin, Polish, Portuguese, Spanish, Swedish, Tone, and Welsh, and top ten lists of mispronunciations, pronunciation complaints, and most frequently asked pronunciations. They appear in the appropriate place in the alphabet in the A-Z text.

These brief discussions are based on language notes put together by past and present members of the Pronunciation Unit. Native speakers and various reference books were also consulted. The panels are intended to provide an overview of the pronunciation of the language in question, giving some specific pronunciation tips and spelling-to-sound conversions where possible, in line with our anglicization policy. They are not intended to give a complete account of that language. We often refer to these panels in the main text, when we feel that the context they provide can be of interest and help clarify a recommendation, for example in the many Latin entries.

Respelling

The BBC Pronunciation Unit uses an in-house phonetic spelling system for all written recommendations. It is based on English spelling conventions and should be easily understood by anyone whose native language is English. We do not expect programme makers to be able to use the alphabet of the International Phonetic Association (IPA).

The phonetic respelling used in this dictionary is based on that used in the *Pocket Oxford English Dictionary*, but is similar to the BBC in-house system in many ways. As with the BBC system, it is based on the sounds of English with the addition of some common non-English sounds such as the front rounded vowels found in French and German.

Consonants

b as in *bat*

ch or tch as in *church*

d as in *day*

f as in *fat*

g as in *get*

h as in *hat*

hl as in Welsh *llan*

j as in *jam*

k as in *king*

kh as in Scottish *loch* or German *ich* (IPA will disambiguate)

l as in *leg*

m as in *man*

n as in *not*

ng as in *sing*

ng-g as in *finger*

nk as in *thank*

p as in *pen*

r as in *red*

s as in *sit*

sh as in *shop*

t as in *top*

th as in *thin*

th as in *this*

v as in *van*

w as in *will*

y as in *yes*

z as in *zebra*

zh as in *vision*

Vowels

a as in *cat*

e as in *bed*

i as in *pin*

o as in *top*

u as in *cup*

uu as in *book*

uh as in *along* ('schwa')

ah as in *calm*

ar as in *bar*

air as in *hair*

aw as in *law*

ee as in *meet*

oo as in *soon*

ur as in *fur*

ay as in *say*
eer as in *beer*
oh as in *most*
oor as in *poor*
or as in *corn*
ow as in *cow*
oy as in *boy*
y as in *cry*

oe as in French *peu*
  or *coeur* (IPA will
  disambiguate)
oey as in French
  fauteuil
ue as in French *vu*
  or German *fünf*
  (IPA will disam-
  biguate)

(ng) after a vowel
  indicates that it is
  nasalized.
a(ng) as in French
  vin
ah(ng) as in French
  blanc
o(ng) as in French
  bon
oe(ng) as in French
  un

Our respellings, unlike many which appear in dictionaries, acknowledge word-final or pre-consonantal R, as in words like *hair* and *party*, which is pronounced in some varieties of English (rhotic accents) and not in others (non-rhotic accents). The BBC Pronunciation Unit's written advice has always included R where it appears in the spelling, on the assumption that this will be pronounced by those with rhotic accents, and not by those with non-rhotic accents. Therefore *Parker* is transcribed as **par**-kuhr, not **pah**-kuh.

Stress and syllables

Syllables are separated by hyphens, and stressed syllables are marked in bold. Secondary stresses are not given. In unusually long names and words more than one syllable may be marked with stress, and in those cases the IPA will indicate which is primary and which is secondary stress.

The way the words are broken into syllables in the respelling is not an attempt to reflect actual syllabification in a given language. Rather, it is a tool to reinforce vowel pronunciations and to ensure the most intuitive transcription.

When a vowel is long (a long monophthong or a diphthong) or is schwa (uh), the consonant which follows it is placed at the start of the following syllable, if there is one: for example, **pee**-tuhr for *Peter* and puh-**tay**-toh for *potato*. When a vowel is short, however, the consonant which follows is placed in the same syllable. The place name *Reading*, for example, would be transcribed **red**-ing, not **re**-ding, which might be confused with the pronunciation **ree**-ding. When there are two consonants we split them between the syllables: *football* is **fuut**-bawl.

We double S in contexts where an English speaker might otherwise pronounce it as z, as in hanss for German *Hans*. We also double R when it is preceded by a short vowel and followed by another vowel, as in **marr**-i for *marry*, **merr**-i for *merry*, **sorr**-i for *sorry*, **mirr**-uhr for *mirror*, and **hurr**-i for *hurry*, in order to avoid confusion with, for example, **ar**-i-uh for *aria*.

IPA

The pronunciation of each entry is also represented using the alphabet of the International Phonetic Association (IPA). These phonemic transcriptions are enclosed by slashes: / /. The IPA transcription represents exactly the same pronunciation that is given in the respelling. However, because a slightly larger range of symbols is used, some sounds can be expressed more precisely in the IPA. For instance, the sound represented as kh in the respelling could either be as in Scottish *loch* or as in German *ich*. The IPA uses two different symbols (x and ç) for these two sounds, and so it serves to disambiguate the pronunciation.

As with the respelling, the set of sounds used in the IPA transcriptions consists of the basic sounds of English with the addition of a small number of other sounds. The IPA transcriptions also acknowledge word-final or pre-consonantal R. Because this sound is pronounced in some accents of English and not in others, it appears in brackets in the IPA transcription. Our IPA transcription is a little more basic than some others which appear in larger pronouncing dictionaries. We do not indicate any other optional sounds by bracketing, italicization, or superscription, and we do not allow for syllabic consonants. In other respects the model of transcription we have applied in this book is that used in all current larger Oxford dictionaries.

When the pronunciation given is an established anglicization a second IPA transcription is often included. This gives a native pronunciation for the benefit of those familiar with the IPA. These pronunciations are enclosed by square brackets: [ ]. In these transcriptions the symbol r is used to denote all r sounds, including the French uvular and the Spanish alveolar trill.

The set of symbols used for the main IPA transcriptions are:

Consonants

b as in *bat*	p as in *pen*	ð as in *this*
d as in *day*	r as in *red*	ʃ as in *shop*
f as in *fat*	s as in *sit*	ʒ as in *vision*
g as in *get*	t as in *top*	tʃ as in *church*
h as in *hat*	v as in *van*	dʒ as in *jam*
j as in *yes*	w as in *will*	
k as in *king*	z as in *zebra*	ɫ as in Welsh *llan*
l as in *leg*		x as in Scottish *loch*
m as in *man*	ŋ as in *sing*	ç as in German *ich*
n as in *not*	θ as in *thin*	

Vowels

a as in *cat*	ɔː as in *law*	y as in French *vu*
ɛ as in *bed*	uː as in *soon*	ʏ as in German
ɪ as in *pin*		*fünf*
i as in *cosy*	ʌɪ as in *cry*	ø as in French *peu*
ɒ as in *top*	aʊ as in *cow*	œ as in French
ʌ as in *cup*	eɪ as in *say*	*coeur*
ʊ as in *book*	əʊ as in *most*	œɪ as in French
ə as in *along*	ɔɪ as in *boy*	*fauteuil*
	ɪə as in *beer*	
ɑː as in *calm*	ʊə as in *poor*	ɛ̃ as in French *vin*
ɛː as in *hair*	ʌɪə as in *fire*	ɑ̃ as in French *blanc*
əː as in *fur*	aʊə as in *hour*	ɔ̃ as in French *bon*
iː as in *meet*		œ̃ as in French *un*

The symbol ː after a vowel indicates that the vowel is long.
The symbol ˜ above a vowel indicates that it is nasalized.

Stress

Primary stress is marked with ' preceding the stressed syllable. If there is also a secondary stress this is marked with a preceding , .

A

aa basaltic lava
ah-ah /ˈɑːɑː/

Aachen city, Germany
ah-khuhn /ˈɑːxən/

Aaiún, el- city, Western Sahara
uhl y-**oon** /əl ʌɪˈuːn/

Aalborg see Ålborg

Aaliyah American singer
ah-**lee**-yuh /ɑːˈliːjə/

Aalsmeer village, Netherlands
ahlss-**meer** /ɑːlsˈmɪə(r)/

Aalst city, Belgium
ahlst /ɑːlst/

This is the Flemish name. The French name
is Alost, pronounced al-**ost**.

Aalto, Alvar Finnish architect and
designer
al-var **ahl**-toh /ˌalvɑː(r) ˈɑːltəʊ/

Aarhus see Århus

Aaron biblical name
air-uhn /ˈɛːrən/

Abaco island, Bahamas
ab-uh-koh /ˈabəkəʊ/

Abadan port, Iran
ab-uh-**dahn** /abəˈdɑːn/

Abagnale Jr, Frank American conman
ab-uhg-nayl /ˈabəgneɪl/

Abakan city, Russia
ab-uh-**kahn** /abəˈkɑːn/

abalone edible mollusc
ab-uh-**loh**-ni /ˌabəˈləʊni/

Abancay city, Peru
ab-an-**ky** /abanˈkʌɪ/

Abbas, Ferhat Algerian nationalist
leader
fuhr-**hat** uh-**bass** /fə(r)ˌhat əˈbas/

Abbas, Mahmoud Palestinian
president
makh-**mood** ab-**ahss** /max.muːd
əˈbɑːs/

Abbe, Ernst German physicist
airnst ab-uh /ˌɛː(r)nst ˈabə/

abbé abbot or other cleric
ab-ay /ˈabeɪ/

Abbeville town, France
ab-**veel** /abˈviːl/

Abbeville city, US
ab-i-vil /ˈabivɪl/

abducens nerve cranial nerve
ab-**dyoo**-suhnz /abˈdjuːsənz/

Abdullah II King of Jordan
ab-**dul**-uh /abˈdʌlə/

Abdul Rahman, Tunku Malayan
statesman
tuunk-oo ab-**duul rah**-muhn /ˌtʊŋkuː
ˌabdʊl ˈrɑːmən/

Abednego biblical name
ab-ed-**nee**-goh /abɛdˈniːgəʊ/

Commonly also uh-**bed**-nuh-goh.

Abel, Karl Friedrich German
composer
karl freed-rikh **ah**-buhl /ˌkɑː(r)l
ˌfriːdrɪç ˈɑːbəl/

Abel, Niels Henrik Norwegian
mathematician
neelss hen-rik **ah**-buhl /ˌniːls ˌhɛnrɪk
ˈɑːbəl/

Abeokuta city, Nigeria
ab-**ay**-ok-oo-tah /aˈbeɪkuːˌtɑː/

Sometimes anglicized to ab-i-oh-**koo**-tuh.

Aberdonian relating to Aberdeen
ab-uhr-**doh**-ni-uhn /ˌabə(r)ˈdəʊniən/

Aberfan village, Wales
ab-uhr-**van** /abə(r)ˈvan/

aberrant departing from accepted
standard
uh-**berr**-uhnt /əˈbɛrənt/

Abertawe Welsh name for Swansea
ab-uhr-**tow**-ay /ˌabər'taʊeɪ/

Aberystwyth town, Wales
ab-uhr-**ist**-with /ˌabərˈɪstwɪθ/

Abia state, Nigeria
ab-i-uh /ˈabiə/

Abidjan port, Côte d'Ivoire
ab-ij-**ahn** /ˌabɪˈdʒɑːn/

Abitur German examinations
ab-it-**oor** /ˌabɪˈtʊə(r)/

Abizaid, John American general
uh-biz-**ayd** /əbɪˈzeɪd/

Abkhazia autonomous region, Georgia
uhp-**khah**-zi-uh /əpˈxɑːziə/

ablative grammatical case
ab-luh-tiv /ˈablətɪv/

Åbo see **Turku**

aborigine Australian indigenous person
ab-uh-**rij**-in-i /abəˈrɪdʒɪni/

Aboukir bay, Egypt
ab-oo-**keer** /ˌabuːˈkɪə(r)/

Abraham Hebrew patriarch
ay-bruh-ham /ˈeɪbrəham/

Abramovich, Roman Russian owner
of Chelsea FC
ruh-**mahn** ab-ruh-**moh**-vitch /rəˌmɑːn
abrəˈməʊvɪtʃ/

This is the Russian pronunciation, and the
one Mr Abramovich uses, but
ab-**ram**-uh-vitch is often heard.

Abruzzi region, Italy
ab-**ruut**-si /aˈbrʊtsi/

abscissa pl. **abscissae** mathematical term
ab-**siss**-uh pl. ab-**siss**-ee /abˈsɪsə/, pl.
/-siː/
• Standard -s plural is also possible.

abseil mountaineering term
ab-sayl /ˈabseɪl/

The German pronunciation **ab**-zyl is also
possible.

absinth plant and alcoholic liqueur
ab-sinth /ˈabsɪnθ/

Abu Dhabi state, United Arab Emirates
ab-oo **dah**-bi /ˌabuːˈdɑːbi/

Abu Dis district of Jerusalem, Israel
ab-oo **deess** /ˌabuːˈdiːs/

Abu Ghraib prison in Baghdad, Iraq
ab-oo **grayb** /ˌabuːˈɡreɪb/, [ˌabu
ˈɣrɛɪb]
• See **ARABIC** panel.

Abuja city, Nigeria
uh-**boo**-juh /əˈbuːdʒə/

abulia absence of willpower
uh-**boo**-li-uh /əˈbuːliə/

Abu Musa island, Iran
ab-oo **moo**-suh /ˌabuːˈmuːsə/

Abuna title in the Ethiopian Orthodox
Church
uh-**boo**-nuh /əˈbuːnə/

Abu Rudeina, Nabil Palestinian
politician
nab-**eel** **ab**-oo roo-**day**-nuh /nabˌiːl
ˌabuːˈruːˈdeɪnə/

Abu Sayyaf militant Islamic group,
SE Asia
ab-oo sy-**yahf** /ˌabuː saɪˈjɑːf/

Abu Simbel site of temples, Egypt
ab-oo **sim**-buhl /ˌabuːˈsɪmbəl/

abyss deep chasm
uh-**biss** /əˈbɪs/

acacia tree
uh-**kay**-shuh /əˈkeɪʃə/

academe academic community
ak-uh-**deem** /ˈakədiːm/

academia academic community
ak-uh-**dee**-mi-uh /ˌakəˈdiːmiə/

acanthus herbaceous plant
uh-**kan**-thuhss /əˈkanθəs/

a cappella sung without instrumental
accompaniment
ak-uh-**pel**-uh /ˌakəˈpɛlə/

Acapulco port, Mexico
ak-uh-**puul**-koh /akəˈpʊlkəʊ/

ACAS Advisory, Conciliation, and
Arbitration Service
ay-kass /ˈeɪkas/

accede agree to a demand
uhk-**seed** /əkˈsiːd/

accelerando musical term
ak-sel-uh-**ran**-doh /akˌsɛləˈrandəʊ/

The Italian pronunciation
atch-el-uh-**ran**-doh is also used.

accidie mental sloth
ak-sid-i /ˈaksɪdi/

accipiter hawk
ak-**sip**-it-uhr /akˈsɪpɪtə(r)/

accouchement childbirth
uh-**koosh**-mo(ng) /əˈkuːʃmõ/

Accra capital of Ghana
uh-**krah** /əˈkrɑː/

Accurist watch company
ak-yuu-rist /ˈakjʊrɪst/

accursed under a curse
uh-**kur**-suhd /əˈkəː(r)səd/

Commonly also uh-**kurst**.

accusative grammatical case
uh-**kyoo**-zuh-tiv /əˈkjuːzətɪv/

accusatory suggesting wrong-doing
uh-**kyoo**-zuh-tuh-ri /əˈkjuːzətəri/

Less commonly also ak-yoo-**zay**-tuh-ri.

Acebes, Ángel Spanish politician
an-khel ath-**ay**-bess /ˌaŋxɛl aˈθeɪbɛs/

Accents

This is not a discussion about dialects, but rather a short account of how acute and grave accents as diacritics over letters have different implications for pronunciation in different languages. It is common to assume that they indicate where stress should fall, but accents have a range of functions:

Vowel quality
In French, for example, the vowel E has two different pronunciations, depending on whether it has an acute or a grave accent. An acute accent over E makes a sound close to ay (although it is not diphthongal in French). For example, *André* is pronounced ah(ng)-**dray**. A grave accent over E is pronounced as in English *bed*. *Irène* is ee-**ren**.

Vowel length
In Czech, Slovak, and Hungarian, for example, any vowel with an acute accent over it is long, and a vowel without an accent is short. This length difference is often confused with stress, even though stress invariably falls on the first syllable in all three of these languages. The name of the Hungarian composer *Esterházy* is pronounced **est**-uhr-hah-zi, with stress on the first syllable, and a long ah in the third.

Stress
In Spanish, for example, if a vowel has an acute accent, it means that vowel is stressed, so *José* is pronounced khoss-**ay**, and the film director *Pedro Almodóvar* is al-moh-**doh**-var.

Consonants
Accents do not appear just on vowels. In Serbo-Croat languages, a Ć is pronounced ch, as in *Slobodan Milošević*, pronounced mil-**osh**-uh-vitch. Accents over consonants are also found in Polish, where they can appear on Ć, Ń, Ś, and Ź, pronounced ch, ny (as in *onion*, in word final position), sh, and zh respectively.

Tone
When tone languages like Chinese are transliterated into the Roman alphabet, an acute accent is sometimes used to represent a rising or high tone, and a grave accent is used to indicate a low or falling tone.

In English
A grave accent is occasionally used in English, especially in poetry, to indicate pronunciation of a vowel that would normally be silent. *Blessèd*, for example, is pronounced **bless**-uhd.

Aceh province, Indonesia
atch-**ay** /ˈatʃeɪ/

Acehnese (also **Achinese**) relating
to Aceh
atch-uh-**neez** /atʃəˈniːz/

acer tree or shrub
ay-suhr /ˈeɪsə(r)/

acerola fruit
ass-uh-**roh**-luh /asəˈrəʊlə/

acetaminophen North American term
for paracetamol
uh-see-tuh-**min**-uh-fen
/ə,siːtəˈmɪnəfɛn/

Also uh-set-uh-**min**-uh-fen.

acetate chemical substance
ass-uh-tayt /ˈasəteɪt/

acetic acid acid in vinegar
uh-**see**-tik /əˈsiːtɪk/

Commonly also uh-**set**-ik.

acetylene colourless hydrocarbon gas
uh-**set**-il-een /əˈsɛtɪliːn/

acetylsalicylic acid chemical name for
aspirin
ass-uh-tyl-sal-uh-**sil**-ik
/,asətʌɪl,saləˈsɪlɪk/

Achaea region of ancient Greece
uh-**kee**-uh /əˈkiːə/

Achaemenid dynasty of ancient Persia
uh-**kee**-muh-nid /əˈkiːmənɪd/

Acharavi resort, Corfu
akh-uh-**rah**-vi /axəˈrɑːvi/

Achates Greek mythological character
uh-**kay**-teez /əˈkeɪtiːz/

Achebe, Chinua Nigerian writer
chee-noo-uh uh-**chay**-bay /,tʃiːnʊə
əˈtʃeɪbeɪ/

Achernar star
ay-kuhr-nar /ˈeɪkə(r)nɑː(r)/

Acheron Greek mythological character
ak-uh-ron /ˈakərɒn/

Acheulian archaeological term
uh-**shoo**-li-uhn /əˈʃuːliən/

Achilles Greek mythological character
uh-**kil**-eez /əˈkɪliːz/

Achinese see **Achenese**

Acholi Ugandan ethnic group
uh-**choh**-li /əˈtʃəʊli/

achondrite stony meteorite
uh-**kon**-dryt /əˈkɒndrʌɪt/

achromatic without colour

ak-roh-**mat**-ik /,akrəʊˈmatɪk/

acidophilus bacterium in yogurt
ass-id-**of**-il-uhss /,asɪˈdɒfɪləs/

ackee (also **akee**) West African tree
ak-i /ˈaki/

acme most highly developed point
ak-mi /ˈakmi/

Acol bridge term
ak-ol /ˈakɒl/

acolyte person assisting a priest
ak-uh-lyt /ˈakəlʌɪt/

Aconcagua mountain, on the border
between Chile and Argentina
ak-on-**kag**-wuh /,akɒnˈkagwə/

aconite poisonous plant
ak-uh-nyt /ˈakənʌɪt/

acoustic relating to sound
uh-**koo**-stik /əˈkuːstɪk/

Formerly uh-**kow**-stik.

acquiesce accept
ak-wi-**ess** /,akwiˈɛs/

acreage area of land
ayk-uh-rij /ˈeɪkərɪdʒ/

acrid unpleasantly bitter or pungent
ak-rid /ˈakrɪd/

acrimony ill feeling
ak-rim-uh-ni /ˈakrɪməni/

acronym word formed from the initial
letters of other words
ak-ruh-nim /ˈakrənɪm/

acrophobia fear of heights
ak-ruh-**foh**-bi-uh /,akrəˈfəʊbiə/

acropolis fortified part of an ancient
Greek city
uh-**krop**-uh-liss /əˈkrɒpəlɪs/

Acrux star
ay-kruks /ˈeɪkrʌks/

Actaeon Greek mythological character
ak-**tee**-uhn /akˈtiːən/

Acteal village, Mexico
ak-tay-al /akteɪˈal/

actinium chemical element
ak-**tin**-i-uhm /akˈtɪniəm/

Actium, Battle of ancient naval battle
ak-ti-uhm /ˈaktiəm/

acuity sharpness
uh-**kyoo**-it-i /əˈkjuːɪti/

acumen ability to make good judgements
ak-yuum-uhn /ˈakjʊmən/

Less commonly also uh-**kyoo**-muhn.

acupuncture complementary medicine using needles
ak-yoo-**punk**-chuhr /'akjʊˌpʌŋktʃə(r)/

acyclovir antiviral drug
ay-**syk**-loh-veer /eɪ'sʌɪkləʊˌvɪə(r)/

adage proverb
ad-ij /'adɪdʒ/

adagio musical term
uh-**dah**-joh /ə'dɑːdʒəʊ/

Adam, Ansel American photographer
an-suhl /'ansəl/

adamantine unable to be broken
ad-uh-**man**-tyn /ˌadə'mantʌɪn/

Adamkus, Valdas Lithuanian president
val-dass ad-**am**-kuuss /ˌvaldas
a'damkʊs/

Adams, John Couch English astronomer
kootch /kuːtʃ/

Adana town and province, Turkey
ad-uh-nuh /'adənə/

Adar Jewish month
ad-**ar** /a'dɑː(r)/

ADAS Agricultural Development Advisory Service
ay-**dass** /'eɪdas/

Addis Ababa capital of Ethiopia
ad-iss **ab**-uh-buh /ˌadɪs 'abəbə/

Adelaide city, Australia
ad-uh-layd /'adəleɪd/

Adélie Land region of the Antarctic
uh-**day**-li /ə'deɪli/

The Adélie penguin is pronounced in the same way.

Aden port, Yemen
ay-duhn /'eɪdən/
• Established anglicization.

Adenauer, Konrad German statesman
kon-raht **ah**-duhn-ow-uhr /ˌkɒnrɑːt
'ɑːdənaʊə(r)/

à deux for two people
ah **doe** /ɑː 'dø/

ad hoc for the purpose in hand
ad **hok** /ˌad 'hɒk/

ad hominem relating to a particular person
ad **hom**-in-em /ˌad 'hɒmɪnɛm/

Adichie, Chimamanda Ngozi Nigerian author
chim-uh-**man**-duh uhng-**goh**-zi

ad-**ee**-chi /tʃɪməˌmandə əŋˌgəʊzi
a'diːtʃi/

Adidas German sports equipment company
ad-id-ass /'adɪdas/

This is the German pronunciation. Less commonly also uh-**dee**-dass in English.

Adi Granth Sikh scripture
ah-di **grunt** /ˌɑːdi 'grʌnt/

ad infinitum 'to infinity' (Latin)
ad in-fin-y-tuhm /ˌad ɪnfɪ'nʌɪtəm/

adios 'goodbye' (Spanish)
ad-i-**oss** /adi'ɒs/

Adirondack range of mountains, US
ad-irr-**on**-dak /ˌadɪ'rɒndak/

adit passage leading into a mine
ad-it /'adɪt/

Adjara autonomous republic, Georgia
aj-**ar**-uh /a'dʒɑːrə/

This is the Georgian form. The Russian name is Ajaria, pronounced uh-**jar**-i-uh.

adjourn pause
uh-**jurn** /ə'dʒɜː(r)n/

adjunct thing added as a supplementary part
aj-unkt /'adʒʌŋkt/

adjutant military officer
aj-uut-uhnt /'adʒʊtənt/

admonitory giving a warning or reprimand
uhd-**mon**-it-uh-ri /əd'mɒnɪtəri/

ad nauseam 'to a disgusting extent' (Latin)
ad **naw**-zi-am /ad 'nɔːziam/

Adnyamathanha Aboriginal language
ad-nyuh-mud-uh-nuh
/'adnjəˌmʌdənə/

adobe clay used as a building material
uh-**doh**-bi /ə'dəʊbi/

Adonai Hebrew name for God
ad-on-**y** /ˌadɒ'nʌɪ/

This is the Hebrew pronunciation. Less commonly also a more anglicized pronunciation ad-on-**ay**-y.

Adonis Greek mythological character
uh-**doh**-niss /ə'dəʊnɪs/

Adorno, Theodor German philosopher
tay-dor uh-**dor**-noh /ˌteɪədɔː(r)
ə'dɔː(r)nəʊ/

adrenal relating to glands situated above the kidneys
uh-**dree**-nuhl /ə'driːnəl/

Adriatic sea and islands, Europe
ay-dri-**at**-ik /ˌeɪdri'atɪk/

adroit clever or skilful
uh-**droyt** /ə'drɔɪt/

aduki small edible bean; also called
adzuki
uh-**doo**-ki /ə'duːki/

adulate praise excessively
ad-yuul-ayt /'adjʊleɪt/

adumbrate represent in outline
ad-um-brayt /'adʌmbreɪt/

Adur river and district, England
ay-duhr /'eɪdə(r)/

advent arrival
ad-vent /'advɛnt/

adversarial involving conflict
ad-vur-**sair**-i-uhl /ˌadvə:(r)'sɛːriəl/

adversary opponent
ad-vuhr-suh-ri /'advə(r)səri/

Sometimes also ad-**vur**-suh-ri.

advocaat Dutch liqueur
ad-vuh-kaht /'advəkɑːt/

Adygeya autonomous republic, Russia
ad-ig-**yay**-uh /adɪ'gjeɪə/

adytum pl. **adyta** sanctuary of ancient
Greek temple
ad-it-uhm, pl. **ad**-it-uh /'adɪtəm/, pl.
/-tə/

adze tool similar to an axe
adz /adz/

adzuki small edible bean; also called
aduki
uhd-**zoo**-ki /əd'zuːki/

Aegean sea, Europe
ee-**jee**-uhn /iː'dʒiːən/

Aegeus Greek mythological character
eej-yooss /'iːdʒuːs/

Aegina island, Greece
ee-**jyn**-uh /iː'dʒʌɪnə/, ['eɣina]
• Established anglicization.

aegis protection
ee-jiss /'iːdʒɪs/

The same pronunciation is used for the
Aegis Trust.

Aegisthus Greek mythological character
ee-**jiss**-thuhss /iː'dʒɪsθəs/

aegrotat university certificate
y-groh-tat /'ʌɪɡrəʊtat/

Commonly also **ee**-groh-tat and
ee-**groh**-tat.

Aelfric Anglo-Saxon monk and writer
al-frik /'alfrɪk/

Aeneas Greek and Roman mythological
character
in-**ee**-uhss /ɪ'niːəs/

Aeneid epic poem by Virgil
ee-ni-id /'iːnɪɪd/

Sometimes also in-**ee**-id.

Aeolus Greek god
ee-uh-luhss /'iːələs/

aeon long period of time
ee-on /'iːɒn/

aerobics method of exercise
air-**oh**-biks /ɛː'rəʊbɪks/

Aeroflot Russian airline
air-oh-flot /'ɛːrəʊflɒt/, [aɪra'flɔt]
• Established anglicization.

Aeschines Greek orator and statesman
ee-skin-eez /'iːskɪniːz/

Aeschylus Greek dramatist
ee-skil-uhss /'iːskɪləs/

Æsir Scandinavian mythological name
ee-suhr /'iːsə(r)/

Aesop Greek storyteller
ee-sop /'iːsɒp/

aesthetic concerned with beauty
eess-**thet**-ik /iːs'θɛtɪk/

Commonly also ess-**thet**-ik.

Afar Djiboutian and Ethiopian ethnic
group
af-ar /'afɑː(r)/

AFASIC Association For All Speech
Impaired Children
ay-**fay**-zik /eɪ'feɪzɪk/
• Play on the word *aphasic*.

affenpinscher dog of a small breed
af-**uhn**-pinsh-uhr /'afən,pɪnʃə(r)/

affidavit written statement
af-id-**ay**-vit /ˌafɪ'deɪvɪt/

affricate phonetic manner of articulation
af-rik-uht /'afrɪkət/

Afghan relating to Afghanistan
af-gan /'afgan/

afghani currency unit, Afghanistan
af-**gah**-ni /af'gɑːni/

Afghanistan country
af-**gan**-ist-ahn /af'ganɪstɑːn/,
[af'ɣanɪstan]
• Established anglicization.

aficionado knowledgeable person
uh-fish-i-uh-**nah**-doh /əˌfɪʃiə'nɑːdəʊ/

Less commonly also uh-fiss-i-uh-**nah**-doh.

Afrikaans South African language
af-rik-**ahnss** /ˌafrɪˈkɑːns/

Afrikander South African breed of cattle
af-rik-**an**-duhr /ˌafrɪˈkandə(r)/

Afrikaner Afrikaans-speaking South
African
af-rik-**ahn**-uhr /ˌafrɪˈkɑːnə(r)/

Afyonkarahisar province and city,
Turkey
af-**yon**-karr-uh-hiss-**ar**
/afˌjɒnkarəhɪˈsɑː(r)/

Aga trademark type of stove
ah-guh /ˈɑːɡə/

Agadir port, Morocco
ag-uh-**deer** /ˌaɡəˈdɪə(r)/

again another time
uh-**gen** /əˈɡɛn/

Less commonly also uh-**gayn**.

against in opposition to
uh-**genst** /əˈɡɛnst/

Less commonly also uh-**gaynst**.

Aga Khan spiritual leader of the Nizari
sect of Ismaili Muslims
ah-guh **kahn** /ˌɑːɡə ˈkɑːn/

Agamemnon Greek mythological
character
ag-uh-**mem**-nuhn /ˌaɡəˈmɛmnən/

agapanthus a South African plant
ag-uh-**pan**-thuhss /ˌaɡəˈpanθəs/

agape Christian love
ag-uh-pi /ˈaɡəpi/

agar gelatinous substance
ay-gar /ˈeɪɡɑː(r)/

agaric fungus
ag-uh-rik /ˈaɡərɪk/

Sometimes also uh-**gar**-ik.

Agartala city, India
ug-ar-tul-uh /ʌˈɡɑː(r)tʌlə/

Agassi, André American tennis player
ahn-dray ag-uh-si /ˌɑːndreɪ ˈaɡəsi/

Agassiz, Louis Swiss-born American
zoologist
lwee ag-uh-si /ˌlwiː ˈaɡəsi/

agate ornamental stone
ag-uht /ˈaɡət/

agave succulent plant
uh-**gay**-vi /əˈɡeɪvi/

Agen city, France

azh-**a(ng)** /aˈʒɛ̃/

agent provocateur person assigned to
provoke unrest
azh-o(ng) pruh-vok-uh-**tur**
/ˌaʒɒ̃ prəˌvɒkəˈtə:(r)/, French [aʒɑ̃
prɔvɔkatœːr]

Sometimes anglicized further to **ayj**-uhnt.

aggregate formed of several separate
elements
ag-ruh-guht /ˈaɡrəɡət/

aggregate form into a cluster
ag-ruh-gayt /ˈaɡrəɡeɪt/

Aghios Nikolaos port, Greece
ag-i-oss nik-uh-**ly**-oss /ˌaɡɪɒs
nɪkəˈlʌɪɒs/

Agincourt, Battle of battle in France
in 1415
aj-in-kor /ˈadʒɪnˌkɔː(r)/
• Established anglicization.

agitato musical term
aj-it-**ah**-toh /ˌadʒɪˈtɑːtəʊ/

agitprop political propaganda
aj-it-prop /ˈadʒɪtprɒp/

Agnesi, Maria Gaetana Italian
mathematician and philosopher
muh-**ree**-uh gah-uh-**tah**-nuh
an-**yay**-zi /məˌriːə ɡɑːəˌtɑːnə anˈjeɪzi/

Agni Vedic god of fire
ag-ni /ˈaɡni/

Agnus Dei section of the Mass
ag-nuuss **day**-ee /ˌaɡnʊs ˈdeɪiː/

Sometimes also **ahn**-yuuss; see LATIN panel.

agoraphobia fear of open or public
places
ag-uh-ruh-**foh**-bi-uh /ˌaɡərəˈfəʊbiə/

Agostini, Giacomo Italian racing
motorcyclist
jah-kuh-moh ag-uh-**stee**-ni
/ˌdʒɑːkəməʊ aɡəˈstiːni/

agouti long-legged burrowing rodent
uh-**goo**-ti /əˈɡuːti/

Agra city, India
ahg-ruh /ˈɑːɡrə/

Agricola, Gnaeus Julius Roman
general
nee-uhss jool-i-uhss uh-**grik**-uh-luh
/ˌniːəs ˌdʒuːliəs əˈɡrɪkələ/
• See LATIN panel.

Ağri province, Turkey
ar-i /ˈɑːri/

Agrippa, Marcus Roman general
mar-kuhss uh-**grip**-uh /ˌmɑ:(r)kəs
ə'grɪpə/

Agropoli city, Italy
ag-**rop**-ol-i /aɡ'rɒpɒli/

Aguascalientes state, Mexico
ag-wask-al-**yen**-tess
/ˌaɡwaskə'ljɛntɛs/

ague illness involving fever and shivering
ay-gyoo /'eɪɡju:/

Aguilera, Christina American pop
singer
krist-ee-nuh ag-yil-**air**-uh /krɪsˌti:nə
aɡjɪ'lɛːrə/

Agulhas, Cape most southerly point of
Africa
uh-**gul**-uhss /ə'ɡʌləs/

Agung mountain, Indonesia
ah-**guung** /'ɑ:ɡʊŋ/

Agusan province and river, Philippines
ag-**oo**-san /a'ɡu:san/

A-Ha Norwegian pop group
ah-**hah** /ɑ:'hɑ:/

Ahab, Captain character in *Moby Dick*
ay-hab /'eɪhab/

Aherne, Bertie Irish prime minister
uh-**hurn** /ə'həː(r)n/

Ahmadabad city, India
ah-muh-duh-bad /'ɑ:mədəbad/

Ahmići village, Bosnia
akh-mee-chi /'axmi:tʃi/

aholehole Hawaiian fish
uh-hoh-li-**hoh**-li /əˌhəʊli'həʊli/

Ahriman evil spirit in Zoroastrianism
ar-im-uhn /'ɑ:rɪmən/

Ahura Mazda creator god of
Zoroastrianism
uh-**hoor**-uh **maz**-duh /əˌhʊərə 'mazdə/

Ahvaz (also **Ahwaz**) town, Iran
ahkh-**vahz** /ɑ:x'vɑ:z/

Ahvenanmaa island and province,
Finland
akh-ven-an-mah /'axvɛnanmɑ:/

This is the Finnish name. The Swedish
name is Åland, pronounced **aw**-land.

Aïda opera by Verdi
ah-ee-duh /ɑ:'i:də/

aide-de-camp military assistant to a
senior officer
ayd duh kahmp /ˌeɪd də 'kɑ:mp/

Aigues river, France

eg /ɛɡ/

aiguille pinnacle of rock in a mountain
range
ayg-**weel** /'eɪɡwi:l/

Aiguille du Midi peak in the Mont
Blanc massif, France
ay-gwee due mee-dee /eɪˌɡwi: dy
mi:'di:/

aikido Japanese martial art
y-kee-doh /ʌɪ'ki:dəʊ/

Aileen English girl's name
y-leen, ay-leen /'ʌɪli:n/, /'ɛɪli:n/

Ailly town, France
y-yee /ʌɪ'ji:/

Ailsa Craig island, Scotland
ayl-suh krayg /ˌeɪlsə 'kreɪɡ/

ailurophobia fear of cats
yl-yuu-ruh-**foh**-bi-uh /ˌʌɪljʊrə'fəʊbiə/

Ain department, France
a(ng) /ɛ̃/

Aintree site of Grand National
racecourse
ayn-tree /'eɪntri:/

Ainu Japanese ethnic group
y-noo /'ʌɪnu:/

aioli mayonnaise seasoned with garlic
y-**oh**-li /ʌɪ'əʊli/

Aisne department and river, France
en /ɛn/

ait island in a river; also called **eyot**
ayt /eɪt/

Aix-en-Provence city, France
eks ah(ng) prov-**ah(ng)ss** /ˌɛks ɑ̃
prɒ'vɑ̃s/

Ajaccio Corsican port, France
aj-**ass**-i-oh /a'dʒasiəʊ/, [aʒaksjo]
• Established anglicization.

Ajanta Caves series of caves, India
uh-**junt**-uh /ə'dʒʌntə/

Ajaria see **Adjara**

Ajax Greek mythological character
ay-jaks /'eɪdʒaks/

Ajax Dutch football club
y-aks /'ʌɪaks/

Ajman states, United Arab Emirates
aj-**mahn** /adʒ'mɑ:n/

Ajmer city, India
uj-**meer** /ʌdʒ'mɪə(r)/

Akan Ghanaian ethnic group
ak-**ahn** /a'kɑ:n/

Akayev, Askar Kyrgyz statesman
ask-ar uh-**ky**-uhf /asˌkɑ:(r) ə'kʌɪəf/

Akbar, Muhammad Mogul emperor
muu-**ham**-uhd **ak**-bar /mʊˌhaməd ˈakbɑː(r)/

akee see ackee

Akela character from the Jungle Book
ah-**kay**-luh /ɑːˈkeɪlə/

Akhbar, al- Egyptian newspaper
uhl ukh-**bar** /əl ʌxˈbɑː(r)/

Akhenaten (also **Akhenaton**) Egyptian pharaoh
ak-uh-**nah**-tuhn /ˌakəˈnɑːtən/

Akhmatova, Anna Russian poet
an-uh ak-**mah**-tuh-vuh /ˌanə akˈmɑːtəvə/

Akihito emperor of Japan
ah-**kee**-hit-oh /ɑːˈkiːhɪtəʊ/

Another common anglicization is ak-i-**hee**-toh; see JAPANESE panel.

akimbo with hands on the hips and elbows turned outwards
uh-**kim**-boh /əˈkɪmbəʊ/

Akkad Mesopotamian kingdom
ak-ad /ˈakad/

Akkadian relating to Akkad
uh-**kay**-di-uhn /əˈkeɪdiən/

Akron city, US
ak-ruhn /ˈakrən/

Aksai Chin region of the Himalayas
ak-sy chin /ˌaksʌɪ ˈtʃɪn/

Aksum (also **Axum**) town, Ethiopia
ak-suum /ˈaksʊm/

Aktyubinsk city and oblast, Kazakhstan
ak-**tyoo**-binsk /akˈtjuːbɪnsk/

Akwa-Ibom state, Nigeria
ak-**wah** ee-buum /akˌwɑː iːˈbʊm/

al- For Arabic names beginning with the article *al-*, look under the spelling of the main part of the name: for example *Qaeda, al-*.

Alabama state, US
al-uh-**bam**-uh /ˌaləˈbamə/

alabaster translucent form of gypsum or calcite
al-uh-**bast**-uhr /aləˈbastə(r)/

Less commonly also al-uh-**bah**-stuhr.

alacrity brisk and cheerful readiness
uh-**lak**-rit-i /əˈlakrɪti/

Alagiah, George BBC journalist
al-uh-**gy**-uh /aləˈɡʌɪə/

Alagoas state, Brazil

al-uh-goh-uhss /ˌaləˈɡəʊəs/

Alain-Fournier French novelist
al-**a(ng)** foorn-**yay** /aˌlɛ̃ fʊə(r)ˈnjeɪ/

Alam, Faria English celebrity
fuh-**ree**-uh uh-**lam** /fəˌriːə əˈlam/

Alamein, el- town, Egypt
uhl **al**-uh-mayn /əl ˈaləmeɪn/

Alamo site of battle during the Texas revolution
al-uh-moh /ˈaləməʊ/

Alamosa county and city, US
al-uh-**moh**-suh /aləˈməʊsə/

Åland see Ahvenanmaa

Al-Anon support organization for the families and friends of alcoholics
al uh-**non** /ˌal əˈnɒn/

Alarcón, Pedro de Spanish novelist
ped-roh day al-ar-**kon** /ˌpɛdrəʊ deɪ alɑː(r)ˈkɒn/

Alaric king of the Visigoths
al-uh-rik /ˈalərɪk/

Albacete city and province, Spain
al-bath-**ay**-tay /albaˈθeɪteɪ/

albacore type of tuna fish
al-buh-kor /ˈalbəkɔː(r)/

Alba Iulia city, Romania
al-buh **yoo**-li-uh /ˌalbə ˈjuːliə/

Alban, St British Christian martyr
awl-buhn /ˈɔːlbən/

Albania country
al-**bay**-ni-uh /alˈbeɪniə/

Albano lake, Italy
al-**bah**-noh /alˈbɑːnəʊ/

Albany city, US
awl-buh-ni /ˈɔːlbəni/

Albarn, Damon English pop singer
awl-barn /ˈɔːlbɑː(r)n/

Albee, Edward American dramatist
awl-bee /ˈɔːlbiː/

albeit though
awl-**bee**-it /ɔːlˈbiːɪt/

Albena resort, Bulgaria
al-**bay**-nuh /alˈbeɪnə/

Albéniz, Isaac Spanish composer
ee-sah-**ak** al-**bay**-neeth /iːsɑːˌak alˈbeɪniːθ/

Albert, Prince Prince of Monaco
al-buhrt /ˈalbə(r)t/, French [albɛːr]
• Established anglicization.

Alberti, Leon Battista Italian architect
lay-on bat-**eest**-uh al-**bair**-ti /ˌleɪɒn
baˈtiːstə alˈbɛː(r)ti/

Albertus Magnus, St Dominican
theologian
al-**bur**-tuhss **mag**-nuhss /alˌbəː(r)təs
ˈmagnəs/

albino person or animal with absence of
pigment
al-**bee**-noh /alˈbiːnəʊ/

AM is al-**by**-noh.

Albinoni, Tomaso Italian composer
tom-**ah**-zoh al-bin-**oh**-ni /tɒˌmɑːzəʊ
ˌalbɪˈnəʊni/

Albion literary term for Britain or
England
al-bi-uhn /ˈalbiən/

Alborán island, Spain
al-borr-**an** /albɒˈran/

Ålborg (also **Aalborg**) city, Denmark
awl-bor /ˈɔːlbɔː(r)/

Albufeira resort, Portugal
al-boo-**fair**-uh /albuːˈfɛːrə/

albumen egg white protein
al-byoo-muhn /ˈalbjʊmən/

Albuquerque city, US
al-buh-kur-ki /ˈalbəˌkəː(r)ki/

Alcaeus Greek lyric poet
al-**see**-uhss /alˈsiːəs/
• See GREEK panel.

Alcalá de Henares city, Spain
al-kal-**ah** day en-**arr**-ess /ˌalkaˈlɑː deɪ
ɛˈnarɛs/

Alcántara town, Spain
al-**kan**-tarr-uh /alˈkantarə/

Alcatraz island and prison, US
al-kuh-traz /ˈalkətraz/

alcazar Spanish palace of Moorish origin
al-kuh-**zar** /ˌalkəˈzɑː(r)/

Alcestis Greek mythological character
al-**sest**-iss /alˈsɛstɪs/

alchemy medieval forerunner of
chemistry
al-kuh-mi /ˈalkəmi/

Alcibiades Athenian general and
statesman
al-si-**by**-uh-deez /ˌalsɪˈbʌɪədiːz/

Alcmene Greek mythological character
alk-**mee**-ni /alkˈmiːni/

Alcott, Louisa May American novelist
awl-kot /ˈɔːlkɒt/

Alcudia resort, Majorca
al-**kooth**-yuh /alˈkuːðjə/

Alcuin English scholar
al-kwin /ˈalkwɪn/

Alda, Alan American actor
awl-duh /ˈɔːldə/

Aldabra island group, Seychelles
al-**dab**-ruh /alˈdabrə/

Aldebaran star
al-**deb**-uh-ruhn /alˈdɛbərən/

Aldeburgh town, England
awld-bruh /ˈɔːldbrə/

al dente cooked so as to be still firm
when bitten
al **den**-tay /al ˈdɛnteɪ/

alder tree
awl-duhr /ˈɔːldə(r)/

Alder Hay hospital, England
awl-duhr-**hay** /ˌɔːldə(r) ˈheɪ/

Alderney island, England
awld-uhr-ni /ˈɔːldə(r)ni/

Aldi German discount store chain
al-di /ˈaldi/

Aldis lamp trademark signalling lamp
awl-diss /ˈɔːldɪs/

Aldiss, Brian English science fiction
writer
awl-diss /ˈɔːldɪs/

Alegranza island, Spain
al-eg-**ran**-thuh /alɛˈɡranθə/

aleikum esalaam Arabic greeting
uh-**lay**-kuum ess-uh-**lahm** /əˌleɪkʊm
ɛsəˈlɑːm/

Alençon town, France
al-ah(ng)-**so(ng)** /alɑ̃ˈsõ/

Alentejo region and former province,
Portugal
al-en-**tay**-zhoo /alɛnˈteɪʒuː/

aleph letter of the Hebrew alphabet
ah-lef /ˈɑːlɛf/

Aleppo city, Syria
uh-**lep**-oh /əˈlɛpəʊ/

Established anglicization. The Arabic name
is Halab, pronounced **hah-lahb**.

Alesi, Jean French racing driver
zhah(ng) al-**ay**-zi /ˌʒɑ̃ aˈleɪzi/

Aletschhorn mountain, Switzerland
ah-letch-horn /ˈɑːlɛtʃˌhɔː(r)n/

Aleut ethnic group inhabiting the
Aleutian Islands
al-i-oot /ˈaliuːt/

Aleutian Islands islands, US
uh-**loo**-shuhn /əˈluːʃən/

Alexandre, Boniface Haitian president
bon-if-**ass** al-uhk-**sah(ng)d**-ruh
/ˌbɒnɪˌfas aləkˈsãdrə/

Alexandria port, Egypt
al-eg-**zahn**-dri-uh /ˌalɛgˈzɑːndriə/
• Established anglicization.

alfalfa leguminous plant
al-**fal**-fuh /alˈfalfə/

Alfa Romeo car manufacturer
al-fuh ruh-**may**-oh /ˌalfə rəˈmeɪəʊ/

Alfvén, Hannes Swedish physicist
han-uhss al-**vayn** /ˌhanəs alˈveɪn/

algae sing. **alga** sea-weed
al-jee, sing. al-guh /ˈaldʒiː, sing. ˈalgə/

The plural is commonly also **al-gee**.

Algarve province, Portugal
al-**garv** /alˈgɑː(r)v/, [alˈgarvə]
• Established anglicization.

algebra area of mathematics
al-juh-bruh /ˈaldʒəbrə/

Algeciras port, Spain
al-juh-**sirr**-uhss /ˌaldʒəˈsɪrəs/,
[alxeˈθiras]
• Established anglicization.

Algeria country
al-**jeer**-i-uh /alˈdʒɪəriə/
• Established anglicization.

Algiers capital of Algeria
al-**jeerz** /alˈdʒɪə(r)z/
• Established anglicization.

Algol star
al-gol /ˈalgɒl/

Algonquin American Indian ethnic
group
al-**gonk**-win /alˈgɒŋkwɪn/

Algren, Nelson American novelist
awl-gruhn /ˈɔːlgrən/

alhaji Muslim who has been to Mecca
uhl-**haj**-i /əlˈhadʒi/

Alhambra fortified Moorish palace
al-**ham**-bruh /alˈhambrə/

Ali, Laila American boxer
lay-luh ah-**lee** /ˌleɪlə ɑːˈliː/

Ali, Muhammad American boxer
muh-**ham**-uhd ah-**lee** /məˌhaməd
ɑːˈliː/

Alicante port, Spain
al-ik-**an**-ti /alɪˈkanti/, [aliˈkante]
• Established anglicization.

Aligarh city, India
ul-ig-**ar** /ʌlɪˈgɑː(r)/

Alighieri, Dante Italian poet and writer
dan-tay al-ig-**yair**-i /ˌdanteɪ alɪˈgjɛːri/

Aline loch and river, Scotland
al-in /ˈalɪn/

Alitalia Italian airline
al-it-**ahl**-i-uh /alɪˈtɑːliə/

aliyah immigration to Israel
uh-**lee**-yuh /əˈliːjə/

Aliyev, Heydar Azerbaijani statesman
hay-dar al-**ee**-yef /ˌheɪdɑː(r) aˈliːjɛf/

Allah 'God' (Arabic)
uh-**lah** /əˈlɑː/

A more anglicized pronunciation, **al-uh**, is
sometimes also used.

Allahabad city, India
al-uh-huh-**bahd** /ˌaləhəˈbɑːd/

Allawi, Iyad Iraqi politician
y-ad uh-**lah**-wi /ˌʌɪad əˈlɑːwi/

allay diminish
uh-**lay** /əˈleɪ/

Allegheny city, river, mountain, and
college, US
al-uh-**gayn**-i /ˌaləˈgeɪni/

allegretto musical term
al-uh-**gret**-oh /ˌaləˈgrɛtəʊ/

Allegri, Gregorio Italian priest and
composer
greg-**awr**-i-oh al-**eg**-ri /grɛˌgɔːriəʊ
aˈlɛgri/

allegro musical term
uh-**leg**-roh /əˈlɛgrəʊ/

allemande German dance
al-mahnd /ˈalmɑːnd/

Allende, Salvador Chilean statesman
sal-vad-**or** al-**yend**-ay /salvaˌdɔː(r)
aˈjɛndeɪ/

allergen substance that causes an
allergic reaction
al-uhr-juhn /ˈalə(r)dʒən/

Allerød geological stage
al-uh-roed /ˈalərøːd/

Allier river, France
al-**yay** /alˈjeɪ/

Alliot-Marie, Michèle French defence
minister
mee-**shel** al-i-**oh** marr-ee /miːˌʃɛl
aliˌəʊ maˈriː/

allosaurus carnivorous dinosaur
al-uh-**sawr**-uhss /ˌaləˈsɔːrəs/

alloy metal
al-oy /'alɔɪ/

alloy mix to make an alloy
uh-**loy** /ə'lɔɪ/

Almagest astronomical treatise
al-muh-jest /'almədʒest/

almanac annual calendar
awl-muh-nak /'ɔːlmənak/

Commonly also **ol**-muh-nak and
al-muh-nak.

Almaty city, Kazakhstan
al-**mah**-tuh /al'mɑːtə/

Almeria town and province, Spain
al-merr-**ee**-uh /ˌalmɛ'riːə/

almirah cupboard or wardrobe
al-**my**-ruh /al'mʌɪrə/

Almirante Brown city, Argentina
al-mirr-**an**-tay **brown** /almɪˌranteɪ 'braʊn/

Almodóvar, Pedro Spanish film
director
ped-roh **al**-mod-**oh**-var /ˌpɛdrəʊ almɒ'dəʊvɑː(r)/

Almond, Marc English singer
ah-muhnd /'ɑːmənd/

almond nut
ah-muhnd /'ɑːmənd/

Less commonly also **ahl**-muhnd or
al-muhnd.

alms money or food given to poor people
ahmz /ɑːmz/

Almqvist, Carl Jonas Love Swedish
novelist
karl yoo-nuhss **loo**-vuh **alm**-kvist /ˌkɑə(r)l ˌjuːnəs ˌluːvə 'almkvɪst/

aloe vera gelatinous substance
al-oh **veer**-uh /ˌaləʊ 'vɪərə/

aloha Hawaiian greeting
uh-**loh**-huh /ə'ləʊhə/

alopecia partial or complete absence
of hair
al-uh-**pee**-shuh /ˌalə'piːʃə/

Alor Setar city, Malaysia
ah-lor suh-**tar** /ˌɑːlɔː(r) sə'tɑː(r)/

Alost see Aalst

Aloysius British boy's name
al-oh-**ish**-uhss /aləʊ'ɪʃəs/

alpaca South American mammal related
to the llama
al-**pak**-uh /al'pakə/

Alpe d'Huez mountain, France

alp **dwez** /ˌalp 'dwɛz/

Alpha Centauri star
al-fuh sen-**taw**-ry /ˌalfə sɛn'tɔːrʌɪ/

Alphaeus biblical name
al-**fee**-uhss /al'fiːəs/

Alpheus Greek god
al-**fee**-uhss /al'fiːəs/

Alpujarras mountainous region, Spain
al-poo-**kharr**-ass /alpu:'xaras/

Alsace region, France
al-**zass** /al'zas/

Alstom French engineering firm
al-stom /'alstɒm/

Altai (also **Altay**) region, Russia
al-**ty** /al'tʌɪ/

Altair star
al-**tair** /'altɛː(r)/

Altamura town, Italy
al-tuh-**moor**-uh /altə'mʊərə/

Altdorfer, Albrecht German painter
alt-brekht **alt**-dor-fuhr /ˌalbrɛçt 'altdɔː(r)fə(r)/

Althing Icelandic parliament
awl-thing /'ɔːlθɪŋ/

Althorp family home of the Earl Spencer
awl-thorp /'ɔːlθɔː(r)p/

The family pronunciation has traditionally
always been **awl**-truhp, although **awl**-thorp
was usual for the village. In 2000 the estate
released a press statement saying that
henceforth it would be known as **awl**-thorp,
and we changed our recommendation
accordingly.

Althusser, Louis French philosopher
lwee al-tue-**sair** /ˌlwiː alty'sɛː(r)/

altimeter instrument for recording
altitude
al-ti-**mee**-tuhr /'altɪmiːtə(r)/

Altman, Robert American film director
awlt-muhn /'ɔːltmən/

alto singing voice
al-toh /'altəʊ/

altruism selfless concern for others
al-troo-iz-uhm /'altrʊɪzəm/

aluminium metal
al-**oo**-**min**-i-uhm /alu:'mɪniəm/

AM is usually *aluminum*, pronounced
uh-**loo**-min-uhm.

alumna pl. **alumnae** female former
student
uh-**lum**-nuh, pl. uh-**lum**-nee /ə'lʌmnə/,
pl. /-niː/

alumnus pl. **alumni** male former student
uh-**lum**-nuhss, pl. uh-**lum**-ni
/ə'lʌmnəs/, pl. /-ni/

alveolus small cavity, pit, or hollow
al-vi-**oh**-luhss /ˌalvi'əʊləs/

Alwyn, William English composer
al-win /'alwɪn/

Alzheimer's disease progressive
mental deterioration
alts-hy-muhrz /'altshʌɪmə(r)z/

Amalfi port, Italy
uh-**mal**-fi /ə'malfi/

amalgam a mixture or blend
uh-**mal**-guhm /ə'malgəm/

Amalthea moon of Jupiter
am-uhl-**thee**-uh /aməl'θiːə/

Amapá state, Brazil
am-uh-**pah** /ˌamə'pɑː/

Amarah, al- town, Iraq
uhl uh-**mar**-uh /əl ə'mɑːrə/

amaretti Italian biscuits
am-uh-**ret**-i /ˌamə'rɛti/

Amarillo city, US
am-uh-**ril**-oh /amə'rɪləʊ/

Amaterasu Shinto god
uh-mah-tuh-**rah**-soo /əˌmɑːtə'rɑːsuː/

Amati Italian violin-maker
uh-**mah**-ti /ə'mɑːti/

Amatola mountain range, South Africa
am-uh-**toh**-luh /amə'təʊlə/

Amazon river, South America
am-uh-zuhn /'aməzən/

Amazonas state, Brazil
am-uh-**zohn**-uhss /ˌamə'zəʊnəs/

Ambala city and district, India
uhm-**bah**-luh /əm'bɑːlə/

Ambanja town, Madagascar
uhm-**bahn**-juh /əm'bɑːndʒə/

Ambato town, Ecuador
am-**bah**-toh /am'bɑːtəʊ/

Ambès town, France
ah(ng)-**bess** /ɑ̃'bɛs/

Ambohimanga city, Madagascar
am-buu-hi-**mang**-guh
/amˌbʊhi'maŋgə/

Ambon island, Indonesia
am-**bon** /am'bɒn/

Amchitka island, US
am-**chit**-kuh /am'tʃɪtkə/

Amec British engineering company
am-ek /'amɛk/

ameliorate make better
uh-**mee**-li-uh-rayt /ə'miːliəreɪt/

amen uttered at the end of a prayer
ah-**men** /ɑ'mɛn/

Commonly also ay-**men**.

Amenábar, Alejandro Spanish film
director
al-ekh-**and**-roh am-en-**ah**-bar
/alɛ'xandrəʊ amɛ'nɑːbɑː(r)/

Amenhotep Egyptian pharaoh
ah-muhn-**hoh**-tep /ˌɑːmən'həʊtɛp/

americium chemical element
am-uh-**riss**-i-uhm /ˌamə'rɪsiəm/

Ames city, Iowa
eymz /eɪmz/

Ameslan American Sign Language
am-uhss-lan /'aməslan/

amethyst precious stone
am-uh-thist /'aməthɪst/

Amharic Ethiopian language
am-**harr**-ik /am'harɪk/

Amherst town, US
am-uhrst /'amə(r)st/

Amicus trade union for manufacturing
and technical workers
am-ik-uhss /'amɪkəs/

amicus curiae pl. **amici curiae** 'friends
of the court' (Latin)
uh-**my**-kuhss **kyoor**-i-ee, pl.
uh-**mee**-see /əˌmʌɪkəs 'kjʊəriiː/, pl.
/əˌmiːsiː/

Legal Latin is often anglicized; see LATIN
panel. A more classical pronunciation,
uh-**mee**-kuhss **kyoor**-i-y, pl. uh-**mee**-ki, is
also possible.

Amiens town, France
am-**ya(ng)** /am'jɛ̃/

Amin, Idi Ugandan dictator
ee-di uh-**meen** /ˌiːdi ə'miːn/

Amindivi Islands group of islands,
India
am-in-**dee**-vi /ˌamɪn'diːvi/

amino class of acids
uh-**mee**-noh /ə'miːnəʊ/

Less commonly also uh-**myn**-oh.

amir Muslim title
uh-**meer** /ə'mɪə(r)/

Amirante Islands group of islands,
Seychelles
am-irr-ant /'amɪrant/

Amis, Kingsley English writer
king-zli **ay**-miss /ˌkɪŋzli ˈeɪmɪs/

Amish Christian sect
ah-mish /ˈɑːmɪʃ/

Amman capital of Jordan
uh-**mahn** /əˈmɑːn/

ammeter instrument for measuring electric current
am-muh-tuhr /ˈamətə(r)/

amniocentesis process in which amniotic fluid is sampled
am-ni-oh-sen-**tee**-siss /ˌamnɪəʊsenˈtiːsɪs/

Amoco British oil company
am-uh-koh /ˈaməkəʊ/

amoeba pl. **amoebae** single-celled animal
uh-**mee**-buh, pl. uh-**mee**-bee /əˈmiːbə/, pl. /-biː/
• Standard -s plural is also possible.

amontillado Spanish sherry
uh-mon-til-**ah**-doh /əˌmɒntɪˈlɑːdəʊ/, [amontiˈʎaðo]
• Established anglicization.

Amos Hebrew prophet
ay-moss /ˈeɪmɒs/

Amos, Baroness Guyanese-born politician
ay-moss /ˈeɪmɒs/

amoxicillin penicillin
uh-moks-i-**sil**-in /əˌmɒksiˈsɪlɪn/

Amoy another name for **Xiamen**
uh-**moy** /əˈmɔɪ/

Ampère, André-Marie French physicist
ah(ng)-**dray** marr-ee ah(ng)-**pair** /ã,dreɪ maˌriː ãˈpɛː(r)/

ampere unit of electric current
am-pair /ˈampɛː(r)/

ampersand sign &
am-puhr-sand /ˈampə(r)sand/

amphibious suited for both land and water
am-**fib**-i-uhss /amˈfɪbiəs/

Amphitrite Greek goddess
am-fit-**ry**-ti /ˌamfɪˈtrʌɪti/

amphora pl. **amphorae** ancient Greek or Roman jug
am-fuh-ruh, pl. am-fuh-ree /ˈamfərə/, pl. /-riː/
• Standard -s plural is also possible.

ampoule glass capsule containing a liquid

am-pool /ˈampuːl/

Sometimes also **amp-yool**.

AMRAAM Advanced Medium Range Air-to-Air Missile
am-ram /ˈamram/

Amritsar city, India
um-**rit**-suhr /ʌmˈrɪtsə(r)/

Amstel river, Netherlands
am-stuhl /ˈamstəl/
• Established anglicization.

Amsterdam capital of the Netherlands
am-stuhr-dam /ˈamstə(r)dam/, [ˌamstərˈdɑm]

Established anglicization. A more Dutch pronunciation, with stress on the last syllable, is also common.

Amu Darya river, central Asia
ah-moo **dar**-i-uh /ˌɑːmuː ˈdɑːriə/

amulet small piece of jewellery
am-yoo-luht /ˈamjʊlət/

Amun-Ra ancient Egyptian god
am-uhn **rah** /ˌamən ˈrɑː/

Amundsen, Roald Norwegian explorer
roo-al **ah**-muun-suhn /ˌruːal ˈɑːmʊnsən/

Amur river, NE Asia
uh-**moor** /əˈmʊə(r)/

amygdala pl. **amygdalae** part of the brain
uh-**mig**-duh-luh, pl. uh-**mig**-duh-lee /əˈmɪgdələ/, pl. /-liː/

Anabaptism doctrine that baptism should only be administered to believing adults
an-uh-**bap**-tiz-uhm /ˌanəˈbaptɪzəm/

anachronism thing appropriate to a period other than that in which it exists
uh-**nak**-ruh-niz-uhm /əˈnakrəˌnɪzəm/

Anacreon Greek poet
uh-**nak**-ri-uhn /əˈnakriən/

Anadyr city and river, Russia
uh-**nad**-eer /əˈnadɪə(r)/

anaemia deficiency of red cells or of haemoglobin in the blood
uh-**nee**-mi-uh /əˈniːmiə/

anaesthesia insensitivity to pain
an-iss-**thee**-zi-uh /ˌanɪsˈθiːziə/

anaesthetic substance that induces insensitivity to pain
an-iss-**thet**-ik /ˌanɪsˈθɛtɪk/

anaesthetist one who administers anaesthetics
uh-**neess**-thuh-tist /əˈniːsθətɪst/

Anaglypta trademark type of wallpaper
an-uh-**glip**-tuh /ˌanəˈɡlɪptə/

Anah, al- town, Iraq
uhl **an**-uh /əl ˈanə/

Anaheim city, US
an-uh-hym /ˈanəhʌɪm/

analgesia inability to feel pain
an-uhl-**jee**-zi-uh /ˌanəlˈdʒiːziə/

analogue a person or thing seen as comparable to another
an-uh-log /ˈanəlɒɡ/

Anambra state, Nigeria
an-**am**-bruh /aˈnambrə/

ananda extreme happiness
ah-**nun**-duh /ɑːˈnʌndə/

Ananias biblical name
an-uh-**ny**-uhss /ˌanəˈnʌɪəs/

Anantnag province, Kashmir
uh-**nunt**-nuhg /əˈnʌntnəɡ/

anapaest metrical foot
an-uh-peest /ˈanəpiːst/

Commonly also **an**-uh-pest.

anaphora use of a word referring back to a word used earlier
uh-**naf**-uh-ruh /əˈnafərə/

anaphylaxis extreme allergic reaction
an-uh-fil-**ak**-siss /ˌanəfɪˈlaksɪs/

anaptyxis insertion of a vowel to aid pronunciation
an-uhp-**tik**-siss /ˌanəpˈtɪksɪs/

Anastacia American pop singer
an-uh-**stay**-zhuh /anəˈsteɪʒə/

Anastasia Russian princess
an-uh-**stah**-si-uh /anəˈstɑːsiə/

anastrozole breast cancer drug
uh-**nast**-ruh-zohl /əˈnastrəzəʊl/

Anatolia western peninsula of Asia
an-uh-**toh**-li-uh /ˌanəˈtəʊliə/

Anaxagoras Greek philosopher
an-ak-**sag**-uh-ruhss /ˌanakˈsaɡərəs/

Anaximander Greek scientist
an-ak-sim-**and**-uhr /aˌnaksɪˈmandə(r)/

Anaximenes Greek philosopher
an-ak-**sim**-uh-neez /ˌanakˈsɪməniːz/

Anbar, al- province, Iraq
uhl uhn-**bar** /əl ənˈbɑː(r)/

Anchises Greek mythological character

an-**ky**-seez /anˈkʌɪsiːz/

anchorite religious recluse
ank-uh-ryt /ˈaŋkərʌɪt/

anchovy small shoaling fish
an-chuh-vi /ˈantʃəvi/

The old-fashioned pronunciation an-**choh**-vi is rarely heard now.

ancillary providing support to the primary activities of an organization
an-**sil**-uh-ri /anˈsɪləri/

Ancona port, Italy
ank-**oh**-nuh /aŋˈkəʊnə/

Ancre river, France
ah(ng)-kruh /ˈɑ̃krə/

Andalusia region, Spain
an-duh-**loo**-si-uh /ˌandəˈluːsiə/

Established anglicization. The Spanish form is Andalucia, and is pronounced an-dal-oo-**see**-uh locally, and an-dal-oo-**thee**-uh in standard Spanish.

Andalusian relating to Andalusia
an-duh-**loo**-si-uhn /ˌandəˈluːsiən/

Andaman and Nicobar Islands groups of islands, Bay of Bengal
and-uh-muhn **nik**-uh-bar /ˈandəmən ˈnɪkəbɑː(r)/

andante musical term
an-**dan**-tay /anˈdanteɪ/

Andean relating to the Andes
an-**dee**-uhn /anˈdiːən/

Sometimes also **an**-di-uhn.

Andelfingen district, Switzerland
an-duhl-fing-uhn /ˈandəlˌfɪŋən/

Andersen, Hans Christian Danish author
hanz **krist**-yuhn an-**duhr**-suhn /ˌhanz ˌkrɪstjən ˈandə(r)sən/
• Established anglicization.

Andes mountain system, South America
and-eez /ˈandiːz/
• Established anglicization.

Andhra Pradesh state, India
ahn-druh pruh-**daysh** /ˌɑːndrə prəˈdeɪʃ/

Andijan city, Uzbekistan
uhn-dij-**ahn** /əndɪˈdʒɑːn/

andiron metal stand
an-dy-uhn /ˈandʌɪən/

Andorra autonomous principality between France and Spain
an-**dawr**-uh /anˈdɔːrə/

Commonly also an-**dorr**-uh.

andouille type of pork sausage
o(ng)-**dwee** /ŏ'dwiː/, French [ɑ̃'duj]

Andress, Ursula Swiss actress
ur-**syuul**-uh **and**-ress /ˌəː(r)sjʊlə 'andres/
• Established anglicization.

Andrić, Ivo Bosnian writer
ee-voh **and**-ritch /ˌiːvəʊ 'andrɪtʃ/

Androcles Roman fictional name
and-ruh-kleez /'andrəkliːz/

androgen male sex hormone
and-ruh-juhn /'andrədʒən/

Andromache Greek mythological character
an-**drom**-uh-ki /an'drɒməki/

Andromeda Greek mythological character
an-**drom**-uh-duh /an'drɒmədə/

Andropov, Yuri Soviet statesman
yoor-i an-**drop**-uhf /ˌjʊəri an'drɒpəf/

anechoic free from echo
an-ek-**oh**-ik /ˌanɛ'kəʊɪk/

anemometer instrument for measuring wind speed
an-uh-**mom**-it-uhr /ˌanə'mɒmɪtə(r)/

anemone plant
uh-**nem**-uh-ni /ə'nɛməni/

aneurysm swelling of the wall of an artery
an-yuu-riz-uhm /'anjʊrɪzəm/

Angelico, Fra Italian painter
frah an-**jel**-ik-oh /ˌfrɑː an'dʒɛlɪkəʊ/

Angelou, Maya American novelist and poet
my-uh an-**juh**-loo /ˌmʌɪə 'andʒəluː/

Angers town, France
ah(ng)-**zhay** /ɑ̃'ʒeɪ/

Angers, Avril English actress
av-reel ang-**guhrz** /ˌavriːl 'aŋgə(r)z/

Angevin dynasty of English kings
an-juh-vin /'andʒəvɪn/
• Established anglicization.

Angharad Welsh girl's name
ang-**harr**-ad /aŋ'harad/

angina medical condition
an-**jy**-nuh /an'dʒʌɪnə/

angioplasty surgical unblocking of a blood vessel
an-ji-oh-plast-i /'andʒiəʊˌplasti/

Angkor capital of the ancient kingdom of Khmer

ang-kor /'aŋkɔː(r)/

Anglesey island and county, Wales
ang-guhl-si /'aŋgəlsi/

Angola country
ang-**goh**-luh /aŋ'gəʊlə/

angora cat, goat, or rabbit of a long-haired breed
ang-**gawr**-uh /aŋ'gɔːrə/

Ångström, Anders Jonas Swedish physicist
an-**duhrsh** yoo-nuhss **ong**-stroem /ˌandə(r)ʃ ˌjuːnəs 'ɒŋstrøm/

angstrom unit of length
ang-struhm /'aŋstrəm/

Anguilla island, the Caribbean
ang-**gwil**-uh /aŋ'gwɪlə/

Anhui province, China
an-**khway** /ˌan'xweɪ/

animadversion criticism or censure
an-im-uhd-**vur**-shuhn /ˌanɪmədˈvəː(r)ʃən/

animatronics technique of making and operating lifelike robots
an-im-uh-**tron**-iks /ˌanɪmə'trɒnɪks/

animé Japanese animation
an-im-ay /'anɪmeɪ/

anion negatively charged ion
an-y-uhn /'anʌɪən/

anise Mediterranean plant
an-iss /'anɪs/

Anisoptera group of insects
an-y-**zop**-tuh-ruh /ˌanʌɪ'zɒptərə/

Anjou former province, France
ah(ng)-**zhoo** /ɑ̃'ʒuː/

Ankara capital of Turkey
ank-uh-ruh /'aŋkərə/

ankh cross-like design
ank /aŋk/

ankylosaur herbivorous dinosaur
ank-il-uh-sor /'aŋkɪləsɔː(r)/

ankylosis stiffening of a joint
ank-il-**oh**-siss /ˌaŋkɪ'ləʊsɪs/

Annaba port, Algeria
an-uh-buh /'anəbə/

Anna Karenina novel by Tolstoy
an-uh kuh-**ren**-in-uh /ˌanə kə'rɛnɪnə/
• Established anglicization.

Annan, Kofi Ghanaian Secretary General of the United Nations
koh-fi **an**-an /ˌkəʊfi 'anan/

Annapolis city, US
uh-**nap**-uh-liss /ə'napəlɪs/

Anglicization

When the Pronunciation Unit advises on the pronunciation of foreign names, words, and phrases, we make recommendations which are as close as possible to the original language. However, we do not expect a perfect reproduction of all non-English sounds. This would be confusing and disruptive for audiences and would also be quite a challenge for broadcasters! Therefore, our recommendations include anglicizations which make speaking and understanding easier. Some simplification is also necessary to give written advice for pronunciations using a respelling system. Our respelling system includes English sounds and also some other consonant and vowel sounds, for instance the Welsh hl as in *llan* and the French oe as in *coeur*.

Established anglicization of names

Many names of foreign countries, rivers, and cities have established anglicizations: that is, standard ways in which they are pronounced or spelled when they are referred to in English. These established anglicizations are those listed in gazetteers, atlases, and dictionaries. Examples include **parr**-iss (not parr-**ee**) for *Paris* and tib-**lee**-si for *Tbilisi*. Examples of established anglicized spellings (for which the pronunciations also differ, of course) include *Turin* for *Torino*, *Munich* for *München*, and *Lyons* for *Lyon*. Where these names appear in this book the native version and an approximate pronunciation is given in a usage note. It is important to note that established anglicizations are not invariably used in an English-language context: for example, the football team of the city *Basle* is called *FC Basel*.

The Pronunciation Unit's recommendations take all these established anglicizations into account. Anglicizations for major place names are usually uncontroversial, but can change over time (e.g. *Marseilles*, *Niger*, *Majorca*). Official spellings or transliterations of names can also change (e.g. *Kolkata*, *Beijing*), which can lead to further changes in established anglicized pronunciations. Less commonly, anglicization can apply to people's names as well as place names (e.g. *Michael Schumacher*); this is particularly common with high-profile people in the areas of international sport, showbusiness, and politics. We research the level of anglicization which a particular person prefers for their name before making recommendations.

Established anglicization of words and phrases

Words and phrases in languages other than English often appear in an English-language context. Topics such as music, science, literature, food and drink, dance, and sport provide many examples. When these words are treated as foreign the Pronunciation Unit makes recommendations which are as close as possible to the original language, subject to the usual simplifications. However, when these words and phrases are taken into English they are generally pronounced using only English sounds, and in such cases a more anglicized recommendation is more appropriate. For example, the French phrase *trompe l'œil* is usually pronounced tromp **loy** in English, rather than tro(ng)p **loey**. As with place names, these anglicizations too can change over time. The title of the Spanish novel *Don Quixote* used to be anglicized to don **kwik**-sot, but this is now rather dated, and don kee-**hoh**-ti is the anglicization we now recommend. Words borrowed from other languages are often initially given foreign pronunciations, and then anglicizations become established: *sudoku* is an excellent example of this.

Annapurna mountain, Nepal
an-uh-**poor**-nuh /ˌanəˈpʊə(r)nə/

Sometimes anglicized to an-uh-**pur**-nuh.

annatto orange-red dye
uh-**nat**-oh /əˈnatəʊ/

anneal heat and then cool slowly
uh-**neel** /əˈniːl/

Annecy town, France
an-**see** /anˈsiː/

Annigoni, Pietro Italian painter
pyet-roh an-ig-**oh**-ni /ˌpjɛtrəʊ anɪˈɡəʊni/

annihilate destroy utterly
uh-**ny**-il-ayt /əˈnʌɪɪleɪt/

Annobón island, Equatorial Guinea
an-uh-**bon** /anəˈbɒn/

Anno Domini 'in the year of the Lord'
(Latin)
an-oh **dom**-in-y /ˌanəʊ ˈdɒmɪnʌɪ/

annus horribilis 'disastrous year'
(Latin)
an-uhss horr-**ee**-bil-iss /ˌanəs hɒˈriːbɪlɪs/

annus mirabilis 'auspicious year'
(Latin)
an-uhss mirr-**rah**-bil-iss /ˌanəs mɪˈrɑːbɪlɪs/

anode positively charged electrode
an-ohd /ˈanəʊd/

anodyne not likely to cause offence
an-uh-dyn /ˈanədʌɪn/

anomaly deviates from what is standard
uh-**nom**-uh-li /əˈnɒməli/

anopheles mosquito
uh-**nof**-il-eez /əˈnɒfɪliːz/

anorexia nervosa pathological
slimming compulsion
an-uh-**rek**-si-uh nur-**voh**-suh
/ˌanəˌrɛksɪə nəˈ(r)ˈvəʊsə/

Anouilh, Jean French dramatist
zhah(ng) an-**wee** /ˌʒɑ̃ anˈwiː/, [anuj]

ANOVA statistical analysis of variance
an-**oh**-vuh /aˈnəʊvə/

Ansar al-Islam Iraqi militant group
un-**sar** uhl iss-**lahm** /ʌnˈsɑː(r) əl ɪsˈlɑːm/

Anschluss annexation of Austria by
Germany in 1938
an-**shluuss** /ˈanʃlʊs/

Anselm, St Italian-born philosopher
and theologian
an-selm /ˈansɛlm/

Anshan city, China
an-**shan** /ˌanˈʃan/

Antabuse trademark for disulfiram
ant-uh-byooss /ˈantəbjuːs/

antacid preventing acidity
an-**tass**-id /anˈtasɪd/

Antaeus Greek mythological character
an-**tee**-uhss /anˈtiːəs/

Antalya port, Turkey
an-**tal**-yuh /anˈtaljə/

Antananarivo capital of Madagascar
un-**tun**-uh-nuh-**ree**-voo
/ʌnˌtʌnənəˈriːvuː/

Antares star
an-**tar**-eez /anˈtɑːriːz/

antebellum occurring before a war
an-ti-**bel**-uhm /ˌantiˈbɛləm/

antecedent thing that precedes another
an-**tiss**-ee-duhnt /ˌantɪˈsiːdənt/

antepenult the last syllable but two
in a word
an-tip-uh-**nult** /ˌantɪpəˈnʌlt/

Anthemius Greek mathematician
an-**thee**-mi-uhss /anˈθiːmiəs/

anthracite coal of a hard variety
an-thruh-syt /ˈanθrəsʌɪt/

anthrax serious bacterial disease
an-thraks /ˈanθraks/

Antibes port and resort, France
ah(ng)-**teeb** /ãˈtiːb/

anticipatory happening in anticipation
of something
an-**tiss**-ip-uh-tuh-ri /anˈtɪsɪpəˌtəri/

Antigone Greek mythological character
an-**tig**-uh-ni /anˈtɪɡəni/

Antigua town, Guatemala
an-**teeg**-wuh /anˈtiːɡwə/

Antigua and Barbuda island state,
Leeward Islands
an-**tee**-guh /anˈtiːɡə/

Antilles group of islands, West Indies
an-**til**-eez /anˈtɪliːz/

antimacassar piece of cloth put over the
back of a chair
an-ti-muh-**kass**-uhr /ˌantiməˈkasə(r)/

antimony chemical element
an-tim-uh-ni /ˈantɪməni/

Antioch city, Turkey
ant-i-ok /ˈantɪɒk/

antipathy feeling of aversion
an-**tip**-uh-thi /anˈtɪpəθi/

antiphon short sentence sung before or
after a psalm
an-tif-uhn /ˈantɪfən/

Antipodes Australia and New Zealand
an-**tip**-uh-deez /anˈtɪpədiːz/

Antisthenes Greek philosopher and
teacher
an-**tiss**-thuh-neez /anˈtɪsθəniːz/

antithesis pl. **antitheses** opposite
an-**tith**-uh-siss, pl. an-**tith**-uh-seez
/anˈtɪθəsɪs/, pl. -siːz/

Antlia constellation
an-tli-uh /ˈantliə/

Antofagasta port, Chile
ant-of-ag-**ast**-uh /ˌantɒfaˈɡastə/

Antoninus Pius Roman emperor
an-tuh-**ny**-nuhss **py**-uhss /ˌantəˌnʌɪnəs
ˈpʌɪəs/

Antonioni, Michelangelo Italian film
director
meek-uh-**lan**-juh-loh an-toh-ni-**oh**-ni
/miːkəˌlandʒələʊ antəʊniˈəʊni/

Antwerp port, Belgium
ant-wurp /ˈantwə(r)p/

> Established anglicization. The Flemish
> name is Antwerpen, pronounced
> **unt**-wairp-uhn, and the French form is
> Anvers, pronounced ah(ng)-**vair**.

Anubis Egyptian god of the dead
uh-**nyoo**-biss /əˈnjuːbɪs/

Anuradhapura city and district,
Sri Lanka
an-uu-rahd-uh-**poor**-uh
/ˌanuˈrɑːdəˈpʊərə/

Anvers see **Antwerp**

Anwar, Mina English actress
mee-nuh an-war /ˌmiːnə ˈanwɑː(r)/

Anzoátegui state, Venezuela
an-**swat**-eg-ee /ansˈwatɛɡi:/

ao dai Vietnamese long-sleeved tunic
ow dy /ˈaʊ ˌdʌɪ/

Aoraki official name for Mount Cook,
New Zealand
ow-**rak**-i /aʊˈraki/

aorta main artery of the body
ay-**or**-tuh /eɪˈɔː(r)tə/

Aosta city, Italy
ah-**ost**-uh /ɑːˈɒstə/

Aotearoa Maori name for New Zealand
ow-tay-uh-**roh**-uh /aʊˌteɪəˈrəʊə/

Aozou Strip disputed desert land, Chad
ow-**zoo** /aʊˈzuː/

Apache American Indian ethnic group
uh-**patch**-i /əˈpatʃi/

apartheid South African policy of
segregation
uh-**part**-hayt /əˈpɑː(r)theɪt/

> This is the Afrikaans pronunciation, and the
> one most common in English. Less common
> is uh-**part**-hyd.

apatosaurus herbivorous dinosaur
uh-pat-uh-**sawr**-uhss /əˌpatəˈsɔːrəs/

APEC Asia-Pacific Economic
Co-operation
ay-pek /ˈeɪpɛk/

Apeldoorn town, Netherlands
ap-uhl-dorn /'apəldɔː(r)n/

Apelles Greek painter
uh-**pel**-eez /əˈpɛliːz/

Apennines mountain range, Italy
ap-uh-nynz /'apənʌɪnz/

Established anglicization. The Italian name
is Appennino, pronounced ap-en-**ee**-noh.

aperitif alcoholic drink taken before
a meal
uh-perr-it-**eef** /əˌpɛrɪˈtiːf/

aphasia impaired speech after brain
damage
uh-**fay**-zi-uh /əˈfeɪzɪə/

aphelion pl. **aphelia** point furthest from
the sun
ap-**hee**-li-uhn, pl. ap-**hee**-li-uh
/apˈhiːliən/, pl. /-liə/

aphorism pithy observation
af-uh-riz-uhm /'afərɪzəm/

aphrodisiac substance that stimulates
sexual desire
af-ruh-**diz**-i-ak /ˌafrəˈdɪziak/

Aphrodisias ancient city of Asia Minor
af-ruh-**diss**-i-uhss /ˌafrəˈdɪsiəs/

Aphrodite Greek goddess
af-ruh-**dy**-ti /ˌafrəˈdʌɪti/

Api mountain, Nepal
ah-pi /'ɑːpi/

Apia capital of Samoa
ah-**pee**-uh /ɑːˈpiːə/

apiary place where bees are kept
ay-pi-uh-ri /'eɪpɪəri/

apical relating to an apex
ap-ik-uhl /'apɪkəl/

Sometimes also **ay**-pik-uhl.

Apis Egyptian mythological god
ah-piss /'ɑːpɪs/

apnoea temporary cessation of breathing
ap-**nee**-uh /apˈniːə/

Sometimes also **ap**-ni-uh.

apocalypse destruction on a
catastrophic scale
uh-**pok**-uh-lips /əˈpɒkəlɪps/

apocope omission of the final sound
of a word
uh-**pok**-uh-pi /əˈpɒkəpi/

apocrine relating to a type of skin cell
ap-uh-kryn /'apəkrʌɪn/

Apocrypha biblical writings not forming

part of the accepted canon of Scripture
uh-**pok**-rif-uh /əˈpɒkrɪfə/

apogee highest point
ap-uh-jee /'apədʒiː/

Apollinaire, Guillaume French poet
gee-**yohm** ap-ol-ee-**nair** /ɡiːˌjəʊm
apɒliːˈnɛː(r)/

Apollinaris bishop of Laodicea in Asia
Minor
uh-pol-in-**air**-iss /əˌpɒlɪˈnɛːrɪs/

Apollonius Greek mathematician
ap-uh-**loh**-ni-uhss /ˌapəˈləʊniəs/

Apollyon name for the Devil
uh-**pol**-yuhn /əˈpɒljən/

apophthegm concise saying or maxim
ap-uh-them /'apəθɛm/

apoplectic overcome with anger
ap-uh-**plek**-tik /ˌapəˈplɛktɪk/

apostasy abandonment of a religious or
political belief
uh-**post**-uh-si /əˈpɒstəsi/

apostolic relating to the Apostles
ap-uh-**stol**-ik /ˌapəˈstɒlɪk/

apostrophe punctuation mark
uh-**post**-ruh-fi /əˈpɒstrəfi/

apothecary person who prepared and
sold medicines
uh-**poth**-uh-kuh-ri /əˈpɒθəkəri/

apotheosis highest point
uh-poth-i-**oh**-siss /əˌpɒθiˈəʊsɪs/

Appalachian Mountains mountain
system, North America
ap-uh-**lay**-chuhn /ˌapəˈleɪtʃən/

Appaloosa North American breed
of horse
ap-uh-**loo**-suh /ˌapəˈluːsə/

appellant person who appeals to a
higher court
uh-**pel**-uhnt /əˈpɛlənt/

appellation name or title
ap-uh-**lay**-shuhn /ˌapəˈleɪʃən/

appendectomy removal of the appendix
ap-en-**dek**-tuh-mi /ˌapənˈdɛktəmi/

Appenzell canton, Switzerland
ap-uhn-tsel /'apəntsɛl/

Appian Way road southward from
Rome
ap-i-uhn /'apiən/

appliqué ornamental needlework
uh-**plee**-kay /əˈpliːkeɪ/

appoggiatura musical term
uh-poj-uh-**tyoor**-uh /əˌpɒdʒəˈtjʊərə/

apricot fruit
ay-prik-oht /ˈeɪprɪkɒt/

Sometimes also **ap**-rik-ot.

a priori knowledge which comes from
theoretical deduction
ay pry-**aw**-ry /ˌeɪ prʌɪˈɔːrʌɪ/

Also ah pri-**aw**-ri.

apropos with reference to
a-pruh-**poh** /ˌaprəˈpəʊ/

Apuleius Roman writer
ap-yuul-**ee**-uhss /ˌapjʊˈliːəs/

Apulia region, Italy
uh-**pyoo**-li-uh /əˈpjuːliə/

Established anglicization. The Italian name
is Puglia, pronounced **pool**-yuh [ˈpuʎʎa].

Apurimac region, Peru
ap-oo-**ree**-mak /apuˈriːmak/

Apus constellation
ay-puhss /ˈeɪpəs/

Aqaba port, Jordan
ak-uh-buh /ˈakəbə/

Aqsa, al- Palestinian militant group
uhl **uk**-suh /əl ˈʌksə/

Aquae Sulis Roman name for Bath
ak-wy **soo**-liss /ˌakwʌɪ ˈsuːlɪs/

aquamanile water container
ak-wuh-muh-**ny**-li /ˌakwəməˈnʌɪli/

Aquarius constellation
uh-**kwair**-i-uhss /əˈkwɛːriəs/

aquatic relating to water
uh-**kwat**-ik /əˈkwatɪk/

Less commonly also uh-**kwot**-ik.

aquavit Scandinavian spirit
ak-wuh-**veet** /akwəˈviːt/

aqua vitae spirit
ak-wuh **vy**-tee /ˌakwə ˈvʌɪtiː/

Sometimes also **vee**-ty; see **Latin** panel.

aqueous of or containing water
ay-kwi-uhss /ˈeɪkwiəs/

Aquila constellation
ak-wil-uh /ˈakwɪlə/

Aquila city, Italy
ak-wee-luh /ˈakwiːlə/

Aquinas, St Thomas Italian
philosopher
uh-**kwyn**-uhss /əˈkwʌɪnəs/

Aquitaine region and former province,
France
ak-wi-**tayn** /ˌakwɪˈteɪn/, [akitɛn]

• Established anglicization.

Ara constellation
ar-uh /ˈɑːrə/

Arabiyah, al- Arabic TV station
uhl arr-ab-**ee**-yuh /əl araˈbiːjə/

Aracajú port, Brazil
arr-uh-kuh-**zhoo** /ˌarəkəˈʒuː/

Arachne Greek mythological character
uh-**rak**-ni /əˈrakni/

arachnophobia fear of spiders
uh-rak-nuh-**foh**-bi-uh /əˌraknəˈfəʊbiə/

Arafat, Mount Mountain, Saudi Arabia
arr-uh-fat /ˈarəfat/, Arabic [ʔaraˈfæːt]
• Established anglicization.

Arafat, Yasser Palestinian statesman
yah-sirr **arr**-uh-fat /ˌjɑːsɪr ˈarəfat/,
Arabic [ˌjæːsɪr ʔaraˈfæːt]
• Established anglicization.

Arafura Sea sea between Australia,
Indonesia, and New Guinea
arr-uh-**foor**-uh /ˌarəˈfʊərə/

Aragon autonomous region, Spain
arr-uh-guhn /ˈarəgən/

Aragorn character from *The Lord
of the Rings*
arr-uh-gorn /ˈarəgɔː(r)n/

Aral Sea inland sea, central Asia
arr-uhl /ˈarəl/

Aramaic ancient Semitic language
arr-uh-**may**-ik /ˌarəˈmeɪk/

Aramis character in *The Three
Musketeers*
arr-uh-miss /ˈarəmɪs/

Aranyaka Hindu sacred treatise
arr-uhn-**yak**-uh /ˌarəˈnjakə/

Arapaho North American Indian people
uh-**rap**-uh-hoh /əˈrapəhəʊ/

Ararat, Mount volcanic peaks, Turkey
arr-uh-rat /ˈarərat/

araucaria tree
arr-aw-**kair**-i-uh /ˌarɔːˈkɛːriə/

Arawak South American ethnic group
arr-uh-wak /ˈarəwak/

Arbil see **Erbil**

arbitrage simultaneous buying and
selling in different markets
ar-bit-**rahzh** /ˈɑː(r)bɪtrɑːʒ/

Sometimes also **ar**-bit-rij.

arbitrary random
ar-bit-ruh-ri /ˈɑː(r)bɪtrəri/

Arabic

Arabic belongs to the Semitic family of languages. With over 150 million native speakers, it is one of the world's major languages. There are two main forms of Arabic, literary Arabic and colloquial Arabic. Literary Arabic is the standard form: it is the language of the Koran, and is used in the media. Colloquial Arabic comprises the various spoken dialects in everyday usage.

Giving recommendations for Arabic pronunciation is complicated by the fact that there is so much variation between different forms of Arabic. Also, our advice is based on spellings transliterated into the Roman alphabet, but the transliterations used can be inconsistent and arbitrary. The Arabic given here is, as always, somewhat anglicized in line with BBC policy and the constraints of phonetic respelling.

Vowels

Literary Arabic has three vowels, which can be either long or short, although the quality of these vowels, particularly A, can be realized in many different ways.

A is generally pronounced a when short and ah when long. *Mohammed* is moh-**ham**-uhd, and *Talabani* is tah-luh-**bah**-ni.

Short A is sometimes closer to u, next to certain consonants. *Qadri* is **kud**-ri.

Long A is sometimes closer to air, but when no R is present in the orthography, we render this sound as ah. This retains the length (which determines stress), but compromises the quality.

I is pronounced i when short and ee when long.

U is pronounced uu when short and oo when long.

Colloquial Arabic also allows for E and O.

E is pronounced e when short and close to ay when long.

O is pronounced o when short, and close to oh or aw when long.

Some of these vowel qualities are commonly reduced to schwa (uh) in anglicized Arabic.

Arabic has two diphthongs. Variously transliterated as AI, AY, EI, or EI, the first of these is commonly pronounced y in literary Arabic, and ay in colloquial Arabic. This why it is so common to hear names like *Mohamed ElBaradei* pronounced both **barr**-uh-dy and **barr**-uh-day. The other diphthong is transliterated AU or AW, and is pronounced ow in literary Arabic, and oh in colloquial Arabic.

Consonants

The Arabic alphabet contains all the consonant sounds of English apart from g, p, and v. There are also many sounds which do not occur in English, some of which are difficult to represent in the respelling.

All instances of kh refers to the sound in Scottish *loch*, never to that of German *ich*.

B, D, F, K, L, M, N, T, and Z are pronounced as in English in anglicized Arabic.

DH is pronounced *th* as in *there*.

GH is pronounced as kh, but with added voicing (i.e. pronounced with vibration of the vocal chords. IPA is [ɣ]). This sound is always anglicized to g.

H is pronounced as h, but can appear in any position in Arabic. We try to reflect this in names such as *Ahmed*, although due to the restrictions of the respellings we represent this sound as kh in this dictionary. This is not ideal, but is better than leaving it out altogether.

J and DJ are pronounced j. In North African dialects, where there is influence from French, J is often pronounced zh.

KH is pronounced kh.

Q is pronounced as k, but further back in the mouth (IPA is [q]). This sound is always anglicized to k.

SH is pronounced sh, but beware of syllable breaks between S and H. *Isham* is iss-**hahm**.

TH is pronounced th.

' is a voiced pharyngeal fricative (IPA is [ʕ]). This is not always transcribed, and is sometimes expressed as an A in the spelling instead, for example *Ba'th* or *Baath*. This is not a sound we can retain in anglicized pronunciations.

The L in the article *al/el* is silent before the so-called sun letters, i.e. the sounds t, th, d, *th*, z, s, sh, l, n, and zh. *Al-Zarqawi* is uh-zuhr-**kah**-wi.

In a native pronunciation the initial consonant of the following word is doubled to compensate (see more about long Arabic consonants below).

This phenomenon is sometimes reflected in the transliteration, and so the Iraqi city *Najaf* may be spelt *an-Najaf* as well as *al-Najaf.*

Stress

Stress is determined by syllable length and structure, but as a general guide stress is placed on the last syllable containing a long vowel or on the vowel immediately preceding a doubled consonant. As with Italian, the double consonant is not a feature we can retain.

Faruq is farr-**ook** and *Muammar* is moo-**um**-uhr.

If all vowels and consonants are short, and the word has more than two syllables, stress falls on the antepenultimate syllable. *Hanafi* is **han**-af-i.

Arbois city, France
ar-**bwah** /ɑ:(r)ˈbwɑ:/

arboreal living in trees
ar-**baw**-ri-uhl /ɑ:(r)ˈbɔ:riəl/

Arbuthnot, John Scottish physician and writer
ar-**buth**-nuht /ɑ:(r)ˈbʌθnət/

Arcadia mountainous district, Greece
ar-**kay**-di-uh /ɑ:(r)ˈkeɪdiə/
• Established anglicization.

Arcady ideal rustic paradise
ar-kuh-di /ˈɑ:(r)kədi/

arcana secrets or mysteries
ar-**kay**-nuh /ɑ:(r)ˈkeɪnə/

Arc de Triomphe ceremonial arch in Paris
ark duh tree-**o(ng)f** /ˌɑ:(r)k də tri:ˈɔ̃f/

Archaean geological term
ar-**kee**-uhn /ɑ:(r)ˈki:ən/

archaeopteryx prehistoric bird
ar-ki-**op**-tuh-riks /ˌɑ:(r)kiˈɒptərɪks/

archaic old or old-fashioned
ar-**kay**-ik /ɑ:(r)ˈkeɪk/

Archangel port, Russia
ark-ayn-juhl /ˈɑ:(r)keɪndʒəl/

Established anglicization. The Russian name is Arkhangelsk, pronounced ar-**khan**-guhlsk [arˈxanɡʲlʲsk].

archangel angel of greater than ordinary rank
ark-ayn-juhl /ˈɑ:(r)keɪndʒəl/

Sometimes also ark-**ayn**-juhl.

Archilochus Greek poet
ar-**kil**-uh-kuhss /ɑ:(r)ˈkɪləkəs/

Archimedes Greek mathematician
ar-kim-**ee**-deez /ˌɑ:(r)kɪˈmi:di:z/

archipelago group of islands
ar-kip-**el**-uh-goh /ˌɑ:(r)kɪˈpɛləɡəʊ/

archivist person who maintains archives
ar-kiv-ist /ˈɑ:(r)kɪvɪst/

archosaur reptile
ar-kuh-sor /ˈɑ:(r)kəsɔ:(r)/

ARCIC Anglican Roman Catholic International Commission
ar-kik /ˈɑ:(r)kɪk/

Arctogaea zoogeographical area
ark-tuh-**jee**-uh /ˌɑ:(r)ktəˈdʒi:ə/

Arcturus star
ark-**tyoor**-uhss /ɑ:(r)kˈtjʊərəs/

Ardea village, Italy

ar-day-uh /ˈɑ:(r)deɪə/

Ardèche river and department, France
ar-**desh** /ɑ:(r)ˈdɛʃ/

Ardennes forested region in Belgium, France, and Luxembourg
ar-**den** /ɑ:(r)ˈdɛn/

Ard Fheis an Irish party political conference
ard esh /ɑ:(r)d ˈɛʃ/

Ardizzone, Edward British artist
ar-diz-**oh**-ni /ˌɑ:(r)dɪˈzəʊni/

Ardnamurchan peninsula, Scotland
ard-nuh-**murkh**-uhn /ˌɑ:(r)dnəˈmə:(r)xən/

are unit of measurement
ar /ɑ:(r)/

Arenal, Mount volcano, Spain
arr-en-**al** /arɛˈnal/

Arendt, Hannah German-born American philosopher
ar-uhnt /ˈɑ:rənt/

areola pl. **areolae** small circular area
uh-**ree**-uh-luh, pl. uh-**ree**-uh-lee /əˈri:ələ/, pl. /-li:/

Areopagitica poem by Milton
arr-i-op-uh-**jit**-ik-uh /ˌarɪɒpəˈdʒɪtɪkə/

Commonly also arr-i-op-uh-**git**-ik-uh.

Arequipa city, Peru
arr-ek-**ee**-puh /ˌarɛˈki:pə/

Ares Greek god
air-eez /ˈɛ:ri:z/

arête sharp mountain ridge
uh-**ret** /əˈrɛt/

Arezzo city and football club, Italy
uh-**ret**-soh /əˈrɛtsəʊ/

Argelès-Gazost resort, France
ar-zhuh-**less** gaz-**ost** /ɑ:(r)ʒəˌlɛs gaˈzɒst/

argent silver
ar-juhnt /ˈɑ:(r)dʒənt/

Argenta town, Italy
ar-**jent**-uh /ɑ:(r)ˈdʒɛntə/

Argentière village, France
ar-zhah(ng)-**tyair** /ɑ:(r)ʒɑ̃ˈtjɛ:(r)/

Argentina country
ar-juhn-**tee**-nuh /ˌɑ:(r)dʒənˈti:nə/, Spanish [arxenˈtina]
• Established anglicization.

Argentine relating to Argentina
ar-juhn-tyn /ˈɑ:(r)dʒəntʌɪn/

Argentinian relating to Argentina
ar-juhn-tin-i-uhn /ˌɑː(r)dʒənˈtɪniən/

Argeş river, Romania
ar-jesh /ˈɑː(r)dʒeʃ/

Argo constellation
ar-goh /ˈɑː(r)ɡəʊ/

argon chemical element
ar-gon /ˈɑː(r)ɡɒn/

Argonauts Greek mythological
characters
ar-guh-nawts /ˈɑː(r)ɡənɔːts/

Argos city, Greece
ar-goss /ˈɑː(r)ɡɒs/

argosy large merchant ship
ar-guh-si /ˈɑː(r)ɡəsi/

argot jargon of a particular group
ar-goh /ˈɑː(r)ɡəʊ/

Argyll and Bute council area, Scotland
ar-gyl byoot /ɑː(r)ˈɡʌɪl ˈbjuːt/

Århus (also **Aarhus**) city, Denmark
or-hooss /ˈɔː(r)huːs/

Ariadne Greek mythological character
arr-i-ad-ni /ˌari'adni/

Arica city, Chile
arr-ee-kuh /a'riːkə/

Ariège river and department, France
arr-i-ezh /ari'ɛʒ/

Ariel moon of Uranus
air-i-uhl /ˈɛːriəl/

Aries constellation
air-eez /ˈɛːriːz/

Arimidex trademark drug
uh-rim-id-eks /ə'rɪmɪdɛks/

arioso musical term
arr-i-oh-zoh /ˌarɪ'əʊzəʊ/

Ariosto, Ludovico Italian poet
lood-uh-veek-oh arr-i-ost-oh
/luːdə,viːkəʊ ari'ɒstəʊ/

Aristarchus Greek scholar
arr-ist-ar-kuhss /ˌarɪ'stɑː(r)kəs/

Aristide, Jean-Bertrand Haitian
statesman
zhah(ng) bair-trah(ng) arr-ist-eed
/ʒɑ̃ bɛː(r),trɑ̃ arɪs'tiːd/

Aristides Greek statesman and general
arr-ist-y-deez /ˌarɪ'stʌɪdiːz/

Aristippus Greek philosopher
arr-ist-ip-uhss /ˌarɪ'stɪpəs/

Aristophanes Greek comic dramatist
arr-ist-of-uh-neez /ˌarɪ'stɒfəniːz/

Aristotelian relating to Aristotle
arr-ist-uh-tee-li-uhn /ˌarɪstə'tiːliən/

Aristotle Greek philosopher and
scientist
arr-ist-ot-uhl /ˈarɪstɒtəl/

arithmetic branch of mathematics
uh-rith-muh-tik /ə'rɪθmətɪk/

arithmetic relating to arithmetic
arr-ith-met-ik /ˌarɪθ'mɛtɪk/

Arkansas city and state, US
ark-uhn-saw /ˈɑː(r)kənsɔː/

The river Arkansas in Kansas, however, is
ar-**kan**-zuhss.

Arkhangelsk see **Archangel**

Arlanda airport, Sweden
ar-lan-duh /ˈɑː(r)landə/

Arles city, France
arl /ɑː(r)l/

Arlon town, Belgium
ar-lo(ng) /ɑː(r)'lõ/

armadillo insectivorous mammal
ar-muh-dil-oh /ˌɑː(r)mə'dɪləʊ/

Armageddon last battle before the Day
of Judgement
ar-muh-ged-uhn /ˌɑː(r)mə'ɡɛdən/

Armagh county, Northern Ireland
ar-mah /ɑː(r)'mɑː/

Armagnac French brandy
ar-muhn-yak /ˈɑː(r)mənjak/

Armani, Giorgio Italian fashion
designer
jor-joh ar-mah-ni /ˈdʒɔː(r)dʒəʊ
ɑː(r)'mɑːni/

Armenia country
ar-mee-ni-uh /ɑː(r)'miːniə/
• Established anglicization.

Armenian, Raffi Canadian composer
and conductor
raf-i ar-mee-ni-uhn /ˈrafi
ɑː(r)'miːniən/

armistice agreement to stop fighting
ar-mist-iss /ˈɑː(r)mɪstɪs/

Armitage, Richard American
politician
ar-mit-ij /ˈɑː(r)mɪtɪdʒ/

armoire cupboard or wardrobe
ar-mwar /ɑː(r)'mwɑː(r)/

Armstrong, Louis American jazz
musician
loo-iss /ˈluːɪs/

This was his preferred pronunciation,
despite the popular pronunciation of his
name as **loo-i**.

Arne, Thomas English composer
arn /ɑː(r)n/

Arnhem town, Netherlands
ar-**nuhm** /'ɑː(r)nəm/

Arno river, Italy
ar-**noh** /'ɑː(r)nəʊ/

arpeggio musical term
ar-**pej**-oh /ɑː(r)'pedʒəʊ/

Arquette family name of American
actors Patricia, Rosanna, and David
ar-**ket** /ɑː(r)'kɛt/

Arras town, France
arr-uhss /'arəs/, [aras]
• Established anglicization.

Arrhenius, Svante Swedish chemist
svan-tuh arr-**ay**-ni-uuss /'svantə
a'reniʊs/

arrhythmia irregular heartbeat
uh-**rith**-mi-uh /ə'rɪðmiə/

arrivederci 'goodbye' (Italian)
arr-iv-ed-**air**-chi /arɪveˈdɛ:(r)tʃi/

arriviste ambitious or self-seeking
person
arr-i-**veest** /ˌari'viːst/

arrondissement subdivision of a
French department
arr-on-**deess**-mo(ng) /ˌarɒn'diːsmɒ̃/,
[arɔ̃dismɑ̃]
• Established anglicization.

Arroyo, Gloria Macapagal-
Philippine president
glaw-ri-uh mak-uh-puh-**gal**
arr-**oy**-oh /ˌglɔ:riə makəpəˌgal a'rɔɪəʊ/

arsenic chemical element
ar-suh-nik /'ɑː(r)sənɪk/

Artaud, Antonin French actor
ah(ng)-toh-**na(ng)** ar-**toh** /ãtəʊ'nɛ̃
ɑ:(r)'təʊ/

Artaxerxes king of ancient Persia
ar-tuh-**zurk**-seez /ˌɑ:(r)tə'zə:(r)ksi:z/

art deco decorative art style
art **dek**-oh /ˌɑ:(r)t 'dɛkəʊ/

Artemis Greek goddess
art-im-iss /'ɑ:(r)tɪmɪs/

Arte Povera Italian artistic movement
ar-tay **pov**-uh-ruh /ˌɑ:(r)teɪ 'pɒvərə/

arthritis painful inflammation of the
joints
arth-**ry**-tiss /ɑ:(r)'θrʌɪtɪs/

Arthropoda phylum of invertebrate
animals
ar-thruh-**poh**-duh /ˌɑ:(r)θrə'pəʊdə/

articulatory relating to the formation of
speech sounds
ar-**tik**-yuul-uh-tuh-ri /ɑ:(r)'tɪkjʊlətəri/

Sometimes also ar-tik-yoo-**lay**-tuh-ri.

artifice clever devices or expedients
ar-tif-iss /'ɑ:(r)tɪfɪs/

artisan worker in a skilled trade
ar-**tiz-an** /ˌɑ:(r)tɪ'zan/

Sometimes also **ar**-tiz-an.

art nouveau style of decorative art and
design
art noo-**voh** /ˌɑ:(r)t nuː'vəʊ/

Artois region and former province,
France
ar-**twah** /ɑ:(r)'twɑ:/

Aruba island, Caribbean
uh-**roo**-buh /ə'ruːbə/

arugula rocket plant
uh-**roo**-guh-luh /ə'ruːgələ/

Arunachal Pradesh state, India
arr-oo-**nah**-chuhl pruh-**daysh**
/aruːˌnɑːtʃəl prə'deɪʃ/

Arundel town, England
arr-uhn-duhl /'arəndəl/

Arwen character from *The Lord
of the Rings*
ar-wen /'ɑ:(r)wɛn/

Aryabhata Indian astronomer
ar-yuh-**bah**-tuh /ˌɑ:(r)jə'bɑːtə/

Aryan ethnic group
air-i-uhn /'ɛːriən/

arytenoid cartilage at the back of
the larynx
arr-it-**ee**-noyd /arɪ'tiːnɔɪd/

as ancient Roman coin
ass /as/

asana yoga posture
ah-suh-nuh /'ɑːsənə/

Asansol city, India
ass-uhn-**sohl** /ˌasən'səʊl/

Asante see **Ashanti**

ASBO Anti-Social Behaviour Order
az-boh /'azbəʊ/

ascetic characterized by self-discipline
uh-**set**-ik /ə'sɛtɪk/

Ascham, Roger English scholar and
writer
ask-uhm /'askəm/

ASCII American Standard Code for
Information Interchange
ask-i /'aski/

Asclepius Greek mythological character
uh-**sklee**-pi-uhss /əˈskliːpiəs/

Ascot town, England
ask-uht /ˈaskət/

ASEAN Association of South-East Asian
Nations
ass-i-an /ˈasian/

Asgard world in Scandinavian mythology
ass-gard /ˈasɡɑː(r)d/

Ashanti (also **Asante**) region, Ghana
uh-**shan**-ti /əˈʃanti/

Ashdod seaport, Israel
ash-**dod** /aʃˈdɒd/

Asher Hebrew patriarch
ash-uhr /ˈaʃə(r)/

Ashgabat (also **Ashkhabad**) capital of
Turkmenistan
ash-khuh-**bat** /aʃxəˈbat/

Ashkenazi Jew of central or eastern
European descent
ash-kuh-**nah**-zi /ˌaʃkəˈnɑːzi/

Ashkenazy, Vladimir Russian-born
pianist
vluh-**dee**-meer ash-kuh-**nah**-zi
/vləˌdiːmɪə(r) ˌaʃkəˈnɑːzi/

ashlar masonry made of large square-cut
stones
ash-luhr /ˈaʃlə(r)/

Ashmolean Museum museum in
Oxford
ash-**moh**-li-uhn /aʃˈməʊliən/

Ashoka (also **Asoka**) Indian emperor
uh-**shoh**-kuh /əˈʃəʊkə/

Ashqelon (also **Ashkelon**) ancient city,
Israel
ash-kuh-**lohn** /aʃkəˈləʊn/

ashtanga type of yoga
ash-**tang**-guh /aʃˈtaŋɡə/

Ashura Muslim holy day
ash-**oor**-uh /aˈʃʊərə/

Asia continent
ay-shuh /ˈeɪʃə/

Commonly also **ay**-zhuh.

Asiago city, Italy
az-**yah**-goh /azˈjɑːɡəʊ/

Asimov, Isaac Russian-born American
writer and scientist
y-zuhk **az**-im-of /ˌʌɪzək ˈazɪmɒf/

Asir Mountains range of mountains,
Saudi Arabia
uh-**seer** /əˈsɪə(r)/

ASLEF Associated Society of Locomotive
Engineers and Firemen
az-lef /ˈazlɛf/

Asmara capital of Eritrea
ass-**mar**-uh /asˈmɑːrə/

Asoka see **Ashoka**

aspartame sweet substance
uh-**spar**-taym /əˈspɑː(r)teɪm/

Asperger's syndrome autistic disorder
asp-ur-guhrz /ˈaspə(r)ɡə(r)z/
• This is the pronunciation preferred by
the National Autistic Society.

asphalt mixture of dark bituminous
pitch with sand or gravel
ass-falt /ˈasfalt/

asphyxia lack of oxygen in the blood
uhss-**fik**-si-uh /əsˈfɪksiə/

Aspromonte Mountains mountain
range, Italy
asp-roh-**mon**-tay /ˌasprəʊˈmɒnteɪ/

Assad, Bashar al- Syrian president
buh-**shar** uhl **uss**-uhd /bəˈʃɑː(r) əl
ˈʌsəd/

Assad, Hafiz al- former Syrian
president
hah-fiz uhl **uss**-uhd /ˌhɑːfɪz əl ˈʌsəd/

assai musical term
ass-**y** /aˈsʌɪ/

Assam state, India
ass-**am** /aˈsam/

assay testing of a metal
uh-**say** /əˈseɪ/

assegai spear
ass-uh-gy /ˈasəɡʌɪ/

Assiniboine river, Canada
uh-**sin**-ib-oyn /əˈsɪnɪbɔɪn/

Assisi town, Italy
uh-**see**-si /əˈsiːsi/

Assur ancient Mesopotamian city
ass-oor /ˈasʊə(r)/

Assyria ancient country
uh-**sirr**-i-uh /əˈsɪriə/

Astana city, Kazakhstan
ast-uh-**nah** /astəˈnɑː/

Astarte Phoenician goddess
uh-**star**-ti /əˈstɑː(r)ti/

astatine chemical element
ast-uh-teen /ˈastətiːn/

asthma respiratory condition
ass-muh /ˈasmə/

astigmatism defect in the eye
uh-**stig**-muh-tiz-uhm /əˈstɪɡmətɪzəm/

Astrakhan city, Russia
ast-ruh-khan /'astrəxan/

Asturias autonomous region, Spain
ast-oor-i-uhss /a'stʊəriəs/

Asunción capital of Paraguay
ass-oon-syon /asu:n'sjɒn/

Aswan city, Egypt
ass-wahn /as'wɑ:n/

Atacama Desert arid region, Chile
at-ak-ah-muh /ˌata'kɑ:mə/

Atahualpa Inca king
at-uh-wal-puh /atə'walpə/

Atalanta Greek mythological character
at-uh-lan-tuh /ˌatə'lantə/

Ataman, Kutluğ Turkish artist
kuut-loo at-uh-man /ˌkʊtlu: atə'man/

Atatürk, Kemal Turkish general and statesman
kuh-mal at-uh-turk /kə,mal 'atətə:(r)k/
• Established anglicization.

atelier workshop or studio
uh-tel-i-ay /ə'tɛlieɪ/

Aten Egyptian god
ah-tuhn /'ɑ:tən/

atenolol beta blocker
uh-ten-uh-lol /ə'tɛnəlɒl/

Athanasius, St Greek theologian
ath-uh-nay-shuhss /ˌaθə'neɪʃəs/

Atharva Veda Hindu text
uh-tar-vuh vay-duh /ə,tɑ:(r)və 'veɪdə/

atheism theory that God does not exist
ay-thi-iz-uhm /'eɪθɪɪzəm/

atheling Anglo-Saxon prince
ath-uh-ling /'aθəlɪŋ/

Athelstan king of England
ath-uhl-stuhn /'aθəlstən/

Athena Greek goddess
uh-theen-uh /ə'θi:nə/

Athenaeum London gentlemen's club; also used in the names of libraries
ath-uh-nee-uhm /ˌaθə'ni:əm/

Athens capital of Greece
ath-uhnz /'aθənz/

Established anglicization. The Greek name is Athina, pronounced ath-ee-nuh.

Athos, Mount mountainous peninsula, Greece
ath-oss /'aθɒs/

Atitlán town, lake, and volcano, Guatemala
at-eet-lan /ati:t'lan/

Atletico Madrid Spanish football team
at-let-ik-oh muh-drid /at,lɛtɪkəʊ mə'drɪd/
• Established anglicization.

Atocha Madrid train station, Spain
at-otch-uh /a'tɒtʃə/

ATOL Air Travel Organizer's Licence
at-ol /'atɒl/

atoll island formed of coral
at-ol /'atɒl/

Commonly also uh-tol.

atomoxetine ADHD drug
at-oh-moks-uh-teen /ˌatəʊ'mɒksəti:n/

Atreus Greek mythological character
ay-tri-uhss /'eɪtrɪəs/

atrophia wasting disease
uh-troh-fi-uh /ə'trəʊfiə/

atrophy waste away
at-ruh-fi /'atrəfi/

atropine poisonous compound
at-ruh-peen /'atrəpi:n/

Atropos Greek mythological character
at-ruh-poss /'atrəpɒs/

ATSIC Aboriginal and Torres Strait Islander Commission
at-sik /'atsɪk/

attaché person on the staff of an ambassador
uh-tash-ay /ə'taʃeɪ/

Attica ancient department of Greece
at-ik-uh /'atɪkə/

Attila king of the Huns
uh-til-uh /ə'tɪlə/

Established anglicization. The Hungarian boy's name is pronounced ot-il-uh.

Attlee, Clement English prime minister
at-li /'atli/

aubade musical announcement of dawn
oh-bahd /əʊ'bɑ:d/

Aube river and department, France
ohb /əʊb/

auberge inn in a French-speaking country
oh-bairzh /əʊ'bɛ:(r)ʒ/

aubergine egg-shaped fruit
oh-buhr-zheen /'əʊbə(r)ʒi:n/

auburn reddish-brown colour
aw-buhrn /'ɔ:bə(r)n/

Aubusson town, France; also carpet made there
oh-byoo-son /'əʊbjusɒn/, [obysɔ̃]

• Established anglicization.

Auchterarder town, Scotland
okh-tuhr-**ar**-duhr /ˌɒxtə(r)'ɑː(r)də(r)/

Auckland city, New Zealand
awk-luhnd /'ɔːklənd/

au courant aware of what is going on
oh koo-**ro(ng)** /ˌəʊ kuː'rɒ̃/, French [o
kurɑ̃]

Auden, W. H. English-born American
poet
aw-duhn /'ɔːdən/

Audubon, John James American
naturalist and artist
aw-duh-buhn /'ɔːdəbən/

Auerbach, Frank German-born
English painter
ow-uhr-bakh /'aʊə(r)bax/

au fait having a good knowledge of
oh **fay** /ˌəʊ 'feɪ/

Augean relating to Augeas
aw-**jee**-uhn /ɔː'dʒiːən/

Augeas Greek mythological character
aw-**jee**-uhss /ɔː'dʒiːəs/

augment change
awg-**ment** /ɔːg'mɛnt/

Augrabies Falls series of waterfalls,
South Africa
uh-**grah**-beez /ə'grɑːbiːz/

Augsburg city, Germany
owks-boork /'aʊksbʊə(r)k/

augury sign of what will happen in
the future
aw-gyuu-ri /'ɔːgjʊri/

august respected and impressive
aw-**gust** /ɔː'gʌst/

Augusta resort, US
aw-**gust**-uh /ɔː'gʌstə/

Augustine, St doctor of the Church
aw-**gust**-in /ɔː'gʌstɪn/

Augustus Roman emperor
aw-**gust**-uhss /ɔː'gʌstəs/

auk seabird
awk /ɔːk/

auld lang syne times long past
awld lang **syn** /ˌɔːld laŋ 'sʌɪn/

aumbry recess or cupboard in a church
awm-bri /'ɔːmbri/

Aung San Burmese nationalist leader
owng **san** /ˌaʊŋ 'san/

Aung San Suu Kyi Burmese political
leader
owng **san** soo **chee** /aʊŋ ˌsan suː 'tʃiː/

Aurangzeb Mogul emperor
aw-**ruhng**-zeb /'ɔːrəŋzɛb/

Aurelian Roman emperor
aw-**ree**-li-uhn /ɔː'riːliən/

Aurelius, Marcus Roman emperor
mar-kuhss aw-**ree**-li-uhss /ˌmɑː(r)kəs
ɔː'riːliəs/
• See LATIN panel.

aureole circle of light
aw-ri-ohl /'ɔːriəʊl/

Auric, Georges French composer
zhorzh orr-**eek** /ˌʒɔː(r)ʒ ɒ'riːk/

auricular relating to the ear
aw-**rik**-yuul-uhr /ɔː'rɪkjʊlə(r)/

Auriga constellation
aw-**ry**-guh /ɔː'rʌɪgə/

Aurora goddess of the dawn
aw-**raw**-ruh /ɔː'rɔːrə/

Aurora Australis southern lights
aw-**raw**-ruh aw-**strah**-liss /ɔːˌrɔːrə
ɔː'strɑːlɪs/

Aurora Borealis northern lights
aw-**raw**-ruh borr-i-**ah**-liss /ɔːˌrɔːrə
bɒri'ɑːlɪs/

Auschwitz Nazi concentration camp
in Poland
owsh-vits /'aʊʃvɪts/

Auslese German white wine
owss-lay-zuh /'aʊsleɪzə/

auspicious conducive to success
aw-**spish**-uhss /ɔː'spɪʃəs/

austere severe or strict
ost-**eer** /ɒ'stɪə(r)/

Austerlitz, Battle of battle in 1805
aw-stuhr-lits /'ɔːstə(r)lɪts/

Austin city, US
ost-in /'ɒstɪn/

Australasia region, South Pacific
ost-ruh-**lay**-shuh /ˌɒstrə'leɪʃə/

Australopithecus bipedal primate
ost-ruh-loh-**pith**-ik-uhss
/ˌɒstrələʊ'pɪθɪkəs/

Austria country
ost-ri-uh /'ɒstriə/

The pronunciation **awst**-ri-uh is less
common now. This is an established
anglicization; the German name is
Österreich, pronounced **oest**-uhr-rykh
['øːstəraɪç].

autarch ruler with absolute power
aw-tark /'ɔːtɑː(r)k/

authoritative able to be trusted as being
accurate
aw-**thorr**-it-uh-tiv /ɔːˈθɒrɪtətɪv/

Less commonly also aw-**thorr**-it-ay-tiv.

autism mental condition
aw-tiz-uhm /ˈɔːtɪzəm/

Autobahn German motorway
ow-toh-bahn /ˈaʊtəʊbɑːn/

Commonly also anglicized to **aw**-toh-bahn.

autodidact self-taught person
aw-toh-did-akt /ˈɔːtəʊdɪdakt/

automaton pl. **automata** mechanical
device made in imitation of a human
being
aw-**tom**-uh-tuhn, pl. aw-**tom**-uh-tuh
/ɔːˈtɒmətən/, pl. /-tə/
• Standard -s plural is also possible.

automotive relating to motor vehicles
aw-tuh-**moh**-tiv /ˌɔːtəˈməʊtɪv/

autopista Spanish motorway
ow-toh-**peest**-uh /ˌaʊtəʊˈpiːstə/

Commonly also anglicized to
aw-toh-**peest**-uh.

autopsy post-mortem examination
aw-top-si /ˈɔːtɒpsi/

Less commonly also aw-**top**-si.

autostrada Italian motorway
ow-toh-**strah**-duh /ˌaʊtəʊˈstrɑːdə/

Commonly also anglicized to
aw-toh-strah-duh.

Auvergne region, France
oh-**vairn** /əʊˈvɛː(r)n/

Auxerre town, France
oh-**sair** /əʊˈsɛː(r)/

Sometimes erroneously awk-**sair**.

auxiliary providing additional help and
support
awg-**zil**-i-uh-ri /ɔːɡˈzɪliəri/

Commonly also awk-**sil**-i-uh-ri.

avalanche mass of snow falling rapidly
down a mountainside
av-uh-lahnsh /ˈavəlɑːnʃ/

Avalon mythical place
av-uh-lon /ˈavəlɒn/

avant-garde new and experimental
ideas
av-ong **gard** /ˌavɒŋ ˈɡɑː(r)d/, French
[avɑ̃ gard]

avast stop!
uh-**vahst** /əˈvɑːst/

Avastin cancer drug
ay-**vast**-in /eɪˈvastɪn/

avatar manifestation of a deity in
bodily form
av-uh-tar /ˈavətɑː(r)/

Avebury village, England
ayv-buh-ri /ˈeɪvbəri/

Aveda American hair and skin care
company
uh-**vay**-duh /əˈveɪdə/

Avedon, Richard American
photographer
av-uh-duhn /ˈavədən/

Avellino town and province, Italy
av-el-**ee**-noh /avɛˈliːnəʊ/

Ave Maria Catholic prayer
ah-vay muh-**ree**-uh /ˌɑːveɪ məˈriːə/

Aventine Hill one of the seven hills of
Rome
av-uhn-tyn /ˈavəntʌɪn/

aver state or assert
uh-**vur** /əˈvəː(r)/

Avernus Roman mythological name
uh-**vur**-nuhss /əˈvəː(r)nəs/

Averroës Spanish-born Islamic
philosopher
uh-**verr**-oh-eez /əˈvɛrəʊiːz/

Aves class of vertebrates
ay-veez /ˈeɪviːz/

Avesta sacred texts of Zoroastrianism
uh-**vest**-uh /əˈvɛstə/

avian relating to birds
ay-vi-uhn /ˈeɪviən/

aviatrix pl. **aviatrices** female pilot
ay-vi-**ay**-triks, pl. ay-vi-**ay**-triss-eez
/ˌeɪviˈeɪtrɪks/, pl. /-trɪsiːz/

Avicenna Persian-born Islamic
philosopher
av-iss-**en**-uh /ˌavɪˈsɛnə/

Avignon city, France
av-een-**yoh(ng)** /aviːnˈjɔ̃/

avocet wading bird
av-uh-set /ˈavəsɛt/

Avogadro, Amedeo Italian chemist
and physicist
am-uh-**day**-oh av-uh-**gahd**-roh
/aməˌdeɪəʊ avəˈɡɑːdrəʊ/

avoirdupois system of weights
av-war-dyoo-pwah
/ˌavwɑː(r)djuːˈpwɑː/

Avoriaz ski resort, France
av-orr-i-ah /avɒriˈɑː/

avuncular kind towards a less
experienced person
uh-**vunk**-yuul-uhr /əˈvʌŋkjʊlə(r)/

AWACS Airborne Warning And Control
System
ay-waks /ˈeɪwaks/

Awarua southern tip of New Zealand
ah-wuh-**roo**-uh /ɑːwəˈruːə/

AWOL Absent WithOut Leave
ay-wol /ˈeɪwɒl/

awry away from the expected course
uh-**ry** /əˈrʌɪ/

axilla pl. **axillae** armpit
ak-**sil**-uh, pl. ak-**sil**-ee /akˈsɪlə/, pl.
/-liː/

axiom accepted statement
ak-si-uhm /ˈaksɪəm/

axiomatic self-evident
ak-si-uh-**mat**-ik /ˌaksɪəˈmatɪk/

Axminster kind of patterned carpet
aks-min-stuhr /ˈaksmɪnstə(r)/

axolotl Mexican salamander
ak-suh-lot-uhl /ˈaksəlɒtəl/

Axum see **Aksum**

Ayacucho city, Peru
y-ak-**oo**-choh /ˌʌɪaˈkuːtʃəʊ/

ayah nanny employed by Europeans
in India
y-uh /ˈʌɪə/

ayahuasca tropical vine
y-uh-**wask**-uh /ˌʌɪəˈwaskə/

ayatollah religious leader among Shiite
Muslims
y-uh-**tol**-luh /ˌʌɪəˈtɒlə/
• Established anglicization.

Ayckbourn, Alan English dramatist
ayk-born /ˈeɪkbɔː(r)n/

aye-aye Madagascan primate
y y /ˈʌɪ ʌɪ/

Ayer, A. J. English philosopher
air /ɛː(r)/

Ayers Rock red rock mass, Australia
airz /ɛː(r)z/

Ayia Napa resort, Cyprus
y-uh **nap**-uh /ˌʌɪə ˈnapə/

Aylesbury town, England

aylz-buh-ri /ˈeɪlzbəri/

Aymará South American ethnic group
y-muh-**rah** /ʌɪməˈrɑː/

Ayodhya town, India
ah-**yohd**-yuh /ɑːˈjəʊdjə/

Ayr port, Scotland
air /ɛː(r)/

Ayurveda traditional Hindu system of
medicine
y-yuhr-**vay**-duh /ʌɪjə(r)ˈveɪdə/

Azad Kashmir autonomous state,
Pakistan
ah-zad kash-**meer** /ˌɑːzad kaʃˈmɪə(r)/

azalea shrub
uh-**zay**-li-uh /əˈzeɪlɪə/

azan Muslim call to ritual prayer
uh-**zahn** /əˈzɑːn/

Azerbaijan country
az-uhr-by-**jahn** /ˌazə(r)bʌɪˈdʒɑːn/

Azeri Turkic ethnic group
uh-**zair**-i /əˈzɛːri/

Azikiwe, Nnamdi (also **Azikwi**)
Nigerian statesman
nam-di uh-**zik**-wi /ˌnamdi əˈzɪkwi/

Azilian relating to an early Mesolithic
culture
uh-**zil**-i-uhn /əˈzɪlɪən/

azimuth astronomical term
az-im-uhth /ˈazɪməθ/

Aziz, Tariq Iraqi politician
tar-ik uh-**zeez** /ˌtɑːrɪk əˈziːz/

Aznar, José Maria Spanish politician
khoss-**ay** marr-ee-uh ath-**nar** /xɒˌseɪ
maˌriːə aθˈnɑː(r)/

Azores group of volcanic islands, Atlantic
Ocean
uh-**zorz** /əˈzɔː(r)z/

Azov, Sea of inland sea, Russia and
Ukraine
ah-**zov** /ˈɑːzɒv/, Russian [ʌˈzɒf]
• Established anglicization.

Azrael Jewish archangel
az-rayl /ˈazreɪl/

AZT AIDS drug
ay-zed-**tee** /ˌeɪzɛdˈtiː/

AM is **ay-zee-tee**.

Aztec Mexican ethnic group
az-tek /ˈaztɛk/

azure bright blue colour
azh-uhr /ˈaʒə(r)/

Commonly also uh-**zyoor**.

B

ba soul of a person or god in ancient Egypt
bah /bɑː/

Baade, Walter German-born American astronomer
bah-duh /'bɑːdə/

Baader-Meinhof Group West German left-wing anarchist group
bah-duhr **myn**-hof /ˌbɑːdə(r) 'mʌɪnhɒf/

Baal ancient Phoenician god
bahl /bɑːl/

Baalbek town, Lebanon
bahl-bek /'bɑːlbɛk/

Baath Party (also **Ba'ath Party**) pan-Arab political party
bahth /bɑːθ/, [ba'ʕθ]
• Established anglicization.

baba rich sponge cake
bah-bah /'bɑːbɑː/

baba 'father' (Hindi)
bah-bah /'bɑːbɑː/

baba ganouj aubergine spread
bah-buh gan-**oozh** /ˌbɑːbə gaˈnuːʒ/

babassu (also **babaçú**) oil palm
bab-uh-**soo** /ˌbabəˈsuː/

Baba Yaga sorceress in Russian folk tales
bah-buh **yah**-guh /ˌbɑːbə ˈjɑːgə/

Babel biblical tower
bay-buhl /'beɪbəl/

Babi adherent of Babism
bah-bi /'bɑːbi/

babiche raw hide formed into strips
buh-**beesh** /bəˈbiːʃ/

Babism religion
bahb-iz-uhm /'bɑːbɪzəm/

babouche heelless slipper
buh-**boosh** /bəˈbuːʃ/

Babruisk river port, Belarus
buh-**broo**-isk /bəˈbruːɪsk/

Babur first Mogul of India
bah-buhr /'bɑːbə(r)/

babushka 'grandmother' (Russian)

bah-buush-kuh /'bɑːbʊʃkə/

A more anglicized pronunciation, buh-**boosh**-kuh, is often heard.

Babuyan Islands group of volcanic islands, Philippines
bah-buu-**yahn** /ˌbɑːbʊˈjɑːn/

Babylon ancient city, Mesopotamia
bab-il-on /'babɪlɒn/

Babylonia ancient region, Mesopotamia
bab-il-**oh**-ni-uh /ˌbabɪˈləʊniə/

bacalao salted codfish
bak-uh-**low** /ˌbakəˈlaʊ/

Baca county, US
bay-kuh /'beɪkə/

Bacall, Lauren American actress
lorr-uhn buh-**kawl** /ˌlɒrən bəˈkɔːl/

Bacău city, Romania
buh-**kow** /bəˈkaʊ/, [baˈkəu]
• Established anglicization.

baccalaureate examination
bak-uh-**lawr**-i-uht /ˌbakəˈlɔːriət/

baccarat card game
bak-uh-rah /'bakərɑː/

Bacchae play by Euripides
bak-y /'bakʌɪ/

Commonly also bak-ee.

bacchanal wild celebration
bak-uh-nuhl /'bakənəl/

Bacchus Roman god of wine
bak-uhss /'bakəs/

Bach trademark flower remedies
batch /batʃ/

Bach, Johann Sebastian German composer
yoh-han zuh-**bast**-i-uhn **bahkh** /ˌjəʊhan zəˌbastiən ˈbɑːx/, [bax]

Bacharach, Burt American songwriter
bak-uh-rak /'bakərak/

Bachelet, Michelle Chilean president
mee-**chel** batch-el-et /miːˌtʃɛl batʃɛˈlɛt/

bacillus pl. **bacilli** bacterium
buh-**sil**-uhss, pl. buh-**sil**-y /bə'sɪləs/, pl.
/-lʌɪ/

Bacolod city, Philippines
bah-**kol**-od /ba:'kɒlɒd/

Baconian relating to Francis Bacon
bay-**koh**-ni-uhn /beɪ'kəʊnɪən/

bactericide substance which kills
bacteria
bak-**teer**-iss-yd /bak'tɪərɪsʌɪd/

bacterium pl. **bacteria** microscopic
single-celled organism
bak-**teer**-i-uhm, pl. bak-**teer**-i-uh
/bak'tɪərɪəm/, pl. /-rɪə/

Bactria ancient country in central Asia
bak-tri-uh /'baktrɪə/

baculovirus virus
bak-yuul-oh-**vy**-ruhss
/'bakjʊləʊˌvʌɪrəs/

Badajoz city and province, Spain
bad-akh-**oth** /bada'xɒθ/

Badakhshan province, Afghanistan
bad-akh-**shahn** /badax'ʃɑːn/

Badawi, Abdullah Ahmad Malaysian
prime minister
ab-**duul**-uh **akh**-muhd buh-**dah**-wi
/abˌdʊlə ˌaxməd bə'dɑːwi/

Badawi, Zeinab BBC journalist
zay-nab buh-**dah**-wi /ˌzeɪnab
bə'dɑːwi/

baddeleyite mineral
bad-uh-li-yt /'badəlɪʌɪt/

Baddiel, David English comedian
buh-**deel** /bə'diːl/

bade past tense of bid
bad /bad/

Commonly also bayd.

Baden spa town, Austria
bah-duhn /'bɑːdən/

Baden-Baden spa town, Germany
bah-duhn bah-duhn /ˌbɑːdən 'bɑːdən/

Baden-Powell, Olave wife of Lord
Baden-Powell
oh-layv bay-duhn poh-uhl /ˌəʊleɪv
ˌbeɪdən 'pəʊəl/

**Baden-Powell, Robert Stephenson
Smyth** English founder of the Boy Scout
movement
smith bay-duhn poh-uhl /ˌsmɪθ
ˌbeɪdən 'pəʊəl/

Baden-Württemberg state, Germany

bah-duhn **vuer**-tuhm-bairk /ˌbɑːdən
'vʊ(r)təmbɛ:(r)k/

Bader, Douglas English airman
bah-duhr /'bɑːdə(r)/

Badghis province, Afghanistan
bad-**geess** /bad'giːs/

badinage humorous conversation
bad-in-ahzh /'badɪnɑːʒ/

Bad Ischl spa town, Germany
baht ish-uhl /ˌbɑːt 'ɪʃəl/

Badon Hill, Battle of ancient British
battle
bay-duhn /'beɪdən/

Badu, Erykah American singer
err-ik-uh bah-**doo** /ˌɛrɪkə bɑː'duː/

Baedeker, Karl German publisher
karl bay-duhk-uhr /ˌkɑː(r)l
'beɪdəkə(r)/

Baer, Karl Ernest von German
biologist
karl air-nest fon bair /ˌkɑː(r)l ˌɛː(r)nɛst
fɒn bɛ:(r)/

Baeyer, Adolph von German organic
chemist
ah-dolf fon by-uhr /ˌɑːdɒlf fɒn
'bʌɪə(r)/

Baez, Joan American folk singer
by-ez /'bʌɪɛz/

Bafatá city, Guinea-Bissau
baf-uh-tah /bafə'tɑː/

BAFTA British Academy of Film and
Television Arts
baf-tuh /'baftə/

bafta coarse fabric
bahf-tuh /'bɑːftə/

Baganda Ugandan ethnic group
buh-**gan**-duh /bə'gandə/

Bagehot, Walter English economist
and journalist
baj-uht /'badʒət/

This British surname is variously
pronounced **baj**-uht and **bag**-uht,
depending on individual preference.

Baggio, Roberto Italian footballer
rob-air-toh baj-oh /rɒˌbɛ:(r)təʊ
'badʒəʊ/

Baghdad capital of Iraq
bag-dad /bag'dad/, Arabic [baɣ'da:d]

Established anglicization. Sometimes also
bag-dad.

Baghlan province, Afghanistan
bag-**lahn** /bagˈlɑːn/

ba gua Chinese religious motif
bah **gwah** /ˌbɑːˈgwɑː/

bahadur great man
bah-huh-**door** /ˌbɑːhəˈdʊə(r)/

Baha'i (also **Bahai**) religion
bah-**hah**-i /bɑːˈhɑːi/

Bahamas country
buh-**hah**-muhz /bəˈhɑːməz/

Bahamian relating to Bahamas
buh-**hay**-mi-uhn /bəˈheɪmiən/

Bahasa variety of Malay
buh-**hah**-suh /bəˈhɑːsə/

Bahawalpur city, Pakistan
buh-**hah**-wuhl-poor
/bəˈhɑːwəl,pʊə(r)/

Bahia (also **Baia**) state, Brazil
bah-**ee**-uh /bɑːˈiːə/

Bahia Blanca port, Argentina
bah-**ee**-uh **blank**-uh /bɑːˌiːə ˈblaŋkə/

Bahrain country
bar-**ayn** /bɑːˈreɪn/

baht currency unit, Thailand
baht /bɑːt/

Baikal lake, Russia
by-**kahl** /bʌɪˈkɑːl/

Baikonur town, Kazakhstan
by-kuh-**noor** /ˌbʌɪkəˈnʊə(r)/

Baile Átha Cliath Irish name for
Dublin
blah **klee**-uh /ˌblɑː ˈkliːə/

bailie Scottish municipal officer and
magistrate
bay-li /ˈbeɪli/

bain-marie pan of hot water
ban muh-**ree** /ˌban məˈriː/

Bairam Muslim festival
by-ram /ˈbʌɪram/

Baird, John Logie Scottish pioneer of
television
loh-gi baird /ˌləʊgi ˈbɛː(r)d/

Baisakhi Sikh festival
by-**sah**-ki /bʌɪˈsɑːki/

baize woollen material
bayz /beɪz/

Baja California peninsula, Mexico
bah-hah /ˈbɑːhɑː/, Spanish [ˈbaxa]
• Established anglicization.

Bajan informal term for Barbadian
bay-juhn /ˈbeɪdʒən/

Bajazet opera by Vivaldi
by-uhd-**zet** /bʌɪəˈdzɛt/

bajra pearl millet
bahj-rah /ˈbɑːdʒrɑː/

baju Malaysian short jacket
bah-joo /ˈbɑːdʒuː/

Baka Cameroonian ethnic group
bak-uh /ˈbakə/

Bakassi peninsula, West Africa
buh-**kass**-i /bəˈkasi/

Bakau town, Gambia
buh-**kow** /bəˈkaʊ/

Bakelite trademark early form of plastic
bayk-uh-lyt /ˈbeɪkəlʌɪt/

baklava Middle Eastern dessert
bak-luh-vuh /ˈbakləvə/

baksheesh small sum of money given
as tip
bak-**sheesh** /bakˈʃiːʃ/

Baku capital of Azerbaijan
bah-**koo** /bɑːˈkuː/

Bakuba see **Baquba**

Bakunin, Mikhail Russian anarchist
mee-khuh-**eel** bak-**oo**-nin /miːxəˌiːl
bəˈkuːnɪn/

Balaclava, Battle of battle in the
Crimean War
bal-uh-**klah**-vuh /ˌbaləˈklɑːvə/

The same pronunciation is used for the head
garment.

balafon large xylophone
bal-uh-fon /ˈbaləfɒn/

Balad city, Iraq
bal-uhd /ˈbaləd/

Balakirev, Mily Alekseyevich
Russian composer
mee-li al-uhk-**say**-uh-vitch
buh-**lak**-irr-uhf /ˌmiːli aləkˌseɪəvɪtʃ
bəˈlakɪrəf/

balalaika Russian musical instrument
bal-uh-**ly**-kuh /ˌbaləˈlʌɪkə/

Balanchine, George Georgian-born
American ballet dancer and
choreographer
bal-uhn-**sheen** /balənˈʃiːn/

Balaton lake, Hungary
bal-uh-ton /ˌbɒləˈtɒn/, [ˈbɒlɒton]
• Established anglicization.

Balboa, Vasco Núñez de Spanish explorer
vask-oh **noon**-yeth day bal-**boh**-uh /ˌvaskəʊ ˌnuːnjɛθ deɪ balˈbəʊə/

balboa currency unit, Panama
bal-**boh**-uh /balˈbəʊə/

balbriggan knitted cotton fabric
bal-**brig**-uhn /balˈbrɪgən/

Balcon, Michael English film producer
bawl-kuhn /ˈbɔːlkən/

baldachin ceremonial canopy
bal-duh-kin /ˈbaldəkɪn/

Balder Scandinavian mythological character
bawl-duhr /ˈbɔːldə(r)/

baldric belt for a sword
bawl-drik /ˈbɔːldrɪk/

Bâle see **Basle**

Balearic Islands group of islands, Spain
bal-i-**arr**-ik /ˌbaliˈarɪk/

baleen whalebone
buh-**leen** /bəˈliːn/

Balenciaga, Cristóbal Spanish couturier
krist-**oh**-bal bal-en-thi-**ah**-guh /krɪsˈtəʊbal baˌlɛnθiˈɑːgə/

Balfour Beatty British engineering company
bal-for **bee**-ti /ˌbalfɔː(r) ˈbiːti/

Bali island, Indonesia
bah-li /ˈbɑːli/

Balıkesir city and province, Turkey
bah-**lik**-ess-eer /bɑːˈlɪkɛsɪə(r)/

Balinese relating to Bali
bah-lin-**eez** /ˌbɑːlɪˈniːz/

Balkans range of mountains, eastern Europe
bawl-kuhnz /ˈbɔːlkənz/

Balkenende, Jan Peter Dutch prime minister
yun **pay**-tuhr **bulk**-uh-nen-duh /ˌjʌn ˌpeɪtə(r) ˈbalkənɛndə/

Ballack, Michael German footballer
mikh-uh-el **bal**-uhk /ˌmɪçəɛl ˈbalək/

ballade type of poem
bal-**ahd** /baˈlɑːd/

balladeer singer or composer of ballads
bal-uh-**deer** /ˌbaləˈdɪə(r)/

Ballantyne, R. M. Scottish author
bal-uhn-tyn /ˈbaləntʌɪn/

Ballarat city, Australia
bal-uh-rat /ˈbalarat/

Ballesteros, Sevvy Spanish golfer
sev-i bal-yest-**air**-oss /ˌsɛvi baljɛˈstɛːrɒs/

ballista catapult
buh-**list**-uh /bəˈlɪstə/

Ballymena town, Northern Ireland
bal-i-**mee**-nuh /ˌbaliˈmiːnə/

Balmoral royal estate, Scotland
bal-**morr**-uhl /balˈmɒrəl/

balneology study of medicinal springs
bal-ni-**ol**-uh-ji /ˌbalniˈɒlədʒi/

Balochistan see **Baluchistan**

BALPA British AirLine Pilots' Association
bal-puh /ˈbalpə/

Balkhash lake, Kazakhstan
bal-**khahsh** /balˈxɑːʃ/

balsa lightweight timber
bawl-suh /ˈbɔːlsə/

Baltacha, Elena Ukrainian-born English tennis player
el-**ay**-nuh bal-**tash**-uh /ɛˌleɪnə balˈtaʃə/

Balthasar one of the three Magi
bal-thuh-zar /ˈbalθəzɑː(r)/

Balthazar large wine bottle
bal-**thaz**-uhr /balˈθazə(r)/

balti type of Pakistani cuisine
bawl-ti /ˈbɔːlti/

Baltic relating to the Baltic Sea
bawl-tik /ˈbɔːltɪk/

Baltimore port, US
bawl-tim-or /ˈbɔːltɪmɔː(r)/

Baltistan region in the Himalayas
bawl-ti-stahn /ˌbɔːltiˈstɑːn/

Baluchi relating to Baluchistan
buh-**loo**-chi /bəˈluːtʃi/

Baluchistan (also **Balochistan**) mountainous region, western Asia
buh-loo-chi-**stahn** /bəˌluːtʃiˈstɑːn/

balun type of electrical transformer
bal-un /ˈbalʌn/

baluster decorative pillar
bal-uh-stuhr /ˈbaləstə(r)/

Balzac, Honoré de French novelist
on-uh-**ray** duh bal-**zak** /ɒnəˌreɪ də balˈzak/
• See FRENCH panel.

Bam town, Iran
  bam /bam/

Bamako capital of Mali
  bam-uh-koh /'baməkəʊ/

Bambara African ethnic group
  bam-**bar**-uh /bam'bɑːrə/

bambino baby or young child
  bam-**bee**-noh /bam'biːnəʊ/

Bamian city and province, Afghanistan
  bahm-**yahn** /bɑːm'jɑːn/

Banaba island, western Pacific
  buh-**nab**-uh /bə'nabə/

banausic mundane or mechanical
  buh-**naw**-sik /bə'nɔːsɪk/

Bada Aceh city, Indonesia
  ban-duh **atch**-ay /ˌbandə 'atʃeɪ/

Bakuba see Baquba

Banda, Hastings Kamuzu Malawian
  statesman
  kuh-**moo**-zoo ban-duh /kəˌmuːzuː
  'bandə/

Bandaranaike, Sirimavo Sinhalese
  stateswoman
  sirr-im-uh-**voh** ban-duh-ruh-**ny**-ik-uh
  /sɪrɪməˌvəʊ ˌbandərə'nʌɪɪkə/

Bandar Lampung city, Indonesia
  band-uhr **lamp**-uung /ˌbandə(r)
  'lampʊŋ/

Bandar Seri Begawan capital of
  Brunei
  band-uhr **serr**-i buh-**gah**-wuhn
  /ˌbandə(r) ˌsɛri bə'gɑːwən/

bandeau band worn round the head
  ban-doh /'bandəʊ/

Banderas, Antonio Spanish actor
  an-**tohn**-yoh ban-**dair**-ass /anˌtəʊniəʊ
  ban'dɛːras/

bandersnatch mythical creature
  band-uhr-snatch /'bandə(r)snatʃ/

bandicoot marsupial
  ban-dik-oot /'bandɪkuːt/

bandolier shoulder belt for cartridges
  ban-duh-**leer** /ˌbandə'lɪə(r)/

bandoneón type of concertina
  ban-don-ay-**on** /ˌbandɒneɪ'ɒn/

bandora bass lute
  ban-**dawr**-uh /ban'dɔːrə/

Bandung city, Indonesia
  ban-duung /'bandʊŋ/

bandura Ukrainian stringed instrument
  ban-**doo**-ruh /ban'duːrə/

Banffshire former county, Scotland
  banf-shuhr /'banfʃə(r)/

Bangalore city, India
  ban-guh-**lor** /ˌbaŋgə'lɔː(r)/

Bangkok capital of Thailand
  bang-**kok** /baŋ'kɒk/

Bangladesh country
  bang-gluh-**desh** /ˌbaŋglə'dɛʃ/

Bangui capital of the Central African
  Republic
  bah(ng)-**gee** /bɑ̃'giː/

Banja Luka town, Bosnia-Herzegovina
  ban-yuh **loo**-kuh /ˌbanjə 'luːkə/

Banjarmasin port, Indonesia
  ban-juhr-**mah**-sin /ˌbandʒə'mɑːsɪn/

Banjul capital of Gambia
  ban-**jool** /ban'dʒuːl/

banjulele stringed musical instrument
  ban-juh-**lay**-lee /bandʒə'leɪli/

Bánk Bán opera by Ferenc Erkel
  bahnk **bahn** /ˌbɑːŋk 'bɑːn/

banksia Australian shrub
  bank-si-uh /'baŋksiə/

banneret knight
  ban-uh-ruht /'banərət/

Bannockburn, Battle of battle in
  Scotland
  ban-uhk-burn /'banəkbəː(r)n/

banquet formal evening feast
  bank-wit /'baŋkwɪt/

banquette upholstered bench
  bank-**et** /baŋ'kɛt/

banshee female spirit
  ban-shee /'banʃiː/

bansuri Indian bamboo flute
  ban-**soor**-i /ban'sʊəri/

banteng Asian forest ox
  ban-teng /'bantɛŋ/

Banton, Buju Jamaican ragga artist
  buuj-oo ban-**tuhn** /ˌbʊdʒuː 'bantən/

Bantu African language group
  ban-**too** /ban'tuː/

banyan Indian fig tree
  ban-yuhn /'banjən/

banzai Japanese acclamation
  ban-**zy** /ban'zʌɪ/

baobab short tree
  bay-oh-bab /'beɪəʊbab/

Baquba (also **Bakuba**) town, Iraq
  bah-**koo**-buh /bɑː'kuːbə/

Barabbas biblical name
buh-**rab**-uhss /bəˈrabəs/

bara brith traditional Welsh bread
barr-uh **brith** /ˌbarə ˈbrɪθ/

Baradei, Mohamed el- see **ElBaradei,
Mohamed**

Barajas site of Madrid International
Airport, Spain
barr-**akh**-ass /baˈraxas/

Barat, Carl English singer and guitarist
barr-uht /ˈbarət/

barathea fine woollen cloth
barr-uh-**thee**-uh /ˌbarəˈθiːə/

baraza public meeting place
buh-**rah**-zuh /bəˈrɑːzə/

Barbadian relating to Barbados
bar-**bay**-di-uhn /bɑː(r)ˈbeɪdiən/

Barbados island, Caribbean
bar-**bay**-doss /bɑː(r)ˈbeɪdɒs/

Barbarossa Barbary pirate; also Second
World War Nazi military campaign
bar-buh-**ross**-uh /ˌbɑː(r)bəˈrɒsə/

Barbary former North African region
bar-buh-ri /ˈbɑː(r)bəri/

barbell piece of fitness equipment
bar-bel /ˈbɑː(r)bɛl/

barbet fruit-eating bird
bar-bit /ˈbɑː(r)bɪt/

barbican outer defence
bar-bik-uhn /ˈbɑː(r)bɪkən/

Barbirolli, John English conductor
bar-birr-**ol**-i /ˌbɑː(r)bɪˈrɒli/

barbitone sleep-inducing drug
bar-bit-ohn /ˈbɑː(r)bɪtəʊn/

barbiturate drug group
bar-**bit**-yuu-ruht /bɑː(r)ˈbɪtjʊrət/

Barbour trademark type of waxed jacket
bar-buhr /ˈbɑː(r)bə(r)/

Barbour, John Scottish poet
bar-buhr /ˈbɑː(r)bə(r)/

barcarole song sung by Venetian
gondoliers
bar-kuh-**rohl** /bɑː(r)kəˈrəʊl/

Barça familiar name for FC Barcelona
bar-suh /ˈbɑː(r)sə/

Barcelona city, Spain
bar-suh-**loh**-nuh /ˌbɑː(r)səˈləʊnə/,
[barθeˈlona]
• Established anglicization.

Bar-Cochba Jewish rebel leader
bar **kok**-buh /bɑː(r) ˈkɒkbə/

Bardolino Italian red wine
bar-duh-**lee**-noh /ˌbɑː(r)dəˈliːnəʊ/

Bárdos, Lajos Hungarian composer
loy-osh **bar**-dosh /ˌlɔɪʃ ˈbɑː(r)dɒʃ/

Bardot, Brigitte French actress
bree-**zheet** bar-**doh** /briːˌʒiːt
bɑː(r)ˈdəʊ/

barège dress fabric
buh-**rayzh** /bəˈreɪʒ/

Bareilly city, India
buh-**ray**-li /bəˈreɪli/

Bareilly strain of salmonella
buh-**ree**-li /bəˈriːli/

Barenboim, Daniel Israeli pianist
dan-yuhl **barr**-uhn-boym /ˌdanjəl
ˈbarənbɔɪm/

Barents Sea sea, Arctic
barr-uhnts /ˈbarənts/
• Established anglicization.

Bargello kind of embroidery
bar-**jel**-oh /bɑː(r)ˈdʒɛləʊ/

Barghouti, Marwan Palestinian
politician
mar-**wan** bar-**goo**-ti /mɑː(r)ˌwan
bɑː(r)ˈguːti/

Bargoed town, Wales
bar-goyd /ˈbɑː(r)ɡɔɪd/

Bari port, Italy
bar-i /ˈbɑːri/

Barinas town and state, Venezuela
barr-**ee**-nass /baˈriːnas/

barium chemical element
bair-i-uhm /ˈbɛːriəm/

bar mitzvah initiation ceremony for a
Jewish boy
bar **mits**-vuh /ˌbɑː(r) ˈmɪtsvə/

Barnabas biblical name
bar-nuh-buhss /ˈbɑː(r)nəbəs/

Barnardo, Thomas John Irish-born
doctor
buhr-**nar**-doh /bə(r)ˈnɑː(r)dəʊ/
• The same pronunciation is used for the
children's charity named after him.

Barnaul city, Russia
bar-nuh-**ool** /ˌbɑː(r)nəˈuːl/

Barnier, Michel French politician
mee-**shell** bar-ni-**ay** /miːˌʃɛl
bɑː(r)niˈeɪ/

Barnum, P. T. American showman
bar-nuhm /ˈbɑː(r)nəm/

Baroda former state, India
buh-**roh**-duh /bəˈrəʊdə/

Barolo Italian red wine
buh-**roh**-loh /bəˈrəʊləʊ/

baroque style of art
buh-**rok** /bəˈrɒk/

barotitis inflammation in the ear
barr-oh-**ty**-tiss /ˌbarəʊˈtʌɪtɪs/

Barquisimeto city, Venezuela
bar-kee-sim-**ay**-toh
/ˌbɑː(r)kiːsɪˈmeɪtəʊ/

Barra island, Scotland
barr-uh /ˈbarə/

barramundi fish
barr-uh-**mun**-di /ˌbarəˈmʌndi/

barranca narrow river gorge
buh-**rank**-uh /bəˈraŋkə/

Barranquilla port, Colombia
barr-ank-**eel**-yuh /baraŋˈkiːljə/

Barrault, Jean-Louis French actor
and director
zhah(ng) **lwee** barr-**oh** /ʒɑ̃ ˌlwiː
baˈrəʊ/

barré method of playing the guitar
barr-ay /ˈbareɪ/

Barrichello, Rubens Brazilian
Formula 1 driver
roo-ba(ng)ss barr-i-**kel**-oo /ˌruːbɛs
bariˈkɛluː/

An anglicized pronunciation, **roo**-buhnz
barr-ik-**el**-oh, is often used.

barrio Spanish district of a town
barr-i-oh /ˈbariəʊ/

barrique wine barrel
buh-**reek** /bəˈriːk/

Barroso, José Manuel Durão
Portuguese politician
zhuuz-**ay** muhn-**wel** duu-row(ng)
buh-**roh**-zoo /ʒuˌzeɪ mənˌwɛl dʊˌrãʊ
bəˈrəʊzuː/

Barsac district, France
bar-**sak** /bɑː(r)ˈsak/

Barschak, Aaron English stand-up
comedian
air-uhn bar-**shak** /ˌɛːrən ˈbɑː(r)ʃak/

Barth, John American novelist
barth /bɑː(r)θ/

Barth, Karl Swiss Protestant theologian
karl bart /ˌkɑː(r)l ˈbɑː(r)t/

Barthes, Roland French writer and
critic

rol-**ah(ng)** bart /rɒˌlɑ̃ ˈbɑː(r)t/

Bartholdi, Auguste French sculptor
oh-**guest** bar-tol-**dee** /əʊˌgyst
bɑː(r)tɒlˈdiː/

Bartók, Béla Hungarian composer
bay-luh **bar**-tok /ˌbeɪlə ˈbɑː(r)tɒk/

Bartolommeo, Fra Italian painter
frah bar-tol-uh-**may**-oh /frɑː
ˌbɑː(r)tɒləˈmeɪəʊ/

Baruch book of the Bible
bar-**uuk** /ˈbɑːrʊk/

baryon subatomic particle
barr-i-on /ˈbarɪɒn/

Baryshnikov, Mikhail Latvian-born
American ballet dancer
mee-khuh-**eel** buh-**rish**-nik-uhf
/miːxəˌiːl bəˈrɪʃnɪˌkəf/

baryte mineral
barr-yt /ˈbarʌɪt/

baryton stringed instrument
barr-it-on /ˈbarɪtɒn/

bascule type of bridge
bask-yool /ˈbaskjuːl/

Basel see **Basle**

basenji hunting dog
buh-**sen**-ji /bəˈsɛndʒi/

Bashir, Abu Bakar Indonesian
Muslim cleric
ab-oo buh-**kar** bah-**sheer** /ˌabu
bəˌkɑː(r) bɑːˈʃiə(r)/

Bashir, Omar Hassan al- Sudanese
president
oh-**mar** **huss**-uhn uhl buh-**sheer**
/ˌəʊmɑː(r) ˌhʌsən əl bəˈʃiə(r)/

Bashir, Martin English journalist
buh-**sheer** /bəˈʃiə(r)/

Bashkir relating to Bashkiria
bash-**keer** /baʃˈkɪə(r)/

Bashkiria autonomous republic, Russia
bash-**keer**-i-uh /baʃˈkɪəriə/

Basie, Count American jazz pianist
bay-si /ˈbeɪsi/

basil aromatic plant
baz-uhl /ˈbazəl/

AM is **bay**-zil.

Basildon town, England
baz-il-duhn /ˈbazɪldən/

basilica large oblong hall or building
buh-**sil**-ik-uh /bəˈsɪlɪkə/

Basilicata region, Italy
buh-sil-ik-**ah**-tuh /bə‚sɪlɪˈkɑːtə/

basilisk mythical reptile
baz-il-isk /ˈbazɪlɪsk/

basinet steel headpiece of a suit of armour
bass-in-et /ˈbasɪnɛt/

Basinger, Kim American actress
bay-sing-uhr /ˈbeɪsɪŋə(r)/

Basle city, Switzerland
bahl /bɑːl/

Established anglicization. The German name is Basel, pronounced **bah**-zuhl, and the French form is Bâle, pronounced bahl.

Basotho South African ethnic group
buh-**soo**-too /bəˈsuːtuː/

Basque ethnic group and language
bask /bask/

Less commonly also bahsk.

Basra city and province, Iraq
baz-ruh /ˈbazrə/, Arabic [ˈbɑsrɑ]
• Established anglicization.

Bas-Rhin department, France
bah **ra(ng)** /‚bɑː ˈrɛ̃/

bass singing voice
bayss /beɪs/

bass freshwater perch
bass /bas/

Bassein port, Burma
bass-**ayn** /baˈseɪn/

Basse-Normandie region, France
bass **nor**-muhn-di /bas ˈnɔː(r)məndi/, [bas nɔrmɑ̃di]
• Established anglicization.

Basseterre capital of St Kitts and Nevis, Leeward Islands
bast-**air** /basˈtɛː(r)/

Basse-Terre main island of Guadeloupe, Caribbean
ba **stair** /bas ˈtɛː(r)/

Bass Strait channel separating Tasmania from Australia
bass /bas/

Bastet ancient Egyptian goddess
bast-et /ˈbastɛt/

Bastia port, Corsica
bast-yuh /ˈbastjə/

bastide French country house
bast-**eed** /baˈstiːd/

Bastille fortress in Paris

bast-**eel** /baˈstiːl/, French [bastij]
• Established anglicization.

basuco impure cocaine
buh-**soo**-koh /bəˈsuːkəʊ/

Bata port, Equatorial Guinea
bah-tuh /ˈbɑːtə/

Batak Indonesian ethnic group
bat-uhk /ˈbatək/

Batan Islands islands, Philippines
buh-**tahn** /bəˈtɑːn/

Bathsheba biblical name
bath-**shee**-buh /baθˈʃiːbə/

Sometimes also **bath**-shib-uh.

batik method of dyeing textiles
buh-**teek** /bəˈtiːk/

Batista, Fulgencio Cuban statesman
fool-**khenss**-yoh bat-**ee**-stuh /fuːlˌxɛnsjəʊ baˈtiːstə/

bat mitzvah initiation ceremony for a Jewish girl
baht **mits**-vuh /‚bɑːt ˈmɪtsvə/

Baton Rouge city, US
bat-uhn **roozh** /‚batən ˈruːʒ/

Battambang city and province, Cambodia
bat-uhm-bang /ˈbatəmbaŋ/

battement ballet movement
bat-**mah(ng)** /batˈmɑ̃/

batterie ballet movement
bat-**ree** /batˈriː/

Batticaloa city, Sri Lanka
bat-ik-uh-**loh**-uh /‚batɪkəˈləʊə/

Baucis Greek mythological character
baw-siss /ˈbɔːsɪs/

Baudelaire, Charles French poet
sharl bohd-**lair** /‚ʃɑː(r)l bəʊdˈlɛː(r)/

Baudrillard, Jean French sociologist
zhah(ng) boh-dree-**yar** /‚ʒɑ̃ bəʊdriːˈjɑː(r)/

Bauer, Harold English-born American pianist
bow-uhr /ˈbaʊə(r)/

Bauhaus school of applied arts
bow-howss /ˈbaʊhaʊs/

Bauhinia orchid; symbol of Hong Kong
baw-**hin**-i-uh /bɔːˈhɪniə/

Bavaria state, Germany
buh-**vair**-i-uh /bəˈvɛːriə/

Established anglicization. The German name is Bayern, pronounced **by**-uhrn.

Bayaka African pygmy ethnic group
by-**ak**-uh /bʌɪˈakə/

Bayelsa state, Nigeria
by-**el**-suh /bʌɪˈɛlsə/

Bayeux city, France
by-**oe** /bʌɪˈə/

Bayji town, Iraq
bay-**ji** /ˈbeɪdʒi/

bayou marshy outlet of a lake or river
by-**oo** /ˈbʌɪuː/

Bayreuth town, Germany
by-**royt** /bʌɪˈrɔɪt/

bdellium fragrant resin
del-i-uhm /ˈdɛlɪəm/

bealach Scottish narrow mountain pass
bel-akh /ˈbɛlax/

Beamon, Bob American long-jumper
bee-muhn /ˈbiːmən/

Béarnaise tarragon-flavoured sauce
bay-uhr-**nayz** /ˌbeɪə(r)ˈneɪz/

Beas (also **Bias**) river, India
bee-**ahss** /biˈɑːs/

beatification process of being declared
blessed by the pope
bi-at-if-ik-**ay**-shuhn /bɪˌatɪfɪˈkeɪʃən/

Beatrix, Queen queen of the
Netherlands
bay-uh-triks /ˈbeɪətrɪks/

Beatty, Earl British admiral
bee-ti /ˈbiːti/

Beatty, Warren American actor
bay-ti /ˈbeɪti/

Beaucaire town, France
boh-**kair** /bəʊˈkɛː(r)/

Beaufort scale scale of wind speed
boh-fuhrt /ˈbəʊfə(r)t/

beau geste noble and generous act
boh **zhest** /ˌbəʊ ˈʒɛst/

Beaujolais district, France; also a type of
wine
boh-**zhuh**-lay /ˈbəʊʒəleɪ/

Beaumont, Francis English dramatist
boh-mont /ˈbəʊmɒnt/

Beaune region, France; also a type of
wine
bohn /bəʊn/

beaux arts fine arts
bohz ar /ˌbəʊz ˈɑː(r)/

béchamel rich sauce made with milk
bay-shuh-**mel** /beɪʃəˈmɛl/

bêche-de-mer large sea cucumber
besh duh **mair** /ˌbɛʃ də ˈmɛː(r)/

Bechstein, Friedrich German
piano-builder
freed-rikh **bekh**-shtyn /ˌfriːdrɪç
ˈbɛçʃtʌɪn/

The piano firm is often anglicized to
bek-styn.

Beckenbauer, Franz German
footballer
frants **bek**-uhn-bow-uhr /ˌfrants
ˈbɛkənˌbaʊə(r)/

Becker, Boris German tennis player
borr-iss **bek**-uhr /ˌbɒrɪs ˈbɛkə(r)/

Becket, St Thomas à English prelate
and statesman
uh **bek**-it /ə ˈbɛkɪt/

Beckett, Samuel Irish dramatist,
novelist, and poet
bek-it /ˈbɛkɪt/

Becquerel, Antoine-Henri French
physicist
ah(ng)-**twahn** ah(ng)-**ree** bek-**rel**
/ɑ̃ˌtwɑːn ɑ̃ˌriː bɛkˈrɛl/

becquerel SI unit of radioactivity
bek-uh-rel /ˈbɛkərɛl/

Bede, St English theologian
beed /biːd/

bedel official with ceremonial duties
bee-duhl /ˈbiːdəl/

Bedouin (also **Beduin**) nomadic Arab of
the desert
bed-uu-in /ˈbɛdʊɪn/

Beelzebub devil or demon
bee-el-zuh-bub /biːˈɛlzəbʌb/

Beerbohm, Max English caricaturist,
essayist, and critic
beer-bohm /ˈbɪə(r)bəʊm/

Beerenauslese German white wine
bair-uhn-owss-lay-zuh
/ˈbɛːrənˌaʊsleɪzə/

Beersheba town, Israel
beer-**shee**-buh /ˌbɪə(r)ˈʃiːbə/

Beethoven, Ludwig van German
composer
loot-vikh van **bayt**-hoh-vuhn /ˌluːtvɪç
van ˈbeɪtˌhəʊvən/

The first name is often anglicized to
luud-vig.

Begin, Menachem Israeli statesman
muh-**nah**-khuhm **beg**-in /məˌnɑːxəm
ˈbɛɡɪn/

BBC English and Received Pronunciation

In the preface to a BBC Pronouncing Dictionary of 1971 one of our predecessors in the Pronunciation Unit wrote, 'Although the BBC does not, and never did, impose pronunciations of its own on English words, the myth of BBC English dies hard. It owed its birth no doubt to the era before the Second World War, when all announcers spoke Received Pronunciation.' This usefully summarizes the relationship between the two terms.

Received Pronunciation (RP)

Received Pronunciation is an accent of spoken English, identified more with a particular social group than a particular region, although it has connections with the accent of southern England and is associated with educated speakers and formal speech. It is used as a model for the teaching of English as a foreign language and is still the accent generally represented in dictionaries which give pronunciations. (For the English pronunciations in this book, we use an accent which could broadly be described as RP; see the introduction for a fuller discussion.) Perhaps for this reason, RP is often thought of as an unchanging accent, a standard against which other accents can be measured or judged. In fact, there is considerable variation within groups of people who are said to speak RP, the term is differently interpreted by different people, and RP itself has changed considerably over time.

BBC English

RP is closely associated in people's minds with broadcasting in general, and the BBC in particular. It is widely believed that the BBC traditionally employed as newsreaders and broadcasters only people who could speak RP. If 'BBC English' were taken literally, it would just mean English as spoken on the BBC—which today would mean virtually every kind of English from all around the world. However, what is usually understood by 'BBC English' is RP, perhaps even the RP stereotypically used by pre-war radio announcers. This term is now used by some linguists and lexicographers as well as by the general public, and reinforces the view that the BBC has a particular responsibility to champion one accent of English, or hold back the tide of language change. In fact, the BBC doesn't require any of its broadcasters to speak with any particular accent, and the advice given by the Pronunciation Unit is broadly suitable for all accents of English.

The Pronunciation Unit advises on the correct pronunciation of words, names, and phrases in all languages (including English), but where two possible pronunciations of an English word exist, it is not part of our remit to enforce the use of one over the other. We can advise programme makers on which pronunciations are permissible by consulting pronunciation dictionaries and other published sources, and may also advise on which form is more common or more traditional in British English, but we do not prohibit any acceptable forms. (A small number of these variant words are commonly the subject of complaints: see the Top Ten Complaints panel.)

---

beguine Caribbean dance
bay-**geen** /beɪˈgiːn/

begum Muslim woman of high rank
bay-**guhm** /ˈbeɪgəm/

Behan, Brendan Irish poet
bee-uhn /ˈbiːən/

behemoth mythological creature
buh-**hee**-moth /bəˈhiːmɒθ/

Behn, Aphra English writer
af-ruh **bayn** /ˌafrə ˈbeɪn/

Behn, Ari Norwegian writer
ar-i **bayn** /ˌɑːri ˈbeɪn/

Behrens, Peter German architect and designer
pay-tuhr bay-ruhnss /ˌpeɪtə(r) ˈbeɪrəns/

Beidaihe resort, China
bay-dy-**khuh** /ˌbeɪdaɪˈxə/

Beiderbecke, Bix American jazz musician and composer
biks by-duhr-bek /ˌbɪks ˈbaɪdə(r)bek/

Beijing capital of China
bay-**jing** /ˌbeɪˈdʒɪŋ/

The pronunciation bay-**zhing** is common, but not correct. A Chinese *j* is never pronounced zh.

Beira port, Mozambique
by-ruh /ˈbaɪrə/

beira antelope
bay-ruh /ˈbeɪrə/

Beirut capital of Lebanon
bay-**root** /beɪˈruːt/

Beit Hanoun town, Palestine
bayt han-**oon** /ˌbeɪt haˈnuːn/

Beja Egyptian nomadic ethnic group
bej-uh /ˈbɛdʒə/

Béjart, Maurice French choreographer
morr-**eess** bay-**zhar** /mɒˈriːs beɪˈʒɑː(r)/

Bekaa valley, Lebanon
bek-**ah** /bɛˈkɑː/

Belafonte, Harry American singer
bel-uh-**fon**-ti /bɛləˈfɒnti/

Belarus country
bel-uh-**rooss** /ˌbɛləˈruːs/
• Established anglicization.

bel canto musical term
bel **kan**-toh /ˌbɛl ˈkantəʊ/

Belém port, Brazil
bel-em /bɛˈlɛm/, Portuguese [beˈlẽi]
• Established anglicization.

Belfast city, Northern Ireland
bel-fahst /ˈbɛlfɑːst/

Belgaum city, India
bel-gowm /ˈbɛlgaʊm/

Belgorod city, Russia
byel-guh-ruht /ˈbjɛlgərət/

Belgrade capital of Serbia
bel-**grayd** /bɛlˈgreɪd/

Established anglicization. The Serbian name is Beograd, pronounced bay-**og**-rat [bɛˈɔɡrat].

Belial name for the devil
bee-li-uhl /ˈbiːliəl/

Belitung island, Indonesia
buh-**lee**-tuung /bə'li:tʊŋ/

Belize country
bel-**eez** /bɛ'li:z/

Belizean relating to Belize
bel-**eez**-i-uhn /bɛ'li:ziən/

Belleek village, Northern Ireland; also the pottery made there
buh-**leek** /bə'li:k/

Bellerophon Greek mythological character
buh-**lerr**-uh-fuhn /bə'lɛrəfən/

Bellingshausen Sea part of the Pacific
bel-ingz-how-zuhn /'bɛlɪŋz,haʊzən/

Bellini, Giovanni Italian painter
juh-**vah**-ni bel-**ee**-ni /dʒə'vɑːni bɛ'li:ni/

Bellini cocktail
bel-**ee**-ni /bɛ'li:ni/

Belloc, Hilaire French-born British writer
ee-**lair** bel-ok /i:ˌlɛː(r) 'bɛlɒk/

Belmopan capital of Belize
bel-moh-**pan** /ˌbɛlməʊ'pan/

Belo Horizonte city, Brazil
bel-oo orr-iz-**on**-ti /ˌbɛlu: ɒrɪ'zɒnti/

Bělohlávek, Jiři Czech conductor
yeer-zhee **byel**-oh-hlah-vek /ˌjɪə(r)ʒi: 'bjɛləʊhlɑːvɛk/

Belorussia former name for Belarus; also called **Byelorussia**
bel-uh-**rush**-uh /ˌbɛlə'rʌʃə/

Bel Paese trademark Italian cheese
bel pah-**ay**-zay /ˌbɛl pɑː'eɪzeɪ/

Belsen Nazi concentration camp; also called **Bergen-Belsen**
bel-suhn /'bɛlsən/, ['bɛlzn]
• Established anglicization.

Belshazzar biblical name; also opera by Handel
bel-**shaz**-uhr /bɛl'ʃazə(r)/

Beltane ancient Celtic festival
bel-tayn /'bɛlteɪn/

Bemba Zambian ethnic group
bem-buh /'bɛmbə/

Benares former name for Varanasi
buh-**nar**-iz /bə'nɑːrɪz/

Benatar, Pat American rock singer
ben-uh-tar /'bɛnətɑː(r)/

Benbecula island, Scotland
ben-**bek**-yuul-uh /bɛn'bɛkjʊlə/

Bendigo town, Australia
ben-dig-oh /'bɛndɪɡəʊ/

Benecol trademark cholesterol-lowering range of foods
ben-uh-kol /'bɛnəkɒl/

Benedict, St Italian hermit
ben-uh-dikt /'bɛnədɪkt/

Benedictine Christian religious order
ben-uh-**dik**-tin /ˌbɛnə'dɪktɪn/

Benedictus part of the Mass
ben-uh-**dik**-tuuss /ˌbɛnə'dɪktʊs/

Benelux Belgium, the Netherlands, and Luxembourg
ben-uh-luks /'bɛnəlʌks/

Beneš, Edvard Czechoslovak statesman
ed-uu-art **ben**-esh /ˌɛdʊɑː(r)t 'bɛnɛʃ/

Benét, Eric American singer
ben-**ay** /bɛ'neɪ/

Benfica Portuguese football team
ben-**fee**-kuh /bɛn'fi:kə/, [bē'fikɐ]
• Established anglicization.

Bengal region of the Indian subcontinent
beng-**gawl** /bɛŋ'ɡɔːl/

Bengali relating to Bengal
beng-**gaw**-li /bɛŋ'ɡɔːli/

Benghazi port, Libya
beng-**gah**-zi /bɛŋ'ɡɑːzi/

Benguela port, Angola
beng-**gel**-uh /bɛŋ'ɡɛlə/

Bengkulu province, Indonesia
buhng-**koo**-loo /bəŋ'ku:lu:/

Ben-Gurion, David Israeli statesman
day-vid ben **goor**-i-uhn /ˌdeɪvɪd bɛn 'ɡʊəriən/
• Established anglicization.

benign gentle or mild
buh-**nyn** /bə'nʌɪn/

Benin country
ben-**een** /bɛ'ni:n/

Bening, Anette American actress
ben-ing /'bɛnɪŋ/

Benitez, Rafael Spanish manager of Liverpool FC
raf-uh-**el** ben-**ee**-teth /rafəˌɛl bɛ'ni:tɛθ/

benne US term for sesame
ben-i /'bɛni/

Bennett, Jana BBC director of television
jay-nuh **ben**-it /ˌdʒeɪnə 'bɛnɪt/

Ben Nevis mountain, Scotland
ben **nev**-iss /ˌbɛn ˈnɛvɪs/

Benoni city, South Africa
buh-**noh**-ni /bəˈnəʊni/

Bentham, Jeremy English philosopher
ben-thuhm /ˈbɛnθəm/

Benue-Congo branch of the
Niger–Congo family of languages
ben-**way** /ˈbɛnweɪ/

Ben Wyvis mountain, Scotland
ben **wiv**-iss /ˌbɛn ˈwɪvɪs/

Benxi city, China
ben-**shee** /ˌbɛnˈʃiː/

Benz, Karl Friedrich German motor
manufacturer
karl freed-rikh bents /ˌkɑː(r)l ˌfriːdrɪç
ˈbɛnts/

The make of car is anglicized to benz; see
MERCEDES BENZ.

Benzedrine trademark drug
ben-zid-reen /ˈbɛnzɪdriːn/

benzodiazepine group of tranquillizing
drugs
ben-zoh-dy-**ayz**-uh-peen
/ˌbɛnzəʊdʌɪˈeɪzəpiːn/

Commonly also **ben**-zoh-dy-**az**-uh-peen.

Beograd see **Belgrade**

Beowulf Old English epic poem
bay-uh-wuulf /ˈbeɪəwʊlf/

Berardi, Antonio English fashion
designer
an-**toh**-ni-oh buh-**rar**-di /anˌtəʊniəʊ
bəˈrɑː(r)di/

Berber North African ethnic group and
language
bur-buhr /ˈbəː(r)bə(r)/

Berbera port, Somalia
bur-buh-ruh /ˈbəː(r)bərə/

Berchtesgaden town, Germany
bairkh-tuhss-**gah**-duhn
/ˌbɛː(r)çtəsˈgɑːdən/

Berenger, Tom American actor
berr-uhn-juhr /ˈbɛrəndʒə(r)/

Berenice ancient Egyptian queen
berr-uh-**ny**-si /ˌbɛrəˈnʌɪsi/

Bereshit book of the Torah
berr-**ay**-shit /bɛˈreɪʃɪt/

Berg, Alban Austrian composer
al-buhn bairk /ˌalbən ˈbɛː(r)k/

Bergamo town and province, Italy
bair-guh-moh /ˈbɛː(r)gəməʊ/

bergamot fragrant plant
bur-guh-mot /ˈbəː(r)gəmɒt/

Bergen port, Norway
bur-guhn /ˈbəː(r)gən/, [ˈbærgən]
• Established anglicization.

Bergen-Belsen Nazi concentration
camp
bair-guhn bel-zuhn /ˌbɛː(r)gən
ˈbɛlzən/

bergenia evergreen Asian plant
buhr-**gee**-ni-uh /bəˈgiːniə/

Bergerac region, France
bair-zhuh-**rak** /bɛː(r)ʒəˈrak/

Berger, Óscar Guatemalan president
osk-ar bair-**khair** /ˌɒskɑː(r)
bɛː(r)ˈxɛː(r)/

Bergman, Ingmar Swedish film
director
ing-mar **bairg**-muhn /ˌɪŋmɑː(r)
ˈbɛː(r)gmən/, [ˈbærjman]

Bergman, Ingrid Swedish actress
ing-rid **bairg**-muhn /ˌɪŋrɪd
ˈbɛː(r)gmən/, [ˈbærjman]

beriberi vitamin deficiency disease
berr-i-**berr**-i /ˌbɛriˈbɛri/

Bering, Vitus Danish navigator and
explorer
vee-tuuss **bair**-ing /ˌviːtʊs ˈbɛːrɪŋ/

Berio, Luciano Italian composer
loo-**chah**-noh **bair**-i-oh /luːˌtʃɑːnəʊ
ˈbɛːriəʊ/

Berkeley city, US
bur-kli /ˈbəː(r)kli/

Berkeley, Busby American film director
buz-bi bur-kli /ˌbʌzbi ˈbəː(r)kli/

Berkeley, George Irish philosopher and
bishop
bar-kli /ˈbɑː(r)kli/

Berkeley, Lennox English composer
bar-kli /ˈbɑː(r)kli/

berkelium chemical element
bur-kli-uhm /ˈbəː(r)kliəm/

Sometimes also bur-**kee**-li-uhm, although
the element takes its name from the US city
Berkeley.

Berkoff, Steven English dramatist
bur-kof /ˈbəː(r)kɒf/

Berkshire county, England
bark-shuhr /ˈbɑː(r)kʃə(r)/

Berkshire county, US
burk-shuhr /'bəː(r)kʃə(r)/

Berlin capital of Germany
bur-**lin** /bəː(r)'lɪn/, [bɛr'liːn]
• Established anglicization.

Berliner, Der German newspaper
dair bair-**lee**-nuhr /dɛː(r)
bɛː(r)'liːnə(r)/

Berlingske Tidende Danish newspaper
bair-ling-skuh **tee**-duhn-duh
/ˌbɛː(r)lɪŋskə 'tiːdəndə/

Berlin, Irving Russian-born American
songwriter
bur-**lin** /bəː(r)'lɪn/

Berlioz, Hector French composer
ek-**tor bair**-li-ohz /ɛkˌtɔː(r)
'bɛː(r)liəʊz/

Berlusconi, Silvio Italian prime
minister
seel-vi-oh bair-loo-**skoh**-ni /ˌsiːlviəʊ
ˌbɛː(r)luːˈskəʊni/

Bermuda country
buhr-**myoo**-duh /bə(r)'mjuːdə/

Bermudian relating to Bermuda
buhr-**myoo**-di-uhn /bə(r)'mjuːdiən/

Bern (also **Berne**) capital of Switzerland
burn /bəː(r)n/, German [bɛrn], French
[bɛrn]
• Established anglicization.

Bernadotte, Jean Baptiste French
soldier; king of Sweden as Charles XIV
zhah(ng) bat-**eest** bair-nad-**ot** /ʒɑ̃
baˌtiːst bɛː(r)naˈdɒt/

Bernhardt, Sarah French actress
sair-uh **bairn**-hart /ˌsɛːrə
'bɛː(r)nhaː(r)t/, French [sara bɛrnar]
• Established anglicization.

Bernini, Gian Lorenzo Italian painter
and architect
jan lorr-**ent**-soh bair-**nee**-ni /dʒan
lɒˌrɛntsəʊ bɛː(r)'niːni/

Bernstein, Leonard American
composer, conductor, and pianist
burn-styn /'bəː(r)nstʌɪn/

Berra, Yogi American baseball player
yoh-gi **berr**-uh /ˌjəʊgi 'bɛrə/

Berry, Halle American actress
hal-i **berr**-i /ˌhali 'bɛri/

Bertolucci, Bernardo Italian film
director
bair-**nar**-doh bair-tuh-**loo**-chi
/ˌbɛː(r)ˌnaː(r)dəʊ bɛː(r)tə'luːtʃi/

Berwald, Franz Swedish composer
franss bair-**vald** /ˌfrans 'bɛː(r)vald/

Berwickshire former county, Scotland
berr-ik-shuhr /'bɛrɪkʃə(r)/

beryllium chemical element
buh-**ril**-i-uhm /bə'rɪliəm/

Besançon city, France
buh-**zah(ng)**-**so(ng)** /bəzɑ̃'sɔ̃/

Besant, Annie English theosophist,
writer, and politician
bess-uhnt /'bɛsənt/

Beşiktaş part of Istanbul; also football
team
besh-ik-**tash** /bɛ'ʃɪktaʃ/

Beslan town, Russia
buh-**slahn** /bə'slaːn/

Bessarabia region, eastern Europe
bess-uh-**ray**-bi-uh /ˌbɛsə'reɪbiə/

Bessemer, Henry English engineer and
inventor
bess-uh-muhr /'bɛsəmə(r)/

Besson, Luc French film director
luek bess-**o(ng)** /ˌlyk bɛ'sɔ̃/

beta letter of the Greek alphabet
bee-tuh /'biːtə/

Betelgeuse star
bee-tuhl-ju(r)z /'biːtəlˌdʒəːz/

Beth Din Jewish court of law
bayt **deen** /ˌbeɪt 'diːn/

Bethlehem town, West Bank
beth-luh-hem /'bɛθləhɛm/

Betjeman, John English poet
betch-uh-muhn /'bɛtʃəmən/

beurré class of pear
byoor-i /'bjʊəri/

Bewick, Thomas English artist
byoo-ik /'bjuːɪk/

bey governor of a district in the Ottoman
Empire
bay /beɪ/

Beyoncé American pop singer
bee-**yon**-say /biː'jɒnseɪ/

bezique card game for two
buh-**zeek** /bə'ziːk/

Bhagwan Hindu god
bug-**wahn** /bʌg'waːn/

bhaji Indian small cake or ball of
vegetables
bah-ji /'baːdʒi/

bhangra type of Punjabi pop music
bung-gruh /ˈbʌŋgrə/

bharal Himalayan wild sheep
burr-uhl /ˈbʌrəl/

Bharat Hindi name for India
burr-uht /ˈbʌrət/

Bhaskar, Sanjeev English comedian
and actor
sun-jeev busk-uhr /sʌnˌdʒiːv
ˈbʌskə(r)/

Bhavnagar port, India
buv-nug-uhr /bʌvˈnʌgə(r)/

Bhel Poori Indian dish
bel poor-i /ˌbɛl ˈpʊəri/

Bhil (also **Bheel**) Indian ethnic group
beel /biːl/

Bhili relating to the Bhils
bee-li /ˈbiːli/

bhindi Indian term for okra
bin-dee /ˈbɪndiː/

Bhojpuri Indian group of languages
bohj-poor-i /ˌbəʊdʒˈpʊəri/

Bhopal city, India
boh-pahl /bəʊˈpɑːl/

Bhubaneswar city, India
boo-buh-naysh-wuhr
/ˌbuːbəˈneɪʃwə(r)/

bhuna (also **bhoona**) Bengali curry
boo-nuh /ˈbuːnə/

Bhutan independent kingdom
boo-tahn /buːˈtɑːn/

Bhutto, Benazir Pakistani stateswoman
ben-uh-zeer boo-toh /ˌbɛnəˌzɪə(r)
ˈbuːtəʊ/

Bhutto, Zulfikar Ali Pakistani
statesman
zuul-fik-ar ah-li boo-toh /ˌzʊlfɪkɑː(r)
ˌɑːli ˈbuːtəʊ/

Biafra, Bight of bay in the Gulf of
Guinea
bi-af-ruh /biˈafrə/

Białystok city, Poland
byow-ist-ok /bjaʊˈɪstɒk/

Biarritz resort, France
beer-its /ˌbɪəˈrɪts/, [bjarits]
• Established anglicization.

Bias see **Beas**

Biber, Heinrich German-Bohemian
composer
hyn-rikh bee-buhr /ˌhʌɪnrɪç ˈbiːbə(r)/

bice blue-green pigment

byss /bʌɪs/

bicentenary two-hundredth anniversary
by-sen-tee-nuh-ri /ˌbʌɪsɛnˈtiːnəri/

bichon frise small dog
bee-shuhn freez /ˌbiːʃən ˈfriːz/

Bielefeld city, Germany
bee-luh-felt /ˈbiːləˌfɛlt/

biennale large art exhibition or music
festival
bee-en-ah-lay /ˌbiːɛˈnɑːleɪ/

biennium pl. **biennia** period of two years
by-en-i-uhm, pl. **by-en-i-uh**
/bʌɪˈɛniəm/, pl. /-niə/
• Standard -s plural is also possible.

Bierce, Ambrose American writer
beers /bɪə(r)s/

BIFU Banking, Insurance, and Finance
Union
bif-yoo /ˈbɪfjuː/

Big Sur resort, US
big sur /ˌbɪg ˈsə:(r)/

Bihar state, India
bi-har /bɪˈhɑː(r)/

Bihari relating to Bihar
bi-har-i /bɪˈhɑːri/

Biko, Steve South African radical leader
bee-koh /ˈbiːkəʊ/

Bilbao port, Spain
bil-bow /bɪlˈbaʊ/

Bild German newspaper
bilt /bɪlt/

Bildad biblical name
bil-dad /ˈbɪldad/

bindi Indian decorative mark on the
forehead
bin-dee /ˈbɪndiː/

Binet, Alfred French psychologist
al-fred bee-nay /alˌfrɛd biːˈneɪ/

Bin Laden, Osama Saudi-born Islamic
dissident
uu-sah-muh bin lah-duhn /ʊˌsɑːmə
bɪn ˈlɑːdən/

Binoche, Juliet French actress
zhuel-yet bee-nosh /ʒylˌjɛt biːˈnɒʃ/

Bioko island, Equatorial Guinea
bi-oh-koh /biˈəʊkəʊ/

biome community of flora and fauna
by-ohm /ˈbʌɪəʊm/

biopic biographical film
by-oh-pik /ˈbʌɪəʊˌpɪk/

biopsy examination of tissue
by-op-si /ˈbaɪɒpsi/

BIOS set of computer instructions
by-oss /ˈbaɪɒs/

biotin vitamin of the B complex
by-uh-tin /ˈbaɪətɪn/

bipedal using only two legs for walking
by-pee-duhl /baɪˈpiːdəl/

bireme ancient warship
by-reem /ˈbaɪriːm/

biretta square cap worn by Roman
Catholic clergymen
birr-et-uh /bɪˈrɛtə/

Birgitta, St variant spelling of St Bridget
beer-git-uh /ˌbɪə(r)ˈɡɪtə/

biriani Indian dish
birr-i-ah-ni /ˌbɪriˈɑːni/

Birkbeck college in London
burk-bek /ˈbɜː(r)kbɛk/

Birkenau part of Auschwitz
concentration camp
beer-kuh-now /ˈbɪə(r)kənaʊ/

Birkenhead town, England
bur-kuhn-hed /ˌbɜː(r)kənˈhɛd/

Birman cat of a long-haired breed
bur-muhn /ˈbɜː(r)mən/

birr currency unit, Ethiopia
beer /bɪə(r)/

bis musical term
biss /bɪs/

Biscay, Bay of part of the North Atlantic
bisk-ay /ˈbɪskeɪ/

biscotti Italian biscuits
bisk-ot-i /bɪˈskɒti/

Bishkek capital of Kyrgyzstan
bish-kek /bɪʃˈkɛk/

Bisho town, South Africa
bee-shoh /ˈbiːʃəʊ/

bishopric office or rank of a bishop
bish-uh-prik /ˈbɪʃəprɪk/

Bislama Vanuatan pidgin language
bish-luh-mah /ˈbɪʃləˌmɑː/

Bismarck city, US
biz-mark /ˈbɪzmɑː(r)k/

Bismarck, Otto von German
statesman
ot-oh fon biz-mark /ˌɒtəʊ fon
ˈbɪzmɑː(r)k/, German [ˈbɪsmark]
• Established anglicization.

bismillah 'in the name of God' (Arabic)
biss-mil-uh /bɪsˈmɪlə/

bismuth chemical element
biz-muhth /ˈbɪzməθ/

bison shaggy-haired wild ox
by-suhn /ˈbaɪsən/

bisque shellfish soup
bisk /bɪsk/

Bissagos Islands group of islands,
Guinea-Bissau
biss-ag-guush /bɪˈsaɡʊʃ/

Bissau capital of Guinea-Bissau
biss-ow /bɪˈsaʊ/

Bisset, Jacqueline English actress
biss-it /ˈbɪsɪt/

bistoury surgical knife
bist-uu-ri /ˈbɪstʊri/

bistre brownish-yellow pigment
bist-uhr /ˈbɪstə(r)/

Bithynia ancient region in Asia Minor
bith-in-i-uh /bɪˈθɪniə/

Bitrex trademark bitter-tasting synthetic
organic compound
bit-reks /ˈbɪtrɛks/

bivouac temporary camp
biv-oo-ak /ˈbɪvuak/

Bizerta port, Tunisia
biz-ur-tuh /bɪˈzɜː(r)tə/

Bizet, Georges French composer
zhorzh bee-zay /ˌʒɔː(r)ʒ biˈzeɪ/

Bjelovar town, Croatia
byel-uh-var /ˈbjɛləvɑː(r)/

Björk Icelandic singer
byoerk /bjœːk/

blackguard dishonourable man
blag-ard /ˈblaɡɑː(r)d/

blaeberry Scottish and northern English
term for bilberry
blay-buh-ri /ˈbleɪbəri/

Blaenau Gwent county borough, Wales
bly-ny gwent /ˌblaɪnaɪ ˈɡwɛnt/

Blahnik, Manolo Spanish shoe
designer
muh-noh-loh blah-nik /məˌnəʊləʊ
ˈblɑːnɪk/

Blair, Cherie English lawyer; wife of
Tony Blair
shuh-ree /ʃəˈriː/

Blanchett, Cate Australian actress
kayt blan-chuht /ˌkeɪt ˈblantʃət/

blancmange gelatinous dessert
bluh-monzh /bləˈmɒnʒ/

Blantyre city, Malawi
blan-ty-uhr /ˈblantʌɪə(r)/

blasé unimpressed or indifferent
blah-zay /ˈblɑːzeɪ/

blaspheme speak irreverently about
sacred things
blass-**feem** /blasˈfiːm/

blasphemous sacrilegious
blass-fuh-muhss /ˈblasfəməs/

Blatter, Sepp Swiss president of FIFA
sep blat-uhr /ˌsɛp ˈblatə(r)/

Blaue Reiter group of German
expressionist painters
blow-uh **ryt**-uhr /ˌblaʊə ˈrʌɪtə(r)/

Blears, Hazel English politician
bleerz /blɪə(r)z/

Blenheim palace, England
blen-uhm /ˈblɛnəm/

bleomycin antibiotic
blee-oh-**my**-sin /ˌbliːəʊˈmʌɪsɪn/

blepharitis inflammation of the eyelid
blef-uh-**ry**-tiss /ˌblɛfəˈrʌɪtɪs/

Blériot, Louis French aviation pioneer
lwee blerr-i-**oh** /ˌlwiː blɛrɪˈəʊ/

blesbok antelope
bless-bok /ˈblɛsbɒk/

blessed made holy
bless-id /ˈblɛsɪd/

blessed past tense of bless
blest /blɛst/

Blethyn, Brenda English actress
bleth-in /ˈblɛðɪn/

Blige, Mary J. American singer
blyj /blʌɪdʒ/

Bligh, William British naval officer
bly /blʌɪ/

blini Russian pancakes
blee-ni /ˈbliːni/

blitzkrieg intense military campaign
blits-kreeg /ˈblɪtskriːg/

Blix, Hans Swedish diplomat and
politician
hahnss bliks /ˌhɑːns ˈblɪks/

Bloch, Ernest Swiss-born American
composer
air-nest blokh /ˌɛː(r)nɛst ˈblɒx/

Bloemfontein city, South Africa
bloom-fuhn-tayn /ˈbluːmfən,teɪn/

Blois city, France
blwah /blwɑː/

Blondin, Charles French acrobat

blon-din /ˈblɒndɪn/, [blɔ̃dɛ̃]
• Established anglicization.

Blum, Léon French statesman
lay-**o(ng) bloom** /leɪ,ɔ̃ ˈbluːm/

Blumenbach, Johann Friedrich
German physiologist and anatomist
yoh-han **freed**-rikh **bloo**-muhn-bakh
/ˌjəʊhan ˌfriːdrɪç ˈbluːmənbax/

B'nai B'rith Jewish organization
bnay brith /ˌbneɪ ˈbrɪθ/

Boadicea queen of the Iceni; also called
Boudicca
boh-uh-diss-ee-uh /ˌbəʊədɪˈsiːə/

Boateng, Paul English politician
bwah-teng /ˈbwɑːtɛŋ/

boatswain ship's officer
boh-suhn /ˈbəʊsən/

Boa Vista town, Brazil
boh-uh **vist**-uh /ˌbəʊə ˈvɪstə/

bocage pastureland
buh-**kahzh** /bəˈkɑːʒ/

Boccaccio, Giovanni Italian writer
and poet
juh-**vah**-ni buh-**katch**-oh /dʒə,vɑːni
bəˈkatʃəʊ/

bocce Italian game; also called **boccia**
botch-ay /ˈbɒtʃeɪ/

Boccherini, Luigi Italian composer
luu-**ee**-ji buh-kuh-**ree**-ni /lʊ,iːdʒi
ˌbʊkəˈriːni/

boccia Italian game; also called **bocce**
botch-uh /ˈbɒtʃə/

bocconcini small balls of mozzarella
cheese
bok-on-**chee**-ni /ˌbɒkɒnˈtʃiːni/

Bocelli, Andrea Italian tenor
an-**dray**-uh botch-**el**-i /an,dreɪə
bɒˈtʃɛli/

Bochum city, Germany
boh-khuum /ˈbəʊxʊm/

Bocquet, Kevin BBC journalist
buh-**kay** /bəˈkeɪ/

bodega cellar or shop selling wine
buh-**day**-guh /bəˈdeɪgə/

Bodensee see **Constance**

Bodhgaya Buddhist place of
enlightenment
bohd-guh-yuh /ˈbəʊdgəjə/

bodhisattva (in Buddhism) person
worthy of nirvana
boh-di-**sut**-vuh /ˌbəʊdɪˈsʌtvə/

bodhrán Irish drum
bow-**rahn** /baʊˈrɑːn/

Bodleian Library library of Oxford
University
bod-li-uhn /ˈbɒdliən/

Bodoni, Giambattista Italian printer
jam-bat-**eest**-uh buh-**doh**-ni
/dʒambaˌtiːstə bəˈdəʊni/

Bodrum resort, Turkey
bod-ruhm /ˈbɒdrəm/

Boeing aircraft manufacturers
boh-ing /ˈbəʊɪŋ/

Boeotia department, Greece
bi-**oh**-shi-uh /biˈəʊʃiə/

Boer Dutch population which settled in
southern Africa
bawr /bɔː(r)/

Commonly also **boh-uhr** and boor.

boeremusiek traditional Afrikaner
music
boor-uh-myoo-sik /ˈbʊərəˌmjuːsɪk/

**Boethius, Anicius Manlius
Severinus** Roman statesman and
philosopher
an-**iss**-i-uhss man-li-uhss
sev-uh-**ry**-nuhss boh-**ee**-thi-uhss
/aˌnɪsiəs ˌmanliəs sɛvəˈrʌɪnəs
bəʊˈiːθiəs/

boeuf bourguignon dish of beef stewed
in red wine
boef bor-gin-yon /ˌbœf bɔː(r)ɡɪnˈjɒn/,
French [bœf burɡinjõ]

Bofors Swedish steel and armaments
company
boh-fuhrz /ˈbəʊfə(r)z/, [bʊˈfɔʂ]
• Established anglicization.

bogan boringly conventional or
old-fashioned person
boh-guhn /ˈbəʊɡən/

Bogarde, Dirk British actor and writer
boh-gard /ˈbəʊɡɑː(r)d/

Bogart, Humphrey American actor
boh-gart /ˈbəʊɡɑː(r)t/

bogle phantom or goblin
boh-guhl /ˈbəʊɡəl/

bogong large Australian moth
boh-gong /ˈbəʊɡɒŋ/

Bogotá capital of Colombia
bog-ot-**ah** /bɒɡɒˈtɑː/

Bo Hai large inlet of the Yellow Sea,
China

boh **khy** /ˌbəʊ ˈxʌɪ/

bohea black China tea
boh-**hee** /bəʊˈhiː/

Bohemia region, Czech Republic
boh-**hee**-mi-uh /bəʊˈhiːmiə/

Böhm, Georg German organist
gay-ork boem /ˌɡeɪɔː(r)k ˈbøːm/

Bohol island, Philippines
boh-**hol** /bəʊˈhɒl/

bohrium chemical element
bawr-i-uhm /ˈbɔːriəm/

Boileau, Nicholas French critic and
poet
nee-kol-**ah** bwal-oh /niːkɒˌlɑː
bwaˈləʊ/

boilie type of flavoured fishing bait
boy-li /ˈbɔɪli/

Boise city, Idaho
boy-si /ˈbɔɪsi/

Bokassa, Jean Bédel African
statesman and military leader
zhah(ng) buh-**del** buh-**kass**-uh /ʒɑ̃
bəˌdɛl bəˈkasə/

bokken wooden sword
bok-uhn /ˈbɒkən/

Bokmål one of two standard forms of
Norwegian
book-mawl /ˈbuːkmɔːl/

bolection architectural feature
buh-**lek**-shuhn /bəˈlɛkʃən/

bolero Spanish dance
buh-**lair**-oh /bəˈlɛːrəʊ/

The *bolero* jacket can also be pronounced
bol-uh-roh.

Boleyn, Anne second wife of Henry
VIII
buh-**lin** /bəˈlɪn/

Bolger, James New Zealand statesman
bol-juhr /ˈbɒldʒə(r)/

bolide large meteor
boh-lyd /ˈbəʊlʌɪd/

Bolingbroke surname of Henry IV
bol-ing-bruuk /ˈbɒlɪŋbrʊk/

Bolívar, Simón Venezuelan patriot
and statesman
see-mon bol-**ee**-var /siːˌmɒn
bɒˈliːvɑː(r)/

bolivar currency unit, Venezuela
bol-**ee**-var /bɒˈliːvɑː(r)/

Bolivia country
buh-**liv**-i-uh /bə'lɪvɪə/, Spanish
[bo'liβja]
• Established anglicization.

boliviano currency unit, Bolivia
buh-liv-i-**ah**-noh /bə,lɪvɪ'ɑːnəʊ/

Böll, Heinrich German novelist
hyn-rikh **boel** /,hʌɪnrɪç 'bœl/

Bollinger brand of champagne
bol-in-juhr /'bɒlɪndʒə(r)/

bollito misto Italian dish
bol-**ee**-toh **mist**-oh /bɒ,liːtəʊ 'mɪstəʊ/

Bologna city, Italy
buh-**lon**-yuh /bə'lɒnjə/

bolometer instrument for measuring
radiant energy
buh-**lom**-it-uhr /bə'lɒmɪtə(r)/

Bolshevik Russian political party
bol-shuh-vik /'bɒlʃəvɪk/

Bolshoi Ballet Russian ballet company
buhl-**shoy** /bəl'ʃɔɪ/

Bolzano city, Italy
bol-**tsah**-noh /bɒl'tsɑːnəʊ/

bomarc anti-aircraft missile
boh-mark /'bəʊmɑː(r)k/

bombard cannon
bom-bard /'bɒmbɑː(r)d/

bombarde wind instrument
bom-bard /'bɒmbɑː(r)d/

bombardier rank of non-commissioned
officer
bom-buh-**deer** /,bɒmbə'dɪə(r)/

bombardon bass tuba
bom-bar-duhn /'bɒmbɑː(r)dən/

bombazine twilled dress fabric
bom-buh-zeen /'bɒmbəziːn/

bombe frozen dome-shaped dessert
bomb /bɒmb/

bombora type of wave
bom-**bawr**-uh /bɒm'bɔːrə/

Bon Japanese Buddhist festival
bon /bɒn/

bona fide genuine
boh-nuh **fy**-di /,bəʊnə 'fʌɪdi/

Bonaire island, Netherlands Antilles
bon-air /bɒ'nɛː(r)/

Bonaparte Corsican family name
boh-nuh-part /'bəʊnəpɑː(r)t/

bona vacantia goods without an
apparent owner
boh-nuh vuh-**kant**-i-uh /,bəʊnə
və'kantɪə/

Bonaventura, St Franciscan theologian
bon-uh-ven-**tyoor**-uh
/,bɒnəvɛn'tjʊərə/

Bondi resort, Australia
bon-dy /'bɒndʌɪ/

bonhomie cheerful friendliness
bon-uh-mee /'bɒnəmiː/

boniato variety of sweet potato
bon-i-**ah**-toh /,bɒni'ɑːtəʊ/

Boniface, St Anglo-Saxon missionary
bon-if-ayss /'bɒnɪfeɪs/

bonito small tuna
buh-**nee**-toh /bə'niːtəʊ/

Bon Jovi American rock band
bon joh-vi /,bɒn 'dʒəʊvi/

bon mot witty remark
bo(ng) **moh** /,bɒ̃ 'məʊ/

Bonnard, Pierre French painter
pyair bon-ar /,pjɛː(r) bɒ'nɑː(r)/

Bono Irish singer
bon-oh /'bɒnəʊ/

Bono, Sonny American singer and
politician
sun-i **boh**-noh /,sʌni 'bəʊnəʊ/

bonobo chimpanzee
buh-**noh**-boh /bə'nəʊbəʊ/

bonsai art of growing miniature trees
bon-sy /'bɒnsʌɪ/

bontebok antelope
bon-tuh-bok /'bɒntəbɒk/

bon voyage 'pleasant journey' (French)
bo(ng) voy-**yahzh** /,bɒ̃ vɔɪ'jɑːʒ/, [bɔ̃
vwaja:ʒ]

bonxie great skua
bonk-si /'bɒŋksi/

Bonynge, Richard Australian
conductor
bon-ing /'bɒnɪŋ/

bonze Japanese or Chinese Buddhist
teacher
bonz /bɒnz/

boojum mythological dangerous animal
boo-juhm /'buːdʒəm/

Boolean relating to the work of
mathematician George Boole
boo-li-uhn /'buːlɪən/

boor rough and bad-mannered person
bor /bɔː(r)/

Less commonly also boor.

Boötes northern constellation
boh-**oh**-teez /bəʊˈəʊtiːz/

Booth, Cherie English lawyer; wife of
Tony Blair
shuh-ree **booth** /ʃəˌriː ˈbuːð/

This British surname is variously
pronounced boo*th* and boo*th*, depending
on individual preference.

Boothia, Gulf of gulf in the Canadian
Arctic
booth-i-uh /ˈbuːðɪə/

Bophuthatswana region, South Africa
boh-poo-tuht-**swah**-nuh
/ˌbəʊpuːtət'swɑːnə/

bora strong, cold wind
baw-ruh /ˈbɔːrə/

Bora-Bora island, French Polynesia
baw-ruh **baw**-ruh /ˌbɔːrə ˈbɔːrə/

boracic consisting of boric acid
buh-**rass**-ik /bəˈrasɪk/

borage herbaceous plant
borr-ij /ˈbɒrɪdʒ/

Borås city, Sweden
buu-**rawss** /bʊˈrɔːs/

Borazon trademark industrial abrasive
baw-ruh-zon /ˈbɔːrəzɒn/

Borbón y Borbón, Juan Carlos de
king of Spain
khwan **kar**-lohss day bor-**bon** ee
bor-**bon** /xwan ˌkɑː(r)lɒʊs deɪ
bɔː(r)ˌbɒn iː bɔː(r)ˈbɒn/

borborygmus rumbling noise in the
intestines
bor-buh-**rig**-muhss /ˌbɔː(r)bəˈrɪgməs/

Bordeaux port, France
bor-**doh** /bɔː(r)ˈdəʊ/

bordelaise served with a sauce of red
wine and onions
bor-duh-**layz** /ˌbɔː(r)dəˈleɪz/

Bordet, Jules Belgian bacteriologist and
immunologist
zhuel bor-**day** /ʒyl bɔː(r)ˈdeɪ/

boreal relating to the climatic zone south
of the Arctic
baw-ri-uhl /ˈbɔːrɪəl/

boreen Irish narrow country road
baw-**reen** /bɔːˈriːn/

Borg, Björn Swedish tennis player
byoern borg /ˌbjœː(r)n ˈbɔː(r)g/,
[ˌbjœːɳ ˈbɔrj]

borgata branch of the Mafia

bor-gah-tuh /bɔː(r)ˈgɑːtə/

Borgia, Cesare Italian statesman
chez-uh-ray bor-**juh** /ˌtʃɛzəreɪ
ˈbɔː(r)dʒə/

Borgia, Lucrezia Italian noblewoman
loo-**kret**-si-uh **borj**-uh /luːˌkrɛtsiə
ˈbɔː(r)dʒə/

Boris Godunov opera by Mussorgsky
borr-iss **god**-uun-of /ˌbɒrɪs ˌgɒdʊnɒf/,
Russian [bʌˌrʲis gəʌdʊˈnɔf]
• Established anglicization.

Borlaug, Norman American scientist
bor-lawg /ˈbɔː(r)lɔːg/

borlotti bean type of kidney bean
bor-**lot**-i /bɔː(r)ˈlɒti/

Bormann, Martin German Nazi
politician
mar-teen bor-**man** /ˌmɑː(r)tiːn
ˈbɔː(r)man/

Borneo island, divided between
Indonesia, Malaysia, and Brunei
bor-ni-oh /ˈbɔː(r)niəʊ/

Bornholm island, Denmark
born-hohm /ˈbɔː(r)nhəʊm/,
[ˈbɒɐnhɔlm]
• Established anglicization.

Borobudur Buddhist monument in Java
borr-oh-buud-**oor** /ˌbɒrəʊbʊˈdʊə(r)/

Borodin, Aleksandr Russian composer
al-uhk-**sahn**-duhr **borr**-uh-din
/aləkˌsɑːndə(r) ˈbɒrədɪn/

Borodino, Battle of battle in 1812 in
Russia
borr-uh-**dee**-noh /ˌbɒrəˈdiːnəʊ/
• Established anglicization.

boron chemical element
baw-ron /ˈbɔːrɒn/

Borrell, Josep Spanish politician
zhuuz-**ep** borr-**el** /ˌʒʊzɛp bʊˈrɛl/

Borromini, Francesco Italian
architect
fran-**chesk**-oh borr-uh-**mee**-ni
/franˌtʃɛskəʊ ˌbɒrəˈmiːni/

Borsalino trademark wide-brimmed hat
bor-suh-**lee**-noh /ˌbɔː(r)səˈliːnəʊ/

borscht Russian or Polish soup
borsht /bɔː(r)ʃt/

borzoi Russian wolfhound
bor-zoy /ˈbɔː(r)zɔɪ/

boscage mass of trees or shrubs
bosk-ij /ˈbɒskɪdʒ/

Boscastle village, England
boss-kah-suhl /ˈbɒskɑːsəl/

Bosnia-Herzegovina country
boz-ni-uh hurt-suh-**gov**-in-uh
/ˌbɒznɪə hɜː(r)tsəˈgɒvɪnə/

Established anglicization. The Bosnian name is Bosna I Hertsegovina, pronounced **boss**-nuh ee **hairt**-suh-**gov**-in-uh.

Bosphorus the Bosporus
boss-fuh-ruhss /ˈbɒsfərəs/

Bosporus strait connecting the Black Sea with the Sea of Marmara
bosp-uh-ruhss /ˈbɒspərəs/

bossa nova Brazilian dance
boss-uh **noh**-vuh /ˌbɒsə ˈnəʊvə/

Botha, P. W. South African statesman
boo-uh-tuh /ˈbuətə/
• This is the Afrikaans pronunciation.

Botham, Ian English cricketer
bohth-uhm /ˈbəʊθəm/

This British surname is variously pronounced **both**-uhm and **bohth**-uhm, depending on individual preference.

Bothnia, Gulf of part of the Baltic Sea
both-ni-uh /ˈbɒθnɪə/

Bothwell, Earl of Scottish nobleman
both-wel /ˈbɒθwɛl/

bothy (also **bothie**) small hut or cottage
both-i /ˈbɒθi/

Botox trademark drug prepared from botulin
boh-toks /ˈbəʊtɒks/

Botswana country
bot-**swah**-nuh /bɒˈtswɑːnə/

Botticelli, Sandro Italian painter
san-droh bot-**itch**-**el**-i /ˌsandrəʊ bɒtɪˈtʃɛli/

botulin bacterial toxin
bot-yuul-in /ˈbɒtjʊlɪn/

botulism food poisoning
bot-yuul-iz-uhm /ˈbɒtjʊlɪzəm/

bouchée small pastry
boo-shay /ˈbuːʃeɪ/

Boucher, François French painter
frah(ng)-**swah** boo-**shay** /frɑ̃swɑːbuːˈʃeɪ/

Boudicca queen of the Iceni; also called **Boadicea**
boo-dik-uh /ˈbuːdɪkə/

boudin French black pudding
boo-da(ng) /ˈbuːdɛ̃/

Bougainville island, Papua New Guinea
boo-guhn-vil /ˈbuːgənvɪl/

Bougainville, Louis Antoine de French explorer
lwee ah(ng)-**twahn** duh
boo-ga(ng)-**veel** /lwiː ɑ̃ˌtwɑːn də buːgɛ̃viːl/

bougie surgical instrument
boo-zhi /ˈbuːʒi/

bouillabaisse fish soup
boo-yuh-**bess** /buːjəˈbɛs/

boule French form of bowls
bool /buːl/

Boulez, Pierre French composer and conductor
pyair boo-**lez** /pjɛː(r) buːˈlɛz/

Boulogne port, France
buul-**oyn** /bʊˈlɔɪn/, [bulɔn]
• Established anglicization.

Boult, Adrian English conductor
bohlt /bəʊlt/

Boulting, John and Roy English film producers and directors
bohl-ting /ˈbəʊltɪŋ/

Boulton, Matthew English engineer
bohl-tuhn /ˈbəʊltən/

Bourbaki name of a group of mathematicians
boor-**bah**-ki /ˌbʊə(r)ˈbɑːki/

Bourbon European royal house
boor-buhn /ˈbʊə(r)bən/, French [burbɔ̃]
• Established anglicization.

Bourbon chocolate-flavoured biscuit
bor-buhn /ˈbɔː(r)bən/

bourbon American whisky
bur-buhn /ˈbɜː(r)bən/

Bourbonnais province, France
boor-bon-**ay** /ˌbʊə(r)bɒˈneɪ/

bourgeois characteristic of the middle class
boor-zhwah /ˈbʊə(r)ʒwɑː/

bourgeoisie middle class
boor-zhwah-**zee** /ˌbʊə(r)ʒwɑːˈziː/

Bourguiba, Habib ibn Ali Tunisian nationalist and statesman
huh-**beeb** ib-uhn al-ee boor-**gee**-buh
/həˌbiːb ˌɪbən aˌliː bʊə(r)ˈgiːbə/

bourrée French dance
boor-**ay** /bʊəˈreɪ/

bourse French stock market
boorss /bʊə(r)s/

Boursin trademark kind of French soft cheese
boor-**sa(ng)** /bʊə(r)'sɛ̃/

Boutros-Ghali, Boutros Egyptian diplomat and politician
boo-tross boo-tross gah-li /,bu:trɒs ,bu:trɒs 'gɑ:li/

Bouvet Island Norwegian island in the South Atlantic
boo-**vay** /bu:'veɪ/

bouzouki Greek musical instrument
buuz-**oo**-ki /bʊ'zu:ki/

bovid mammal of the cattle family
boh-vid /'bəʊvɪd/

bovine relating to cattle
boh-vyn /'bəʊvʌɪn/

bovine spongiform encephalopathy disease of cattle; 'mad cow disease'
boh-vyn **spun**-ji-form en-kef-uh-**lop**-uh-thi /,bəʊvʌɪn ,spʌndʒɪfɔ:(r)m ,ɛŋkɛfə'lɒpəθi/

Bow, Clara American actress
boh /bəʊ/

Bowen, Elizabeth Irish-born British novelist
boh-uhn /'bəʊən/

Bowery street and district in New York City
bow-uh-ri /'baʊəri/

bowhead Arctic whale
boh-hed /'bəʊhɛd/

Bowie, David English singer
boh-i /'bəʊi/

Bowie, Jim American frontiersman
boo-i /'bu:i/

bowie knife long type of knife
boh-i /'bəʊi/

AM is **boo**-i.

Bowles, Paul American writer and composer
bohlz /bəʊlz/

Bowness town, England
boh-**ness** /bəʊ'nɛs/

Bow Street location in London
boh /bəʊ/

Brabant former duchy, western Europe
bruh-**bant** /brə'bant/

Brachiopoda phylum of marine invertebrates

brak-i-uh-**poh**-duh /,brakiə'pəʊdə/

brachytherapy treatment of cancer
brak-i-**therr**-uh-pi /,braki'θɛrəpi/

bradawl tool for boring holes
brad-awl /'bradɔ:l/

Bradenham ham trademark dark sweet-cured ham
brad-uhn-uhm /'bradənəm/

bradycardia abnormally slow heart action
brad-i-**kar**-di-uh /,bradi'kɑ:(r)diə/

brae steep bank or hillside
bray /breɪ/

Braeburn dessert apple
bray-burn /'breɪbə:(r)n/

Braga city, Portugal
brah-guh /'brɑ:gə/

Braganza city, Portugal
bruh-**gan**-zuh /brə'ganzə/

braggadocio boastful or arrogant behaviour
brag-uh-**doh**-choh /,bragə'dəʊtʃəʊ/

Brahe, Tycho Danish astronomer
ty-koh **brah**-hi /,tʌɪkəʊ 'brɑ:hi/, [,ty:ko 'brɑ:ə]
• Established anglicization.

Brahma Hindu god
brah-muh /'brɑ:mə/

Brahman member of the highest Hindu caste
brah-muhn /'brɑ:mən/

Brahmanism post-Vedic Indian religion
brah-muh-niz-uhm /'brɑ:mə,nɪzəm/

Brahmaputra river, southern Asia
brah-muh-**poot**-ruh /,brɑ:mə'pu:trə/

Brahms, Johannes German composer
yoh-**han**-uhss brahmz /jəʊ,hanəs 'brɑ:mz/, [,'brɑ:ms]
• Established anglicization.

Brahui Pakistani ethnic group
bruh-**hoo**-i /brə'hu:i/

Brăila city, Romania
bruh-**ee**-luh /brə'i:lə/

Braille, Louis French educationist
lwee bry /,lwi: 'brʌɪ/

Braille written language for the blind
brayl /breɪl/

Bramah, Joseph English inventor
bram-uh /'bramə/

Bramante, Donato Italian architect
don-ah-toh bram-an-tay /dɒˌnɑːtəʊ
brəˈmanteɪ/

Branagh, Kenneth English actor,
producer, and director
bran-uh /ˈbranə/

Brâncuși, Constantin Romanian
sculptor
kon-stuhn-teen brank-oo-zi
/ˌkɒnstantiːn branˈkuːzi/, [kɔnstanˈtin
brəŋˈkuʃj]
• Established anglicization.

Brandenburg state, Germany
bran-duhn-burg /ˈbrandənˌbəː(r)g/,
[ˈbrandənˌburk]
• Established anglicization.

Brandt, Bill German-born British
photographer
brant /brant/

Brandt, Willy German statesman
vil-i brant /ˌvɪli ˈbrant/

Braque, Georges French painter
zhorzh brak /ˌʒɔː(r)ʒ ˈbrak/

Brasilia capital of Brazil
bruh-zil-i-uh /brəˈzɪliə/

Brașov city, Romania
brash-ov /braˈʃɒv/

brassard band worn on the sleeve
brass-ard /ˈbrasɑː(r)d/

brassica plant
brass-ik-uh /ˈbrasɪkə/

brassiere undergarment
braz-i-air /ˈbrazɪɛː(r)/

Bratislava capital of Slovakia
brat-iss-lah-vuh /ˌbratɪˈslɑːvə/,
[ˈbratʲislava]
• Established anglicization.

bratwurst type of German pork sausage
brat-vurst /ˈbratvəː(r)st/, [ˈbraːtvʊrst]

Braun electrical appliances company
brawn /brɔːn/

Braun, Eva German mistress of Adolf
Hitler
ay-vuh brown /ˌeɪvə ˈbraʊn/

braw fine, good, or pleasing
braw /brɔː/

Brazil country
bruh-zil /brəˈzɪl/

Established anglicization. The Portuguese
form is Brasil, pronounced braz-ee-oo
[braˈziw].

Brazzaville capital of Congo
braz-uh-vil /ˈbrazəvɪl/

Brecht, Bertolt German dramatist
and poet
bair-tolt brekht /ˌbɛː(r)tɒlt ˈbrɛçt/

Breda town, Netherlands
bray-duh /ˈbreɪdə/

Bregenz city, Austria
bray-gents /ˈbreɪgɛnts/

Brel, Jacques Belgian singer and
composer
zhahk brel /ˌʒɑːk ˈbrɛl/

Bremen state, Germany
bray-muhn /ˈbreɪmən/

Brenner Pass Alpine pass
bren-uhr /ˈbrɛnə(r)/

bresaola Italian dish
bress-ow-luh /brɛˈsaʊlə/

Brescia city, Italy
bresh-uh /ˈbrɛʃə/

Bresson, Robert French film director
rob-air bress-o(ng) /rɒˌbɛː(r) brɛˈsɔ̃/

Brest port, France
brest /brɛst/

Bretagne French name for Brittany
bruh-tan-yuh /brəˈtanjə/, [brətanj]

Breton relating to Brittany
bret-uhn /ˈbrɛtən/

Breton, André French poet, essayist,
and critic
ah(ng)-dray bruh-to(ng) /ɑ̃ˌdreɪ
brəˈtɔ̃/

Brezhnev, Leonid Soviet statesman
lay-uh-need brezh-nyef /leɪəˌniːd
ˈbrɛʒnjɛf/

Brie cheese
bree /briː/

Briers, Richard English actor
bry-uhrz /ˈbrʌɪə(r)z/

This British family name is variously
pronounced breerz and bry-uhrz,
depending on individual preference.

brigand bandit
brig-uhnd /ˈbrɪg(ə)nd/

brigandine coat of mail
brig-uhn-deen /ˈbrɪgəndiːn/

brigantine two-masted sailing ship
brig-uhn-teen /ˈbrɪgantiːn/

Brignoles town, France
breen-yol /briːnˈjɒl/

Brindisi port, Italy
brin-diz-i /'brɪndɪzi/

brinjal Anglo-Indian name for aubergine
brin-jawl /'brɪndʒɔːl/

brio vivacity of style or performance
bree-oh /'briːəʊ/

brioche kind of bread
bree-**osh** /briːˈɒʃ/

Brisbane city, Australia
briz-buhn /'brɪzbən/

brisé ballet jump
bree-**zay** /briːˈzeɪ/

brisling sardine-like fish
briss-ling /'brɪslɪŋ/

Brno city, Czech Republic
bur-noh /'bɜː(r)nəʊ/, ['bɾnɔ]
• Established anglicization.

Brobdingnagian huge
brob-ding-**nag**-i-uhn
/ˌbrɒbdɪŋˈnæɡiən/

Broca's area part of the brain
broh-kuhz /'brəʊkəz/

broch Scottish prehistoric circular stone
tower
brokh /brɒx/

brochette barbecue or grill skewer
brosh-**et** /brɒˈʃet/

brochure small book or magazine
broh-shuhr /'brəʊʃə(r)/

Less commonly also brosh-**oor**.

Brocken mountain, Germany
brok-uhn /'brɒkən/

bromine chemical element
broh-meen /'brəʊmiːn/

bromocriptine drug
broh-moh-**krip**-teen
/ˌbrəʊməʊˈkrɪptiːn/

bronchiectasis abnormal widening of
the bronchi
bronk-i-**ek**-tuh-siss /ˌbrɒŋkiˈektəsɪs/

bronchiole minute branches into which
a bronchus divides
bron-ki-ohl /'brɒŋkiəʊl/

bronchiolitis inflammation of the
bronchioles
bron-ki-uh-**ly**-tiss /ˌbrɒŋkiəˈlaɪtɪs/

bronchoscopy method of investigating
the bronchial tubes
bron-**kosk**-uh-pi /brɒnˈkɒskəpi/

Brontë family of English authors
bron-ti /'brɒnti/

Bronx borough in New York City
bronks /brɒŋks/

Bronzino, Agnolo Italian painter
an-yoh-loh brond-**zee**-noh /ˌanjəʊləʊ
brɒnˈdziːnəʊ/

Bros brothers
bross /brɒs/

brose kind of porridge
brohz /brəʊz/

brougham horse-drawn carriage
broo-uhm /'bruːəm/

Brougham British family name
broo-uhm, bruum, **broh**-uhm, brohm
/'bruːəm/, /bruːm/, /'brəʊəm/, /brəʊm/

Brouwer, Adriaen Flemish painter
ah-dri-ahn **brow**-uhr /ˌɑːdriɑːn
'braʊə(r)/

Brown, Mather American painter
math-uhr /'maðə(r)/

Brubeck, Dave American jazz pianist
and composer
broo-bek /'bruːbek/

brucellosis bacterial disease
broo-suh-**loh**-siss /ˌbruːsəˈləʊsɪs/

Bruckner, Anton Austrian composer
and organist
an-tohn **bruuk**-nuhr /ˌantəʊn
'brʊknə(r)/

Bruegel (also **Brueghel**) Flemish family
of artists
broy-guhl /'brɔɪɡəl/, ['brøːxəl]
• Established anglicization.

Bruges city, Belgium
broozh /bruːʒ/

This is the French form. The Flemish name
is Brugge, pronounced **bruekh**-uh
['bryːxə].

Brummell, George Bryan English
dandy
brum-uhl /'brʌməl/

Brundtland, Gro Harlem Norwegian
stateswoman
groo har-luhm **bruunt**-lan /ˌgruː
ˌhɑː(r)ləm 'brʊntlan/

Brunei sultanate
broo-**ny** /bruːˈnaɪ/

Brunel, Isambard Kingdom English
engineer
iz-uhm-bard bruun-**el** /ˌɪzəmbɑː(r)d
brʊˈnel/

Brunhild German mythological name
broon-hilt /'bruːnhɪlt/

bruschetta toasted Italian bread
bruusk-**et**-uh /brʊ'skɛtə/

Brussels capital of Belgium
bruss-uhlz /'brʌsəlz/

Established anglicization. The Flemish
name is Brussel, pronounced **bruess**-uhl
['brysəl], and the French name is
Bruxelles, pronounced brue-**sel** [brysɛl].

Bryansk city, Russia
bri-**ansk** /bri'ansk/

Bual variety of wine grape
boo-al /'buːal/

Bublé, Michael Canadian singer
my-kuhl **boob**-lay /ˌmaɪkəl 'buːbleɪ/

bucatini small hollow tubes of pasta
buuk-uh-**tee**-ni /ˌbʊkə'tiːni/

buccaneer pirate
buk-uh-**neer** /ˌbʌkə'nɪə(r)/

Bucephalus favourite horse of
Alexander the Great
byoo-**sef**-uh-luhss /bjuː'sɛfələs/

Buchan, John Scottish novelist
bukh-uhn /'bʌxən/

Buchanan, James American statesman
byoo-**kan**-uhn /bjuː'kanən/

Bucharest capital of Romania
boo-kuh-**rest** /ˌbuːkə'rɛst/

Established anglicization, sometimes also
boo-kuh-rest. The Romanian name is
Bucureşti, pronounced boo-koo-**resh**-ti
[buku'rɛʃti].

Buchenwald Nazi concentration camp
bookh-uhn-valt /'buːxənvalt/

Budapest capital of Hungary
byoo-duh-**pest** /bjuːdə'pɛst/,
['budɒpɛʃt]

Established anglicization, sometimes also
boo-duh-pest.

Buddha founder of Buddhism
buud-uh /'bʊdə/

Buddhism religion
buud-diz-uhm /'bʊdɪzəm/

Buenaventura port, Colombia
bway-nuh-ven-**toor**-uh
/ˌbweɪnəvɛn'tʊərə/

Buenos Aires capital of Argentina
bway-noss y-reez /ˌbweɪnəs 'ʌɪriːz/,
Spanish /ˌbwenos 'ajres/

• Established anglicization.

Buerk, Michael BBC journalist
burk /bəː(r)k/

buffet meal consisting of several dishes
buuf-ay /'bʊfeɪ/

Commonly also **buf**-ay.

buffet strike
buf-it /'bʌfɪt/

Buganda former kingdom of East Africa
boo-**gan**-duh /buː'gandə/

Bujumbura capital of Burundi
buuj-uum-**boor**-uh /ˌbʊdʒʊm'bʊərə/

Bulawayo city, Zimbabwe
boo-luh-**way**-oh /ˌbuːlə'weɪəʊ/

bulgar cereal food made from whole
wheat
bul-guhr /'bʌlgə(r)/

Bulgari Italian jewellery and perfume
house
buul-guh-ri /'bʊlgəri/

bulimia nervosa eating disorder
buul-**im**-i-uh nur-**voh**-suh /bʊˌlɪmiə
nəː(r)'vəʊsə/

Bulsara, Farookh real name of Freddie
Mercury
fuh-**rook** buul-**sar**-uh /fəˌruːk
bʊl'sɑːrə/

Bundesbank central bank of Germany
buun-duhss-bank /'bʊndəsˌbaŋk/

Bundesrat German upper house of
Parliament
buun-duhss-raht /'bʊndəsˌrɑːt/

Bundestag German lower house of
Parliament
buun-duhss-tahk /'bʊndəsˌtɑːk/

Bunsen, Robert German chemist
roh-bairt **buun**-zuhn /ˌrəʊbɛː(r)t
'bʊnzən/

The Bunsen burner is pronounced
bun-suhn.

Bunyan, John English writer
bun-yuhn /'bʌnjən/

bunyip mythical amphibious monster
bun-yip /'bʌnjɪp/

BUPA British United Provident
Association
boo-puh /'buːpə/

bupropion trademark antidepressant drug
byoo-**proh**-pi-uhn /bjuː'prəʊpiən/

Burbank city, California
  bur-bank /'bəː(r)baŋk/

Burberry trademark English fashion label
  bur-buh-ri /'bəː(r)bəri/

burfi Indian sweet
  bur-fi /'bəː(r)fi/

Burgas port, Bulgaria
  boor-**gass** /buə(r)'gas/

Burgenland state, Austria
  boor-guhn-lant /'buə(r)gən‚lant/

Burghley, William Cecil English
  statesman
  bur-li /'bəː(r)li/

Burgos town, Spain
  boor-goss /'buə(r)gɒs/

Burgoyne, John English general and
  dramatist
  bur-**goyn** /bəː(r)'gɔɪn/

burka Muslim garment
  bur-kuh /'bəː(r)kə/
  • Established anglicization.

Burkina Faso country
  bur-**kee**-nuh **fass**-oh /bəː(r)‚kiːnə
  'fasəu/

Established anglicization; a more native
pronunciation would be boor-**kee**-nuh.

Burma country
  bur-muh /'bəː(r)mə/

Burnett, Frances Hodgson
  British-born American novelist
  bur-**net** /bəː(r)'nɛt/

This British surname is variously
pronounced bur-**net** and bur-nuht,
depending on individual preference.

Burrell, Paul ex-butler of Princess
  Diana
  burr-uhl /'bʌrəl/

burrito Mexican dish
  buh-**ree**-toh /bə'riːtəu/

Bursa city, Turkey
  boor-suh /'buə(r)sə/

Burundi country
  buu-**ruun**-di /bu'rundi/

Buryatia autonomous republic, Russia
  boor-**yah**-ti-uh /‚buə(r)'jɑːtiə/

Buscemi, Steve American actor
  buush-**em**-i /bu'ʃɛmi/

bushel measure of capacity
  buush-uhl /'buʃəl/

bushido Japanese samurai code of
  honour
  boosh-id-oh /'buːʃɪdəu/

Bushnell, Candace American author
  kan-diss buush-**nel** /‚kandɪs buʃ'nɛl/

Busoni, Ferruccio Italian composer,
  conductor, and pianist
  fuh-**roo**-choh boo-**zoh**-ni /fə‚ruːtʃəu
  buː'zəuni/

Bussell, Darcey English ballet dancer
  buss-uhl /'bʌsəl/

butane flammable hydrocarbon gas
  byoo-tayn /'bjuːteɪn/

butanol isomeric liquid alcohols used
  as solvents
  byoo-tuh-nol /'bjuːtənɒl/

Buteyko denoting a technique of
  controlled breathing
  boo-**tay**-koh /buː'teɪkəu/

Buthelezi, Mangosuthu (Gatsha)
  South African politician
  mang-**goh**-soo-too boo-tuh-**lay**-zi
  (**gatch**-uh) /maŋ‚gəusuːtuː buːtə'leɪzi
  ('gatʃə)/

Buxtehude, Dietrich Danish organist
  and composer
  deet-rikh buuk-stuh-hoo-duh /‚diːtrɪç
  'bukstəhuːdə/

Byblos ancient Mediterranean seaport
  bib-loss /'bɪblɒs/

Bydgoszcz city, Poland
  bid-goshtch /'bɪdgɒʃtʃ/

Byelorussia former name for Belarus;
  also called **Belorussia**
  byel-uh-**rush**-uh /bjɛlə'rʌʃə/

byssinosis lung disease
  biss-in-**oh**-siss /‚bɪsɪ'nəusɪs/

byte group of binary digits or bits
  byt /bʌɪt/

Bytom city, Poland
  bit-uhm /'bɪtəm/

Byzantine relating to Byzantium
  biz-**an**-tyn /bɪ'zantʌɪn/

Sometimes also by-**zan**-tyn.

Byzantium ancient Greek city
  biz-**ant**-i-uhm /bɪ'zantiəm/

Sometimes also by-**zan**-ti-uhm.

C

C3PO character from the *Star Wars* films
see-**three**-pee-oh /siːˈθriːpiːəʊ/

Caaba see **Kaaba**

Caan, James American actor
kahn /kɑːn/

cabal secret faction
kuh-**bal** /kəˈbal/

cabaletta simple aria
kab-uh-**let**-uh /ˌkabəˈlɛtə/

Caballé, Montserrat Spanish soprano
mont-serr-**at** kab-al-**yay** /mɒntsɛˌrat kabaˈljeɪ/

caballero Spanish gentleman
kab-al-**yair**-oh /ˌkabaˈljɛːrəʊ/

cabaret entertainment held in a
nightclub
kab-uh-**ray** /ˈkabəreɪ/

Commonly also kab-uh-**ray**.

Cabbala (also **Kabbalah**) mystic Hebrew
interpretation of the Old Testament
kuh-**bah**-luh /kəˈbɑːlə/

Less commonly also **kab**-uh-luh.

cabbalistic relating to Cabbala
kab-uh-**list**-ik /kabəˈlɪstɪk/

Cabernet Sauvignon black wine grape
kab-uhr-nay soh-veen-**yo(ng)**
/ˌkabə(r)neɪ səʊviːnˈjɒ̃/

Cabinda autonomous district of Angola
kuh-**bin**-duh /kəˈbɪndə/

caboclo American Indian ethnic group
kuh-**bohk**-loh /kəˈbəʊkləʊ/

Caborn, Richard English politician
kay-born /ˈkeɪbɔː(r)n/

Cabo Roig resort, Spain
kab-oh royg /ˌkabəʊ ˈrɔɪg/

Cabot, John Italian navigator
kab-uht /ˈkabət/

cabriole ballet jump
kab-ri-ohl /ˈkabriəʊl/

cabriolet car with a roof that folds down
kab-ri-uh-lay /ˈkabriəleɪ/

cacao bean-like seeds
kuh-**kah**-oh /kəˈkɑːəʊ/

Cáceres province and city, Spain
kath-err-ayss /ˈkaθereɪs/

cachaca Brazilian rum
kuh-**shah**-kuh /kəˈʃɑːkə/

cachexia weakness and wasting
of the body
kuh-**kek**-si-uh /kəˈkɛksiə/

cachucha Spanish dance
katch-**oo**-chuh /kaˈtʃuːtʃə/

Caddoan group of American Indian
ethnic groups
kad-oh-uhn /ˈkadəʊən/

Cadiz city, Spain
kuh-**diz** /kəˈdɪz/

Established anglicization. The Spanish form
is Cádiz, pronounced **kath**-eeth.

Cadmean relating to Cadmus
kad-**mee**-uhn /kadˈmiːən/

cadmium chemical element
kad-mi-uhm /ˈkadmiəm/

Cadmus Greek mythological character
kad-muhss /ˈkadməs/

Caedmon Anglo-Saxon monk and poet
kad-muhn /ˈkadmən/

Caelian Hill one of the seven hills of
Rome
see-li-uhn /ˈsiːliən/

Caelum constellation
see-luhm /ˈsiːləm/

Caen city, France
kah(ng) /kɑ̃/

Less commonly also anglicized to kahn.

Caerdydd Welsh name for Cardiff
kyr-**deeth** /kaɪrˈdiːð/

Caernarfon (also **Caernarvon**) town,
Wales
kuhr-**nar**-vuhn /kə(r)ˈnɑː(r)vən/,
[kaɪrˈnarvɒn]
• Established anglicization.

Caerphilly mild white cheese
kuhr-**fil**-i /kə(r)ˈfɪli/

Caesar title of Roman emperors
see-zuhr /ˈsiːzə(r)/
• See LATIN panel.

Caesarea ancient port, Israel
see-zuh-**ree**-uh /ˌsiːzəˈriːə/

Caesarean section delivery of a child by cutting through the walls of the abdomen
siz-**air**-i-uhn /sɪˈzɛːriən/

caesium chemical element
see-zi-uhm /ˈsiːziəm/

cafe (also **café**) small restaurant
kaf-ay /ˈkafeɪ/

Commonly also kaf-**ay**.

cafetière coffee pot
kaf-uh-**tyair** /ˌkafəˈtjɛː(r)/

caffè latte drink
kaf-ay lat-ay /ˌkafeɪ ˈlateɪ/

The pronunciation **lah**-tay is widespread, especially in AM, but deprecated because it is felt to be less like the Italian.

caffè macchiato drink
kaf-ay mak-i-**ah**-toh /ˌkafeɪ makiˈɑːtəʊ/

CAFOD CAtholic Fund for Overseas Development
kaf-od /ˈkafɒd/

Cagayan Islands group of islands, Philippines
kag-uh-**yahn** /ˌkagəˈjɑːn/

Cagliari capital of Sardinia
kal-yuh-ri /ˈkaljəri/

cagoule waterproof jacket
kuh-**gool** /kəˈɡuːl/

cahoots secret partnership
kuh-**hoots** /kəˈhuːts/

Cahora Bassa lake, Mozambique
kuh-**haw**-ruh bass-uh /kəˌhɔːrə ˈbasə/

Caicos see **Turks and Caicos Islands**

caipirinha Brazilian cocktail
ky-pirr-**in**-yuh /ˌkaɪpɪˈrɪnjə/

Cairns town, Australia
kairnz /kɛː(r)nz/

Cairo capital of Egypt
ky-roh /ˈkaɪrəʊ/

Established anglicization. The Arabic name is El Qahira, pronounced uhl kah-hi-ruh [əl ˈqɑːhira:].

Cairo city, US
kair-oh /ˈkɛːrəʊ/

Caithness former county, Scotland
kayth-nuhss /ˈkeɪθnəs/

Cajun native of Louisiana, of Acadian-French descent
kay-juhn /ˈkeɪdʒən/

Calabar port, Nigeria
kal-uh-**bar** /kaləˈbɑː(r)/

Calabria region, Italy
kuh-**lab**-ri-uh /kəˈlabriə/

Calais port, France
kal-ay /ˈkaleɪ/, [kalɛ]
• Established anglicization.

calamari squid
kal-uh-**mar**-i /ˌkaləˈmɑːri/

calciferol D vitamin
kal-**sif**-uh-rol /kalˈsɪfərɒl/

calculus pl. **calculi** branch of mathematics
kal-kyuul-uhss, pl. **kal**-kyuul-y /ˈkalkjʊləs/, pl. /-lʌɪ/
• See **LATIN** panel.

Calcutta former name for Kolkata
kal-**kut**-uh /kalˈkʌtə/

Caldecott, Randolph English artist
kawl-dik-ot /ˈkɔːldɪkɒt/

Calder, Alexander American sculptor
kawl-duhr /ˈkɔːldə(r)/

Calderón de la Barca, Pedro Spanish dramatist
ped-roh kal-derr-**on** day lah bar-kuh /ˌpedrəʊ kaldɛˌrɒn deɪ lɑː ˈbɑː(r)kə/

Caldwell, Erskine American novelist
ur-skin **kawld**-wel /ˌəː(r)skɪn ˈkɔːldwɛl/

Caledonian relating to Scotland
kal-uh-**doh**-ni-uhn /ˌkaləˈdəʊniən/

calends first day of the month in the ancient Roman calendar
kal-endz /ˈkalɛndz/

Calgary city, Canada
kal-guh-ri /ˈkalɡəri/

Cali city, Colombia
kah-li /ˈkɑːli/

Calicut port, India
kal-ik-ut /ˈkalɪkʌt/

californium chemical element
kal-if-**or**-ni-uhm /ˌkalɪˈfɔː(r)niəm/

Caligula Roman emperor
kuh-**lig**-yuul-uh /kəˈlɪɡjʊlə/

caliph chief Muslim civil and religious ruler
kay-lif /ˈkeɪlɪf/

Commonly also kal-**if** or kuh-**leef**.

Callanetics trademark system of physical exercises
kal-uh-**net**-iks /ˌkaləˈnɛtɪks/

Callao port, Peru
kal-**yah**-oh /kə'ljɑːəʊ/

Callas, Maria American-born operatic soprano
muh-**ree**-uh kal-**ass** /məˌriːə 'kaləs/

Callicrates Greek architect
kuh-**lik**-ruh-teez /kə'lɪkrətiːz/

Callimachus Greek poet and scholar
kuh-**lim**-uh-kuhss /kə'lɪməkəs/

Calliope Greek mythological character
kuh-**ly**-uh-pi /kə'lʌɪəpi/

Callisto Greek mythological character
kuh-**list**-oh /kə'lɪstəʊ/

calmative having a sedative effect
kahm-uh-tiv /'kɑːmətɪv/

Sometimes also **kal**-muh-tiv.

Calor gas trademark liquefied butane
kal-uhr /'kalə(r)/

calorimeter apparatus for measuring the amount of heat
kal-uh-**rim**-uh-tuhr /ˌkalə'rɪmətə(r)/

caltrop spiked metal ball
kal-truhp /'kaltrəp/

calumet peace pipe
kal-yuum-et /'kaljʊmɛt/

Calvados region, France; also brandy made there
kal-vuh-doss /'kalvədɒs/

Calvary hill on which Christ was crucified
kal-vuh-ri /'kalvəri/

Calvino, Italo Italian writer
ee-tal-oh kal-**vee**-noh /ˌiːtaləʊ kal'viːnəʊ/

Calypso Greek mythological character
kuh-**lip**-soh /kə'lɪpsəʊ/

calypso West Indian music
kuh-**lip**-soh /kə'lɪpsəʊ/

calzone folded pizza
kal-**tsoh**-nay /kal'tsəʊneɪ/

Camargue region, France
kam-**arg** /ka'mɑː(r)g/

Cambay, Gulf of inlet of the Arabian Sea, India
kam-**bay** /kam'beɪ/

Cambodia country
kam-**boh**-di-uh /kam'bəʊdiə/

cambozola (also **cambazola**) trademark German blue soft cheese
kam-buh-**zoh**-luh /ˌkambə'zəʊlə/

Cambrian relating to Wales

kam-bri-uhn /'kambriən/

Cambyses king of Persia
kam-**by**-seez /kam'bʌɪsiːz/

camelopard giraffe
kam-uhl-uh-pard /'kaməlapɑː(r)d/

Sometimes also kuh-**mel**-uh-pard.

Camelopardalis constellation
kuh-mel-oh-**par**-duh-liss /kəˌmɛləʊ'pɑː(r)dəlɪs/

Camelot place where King Arthur held his court
kam-uh-lot /'kamələt/

Camembert soft, creamy cheese
kam-uhm-bair /'kaməmbɛː(r)/

Cameroon country
kam-uh-**roon** /ˌkamə'ruːn/

camisole undergarment
kam-iss-ohl /'kamɪsəʊl/

Camões, Luis de (also **Camoëns**) Portuguese poet
luu-**eesh** duh kuh-**moy(ng)sh** /lʊˌiːʃ də kə'mɔɪʃ/

camogie Irish game
kam-oh-gi /'kaməʊgi/

Campania region, Italy
kam-**pahn**-yuh /kam'pɑːnjə/

Campari trademark aperitif
kam-**par**-i /kam'pɑːri/

Campeche state, Mexico
kam-**petch**-ay /kam'pɛtʃeɪ/

Campbell, Menzies Scottish politician
ming-iss /'mɪŋɪs/

Campbell, Naomi English model
nay-oh-mi /'neɪəʊmi/

Campbell, Neve American actress
nev /nɛv/

Campinas city, Brazil
kuhm-**pee**-nass /kəm'piːnas/

Campion, Jane New Zealand film director
kamp-i-uhn /'kampiən/

Campobasso city, Italy
kam-poh-**bass**-oh /ˌkampəʊ'basəʊ/

Campo Grande city, Brazil
kam-poo gran-di /ˌkampuː 'grandi/

campylobacter bacterium
kam-pil-oh-bak-tuhr /'kampɪləʊˌbaktə(r)/

CAMRA CAMpaign for Real Ale
kam-ruh /'kamrə/

Camulodunum Roman name for Colchester
kam-yuul-uh-**dyoo**-nuhm
/ˌkamjʊlə'djuːnəm/

Camus, Albert French novelist
al-**bair** kam-ue /alˌbɛː(r) ka'my/

Cana ancient town in Galilee
kay-nuh /'keɪnə/

Canaan biblical place name
kay-nuhn /'keɪnən/

Canadien French Canadian
kan-ad-**ya(ng)** /ˌkana'djɛ̃/

Canaletto Italian painter
kan-uh-**let**-oh /ˌkanə'lɛtəʊ/

canapé small piece of bread or pastry with a savoury topping
kan-uh-pay /'kanəpeɪ/

canasta card game
kuh-**nast**-uh /kə'nastə/

Canaveral, Cape cape in Florida, US
kuh-**nav**-ruhl /kə'navrəl/

Canberra capital of Australia
kan-buh-ruh /'kanbərə/

Cancún resort, Mexico
kank-**oon** /kaŋ'kuːn/

Candanchú resort, Spain
kan-dan-**choo** /kandan'tʃuː/

candela SI unit of luminous intensity
kan-**dee**-luh /kan'diːlə/

Commonly also kan-**del**-uh.

---

candelabrum pl. **candelabra** candlestick
kan-duh-**lah**-bruhm, pl.
kan-duh-**lah**-bruh /ˌkandə'lɑːbrəm/, pl.
/-brə/

candida parasitic fungus
kan-did-uh /'kandɪdə/

Candide novel by Voltaire
kah(ng)-**deed** /kɑ̃'diːd/

candidiasis infection with candida
kan-did-**y**-uh-siss /ˌkandɪ'dʌɪəsɪs/

Candlemas Christian festival
kan-duhl-mass /'kandəlmas/

candomblé Brazilian sect
kan-dom-**blay** /ˌkandɒm'bleɪ/

CANDU nuclear reactor
kan-doo /'kanduː/

Canes Venatici constellation
kay-neez vuh-**nat**-iss-y /ˌkeɪniːz və'natɪsʌɪ/

Canetti, Elias Bulgarian-born British writer
ay-**lee**-ass kuh-**net**-i /eɪˌliːas kə'nɛti/

canine relating to dogs
kay-nyn /'keɪnʌɪn/

Canis Major constellation
kay-niss **may**-juhr /ˌkeɪnɪs 'meɪdʒə(r)/

Canis Minor constellation
kay-niss **my**-nuhr /ˌkeɪnɪs 'mʌɪnə(r)/

cannabis indica hemp
kan-uh-biss **in**-dik-uh /ˌkanəbɪs 'ɪndɪkə/

cannellini bean
kan-uh-**lee**-ni /ˌkanə'liːni/

cannelloni rolls of pasta
kan-uh-**loh**-ni /ˌkanə'ləʊni/

Cannes resort, France
kan /kan/

cannoli dessert
kan-**oh**-li /ka'nəʊli/

canola oilseed rape
kuh-**noh**-luh /kə'nəʊlə/

Canopic jar ancient Egyptian urn
kuh-**noh**-pik /kə'nəʊpɪk/

Canopus star
kuh-**noh**-puhss /kə'nəʊpəs/

Canova, Antonio Italian sculptor
an-**tohn**-yoh kan-**oh**-vuh /anˌtəʊnjəʊ ka'nəʊvə/

Cantab of Cambridge University
kan-tab /'kantab/

cantabile musical term
kan-**tah**-bil-ay /kan'tɑːbɪleɪ/

Cantabria autonomous region, Spain
kan-**tab**-ri-uh /kan'tabriə/

Cantabrigian relating to Cambridge
kant-uh-**brij**-i-uhn /ˌkantə'brɪdʒiən/

Cantal department, France
kah(ng)-**tal** /kɑ̃'tal/

The cheese made there is sometimes anglicized further, to **kan**-tahl.

---

cantaloupe melon
kan-tuh-loop /'kantəluːp/

cantata piece of music
kan-**tah**-tuh /kan'tɑːtə/

Canteloube, Joseph French composer
zhoh-**zef** kah(ng)-tuh-**loob** /ʒəʊˌzɛf kɑ̃tə'luːb/

canthus pl. **canthi** corner of the eye
kan-thuhss, pl. **kan**-thy /'kanθəs/, pl. /-θʌɪ/

canticle hymn or chant
kan-tik-uhl /'kantɪkəl/

cantina bar
kan-**tee**-nuh /kanˈtiːnə/

canto section of a poem
kan-toh /ˈkantəʊ/

Cantona, Éric French footballer
err-**eek** kan-ton-**ah** /ɛˌriːk kantɒˈnɑː/

Cantor, Georg Russian-born German mathematician
gay-ork **kan**-tor /ˌɡeɪɔː(r)k ˈkantɔː(r)/

Canute (also **Cnut** or **Knut**) Danish king of England
kuh-**nyoot** /kəˈnjuːt/

The Danish pronunciation of the name Knut is knood.

canzone pl. **canzoni** Italian or Provençal song
kant-**soh**-nay, pl. kant-**soh**-ni /kanˈtsəʊneɪ, pl. /-ni/

Capablanca, José Raúl Cuban chess player
khoss-**ay** rah-**ool** kap-ab-**lank**-uh /xɒˌseɪ rɑːˌuːl kapaˈblaŋkə/

Čapek, Karel Czech novelist
karr-el **chap**-ek /ˌkarɛl ˈtʃapɛk/

Capella star
kuh-**pel**-uh /kəˈpɛlə/

capellini pasta
kap-uh-**lee**-ni /ˌkapəˈliːni/

Cape Verde Islands country
kayp **vurd** /ˌkeɪp ˈvɜː(r)d/

Established anglicization. The Portuguese name is Ilhas do Cabo Verde, pronounced **eel**-yuhsh doo **kab**-oo **vair**-di.

capillary fine branching blood vessels
kuh-**pil**-uh-ri /kəˈpɪləri/

Capitoline Hill one of the seven hills of Rome
kuh-**pit**-uh-lyn /kəˈpɪtəlʌɪn/

capoeira Brazilian dance
kap-uu-**ay**-ruh /ˌkapʊˈeɪrə/

caponata Italian dish
kap-oh-**nah**-tuh /ˌkapəʊˈnɑːtə/

Capone, Al American gangster
kuh-**pohn** /kəˈpəʊn/

Capote, Truman American writer
troo-muhn kuh-**poh**-ti /ˌtruːmən kəˈpəʊti/

Cappadocia ancient region of Asia Minor
kap-uh-**doh**-shuh /ˌkapəˈdəʊʃə/

cappelletti pasta dish

kap-uh-**let**-i /ˌkapəˈlɛti/

cappuccino type of coffee
kap-oo-**chee**-noh /ˌkapuˈtʃiːnəʊ/

Capra, Frank Italian-born American film director
kap-ruh /ˈkaprə/

Capri island, Italy
kuh-**pree** /kəˈpriː/, [ˈkaːpri]
• Established anglicization.

Capriati, Jennifer American tennis player
kap-ri-**ah**-ti /kapriˈɑːti/

Capricornus constellation
kap-rik-**or**-nuhss /ˌkaprɪˈkɔː(r)nəs/

capri pants trousers
kuh-**pree** /kəˈpriː/

Caprivi Strip narrow strip, Namibia
kuh-**pree**-vi /kəˈpriːvi/

captious finding fault
kap-shuhss /ˈkapʃəs/

capybara South American mammal
kap-ib-**ar**-uh /ˌkapɪˈbɑːrə/

Caracalla Roman emperor
karr-uh-**kal**-uh /ˌkarəˈkalə/

Caracas capital of Venezuela
kuh-**rak**-uhss /kəˈrakəs/

Carajás region, Brazil
karr-azh-**ass** /ˌkaraˈʒas/

carambola fruit
karr-uhm-**boh**-luh /ˌkarəmˈbəʊlə/

Caractacus British chieftain
kuh-**rak**-tuh-kuhss /kəˈraktəkəs/

Caravaggio, Michelangelo Merisi da Italian painter
meek-uh-**lan**-juh-loh merr-**ee**-zi dah karr-uh-**vaj**-oh /miːkəˌlandʒələʊ mɛˌriːzi dɑː karəˈvadʒəʊ/

carbine automatic rifle
kar-byn /ˈkɑː(r)bʌɪn/

carbonado diamond
kar-buh-**nay**-doh /ˌkɑː(r)bəˈneɪdəʊ/

carbonara pasta sauce
kar-buh-**nar**-uh /ˌkɑː(r)bəˈnɑːrə/

Carboniferous geological era
kar-buh-**nif**-uh-ruhss /ˌkɑː(r)bəˈnɪfərəs/

carbuncle abscess
kar-bunk-uhl /ˈkɑː(r)bʌŋkəl/

carburettor engine device
kar-buh-**ret**-uhr /kɑː(r)bəˈrɛtə(r)/

AM is **kar**-buh-**ray**-tuhr.

Carcassonne city, France
kar-kuh-son /ˌkɑː(r)kəˈsɒn/

Carchemish ancient city on the upper
Euphrates
kar-kuh-mish /ˈkɑː(r)kəmɪʃ/

carcinogenic causing cancer
kar-sin-uh-jen-ik /ˌkɑː(r)sɪnəˈdʒɛnɪk/

carcinoma pl. **carcinomata** type of
cancer
kar-sin-oh-muh, pl.
kar-sin-oh-muh-tuh /ˌkɑː(r)sɪˈnəʊmə/,
pl. /-mətə/
• Standard -s plural is also possible.

cardamom (also **cardamum**) spice
kar-duh-muhm /ˈkɑː(r)dəməm/

Cardin, Pierre French couturier
pyair kar-da(ng) /ˌpjɛː(r) kɑː(r)ˈdɛ̃/

cardiomegaly enlargement of the heart
kar-di-oh-meg-uh-li
/ˌkɑː(r)diəʊˈmɛɡəli/

Carentan city, France
karr-ah(ng)-tah(ng) /karɑ̃ˈtɑ̃/

The Second World War battle here is
sometimes pronounced in a more anglicized
manner, as **karr-uhn-tan.**

caret mark placed in writing (^, ʌ)
karr-uht /ˈkarət/

Carey, Mariah American singer
muh-ry-uh kair-i /məˌrʌɪə ˈkɛːri/

Caria ancient region of Asia Minor
kair-i-uh /ˈkɛːriə/

Carib South American ethnic group
karr-ib /ˈkarɪb/

Cariban South American language
family
karr-ib-uhn /ˈkarɪbən/

Caribbean region
karr-ib-ee-uhn /ˌkarɪˈbiːən/

Less commonly also **kuh-rib-i-uhn.**

caribou reindeer
karr-ib-oo /ˈkarɪbuː/

CARICOM Caribbean Community and
Common Market
karr-ik-om /ˈkarɪkɒm/

Carina constellation
kuh-ryn-uh /kəˈrʌɪnə/

Carinthia state, Austria
kuh-rinth-i-uh /kəˈrɪnθiə/

Established anglicization. The German
name is Kärnten, pronounced **kairn-tuhn.**

carioca native of Rio de Janeiro
karr-i-oh-kuh /ˌkariˈəʊkə/

caritas Christian love of humankind
karr-it-ahss /ˈkarɪtɑːs/

Carlisle city, England
kar-lyl /kɑː(r)ˈlʌɪl/

The local pronunciation is **kar-lyl.**

Carlow county, Republic of Ireland
kar-loh /ˈkɑː(r)ləʊ/

Carlyle, Thomas Scottish historian and
political philosopher
kar-lyl /kɑː(r)ˈlʌɪl/

This British surname is variously
pronounced **kar-**lyl and kar-**lyl**, depending
on individual preference.

Carmarthen town, Wales
kuh-mar-thuhn /kəˈmɑː(r)ðən/

Carmel, Mount group of mountains,
Israel
kar-muhl /ˈkɑː(r)məl/

Carmen opera by Bizet
kar-men /ˈkɑː(r)mɛn/

carmine crimson colour
kar-myn /ˈkɑː(r)mʌɪn/

Carnap, Rudolf German-born
American philosopher
roo-dolf kar-nap /ˌruːdɒlf ˈkɑː(r)nap/

Carné, Marcel French film director
mar-sel kar-nay /mɑː(r)ˌsɛl kɑː(r)ˈneɪ/

Carnegie, Andrew Scottish-born
American industrialist
kar-nay-gi /kɑː(r)ˈneɪɡi/

This British surname is variously
pronounced kar-**neg**-i, kar-**nay**-gi,
kar-**nee**-gi, and **kar**-nuh-gi, depending on
individual preference. Carnegie Hall in New
York is **kar-nuh-gi.**

carnet book of tickets
kar-nay /ˈkɑː(r)neɪ/

Carnivora order of mammals
kar-niv-uh-ruh /kɑː(r)ˈnɪvərə/

carob trea
karr-uhb /ˈkarəb/

Caroline relating to the reigns of
Charles I and II
karr-uh-lyn /ˈkarəlʌɪn/

carotene orange or red plant pigment
karr-uh-teen /ˈkarətiːn/

Carothers, Wallace Hume American
industrial chemist
kuh-ruth-uhrz /kəˈrʌðə(r)z/

Carpaccio, Vittore Italian painter
vit-**aw**-ray kar-**patch**-oh /vɪˌtɔːreɪ
kɑː(r)'patʃəʊ/

carpaccio Italian hors d'oeuvre
kar-**patch**-oh /kɑː(r)'patʃəʊ/

Carpathian Mountains mountain
system, Europe
kar-**pay**-thi-uhn /kɑː(r)'peɪθɪən/

carpe diem 'seize the day' (Latin)
kar-pay **dee**-em /ˌkɑː(r)peɪ 'diːɛm/

Carpentaria, Gulf of bay, Australia
kar-puhn-**tair**-i-uh /ˌkɑː(r)pən'tɛːriə/

Carracci family of Italian painters
karr-**atch**-i /ka'ratʃi/

carrageen (also **carragheen**) edible
seaweed
karr-uh-geen /'karəgiːn/

Carrara town, Italy
kuh-**rar**-uh /kə'rɑːrə/

Carradine, David American actor
karr-uh-deen /'karədiːn/

Carreras, José Spanish tenor
khoss-**ay** karr-**air**-ass /xɒˌseɪ ka'rɛːras/

Carrey, Jim American actor
kair-i /'kɛːri/

Cartagena port, Spain
kar-takh-**ay**-nuh /ˌkɑː(r)ta'xeɪmə/

A more anglicized form, kart-uh-**jee**-nuh, is
less common now.

carte blanche complete freedom
kart **blahnsh** /ˌkɑː(r)t 'blɑːnʃ/

Cartesian relating to Descartes
kar-**tee**-zi-uhn /kɑː'tiːzɪən/

Carthage ancient city, North Africa
kar-thij /'kɑː(r)θɪdʒ/

Cartier, Jacques French explorer
zhahk kart-**yay** /ˌʒɑːk kɑː(r)'tjeɪ/

Cartier French jeweller and watchmaker
kart-i-ay /'kɑː(r)tieɪ/, [kartje]
• Established anglicization.

Caruso, Enrico Italian tenor
en-**ree**-koh kuh-**roo**-zoh /ɛnˌriːkəʊ
kə'ruːzəʊ/

Carvalho, João de Sousa Portuguese
composer
zhuu-**ow(ng)** duh **soh**-zuh
kuhr-**val**-yoo /ʒʊˌãʊ də ˌsəʊzə
kə(r)'valjuː/

Carys Welsh girl's name
karr-iss /'karɪs/

Casablanca city, Morocco
kass-uh-**blank**-uh /ˌkasə'blaŋkə/

Casals, Pablo Spanish composer
pab-loh kuh-**zalss** /ˌpabləʊ kə'zals/

Casanova, Giovanni Italian adventurer
juh-**vah**-ni kass-uh-**noh**-vuh /jəˌvɑːni
ˌkasə'nəʊvə/

cascabel red chilli pepper
kask-uh-bel /'kaskəbɛl/

caseation condition characteristic of
tuberculosis
kay-si-**ay**-shuhn /ˌkeɪsi'eɪʃən/

casein protein present in milk
kay-seen /'keɪsiːn/

cashew nut
kash-oo /'kaʃuː/

Commonly also kuh-**shoo**.

cashmere fine wool; also shawl made
from it
kash-meer /'kaʃmɪə(r)/

Caspar one of the three Magi
kasp-uhr /'kaspə(r)/

Caspian Sea salt lake, central Asia
kasp-i-uhn /'kaspɪən/

Cassandra Greek mythological character
kuh-**san**-druh /kə'sandrə/

Commonly also kuh-**sahn**-druh.

cassata ice cream
kuh-**sah**-tuh /kə'sɑːtə/

Cassatt, Mary American painter
kuh-**sat** /kə'sat/

Cassavetes, John American actor
kass-uh-**vee**-teez /kasə'viːtiːz/

cassia tree
kass-i-uh /'kasiə/

Cassini, Giovanni Italian-born French
astronomer
juh-**vah**-ni kass-ee-ni /dʒəˌvɑːni
ka'siːni/

Cassiopeia Greek mythological
character
kass-i-oh-**pee**-uh /ˌkasiəʊ'piːə/

cassis blackcurrant liqueur
kass-**eess** /ka'siːs/

Cassis region, France
kass-**ee** /ka'siː/

Cassius, Gaius Roman general
gy-uhss **kass**-i-uhss /ˌgʌɪəs 'kasiəs/

cassoulet French stew
kass-oo-**lay** /kasʊ'leɪ/

Castalia Greek mythological place name
kast-**ay**-li-uh /ka'steɪliə/

Castel Gandolfo summer residence of the Pope
kast-**el** gan-**dol**-foh /kasˌtɛl ganˈdɒlfəʊ/

Castellón city and province, Spain
kast-el-**yon** /kastɛˈljɒn/

Castile region, Spain
kast-**eel** /kaˈstiːl/

Established anglicization. The Spanish name is Castilla, pronounced kast-**eel**-yuh [kasˈtiʎa].

Castilian relating to Castile
kast-**il**-i-uhn /kaˈstɪliən/

Castilla-La Mancha autonomous region, Spain
kast-**eel**-yuh lam-**an**-chuh /kaˌstiːljə la ˈmantʃə/

Castilla-León autonomous region, Spain
kast-**eel**-yuh lay-**on** /kaˌstiːljə leɪˈɒn/

Castlebar town, Republic of Ireland
kah-suhl-**bar** /ˌkɑːsəlˈbɑː(r)/

Castlereagh, Robert Stewart Irish-born British statesman
kah-suhl-ray /ˈkɑːsəlreɪ/

Castor Greek mythological character
kah-stuhr /ˈkɑːstə(r)/

Castries capital of St Lucia
kast-**reess** /kaˈstriːs/

Castro, Fidel Cuban statesman
fee-**del** kast-roh /fiːˌdɛl ˈkastrəʊ/, Spanish [fiˌðel ˈkastro]

casual relaxed
kazh-oo-uhl /ˈkaʒuəl/

The pronunciation kaz-yoo-uhl is less common now.

catachresis pl. **catachreses** use of a word in an incorrect way
kat-uh-**kree**-siss, pl. kat-uh-**kree**-seez /ˌkatəˈkriːsɪs, pl. -siːz/

cataclysm large-scale violent event
kat-uh-kliz-uhm /ˈkatəˌklɪzəm/

catacomb underground cemetery
kat-uh-koom /ˈkatəkuːm/

Catalan relating to Catalonia
kat-uh-lan /ˈkatəlan/

catalepsy medical condition
kat-uh-lep-si /ˈkatəlɛpsi/

Catalonia autonomous region, Spain
kat-uh-**loh**-ni-uh /ˌkatəˈləʊniə/

Established anglicization. The Spanish name is Cataluña, and the Catalan is Catalunya; both are pronounced kat-al-**oon**-yuh.

Catania port, Sicily
kuh-**tah**-ni-uh /kəˈtɑːniə/

cataphora grammatical term
kuh-**taf**-uh-ruh /kəˈtafərə/

cataplexy medical condition
kat-uh-plek-si /ˈkatəˌplɛksi/

cataract large waterfall
kat-uh-rakt /ˈkatərakt/

catarrh build-up of mucus in the nose or throat
kuh-**tar** /kəˈtɑː(r)/

catawba North American variety of grape
kuh-**taw**-buh /kəˈtɔːbə/

catechesis religious instruction
kat-uh-**kee**-siss /ˌkatəˈkiːsɪs/

catechetical relating to religious instruction
kat-uh-**ket**-ik-uhl /ˌkatəˈkɛtɪkəl/

catechism questions and answers about Christian religion
kat-uh-kiz-uhm /ˈkatəkɪzəm/

catechu vegetable extract
kat-uh-choo /ˈkatətʃuː/

catechumen person who is receiving religious instruction
kat-uh-**kyoo**-men /ˌkatəˈkjuːmɛn/

Cathay China
kath-**ay** /kaˈθeɪ/

Cather, Willa American novelist
wil-uh k**ath**-uhr /ˌwɪlə ˈkaðə(r)/

catheter tube inserted into a body cavity
kath-uh-tuhr /ˈkaθətə(r)/

Catholicism religion
kuh-**thol**-iss-iz-uhm /kəˈθɒlɪsɪzəm/

Catiline Roman nobleman and conspirator
kat-il-yn /ˈkatɪlʌɪn/

cation positively charged ion
kat-y-uhn /ˈkatʌɪən/

Cato, Marcus Roman statesman
mar-kuhss **kay**-toh /ˌmɑː(r)kəs ˈkeɪtəʊ/

Catskill Mountains range of mountains, US
kat-skil /ˈkatskɪl/

Catullus, Gaius Valerius Roman poet
gy-uhss vuh-**leer**-i-uhss kuh-**tul**-uhss
/ˌɡAIəs vəˌlɪəriəs kəˈtʌləs/

caubeen Irish beret
kaw-**been** /kɔːˈbiːn/

Caucasian relating to the Caucasus
kaw-**kay**-zhuhn /kɔːˈkeɪzən/

Caucasus mountainous region, Europe
kaw-kuh-suhss /ˈkɔːkəsəs/

caul amniotic membrane enclosing a
foetus
kawl /kɔːl/

Cauvery river, India
kaw-vuh-ri /ˈkɔːvəri/

cava Spanish sparkling wine
kah-vuh /ˈkɑːvə/

Cavafy, Constantine Greek poet
kon-stan-tyn kuh-**vah**-fi /ˌkɒnstantʌɪn
kəˈvɑːfi/

Cavan county, Republic of Ireland
kav-uhn /ˈkavən/

cavaquinho type of guitar
kav-ak-**een**-yoh /ˌkavaˈkiːnjəʊ/

cave look out!
kay-vi /ˈkeɪvi/

See LATIN panel.

caveat warning of specific stipulations
kav-i-at /ˈkaviat/

Cavell, Edith English nurse
kav-uhl /ˈkavəl/

caviar pickled fish roe
kav-i-ar /ˈkavɪɑː(r)/

Sometimes also kav-i-ar.

Caviezel, Jim American actor
kuh-**vee**-zuhl /kəˈviːzəl/

cavil make petty objections
kav-uhl /ˈkavəl/

Cavour, Camillo Benso Italian
statesman
kuh-**mee**-loh ben-soh kuh-**voor**
/kəˌmiːləʊ ˌbɛnsəʊ kəˈvʊə(r)/

Cawnpore see Kanpur

Cayenne capital of French Guiana
kay-**en** /keɪˈɛn/, French [kajɛn]
• Established anglicization. The same
pronunciation is used for cayenne pepper.

Cayman Islands group of islands,
Caribbean Sea
kay-muhn /ˈkeɪmən/

Cayuga American Indian ethnic group

kay-**yoo**-guh /keɪˈjuːɡə/

Cayuse American Indian ethnic group
ky-yooss /ˈkʌɪjuːs/

Cazale, John American actor
kuh-**zahl** /kəˈzɑːl/

Ceará state, Brazil
say-uh-**rah** /ˌseɪəˈrɑː/

Ceauşescu, Elena wife of Nicolae
Ceauşescu
uh-**lay**-nuh chow-**shesk**-oo /əˌlɛmə
tʃaʊˈʃɛsku:/

Ceauşescu, Nicolae Romanian
statesman
nik-uh-**ly** chow-**shesk**-oo /nɪkəˌlʌɪ
tʃaʊˈʃɛsku:/

Cebu island, Philippines
suh-**boo** /səˈbuː/

Cecilia, St Roman martyr
suh-**seel**-yuh /səˈsiːljə/

cedi currency unit, Ghana
see-di /ˈsiːdi/

cedilla diacritic (ˌ)
suh-**dil**-uh /səˈdɪlə/

Ceefax trademark BBC teletext service
see-faks /ˈsiːfaks/

ceilidh Scottish or Irish social event
kay-li /ˈkeɪli/

Celebra trademark drug
suh-**leb**-ruh /səˈlɛbrə/

celesta musical instrument
suh-**lest**-uh /səˈlɛstə/

Céline, Louis-Ferdinand French
novelist
lwee fair-dee-**nah(ng)** say-**leen** /lwiː
fɛː(r)diːˌnɑ̃ seɪˈliːn/

Cellini, Benvenuto Italian goldsmith
and sculptor
ben-vuh-**noo**-toh chel-**ee**-ni
/bɛnvəˌnuːtəʊ tʃɛˈliːni/

cello musical instrument
chel-oh /ˈtʃɛləʊ/

cellulite subcutaneous fat
sel-yuul-yt /ˈsɛljʊlʌɪt/

Celsius, Anders Swedish astronomer
an-duhrsh **sel**-si-uuss /ˌandə(r)ʃ
ˈsɛlsiʊs/

Celsius scale of temperature
sel-si-uhss /ˈsɛlsiəs/

Celt pre-Roman ethnic group
kelt /kɛlt/

Less commonly also selt.

Celtic relating to the Celts
kel-tik /ˈkɛltɪk/

Less commonly also **sel**-tik. The Scottish football club, however, is always **sel**-tik.

cembalo harpsichord
chem-buh-loh /ˈtʃɛmbələʊ/

cenotaph monument
sen-uh-tahf /ˈsɛnətɑːf/

Cenozoic geological era
see-nuh-**zoh**-ik /ˌsiːnəˈzəʊɪk/

censure express disapproval
sen-shuhr /ˈsɛnʃə(r)/

The pronunciation **sen**-syoor is now less commonly heard.

centaur Greek mythological creature
sen-tor /ˈsɛntɔː(r)/

Centaurus constellation
sen-**taw**-ruhss /sɛnˈtɔːrəs/

centenarian person who is a hundred years old
sen-tuh-**nair**-i-uhn /ˌsɛntəˈnɛːriən/

centenary hundredth anniversary
sen-**tee**-nuh-ri /sɛnˈtiːnəri/

centesimal relating to division into hundredths
sen-**tess**-im-uhl /sɛnˈtɛsɪməl/

Centre region, France
sah(ng)-truh /ˈsɑ̃trə/

Centrica holding company for British Gas
sen-trik-uh /ˈsɛntrɪkə/

centrifugal moving away from a centre
sen-trif-**yoo**-guhl /ˌsɛntrɪˈfjuːɡəl/

Sometimes also sen-**trif**-yuug-uhl, especially in AM.

centripetal moving towards a centre
sen-trip-**ee**-tuhl /ˌsɛntrɪˈpiːtəl/

Sometimes also sen-**trip**-it-uhl, especially in AM.

centurion commander in the ancient Roman army
sent-**yoor**-i-uhn /sɛnˈtjʊəriən/

cep mushroom
sep /sɛp/

cephalic relating to the head
kef-**al**-ik /kɛˈfalɪk/

Commonly also suh-**fal**-ik.

Cephalonia island, Greece
sef-uh-**loh**-ni-uh /ˌsɛfəˈləʊniə/

Established anglicization. The Greek name is Kefallinia, pronounced kef-al-ee-**nee**-uh.

Cephalosporin antibiotic drug
kef-uh-loh-**spaw**-rin /ˌkɛfələʊˈspɔːrɪn/

Cepheus constellation
see-fi-uhss /ˈsiːfɪəs/

Ceram Sea part of the western Pacific Ocean
say-ruhm /ˈseɪrəm/

Cerberus Greek mythological creature
sur-buh-ruhss /ˈsəː(r)bərəs/

cerebral of the cerebrum of the brain
suh-**ree**-bruhl /səˈriːbrəl/

Commonly also **serr**-uhb-ruhl.

cerebrum pl. **cerebra** part of the brain
suh-**reeb**-ruhm, pl. suh-**reeb**-ruh /səˈriːbrəm/, pl. /-brə/

Commonly also **serr**-uhb-ruhm, pl. **serr**-uhb-ruh.

Ceredigion county, Wales
kerr-uh-**dig**-yon /ˌkɛrəˈdɪɡjɒn/

cereology study of crop circles
seer-i-**ol**-uh-ji /ˌsɪəriˈɒlədʒi/

Ceres Roman goddess of agriculture
seer-eez /ˈsɪəriːz/

cerise clear red colour
suh-**reess** /səˈriːs/

cerium chemical element
seer-i-uhm /ˈsɪəriəm/

CERN European Organization for Nuclear Research
surn /səː(r)n/

ceroc dance
serr-**ok** /sɛˈrɒk/

The name is a contraction of the French phrase 'C'est le roc(k)!'

Cerruti Italian fashion label
cherr-**oo**-ti /tʃɛˈruːti/

cerumen earwax
suh-**roo**-muhn /səˈruːmən/

Cervantes, Miguel de Spanish novelist and dramatist
mee-**gel** day sur-**van**-teez /miːˌɡɛl deɪ səː(r)ˈvantiːz/, /ˌmiːˌɣel de θerˈβantes/
• Established anglicization.

cervical relating to the cervix
sur-vik-uhl /ˈsəː(r)vɪkəl/

The pronunciation **sur**-**vy**-kuhl is also common, particularly in the medical profession.

cervix pl. **cervices** neck of the womb
sur-viks, pl. **sur**-viss-eez /'sə:(r)vɪks/,
pl. /-vɪsiːz/

Cesarewitch English horse race
suh-**zarr**-uh-witch /sə'zarəwɪtʃ/

České Budějovice city, Czech Republic
chesk-ay buud-yuh-yov-it-suh
/ˌtʃɛskeɪ 'bʊdjəjɒvɪtsə/

Cetacea order of marine mammals
suh-**tay**-shuh /sə'teɪʃə/

Cetshwayo Zulu king
set-**shway**-oh /sɛ'tʃweɪəʊ/

Cetus constellation
see-tuhss /'siːtəs/

Ceuta Spanish enclave, Morocco
syoo-tuh /'sjuːtə/, Spanish ['θeuta]
• Established anglicization.

Cévennes mountain range, France
say-**ven** /seɪ'vɛn/

ceviche South American fish dish
sev-**ee**-chay /sɛ'viːtʃeɪ/

Ceylon former name for Sri Lanka
suh-**lon** /sə'lɒn/

Cézanne, Paul French painter
pol say-**zan** /ˌpɒl seɪ'zan/

Chablis village, France; also wine
made there
shab-**lee** /ʃab'liː/

Chabrol, Claude French film director
klohd shab-**rol** /ˌkləʊd ʃa'brɒl/

cha-cha ballroom dance
chah-chah /'tʃɑːtʃɑː/

chacham see **haham**

Chaco War dispute between Bolivia and
Paraguay
chah-koh /'tʃɑːkəʊ/

Chad country
chad /tʃad/

chador piece of cloth worn by Muslim
women
chud-uhr /'tʃʌdə(r)/

chaebol business conglomerate
chay-bol /'tʃeɪbɒl/

Chagall, Marc Russian-born French
painter
mark shag-**al** /ˌmɑː(r)k ʃa'gal/

Chagos Archipelago group of islands,
Indian Ocean
chah-gohss /'tʃɑːgəʊs/

chai tea
chy /tʃʌɪ/

chaîné ballet step
shen-**ay** /ʃɛ'neɪ/

chaise-longue type of sofa
shez-**long** /ʃɛz'lɒŋ/

Chaka see **Shaka**

chakra centre of spiritual power
in the body
chuk-ruh /'tʃʌkrə/

Chalabi, Ahmad al- Iraqi politician
akh-muhd uhl chal-uh-bi /ˌaxməd əl
'tʃaləbi/

Chalayan, Hussein Cypriot fashion
designer
huu-**sayn** chuh-**ly**-uhn /hʊˌseɪn
tʃə'lʌɪən/

Chalcedon former city, Asia Minor
kal-suh-don /'kalsədɒn/

chalcedony precious stone
kal-**sed**-uh-ni /kal'sɛdəni/

Chalcis town, Greece
kal-siss /'kalsɪs/

Established anglicization. The Greek name
is Khalkis, pronounced khal-**keess**.

Chaldea ancient country, Iraq
kal-**dee**-uh /kal'diːə/

Chaldee language of the ancient
Chaldeans
kal-dee /'kaldiː/

chalet wooden house
shal-ay /'ʃaleɪ/

Chaliapin, Fyodor Russian operatic
bass
fyod-uhr shal-**yah**-pin /ˌfjɒdə(r)
ʃa'ljɑːpɪn/

challis clothing fabric
chal-iss /'tʃalɪs/

chalumeau musical instrument
shal-**uum**-oh /'ʃalʊməʊ/

Cham indigenous ethnic group of
Vietnam and Cambodia
cham /tʃam/

Chamaeleon constellation
kuh-**mee**-li-uhn /kə'miːliən/

Chamberlain, Neville British
statesman
chaym-buhr-lin /'tʃeɪmbə(r)lɪn/

Chambertin French red wine
shah(ng)-bair-**ta(ng)** /ʃɑ̃bɛː(r)'tɛ̃/

Chambéry town, France
shah(ng)-berr-ee /ʃɑ̃bɛ'riː/

chameleon lizard-like creature
kuh-**mee**-li-uhn /kə'miːliən/

chametz food prohibited during
Passover
khah-mets /'xɑːmɛts/

Chamonix resort, France
sham-uh-nee /'ʃaməniː/

Chamorro indigenous ethnic group
of Guam
chuh-**morr**-oh /tʃə'mɒrəʊ/

Champagne region, France
shah(ng)-**pan**-yuh /ʃãˈpanjə/,
[ʃãpanj]

champagne sparkling wine
sham-**payn** /ʃamˈpeɪn/

Champaign city and county, US
sham-**payn** /ʃamˈpeɪn/

champaign open level countryside
cham-payn /'tʃampeɪn/

Champlain, Samuel de French
explorer
sam-ue-**el** duh shah(ng)-**pla(ng)**
/samyˌɛl də ʃãˈplɛ̃/

Champs Élysées avenue in Paris
shonz uh-**lee**-zay /ˌʃɒnz əˈliːzeɪ/,
French [ʃãz elize]
• Established anglicization.

Chan Chan capital of the pre-Inca
civilization of the Chimu
chan chan /tʃan 'tʃan/

chancre ulcer
shank-uhr /'ʃaŋkə(r)/

chandelier hanging light
shan-duh-**leer** /ˌʃandə'lɪə(r)/

Chandigarh city, India
chun-**dee**-guhr /tʃʌn'diːɡə(r)/

Chandragupta Maurya Indian
emperor
chun-druh-**guup**-tuh **mow**-ri-uh
/ˌtʃʌndrəˌɡʊptə 'maʊriə/

Chanel, Coco French couturière
koh-koh shuh-**nel** /ˌkəʊkəʊ ʃəˈnɛl/

Chaney, Lon American actor
lon chay-ni /ˌlɒn 'tʃeɪni/

Changchun city, China
chang-**chuun** /ˌtʃaŋ'tʃʊn/

Chang Jiang see **Yangtze**

Changsha city, China
chang-**shah** /ˌtʃaŋ'ʃɑː/

Chania (also **Khaniá**) port, Crete
khan-**yah** /xa'njɑː/

chanterelle mushroom
shan-tuh-**rel** /ʃantəˈrɛl/

chanteuse female singer
shahn-**tu(r)z** /ʃɑːnˈtəːz/

Chanukkah see **Hanukkah**

Chao Phraya river, Thailand
chow pruh-**yah** /ˌtʃaʊ prə'jɑː/

chaparajos (also **chaparejos**) leather
trousers
chap-uh-**ray**-hohss /ˌtʃapə'reɪhəʊs/

chapatti thin pancake
chuh-**pat**-i /tʃə'pati/

Chapman, Dinos English artist
dee-noss **chap**-muhn /ˌdiːnɒs
'tʃapmən/

Chappaquiddick Island island, US
chap-uh-**kwid**-ik /ˌtʃapə'kwɪdɪk/

Chappell, Greg Australian cricketer
chap-uhl /'tʃapəl/

charango musical instrument
chuh-**rang**-goh /tʃə'raŋɡəʊ/

charas cannabis resin
char-uhss /'tʃɑːrəs/

Charcot, Jean-Martin French
neurologist
zhah(ng) mar-**ta(ng)** shar-**koh** /ʒã
mɑː(r),tɛ̃ ʃɑː(r)'kəʊ/

Chardonnay variety of white wine grape
shar-duh-nay /'ʃɑː(r)dəneɪ/

Charente river, France
sharr-**ah(ng)t** /ʃa'rãt/

charisma pl. **charismata** charm
kuh-**riz**-muh, pl. kuh-**riz**-muh-tuh
/kə'rɪzmə/, pl. /-mətə/

Charlemagne king of the Franks
shar-luh-mayn /'ʃɑː(r)ləmeɪn/, French
[ʃarləmanj]

Charleroi city, Belgium
sharl-**rwah** /ʃɑː(r)l'rwɑː/

charlock wild mustard
char-lok /'tʃɑː(r)lɒk/

Charlotte Amalie capital of the Virgin
Islands
shar-luht uh-**mahl**-yuh /ˌʃɑː(r)lət
ə'mɑːljə/

Charon Greek mythological character
kair-uhn /'kɛːrən/

Chartres city, France
shart-ruh /'ʃɑː(r)trə/

chartreuse liqueur
shar-**troez** /ʃɑː(r)'trøːz/

Charybdis Greek mythological whirlpool
kuh-**rib**-diss /kə'rɪbdɪs/

Chase, Chevy American actor
chev-i chayss /ˌtʃɛvi ˈtʃeɪs/

Chasid see **Hasid**

Chasidic see **Hasidic**

Chasidism see **Hasidism**

chasm deep fissure in the earth's surface
kaz-uhm /ˈkazəm/

chassé dancing step
shass-ay /ˈʃaseɪ/

Chasselas variety of white grape
shass-uh-lah /ʃasəˈlɑː/

chateaubriand beef steak
shat-oh-bree-o(ng) /ˌʃatəʊbriːˈõ/,
French [ʃatobrijɑ̃]

Chaucer, Geoffrey English poet
chaw-suhr /ˈtʃɔːsə(r)/

Chaumes French cheese
shohm /ʃəʊm/

Chávez-Frias, Hugo Venezuelan
president
oo-goh chav-ess free-ass /ˌuːgəʊ
ˌtʃavess ˈfriːas/

Chavin ancient Peruvian civilization
chav-een /tʃaˈviːn/

Cheboksary city, Russia
chuh-buhk-sar-i /tʃəbəkˈsɑːri/

Chechen relating to Chechnya
chetch-en /ˈtʃɛtʃɛn/

Chechnya (also **Chechenia**)
autonomous republic, Russia
chetch-nyah /ˌtʃɛtʃˈnjɑː/

cheder (also **heder**) pl. **chedarim** Jewish
school
khed-uhr, pl. khed-ar-im /ˈxɛdə(r)/, pl.
/-ˈdɑːrɪm/
• Standard -s plural is also possible.

Cheka Soviet organization
chek-uh /ˈtʃɛkə/

Chekhov, Anton Russian dramatist
an-ton chek-of /ˌantɒn ˈtʃɛkɒf/

Cheltenham town, England
chelt-uhn-uhm /ˈtʃɛltənəm/

Chela, Juan Ignacio Argentine tennis
player
khwan eeg-nass-yoh chay-luh /xwan
iːgˌnasjəʊ ˈtʃeɪlə/

Chelyabinsk city, Russia
chuhl-yah-binsk /tʃəlˈjaːbɪnsk/

chemise dress
shuh-meez /ʃəˈmiːz/

Chemnitz city, Germany

kem-nits /ˈkɛmnɪts/

chemotherapy treatment of disease
kee-moh-**therr**-uh-pi /ˌkiːməʊˈθɛrəpi/

Chenab river, India and Pakistan
chuh-**nahb** /tʃəˈnɑːb/

Cheney, Richard (**Dick**) American
politician
chay-ni /ˈtʃeɪmi/

This surname is variously pronounced
chee-ni and chay-ni, depending on
individual preference.

Chengdu city, China
cheng-doo /ˌtʃɛŋˈduː/

chenille yarn
shuh-neel /ʃəˈniːl/

Chennai official name for Madras
chen-y /ˈtʃɛnʌɪ/

Cheops Egyptian pharaoh
kee-ops /ˈkiːɒps/

Cher river, France
shair /ʃɛː(r)/

Cher American singer and actress
shair /ʃɛː(r)/

Cherbourg port, France
shair-boorg /ˈʃɛː(r)bʊə(r)g/, [ʃɛrbur]
• Established anglicization.

Cherepovets city, Russia
cherr-uh-puh-vyets /ˌtʃɛrəpəˈvjɛts/

cherimoya apple
cherr-im-oy-uh /ˌtʃɛrɪˈmɔɪə/

Cherkasy port, Ukraine
chuhr-kass-i /tʃəˈ(r)ˈkasi/

Cherkessk city, Russia
chuhr-kyesk /tʃə(r)ˈkjɛsk/

Chernenko, Konstantin Soviet
statesman
kon-stuhn-teen chuhrn-yen-koh
/kɒnstənˌtiːn tʃə(r)ˈnjɛnkəʊ/

Chernihiv port, Ukraine
chair-nee-hiv /tʃɛː(r)ˈniːhɪv/

Chernivtsi city, Ukraine
chur-nivt-si /tʃə(r)ˈnɪvtsi/

Chernobyl town, Ukraine
chuhr-nob-il /tʃə(r)ˈnɒbɪl/

Cherokee American Indian ethnic group
cherr-uh-kee /ˌtʃɛrəˈkiː/

cheroot cigar
shuh-root /ʃəˈruːt/

Cherso island, Italy
kair-soh /ˈkɛː(r)səʊ/

Cherubini, Maria Luigi Italian
composer
mu-**ree**-uh luu-**ee**-ji kerr-uub-**ee**-ni
/məˌriːə luˌiːdʒi kɛrʊˈbiːni/

Cherwell, Frederick German-born
British physicist
char-wel /ˈtʃɑː(r)wɛl/
• The same pronunciation is used for the
River Cherwell in Oxford.

Chesapeake Bay inlet of the North
Atlantic, US
chess-uh-peek /ˈtʃɛsəpiːk/

Cheshire county, England
chesh-uhr /ˈtʃɛʃə(r)/

Chesil Beach shingle beach, England
chez-il /ˈtʃɛzɪl/

Chetumal port, Mexico
chet-uum-**al** /ˌtʃɛtʊˈmal/

Chevalier, Maurice French singer
and actor
morr-**eess** shuh-val-**yay** /mɒˌriːs
ʃəvaˈljeɪ/

Cheviot Hills range of hills on the
border between England and Scotland
cheev-i-uht /ˈtʃiːviət/

Sometimes also **chev**-i-uht, both for the
place and for the breed of sheep.

chèvre French cheese
shev-ruh /ˈʃɛvrə/

Cheyenne city, US
shy-**an** /ʃʌɪˈan/

Commonly also shy-**en**.

Chhattisgarh state, India
chat-iz-**gar** /ˌtʃatɪzˈgɑː(r)/

chi letter of the Greek alphabet
ky /kʌɪ/

chi see **qi**

Chiang Kai-shek Chinese statesman
chang ky-**shek** /ˌtʃaŋ kʌɪˈʃɛk/
• Established anglicization.

Chiangmai city, Thailand
cheng-**my** /tʃɛŋˈmʌɪ/

Chianti Italian red wine
ki-**an**-ti /kiˈanti/

Chiapas state, Mexico
chi-**ap**-ass /tʃiˈapas/

Chiba city, Japan
chee-buh /ˈtʃiːbə/

Chibcha Colombian ethnic group
chib-chuh /ˈtʃɪbtʃə/

chibouk Turkish tobacco pipe
chib-**ook** /tʃɪˈbuːk/

chic stylishly fashionable
sheek /ʃiːk/

chicane double bend
shik-**ayn** /ʃɪˈkeɪn/

Chichén Itzá Mayan empire centre,
Mexico
chee-**chen** eet-**sah** /tʃiːˌtʃɛn iːtˈsɑː/

Chichester city, England
chitch-uh-stuhr /ˈtʃɪtʃəstə(r)/

The pronunciation of Chichester in Tyne
and Wear, however, is **chy**-chuh-stuhr.

Chichester, Francis English
yachtsman
chitch-uh-stuhr /ˈtʃɪtʃəstə(r)/

Chickasaw American Indian ethnic
group
chik-uh-saw /ˈtʃɪkəsɔː/

chicory plant
chik-uh-ri /ˈtʃɪkəri/

Chicoutimi river, city, and county,
Canada
shik-**oo**-tim-i /ʃɪˈkuːtɪmi/

Chihuahua state, Mexico
chee-**wah**-wuh /tʃiːˈwɑːwə/

chikungunya viral disease
chik-uung-**guun**-yuh /ˌtʃɪkʊŋˈɡʊnjə/

Childermas Christian festival
child-uhr-mass /ˈtʃɪldə(r)mas/

Childers, Erskine English-born Irish
writer and political activist
ur-skin **child**-uhrz /ˌəː(r)skɪn
ˈtʃɪldə(r)z/

Chile country
chil-i /ˈtʃɪli/, Spanish [ˈtʃile]
• Established anglicization.

Chilean relating to Chile
chil-i-uhn /ˈtʃɪliən/

chillum hookah
chil-uhm /ˈtʃɪləm/

Chilpancingo city, Mexico
cheel-pal-**seeng**-goh
/ˌtʃiːlpanˈsiːŋɡəʊ/

Chiltern Hills range of chalk hills,
England
chilt-uhrn /ˈtʃɪltə(r)n/

Chimborazo mountain, Ecuador
cheem-boh-**rah**-soh /ˌtʃiːmbəʊˈrɑːsəʊ/

chimera (also **chimaera**) mythological
monster
ky-**meer**-uh /kʌɪˈmɪərə/

chimichanga deep-fried tortilla
cheem-i-**chang**-guh /ˌtʃiːmiˈtʃaŋɡə/

Chimú Peruvian ethnic group
chee-**moo** /tʃi:'mu:/

Chindwin river, Burma
chind-**win** /tʃɪn'dwɪn/

chino cotton twill fabric
chee-**noh** /'tʃi:nəʊ/

Chinook American Indian ethnic group
shin-**uuk** /ʃɪ'nʊk/
• The same pronunciation is used for the helicopter.

Chios island, Greece
ky-oss /'kaɪɒs/

Established anglicization. The Greek name is Khios, pronounced **khee**-oss ['xíɔs].

Chipewyan Canadian ethnic group
chip-uh-**wy**-uhn /,tʃɪpə'waɪən/

Chirac, Jacques French president
zhahk sheer-**ak** /,ʒɑːk ʃɪə'rak/

Chirico, Giorgio de Greek-born Italian painter
jor-joh day **keer**-ik-oh /,dʒɔː(r)dʒəʊ deɪ 'kɪərɪkəʊ/

chiromancy interpretation of the lines on the palms
ky-roh-man-si /'kaɪrəʊmansi/

Chiron Greek mythological character
ky-ron /'kaɪrɒn/

chiropody treatment of the feet
kirr-**op**-uh-di /kɪ'rɒpədi/

chiropractic system of complementary medicine
ky-roh-**prak**-tik /,kaɪrəʊ'praktɪk/

Chişinău capital of Moldova
kish-in-**ow** /,kɪʃɪ'naʊ/

chitarrone lute
kee-tuh-**roh**-nay /,kiːtə'rəʊneɪ/

Chittagong seaport, Bangladesh
chit-uh-**gong** /tʃɪtə'gɒŋ/

chlamydia pl. same or **chlamydiae** parasitic bacterium
kluh-**mid**-i-uh, pl. kluh-**mid**-i-ee /klə'mɪdiə/, pl. /-diː/

chlorambucil cancer drug
klaw-**ram**-byoo-sil /klɔː'rambjuːsɪl/

chlorine chemical element
klaw-reen /'klɔːriːn/

chlorophyll pigment
klorr-uh-fil /'klɒrəfɪl/

Commonly also **klaw**-roh for words beginning with *chloro*-.

chlorpromazine tranquillizer
klor-**proh**-muh-zeen /klɔː(r)'prəʊməziːn/

Choctaw American Indian ethnic group
chok-taw /'tʃɒktɔː/

Chokwe African ethnic group
chok-way /'tʃɒkweɪ/

cholelithiasis formation of gallstones
kol-uh-lith-**y**-uh-siss /,kɒləlɪ'θaɪəsɪs/

cholera bacterial disease
kol-uh-ruh /'kɒlərə/

choleraic infected with cholera
kol-uh-**ray**-ik /,kɒlə'reɪɪk/

choleric bad-tempered
kol-uh-rik /'kɒlərɪk/

choli bodice worn under a sari
choh-li /'tʃəʊli/

Chomolungma Tibetan name for Mount Everest
choh-moh-**luung**-muh /tʃəʊməʊ'lʊŋmə/

Chomsky, Noam American linguist
nohm chom-ski /,nəʊm 'tʃɒmski/

Chongjin port, North Korea
chong-**jin** /tʃɒŋ'dʒɪn/

Chongqing city, China
chuung-**ching** /,tʃʊŋ'tʃɪŋ/

Chopin, Frédéric Polish-born French composer
fray-day-**reek** shop-a**(ng)** /freɪdeɪ,riːk ʃɒ'pɛ̃/

An anglicized pronunciation, **shoh**-pa(ng), is also common.

Chopin, Kate American novelist
shoh-pan /'ʃəʊpan/

chop suey Chinese dish
chop **soo**-i /,tʃɒp'suːi/

Chordata phylum of animals
kor-**day**-tuh /kɔː(r)'deɪtə/

chordophone stringed instrument
kor-duh-fohn /'kɔː(r)dəfəʊn/

chorea neurological disorder
korr-**ee**-uh /kɒ'riːə/

chorine chorus girl
kaw-reen /'kɔːriːn/

chorizo Spanish pork sausage
chuh-**ree**-zoh /tʃə'riːzəʊ/, [tʃɒ'riθɒ]

Often also (erroneously) chuh-**rits**-oh.

chorten Buddhist shrine
chor-tuhn /'tʃɔː(r)tən/

choux pastry
shoo /ʃuː/

chow mein Chinese dish
chow **mayn** /ˌtʃaʊ ˈmeɪn/

Chrétien, Jean Canadian statesman
zhah(ng) krayt-**ya(ng)** /ˌʒɑ̃ kreɪˈtjɛ̃/

Christian relating to Christianity
kriss-chuhn /ˈkrɪstʃən/

The pronunciation **krist**-i-uhn is less
common now.

chrysalis insect pupa
kriss-uh-liss /ˈkrɪsəlɪs/

chrysanthemum plant
kriss-**anth**-uh-muhm /krɪˈsanθəməm/

Chrysostom, St John bishop of
Constantinople
kriss-uhst-uhm /ˈkrɪsəstəm/

Chubu region, Japan
choo-boo /ˈtʃuːbuː/

Chugoku region, Japan
chuung-ok-oo /ˈtʃʊŋɒkuː/
• See **JAPANESE** panel.

Chukchi Sea part of the Arctic Ocean
chuuk-chee /ˈtʃʊktʃiː/

This pronunciation is also suitable for the
Siberian ethnic group of the same name.

Chumash American Indian people
choo-mash /ˈtʃuːmaʃ/

Chur city, Switzerland
koor /kʊə(r)/

This is the German name; the French form
is Coire, pronounced **kwar.**

churidars Indian trousers
chuu-rid-arz /ˈtʃʊrɪdɑː(r)z/

churrasco South American dish
chuu-**rask**-oh /tʃʊˈraskəʊ/

chutzpah self-confidence
khuuts-puh /ˈxʊtspə/

Chuvashia autonomous republic, Russia
choo-**vah**-shi-uh /tʃuːˈvɑːʃiə/

chyme acidic fluid in the stomach and
the small intestine
kym /kʌɪm/

chypre perfume
sheep-ruh /ˈʃiːprə/

ciabatta Italian bread
chuh-**bat**-uh /tʃəˈbatə/

Ciampi, Carlo Azeglio Italian
president
kar-loh ad-**zel**-yoh **champ**-i /ˌkɑː(r)ləʊ
aˌdzɛljəʊ ˈtʃampi/

ciao Italian greeting
chow /tʃaʊ/

Ciampino airport, Rome
champ-**ee-noh** /tʃamˈpiːnəʊ/

Cian Irish boy's name
kee-uhn /ˈkiːən/

Ciara Irish girl's name
keer-uh /ˈkɪərə/

Ciara American singer
si-**air-uh** /siˈɛːrə/

Cibber, Colley English dramatist
sib-uhr /ˈsɪbə(r)/

cicely plant
siss-i-li /ˈsɪsɪli/

Ciccone, Madonna full name of
American singer Madonna
chik-**oh-ni** /tʃɪˈkəʊni/

Cicero, Marcus Tullius Roman
statesman
mar-kuhss tul-i-uhss siss-uh-roh
/ˌmɑː(r)kəs ˌtʌlɪəs ˈsɪsərəʊ/
• See **LATIN** panel.

Cieszyn city, Poland
chesh-in /ˈtʃɛʃɪn/

cilantro coriander
sil-**ant-roh** /sɪˈlantrəʊ/

cilice haircloth
sil-iss /ˈsɪlɪs/

Cilicia ancient region, Asia Minor
sil-**ish-uh** /sɪˈlɪʃə/

cimbalom musical instrument
sim-buh-luhm /ˈsɪmbələm/

cimetidine antihistamine drug
sy-**met-id-een** /sʌɪˈmɛtɪdiːn/

Cimmerian ancient nomadic ethnic
group
sim-**eer-i-uhn** /sɪˈmɪəriən/

Cincinnati city, US
sin-sin-**at-i** /ˌsɪnsɪˈnati/

cineraria plant
sin-uh-**rair-i-uh** /ˌsɪnəˈrɛːriə/

cinerary urn urn for holding ashes
sin-uh-ruh-ri /ˈsɪnərəri/

cinquecento period of Italian art
chink-wi-**chen-toh** /ˌtʃɪŋkwɪˈtʃɛntəʊ/

cinquefoil plant
sink-foyl /ˈsɪŋkfɔɪl/

Cinque Ports group of medieval ports,
England
sink **ports** /ˌsɪŋk ˈpɔː(r)ts/

Cintra see **Sintra**

circadian relating to twenty-four hour rhythm
sur-kay-di-uhn /sə:(r)ˈkeɪdiən/

Circassian Caucasian ethnic group
sur-**kass**-i-uhn /sə:(r)ˈkasiən/

Circe Greek mythological character
sur-si /ˈsə:(r)si/

Circinus constellation
sur-sin-uhss /ˈsə:(r)sɪnəs/

ciré fabric
see-ray /ˈsiːreɪ/

Cirencester town, England
sy-ruhn-sest-uhr /ˈsʌɪrənˌsɛstə(r)/

Cirque du Soleil Canadian circus
seerk due sol-**ay** /ˌsɪə(r)k dy sɒˈleɪ/

cirrhosis liver disease
sirr-**oh**-siss /sɪˈrəʊsɪs/

cirrocumulus cloud
sirr-oh-**kyoo-myuul**-uhss
/ˌsɪrəʊˈkjuːmjʊləs/

cirrostratus cloud
sirr-oh-**strah**-tuhss /ˌsɪrəʊˈstrɑːtəs/

Commonly also sirr-oh-**stray**-tuhss.

cirrus pl. **cirri** cloud
sirr-uhss, pl. **sirr**-y /ˈsɪrəs, pl. /-rʌɪ/

cisalpine on the southern side of the Alps
siss-**al**-pyn /sɪsˈalpʌɪn/

Ciskei former Xhosa homeland, South Africa
sisk-y /ˈsɪskʌɪ/

cisplatin cancer drug
sisp-**lat**-in /sɪsˈplatɪn/

cispontine on the north side of the Thames
sisp-**on**-tyn /sɪsˈpɒntʌɪn/

citadel fortress
sit-uh-duhl /ˈsɪtədəl/

CITES Convention on International Trade in Endangered Species
sy-teez /ˈsʌɪtiːz/

Citlaltépetl mountain, Mexico
seet-lal-**tay**-pet-uhl /ˌsiːtlalˈteɪpɛtəl/

citole stringed instrument
sit-**ohl** /sɪˈtəʊl/

Citroën French car manufacturers
sit-ruhn /ˈsɪtrən/, [sɪtrɔɛn]
• Established anglicization.

cittern stringed instrument
sit-uhrn /ˈsɪtə(r)n/

Ciudad Bolívar city, Venezuela
syoo-**dath** bol-**ee**-var /sjuːˌdað bɒˈliːvɑː(r)/

Ciudad Victoria city, Mexico
syoo-**dath** veek-**tor**-yuh /sjuːˌdað viːkˈtɔːrjə/

civet carnivorous mammal
siv-it /ˈsɪvɪt/

clachan small village or hamlet
klakh-uhn /ˈklaxən/

Clackmannanshire former county, Scotland
klak-**man**-uhn-sheer /klakˈmanənʃɪə(r)/

Clactonian lower palaeolithic culture
klak-**toh**-ni-uhn /klakˈtəʊniən/

Claddagh ring Irish ring
klad-uh /ˈkladə/

clafoutis flan made of fruit
klaf-**oo**-ti /klaˈfuːti/

Clair, René French film director
ruh-**nay klair** /rəˈneɪ ˈklɛː(r)/

clair-de-lune blue-grey colour
klair duh **loon** /ˌklɛː(r) də ˈluːn/, French [ˌklɛːr də ˈlyn]

clamant demanding attention
klay-muhnt /ˈkleɪmənt/

Sometimes also **klam**-uhnt.

clandestine kept secret
klan-**dest**-in /klanˈdɛstɪn/

Commonly also **klan**-dest-yn.

Clarenceux heraldic title
klarr-uhn-soo /ˈklarənsuː/

claret French red wine
klarr-uht /ˈklarət/

clarsach Irish harp
klar-suhkh /ˈklɑː(r)səx/

clary herbaceous plant
klair-i /ˈklɛːri/

Claude Lorrain French painter
klohd lorr-**a(ng)** /ˌkləʊd lɒˈrɛ̃/

Claudius Roman emperor
klaw-di-uhss /ˈklɔːdiəs/
• See LATIN panel.

Clausewitz, Karl von Prussian general
karl-fon klow-zuh-vits /ˌkɑː(r)l fɒn ˈklaʊzəvɪts/

Clausius, Rudolf German physicist
roo-dolf klow-zi-uuss /ˌruːdɒlf ˈklaʊziʊs/

claustrophobia fear of confined places
klost-ruh-**foh**-bi-uh /ˌklɒstrəˈfəʊbiə/

claves musical instrument
klayvz /kleɪvz/

Commonly also klahvz.

clavichord keyboard instrument
klav-ik-ord /ˈklavɪkɔː(r)d/

clavicle collarbone
klav-ik-uhl /ˈklavɪkəl/

clavier keyboard instrument
kluh-veer /kləˈvɪə(r)/

Sometimes also klav-i-uhr.

Clayderman, Richard French pianist
ritch-uhrd klay-duhr-muhn /ˌrɪtʃə(r)d
ˈkleɪdə(r)mən/
• Established anglicization.

Cleisthenes Athenian statesman
klyss-thuh-neez /ˈklaɪsθəniːz/

Clemenceau, Georges French
statesman
zhorzh klem-ah(ng)-soh /ˌʒɔː(r)ʒ
klɛmãˈsəʊ/

clementine tangerine
klem-uhn-tyn /ˈklɛməntʌɪn/

Commonly also klem-uhn-teen.

clenbuterol asthma drug
klen-byoo-tuh-rol /klɛnˈbjuːtərɒl/

Cleopatra queen of Egypt
klee-uh-pat-ruh /ˌkliːəˈpatrə/

clepsydra pl. **clepsydrae** ancient
time-measuring device
klep-sid-ruh, pl. klep-sid-ree
/ˈklɛpsɪdrə/, pl. /-driː/
• Standard -s plural is also possible.

clerk administrative person in an office
klark /klɑː(r)k/

AM is klurk.

Clermont-Ferrand city, France
klair-mo(ng) ferr-ah(ng) /ˌklɛː(r)mɔ̃
fɛˈrã/

Cleveland former county, England
kleev-luhnd /ˈkliːvlənd/

Clift, Montgomery American actor
muhnt-gum-uh-ri klift /məntˌɡʌməri
ˈklɪft/

Clijsters, Kim Belgian tennis player
kim klyst-uhrss /ˌkɪm ˈklʌɪstə(r)s/

climacteric critical period
kly-mak-tuh-rik /klʌɪˈmaktərɪk/

Commonly also kly-mak-terr-ik.

Climbié, Victoria 8-year-old girl from

Côte d'Ivoire, subjected to severe abuse
and neglect
klim-bi-ay /ˈklɪmbieɪ/

clime region considered with reference to
its climate
klym /klʌɪm/

Cline, Patsy American country singer
klyn /klʌɪn/

Clio Greek mythological character
kly-oh /ˈklʌɪəʊ/

Sometimes also klee-oh, and always for the
Renault car model.

clique close-knit group of people
kleek /kliːk/

clitoris part of the female genitals
klit-uh-riss /ˈklɪtərɪs/

Less commonly in AM also klit-aw-riss.

clomiphene fertility drug
kloh-mif-een /ˈkləʊmɪfiːn/

Clonmel town, Republic of Ireland
klon-mel /klɒnˈmɛl/

clostridium difficile bacterium
klost-rid-i-uhm dif-iss-il /klɒˌstrɪdiəm
ˈdɪfɪsɪl/

This pronunciation is in line with the usage
of the various microbiology and infection
control experts the BBC has consulted.
Medical Latin is commonly anglicized; see
LATIN panel.

Clotho Greek mythological character
kloh-thoh /ˈkləʊθəʊ/

clou musical term
kloo /kluː/

Clough town, northern Ireland
klokh /klɒx/

clough ravine
kluf /klʌf/

Clough, Arthur Hugh English poet
kluf /klʌf/

Clough, Brian English football manager
kluf /klʌf/

Clovis king of the Franks
kloh-viss /ˈkləʊvɪs/

clozapine sedative drug
kloh-zuh-peen /ˈkləʊzəpiːn/

Cluj–Napoca city, Romania
kloozh nap-ok-uh /ˌkluːʒ naˈpɒkə/

Cluniac relating to a Benedictine
monastic order founded at Cluny
kloon-i-ak /ˈkluːniak/

Clicks

Clicks are a certain kind of consonant found in many African languages. English consonants are made by interrupting or constricting the flow of air coming out of the lungs. Click consonants, by contrast, are made by air being sucked into the mouth. Although these sounds do not occur as consonants in English (or any other European language), English speakers can still make some click sounds, and sometimes even use them, as signals, in speech. For example, the 'tutting' noise we use to convey disapproval is in fact a dental click. Another example of a click consonant is the 'kissing' noise (bilabial click), and yet another is the 'gee-up' noise we might use to encourage a horse to move forward (lateral click).

We do not expect BBC announcers to be able to reproduce clicks in African names, and we anglicize as best we can, substituting clicks with the nearest English consonant. Wherever possible we try to consult with the owner of the name to establish their preferred anglicized pronunciation. *Welshman Ncube*, a Zimbabwean politician, told a BBC reporter that he would rather have his name pronounced without a click altogether, rather than with an attempted click or with an English consonant instead. The C in *Ncube* represents a dental click (the 'tutting' sound), and we now advise programme makers to say **noo**-bay, rather than, for instance, n-**too**-bay.

Cluny town, France
klue-**nee** /kly'niː/

Clutha river, New Zealand
kloo-thuh /'kluːθə/

Clwyd former county, Wales
kluu-id /'klʊɪd/

Cnut see Canute

Clytemnestra Greek mythological character
kly-tuhm-**nest**-ruh /ˌklʌɪtəm'nɛstrə/

Cnidaria phylum of aquatic invertebrate animals
kny-**dair**-i-uh /knʌɪ'dɛːriə/

coagulate change to a solid or semi-solid state
koh-**ag**-yuul-ayt /kəʊ'agjʊleɪt/

Coahuila state, Mexico
koh-ah-**weel**-uh /ˌkəʊɑː'wiːlə/

coalesce come together to form one mass
koh-uh-**less** /ˌkəʊə'lɛs/

coaxial having a common axis
koh-**ak**-si-uhl /kəʊ'aksiəl/

Cobain, Kurt American rock singer
kuh-**bayn** /kə'beɪn/

cobalt chemical element
koh-bawlt /'kəʊbɔːlt/

Commonly also **koh**-bolt.

COBE NASA satellite
koh-bi /'kəʊbi/

coble fishing boat
koh-buhl /'kəʊbəl/

COBOL computer programming language
koh-bol /'kəʊbɒl/

Coburg city, Germany
koh-burg /'kəʊbə(r)g/, ['koːbʊrk]
• Established anglicization.

coca tropical American shrub
koh-kuh /'kəʊkə/

cocaine drug
koh-kayn /kəʊˈkeɪn/

Cochabamba city, Bolivia
kotch-uh-bamb-uh /ˌkɒtʃəˈbambə/

Cochin port, India
koh-chin /ˈkəʊtʃɪn/

cochlea pl. **cochleae** cavity of the inner
ear
kok-li-uh, pl. **kok-li-ee** /ˈkɒkliə/, pl.
/-kliiː/

Cochran, Charles Blake English
theatrical producer
kok-ruhn /ˈkɒkrən/

This British surname is variously
pronounced **kok-ruhn** and **kokh-ruhn**,
depending on individual preference.

Cochran, Eddie American
rock-and-roll singer
kok-ruhn /ˈkɒkrən/

Cochran, Jacqueline American aviator
kok-ruhn /ˈkɒkrən/

cockatiel parrot
kok-uh-teel /ˌkɒkəˈtiːl/

cockatoo parrot
kok-uh-too /ˌkɒkəˈtuː/

Cocos Islands group of islands, Indian
Ocean
koh-kuhss /ˈkəʊkəs/

cocotte heatproof dish
kok-ot /kɒˈkɒt/

Cocteau, Jean French dramatist
zhah(ng) kok-toh /ˌʒɑ̃ kɒkˈtəʊ/

coda musical term
koh-duh /ˈkəʊdə/

codec device that compresses data
koh-dek /ˈkəʊdɛk/

codeine analgesic drug
koh-deen /ˈkəʊdiːn/

codex pl. **codices** ancient manuscript text
koh-deks, pl. **koh-diss-eez** /ˈkəʊdɛks/,
pl. /-dɪsiːz/
• Standard -es plural is also possible.

codex calixtinus 12th-century
manuscript
koh-deks kal-ik-stee-nuhss /ˌkəʊdɛks
kalɪkˈstiːnəs/

codicil supplement to a will
kod-iss-il /ˈkɒdɪsɪl/

Coe, Sebastian English athlete and
politician
koh /kəʊ/

Coelho, Paulo Brazilian writer
pow-loo kuu-el-yoo /ˌpaʊlu: kʊˈɛljuː/

coeliac relating to the abdomen
seel-i-ak /ˈsiːliak/

coelurosaur dinosaur
sil-yoor-uh-sor /sɪˈljʊərəsɔː(r)/

Coen, Joel and Ethan American film
directors
koh-uhn /ˈkəʊən/

coenobite member of a monastic
community
see-nuh-byt /ˈsiːnəbʌɪt/

coerce persuade
koh-urss /kəʊˈə:(r)s/

Coetzee, J. M. South African novelist
kuut-see /kʊtˈsiː/

This pronunciation was confirmed in a letter
to the Pronunciation Unit from Mr Coetzee.
The family name is pronounced
kuut-see-uh in Afrikaans.

cogitate think deeply
koj-it-ayt /ˈkɒdʒɪteɪt/

cogito ergo sum 'I think, therefore I
am' (Latin)
kog-it-oh air-goh suum /ˌkɒgɪtəʊ
ˌɛ:(r)gəʊ ˈsʊm/

Commonly also **ur-goh sum**; see LATIN
panel.

cognac brandy
kon-yak /ˈkɒnjak/

cognizant having knowledge
kog-niz-uhnt /ˈkɒgnɪzənt/

cognize know
kog-nyz /kɒgˈnʌɪz/

cognoscenti well-informed people
kog-nuh-shen-ti /ˌkɒgnəˈʃɛnti/

Commonly also **kon-yuh-shen-ti**.

Cohen, Leonard Canadian singer
len-uhrd koh-uhn /ˌlɛnə(r)d ˈkəʊən/

cohere form a unified whole
koh-heer /kəʊˈhɪə(r)/

cohesion action of forming a united
whole
koh-hee-zhuhn /kəʊˈhiːʒən/

Cohn, Ferdinand German botanist
fair-din-ant kohn /ˌfɛ:(r)dɪnant ˈkəʊn/

cohort ancient Roman military unit
koh-hort /ˈkəʊhɔ:(r)t/

coiffeur hairdresser
kwaf-ur /kwaˈfə:(r)/

Coimbatore city, India
koym-buh-tor /ˌkɔɪmbə'tɔː(r)/

Coimbra city, Portugal
kweem-bruh /'kwiːmbrə/

Cointreau trademark liqueur
kwon-troh /'kwɒntrəʊ/, French
[kwɛ̃tro]

Coire city, Switzerland
kwar /kwɑː(r)/

This is the French name; the German form is Chur, pronounced koor.

coitus sexual intercourse
koh-it-uhss /'kəʊɪtəs/

Coke, Peter English actor
kuuk /kʊk/

This British surname is variously pronounced kohk and kuuk, depending on individual preference.

colander perforated bowl
kol-uhn-duhr /'kɒləndə(r)/

Sometimes also kul-uhn-duhr.

Colbert, Jean Baptiste French statesman
zhah(ng) bat-eest kol-bair /ʒ̃ɑ baˌtiːst kɒl'bɛː(r)/

colcannon Irish and Scottish dish
kol-kan-uhn /kɒl'kanən/

Colchester town, England
kohl-chuhst-uhr /'kəʊltʃəstə(r)/

Colchis ancient region, Caucasus
kol-kiss /'kɒlkɪs/

Colditz medieval castle, Germany
kohl-dits /'kəʊldɪts/, ['kɔldɪts]
• Established anglicization.

colectomy surgical removal of the colon
koh-lek-tuh-mi /kəʊ'lɛktəmi/

Coleraine town, Northern Ireland
kohl-rayn /kəʊl'reɪn/

Coleridge, Samuel Taylor English poet, critic, and philosopher
kohl-uh-rij /'kəʊlərɪdʒ/

Colette French novelist
kol-et /kɒ'lɛt/

Colima state, Mexico
kol-ee-muh /kɒ'liːmə/

coliseum (also **colosseum**) large theatre
kol-uh-see-uhm /ˌkɒlə'siːəm/

colitis inflammation of the lining of the colon
kuh-ly-tiss /kə'lʌɪtɪs/

collage form of art
kol-ahzh /kɒ'lɑː3/

Commonly also kol-ahzh.

collagen structural protein
kol-uh-juhn /'kɒlədʒən/

collapsar old star that has collapsed
kuh-lap-sar /kə'lapsɑː(r)/

collect short prayer
kol-ekt /'kɒlɛkt/

collegian member of a college
kuh-lee-ji-uhn /kə'liːdʒiən/

Colles' fracture broken wrist
kol-iss /'kɒlɪs/

colliculus pl. **colliculi** swelling in the roof of the midbrain
kuh-lik-yuul-uhss, pl. **kuh-lik-yuul-y** /kə'lɪkjʊləs/, pl. /-lʌɪ/

collier coal miner
kol-i-uhr /'kɒlɪə(r)/

collocutor person who takes part in a conversation
kuh-lok-yuut-uhr /kə'lɒkjʊtə(r)/

Commonly also kol-uh-kyoot-uhr.

colloquial used in ordinary or familiar conversation
kuh-loh-kwi-uhl /kə'ləʊkwiəl/

colloquium pl. **colloquia** academic conference
kuh-loh-kwi-uhm, pl. **ku-loh-kwi-uh** /kə'ləʊkwiəm/, /-kwiə/
• Standard -s plural is also possible.

collude come to a secret understanding
kuh-lood /kə'luːd/

Less commonly also kuh-lyood.

colobus African monkey
kol-uh-buhss /'kɒləbəs/

Cologne city, Germany
kuh-lohn /kə'ləʊn/

Established anglicization. The German name is Köln, pronounced koeln ['kœln].

cologne scented toilet water
kuh-lohn /kə'ləʊn/

Colombia country
kuh-lomb-i-uh /kə'lɒmbiə/

Colombo capital of Sri Lanka
kuh-lum-boh /kə'lʌmbəʊ/

Colón port, Panama
kol-on /kɒ'lɒn/

colon part of the intestine
ko-luhn /ˈkəʊlən/

Commonly also **koh**-lon. The same
pronunciations are used for the punctuation
mark.

colón pl. **colones** currency unit, Costa
Rica and El Salvador
kol-on, pl. **kol**-on-ess /kɒˈlɒn/, pl.
/-ˈlɒnɛs/

colonel rank of officer
ku(r)-nuhl /ˈkəː(r)nəl/

colonic relating to the colon
kuh-**lon**-ik /kəˈlɒnɪk/

Colorado state and river, US
kol-uh-**rah**-doh /ˌkɒləˈrɑːdəʊ/

Colosseum amphitheatre in Rome
kol-uh-**see**-uhm /ˌkɒləˈsiːəm/

Colossians book of the Bible
kuh-**losh**-uhnz /kəˈlɒʃənz/

colostomy surgical shortening of the
colon
kuh-**lost**-uh-mi /kəˈlɒstəmi/

Colt, Samuel American inventor
kohlt /kəʊlt/
• The same pronunciation is used for the
type of revolver.

colt young uncastrated male horse
kohlt /kəʊlt/

Coltrane, John American jazz
saxophonist
kol-**trayn** /kɒlˈtreɪn/

Columba constellation
kuh-**lum**-buh /kəˈlʌmbə/

Columbia river, North America
kuh-**lum**-bi-uh /kəˈlʌmbiə/

Columbine High School scene of
school shooting in 1999
kol-uhm-byn /ˈkɒləmbʌɪn/

columbite mineral
kuh-**lum**-byt /kəˈlʌmbʌɪt/

Coma Berenices constellation
koh-muh berr-in-**y**-seez /ˌkəʊmə
ˌbɛrɪˈnʌɪsiːz/

Comanche American Indian ethnic
group
kuh-**man**-chi /kəˈmantʃi/

Comaneci, Nadia Romanian-born
American gymnast
nah-dyuh kom-uhn-**etch** /ˌnɑːdjə
ˌkɒməˈnɛtʃ/

combatant person engaged in fighting
kom-buh-tuhnt /ˈkɒmbətənt/

Sometimes also **kum**-buh-tuhnt.

combe short valley
koom /kuːm/

combine group of people acting together
for a commercial purpose
kom-byn /ˈkɒmbʌɪn/

combine harvest a crop
kom-byn /ˈkɒmbʌɪn/

Combs, Sean American rap artist
shawn kohmz /ˌʃɔːn ˈkəʊmz/

Comecon economic association of
eastern European countries
kom-ik-on /ˈkɒmɪkɒn/

comfit sweet
kum-fit /ˈkʌmfɪt/

comfrey plant of the borage family
kum-fri /ˈkʌmfri/

Comice dessert pear
kom-iss /ˈkɒmɪs/

Comino island, Malta
kom-**ee**-noh /kɒˈmiːnəʊ/

COMINT COMmunications
INTelligence
kom-int /ˈkɒmɪnt/

Comintern communist organization
kom-in-turn /ˈkɒmɪntəː(r)n/

comme ci, comme ça neither very
good nor very bad
kom see kom sah /kɒm ˌsiː kɒm ˈsɑː/

commensurable measurable by the
same standard
kuh-**men**-shuh-ruh-buhl
/kəˈmɛnʃərəbəl/

commensurate corresponding in size
or degree
kuh-**men**-shuh-ruht /kəˈmɛnʃərət/

commis junior chef
kom-i /ˈkɒmi/

commissaire senior police officer in
France
kom-iss-**air** /ˌkɒmɪˈsɛ(r)/

commissar official of the Communist
Party
kom-miss-**ar** /ˌkɒmɪˈsɑː(r)/

Commerzbank Frankfurt-based
international bank
kom-airts-bank /ˈkɒmɛː(r)tsbaŋk/

commissary deputy or delegate
kom-iss-uh-ri /ˈkɒmɪsəri/

commodious comfortable
kuh-**moh**-di-uhss /kəˈməʊdiəs/

Top ten complaints about pronunciations

The Pronunciation Unit sometimes receives complaints from viewers and listeners about specific pronunciations. The following words and names are examples of these. Some complaints are justified, and some perhaps less so. Look up each individual entry for our recommendation, and a note on the possible variations!

clostridium difficile	harass
controversy	kilometre
Davos	Kuwait
debris	New Orleans
the letter H	schedule

---

commodore naval rank
kom-uh-dor /ˈkɒmədɔː(r)/

communal shared by members of a community
kom-yuun-uhl /ˈkɒmjʊnəl/

Commonly also kuh-**myoo**-nuhl.

commune group of people living together
kom-yoon /ˈkɒmjuːn/

commune interact
kuh-**myoon** /kəˈmjuːn/

communiqué official announcement
kuh-**myoo**-nik-ay /kəˈmjuːnɪkeɪ/

Como lake, Italy
koh-moh /ˈkəʊməʊ/

Comodoro Rivadavia port, Argentina
kom-od-**aw**-roh ree-vad-**ah**-vyuh /ˌkɒmɒˌdɔːrəʊ riːvaˈdɑːvjə/

Comorin cape, India
kom-uh-rin /ˈkɒmərɪn/

Comoros country
kom-uh-rohz /ˈkɒmərəʊz/

Sometimes also kuh-**maw**-rohz.

compadre friend or companion
kom-**pah**-dray /kɒmˈpɑːdreɪ/

comparable able to be likened to another

kom-puh-ruh-buhl /ˈkɒmpərəbəl/

Commonly also kuhm-**parr**-uh-buhl.

comparative pertaining to comparison
kuhm-**parr**-uh-tiv /kəmˈparətɪv/

compeer person of equal rank
kuhm-**peer** /kəmˈpɪə(r)/

compère person who introduces performers
kom-pair /ˈkɒmpɛː(r)/

comport conduct oneself
kuhm-**port** /kəmˈpɔː(r)t/

composite made up of several parts
kom-puh-zit /ˈkɒmpəzɪt/

compos mentis having full control of one's mind
kom-puhss **men**-tiss /ˌkɒmpəs ˈmɛntɪs/

compote fruit preserved in syrup
kom-poht /ˈkɒmpəʊt/

Compton-Burnett, Ivy English novelist
kump-tuhn **bur**-nuht /ˌkʌmptən ˈbəː(r)nət/

Comte, Auguste French philosopher
oh-**guest** ko(ng)t /əʊˌgyst ˈkɔ̃t/

Conakry capital of Guinea
kon-uh-kri /ˈkɒnəkri/

con amore musical term
  kon am-**aw**-ray /ˌkɒn aˈmɔːreɪ/

Conan Doyle, Arthur Scottish author
  koh-nuhn **doyl** /ˌkəʊnən ˈdɔɪl/

con brio musical term
  kon **bree**-oh /ˌkɒn ˈbriːəʊ/

concave curved inwards
  kon-**kayv** /kɒnˈkeɪv/

Concepción city, Chile
  kon-sep-**syon** /kɒnsɛpˈsjɒn/

concertina musical instrument
  kon-suhr-**tee**-nuh /ˌkɒnsə(r)ˈtiːnə/

concerto musical composition
  kuhn-**chair**-toh /kənˈtʃɛː(r)təʊ/

conciliar relating to a council
  kuhn-**sil**-i-uhr /kənˈsɪliə(r)/

conclave private meeting
  konk-layv /ˈkɒŋkleɪv/

Concord city, US
  konk-ord /ˈkɒŋkɔː(r)d/

Concorde airliner
  konk-ord /ˈkɒŋkɔː(r)d/

concubinage practice of keeping a concubine
  kon-**kyoo**-bin-ij /kɒnˈkjuːbɪnɪdʒ/

concubine woman who cohabits with a man without being his wife
  konk-yuub-yn /ˈkɒŋkjʊbʌɪn/

Condé Nast magazine publishers
  kon-day nahst /ˌkɒndeɪ ˈnɑːst/

conductus pl. **conducti** musical setting of a metrical Latin text
  kuhn-**duk**-tuhss, pl. kuhn-**duk**-ty /kənˈdʌktəs/, pl. /-tʌɪ/
  • See LATIN panel.

conduit channel for conveying water
  kon-dyoo-it /ˈkɒndjʊɪt/

confect make from various elements
  kuhn-**fekt** /kənˈfɛkt/

confidant (also **confidante**) person with whom one shares a private matter
  kon-fid-ant /ˈkɒnfɪdant/

Sometimes also kon-fid-**ahnt**.

confine boundaries of a place
  kon-fyn /ˈkɒnfʌɪn/

confine restrict
  kuhn-**fyn** /kənˈfʌɪn/

confit meat cooked slowly in its own fat
  kon-fi /ˈkɒnfi/

confrère fellow member of a profession
  kon-frair /ˈkɒnfrɛː(r)/

Confucianism doctrines of Confucius
  kuhn-**fyoo**-shuh-niz-uhm /kənˈfjuːʃənɪzəm/

Confucius Chinese philosopher
  kuhn-**fyoo**-shuhss /kənˈfjuːʃəs/

congee porridge made from rice
  kon-jee /ˈkɒndʒiː/

congener member of the same kind or class as another
  kuhn-**jeen**-uhr /kənˈdʒiːnə(r)/

conger edible eel
  kong-guhr /ˈkɒŋɡə(r)/

congeries disorderly collection
  kon-**jeer**-eez /kɒnˈdʒɪəriːz/

Congo river, central Africa
  kong-goh /ˈkɒŋɡəʊ/

Congolese relating to Congo or the Democratic Republic of Congo
  kong-guh-**leez** /ˌkɒŋɡəˈliːz/

congregant member of a congregation
  kong-grig-uhnt /ˈkɒŋɡrɪɡənt/

Congreve, William English dramatist
  kong-greev /ˈkɒŋɡriːv/

congruent in agreement
  kong-groo-uhnt /ˈkɒŋɡruənt/

congruous in agreement
  kong-groo-uhss /ˈkɒŋɡruəs/

conic of a cone
  kon-ik /ˈkɒnɪk/

conifer tree
  kon-if-uhr /ˈkɒnɪfə(r)/

coniform having the shape of a cone
  kohn-if-orm /ˈkəʊnɪfɔː(r)m/

coniine poisonous compound
  koh-ni-een /ˈkəʊniiːn/

conjugate related
  kon-juug-uht /ˈkɒndʒʊɡət/

conjugate give the different forms of a verb
  kon-juug-ayt /ˈkɒndʒʊɡeɪt/

conjunctiva membrane that covers the front of the eye
  kon-junk-**ty**-vuh /ˌkɒndʒʌŋkˈtʌɪvə/

conjunctivitis inflammation of the conjunctiva
  kuhn-junk-tiv-**y**-tiss /kənˌdʒʌŋktɪˈvʌɪtɪs/

con moto musical term
  kon **moh**-toh /ˌkɒn ˈməʊtəʊ/

Connacht (also **Connaught**) province, Republic of Ireland
  kon-awt /ˈkɒnɔːt/

connate existing in a person from birth
kon-ayt /'kɒneɪt/

Connecticut state, US
kuh-**net**-ik-uht /kə'nɛtɪkət/

Connemara region, Republic of Ireland
kon-i-**mar**-uh /ˌkɒni'mɑːrə/

connoisseur expert
kon-uh-**sur** /ˌkɒnə'sə:(r)/

connote imply or suggest
kuh-**noht** /kə'nəʊt/

connubial relating to marriage
kuh-**nyoo**-bi-uhl /kə'nju:biəl/

conquistador pl. **conquistadores**
conqueror
kon-**kwist**-uh-dor, pl.
kon-**kwist**-uh-**daw**-rayz
/kɒn'kwɪstədɔ:(r)/, pl. /-'dɔ:reɪz/
• Standard -s plural is also possible.

consensual relating to consent
kuhn-**sen**-shoo-uhl /kən'sɛnʃuəl/

conservatoire musical school
kuhn-**sur**-vuh-twar
/kən'sə:(r)vətwɑ:(r)/

conservator person responsible for
repair and preservation
kuhn-**sur**-vuh-tuhr /kən'sə:(r)vətə(r)/

Sometimes also kon-suhr-**vay**-tuhr.

consigliere member of a Mafia family
kon-sil-**yair**-ay /ˌkɒnsɪ'ljɛːreɪ/

console unit accommodating a set of
controls for electronic equipment
kon-sohl /'kɒnsəʊl/

Consols government securities of Great
Britain
kon-suhlz /'kɒnsəlz/

consommé soup
kon-**som**-ay /kɒn'sɒmeɪ/

con sordino musical term
kon sor-**dee**-noh /ˌkɒn sɔ:(r)'di:nəʊ/

consortium pl. **consortia** association
kuhn-**sor**-ti-uhm, pl. kuhn-**sor**-ti-uh
/kən'sɔ:(r)tiəm/, pl. /-tiə/
• Standard -s plural is also possible.

Constable, John English painter
kun-stuh-buhl /'kʌnstəbəl/

This British surname is variously
pronounced **kun**-stuh-buhl and
kon-stuh-buhl, depending on individual
preference.

constable police officer
kun-stuh-buhl /'kʌnstəbəl/

Commonly also **kon**-stuh-buhl.

Constance lake and port, Germany
kon-stuhnss /'kɒnstəns/

Established anglicization. The German
name for the city is Konstanz, pronounced
kon-stants, and the lake is Bodensee,
pronounced **boh**-duhn-zay.

Constanţa (also **Constanza**) port,
Romania
kon-**stant**-suh /kɒn'stantsə/

Constantine city, Algeria
kon-stuhn-tyn /'kɒnstəntʌɪn/

Constantine Roman emperor
kon-stuhn-tyn /'kɒnstəntʌɪn/

Constantinople former name for
Istanbul
kon-stan-tin-**oh**-puhl
/ˌkɒnstantɪ'nəʊpəl/

consternate fill with anxiety
kon-stuhr-nayt /'kɒnstə(r)neɪt/

consubstantiation Christian doctrine
kon-suhb-stan-shi-**ay**-shuhn
/ˌkɒnsəbstanʃi'eɪʃən/

consuetude custom
kon-swit-yood /'kɒnswɪtju:d/

contagion spread of disease by close
contact
kuhn-**tay**-juhn /kən'teɪdʒən/

contemplative involving prolonged
thought
kuhn-**tem**-pluh-tiv /kən'tɛmplətɪv/

contemporaneous existing at the same
period of time
kuhn-tem-puh-**ray**-ni-uhss
/kənˌtɛmpə'reɪniəs/

contiguous sharing a common border
kuhn-**tig**-yoo-uhss /kən'tɪgjuəs/

contingency possible future
circumstance
kuhn-**tin**-juhn-si /kən'tɪndʒənsi/

contralto singing voice
kuhn-**tral**-toh /kən'traltəʊ/

contrariety contrary opposition
kon-truh-**ry**-uh-ti /ˌkɒntrə'rʌɪəti/

contrary opposite
kon-truh-ri /'kɒntrəri/

contrary perverse
kuhn-**trair**-i /kən'trɛːri/

contretemps dispute
kon-truh-to(ng) /'kɒntrətɒ̃/, [kɔ̃trətɑ̃]

contribute give
kuhn-**trib**-yoot /kən'trɪbjuːt/

Commonly also **kon**-trib-yoot.

contributor person who gives
kuhn-**trib**-yuut-uhr /kən'trɪbjʊtə(r)/

controversy dispute
kon-truh-vur-si /'kɒntrəvəː(r)si/

This is the traditional pronunciation, but kuhn-**trov**-uhr-si is equally, if not more, common, and equally acceptable. AM is **kon**-truh-vur-si.

contuse injure
kuhn-**tyooz** /kən'tjuːz/

conundrum problem
kuh-**nun**-druhm /kə'nʌndrəm/

convalesce recover
kon-vuh-**less** /ˌkɒnvə'lɛs/

convex curved like the exterior of a circle
kon-**veks** /kɒn'vɛks/

Conwy (also **Conway**) town, Wales
kon-wi /'kɒnwi/

Coolidge, Calvin American statesman
koo-lij /'kuːlɪdʒ/

cooncan card game
koon-kan /'kuːnkan/

co-op cooperative business
koh-op /'kəʊɒp/

Copacabana Beach resort, Brazil
kop-uh-kab-**an**-uh /ˌkɒpəka'banə/

Copán ancient Mayan city, Honduras
koh-**pan** /kəʊ'pan/

Copenhagen capital of Denmark
koh-puhn-**hay**-guhn /ˌkəʊpən'heɪgən/

Established anglicization. The Danish name is København, pronounced koe-buhn-**hown** [købən'haʊʔn].

Copernicus, Nicolaus Polish astronomer
nik-ol-**ay**-uhss kuh-**pur**-nik-uhss /ˌnɪkɒˌleɪəs kə'pəː(r)nɪkəs/

This is the Latinized form. The Polish name is Mikołaj Kopernik, pronounced mee-**koh**-y kop-**air**-neek [miˌkɔwaj kɔ'pɛrnik].

Copland, Aaron American composer
air-uhn **kohp**-luhnd /ˌɛːrən 'kəʊplənd/

Copley, John Singleton American painter
kop-li /'kɒpli/

Coppola, Francis Ford American film director
koh-puh-luh /'kəʊpələ/

coprolalia involuntary use of obscene language
kop-roh-**lay**-li-uh /ˌkɒprəʊ'leɪliə/

Copt native Egyptian in the Hellenistic and Roman periods
kopt /kɒpt/

coq au vin chicken casserole
kok oh **va(ng)** /ˌkɒk əʊ 'vɛ̃/

coquetry flirtatious behaviour
kok-uht-ri /'kɒkətri/

Cora American Indian ethnic group
kaw-ruh /'kɔːrə/

cor anglais woodwind instrument
kor **ong**-glay /kɔːr 'ɒŋgleɪ/

Sometimes also kor **ahng**-glay.

Corcovado mountain, Brazil
kor-kov-**ah**-doo /ˌkɔː(r)kɒ'vɑːduː/

Corcyra ancient Greek name for Corfu
kor-**sy**-ruh /kɔː(r)'sʌɪrə/

cordate heart-shaped
kor-dayt /'kɔː(r)deɪt/

Corday, Charlotte French political assassin
shar-**lot** kor-**day** /ʃɑː(r)ˌlɒt kɔː(r)'deɪ/

Córdoba (also **Cordova**) city, Argentina
kor-duh-buh /'kɔː(r)dəbə/, ['kɔrðoβa]

Established anglicization. Use also for Córdoba in Spain, and the currency unit of Nicaragua.

cordon bleu of high-class cooking
kor-**do(ng) bleu** /ˌkɔː(r)dɔ̃ 'blə/

Cordura trademark synthetic fabric
kor-**dyoor**-uh /kɔː(r)'djʊərə/

corduroy cotton fabric
kor-duh-roy /'kɔː(r)dərɔɪ/

Corea, Chick American composer
chik kuh-**ree**-uh /ˌtʃɪk kə'riːə/

Corelli, Arcangelo Italian composer
ar-**kan**-juh-loh kuh-**rel**-i /ɑː(r)ˌkandʒələʊ kə'rɛli/

Corelli, Marie English writer
kuh-**rel**-i /kə'rɛli/

Corfu island, Greece
kor-**foo** /kɔː(r)'fuː/

This is the Italian name, adopted in English. The Greek name is Kérkira, pronounced **kair**-kirr-uh ['kɛrkira].

Coria, Guillermo Argentine tennis player
geel-**yair**-moh **korr**-i-uh /ɡiːl.jɛː(r)məʊ 'kɒriə/

coriander plant
korr-i-**an**-duhr /ˌkɒrɪ'andə(r)/

Corinth city, Greece
korr-inth /'kɒrɪnθ/

Established anglicization. The Greek name is Kórinthos, pronounced **korr**-in-thoss.

Coriolanus, Gaius Marcius Roman general
gy-uhss **marsh**-uhss
korr-i-uh-**lay**-nuhss /ˌɡaɪəs ˌmɑː(r)ʃəs ˌkɒriə'leɪnəs/

cornea layer covering the eye
kor-ni-uh /'kɔː(r)niə/

Corneille, Pierre French dramatist
pyair kor-**nay** /ˌpjɛː(r) kɔː(r)'neɪ/

cornetto woodwind instrument
kor-**net**-oh /kɔː(r)'nɛtəʊ/

cornucopia the horn of plenty
kor-nyuuk-**oh**-pi-uh /ˌkɔː(r)njʊ'kəʊpiə/

corolla petals of a flower
kuh-**rol**-uh /kə'rɒlə/

corollary proposition
kuh-**rol**-uh-ri /kə'rɒləri/

Coromandel Coast southern part of the east coast of India
korr-uh-**man**-duhl /ˌkɒrə'mandəl/

Corona Australis constellation
kuh-**roh**-nuh aw-**strah**-liss /kəˌrəʊnə ɔː'strɑːlɪs/

Corona Borealis constellation
kuh-**roh**-nuh borr-i-**ah**-liss /kəˌrəʊnə ˌbɒrɪ'ɑːlɪs/

coronach funeral song
korr-uhn-akh /'kɒrənax/

coronal garland for the head
korr-uh-nuhl /'kɒrənəl/

coronal relating to a crown or coronation
korr-**oh**-nuhl /kɒ'rəʊnəl/

Commonly also **korr**-uh-nuhl.

Corot, Camille French painter
kam-**ee** korr-**oh** /ka,mi: kɒ'rəʊ/

corporeal relating to a person's body
kor-**paw**-ri-uhl /kɔː(r)'pɔːriəl/

corps pl. **corps** main subdivision of an army
kor, pl. korz /kɔː(r)/, pl. /kɔː(r)z/

Corpus Christi feast of the blessed sacrament or body of Christ
kor-**puhss krist**-i /ˌkɔː(r)pəs 'krɪsti/

corral pen for livestock
kuh-**rahl** /kə'rɑːl/

Correggio, Antonio Italian painter
an-**tohn**-yoh korr-**ej**-oh /an,təʊnjəʊ kɒ'rɛdʒəʊ/

Corrèze department, France
korr-**ez** /kɒ'rɛz/

Corriedale breed of sheep
korr-i-dayl /'kɒrideɪl/

Corrientes province and city, Argentina
korr-i-**en**-tess /kɒri'entes/

Corsica island, France
kor-sik-uh /'kɔː(r)sɪkə/

The French name is Corse, pronounced korss.

cortège procession
kor-**tezh** /kɔː(r)'tɛʒ/

Cortes legislative assembly, Spain
kor-**tess** /'kɔː(r)tɛs/

Cortés, Joaquin Spanish flamenco dancer
khoh-ak-**een** kort-**ayss** /xəʊa,ki:n kɔː(r)'teɪs/

cortisone hormone
kor-tiz-ohn /'kɔː(r)tɪzəʊn/

Corunna port, Spain
kuh-**run**-uh /kə'rʌnə/

Established anglicization, although somewhat old-fashioned. The Spanish name is La Coruña, pronounced lah korr-**oon**-yuh [la ko'ruɲa].

corvette warship
kor-**vet** /kɔː(r)'vɛt/

corvina Italian variety of wine grape
kor-**vee**-nuh /kɔː(r)'vi:nə/

Corvus constellation
kor-vuhss /'kɔː(r)vəs/

Cos see Kos

cos lettuce
koss /kɒs/

Cosa Nostra American criminal organization
koh-zuh **nost**-ruh /ˌkəʊzə 'nɒstrə/

Cosimo de' Medici Italian statesman and banker
koz-ee-moh day **med**-itch-i /'kɒzi:məʊ deɪ 'mɛdɪtʃi/

cosmogeny evolution of the universe
koz-**moj**-uh-ni /kɒz'mɒdʒəni/

cosmogony branch of science that deals with the evolution of the universe
koz-**mog**-uh-ni /ˈkɒzˈmɒgəni/

Cosi Fan Tutte opera by Mozart
koh-**see** fan **too**-tay /ˈkəʊˌsiː fan ˈtuːteɪ/

cosmopolis cosmopolitan city
koz-**mop**-uh-liss /ˈkɒzˈmɒpəlɪs/

COSPAR Committee on Space Research
koh-spar /ˈkəʊspɑː(r)/

Cossack Russian ethnic group
koss-ak /ˈkɒsak/

Costa Blanca resort, Spain
kost-uh **blank**-uh /ˌkɒstə ˈblaŋkə/

Costa Brava resort, Spain
kost-uh **brah**-vuh /ˌkɒstə ˈbrɑːvə/

Costa del Sol resort, Spain
kost-uh del **sol** /ˌkɒstə dɛl ˈsɒl/

Costard cooking apple
kust-uhrd /ˈkʌstə(r)d/

Commonly also **kost**-uhrd.

Costa Rica country
kost-uh **ree**-kuh /ˌkɒstə ˈriːkə/

Côte d'Azur region, France
koht duh-**zyoor** /ˌkəʊt dəˈzjʊə(r)/, [kot dazy:r]
• Established anglicization.

Côte d'Ivoire country
koht dee-**vwar** /ˌkəʊt diːˈvwɑː(r)/

Cotonou city, Benin
kot-uh-**noo** /ˌkɒtəˈnuː/

Cotopaxi volcano, Ecuador
kot-op-**ak**-si /ˌkɒtɒˈpaksi/

Cotswold breed of sheep
kots-wohld /ˈkɒtswəʊld/

Cottbus city, Germany
kot-buuss /ˈkɒtbʊs/

cotyledon embryonic leaf
kot-il-**ee**-duhn /ˌkɒtɪˈliːdən/

couch grass
kowtch /kaʊtʃ/

Sometimes also **kootch**.

couchant heraldic term
kow-chuhnt /ˈkaʊtʃənt/

cougar North American term for puma
koo-guhr /ˈkuːgə(r)/

coulibiac Russian dish
koo-lib-**yak** /ˌkuːlɪˈbjak/

coulis vegetable or fruit purée
koo-li /ˈkuːli/

Coulomb, Charles Augustin de
French physicist
sharl oh-guest-**a(ng)** duh koo-**lo(ng)** /ˌʃɑː(r)l əʊgysˌtɛ̃ də kuːˈlõ/

coulomb SI unit of electric charge
koo-lom /ˈkuːlɒm/

coulrophobia fear of clowns
kol-ruh-**foh**-bi-uh /ˌkɒlrəˈfəʊbiə/

Coulthard, David Scottish Formula 1 racing driver
kohl-thard /ˈkəʊlθɑː(r)d/

This British surname is variously pronounced **kohl**-thard and **kool**-tard, depending on individual preference.

coumarin vanilla-scented compound
koo-muh-rin /ˈkuːmərɪn/

coup pl. **coups** seizure of power from a government
koo, pl. kooz /kuː/, pl. /kuːz/

coupe glass dish
koop /kuːp/

coupé type of car
koo-pay /ˈkuːpeɪ/

Couperin, François French composer
frah(ng)-**swah** koo-puh-**ra(ng)** /frãˌswɑː kuːpəˈrɛ̃/

Courbet, Gustave French painter
gue-**stahv** koor-**bay** /gyˌstɑːv kəʊ(r)ˈbeɪ/

Courrèges, André French fashion designer
ah(ng)-**dray** koor-**ezh** /ãˌdreɪ kʊəˈrɛʒ/

Courtauld, Samuel English industrialist
kor-tohld /ˈkɔː(r)təʊld/

Coupland, Diana English actress
koop-luhnd /ˈkuːplənd/

Coupland, Douglas Canadian author
kohp-luhnd /ˈkəʊplənd/

Courier, Jim American tennis player
koor-i-uhr /ˈkʊəriə(r)/

courtier companion to the king or queen
kor-ti-uhr /ˈkɔː(r)tiə(r)/

couscous North African semolina
kuuss-kuuss /ˈkʊskʊs/

Cousteau, Jacques-Yves French oceanographer and film director
zhahk **eev** koo-**stoh** /zɑːk ˌiːv kuːˈstəʊ/

couth cultured and refined
kooth /kuːθ/

Coventry city, England
kov-uhn-tri /ˈkɒvəntri/

Coverdale, Miles English biblical scholar
kuv-uhr-dayl /ˈkʌvə(r)deɪl/

covert shelter
kuv-uhrt /ˈkʌvə(r)t/

covert not openly
kuv-uhrt /ˈkʌvə(r)t/

Commonly also **koh**-vurt.

covet yearn to possess
kuv-uht /ˈkʌvət/

Cowdrey, Colin English cricketer
kow-dri /ˈkaʊdri/

Cowes town, England
kowz /kaʊz/

Cowichan sweater thick sweater
kow-itch-uhn /ˈkaʊɪtʃən/

Cowper, William English poet
koop-uhr /ˈkuːpə(r)/

This British surname is variously pronounced **koop**-uhr and **kow**-puhr, depending on individual preference.

coxswain person who steers a ship's boat
kok-suhn /ˈkɒksən/

Coyoacán region, Mexico
koy-oh-ak-**an** /ˌkɔɪəʊakˈan/

coyote North American wild dog
koy-**oh**-ti /kɔɪˈəʊti/

Sometimes also **koy**-oht.

cozen trick or deceive
kuz-uhn /ˈkʌzən/

Cozumel island, Caribbean
koss-oo-**mel** /kɒsuːˈmɛl/

Crabbe, George English poet
krab /krab/

Cracow city, Poland
krak-of /ˈkrakɒf/

Established anglicization; sometimes also **krak**-ow, especially in AM. The Polish name is Kraków, pronounced **krak**-oof.

Craiova city, Romania
kruh-**yoh**-vuh /krəˈjəʊvə/

Cranach, Lucas German painter
loo-kass **krah**-nakh /ˌluːkas ˈkrɑːnax/

cranium pl. **crania** skull
kray-ni-uhm, pl. **kray**-ni-uh /ˈkreɪnɪəm/, pl. /-nɪə/
• Standard -s plural is also possible.

crannog ancient fortified dwelling
kran-uhg /ˈkranəɡ/

Crassus, Marcus Licinius Roman politician
mar-kuhss ly-**sin**-i-uhss **krass**-uhss /ˌmɑː(r)kəs lʌɪˌsɪnɪəs ˈkrasəs/

Crater constellation
kray-tuhr /ˈkreɪtə(r)/

craton block of the earth's crust
krat-on /ˈkratɒn/

creatine compound formed in protein metabolism
kree-uh-teen /ˈkriːətiːn/

creatinine compound which is produced by metabolism of creatine
kri-**at**-in-een /krɪˈatɪniːn/

crèche nursery
kresh /krɛʃ/

credulity tendency to believe that something is true
kruh-**dyoo**-luh-ti /krəˈdjuːləti/

credulous showing too great a readiness to believe things
kred-yuul-uhss /ˈkrɛdjʊləs/

Cree American Indian ethnic group
kree /kriː/

crème brûlée dessert
krem broo-**lay** /ˌkrɛm bruːˈleɪ/

Cremona city, Italy
kruh-**moh**-nuh /krəˈməʊnə/

Creole language formed from a pidgin
kree-ohl /ˈkriːəʊl/

crêpe thin fabric
krayp /kreɪp/

crescendo pl. **crescendi** musical term
kruh-**shen**-doh, pl. kruh-**shen**-di /krəˈʃɛndəʊ/, pl. /-di/
• Standard -s plural is also possible.

Cressida Shakespearean character
kress-id-uh /ˈkrɛsɪdə/

Cretaceous geological period
kruh-**tay**-shuhss /krəˈteɪʃəs/

Crete island, Greece
kreet /kriːt/

Established anglicization. The Greek name is Kriti, pronounced **kree**-ti.

cretic metrical foot
kree-tik /ˈkriːtɪk/

cretin stupid person
kret-in /ˈkrɛtɪn/

Creutzfeldt–Jakob disease degenerative disease
kroyts-felt **yak**-ob /ˌkrɔɪtsfɛlt ˈjakɒb/

Crichton, James Scottish adventurer
kry-tuhn /ˈkrʌɪtən/

Crimea peninsula, Ukraine
kry-**mee**-uh /krʌɪˈmiːə/

Established anglicization. The Ukrainian name is Krym, pronounced krim [krɪm].

crimplene trademark synthetic fabric
krimp-leen /ˈkrɪmpliːn/

crimson deep red colour
krim-zuhn /ˈkrɪmzən/

crinoline petticoat
krin-uh-lin /ˈkrɪnəlɪn/

Criseyde see **Troilus and Criseyde**

Croat native of Croatia
kroh-at /ˈkrəʊat/

Croatia country
kroh-**ay**-shuh /krəʊˈeɪʃə/

Established anglicization. The Croatian name is Hrvatska, pronounced **hur**-vaht-skah [ˈhrvaːtskaː].

Croce, Benedetto Italian philosopher and politician
ben-uh-**det**-oh **kroh**-chay /bɛnəˌdɛtəʊ ˈkrəʊtʃeɪ/

crochet handicraft
kroh-shay /ˈkrəʊʃeɪ/

crocus pl. **croci** plant
kroh-kuhss, pl. **kroh**-ky /ˈkrəʊkəs/, pl. /-kʌɪ/
• Standard -es plural also possible.

croeso 'welcome' (Welsh)
kroy-saw /ˈkrɔɪsɔː/

Croesus last king of Lydia
kree-suhss /ˈkriːsəs/

Crohn's disease disease of the intestines
krohnz /krəʊnz/

croissant French roll
krwass-o(ng) /ˈkrwasɒ̃/

Commonly also **kwass**-o(ng).

Cro-Magnon earliest form of modern human
kroh-**man**-yon /ˌkrəʊˈmanjɒn/

Commonly also kroh-**mag**-nuhn.

Cromarty Firth inlet of the Moray Firth, Scotland
krom-uhr-ti /ˈkrɒmə(r)ti/

Cromerian geological period
kroh-**meer**-i-uhn /krəʊˈmɪəriən/

cromlech tomb

krom-lek /ˈkrɒmlɛk/

Cronin, A. J. Scottish novelist
kroh-nin /ˈkrəʊnɪn/

Cronus (also **Kronos**) Greek mythological character
kroh-nuhss /ˈkrəʊnəs/

croquembouche dessert
krok-om-**boosh** /ˌkrɒkɒmˈbuːʃ/

croquet game
kroh-kay /ˈkrəʊkeɪ/

crostini Italian starter
krost-**ee**-ni /krɒˈstiːni/

croup inflammation of the larynx and trachea in children
kroop /kruːp/

croupier person in charge of a gaming table
kroo-pi-ay /ˈkruːpieɪ/

croustade pastry hollowed to receive a savoury filling
kruust-**ahd** /kruːˈstɑːd/

croute piece of toasted bread
kroot /kruːt/

crouton small piece of toasted bread
kroo-ton /ˈkruːtɒn/

Crozet Islands group of islands, Indian Ocean
kroh-**zay** /krəʊˈzeɪ/

Crudup, Billy American actor
kroo-dup /ˈkruːdʌp/

Cruft, Charles English showman
kruft /krʌft/

Cruikshank, George English painter, illustrator, and caricaturist
kruuk-shank /ˈkrʊkʃaŋk/

Crustacea group of aquatic arthropods
krust-**ay**-shuh /krʌˈsteɪʃə/

Crux constellation
kruks /krʌks/

Cruyff, Johan Dutch footballer
yoh-hun **kroeyf** /ˌjəʊhʌn ˈkrœɪf/

Cruz, Penélope Spanish actress
pen-**el**-op-ay **krooth** /pɛˌnɛlɒpeɪ ˈkruːθ/

A more anglicized pronunciation, puh-**nel**-uh-pi **krooz**, is very common.

Cryptozoic geological period
krip-tuh-**zoh**-ik /ˌkrɪptəˈzəʊɪk/

crystalline having the form of a crystal
krist-uh-lyn /ˈkrɪstəlʌɪn/

csárdás Hungarian dance
char-dahsh /ˈtʃɑː(r)dɑːʃ/

Ctesiphon ancient city on the Tigris
tess-if-uhn /ˈtɛsɪfən/

cuatro small guitar
kwat-roh /ˈkwatrəʊ/

Cuba country
kyoo-buh /ˈkjuːbə/, Spanish [ˈkuβa]
• Established anglicization.

cueca South American dance
kway-kuh /ˈkweɪkə/

Cuenca city, Ecuador
kwenk-uh /ˈkwɛŋkə/

Cuernavaca resort, Mexico
kwair-nav-ak-uh /ˌkwɛː(r)naˈvakə/

Cuiabá port, Brazil
koo-yuh-bah /ˌkuːjəˈbɑː/

Culdee Irish or Scottish monk
kul-dee /kʌlˈdiː/

cul-de-sac street closed at one end
kul duh sak /ˈkʌl də sak/

Commonly also **kuul duh sak**.

Culiacán Rosales city, Mexico
kool-yak-an roh-sah-less /kuːljaˌkan
rəʊˈsɑːlɛs/

Culkin, Macaulay American actor
muh-kaw-li kulk-in /məˌkɔːli ˈkʌlkɪn/

Culloden, Battle of battle in the
Jacobite uprising
kuh-lod-uhn /kəˈlɒdən/

Cumberland former county, England
kumb-uhr-luhnd /ˈkʌmbə(r)lənd/

Cumbernauld town, Scotland
kumb-uhr-nawld /ˌkʌmbə(r)ˈnɔːld/

cumbia Colombian dance
kuum-bi-uh /ˈkʊmbiə/

Cumbria county, England
kumb-ri-uh /ˈkʌmbriə/

cumin seed
kyoo-min /ˈkjuːmɪn/

cum laude 'with distinction' (Latin)
kum law-di /ˌkʌm ˈlɔːdi/

Commonly also **kuum low-day**; see LATIN
panel.

cumulonimbus pl. **cumulonimbi** cloud
kyoo-myuul-oh-nim-buhss,
pl. **kyoo-myuul-oh-nim-by**
/ˌkjuːmjʊləʊˈnɪmbəs/, pl. /-bʌɪ/

cumulus pl. **cumuli** cloud
kyoo-myuul-uhss, pl. **kyoo-myuul-y**
/ˈkjuːmjʊləs/, pl. /-lʌɪ/

Cunard, Samuel Canadian-born British
shipowner
kyoo-nard /kjuːˈnɑː(r)d/

Cunene river, Angola
kuun-en-uh /kʊˈnɛnə/

cupola rounded dome
kyoo-puh-luh /ˈkjuːpələ/

Curaçao island, Netherlands Antilles
kyoor-uh-sow /ˌkjʊərəˈsaʊ/

Commonly also **kyoor-uh-soh**. The same
pronunciations are used for the liqueur.

curate assistant to a vicar, rector, or
parish priest
kyoor-uht /ˈkjʊərət/

curate organize an exhibition
kyuu-rayt /kjʊˈreɪt/

Curie, Marie Polish-born French
physicist
marr-i kyoor-i /ˌmari ˈkjʊəri/, French
[mari kyri]

Established anglicization. She was born
Maria Skłodowska, pronounced **marr-i-uh
skwod-of-skuh**.

curie unit of radioactivity
kyoor-i /ˈkjʊəri/

Curitiba city, Brazil
koor-it-ee-buh /ˌkʊərɪˈtiːbə/

curium chemical element
kyoor-i-uhm /ˈkjʊəriəm/

curragh marshy waste ground
kurr-uh /ˈkʌrə/

Sometimes also **kurr-ukh** [ˈkʌrəx].

curriculum vitae account of a person's
qualifications
kuh-rik-yuul-uhm vee-ty /kəˌrɪkjʊləm
ˈviːtʌɪ/

cursed under a curse
kur-suhd /ˈkəː(r)səd/

Sometimes also **kurst**.

Cusack, Niamh Irish actress
neev kyoo-sak /ˌniːv ˈkjuːsak/

cusec unit of flow
kyoo-sek /ˈkjuːsɛk/

Cush biblical name
 kuush /kʊʃ/

cutaneous relating to the skin
 kyoo-**tay**-ni-uhss /kjuːˈteɪniəs/

cuvée type of wine
 kyoo-vay /ˈkjuːveɪ/, French [kyve]

Cuzco city, Peru
 koosk-oh /ˈkuːskəʊ/

cwm valley
 kuum /kʊm/

Cwmbran town, Wales
 kuum-**brahn** /kʊmˈbrɑːn/

cyan greenish-blue colour
 sy-uhn /ˈsaɪən/

cyanide salt of hydrocyanic acid
 sy-uh-nyd /ˈsaɪənʌɪd/

cyanogen poisonous gas
 sy-**an**-uh-juhn /sʌɪˈanədʒən/

Cybele mythological mother goddess
 sib-il-i /ˈsɪbɪli/

cyborg person with mechanical elements
 built into the body
 sy-borg /ˈsaɪbɔː(r)g/

cycad palm-like plant
 sy-kad /ˈsaɪkad/

Cyclades group of islands, Aegean Sea
 sik-luh-deez /ˈsɪklədiːz/

Established anglicization. The Greek name
is Kikládhes, pronounced kee-**klath**-ess.

Cycladic relating to the Cyclades
 sik-**lad**-ik /sɪˈkladɪk/

cyclamen plant
 sik-luh-muhn /ˈsɪkləmən/

cyclical relating to a cycle
 sik-lik-uhl /ˈsɪklɪkəl/

Sometimes also **syk**-lik-uhl.

cyclone climatic condition
 sy-klohn /ˈsaɪkləʊn/

Cyclops pl. **Cyclopes** Greek mythological
 character
 sy-klops, pl. sy-**kloh**-peez /ˈsaɪklɒps/,
 pl. /sʌɪˈkləʊpiːz/
 • Standard -es plural is also possible.

Cygnus constellation
 sig-nuhss /ˈsɪgnəs/

Cymbeline British chieftain
 sim-buh-leen /ˈsɪmbəliːn/

Cymric relating to Wales
 kum-rik /ˈkʌmrɪk/, [ˈkəmrɪk]

Cymru Welsh name for Wales
 kum-ri /ˈkʌmri/, [ˈkəmri]

Cyprian, St Carthaginian bishop
 and martyr
 sip-ri-uhn /ˈsɪpriən/

Cyprus country
 syp-ruhss /ˈsʌɪprəs/
 • Established anglicization.

Cyrano de Bergerac, Savinien
 French soldier, duellist, and writer
 sav-in-ya(ng) **sirr**-uh-noh duh
 bur-zhuh-rak /savɪˌnjɛ̃ ˌsɪrənəʊ də
 ˈbəː(r)ʒərak/, [savinjɛ̃ sirano də
 bɛrʒərak]
 • Established anglicization.

Cyrenaica region of Libya
 sy-ruh-**nay**-ik-uh /ˌsʌɪrəˈneɪkə/

Cyrene ancient Greek city
 sy-**ree**-ni /sʌɪˈriːni/

Cyrillic alphabet used in many Slavonic
 languages
 sirr-il-lik /sɪˈrɪlɪk/

Cyrus king of Persia
 sy-ruhss /ˈsʌɪrəs/

cystitis bladder inflammation
 sist-**y**-tiss /sɪˈstʌɪtɪs/

Cytherea another name for Aphrodite
 sith-uh-**ree**-uh /ˌsɪθəˈriːə/

Cytherean relating to the planet Venus
 sith-uh-**ree**-uhn /ˌsɪθəˈriːən/

czar see **tsar**

Czech relating to the Czech Republic
 chek /tʃɛk/

Czechoslovakia former country
 chek-uh-sluh-**vak**-i-uh
 /ˌtʃɛkəsləˈvakiə/

Czerny, Karl Austrian composer
 karl chair-ni /ˌkɑː(r)l ˈtʃɛː(r)ni/

Częstochowa city, Poland
 chen-stokh-**ov**-uh /ˌtʃɛnstɒˈxɒvə/,
 [tʃɛ̃stɔˈxɔva]

Czech

The Czech language (*Čeština*, pronounced **chesh**-tin-uh, in Czech) is very similar to Slovak, and belongs to the Slavonic language family. To English speakers, written Czech can look daunting because of the accents and the long sequences of consonants. However, the pronunciations are entirely predictable once you apply the rules.

In Czech L, R, N, and M can function as vowels. For example, the L in the word *vlk* (*wolf*) functions rather like the L in English *apple*. When we are giving pronunciations for Czech words that include these consonants we sometimes insert a vowel to make them easier to read: for the place name *Brno* we give **bur**-noh, although there is really no U in the first syllable.

Stress

Stress in Czech is very easy: it falls invariably on the first syllable. The surname *Janáček* is pronounced **yan**-ah-chek in Czech, although for the composer there is also an established anglicization, **yan**-uh-chek.

Vowels

Acute accents on vowels simply indicate that the vowel is long. When we are giving pronunciation advice we reflect this by choosing the closest long vowel or diphthong in English. So for A we advise a, while for Á we advise ah. E is e, and for É we advise ay. Ě is pronounced ye. I and Y are i, and Í and Ý are ee. O is o and Ó is oh or aw, U is uu, and Ú or Ů are oo.

Consonants

Consonants in Czech can appear plain, with a v-shaped diacritic mark called a háček, or with a following apostrophe.

C is pronounced ts, and Č is pronounced ch.

Ď (or D') is dy, as in *dune*, and Ť (or T') is ty as in *tune*.

Ň is ny as in *onion*.

Ř is a tricky sound, pronounced rzh between vowels and rsh after P, T, and K or at the end of a word.

Š is pronounced sh, and Ž is pronounced zh.

D

da capo musical term
dah **kah**-poh /dɑː ˈkɑːpəʊ/

Dacca see **Dhaka**

dacha Russian country house
datch-uh /ˈdatʃə/

Dachau German Nazi concentration camp
dakh-ow /ˈdaxaʊ/

dachshund breed of dog
dak-suhnd /ˈdaksənd/, German [ˈdakʃʊnt]

dactyl metrical foot
dak-til /ˈdaktɪl/

Dada art movement
dah-dah /ˈdɑːdɑː/

Dadra and Nagar Haveli union territory, India
dahd-ruh **nug**-uhr huh-**vay**-li /ˈdɑːdrə ˌnʌgə(r) həˈveɪli/

Daedalic relating to Daedalus
dee-duh-lik /ˈdiːdəlɪk/

Daedalus Greek mythological character
dee-duh-luhss /ˈdiːdələs/

AM is **ded**-uh-luhss.

Daegu (also **Taegu**) city, South Korea
teg-oo /ˈtɛguː/

daemon semi-divine being
dee-muhn /ˈdiːmən/

Daewoo Korean car manufacturer
day-oo /ˈdeɪuː/, [dɛuː]
• Established anglicization.

Dafoe, Willem American actor
wil-uhm duh-**foh** /ˌwɪləm dəˈfəʊ/

Dafydd Welsh boy's name
dav-ith /ˈdavɪð/

da Gama, Vasco Portuguese explorer
vask-oh duh **gah**-muh /ˌvaskəʊ də ˈgɑːmə/

Dagens Nyheter Swedish newspaper
dah-guhnss **nue**-hay-tuhr /ˌdɑːgəns ˈnyːheɪtə(r)/

Dagestan autonomous republic, Russia
dah-guh-**stahn** /ˌdɑːgəˈstɑːn/, [dəgʲɪˈstan]

• Established anglicization.

Dagestanian relating to Dagestan
dah-guh-**stah**-ni-uhn /ˌdɑːgəˈstɑːniən/

Dagon ancient Philistine god
day-gon /ˈdeɪgɒn/

Daguerre, Louis-Jacques-Mandé French physicist
lwee **zhahk** mah(ng)-**day** dag-**air** /lwiː ˌʒɑːk mɑ̃ˌdeɪ daˈgɛː(r)/

daguerreotype photographic process
duh-**gerr**-uh-typ /dəˈgɛrətʌɪp/

Dahl, Roald British writer, of Norwegian descent
roo-al **dahl** /ˌruːal ˈdɑːl/

dahlia plant
day-li-uh /ˈdeɪliə/

Dahmer, Jeffrey American serial killer
dah-muhr /ˈdɑːmə(r)/

Dahomey former name for Benin
duh-**hoh**-mi /dəˈhəʊmi/

Dáil Irish lower house of Parliament
doyl /dɔɪl/

Daimler, Gottlieb German motor manufacturer
got-leep **dym**-luhr /ˌgɒtliːp ˈdʌɪmlə(r)/

An anglicized pronunciation, **daym**-luhr, is used for the make of car.

daiquiri cocktail
dak-irr-i /ˈdakɪri/

Sometimes also **dy**-kirr-i.

Dakar capital of Senegal
dak-ar /ˈdakɑː(r)/

Dakota former territory, US
duh-**koh**-tuh /dəˈkəʊtə/

dal see **dhal**

Dalai Lama spiritual head of Tibetan Buddhism
dal-y **lah**-muh /ˌdalʌɪ ˈlɑːmə/

Dalarna province, Sweden
dahl-uhr-nuh /ˈdɑːlə(r)nə/

There is an English form, Dalecarlia, pronounced **dahl**-uh-**kar**-li-uh, which is sometimes used.

dalasi currency unit, Gambia
dah-**lah**-see /dɑːˈlɑːsiː/

dalek character from *Dr Who*
dah-lek /ˈdɑːlɛk/

d'Alembert, Jean le Rond French mathematician
zhah(ng) luh **ro(ng)** dal-ah(ng)-**bair**
/ʒɑ̃ lə ˌrɔ̃ dalɑ̃ˈbɛː(r)/

Dalglish, Kenny Scottish footballer
dal-**gleesh** /dalˈɡliːʃ/

Dalhousie, James British colonial administrator
dal-**how**-zi /dalˈhaʊzi/

Dalí, Salvador Spanish painter
sal-vuh-dor dah-li /ˌsalvədɔː(r) ˈdɑːli/,
[salβaˌðor daˈli]
• Established anglicization.

Dalian port, China
dahl-**yan** /ˌdɑːˈljan/

Dalit Indian caste
dul-it /ˈdʌlɪt/

Dallapiccola, Luigi Italian composer
luu-**ee**-ji dal-uh-**pee**-kol-uh /luˌiːdʒi
ˌdaləˈpiːkɒlə/

Dallaglio, Lawrence English rugby player
duh-**lal**-i-oh /dəˈlaliəʊ/

Dall sheep breed of sheep
dahl /dɑːl/

Dalmatia ancient region in what is now Croatia
dal-**may**-shuh /dalˈmeɪʃə/

dalmatic garment worn by bishops, and by monarchs at their coronation
dal-**mat**-ik /dalˈmatɪk/

Dalriada ancient Gaelic kingdom
dal-**ree**-uh-duh /dalˈriːədə/

dal segno musical term
dal sen-yoh /dal ˈsɛnjəʊ/

dalton chemical unit
dawl-tuhn /ˈdɔːltən/

Dalziel British family name
dee-el, dal-zeel /diːˈɛl/, /ˈdalziːl/

The TV character in *Dalziel and Pascoe* is pronounced dee-el.

Daman and Diu union territory, India
duh-**mahn** dee-oo /dəˈmɑːn ˈdiːuː/

Damara Namibian ethnic group
duh-**mar**-uh /dəˈmɑːrə/

Damaraland region, Namibia
duh-**mar**-uh-land /dəˈmɑːrəland/

Damascene relating to Damascus
dam-uh-seen /ˈdaməsiːn/

Damascus capital of Syria
duh-**mask**-uhss /dəˈmaskəs/

Established anglicization; sometimes also duh-**mahsk**-uhss. The Arabic name is Dimashq, pronounced dim-**ashk** [diˈmaʃq].

damask silk or linen fabric
dam-uhsk /ˈdaməsk/

Damazer, Mark controller of BBC Radio 4 and BBC 7
dam-uh-zuhr /ˈdaməzə(r)/

Damietta eastern branch of the Nile delta
dam-i-**et**-uh /ˌdamiˈɛtə/

Established anglicization. The Arabic name is Dumyat, pronounced duum-**yaht**.

damnatory causing damnation
dam-nuh-tuh-ri /ˈdamnəˌtəri/

Damocles Greek mythological character
dam-uh-kleez /ˈdaməkliːz/

Dampier, William English explorer
dam-peer /ˈdampɪə(r)/

Dana, James Dwight American naturalist
day-nuh /ˈdeɪnə/

This name is variously pronounced day-nuh, dah-nuh, and dan-uh, depending on individual preference.

Dana, Richard Henry American adventurer
day-nuh /ˈdeɪnə/

Danaë Greek mythological character
dan-i-ee /ˈdaniiː/

Da Nang city, Vietnam
dah nung /ˌdɑːˈnʌŋ/

Dandong port, China
dan-**duung** /ˌdanˈdʊŋ/

Danegeld Anglo-Saxon land tax
dayn-geld /ˈdeɪnɡɛld/

Danelaw part of England formerly occupied by Danes
dayn-law /ˈdeɪnlɔː/

danewort plant
dayn-wurt /ˈdeɪnwə(r)t/

Danna, Mychael American composer
my-kuhl dan-uh /ˌmʌɪkəl ˈdanə/

Danner, Blythe American actress
blyth dan-uhr /ˌblʌɪð ˈdanə(r)/

d'Annunzio, Gabriele Italian novelist
gab-ri-**ay**-lay dan-**uunt**-syoh
/ˌɡabriˌeɪleɪ daˈnʊntsjəʊ/

Dante Italian poet
dan-tay /ˈdanteɪ/

Dantean relating to Dante
dant-i-uhn /ˈdantiən/

Sometimes also dan-**tee**-uhn.

Danton, Georges French revolutionary
zhorzh dah(ng)-**to(ng)** /ˌʒɔː(r)ʒ dãˈtõ/

Danube river, Europe
dan-yoob /ˈdanjuːb/

Established anglicization. Other languages
are: German: Donau **doh**-now [ˈdoːnau];
Czech: Dunaj **duun**-y [ˈdunaj];
Hungarian: Duna **duun**-uh [ˈdunɒ];
Serbo-Croat: Dunav **doo**-nav [ˈdunav];
Bulgarian: Dunaw **doo**-nuhf [ˈdunɐf];
Russian: Dunay doo-**ny** [duˈnaj];
Romanian: Dunărea **doon**-uhr-yuh
[ˈdunərja].

Danzig see **Gdańsk**

Daphne Greek mythological character
daf-ni /ˈdafni/

Daphnis Greek mythological character
daf-niss /ˈdafnɪs/

Da Ponte, Lorenzo Italian poet and
librettist
lorr-**ent**-soh dah **pont**-ay /lɒˌrɛntsəʊ
dɑː ˈpɒnteɪ/

Dapsang another name for the
mountain K2
dup-sung /dʌpˈsʌŋ/

Daqing city, China
dah-ching /ˌdɑːˈtʃɪŋ/

Darabont, Frank American film
director
darr-uh-bont /ˈdarəbɒnt/

Dardanelles strait between Europe and
Asiatic Turkey
dar-duh-nelz /ˌdɑː(r)dəˈnɛlz/

Dardenne, Sabine Belgian kidnap
victim
sab-**een** dar-**den** /saˌbiːn dɑː(r)ˈdɛn/

Dar es Salaam port, Tanzania
dar ess suh-lahm /ˌdɑːr ɛs səˈlɑːm/

Darfur region, Sudan
dar-**foor** /dɑː(r)ˈfʊə(r)/

Dari Afghan language
darr-ee /daˈriː/

Darién province, Panama
darr-i-en /dariˈɛn/

dariole cooking mould
darr-i-ohl /ˈdariəʊl/

Darius name of three ancient
kings of Persia
duh-**ry**-uhss /dəˈrʌɪəs/

Darjeeling hill station, India
dar-**jee**-ling /dɑː(r)ˈdʒiːlɪŋ/
• Use also for the tea grown there.

Darkhan city, Mongolia
dar-**khan** /dɑː(r)ˈxɑːn/

Darmstadt town, Germany
darm-shtat /ˈdɑː(r)mʃtat/

DARPA Defense Advanced Research
Projects Agency
dar-puh /ˈdɑː(r)pə/

Dartmoor moorland district, England
dart-mor /ˈdɑː(r)tmɔː(r)/

Sometimes also **dart**-moor.

Dartmouth port, England
dart-muhth /ˈdɑː(r)tməθ/

Daschle, Tom American politician
dash-uhl /ˈdaʃəl/

Dasehra see **Dussehra**

dashiki loose shirt or tunic
dah-shik-i /dɑːˈʃɪki/

da Silva, Luiz Inácio Lula Brazilian
president
luu-**eess** ee-**nass**-yoo **loo**-luh duh
seel-vuh /lʊˌiːs iːˌnasju ˌluːlə də ˈsiːlvə/

Das Rheingold opera by Wagner
dass **ryn**-golt /das ˈrʌɪŋɡɒlt/

dative grammatical case
day-tiv /ˈdeɪtɪv/

Datong city, China
dah-**tuung** /ˌdɑːˈtʊŋ/

Datuk title of respect
dah-tuhk /ˈdɑːtək/

datum piece of information
day-tuhm /ˈdeɪtəm/

daube meat stew
dohb /dəʊb/

Daubenton kind of bat
daw-buhn-tuhn /ˈdɔːbəntən/

Equally commonly also daw-**bent**-uhn;
both pronunciations are in use among
British naturalists.

Daubigny, Charles François French
painter
sharl frah(ng)-**swah** doh-bin-**yee**
/ʃɑː(r)l frãˌswɑː dəʊbɪnˈjiː/

Daudet, Alphonse French novelist
al-**fo(ng)ss** doh-**day** /al,fɔs dəʊ'deɪ/

Daumier, Honoré French painter
on-orr-**ay** dohm-**yay** /ɒnɒ,reɪ
dəʊ'mjeɪ/

daunorubicin antibiotic
daw-noh-**roo**-biss-in /,dɔːnəʊ'ruːbɪsɪn/

dauphin eldest son of the King of France
doh-fa(ng) /'dəʊfɛ̃/

Sometimes also **daw-fin.**

Dauphiné region, France
doh-fin-**ay** /dəʊfɪ'neɪ/

Davao port, Philippines
dav-**ah**-oh /da'vɑːəʊ/

David, Jacques-Louis French painter
zhahk **lwee** dav-**eed** /ʒɑːk ,lwiː
da'viːd/

Davies, Alan English actor
day-veez /'deɪviːz/

Davies, Wyre BBC reporter
wirr-uh **day**-viss /,wɪrə 'deɪvɪs/

Davis, Bette American actress
bet-i **day**-viss /,beti 'deɪvɪs/

Davos resort, Switzerland
dav-ohss /da'vəʊs/, German [da'voːs]

When referring to the World Economic
Forum held there, it is common to use an
'international', anglicized pronunciation,
dav-oss. Our BBC business reporters tell us
that the name has transcended geography,
as the WEF is know by this name even when
it is held in other countries. The Swiss
pronunciation should be used in all other
contexts.

Dayak (also **Dyak**) ethnic group in
Borneo
dy-ak /'dʌɪak/

Dayan, Moshe Israeli statesman and
general
mosh-**ay** dy-**ahn** /mɒ,ʃeɪ dʌɪ'ɑːn/

dayan pl. **dayanim** senior rabbi
dy-**ahn**, pl. dy-**ah**-nim /dʌɪ'ɑːn/, pl.
/dʌɪ'ɑːnɪm/

Dayton city, US
day-tuhn /'deɪtən/

Daytona Beach resort, US
day-**toh**-nuh /deɪ'təʊnə/

deacon ordained minister
dee-kuhn /'diːkən/

Deakin, Alfred Australian statesman
dee-kin /'diːkɪn/

Deayton, Angus English comedian
dee-tuhn /'diːtən/

debacle sudden disastrous collapse or
defeat
day-**bah**-kuhl /deɪ'bɑːkəl/

de Beauvoir, Simone French
philosopher
see-**mon** duh boh-**vwar** /siː,mɒn də
bəʊ'vwɑː(r)/

De Beers South African mining
company
duh **beerz** /də 'bɪə(r)z/

Debrecen city and football team,
Hungary
deb-ret-sen /'dɛbrɛtsɛn/

Debrett, John English publisher
duh-**bret** /də'brɛt/

debris pieces of rubbish or remains
deb-ree /'dɛbriː/

Less commonly also **day-bree.** The form
duh-**bree** is now used more commonly in
BR, but is still regarded as the AM
pronunciation.

de Burgh, Chris Irish singer
duh **burg** /də 'bɜː(r)g/

Debussy, Claude French composer
klohd duh-bue-**see** /,kləʊd dəby'si/

Commonly also anglicized to duh-**boo**-si.

debut first appearance
day-byoo /'deɪbjuː/

Commonly also **deb**-yoo.

debutant man making his first
appearance
deb-yoo-to(ng) /'dɛbjuːtɒ̃/, French
[debytɑ̃]

debutante woman making her first
appearance
deb-yuh-tahnt /'dɛbjətɑːnt/, French
[debytɑ̃t]

Debye, Peter Dutch-born American
chemical physicist
duh-**by** /də'bʌɪ/

decade period of ten years
dek-ayd /'dɛkeɪd/

Less commonly also dek-**ayd.**

decagon figure with ten straight sides
dek-uh-guhn /'dɛkəgən/

decahedron figure with ten plane faces
dek-uh-**hee**-druhn /,dɛkə'hiːdrən/

Sometimes also dek-uh-**hed**-ruhn.

Decalogue Ten Commandments
dek-uh-log /'dɛkəlɒg/

Decameron work by Boccaccio
dek-**am**-uh-ruhn /dɛ'kamərən/

decanal relating to a dean
duh-**kay**-nuhl /də'keɪməl/

Sometimes also dek-uh-nuhl.

decathlon athletic event
dek-**ath**-lon /dɛ'kaθlɒn/

Deccan plateau, India
dek-**uhn** /'dɛkən/

deciduous shedding its leaves annually
duh-**sid**-yoo-uhss /də'sɪdjuəs/

Decius, Gaius Messius Quintus Trajanus Roman emperor
gy-uhss mess-i-uhss **kwint**-uhss truh-**jay**-nuhss dee-si-uhss /ˌgʌɪəs ˌmɛsɪəs ˌkwɪntəs trəˌdʒeɪnəs 'diːsɪəs/

declarative making a declaration
duh-**klarr**-uh-tiv /də'klarətɪv/

de Clerambault's syndrome erotomania
duh **klerr**-uhm-bohz /də 'klɛrəmbəʊz/

declivity downward slope
duh-**kliv**-it-i /də'klɪvɪti/

decollate behead
duh-**kol**-ayt /də'kɒleɪt/

Sometimes also dek-uh-layt.

decollate separate sheets of paper into different piles
dee-kuh-**layt** /ˌdiːkə'leɪt/

décolletage low neckline
day-kol-**tahzh** /ˌdeɪkɒl'tɑːʒ/

décolleté (also **décolletée**) having a low neckline
day-**kol**-tay /deɪ'kɒlteɪ/

decor decoration of a room
day-**kor** /'deɪkɔː(r)/

Commonly also dek-or.

Decretum collection of judgements in canon law
duh-**kree**-tuhm /də'kriːtəm/

decry publicly denounce
duh-**kry** /də'krʌɪ/

Dedekind, Richard German mathematician
rikh-art day-duh-kint /ˌrɪçɑː(r)t 'deɪdəkɪnt/

de facto in fact

day **fak**-toh /ˌdeɪ 'faktəʊ/

de Falla, Manuel Spanish composer
man-**wel** day fal-yuh /manˌwɛl deɪ 'faljə/

Defoe, Daniel English novelist
duh-**foh** /də'fəʊ/

dégagé unconcerned or unconstrained
day-gah-zhay /deɪgɑːʒeɪ/

Degas, Edgar French painter and sculptor
ed-gar duh-**gah** /ˌɛdgɑː(r) də'gɑː/

de Gaulle, Charles French statesman
sharl duh **gohl** /ˌʃɑː(r)l də 'gəʊl/

degenerate immoral or corrupt person
duh-**jen**-uh-ruht /də'dʒɛnərət/

DeGeneres, Ellen American comedian
duh-**jen**-uh-ruhss /də'dʒɛnərəs/

de Havilland, Geoffrey English aircraft designer
duh **hav**-il-uhnd /də 'havɪlənd/

de Hooch, Pieter (also **de Hoogh**) Dutch painter
pee-tuhr duh **hohkh** /ˌpiːtə(r) də 'həʊx/

de Hoop Scheffer, Jaap Dutch secretary general of NATO
yahp duh **hohp skhef**-uhr /ˌjɑːp də ˌhəʊp 'sxɛfə(r)/

Dehra Dun city, India
dair-uh doon /ˌdɛːrə 'duːn/

dehydrate cause something to lose a large amount of water
dee-**hy**-drayt /diː'hʌɪdreɪt/

Commonly also dee-hy-**drayt**.

Deianira Greek mythological character
dee-uh-**ny**-ruh /ˌdiːə'nʌɪrə/

deicide killing of a god
day-iss-yd /'deɪɪsʌɪd/

Deighton, Len English writer
day-tuhn /'deɪtən/

This British surname is variously pronounced day-tuhn and dy-tuhn, depending on individual preference. The Yorkshire place names, however, are dee-tuhn.

Dei gratia by the grace of God
day-ee grah-ti-uh /ˌdeɪɪ: 'grɑːtɪə/

Deimos moon of Mars
day-moss /'deɪmɒs/

deinonychus dinosaur
dy-**non**-ik-uhss /dʌɪ'nɒnɪkəs/

deism belief in the existence of a supreme being
day-iz-uhm /'deɪɪzəm/

deity god or goddess
day-it-i /'deɪɪti/

déjà vu feeling of having already experienced the present situation
day-zhah voo /ˌdeɪʒɑː 'vuː/, French /deʒa vy/

de Klerk, F. W. South African statesman
duh klairk /də 'klɛː(r)k/

de Kooning, Willem Dutch-born American painter
wil-uhm duh koo-ning /ˌwɪləm də 'kuːnɪŋ/

Delacroix, Eugène French painter
oe-zhen del-ah-krwah /øˌʒɛn dɛlɑː'krwɑː/

de la Mare, Walter English poet
del uh mair /dɛ lə 'mɛː(r)/

Delaunay, Robert French painter
rob-air duh-loh-nay /rɒˌbɛː(r) dələʊ'neɪ/

Delaunay-Terk, Sonia Russian-born French painter
son-yuh duh-loh-nay tairk /ˌsɒnjə dələʊˌneɪ 'tɛː(r)k/

Delaware river, US
del-uh-wair /'dɛləwɛː(r)/

de Leeuw, Ton Dutch composer
ton duh lay-oo /ˌtɒn də 'leɪuː/

de Lempica, Tamara Polish-born American artist
tuh-mar-uh duh lem-pik-uh /təˌmɑːrə də 'lɛmpɪkə/

This is the pronunciation used by the family. The Polish pronunciation is lem-pit-suh.

Delfont, Bernard Russian-born British impresario
del-font /'dɛlfɒnt/

Delft town, Netherlands
delft /dɛlft/

Delhi state, India
del-i /'dɛli/

Delibes, Léo French composer
lay-oh duh-leeb /ˌleɪəʊ də'liːb/

delicatessen shop selling prepared foods
del-ik-uh-tess-uhn /ˌdɛlɪkə'tɛsən/

Delilah biblical name
duh-ly-luh /də'lʌɪlə/

delirium tremens psychotic condition
duh-lirr-i-uhm tree-menz /dəˌlɪriəm 'triːmɛnz/

Delius, Frederick English composer
dee-li-uhss /'diːliəs/

della Quercia, Jacopo Italian sculptor
yah-kuh-poh del-uh kwair-chuh /ˌjɑːkəpəʊ ˌdɛlə 'kwɛː(r)tʃə/

della Robbia, Luca Italian sculptor
loo-kuh del-uh rob-yuh /ˌluːkə ˌdɛlə 'rɒbjə/

Dell'Olio, Nancy Italian lawyer; girlfriend of Sven-Göran Eriksson
nan-si del-ol-yoh /ˌnansi dɛl'ɒljəʊ/

Delors, Jacques French politician
zhahk duh-lor /ˌʒɑːk də'lɔː(r)/

Delos island, Greece
dee-loss /'diːlɒs/

Established anglicization. The Greek name is Dhilos, pronounced **thee**-loss.

Delphi ancient Greek religious sanctuary
del-fy /'dɛlfʌɪ/

Established anglicization. Commonly also del-fi; see GREEK panel. The Greek name is Dhelfoi, pronounced thel-**fee**.

Delphinus constellation
del-fy-nuhss /dɛl'fʌɪnəs/

Delpy, Julie French actress
zhue-lee del-pee /ʒyˌliː dɛl'piː/

Delray Beach resort, US
del-ray /'dɛlreɪ/

delude make believe something that is not true
duh-lood /də'luːd/

The pronunciation duh-lyood is less common now.

de luxe luxurious
duh luks /də 'lʌks/

Sometimes also luuks or looks.

deme ancient Greek political division
deem /diːm/

de Menezes, Jean Charles Brazilian man, shot dead by police in London
zhee-uh(ng) shar-liss ji men-ez-iss /ˌʒiːə ˌʃɑː(r)lɪs dʒi mɛ'nɛzɪs/
• See PORTUGUESE panel.

dementia mental disorder
duh-men-shuh /də'mɛnʃə/

Demerara river, Guyana
dem-uh-rar-uh /ˌdɛmə'rɑːrə/

The pronunciation dem-uh-**rair**-uh is also sometimes used, especially for the brown sugar from Guyana.

Demerol trademark pethidine
dem-uh-rol /ˈdɛmərɒl/

demesne land attached to a manor
duh-**mayn** /dəˈmeɪn/

Demeter Greek goddess
duh-**mee**-tuhr /dəˈmiːtə(r)/

de Mille, Cecil B. American film producer and director
duh **mil** /də ˈmɪl/

Demme, Jonathan American film director
dem-i /ˈdɛmi/

Democritus Greek philosopher
duh-**mok**-rit-uhss /dəˈmɒkrɪtəs/

de Moivre's theorem mathematical theorem
duh **mwah**-vruh /də ˈmwɑːvrə/

demonolatry worship of demons
dee-muh-**nol**-uh-tri /ˌdiːməˈnɒlətri/

de Morales, Cristóbal Spanish composer
kree-**stoh**-bal day morr-**ah**-less /kriːˌstəʊbal deɪ mɒˈrɑːlɛs/

De Mornay, Rebecca American actress
duh **mor**-nay /də ˈmɔː(r)neɪ/

Demosthenes Greek orator and statesman
duh-**moss**-thuh-neez /dəˈmɒsθəniːz/

demulcent relieving inflammation
duh-**mul**-suhnt /dəˈmʌlsənt/

demur raise objections
duh-**mur** /dəˈmə:(r)/

demure reserved and shy
duh-**myoor** /dəˈmjʊə(r)/

Commonly also duh-**myor**.

Denali mountain, US
duh-**nah**-li /dəˈnɑːli/

denar currency unit, Macedonia
den-ar /ˈdɛnɑː(r)/

denarius pl. **denarii** ancient Roman silver coin
duh-**nair**-i-uhss, pl. duh-**nair**-i-y /dəˈnɛːriəs, pl. /-riʌɪ/

Denbighshire county, Wales
den-bish-uhr /ˈdɛnbɪʃə(r)/

dendrite extension of a nerve cell
den-dryt /ˈdɛndrʌɪt/

Dene American Indian ethnic group

den-ay /ˈdɛneɪ/

dene vale
deen /diːn/

Deneb star
den-eb /ˈdɛnɛb/

Denebola star
duh-**neb**-uh-luh /dəˈnɛbələ/

Deneuve, Catherine French actress
kath-uh-rin duh-**noev** /ˈkaθərɪn dəˈnœv/, [katrin]
• First name anglicized.

dengue fever viral disease
deng-gi /ˈdɛŋgi/

Deng Xiaoping Chinese statesman
dung shi-ow-**ping** /ˌdʌŋ ʃiˌaʊˈpɪŋ/

Den Haag see Hague, The

Denholm British family name
den-uhm /ˈdɛnəm/

This is also the usual pronunciation for British place names with the same spelling. Denholm in West Yorkshire, however, is **den**-holm.

denier unit of weight
den-i-uhr /ˈdɛniə(r)/

De Niro, Robert American actor
duh **neer**-oh /də ˈnɪərəʊ/

Denis, Maurice French painter
morr-**eess** duh-**nee** /mɒˌriːs dəˈniː/

Denpasar city, Indonesia
den-pass-ar /ˈdɛnˈpasɑː(r)/

densimeter instrument for measuring density
den-sim-uh-tuhr /ˈdɛnsɪmətə(r)/

dentalium tusk shells
den-tay-li-uhm /dɛnˈteɪliəm/

dentine tooth tissue
den-teen /ˈdɛntiːn/

Deo gratias 'thanks be to God' (Latin)
day-oh grah-ti-uhss /ˌdeɪəʊ ˈɡrɑːtiəs/
• See LATIN panel.

Deo volente 'God willing' (Latin)
day-oh vol-en-tay /ˌdeɪəʊ vɒˈlɛnteɪ/

De Palma, Brian American film director
duh **pahl**-muh /də ˈpɑːlmə/

Depardieu, Gérard French actor
zhay-**rar** duh-par-**dyoe** /ʒeiˌrɑː(r) dəpɑː(r)ˈdjø/

depilatory used to remove unwanted hair
duh-**pil**-uh-tuh-ri /dəˈpɪlətəri/

Depeche Mode English pop group
duh-**pesh** mohd /dəˌpɛʃ ˈməʊd/

de profundis 'out of the depths' (Latin)
day pruh-**fuun**-diss /ˌdeɪ prəˈfʊndɪs/

De Quincey, Thomas English essayist
and critic
duh **kwin**-si /də ˈkwɪnsi/

Derain, André French painter
ah(ng)-**dray** duh-**ra(ng)** /ɑ̃ˌdreɪ dəˈrɛ̃/

Derbent city, Russia
duhr-**bent** /də(r)ˈbɛnt/

Derby city, England
dar-bi /ˈdɑː(r)bi/

Derby annual horse-race
dar-bi /ˈdɑː(r)bi/

AM is **dur**-bi.

derecho climactic condition
duh-**ray**-choh /dəˈreɪtʃəʊ/

dermatitis skin condition
dur-muh-**ty**-tiss /ˌdɜː(r)məˈtaɪtɪs/

Derrida, Jacques French philosopher
zhahk derr-ee-**dah** /ˌʒɑːk dɛriˈdɑː/

Der Ring des Nibelungen series of
operas by Wagner
dair **ring** dess **nee**-buhl-uung-uhn
/dɛː(r) ˌrɪŋ dɛs ˈniːbəlʊŋən/

derringer pistol
derr-in-juhr /ˈdɛrɪndʒə(r)/

Der Rosenkavalier opera by Richard
Strauss
dair **roh**-zuhn-kav-uh-leer /dɛː(r)
ˈrəʊzənkavəliə(r)/

Der Spiegel German magazine
dair **shpee**-guhl /dɛː(r) ˈʃpiːɡəl/

dervish Muslim friar
dur-vish /ˈdɜː(r)vɪʃ/

Desai, Anita Indian-born British writer
uh-**nee**-tuh dess-**y** /əˈniːtə dɛˈsaɪ/

Descartes, René French philosopher
ruh-**nay** day-**kart** /rəˌneɪ deɪˈkɑː(r)t/

desi local or indigenous
day-si /ˈdeɪsi/

De Sica, Vittorio Italian film director
and actor
vi-**taw**-ri-oh day **see**-kuh /viˌtɔːriəʊ
deɪ ˈsiːkə/

desideratum pl. **desiderata** something
that is needed or wanted
duh-zid-uh-**rah**-tuhm, pl.
duh-zid-uh-**rah**-tuh /dəˌzɪdəˈrɑːtəm/,
pl. /-tə/

Desiree potato
dez-**eer**-ay /ˈdɛˈzɪəreɪ/

Des Moines city, US
duh **moyn** /də ˈmɔɪn/

despicable deserving contempt
duh-**spik**-uh-buhl /dəˈspɪkəbəl/

Sometimes also **desp**-ik-uh-buhl.

despot ruler
desp-ot /ˈdɛspɒt/

des Prez, Josquin (also **des Prés** or
Deprez) Flemish composer
zhosk-a(ng) day **pray** /ʒɒsˌkɛ̃ deɪ ˈpreɪ/

desquamate come off in scales or flakes
desk-wuh-**mayt** /ˈdɛskwəmeɪt/

Dessau city, Germany
dess-ow /ˈdɛsaʊ/

de Staël, Madame French novelist
and critic
mad-**am** duh **stahl** /madˌam də ˈstɑːl/

De Stijl Dutch art movement
duh **styl** /də ˈstʌɪl/
• See **DUTCH** panel.

destrier medieval knight's warhorse
dest-ri-uhr /ˈdɛstriə(r)/

desuetude state of disuse
dess-wi-tyood /ˈdɛswɪtjuːd/

Sometimes also duh-**syoo**-uh-tyood.

desultory lacking purpose
dess-uhl-tuh-ri /ˈdɛsəltəri/

detritus waste
duh-**try**-tuhss /dəˈtraɪtəs/

Detroit city, US
duh-**troyt** /dəˈtrɔɪt/

de trop not wanted
duh **troh** /də ˈtrəʊ/

Dettol trademark household disinfectant
det-ol /ˈdɛtɒl/

Dettori, Frankie Italian-born jockey
det-**aw**-ri /dɛˈtɔːri/

Deucalion Greek mythological character
dyoo-**kay**-li-uhn /djuːˈkeɪliən/

deus ex machina unexpected event
saving a hopeless situation
day-uuss eks **mak**-i-nuh /ˌdeɪʊs ɛks
ˈmakɪnə/
• See **LATIN** panel.

deuteranopia colour blindness
dyoo-tuh-ruh-**noh**-pi-uh
/ˌdjuːtərəˈnəʊpiə/

Deutero-Isaiah supposed author of
Isaiah 40–55
dyoo-tuh-roh y-**zy**-uh /ˌdjuːtərəʊ
ʌɪˈzʌɪə/

Deuteronomy book of the Bible
dyoo-tuh-**ron**-uh-mi /ˌdjuːtəˈrɒnəmi/

Deutsche Börse German stock
exchange
doytch-uh **boer**-zuh /ˌdɔɪtʃə ˈbœ(r)zə/

Deutsche Mark former currency unit,
Germany; also called **Deutschmark**
doytch-uh **mark** /ˌdɔɪtʃə ˈmɑː(r)k/

Deutschland German name for
Germany
doytch-lant /ˈdɔɪtʃlant/

Deutschmark former currency unit,
Germany; also called **Deutsche Mark**
doytch-mark /ˈdɔɪtʃmɑː(r)k/

Deva Hindu god
day-vuh /ˈdeɪvə/

devadasi dancer in a Hindu temple
day-vuh-**dah**-si /ˌdeɪvəˈdɑːsi/

de Valera, Eamon American-born Irish
statesman
ay-muhn duh vuh-**lair**-uh /ˌeɪmən də
vəˈlɛːrə/

de Valois, Ninette Irish ballet dancer
nin-**et** duh **val**-wah /nɪˌnɛt də ˈvalwɑː/

Devanagari Indian alphabet
day-vuh-**nah**-guh-ri /ˌdeɪvəˈnɑːɡəri/

développé ballet movement
dev-lop-**ay** /ˌdɛvlɒˈpeɪ/

Devensian geological period
duh-**ven**-zi-uhn /dəˈvɛnziən/

Devereux British family name
dev-uh-ruh, **dev**-uh-roo,
dev-uh-rooks, **dev**-uh-reks,
dev-uh-roh /ˈdɛvərə/, /ˈdɛvəruː/,
/ˈdɛvəruːks/, /ˈdɛvərɛks/, /ˈdɛvərəʊ/

Devi Hindu goddess
day-vi /ˈdeɪvi/

de Villepin, Dominique French prime
minister
dom-ee-**neek** duh veel-**pa(ng)**
/dɒmiːˌniːk də viːlˈpɛ̃/

devolution transfer of power to a lower
level
dee-vuh-**loo**-shuhn /ˌdiːvəˈluːʃən/

Commonly also dev-uh-**loo**-shuhn.

Devonian relating to Devon
dev-**oh**-ni-uhn /dɛˈvəʊniən/

devoré velvet fabric
duh-**vaw**-ray /dəˈvɔːreɪ/

de Vries, Adriaen Dutch sculptor
ah-dri-ahn duh **vreess** /ˌɑːdriɑːn də
ˈvriːs/

de Vries, Hugo Dutch botanist
hue-khoh duh **vreess** /ˌhyxəʊ də
ˈvriːs/

de Waart, Edo Dutch conductor
ay-doh duh **wart** /ˌeɪdəʊ də ˈwɑː(r)t/

Dewar, James Scottish chemist and
physicist
dyoo-uhr /ˈdjuːə(r)/

Dewey, John American philosopher
dyoo-i /ˈdjuːi/

Dewi Welsh name for St David
de-wi /ˈdɛwi/

Dewsbury town, England
dyooz-buh-ri /ˈdjuːzbəri/

dexamethasone drug
dek-suh-**meth**-uh-sohn
/ˌdɛksəˈmɛθəsəʊn/

Dexedrine drug
dek-suh-dreen /ˈdɛksədriːn/

Dhaka (also **Dacca**) capital of
Bangladesh
dak-uh /ˈdakə/

dhal (also **dal**) split pulses
dahl /dɑːl/

Dhanbad city, India
dun-bad /ˈdʌnbad/

dhansak Indian dish
dun-sahk /ˈdʌnsɑːk/

Dharamsala Indian residence of the
Dalai Lama
durr-uhm-**sah**-luh /ˌdʌrəmˈsɑːlə/

dharma Buddhist and Hindu moral law
dar-muh /ˈdɑː(r)mə/

Dharuk Australian aboriginal language
durr-uuk /ˈdʌrʊk/

Dhaulagiri mountain massif, Himalayas
dow-luh-**girr**-i /ˌdaʊləˈɡɪri/

Dhelfoi see **Delphi**

Dhilos see **Delos**

Dhofar province, Oman
doh-**far** /dəʊˈfɑː(r)/

dhol Indian drum
dohl /dəʊl/

dholak type of dhol
doh-luhk /ˈdəʊlək/

dhole Asian wild dog
dohl /dəʊl/

dhoti loincloth
doh-ti /ˈdəʊti/

dhurrie Indian cotton rug
durr-i /ˈdʌri/

Diabaté, Toumani Malian kora player
too-**mah**-ni dee-ab-at-**ay** /tuːˌmɑːni diːabaˈteɪ/

diabetes insipidus form of diabetes
dy-uh-**bee**-teez in-**sip**-id-uhss /dʌɪəˌbiːtiːz ɪnˈsɪpɪdəs/

diabetes mellitus commonest form of diabetes
dy-uh-**bee**-teez muh-**ly**-tuhss /dʌɪəˌbiːtiːz məˈlʌɪtəs/

diabolism devil worship
dy-**ab**-uh-liz-uhm /dʌɪˈabəlɪzəm/

diacetylmorphine technical term for heroin
dy-**ass**-uh-tyl-**mor**-feen /dʌɪˌasətʌɪlˈmɔː(r)fiːn/

diaconal relating to a deacon
dy-**ak**-uh-nuhl /dʌɪˈakənəl/

diaconate office of deacon
dy-**ak**-uh-nayt /dʌɪˈakəneɪt/

diacritic sign, such as an accent
dy-uh-**krit**-ik /ˌdʌɪəˈkrɪtɪk/

diadem jewelled crown or headband
dy-uh-dem /ˈdʌɪədɛm/

Diadochi Macedonian generals
dy-**ad**-uh-ki /dʌɪˈadəki/

diaeresis pl. **diaereses** mark (¨)
dy-**eer**-iss-iss, pl. dy-**eer**-iss-eez /dʌɪˈɪərɪsɪs/, pl. /-siːz/

Commonly also dy-**err**-iss-iss, dy-uh-**ree**-siss.

Diaghilev, Sergei Russian ballet dancer
suhr-**gay** di-**ag**-il-ef /sə(r)ˌgeɪ diˈagɪlɛf/

Diageo beer, wine, and spirits company
di-**aj**-i-oh /diˈadʒiəʊ/

diagnose identify an illness
dy-uhg-nohz /ˈdʌɪəgnəʊz/

Commonly also dy-uhg-**nohz**.

dialyse purify by means of dialysis
dy-uh-lyz /ˈdʌɪəlʌɪz/

dialysis pl. **dialyses** medical treatment
dy-**al**-iss-iss, pl. dy-**al**-iss-eez /dʌɪˈalɪsɪs/, pl. /-siːz/

diamanté imitation diamond trimming
dee-uh-**mon**-tay /diːəˈmɒnteɪ/

Less commonly also dy-uh-**mant**-i.

diamantine made from diamonds
dy-uh-**man**-teen /ˌdʌɪəˈmantiːn/

Diana Roman goddess
dy-**an**-uh /dʌɪˈanə/

dianthus plant
dy-**an**-thuhss /dʌɪˈanθəs/

diaphanous delicate and translucent
dy-**af**-uh-nuhss /dʌɪˈafənəs/

diaphoresis sweating
dy-uh-fuh-**ree**-siss /ˌdʌɪəfəˈriːsɪs/

diarchy government by two independent authorities
dy-ar-ki /ˈdʌɪɑː(r)ki/

Dias, Bartolomeu Portuguese explorer
bar-tol-uh-**may**-oo dee-uhsh /bɑː(r)tʊləˌmeɪuː ˈdiːəʃ/

diaspora dispersion of the Jews beyond Israel
dy-**asp**-uh-ruh /dʌɪˈaspərə/

diastole phase of the heartbeat
dy-**ast**-uh-li /dʌɪˈastəli/

diathermy medical and surgical technique
dy-uh-thur-mi /ˈdʌɪəˌθəː(r)mi/

Diaz, Porfirio Mexican statesman
por-**feer**-i-oh dee-**ass** /pɔː(r)ˌfɪəriəʊ ˈdiːas/

diazepam drug of the benzodiazepine group
dy-**ayz**-uh-pam /dʌɪˈeɪzəpam/

As with other drugs in this group, the pronunciation -**az**-uh-pam is also common.

Dibnah, Fred English steeplejack and broadcaster
dib-nuh /ˈdɪbnə/

DiCaprio, Leonardo American actor
lee-uh-**nar**-doh dik-**ap**-ri-oh /liːəˌnɑː(r)dəʊ dɪˈkapriəʊ/

dichotomy contrast between two things
dy-**kot**-uh-mi /dʌɪˈkɒtəmi/

Sometimes also dik-**ot**-uh-mi.

Dickensian relating to Charles Dickens
dik-**en**-zi-uhn /dɪˈkɛnziən/

dictum pl. **dicta** formal pronouncement
dik-tuhm, pl. **dik**-tuh /ˈdɪktəm/, pl. /-tə/
• Standard -s plural is also possible.

didactic intended to teach
dy-**dak**-tik /dʌɪˈdaktɪk/

Sometimes also did-**ak**-tik.

dideoxycytidine Aids drug
dy-di-oks-i-**sy**-tid-een
/ˌdʌɪdɪɒksiˈsʌɪtɪdiːn/

dideoxyinosine Aids drug
dy-di-oks-i-**in**-oh-seen
/ˌdʌɪdɪɒksiˈnəʊsiːn/

Diderot, Denis French philosopher
duh-**nee** dee-duh-**roh** /dəˌniː
diːdəˈrəʊ/

didgeridoo (also **didjeridu**) Australian
Aboriginal musical instrument
dij-uh-rid-**oo** /ˌdɪdʒərɪˈduː/

Dido Roman mythological name
dy-doh /ˈdʌɪdəʊ/

Dido English singer
dy-doh /ˈdʌɪdəʊ/

Didyma ancient sanctuary, Asia Minor
did-im-uh /ˈdɪdɪmə/

Die Fledermaus operetta by Strauss
dee **flay**-duhr-mowss /diː
ˈfleɪdə(r)maʊs/

Diego Garcia island, Chagos
Archipelago
di-**ay**-goh gar-**see**-uh /diˌeɪgəʊ
gɑː(r)ˈsiːə/

Dien Bien Phu town, Vietnam
dee-uhn **bee**-uhn **foo** /ˌdiːən ˌbiːən
ˈfuː/

Dieppe port, France
dyep /djɛp/

Diesel, Rudolf French-born German
engineer
roo-dolf **dee**-zuhl /ˌruːdɒlf ˈdiːzəl/

Dies Irae 'Day of Wrath' (Latin)
dee-ez **eer**-y /ˌdiːɛz ˈɪərʌɪ/
• See LATIN panel.

Dietrich, Marlene German-born
American actress and singer
mar-**lay**-nuh **dee**-trik /mɑː(r)ˌleɪnə
ˈdiːtrɪk/, German [ˈdiːtrɪç]
• Family name anglicized.

Dieu et mon droit 'God and my right'
(French), the motto of the British
monarch
dyoe ay mo(ng) **drwah** /ˌdjø eɪ mɔ̃
ˈdrwɑ/

Die Walküre opera by Wagner
dee val-**kue**-ruh /diː valˈkyːrə/

Sometimes also dee **val**-kue-ruh; the
English version of the title is *The Valkyrie*.

Die Welt German newspaper
dee **velt** /diː ˈvɛlt/

Die Zauberflöte opera by Mozart; 'the
magic flute'
dee **tsow**-buhr-floe-tuh /diː
ˈtsaʊbə(r)ˌfløːtə/

digamma letter of the Greek alphabet
dy-**gam**-uh /dʌɪˈgamə/

digest summary of information
dy-jest /ˈdʌɪdʒɛst/

digest break down
dy-**jest** /dʌɪˈdʒɛst/

Sometimes also dij-**est**.

digestif drink
dee-zhest-**eef** /ˌdiːʒɛˈstiːf/

digitalis drug
dij-it-**ay**-liss /ˌdɪdʒɪˈteɪlɪs/

diglossia situation in which two
languages are used under different
conditions
dy-**gloss**-i-uh /dʌɪˈglɒsiə/

digraph combination of two letters
representing one sound
dy-grahf /ˈdʌɪgrɑːf/

dihedral having two plane faces
dy-**hee**-druhl /dʌɪˈhiːdrəl/

Dijla see **Tigris**

Dijon city, France
dee-**zho(ng)** /diːˈʒɔ̃/

dilate make wider
dy-**layt** /dʌɪˈleɪt/

Sometimes also dil-**ayt**.

dilatory slow to act
dil-uh-tuh-ri /ˈdɪlətəri/

dilemma situation with a difficult choice
dil-**em**-uh /dɪˈlɛmə/

Commonly also dy-**lem**-uh.

Dili port, Indonesia
dee-lee /ˈdiːliː/

dilophosaurus dinosaur
dy-**loh**-fuh-**saw**-ruhss
/dʌɪˌləʊfəˈsɔːrəs/

DiMaggio, Joe American baseball
player
dim-**aj**-i-oh /dɪˈmadʒiəʊ/

dimension measurable extent
dy-**men**-shuhn /dʌɪˈmɛnʃən/

Sometimes also dim-**en**-shuhn.

dimissory denoting formal permission
from a bishop
dim-iss-uh-ri /ˈdɪmɪsəri/

dimity cotton fabric
dim-it-i /'dɪmɪti/

dim sum Chinese dish
dim **sum** /ˌdɪm 'sʌm/

dinar currency unit, Bosnia and Serbia
dee-nar /'diːnɑː(r)/

Dinaric Alps mountain range, Balkans
din-**arr**-ik /dɪ'narɪk/

dinero money
din-**air**-oh /dɪ'nɛːrəʊ/

Ding an sich 'thing in itself' (German)
ding an **zikh** /ˌdɪŋ an 'zɪç/

dinghy small boat
ding-i /'dɪŋi/

Sometimes also **ding**-gi.

Dinka Sudanese ethnic group
dink-uh /'dɪŋkə/

diocesan relating to a diocese
dy-**oss**-uh-suhn /dʌɪ'ɒsəsən/

diocese pl. **dioceses** district under the
jurisdiction of a bishop
dy-uh-siss, pl. **dy**-uh-seez /'dʌɪəsɪs/, pl.
/-siːz/

Diocletian Roman emperor
dy-uh-**klee**-shuhn /ˌdʌɪə'kliːʃən/

diode semiconductor device
dy-ohd /'dʌɪəʊd/

Diogenes Greek philosopher
dy-**oj**-uh-neez /dʌɪ'ɒdʒəniːz/

Diomedes Greek mythological character
dy-uh-**mee**-deez /dʌɪə'miːdiːz/

Dione moon of Saturn
dy-**oh**-ni /dʌɪ'əʊni/

Dionysiac relating to Dionysus
dy-uh-**niz**-i-ak /ˌdʌɪə'nɪziak/

Dionysius name of two rulers of
Syracuse
dy-uh-**niss**-i-uhss /ˌdʌɪə'nɪsiəs/

Dionysius Exiguus Scythian monk and
scholar
dy-uh-**niss**-i-uhss eg-**zig**-yoo-uhss
/ˌdʌɪəˌnɪsiəs ɛg'zɪgjuəs/

Dionysius the Areopagite Greek
churchman
dy-uh-**niss**-i-uhss arr-i-**op**-uh-gyt
/ˌdʌɪəˌnɪsiəs ˌarɪ'ɒpəgʌɪt/

Dionysus Greek god
dy-uh-**ny**-suhss /ˌdʌɪə'nʌɪsəs/

Diophantus Greek mathematician
dy-uh-**fan**-tuhss /ˌdʌɪə'fantəs/

Dior, Christian French couturier

krist-i-uhn di-**or** /ˌkrɪstiən di'ɔː(r)/,
French [kristjɑ̃ djɔːr]
• Established anglicization.

Dioscuri Greek mythological characters
dy-**osk**-yuu-ri /dʌɪ'ɒskjʊri/

diphtheria bacterial disease
dif-**theer**-i-uh /dɪf'θɪəriə/

Commonly also dip-**theer**-i-uh.

---

diphthong two vowel sounds combined
in a single syllable
dif-thong /'dɪfθɒŋ/

Commonly also **dip**-thong.

---

diplococcus pl. **diplococci** bacterium
dip-loh-**kok**-uhss, pl. dip-loh-**kok**-y
/ˌdɪpləʊ'kɒkəs/, pl. /-kʌɪ/

Plural is sometimes also -**kok**-sy; see LATIN
panel.

---

diplodocus dinosaur
dip-**lod**-uh-kuhss /dɪ'plɒdəkəs/

Commonly also dip-loh-**doh**-kuhss.

Dirac, Paul English physicist
dirr-**ak** /dɪ'rak/

direct straight
dy-**rekt** /dʌɪ'rɛkt/

Commonly also duh-**rekt**, especially in AM.

---

direction guidance
dy-**rek**-shuhn /dʌɪ'rɛkʃən/

Commonly also duh-**rek**-shuhn.

---

dirge lament for the dead
durj /dəː(r)dʒ/

dirham currency unit, Morocco and the
United Arab Emirates
deer-huhm /'dɪə(r)həm/

dirigible airship
dirr-ij-ib-uhl /'dɪrɪdʒɪbəl/

diriment impediment factor which
invalidates a marriage
dirr-im-uhnt im-**ped**-im-uhnt
/ˌdɪrɪmənt ɪm'pɛdɪmənt/

dirk dagger
durk /dəː(r)k/

disinter dig up
diss-in-**tur** /ˌdɪsɪn'təː(r)/

disinvoltura self-assurance
diss-in-vol-**tyoor**-uh /ˌdɪsɪnvɒl'tjʊərə/

Disko island, Greenland
disk-oh /'dɪskəʊ/

Dismas biblical name
diss-muhss /'dɪsməs/

disomy chromosomal condition
dy-**soh**-mi /dʌɪ'səʊmi/

Dispur city, India
disp-**oor** /dɪs'pʊə(r)/

Disraeli, Benjamin English statesman
diz-**ray**-li /dɪz'reɪli/

dissect cut up
dy-**sekt** /dʌɪ'sɛkt/

Commonly also diss-**ekt**.

distaff spindle
dist-ahf /'dɪstɑːf/

Di Stefano, Alfredo Argentinian-born
Spanish footballer
al-**fray**-*th*oh di **stef**-uh-noh /al,freɪðəʊ
di 'stɛfənəʊ/

Di Stefano, Giovanni Italian-English
lawyer
juh-**vah**-ni di **stef**-uh-noh /dʒə,vɑːni di
'stɛfənəʊ/

Distel, Sasha French singer
sash-uh dist-**el** /,saʃə dɪs'tɛl/

distich pair of verse lines
dist-ik /'dɪstɪk/

distribute deal out
dist-**rib**-yoot /dɪ'strɪbjuːt/

Sometimes also dist-rib-yoot.

disulfiram drug used in the treatment of
alcoholism
dy-**sul**-firr-am /dʌɪ'sʌlfɪram/

divagate stray or digress
dy-vuh-gayt /'dʌɪvəgeɪt/

divan bed
div-**an** /dɪ'van/

diverse showing variety
dy-**vurss** /dʌɪ'vəː(r)s/

Sometimes also **dy**-vurss.

diversity state of being diverse
dy-**vur**-sit-i /dʌɪ'vəː(r)sɪti/

Sometimes also **dy**-**ur**-sit-i.

Dives river, France
deev /diːv/

Dives 'rich man' (Latin)
dy-veez /'dʌɪviːz/
• See LATIN panel.

divisi musical term
div-**ee**-si /dɪ'viːsi/

divorcee (also **divorcé** or **divorcée**)
divorced person
div-or-**see** /,dɪvɔː(r)'siː/

Sometimes also div-or-**say**.

divulge make known
dy-**vulj** /dʌɪ'vʌldʒ/

Sometimes also div-**ulj**.

Diwali Hindu festival
di-**wah**-li /di'wɑːli/

diwan administrative office
di-**wahn** /di'wɑːn/

diya oil lamp
dee-yuh /'diːjə/

Diyarbakır city and province, Turkey
di-**yar**-buh-kur /di'jɑː(r)bə,kə:(r)/

Djakarta see **Jakarta**

djellaba (also **djellabah** or **jellaba**)
hooded cloak
jel-uh-buh /'dʒɛləbə/

Djerba (also **Jerba**) island, Tunisia
jair-buh /'dʒɛː(r)bə/

Djibouti (also **Jibuti**) country
jib-**oo**-ti /dʒɪ'buːti/

Djindjić, Zoran Serbian statesman
zorr-an **jin**-jitch /,zɒran 'dʒɪndʒɪtʃ/

Djurgården island in Stockholm; also a
football team
yoor-gor-duhn /'jʊə(r),gɔː(r)dən/

Dnieper river, eastern Europe
dnee-puhr /'dniːpə(r)/

Established anglicization. The Russian
name is Dnepr, pronounced **dnyep**-uhr
[dʲnʲɛpr].

Dniester river, eastern Europe
dnee-stuhr /'dniːstə(r)/

Established anglicization. The Russian
name is Dnestr, pronounced **dnyest**-uhr
[dʲnʲɛstr].

Dniprodzerzhinsk city, Ukraine
dnee-pruhd-zuhr-**zhinsk**
/,dniːprədzə(r)'ʒɪnsk/

Dnipropetrovsk city, Ukraine
dnee-pruh-puht-**rofsk**
/,dniːprəpə'trɒfsk/

Dobermann pinscher breed of dog
doh-buhr-muhn **pinsh**-uhr
/,dəʊbə(r)mən 'pɪnʃə(r)/

dobra currency unit, São Tomé and
Principe
dob-ruh /'dɒbrə/

Dobrich city, Bulgaria
dob-ritch /'dɒbrɪtʃ/

dobro trademark acoustic guitar
doh-broh /'dəʊbrəʊ/

Dobruja district, Romania and Bulgaria
dob-ruu-yuh /'dɒbrʊjə/

docent member of university teaching
staff
doh-suhnt /'dəʊsənt/

doctorate the highest degree awarded by
a university faculty
dok-tuh-ruht /'dɒktərət/

Doctor Faustus play by Marlowe
fow-stuhss /'faʊstəs/

Sometimes also **faw**-stuhss.

Doctor Jekyll fictional character
jek-uhl /'dʒɛkəl/

The pronunciation used in the 1932 film *Dr
Jekyll and Mr Hyde*, however, is **jee**-kuhl.

Doctor Zhivago novel by Pasternak
zhiv-**ah**-goh /ʒɪ'vɑːɡəʊ/

doctrinal relating to a doctrine
dok-**try**-nuhl /dɒk'trʌɪnəl/

dodecagon plane figure with twelve
straight sides
doh-**dek**-uh-guhn /dəʊ'dɛkəɡən/

dodecahedron pl. **dodecahedra**
three-dimensional shape with twelve
plane faces
doh-dek-uh-**hee**-druhn,
pl. doh-dek-uh-**hee**-druh
/ˌdəʊdɛkə'hiːdrən/, pl. /-drə/

Sometimes also doh-dek-uh-**hed**-ruhn;
standard -s plural is also possible.

Dodecanese islands, Greece
doh-dek-uh-**neez** /ˌdəʊdɛkə'niːz/

dodo extinct flightless bird
doh-doh /'dəʊdəʊ/

Dodoma capital of Tanzania
doh-**doh**-muh /dəʊ'dəʊmə/

doggerel comic verse
dog-uh-ruhl /'dɒɡərəl/

Dogrib Canadian ethnic group
dog-rib /'dɒɡrɪb/

Doha capital of Qatar
doh-hah /'dəʊhɑː/

Doherty, Pete English musician
dokh-uhr-ti /'dɒxə(r)ti/

This British surname is variously
pronounced **dokh**-uhr-ti, **do**-huhr-ti,
doh-huhr-ti, **doh**-uhr-ti, and **dok**-uhr-ti,
depending on individual preference.

Dohnányi, Ernő Hungarian musician
air-noe **dokh**-nahn-yi /ˌɛ:(r)nøː
'dɒxnɑːnji/

Doisneau, Robert French
photographer
rob-**air** dwan-oh /rɒ,bɛ:(r) dwa'nəʊ/

dojo judo hall
doh-joh /'dəʊdʒəʊ/

Dokić, Jelena Serbian-born Australian
tennis player
yuh-**lay**-nuh **dok**-itch /jə'leɪnə 'dɒkɪtʃ/

Dolby trademark electronic
noise-reduction system
dol-bi /'dɒlbi/

dolce musical term
dol-chay /'dɒltʃeɪ/

Dolcelatte trademark Italian cheese
dol-chuh-**lah**-tay /ˌdɒltʃə'lɑːteɪ/

dolce vita life of pleasure and luxury
dol-chay vee-tuh /ˌdɒltʃeɪ 'viːtə/

doldrums state of stagnation or
depression
dol-druhmz /'dɒldrəmz/

doli capax legal term
dol-i **kap**-aks /ˌdɒli 'kapaks/

Dolin, Anton English ballet dancer
an-tuhn **dol**-in /ˌantən 'dɒlɪn/

D'Oliveira, Basil South African-born
English cricketer
dol-iv-**eer**-uh /dɒlɪ'vɪərə/

Dollfuss, Engelbert Austrian
statesman
eng-uhl-bairt **dol**-fooss /ˌɛŋəlbɛ:(r)t
'dɒlfuːs/

dolma pl. **dolmades** Greek and Turkish
dish
dol-muh, pl. dol-**mah**-*thez* /'dɒlmə,
pl. /-'mɑːðɛz/
• Standard -s plural is also possible.

dolman Turkish robe
dol-muhn /'dɒlmən/

dolmen megalithic tomb
dol-men /'dɒlmɛn/

dolmus shared taxi
dol-muush /'dɒlmʊʃ/

dolorimeter instrument for measuring
pain
dol-uh-**rim**-uh-tuhr /ˌdɒlə'rɪmətə(r)/

dolorous expressing sorrow or distress
dol-uh-ruhss /'dɒlərəs/

dolour state of sorrow or distress
dol-uhr /'dɒlə(r)/

domaine vineyard
duh-**mayn** /də'meɪn/

dombra musical instrument
dom-bruh /'dɒmbrə/

Domesday Middle English spelling of doomsday
doomz-day /'duːmzdeɪ/

domicile country that a person treats as their permanent home
dom-i-syl /'dɒmɪsʌɪl/

dominatrix pl. **dominatrices** dominating woman
dom-in-**ay**-triks,
pl. dom-in-**ay**-triss-eez
/ˌdɒmɪ'neɪtrɪks/, pl. /-'trɪsiːz/
• Standard -es plural is also possible.

Domingo, Placido Spanish tenor
plass-id-oh dom-**eeng**-goh /ˌplasɪdəʊ dɒ'mɪŋɡəʊ/

Dominic, St Spanish priest and friar
dom-in-ik /'dɒmɪnɪk/

Dominica island, Caribbean
dom-in-**ee**-kuh /ˌdɒmɪ'niːkə/

dominical relating to Sundays
duh-**min**-ik-uhl /də'mɪnɪkəl/

Dominican Roman Catholic order
duh-**min**-ik-uhn /də'mɪnɪkən/

Dominican relating to the island of Dominica
dom-in-**ee**-kuhn /ˌdɒmɪ'niːkən/

Dominican Republic country
duh-**min**-ik-uhn /də'mɪnɪkən/

dominie schoolmaster
dom-in-i /'dɒmɪni/

Domino, Fats American pianist
dom-in-oh /'dɒmɪnəʊ/

Domitian Roman emperor
duh-**mish**-uhn /də'mɪʃən/

Don river, Russia
don /dɒn/

Donatello Italian sculptor
don-uh-**tel**-oh /ˌdɒnə'tɛləʊ/

Donati, Giambattista Italian astronomer
jam-bat-**ee**-stuh don-**ah**-ti /dʒambaˌtiːstə dɒ'nɑːti/

Donatus, Aelius Roman grammarian
ee-li-uhss duh-**nay**-tuhss /ˌiːlɪəs

də'neɪtəs/

Donau see Danube

Doncaster town, England
donk-uh-stuhr /'dɒŋkəstə(r)/

Donegal county, Republic of Ireland
don-uh-**gawl** /ˌdɒnə'ɡɔːl/

Commonly also dun-uh-**gawl**.

doner kebab Turkish dish
don-uhr /'dɒnə(r)/

Established anglicization. The Turkish word is *döner*, pronounced doen-**air**.

Donets river, eastern Europe
don-**yets** /dɒ'njɛts/

Donetsk city, Ukraine
don-**etsk** /dɒ'nɛtsk/

This is the Ukrainian pronunciation; the Russian is don-**yetsk**.

Don Giovanni opera by Verdi
don juh-**vah**-ni /dɒn dʒə'vɑːni/

Dönitz, Karl German Second World War admiral
karl doe-nits /ˌkɑː(r)l 'dəːnɪts/

Donizetti, Gaetano Italian composer
gah-uh-**tah**-noh don-it-**set**-i /ɡɑːəˌtɑːnəʊ dɒnɪ'tsɛti/

donjon tower or innermost keep of a castle
don-juhn /'dɒndʒən/

Don Juan legendary Spanish nobleman
don **hwahn** /dɒn 'hwɑːn/, [dɒŋ 'xwan]

Established anglicization. There is also an old-fashioned anglicized version, don **joo**-uhn.

Donne, John English poet and preacher
dun /dʌn/

donnée (also **donné**) subject or theme of a narrative
don-ay /'dɒneɪ/

Donohoe, Amanda English actress
don-uh-hoh /'dɒnəhəʊ/

This British surname is variously pronounced **don**-uh-hoh and **dun**-uh-hoo, depending on individual preference.

Don Quixote novel by Cervantes
don kee-**hoh**-ti /dɒn kiː'həʊti/, Spanish [don ki'xote]

Established anglicization. There is also an old-fashioned anglicized version, don **kwik**-sot.

Doornik see **Tournai**

dopamine compound present in the body
doh-puh-meen /'dəʊpəmi:n/

dopiaza Indian dish
doh-pi-ah-zuh /'dəʊpiɑːzə/

doppelgänger apparition or double of a living person
dop-uhl-geng-uhr /'dɒpəl,gɛŋə(r)/

This word often appears in English as *doppelganger*, pronounced dop-uhl-gang-uhr.

Doppler, Johann Christian Austrian physicist
yoh-han krist-i-an dop-luhr /,jəʊhan ,krɪstian 'dɒplə(r)/

dor beetle
dor /dɔː(r)/

Dorado constellation
duh-rah-doh /də'rɑːdəʊ/

Dorchester town, England
dor-chist-uhr /'dɔː(r)tʃɪstə(r)/

Dordogne river and department, France
dor-doyn /dɔː(r)'dɔɪn/, [dɔrdɔɲ]
• Established anglicization.

Dordrecht city, Netherlands
dor-drekht /'dɔː(r)drɛxt/

Also known as Dort, pronounced dort.

Doré, Gustave French book illustrator
gue-stahv daw-ray /gy,stɑːv dɔː'reɪ/

dorje Buddhist symbol
dor-jay /'dɔː(r)dʒeɪ/

Dormobile trademark motor caravan
dor-muh-beel /'dɔː(r)məbiːl/

doronicum plant
duh-ron-ik-uhm /də'rɒnɪkəm/

Dorset county, England
dor-suht /'dɔː(r)sət/

Dort see **Dordrecht**

Dortmund city, Germany
dort-muunt /'dɔː(r)tmʊnt/

dory small rowing boat
daw-ri /'dɔːri/

dosa pl. **dosai** type of pancake
doh-suh, pl. doh-sy /'dəʊsə/, pl. /-sʌɪ/
• Standard -s plural is also possible.

do-si-do dance step
doh si doh /,dəʊ si 'dəʊ/

Dos Passos, John American novelist
doss pass-oss /dɒs 'pasɒs/

dossal ornamental cloth
doss-uhl /'dɒsəl/

Dos Santos, José Eduardo president of Angola
zhuuz-ay uhd-war-doo duush
sant-uush /ʒʊ,zeɪ əd,wɑː(r)dəʊ dʊʃ 'santʊʃ/

dossier collection of documents
doss-i-ay /'dɒsieɪ/

Sometimes also doss-i-uhr.

dost archaic second person singular present of do
dust /dʌst/

Dostoevsky, Fyodor (also **Dostoyevsky**) Russian novelist
fyod-uhr dost-uh-yef-ski /,fjɒdə(r) ,dɒstə'jɛfski/

doth archaic third person singular present of do
duth /dʌθ/

Douala city, Cameroon
doo-ah-luh /du:'ɑːlə/

Douay Bible translation of the Bible
dow-ay /'daʊeɪ/

The place in France, now spelt Douai, is pronounced doo-ay.

Doubs river and department, France
doo /du:/

douce sober and sedate
dooss /du:s/

douceur financial inducement
doo-sur /du:'sə:(r)/

Douglas-Home, Alec British statesman
dug-luhss hyoom /,dʌgləs 'hju:m/

doula woman giving support to another woman during childbirth
doo-luh /'du:lə/

Doulton trademark type of pottery or porcelain
dohl-tuhn /'dəʊltən/

dour severe and gloomy
door /'dʊə(r)/

Commonly also dow-uhr.

Douro river, Portugal
door-oh /'dʊərəʊ/, ['doru]

Established anglicization. The Spanish name is Duero, pronounced dwair-oh.

Dowding, Hugh British Marshal of the RAF
dow-ding /'daʊdɪŋ/

dower widow's share for life of her husband's estate
dow-uhr /'daʊə(r)/

Dow Jones index New York Stock Exchange shares index
dow **johnz** /daʊ 'dʒəʊnz/

Dowson, Ernest English poet
dow-suhn /'daʊsən/

doxycycline antibiotic
dok-si-**sy**-kleen /ˌdɒksi'saɪkliːn/

Doyle, Arthur Conan Scottish novelist
koh-nuhn **doyl** /ˌkəʊnən 'dɔɪl/

D'Oyly Carte, Richard English impresario and producer
doy-li **kart** /ˌdɔɪli 'kɑː(r)t/

dracaena shrub or tree
druh-**see**-nuh /drə'siːnə/

drachm unit of weight
dram /dram/

drachma pl. **drachmae** former currency unit, Greece
drak-muh, pl. **drak**-mee /'drakmə/, pl. /-miː/
• Standard -s plural is also possible.

Draco Athenian legislator
dray-koh /'dreɪkəʊ/

draconian harsh and severe
druh-**koh**-ni-uhn /drə'kəʊniən/

Dracula novel by Bram Stoker
drak-yuul-uh /'drakjʊlə/

dragée sweet
drah-zhay /'drɑːʒeɪ/

Draghi, Giovanni Italian composer
juh-**vah**-ni **drah**-gi /dʒə,vɑːni 'drɑːgi/

dragoman interpreter or guide
drag-oh-muhn /'dragəʊmən/

dragonnade persecution by Louis XIV against French Protestants
drag-uh-**nayd** /ˌdragə'neɪd/

dragoon cavalry soldier
druh-**goon** /drə'guːn/

Drakensberg Mountains range of mountains, southern Africa
drah-kuhnz-burg /'drɑːkənz,bə:(r)g/

Dralon trademark synthetic textile
dray-lon /'dreɪlɒn/

dram small drink of whisky or other spirits
dram /dram/

dram currency unit, Armenia
drahm /drɑːm/

Dramamine trademark antihistamine
dram-uh-meen /'draməmiːn/

Drambuie trademark Scotch whisky liqueur
dram-**byoo**-i /dram'bjuːi/

Drammen port, Norway
dram-uhn /'dramən/

Drang nach Osten former German policy of eastward expansion
drang nahkh **ost**-uhn /ˌdraŋ nɑːx 'ɒstən/

Dravidian family of languages spoken in India and Sri Lanka
druh-**vid**-i-uhn /drə'vɪdiən/

dreidel four-sided spinning top with a Hebrew letter on each side
dray-duhl /'dreɪdəl/

Dreiser, Theodore American novelist
dry-suhr /'draɪsə(r)/

Drenthe province, Netherlands
dren-tuh /'drɛntə/

Dresden city, Germany
drez-duhn /'drɛzdən/, ['dre:sdn]
• Established anglicization.

dressage art of riding and training a horse
dress-ahzh /'drɛsɑːʒ/

Dreux town, France
droe /drø/

Dreyfus, Alfred French army officer
al-fruhd **dray**-fuhss /ˌalfrəd 'dreɪfəs/, [alfrɛd drɛfys]
• Established anglicization.

Dreyfuss, Richard American actor
dry-fuhss /'draɪfəs/

Dr see Doctor

Drogheda port, Republic of Ireland
droy-uh-duh /'drɔɪədə/

drogue device towed behind a boat or aircraft
drohg /drəʊg/

droid robot
droyd /drɔɪd/

dromaeosaur dinosaur; also called **dromaeosaurid**
droh-mi-oh-sor /'drəʊmiəʊsɔː(r)/

dromaeosaurid dinosaur; also called **dromaeosaur**
droh-mi-oh-**saw**-rid /ˌdrəʊmiəʊ'sɔːrɪd/

dromedary Arabian camel
drom-uh-duh-ri /'drɒmədəri/

Sometimes also **drum-uh-duh-ri**.

dromond medieval ship
drom-uhnd /'drɒmənd/

Sometimes also **drum-uhnd**.

dromos pl. **dromoi** passage leading into
an ancient Greek temple or tomb
drom-oss, pl. **drom-oy** /'drɒmɒs/, pl.
/-mɔɪ/

droshky Russian carriage
drosh-ki /'drɒʃki/

Drouzhba resort, Bulgaria
droozh-buh /'druːʒbə/

drugget floor covering
drug-it /'drʌgɪt/

Druid priest in the ancient Celtic religion
droo-id /'druːɪd/

Drumcondra suburb of Dublin
drum-kond-ruh /drʌm'kɒndrə/

drumlin small hill
drum-lin /'drʌmlɪn/

drupe fruit
droop /druːp/

drupel individual drupes forming a fruit
such as a raspberry
droo-puhl /'druːpəl/

Drury Lane site in London
droor-i /'drʊəri/

Druze political and religious sect of
Islamic origin
drooz /druːz/

dryad nymph
dry-ad /'drʌɪad/

dryas plant
dry-uhss /'drʌɪəs/

Dryopithecus fossil anthropoid ape
dry-uh-pith-uh-kuhss /ˌdrʌɪə'pɪθəkəs/

Dubai state, United Arab Emirates
doo-by /duː'bʌɪ/

Du Barry, Jeanne Bécu French
courtier
zhan bay-kue due barr-ee /ˌʒan beɪˌky
dy ba'riː/

Dubček, Alexander Czechoslovak
statesman
al-ek-san-duhr duub-chek
/ˌaləksandə(r) 'dʊbtʃɛk/

dubiety state of being doubtful
dyoo-by-it-i /djuː'bʌɪti/

dubnium chemical element
dub-ni-uhm /'dʌbniəm/

Dubno city, Ukraine
doob-nuh /'duːbnə/

Du Bois, W. E. B. American writer
doo boyz /duː'bɔɪz/

Dubonnet trademark French red
vermouth
dyoo-bon-ay /djuː'bɒneɪ/, [dybɔnɛ]
• Established anglicization.

Dubrovnik port, Croatia
duub-rov-nik /dʊ'brɒvnɪk/

Dubuffet, Jean French painter
zhah(ng) due-bue-fay /ˌʒɑ̃ dyby'feɪ/

Dubuque city, US
duh-byook /də'bjuːk/

ducat gold coin
duk-uht /'dʌkət/

Duccio Italian painter
doo-choh /'duːtʃəʊ/

Duce title assumed by Benito Mussolini
doo-chay /'duːtʃeɪ/

Ducett, Lyse Canadian BBC journalist
leez doo-set /ˌliːz duː'sɛt/

Duchamp, Marcel French-born
American artist
mar-sel due-shah(ng) /mɑː(r)ˌsɛl
dy'ʃɑ̃/

Duchenne form of muscular dystrophy
doo-shen /duː'ʃɛn/

duchesse satin
doo-shess /duː'ʃɛs/

duduk woodwind instrument
duud-ook /dʊ'duːk/

duende quality of passion and
inspiration
doo-en-day /duː'ɛndeɪ/

duenna governess
doo-en-uh /duː'ɛnə/

Duero see **Douro**

Dufay, Guillaume French composer
gee-yohm due-fay /giːˌjəʊm dy'feɪ/

Dufy, Raoul French painter and textile
designer
rah-ool due-fee /rɑːˌuːl dy'fiː/

dugite venomous snake
dyoo-gyt /'djuːgʌɪt/

duiker African antelope
dy-kuhr /'dʌɪkə(r)/

Duisburg city, Germany
dyooz-burg /ˈdjuːzbə(r)g/, German
[ˈdyːsbʊrk]
• Established anglicization.

Duisenberg, Wim Dutch banker and
politician
wim dow-suhn-bairkh /ˌwɪm
ˈdaʊsənbɛː(r)x/, [ˈdœɪsənbɛrx]
• This is the usual pronunciation in
English.

Dujail, al- town, Iraq
uh-**duu**-jyl /ədʊˈdʒʌɪl/
• See ARABIC panel.

Dukas, Paul French composer
pol due-**kass** /ˌpɒl dyˈkas/

dukun traditional healer
doo-kun /ˈduːkʌn/

dulcamara extract of woody nightshade
dul-kuh-**mair**-uh /ˌdʌlkəˈmɛːrə/

dulcet sweet and soothing
dul-suht /ˈdʌlsət/

dulcian musical instrument
dul-si-uhn /ˈdʌlsiən/

dulciana organ stop
dul-si-**ah**-nuh /ˌdʌlsiˈɑːnə/

dulcimer musical instrument
dul-sim-uhr /ˈdʌlsɪmə(r)/

dulcitone musical instrument
dul-sit-ohn /ˈdʌlsɪtəʊn/

dulia reverence accorded to saints
and angels
dyuul-y-uh /djʊˈlʌɪə/

Dulles airport in Washington DC
dul-uhss /ˈdʌləs/

dulse edible seaweed
dulss /dʌls/

Duluth port, US
duh-**looth** /dəˈluːθ/

Duma lower house of the Russian
parliament
doo-muh /ˈduːmə/

Dumas, Alexandre (fils) French
novelist
al-ek-**sah(ng)**-druh due-**mah (feess)**
/alɛkˌsɑ̃drə dyˈmɑː (fiːs)/

More anglicized pronunciations, such as
dyoo-mah or **doo**-mah, are also common.

Du Maurier, Daphne English novelist
doo **morr**-i-ay /duː ˈmɒrieɪ/

Dumbarton town, Scotland
dum-**bar**-tuhn /dʌmˈbɑː(r)tən/

Dumfries town, Scotland
dum-**freess** /dʌmˈfriːs/

dumka pl. **dumky** Slavic music
duum-kuh, pl. **duum**-ki /ˈdʊmkə/, pl.
/ˈdʊmki/
• Standard -s plural is also possible.

Dumyat see **Damietta**

Dunajec river, Poland
doo-**ny**-ets /duːˈnʌɪɛts/

dunam measure of land area in the
former Turkish empire
duun-uhm /ˈdʊnəm/

Dunbar, William Scottish poet
dun-**bar** /dʌnˈbɑː(r)/

Dunbartonshire former county,
Scotland
dun-**bar**-tuhn-shuhr
/dʌnˈbɑː(r)tənʃə(r)/

Dunblane town, Scotland
dun-**blayn** /dʌnˈbleɪn/

Dundalk town, Republic of Ireland
dun-**dawk** /dʌnˈdɔːk/

Dunedin city, New Zealand
dun-**ee**-din /dʌˈniːdɪn/

Dunfermline town, Scotland
dun-**furm**-lin /dʌnˈfəː(r)mlɪn/

Dungarvan town, Republic of Ireland
dun-**gar**-vuhn /dʌnˈgɑː(r)vən/

Dungeness crab type of crab
dun-juh-**ness** /ˌdʌndʒəˈnɛs/

Dunhuang town, China
duun-**khwang** /ˌdʊnˈxwaŋ/

Dunker sect of Baptist Christians
dunk-uhr /ˈdʌŋkə(r)/

Dunkirk port, France
dun-**kurk** /dʌnˈkəː(r)k/

Established anglicization. The French name
is Dunkerque, pronounced doe(ng)-**kairk**
[dœ̃kɛrk].

Dun Laoghaire port, Republic of
Ireland
dun **leer**-i /dʌn ˈlɪəri/

Dunlop, John Boyd Scottish inventor
dun-lop /ˈdʌnlɒp/

This British surname is variously
pronounced dun-**lop** and **dun**-lop,
depending on individual preference. The
Scottish place name is dun-**lop**, and the tyre
and sports goods company is **dun**-lop.

Dunmow, Great town, England
dun-moh /ˈdʌnməʊ/

Duns Scotus, John Scottish theologian and scholar
dunz **skoh**-tuhss /dʌnz 'skəʊtəs/

Dunst, Kirsten American actress
keer-stuhn dunst /ˌkɪə(r)stən 'dʌnst/

Dunstable, John English composer
dun-stuh-buhl /'dʌnstəbəl/

Dunstan, St Anglo-Saxon prelate
dun-stuhn /'dʌnstən/

duodenary based on the number twelve
dyoo-uh-**dee**-nuh-ri /ˌdjuːə'diːnəri/

duodenum pl. **duodena** part of the small intestine
dyoo-uh-**dee**-nuhm,
pl. dyoo-uh-**dee**-nuh /ˌdjuːə'diːnəm/,
pl. /-'diːnə/
• Standard -s plural is also possible.

duomo Italian cathedral
dwoh-moh /'dwəʊməʊ/

Duparc, Henri French composer
ah(ng)-ree due-**park** /ˌɑ̃ˌriː dyˈpɑː(r)k/

dupatta Indian scarf
duup-**ut**-uh /dʊˈpʌtə/

dupion silk fabric
dyoo-pi-uhn /'djuːpiən/

duple musical term
dyoo-puhl /'djuːpəl/

dupondius pl. **dupondii** Roman coin
dyoo-**pon**-di-uhss, dyoo-**pon**-di-y /djuːˈpɒndiəs/, pl. /-diaɪ/

du Pré, Jacqueline English cellist
zhak-leen due **pray** /ˌʒaklin dy 'preɪ/

Dupuytren, Guillaume French surgeon
gee-**yohm** due-pwee-**tra(ng)** /giːˌjəʊm dypwiːˈtrɛ̃/

Dupuytren's contracture medical condition
doop-**wee**-truhnss /duːˈpwiːtrəns/

Duque de Caxias city, Brazil
doo-ki ji kuh-**shee**-uhss /ˌduːki dʒi kəˈʃiːəs/

Duralumin trademark alloy of aluminium
dyuu-**ral**-yuum-in /djʊˈraljʊmɪn/

dura mater membrane enveloping the brain and spinal cord
dyoor-uh **may**-tuhr /ˌdjʊərə 'meɪtə(r)/

Duran Duran English pop group
dyuu-**ran** dyuu-**ran** /djʊˌran djʊ'ran/

Durango state, Mexico
doo-**rang**-goh /duːˈraŋgəʊ/

Durão Barroso, José Manuel Portuguese politician
zhuuz-**ay** muhn-**wel** duu-**row(ng)** buh-**roh**-zoo /ʒʊˌzeɪ mənˌwɛl dʊˌrãʊ bəˈrəʊzuː/
• See **PORTUGUESE** panel.

Duras, Marguerite French novelist
mar-guh-**reet** due-**rahss** /mɑːˌ(r)gəˌriːt dyˈrɑːs/

Durazzo see **Durrës**

durbar court of an Indian ruler
dur-bar /'dəː(r)bɑː(r)/

Dürer, Albrecht German engraver and painter
al-brekht **due**-ruhr /ˌalbrɛçt 'dyːrə(r)/

A more anglicized pronunciation, **dyoor**-uhr, is also very common.

duress threats or violence
dyuu-**ress** /djʊ'rɛs/

Durey, Louis French composer
lwee due-**ray** /ˌlwiː dyˈreɪ/

Durga Hindu goddess
door-guh /'dʊə(r)gə/

Durgapur city, India
door-guh-**poor** /ˌdʊə(r)gəˈpʊə(r)/

Durham city, England
durr-uhm /'dʌrəm/

durian tropical fruit
door-i-uhn /'dʊəriən/

Durkheim, Émile French sociologist
ay-**meel** durk-**hym** /eɪˌmiːl 'dəː(r)khʌɪm/, [emil dyrkɛm]
• Established anglicization.

durra kind of corn
duu-ruh /'dʊrə/

Durrell, Gerald English zoologist and writer
durr-uhl /'dʌrəl/
• The same pronunciation is used for his brother, the writer Lawrence Durrell.

Durrës port, Albania
duu-ruhss /'dʊrəs/

The Italian name is Durazzo, pronounced duu-**rat**-soh.

durum a kind of wheat
dyoor-uhm /'djʊərəm/

Duse, Eleonora Italian actress
el-ay-on-**aw**-ruh **doo**-zay /ɛleɪˌɒnɔːrə 'duːzeɪ/

Dushanbe capital of Tajikistan
doo-shan-**bay** /duːʃanˈbeɪ/

Dutch

Dutch (*Nederlands* in Dutch, pronounced **nay**-duhr-luntss) is a West Germanic language spoken by about 22 million people, mainly in the Netherlands and Belgium. It is also the official language of Surinam and of the Netherlands Antilles. Dutch spoken in Belgium is more commonly known as Flemish, but the two are considered a single language. The Dutch given here is, as always, somewhat anglicized in line with BBC policy and the constraints of the phonetic respelling.

Vowels

Dutch vowels are short before two or more consonants, and before one consonant at the end of a word. They are commonly long before a single consonant followed by another vowel, and often also before R.

A is pronounced u when short, as in vun for *Van*. It is pronounced ah when long.

AA is pronounced ah. *Haarlem* is **har**-luhm.

E is pronounced e when short, and close to ay (although not diphthongal in Dutch) or air when long.

EE is pronounced close to ay.

EU is pronounced oe (as in French *peu*).

I is pronounced i when short, and ee when long.

IE is pronounced ee.

O is pronounced o when short, and close to oh (although not diphthongal in Dutch) or aw when long.

OE is pronounced oo. *Bloem* is bloom.

OO is pronounced oh or aw. *Boom* is bohm.

U is pronounced ue (as in German *fünf*) when short, and ue (as in French *vu*) when long. The short version is often pronounced as uu in English.

UU is pronounced ue (as in French *vu*).

Y is pronounced ee. Y is sometimes found in old spellings, corresponding to the modern IJ, in which case it should be pronounced as IJ—see below.

Some of these vowels may be reduced to schwa (uh) in unstressed syllables in Dutch, and perhaps more so in anglicized Dutch.

AAI is pronounced close to y (as in *cry*).

AAU, AU, and OU are pronounced close to ow.

EEU is pronounced as long E followed by w. In anglicized Dutch the closest we can get is **ay**-oo.

EI and IJ are pronounced between English y and ay. Traditionally this diphthong is treated as y in English, which is also the case in this dictionary. *Van Dijk* is dyk.

IEU is pronounced as ee followed by w. In anglicized Dutch the closest we can get is yoo. *Nieuw* is nyoo.

OEI is pronounced as oo followed by y. The closest we can get is **oo**-i.

OOI is pronounced close to oy.

UI and UY are pronounced oey (as in French *fauteuil*). Pronunciation of this diphthong has proven particularly difficult for English speakers, and in some anglicizations it is treated as ow, as in **dow**-suhn-bairkh for *Wim Duisenberg*. Sometimes it is treated as y, as in zy-duhr for *Zuider Zee*. And sometimes oy or ay are used too!

Consonants

B, D, F, H, K, M, P, T, and Z are pronounced as in English, although B, D, and Z are pronounced p, t, and s at the end of a word.

C is pronounced k before A, O, and U, and before all consonants except H. It is pronounced s before E, I, and Y.

CH is usually pronounced kh (always as in Scottish *loch* in Dutch, never German *ich*). Sometimes it is sh, and in initial position in personal names it may also be k. *Echt* is ekht, *Chinees* is shee-**nayss**, and *Christus* is **krist**-uess.

G is pronounced as kh, or as kh with added voicing (i.e. pronounced with vibration of the vocal cords. IPA is [ɣ]).

J is pronounced y.

N is pronounced as n, but can be silent at the end of a word.

NG is pronounced ng, never ng-g. The combination INGA is ing-khah.

PH is pronounced f.

QU is pronounced kw.

SCH is pronounced skh. *Schiphol* is **skhip**-hol. At the end of a word it is pronounced s. *Bosch* is boss.

SJ and STJ are pronounced sh.

TH is pronounced t.

V is pronounced v, but with weak voicing, so f is sometimes preferred. We treat this sound as v.

W is pronounced like v, but with much lighter contact between lip and teeth. We treat this sound as w.

Stress

Stress usually falls on the first syllable. The following prefixes, however, are always unstressed: BE-, GE-, ER-, HER-, VER-, and ONT-. *Bedenken* is buh-**denk**-uhn.

Dussehra (also **Dasehra**) Hindu festival
dush-uh-ruh /'dʌʃərə/

Düsseldorf city, Germany
duuss-uhl-dorf /'dʊsəldɔː(r)f/,
['dʏsldɔrf]
• Established anglicization.

duumvir officials holding a joint office
dyoo-**um**-vuhr /djuː'ʌmvə(r)/

duumvirate coalition of two people
having joint authority
dyoo-**um**-virr-uht /djuː'ʌmvɪrət/

Duvalier, François Haitian statesman
frah(ng)-**swah** due-val-**yay** /frɑ̃,swɑː
dyval'jeɪ/

dux pl. **duces** top pupil in a school or class
duks, pl. **dyoo**-seez /dʌks/, pl.
/'djuːsiːz/

Dvořák, Antonín Czech composer
an-tuh-neen **dvor**-zhahk /,antəniːn
'dvɔː(r)ʒɑːk/

dwam state of semi-consciousness
dwahm /dwɑːm/

Dyak see **Dayak**

dybbuk pl. **dybbukim** wandering spirit
dib-uuk, pl. **dib**-uuk-im /'dɪbʊk/, pl.
/-kɪm/
• Standard -s plural is also possible.

Dyfed former county, Wales
duv-ed /'dʌvɛd/, ['dəvɛd]

Dynamo part of the name of several
European football teams
dy-nuh-moh /'dʌɪnəməʊ/

This is the usual anglicization. The German
pronunciation, for example, is
due-**nah**-moh [dy'naːmo] and the Russian
is din-**ah**-muh [dɪ'nama].

dynast member of a powerful family
din-uhst /'dɪnəst/

Commonly also **dy**-nuhst.

dynasty line of hereditary rulers of a
country
din-uh-sti /'dɪnəsti/

Commonly also **dy**-nuh-sti.

dyne unit of force
dyn /dʌɪn/

dynode intermediate electrode
dy-nohd /'dʌɪnəʊd/

dysarthria difficult or unclear
articulation of speech
diss-**ar**-thri-uh /dɪs'ɑː(r)θriə/

dyscrasia abnormal or disordered state
of the body or of a bodily part
disk-**ray**-zi-uh /dɪs'kreɪziə/

dysentery infection of the intestines
diss-uhn-tri /'dɪsəntri/

dysgraphia inability to write coherently
diss-**graf**-i-uh /dɪs'grafiə/

dyskinesia abnormality or impairment
of voluntary movement
disk-in-**ee**-zi-uh /,dɪskɪniːziə/

dyslalia inability to articulate
comprehensible speech
diss-**lay**-li-uh /dɪs'leɪliə/

dyslexia reading disorder
diss-**lek**-si-uh /dɪs'lɛksiə/

dysphasia language disorder
diss-**fay**-zi-uh /dɪs'feɪziə/

dysphemism derogatory or unpleasant
term
diss-fuh-miz-uhm /'dɪsfəmɪzəm/

dyspnoea difficult or laboured breathing
disp-**nee**-uh /dɪsp'niːə/

dyspraxia developmental disorder
disp-**rak**-si-uh /dɪs'praksiə/

dysprosium chemical element
disp-**roh**-zi-uhm /dɪs'prəʊziəm/

dysthymia depression
diss-**thy**-mi-uh /dɪs'θʌɪmiə/

dystocia difficult birth
dist-**oh**-shuh /dɪs'təʊʃə/

dystrophy disorder in which an organ
wastes away
dist-ruh-fi /'dɪstrəfi/

Dzaoudzi city, Mayotte and the Comoros
dzowd-zi /'dzaʊdzi/

Dzerzhinsk city, Russia
dzuhr-**zhinsk** /dzə(r)'ʒɪnsk/

Dzerzhinsky, Feliks Russian Bolshevik
leader
fay-liks dzuhr-**zhin**-ski /,feɪlɪks
dzə(r)'ʒɪnski/

dzo (also **dzho** or **zho**) hybrid of a cow
and a yak
zhoh /ʒəʊ/

Dzongkha official language of Bhutan
dzong-kuh /'dzʊŋkə/

E

Eadwig king of England; also called
Edwy
ay-uhd-wi /ˈeɪədwi/

Sometimes also **ed**-wig.

Eakins, Thomas American painter and
photographer
ee-kinz /ˈiːkɪnz/

Earhart, Amelia American aviator
uh-**mee**-li-uh **air**-hart /əˌmiːliə
ˈɛː(r)hɑː(r)t/

Earp, Wyatt American gambler and
marshal
wy-uht **urp** /ˌwʌɪət ˈəː(r)p/

East Kilbride town, Scotland
eest kil-**bryd** /ˌiːst kɪlˈbrʌɪd/

eau de cologne toilet water
oh duh kuh-**lohn** /ˌəʊ də kəˈləʊn/

eau de Nil pale green
oh duh **neel** /ˌəʊ də ˈniːl/

eau de toilette dilute perfume
oh duh twah-**let** /ˌəʊ də twɑːˈlɛt/

eau de vie brandy
oh duh **vee** /ˌəʊ də ˈviː/

Ebadi, Shirin Iranian activist and
Nobel laureate
shirr-**een** eb-uh-**dee** /ʃɪˌriːn ɛbəˈdiː/

Ebola fever infectious disease
ee-**boh**-luh /iːˈbəʊlə/

Ebonics American Black English
eb-**on**-iks /ɛˈbɒnɪks/

Eboracum Roman name for York
ee-**borr**-uh-kuhm /iːˈbɒrəkəm/

Ebro river, Spain
ee-broh /ˈiːbrəʊ/, [ˈeβɾo]
• Established anglicization.

ebullient cheerful and full of energy
uh-**bul**-yuhnt /əˈbʌljənt/

Sometimes also uh-**buul**-yuhnt.

Ecce Homo painting of Christ
ek-ay **hoh**-moh /ˌɛkeɪ ˈhəʊməʊ/

ecchymosis pl. **ecchymoses** skin
discoloration
ek-im-**oh**-siss, pl. ek-im-**oh**-seez
/ˌɛkɪˈməʊsɪs/, pl. /-siːz/

Ecclesiastes book of the Bible
uh-klee-zi-**ast**-eez /əˌkliːziˈastiːz/

ecdysis shedding of skin
ek-diss-iss /ˈɛkdɪsɪs/

echelon level or rank
esh-uh-lon /ˈɛʃəlɒn/

echeveria succulent plant
etch-uh-**veer**-i-uh /ˌɛtʃəˈvɪəriə/

echidna spiny egg-laying mammal
ek-**id**-nuh /ɛˈkɪdnə/

echinacea flower used in herbal
medicine
ek-in-**ay**-shuh /ˌɛkɪˈneɪʃə/

echocardiogram medical test of
the heart
ek-oh-**kar**-di-oh-gram
/ˌɛkəʊˈkɑː(r)diəʊgram/

echolalia meaningless repetition of
words and phrases
ek-oh-**lay**-li-uh /ˌɛkəʊˈleɪliə/

echt authentic and typical
ekht /ɛxt/, German [ɛçt]

eclampsia convulsive disorder
ek-**lamp**-si-uh /ɛˈklampsiə/

éclat brilliant display or effect
ay-**klah** /eɪˈklɑː/

eclogue short pastoral poem
ek-log /ˈɛklɒg/

Eco, Umberto Italian novelist and
semiotician
oom-**bair**-toh **ay**-koh /uːmˌbɛː(r)təʊ
ˈeɪkəʊ/

E. coli bacterium which can cause food
poisoning
ee **koh**-ly /ˌiː ˈkəʊlʌɪ/

ecology branch of biology
ek-**ol**-uh-ji /ɛˈkɒlədʒi/

Commonly also ee-**kol**-uh-ji.

economic relating to economics or the
economy
ek-uh-**nom**-ik /ˌɛkəˈnɒmɪk/

Commonly also ee-kuh-**nom**-ik.

ecossaise country dance
ek-oss-**ayz** /ˌɛkɒˈseɪz/

écru light fawn colour
ay-kroo /ˈeɪkru:/

ECOWAS Economic Community of West African States
ek-**oh**-uhss /ɛˈkəʊəs/

ectomorph lightly built person
ek-toh-morf /ˈɛktəʊmɔ:(r)f/

ectopic in an abnormal place or position
ek-**top**-ik /ɛkˈtɒpɪk/

ecu (also **ECU**) European Currency Unit, former term for the euro
ek-yoo /ˈɛkju:/

Many pronunciations were used, including **ayk**-yoo, **eek**-yoo and ayk-**yoo**.

Ecuador country
ek-wuh-dor /ˈɛkwədɔ:(r)/, Spanish [ekwaˈðor]
• Established anglicization.

ecumenical representing a number of different Christian churches
ek-yoo-**men**-ik-uhl /ɛkju:ˈmɛnɪkəl/

Sometimes also eek-yoo-**men**-ik-uhl.

eczema skin condition
eks-uh-muh /ˈɛksəmə/

Sometimes pronounced uhg-**zee**-muh in AM.

Edam Dutch cheese
ee-dam /ˈi:dam/, [eːˈdɑm]
• Established anglicization.

edamame Japanese soybean dish
ed-uh-**mam**-ay /ˌɛdəˈmameɪ/

Edda collection of Old Norse poems
ed-uh /ˈɛdə/

edelweiss European mountain plant
ay-duhl-vyss /ˈeɪdəlvaɪs/

Edexcel British examination board
ed-ek-**sel** /ˌɛdɛkˈsɛl/

Eden biblical paradise
ee-duhn /ˈi:dən/

edh see **eth**

Ediacaran period of geological time
ee-di-**ak**-uh-ruhn /ˌi:diˈakərən/

edict official order or proclamation
ee-dikt /ˈi:dɪkt/

edify instruct intellectually
ed-i-fy /ˈɛdɪfʌɪ/

Edinburgh capital of Scotland
ed-in-buh-ruh /ˈɛdɪnbərə/

Commonly also **ed**-in-bruh.

Edirne city and province, Turkey
ed-**eer**-nuh /ɛˈdɪə(r)nə/

Edison, Thomas American inventor
ed-iss-uhn /ˈɛdɪsən/

Edmonton city, Canada
ed-muhn-tuhn /ˈɛdməntən/

Edo former name for Tokyo
ed-oh /ˈɛdəʊ/

Edwardiana articles from the reign of Edward VII
ed-wor-di-**ah**-nuh /ɛdˌwɔ:(r)diˈɑ:nə/

Edwy king of England; also called **Eadwig**
ed-wi /ˈɛdwi/

eejit 'idiot' (Irish and Scottish)
ee-jit /ˈi:dʒɪt/

Egeland, Jan Norwegian UN official
yahn **ay**-guh-lan /ˌjɑ:n ˈeɪɡələn/

Eelam proposed Tamil homeland in Sri Lanka
ee-luhm /ˈi:ləm/

e'en literary form of 'even'
een /i:n/

e'er literary form of 'ever'
air /ɛ:(r)/

effendi man of high social standing in an Arab country
ef-**en**-di /ɛˈfɛndi/

effete over-refined
ef-**eet** /ɛˈfi:t/

efficacy ability to produce a desired result
ef-ik-uh-si /ˈɛfɪkəsi/

effleurage form of massage
ef-luh-**rahzh** /ˌɛfləˈrɑ:ʒ/

effulgent shining brightly
ef-**ul**-juhnt /ɛˈfʌldʒənt/

Sometimes also ef-**uul**-juhnt.

EFTPOS Electronic Funds Transfer at Point Of Sale
eft-poz /ˈɛftpɒz/

egad expression of surprise
ee-**gad** /i:ˈɡad/

Eger town, Hungary
eg-air /ˈɛɡɛ:(r)/

ego a person's sense of self-esteem
ee-goh /ˈi:ɡəʊ/

Also pronounced **eg**-oh; both pronunciations are also possible in words such as *egocentric*, *egoism*, etc.

egregious outstandingly bad
uhg-**ree**-juhss /ə'gri:dʒəs/

egress going out
ee-gress /'i:grɛs/

egressive type of speech sound
ig-**ress**-iv /ɪ'grɛsɪv/

egret white heron
ee-gruht /'i:grət/

Ehle, Jennifer British actress
ee-li /'i:li/

Ehrlich, Paul German medical scientist
powl air-likh /,paʊl 'ɛ:(r)lɪç/

Eichmann, Adolf German Nazi leader
ah-dolf **ykh**-man /,ɑ:dɒlf 'ʌɪçman/

Eid (also **Id**) Muslim festival
eed /i:d/

Eid-ul-Fitr, pronounced **eed** uhl **fit**-uhr,
marks the end of Ramadan. Eid-ul-Adha,
pronounced **eed** uhl **ud**-huh, marks the
culmination of the hajj.

eidos philosophical term
y-doss /'ʌɪdɒs/

This pronunciation is also used for the
computer game company of the same name.

Eiffel, Gustave French engineer
gue-**stahv** ef-el /gys,tɑ:v ɛ'fɛl/

An anglicized pronunciation, **y-fuhl**, is used
for the Eiffel Tower.

Eiger mountain peak, Switzerland
y-guhr /'ʌɪgə(r)/

Eigg island, Scotland
eg /ɛg/

Eilat (also **Elat**) port, Israel
ay-lat /eɪ'lat/

Eilidh Gaelic girl's name
ay-li /'eɪli/

Eindhoven city, Netherlands
ynd-hoh-vuhn /'ʌɪnd,həʊvən/,
[ˈɛintho:vəˈ(n)]
• Established anglicization; see DUTCH
panel.

Einfühlung empathy
yn-fue-luung /'ʌɪn,fy:lʊŋ/

Einstein, Albert German-born
American theoretical physicist
yn-styn /'ʌɪnstʌɪn/

Established anglicization; the German
pronunciation is **yn-shtyn**.

einsteinium chemical element
yn-**sty**-ni-uhm /ʌɪn'stʌɪniəm/

Éire Gaelic name for Ireland
air-uh /'ɛ:rə/

Eirene Greek goddess
y-ree-ni /ʌɪ'ri:ni/

Eisenhower, Dwight David American
president
y-zuhn-how-uhr /'ʌɪzən,haʊə(r)/

Eisenstadt city, Austria
y-zuhn-shtat /'ʌɪzən,ʃtat/

eisteddfod, pl. **eisteddfodau** Welsh
festival of music and poetry
y-steth-vod, pl. y-steth-**vod**-y
/ʌɪ'stɛðvɒd/, pl. /ʌɪstɛð'vɒdʌɪ/

either one of two
y-thuhr /'ʌɪðə(r)/

Equally commonly ee-thuhr. Traditionally,
BR is y-thuhr and AM is ee-thuhr.

ejido Mexican communally farmed land
ekh-ee-thoh /ɛ'xi:ðəʊ/

Ejiofor, Chiwetel British actor
chee-wuh-tel ee-ji-uh-for /,tʃi:wətɛl
'i:dʒiəfɔ:(r)/

Ekaterinburg (also **Yekaterinburg**)
town, Russia
yuh-kat-uh-**reen**-burg
/jə,katə'ri:nbə:(r)g/, [jɛkətʲɪrʲɪnˈburk]
• Established anglicization.

eke make something last longer
eek /i:k/

élan style
ay-**lan** /eɪ'lan/

eland antelope
ee-luhnd /'i:lənd/

Elat see Eilat

Elba island, Italy
el-buh /'ɛlbə/

ElBaradei, Mohamed Egyptian
director of the International Atomic
Energy Agency
muh-**ham**-uhd uhl **barr**-uh-dy
/mə,haməd əl 'barədʌɪ/
• This is his preferred anglicization.

Elbasan town, Albania
el-buh-**san** /,ɛlbə'san/

Elbe river, central Europe
el-buh /'ɛlbə/

There is also an older anglicization, elb.

Elbrus mountain, Caucasus
el-**brooss** /ɛl'bru:s/

Elche town, Spain
el-chay /'ɛltʃeɪ/

El Dorado fictitious place
el duh-**rah**-doh /ˌɛl dəˈrɑːdəʊ/

electoral relating to an election
uh-**lek**-tuh-ruhl /əˈlɛktərəl/

Electra Greek mythological character
uh-**lek**-truh /əˈlɛktrə/

electrolysis chemical decomposition
el-ek-**trol**-uh-siss /ˌɛlɛkˈtrɒlǝsɪs/

eleemosynary relating to charity
el-i-ee-**moz**-in-uh-ri /ˌɛliːˈmɒzɪnəri/

elegiac relating to an elegy
el-uh-**jy**-uhk /ˌɛləˈdʒʌɪək/

elemi resin used in varnishes
el-uh-mi /ˈɛləmi/

elephantiasis swelling of a limb
el-uh-**fuhn**-ty-uh-siss /ˌɛləfənˈtʌɪəsɪs/

elephantine characteristic of elephants
el-uh-**fan**-tyn /ɛləˈfantʌɪn/

Elgar, Edward British composer
el-gar /ˈɛlgɑː(r)/

Elgin town, Scotland
el-gin /ˈɛlgɪn/

This is also the appropriate pronunciation for the Elgin Marbles from the Parthenon. Many American towns of the same name are pronounced **el**-jin.

El Greco Cretan-born Spanish painter
el **grek**-oh /ɛl ˈgrɛkəʊ/

Eli biblical character
ee-ly /ˈiːlʌɪ/

eligible having the right to do something
el-ij-uh-buhl /ˈɛlɪdʒəbəl/

Elijah Hebrew prophet
uh-**ly**-juh /əˈlʌɪdʒə/

Elisha Hebrew prophet
uh-**ly**-shuh /əˈlʌɪʃə/

elision the omission of a sound when speaking
uh-**lizh**-uhn /əˈlɪʒən/

Elista city, Russia
el-**ee**-stuh /ɛˈliːstə/

elixir potion
el-**ik**-seer /ɛˈlɪksɪə(r)/

Ellan Vannin Manx name for the Isle of Man
el-yuhn **van**-in /ˌɛljən ˈvanɪn/

El Niño climatic phenomenon
el neen-yoh /ɛl ˈniːnjəʊ/

Ellesmere Island Canada
elz-meer /ˈɛlzmɪə(r)/

El Pais Spanish newspaper

el py-**eess** /ɛl pʌɪˈiːs/, [el paˈis]

El Paso city, Texas
el **pass**-oh /ɛl ˈpasəʊ/

El Salvador country
el **sal**-vuh-dor /ɛl ˈsalvadɔː(r)/, Spanish [el salβaˈðor]
• Established anglicization.

Elsinore port, Denmark
el-sin-or /ˈɛlsɪnɔː(r)/

Established anglicization. The Danish name is Helsingør, pronounced hel-sing-**oer** [hɛlsɪŋˈøːʔr].

Éluard, Paul French poet
pol ayl-**war** /ˌpɒl eɪlwɑː(r)/

Elul Jewish month
el-**ool** /ɛˈluːl/

Ely city, England
ee-li /ˈiːli/

Elysée Palace building in Paris
ay-lee-**zay** /eɪˈliːzeɪ/, [elize]
• Established anglicization.

Elysium Greek mythological paradise
uh-**liz**-i-uhm /əˈlɪziəm/

emanate issue
em-uh-nayt /ˈɛməneɪt/

embarras de richesses more resources than one knows what to do with
o(ng)-**barr**-ah duh ree-**shess** /ˌɒ̃baˌrɑː də riːˈʃɛs/, French [ɑ̃bara də riʃɛs]

embolism obstruction of an artery
em-buh-liz-uhm /ˈɛmbəlɪzəm/

embouchure musical term
om-**buush**-oor /ˌɒmbʊˈʃʊə(r)/

embrasure architectural feature
em-**bray**-zhuhr /ɛmˈbreɪʒə(r)/

emcee master of ceremonies
em-**see** /ɛmˈsiː/

E=mc2 Einstein's formula
ee **eek**-wuhlz emm **see** skwaird /ˌiː ˌiːkwəlz ɛm ˈsiː skwɛː(r)d/

This formula is often pronounced with stress on the *m* and the *squared* rather than the *c*. However, this stress pattern may suggest, wrongly, that both *m* and *c* should be squared, when it is in fact only the individual quantity *c* which is squared.

emeritus honorary title
uh-**merr**-it-uhss /əˈmɛrɪtəs/

emery abrasive
em-uh-ri /ˈɛməri/

emetic causing vomiting
uh-**met**-ik /ə'mɛtɪk/

emic anthropological term
ee-mik /'i:mɪk/

émigré migrant
em-i-gray /'ɛmɪgreɪ/

Emi Koussi mountain, Chad
ay-mi **koo**-si /ˌeɪmi 'ku:si/

Emilia-Romagna region, Italy
em-**eel**-yuh roh-**mah**-nyuh /ɛˌmi:ljə
rəʊ'mɑ:njə/

Emin, Tracey English artist
em-in /'ɛmɪn/

Eminem American singer
em-in-em /ˌɛmɪn'ɛm/

emir Arab title
em-**eer** /ɛ'mɪə(r)/

emirate lands of an emir
em-irr-uht /'ɛmɪrət/

Emmanuel name given to Christ
uh-**man**-yoo-uhl /ə'manjuəl/

Emmental (also **Emmenthal**) Swiss
cheese
em-uhn-tahl /'ɛməntɑ:l/

Emmerich, Roland German film
director
roh-lant em-uh-rikh /ˌrəʊlant 'ɛmərɪç/

emo style of rock music
ee-moh /'i:məʊ/

emolument salary
em-**ol**-yuum-uhnt /ɛ'mɒljʊmənt/

emoticon representation of a facial
expression used in electronic
communications
uh-**moh**-tik-on /ə'məʊtɪkɒn/

empanada Spanish savoury pastry
turnover
em-puh-**nah**-duh /ˌɛmpə'nɑ:də/

Empedocles Greek philosopher
em-**ped**-uh-kleez /ɛm'pɛdəkli:z/

emphysema lung disease
em-fuh-**see**-muh /ˌɛmfə'si:mə/

empyema collection of pus in a cavity
in the body
em-py-**ee**-muh /ˌɛmpʌɪ'i:mə/

empyreal relating to heaven
em-py-**ree**-uhl /ˌɛmpʌɪ'ri:əl/

Less commonly also em-**pirr**-i-uhl.

en bloc all together
on **blok** /ˌɒn 'blɒk/

The word *en*, here and in other phrases, can
also be pronounced in the French manner,
as ah(ng).

Encaenia annual celebration at Oxford
University
en-**see**-ni-uh /ɛn'si:niə/

enceinte pregnant
on-sant /ɒn'sant/

Can also be pronounced in the French
manner, as ah(ng)-**sa(ng)t**.

Enceladus moon of Saturn
en-**sel**-uh-duhss /ɛn'sɛlədəs/

encephalitis inflammation of the brain
en-kef-uh-**ly**-tiss /ɛnˌkɛfə'lʌɪtɪs/

The element -*cephal*- can also be
pronounced **sef**-uhl, here and in other
words.

enchilada filled tortilla
en-chil-**ah**-duh /ˌɛntʃɪ'lɑ:də/

enchiridion book containing essential
information on a subject
en-ky-**rid**-i-uhn /ˌɛnkʌɪ'rɪdiən/

enclave enclosed territory
en-klayv /'ɛnkleɪv/

Sometimes also **onk**-layv.

encomium praise
en-**koh**-mi-uhm /ɛn'kəʊmiəm/

encompass surround
en-**kum**-puhss /ɛn'kʌmpəs/

en croute in a pastry crust
on **kroot** /ˌɒn 'kru:t/

encyclical papal letter
en-**sik**-lik-uhl /ɛn'sɪklɪkəl/

encyclopedia (also **encyclopaedia**)
book giving information on many
subjects
en-sy-kluh-**pee**-di-uh
/ɛnˌsʌɪklə'pi:diə/

endemic regularly found among
particular people
en-**dem**-ik /ɛn'dɛmɪk/

Endemol Dutch television production
company
en-duh-mol /'ɛndəmɒl/

Enderby Land part of Antarctica
end-uhr-bi /'ɛndə(r)bi/

endive salad leaves
en-dyv /'ɛndʌɪv/

endocrine relating to hormonal glands
en-duh-kryn /'ɛndəkrʌɪn/

Sometimes also pronounced en-duh-krin or
en-duh-kreen.

endogamy marrying within a
community
en-**dog**-uh-mi /ɛn'dɒgəmi/

endogenous having an internal cause
en-**doj**-uh-nuhss /ɛn'dɒdʒənəs/

endometriosis gynaecological condition
en-duh-mee-tri-**oh**-siss
/ˌɛndəˌmiːtri'əʊsɪs/

endorphin hormone
en-**dor**-fin /ɛn'dɔː(r)fɪn/

endoscopy internal medical
investigation
en-**dosk**-uh-pi /ɛn'dɒskəpi/

endow give
en-**dow** /ɛn'daʊ/

Endymion Greek mythological character
en-**dim**-i-uhn /ɛn'dɪmiən/

Eneolithic archaeological period
ee-ni-uh-**lith**-ik /ˌiːniə'lɪθɪk/

enfant terrible controversial person
on-fon terr-**ee**-bluh /ˌɒnfɒn tɛ'riːblə/

Enfant can also be pronounced in the
French manner, as ah(ng)-**fah(ng)**.

enfeoff give property in exchange for
service
en-**feef** /ɛn'fiːf/

enfranchise permit to vote
en-**fran**-chyz /ɛn'frantʃaɪz/

Engels, Friedrich German philosopher
freed-rikh **eng**-uhlss /ˌfriːdrɪç 'ɛŋəls/

Enisey see **Yenisei**

Eniwetok island in the North Pacific
en-i-**wee**-tok /ˌɛni'wiːtɒk/

enjambement (also **enjambment**)
poetic term
en-**jamb**-muhnt /ɛn'dʒambmənt/

en masse in a group
on **mass** /ˌɒn 'mas/

ennead group of nine
en-i-ad /'ɛniad/

Enniskillen town, Northern Ireland
en-isk-**il**-uhn /ˌɛnɪs'kɪlən/

Ennius, Quintus Roman poet and
dramatist
kwint-uhss **en**-i-uhss /ˌkwɪntəs 'ɛniəs/

ennui listlessness
on-**wee** /ɒn'wiː/

Eno, Brian English musician
ee-noh /'iːnəʊ/

Enoch biblical character
ee-nok /'iːnɒk/

enoki Japanese mushroom
en-**oh**-ki /ɛ'nəʊki/

Enola Gay American plane which
dropped the first atomic bomb on
Hiroshima
uh-**noh**-luh **gay** /əˌnəʊlə 'geɪ/

enosis hypothetical political union of
Cyprus and Greece
en-uh-siss /'ɛnəsɪs/

en papillote cooked and served in a
paper wrapper
on pap-i-**yot** /ɒn papi'jɒt/

Enron American energy company
en-ron /'ɛnrɒn/

Enschede city, Netherlands
enss-khuh-day /'ɛnsxədeɪ/

ensemble group of musicians
on-**som**-buhl /ɒn'sɒmbəl/

en suite adjoining a bedroom
on **sweet** /ɒn 'swiːt/

Entebbe town, Uganda
en-**teb**-i /ɛn'tɛbi/

entelechy realization of potential
en-**tel**-uh-ki /ɛn'tɛləki/

entente cordiale friendly
understanding between states
on-**tont** kor-di-**ahl** /ɒn'tɒnt
kɔː(r)di'ɑːl/

Can also be pronounced in the French
manner, as ah(ng)-**tah(ng)**t kord-**yal**.

enteritis inflammation of the intestine
en-tuh-**ry**-tiss /ˌɛntə'raɪtɪs/

enthalpy thermodynamics term
en-**thuhl**-pi /'ɛnθəlpi/

enthral fascinate
en-**thrawl** /ɛn'θrɔːl/

entomology study of insects
en-tuh-**mol**-uh-ji /ˌɛntə'mɒlədʒi/

entr'acte interval between two acts of a
play or opera
on-**trakt** /ɒn'trakt/

en travesti cross-dressed
on trav-est-**ee** /ˌɒn travɛ'stiː/

entrecôte boned steak
on-truh-koht /'ɒntrəkəʊt/

entrée main course
on-tray /'ɒntreɪ/

entremets light dish served between
courses
ont-ruh-**may** /ɒntrə'meɪ/

entrepreneur businessperson
on-truh-pruh-**nur** /ˌɒntrəprəˈnəː(r)/

entropy thermodynamics term
en-truh-pi /ˈɛntrəpi/

enuresis involuntary urination
en-yoor-**ee**-siss /ˌɛnjʊəˈriːsɪs/

envelope flat paper container with a flap
en-vuh-lohp /ˈɛnvələʊp/

Less commonly also **on**-vuh-lohp.

Enver Pasha Turkish political and
military leader
en-vuhr **pash**-uh /ˌɛnvə(r) ˈpaʃə/

environs surrounds
en-**vy**-ruhnz /ɛnˈvʌɪrənz/

envoi (also **envoy**) a short stanza
concluding a poem
en-voy /ˈɛnvɔɪ/

Enya Irish composer
en-yuh /ˈɛnjə/

Enzed New Zealand or a New Zealander
en-**zed** /ɛnˈzɛd/

enzyme biochemical substance
en-zym /ˈɛnzʌɪm/

Eocene geological epoch
ee-oh-seen /ˈiːəʊsiːn/

Eoin Irish boy's name
oh-in /ˈəʊɪn/

Eos Greek goddess
ee-oss /ˈiːɒs/

Eowyn character from *The Lord of the
Rings*
ay-oh-win /ˈeɪəʊwɪn/

eparchy province of the Orthodox
Church
ep-ar-ki /ˈɛpɑː(r)ki/

épater shock conventional people
ep-at-**ay** /ɛpaˈteɪ/

epaulette shoulder piece on clothing
ep-uh-**let** /ɛpəˈlɛt/

épée fencing sword
ep-ay /ˈɛpeɪ/

epenthesis pl. **epentheses** insertion of a
sound or an unetymological letter
ep-**en**-thuh-siss, pl. ep-**en**-thuh-seez
/ɛˈpɛnθəsɪs/, pl. /-siːz/

ephedra shrub
ef-**ed**-ruh /ɛˈfɛdrə/

ephedrine stimulant drug
ef-uh-dreen /ˈɛfədriːn/

ephemeral transient
ef-**em**-uh-ruhl /ɛˈfɛmərəl/

Sometimes also ef-**ee**-muh-ruhl.

Ephesians book of the New Testament
ef-**eezh**-uhnz /ɛˈfiːʒənz/

Ephesus ancient Greek city
ef-uh-suhss /ˈɛfəsəs/

epicene having characteristics of both or
neither sex
ep-iss-een /ˈɛpɪsiːn/

Epictetus Greek philosopher
ep-ik-**tee**-tuhss /ˌɛpɪkˈtiːtəs/

Epicurus Greek philosopher
ep-ik-**yoor**-uhss /ˌɛpɪˈkjʊərəs/

epidemiology study of epidemics
ep-id-ee-mi-**ol**-uh-ji /ˌɛpɪdiːmiˈɒlədʒi/

epidural spinal anaesthetic
ep-id-**yoor**-uhl /ˌɛpɪˈdjʊərəl/

epigeal growing on the ground
ep-ij-**ee**-uhl /ˌɛpɪˈdʒiːəl/

epilepsy neurological disorder
ep-il-ep-si /ˈɛpɪlɛpsi/

epilogue concluding section
ep-il-og /ˈɛpɪlɒg/

epiphany revelation
uh-**pif**-uh-ni /əˈpɪfəni/

Epirus region, Greece
uh-**py**-ruhss /əˈpʌɪrəs/

episcopalian of or advocating
government of a Church by bishops
ep-isk-uh-**pay**-li-uhn /ɛˌpɪskəˈpeɪliən/

episiotomy obstetric procedure
ep-ee-zi-**ot**-uh-mi /ɛˌpiːziˈɒtəmi/

epistemology theory of knowledge
ep-ist-im-**ol**-uh-ji /ɛˌpɪstɪˈmɒlədʒi/

epistle letter
uh-**piss**-uhl /əˈpɪsəl/

epistolary relating to letters
uh-**pist**-uh-luh-ri /əˈpɪstələri/

epithalamium song or poem celebrating
a marriage
ep-ith-uh-**lay**-mi-uhm
/ˌɛpɪθəˈleɪmiəm/

epithet phrase
ep-ith-et /ˈɛpɪθɛt/

epitome perfect example
ep-**it**-uh-mi /ɛˈpɪtəmi/

e pluribus unum 'one out of many'
(Latin), the motto of the US
ay **ploor**-ib-uuss **oo**-nuum /eɪ
ˌplʊərɪbʊs ˈuːnʊm/

epoch period of time
ee-pok /ˈiːpɒk/

AM is commonly **ep**-ok.

epode lyric poem
ep-ohd /ˈɛpəʊd/

eponymous giving their name to something
uh-**pon**-im-uhss /əˈpɒnɪməs/

EPOS electronic point of sale
ee-poss /ˈiːpɒs/

epoxy polymer
ep-**ok**-si /ɛˈpɒksi/

epsilon letter of the Greek alphabet
ep-sil-on /ˈɛpsɪlɒn/

Sometimes also ep-**sy**-lon.

Epstein, Brian English manager of the Beatles
ep-styn /ˈɛpstʌɪn/

Epstein, Jacob American-born sculptor
ep-styn /ˈɛpstʌɪn/

equatorial at or near the equator
ek-wuh-**taw**-ri-uhl /ˌɛkwəˈtɔːriəl/

equerry royal servant
uh-**kwerr**-i /əˈkwɛri/

Sometimes also ek-wuh-ri.

equine relating to horses
ek-wyn /ˈɛkwʌɪn/

equinox time when day and night are of equal length
ek-win-oks /ˈɛkwɪnɒks/

The *equi*- element can also be pronounced eek-wi, here and in some other words such as *equilibrium, equilateral*, etc.

equitable fair and impartial
ek-wi-tuh-buhl /ˈɛkwɪtəbəl/

equivocate use ambiguous language
uh-**kwiv**-uh-kayt /əˈkwɪvəkeɪt/

era period of history
eer-uh /ˈɪərə/

AM is sometimes also **err**-uh.

Erasmus, Desiderius Dutch humanist and scholar
dess-id-**air**-i-uuss err-**ass**-muuss
/ˌdɛsɪˌdɛːriʊs ɛˈrasmʊs/

A more anglicized pronunciation, uh-**raz**-muhss, is also sometimes heard.

Erato Greek mythological character
err-uh-toh /ˈɛratəʊ/

Eratosthenes Greek scholar and astronomer
err-uh-**toss**-thuh-neez /ˌɛrəˈtɒsθəniːz/

Erbil (also **Arbil, Irbil**) town, Iraq
air-beel /ɛː(r)ˈbiːl/

erbium chemical element
ur-bi-uhm /ˈəː(r)biəm/

Erdoğan, Recep Tayyıp Turkish prime minister
rej-ep **ty**-ip air-doh-uhn /ˌrɛdʒɛp ˌtʌɪp ˈɛː(r)dəʊən/

ere before
air /ɛː(r)/

Erebus Greek god
err-uh-buhss /ˈɛrəbəs/

Erekat, Saeb Palestinian politician
sah-eb err-uh-**kaht** /ˌsɑːɛb ɛrəˈkɑːt/

eremite Christian recluse
err-uh-myt /ˈɛrəmʌɪt/

Erevan see **Yerevan**

Erfurt city, Germany
air-foort /ˈɛː(r)fʊə(r)t/

ergometer apparatus which measures energy expended
ur-**gom**-uh-tuhr /əː(r)ˈgɒmətə(r)/

ergot cereal disease
ur-got /ˈəː(r)gɒt/

erhu (also **erh hu**) Chinese two-stringed musical instrument
ur-**khoo** /ˌəː(r)ˈxuː/

Ericsson Swedish mobile telecommunications company
err-ik-suhn /ˈɛrɪksən/, [ˈeːrɪksɔn]
• Established anglicization.

Eridanus constellation
err-id-uh-nuhss /ɛˈrɪdənəs/

Erie, Lake lake, US–Canada border
eer-i /ˈɪəri/

Eriksson, Sven-Göran Swedish football manager
sven **yoer**-an ay-rik-son /svɛn ˌjœːran ˈeɪrɪksɒn/

Erin literary name for Ireland
err-in /ˈɛrɪn/

Erinyes Greek mythological characters
err-in-i-eez /ɛˈrɪniiːz/

Eriskay island, Scotland
err-isk-ay /ˈɛrɪskeɪ/

Erith district of London
eer-ith /ˈɪərɪθ/

Eritrea autonomous state, east Africa
err-it-**ray**-uh /ˌɛrɪˈtreɪə/

Ekel, Ferenc Hungarian composer
ferr-ents **air**-kel /ˌfɛrɛnts ˈɛːkɛl/

Erlangen town, Germany
air-lang-uhn /ˈɛː(r)laŋən/

ermine stoat
ur-min /ˈəː(r)mɪn/

Ernst, Max German artist
maks **airnst** /ˌmaks ˈɛː(r)nst/

Eros Greek god
eer-oss /ˈɪərɒs/

Eroica symphony by Beethoven
err-**oh**-ik-uh /ɛˈrəʊɪkə/

err be mistaken
ur /əː(r)/

errant straying
err-uhnt /ˈɛrənt/

ersatz substitute
air-**zats** /ɛː(r)ˈzats/

Sometimes also **ur**-zats.

Erse Gaelic language
urss /əː(r)s/

Erté Russian-born French fashion
designer
air-**tay** /ɛː(r)ˈteɪ/

erudite showing great knowledge
err-uud-yt /ˈɛrʊdʌɪt/

eruv pl. **eruvim** area which symbolically
extends the private domain of Jewish
households
err-uuv, pl. **err**-uuv-im /ˈɛrʊv/, pl.
/-vɪm/

erythema reddening of the skin
err-ith-**ee**-muh /ˌɛrɪˈθiːmə/

Eryri Welsh name for Snowdonia
err-**urr**-i /ɛˈrʌri/

Erzgebirge mountain range,
Germany–Czech Republic border
airts-guh-beer-guh
/ˈɛː(r)tsɡəˌbɪə(r)ɡə/

Erzurum city, Turkey
air-**zuu**-ruum /ˈɛː(r)zʊrʊm/

Esau biblical character
ee-saw /ˈiːsɔː/

Esbjerg port, Denmark
ess-byair /ˈɛsbjɛː(r)/

escalope thin slice of meat
esk-**al**-uhp /ɛˈskaləp/

Sometimes also **esk**-uh-lop.

escargot edible snail
esk-**ar**-goh /ɛˈskɑː(r)ɡəʊ/, French
[ɛskaʁɡo]

escarole salad leaf

esk-uh-rohl /ˈɛskərəʊl/

eschatology theological term
esk-uh-**tol**-uh-ji /ˌɛskəˈtɒlədʒi/

Escaut see **Scheldt**

escheat reversion of property on the
owner's death
ess-**cheet** /ɛsˈtʃiːt/

eschew deliberately avoid
ess-**choo** /ɛsˈtʃuː/

Escoffier, Georges-Auguste French
chef
zhorzh oh-**guest** esk-of-**yay** /ˌʒɔː(r)ʒ
əʊˌɡyst ɛskɒˈfjeɪ/

escolar large fish
esk-uh-**lar** /ˌɛskəˈlɑː(r)/

Escorial monastery and palace in Spain
esk-orr-i-**al** /ˌɛskɒriˈal/

escritoire small writing desk
esk-ri-**twar** /ˌɛskriˈtwɑː(r)/

escrow US legal term
esk-roh /ˈɛskrəʊ/

escutcheon shield
esk-**utch**-uhn /ɛˈskʌtʃən/

Esfahan (also **Isfahan**) city, Iran
ess-fuh-**hahn** /ˌɛsfəˈhɑːn/

Esher town, England
ee-shuhr /ˈiːʃə(r)/

Eskişehir city, Turkey
esk-**ish**-uh-heer /ɛsˈkɪʃəhɪə(r)/

esoteric likely to be understood by only a
small number of people
ee-suh-**terr**-ik /ˌiːsəˈtɛrɪk/

Sometimes also ess-uh-**terr**-ik.

espada fish
esp-**ah**-duh /ɛˈspɑːdə/

espadrille canvas shoe
esp-uh-dril /ˈɛspədrɪl/

espalier tree trained to grow against
a wall
esp-**al**-yuhr /ɛˈspaljə(r)/

Sometimes also esp-**al**-yay.

Esperanto artificial language
esp-uh-**ran**-toh /ˌɛspəˈrantəʊ/

Espirito Santo state, Brazil
esp-**ee**-rit-oo **san**-too /ɛˌspiːrɪtuː
ˈsantuː/

esplanade open area
esp-luh-**nayd** /ˌɛspləˈneɪd/

Sometimes also esp-luh-**nahd**.

espouse support a cause
esp-**owz** /ɛˈspaʊz/

espressivo musical term
esp-ress-**ee**-voh /ˌɛsprɛˈsiːvəʊ/

espresso coffee
esp-**ress**-oh /ɛˈsprɛsəʊ/

Sometimes erroneously pronounced eks-**press**-oh.

esprit de corps mutual loyalty
esp-**ree** duh kor /ɛˌspriː də ˈkɔː(r)/

Esquiline one of the seven hills of Rome
esk-wil-yn /ˈɛskwɪlʌɪn/

Esquipulas town, Guatemala
esk-ee-**poo**-lass /ˌɛskiːˈpuːlas/

esquire title appended to a man's name
esk-**wy**-uhr /ɛˈskwʌɪə(r)/

Essen city, Germany
ess-uhn /ˈɛsən/

Essequibo river, Guyana
ess-uh-**kee**-boh /ˌɛsəˈkiːbəʊ/

Estádio da Luz football stadium, Lisbon
ish-**taj**-oo duh **loosh** /ɪʃˌtadʒuː də ˈluːʃ/

Estadio Santiago Bernabeu football stadium, Madrid
est-**ath**-yoh sant-**yag**-oh bair-nab-**ay**-oo /ɛˈstaðjəʊ sanˈtjagəʊ bɛː(r)naˈbeɪu:/

estancia cattle ranch
est-**anss**-i-uh /ɛˈstansiə/

Estefan, Gloria Cuban singer
glaw-ri-uh est-**ef**-an /ˌglɔːriə ɛˈstɛfan/

Estée Lauder American cosmetics company
est-ay **law**-duhr /ˌɛsteɪ ˈlɔːdə(r)/

Esterházy, Pál Hungarian composer
pahl est-uhr-**hah**-zi /ˌpɑːl ˈɛstə(r)hɑːzi/

Estevez, Emilio American actor
uh-**meel**-i-oh est-uh-vez /əˌmiːliəʊ ˈɛstəvɛz/

Estima potato variety
est-**ee**-muh /ɛˈstiːmə/

Estonia country
est-**oh**-ni-uh /ɛˈstəʊniə/

Established anglicization. The Estonian name is Eesti, pronounced **ay**-sti [ˈeːsti].

Estoril town, Portugal
ish-tuh-**reel** /ɪʃtəˈriːl/

Sometimes anglicized to est-uh-**ril**.

Estremadura region, Portugal
ish-truh-muh-**doo**-ruh /ˌɪʃtrəməˈduːrə/

Esztergom town, Hungary
est-uhr-gom /ˈɛstə(r)gɒm/

ETA Estimated Time of Arrival
ee-tee-**ay** /ˌiːtiːˈeɪ/

ETA Basque separatist movement
et-uh /ˈɛtə/

eta letter of the Greek alphabet
ee-tuh /ˈiːtə/

étagère furniture
et-uh-**zhair** /ɛtəˈʒɛː(r)/

et al. 'and others' (Latin)
et **al** /ɛt ˈal/

et cetera (also **etcetera**) 'and so on' (Latin)
et-**set**-uh-ruh /ɛtˈsɛtərə/

Sometimes erroneously pronounced ek-**set**-uh-ruh.

eth (also **edh**) Old English letter
eth /ɛð/

ethane flammable gas
ee-**thayn** /ˈiːθeɪn/

Sometimes also **eth**-ayn.

ethanol ethyl alcohol
eth-uh-nol /ˈɛθənɒl/

Ethelred English king
eth-uhl-red /ˈɛθəlrɛd/

ether flammable liquid
ee-thuhr /ˈiːθə(r)/

ethereal unworldly
uh-**theer**-i-uhl /əˈθɪəriəl/

Ethiopia country
ee-thi-**oh**-pi-uh /ˌiːθiˈəʊpiə/

ethology science of animal behaviour
ee-**thol**-uh-ji /iːˈθɒlədʒi/

ethos spirit of a culture, era, or community
ee-thoss /ˈiːθɒs/

AM is sometimes also **eth**-oss.

ethyl derived from ethane
ee-thyl /ˈiːθʌɪl/

Sometimes also **eth**-il.

Etna, Mount volcano, Italy
et-nuh /ˈɛtnə/

Eton College boys' public school, England
ee-tuhn /ˈiːtən/

étouffée spicy Cajun stew
ay-too-**fay** /ˌeɪtuːˈfeɪ/

Etruscan relating to an ancient Italian state
uh-**trusk**-uhn /ə'trʌskən/

étude short musical composition
ay-**tyood** /eɪ'tjuːd/, French [etyd]

etymology study of the origin of words
et-im-**ol**-uh-ji /ˌɛtɪ'mɒlədʒi/

Euboea island, Greece
yoo-**bee**-uh /juː'biːə/

Established anglicization. The Greek name is Έύvοια, pronounced **ev**-yuh.

Eucharist Christian sacrament
yoo-kuh-rist /'juːkərɪst/

euchre card game
yoo-kuhr /'juːkə(r)/

Euclid Greek mathematician
yoo-klid /'juːklɪd/

Euclidean system of geometry
yoo-**klid**-i-uhn /juː'klɪdiən/

Eugene Onegin opera by Tchaikovsky
yoo-jeen on-**yay**-gin /ˌjuː'dʒiːn ɒn'jeɪgɪn/
• Established anglicization.

eugenics selective breeding
yoo-**jen**-iks /juː'dʒɛnɪks/

Eugénie wife of Napoleon III
yoo-**zhay**-ni /juː'ʒeɪmi/, French [øʒeni]
• Established anglicization.

Eugenie, Princess member of the UK royal family
yoo-zhuh-ni /'juːʒəni/

eukaryote organism
yoo-**karr**-i-oht /juː'kariəʊt/

Euler, Leonhard Swiss mathematician
lay-on-hart **oy**-luhr /ˌleɪɒnhɑː(r)t 'ɔɪlə(r)/

eulogy praise
yoo-luh-ji /'juːlədʒi/

Eumenides Greek mythological characters
yoo-**men**-id-eez /juː'mɛnɪdiːz/

euphonious pleasing to the ear
yoo-**foh**-ni-uhss /juː'fəʊniəs/

euphorbia plant
yoo-**for**-bi-uh /juː'fɔː(r)biə/

Euphrates river, Iraq
yoo-**fray**-teez /juː'freɪtiːz/
• Established anglicization.

Eurasia Europe and Asia combined
yoor-**ay**-zhuh /ˌjʊə'reɪʒə/

Euratom European Atomic Energy Community
yoor-**at**-uhm /jʊə'ratəm/

eureka cry of joy
yoor-**ee**-kuh /jʊə'riːkə/

Euridice opera by Peri
ay-oor-id-**ee**-chay /eɪʊərɪ'diːtʃeɪ/

This Italian pronunciation of Eurydice is also appropriate for several other operas.

Euripides Greek dramatist
yoor-**ip**-id-eez /ˌjʊə'rɪpɪdiːz/

euro currency unit
yoor-oh /'jʊərəʊ/
• Established anglicization.

europium chemical element
yoor-**oh**-pi-uhm /jʊər'əʊpiəm/

Europoort port, Netherlands
yoor-oh-port /'jʊərəʊpɔː(r)t/, ['øːroːpoːrt]
• Established anglicization.

Eurydice Greek mythological character
yoor-**id**-iss-i /jʊə'rɪdisi/

Eurynome Greek mythological character
yoor-**in**-uh-mi /jʊə'rɪnəmi/

Eusebius Syrian bishop
yoo-**see**-bi-uhss /juː'siːbiəs/

Eustachian tube passage leading from the pharynx to the ear
yoo-**stay**-shuhn /juː'steɪʃən/

Euterpe Greek mythological character
yoo-**tur**-pi /juː'tə(r)pi/

evanesce pass out of sight
ev-uh-**ness** /ɛvə'nɛs/

Sometimes also ee-vuh-**ness**.

Evelyn, John English diarist
eev-lin /'iːvlɪn/

The British boy's or girl's name Evelyn is variously pronounced **eev**-lin and **ev**-uh-lin, depending on individual preference.

Everest, Mount mountain, Himalayas
ev-uh-ruhst /'ɛvərəst/

Curiously, explorer Sir George Everest (after whom the mountain was named) pronounced his name **eev**-uh-rest.

Evian trademark mineral water
ev-yah(ng) /'ɛvjã/

evolution biological process
ev-uh-**loo**-shuhn /ˌɛvə'luːʃən/

Commonly also ee-vuh-**loo**-shuhn.

Έύvοια see **Euboea**

Ewe west African ethnic group and language
ay-way /'eɪweɪ/

ewe female sheep
yoo /juː/

Ewelme town, England
yoo-elm /'juːɛlm/

ewer jug
yoo-uhr /'juːə(r)/

exalt speak highly of
eg-**zawlt** /ɛg'zɔːlt/

Commonly also eg-**zolt**. The prefix *ex-* is variously pronounced eks or egz.

Excalibur legendary sword
ek-**skal**-ib-uhr /ɛks'kalɪbə(r)/

ex cathedra with full authority
eks kuh-**thee**-druh /ˌɛks kə'θiːdrə/

excelsior hotel name
ek-**sel**-si-or /ɛk'sɛlsiɔː(r)/

exchequer treasury
eks-**chek**-uhr /ɛks'tʃɛkə(r)/

excoriate scar
ek-**skaw**-ri-ayt /ɛk'skɔːrieɪt/

exeat permission for temporary absence
eks-i-at /'ɛksiat/

exegesis , pl. **exegeses** critical interpretation of a text
ek-sij-**ee**-siss, pl. ek-sij-**ee**-seez /ˌɛksɪ'dʒiːsɪs/, pl. /-siːz/

exequy funeral rites
ek-suh-kwi /'ɛksəkwi/

Exeter city, England
ek-suh-tuhr /'ɛksətə(r)/

exeunt stage direction
ek-si-unt /'ɛksiʌnt/

ex gratia done as a favour and not under compulsion
eks **gray**-shuh /ˌɛks 'greɪʃə/

exigency urgent need
ek-sij-uhn-si /'ɛksɪdʒənsi/

Sometimes also ek-**sij**-uhn-si.

ex libris bookplate inscription
eks **leeb**-riss /ˌɛks 'liːbrɪs/

ex nihilo out of nothing
eks **ny**-hil-oh /ˌɛks 'nʌɪhɪləʊ/

Exocet trademark missile
ek-suh-set /'ɛksəsɛt/

exodus mass departure
ek-suh-duhss /'ɛksədəs/

exogamy marrying outside a community
ek-**sog**-uh-mi /ɛk'sɒgəmi/

expatiate speak in detail about
ek-**spay**-shi-ayt /ɛk'speɪʃieɪt/

expiate make reparation for
ek-spi-ayt /'ɛkspieɪt/

expletive swear word
eks-**plee**-tiv /ɛk'spliːtɪv/

AM is eks-**pluh**-tiv.

exposé media revelation
ek-**spoh**-zay /ɛk'spəʊzeɪ/

AM is ek-spoh-**zay**.

expurgate bowdlerize
ek-spur-gayt /'ɛkspɔː(r)geɪt/

exquisite beautiful and delicate
eks-**kwiz**-it /ɛk'skwɪzɪt/

Sometimes also **eks**-kwuh-zit.

extant still in existence
ek-stant /'ɛk'stant/

Sometimes also ek-**stuhnt**.

extol praise
ek-**stohl** /ɛk'stəʊl/

extrados architectural term
eks-**tray**-doss /ɛk'streɪdɒs/

extrasystole arrhythmic heartbeat
eks-truh-**sist**-uh-li /ˌɛkstrə'sɪstəli/

Extremadura region, Spain
eks-tray-muh-**door**-uh /ˌɛkstreɪmə'dʊərə/

Exuma islands, Bahamas
ek-**soo**-muh /ɛk'suːmə/

ex-voto offering
eks **voh**-toh /ˌɛks 'vəʊtəʊ/

Exxon Mobil company name
ek-son **moh**-bil /ˌɛksɒn 'məʊbɪl/

eyot island in a river; also called **ait**
ay-uht /'eɪət/

eyre medieval court
air /ɛː(r)/

eyrie eagle's nest
eer-i /'ɪəri/

Sometimes also **y**-ri or **air**-i.

Ezekiel Hebrew prophet
uh-**zee**-ki-uhl /ə'ziːkiəl/

Ezra Hebrew prophet
ez-ruh /'ɛzrə/

F

faba broad bean; also called **fava**
fah-buh /ˈfɑːbə/

Faber & Faber book publishers
fay-buhr /ˌfeɪbə(r)/

Faber, Johann German composer
yoh-han fah-buhr /ˌjəʊhan ˈfɑːbə(r)/

Fabergé, Carl Russian goldsmith and jeweller
karl fab-uhr-zhay /ˌkɑː(r)l ˈfabə(r)ʒeɪ/

Fabian Society socialist organization
fay-bi-uhn /ˈfeɪbɪən/

Fabius Roman general and statesman
fay-bi-uhss /ˈfeɪbɪəs/

Fabre, Jean Henri French entomologist
zhah(ng) ah(ng)-ree fab-ruh /ʒɑ̃ ɑ̃ˌriː ˈfabrə/

Fabricius, David German astronomer
dah-vit fab-reet-si-uuss /ˌdɑːvɪt fabˈriːtsɪʊs/

fabulate relate invented stories
fab-yuul-ayt /ˈfabjʊleɪt/

facile ignoring the true complexities of an issue
fass-yl /ˈfasʌɪl/

AM usually **fass**-il.

---

facsimile exact copy
fak-sim-il-i /fakˈsɪmɪli/

factotum employee who does all kinds of work
fak-toh-tuhm /fakˈtəʊtəm/

factual concerned with facts
fak-choo-uhl /ˈfaktʃʊəl/

The pronunciation **fak-tyoo-uhl** is less common now.

---

facula pl. **faculae** bright region on the surface of the Sun
fak-yuul-uh, pl. fak-yuul-ee /ˈfakjʊlə/, pl. /-liː/

fado type of Portuguese music
fad-oo /ˈfaduː/

Faenza town, Italy
fah-ent-suh /fɑːˈɛntsə/

Faeroe Islands see **Faroe Islands**

Fahrenheit scale of temperature
farr-uhn-hyt /ˈfarənhʌɪt/

Less commonly also **far**-uhn-hyt.

---

faience glazed ceramic ware
fy-o(ng)ss /fʌɪˈɒ̃s/, French [fajɑ̃ːs]

faille light-woven fabric
fayl /feɪl/

fáilte 'welcome' (Irish Gaelic)
fawl-chuh /ˈfɔːltʃə/

Faisal name of two kings of Iraq
fy-suhl /ˈfʌɪsəl/

Faisalabad city, Pakistan
fy-suh-luh-bad /ˈfʌɪsələˌbad/

fait accompli thing that has already happened
fayt uh-kom-pli /ˌfeɪt əˈkɒmpli/, French /fɛt akɔ̃pli/

Faizabad city, India
fy-zuh-bad /ˈfʌɪzəbad/

fajitas Mexican dish
fuh-hee-tuhz /fəˈhiːtəz/, Spanish [faˈxitas]

fakir (also **faquir**) Muslim religious ascetic
fay-keer /ˈfeɪkɪə(r)/

Commonly also **fuh-keer**.

Falabella horse of a miniature breed
fal-uh-bel-uh /ˌfaləˈbɛlə/

falafel (also **felafel**) Middle Eastern dish
fuh-laf-uhl /fəˈlafəl/

Falange Spanish Fascist movement
fal-an-khay /faˈlaŋxeɪ/

A more anglicized pronunciation, **fuh-lanj**, is also common.

---

falangist member of the Falange party
fuh-lan-jist /fəˈlandʒɪst/

falchion sword
fawl-chuhn /ˈfɔːltʃən/

falciparum most severe form of malaria
fal-sip-uh-ruhm /falˈsɪpərəm/

falcon bird of prey
fawl-kuhn /ˈfɔːlkən/

Commonly also **fol**-kuhn and **fal**-kuhn.

Falconer, Lord Scottish politician
folk-uh-nuhr /ˈfɒlkənə(r)/

Falconio, Peter English backpacker
who disappeared in Australia
fal-**koh**-ni-oh /falˈkəʊniəʊ/

Faldo, Nick English golfer
fal-doh /ˈfaldəʊ/

Faliraki resort, Rhodes
fal-i-**rak**-i /faliˈraki/

Falkirk town, Scotland
fawl-kurk /ˈfɔːlkə(r)k/

Commonly also **fol**-kurk.

Falkland Islands group of islands,
South Atlantic
fawl-kluhnd /ˈfɔːlklənd/

Commonly also **folk**-luhnd.

Falla, Manuel de Spanish composer
man-**wel** day **fal**-yuh /man,wɛl deɪ
ˈfaljə/

Fallopian tube part of the female
reproductive system
fuh-**loh**-pi-uhn /fəˈləʊpiən/

Falluja, al- city, Iraq
uhl fuh-**loo**-juh /əl fəˈluːdʒə/

Falmouth port, England
fal-muhth /ˈfalməθ/

Falstaffian relating to the
Shakespearean character Falstaff
fawl-**stah**-fi-uhn /fɔːlˈstɑːfiən/

Commonly also fol-**staf**-i-uhn.

Falster island, Denmark
fal-stuhr /ˈfalstə(r)/

Fältskog, Agnetha Swedish singer
ang-**nay**-tuh **felt**-skoog /aŋ,neɪtə
ˈfɛltskuːg/

Falun Gong Chinese meditation regime
fah-luun **guung** /ˌfɑːlʊn ˈgʊŋ/

famulus pl. **famuli** assistant or servant
fam-yuul-uhss, pl. **fam**-yuul-y
/ˈfamjʊləs, pl. -lʌɪ/

Fanakalo (also **Fanagalo**) South African
lingua franca
fun-uh-kuh-**loh** /ˌfʌnəkəˈləʊ/

fandango Spanish dance
fan-**dang**-goh /fanˈdaŋgəʊ/

Fangio, Juan Manuel Argentine
motor-racing driver
khwan man-**wel fan**-ji-oh /xwan
man,wɛl ˈfandʒiəʊ/

fantasia musical composition
fan-**tay**-zi-uh /fanˈteɪziə/

Commonly also fan-tuh-**zee**-uh.

Fante (also **Fanti**) Ghanaian people
fan-ti /ˈfanti/

faquir see **fakir**

farad SI unit of electrical capacitance
farr-ad /ˈfarad/

faraday unit of electric charge
farr-uh-day /ˈfarədeɪ/

Faramir character from *The Lord of the
Rings*
farr-uh-meer /ˌfarəmɪə(r)/

farandole Provençal dance
farr-uhn-**dohl** /ˌfarənˈdəʊl/

farang Thai term for a European
farr-**ang** /faˈraŋ/

FARC Fuerzas Armadas Revolucionarias
de Colombia (Revolutionary Armed
Forces of Colombia)
fark /fɑː(r)k/

fardel bundle or collection
far-duhl /ˈfɑː(r)dəl/

farfalle type of pasta
far-**fal**-ay /fɑː(r)ˈfaleɪ/

Faridabad city, northern India
fuh-**ree**-duh-bad /fəˈriːdəbad/

farina type of flour
fuh-**ree**-nuh /fəˈriːnə/

Sometimes also fuh-**ry**-nuh.

Farkas, Ferenc Hungarian composer
ferr-ents **for**-kosh /ˌfɛrɛnts ˈfɔː(r)kɒʃ/

Farnborough town, England
farn-buh-ruh /ˈfɑː(r)nbərə/

Farne Islands group of islands, England
farn /fɑː(r)n/

Farnese, Alessandro Italian general
and statesman
al-ess-**an**-droh far-**nay**-say
/alɛ,sandrəʊ fɑː(r)ˈneɪseɪ/

Faro port, Portugal
farr-oo /ˈfaruː/

faro card game
fair-oh /ˈfɛːrəʊ/

Fårö island, Sweden
faw-roe /ˈfɔːrøː/

Faroe Islands (also **Faeroe Islands**)
group of islands, North Atlantic
fair-oh /ˈfɛːrəʊ/

Faroese (also **Faeroese**) relating to the Faroe Islands
fair-oh-**eez** /ˌfɛːrəʊˈiːz/

farouche sullen or shy in company
fuh-**roosh** /fəˈruːʃ/

Farouk king of Egypt
fuh-**rook** /fəˈruːk/

Farquhar islands, Seychelles
far-kuhr /ˈfɑː(r)kə(r)/

Farquhar, David New Zealand composer
fark-war /ˈfɑː(r)kwɑː(r)/

Farquhar, George Irish dramatist
far-kuhr /ˈfɑː(r)kə(r)/

farrago confused mixture
fuh-**rah**-goh /fəˈrɑːgəʊ/

Farrell, Colin Irish actor
farr-uhl /ˈfarəl/

farrier smith who shoes horses
farr-i-uhr /ˈfariə(r)/

farruca type of flamenco dance
fuh-**roo**-kuh /fəˈruːkə/

Farsi official language of Iran
far-si /ˈfɑː(r)si/

fartlek system of athletic training
fart-lek /ˈfɑː(r)tlɛk/

fasces Roman emblem of power
fass-eez /ˈfasiːz/

fascia sheath of tissue enclosing a muscle
fash-uh /ˈfaʃə/

fascicle separately published instalment of a book
fass-ik-uhl /ˈfasɪkəl/

fasciitis inflammation of the fascia
fash-i-**y**-tiss /ˌfaʃɪˈʌɪtɪs/

fascioliasis liver fluke infection
fass-i-uh-**ly**-uh-siss /ˌfasɪəˈlʌɪəsɪs/

Fashanu, John English footballer
fash-uh-noo /ˈfaʃənuː/

fashionista designer of haute couture
fash-uh-**neest**-uh /ˌfaʃəˈniːstə/

Faslane bay, Scotland
faz-**layn** /fazˈleɪn/

Fassbinder, Rainer Werner German film director
ry-nuhr **vair**-nuhr **fass**-bind-uhr /ˌrʌɪnə(r) ˌvɛː(r)nə(r) ˈfasbɪndə(r)/

Fastnet rocky islet, Republic of Ireland
fahst-net /ˈfɑːstnɛt/

Fatah, al- Palestinian political and military organization

uhl **fut**-uh /əl ˈfʌtə/

Fata Morgana mirage
fah-tuh mor-**gah**-nuh /ˌfɑːtə mɔː(r)ˈgɑːnə/

Fatiha (also **Fatihah**) short first sura of the Koran
fah-ti-uh /ˈfɑːtiə/

Fatima youngest daughter of the prophet Muhammad
fat-im-uh /ˈfatɪmə/

Fátima village, Portugal
fat-im-uh /ˈfatɪmə/

Fatimid descended from Fatima
fat-im-id /ˈfatɪmɪd/

fatoush Middle Eastern dish
fat-**oosh** /faˈtuːʃ/

fatuous silly and pointless
fat-yoo-uhss /ˈfatjʊəs/

fatwa legal Islamic pronouncement
fat-wah /ˈfatwɑː/

faubourg suburb, especially one in Paris
foh-boor /ˈfəʊbʊə(r)/

fauces opening at the back of the mouth leading to the pharynx
faw-seez /ˈfɔːsiːz/

faucet tap
faw-suht /ˈfɔːsət/

faujdar (also **faujidar**) Indian police officer
faw-jid-ar /ˈfɔːdʒɪdɑː(r)/

Faulkner, William American novelist
fawk-nuhr /ˈfɔːknə(r)/

Faulks, Sebastian English writer
fohks /fəʊks/

faun Roman god
fawn /fɔːn/

fauna pl. **faunae** animals of a region
faw-nuh, pl. **faw**-nee /ˈfɔːnə, pl. /-niː/
• Standard -s plural is also possible.

Fauntleroy excessively well-mannered young boy
font-luh-roy /ˈfɒntlərɔɪ/

Faunus Roman mythological god
faw-nuhss /ˈfɔːnəs/

Fauré, Gabriel French composer and organist
gab-ri-**el** faw-**ray** /ˌgabriˌɛl fɔːˈreɪ/

Faust German astronomer and necromancer
fowst /faʊst/

Faustus, Dr see **Doctor Faustus**

faute de mieux 'for want of better'
(French)
foht duh **myoe** /ˌfəʊt də 'mjøː/

Fauve group of painters who favoured
fauvism
fohv /fəʊv/

fauvism style of painting
foh-viz-uhm /'fəʊvɪzəm/

faux pas embarrassing or tactless act
foh **pah** /fəʊ 'pɑː/

fava broad bean; also called **faba**
fah-vuh /'fɑːvə/

favela Brazilian shack or shanty town
fav-**el**-uh /fa'vɛlə/

favrile glass coloured iridescent glass
fuh-**vreel** /fə'vriːl/

Fawcett, Farrah American actress
farr-uh **faw**-suht /ˌfarə 'fɔːsət/

Fawkes, Guy English conspirator
fawks /fɔːks/

Fayed, Emad 'Dodi' son of Mohamed
Al Fayed
ee-mad **doh**-di **fy**-uhd /ˌiːmad ˌdəʊdi
'fʌɪəd/

Fayed, Mohamed Al Egyptian
chairman of Harrods
muh-**ham**-uhd uhl **fy**-uhd /məˌhaməd
əl 'fʌɪəd/

fazenda Portuguese estate or large farm
fuh-**zen**-duh /fə'zɛndə/

fazendeiro person who owns a fazenda
faz-en-**day**-roo /ˌfazɛn'deɪruː/

Featherstonehaugh British family
name
feth-uhr-stuhn-haw, **fan**-shaw,
fest-uhn-haw, **fee**-suhn-hay,
feer-stuhn-haw /'fɛðə(r)stənhɔː/,
/'fanʃɔː/, /'fɛstənhɔː/, /'fiːsənheɪ/,
/'fɪə(r)stənhɔː/

febrifuge medicine used to reduce fever
feb-rif-yooj /'fɛbrɪfjuːdʒ/

February month
feb-roo-uh-ri /'fɛbruəri/

Commonly also **feb**-yoo-uh-ri, and
sometimes also **feb**-ruu-ri or **feb**-yuu-ri.

Fechner, Gustav German physicist and
psychologist
guust-ahf **fekh**-nuhr /ˌgʊstɑːf
'fɛçnə(r)/

fedayeen (also **fidayeen**) Arab guerrillas
fed-uh-**yeen** /ˌfɛdə'jiːn/

Federer, Roger Swiss tennis player
roj-uhr **fed**-uh-ruhr /ˌrɒdʒə(r)
'fɛdərə(r)/, German ['feːdərɐ]

This is his own anglicized pronunciation.

Federline, Kevin American dancer
fed-uhr-lyn /'fɛdə(r)lʌɪn/

fedora felt hat
fuh-**daw**-ruh /fə'dɔːrə/

feijoada Brazilian or Portuguese dish
fay-**zhwad**-uh /feɪ'ʒwadə/

feis pl. **feiseanna** Irish or Scottish music
festival
fesh, pl. **fesh**-uh-nuh /fɛʃ/, pl. /'fɛʃənə/

felafel see falafel

felid mammal of the cat family
fee-lid /'fiːlɪd/

felix culpa 'fortunate fault' (Latin)
fay-liks **kuul**-puh /ˌfeɪlɪks 'kʊlpə/
• See LATIN panel.

Felixstowe port, England
fee-lik-stoh /'fiːlɪkstəʊ/

fellah pl. **fellahin** Egyptian peasant
fel-uh, pl. fel-uh-**heen** /'fɛlə/, pl.
/fɛlə'hiːn/

Fellini, Federico Italian film director
fed-uh-**ree**-koh fel-**ee**-ni /ˌfɛdə,riːkəʊ
fɛ'liːni/

felo de se suicide
fee-loh dee **see** /ˌfiːləʊ di: 'siː/

felucca small boat
fel-**uk**-uh /fɛ'lʌkə/

femme fatale seductive woman
fam fuh-**tahl** /ˌfam fə'tɑːl/

femur pl. **femora** bone of the thigh
fee-muhr, pl. **fem**-uh-ruh /'fiːmə(r)/,
pl. /'fɛmərə/
• Standard -s plural is also possible.

fenestella niche in a church
fen-uh-**stel**-uh /ˌfɛnə'stɛlə/

fenestra pl. **fenestrae** hole or opening
fuh-**nest**-ruh, pl. fuh-**nest**-ree
/fə'nɛstrə/, pl. /-triː/

feng shui Chinese system of laws in
relation to the flow of energy
fung **shway** /ˌfʌŋ 'ʃweɪ/

A more anglicized pronunciation, feng
shwee, is also heard.

Fenian member of the Irish Republican
Brotherhood
fee-ni-uhn /'fiːnɪən/

fennec small fox
fen-ek /ˈfɛnɛk/

Fennoscandia land mass in NW Europe
fen-oh-**skan**-di-uh /ˌfɛnəʊˈskandiə/

fenugreek plant
fen-**yoo**-greek /ˈfɛnjuːɡriːk/

feral in a wild state
ferr-uhl /ˈfɛrəl/

fer de lance viper
fair duh lahnss /ˌfɛː(r) də ˈlɑːns/

feretory shrine containing the relics
of a saint
ferr-uh-tuh-ri /ˈfɛrətəri/

Fergana city, Uzbekistan
fuhr-**gah**-nuh /fə(r)ˈɡɑːnə/

This is the Uzbek pronunciation. A
Russified pronunciation, fyuhr-guh-**nah**, is
also heard.

feria Spanish fair
ferr-i-uh /ˈfɛriə/

ferial denoting an ordinary weekday
feer-i-uhl /ˈfɪəriəl/

Ferlinghetti, Lawrence American
poet and publisher
fur-ling-**get**-i /ˌfəː(r)lɪŋˈɡɛti/

Fermanagh county, Northern Ireland
fuhr-**man**-uh /fə(r)ˈmanə/

Fermat, Pierre de French
mathematician
pyair duh fair-**mah** /ˌpjɛː(r) də
fɛː(r)ˈmɑː/

fermata musical term
fur-**mah**-tuh /fəː(r)ˈmɑːtə/

Fermi, Enrico Italian-born American
atomic physicist
en-**ree**-koh **fur**-mi /ɛnˌriːkəʊ ˈfəː(r)mi/

fermi unit of length
fur-mi /ˈfəː(r)mi/

fermium chemical element
fur-mi-uhm /ˈfəː(r)miəm/

ferox trout
ferr-oks /ˈfɛrɒks/

Ferranti, Sebastian English electrical
engineer
fuh-**ran**-ti /fəˈranti/

Ferrara city and province, Italy
ferr-ar-uh /fɛˈrɑːrə/

Ferrari, Enzo Italian car designer and
manufacturer
ent-soh ferr-ar-i /ˌɛntsəʊ fɛˈrɑːri/

The make of car is fuh-**rar**-i.

Ferreira, Wayne South African tennis
player
fuh-**rair**-uh /fəˈrɛːrə/

Ferrer, Ibrahim Cuban singer
eeb-rah-**eem** ferr-air /iːbrɑːˌiːm
fɛˈrɛː(r)/

Ferrero, Juan Carlos Spanish tennis
player
khwan **kar**-loss ferr-**air**-oh /xwan
ˌkɑː(r)lɒs fɛˈrɛːrəʊ/

Ferrier, Kathleen English contralto
ferr-i-uhr /ˈfɛriə(r)/

ferrous containing iron
ferr-uhss /ˈfɛrəs/

ferruginous containing rust
ferr-**oo**-jin-uhss /fɛˈruːdʒɪnəs/

Fès see Fez

Fessenden, Reginald Aubrey
Canadian-born American pioneer of
radio-telephony
fess-uhn-duhn /ˈfɛsəndən/

festoon garland of flowers
fest-**oon** /fɛˈstuːn/

feta (also **fetta**) Greek cheese
fet-uh /ˈfɛtə/

fête public function
fayt /feɪt/

fetid (also **foetid**) smelling extremely
unpleasant
fet-id /ˈfɛtɪd/

Commonly also **fee**-tid.

fetor a strong, foul smell
fee-tuhr /ˈfiːtə(r)/

fettuccine (also **fettucini**) type of pasta
fet-uu-**chee**-ni /ˌfɛtʊˈtʃiːni/

Feuerbach, Ludwig German
philosopher
loot-vikh **foy**-uhr-bakh /ˌluːtvɪç
ˈfɔɪə(r)bax/

Feydeau, Georges French dramatist
zhorzh fay-**doh** /ˌzɔː(r)ʒ feɪˈdəʊ/

Feyenoord Dutch football team and
suburb of Rotterdam
fy-uhn-ort /ˈfʌɪənɔː(r)t/
• See DUTCH panel.

Feynman, Richard Phillips American
physicist
fyn-muhn /ˈfʌɪnmən/

Fez (also **Fès**) city, Morocco
fez /fɛz/

fez Turkish hat
fez /fɛz/

fiancé (also **fiancée**) person to whom one is engaged to be married
fi-**on**-say /fɪ'ɒnseɪ/

Commonly also fi-**ahn**-say, and in AM also fee-ahn-**say**.

fianchetto chess move
fyan-**ket**-oh /fjan'kɛtəʊ/

Fianna Fáil Irish political party
fee-uh-nuh **foyl** /ˌfiːənə 'fɔɪl/,
Irish Gaelic [ˌfˠiənə 'faːlʲ]
• Established anglicization.

Fibonacci, Leonardo Italian mathematician
lay-oh-**nar**-doh fee-boh-**nah**-chi
/leɪəʊˌnɑː(r)dəʊ ˌfiːbəʊ'nɑːtʃi/

fibroma pl. **fibromata** benign fibrous tumour
fy-**broh**-muh, fy-**broh**-muh-tuh
/fʌɪ'brəʊmə/, pl. /-mətə/
• Standard -s plural is also possible.

fibromyalgia rheumatic condition
fy-broh-my-**al**-ji-uh
/ˌfʌɪbrəʊmʌɪ'aldʒiə/

fibula pl. **fibulae** leg bone
fib-yuul-uh, pl. **fib**-yuul-ee /'fɪbjʊlə/,
pl. /-liː/
• Standard -s plural is also possible.

Fichte, Johann Gottlieb German philosopher
yoh-han **got**-leep **fikh**-tuh /ˌjəʊhan
ˌgɒtliːp 'fɪçtə/

ficus plant
fy-**kuhss** /'fʌɪkəs/

Commonly also **fee**-kuhss; see LATIN panel.

fidayeen see fedayeen

FIDE world chess federation
fee-day /'fiːdeɪ/

Fiennes, Ralph English actor
rayf fynz /ˌreɪf 'fʌɪnz/

Fiennes, Ranulph English explorer
ran-uhlf **fynz** /ˌranəlf 'fʌɪnz/

FIFA Fédération Internationale de Football Association
fee-fuh /'fiːfə/

Figaro character in Mozart's opera *The Marriage of Figaro*
fee-guh-roh /'fiːɡərəʊ/

Fiji country
fee-jee /'fiːdʒiː/

Fijian relating to Fiji
fee-**jee**-uhn /fiː'dʒiːən/

filariasis tropical disease
fil-uh-**ry**-uh-siss /ˌfɪlə'rʌɪəsɪs/

filet mignon tender piece of beef
fil-ay **meen**-yo(ng) /ˌfɪleɪ 'miːnjõ/

AM is fil-**ay** min-**yawn**.

Filipino relating to the Philippines
fil-ip-**ee**-noh /ˌfɪlɪ'piːnəʊ/

film noir film genre
film **nwar** /ˌfɪlm 'nwɑː(r)/

filo (also **phyllo**) pastry
fee-loh /'fiːləʊ/

filovirus virus
fee-loh-vy-ruhss /'fiːləʊˌvʌɪrəs/

fils used to distinguish a son from a father of the same name
feess /fiːs/

finale last part of an event
fin-**ah**-li /fɪ'nɑːli/

finance management of money
fy-nanss /'fʌɪnans/

Less commonly also fy-**nanss** and fin-**anss**.

financial relating to finance
fy-**nan**-shuhl /fʌɪ'nanʃəl/

Less commonly also fin-**an**-shuhl.

fin de siècle relating to the end of a century
fa(ng) duh **syek**-luh /ˌfɛ̃ də 'sjɛklə/

fine French brandy
feen /fiːn/

fine musical term
fee-nay /'fiːneɪ/

Fine Gael Irish political party
fin-uh **gayl** /ˌfɪnə 'ɡeɪl/, Irish Gaelic
[ˌfˠinʲə 'ɡeːl]

Finisterre, Cape promontory, Spain
fin-ist-**air** /ˌfɪnɪ'stɛː(r)/

Finland country
fin-luhnd /'fɪnlənd/

Established anglicization. The Finnish name is Suomi, pronounced **soo**-om-i.

Finn MacCool (also **Finn Mac Cumhaill**) Irish mythological character
fin muh-**kool** /ˌfɪn mə'kuːl/

Finno-Ugric group of languages
fin-oh-**yoo**-grik /ˌfɪnəʊ'juːɡrɪk/

fino sherry
fee-noh /'fiːnəʊ/

Finucane, Patrick Northern Irish lawyer
fin-**oo**-kuhn /fɪ'nuːkən/

Fiorentina Italian football club
fyorr-en-**tee**-nuh /fjɔrɛn'tiːnə/

fioritura pl. **fioriture** musical term
fi-aw-ri-**toor**-uh, pl. fi-aw-ri-**toor**-ay
/fi,ɔːri'tʊərə/, pl. /-reɪ/

fiqh philosophy of Islamic law
feek /fiːk/

Firenze see **Florence**

firn crystalline or granular snow
feern /'fɪən/

firni Indian dish
feer-ni /'fɪə(r)ni/

Fischer-Dieskau, Dietrich German
baritone
deet-rikh fish-uhr **dee**-skow /,diːtrɪç
,fɪʃə(r) 'diːskaʊ/

Fischer, Joschka German politician
yosh-kuh fish-uhr /,jɒʃkə 'fɪʃə(r)/

Fish Hoek suburb of Cape Town
fish huuk /'fɪʃ hʊk/

fistula pl. **fistulae** abnormal or surgically
made passage
fist-yuul-uh, pl. **fist**-yuul-ee /'fɪstjʊlə/,
pl. /-liː/
• Standard -s plural is also possible.

FISU International University Sports
Federation
fee-zoo /'fiːzuː/

fitché heraldic term
fitch-ay /'fɪtʃeɪ/

Fiume see **Rijeka**

fjord deep inlet of the sea between high
cliffs
fyord /fjɔː(r)d/, Norwegian [fjuːr]

flageolet French kidney bean
flaj-uh-**let** /fladʒə'lɛt/, [flaʒɔlɛ]

Commonly also flaj-uh-**lay**. The same
pronunciations are used for the musical
instrument.

flagon container in which drink is served
flag-uhn /'flagən/

Flaine resort, France
flen /flɛn/

flambé covered with spirits and set alight
briefly
flom-bay /'flɒmbeɪ/, French [flãbe]

Flamborough Head promontory,
England
flam-buh-ruh /'flambərə/

Flamengo Brazilian football club
fluh-**meng**-goo /flə'mɛŋguː/

Flamsteed, John English astronomer
flam-steed /'flamstiːd/

Flanagan, Fionnula Irish actress
fin-**oo**-luh /fɪ'nuːlə/

Flanders region, divided between
Belgium, France, and the Netherlands
flahn-duhrz /'flɑːndə(r)z/

Established anglicization. The Flemish
name is Vlaanderen, pronounced
vlahn-duh-ruh(n), and the French name is
Flandre (or Flandres), both pronounced
flah(ng)-druh.

Flandrian geological stage
flahn-dri-uhn /'flɑːndriən/

Flaubert, Gustave French novelist
gue-**stahv** floh-bair /gy,stɑːv
fləʊ'bɛː(r)/

Flavian dynasty of Roman emperors
flay-vi-uhn /'fleɪviən/

flavin pigment
flay-vin /'fleɪvɪn/

fleadh Irish music festival
flah /flɑː/

Fleming native of Flanders
flem-ing /'flɛmɪŋ/

Flemish relating to Flanders
flem-ish /'flɛmɪʃ/

Flensburg city, Germany
flenss-boork /'flɛnsbʊə(r)k/

fleur-de-lis lily
flur-duh-**lee** /,fləː(r)də'liː/

fleury decorated with fleurs-de-lis;
also **flory**
floor-i /'flʊəri/

Flevoland province, Netherlands
flay-voh-lunt /'fleɪvəʊlʌnt/

floccinaucinihilipilification action of
estimating something as worthless
flok-sin-aw-si-**ni**-hil-ip-il-if-ik-**ay**-
shuhn /,flɒksɪ,nɔːsɪ,nihɪlɪ,pɪlɪfɪ'keɪʃən/

floccus pl. **flocci** tuft of wool
flok-uhss, pl. **flok**-y /'flɒkəs/, pl. /-kʌɪ/

Plural is sometimes also flok-sy.

flokati Greek rug
flok-**ah**-ti /flɒ'kɑːti/

Florence city, Italy
florr-uhnss /'flɒrəns/

Established anglicization. The Italian name
is Firenze, pronounced firr-**ent**-say.

Florentine relating to Florence
florr-uhn-tyn /ˈflɒrəntʌɪn/

Flores island, Indonesia
flaw-ress /ˈflɔːrɛs/

Flores island, the Azores
florr-uhsh /ˈflɒrəʃ/

Floriano city, Brazil
florr-i-**an**-oo /flɒriˈanuː/

Florianópolis city, Brazil
florr-i-uh-**nop**-uul-iss /ˌflɒriəˈnɒpʊlɪs/

floriferous producing many flowers
florr-**if**-uh-ruhss /flɒˈrɪfərəs/

florilegium pl. **florilegia** collection of
literary extracts
florr-il-**ee**-ji-uhm, pl. florr-il-**ee**-ji-uh
/ˌflɒrɪˈliːdʒɪəm/, pl. /-dʒɪə/
• Standard -s plural is also possible.

florin former British coin
florr-in /ˈflɒrɪn/

Florio, John English lexicographer
flaw-ri-oh /ˈflɔːriəʊ/

flory decorated with fleurs-de-lis; also
fleury
flaw-ri /ˈflɔːri/

flotilla small fleet of ships
fluh-**til**-uh /fləˈtɪlə/

Flotow, Friedrich German composer
freed-rikh **floh**-toh /ˌfriːdrɪç ˈfləʊtəʊ/

flotsam wreckage of a ship
flot-suhm /ˈflɒtsəm/

floweret floret
flow-uh-ruht /ˈflaʊərət/

flugelhorn musical instrument
floo-guhl-horn /ˈfluːɡəlhɔː(r)n/

Fluminense Brazilian football club
floo-min-**e(ng)**-si /fluːmɪˈnẽsi/

fluoresce shine or glow brightly
flaw-**ress** /flɔːˈrɛs/

Sometimes also floo-uh-**ress**.

fluoride chemical compound
floor-yd /ˈflʊərʌɪd/

Commonly also **flaw-ryd**.

fluorine chemical element
floor-een /ˈflʊəriːn/

Commonly also **flaw-reen**.

Fluoxetine trademark antidepressant drug
floo-**ok**-suh-teen /fluːˈɒksətiːn/

Flushing port, Netherlands
flush-ing /ˈflʌʃɪŋ/

Established anglicization. The Dutch name
is Vlissingen, pronounced **vliss**-ing-uh(n).

fluvial relating to rivers
floo-vi-uhl /ˈfluːvɪəl/

fluvoxamine antidepressant drug
floo-**voks**-uh-meen /fluːˈvɒksəmiːn/

Fo, Dario Italian writer
dar-i-oh **foh** /ˌdɑːriəʊ ˈfəʊ/

Foça city, Turkey
fotch-uh /ˈfɒtʃə/

focaccia Italian bread
fuh-**katch**-uh /fəˈkatʃə/

Foch, Ferdinand French general
fair-dee-**nah(ng)** **fosh** /fɛː(r)diːˌnã
ˈfɒʃ/

foetid see fetid

Foggia town, Italy
foj-uh /ˈfɒdʒə/

Fogh Rasmussen, Anders see
Rasmussen, Anders Fogh

fogou Cornish earth-house
foh-goo /ˈfəʊɡuː/

föhn (also **foehn**) hot wind
foen /fəːn/

foie gras short for pâté de foie gras
fwah **grah** /ˌfwɑː ˈɡrɑː/

Fokine, Michel Russian-born American
dancer
mee-**shel** fuh-**keen** /miːˌʃɛl fəˈkiːn/

Fokker, Anthony Dutch-born
American aircraft designer
fok-uhr /ˈfɒkə(r)/

The same pronunciation is used for the
make of aircraft.

folacin another term for folic acid
fohl-uh-sin /ˈfəʊləsɪn/

folic acid vitamin of the B complex
foh-lik /ˈfəʊlɪk/

Sometimes also **fol-ik**.

folio individual leaf of paper or
parchment
foh-li-oh /ˈfəʊliəʊ/

Folketing Danish parliament
fol-kuh-ting /ˈfɒlkətɪŋ/

Folkestone port, England
fohk-stuhn /ˈfəʊkstən/

follis Roman coin
fol-iss /ˈfɒlɪs/

Folsom Palaeo-Indian culture
fohl-suhm /ˈfəʊlsəm/

Fomalhaut star
foh-muhl-hawt /ˈfəʊməlˌhɔːt/

foment instigate or stir up
foh-**ment** /fəʊˈment/

fomites objects or materials which are likely to carry infection
foh-mit-eez /ˈfəʊmɪtiːz/

fondant thick paste made of sugar and water
fon-duhnt /ˈfɒndənt/

fondue French dish
fon-doo /ˈfɒnduː/, [fɔ̃dy]

fontanelle space between the bones of the skull in an infant
fon-tuh-**nel** /ˌfɒntəˈnɛl/

Fonteyn, Margot English ballet dancer
mar-goh fon-**tayn** /ˌmɑː(r)gəʊ fɒnˈteɪn/

fontina Italian cheese
fon-**tee**-nuh /fɒnˈtiːnə/

foo yong Chinese dish
foo yong /ˌfuːˈjɒŋ/

foramen pl. **foramina** opening or passage
fuh-**ray**-men, pl. fuh-**ram**-in-uh /fəˈreɪmɛn, pl. /-ˈramɪnə/

forastero cacao tree
forr-uh-**stair**-oh /ˌfɒrəˈstɛːrəʊ/

foray sudden attack
forr-ay /ˈfɒreɪ/

Forbes American magazine
forbz /fɔː(r)bz/

The British surname is variously pronounced **for**-buhss and forbz, depending on individual preference.

fordo (also **foredo**) kill
for-**doo** /fɔː(r)ˈduː/

forehead part of the face
fawr-hed /ˈfɔː(r)hɛd/

Less commonly also **forr**-id.

Forfar town, Scotland
for-fuhr /ˈfɔː(r)fə(r)/

forfeit lose or be deprived
for-fit /ˈfɔː(r)fɪt/

forint currency unit, Hungary
forr-int /ˈfɒrɪnt/

formaldehyde gas, used in solution as a preservative
for-**mal**-duh-hyd /fɔː(r)ˈmaldəhʌɪd/

Forman, Milos Czech-born American film director
mee-losh **for**-muhn /ˌmiːlɒʃ ˈfɔː(r)mən/

Formentera island, Mediterranean
for-men-**tair**-uh /ˌfɔː(r)mɛnˈtɛːrə/

Formica trademark plastic laminate
for-**my**-kuh /fɔː(r)ˈmʌɪkə/

formicarium ant's nest
for-mik-**air**-i-uhm /ˌfɔː(r)mɪˈkɛːriəm/

formidable inspiring fear or respect
for-mid-uh-buhl /ˈfɔː(r)mɪdəbəl/

Commonly also for-**mid**-uh-buhl.

Formosa former name for Taiwan
for-**moh**-suh /fɔː(r)ˈməʊsə/

formula pl. **formulae** mathematical rule
for-myuul-uh, pl. **for**-myuul-ee /ˈfɔː(r)mjʊlə, pl. /-liː/
• Standard -s plural is also possible.

formulary collection of set forms
for-myuul-uh-ri /ˈfɔːmjʊləri/

Fornax constellation
for-naks /ˈfɔː(r)naks/

Fornells resort, Menorca
for-**nelss** /fɔː(r)ˈnɛls/

Forster, E. M. English novelist
for-stuhr /ˈfɔː(r)stə(r)/

Forsyth, Frederick English novelist
for-**syth** /fɔː(r)ˈsʌɪθ/

Forsyth, Bruce English entertainer
for-syth /ˈfɔː(r)sʌɪθ/

forsythia shrub
for-**sy**-thi-uh /fɔː(r)ˈsʌɪθiə/

Fortaleza port, Brazil
for-tuh-**lay**-zuh /ˌfɔː(r)təˈleɪzə/

Fort-de-France capital of Martinique
for-duh-**frah(ng)ss** /ˌfɔː(r)dəˈfrɑ̃s/

forte thing at which someone excels
for-tay /ˈfɔː(r)teɪ/

Sometimes also **fort**-i, but fort is less common now.

forte musical term
for-tay /ˈfɔː(r)teɪ/

fortepiano type of piano
for-tay-**pyan**-oh /ˌfɔː(r)teɪˈpjanəʊ/

forthwith immediately
forth-**with** /fɔːθˈwɪθ/

Sometimes also forth-**with**.

fortis strongly articulated
for-tiss /ˈfɔː(r)tɪs/

fortissimo pl. **fortissimi** musical term
for-**tiss**-i-moh, pl. for-**tiss**-im-i
/fɔː(r)ˈtɪsɪməʊ, pl. /-mi/
• Standard -s plural is also possible.

Fort Knox military reservation, US
noks /nɒks/

Fort Lamy former name for **N'Djamena**
for **lam**-ee /ˌfɔː(r) ˈlami/

Fortuyn, Pim Dutch politician
pim for-**toeyn** /ˌpɪm fɔː(r)ˈtœɪn/

Forza Italia Italian political party
fort-suh ee-**tahl**-yuh /ˌfɔː(r)tsə
iːˈtɑːljə/

Fosbury, Richard American
high-jumper
foz-buh-ri /ˈfɒzbəri/

fossa pl. **fossae** hollow
foss-uh, pl. **foss**-ee /ˈfɒsə, pl. /-siː/

Fosse, Bob American theatre and film
director
foss-i /ˈfɒsi/

fosse narrow trench or excavation
foss /fɒs/

fossiliferous containing fossils
foss-il-if-uh-ruhss /ˌfɒsɪˈlɪfərəs/

Foucault, Michel French philosopher
mee-**shel** foo-**koh** /miːˌʃɛl fuːˈkəʊ/

Foulah see **Fula**

foulard material of silk or silk and cotton
foo-lard /ˈfuːlɑː(r)d/

Foulkes, Imogen BBC journalist
fohks /fəʊks/

This British surname is variously
pronounced fohks and fowks, depending
on individual preference.

Fourier, Joseph French mathematician
zhoh-**zef** foor-i-**ay** /ˌʒəʊˌzɛf fʊəriˈeɪ/

The same pronunciation is used for Fourier
analysis.

fovea pl. **foveae** depression in the retina
foh-vi-uh, pl. **foh**-vi-ee /ˈfəʊviə, pl.
/-viː/

Fowles, John English novelist
fowlz /faʊlz/

Fox, Vivica American actress
viv-ik-uh /ˈvɪvɪkə/

Fox Quesada, Vicente Mexican
president
vee-**sen**-tay foks kay-**sah**-*th*uh
/viːˌsɛnteɪ ˌfɒks keɪˈsɑːðə/

foyer entrance hall

foy-ay /ˈfɔɪeɪ/

Fra title given to an Italian monk or friar
frah /frɑː/

fracas disturbance or quarrel
frak-ah /ˈfrɑkɑː/

Fragonard, Jean-Honoré French
painter
zhah(ng) on-orr-**ay** frag-on-**ar** /ʒɑ̃
ɒnɒˌreɪ fragɒˈnɑː(r)/

franc former currency unit, France
frank /fraŋk/, [frɑ̃]

France country
frahnss /frɑːns/, [frɑ̃s]
• Established anglicization.

Franche-Comté region, France
frah(ng)sh ko(ng)-**tay** /ˌfrɑ̃ʃ kɔ̃ˈteɪ/

francium chemical element
fran-si-uhm /ˈfransiəm/

Franck, César Belgian-born French
composer
say-**zar frah(ng)k** /seɪˌzɑː(r) ˈfrɑ̃k/

Franconia medieval duchy, Germany
frank-**oh**-ni-uh /fraŋˈkəʊniə/

francophone French-speaking
frank-oh-fohn /ˈfraŋkəʊfəʊn/

Frankenstein novel by Mary Shelley
frank-uhn-styn /ˈfraŋkənstʌɪn/

Frankfort city, US
frank-fuhrt /ˈfraŋkfə(r)t/

Frankfurt city, Germany
frank-furt /ˈfraŋkfə(r)t/, German
/ˈfraŋkfʊrt/
• Established anglicization.

Franklin, Aretha American singer
uh-**ree**-thuh **frank**-lin /əˌriːθə
ˈfraŋklɪn/

Franz Josef emperor of Austria
frants yoh-zef /ˌfrants ˈjəʊzɛf/

frappé iced drink
frap-**ay** /fraˈpeɪ/

Frascati region, Italy; also white wine
made there
frask-**ah**-ti /fraˈskɑːti/

frater refectory of a monastery
fray-tuhr /ˈfreɪtə(r)/

Frattini, Franco Italian politician
frank-oh frat-**ee**-ni /ˌfraŋkəʊ fraˈtiːni/

Frau pl. **Frauen** German title for a
woman
frow, pl. **frow**-uhn /fraʊ, pl. /ˈfraʊən/

Fräulein German title for a young woman
froy-lyn /ˈfrɔɪlʌɪn/

Fray Bentos port, Uruguay
fray **bent**-oss /ˌfreɪ ˈbɛntɒs/

Frazier, Joe American boxer
fray-zi-uhr /ˈfreɪzɪə(r)/

This surname can also be pronounced **fray**-zhuhr in AM.

Fredericton city, Canada
fred-rik-tuhn /ˈfrɛdrɪktən/

freesia plant
free-zhuh /ˈfriːʒə/

Commonly also **free**-zi-uh.

Frege, Gottlob German philosopher
got-lohp **fray**-guh /ˌɡɒtləʊp ˈfreɪɡə/

Freiburg city, Germany
fry-boork /ˈfrʌɪbʊə(r)k/

Frelimo Mozambican political party
frel-**ee**-moh /frɛˈliːməʊ/

Fremantle port, Australia
free-mant-uhl /ˈfriːmantəl/

Frémont, John Charles American explorer
free-mont /ˈfriːmɒnt/

freon trademark aerosol propellant
free-on /ˈfriːɒn/

Frescobaldi, Girolamo Italian composer
jirr-**ol**-uh-moh fresk-oh-**bal**-di /dʒɪˌrɒləməʊ frɛskəʊˈbaldi/

Fresno city, US
frez-noh /ˈfrɛznəʊ/

Freud, Lucian German-born British painter
loo-si-uhn froyd /ˌluːsɪən ˈfrɔɪd/

Freud, Sigmund Austrian psychotherapist
zeek-muunt froyd /ˌziːkmʊnt ˈfrɔɪd/

Frey Norse god
fray /freɪ/

Freya Norse goddess
fray-uh /ˈfreɪə/

fricative type of speech sound
frik-uh-tiv /ˈfrɪkətɪv/

Friedan, Betty American feminist and writer
free-duhn /ˈfriːdən/

Friedman, Milton American economist
freed-muhn /ˈfriːdmən/

Friedrich, Caspar David German painter
kasp-ar **dah**-vit **freed**-rikh /ˌkaspɑː(r) ˌdɑːvɪt ˈfriːdrɪç/

Friel, Anna English actress
freel /friːl/

Friesian breed of cow
free-zhuhn /ˈfriːʒən/

Friesland province, Netherlands
freez-luhnd /ˈfriːzlənd/, [ˈfriːslɑnt]
• Established anglicization.

Frigga Norse mythological character
frig-uh /ˈfrɪɡə/

frijoles beans
fri-**hoh**-less /friˈhəʊlɛs/

Frisia ancient region, Europe
free-zhuh /ˈfriːʒə/

Commonly also **friz**-i-uh.

frittata Italian dish
frit-**ah**-tuh /frɪˈtɑːtə/

fritto misto Italian mixed dish
free-toh **mist**-oh /ˌfriːtəʊ ˈmɪstəʊ/

Friuli historic region, Europe
fri-**oo**-li /friˈuːli/

Friuli-Venezia Giulia region, Italy
fri-**oo**-li ven-**ets**-i-uh **joo**-li-uh /friˌuːli vɛˌnɛtsɪə ˈdʒuːlɪə/

frizzante semi-sparkling
frit-**san**-tay /frɪtˈsanteɪ/

Frobisher, Martin English explorer
froh-bish-uhr /ˈfrəʊbɪʃə(r)/

Frodo character from *The Lord of the Rings*
froh-doh /ˈfrəʊdəʊ/

Fröhliche Weihnachten 'Happy Christmas' (German)
froe-likh-uh **vy**-nakh-tuhn /ˌfrøːlɪçə ˈvʌɪnaxtən/

fromage frais soft cheese
from-**ahzh** fray /frɒˌmɑːʒ ˈfreɪ/

Fronde series of civil wars, France
fro(ng)d /frɔ̃d/

frontier border separating two countries
frun-teer /ˈfrʌntɪə(r)/

Commonly also frun-**teer**.

Frostrup, Mariella Norwegian-born English television presenter
marr-i-**el**-uh **frost**-ruup /mariˌɛlə ˈfrɒstrʊp/

French

French is a Romance language, spoken by over 100 million people as their mother tongue. It is an official language in many countries, such as Belgium, Switzerland, Canada, and numerous African countries. French pronunciation is difficult because it is unpredictable. Like English—although less so—the pronunciation does not always reflect the spelling. You may get different sounds represented by the same letter, and there are letters which are sometimes pronounced and sometimes silent. For example, should the S in the family name *Ramus* be pronounced? As it happens, both forms are used and not even a native French speaker could be sure without checking with the owner of the name first! Having said that, here are some general pronunciation tips.

Stress

French does not have stressed syllables in the same way as English. In a French word all syllables are given more or less equal weight, while the last syllable in a sentence is pronounced with a little more force. This sentence-level tonal pattern is sometimes mistaken for word-final stress.

Despite this, when giving advice on how to pronounce French names in an English context it becomes necessary to use stress. Traditionally, English speakers like to stress the first syllable of French words, and will say **kal**-ay and **shat**-oh for *Calais* and *château*. The BBC sometimes gets complaints about this, as it is perceived as less 'French'. These days, when we research French names for our broadcasters we often give last-syllable stress, as you will see in the many French entries in this dictionary.

Accents

Accents in French therefore do not indicate stress, but vowel quality. An acute accent over E makes a sound close to ay (although not diphthongal in French). *André*, for example, is pronounced ah(ng)-**dray**. A grave accent over E is pronounced as in English *bed*. *Irène* is ee-**ren**.

Nasalized vowels

Vowels are nasalized before N or M at the end of a word or when N or M is followed by another consonant. Otherwise, the vowel is not nasalized and the N or M is pronounced. So *bon* is pronounced bo(ng), and *bonne* is bon. The letter E can be pronounced either ah(ng) or a(ng) when nasalized. Contrary to popular belief, the composer *Poulenc* is in fact pronounced poo-**la(ng)k**, not poo-**lah(ng)k**.

Liaison

The letters S, Z, X, T, D, N, M, R, P, and G are usually silent at the end of a word, but if the next word begins with a vowel sound they are generally pronounced. *Petit* is puh-**tee**, but *petit enfant* is puh-**teet** ah(ng)-**fah(ng)**. This phenomenon is known as liaison. There are many rules governing the occurrence of liaison in French. For example, it is more common in formal language than in an informal, colloquial context.

Some other letters

C is pronounced s before the letters I, E, and Y. It is pronounced k before A, U, O, and all consonants. Ç is always pronounced s. CH is always sh.

G is pronounced zh before I, E, and Y. It is pronounced g before A, O, U, and all consonants.

H in word-initial position is always silent, although there are two kinds of silent H. One kind, known in French as H aspiré, prevents liaison taking place. Loanwords from other languages (*hi-fi*, *hot-dog*) are likely to be H aspiré.

J is always pronounced zh.

O can be either oh or o. Ô is always oh.

Q is always k.

S is usually s. Between vowels and in a liaison it is voiced z.

U is always ue, the close, rounded vowel you find in French *vu*.

W can be either v or w, more usually v.

X can be pronounced in different ways, usually ks, but gz between vowels. In some cases it is also pronounced s, as in the place name *Auxerre*.

Y is ee as a vowel, and y as a consonant.

Frottola Italian madrigal
 frot-oh-luh /'frɒtəʊlə/

fructose sugar
 fruk-tohz /'frʌktəʊz/

FTSE London stock exchange index
 fuut-si /'fʊtsi/

Fuad name of two kings of Egypt
 foo-ad /'fuːad/

Fuchs, Klaus German-born British physicist
 klowss fuuks /ˌklaʊs 'fʊks/

Fuchs, Vivian English geologist and explorer
 fuuks /fʊks/

fuchsia shrub
 fyoo-shuh /'fjuːʃə/

fuchsin (also **fuchsine**) red synthetic dye
 fook-seen /'fuːksiːn/

fuehrer see **führer**

Fuentes, Carlos Mexican writer
 kar-loss fwent-ess /ˌkɑː(r)lɒs 'fwɛntɛs/

Fuerteventura island, Canary Islands
 fwair-tay-ven-toor-uh /ˌfwɛː(r)teɪvɛn'tʊərə/

Fugard, Athol South African dramatist
 ath-uhl fyoo-gard /ˌaθəl 'fjuːgɑː(r)d/

fugato musical term
 foo-gah-toh /fuː'gɑːtəʊ/

fugu poisonous pufferfish
 foo-goo /'fuːguː/

fugue musical composition
fyoog /ˈfjuːg/

führer (also **fuehrer**) tyrannical leader
fyoor-uhr /ˈfjʊərə(r)/, German [ˈfyːrɐ]

Fujairah state, United Arab Emirates
foo-**jy**-ruh /fuːˈdʒʌɪrə/

Fuji, Mount volcano, Japan
foo-ji /ˈfuːdʒi/

Fujian province, China
foo-ji-an /ˌfuːdʒiˈan/

The strain of influenza of the same name, however, is usually pronounced **foo**-ji-uhn.

Fujitsu Japanese company
foo-**jit**-soo /fuːˈdʒɪtsuː/
• Established anglicization; see JAPANESE panel.

Fukuoka city, Japan
foo-koo-**oh**-kuh /ˌfuːkuːˈəʊkə/

Fula (also **Foulah**) Fulani language
foo-luh /ˈfuːlə/

Fulani West African ethnic group
foo-**lah**-ni /fuːˈlɑːni/

fulvous reddish yellow
ful-vuhss /ˈfʌlvəs/

Sometimes also **fuul**-vuhss.

fumarole opening in a volcano
fyoo-muh-rohl /ˈfjuːmərəʊl/

Funafuti capital of Tuvalu
foo-nuh-**foo**-ti /ˌfuːnəˈfuːti/

Funchal port, Madeira
fuun-**shal** /fʊnˈʃal/, Portuguese [fũˈʃal]
• Established anglicization.

fundus pl. **fundi** part of a hollow organ
fun-duhss, pl. **fun**-dy /ˈfʌndəs/, pl. /-dʌɪ/

Funen island, Denmark
fyoo-nuhn /ˈfjuːnən/

Established anglicization. The Danish name is Fyn, pronounced fuen [fyːn].

fungus pl. **fungi** mushroom
fung-guhss, pl. **fung**-gy /ˈfʌŋgəs/, pl. /-gʌɪ/

Plural less commonly also **fun**-jy; standard -es plural is also possible.

Fur Sudanese ethnic group
foor /fʊə(r)/

Für Elise piano piece by Beethoven
fuer el-**ee**-zuh /ˌfyː(r) ɛˈliːzə/

furioso musical term
fyoor-i-**oh**-zoh /ˌfjʊəriˈəʊzəʊ/

Furneaux Islands group of islands, Tasmania
fur-noh /ˈfəː(r)nəʊ/

furore outbreak of public anger or excitement
fyoo-**raw**-ri /ˌfjʊˈrɔːri/

Sometimes also **fyoor**-or. AM is **fyoor**-uhr.

Furtwängler, Wilhelm German conductor
vil-helm **foort**-veng-luhr /ˌvɪlhɛlm ˈfʊə(r)tˌvɛŋlə(r)/

fuscous dark and sombre in colour
fusk-uhss /ˈfʌskəs/

fuselage main body of an aircraft
fyoo-zuh-lahzh /ˈfjuːzəlɑːʒ/

Commonly also **fyoo**-zuh-lij.

Fuseli, Henry Swiss-born British painter
fyoo-zuh-li /ˈfjuːzəli/

Very commonly also fyoo-**zel**-i.

fusel oil mixture of several alcohols
fyoo-zuhl /ˈfjuːzəl/

Fushun city, China
foo-**shuun** /fuːˈʃʊn/

fusilier member of various British regiments
fyoo-zil-**eer** /ˌfjuːzɪˈlɪə(r)/

fusillade series of shots fired
fyoo-zil-**ayd** /ˌfjuːzɪˈleɪd/

Sometimes also fyoo-zil-**ahd**.

fusilli type of pasta
foo-**zee**-li /fuːˈziːli/

fustanella Greek and Albanian kilt
fust-uh-**nel**-uh /ˌfʌstəˈnɛlə/

futhark runic alphabet
foo-thark /ˈfuːθɑː(r)k/

futon type of mattress
foo-ton /ˈfuːtɒn/

Futuna see **Wallis and Futuna Islands**

Fuxin city, China
foo-**shin** /fuːˈʃɪn/

Fuzhou port, China
foo-**joh** /fuːˈdʒəʊ/

fylfot swastika
fil-fot /ˈfɪlfɒt/

Fyn see **Funen**

fyrd English militia before 1066
furd /fəː(r)d/

Sometimes also **feerd**.

G

Ga Ghanaian language
gah /gɑː/

Gaarder, Jostein Norwegian writer
yoo-stayn gor-duhr /ˌjuːsteɪn ˈɡɔː(r)də(r)/

gaberdine worsted or cotton cloth
gab-uhr-deen /ˌɡabə(r)ˈdiːn/

Gabès (also **Qabis**) port, Tunisia
gah-biss /ˈɡɑːbɪs/

Gabo, Naum Russian-born American sculptor
nawm gab-oh /ˌnɔːm ˈɡabəʊ/

Gabon country
guh-bon /ɡəˈbɒn/, French [ɡabɔ̃]

Established anglicization; sometimes also **gab**-on.

Gabonese relating to Gabon
gab-uh-neez /ɡabəˈniːz/

Gaboon viper snake
guh-boon /ɡəˈbuːn/

Gabor, Zsa Zsa Hungarian-born American actress
zhah zhah gab-or /ˌʒɑː ʒɑː ɡəˈbɔː(r)/

The pronunciation of the Hungarian surname Gábor is **gah**-bor.

Gaborone capital of Botswana
gab-uh-roh-ni /ˌɡabəˈrəʊni/

Established anglicization. A more native pronunciation, khab-uu-**roo**-ni, is also heard.

Gabriel biblical name
gay-bri-uhl /ˈɡeɪbrɪəl/

Gabrieli, Giovanni Italian composer and organist
juh-vah-ni gab-ri-ay-li /dʒəˌvɑːni ɡabriˈeɪli/

Gad biblical name
gad /ɡad/

Gaddafi, Mu'ammer (also **Qaddafi**) Libyan head of state
muu-um-uhr guh-dah-fi /mʊˌʌmə(r) ɡəˈdɑːfi/, Arabic [muˈʌmmə(r) qaðˈdæːfi]

• Established anglicization; see **ARABIC** panel.

Gade, Niels Danish composer
neelss gay-thuh /ˌniːls ˈɡeɪðə/, [ˈɡɛːðə]

gadolinium chemical element
gad-uh-lin-i-uhm /ˌɡadəˈlɪniəm/

Gaea Greek mythological character; also called **Gaia**
jee-uh /ˈdʒiːə/

Gael Gaelic-speaking person
gayl /ɡeɪl/

Gaelic relating to the Gaels or their language
gay-lik, gal-ik /ˈɡeɪlɪk/, /ˈɡalɪk/

Irish Gaelic is usually pronounced **gay**-lik, while Scottish Gaelic is more commonly **gal**-ik.

Gaeltacht region, Ireland
gayl-tuhkht /ˈɡeɪltəxt/

Gagarin, Yuri Russian cosmonaut
yoor-i guh-gar-in /ˌjʊəri ɡəˈɡɑːrɪn/

Gagauz Moldovan ethnic group
gag-uh-ooz /ɡaɡəˈuːz/

Gaia Greek mythological character; also called **Gaea**
gy-uh /ˈɡʌɪə/

gaijin Japanese word for a foreigner
gy-jin /ɡʌɪˈdʒɪn/

gaillardia plant of the daisy family
gay-lar-di-uh /ɡeɪˈlɑː(r)diə/

Gainsborough, Thomas English painter
gaynz-buh-ruh /ˈɡeɪnzbərə/

Gainsbourg, Serge French singer
sairzh ga(ng)z-boor /ˌsɛː(r)ʒ ˈɡɛ̃zbʊə(r)/

gaita bagpipe
gy-tuh /ˈɡʌɪtə/

Gaitskell, Hugh English statesman
gayt-skuhl /ˈɡeɪtskəl/

gala social occasion
gah-luh /ˈɡɑːlə/

Sometimes also, and commonly in AM, **gay**-luh.

Gaelic

Irish Gaelic (usually pronounced **gay**-lik, and sometimes just called Irish) and Scottish Gaelic (usually pronounced **gal**-ik) are two distinct languages. However, they are closely related to one another, and it is possible to generalize about the pronunciation that should be used when words or names from either language are being spoken in an English-language context. The BBC broadcasts in both Scottish Gaelic (see http://www.bbc.co.uk/scotland/alba) and Irish (see http://www.bbc.co.uk/northernireland/irish), and we usually consult native speakers working within the BBC to verify our recommendations. As always, these are anglicized in line with our policy and the constraints of the respelling.

There can be a considerable level of anglicization of Gaelic place names, since English is usually also spoken. There is also some regional variation between speakers of Gaelic. Our consultation with native speakers allows us to gauge the appropriate level of anglicization, as well as giving us guidance with the more complex areas of Gaelic pronunciation. A few broad guidelines are listed below.

Stress in Gaelic generally falls on the first syllable, with a few specific exceptions.

Vowels

An acute accent (called a *fada* in Irish Gaelic) indicates that a vowel is long. In our recommendations we advise that A is pronounced uh and Á is aw; E is pronounced e and É is ay; I is pronounced i and Í is ee; O is pronounced o and Ó is oh; and U is pronounced u and Ú is oo. Other vowel pronunciations such as diphthongs are more complex, and we consult native speakers for guidance.

Consonants

B, C, F, L, M, and R are pronounced approximately as in English. D, G, L, N, S, and T are as in English before A, O, or U, but they change before E or I; D becomes j, G is gy, L is ly, N is ny, S is sh, and T is ch. For example, the Gaelic toast *Sláinte* can be pronounced **slahn**-chuh.

H at the beginning of a word is pronounced h, but H after a consonant indicates a pronunciation change. BH and MH are usually both pronounced v. For example, the Scottish name *Mhairi* can be pronounced **vah**-ri (although **mar**-i is also used), and the Irish name *Siobhán* is shiv-**awn**. DH and GH are both pronounced similarly to kh (as in *loch*) before A, O, or U, and y before E or I or in the middle of a word. PH is pronounced f, CH is pronounced kh (as in *loch*), and SH and TH are both pronounced h. Sequences of consonants with H can also become completely silent; we consult dictionaries and native speakers for further guidance.

galactagogue food or drug promoting flow of a mother's milk
guh-**lakt**-uh-gog /gəˈlaktəgɒg/

Galadriel character from *The Lord of the Rings*
gal-**ad**-ri-el /gəˈladriɛl/

galago bushbaby
guh-**lay**-goh /gəˈleɪgəʊ/

Galahad knight
gal-uh-had /ˈgaləhad/

galangal herb
gal-uhng-gal /ˈgaləŋgal/

galant musical term
gal-**ant** /gəˈlant/

galantine dish of white meat or fish
gal-uhn-teen /ˈgalantiːn/

Galapagos Islands islands, Pacific Ocean
guh-**lap**-uh-goss /gəˈlapəgɒs/

Galatas resort, Crete
gal-**at**-**ass** /galaˈtas/

Galatea Greek mythological character
gal-uh-**tee**-uh /ˌgaləˈtiːə/

Galatasaray Turkish football club
guh-**lat**-uh-suh-ry /gəˌlatəsəˈrʌɪ/

Galați city, Romania
gal-**ats** /gaˈlats/

Galatia ancient region, Asia Minor
guh-**lay**-shuh /gəˈleɪʃə/

Galatians book of the New Testament
guh-**lay**-shuhnz /gəˈleɪʃənz/

Galba Roman emperor
gal-buh /ˈgalbə/

Galbraith, John Kenneth Canadian-born American economist
gal-brayth /ˈgalbreɪθ/

The BR pronunciation of this surname is gal-**brayth**.

Galeão airport, Rio de Janeiro
gal-i-**ow(ng)** /galiˈãʊ/

Galen Greek physician
gay-luhn /ˈgeɪlən/

galenic relating to Galen
guh-**len**-ik /gəˈlɛnɪk/

galette savoury pancake
guh-**let** /gəˈlɛt/

galia melon small melon
gah-li-uh /ˈgɑːliə/

Galicia autonomous region, Spain
guh-**liss**-i-uh /gəˈlɪsiə/, [gaˈliθja]

Established anglicization. Also known as Galiza in Galician, pronounced gal-**ee**-thuh.

Galilean relating to Galileo
gal-il-**ay**-uhn /ˌgalɪˈleɪən/

Galilean relating to Galilee
gal-il-**ee**-uhn /ˌgalɪˈliːən/

Galilee region, ancient Palestine
gal-il-ee /ˈgalɪliː/

Galileo Galilei Italian astronomer
gal-il-**ay**-oh gal-il-**ay**-i /ˌgalɪˈleɪəʊ ˌgalɪˈleɪi/

Galiza see **Galicia**

gall impudent behaviour
gawl /gɔːl/

Gallagher, Liam and Noel English musicians
gal-uh-guhr /ˈgaləgə(r)/

This British surname is variously pronounced gal-uh-huhr, gal-uh-khuhr, and gal-uh-guhr, depending on individual preference.

gallant charming man
guh-**lant** /gəˈlant/

Galle port, Sri Lanka
gawl /gɔːl/
• Established anglicization.

galleria collection of shops under a single roof
gal-uh-**ree**-uh /ˌgaləˈriːə/

Gallia Narbonensis Roman province
gal-i-uh nar-buh-**nen**-siss /ˌgaliə ˌnɑː(r)bəˈnɛnsɪs/

Galliano Italian liqueur
gal-i-**ah**-noh /ˌgaliˈɑːnəʊ/

galliard dance
gal-i-ard /ˈgaliɑː(r)d/

Gallic relating to France
gal-ik /ˈgalɪk/

Gallican relating to the ancient Church of Gaul or France
gal-ik-uhn /ˈgalɪkən/

Gallicism French idiom
gal-iss-iz-uhm /ˈgalɪˌsɪzəm/

galligaskins breeches, trousers, or gaiters
gal-ig-**ask**-inz /ˌgalɪˈgaskɪnz/

gallimimus dinosaur
gal-im-**y**-muhss /ˌgalɪˈmʌɪməs/

galliot ship
gal-i-uht /ˈgaliət/

Gallipoli peninsula, Turkey
guh-**lip**-uh-li /gəˈlɪpəli/

gallium chemical element
gal-i-uhm /ˈgaliəm/

galliwasp lizard
gal-i-wosp /ˈgaliwɒsp/

galloglass mercenary
gal-oh-glahss /ˈgaləʊglɑːs/

gallon unit of volume
gal-uhn /ˈgalən/

galloon ornamental strip of fabric
guh-**loon** /gəˈluːn/

Galloway area, Scotland
gal-uh-way /ˈgaləweɪ/

gallstone hard mass formed in the gall
bladder
gawl-stohn /ˈgɔːlstəʊn/

Gallup poll trademark assessment of
public opinion
gal-uhp /ˈgaləp/

Galois, Évariste French mathematician
ay-varr-**eest** gal-**wah** /eɪvaˌriːst
galˈwɑː/

galop ballroom dance
gal-uhp /ˈgaləp/

Sometimes also gal-**op**.

galosh waterproof overshoe
guh-**losh** /gəˈlɒʃ/

Galsworthy, John English novelist
gawlz-wur-*thi* /ˈgɔːlzwəː(r)ði/

Galtieri, Leopoldo Argentinian
politician
lay-op-**ol**-doh galt-**yair**-i /leɪɒpˌɒldəʊ
ˌgaltjˈɛːri/

Galton, Francis English scientist
gawl-tuhn /ˈgɔːltən/

Galvani, Luigi Italian anatomist
luu-**ee**-ji gal-**vah**-ni /lʊˌiːdʒi galˈvɑːni/

galvanic relating to electric currents
produced by chemical action
gal-**van**-ik /galˈvanɪk/

galvanize shock someone into taking
action
gal-vuh-nyz /ˈgalvənʌɪz/

galvanometer instrument for
measuring electric currents
gal-vuh-**nom**-it-uhr /ˌgalvəˈnɒmɪtə(r)/

Galveston port, US
gal-vuh-stuhn /ˈgalvəstən/

Galway county, Republic of Ireland
gawl-way /ˈgɔːlweɪ/

Gama, Vasco da see **da Gama, Vasco**

Gamay variety of black wine grape
gam-ay /ˈgameɪ/

gamba see **viola da gamba**

Gambia country
gam-bi-uh /ˈgambiə/

Gambier Islands group of coral islands,
South Pacific
gam-bi-uhr /ˈgambiə(r)/

Gambon, Michael Irish-born British
actor
gam-bon /ˈgambɒn/

gamelan traditional Indonesian
instrumental ensemble
gam-uh-lan /ˈgaməlan/

gamgee surgical dressing
gam-ji /ˈgamdʒi/

Gamla Stan historic area of Stockholm
gam-luh **stahn** /ˌgamlə ˈstɑːn/

gamma letter of the Greek alphabet
gam-uh /ˈgamə/

Gamow, George Russian-born
American physicist
gay-moh /ˈgeɪməʊ/

gamut complete range of something
gam-uht /ˈgamət/

Gan dialect of Chinese
gan /gan/

ganache whipped filling of chocolate
and cream
guh-**nash** /gəˈnaʃ/

Ganapati another name for Ganesh
gun-uh-**put**-i /ˌgʌnəˈpʌti/

Gäncä city, Azerbaijan
guhn-juh /ˈgəndʒə/

Gance, Abel French film director
ab-**el** gah(ng)ss /aˌbɛl ˈgɑːs/

Gand see **Ghent**

Gandalf character from *The Lord of
the Rings*
gan-dalf /ˈgandalf/

Gander town, Newfoundland
gan-duhr /ˈgandə(r)/

gander male goose
gan-duhr /ˈgandə(r)/

Gandhi, Indira Indian stateswoman
in-dirr-uh **gahn**-di /ˌɪndɪrə ˈgɑːndi/

Gandhi, Mahatma Indian nationalist
and spiritual leader
muh-**haht**-muh **gahn**-di /məˌhɑːtmə
ˈgɑːndi/

Gandhi, Rajiv Indian statesman
rah-**jeev** **gahn**-di /ˌrɑːˌdʒiːv ˈɡɑːndi/

Gandhi, Sonia Italian-born Indian politician
son-yuh **gahn**-di /ˌsɒnjə ˈɡɑːndi/

Gandhinagar city, India
gahn-di-**nug**-uhr /ˌɡɑːndiˈnʌɡə(r)/

Ganesh Hindu god; also called **Ganesha**
guh-**naysh** /ɡəˈneɪʃ/

Ganesha Hindu god; also called **Ganesh**
guh-**nay**-shuh /ɡəˈneɪʃə/

Ganges river, India and Bangladesh
gan-jeez /ˈɡandʒiːz/

Established anglicization. The Hindi name is Ganga, pronounced **gung**-guh.

gangrene death and decomposition of body tissue
gang-green /ˈɡaŋɡriːn/

Gangtok city, India
gang-**tok** /ɡaŋˈtɒk/

ganja cannabis
gan-juh /ˈɡandʒə/

Gansu province, China
gan-**soo** /ɡanˈsuː/

Ganymede Greek mythological character
gan-im-eed /ˈɡanɪmiːd/

garage building for housing vehicles
garr-ij /ˈɡarɪdʒ/

Very commonly also **garr**-ahj and **garr**-ahzh. AM is usually guh-**rahzh**.

Garai, Romola English actress
ruh-**moh**-luh guh-**ry** /rəˌməʊlə ɡəˈrʌɪ/

garam masala Indian spice mixture
gurr-uhm muh-**sah**-luh /ˌɡʌrəm məˈsɑːlə/

garand rifle
garr-uhnd /ˈɡarənd/

garbanzo bean chickpea
gar-**ban**-zoh /ɡɑː(r)ˈbanzəʊ/

Garbarek, Jan Norwegian jazz musician
yahn guhr-**bar**-ek /ˌjɑːn ɡə(r)ˈbɑːrɛk/

Garbo, Greta Swedish actress
gret-uh **gar**-boh /ˌɡrɛtə ˈɡɑː(r)bəʊ/, [ˌɡreːtə ˈɡarbʊ]

Established anglicization. Her real name was Greta Gustafsson, pronounced **guust**-af-son.

Garcia Bernal, Gael Mexican actor

gah-**el** gar-**see**-uh bair-**nal** /ɡɑːˌɛl ɡɑː(r)ˌsiːə bɛː(r)ˈnal/

Garcia Márquez, Gabriel Colombian novelist
gab-ri-**el** gar-**see**-uh mar-**kess** /ˌɡabriˌɛl ɡɑː(r)ˌsiːə ˈmɑː(r)kɛs/

garçon waiter in a French restaurant or hotel
gar-son /ˈɡɑː(r)sɒn/, [ɡarsɔ̃]

Garda pl. **Gardai** Irish state police force
gar-duh, pl. gar-**dee** /ˈɡɑː(r)də/, pl. /ˌˈdiː/

Garda, Lake lake, Italy
gar-duh /ˈɡɑː(r)də/

Gardena city, US
gar-**dee**-nuh /ɡɑː(r)ˈdiːnə/

gardenia tree or shrub
gar-**dee**-ni-uh /ɡɑː(r)ˈdiːniə/

garderobe toilet in a medieval building
gar-drohb /ˈɡɑː(r)drəʊb/

gargantuan enormous
gar-**gan**-tyoo-uhn /ɡɑː(r)ˈɡantjuən/

gargoyle grotesque carved human or animal face
gar-goyl /ˈɡɑː(r)ɡɔɪl/

Garibaldi, Giuseppe Italian military leader
juuz-**ep**-ay garr-ib-**al**-di /dʒʊˌzɛpeɪ ɡariˈbaldi/

garibaldi biscuit
garr-ib-**awl**-di /ˌɡarɪˈbɔːldi/

Garmisch-Partenkirchen town, Germany
gar-mish par-tuhn-**keer**-khuhn /ˌɡɑː(r)mɪʃ pɑː(r)tən̩ˈkɪə(r)çən/

Garonne river, France
garr-**on** /ɡaˈrɒn/

Garoua port, Cameroon
garr-**oo**-uh /ɡaˈruːə/

garron Highland pony
garr-uhn /ˈɡarən/

Garros, Roland French aviator
rol-**ah(ng)** garr-**oss** /rɒˌlɑ̃ ɡaˈrɒs/

The same pronunciation is used for the Roland-Garros sports stadium in Paris.

garrotte kill by strangulation
guh-**rot** /ɡəˈrɒt/

garrulous excessively talkative
garr-uh-luhss /ˈɡarələs/

Garuda mythical bird in Hinduism
garr-uud-uh /ˈɡarʊdə/

Garvey, Marcus Jamaican political
activist
gar-vi /ˈgɑː(r)vi/

Gascoigne, Paul English footballer
gask-oyn /ˈgaskɔɪn/

Gascon relating to Gascony
gask-uhn /ˈgaskən/

Gascony region, France
gask-uh-ni /ˈgaskəni/

Established anglicization. The French name
is Gascogne, pronounced gask-**on**-yuh
[gaskɔnj].

gaseous relating to gas
gass-i-uhss /ˈgasiəs/

Sometimes also **gay**-si-uhss.

Gaskell, Elizabeth English novelist
gask-uhl /ˈgaskəl/

Gassendi, Pierre French astronomer
and philosopher
pyair gass-a(ng)-**dee** /ˌpjɛː(r) gasɛ̃ˈdiː/

Gastarbeiter guest worker
gast-ar-by-tuhr /ˈgastˌɑː(r)bʌɪtə(r)/

Gasthaus pl. **Gasthäuser** German
inn or hotel
gast-howss, pl. **gast**-hoy-zuhr
/ˈgasthaʊs, pl. -ˌhɔɪzə(r)/

Gasthof pl. **Gasthöfe** German hotel
gast-hohf, pl. **gast**-hoe-fuh
/ˈgasthəʊf, pl. -ˌhøːfə/
• Standard -s plural is also possible.

Gastornis extinct flightless bird
gast-**or**-niss /gaˈstɔː(r)nɪs/

gastrectomy surgical removal of the
stomach
gast-**rek**-tuh-mi /gaˈstrɛktəmi/

gastritis inflammation of the lining of
the stomach
gast-**ry**-tiss /gaˈstrʌɪtɪs/

gastronome gourmet
gast-ruh-nohm /ˈgastrənəʊm/

Gastropoda class of molluscs
gast-**rop**-uh-duh /gasˈtrɒpədə/

gateau cake
gat-oh /ˈgatəʊ/

Gatha poem attributed to Zoroaster
gah-thah /ˈgɑːθɑː/

gauche unsophisticated
gohsh /gəʊʃ/

Gaucher's disease hereditary disease
goh-**shayz** /gəʊˈʃeɪz/

gaucho cowboy
gow-choh /ˈgaʊtʃəʊ/

Gaudí, Antonio Spanish architect
an-**tohn**-yoh gow-**dee** /anˈtəʊnjəʊ
gaʊˈdiː/, [gauˈði]

Gaudier-Brzeska, Henri French
sculptor
ah(ng)-**ree** goh-**dyay bzhesk**-uh /ãˌriː
gəʊˌdjeɪ ˈbʒɛskə/

gauge instrument
gayj /geɪdʒ/

Gauguin, Paul French painter
pol goh-**ga(ng)** /ˌpɒl gəʊˈgɛ̃/

Gauhati city, India
gow-**hah**-ti /gaʊˈhɑːti/

Gaul ancient region, Europe
gawl /gɔːl/

Gauleiter official under Nazi rule
gow-ly-tuhr /ˈgaʊlʌɪtə(r)/

Gaulle, Charles de see de Gaulle,
Charles

Gaullism principles and policies of
Charles de Gaulle
goh-liz-uhm /ˈgəʊlɪzəm/

Gaultier, Jean-Paul French fashion
designer
zhah(ng) pol goh-**tyay** /ʒã ˌpɒl
gəʊˈtjeɪ/

gaur wild ox
gow-uhr /ˈgaʊə(r)/

Gauss, Karl Friedrich German
mathematician
karl freed-rikh **gowss** /ˌkɑː(r)l ˌfriːdrɪç
ˈgaʊs/

gauss unit of magnetic induction
gowss /gaʊs/

Gautama see Siddhartha Gautama

Gauteng province, South Africa
khow-teng /ˈxaʊtɛŋ/

gauze transparent fabric
gawz /gɔːz/

gavage administration of food or drugs
by force
gav-**ahzh** /gaˈvɑːʒ/

Gavaskar, Sunil Indian cricketer
soo-**neel** gah-**vuhsk**-uhr /suːˌniːl
ˈgɑːvəskə(r)/

gavel auctioneer's hammer
gav-uhl /ˈgavəl/

gavelkind system of inheritance
gav-uhl-kynd /ˈgavəlkʌɪnd/

Gävle city, Sweden
yay-vluh /'jeɪvlə/, ['jɛːvlə]

gavotte French dance
guh-**vot** /gə'vɒt/

Gawain knight in Arthurian legend
gah-wayn /'gɑːweɪn/

Commonly also guh-**wayn**.

Gaya city, India
gy-uh /'gʌɪə/

gayal ox
gy-**al** /gʌɪ'al/

Gazankulu former Tsonga homeland,
South Africa
gaz-ank-**oo**-loo /,gazaŋ'kuːluː/

gazar kind of silk fabric
guh-**zar** /gə'zɑː(r)/

Gaza Strip strip of territory, Palestine
gah-zuh /'gɑːzə/

gazebo small building
guh-**zee**-boh /gə'ziːbəʊ/

gazetteer geographical index or
dictionary
gaz-uh-**teer** /,gazə'tɪə(r)/

Gaziantep city, Turkey
gah-**zee**-an-tep /gɑː'ziːanˌtɛp/

gazpacho Spanish dish
gaz-**patch**-oh /gaz'patʃəʊ/, [gaθ'patʃo]

Gdańsk port, Poland
guh-**dansk** /gə'dansk/, [gdaĩsk]

Established anglicization. The German
name is Danzig, pronounced **dant**-sikh
['dantsɪç].

Gdynia port, Poland
guh-**din**-yuh /gə'dɪnjə/

gean cherry
geen /giːn/

Geber Arab chemist
jee-buhr /'dʒiːbə(r)/

gecko lizard
gek-oh /'gɛkəʊ/

Geechee English creole spoken in South
Carolina and Georgia
gee-chee /'giːtʃiː/

Geelong port, Australia
jee-**long** /dʒiː'lɒŋ/

Ge'ez ancient Semitic language of
Ethiopia
gee-ez /'giːɛz/

gefilte fish Jewish dish
guh-**fil**-tuh /gə'fɪltə/

gegenschein light seen in the night sky
opposite the position of the sun
gay-guhn-shyn /'geɪgənˌʃʌɪn/

Gehenna hell
guh-**hen**-uh /gə'hɛnə/

Gehrig, Lou American baseball player
gerr-ig /'gɛrɪg/

Gehry, Frank Canadian-born American
architect
gair-i /'gɛːri/

Geiger, Hans Wilhelm German
nuclear physicist
hanss vil-**helm gy**-guhr /,hans
ˌvɪlhɛlm 'gʌɪgə(r)/

Geikie, Archibald Scottish geologist
gee-ki /'giːki/

geisha Japanese hostess
gay-shuh /'geɪʃə/

geist spirit
gyst /gʌɪst/

Gejiu (also **Geju**) city, China
gej-**oo** /gɛ'dʒuː/

gelada baboon
juh-**lah**-duh /dʒə'lɑːdə/

gelato pl. **gelati** Italian ice cream
juh-**lah**-toh, pl. juh-**lah**-ti /dʒə'lɑːtəʊ/,
pl. /dʒə'lɑːti/

Gelderland province, Netherlands
gel-duhr-land /'gɛldə(r)land/,
['ɣɛldərlɑnt]
• Established anglicization.

Geldof, Bob Irish musician
gel-dof /'gɛldɒf/

Geller, Uri Israeli celebrity
oor-i **gel**-uhr /,ʊəri 'gɛlə(r)/

Gell-Mann, Murray American
theoretical physicist
gel-**man** /gɛl'man/

Gelsenkirchen city, Germany
gel-zuhn-**keer**-khuhn
/,gɛlzən'kɪə(r)çən/

gematria Cabbalistic method of
interpreting the Hebrew scriptures
gee-**may**-tri-uh /giː'meɪtriə/

Gemayel, Pierre Lebanese political
leader
pyair juh-**my**-uhl /,pjɛː(r) dʒə'mʌɪəl/

Gemeinschaft social relations between
individuals
guh-**myn**-shaft /gə'mʌɪnʃaft/

geminate identical adjacent speech
sounds
jem-in-uht /'dʒɛmɪnət/

geminate double a speech sound
jem-in-ayt /'dʒɛmɪneɪt/

Gemini constellation
jem-in-y /'dʒɛmɪnʌɪ/

gemsbok antelope
khemz-bok /'xɛmzbɒk/

gendarme French police officer
zhah(ng)-**darm** /ʒɑ̃n'dɑː(r)m/

genealogy study of lines of descent
jee-ni-**al**-uh-ji /dʒiːni'alədʒi/

generalissimo commander
jen-uh-ruh-**liss**-im-oh
/ˌdʒɛnərə'lɪsɪməʊ/

Genesis book of the Bible
jen-uh-siss /'dʒɛnəsɪs/

Genet, Jean French novelist
zhah(ng) zhuh-**nay** /ˌʒɑ̃ ʒə'neɪ/

Geneva city, Switzerland
juh-**nee**-vuh /dʒə'niːvə/

Established anglicization. The French name is Genève, pronounced zhuh-**nev**, and the German name is Genf, pronounced genf.

genever Dutch gin
juh-**nee**-vuhr /dʒə'niːvə(r)/

Genghis Khan Mongol emperor
jeng-giss **kahn** /ˌdʒɛŋgɪs 'kɑːn/

genic relating to genes
jen-ik /'dʒɛnɪk/

Commonly also **jee**-nik.

genizah room attached to a synagogue
gen-**ee**-zuh /gɛ'niːzə/

Genoa port, Italy
jen-oh-uh /'dʒɛnəʊə/

Established anglicization. The Italian name is Genova, pronounced **jay**-nov-uh ['dʒɛːnova].

genocide killing of a large group of people
jen-uh-syd /'dʒɛnəsʌɪd/

genotype genetic constitution of an organism
jen-uh-typ /'dʒɛnətʌɪp/

Commonly also **jee**-nuh-typ.

genre style or category
zhon-ruh /'ʒɒnrə/

Gent see **Ghent**

gentamicin antibiotic
jen-tuh-**my**-sin /ˌdʒɛntə'mʌɪsɪn/

Gentile da Fabriano Italian painter

jen-**tee**-lay dah fab-ri-**ah**-noh
/ˌdʒɛnˌtiːleɪ dɑː ˌfabrɪ'ɑːnəʊ/

gentoo penguin
jen-**too** /dʒɛn'tuː/

genus pl. **genera** grouping of organisms
jee-nuhss, pl. **jen**-uh-ruh /'dʒiːnəs/, pl. /'dʒɛnərə/

georgette dress fabric
jor-**jet** /dʒɔː(r)'dʒɛt/

Gera city, Germany
gay-ruh /'geɪrə/

Geraldton port, Australia
jerr-uhl-tuhn /'dʒɛrəltən/

geranial fragrant oil
juh-**ray**-ni-uhl /dʒə'reɪnɪəl/

geranium plant
juh-**ray**-ni-uhm /dʒə'reɪnɪəm/

gerbera plant
jur-buh-ruh /'dʒəː(r)bərə/

Sometimes also **gur**-buh-ruh.

gerbil rodent
jur-bil /'dʒəː(r)bɪl/

gerenuk antelope
gerr-uh-nuuk /'gɛrənʊk/

Géricault, Théodore French painter
tay-od-**or** zherr-ik-**oh** /teɪɒˌdɔː(r) ʒɛrɪ'kəʊ/

germanium chemical element
jur-**may**-ni-uhm /dʒəː(r)'meɪnɪəm/

Germiston city, South Africa
jur-mist-uhn /'dʒəː(r)mɪstən/

Gerona city, Spain
kherr-**oh**-nuh /xɛ'rəʊnə/

Geronimo Apache chief
juh-**ron**-im-oh /dʒə'rɒnɪməʊ/

Gershwin, George and Ira American songwriters
y-ruh **gursh**-win /ˌʌɪrə 'gəː(r)ʃwɪn/

gerund grammatical term
jerr-uhnd /'dʒɛrənd/

gerundive grammatical term
juh-**rund**-iv /dʒə'rʌndɪv/

Gervais, Ricky English comedian
juhr-**vayss** /dʒə(r)'veɪs/

Gestapo Nazi secret police
gest-**ah**-poh /gɛ'stɑːpəʊ/, German [ge'sta:po] or [gə'ʃta:po]

gesundheit used to wish good health to a person who has just sneezed
guh-**zuunt**-hyt /gə'zʊnthʌɪt/

German

German (*Deutsch*, pronounced doytsh, in German) is spoken in Austria, Germany, Switzerland, and neighbouring countries, and is one of the three official languages of the EU. There are a number of German loan-words in English (e.g. *doppelgänger* and *Schadenfreude*), and others from Yiddish, which was originally a dialect of German. Stress in German is not always predictable, and a good German dictionary should be consulted for word-specific stress information.

Vowels

German vowels are either short or long. The rules governing this are complicated and subject to exceptions. As a rough guideline, vowels followed by two or more consonants (as in *Punkt*, pronounced puunkt) are short. Where vowels are doubled (as in *Saal*, pronounced zahl) or followed by H (as in *sehr*, pronounced zair), they are long, and they are usually also long when followed by just one consonant or where they are at the end of a word and stressed (as in *Büro*, pronounced bue-**roh**). As with stress, it is best to consult a good German dictionary for word-specific information.

In our anglicized recommendations we advise that A is pronounced a if short, ah if long. Ä (sometimes spelled AE) is e if short, or ay if long. AU is ow, and ÄU (or AEU) is oy: so *frau* is frow, and *fräulein* is **froy**-lyn. E is pronounced e if short, ay if long, and I is pronounced i if short, or ee if long. IE is pronounced ee, and EI is pronounced y: so *Kiel* is keel and *Rhein* is ryn. O is pronounced o if short, oh or aw if long, and Ö (sometimes spelled OE) is oe, either as in French *peu* or *coeur*. U is pronounced uu if short, oo if long, and Ü (or UE) is ue as in French *vu* or German *fünf*.

Consonants

B, D, and G are pronounced as b, d, and g, except at the end of a word, where they become devoiced to p, t, and k. Therefore *Tage* is **tah**-guh, but *Tag* is tahk.

C appears only in foreign words in German, and is pronounced k before A and O, and ts before E, I, and Y.

CH is pronounced kh as in *loch* after A, O, and U, and kh as in German *ich* in most other positions. This latter sound is close to the hy sound at the start of English *Hugh*. CH appears at the beginning only of foreign words in German, and may be pronounced sh, kh, or k depending on the word.

H is silent after a consonant: *Goethe* is pronounced **goe**-tuh.

J is pronounced y as in *yes*. K and P are always pronounced even in consonant sequences (i.e. in words like *Knecht* and *Pfeffer*).

NG is pronounced ng (not ng-g). QU is pronounced kv.

S is usually z: *Sieg* is pronounced zeek. S becomes devoiced to s at the end of words and before K. Before P and T, S becomes sh, and the sequence SCH is also pronounced sh.

TH appears sometimes in older spellings of German, and is pronounced t.

V is pronounced f at the beginning of words, otherwise v. W is pronounced v.

X is pronounced ks, Y appears only as a vowel and is pronounced ue or occasionally ee, and Z is pronounced ts.

Gethsemane, Garden of garden between Jerusalem and the Mount of Olives
geth-**sem**-uh-ni /gɛθ'sɛməni/

Gettysburg town, US
get-iz-burg /'gɛtɪzbə:(r)g/

Gewürztraminer variety of white grape
guh-**vuerts**-tram-ee-nuhr /gəˈvʏ(r)tstra‚miːnə(r)/

geyser hot spring
gay-suhr /'geɪsə(r)/

Commonly also **gy**-zuhr or **gee**-zuhr.

Ghali, Boutros Boutros see **Boutros-Ghali, Boutros**

Ghana country
gah-nuh /'gɑːnə/

Ghanaian relating to Ghana
gah-**nay**-uhn /gɑːˈneɪən/

gharara Indian trousers
gurr-**ar**-uh /gʌ'rɑːrə/

ghatam Indian musical instrument
gah-tum /'gɑːtʌm/

Ghats mountain ranges, India
gahts /gɑːts/

ghazal lyric poem
guz-ul /'gʌzʌl/

Ghazi Muslim fighter against non-Muslims
gah-zi /'gɑːzi/

Ghaziabad city, India
gah-zi-uh-bad /'gɑːziəbad/

Ghaznavid Turkish Muslim dynasty
gaz-**nah**-vid /gaz'nɑːvɪd/

ghee clarified butter

gee /giː/

Gheg Albanian ethnic group
geg /gɛg/

Ghent city, Belgium
gent /gɛnt/

Established anglicization. The Flemish name is Gent, pronounced khent [xɛnt], and the French name is Gand, pronounced gah(ng) [gɑ̃].

Gheorghiu, Angela Romanian soprano
an-**jel**-uh gyor-**gyoo** /an‚dʒɛlə gjɔ:(r)'gjuː/

Ghibelline faction in Italian medieval politics
gib-uh-lyn /'gɪbəlʌɪn/

Ghiberti, Lorenzo Italian sculptor and goldsmith
lorr-**ent**-soh gee-**bair**-ti /lɒ‚rɛntsəʊ giː'bɛː(r)ti/

Ghibli Japanese animation film studio
jeeb-li /'dʒiːbli/

ghibli hot southerly wind of North Africa
gib-li /'gɪbli/

Ghirlandaio Italian painter
geer-lan-**dy**-oh /ˌgɪə(r)lan'dʌɪəʊ/

ghoul evil spirit or phantom
gool /guːl/

Ghulghuleh ancient city, Afghanistan
guul-**guul**-uh /gʊl'gʊlə/

gi jacket worn in judo
gee /giː/

Giacometti, Alberto Swiss sculptor and painter
al-**bair**-toh jak-uh-**met**-i /alˌbɛː(r)təʊ ‚dʒakə'mɛti/

Giamatti, Paul American actor
jee-uh-mat-i /dʒiːəˈmati/

gibberish meaningless speech or writing
jib-uh-rish /ˈdʒɪbərɪʃ/

Less commonly also **gib-uh-rish**.

giblets liver, heart, gizzard, and neck of a
chicken
jib-lits /ˈdʒɪblɪts/

Gibraltar British dependency, Iberian
peninsula
jib-rawl-tuhr /dʒɪˈbrɔːltə(r)/

Gibraltarian relating to Gibraltar
jib-rawl-tair-i-uhn /dʒɪbrɔːlˈtɛːriən/

Gibran, Khalil Lebanese-born
American writer
kuh-leel zhib-rahn /kəˌliːl ʒɪˈbrɑːn/

gibus top hat
jy-buhss /ˈdʒaɪbəs/

gid disease of sheep and goats
gid /gɪd/

Gide, André French novelist
ah(ng)-dray zheed /ãˌdreɪ ˈʒiːd/

Gideon biblical name
gid-i-uhn /ˈgɪdiən/

Gielgud, John English actor and
director
geel-guud /ˈgiːlgʊd/

Gifu city, Japan
gee-foo /ˈgiːfuː/

gigabyte unit of information
gig-uh-byt /ˈgɪgəbʌɪt/

Gigli, Beniamino Italian tenor
ben-yam-ee-noh jeel-yi /benjaˌmiːnəʊ
ˈdʒiːlji/

gigolo young man financially supported
by a woman
jig-uh-loh /ˈdʒɪgələʊ/

Sometimes also **zhig-uh-loh**.

gigot leg of mutton or lamb
jig-uht /ˈdʒɪgət/

gigue musical composition
zheeg /ʒiːg/

Gijón city, Spain
khee-khon /xiːˈxɒn/

Gila river, US
hee-luh /ˈhiːlə/

The same pronunciation is used for the Gila
lizard.

gilet sleeveless padded jacket
zhee-lay /ˈʒiːleɪ/

Gilgamesh legendary king
gil-guh-mesh /ˈgɪlgəmɛʃ/

Gill, Eric English sculptor
gil /gɪl/

gill unit of liquid measure
jil /dʒɪl/

gill deep ravine
gil /gɪl/

gill female ferret
jil /dʒɪl/

Gillespie, Dizzy American jazz
musician
gil-esp-i /gɪˈlɛspi/

Gilliam, Terry American cartoonist and
film director
gil-i-uhm /ˈgɪliəm/

Gillingham town, England
jil-ing-uhm /ˈdʒɪlɪŋəm/

The village in Dorset is pronounced
gil-ing-uhm. This is also a British surname,
variously pronounced **jil-ing-uhm** and
gil-ing-uhm, depending on individual
preference.

Gimli character from *The Lord of the
Rings*
gim-li /ˈgɪmli/

gimp twisted silk, worsted, or cotton
gimp /gɪmp/

Ginastera, Alberto Argentine
composer
al-bair-toh khee-nast-air-uh
/alˌbɛː(r)təʊ xiːˈnastɛːrə/

gingham checked cotton cloth
ging-uhm /ˈgɪŋəm/

gingival concerned with the gums
jin-jy-vuhl /dʒɪnˈdʒʌɪvəl/

gingivitis inflammation of the gums
jin-jiv-y-tiss /ˌdʒɪndʒɪˈvʌɪtɪs/

ginkgo (also **gingko**) Chinese tree
gink-oh /ˈgɪŋkəʊ/

Ginsberg, Allen American poet
ginz-burg /ˈgɪnzbəː(r)g/

ginseng plant
jin-seng /ˈdʒɪnsɛŋ/

Giorgione Italian painter
jor-joh-nay /ˌdʒɔː(r)ˈdʒəʊneɪ/

Giotto Italian painter
jot-oh /ˈdʒɒtəʊ/

girandole candlestick
jirr-uhn-dohl /ˈdʒɪrəndəʊl/

giro system of electronic credit transfer
jy-roh /ˈdʒʌɪrəʊ/

Gironde river estuary, France
zhee-**ro(ng)d** /ʒiːˈrɒd/

Girondist member of the French
moderate republican party
jirr-**on**-dist /dʒɪˈrɒndɪst/

Gisborne port, New Zealand
giz-buhrn /ˈɡɪzbə(r)n/

Giscard d'Estaing, Valéry French
statesman
val-air-**ee** zhee-**skar** dest-**a(ng)**
/valɛːˌriː ʒiːˌskɑː(r) dɛˈstɛ̃/

Gish, Lillian American actress
gish /ɡɪʃ/

Gissing, George English novelist
giss-ing /ˈɡɪsɪŋ/

gîte French holiday house
zheet /ʒiːt/

gittern medieval stringed instrument
git-urn /ˈɡɪtə(r)n/

Giuliani, Rudy American politician
joo-li-**ah**-ni /dʒuːliˈɑːni/

Givenchy French fashion house
zhee-vah(ng)-**shee** /ʒiːvãˈʃiː/

Giza city, Egypt
gee-zuh /ˈɡiːzə/

glabrous free from hair
glay-bruhss /ˈɡleɪbrəs/

glacé preserved in sugar
glass-ay /ˈɡlaseɪ/

glacial relating to ice
glay-shuhl /ˈɡleɪʃəl/

The pronunciation **glay**-si-uhl is less
common now.

glacier mass of ice
glass-i-uhr /ˈɡlasiə(r)/

Sometimes also **glay**-si-uhr.

gladiolus pl. **gladioli** plant of the iris
family
glad-i-**oh**-luhss, pl. glad-i-**oh**-ly
/ˌɡladiˈəʊləs, pl. -lʌɪ/
• Standard -es plural is also possible.

Glagolitic alphabet based on Greek
minuscules
glag-uh-**lit**-ik /ˌɡlaɡəˈlɪtɪk/

glaive sword
glayv /ɡleɪv/

Glamorgan former county, South Wales
gluh-**mor**-guhn /ɡləˈmɔː(r)ɡən/

glandular relating to glands
glan-juul-uhr /ˈɡlandʒʊlə(r)/

The pronunciation **gland**-yuul-uhr is less
common now.

Glasgow city, Scotland
glahz-goh /ˈɡlɑːzɡəʊ/

This is a standardized version of the place
name; locally, the pronunciation is
glaz-goh.

Glashow, Sheldon Lee American
physicist
glash-ow /ˈɡlaʃaʊ/

glasnost policy of more open
consultative government
glass-nost /ˈɡlasnɒst/, Russian
[ˈɡlasnəsʲtʲ]

glassine glossy transparent paper
glah-seen /ˈɡlɑːsiːn/

Glastonbury town, England
glast-uhn-buh-ri /ˈɡlastənbəri/

Commonly also **glah**-stuhn-buh-ri; both
pronunciations are used locally.

Glaswegian relating to Glasgow
glaz-**wee**-juhn /ɡlazˈwiːdʒən/

Sometimes also glahz-**wee**-juhn.

glaucoma disease of the eye
glaw-**koh**-muh /ɡlɔːˈkəʊmə/

glaucous greyish-green or blue colour
glaw-kuhss /ˈɡlɔːkəs/

Glazunov, Aleksandr Russian
composer
al-uhk-**sahn**-duhr glaz-**uun**-of
/aˌləkˌsɑːndə(r) ˈɡlazʊnɒf/, [ɡləzuˈnɔf]
• Established anglicization.

Gleichschaltung standardization of
political, economic, and cultural
institutions
glykh-shal-tuung /ˈɡlʌɪçˌʃaltʊŋ/

Glendower, Owen Welsh chief
glen-**dow**-uhr /ɡlɛnˈdaʊə(r)/

Established anglicization. The Welsh name
is Owain Glyndwr, pronounced **oh**-yn
glin-**door**.

Gleneagles valley, Scotland
glen-**ee**-guhlz /ɡlɛnˈiːɡəlz/

Glenmorangie whisky distillery
glen-**morr**-uhn-ji /ɡlɛnˈmɒrəndʒi/

Glenrothes town, Scotland
glen-**roth**-uhss /ɡlɛnˈrɒθəs/

Glevum Roman name for Gloucester
glee-vuhm /ˈgliːvəm/

glia connective tissue of the nervous system
gly-uh /ˈglʌɪə/

Glinka, Mikhail Russian composer
mee-khuh-**eel glin**-kuh /miːxəˌiːl ˈglɪŋkə/

glioma pl. **gliomata** tumour
gly-**oh**-muh, pl. gly-**oh**-muh-tuh /glʌɪˈəʊmə/, pl. /-mətə/
• Standard -s plural is also possible.

glissando pl. **glissandi** musical term
gliss-**an**-doh, pl. gliss-**an**-di /glɪˈsandəʊ/, pl. /-di/
• Standard -s plural is also possible.

glissé ballet movement
glee-**say** /gliːˈseɪ/

Glittertind mountain, Norway
glit-uhr-tin /ˈglɪtə(r)tɪn/

Gliwice city, Poland
glee-**veet**-suh /gliːˈviːtsə/

globular globe-shaped
glob-yuul-uhr /ˈglɒbjʊlə(r)/

globulin protein found in blood
glob-yuul-in /ˈglɒbjʊlɪn/

glockenspiel musical instrument
glok-uhn-shpeel /ˈglɒkənʃpiːl/

glögg Scandinavian mulled wine
gloeg /glœg/

Gloriana Queen Elizabeth I
glaw-ri-**ah**-nuh /ˌglɔːriˈɑːnə/

Gloucester city, England
glost-uhr /ˈglɒstə(r)/

Glover, Fi BBC journalist
fee gluv-uhr /ˌfiː ˈglʌvə(r)/

glower have an angry look on one's face
glow-uhr /ˈglaʊə(r)/

gloxinia plant
glok-**sin**-i-uh /glɒkˈsɪniə/

Gluck, Christoph Willibald von German composer
krist-of **vil**-ib-alt fon **gluuk** /ˌkrɪstɒf ˌvɪlɪbalt fɒn ˈglʊk/

glucose simple sugar
gloo-kohz /ˈgluːkəʊz/

Glühwein German mulled wine
glue-vyn /ˈglyːvʌɪn/

gluten protein
gloo-tuhn /ˈgluːtən/

glycaemia presence of glucose in the blood

gly-**see**-mi-uh /glʌɪˈsiːmiə/

glycerine syrupy liquid
gliss-uh-reen /ˈglɪsəriːn/

glycogen starch-like substance
gly-kuh-juhn /ˈglʌɪkədʒən/

glycolysis breakdown of glucose
gly-**kol**-iss-iss /glʌɪˈkɒlɪsɪs/

Glyndebourne annual opera festival
glynd-born /ˈglʌɪndbɔː(r)n/

Glyndwr see **Glendower**

glyph hieroglyphic symbol
glif /glɪf/

Gnassingbe Eyadéma, Faure Togolese president
for nyass-**eeng**-bay ay-**ah**-day-muh /ˌfɔː(r) njaˌsiːŋbeɪ eɪˈɑːdeɪmə/

gneiss kind of rock
nyss /nʌɪs/

gnocchi Italian dumplings
nyok-i /ˈnjɒki/

gnome statement of a general truth
nohm /nəʊm/
Sometimes also **noh**-mee.

gnostic relating to knowledge
nost-ik /ˈnɒstɪk/

gnu kind of antelope
noo /nuː/
The pronunciation guh-**noo** is generally only used in jocular contexts.

Goa state, India
goh-uh /ˈgəʊə/

goatee beard
goh-**tee** /gəʊˈtiː/
Commonly also **goh**-tee.

Göbbels, Joseph see **Goebbels**

Gobbi, Tito Italian baritone
tee-toh **gob**-i /ˌtiːtəʊ ˈgɒbi/

Gobi desert, Mongolia and China
goh-bi /ˈgəʊbi/

Gobineau, Joseph Arthur French writer
zhoh-**zef** ar-**tuer gob**-ee-**noh** /ʒəʊˌzef ɑː(r)ˌtyː(r) gɒbiˈnəʊ/

gobo Japanese vegetable root
goh-boh /ˈgəʊbəʊ/

Godard, Jean-Luc French film director
zhah(ng) **luek** god-**ar** /ʒɑ̃ ˌlyk gɒˈdɑː(r)/

Godavari river, India
guh-**dah**-vuh-ri /gəˈdɑːvəri/

Goddard, Robert Hutchings
American physicist
god-ard /ˈɡɒdɑː(r)d/

godetia plant
goh-**dee**-shuh /ɡəʊˈdiːʃə/

Godhavn town, Greenland
god-hah-vuhn /ˈɡɒd,hɑːvən/, Danish
[ˈɡoðhɑwn]
• Established anglicization.

Godiva, Lady English noblewoman
guh-**dy**-vuh /ɡəˈdʌɪvə/

Godunov, Boris tsar of Russia
borr-iss **god**-uun-of /ˌbɒrɪs ˈɡɒdʊnɒf/,
[ba,rʲis ɡadʊˈnɔf]

Established anglicization; also suitable for the opera of the same name by Mussorgsky.

Goebbels, Joseph (also **Göbbels**)
German Nazi leader
yoh-zuhf **goeb**-uhlss /ˌjəʊzəf ˈɡœbəls/

Goering, Hermann (also **Göring**)
German Nazi leader
hair-man **goer**-ing /ˌhɛː(r)man ˈɡøːrɪŋ/

Goes, Hugo van der Flemish painter
hue-khoh vun dair **khooss** /ˌhyːxəʊ
vʌn dɛː(r) ˈxuːs/

goest archaic second person singular
present of go
goh-uhst /ˈɡəʊəst/

goeth archaic third person singular
present of go
goh-uhth /ˈɡəʊəθ/

Goethe, Johann Wolfgang von
German poet
yoh-han **volf**-gang fon **goe**-tuh
/ˌjəʊhan ˌvɒlfɡaŋ fɒn ˈɡøːtə/

Gog and Magog biblical names
gog may-gog /ˈɡɒɡ ˈmeɪɡɒɡ/

Gogol, Nikolai Russian novelist
nik-uh-**ly gog**-uhl /ˌnɪkəˌlʌɪ ˈɡɒɡəl/

Goiânia city, Brazil
goy-**ahn**-yuh /ɡɔɪˈɑːnjə/

Goiás state, Brazil
goy-**ass** /ɡɔɪˈas/

Goidelic group of Celtic languages
goy-**del**-ik /ɡɔɪˈdɛlɪk/

goitre swelling of the neck
goy-tuhr /ˈɡɔɪtə(r)/

Gokhale, Gopal Krishna Indian
political leader
goh-pal **krish**-nuh **goh**-kuh-luh
/ˌɡəʊpal ˌkrɪʃnə ˈɡəʊkələ/

Golan Heights hills, Middle East
goh-**lahn** /ɡəʊˈlɑːn/

Goldberg, Whoopi American actress
wuup-i **gohld**-burg /ˌwʊpi
ˌɡəʊldbə(r)g/

Goldblum, Jeff American actor
gohld-bloom /ˈɡəʊldbluːm/

goldwasser liqueur
golt-vass-uhr /ˈɡɒltvasə(r)/

golem figure in Jewish legend
goh-luhm /ˈɡəʊləm/

Golestan province, Iran
guul-est-**ahn** /ɡʊlɛˈstɑːn/

Golgotha site of the crucifixion of Jesus
gol-guh-thuh /ˈɡɒlɡəθə/

Goliath biblical name
guh-**ly**-uhth /ɡəˈlʌɪəθ/

Gollancz, Victor English publisher
guh-**lants** /ɡəˈlants/

Gollum character from *The Lord of the Rings*
gol-uhm /ˈɡɒləm/

Gomorrah town, ancient Palestine
guh-**morr**-uh /ɡəˈmɒrə/

Gonaïves city, Haiti
gon-ah-**eev** /ɡɒnɑːˈiːv/

Goncharov, Ivan Russian novelist
ee-**vahn** guhn-chuh-**rof** /iːˌvɑːn
ɡənt̩ʃəˈrɒf/

gondola Venetian boat
gon-duh-luh /ˈɡɒndələ/

gondolier person who steers a gondola
gon-duh-**leer** /ˌɡɒndəˈliə(r)/

Gondor place in *The Lord of the Rings*
gond-or /ˈɡɒndɔː(r)/

Gondwana prehistoric continental area
gond-**wah**-nuh /ɡɒnˈdwɑːnə/

gonfalon banner
gon-fuh-luhn /ˈɡɒnfələn/

gonococcus pl. **gonococci** bacteria
gon-uh-**kok**-uhs, pl. gon-uh-**kok**-y
/ˌɡɒnəˈkɒkəs, pl. /-kʌɪ/

Plural is sometimes also **-kok**-sy; see LATIN panel.

gonorrhoea venereal disease
gon-uh-**ree**-uh /ˌɡɒnəˈriːə/

Gooding Jr, Cuba American actor
kyoo-buh /ˈkjuːbə/

googol equivalent to ten raised to the
power of a hundred
goo-gol /ˈɡuːɡɒl/

googolplex equivalent to ten raised to the power of a googol
goo-guhl-pleks /ˈguːgəlplɛks/

goombay drum
goom-bay /ˈguːmbeɪ/

Goossens, Eugene English composer
goo-suhnz /ˈguːsənz/

The Dutch pronunciation of this surname is **khoh-suhnss** [ˈxoːsəns].

gopak Ukrainian dance
goh-pak /ˈgəʊpak/

gopher rodent
goh-fuhr /ˈgəʊfə(r)/

gopura pyramidal tower
goh-puu-ruh /ˈgəʊpʊrə/

Gorakhpur city, India
gaw-ruhk-poor /ˈgɔːrək,pʊə(r)/

goral goat-antelope
gaw-ruhl /ˈgɔːrəl/

Gorbachev, Mikhail Soviet statesman
mee-khuh-eel gor-buh-chof /miːxə,iːl gɔː(r)bəˈtʃɒf/

Gorbacheva, Raisa wife of Mikhail Gorbachev
ruh-ee-suh gor-buh-choh-vuh /rə,iːsə gɔː(r)bəˈtʃəʊvə/

Gorbals district of Glasgow
gor-buhlz /ˈgɔː(r)bəlz/

Gordian knot difficult problem
gor-di-uhn /ˈgɔː(r)diən/

Gordimer, Nadine South African novelist
nuh-deen gor-dim-uhr /nə,diːn ˈgɔː(r)dɪmə(r)/

Gordium ancient city, Asia Minor
gor-di-uhm /ˈgɔː(r)diəm/

gordo variety of grape
gor-doh /ˈgɔː(r)dəʊ/

Górecki, Henryk Polish composer
hen-rik goo-ret-ski /ˌhɛnrɪk guˈrɛtski/

Göreme valley, Turkey
goe-rem-uh /ˈgœˈrɛmə/

Gore-tex trademark waterproof fabric
gor-teks /ˈgɔː(r)tɛks/

gorgon Greek mythological character
gor-guhn /ˈgɔː(r)gən/

gorgoneion pl. **gorgoneia** representation of a gorgon's head
gor-guh-ny-uhn, pl. **gor-guh-ny-uh** /ˌgɔː(r)gəˈnʌɪən/, pl. /-ˈnʌɪə/

Gorgonzola Italian cheese

gor-guhn-zoh-luh /ˌgɔː(r)gənˈzəʊlə/

Göring, Hermann see **Goering**

Gorky, Maxim Russian writer
muhk-seem gor-ki /mək,siːm ˈgɔː(r)ki/

Görlitz city, Germany
goer-lits /ˈgœ(r)lɪts/

Gorno-Altai autonomous republic, Russia
gor-noh al-ty /ˌgɔː(r)nəʊ alˈtʌɪ/

Gorno-Altaisk city, Russia
gor-noh al-tysk /ˌgɔː(r)nəʊ alˈtʌɪsk/

Gorsedd council of Celtic bards and Druids
gor-seth /ˈgɔː(r)sɛð/

gosht Indian term for red meat
gohsht /ˈgəʊʃt/

Gotama see **Siddhartha Gotama**

Goth Germanic ethnic group
goth /gɒθ/

Gotha city, Germany
goh-thuh /ˈgəʊθə/, [ˈgoːta]
• Established anglicization.

Gotham nickname for New York
goth-uhm /ˈgɒθəm/

Gotham village, England
goh-tuhm /ˈgəʊtəm/

Gothenburg port, Sweden
goth-uhn-burg /ˈgɒθənbə:(r)g/

Established anglicization. The Swedish name is Göteborg, pronounced yoe-tuh-**bory** [jœtəˈbɔrj].

Gotland island, Sweden
got-land /ˈgɒtland/

Götterdämmerung opera by Wagner
goet-uhr-dem-uh-ruung /ˈgœtə(r),dɛmərʊŋ/

Göttingen town, Germany
goet-ing-uhn /ˈgœtɪŋən/

Gouda town, Netherlands
gow-duh /ˈgaʊdə/, [ˈxɔuda:]

Established anglicization; also suitable for the cheese of the same name.

gouge chisel
gowj /gaʊdʒ/

Gough Island island, South Atlantic
gof /gɒf/

goujons deep-fried chicken or fish
gooj-uhnz /ˈguːdʒənz/, French [guʒɔ̃]

goulash Hungarian dish
goo-lash /ˈguːlaʃ/

Gould, Glenn Canadian pianist and composer
goold /guːld/

This surname is variously pronounced goold and gohld, depending on individual preference.

Gould, John English artist
goold /guːld/

Gounod, Charles French composer
sharl goo-**noh** /ˌʃɑː(r)l guːˈnəʊ/

gourd fruit
goord /gʊə(r)d/

Commonly also gord.

gourde currency unit, Haiti
goord /gʊə(r)d/

gourmet connoisseur of good food
goor-may /ˈgʊə(r)meɪ/

Commonly also **gor**-may.

gout disease
gowt /gaʊt/

goy pl. **goyim** Jewish name for a non-Jew
goy, pl. **goy**-im /gɔɪ/, pl. /ˈgɔɪɪm/
• Standard -s plural is also possible.

Goya Spanish painter
goy-uh /ˈgɔɪə/

Gozo island, Malta
goh-zoh /ˈgəʊzəʊ/

Gracchus, Tiberius Sempronius Roman tribune
ty-**beer**-i-uhss sem-**proh**-ni-uhss
grak-uhss /tʌɪˌbɪəriəs sɛmˌprəʊniəs ˈgrakəs/

Gracias a Dios cape, Central America
grass-yass ah dyoss /ˌgrasjas ɑː ˈdjɒs/

graduand person receiving an academic degree
graj-oo-and /ˈgradʒuand/

Graecism Greek idiom
gree-siz-uhm /ˈgriːsɪzəm/

Graf, Steffi German tennis player
shtef-i grahf /ˌʃtɛfi ˈgrɑːf/

graffiti sing. **graffito** drawing or writing scratched on a wall
gruh-**fee**-ti, sing. gruh-**fee**-toh /grəˈfiːti/, sing. /-təʊ/

Grainger, Percy Australian-born American composer
grayn-juhr /ˈgreɪndʒə(r)/

gramicidin antibiotic
gram-iss-**y**-din /ˌgramɪˈsʌɪdɪn/

Grammaticas, Damian BBC journalist
gruh-**mat**-ik-uhss /grəˈmatɪkəs/

Grampian former region, Scotland
gram-pi-uhn /ˈgrampiən/

Gramsci, Antonio Italian political theorist
an-**tohn**-yoh gram-shi /anˌtəʊnjəʊ ˈgramʃi/

Granada city, Spain
gruh-**nah**-duh /grəˈnɑːdə/, [graˈnaða]
• Established anglicization.

granadilla passion fruit
gran-uh-**dil**-uh /granəˈdɪlə/

Granados, Enrique Spanish composer
en-**ree**-kay gran-ah-*th*oss /ɛnˌriːkeɪ graˈnɑːðɒs/

Gran Canaria island, Canary Islands
gran kuh-**nair**-i-uh /ˌgran kəˈnɛːriə/, Spanish [ˌgraŋ kaˈnarja]
• Established anglicization.

Gran Chaco plain, South America
gran chak-oh /ˌgran ˈtʃakəʊ/

grandam archaic term for grandmother
gran-dam /ˈgrandam/

Grande Comore island, Comoros
grah(ng)d kuh-mor /ˌgrɑ̃d kəˈmɔː(r)/

grand mal form of epilepsy
gron mal /ˌgrɒn ˈmal/

Grand Marnier trademark liqueur
gron mar-ni-ay /ˌgrɒn ˈmɑː(r)nieɪ/, French [grɑ̃ marnje]

Grand Prix motor-racing contest
gron pree /ˌgrɒn ˈpriː/, French [grɑ̃ pri]

granola kind of breakfast cereal
gruhn-**oh**-luh /grəˈnəʊlə/

Grantha southern Indian alphabet
grun-tuh /ˈgrʌntə/

gran turismo car
gran tuu-**riz**-moh /ˌgran tʊˈrɪzməʊ/

grapheme smallest meaningful unit in a writing system
graf-eem /ˈgrafiːm/

Grappelli, Stephane French jazz violinist
stay-fan gruh-**pel**-i /steɪˌfan grəˈpɛli/

Grasmere village and lake, England
grahss-meer /ˈgrɑːsmɪə(r)/

Grass, Günter German novelist
guen-tuhr grass /ˌgʏntə(r) ˈgras/

Grasse town, France
grass /gras/

gratis without charge
grat-iss /ˈgratɪs/

Sometimes also **grah**-tiss or **gray**-tiss.

gratuitous done without good reason
gruh-**tyoo**-it-uhss /grəˈtjuːɪtəs/

gravad lax Scandinavian dish; also
called **gravlax**
grav-uhd **laks** /ˈgravəd ˌlaks/, Swedish
[ˌgrɑːvad ˈlaks]

gravamen pl. **gravamina** most serious
part of a complaint or accusation
gruh-**vay**-men, pl. gruh-**vay**-min-uh
/grəˈveɪmɛn/, pl. /-mɪnə/

grave accent diacritic (ˋ)
grahv /grɑːv/

Gravenstein apple
grah-vuhn-styn /ˈgrɑːvənˌstʌɪn/

Graves, Robert English poet
grayvz /greɪvz/

Graves district, France; also wine made
there
grahv /grɑːv/

Graves' disease enlargement of the
thyroid
grayvz /greɪvz/

Gravettian Upper Palaeolithic culture
gruh-**vet**-i-uhn /grəˈvɛtiən/

gravitas dignity and seriousness
grav-it-ass /ˈgravɪtas/

gravlax Scandinavian dish; also called
gravad lax
grav-laks /ˈgravlaks/, Swedish
[ˈgrɑːvlaks]

Graz city, Austria
grahts /grɑːts/

grebe waterbird
greeb /griːb/

Greco, El see **El Greco**

Greenland island, Denmark
green-luhnd /ˈgriːnlənd/

Established anglicization. The Danish name
is Grønland, pronounced **groen**-lan
[ˈgrœnlæn], and the Inuit name is
Kalaallit Nunaat, pronounced kuh-**lah**-lit
nuh-**naht**.

Greenock port, Scotland
green-uhk /ˈgriːnək/

Greenwich borough, London
gren-itch /ˈgrɛnɪtʃ/

Greer, Germaine Australian feminist
and author

juhr-mayn greer /dʒə(r)ˌmeɪn ˈgrɪə(r)/

gregarious fond of company
gruh-**gair**-i-uhss /grəˈgɛːriəs/

Gregorian calendar calendar
introduced by Pope Gregory XIII
gruh-**gaw**-ri-uhn /grəˈgɔːriən/

Gregory of Nazianzus, St Doctor of
the Church
naz-i-an-zuhss /ˌnaziˈanzəs/

Gregory of Nyssa, St Doctor of the
Eastern Church
niss-uh /ˈnɪsə/

Gregory of Tours, St Frankish bishop
and historian
toor /tʊə(r)/

Grenache black wine grape
gruh-**nash** /grəˈnaʃ/

Grenada country
gruh-**nay**-duh /grəˈneɪdə/

grenade small bomb
gruh-**nayd** /grəˈneɪd/

Grenadian relating to Grenada
gruh-**nay**-di-uhn /grəˈneɪdiən/

grenadier soldier armed with grenade
gren-uh-**deer** /ˌgrɛnəˈdɪə(r)/

grenadine sweet cordial
gren-uh-deen /ˈgrɛnədiːn/

Grenadine Islands chain of islands,
Caribbean
gren-uh-deen /ˈgrɛnədiːn/

Grendel fictional creature in Beowulf
gren-duhl /ˈgrɛndəl/

Grenfell, Joyce English entertainer and
writer
gren-fuhl /ˈgrɛnfəl/

Grenoble city, France
gruh-**noh**-buhl /grəˈnəʊbəl/, [grənɔbl]
• Established anglicization.

Gresham, Thomas English financier
gresh-uhm /ˈgrɛʃəm/

Gresley, Nigel British railway engineer
grez-li /ˈgrɛzli/

Gretzky, Wayne Canadian ice-hockey
player
gret-ski /ˈgrɛtski/

Greuze, Jean-Baptiste French painter
zhah(ng) bat-**eest groez** /ʒɑ̃ baˌtiːst
ˈgrøːz/

Grieg, Edvard Norwegian composer
ed-vard **greeg** /ˌɛdvɑː(r)d ˈgriːg/

griffon breed of dog
grif-uhn /ˈgrɪfən/

Greek

Greek is a modern European language, and also an ancient language
which was a rich source for the vocabulary of English, producing, for
example, *phobia, tele-, micro-, meta-, eu-,* and *dys-.* Many medical and
scientific terms have Greek roots. Modern Greek and ancient Greek
differ in many respects, including pronunciation.

This panel offers a brief overview of the pronunciation of modern
and ancient Greek, both of which are written using the Greek alphabet.
When we encounter Greek words for which pronunciation advice is
required, they have usually already been transliterated into the Roman
alphabet. The transliteration represents an attempt to supply a
phonetic version, so some aspects of the pronunciation are straightforward. However, other aspects, in particular the correct stress
placement, are not.

Modern Greek

Stress can fall on any of the last three syllables of a word. Although this
is marked with acute accents in the original Greek, these accents are
usually absent from transliterations, so we consult dictionaries and
native speakers for guidance. Most consonants, as they appear in transliterations, are pronounced as in English, except that B is often v, and
D is th, as in *this.* The sequence NT is usually pronounced nd;
Konstantinos is pronounced kon-stan-**dee**-noss. PH is pronounced f,
TH is pronounced th, and KH is pronounced kh as in *loch,* which can
be anglicized to k. G is pronounced g unless it appears before G, K, KS,
or KH, in which case it is ng, or before E or I, in which case it is y: *Agia
Napa* is pronounced **y**-uh **nap**-uh. Vowels are roughly A: a, E: e, I: ee,
O: o and U/Y: oo. Diphthongs EI and OI are both pronounced ee, and
AI is e. Modern Greek does not distinguish between long and short
vowels. Modern Greek pronunciation standards are generally also used
for New Testament and medieval Greek, although liturgical or sung
Greek (e.g. *kyrie eleison*) is usually subject to further anglicization.

Ancient Greek

The precise correct pronunciation of Ancient Greek is a matter of considerable and continuing debate, too complex to rehearse here. Ancient
Greek had pitch accents, indicated with acute, circumflex, and grave
diacritics. As with Modern Greek, accents could fall on any of the last
three syllables and are frequently missing from transliterations. In the
absence of native speakers, dictionaries must be consulted for guidance. Ancient Greek also had diacritics to indicate whether or not an *h*

sound was made before a word-initial vowel. The symbol ' over a vowel indicates rough breathing (i.e. a preceding *h* sound), and the symbol ' indicates smooth breathing (no initial *h* sound).

B is pronounced b and D is pronounced d. PH, TH, and KH are pronounced p, t, and k. (Each of these consonants is strongly aspirated to contrast with the unaspirated consonants P, T, and K. The consonant sequences in the English words *uphill*, *fathead*, and *backhand* may give an idea of how the aspirated consonants should sound. Unaspirated consonants are pronounced as in the English words *spin*, *stick*, and *skin*.) Vowels in ancient Greek were either long or short. In general, when anglicized, A is pronounced a if short, ah if long; E is e if short, ay if long, I is i or ee, O is o or aw, and U or Y is ue (as in German *fünf*) or oo. EI is pronounced as in *feud*.

Names from ancient Greek are generally pronounced as classical Latin, with the same range of systems (see Latin panel). For example, *Bacchae* can be pronounced as anglicized **bak**-ee or as classical **bak**-y, and the C in words like *encephalitis* can be pronounced as anglicized s or classical k.

---

grillage framework forming a foundation for buildings
gril-ij /ˈɡrɪlɪdʒ/

grilse salmon
grilss /ɡrɪls/

grimace twisted expression
grim-uhss /ˈɡrɪməs/

Sometimes also grim-**ayss**.

Grimaldi, Francesco Maria Italian astronomer
fran-**chesk**-oh muh-**ree**-uh grim-**al**-di /franˌtʃɛskəʊ məˌriːə ɡrɪˈmaldi/

Grimaldi, Joseph English circus entertainer
grim-**al**-di /ɡrɪˈmaldi/

grimalkin cat
grim-**al**-kin /ɡrɪˈmalkɪn/

Grimm, Jacob and Wilhelm German philologists and folklorists
yah-kop **vil**-helm grim /ˈjɑːkɒp ˌvɪlhɛlm ˈɡrɪm/

Grimond, Jo Scottish politician
grim-uhnd /ˈɡrɪmənd/

gringo white person from an English-speaking country
gring-goh /ˈɡrɪŋɡəʊ/

grippe old-fashioned term for influenza
grip /ɡrɪp/

Griqua South African ethnic group
greek-wuh /ˈɡriːkwə/

Gris, Juan Spanish painter
khwan greess /ˌxwan ˈɡriːs/

griseofulvin antibiotic
griz-i-oh-**fuul**-vin /ˌɡrɪziəʊˈfʊlvɪn/

grisette mushroom
griz-**et** /ɡrɪˈzɛt/

gris-gris charm or amulet
gree gree /ˈɡriː ɡriː/

griskin lean part of a loin of pork
grisk-in /ˈɡrɪskɪn/

grison South American monkey
griz-uhn /ˈɡrɪzən/

grissini Italian breadsticks
griss-**ee**-ni /ɡrɪˈsiːni/

Grivas, George Greek-Cypriot patriot
gree-vuhss /ˈɡriːvəs/

grivet African monkey
griv-uht /ˈɡrɪvət/

Grobbelaar, Bruce South African-born English footballer
grob-uh-lar /ˈɡrɒbəlɑː(r)/

Groening, Matt American cartoonist
gray-ning /ˈɡreɪnɪŋ/

grogram fabric made of silk
grog-ruhm /ˈɡrɒɡrəm/

Gromyko, Andrei Soviet statesman
an-**dray** gruh-**mee**-koh /an,dreɪ
grə'mi:kəʊ/

Groningen city, Netherlands
groh-ning-uhn /'grəʊnɪŋən/,
['ɣroːnɪŋə(n)]
• Established anglicization.

Grønland see Greenland

Gropius, Walter German-born
American architect
groh-pi-uhss /'grəʊpiəs/

grosbeak songbird
grohss-beek /'grəʊsbiːk/

grosgrain fabric
groh-grayn /'grəʊgreɪn/

Grosjean, Sébastien French tennis
player
say-bast-**ya(ng)** groh-**zhah(ng)**
/seɪbas,tjɛ̃ grəʊ'ʒɑ̃/

Grosseteste, Robert English
churchman
groh-stest /'grəʊstɛst/

Grossglockner mountain, Austria
grohss-glok-nuhr /'grəʊs,glɒknə(r)/

Grosvenor British family name
groh-vnuhr /'grəʊvnə(r)/

Grosz, George German-born American
painter
grohss /grəʊs/

Grotius, Hugo Dutch jurist and
diplomat
hyoo-goh **groh**-shi-uhss /,hju:gəʊ
'grəʊʃiəs/
• Established anglicization.

groupuscule political or religious
splinter group
groo-puh-skyool /'gru:pə,skju:l/

Grozny capital of Chechnya
groz-ni /'grɒzni/

Gruffydd, Ioan Welsh actor
yoh-uhn **grif**-ith /,jəʊən 'grɪfɪð/

Grundig German electronics company
grun-dig /'grʌndɪg/, ['grʊndɪç]
• Established anglicization.

Grünewald, Mathias German painter
mat-**ee**-ass **grue**-nuh-valt /ma,ti:as
'gry:nəvalt/

Grus constellation
gruss /grʌs/

Gruyère cheese
groo-yair /'gru:jɛ:(r)/, French [gryjɛːr]

grysbok antelope

gryss-bok /'grʌɪsbɒk/

Grytviken settlement on the island of
South Georgia, South Atlantic
grit-vee-kuhn /'grɪt,vi:kən/

Gstaad resort, Switzerland
guh-**shtahd** /gə'ʃtɑːd/, German [kʃtaːt]
• Established anglicization.

guacamole avocado dish
gwak-uh-**moh**-li /,gwakə'məʊli/

Guadalajara city, Spain
gwad-al-akh-**ar**-uh /,gwadala'xɑːrə/

Guadalcanal island, Pacific
gwad-al-kan-**al** /,gwadalka'nal/

Guadalquivir river, Spain
gwad-al-kee-**veer** /,gwadalki:'vɪə(r)/

Guadeloupe group of islands, Lesser
Antilles
gwad-uh-**loop** /,gwadə'lu:p/

Guadiana river, Spain and Portugal
gwad-i-**an**-uh /,gwadi'anə/

Guam island, Pacific
gwahm /gwɑːm/

Guanajuato state, Mexico
gwan-akh-**wat**-oh /gwana'xwatəʊ/

Guanche Canary Islands aboriginal
ethnic group
gwan-chay /'gwantʃeɪ/

Guangdong province, China
gwang-**duung** /,gwaŋ'dʊŋ/

Guangxi Zhuang autonomous region,
China
gwang-shee **jwang** /,gwaŋʃi: 'dʒwaŋ/

Guangzhou city, China
gwang-**joh** /,gwaŋ'dʒəʊ/

Guantánamo Bay bay and prison, Cuba
gwan-**tan**-uh-moh /gwan'tanəməʊ/

Guaraní American Indian ethnic group
gwar-uh-**nee** /,gwɑːrə'niː/

guardant heraldic term
gar-duhnt /'gɑː(r)dənt/

Guardi, Francesco Italian painter
fran-**chesk**-oh **gwar**-di /fran,tʃeskəʊ
'gwɑː(r)di/

Guarneri, Giuseppe Italian
violin-maker
juuz-**ep**-ay gwar-**nair**-i /dʒʊ,zɛpeɪ
gwɑː(r)'nɛːri/

Guatemala country
gwat-uh-**mah**-luh /,gwatə'mɑːlə/

guava fruit
gwah-vuh /'gwɑːvə/

Guayaquil port, Ecuador
gwy-ak-eel /gwʌɪəˈkiːl/

Gucci Italian fashion label
goo-chi /ˈguːtʃi/

Guelph faction in Italian medieval politics
gwelf /gwɛlf/

guenon African monkey
guh-non /gəˈnɒn/

Guericke, Otto von German engineer and physicist
ot-oh fon gair-ik-uh /ˌɒtəʊ fɒn ˈgɛːrɪkə/

Guerin, Orla BBC journalist
or-luh geer-in /ˌɔː(r)lə ˈgɪərɪn/

Guerin, Veronica Irish journalist
gair-in /ˈgɛːrɪn/

Guernica town, Spain
gair-nee-kuh /gɛː(r)ˈniːkə/

Guernsey island, English Channel
gurn-zi /ˈgəː(r)nzi/

Guerrero state, Mexico
gerr-air-oh /gɛˈrɛːrəʊ/

guerrilla independent fighter
guh-ril-uh /gəˈrɪlə/

Guevara, Ernesto 'Che' Argentine revolutionary leader
air-nest-oh chay guh-var-uh /ɛː(r),nɛstəʊ ˌtʃeɪ gəˈvɑːrə/

Guggenheim, Meyer Swiss-born American industrialist
my-uhr guug-uhn-hym /ˌmʌɪə(r) ˈgʊgənhʌɪm/

The same pronunciation is used for the Guggenheim museums.

Guiana region, South America
gi-ah-nuh /giˈɑːnə/

Guignol French puppet show
geen-yol /giːˈnjɒl/

guilder former currency unit, Netherlands
gil-duhr /ˈgɪldə(r)/

Guildford town, England
gil-fuhrd /ˈgɪlfə(r)d/

Guilin city, China
gway-lin /ˌgweɪˈlɪn/

Guillain–Barré syndrome nervous disorder
gee-ya(ng) barr-ay /ˌgɪjɛ̃ ˈbareɪ/

guillotine cutting machine
gil-uh-teen /ˈgɪlətiːn/

Guinea country
gin-i /ˈgɪni/

guinea former currency unit, UK
gin-i /ˈgɪni/

Guinea-Bissau country
gin-i biss-ow /ˌgɪnɪ bɪˈsaʊ/

Guinean relating to Guinea
gin-i-uhn /ˈgɪniən/

Guinevere wife of King Arthur
gwin-uh-veer /ˈgwɪnəvɪə(r)/

Guinness, Alec English actor
gin-uhss /ˈgɪnəs/

guiro (also **güiro**) musical instrument
gweer-oh /ˈgwɪərəʊ/

Guiyang city, China
gway-yang /ˌgweɪˈjaŋ/

Guizhou province, China
gway-joh /ˌgweɪˈdʒəʊ/

Gujarat state, India
guuj-uh-raht /ˌgʊdʒəˈrɑːt/

Gujarati relating to Gujarat
guuj-uh-rah-ti /ˌgʊdʒəˈrɑːti/

Gujranwala city, Pakistan
guuj-ruhn-wah-luh /ˌgʊdʒrən'wɑːlə/

Gujrat city, Pakistan
guuj-raht /gʊdʒˈrɑːt/

Gül, Abdullah Turkish politician
ab-duul-uh guel /ab,dʊlə ˈgyl/

gulab jamun Indian sweet
guul-ahb jah-mun /gʊ,lɑːb ˈdʒɑːmʌn/

Gulag system of Soviet labour camps
goo-lag /ˈguːlag/, Russian [guˈlak]
• Established anglicization.

Gulbarga city, India
guul-bar-guh /gʊlˈbɑː(r)gə/

Gulbenkian, Calouste Sarkis Turkish-born British oil magnate and philanthropist
kuh-loost sar-keess guul-benk-i-uhn /kə,luːst sɑː(r),kiːs gʊlˈbɛŋkiən/

gulden guilder
guuld-uhn /ˈgʊldən/

gules heraldic term
gyoolz /gjuːlz/

Gullah American ethnic group
gul-uh /ˈgʌlə/

Gullit, Ruud Dutch footballer
ruet khuul-it /ˌryːt ˈxʊlɪt/

Gunnell, Sally English athlete
gun-uhl /ˈgʌnəl/

Gunter's chain former measuring
instrument
gun-tuhrz /ˈgʌntə(r)z/

Guntur city, India
guun-**toor** /gʊnˈtʊə(r)/

gunwale (also **gunnel**) upper edge of a
ship's side
gun-uhl /ˈgʌnəl/

Inwale, however, is pronounced **in**-wayl.

guppy fish
gup-i /ˈgʌpi/

Gupta Hindu dynasty
guup-tuh /ˈgʊptə/

Gur West African language group
goor /gʊə(r)/

gur type of brown sugar
goor /gʊə(r)/

Gurdjieff, George Russian spiritual
leader and occultist
goor-ji-uhf /ˈgʊə(r)dʒiəf/

gurdwara Sikh place of worship
goor-**dwar**-uh /gʊə(r)ˈdwɑːrə/

Gurkha Nepalese ethnic group
gur-kuh /ˈgəː(r)kə/

Commonly also **goor**-kuh.

Gurkhali Nepali
gur-**kah**-li /gəː(r)ˈkɑːli/

Gurmukhi script used for writing
Punjabi
goor-muuk-i /ˈgʊə(r)mʊki/

guru Hindu spiritual teacher
guu-roo /ˈgʊruː/

Gustavus Adolphus former king of
Sweden
guust-**ah**-vuhss uh-**dolf**-uhss
/gʊˌstɑːvəs əˈdɒlfəs/

Gutenberg, Johannes German printer
yoh-**han**-uhss **goo**-tuhn-bairk
/jəʊˌhanəs ˈguːtənbɛː(r)k/

Guthrie, Woody American folk singer

guth-ri /ˈgʌθri/

Guyana country
gy-**an**-uh /gʌɪˈanə/

Guyenne region, France
gwee-**yen** /gwiːˈjɛn/

Gwalior city, India
gwah-li-or /ˈgwɑːliɔː(r)/

Gwent former county, Wales
gwent /gwɛnt/

Gwynedd county, Wales
gwin-e*th* /ˈgwɪnɛð/

gwyniad fish
gwin-i-ad /ˈgwɪniad/

gyan knowledge
gyahn /gjɑːn/

Gyanendra king of Nepal
gyuh-**nen**-druh /gjəˈnɛndrə/

gymkhana equestrian day event
jim-**kah**-nuh /dʒɪmˈkɑːnə/

Gyllenhaal, Jake and Maggie
American actors
jil-uhn-**hawl** /ˈdʒɪlənhɔːl/

gymnasium pl. **gymnasia** building
equipped for gymnastics
jim-**nay**-zi-uhm, pl. jim-**nay**-zi-uh
/dʒɪmˈneɪziəm/, pl. /-ziə/
• Standard -s plural is also possible.

gynaeceum part of a Greek or Roman
building set apart for women
jy-**nee**-si-uhm /dʒʌɪˈniːsiəm/

Sometimes also gy-**nee**-si-uhm; see GREEK
panel.

gynaecology branch of medicine
gy-nuh-**kol**-uh-ji /ˌgʌɪnəˈkɒlədʒi/

Less commonly also jy-nuh-**kol**-uh-ji.

gyratory circular motion
jy-**ray**-tuh-ri /dʒʌɪˈreɪtəri/

Sometimes also **jy**-ruh-tuh-ri.

Gyumri city, Armenia
gyuum-ri /ˈgjʊmri/

H

H letter of the alphabet
aytch /eɪtʃ/

The pronunciation haytch is the usual pronunciation in Irish English, but often seen as a mispronunciation in BR and AM.

Häagen-Dazs American ice cream company
hah-guhn-dahss /ˈhɑːɡənˌdɑːs/

Commonly also hah-guhn-**dahss**. The name is made up, and not based on any particular language.

Haakon Crown Prince of Norway
haw-kon /ˈhɔːkɒn/

Ha'aretz Israeli newspaper
huh-**ar**-uhts /həˈɑːrəts/

Haarlem city, Netherlands
har-luhm /ˈhɑː(r)ləm/

Habakkuk Hebrew prophet
hab-uh-kuhk /ˈhabəkək/

Hába, Alois Czech composer
al-oyss hah-buh /ˌalɔɪs ˈhɑːbə/

Habana see **Havana**

habanera Cuban dance
ab-an-**air**-uh /ˌabaˈnɛːrə/

Habdalah (also **Havdalah**) Jewish religious ceremony
hav-**dah**-luh /havˈdɑːlə/

haberdasher dealer in sewing items
hab-uhr-dash-uhr /ˈhabə(r)ˌdaʃə(r)/

habergeon coat of mail
hab-uhr-juhn /ˈhabə(r)dʒən/

Sometimes also huh-**bur**-juhn.

Habermas, Jürgen German philosopher
yuer-guhn hah-buhr-mahss /ˌjʏ(r)ɡən ˈhɑːbə(r)mɑːs/

habitué resident
huh-**bitch**-oo-ay /həˈbɪtʃueɪ/

habitus general constitution
hab-it-uhss /ˈhabɪtəs/

haboob desert wind
huh-**boob** /həˈbuːb/

Habsburg (also **Hapsburg**) European dynasty
haps-burg /ˈhapsbəː(r)ɡ/, German [ˈhaːpsbʊrk]
• Established anglicization.

háček diacritic (ˇ)
hah-chek /ˈhɑːtʃɛk/

hachures parallel lines
hash-**yoorz** /haˈʃjʊə(r)z/

hacienda large estate
hass-i-**en**-duh /ˌhasiˈɛndə/, Spanish [aˈθjenda], [aˈsjenda]
• See SPANISH panel.

Hadamar German Nazi concentration camp
had-uh-mar /ˈhadəmɑː(r)/

Hades Greek mythological underworld
hay-deez /ˈheɪdiːz/

Hadhramaut region, Yemen
had-ruh-mowt /ˌhadrəˈmaʊt/

Hadith collection of Muslim traditions
had-**eeth** /haˈdiːθ/

Hadlee, Richard New Zealand cricketer
had-li /ˈhadli/

Hadrian Roman emperor
hay-dri-uhn /ˈheɪdriən/

hadrosaur dinosaur
had-ruh-sor /ˈhadrəsɔː(r)/

haemal concerning the blood
hee-muhl /ˈhiːməl/

haematoma pl. **haematomata** swelling of clotted blood
hee-muh-**toh**-muh, pl. hee-muh-**toh**-muh-tuh /ˌhiːməˈtəʊmə/, pl. /-mətə/
• Standard -s plural is also possible.

haemoglobin protein
hee-muh-**gloh**-bin /ˌhiːməˈɡləʊbɪn/

haemophilia reduced ability of the blood to clot
hee-muh-**fil**-i-uh /ˌhiːməˈfɪliə/

haemorrhage bleeding
hem-uh-rij /ˈhɛmərɪdʒ/

haemorrhoid swollen veins around the
anus
hem-uh-**royd** /'hɛmərɔɪd/

haere mai Maori greeting
hy-ruh **my** /ˌhʌɪrə 'mʌɪ/

hafiz Muslim who knows the Koran by
heart
hah-fiz /'hɑːfɪz/

Haflinger breed of pony
haf-ling-uhr /'haflɪŋə(r)/

hafnium chemical element
haf-ni-uhm /'hafnɪəm/

haft handle of a knife
hahft /hɑːft/

Hagar biblical name
hay-gar /'heɪɡɑː(r)/

Hagen city, Germany
hah-guhn /'hɑːɡən/

Haggai Hebrew prophet
hag-y /'haɡʌɪ/

Hagia Sophia building in Istanbul
y-uh **soh**-**fee**-uh /ˌʌɪə səʊ'fiːə/

Hagiographa books of the Bible
hag-i-**og**-ruh-fuh /ˌhaɡi'ɒɡrəfə/

Hagrid character from the *Harry Potter*
books
hag-rid /'haɡrɪd/

Hague, The city, Netherlands
hayg /heɪɡ/

Established anglicization. The Dutch name
is Den Haag, pronounced den **hahkh** [dɛn
'hɑːx].

Haguenau city, French
ag-**noh** /aɡ'nəʊ/

haham (also **chacham**) person learned in
Jewish law
hah-huhm /'hɑːhəm/

Hahn, Otto German chemist
ot-oh **hahn** /ˌɒtəʊ 'hɑːn/

Haida American Indian ethnic group
hy-duh /'hʌɪdə/

Haifa port, Israel
hy-fuh /'hʌɪfə/

haik North African garment
hyk /hʌɪk/

Haikou capital of Hainan autonomous
region
khy-**koh** /ˌxʌɪ'kəʊ/

haiku Japanese poem
hy-koo /'hʌɪkuː/

Haile Selassie Ethiopian emperor

hy-li **suh**-**lass**-i /ˌhʌɪli sə'lasi/

Hainan autonomous region, China
khy-**nan** /ˌxʌɪ'nan/

Hainault part of London
hayn-awlt /'heɪnɔːlt/

Commonly also **hayn**-olt or **hayn**-awt.

Hainaut province, Belgium
en-**oh** /ɛ'nəʊ/

Haiphong port, Vietnam
hy-**fong** /hʌɪ'fɒŋ/

Haiti country
hay-ti /'heɪti/, French [aiti]
• Established anglicization.

Haitian relating to Haiti
hay-shuhn /'heɪʃən/

Haitink, Bernard Dutch conductor
bair-nart **hy**-tink /ˌbɛː(r)nɑː(r)t
'hʌɪtɪŋk/

hajj (also **haj**) Muslim pilgrimage to
Mecca
haj /hadʒ/

hajji (also **haji**) Muslim who has been to
Mecca
haj-i /'hadʒi/

haka Maori ceremonial war dance
hah-kuh /'hɑːkə/

hakama Japanese garment
hak-am-uh /'hakəmə/

Hakenkreuz swastika
hah-kuhn-kroyts /'hɑːkən,krɔɪts/

hakim governor in Muslim countries and
India
hak-**eem** /ha'kiːm/

Hakka Chinese ethnic group
hak-uh /'hakə/

Hakluyt, Richard English geographer
and historian
hak-loot /'hakluːt/

Hakodate port, Japan
hah-koh-**dah**-tay /ˌhɑːkəʊ'dɑːteɪ/

Halab see Aleppo

Halabjah city, Iraq
hal-uhb-juh /'haləbdʒə/

Halacha Jewish law
hal-ah-**khah** /ˌhalɑː'xɑː/

Halafian prehistoric culture
huh-**lah**-fi-uhn /hə'lɑːfiən/

halal meat prepared as prescribed by
Muslim law
huh-**lahl** /hə'lɑːl/

halberd combined spear and battleaxe
hal-burd /'halbə(r)d/

halberdier man armed with a halberd
hal-buhr-**deer** /ˌhalbə(r)'dɪə(r)/

Haldane, J. B. S. Scottish biologist
hawl-dayn /'hɔːldeɪn/

haldi Indian term for turmeric
hul-di /'hʌldi/

Halesowen town, England
hayl-**zoh**-uhn /heɪlz'əʊən/

Haley, Bill American rock-and-roll
singer
hay-li /'heɪli/

halfpenny former British coin
hayp-ni /'heɪpni/

The British surname Halfpenny is usually
pronounced **hahf**-puh-ni.

halfpennyworth as much as could be
bought for a halfpenny
hay-puhrth /'heɪpə(r)θ/

Sometimes also **hayp**-ni-wuhrth.

halibut fish
hal-ib-uht /'halɪbət/

Halicarnassus ancient Greek city
hal-ik-ar-**nass**-uhss /ˌhalɪkɑː(r)'nasəs/

halitosis bad breath
hal-it-**oh**-siss /ˌhalɪ'təʊsɪs/

Halle city, Germany
hal-uh /'halə/

Hallé, Charles German-born pianist
and conductor
hal-ay /'haleɪ/

Haller, Albrecht von Swiss anatomist
and physiologist
al-brekht fon hal-uhr /ˌalbreçt fɒn
'halə(r)/

Halley, Edmond English astronomer
hal-i /'hali/

The same pronunciation is used for Halley's
comet. This British surname is variously
pronounced **hal**-i, **hay**-li, and **haw**-li,
depending on individual preference.

halloumi Cypriot cheese
huh-**loo**-mi /hə'luːmi/

Hallstatt archaeological phase
hal-shtat /'halʃtat/

hallucinogen drug that causes
hallucinations
huh-**loo**-sin-uh-juhn /hə'luːsɪnədʒən/

hallux pl. **halluces** big toe
hal-uhks, pl. **hal**-yuu-seez /'haləks/, pl.
/-jʊsiːz/
• Standard -es plural is also possible.

halma board game
hal-muh /'halmə/

Halmahera island, Indonesia
hal-muh-**heer**-uh /ˌhalmə'hɪərə/

haloperidol antidepressant drug
hal-oh-**perr**-id-ol /ˌhaləʊ'perɪdɒl/

Hals, Frans Dutch painter
frunss hulss /ˌfrʌns 'hʌls/

Hälsingborg see **Helsingborg**

halva Middle Eastern sweet
hal-vuh /'halvə/

Ham biblical name
ham /ham/

Hama (also **Hamah**) city, Syria
hah-muh /'hɑːmə/

Hamada, Shoji Japanese potter
shoh-ji ham-ad-uh /ˌʃəʊdʒi 'hamadə/

hamadryad Greek mythological
character
ham-uh-**dry**-uhd /ˌhamə'drʌɪəd/

hamadryas baboon
ham-uh-**dry**-uhss /ˌhamə'drʌɪəs/

Hamamatsu city, Japan
ham-uh-**mat**-soo /ˌhamə'matsuː/

hamamelis witch hazel
ham-uh-**mee**-liss /ˌhamə'miːlɪs/

Hamas Palestinian Islamic movement
ham-**ass** /ha'mas/

hamate hand bone
hay-muht /'heɪmət/

Hamburg port, Germany
ham-burg /'hambə:(r)g/, ['hambʊrk]
• Established anglicization.

Hamelin town, Germany
ham-lin /'hamlɪn/

Established anglicization. The German
name is Hameln, pronounced **hah**-muhln.

Hamhung city, North Korea
ham-**hung** /ham'hʌŋ/

Hamilcar Carthaginian general
ham-il-kar /ha'mɪlkɑː(r)/

Commonly also **ham**-il-kar.

Hamite North African ethnic group
ham-yt /'hamʌɪt/

Hamitic group of African languages
huh-**mit**-ik /hə'mɪtɪk/

Hamm city, Germany
ham /ham/

Hammarskjöld, Dag Swedish
diplomat and politician
dahg ham-uhr-shoeld /ˌdɑːg
ˈhamə(r)ˌʃøld/

Hammerfest port, Norway
ham-uhr-fest /ˈhamə(r)fɛst/

Hammerstein, Oscar American
librettist
ham-uhr-styn /ˈhamə(r)staɪn/

Hammett, Dashiell American novelist
dash-eel ham-uht /daˌʃiːl ˈhamət/

Hammurabi king of Babylonia
ham-uu-rah-bi /ˌhamʊˈrɑːbi/

Hamnett, Katharine English fashion
designer
ham-nuht /ˈhamnət/

Hamsun, Knut Norwegian novelist
knoot ham-soon /ˌknuːt ˈhamsuːn/

Hamza, Abu Egyptian-born British
radical Muslim
ab-oo ham-zuh /ˌabuː ˈhamzə/

Handel, George Frederick
German-born English composer
han-duhl /ˈhandəl/

Established anglicization. The German
name is Händel, pronounced **hen-duhl**.

Hang Seng Hong Kong stock exchange
index
hang seng /ˌhaŋ ˈsɛŋ/

Hangzhou city, China
hang-joh /ˌhaŋˈdʒəʊ/

Haniyah, Ismail Palestinian prime
minister
iss-muh-eel han-ee-yuh /ɪsməˌiːl
haˈniːjə/

Hanna-Barbera American cartoon film
makers
han-uh bar-bair-uh /ˌhanə
bɑː(r)ˈbɛːrə/

Hannibal Carthaginian general
han-ib-uhl /ˈhanɪbəl/

Hanoi capital of Vietnam
han-oy /haˈnɔɪ/

Hanover city, Germany
han-oh-vuhr /ˈhanəʊvə(r)/

Established anglicization. The German form
is Hannover, pronounced **han-oh-fuhr**
[haˈnoːfə].

Hanoverian relating to Hanover
han-uh-veer-i-uhn /ˌhanəˈvɪəriən/

Hanse medieval guild of merchants

han-suh /ˈhansə/

Hanseatic League medieval association
of north German cities
han-si-at-ik /ˌhansiˈatɪk/

Hanukkah (also **Chanukkah**) Jewish
festival
han-uh-kuh /ˈhanəkə/, Hebrew
[xanuˈka]

Sometimes also **hon-uh-kuh** or
hah-nuh-kuh.

Hanuman Hindu monkey-like being
hun-uum-ahn /ˌhʌnʊˈmɑːn/

Happisburgh resort, England
hayz-buh-ruh /ˈheɪzbərə/

Hapsburg see Habsburg

hara-kiri ritual samurai suicide
harr-uh-kirr-i /ˌharəˈkɪri/

haram forbidden by Islamic law
har-ahm /hɑːˈrɑːm/

Harappa ancient city of the Indus valley
huh-rap-uh /həˈrapə/

Harare capital of Zimbabwe
huh-rar-i /həˈrɑːri/
• Established anglicization.

harass annoy or pester
harr-uhss /ˈharəs/

This is the traditional British English
pronunciation. The variant huh-**rass** is
gaining ground in BR but still disliked by
many in the UK, and the same applies to the
word *harassment*. AM is huh-**rass**.

Harbin city, China
har-been /ˌhɑː(r)ˈbiːn/

Hardanger district, Norway
har-dang-uhr /hɑː(r)ˈdaŋə(r)/

Hardecanute king of Denmark and
England
har-duh-kuh-nyoot /ˈhɑː(r)dəkənjuːt/

Hardwar city, India
hard-war /hɑː(r)ˈdwɑː(r)/

Hare Krishna religious cult
har-ay krish-nuh /ˌhɑːreɪ ˈkrɪʃnə/

harem part of a Muslim household
reserved for women
har-eem /ˈhɑːriːm/

Commonly also **hair-uhm**.

Hargeisa city, Somalia
har-gay-suh /hɑː(r)ˈgeɪsə/

haricot French bean
harr-ik-oh /ˈharɪkəʊ/

Harijan Hindu group of the lowest social status
hurr-ij-un /ˈhʌrɪdʒʌn/

Haringey part of London
harr-ing-gay /ˈhærɪŋgeɪ/

Hariri, Rafik al- Lebanese politician
ruh-feek uhl huh-ree-ri /rəˌfiːk əl həˈriːri/

harissa North African spicy paste
huh-riss-uh /həˈrɪsə/

Harlech village, Wales
har-lek /ˈhɑː(r)lɛk, [ˈharlɛx]
• Established anglicization.

harmattan dry wind
har-mat-uhn /hɑː(r)ˈmatən/

harpsichord keyboard instrument
harp-sik-ord /ˈhɑː(r)psɪkɔː(r)d/

harquebus gun
har-kwib-uhss /ˈhɑː(r)kwɪbəs/

Harri, Guto BBC journalist
git-oh harr-i /ˌgɪtəʊ ˈhari/

Harrovian member of Harrow School
huh-roh-vi-uhn /həˈrəʊviən/

Harte, Bret American short-story writer
hart /hɑː(r)t/

hartebeest antelope
har-tuh-beest /ˈhɑː(r)təbiːst/

Hartlepool port, England
hart-luh-pool /ˈhɑː(r)tləˌpuːl/

Harun ar-Rashid caliph of Baghdad
harr-oon uh-rash-eed /haˌruːn əraˈʃiːd/
• See ARABIC panel.

haruspex pl. **haruspices** religious official
huh-rusp-eks, pl. **huh-rusp-iss-eez** /həˈrʌspɛks/, pl. /-spɪsiːz/

Harwich port, England
harr-ij /ˈharɪdʒ/

Haryana state, India
hurr-i-ah-nuh /ˌhʌriˈɑːnə/

Harz Mountains range of mountains, Germany
harts /hɑː(r)ts/

Hasdrubal Carthaginian general
haz-druub-uhl /ˈhazdrʊbəl/

Hašek, Jaroslav Czech novelist
yarr-oss-laf hash-ek /ˌjarʊslaf ˈhaʃɛk/

hashish cannabis
hash-ish /ˈhaʃɪʃ/
Commonly also hash-**eesh**.

Hasidic (also **Chasidic** or **Chassidic**)
relating to Hasidism
hass-id-ik /haˈsɪdɪk/

Hasidism (also **Chasidism** or **Chassidism**) mystical Jewish movement
hass-id-iz-uhm /ˈhasɪˌdɪzəm/

Hasmonean Jewish dynasty
haz-muh-nee-uhn /ˌhazməˈniːən/

Hasselt city, Belgium
huss-uhlt /ˈhʌsəlt/

Hasselbaink, Jimmy Floyd Dutch footballer
huss-uhl-bynk /ˈhʌsəlbʌɪŋk/

hassium chemical element
hass-i-uhm /ˈhasiəm/

Hathaway, Anne wife of William Shakespeare
hath-uh-way /ˈhaθəweɪ/

hatha type of yoga
hath-uh /ˈhaθə/
Sometimes also **hut**-uh.

Hathor ancient Egyptian goddess
hath-or /ˈhaθɔː(r)/

Hatshepsut ancient Egyptian queen
hat-shep-suut /hatˈʃɛpsʊt/

Hattusa capital of the ancient Hittite empire
hat-uuss-uh /ˈhatʊsə/

Hauer, Rutger Dutch actor
ruut-guhr how-uhr /ˌrʊtgə(r) ˈhaʊə(r)/

Hau-Hauism Maori religion
how how-iz-uhm /ˈhaʊ ˌhaʊɪzəm/

Hauptmann, Gerhart German dramatist
gair-hart howpt-man /ˌgɛː(r)hɑː(r)t ˈhaʊptman/

haurient heraldic term
haw-ri-uhnt /ˈhɔːriənt/

Hausa Nigerian language and ethnic group
how-suh /ˈhaʊsə/

haute couture fashion design
oht kuu-tyoor /ˌəʊt kʊˈtjʊə(r)/

haute cuisine cooking of high-quality food
oht kwiz-een /ˌəʊt kwɪˈziːn/

hauteur proud haughtiness of manner
oh-tur /əʊˈtə(r)/

havan Hindu ritual burning of offerings
hav-uhn /ˈhavən/

Havana capital of Cuba
huh-van-uh /həˈvanə/

Established anglicization. The Spanish name is Habana, pronounced **ab-an-uh** [a'βana].

Havant town, England
hav-uhnt /'havənt/

Havdalah see **Habdalah**

Havel, Václav Czech dramatist and statesman
vaht-slaf **hav**-el /ˌvɑːtslaf 'havɛl/

Hawaii state, US
huh-**wy**-i /hə'wʌɪi/

hawala Arab system of transferring money
huh-**wah**-luh /hə'wɑːlə/

Hawick town, Scotland
hoyk /hɔɪk/

Haworth, Walter Norman English chemist
how-uhrth /'haʊwə(r)θ/

This British surname is variously pronounced **how**-uhrth and **haw**-uhrth, depending on individual preference.

Haydn, Franz Joseph Austrian composer
frants yoh-zuhf **hy**-duhn /ˌfrants ˌjəʊzəf 'hʌɪdən/

Hayek, Salma Mexican actress
sal-muh **hy**-ek /ˌsalmə 'hʌɪɛk/

Hayward Gallery art gallery in London
hay-wuhrd /'heɪwə(r)d/

Hazchem system of labelling hazardous chemicals
haz-kem /'hazkɛm/

Hazlitt, William English essayist
hayz-lit /'heɪzlɪt/

This is the family pronunciation, but the name is commionly also pronounced **haz**-lit.

HBOS banking group
aytch-boss /'eɪtʃbɒs/

Heaney, Seamus Irish poet
shay-muhss **hee**-ni /ˌʃeɪməs 'hiːni/

hearken listen
har-kuhn /'hɑː(r)kən/

Hearst, William Randolph American newspaper publisher
hurst /həː(r)st/

Heaviside, Oliver English physicist
hev-iss-yd /'hɛvɪsʌɪd/

hebdomadal weekly
heb-**dom**-uh-duhl /hɛb'dɒmədəl/

Hebe Greek mythological character

hee-bi /'hiːbi/

Hebei province, China
khuh-**bay** /ˌxə'beɪ/

hebephrenia form of schizophrenia
hee-buh-**free**-ni-uh /ˌhiːbə'friːniə/

Hebraic relating to Hebrew
huh-**bray**-ik /hə'breɪɪk/

Hebraist scholar of the Hebrew language
heeb-ray-isst /'hiːbreɪɪst/

Hebrew Israeli language
hee-broo /'hiːbruː/

Hebrides group of islands, Scotland
heb-rid-eez /'hɛbrɪdiːz/

Hebron city, West Bank
heb-ron /'hɛbrɒn/

Hecate Greek goddess
hek-uh-ti /'hɛkəti/

hecatomb great public sacrifice
hek-uh-toom /'hɛkətuːm/

Heche, Anne American actress
hesh /hɛʃ/

hectare unit of square measure
hek-tair /'hɛktɛː(r)/

Sometimes also **hek**-tar.

Hector Greek mythological character
hek-tuhr /'hɛktə(r)/

Hecuba Greek mythological character
hek-yuub-uh /'hɛkjʊbə/

heder see **cheder**

hedonism pursuit of pleasure
hee-duh-niz-uhm /'hiːdənɪzəm/

Commonly also **hed**-uh-niz-uhm.

Hefei city, China
khuh-**fay** /ˌxə'feɪ/

Hegel, Georg Wilhelm Friedrich German philosopher
gay-ork **vil**-helm **freed**-rikh **hay**-guhl /ˌɡeɪɔː(r)k ˌvɪlhɛlm ˌfriːdrɪç 'heɪɡəl/

hegemonic dominant
heg-uh-**mon**-ik /ˌhɛɡə'mɒnɪk/

Sometimes also hej-uh-**mon**-ik.

Hegira (also **Hejira**) Muhammad's departure from Mecca to Medina
hej-irr-uh /'hɛdʒɪrə/

heiau ancient Hawaiian temple
hay-oh /'heɪəʊ/

Heidegger, Martin German
philosopher
mar-teen hy-deg-uhr /ˌmɑː(r)tiːn
ˈhʌɪˌdɛgə(r)/

Heidelberg city, Germany
hy-duhl-burg /ˈhʌɪdəlbəː(r)g/,
[ˈhaidəlbɛrk]
• Established anglicization.

Heilbronn city, Germany
hyl-bron /hʌɪlˈbrɒn/

Heilongjiang province, China
khay-luung-ji-ang /ˌxeɪlʊŋdʒiˈaŋ/

Heimat 'homeland' (German)
hy-maht /ˈhʌɪmɑːt/

Heimlich manoeuvre first-aid
procedure
hym-lik /ˈhʌɪmlɪk/, German [ˈhaimlɪç]
• Established anglicization.

Heine, Heinrich German poet
hyn-rikh hy-nuh /ˌhʌɪnrɪç ˈhʌɪnə/

Heinlein, Robert A. American writer
hyn-lyn /ˈhʌɪnlʌɪn/

heinous utterly wicked
hay-nuhss /ˈheɪnəs/

Sometimes also **hee-nuhss**, and erroneously
hee-ni-uhss.

Heinz, Henry John American food
manufacturer
hynz /hʌɪnz/

Heisenberg, Werner Karl German
philosopher
vair-nuhr karl hy-zuhn-bairk
/ˌvɛː(r)nə(r) ˌkɑː(r)l ˈhʌɪzənbɛː(r)k/

hei-tiki Maori neck ornament
hay-tik-i /heɪˈtɪki/

Hejaz (also **Hijaz**) region, Saudi Arabia
huh-jaz /həˈdʒaz/

Hejira see **Hegira**

Hekla volcano, Iceland
hek-luh /ˈhɛklə/

HeLa cells immortal cell line used in
research
hee-luh /ˈhiːlə/

Helena city, US
hel-uh-nuh /ˈhɛlənə/

Helena, St Roman empress
hel-uh-nuh /ˈhɛlənə/
• See also the island of ST HELENA.

Helgoland see **Heligoland**

heliacal relating to the sun
huh-ly-uh-kuhl /həˈlʌɪəkəl/

helianthus plant
hee-li-an-thuhss /ˌhiːliˈanθəs/

helical having the shape of a helix
hel-ik-uhl /ˈhɛlɪkəl/

Sometimes also **hee-lik-uhl**.

helicon musical instrument
hel-ik-uhn /ˈhɛlɪkən/

Helicon, Mount mountain, Greece
hel-ik-uhn /ˈhɛlɪkən/

Heligoland island, Germany
hel-ig-oh-land /ˈhɛlɪgəʊland/

Established anglicization. The German
name is Helgoland, pronounced
hel-goh-lant.

Heliogabalus Roman emperor
hee-li-oh-gab-uh-luhss
/ˌhiːliəˈgabələs/

Heliopolis ancient Egyptian city
hee-li-op-uh-liss /ˌhiːliˈɒpəlɪs/

Helios Greek god
hee-li-uhss /ˈhiːliəs/

helium chemical element
hee-li-uhm /ˈhiːliəm/

helix pl. **helices** spiral form
hee-liks, pl. **hel-iss-eez** /ˈhiːlɪks/, pl.
/ˈhɛlɪsiːz/
• Standard -es plural is also possible.

Helladic Bronze Age cultures of Greece
hel-ad-ik /hɛˈladɪk/

Hellas Greece
hel-ass /ˈhɛlas/

hellebore plant
hel-ib-or /ˈhɛlɪbɔː(r)/

Hellene ancient Greek
hel-een /ˈhɛliːn/

Hellenic Greek
hel-en-ik /hɛˈlɛnɪk/

Hellenize make Greek
hel-uh-nyz /ˈhɛlənʌɪz/

Hellespont ancient name for the
Dardanelles
hel-uhss-pont /ˈhɛləspɒnt/

Helmand river and province,
Afghanistan
hel-mand /hɛlˈmand/

helminthiasis infestation with
parasitic worms
hel-min-thy-uh-siss /ˌhɛlmɪnˈθʌɪəsɪs/

helot serf in ancient Sparta
hel-uht /ˈhɛlət/

Helsingborg (also **Hälsingborg**) port, Sweden
hel-sing-**borg** /ˈhɛlsɪŋˈbɔː(r)ɡ/, [ˌhɛlsɪŋˈbɔrj]
• Established anglicization.

Helsingør see **Elsinore**

Helsinki capital of Finland
hel-sink-i /ˈhɛlsɪŋki/
• Note the stress on the first syllable!

Helvetia Latin name for Switzerland
hel-**vee**-shuh /hɛlˈviːʃə/

hemianopia blindness over half the field of vision
hem-i-uh-**noh**-pi-uh /ˌhɛmiəˈnəʊpiə/

hemiola musical term
hem-i-**oh**-luh /ˌhɛmiˈəʊlə/

hemiplegia paralysis of one side of the body
hem-ip-**lee**-juh /ˌhɛmɪˈpliːdʒə/

hemistich half of a line of verse
hem-ist-ik /ˈhɛmɪstɪk/

Hemkund lake, India
hem-**kuund** /hɛmˈkʊnd/

Henan province, China
khuh-**nan** /ˌxəˈnan/

hendecagon figure with eleven straight sides
hen-**dek**-uh-guhn /hɛnˈdɛkəɡən/

hendiadys grammatical structure
hen-**dy**-uh-diss /hɛnˈdʌɪədɪs/

Hengist and Horsa semi-mythological Jutish leaders
heng-gist **hor**-suh /ˈhɛŋɡɪst ˈhɔː(r)sə/

Henin-Ardenne, Justine Belgian tennis player
zhue-**steen** en-a**(ng)** ar-den /ʒyˈstiːn ɛˌnɛ̃ ɑː(r)ˈdɛn/

Henri, Robert American painter
hen-ri /ˈhɛnri/

Henrician relating to Henry VIII of England
hen-**rish**-uhn /hɛnˈrɪʃən/

Henry, Thierry French footballer
tyerr-**ee** ah(ng)-ree /tjɛˌri: ɑ̃ˈri:/

Henze, Hans Werner German composer
hanss vair-nuhr hent-suh /ˌhans ˌvɛː(r)nə(r) ˈhɛntsə/

heparin compound occurring in the liver
hep-uh-rin /ˈhɛpərɪn/

hepatic relating to the liver
hep-**at**-ik /hɛˈpatɪk/

hepatitis inflammation of the liver
hep-uh-**ty**-tiss /ˌhɛpəˈtʌɪtɪs/

hepatoma pl. **hepatomata** liver cancer
hep-uh-**toh**-muh, pl. hep-uh-**toh**-muh-tuh /ˌhɛpəˈtəʊmə/, pl. /-mətə/
• Standard -s plural is also possible.

Hephaestus Greek god
huh-**fee**-stuhss /huˈfiːstəs/

heptad group or set of seven
hep-tad /ˈhɛptad/

heptagon figure with seven sides
hep-tuh-guhn /ˈhɛptəɡən/

heptahedron figure with seven plane faces
hep-tuh-**hee**-druhn /ˌhɛptəˈhiːdrən/
Sometimes also hep-tuh-**hed**-ruhn.

heptameter line of verse consisting of seven metrical feet
hep-**tam**-uh-tuhr /hɛpˈtamətə(r)/

heptarchy region consisting of seven autonomous regions
hep-tar-ki /ˈhɛptɑː(r)ki/

Heptateuch books of the Bible
hep-tuh-tyook /ˈhɛptətjuːk/

heptathlon athletic event
hep-**tath**-lon /hɛpˈtaθlɒn/

Hera Greek goddess
heer-uh /ˈhɪərə/

Heracles Greek mythological character; also called **Hercules**
herr-uh-kleez /ˈhɛrəkliːz/

Heraclitus Greek philosopher
herr-uh-**kly**-tuhss /ˌhɛrəˈklʌɪtəs/

Heraklion capital, Crete
huh-**rak**-li-uhn /həˈrakliən/

Herat city, Afghanistan
herr-**aht** /hɛˈrɑːt/

herbaceous relating to herbs
hur-**bay**-shuhss /hə(r)ˈbeɪʃəs/

herbarium pl. **herbaria** collection of dried plants
hur-**bair**-i-uhm, pl. hur-**bair**-i-uh /hə(r)ˈbɛːriəm/, pl. /-riə/

herbivore animal that feeds on plants
hur-biv-or /ˈhə(r)bɪvɔː(r)/

Herceptin cancer drug
hur-**sep**-tin /hə(r)ˈsɛptɪn/

Herculaneum ancient Roman town
hur-kyuul-**ay**-ni-uhm /ˌhə(r)kjʊˈleɪniəm/

Herculean requiring great strength
hur-kyuul-**ee**-uhn /ˌhəː(r)kjʊˈliːən/

Sometimes also hur-**kyoo**-li-uhn.

Hercules Greek mythological character;
also called **Heracles**
hur-kyuul-eez /ˈhəː(r)kjʊliːz/

Hereford city, England
herr-uh-fuhrd /ˈhɛrəfə(r)d/

Herero African ethnic group
huh-**rair**-oh /həˈrɛːrəʊ/

Hereward the Wake semi-legendary
Anglo-Saxon leader
herr-uh-wuhrd /ˈhɛrəwə(r)d/

Hergé Belgian cartoonist
air-**zhay** /ɛ:(r)ˈʒeɪ/

hermaphrodite human or animal
having both male and female sex organs
hur-**maf**-ruh-dyt /həː(r)ˈmafrədʌɪt/

Hermaphroditus Greek mythological
character
huhr-maf-ruh-**dy**-tuhss
/həˌmafrəˈdʌɪtəs/

Hermes Greek mythological character
hur-meez /ˈhəː(r)miːz/

Hermès French fashion label
air-**mess** /ɛ:(r)ˈmɛs/

Hermosillo city, Mexico
air-moss-**eel**-yoh /ˌɛ:(r)mɒˈsiːljəʊ/

hernia pl. **herniae** medical condition
hur-ni-uh, pl. **hur**-ni-ee /ˈhəː(r)niə/, pl.
/-niː/
• Standard -s plural is also possible.

Herning city, Denmark
hair-ning /ˈhɛː(r)nɪŋ/

Herod name of several rulers of ancient
Palestine
herr-uhd /ˈhɛrəd/

Herodotus Greek historian
herr-**od**-uh-tuhss /hɛˈrɒdətəs/

Herophilus Greek anatomist
heer-**of**-il-uhss /hɪəˈrɒfɪləs/

Herr pl. **Herren** German title for a man
hair, pl. herr-uhn /hɛː(r)/, pl. /ˈhɛrən/

Herri Batasuna Basque political party
err-i bat-ass-**oo**-nuh /ˌɛri bataˈsuːnə/

Herschel, William German-born
British astronomer
hur-shuhl /ˈhəː(r)ʃəl/

Hertford town, England
hart-fuhrd /ˈhɑː(r)tfə(r)d/

Hertz, Heinrich Rudolf German
physicist

hyn-rikh roo-dolf hairts /ˌhʌɪnrɪç
ˌruːdɒlf ˈhɛː(r)ts/

hertz SI unit of frequency
hurts /həː(r)ts/

Herut Israeli political party
herr-**oot** /hɛˈruːt/

Herzegovina see **Bosnia-Herzegovina**

Herzl, Theodor Hungarian-born
Austrian Zionist leader
hurt-suhl /ˈhəː(r)tsəl/, German
[ˌteːodoːɐ ˈhɛrtsl]
• Established anglicization.

Herzog, Werner German film director
vair-nuhr hairt-sohk /ˌvɛː(r)nə(r)
ˈhɛː(r)tsəʊk/

Heshvan see **Hesvan**

Hesiod Greek poet
hee-si-uhd /ˈhiːsiəd/

Hesperian concerning the Hesperides
hesp-**eer**-i-uhn /hɛˈspɪəriən/

Hesperides Greek mythological
characters
hesp-**err**-id-eez /hɛˈspɛrɪdiːz/

hesperidium pl. **hesperidia** fruit
hesp-uh-**rid**-i-uhm,
pl. hesp-uh-**rid**-i-uh /ˌhɛspəˈrɪdiəm/,
pl. /-diə/

Hesperus name for the planet Venus
hesp-uh-ruhss /ˈhɛspərəs/

Hess, Rudolf German Nazi politician
roo-dolf hess /ˌruːdɒlf ˈhɛs/

Hesse state, Germany
hess /hɛs/

Established anglicization. The German
name is Hessen, pronounced **hess**-uhn.

Hesse, Hermann German-born Swiss
novelist
hair-man hess-uh /ˌhɛː(r)man ˈhɛsə/

Hesvan (also **Heshvan**) Jewish month
hess-vuhn /ˈhɛsvən/

heterogeneous diverse
het-uh-ruh-**jee**-ni-uhss
/ˌhɛtərəˈdʒiːniəs/

Less commonly also het-uh-ruh-**jen**-i-uhss.
Sometimes also spelled *heterogenous*, in
which case the pronunciation
het-uh-**roj**-uh-nuhss is commonly used.

hetman Polish or Cossack military
commander
het-muhn /ˈhɛtmən/

heurige wine from the latest harvest
hoy-rig-uh /ˈhɔɪrɪgə/

heuristic enabling a person to learn
something for themselves
hyoo-uh-**rist**-ik /ˌhjuəˈrɪstɪk/

Heugh British family name
hyoo /hjuː/

The place in Northumberland, however, is
hyoof.

Hewitt, Lleyton Australian tennis
player
lay-tuhn **hyoo**-it /ˌleɪtən ˈhjuːɪt/

hexachord musical scale of six notes
hek-suh-kord /ˈhɛksəkɔː(r)d/

hexad set of six
hek-sad /ˈhɛksad/

hexagon figure with six straight sides
hek-suh-guhn /ˈhɛksəgən/

hexahedron figure with six plane faces
hek-suh-**heed**-ruhn /ˌhɛksəˈhiːdrən/

Sometimes also hek-suh-**hed**-ruhn.

hexamerous having parts arranged in
groups of six
hek-**sam**-uh-ruhss /hɛkˈsamərəs/

hexameter line of verse consisting of six
metrical feet
hek-**sam**-uh-tuhr /hɛkˈsamətə(r)/

Hexateuch books of the Bible
hek-suh-tyook /ˈhɛksətjuːk/

hexavalent having a valency of six
hek-suh-**vay**-luhnt /ˌhɛksəˈveɪlənt/

Heyer, Georgette English novelist
hay-uhr /ˈheɪə(r)/

Heyerdahl, Thor Norwegian
anthropologist
toor hay-uhr-dahl /ˌtʊə(r) ˈheɪə(r)dɑːl/

Heysel football stadium, Belgium
hy-suhl /ˈhʌɪsəl/
• See DUTCH panel.

Hezbollah (also **Hizbullah**) extremist
Shiite Muslim group
hez-buul-**ah** /ˌhɛzbʊˈlɑː/

Hezekiah biblical name
hez-uh-**ky**-uh /hɛzəˈkʌɪə/

hiatus pause
hy-**ay**-tuhss /hʌɪˈeɪtəs/

Hiawatha legendary North American
Indian chieftain
hy-uh-**woth**-uh /ˌhʌɪəˈwɒθə/

hiba Japanese conifer
hee-buh /ˈhiːbə/

hibachi portable cooking apparatus
hib-**atch**-i /hɪˈbatʃi/

hibakusha survivor of either of the
atomic explosions at Hiroshima or
Nagasaki
hib-uh-**koo**-shuh /ˌhɪbəˌkuːˈʃə/

Hibernian relating to Ireland
hy-**bur**-ni-uhn /hʌɪˈbəː(r)nɪən/

The Scottish football team of the same name
is hib-**ur**-ni-uhn.

hibiscus plant
hib-**isk**-uhss /hɪˈbɪskəs/

hic jacet epitaph
hik **jay**-set /ˌhɪk ˈdʒeɪsɛt/

Commonly also **yak**-et.

Hidalgo state, Mexico
ee-**dal**-goh /iːˈdalgəʊ/

Hidatsa American Indian ethnic group
hid-**at**-suh /hɪˈdatsə/

hidrosis sweating
hid-**roh**-siss /hɪˈdrəʊsɪs/

hierarch chief priest or other leader
hy-uh-rark /ˈhʌɪərɑː(r)k/

hierarchy system of ranking
hy-uh-rar-ki /ˈhʌɪərɑː(r)ki/

hieratic concerning priests
hy-uh-**rat**-ik /ˌhʌɪəˈratɪk/

hieroglyph symbol in ancient Egyptian
hy-ruh-glif /ˈhʌɪrəglɪf/

hierophant priest who interprets sacred
mysteries
hy-roh-fant /ˈhʌɪrəʊfant/

Hierro island, Canary Islands
yerr-oh /ˈjɛrəʊ/

hijab head covering worn by some
Muslim women
hij-**ahb** /hɪˈdʒɑːb/

Hijaz see Hejaz

hijra transvestite or eunuch
hij-ruh /ˈhɪdʒrə/

Hildegard of Bingen, St German
abbess
hil-duh-gard **bing**-uhn /ˌhɪldəgɑː(r)d
ˈbɪŋən/

Hildesheim city, Germany
hil-duhss-hym /ˈhɪldəsˌhʌɪm/

Hilfiger, Tommy American fashion
designer
hil-fig-uhr /ˈhɪlfɪgə(r)/

Hilla, al- province and town, Iraq
uhl **hil**-uh /əl ˈhɪlə/

Hilversum town, Netherlands
hil-vuhr-suhm /ˈhɪlvə(r)səm/

Himachal Pradesh state, India
him-**ah**-chuhl pruh-**daysh** /hɪˌmɑːtʃəl prəˈdeɪʃ/

Himalayas mountain system, Asia
him-uh-**lay**-uhz /ˌhɪməˈleɪəz/

Established anglicization. Less commonly also him-**ah**-li-uhz.

himation ancient Greek garment
him-**at**-i-on /hɪˈmatɪɒn/

Himmler, Heinrich German Nazi leader
hyn-rikh **him**-luhr /ˌhʌɪnrɪç ˈhɪmlə(r)/

Hims see **Homs**

Himyarite ancient ethnic group of the Arabian peninsula
him-yuh-ryt /ˈhɪmjərʌɪt/

Hinault, Bernard French racing cyclist
bair-**nar** ee-**noh** /bɛː(r)ˌnɑː(r) iːˈnəʊ/

Hinayana branch of Buddhism
hee-nuh-**yah**-nuh /ˌhiːnəˈjɑːnə/

Hindemith, Paul German composer
powl **hin**-duh-mit /paʊl ˈhɪndəmɪt/

Hindenburg, Paul von German statesman
powl fon **hin**-duhn-boork /ˌpaʊl fɒn ˈhɪndənˌbʊə(r)k/

A more anglicized pronunciation, hin-duhn-burg, is used for the Zeppelin named after him.

Hindi Indian language
hin-di /ˈhɪndi/

Hindley, Myra English murderer
hind-li /ˈhɪndli/

This British surname is variously pronounced **hind**-li and **hynd**-li, depending on individual preference.

Hindu relating to Hinduism
hin-doo /ˈhɪnduː/

Hindu Kush range of mountains, Asia
hin-doo **kuush** /ˌhɪnduː ˈkʊʃ/

Sometimes also **koosh**.

Hindustan historical region, Asia
hin-duust-**ahn** /ˌhɪndʊˈstɑːn/

Hindustani group of Indian languages
hin-duust-**ah**-ni /ˌhɪndʊˈstɑːni/

Hindutva strong sense of Hindu identity

hin-**duut**-vuh /hɪnˈdʊtvə/

hinoki Japanese tree
hin-**oh**-ki /hɪˈnəʊki/

Hingis, Martina Swiss tennis player
mar-**tee**-nuh **hing**-giss /mɑː(r)ˌtiːnə ˈhɪŋɡɪs/

Hipparchus Greek astronomer
hip-**ar**-kuhss /hɪˈpɑː(r)kəs/

hippeastrum amaryllis
hip-i-**ast**-ruhm /ˌhɪpiˈastrəm/

hippocampus pl. **hippocampi** part of the brain
hip-oh-**kam**-puhss, pl. hip-oh-**kamp**-y /ˌhɪpəʊˈkampəs/, pl. /-pʌɪ/

hippocras wine flavoured with spices
hip-uh-krass /ˈhɪpəkras/

Hippocrates Greek physician
hip-**ok**-ruh-teez /hɪˈpɒkrətiːz/

hippogriff mythical creature
hip-oh-grif /ˈhɪpəʊɡrɪf/

Hippolytus Greek mythological character
hip-**ol**-it-uhss /hɪˈpɒlɪtəs/

hippopotamus pl. **hippopotami** African mammal
hip-uh-**pot**-uh-muhss, pl. hip-uh-**pot**-uh-my /ˌhɪpəˈpɒtəməs/, pl. /-mʌɪ/

• Standard -es plural is also possible.

hiragana Japanese writing system
hirr-uh-**gah**-nuh /ˌhɪrəˈɡɑːnə/

hircine relating to goats
hur-syn /ˈhəː(r)sʌɪn/

Hirohito emperor of Japan
hirr-oh-**hee**-toh /ˌhɪrəˈhiːtəʊ/, [çiroçito]

• Established anglicization.

Hiroshima city, Japan
hirr-**osh**-im-uh /hɪˈrɒʃɪmə/

This anglicized pronunciation is closer to the Japanese than the also common pronunciation hirr-uh-**shee**-muh. See JAPANESE panel.

Hispaniola island, Caribbean
isp-an-**yoh**-luh /ˌɪspanˈjəʊlə/

Hispanist expert in Spanish language and culture
hisp-uh-nist /ˈhɪspənɪst/

histamine chemical involved in immune responses
hist-tuh-meen /ˈhɪstəmiːn/

histrionic excessively dramatic
hist-ri-**on**-ik /ˌhɪstrɪˈɒnɪk/

Hitchens, Ivon English painter
y-vuhn **hitch**-uhnz /ˌʌɪvən ˈhɪtʃənz/

Hittite ancient ethnic group of Asia
Minor
hit-yt /ˈhɪtʌɪt/

Hizbullah see **Hezbollah**

Hmong Asian ethnic group; also called
Meo or **Miao**
hmong /hmɒŋ/

Hobart capital of Tasmania, Australia
hoh-bart /ˈhəʊbɑːrt/

Hobbema, Meindert Dutch painter
myn-duhrt **hob**-uh-muh /ˌmʌɪndə(r)t
ˈhɒbəmə/
• See DUTCH panel.

Hobbes, Thomas English philosopher
hobz /hɒbz/

Hoboken city, US
hoh-boh-kuhn /ˈhəʊbəʊkən/

Ho Chi Minh Vietnamese statesman
hoh chee **min** /ˌhəʊ tʃiː ˈmɪn/

Hodeida port, Yemen
huh-**day**-duh /həˈdeɪdə/

hodiernal relating to the present day
hod-i-ur-nuhl /ˌhɒdɪˈəː(r)nəl/

Høeg, Peter Danish writer
pay-duhr hoe /ˌpeɪdə(r) ˈhø/

Hoffa, Jimmy American trade union
leader
hof-uh /ˈhɒfə/

Hofmannsthal, Hugo von Austrian
poet and dramatist
hoo-goh fon **hof**-muhnss-tahl
/ˌhuːɡəʊ fon ˈhɒfmənsˌtɑːl/

hogan Navajo Indian hut
hoh-guhn /ˈhəʊɡən/

Hogarth, William English painter
hoh-garth /ˈhəʊɡɑː(r)θ/

Commonly also **hog**-uhrt.

Hoggar Mountains mountain range,
Algeria
hog-uhr /ˈhɒɡə(r)/

Hogmanay New Year's Eve
hog-muh-nay /ˈhɒɡmᵊneɪ/

Hohenstaufen German dynastic family
hoh-uhn-**shtow**-fuhn /ˌhəʊən'ʃtaʊfən/

Hohenzollern German dynastic family
hoh-uhn-**tsol**-uhrn /ˌhəʊən'tsɒlə(r)n/

A more anglicized pronunciation,
hoh-uhn-zol-uhrn, is also common.

Hohhot capital of Inner Mongolia
autonomous region, China
hoh-**hot** /həʊˈhɒt/
• Established anglicization.

hoisin Chinese cooking sauce
hoy-zin /ˈhɔɪzɪn/

Hokan group of American Indian
languages
hoh-kan /ˈhəʊkan/

hoki fish
hoh-ki /ˈhəʊki/

Hokkaido island, Japan
hok-**y**-doh /hɒˈkʌɪdəʊ/

Hokusai, Katsushika Japanese painter
kat-suu-**shee**-kuh hok-uu-sy
/katsʊˌʃiːkə ˈhɒkʊsʌɪ/

Holarctic zoogeographical region
hoh-**lark**-tik /həʊˈlɑː(r)ktɪk/

Holbein, Hans German painter
hanss hol-byn /ˌhans ˈhɒlbʌɪn/

Holborn part of London
hoh-buhrn /ˈhəʊbə(r)n/

Sometimes also **hohl**-buhrn.

Hölderlin, Friedrich German poet
freed-rikh **hoel**-duhr-leen /ˌfriːdrɪç
ˈhœldə(r)liːn/

Holi Hindu festival
hoh-lee /ˈhəʊliː/

Holinshed, Raphael English
chronicler
hol-in-shed /ˈhɒlɪnʃɛd/

hollandaise sauce creamy sauce
hol-uhn-**dayz** /ˌhɒlən'deɪz/

Hollerith, Herman American engineer
hol-uh-rith /ˈhɒlərɪθ/

Holm island, Scotland
holm /hɒlm/

holm (also **holme**) islet
hohm /həʊm/

holmium chemical element
hohl-mi-uhm /ˈhəʊlmiəm/

holocaust destruction on a mass scale
hol-uh-kawst /ˈhɒləkɔːst/

Holocene the present epoch
hol-uh-seen /ˈhɒləsiːn/

Holofernes biblical name
hol-uh-**fur**-neez /ˌhɒləˈfəː(r)niːz/

Sometimes also huh-**lof**-uhr-neez.

holothurian sea cucumber
hol-oh-**thyoor**-i-uhn /ˌhɒləʊˈθjʊəriən/

Holst, Gustav English composer
guust-ahv **hohlst** /ˌɡʊstɑːv ˈhəʊlst/

Holstein former duchy of Saxony
hol-shtyn /ˈhɒlʃtʌɪn/

Holsteinian geological period
hol-**sty**-ni-uhn /hɒlˈstʌɪnɪən/

holt den of an otter
hohlt /həʊlt/

Holyfield, Evander American boxer
uh-**van**-duhr **hoh**-li-feeld /əˌvandə(r) ˈhəʊlifiːld/

Holyhead port, Wales
hol-i-hed /ˈhɒlɪhɛd/

Holyoake, Keith New Zealand statesman
hoh-li-ohk /ˈhəʊlɪəʊk/

Holyrood Scottish parliament
hol-i-rood /ˈhɒlɪruːd/

homage special honour or respect
hom-ij /ˈhɒmɪdʒ/

hombre 'man' (Spanish)
omb-ray /ˈɒmbreɪ/

homeopath practitioner of homeopathy
hoh-mi-oh-path /ˈhəʊmɪəʊpaθ/

Less commonly also **hom**-i-oh-path.

homeopathy system of complementary medicine
hoh-mi-**op**-uh-thi /ˌhəʊmɪˈɒpəθi/

Less commonly also hom-i-**op**-uh-thi.

Homer Greek epic poet
hoh-muhr /ˈhəʊmə(r)/

Homeric relating to Homer
hoh-**merr**-ik /həʊˈmɛrɪk/

homily religious discourse
hom-il-i /ˈhɒmɪli/

homogamy inbreeding
hom-**og**-uh-mi /hɒˈmɒɡəmi/

homogeneous of the same kind
hom-oh-**jee**-ni-uhss /ˌhɒməʊˈdʒiːnɪəs/

Less commonly also pronounced huh-**moj**-uh-nuhss.

homogeny uniformity
huh-**moj**-uh-ni /həˈmɒdʒəni/

homologate approve for sale
huh-**mol**-uh-gayt /həˈmɒləɡeɪt/

homonym word having the same pronunciation or spelling as another, but a different meaning
hom-uh-nim /ˈhɒmənɪm/

homophone word having the same

pronunciation as another, but a different meaning
hom-uh-fohn /ˈhɒməfəʊn/

Homo sapiens primate species
hoh-moh **sap**-i-enz /ˌhəʊməʊ ˈsapɪɛnz/

Commonly also **hoh**-moh **say**-pi-uhnz.

homosexual sexually attracted to people of one's own sex
hom-oh-**sek**-shoo-uhl /ˌhɒməʊˈsɛkʃʊəl/

Words that contain the prefix *homo-* can usually be pronounced **hom**-oh or **hoh**-moh.

Homs (also **Hims**) city, Syria
homss /hɒms/

homunculus pl. **homunculi** small human or humanoid creature
hom-**unk**-yuul-uhss,
pl. hom-**unk**-yuul-y /hɒˈmʌŋkjʊləs/, pl. /-lʌɪ/
• Standard -es plural is also possible.

Honda, Soichiro Japanese motor manufacturer
soh-**ee**-chirr-oh **hon**-duh /səʊˌiːtʃɪrəʊ ˈhɒndə/

Honduras country
hon-**dyoor**-uhss /hɒnˈdjʊərəs/, Spanish [onˈduras]
• Established anglicization.

Honecker, Erich East German statesman
ay-rikh **hon**-ek-uhr /ˌeɪrɪç ˈhɒnɛkə(r)/

Honegger, Arthur French composer
hon-uhg-uhr /ˈhɒnəɡə(r)/, [artyr ɔnɛɡɛːr]
• Established anglicization.

honewort plant
hohn-wurt /ˈhəʊnwəː(r)t/

hongi Maori greeting
hong-i /ˈhɒŋi/

Honiara capital of the Solomon Islands
hon-i-**ar**-uh /ˌhɒniˈɑːrə/

Honolulu state capital of Hawaii
hon-uh-**loo**-loo /ˌhɒnəˈluːluː/

honorand person to be publicly honoured
on-uh-rand /ˈɒnərand/

Honshu island, Japan
hon-shoo /ˈhɒnʃuː/

Hooghly (also **Hugli**) river, India
hoog-li /ˈhuːɡli/

Hoogstraten, Nicholas van English property magnate
van **hoog**-strah-tuhn /van ˈhuːɡstrɑːtən/

The Dutch pronunciation of this surname is **hohkh**-strah-tuhn.

hookah oriental tobacco pipe
huuk-uh /ˈhʊkə/

hoopoe bird
hoo-poo /ˈhuːpuː/

Hoosier native of Indiana, US
hoo-zhuhr /ˈhuːʒə(r)/

Hopi American ethnic group
hoh-pi /ˈhəʊpi/

hoplite ancient Greek soldier
hop-lyt /ˈhɒplʌɪt/

hora (also **horah**) Romanian or Israeli dance
haw-ruh /ˈhɔːrə/

Horace Roman poet
horr-uhss /ˈhɒrəs/

Established anglicization. The Latin is Horatius, usually pronounced horr-**ay**-shi-uhss; see LATIN panel.

horal relating to hours
haw-ruhl /ˈhɔːrəl/

Horatian relating to Horace
horr-**ay**-shuhn /hɒˈreɪʃən/

horchata drink made from tiger nuts
or-**chah**-tuh /ɔː(r)ˈtʃɑːtə/

Horkheimer, Max German philosopher
maks **hork**-hym-uhr /ˌmaks ˈhɔː(r)kˌhʌɪmə(r)/

Hormuz island, Iran
hor-**mooz** /hɔː(r)ˈmuːz/

Hornung, Ernest William English novelist
hor-nuhng /ˈhɔː(r)nəŋ/

Horologium southern constellation
horr-uh-**loj**-i-uhm /ˌhɒrəˈlɒdʒiəm/

Horowitz, Vladimir Russian-born American pianist
vlad-im-eer **horr**-uh-vits /ˌvladɪmɪə(r) ˈhɒrəvɪts/

horror vacui fear of leaving empty spaces
horr-uhr vak-yoo-y /ˌhɒrə(r) ˈvakjuʌɪ/

hors d'oeuvre small savoury dish
or **durv** /ˌɔː(r) ˈdə:(r)v/, French [ɔr dœːvr]

Horsens port, Denmark
hor-suhnss /ˈhɔː(r)səns/

Horst Wessel Song official song of the Nazi Party in Germany
horst vess-uhl /ˌhɔː(r)st ˈvɛsəl/

Horta, Victor Belgian architect
veek-**tor** or-**tah** /viːkˌtɔː(r) ɔː(r)ˈtɑː/

hortatory aiming to exhort
hor-tuh-tuh-ri /ˈhɔː(r)tətəri/

hortensia plant
hor-**ten**-si-uh /hɔː(r)ˈtɛnsiə/

Horus ancient Egyptian god
haw-ruhss /ˈhɔːrəs/

Hosay Muslim festival
hoh-**zay** /həʊˈzeɪ/

Hosea Hebrew prophet
hoh-**zee**-uh /həʊˈziːə/

hospitable friendly and welcoming
hoss-**pit**-uh-buhl /hɒˈspɪtəbəl/

Sometimes also **hosp**-it-uh-buhl.

hospitaller member of a charitable religious order
hosp-it-uh-luhr /ˈhɒspɪtələ(r)/

hospodar Ottoman governor
hosp-uh-dar /ˈhɒspədɑː(r)/

Höss, Rudolf German Nazi commandant of Auschwitz
roo-**dolf hoess** /ˌruːdɒlf ˈhœs/

Houdini, Harry Hungarian-born American magician
hoo-**dee**-ni /huːˈdiːni/

Houellebecq, Michel French writer
mee-**shel** wel-**bek** /miːˌʃɛl wɛlˈbɛk/

Hough, Stephen English pianist
huf /hʌf/

This British surname is variously pronounced huf, hof, and how, depending on individual preference. Hough End in Manchester is huf.

Houllier, Gérard French football manager
zhay-**rar** ool-**yay** /ʒeɪˌrɑː(r) uːlˈjeɪ/

houmous chickpea spread
huum-uhss /ˈhʊməs/

houngan voodoo priest
hoong-guhn /ˈhuːŋɡən/

houri beautiful young woman
hoor-i /ˈhʊəri/

Housatonic river, US
hoo-suh-**ton**-ik /ˌhuːsəˈtɒnɪk/

Houston port, US (Texas)
hyoo-stuhn /ˈhjuːstən/

There are many US towns called Houston, most of which are pronounced as above. Houston in Delaware and in Georgia, however, are **how**-stuhn. The NASA space centre is in Houston, Texas.

houting fish
how-ting /'haʊtɪŋ/

howdah seat for riding on an elephant or camel
how-duh /'haʊdə/

howitzer gun
how-it-suhr /'haʊɪtsə(r)/

Howrah city, India
how-ruh /'haʊrə/

howtowdie Scottish dish
how-**tow**-di /haʊˈtaʊdi/

Hoxha, Enver Albanian statesman
en-vuhr **hoj**-uh /ˌɛnvə(r) ˈhɒdʒə/

Hoxnian geological period
hoks-ni-uhn /'hɒksniən/

hoya shrub
hoy-uh /'hɔɪə/

Hozier, Clementine maiden name of Clementine Churchill
klem-uhn-teen **hoh**-zi-uhr
/ˌklɛmənti:n ˈhəʊziə(r)/

Hradec Králové town, Czech Republic
hrad-ets **krah**-lov-ay /ˌhradɛts ˈkrɑːlɒveɪ/

Hrodna city, Belarus
hrod-nuh /'hrɒdnə/

Hrvatska see **Croatia**

hryvna (also **hrivna**) currency unit, Ukraine
hreev-nuh /'hriːvnə/

Huainan city, China
khwy-**nan** /ˌxwʌɪˈnan/

Huallaga river, Peru
wal-**yag**-uh /waˈljagə/

Huambo city, Angola
wam-boo /'wambuː/

Huang Hai Yellow Sea
khwang **khy** /ˌxwaŋ ˈxʌɪ/

Huang Ho Yellow River
khwang **hoh** /ˌxwaŋ ˈhəʊ/

huarache sandal
warr-**atch**-ay /waˈratʃeɪ/

Huascarán volcano, Peru
wask-arr-**an** /waskaˈran/

Hubei province, China
khoo-**bay** /ˌxuːˈbeɪ/

Hubli city, India
hoo-bli /'huːbli/

hubris excessive self-confidence
hyoo-briss /'hjuːbrɪs/

huchen type of salmon
hoo-kuhn /'huːkən/

Hué city, Vietnam
hway /hweɪ/

Hugli see **Hooghly**

Hugo, Victor French poet, novelist, and dramatist
vik-tuhr **hyoo**-goh /ˌvɪktə(r) ˈhjuːgəʊ/, [viktɔːr ygo]
• Established anglicization.

Huguenot French Protestant
hyoo-guh-noh /'hjuːgənəʊ/

hui large ceremonial gathering
hoo-i /'huːi/

hula Hawaiian dance
hoo-luh /'huːlə/

Hu Jintao Chinese president
khoo jin-**tow** /ˌxu dʒɪnˈtaʊ/

Hulce, Tom American actor
hulss /hʌls/

Humber estuary, England
humb-uhr /'hʌmbə(r)/

humectant preserving moisture
hyuum-**ek**-tuhnt /hjʊˈmɛktənt/

humerus pl. **humeri** arm bone
hyoo-muh-ruhss, pl. **hyoo**-muh-ry
/'hjuːmərəs, pl. /-rʌɪ/

humidor airtight container
hyoo-mid-or /'hjuːmɪdɔː(r)/

humoral relating to the body fluids
hyoo-muh-ruhl /'hjuːmərəl/

humoresque short piece of music
hyoo-muh-**resk** /ˌhjuːməˈrɛsk/

Humperdinck, Engelbert German composer
eng-uhl-bairt **huum**-puhr-dink
/ˌɛŋəlbɛː(r)t ˈhʊmpə(r)dɪŋk/

The 1970s pop singer Engelbert Humperdinck, who named himself after the German composer, is usually **eng**-guhl-burt **hump**-uhr-dink.

humus organic component of soil
hyoo-muhss /'hjuːməs/

Hunan province, China
khoo-**nan** /ˌxuːˈnan/

Huon pine conifer
hyoo-on /'hjuːɒn/

hurdy-gurdy musical instrument
hur-di-gur-di /ˈhəː(r)diˌɡəː(r)di/

Huron North American ethnic group
hyoor-uhn /ˈhjʊərən/

The same pronunciation is used for Lake Huron.

Hurrian ancient ethnic group
hurr-i-uhn /ˈhʌriən/

hurricane storm
hurr-ik-uhn /ˈhʌrɪkən/

Commonly also **hurr-ik-ayn**.

Husák, Gustáv Czechoslovak statesman
guust-ahf huuss-ahk /ˌɡʊstɑːf ˈhʊsɑːk/

Huss, John Bohemian religious reformer
huss /hʌs/

Established anglicization. The Czech form is Jan Hus, pronounced **yan huuss**.

Hussein, ibn Talal (also **Husain**) former king of Jordan
ib-uhn tuh-lal huuss-ayn /ˌɪbən təˌlal hʊˈseɪn/

Hussein, Saddam (also **Husain**) Iraqi statesman
sad-ahm huuss-ayn /saˌdɑːm hʊˈseɪn/

Husserl, Edmund German philosopher
et-muunt huuss-uhrl /ˌɛtmʊnt ˈhʊsə(r)l/

Hussite follower of John Huss
huss-yt /ˈhʌsʌɪt/

Hutterite Christian sect established in Moravia
hut-uh-ryt /ˈhʌtərʌɪt/

Hutu African ethnic group
hoo-too /ˈhuːtuː/

Huw Welsh boy's name
hyoo /hjuː/

Huygens, Christiaan Dutch physicist, mathematician, and astronomer
krist-i-ahn hy-guhnz /ˌkrɪstiɑːn ˈhʌɪɡənz/, [ˌkrɪstiaːn ˈhœyxəns]

Established anglicization. The space probe named after him is anglicized differently, and is pronounced **hoy-guhnz**!

Huyton area of Liverpool
hy-tuhn /ˈhʌɪtən/

Hwange town, Zimbabwe
hwang-gi /ˈhwaŋɡi/

hwyl feeling of emotional motivation and energy

hoo-il /ˈhuːɪl/

hyacinth plant
hy-uh-sinth /ˈhʌɪəsɪnθ/

Hyacinthus Greek mythological character
hy-uh-**sinth**-uhss /ˌhʌɪəˈsɪnθəs/

Hyades star cluster
hy-uh-deez /ˈhʌɪədiːz/

hyaenodon extinct mammal
hy-ee-nuh-don /hʌɪˈiːnədɒn/

hydatid cyst
hy-duh-tid /ˈhʌɪdətɪd/

Hyderabad city, India
hy-duh-ruh-bad /ˈhʌɪdərəbad/

Hydra Greek mythological creature
hyd-ruh /ˈhʌɪdrə/

hydramnios medical condition
hy-**dram**-ni-oss /hʌɪˈdramnɪɒs/

hydrangea shrub
hy-**drayn**-juh /hʌɪˈdreɪndʒə/

hydria ancient Greek pitcher
hy-dri-uh /ˈhʌɪdriə/

hydropathy treatment of illness through the use of water
hyd-**rop**-uh-thi /hʌɪˈdrɒpəθi/

Hydrus southern constellation
hyd-ruhss /ˈhʌɪdrəs/

hygroscope instrument which measures humidity of the air
hyg-roh-skohp /ˈhʌɪɡrəʊskəʊp/

Hyksos ancient ethnic group
hik-soss /ˈhɪksɒs/

hyoid neck bone
hy-oyd /ˈhʌɪɔɪd/

hypaesthesia diminished physical sensitivity
hy-peess-**thee**-zi-uh /ˌhʌɪpiːˈsˈθiːziə/

Hypatia Greek philosopher
hy-**pay**-shuh /hʌɪˈpeɪʃə/

hyperaemia excessive accumulation of blood
hy-puhr-**ee**-mi-uh /ˌhʌɪpərˈiːmiə/

hyperaesthesia excessive physical sensitivity
hy-puhr-eess-**thee**-zi-uh /ˌhʌɪpəriːsˈθiːziə/

hyperalgesia heightened sensitivity to pain
hy-puhr-al-**jee**-zi-uh /ˌhʌɪpəralˈdʒiːziə/

hyperbaton inversion of the normal order of words
hy-**pur**-buh-ton /hʌɪˈpəː(r)bətɒn/

hyperbole exaggerated statements
hy-**pur**-buh-li /hʌɪˈpəː(r)bəli/

hyperglycaemia excess of glucose in the bloodstream
hy-puhr-gly-**see**-mi-uh /ˌhʌɪpə(r)ɡlʌɪˈsiːmiə/

hypericum plant
hy-**perr**-ik-uhm /hʌɪˈpɛrɪkəm/

Hyperion moon of Saturn
hy-**peer**-i-uhn /hʌɪˈpɪəriən/

hyperlipaemia high concentration of fats in the blood
hy-puhr-lip-**ee**-mi-uh /ˌhʌɪpə(r)lɪˈpiːmiə/

hypermetropia long-sightedness
hy-puhr-muht-**roh**-pi-uh /ˌhʌɪpə(r)məˈtrəʊpiə/

hyperthermia high body temperature
hy-puhr-**thur**-mi-uh /ˌhʌɪpə(r)ˈθəː(r)miə/

hypertrophy enlargement of an organ
hy-**pur**-truh-fi /hʌɪˈpəː(r)trəfi/

hyphen sign (-)
hy-**fuhn** /ˈhʌɪfən/

hypnagogic relating to the state immediately before falling asleep
hip-nuh-**goj**-ik /ˌhɪpnəˈɡɒdʒɪk/

hypnopompic relating to the state immediately preceding waking up
hip-nuh-**pom**-pik /ˌhɪpnəˈpɒmpɪk/

Hypnos Greek god
hip-**noss** /ˈhɪpnɒs/

hypocalcaemia deficiency of calcium in the bloodstream
hy-poh-kal-**see**-mi-uh /ˌhʌɪpəʊkalˈsiːmiə/

hypocaust ancient Roman heating system
hy-poh-**kawst** /ˈhʌɪpəʊkɔːst/

hypochondria chronic anxiety about one's health
hy-puh-**kon**-dri-uh /ˌhʌɪpəˈkɒndriə/

hypochondriacal affected by

hypochondria
hy-poh-kon-**dry**-uh-kuhl /ˌhʌɪpəʊkɒnˈdrʌɪəkəl/

hypogeal underground
hy-poh-**jee**-uhl /ˌhʌɪpəʊˈdʒiːəl/

hypogeum underground chamber
hy-poh-**jee**-uhm /ˌhʌɪpəʊˈdʒiːəm/

hypoglycaemia deficiency of glucose in the bloodstream
hy-poh-gly-**see**-mi-uh /ˌhʌɪpəʊɡlʌɪˈsiːmiə/

hypokalaemia deficiency of potassium in the bloodstream
hy-poh-kuh-**lee**-mi-uh /ˌhʌɪpəʊkəˈliːmiə/

hypomagnesaemia deficiency of magnesium in the blood
hy-poh-mag-niz-**ee**-mi-uh /ˌhʌɪpəʊˌmaɡnɪˈziːmiə/

hypostasis pl. **hypostases** accumulation of fluid in the lower parts of the body
hy-**post**-uh-siss, pl. hy-**post**-uh-seez /hʌɪˈpɒstəsɪs/, pl. /-siːz/

hypostatic relating to the persons of the Trinity
hy-poh-**stat**-ik /ˌhʌɪpəʊˈstatɪk/

hypotaxis grammatical term
hy-poh-**tak**-siss /ˌhʌɪpəʊˈtaksɪs/

hypothermia low body temperature
hy-poh-**thur**-mi-uh /ˌhʌɪpəʊˈθəː(r)miə/

hypoxaemia low concentration of oxygen in the blood
hy-pok-**see**-mi-uh /ˌhʌɪpɒkˈsiːmiə/

hypsilophodont dinosaur
hip-sil-**of**-uh-dont /ˌhɪpsɪˈlɒfədɒnt/

hyson type of green China tea
hy-**suhn** /ˈhʌɪsən/

hyssop plant
hiss-uhp /ˈhɪsəp/

hysterectomy surgical removal of the womb
hist-uh-**rek**-tuh-mi /ˌhɪstəˈrɛktəmi/

Hyundai Korean motor company
hyuun-dy /ˈhjʊndʌɪ/, [hjən dɛ]

Established anglicization, commonly also hy-**un**-dy. AM is usually **hun**-day.

I

iambic poetic metre
y-**am**-bik /ʌɪˈambɪk/

Iannucci, Armando Scottish comedy writer
ar-**man**-doh yan-**oo**-chi /ɑː(r),mandəʊ jaˈnuːtʃi/

Iapetus one of Saturn's moons
y-**ap**-uh-tuhss /ʌɪˈapətəs/

Iaşi city, Romania
yash /jaʃ/

IATA International Air Transport Association
y-**ah**-tuh /ʌɪˈɑːtə/

Ibadan city, Nigeria
ib-**ad**-uhn /ɪˈbadən/

Ibarretxe, Juan José Basque politician
khwan khoss-**ay** ee-barr-**etch**-ay /xwan xɒ,seɪ iːbarˈɛtʃeɪ/

Ibárruri Gómez, Dolores Spanish communist politician
dol-**orr**-ess ee-barr-oo-ri **goh**-meth /dɒ,lɒrɛs iːˈbaruːri ˈgəʊmɛθ/

Iberia peninsula, SW Europe; also Spanish airline
y-**beer**-i-uh /ʌɪˈbɪəriə/
• Established anglicization.

Ibert, Jacques French composer
zhahk ee-**bair** /,ʒɑːk iːˈbɛː(r)/

ibex mountain goat
y-beks /ˈʌɪbɛks/

Ibibio Nigerian ethnic group and language
ib-**ib**-i-oh /ɪˈbɪbiəʊ/

ibid. in the same source
ib-id /ˈɪbɪd/

Ibiza island, Spain
ib-**eeth**-uh /ɪˈbiːθə/

Ibn Batuta Arab explorer
ib-uhn bah-**too**-tah /,ɪbən bɑːˈtuːtɑː/

Ibo (also **Igbo**) Nigerian ethnic group and language
ee-**boh** /ˈiːbəʊ/, [ˈɪgbɒ]
• Established anglicization.

Ibrox Park Glasgow Rangers' football ground
y-broks /ˈʌɪbrɒks/

Ibsen, Henrik Norwegian dramatist
hen-rik ib-**suhn** /,hɛnrɪk ˈɪbsən/

ibuprofen anti-inflammatory drug
y-byoo-**proh**-fuhn /,ʌɪbjuːˈprəʊfən/
Sometimes also y-**byoo**-pruh-fen.

Icarus Greek mythological character
ik-uh-ruhss /ˈɪkərəs/

Iceni tribe of ancient Britain
y-**see**-ny /ʌɪˈsiːnʌɪ/
Sometimes also y-**see**-ni.

ich dien 'I serve' (German); motto of the Prince of Wales
ikh **deen** /,ɪç ˈdiːn/

Ichikawa, Kon Japanese film director
kohn itch-i-**kah**-wuh /,kəʊn ɪtʃiˈkɑːwə/

I Ching ancient Chinese divination manual
ee ching /,iː ˈtʃɪŋ/

ichthus symbol of Christianity
ik-thuhss /ˈɪkθəs/

I-chun see **Yichun**

iconoclasm rejection of cherished beliefs
y-**kon**-uh-klaz-uhm /ʌɪˈkɒnəklazəm/

icosahedron mathematical figure
y-koss-uh-**hee**-druhn /,ʌɪkɒsəˈhiːdrən/
Sometimes also y-koss-uh-**hed**-ruhn.

Ictinus ancient Greek architect
ik-**ty**-nuhss /ɪkˈtʌɪnəs/

id part of the mind
id /ɪd/

Id see **Eid**

Ida mountain, Crete
y-duh /ˈʌɪdə/

Idaho state, US
y-duh-hoh /ˈʌɪdəhəʊ/

idée fixe idea that dominates the mind
ee-day feeks /,iːdeɪ ˈfiːks/

idem used to indicate an author who has just been mentioned
y-dem /ˈʌɪdɛm/

Also pronounced **id**-em.

ideology a system of ideas and ideals
y-di-**ol**-uh-ji /ˌʌɪdɪˈɒlədʒi/

Sometimes also id-i-**ol**-uh-ji.

ides day falling roughly in the middle of
each month
ydz /ʌɪdz/

idigbo West African tree
id-**ig**-boh /ɪˈdɪɡbəʊ/

idiolect speech habits peculiar to a
particular person
id-i-uh-lekt /ˈɪdɪəlɛkt/

idiot savant person who has a mental
disability but is extremely gifted in a
particular way
eed-i-oh sav-**o(ng)** /ˌiːdɪəʊ saˈvɒ̃/,
French [idjo savɑ̃]

Sometimes further anglicized to **id**-i-uht
sav-uhnt.

idli south Indian steamed cake of rice
id-lee /ˈɪdliː/

idolater person who worships idols
y-**dol**-uh-tuhr /ʌɪˈdɒlətə(r)/

Idomeneo opera by Mozart
id-om-uhn-**ay**-oh /ɪdɒməˈneɪəʊ/

Idomeneus Greek mythological
character
y-**dom**-uhn-yooss /ʌɪˈdɒmənjuːs/

idyll peaceful or picturesque situation
id-il /ˈɪdɪl/

Iestyn Welsh boy's name
yest-in /ˈjɛstɪn/

Ieuan Welsh boy's name
yy-uhn /ˈjʌɪən/, [ˈjʌɪan]

Ifans, Rhys Welsh actor
reess ee-vanz /ˌriːs ˈiːvanz/

Ife city, Nigeria
ee-fay /ˈiːfeɪ/

Iftar meal eaten during Ramadan
if-tar /ˈɪftɑː(r)/

Igbo see **Ibo**

Iglesias, Julio Spanish singer
hoo-li-oh ig-**lay**-zi-uhss /ˌhuːliəʊ
ɪˈɡleɪzɪəs/
• Established anglicization.

Iglesias, Enrique Spanish singer
en-**ree**-kay ig-**lay**-zi-uhss /ɛnˌriːkeɪ
ɪˈɡleɪzɪəs/
• Established anglicization.

Ignatius Loyola, St Spanish theologian

ig-**nay**-shuhss loy-**oh**-luh /ɪɡˌneɪʃəs
lɔɪˈəʊlə/

ignominy public shame or disgrace
ig-nuh-min-i /ˈɪɡnəmmi/

Iguaçú (also **Iguazú**) river, South
America
ig-wuh-**soo** /ˌɪɡwəˈsuː/

iguana lizard
ig-**wah**-nuh /ɪˈɡwɑːnə/

iiwi Hawaiian bird
i-**ee**-wi /iˈiːwi/

Iittala Finnish glassware company
ee-tal-uh /ˈiːtalə/

Ijo (also **Ijaw**) Nigerian ethnic group
ee-joh /ˈiːdʒəʊ/

IJssel river, Netherlands
y-suhl /ˈʌɪsəl/

IJsselmeer lake, Netherlands
y-suhl-meer /ˈʌɪsəlmɪə(r)/

Ikaria island, Greece
ik-**air**-i-uh /ɪˈkɛːriə/

ikat fabric
ee-kat /ˈiːkat/

Ikea Swedish furniture retailer
y-**kee**-uh /ʌɪˈkiːə/, [ˈɪˈkeːa]
• Established anglicization.

ikebana Japanese flower arrangement
ik-uh-**bah**-nuh /ˌɪkəˈbɑːnə/

Île-de-France region, France
eel duh **frah(ng)ss** /ˌiːl də ˈfrɑ̃s/

Ilesha city, Nigeria
il-**aysh**-uh /ɪˈleɪʃə/

ileum part of the small intestine
il-i-uhm /ˈɪliəm/

Iliad Greek epic poem
il-i-ad /ˈɪliad/

Iliescu, Ion former Romanian president
yohn il-**yes**-koo /ˌjəʊn ɪlˈjɛskuː/

illegible unreadable
il-**ej**-ib-uhl /ɪˈlɛdʒɪbəl/

Illich, Ivan Austrian-born American
writer
y-vuhn il-**itch** /ˌʌɪvən ˈɪlɪtʃ/

Illinois state, US
il-in-**oy** /ˌɪlɪˈnɔɪ/

illuminati people claiming to possess
special enlightenment
il-oo-min-**ah**-ti /ɪˌluːmɪˈnɑːti/

Illyria ancient region along the coast of
the Adriatic Sea
il-**irr**-i-uh /ɪˈlɪriə/

Iloilo port, Philippines
ee-loh-**ee**-loh /ˌiːləʊˈiːləʊ/

Ilorin city, Nigeria
il-**orr**-in /ɪˈlɒrɪn/

imagism movement in 20th-century
English and American poetry
im-ij-iz-uhm /ˈɪmɪdʒɪzəm/

imago pl. **imagines** the final stage of an
insect
im-**ay**-goh, pl. im-**ay**-jin-eez
/ɪˈmeɪɡəʊ, pl. /ɪˈmeɪdʒɪniːz/

Standard -s plural is also possible. The UK
publishing company of the same name is
im-**ah**-goh.

imam person who leads prayers in a
mosque
im-**ahm** /ɪˈmɑːm/

Iman Somali supermodel
im-**ahn** /ɪˈmɑːn/

Imari a type of Japanese porcelain
im-**ar**-i /ɪˈmɑːri/

IMAX trademark a technique of
widescreen cinematography
y-maks /ˈʌɪmaks/

Imbolc ancient Celtic festival
im-bolk /ˈɪmbɒlk/

imbroglio complicated or embarrassing
situation
im-**broh**-li-oh /ɪmˈbrəʊliəʊ/

Imbros island, Turkey
im-bross /ˈɪmbrɒs/

Established anglicization. The Turkish name
is Imroz, pronounced im-**roz**.

Imbruglia, Natalie Australian singer
and actress
im-**broo**-li-uh /ɪmˈbruːliə/

imbue permeate
im-**byoo** /ɪmˈbjuː/

Imhotep Egyptian architect and scholar
im-**hoh**-tep /ɪmˈhəʊtɛp/

imipramine antidepressant drug
im-**ip**-ruh-meen /ɪˈmɪprəmiːn/

immolate kill or offer as a sacrifice
im-uh-layt /ˈɪməleɪt/

impala antelope
im-**pah**-luh /ɪmˈpɑːlə/

impatiens plant
im-**pat**-i-enz /ɪmˈpatɪɛnz/

Commonly also im-**pay**-shenz

impecunious having little money

im-puh-**kyoo**-ni-uhss /ˌɪmpəˈkjuːnɪəs/

imperator commander
im-puh-**rah**-tor /ˌɪmpəˈrɑːtɔː(r)/

impetigo bacterial skin infection
im-puh-**ty**-goh /ˌɪmpəˈtʌɪɡəʊ/

Imphal city, India
im-**fahl** /ɪmˈfɑːl/

impious showing a lack of respect for
religion
im-pi-uhss /ˈɪmpiəs/

Commonly also im-**py**-uhss.

importune harass
im-por-**tyoon** /ˌɪmpɔː(r)ˈtjuːn/

impresario concert organizer
im-pruh-**sar**-i-oh /ˌɪmprəˈsɑːriəʊ/

imprimatur Catholic licence to print a
religious book
im-prim-**ah**-tuhr /ˌɪmprɪˈmɑːtə(r)/

impugn dispute the truth of
im-**pyoon** /ɪmˈpjuːn/

in absentia not present
in ab-**sen**-ti-uh /ˌɪn abˈsɛntiə/

Inari lake, Finland
in-**arr**-i /ˈɪnari/

Iñaritu, Alejandro González
Mexican film director
al-ekh-**and**-roh gon-**sah**-less
een-**yarr**-ee-too /aleˌxandrəʊ
ɡɒnˌsɑːlɛs iˈnjariːtuː/

incarnadine crimson colour
in-**kar**-nuh-dyn /ɪnˈkɑː(r)nədʌɪn/

inchoate not fully formed or developed
in-**koh**-uht /ɪnˈkəʊət/

Sometimes also in-**koh**-ayt.

Inchon port, South Korea
in-**chon** /ɪnˈtʃɒn/

inclement unpleasant
in-**klem**-uhnt /ɪnˈklɛmənt/

incognito concealing one's true identity
in-kog-**nee**-toh /ˌɪnkɒɡˈniːtəʊ/

Less commonly also in-**kog**-nit-oh.

incommunicado not communicating
in-kuh-myoo-nik-**ah**-doh
/ˌɪnkəmjuːnɪˈkɑːdəʊ/

inconnu unknown person
a(ng)-kon-**ue** /ɛ̃kɒˈny/

incubus pl. **incubi** male demon
ink-yuub-uhss, pl. **ink**-yuu-by
/ˈɪŋkjʊbəs/, pl. /-bʌɪ/

incunabula early printed books
in-kyuu-**nab**-yuul-uh /ˌɪnkjʊˈnabjʊlə/

incus pl. **incudes** small bone in the
middle ear
ink-uhss, pl. **ink**-yuu-deez /ˈɪŋkəs/, pl.
/ˈɪŋkjʊdiːz/

index pl. **indices** alphabetical list
in-deks, pl. in-duh-**seez** /ˈɪndɛks/, pl.
/ˈɪndəsiːz/

Standard -es plural is also possible.

Indiana state, US
in-di-**an**-uh /ˌɪndiˈanə/

Indianapolis city, US
in-di-uh-**nap**-uh-liss /ˌɪndiəˈnapəlɪs/

indict formally charge with a crime
in-**dyt** /ɪnˈdʌɪt/

indigent poor
in-dij-uhnt /ˈɪndɪdʒənt/

Indigirka river, Russia
in-dig-**eer**-kuh /ˌɪndɪˈɡɪə(r)kə/

indigo dye
in-dig-oh /ˈɪndɪɡəʊ/

indium chemical element
in-di-uhm /ˈɪndiəm/

indolent lazy
in-duh-luhnt /ˈɪndələnt/

indomitable impossible to subdue
in-**dom**-it-uh-buhl /ɪnˈdɒmɪtəbəl/

Indonesia country
in-doh-**neezh**-uh /ˌɪndəʊˈniːʒə/

Less commonly also in-doh-**neesh**-uh and
in-doh-**neez**-i-uh.

Indore city, India
in-**dor** /ɪnˈdɔː(r)/

Indre river and department, France
a(ng)d-ruh /ˈɛ̃drə/

Indurain, Miguel Spanish cyclist
mee-**gel** in-doo-ryn /miːˈɡɛl ɪnduːˈrʌɪn/

Indus river, Asia
in-duhss /ˈɪndəs/

ineluctable unable to be avoided
in-uh-**luk**-tuh-buhl /ˌɪnəˈlʌktəbəl/

inexorable impossible to stop
in-**ek**-suh-ruh-buhl /ɪnˈɛksərəbəl/

in extremis in an extremely difficult
situation
in ek-**stree**-miss /ˌɪn ɛkˈstriːmɪs/

inextricable impossible to separate
in-ek-**strik**-uh-buhl /ɪnɛkˈstrɪkəbəl/

Less commonly also in-**eks**-trik-uh-buhl.

infamous well known for a bad quality
or deed
in-fuh-muhss /ˈɪnfəməs/

infarct dead tissue after failure of blood
supply
in-farkt /ˈɪnfɑː(r)kt/

infidel person with no religion
in-fid-uhl /ˈɪnfɪdəl/

infinitesimal extremely small
in-fin-it-**ess**-im-uhl /ˌɪnfɪnɪˈtɛsɪməl/

in flagrante delicto in the act of
wrongdoing
in fluh-**gran**-tay duh-**lik**-toh
/ɪn fləˌɡranteɪ dəˈlɪktəʊ/

infra dig beneath one
in-fruh dig /ˌɪnfrə ˈdɪɡ/

Ingenhousz, Jan Dutch scientist
yun ing-**guhn**-howss /jʌn ˈɪŋɡənhaʊs/
• Established anglicization.

ingénue unsophisticated young woman
a(ng)zh-uh-nue /ˈɛ̃ʒəny/

Commonly also anglicized to
an-zhuh-nyoo.

ingenuity the quality of being original
and inventive
in-juh-**nyoo**-it-i /ˌɪndʒəˈnjuːɪti/

ingenuous innocent and unsuspecting
in-**jen**-yoo-uhss /ɪnˈdʒɛnjuːəs/

Inglis British family name
ing-guhlz, **ing**-gliss /ˈɪŋɡəlz/, /ˈɪŋɡlɪs/

ingot a block of metal
ing-guht /ˈɪŋɡət/

Ingres, Jean Auguste Dominique
French painter
zhah(ng) oh-**guest** dom-in-**eek**
a(ng)g-ruh /ʒɑ̃ əʊˌɡyst dɒmɪˈniːk ˈɛ̃ɡrə/

Ingush relating to Ingushetia
ing-**guush** /ɪŋˈɡʊʃ/

Ingushetia autonomous republic, Russia
ing-guush-**et**-i-uh /ˌɪŋɡʊˈʃetiə/

inherent existing in something as a
permanent attribute
in-**herr**-uhnt /ɪnˈhɛrənt/

Less commonly also in-**heer**-uhnt.

inimical tending to obstruct or harm
in-**im**-ik-uhl /ɪˈnɪmɪkəl/

injera Ethiopian bread
in-jeer-uh /ˈɪndʒɪərə/

Inkatha South African political party
in-**kah**-tuh /ɪnˈkɑːtə/

in loco parentis in the place of a parent
in **loh**-koh puh-**ren**-tiss /ɪn ˌləʊkəʊ pəˈrɛntɪs/

Inmarsat INternational MARitime SATellite organization
in-mar-sat /ˈɪnmɑː(r)sat/

in medias res into the middle of a narrative
in **mee**-di-ass **rayz** /ɪn ˌmiːdias ˈreɪz/

innovative featuring new methods
in-uh-vuh-tiv /ˈɪnəvətɪv/

Sometimes also **in**-uh-vay-tiv and less commonly in-**oh**-vuh-tiv.

Innsbruck city, Austria
inz-bruuk /ˈɪnzbrʊk/, [ˈɪnsbrʊk]
• Established anglicization.

Ino Greek goddess
y-noh /ˈʌɪnəʊ/

inquilab revolution or uprising
ink-il-ahb /ˈɪŋkɪlɑːb/

in re in the legal case of
in **ree** /ɪn ˈriː/

insectivore animal that feeds on insects
in-**sek**-tiv-or /ɪnˈsɛktɪvɔː(r)/

insectivorous feeding on insects
in-sek-**tiv**-uh-ruhss /ˌɪnsɛkˈtɪvərəs/

inshallah 'Allah willing' (Arabic)
in-**shah**-luh /ɪnˈʃɑːlə/, [inˈʃaːʔaˈlaːh]
• Established anglicization.

insidious proceeding in a gradual way
in-**sid**-i-uhss /ɪnˈsɪdiəs/

insignia emblem of military rank
in-**sig**-ni-uh /ɪnˈsɪɡniə/

in situ in the original place
in **sit**-yoo /ɪn ˈsɪtjuː/

insouciance casual lack of concern
in-**soo**-si-uhnss /ɪnˈsuːsiəns/

in statu pupillari under guardianship
in **stat**-yoo pyoo-pil-**ar**-i /ɪn ˌstatjuː ˌpjuːpɪˈlɑːri/

insuperable impossible to overcome
in-**soo**-puh-ruh-buhl /ɪnˈsuːpərəbəl/

The pronunciation in-**syoo**-puh-ruh-buhl is now rather dated.

intaglio design engraved into a material
in-**tal**-yoh /ɪnˈtaljəʊ/

intarsia method of knitting
in-**tar**-si-uh /ɪnˈtɑː(r)siə/

integer whole number
in-tuh-juhr /ˈɪntədʒə(r)/

integral fundamental or included
in-tuh-gruhl /ˈɪntəɡrəl/

Commonly also in-**teg**-ruhl, although not for the mathematical term.

integument outer protective layer
in-**teg**-yuum-uhnt /ɪnˈtɛɡjʊmənt/

intelligentsia intellectuals
in-tel-lij-**ent**-si-uh /ɪnˌtɛlɪˈdʒɛntsiə/

inter alia among other things
int-uhr **ay**-li-uh /ˌɪntər ˈeɪliə/

interdict a prohibition
int-uhr-dikt /ˈɪntə(r)dɪkt/

interdict prohibit
int-uhr-**dikt** /ˌɪntə(r)ˈdɪkt/

Interlagos Formula One racing venue, Brazil
in-tair-**lah**-guuss /ˌɪntɛː(r)ˈlɑːɡʊs/

Interlaken town, Switzerland
int-uhr-**lah**-kuhn /ˈɪntə(r)ˌlɑːkən/

interlocutor person who takes part in a dialogue
int-uhr-**lok**-yuut-uhr /ˌɪntə(r)ˈlɒkjʊtə(r)/

interloper person in a situation where they do not belong
int-uhr-loh-puhr /ˈɪntə(r)ləʊpə(r)/

interment burial
in-**tur**-muhnt /ɪnˈtɜː(r)mənt/

Inter Milan Italian football team
in-tuhr mil-**an** /ˌɪntə(r) mɪˈlan/

Internationale revolutionary song composed in France
in-tuhr-nash-uh-**nahl** /ˌɪntə(r)naʃəˈnɑːl/

internecine destructive to both sides in conflict
in-tuhr-**nee**-syn /ˌɪntə(r)ˈniːsʌɪn/

Interpol international police organization
in-tuhr-pol /ˈɪntə(r)pɒl/

interpolate insert
in-**tur**-puh-layt /ɪnˈtə:(r)pəleɪt/

interregnum period when government is suspended
in-tuhr-**reg**-nuhm /ˌɪntə(r)ˈrɛɡnəm/

interrogative questioning
in-tuhr-**rog**-uh-tiv /ˌɪntə(r)ˈrɒɡətɪv/

interstice intervening space
in-**tur**-stiss /ɪnˈtə:(r)stɪs/

intestate not having made a will before death
in-**test**-ayt /ɪnˈtɛsteɪt/

intestinal relating to the intestines
in-**test**-in-uhl /ɪnˈtɛstɪnəl/

Less commonly also in-test-**y**-nuhl.

intichiuma Aboriginal ceremonies
in-titch-i-**oo**-muh /ˌɪntɪtʃiˈuːmə/

intifada Palestinian uprising
in-ti-**fah**-duh /ˌɪntɪˈfɑːdə/

intrados inner curve of an arch
in-**tray**-doss /ɪnˈtreɪdɒs/

intransigent stubborn
in-**tran**-sij-uhnt /ɪnˈtransɪdʒənt/

intravenous within a vein
in-truh-**vee**-nuhss /ˌɪntrəˈviːnəs/

intricacy detail
in-**trik**-uh-si /ˈɪntrɪkəsi/

introit psalm
in-troyt /ˈɪntrɔɪt/

Sometimes also in-**troh**-it.

intubate insert a tube into
in-**tyuub**-ayt /ˈɪntjʊbeɪt/

intuit understand by instinct
in-**tyoo**-it /ɪnˈtjuːɪt/

Inuit North American and Greenlandic
ethnic group
in-uu-it /ˈɪnʊɪt/

Inuk a member of the Inuit people
in-**uuk** /ˈɪnʊk/

Inuktitut Inuit language
in-**uuk**-tit-uut /ɪˈnʊktɪtʊt/

inundate overwhelm
in-un-dayt /ˈɪnʌndeɪt/

Inupiaq Alaskan ethnic group
in-**oo**-pi-ak /ɪˈnuːpiak/

inure accustom
in-**yoor** /ɪˈnjʊə(r)/

in utero in the uterus
in **yoot**-uh-roh /ɪn ˈjuːtərəʊ/

inveigle persuade by flattery
in-**vay**-guhl /ɪnˈveɪɡəl/

Sometimes also in-**vee**-guhl.

inventory list of items
in-vuhn-tuh-ri /ˈɪnvəntəri/

Invercargill city, New Zealand
in-vuhr-**kar**-gil /ˌɪnvə(r)ˈkɑː(r)ɡɪl/

Inverness city, Scotland
in-vuhr-**ness** /ˌɪnvə(r)ˈnɛs/

Invernessian relating to Inverness
in-vuhr-**neezh**-uhn /ˌɪnvə(r)ˈniːʒən/

inveterate having a long-established
habit
in-**vet**-uh-ruht /ɪnˈvɛtərət/

in vino veritas 'there is truth in wine'
(Latin)
in **vee**-noh **verr**-it-ass /ɪn ˌviːnəʊ
ˈvɛrɪtas/

in vitro in a test tube
in **veet**-roh /ɪn ˈviːtrəʊ/

in vivo in a living organism
in **vee**-voh /ɪn ˈviːvəʊ/

inwale structural piece on the inside of a
boat
in-**wayl** /ˈɪnweɪl/

Gunwale, however, is pronounced **gun**-uhl.

INXS Australian rock band
in-ek-**sess** /ˌɪnɛkˈsɛs/

inyanga traditional healer
in-**yang**-guh /ɪnˈjaŋɡə/

Io Greek mythological character
y-oh /ˈʌɪəʊ/

Ioan Welsh boy's name
yoh-uhn /ˈjəʊən/

iodine chemical element
y-uh-deen /ˈʌɪədiːn/

Sometimes also **y**-uh-dyn.

ion atom or molecule with a net electric
charge
y-uhn /ˈʌɪən/

Iona island, Scotland
y-oh-nuh /ʌɪˈəʊnə/

Ionesco, Eugène Romanian-born
French dramatist
oe-**zhen** ee-uh-**nesk**-oh /øˌʒɛn
iːəˈnɛskəʊ/

Ionic relating to a classical order of
architecture
y-**on**-ik /ʌɪˈɒnɪk/

ionosphere layer of the earth's
atmosphere
y-**on**-uhss-feer /ʌɪˈɒnəsfɪə(r)/

iota letter of the Greek alphabet
y-**oh**-tuh /ʌɪˈəʊtə/

Iowa state, US
y-uh-wuh /ˈʌɪəwə/

Ipatieff, Vladimir Nikolaievich
Russian-born American chemist
vluh-**dee**-meer nik-uh-**ly**-uh-vitch
ip-**at**-i-ef /vlaˌdiːmɪə(r) nɪkəˌlʌɪəvɪtʃ
ɪˈpatiɛf/

ipecacuanha drug
ip-ik-ak-yuu-**an**-uh /ˌɪpɪkakjʊˈanə/

The short form *ipecac* is pronounced
ip-uh-**kak**.

Iphigenia Greek mythological character
if-ij-in-**y**-uh /ˌɪfɪdʒɪˈnʌɪə/

Ipoh city, Malaysia
ee-poh /ˈiːpəʊ/

ippon point scored in martial sports
ip-on /ˈɪpɒn/

ipse dixit unproven statement
ip-say **dik**-sit /ˌɪpseɪ ˈdɪksɪt/

Sometimes also **ip-see**.

ipso facto 'by that very fact' (Latin)
ip-soh **fak**-toh /ˌɪpsəʊ ˈfaktəʊ/

Iqbal, Muhammad Indian poet and
philosopher
muu-**ham**-uhd **ik**-bal /mʊˌhaməd
ˈɪkbal/

Iquitos city, Peru
ik-**ee**-toss /ɪˈkiːtɒs/

Iran country
irr-**ahn** /ɪˈrɑːn/

Less commonly also irr-**an**, although this
sounds less like the Farsi pronunciation.

Iraq country, Middle East
irr-**ahk** /ɪˈrɑːk/

Less commonly also irr-**ak**, although this
sounds less like the Arabic pronunciation.
The pronunciation y-**rak** is sometimes heard
in AM.

irascible easily angered
irr-**ass**-ib-uhl /ɪˈrasɪbəl/

irate feeling great anger
y-**rayt** /ʌɪˈreɪt/

Irbil see **Erbil**

Irenaeus, St Greek theologian
y-rin-**ee**-uhss /ˌʌɪərɪˈniːəs/

Irgun Zionist organization
eer-**guun** /ɪə(r)ˈɡʊn/

Irian Jaya province, Indonesia
irr-i-uhn **jy**-uh /ˌɪrɪən ˈdʒʌɪə/

iridescent showing luminous colours
irr-id-**ess**-uhnt /ˌɪrɪˈdɛsənt/

iridium chemical element
irr-**id**-i-uhm /ɪˈrɪdiəm/

Less commonly also y-**rid**-i-uhm.

irie pleasing
y-ree /ˈʌɪriː/

Irkutsk city, Russia
eer-**kuutsk** /ɪə(r)ˈkʊtsk/

iroko African tree
irr-**oh**-koh /ɪˈrəʊkəʊ/

Iroquois American Indian ethnic group
and place name
irr-uh-**kwoy** /ˈɪrəkwɔɪ/

Irrawaddy river, Burma
irr-uh-**wod**-i /ˌɪrəˈwɒdi/

irrevocable not able to be reversed
irr-**ev**-uh-kuh-buhl /ɪˈrɛvəkəbəl/

Irtysh river, central Asia
eer-**tish** /ɪə(r)ˈtɪʃ/

irukandji Australian jellyfish
irr-uh-**kan**-ji /ɪrəˈkandʒi/

Irvine, Andrew English Arctic explorer
and mountaineer
ur-vin /ˈəː(r)vɪn/

Irvine, Eddie Northern Irish Formula
One racing driver
ur-vyn /ˈəː(r)vʌɪn/

ISA Individual Savings Account
y-suh /ˈʌɪsə/

Isaac Hebrew patriarch
y-zuhk /ˈʌɪzək/

Isaiah Hebrew prophet
y-**zy**-uh /ʌɪˈzʌɪə/

Isar river, Germany
ee-zuhr /ˈiːzə(r)/

ischaemia inadequate blood supply to
an organ
isk-**ee**-mi-uh /ɪˈskiːmiə/

Ischia island, Italy
isk-i-uh /ˈɪskiə/

Ise city, Japan
ee-say /ˈiːseɪ/

Iseabail Gaelic girl's name
ish-uh-bal /ˈɪʃəbal/

Isengard place in *The Lord of the Rings*
y-zuhn-gard /ˈʌɪzənɡɑː(r)d/

Isère department and river, France
ee-**zair** /iːˈzɛ(r)/

Iseult (also **Yseult**) mythological
character; also called **Isolde**
ee-**soolt** /iːˈsuːlt/

Isfahan see **Esfahan**

Ishiguro, Kazuo Japanese-born British
novelist
kaz-oo-oh ish-ig-**oor**-oh /ˌkazuːəʊ
ˌɪʃɪˈɡʊərəʊ/

Ishihara test test for colour blindness
ish-i-**har**-uh /ɪʃɪˈhɑːrə/

Ishmael biblical name
ish-**may**-uhl /ˈɪʃmeɪəl/

Ishtar Babylonian goddess
ish-tar /ˈɪʃtɑː(r)/

Isidore tropical storm
iz-id-or /ˈɪzɪdɔː(r)/

Isildur character from *The Lord of the
Rings*
iss-il-**door** /ˈɪsɪlduə(r)/

isinglass gelatin obtained from fish
y-zing-glahss /ˈʌɪzɪŋˌɡlɑːs/

Isis Egyptian goddess of fertility
y-siss /ˈʌɪsɪs/

Iskandariyah, al- city, Iraq
uhl isk-uhn-duh-**ree**-yuh
/əl ɪskəndəˈriːjə/

Iskenderun port, Turkey
isk-en-duh-roon /ɪsˈkɛndəruːn/

Islam religion
iss-**lahm** /ɪsˈlɑːm/

There are many possible pronunciations of
this word in English. This form is closest to
the Arabic, and is the one recommended by
the British Council of Muslims.

Islamabad capital of Pakistan
iss-**lahm**-uh-bad /ɪsˈlɑːməbad/

Islamic relating to Islam
iss-**lam**-ik /ɪsˈlamɪk/

Islas Malvinas Spanish name for the
Falkland Islands
eess-lass mal-**vee**-nass /ˈiːslas
malˈviːnas/

Islay island, Scotland
y-luh /ˈʌɪlə/

Ismaili member of a branch of Shiite
Muslims
iss-my-**ee**-li /ɪsmʌɪˈiːli/

isobar line indicating pressure on a
weather map
y-soh-bar /ˈʌɪsəʊbɑː(r)/

isochronous occurring at the same time
y-**sok**-ruh-nuhss /ʌɪˈsɒkrənəs/

Isocrates Athenian orator
y-**sok**-ruh-teez /ʌɪˈsɒkrətiːz/

Isolde mythological character; also called
Iseult
iz-**old**-uh /ɪˈzɒldə/

isosceles of a triangle with two sides of
equal length

y-**soss**-uh-leez /ʌɪˈsɒsəliːz/

isotherm line indicating temperature on
a weather map
y-soh-thurm /ˈʌɪsəʊθəː(r)m/

isotope chemical element with a
particular nuclear composition
y-soh-tohp /ˈʌɪsəʊtəʊp/

ispaghula dried seeds of a southern
Asian plantain
isp-uh-**goo**-luh /ˌɪspəˈɡuːlə/

Israel country, Middle East
iz-ray-uhl /ˈɪzreɪl/

Israeli relating to Israel
iz-**ray**-li /ɪzˈreɪli/

Israelite member of the ancient Hebrew
nation
iz-ruh-lyt /ˈɪzrəlʌɪt/

Israfel angel
iz-ruh-fel /ˈɪzrəfɛl/

Issachar Hebrew patriarch
iss-uh-kuhr /ˈɪsəkə(r)/

issei Japanese immigrant to North
America
ee-say /ˈiːseɪ/

Issigonis, Alec Turkish-born British car
designer
iss-ig-**oh**-niss /ˌɪsɪˈɡəʊnɪs/

Istanbul port, Turkey
ist-an-**buul** /ˌɪstanˈbʊl/, [isˈtɑnbul]
• Established anglicization.

isthmus strip of land with sea on either
side
iss-muhss /ˈɪsməs/

Sometimes also **isth**-muhss.

Isuzu Japanese vehicle manufacturer
ee-**soo**-zoo /iːˈsuːzuː/

Sometimes anglicized to y-**soo**-zoo.

Ita Gaelic girl's name
ee-tuh /ˈiːtə/

Itala city, Italy
ee-tuh-luh /ˈiːtələ/

The Itala car manufacturer is commonly
anglicized to it-**ah**-luh.

Itaipu dam, Brazil
ee-ty-poo /iːtʌɪˈpuː/

italic kind of typeface
it-**al**-ik /ɪˈtalɪk/

Itanagar city, India
ee-tuh-**nug**-uhr /ˌiːtəˈnʌɡə(r)/

ITAR-Tass Russian news agency
ee-tar **tass** /ˌiːtɑː(r) ˈtas/

Ithaca Greek island
ith-uh-kuh /ˈɪθəkə/

itinerary planned journey
y-**tin**-uh-ruh-ri /ʌɪˈtɪnərəri/

Ito, Prince Hirobumi Japanese
statesman
hirr-ob-**oo**-mi **ee**-toh /hɪrɒˌbuːmi
ˈiːtəʊ/

Ito, Robert Canadian actor
ee-toh /ˈiːtəʊ/

Ivan various Russian rulers
y-vuhn /ˈʌɪvən/
• Established anglicization.

Ivanišević, Goran Croatian tennis
player
gorr-an ee-van-**eesh**-uh-vitch /ˌɡɒran
iːvanˈiːʃəvɪtʃ/

Ivanov, Sergei Russian defence minister
suhr-**gay** eev-uh-**nof** /sə(r)ˌɡeɪ
iːvəˈnɒf/

Ivanovo city, Russia
ee-**vahn**-uh-voh /iːˈvɑːnəvəʊ/

Ivel river, England
y-vuhl /ˈʌɪvəl/

Iwan, Dafydd president of Plaid Cymru
dav-ith **yoo**-uhn /ˌdavɪð ˈjuːən/

Iwerks, Ub American animator
ub y-wurks /ˌʌb ˈʌɪwə:(r)ks/

iwi Maori ethnic group
ee-wi /ˈiːwi/

Iwo Jima volcanic island, western Pacific
ee-woh **jee**-muh /ˌiːwəʊ ˈdʒiːmə/

Ixion Greek mythological character
ik-**sy**-uhn /ɪkˈsʌɪən/

ixnay used in rejecting something
specified
iks-nay /ˈɪksneɪ/

Ixtaccihuatl volcano, Mexico
ee-stak-**see**-wuh-tuhl /iːstakˈsiːwətəl/

Ixtapa city, Mexico
ee-**stap**-uh /iːsˈtapə/

Iyengar type of yoga
i-**yeng**-gar /iˈjɛŋɡɑː(r)/

Iyyar Hebrew month
ee-yar /ˈiːjɑː(r)/

izard chamois
iz-uhrd /ˈɪzə(r)d/

Izhevsk city, Russia
izh-**efsk** /ɪˈʒɛfsk/

İzmir port, Turkey
iz-meer /ˈɪzmɪə(r)/

İzmit city, Turkey
iz-**mit** /ɪzˈmɪt/

Izvestia (also **Izvestiya**) Russian
newspaper
iz-**vest**-i-uh /ɪzˈvɛstiə/

Izzard, Eddie British comedian
iz-ard /ˈɪzɑː(r)d/

Italian

Italian has retained more similarity to Latin than any of the other
Romance languages. As well as being spoken in Italy, Italian is one of
the official languages of Switzerland, and is also spoken by large communities in America, Argentina, and Brazil. English has numerous
Italian loanwords, particularly in the fields of food and music.

There are many dialects of Italian. One of the standard forms is
commonly referred to as the RAI accent—RAI is the Italian national
broadcaster.

The Italian given here is, as always, somewhat anglicized in line with
BBC policy and the constraints of the phonetic respelling.

Vowels

The Italian vowels A, E, I, O, and U have seven corresponding vowel
sounds, as both E and O can be realized in two different ways.

A, I, and U are generally pronounced a (or ah, depending on length), ee
(or i), and oo.

E can be pronounced either as e or as close to ay (although not diphthongal in Italian). A long Italian e is also pronounced ay.

O can be pronounced either as o or as close to oh (although not diphthongal in Italian). A long Italian o is traditionally often also pronounced oh, although aw is closer to the native pronunciation.

Some of these vowel qualities are commonly reduced to schwa (uh) in
anglicized Italian. We always treat unstressed word-final A as uh
rather than ah. Furthermore, an unstressed U is sometimes treated
as uu in anglicized Italian, particularly when it is followed by a consonant in the same syllable.

Consonants

The Italian consonant sounds themselves offer no difficulty for
English speakers, although they are not always easily predicted from
the spelling.

Our treatment of the Italian double consonants is dealt with below
in the stress section.

The letters B, D, F, L, M, N, P, T, and V are pronounced as in English.

C and CC are pronounced k before the letters A, O, and U, and ch
before E and I. *Enrico* is en-**ree**-koh, and *Pacino* is patch-**ee**-noh.

Please note that although the presence of I turns the pronunciation
of C into ch (and G into j, and GL into ly: see below), the I itself is not
pronounced if another vowel is following. *Luciano* is pronounced

loo-**chah**-noh, not loo-chee-**ah**-noh, and *Giovanni* is pronounced jov-**ah**-ni, not jee-ov-**ah**-ni. The only function of I in this position is to indicate the pronunciation of C, G, and GL.

CH and CCH are always pronounced k. *Greta Scacchi* is **skak**-i.

G and GG are pronounced g before A, O, and U, and j before E and I. *Gondola* is **gon**-dol-uh, and *Gino* is **jee**-noh.

GH is always pronounced g. *Ghetto* is **get**-oh.

GLI is almost always pronounced lyi (or lyee). *Gigli* is **jeel**-yi.

GN is pronounced ny. *Gnocchi* is **nyok**-i.

GU is pronounced gw. *Guido* is **gwee**-doh.

J is pronounced y. *Juventus* is yoo-**ven**-tuuss.

QU is pronounced kw. *Questa* is **kwest**-uh. *Quattrocento* is kwat-roh-**chen**-toh.

S is pronounced s initially, but can be either s or z between two vowels. *Santo* is **san**-toh, *casa* is **kah**-suh, but *paradiso* is parr-uh-**dee**-zoh.

S is always z before B, D, and G. *Sbarco* is **zbar**-koh.

SC is pronounced sk before A, O, and U, and sh before I and E. *Scuola* is **skwoh**-luh, and *scena* is **shay**-nuh.

SCH is always pronounced sk. *Scherzo* is **skairt**-soh.

Z and ZZ are mostly pronounced ts, but can also be dz. *Zio* is **tsee**-oh, but *Donizetti* is don-id-**zet**-i.

Stress

Italian words are commonly stressed on the second-to-last syllable, but stress is variable and it is advisable to check each individual case by consulting an Italian dictionary. The perceived penultimate stress pattern sometimes leads to mispronunciations of names like *Stefano* as stef-**ah**-noh, when it should be **stef**-an-oh. Sometimes stress falls on the last syllable, and this is usually indicated by a grave accent. *Cittá* is chit-**ah**.

It is argued that a stressed syllable must have either a long vowel or a long (double) consonant. Double consonants in Italian words and names, such as the CC in *Scacchi*, are always pronounced as such, but since this does not occur in English it is usually not something we can reflect when giving Italian recommendations to programme makers. It is therefore common to compensate with a long vowel instead, so *pizza* becomes **peet**-suh instead of just **pit**-suh.

J

ja South African term for yes
yah /jɑː/

Jabaliya refugee camp, Middle East
juh-**bah**-li-uh /dʒəˈbɑːliə/

Jabalpur city, India
jub-uhl-**poor** /ˌdʒʌbəlˈpʊə(r)/

jabberwocky invented or meaningless
language
jab-uhr-wok-i /ˈdʒabə(r)ˌwɒki/

jabot frill on the front of a blouse
zhab-oh /ˈʒabəʊ/

jacal thatched hut
huh-**kahl** /həˈkɑːl/

jacamar tropical American bird
jak-uh-mar /ˈdʒakəmɑː(r)/

jacaranda tropical American tree
jak-uh-**ran**-duh /ˌdʒakəˈrandə/

jacinth reddish-orange gem
jass-inth /ˈdʒasɪnθ/

Sometimes also **jay**-sinth.

jackanapes cheeky or impertinent
person
jak-uh-nayps /ˈdʒakəneɪps/

jackeen city-dweller
jak-**een** /dʒaˈkiːn/

Jackson, Mahalia American singer
muh-**hay**-li-uh /məˈheɪliə/

Jacob Hebrew patriarch
jay-kuhb /ˈdʒeɪkəb/

Jacobean relating to the reign of James I
jak-uh-**bee**-uhn /ˌdʒakəˈbiːən/

Jacobethan combining Elizabethan and
Jacobean styles
jak-uh-**beeth**-uhn /ˌdʒakəˈbiːθən/

Jacobi, Derek English actor
jak-uh-bi /ˈdʒakəbi/

Jacobi, Frederick American composer
juh-**koh**-bi /dʒəˈkəʊbi/

Jacobi, Karl Gustav Jacob German
mathematician
karl guust-ahf **yah**-kop yak-**oh**-bi
/ˌkɑː(r)l ˌɡʊstɑːf ˌjɑːkɒp jaˈkəʊbi/

Jacobsen, Arne Danish architect and
furniture designer
ar-nuh **yak**-uhb-suhn /ˌɑːrnə

ˈjakəbsən/

Jacobsen, Howard English author
jay-kuhb-suhn /ˈdʒeɪkəbsən/

jacquard apparatus used in weaving
jak-ard /ˈdʒakɑː(r)d/

jacuzzi trademark bath with underwater
jets of water
juh-**koo**-zi /dʒəˈkuːzi/

Established anglicization. The Italian
inventor, Candido Jacuzzi, is pronounced
kan-did-oh yuh-**koot**-si.

Jadida, el- city, Morocco
uh-zhuh-**dee**-duh /əʒəˈdiːdə/
• See ARABIC panel.

j'adoube term in chess
zhah-**doob** /ʒɑːˈduːb/

Jaeger English fashion label
yay-guhr /ˈjeɪɡə(r)/

jaeger bird
jay-guhr /ˈdʒeɪɡə(r)/

Jaén province and town, Spain
khah-**en** /xɑːˈɛn/

Ja'fari, Ibrahim al- Iraqi prime
minister
ib-ruh-**heem** uhl jah-fuh-ri /ɪbrəˌhiːm
əl ˈdʒɑːfəri/

Jaffa city and port, Israel
jaf-uh /ˈdʒafə/

Jaffna city and port, Sri Lanka
jaf-nuh /ˈdʒafnə/

Jaffrey, Madhur Indian actress and
cookery expert
mad-uhr **jaf**-ri /ˌmadə(r) ˈdʒafri/

Jagannatha form of Krishna; also called
Juggernaut
jag-uh-**nah**-thuh /ˌdʒaɡəˈnɑːθə/

Jagdeo, Bharrat Guyanese president
barr-uht **jag**-day-oh /ˌbarət
ˈdʒaɡdeɪəʊ/

jaggery dark brown sugar
jag-uh-ri /ˈdʒaɡəri/

Jagiełło Polish dynasty
yag-**yay**-woh /jaɡˈjeɪwəʊ/

jaguar large cat
jag-yuu-uhr /ˈdʒaɡjʊə(r)/

AM is **jag**-war.

Jah Rastafarian name for God
jah /dʒɑː/

Jahorina mountain, Bosnia–Herzegovina
yah-horr-een-uh /ˈjɑːhɒriːnə/

Jai 'victory!' (Hindi)
jy /dʒʌɪ/

jai alai Basque game
hy uh-**ly** /ˌhʌɪ əˈlʌɪ/
• Established anglicization.

Jainism religious movement
jy-niz-uhm /ˈdʒʌɪnɪzəm/

Sometimes also **jay**-niz-uhm.

Jaipur city, India
jy-**poor** /dʒʌɪˈpʊə(r)/

Jakarta (also **Djakarta**) capital of Indonesia
juh-**kar**-tuh /dʒəˈkɑː(r)tə/

Jakobson, Roman Russian-born American linguist
ruh-**mahn** yak-uhb-suhn /rəˌmɑːn ˈjakəbsən/

JAL Japan AirLines
jal /dʒal/

Jalalabad city, Afghanistan
juh-**lah**-luh-bad /dʒəˈlɑːləbad/

Jalandhar (also **Jullundur**) city, India
juh-**lun**-duhr /dʒəˈlʌndə(r)/

Jalapa city, Mexico
khal-**ap**-uh /xaˈlapə/

jalapeño green chilli pepper
khal-uh-**payn**-yoh /ˌxaləˈpeɪnjəʊ/

Often anglicized to hal-uh-**payn**-yoh or hal-uh-**pee**-noh.

jalebi Indian sweet
juh-**lay**-bi /dʒəˈleɪbi/

jaleo Spanish dance
khal-**ay**-oh /xaˈleɪəʊ/

jalfrezi Indian dish
jal-**fray**-zi /dʒalˈfreɪzi/

Jalisco state, Mexico
khal-**eesk**-oh /xaˈliːskəʊ/

Jalón town and river, Spain
khal-**on** /xaˈlɒn/

Jamaat-e-Islami Pakistani political party
juh-**mah**-tay iss-**lah**-mi /dʒəˌmɑːteɪ ɪsˈlɑːmi/

jambalaya Cajun dish

jam-buh-**ly**-uh /ˌdʒambəˈlʌɪə/

jamboree large celebration
jam-buh-**ree** /ˌdʒambəˈriː/

Jamelia English singer
juh-**mee**-li-uh /dʒəˈmiːliə/

Jamia district of Baghdad
jam-i-uh /ˈdʒamiə/

Jamieson, Robert Alan Scottish writer
jim-iss-uhn /ˈdʒɪmɪsən/

Jammu town, India
jum-oo /ˈdʒʌmuː/

Jamnagar port, India
jum-**nug**-uhr /dʒʌmˈnʌgə(r)/

Jamshedpur city, India
jum-shed-**poor** /ˌdʒʌmʃɛdˈpʊə(r)/

Jamshid legendary king of Persia
jam-**sheed** /dʒamˈʃiːd/

Janabi, Adnan al- Iraqi politician
ad-**nan** uhl juh-**nah**-bi /adˌnan əl dʒəˈnɑːbi/

Janáček, Leoš Czech composer
lay-osh yan-uh-chek /ˌleɪʊʃ ˈjanətʃɛk/, [ˈjanaːtʃɛk]
• Established anglicization.

jankers punishment for military offence
jank-uhrz /ˈdʒaŋkə(r)z/

Jan Mayen island, Arctic
yan my-uhn /jan ˈmʌɪən/

Jansen, Cornelius Otto Flemish theologian
kor-**nay**-li-uuss ot-oh yun-suhn /kɔː(r)ˌneɪliʊs ˌɒtəʊ ˈjʌnsən/

The Catholic reform movement he founded, Jansenism, has an anglicized pronunciation: jan-suh-niz-uhm.

Janssen, Famke Dutch actress
fum-kuh yun-suhn /ˌfʌmkə ˈjʌnsən/

Jansson, Tove Finnish author
too-vuh yahn-son /ˌtuːvə ˈjɑːnsɒn/

Janus ancient Italian deity
jay-nuhss /ˈdʒeɪnəs/

Janus, Samantha English actress
jan-uhss /ˈdʒanəs/

Japheth biblical name
jay-feth /ˈdʒeɪfɛθ/

japonica Asian shrub
juh-**pon**-ik-uh /dʒəˈpɒnɪkə/

Jaques-Dalcroze, Émile Austrian-born Swiss composer
ay-**meel** zhahk dal-**krohz** /eɪˌmiːl ˌʒɑːk dalˈkrəʊz/

Japanese

Since Japanese has its own writing system, Japanese names and words that appear in an English language context have usually already been transliterated into the Roman alphabet. As with Greek and other transliterated languages, these transliterations attempt to be 'phonetic', so that the pronunciation ought to be more or less predictable from the transliterated spelling.

Stress and syllable structure

There is no syllable stress in Japanese, and each syllable should be given equal weight and length for an authentic-sounding pronunciation. However, because English speakers tend to look for stress in a word, and might apply stress where it sounds worst, we include stress in our anglicized recommendations. We apply stress where it seems least obtrusive, in many cases consulting native speakers for their preference. This is particularly useful in counteracting the English tendency to apply stress on the second-last syllable. For example, *Hiroshima* is better pronounced hirr-**osh**-im-uh than hirr-uh-**shee**-muh. However, when names and words are anglicized, the stress does often fall on the second-last syllable, as in *Toshiba* or *sudoku*.

Japanese has a much simpler syllable structure than English. Each basic syllable element is made up of one of five short vowels (A, E, I, O, and U), either on their own or preceded by a single consonant. There are no consonant clusters, and the only consonant that appears on its own without a vowel is N. When foreign words with consonant clusters are taken into Japanese, vowels are inserted: for example, *strike* becomes *sutoraiku*.

Vowels

The five vowels of Japanese A, E, I, O, and U are approximately a, e, ee, aw or o, and oo. Two vowels can appear in sequence. If the two vowels are different, a diphthong sequence is produced: *sensei* is pronounced sen-**say**. If the two vowels are identical, a long vowel is produced: *hontoo* is pronounced hon-**taw**. In some transliterated spellings these double vowels are written as one vowel with a macron (*hontō*) rather than as a sequence of two vowels, but the pronunciation is the same. Sometimes the macron can be lost, so *Tōkyō* (which has four syllable elements in Japanese, to-o-kyo-o) appears spelled *Tokyo*. The vowels U and I are often whispered when they appear between two voiceless consonants or at the end of a word, and a better English pronunciation can be achieved by missing out these vowels altogether. For example, *daisuki desu* (*I love it*) is best pronounced **dy**-ski **dess**.

Consonants

Most Japanese consonants in transliteration have a similar pronunciation to English consonants. The letter L does not occur in Japanese, and R can be pronounced to sound like either r or l. (It is for this reason that Japanese speakers learning English have particular trouble producing and distinguishing between these two sounds.) G is usually pronounced g, but between vowels it is pronounced ng as in *singer*. H before I is pronounced kh in German *ich*. N is usually n, but it is pronounced m before M, P, and B, and ng before K and G.

Jarama river, Spain
kharr-**am**-uh /xaˈramə/

jarl Norse or Danish chief
yarl /jɑː(r)l/

Jarlsberg trademark Norwegian cheese
yarlz-burg /ˈjɑː(r)lzbəː(r)g/
• Established anglicization.

Jarmusch, Jim American film director
jar-muhsh /ˈdʒɑː(r)məʃ/

Järnefelt, Armas Finnish conductor
ar-mass **yair**-nuh-felt /ˌɑː(r)mas ˈjɛː(r)nəfɛlt/

Jarre, Jean-Michel French composer
zhah(ng) mee-**shel** zhar /ʒã miːˌʃɛl ˈʒɑː(r)/

Jarreau, Al American jazz musician
juh-**roh** /dʒəˈrəʊ/

Jarry, Alfred French dramatist
al-**fred** zharr-ee /alˌfrɛd ʒaˈriː/

Jaruzelski, Wojciech Polish general and statesman
voy-chekh yarr-oo-**zel**-ski /ˌvɔɪtʃɛx jaruˈzɛlski/

Jasenovac Second World War concentration camp, Croatia
yuh-**sen**-uh-vats /jəˈsɛnəvats/

Jasná ski resort, Slovakia
yass-nah /ˈjasnɑː/

Jataka story of the former life of the Buddha
jut-uh-kuh /ˈdʒʌtəkə/

jatha armed Sikh parade
jah-tuh /ˈdʒɑːtə/

JATO Jet Assisted Take-Off
jay-toh /ˈdʒeɪtəʊ/

jaundice medical condition
jawn-diss /ˈdʒɔːndɪs/

Java island, Indonesia
jah-vuh /ˈdʒɑːvə/

Java trademark computer programming language
jah-vuh /ˈdʒɑːvə/

Jawf, al- region and city, Saudi Arabia
uhl **jowf** /əl ˈdʒaʊf/

Jazeera, al- Arabic satellite TV channel
uhl juh-**zeer**-uh /əl dʒəˈzɪərə/

Jean, Wyclef American pop singer
wy-klef **zhahn** /ˌwʌɪklɛf ˈʒɑːn/

Jeddah (also **Jiddah**) seaport, Saudi Arabia
jed-uh /ˈdʒɛdə/

Jedi knight in the *Star Wars* films
jed-y /ˈdʒɛdʌɪ/

Jehoshaphat biblical name
juh-**hosh**-uh-fat /dʒɪˈhɒʃəfat/

Jehovah 'God' (Hebrew)
juh-**hoh**-vuh /dʒəˈhəʊvə/
• Established anglicization.

Jekyll, Dr see Doctor Jekyll

Jekyll, Gertrude English horticulturalist
jee-kuhl /ˈdʒiːkəl/

Jelinek, Elfriede Austrian author
el-**free**-duh **yel**-in-ek /ɛlˌfriːdə ˈjɛlɪnɛk/

jellaba see djellaba

Jemaah Islamiyah south-east Asian Islamic terrorist organization
jem-**ah** iss-luh-**mee**-yuh /dʒɛˌmɑː ɪsləˈmiːjə/

Jena town, Germany
yay-nuh /ˈjeɪnə/

Jenin city, Palestine
juh-**neen** /dʒəˈniːn/

Jenůfa opera by Janáček
yen-oo-fuh /ˈjɛnuːfə/

Jerba see **Djerba**

jerboa desert-dwelling rodent
jur-**boh**-uh /dʒəːˈ(r)ˈbəʊə/

jeremiad long, mournful lamentation
jerr-uh-**my**-ad /ˌdʒɛrəˈmʌɪad/

Jeremiah Hebrew prophet
jerr-uh-**my**-uh /ˌdʒɛrəˈmʌɪə/

Jerez town, Spain
kherr-**eth** /xɛˈrɛθ/

Jericho town, Palestine
jerr-ik-oh /ˈdʒɛrɪkəʊ/

jeroboam large wine bottle
jerr-uh-**boh**-uhm /ˌdʒɛrəˈbəʊəm/

Jèrriais Jersey form of French
zherr-i-ay /ˈʒɛriei/

Jerusalem capital of Israel
juh-**roo**-suh-luhm /dʒəˈruːsələm/
• Established anglicization.

Jervis, John British admiral
jar-viss /ˈdʒɑː(r)vɪs/

Jesse biblical name
jess-i /ˈdʒɛsi/

Jesu archaic form of Jesus
jeez-yoo /ˈdʒiːzjuː/

Sometimes also **yay**-zoo.

jeté ballet-step
zhuh-**tay** /ʒəˈtei/

Jethou island, Channel Islands
jet-oo /ˈdʒɛtuː/

jeunesse dorée gilded youth
zhoe-**ness** daw-**ray** /ʒøˌnɛs dɔːˈrei/

Jewry Jews collectively
joor-i /ˈdʒʊəri/

Jezebel biblical name
jez-uh-bel /ˈdʒɛzəbɛl/

Jhansi city, India
jahn-si /ˈdʒɑːnsi/

Jharkand state, India
jar-kuhnd /ˈdʒɑː(r)kənd/

Jhelum river, Himalayas
jee-luhm /ˈdʒiːləm/

Jiangsu province, China
ji-ang-**soo** /dʒiˌaŋˈsuː/

Jiangxi province, China
ji-ang-**shee** /dʒiˌaŋˈʃiː/

jibba long coat worn by Muslim men

jib-uh /ˈdʒɪbə/

Jibuti see **Djibouti**

Jiddah see **Jeddah**

jihad war against unbelievers
ji-**hahd** /dʒɪˈhɑːd/

Commonly also ji-**had**.

jihadi person involved in a jihad
ji-**hah**-di /dʒɪˈhɑːdi/

jilbab Muslim floor-length robe
jil-**bab** /dʒɪlˈbab/

Jilin province, China
jee-**lin** /ˌdʒiːˈlɪn/

Jimmu legendary first emperor of Japan
jim-oo /ˈdʒɪmuː/

Jin Chinese dynasty
jin /dʒɪn/

Jinan city, China
jee-**nan** /ˌdʒiːˈnan/

Jinnah, Muhammad Ali Indian
statesman
muu-**ham**-uhd al-i **jin**-uh /mʊˌhaməd
ˌali ˈdʒɪnə/

jiu-jitsu see **ju-jitsu**

João Pessoa city, Brazil
zhuu-**ow(ng)** pess-**oh**-uh /ʒʊˌãʊ
pɛˈsəʊə/

Job biblical name
johb /dʒəʊb/

Jobs, Steven American computer
entrepreneur
jobz /dʒɒbz/

Jocasta Greek mythological character
joh-**kast**-uh /dʒəʊˈkastə/

jocose playful or humorous
juh-**kohss** /dʒəˈkəʊs/

Jodhpur city, India
jod-poor /ˈdʒɒdpʊə(r)/

jodhpurs trousers worn for horse riding
jod-puhrz /ˈdʒɒdpə(r)z/

Jodrell Bank site of radio telescope,
England
jod-ruhl /ˈdʒɒdrəl/

Joffre, Joseph Jacques Césaire
French marshal
zhoh-**zef** zhahk say-**zair** zhof-ruh
/ʒəʊˌzɛf ʒɑːk seiˌzɛː(r) ˈʒɒfrə/

Jogjakarta see **Yogyakarta**

Johansson, Lennart Swedish
president of UEFA
len-art **yoo**-han-son /ˌlɛnɑː(r)t
ˈjuːhansɒn/

Johansson, Scarlett American actress
skar-luht joh-**han**-suhn /ˌskɑː(r)lət
dʒəʊˈhansən/

Johansson, Thomas Swedish tennis player
too-mass **yoo**-han-son /ˌtuːmas
ˈjuːhansɒn/

John Menzies Scottish booksellers and stationers
ming-iss /ˈmɪŋɪs/

Often also erroneously **men**-ziss.

Johor (also **Johore**) state, Malaysia
juh-**hor** /dʒəˈhɔː(r)/

Johor Baharu city, Malaysia
juh-**hor bar**-oo /dʒəˌhɔː(r) ˈbaːruː/

joie de vivre exuberant enjoyment of life
zhwah duh **veev**-ruh /ˌʒwɑː də ˈviːvrə/

jojoba oil extracted from an American shrub
hoh-**hoh**-buh /həʊˈhəʊbə/

Jolie, Angelina American actress
an-juh-**lee**-nuh zhoh-**lee** /andʒəˈliːnə
ʒəʊˈliː/

jolie laide attractive woman with ugly features
zhol-ee **led** /ˌʒɒliː ˈlɛd/

Joliot, Jean-Frédéric French nuclear physicist
zhah(ng) fray-day-**reek** zhol-**yoh** /ʒɑ̃
freɪdeɪˌriːk ʒɒlˈjəʊ/

jollof West African rice stew
jol-uhf /ˈdʒɒləf/

Jolson, Al Russian-born American singer and comedian
johl-suhn /ˈdʒəʊlsən/

Jonagold dessert apple
jon-uh-gohld /ˈdʒɒnəˌgəʊld/

Jonah Hebrew prophet
joh-nuh /ˈdʒəʊnə/

Jong, Erica American author
err-ik-uh **jong** /ˌɛrɪkə ˈdʒɒŋ/

Jönköping city, Sweden
yoen-shoep-ing /ˈjɜːnˌʃɜːpɪŋ/

jonquil narcissus
jonk-wil /ˈdʒɒŋkwɪl/

Jonze, Spike American film director
spyk johnz /ˌspʌɪk ˈdʒəʊnz/

Jordaens, Jacob Flemish painter
yah-kop yor-**dahnss** /ˌjɑːkɒp
jɔː(r)ˈdɑːns/

Jorvik (also **Yorvik**) Viking name for York
yor-vik /ˈjɔː(r)vɪk/

Jospin, Lionel French politician
lee-on-**el** zhoss-**pa(ng)** /liːɒˈnɛl ʒɒsˈpɛ̃/

jota Spanish folk dance
khoh-tuh /ˈxəʊtə/

Jotunheim world in Norse mythology
yoh-tuun-haym /ˈjəʊtʊnˌheɪm/

In Germanic contexts commonly also **yoh**-tuhn-hym.

joual non-standard form of Canadian French
zhwal /ʒwal/

jouk turn or bend quickly
jook /dʒuːk/

Joule, James Prescott English physicist
jool /dʒuːl/

joule unit of work or energy
jool /dʒuːl/

Jove Greek god
johv /ˈdʒəʊv/

Jovovich, Milla American actress and model
mee-luh **yoh**-vuh-vitch /ˌmiːlə
ˈjəʊvəvɪtʃ/

Jowell, Tessa English culture minister
jow-uhl /ˈdʒaʊəl/

This British surname is variously pronounced **jow**-uhl and **joh**-uhl, depending on individual preference.

JPEG format for compressing images
jay-peg /ˈjeɪpɛg/

Juan tropical storm name
hwahn /ˈhwɑːn/

Juan Carlos de Borbón y Borbón king of Spain
khwan **kar**-loss day bor-**bon** ee
bor-**bon** /xwan ˌkɑː(r)lɒs deɪ bɔː(r)ˌbɒn
iː bɔː(r)ˈbɒn/

Juárez, Benito Pablo Mexican statesman
ben-**ee**-toh **pab**-loh khwarr-**ess**
/bɛˌniːtəʊ ˌpabləʊ ˈxwarɛs/

Juba city, Sudan
joo-buh /ˈdʒuːbə/

Jubba river, East Africa
juub-uh /ˈdʒʊbə/

Jubilate hundredth psalm
joo-bil-**ah**-tay /ˌdʒuːbɪˈlɑːteɪ/

jubilate show great happines
joo-bil-ayt /'dʒuːbɪleɪt/

Judaea southern part of ancient
Palestine
joo-dee-uh /dʒuːˈdiːə/

Judah Hebrew patriarch
joo-duh /'dʒuːdə/

Judaism religion
joo-day-iz-uhm /'dʒuːdeɪɪzəm/

Judas Maccabaeus Jewish leader
joo-duhss mak-uh-bee-uhss /,dʒuːdəs ,makəˈbiːəs/

Judenrat Jewish council
yoo-duhn-raht /'juːdənrɑːt/

judoka expert in judo
joo-doh-kuh /'dʒuːdəʊkə/

Sometimes also **joo-doh-kuh**.

Jugendstil German term for art nouveau
yoo-guhnt-shteel /'juːɡəntˌʃtiːl/

Juggernaut form of Krishna; also called
Jagannatha
jug-uhr-nawt /'dʒʌɡə(r)nɔːt/

juggernaut large vehicle
jug-uhr-nawt /'dʒʌɡə(r)nɔːt/

jugular of the neck or throat
jug-yuul-uhr /'dʒʌɡjʊlə(r)/

Less commonly also **joog-yuul-uhr**.

ju-jitsu (also **jiu-jitsu** or **ju-jutsu**)
Japanese system of wrestling
joo-jit-soo /dʒuːˈdʒɪtsuː/

jujube fruit of a Eurasian plant
joo-joob /'dʒuːdʒuːb/

Juilliard school of music in New York
joo-li-ard /'dʒuːliɑː(r)d/

julep sweet drink
joo-lep /'dʒuːlɛp/

julienne portion of food cut into short
strips
joo-li-en /,dʒuːliˈɛn/

Jullundur see **Jalandhar**

jumar climbing clamp
joo-muhr /'dʒuːmə(r)/

Jumeirah luxury hotel complex, United
Arab Emirates
joo-my-ruh /dʒuːˈmʌɪrə/

Jumna river, India
jum-nuh /'dʒʌmnə/

Juncker, Jean-Claude prime minister

of Luxembourg
zhah(ng) klohd yuunk-uhr /ʒã ,kləʊd 'jʊŋkə(r)/

Juneau port, Alaska
joo-noh /'dʒuːnəʊ/

Jung, Carl Swiss psychologist
karl yuung /,kɑː(r)l 'jʊŋ/

Junge, Traudl German private secretary
to Hitler
trow-duhl yuung-uh /,traʊdəl 'jʊŋə/

Jungfrau mountain, Switzerland
yuung-frow /'jʊŋfraʊ/

jungli uncultured
jung-gli /'dʒʌŋɡli/

juniper evergreen shrub
joo-nip-uhr /'dʒuːnɪpə(r)/

junket dish of flavoured curds of milk
junk-uht /'dʒʌŋkət/

Juno Roman goddess
joo-noh /'dʒuːnəʊ/

Juno beach D-day landing code name
joo-noh /'dʒuːnəʊ/

junta political group taking power by
force
jun-tuh /'dʒʌntə/, Spanish ['xunta]
• Established anglicization.

Juppé, Alain French politician
al-a(ng) zhue-pay /al,ɛ̃ ʒyˈpeɪ/

Jura mountain ranges, France and
Switzerland
joor-uh /'dʒʊərə/, French [ʒyra]
• Established anglicization.

Jura island, Scotland
joor-uh /'dʒʊərə/

Justinian Byzantine emperor
just-in-i-uhn /dʒʌˈstɪniən/

Jute Germanic ethnic group
joot /dʒuːt/

Jutland peninsula, NW Europe
jut-luhnd /'dʒʌtlənd/
• Established anglicization.

Juvenal Roman satirist
joo-vuh-nuhl /'dʒuːvənəl/

Juventus Italian football club
yoo-ven-tuuss /juːˈvɛntʊs/

Jyväskylä city, Finland
yue-vask-uel-uh /'jyvaskylə/, ['jyvæskylæ]

K

ka spiritual part of a human being or god
kah /kɑː/

Kaaba (also **Caaba**) Muslim shrine in Mecca
kah-buh /ˈkɑːbə/

Kaapenaar inhabitant of Cape Town
kah-puh-nar /ˈkɑːpə,nɑː(r)/

kabaddi sport
kuh-**bad**-i /kəˈbadi/

kabaka ruler of the Baganda people of Uganda
kuh-**bah**-kuh /kəˈbɑːkə/

Kabalega Falls waterfall, Uganda
kab-uh-**lay**-guh /ˌkabəˈleɪgə/

Kabardian relating to Kabardino
kuh-**bar**-di-uhn /kəˈbɑː(r)diən/

Kabardino-Balkaria autonomous republic, Russia
kuh-buhr-**dyee**-nuh buhl-**kar**-i-uh /ˌkəbə(r)ˈdjiːnə bəlˈkɑːriə/

Kabbalah see Cabbala

kabeljou fish
kab-uhl-**yoh** /ˌkabəlˈjəʊ/

Kabila, Laurent-Désiré African politician
lorr-**ah(ng)** day-zee-**ray** kab-ee-luh /lɒˌrɑ̃ deɪziːˌreɪ kaˈbiːlə/

Kabinett German wine
kab-in-**et** /ˌkabɪˈnɛt/

kabloona pl. **kabloonat** person who is not an Inuit
kuhb-**loo**-nuh, pl. kuhb-**loo**-nat /kəˈbluːnə/, pl. /-ˈnat/
• Standard -s plural is also possible.

kabuki traditional form of Japanese drama
kuh-**boo**-ki /kəˈbuːki/

Kabul capital of Afghanistan
kah-buul /ˈkɑːbʊl/

Kabwe town, Zambia
kab-way /ˈkabweɪ/

Kabyle Algerian ethnic group
kuh-**byl** /kəˈbʌɪl/

Kabylia region, Algeria
kuh-**bil**-i-uh /kəˈbɪliə/

Established anglicization. The French name is Kabylie, pronounced kab-il-**ee**.

Kachin Asian ethnic group
katch-in /ˈkatʃɪn/

kachina spirit in the Pueblo Indian mythology
kuh-**chee**-nuh /kəˈtʃiːnə/

kadaitcha Aboriginal mission of vengeance
kuh-**dy**-chuh /kəˈdʌɪtʃə/

Kádár, János Hungarian statesman
yah-nosh **kah**-dar /ˈjɑːnɒʃ ˈkɑːdɑː(r)/

Kaddish Jewish prayer sequence
kad-ish /ˈkadɪʃ/

Established anglicization. The Hebrew spelling of the word is Kaddisch, pronounced kad-**eesh**.

Kadima Israeli political party
kuh-**dee**-muh /kəˈdiːmə/

kaffiyeh see **keffiyeh**

Kafir Afghan ethnic group
kaf-eer /ˈkafɪə(r)/

kafir person who is not a Muslim
kaf-eer /ˈkafɪə(r)/

Kafka, Franz Czech novelist
frants **kaf**-kuh /ˌfrants ˈkafkə/

kaftan long tunic
kaf-tan /ˈkaftan/

Kagame, Paul Rwandan president
pol kuh-**gah**-may /ˌpɒl kəˈgɑːmeɪ/

Kagoshima city, Japan
kag-**osh**-im-uh /kaˈgɒʃɪmə/

kagu bird
kah-goo /ˈkɑːguː/

kahikatea New Zealand tree
ky-kuh-**tee**-uh /ˌkʌɪkəˈtiːə/

Kahlo, Frida Mexican painter
free-duh **kah**-loh /ˌfriːdə ˈkɑːləʊ/

Kahlúa trademark liqueur
kuh-**loo**-uh /kəˈluːə/

kahuna Hawaiian wise man
kuh-**hoo**-nuh /kəˈhuːnə/

Kaifeng city, China
ky-**fung** /ˌkʌɪˈfʌŋ/

kairos propitious moment for decision or action
ky-ross /ˈkaɪrɒs/

Kairouan city, Tunisia
ky-ruu-**ahn** /ˌkaɪrʊˈɑːn/

Kaiser, Georg German dramatist
gay-ork **ky**-zuhr /ˌɡeɪɔː(r)k ˈkaɪzə(r)/

kaiser German emperor
ky-zuhr /ˈkaɪzə(r)/

Kaiserslautern city, Germany
ky-zuhrss-**low**-tuhrn
/ˌkaɪzə(r)sˈlaʊtə(r)n/

kaizen Japanese business philosophy
ky-**zen** /kaɪˈzen/

kakapo parrot
kah-kuh-poh /ˈkɑːkəpəʊ/

kakemono Japanese painting
kak-em-**oh**-noh /ˌkakɛˈməʊnəʊ/

Kakiemon style of Japanese porcelain
kak-ee-em-on /kaˈkiːɛmɒn/

Kalaallit Nunaat see **Greenland**

kala-azar form of leishmaniasis
kah-luh uh-**zar** /ˌkɑːlə əˈzɑː(r)/

Kalahari Desert desert, Africa
kal-uh-**har**-i /ˌkaləˈhɑːri/

kalanchoe plant
kal-uhn-**koh**-i /ˌkalənˈkəʊi/

Kalashnikov rifle
kuh-**lash**-nik-of /kəˈlaʃnɪkɒf/

kale cabbage
kayl /keɪl/

Kalevala Finnish national epic
kal-ev-al-uh /ˈkalevalə/

Kalgoorlie town, Australia
kal-**goor**-li /kalˈɡʊə(r)li/

Kali Hindu goddess
kah-li /ˈkɑːli/

kali saltwort
kay-ly /ˈkeɪlʌi/

Sometimes also **kal**-i.

Kalidasa Indian poet
kal-id-**ah**-suh /ˌkalɪˈdɑːsə/

Kalimantan region, Indonesia
kal-im-**an**-tan /ˌkalɪˈmantan/

kalimba African thumb piano
kuh-**limb**-uh /kəˈlɪmbə/

Kalinin, Mikhail Soviet statesman
mee-khuh-**eel** kuh-**lee**-nin /miːxəˌiːl kəˈliːnɪn/

Kaliningrad port and region, Russia

kuh-**lee**-nin-grat /kəˈliːnɪngrat/

Kalisz city, Poland
kal-eesh /ˈkaliːʃ/

Kalmar port, Sweden
kal-mar /ˈkalmɑː(r)/

kalmia shrub
kal-mi-uh /ˈkalmiə/

Kalmyk Kalmykian ethnic group
kal-mik /ˈkalmɪk/

Kalmykia autonomous republic, Russia
kal-**mik**-i-uh /kalˈmɪkiə/

kalong flying fox
kah-long /ˈkɑːlɒŋ/

kalpa period of time
kal-puh /ˈkalpə/

Kaluga city, Russia
kuh-**loo**-guh /kəˈluːɡə/

Kalyan city, India
kul-**yahn** /kʌlˈjɑːn/

Kama Hindu god
kah-muh /ˈkɑːmə/

kamahi tree
kah-muh-hi /ˈkɑːməhi/

Kama Sutra ancient Sanskrit treatise
kah-muh **soo**-truh /ˌkɑːmə ˈsuːtrə/

Kamba Kenyan ethnic group
kam-buh /ˈkambə/

Kamchatka peninsula, Russia
kam-**chat**-kuh /kamˈtʃatkə/

kameez Indian tunic
kuh-**meez** /kəˈmiːz/

Kamensk-Uralsky city, Russia
kah-muhnsk uu-**ral**-ski /ˌkɑːmənsk ʊˈralski/

Kamerlingh Onnes, Heike Dutch physicist
hy-kuh **kah**-muhr-ling **on**-uhss /ˌhaɪkə ˌkɑːmə(r)lɪŋ ˈɒnəs/

kami divine being in the Shinto religion
kah-mi /ˈkɑːmi/

kamikaze Japanese suicidal aircraft crash
kam-ik-**ah**-zi /ˌkamɪˈkɑːzi/

Kamilaroi Australian Aboriginal ethnic group
kuh-**mil**-uh-roy /kəˈmɪlərɔɪ/

Kampala capital of Uganda
kam-**pah**-luh /kamˈpɑːlə/

kampong Malaysian enclosure or village
kam-pong /kamˈpɒŋ/

Kampuchea former name for Cambodia
kam-puutch-**ee**-uh /kampʊˈtʃiːə/

kana system of Japanese writing
kah-nuh /ˈkɑːnə/

kanaka native of Hawaii
kuh-**nak**-uh /kəˈnakə/

kanamycin antibiotic
kan-uh-**my**-sin /ˌkanəˈmʌɪsɪn/

Kanarese Indian ethnic group
kan-uh-**reez** /ˌkanəˈriːz/

Kanawa, Kiri Te see Te Kanawa, Kiri

Kanchenjunga mountain, Himalayas
kan-chen-**jung**-guh /ˌkantʃɛnˈdʒʌŋgə/

Kandahar city, Afghanistan
kan-duh-**har** /ˌkandəˈhɑː(r)/

Kandinsky, Wassily Russian painter
vuh-**see**-li kan-**din**-ski /vəˌsiːli kanˈdɪnski/

Kandy city, Sri Lanka
kan-dee /ˈkandiː/

Kangar city, Malaysia
kang-gar /ˈkaŋgɑː(r)/

KaNgwane former Swazi homeland, South Africa
kah-uhng-**gwah**-nay /ˌkɑːəŋˈgwɑːneɪ/

kanji Japanese writing system
kan-ji /ˈkandʒi/

Kannada Dravidian language
kan-uh-duh /ˈkanədə/

Kano city, Nigeria
kah-noh /ˈkɑːnəʊ/

Kanpur (also **Cawnpore**) city, India
kahn-**poor** /kɑːnˈpʊə(r)/

Kansas state, US
kan-zuhss /ˈkanzəs/

Kant, Immanuel German philosopher
im-**ahn**-wel kant /ɪˌmɑːnwɛl ˈkant/

Kanto region, Japan
kan-toh /ˈkantəʊ/

KANU Kenya African National Union
kah-noo /ˈkɑːnuː/

kanuka tree
kah-nuuk-uh /ˈkɑːnʊkə/

Kanuri Nigerian language
kuh-**noor**-i /kəˈnʊəri/

kanzu East African robe
kan-zoo /ˈkanzuː/

Kaohsiung port, Taiwan
kow-shi-**uung** /ˌkaʊʃiˈʊŋ/

Kaonde Zambian ethnic group
kah-**on**-day /kɑːˈɒndeɪ/

Kapachira Falls waterfalls, Malawi
kap-uh-**cheer**-uh /ˌkapəˈtʃɪərə/

kapellmeister conductor of an orchestra or choir
kuh-**pel**-my-stuhr /kəˈpɛlˌmʌɪstə(r)/

Kapil Dev Indian cricketer
kap-il **dev** /ˌkapɪl ˈdɛv/

Kaposi's sarcoma form of cancer
kuh-**poh**-siz sar-**koh**-muh /kəˌpəʊsɪz sɑːˈ(r)ˈkəʊmə/

kappa letter of the Greek alphabet
kap-uh /ˈkapə/

Kaprál, Václav Czech composer
vaht-slaf **kap**-rahl /ˌvɑːtslaf ˈkapraːl/

Kapranos, Alex Scottish singer
kuh-**prah**-noss /kəˈprɑːnɒs/

Kaprun resort, Austria
kuh-**proon** /kəˈpruːn/

kapur tree
kap-uhr /ˈkapə(r)/

kaput broken and useless
kuh-**puut** /kəˈpʊt/

Karachai-Cherkessia autonomous republic, Russia
karr-uh-**chy** chair-**kess**-i-uh /karəˌtʃʌɪ tʃɛːˈ(r)ˈkɛsiə/

Karachi city, Pakistan
kuh-**rah**-chi /kəˈrɑːtʃi/

Karaganda see Qaraghandy

karahi (also **karai**) Indian frying pan
kurr-**y** /kʌˈrʌɪ/

Karaite Jewish sect
kair-uh-yt /ˈkɛːrəʌɪt/

Karaj city, Iran
karr-**ahj** /kaˈrɑːdʒ/

Karajan, Herbert von Austrian conductor
hair-bairt fon karr-uh-yahn /ˌhɛː(r)bɛː(r)t fɒn ˈkarəjɑːn/

Karakalpak autonomous republic, Russia
karr-uh-**kal**-pak /ˌkarəˈkalpak/

Karakoram mountain system, central Asia
karr-uh-**kaw**-ruhm /ˌkarəˈkɔːrəm/

karakul breed of sheep
karr-uh-kuul /ˈkarəkʊl/

Kara Kum desert, central Asia
karr-uh koom /ˌkarə ˈkuːm/

karanga Maori ritual chant
karr-ang-uh /ˈkaraŋə/

karaoke Japanese form of entertainment
karr-uh-**oh**-ki /ˌkarəˈəʊki/

Kara Sea part of the Arctic Ocean
kar-uh /ˈkɑːrə/

karate oriental system of unarmed combat
kuh-**rah**-ti /kəˈrɑːti/, Japanese [karate]
• Established anglicization.

karateka practitioner of karate
kuh-**rah**-tik-ah /kəˈrɑːtɪkɑː/

Karbala (also **Kerbala**) city, Iraq
kar-buh-**lah** /kɑː(r)bəˈlɑː/

Karelia region, NE Europe
kuh-**ray**-li-uh /kəˈreɪliə/

Karen Burmese ethnic group
kuh-**ren** /kəˈrɛn/

Kariba lake, central Africa
kuh-**ree**-buh /kəˈriːbə/

Karloff, Boris British-born American actor
kar-lof /ˈkɑː(r)lɒf/

Karlovy Vary town, Czech Republic
kar-lov-i **varr**-i /ˌkɑː(r)lɒvi ˈvari/

Karlsruhe town, Germany
karlss-roo-uh /ˈkɑː(r)lsˌruːə/

Karnak village, Egypt
kar-nak /ˈkɑː(r)nak/

Karnataka state, India
kuhr-**nah**-tuh-kuh /kə(r)ˈnɑːtəkə/

Kärnten see **Carinthia**

Karoo plateau, South Africa
kuh-**roo** /kəˈruː/

karoshi death caused by overwork
karr-**oh**-shi /kaˈrəʊʃi/

Karpov, Anatoli Russian chess player
an-uh-**tol**-i **kar**-puhf /anəˌtɒli ˈkɑː(r)pəf/

Kars city and province, Turkey
karss /kɑː(r)s/

Karsh, Yousuf Armenian-born Canadian photographer
yuuss-uuf **karsh** /ˌjʊsʊf ˈkɑː(r)ʃ/

Kartvelian South Caucasian
kart-**vee**-li-uhn /kɑː(r)tˈviːliən/

karyotype appearance of the chromosomes in a cell nuclei
karr-i-oh-typ /ˈkariəʊtʌɪp/

kasbah citadel of a North African city
kaz-bah /ˈkazbɑː/

Kashmir region, border of India and Pakistan

kash-**meer** /kaʃˈmɪə(r)/

Kashmiri relating to Kashmir
kash-**meer**-i /kaʃˈmɪəri/

kashrut body of Jewish religious laws
kash-**root** /kaʃˈruːt/

Kasparov, Garry Azerbaijani chess player
kuhsp-**ar**-uhf /kəˈspɑːrəf/

Kassel city, Germany
kass-uhl /ˈkasəl/

Kasur city, Pakistan
kuh-**soor** /kəˈsʊə(r)/

kata training exercises in karate
kah-tah /ˈkɑːtɑː/

katakana Japanese writing system
kat-uh-**kah**-nuh /ˌkatəˈkɑːnə/

katana Japanese samurai sword
kuh-**tah**-nuh /kəˈtɑːnə/

Katanga region, Democratic Republic of Congo
kuh-**tang**-guh /kəˈtaŋɡə/

Katangese relating to Katanga
kat-ang-**geez** /ˌkataŋˈɡiːz/

Kathak Indian dance
kut-uhk /ˈkʌtək/

Kathakali Indian dance
kut-uh-**kul**-i /ˌkʌtəˈkʌli/

katharevousa form of modern Greek
kath-uh-**rev**-oo-suh /ˌkaθəˈrɛvuːsə/

katharometer instrument for detecting a gas
kath-uh-**rom**-it-uhr /ˌkaθəˈrɒmɪtə(r)/

Kathiawar peninsula, India
kat-i-uh-**war** /ˌkatiəˈwɑː(r)/

Kathmandu (also **Katmandu**) capital of Nepal
kat-man-**doo** /ˌkatmanˈduː/

katipo venomous spider
kat-ip-oh /ˈkatɪpəʊ/

Katowice city, Poland
kat-ov-**eet**-suh /katɒˈviːtsə/

Katsav, Moshe Israeli statesman
mosh-**ay** kat-**sav** /mɒˌʃeɪ katˈsav/

katsuobushi Japanese dried fish
kat-swoh-**buush**-i /ˌkatswəʊˈbʊʃi/

Kattegat strait between Sweden and Denmark
kat-uh-gat /ˈkatəgat/

katydid insect
kay-tid-id /ˈkeɪtɪdɪd/

Kauai island, Hawaii
kow-**ah**-i /kaʊˈɑːi/

Kauffmann, Angelica Swiss painter
an-**jel**-ik-uh **kowf**-man /anˌdʒɛlɪkə
ˈkaʊfman/

Kaufman, Charlie American
screenwriter
kowf-muhn /ˈkaʊfmən/

This English surname is variously
pronounced **kowf**-muhn and **kawf**-muhn,
depending on individual preference.

kaumatua Maori elder
kow-**mah**-tuu-uh /kaʊˈmɑːtʊə/

Kaunas city, Lithuania
kow-nuhss /ˈkaʊnəs/

Kaunda, Kenneth Zambian statesman
kah-**uun**-duh /kɑːˈʊndə/

kauri forest tree
kow-ri /ˈkaʊri/

kava Polynesian narcotic sedative drink
kah-vuh /ˈkɑːvə/

Kaválla port, Greece
kuh-**val**-uh /kəˈvalə/

Kawabata, Yasunari Japanese novelist
yass-uun-**ar**-i kah-wuh-**bah**-tuh
/jasuˌnɑːri ˌkɑːwəˈbɑːtə/

Kawasaki city, Japan
kah-wuh-**sah**-ki /ˌkɑːwəˈsɑːki/

kayak canoe
ky-ak /ˈkʌɪak/

kayakeet shrub
ky-uh-keet /ˈkʌɪəkiːt/

Kayseri city, Turkey
ky-suh-ri /ˈkʌɪsəri/

kazachoc Slavic dance
kaz-uh-**chok** /ˌkazəˈtʃɒk/

Kazakh relating to Kazakhstan
kuh-**zak** /kəˈzak/

Commonly also **kaz**-ak.

Kazakhstan country
kaz-ak-**stahn** /ˌkazakˈstɑːn/

Kazan port, Russia
kuh-**zahn** /kəˈzɑːn/

Kazan, Elia Turkish-born American
film director
ee-li-uh kuh-**zahn** /ˌiːliə kəˈzɑːn/

kazoo musical instrument
kuh-**zoo** /kəˈzuː/

kea parrot
kee-uh /ˈkiːə/

kebab pieces of meat roasted on a skewer
kuh-**bab** /kəˈbab/

Keble, John English churchman
kee-buhl /ˈkiːbəl/

Kebnekaise mountain, Sweden
keb-nuh-**ky**-suh /ˌkɛbnəˈkʌɪsə/

Kedah state, Malaysia
ked-uh /ˈkɛdə/

kedgeree fish dish
kej-uh-ree /ˈkɛdʒəriː/

keema minced meat
kee-muh /ˈkiːmə/

Keemun Chinese tea
kee-moon /ˈkiːmuːn/

keeshond breed of dog
kayss-hond /ˈkeɪshɒnd/

Kefallinia see Cephalonia

keffiyeh (also **kaffiyeh**) Arab headdress
kuh-**fee**-yuh /kəˈfiːjə/

Keflavik port, Iceland
kef-luh-veek /ˈkɛfləviːk/

keftedes Greek meatballs
kef-**teth**-eez /kɛfˈtɛðiːz/

Kehlstein Hitler's mountain retreat in
the Alps
kayl-shtyn /ˈkeɪlʃtʌɪn/

Keighley town, England
keeth-li /ˈkiːθli/

keiretsu business conglomeration
kay-**ret**-soo /keɪˈrɛtsuː/

Kelantan state, Malaysia
kuh-**lan**-tuhn /kəˈlantən/

Kellogg, Will Keith American food
manufacturer
kel-og /ˈkɛlɒɡ/

keloid irregular tissue formed at a scar
kee-loyd /ˈkiːlɔɪd/

kelpie water spirit of Scottish folklore
kel-pi /ˈkɛlpi/

Kemerovo city, Russia
kyem-uh-ruh-vuh /ˈkjɛmərəvə/

Kendal town, England
ken-duhl /ˈkɛndəl/

kendo Japanese form of fencing
ken-doh /ˈkɛndəʊ/

Keneally, Thomas Australian novelist
kuh-**nee**-li /kəˈniːli/

Kennebec river, US
ken-uh-bek /ˈkɛnəbɛk/

Kennebunkport town, US
ken-uh-**bunk**-port /kɛnəˈbʌŋkpɔː(r)t/

Kennedy, Helena Scottish barrister
huh-**lay**-nuh /həˈleɪnə/

keno game similar to bingo
kee-noh /'ki:nəʊ/

kenosis renunciation of the divine nature
kuh-**noh**-siss /kə'nəʊsɪs/

kente Ghanaian cloth
ken-tuh /'kɛntə/

Kentucky state, US
ken-**tuk**-i /kɛn'tʌki/

Kenya country
ken-yuh /'kɛnjə/

This has been the BBC Pronunciation Unit
recommendation since 1965. The
pronunciation **keen**-yuh is now dated.

Kenyatta, Jomo Kenyan statesman
joh-moh ken-**yat**-uh /ˌdʒəʊməʊ
kɛn'jatə/

kepi French military cap
kep-i /'kɛpi/

Kepler, Johannes German astronomer
yoh-**han**-uhss kep-luhr /jəʊˌhanəs
'kɛplə(r)/

Kerala state, India
kerr-uh-luh /'kɛrələ/

keratectomy surgical removal of a
section of the cornea
kerr-uh-**tek**-tuh-mi /ˌkɛrə'tɛktəmi/

keratin protein
kerr-uh-tin /'kɛrətɪn/

keratinize change into a form
containing keratin
kerr-uh-tin-yz /'kɛrətɪnʌɪz/

Sometimes also kuh-**rat**-in-yz.

keratinous containing keratin
kuh-**rat**-in-uhss /kə'ratɪnəs/

keratitis inflammation of the cornea
kerr-uh-**ty**-tiss /ˌkɛrə'tʌɪtɪs/

keratomileusis surgical reshaping of
the cornea
kerr-uh-toh-my-**loo**-siss
/ˌkɛrətəʊmʌɪ'lu:sɪs/

keratoplasty surgery on the cornea
kerr-uh-toh-plast-i /'kɛrətəʊˌplasti/

keratosis growth on the skin
kerr-uh-**toh**-siss /ˌkɛrə'təʊsɪs/

Kerbala see Karbala

Kerch city, Ukraine
kairtch /kɛ:(r)tʃ/

Keres Pueblo Indian ethnic group
kerr-ess /'kɛrɛs/

Kerguelen Islands group of islands,
Indian Ocean
kur-guh-lin /'kə:(r)gəlɪn/
• Established anglicization.

Kérkira see Corfu

Kerkrade town, Netherlands
kairk-rah-duh /'kɛ:(r)krɑ:də/

Kermadec Islands group of islands,
South Pacific
kur-**mad**-ek /kə:(r)'madɛk/

kermes red dye
kur-miz /'kə:(r)mɪz/

kerosene fuel oil
kerr-uh-seen /'kɛrəsi:n/

Kerouac, Jack American novelist
kerr-oo-ak /'kɛruak/

Kerr, Deborah Scottish actress
deb-uh-ruh kar /ˌdɛbərə 'kɑ:(r)/

This British surname is variously
pronounced kur, kar, and kair, depending
on individual preference.

Kertész, Imre Hungarian author
im-ruh **kair**-tayss /ˌɪmrə 'kɛ:(r)teɪs/

Kesey, Ken American novelist
kee-zi /'ki:zi/

Keswick town, England
kez-ik /'kɛzɪk/

ketamine anaesthetic drug
ket-uh-meen /'kɛtəmi:n/

kewpie doll
kyoo-pi /'kju:pi/

Keynes, John Maynard English
economist
kaynz /keɪnz/

Khabarovsk region, Russia
khuh-**bar**-uhfsk /xə'bɑ:rəfsk/

Khakassia autonomous republic, Russia
khuh-**kass**-i-uh /xə'kasiə/

khaki cotton fabric of a brownish-yellow
colour
kah-ki /'kɑ:ki/

AM is kak-i.

Khalistan proposed independent Sikh
state
kah-li-stahn /'kɑ:listɑ:n/

Khalkha Mongolian ethnic group
kahl-kuh /'kɑ:lkə/

Khalkis see Chalcis

Khalsa body or company of fully
initiated Sikhs
kul-suh /'kʌlsə/

Khama, Seretse Botswanan statesman
suh-**ret**-si kah-muh /sə‚rɛtsi 'kɑːmə/

Khamene'i, Ayatollah Ali Iranian
supreme leader
y-uh-**tol**-uh al-**ee** khah-muh-nuh-**ee**
/ˌʌɪəˌtɒlə aˌli: xɑːmənəˈiː/

khamsin hot Egyptian wind
kam-sin /'kamsɪn/

Khan, Chaka American singer
chak-uh **kahn** /ˌtʃakə 'kɑːn/

Khan, Imran Pakistani cricketer
im-rahn **kahn** /ˌɪmrɑːn 'kɑːn/, Urdu
[xɑːn]
• Established anglicization.

khan Muslim title
kahn /kɑːn/

Khaniá see **Chania**

Khao Lak resort, Thailand
kow **lak** /ˌkaʊ 'lak/

Kharg island, Persian Gulf
kharg /xɑː(r)ɡ/

Kharkiv city, Ukraine
khar-kif /'xɑː(r)kɪf/

Khartoum capital of Sudan
kar-**toom** /kɑː(r)'tuːm/, Arabic
[xar'tuːm]
• Established anglicization.

khat see **qat**

khayal traditional Indian song
kuh-**yahl** /kəˈjɑːl/

Khayelitsha township, South Africa
ky-yuh-**leet**-shuh /ˌkʌɪjəˈliːtʃə/

Khayyam, Omar see **Rubaiyat**

Khazar Turkic ethnic group
kuh-**zar** /kəˈzɑː(r)/

Khedive title of the viceroy of Egypt
kuh-**deev** /kəˈdiːv/

Kherson port, Ukraine
khuhr-**son** /xə(r)'sɒn/

khichri Indian dish
kitch-ree /'kɪtʃriː/

Khios see **Chios**

khir Indian dish
keer /'kɪə(r)/

Khmer ancient kingdom, Asia
kmair /kmɛː(r)/

Khmer Rouge Cambodian guerrilla
organization
kmair **roozh** /ˌkmɛː(r) 'ruːʒ/

Khoikhoi South African ethnic group
koy-koy /'kɔɪkɔɪ/

Khoisan South African ethnic group
koy-sahn /'kɔɪsɑːn/

kho-kho Indian game
koh koh /'kəʊ kəʊ/

Khomeini, Ruhollah Iranian Shiite
Muslim leader
roo-huul-**ah** khom-ay-nee /ruːhʊˌlɑː
xɒmeɪˈniː/

Khonsu Egyptian god
kon-soo /'kɒnsuː/

Khorramshahr port, Iran
khuu-ruhm-**shar** /ˌxʊrəmˈʃɑː(r)/

Khrushchev, Nikita Soviet statesman
nik-ee-tuh **kruush**-chof /nɪˌkiːtə
'krʊʃtʃɒf/, Russian [xruʃ'tʃɒf]
• Established anglicization.

Khufu Egyptian pharaoh
khoo-foo /'xuːfuː/

Khulna city, Bangladesh
kuul-nuh /'kʊlnə/

Khunjerab Pass pass through the
Himalayas
kun-yuh-rahb /'kʌnjərɑːb/

Khyber Pass mountain pass in the
Hindu Kush
ky-buhr /'kʌɪbə(r)/

ki see **qi**

kia ora Maori greeting
kee-uh **aw**-ruh /ˌkiːə 'ɔːrə/

kibbutz pl. **kibbutzim** communal
settlement in Israel
kib-**uuts**, pl. kib-uuts-**eem** /kɪ'bʊts/, pl.
/kɪbʊ'tsiːm/

kibbutznik member of a kibbutz
kib-**uuts**-nik /kɪ'bʊtsnɪk/

kibitz look on and offer unwelcome
advice
kib-its /'kɪbɪts/

Kickapoo American Indian ethnic group
kik-uh-**poo** /'kɪkəpuː/

Kidderminster town, England
kid-uhr-min-stuhr /'kɪdə(r)ˌmɪnstə(r)/

kiddush Jewish ceremony
kid-uush /'kɪdʊʃ/

Kiel port, Germany
keel /kiːl/

kielbasa Polish sausage
keel-**bass**-uh /kiːl'basə/

Kielce city, Poland
kyelt-suh /'kjɛltsə/

Kierkegaard, Søren Danish
philosopher
soer-uhn **keer**-kuh-gor /ˌsœːrən
ˈkɪə(r)kəgɔː(r)/

Kieslowski, Krzysztof Polish film
director
kshish-tof kyesh-**lof**-ski /ˌkʃɪʃtɒf
kjɛʃˈlɒfski/

Kiev capital of Ukraine
kee-ef /ˈkiːɛf/

Established anglicization. The Ukrainian
name is Kyiv, pronounced **ki**-yif [ˈkijɪf].

Kigali capital of Rwanda
kig-**ah**-li /kɪˈɡɑːli/

Kikládhes see **Cyclades**

Kikongo Bantu language
kik-**ong**-goh /kɪˈkɒŋɡəʊ/

Kikuyu Kenyan ethnic group
kik-**oo**-yoo /kɪˈkuːjuː/

Kilauea volcano, Hawaii
kee-low-**ay**-uh /ˌkiːlaʊˈeɪə/

Kildare county, Republic of Ireland
kil-**dair** /kɪlˈdɛː(r)/

kilderkin cask for liquids
kil-duhr-kin /ˈkɪldə(r)kɪn/

kilim Turkish carpet
kil-**eem** /kɪˈliːm/

Kilimanjaro, Mount mountain,
Tanzania
kil-im-uhn-**jar**-oh /ˌkɪlɪmənˈdʒɑːrəʊ/

Kilkenny county, Republic of Ireland
kil-**ken**-i /kɪlˈkɛni/

Killarney town, Republic of Ireland
kil-**ar**-ni /kɪlˈlɑː(r)ni/

Kilmarnock town, Scotland
kil-**mar**-nuhk /kɪlˈmɑː(r)nək/

kilometre unit of measurement
kil-uh-mee-tuhr /ˈkɪləˌmiːtə(r)/

This is the traditional pronunciation, but
kil-**om**-uh-tuhr is equally, if not more,
common, and equally acceptable. AM is
usually kil-**om**-uh-tuhr.

kimchi Korean dish
kim-chi /ˈkɪmtʃi/

Kim Il-sung Korean statesman
kim il sung /ˌkɪm ɪl ˈsʌŋ/

kimono Japanese robe
kim-**oh**-noh /kɪˈməʊnəʊ/

kina currency unit, Papua New Guinea
kee-nuh /ˈkiːnə/

Kinabalu, Mount mountain, Malaysia
kin-uh-**bah**-loo /ˌkɪnəˈbɑːluː/

kinaesthesia sense of muscular effort
kin-uhss-**thee**-zi-uh /ˌkɪnəsˈθiːziə/

Kincardineshire former county,
Scotland
kin-**kar**-din-shuhr /kɪnˈkɑː(r)dɪnʃə(r)/

kine cows collectively
kyn /kʌɪn/

kinematics branch of mechanics
kin-uh-**mat**-iks /ˌkɪnəˈmatɪks/

kinesics study of gestures as non-verbal
communication
kin-**ee**-siks /kɪˈniːsɪks/

kinesis movement
kin-**ee**-siss /kɪˈniːsɪs/

kinetic relating to motion
kin-**et**-ik /kɪˈnɛtɪk/

kinetoscope early motion-picture device
kin-**ee**-toh-skohp /kɪˈniːtəʊskəʊp/

kinin substance formed in body tissue in
response to injury
ky-nin /ˈkʌɪnɪn/

kinkajou racoon-like animal
kink-uh-joo /ˈkɪŋkəˌdʒuː/

Kinki region, Japan
keen-kee /ˈkiːŋkiː/

Kinnear, Greg American actor
kin-**eer** /kɪˈnɪə(r)/

This surname is variously pronounced
kin-**eer** and kin-**air**, depending on
individual preference.

Kinneret, Lake another name for the
Sea of Galilee
kin-uh-ret /ˈkɪnərɛt/

kinnikinnick substitute for tobacco
kin-ik-in-**ik** /ˌkɪnɪkɪˈnɪk/

kino gum
kee-noh /ˈkiːnəʊ/

Kinross-shire former county, Scotland
kin-**ross** shuhr /kɪnˈrɒs ʃə(r)/

Kinsey, Alfred Charles American
zoologist and sex researcher
kin-zi /ˈkɪnzi/

Kinshasa capital of the Democratic
Republic of Congo
kin-**shah**-suh /kɪnˈʃɑːsə/

Kinski, Nastassja German-born actress
nast-**ass**-yuh **kin**-ski /nasˌtasjə ˈkɪnski/

Kintyre peninsula, Scotland
kin-**ty**-uhr /kɪnˈtʌɪə(r)/

kippa Jewish skullcap
kip-**ah** /kɪˈpɑː/

Kipling, Rudyard Indian-born British writer
rud-yuhrd **kip**-ling /ˌrʌdjə(r)d ˈkɪplɪŋ/

Kir trademark alcoholic drink
keer /kɪə(r)/

Kirchhoff, Gustav Robert German physicist
guust-ahf **roh**-bairt **keerkh**-hof /ˌɡʊstɑːf ˌrəʊbɛː(r)t ˈkɪə(r)çhɒf/

Kirchner, Ernst Ludwig German painter
airnst loot-vikh **keerkh**-nuhr /ˌɛː(r)nst ˌluːtvɪç ˈkɪə(r)çnə(r)/

Kirchner, Nestor Argentine president
nest-or **keertch**-nuhr /ˌnɛstɔː(r) ˈkɪə(r)tʃnə(r)/

Kiribati country
kirr-ib-**ass** /ˌkɪrɪˈbas/

A pronunciation closer to the spelling, kirr-ib-**ah**-ti, is also common.

kirk church
kurk /kə:(r)k/

Kirkcaldy town, Scotland
kur-**kod**-i /kə:(r)ˈkɒdi/

Kirkcudbright town, Scotland
kur-**koob**-ri /kə:(r)ˈkuːbri/

kirkman clergyman
kurk-muhn /ˈkə:(r)kmən/

Kirkuk city, Iraq
keer-**kuuk** /kɪə(r)ˈkʊk/

Kirkwall port, Scotland
kurk-wawl /ˈkə:(r)kwɔːl/

Kirman carpet
keer-**mahn** /kɪə(r)ˈmɑːn/

kirpan sword worn by Sikhs
kur-**pahn** /kə:(r)ˈpɑːn/

kirsch cherry brandy
keersh /kɪə(r)ʃ/

kirtan Hindu devotional song
keer-tun /ˈkɪə(r)tʌn/

Kiruna town, Sweden
kirr-uun-uh /ˈkɪrʊnə/

Kirundi language of Burundi
kirr-**uun**-di /kɪˈrʊndi/

Kisangani city, Democratic Republic of Congo
kiss-ang-**gah**-ni /ˌkɪsaŋˈɡɑːni/

kishke beef intestine
kish-kuh /ˈkɪʃkə/

Kislev Jewish month
kiss-lef /ˈkɪslɛf/

kismet destiny
kiz-met /ˈkɪzmɛt/

kissel Russian dessert
kiss-uhl /ˈkɪsəl/

Kissinger, Henry German-born American statesman
kiss-in-juhr /ˈkɪsɪndʒə(r)/

Kiswahili another term for Swahili
kee-swuh-**hee**-li /ˌkiːswəˈhiːli/

kitab the Koran
kit-**ahb** /kɪˈtɑːb/

Kitakyushu port, Japan
kee-tuh-**kyoo**-shoo /ˌkiːtəˈkjuːʃuː/

Kitchener, Herbert British soldier and statesman
kitch-uh-nuhr /ˈkɪtʃənə(r)/

kitenge East African cotton fabric
kit-**eng**-gi /kɪˈtɛŋɡi/

kith one's relations
kith /kɪθ/

kittiwake gull
kit-i-wayk /ˈkɪtiweɪk/

Kitwe city, Zambia
kit-way /ˈkɪtweɪ/

Kitzbühel town, Austria
kits-bue-uhl /ˈkɪtsbyːəl/

kiva underground chamber
kee-vuh /ˈkiːvə/

Kivu, Lake lake, central Africa
kee-voo /ˈkiːvuː/

Kiwanis Club North American society of business and professional people
ki-**wah**-niss /kɪˈwɑːnɪs/

Klagenfurt city, Austria
klah-guhn-foort /ˈklɑːɡənˌfʊə(r)t/

Klaipeda port, Lithuania
kly-puh-duh /ˈklʌɪpədə/

Klamath American Indian ethnic group
klam-uhth /ˈklaməθ/

Klaproth, Martin Heinrich German chemist
mar-teen **hyn**-rikh **klap**-roht /ˌmɑː(r)tiːn ˌhʌɪnrɪç ˈklaprəʊt/

klaxon trademark electric horn
klak-suhn /ˈklaksən/

klebsiella bacterium
kleb-zi-**el**-uh /ˌklɛbziˈɛlə/

Klee, Paul Swiss painter
powl klay /ˌpaʊl ˈkleɪ/

Klein, Calvin American fashion designer
klyn /klʌɪn/

Klein, Melanie Austrian-born psychoanalyst
klyn /klʌɪn/

Klemperer, Otto German-born conductor and composer
ot-oh **klem**-puh-ruhr /ˌɒtəʊ ˈklɛmpərə(r)/

klepht Greek independence fighter
kleft /klɛft/

kleptomania recurrent urge to steal
klep-tuh-**may**-ni-uh /ˌklɛptəˈmeɪniə/

Klerksdorp city, South Africa
klarks-dorp /ˈklɑː(r)ksdɔː(r)p/

kletterschuh climbing boot
klet-uhr-shoo /ˈklɛtə(r)ʃuː/

klezmer traditional Jewish music
klez-muhr /ˈklɛzmə(r)/

klieg light powerful electric lamp
kleeg /kliːg/

Klimt, Gustav Austrian painter
guust-ahf **klimt** /ˌɡʊstɑːf ˈklɪmt/

Klinefelter's syndrome genetic condition
klyn-felt-uhrz /ˈklʌɪnˌfɛltə(r)z/

Klingon alien in *Star Trek*
kling-on /ˈklɪŋɒn/

klipspringer antelope
klip-spring-uhr /ˈklɪpˌsprɪŋə(r)/

Klondike tributary of the Yukon River, Canada
klon-dyk /ˈklɒndʌɪk/

Klosters resort, Switzerland
kloh-stuhrz /ˈkləʊstə(r)z/, German /ˈkloːstɐs/
• Established anglicization.

Kluxer member of the Ku Klux Klan
kluk-suhr /ˈklʌksə(r)/

knackwurst German sausage
nak-vurst /ˈnakvə:(r)st/, [ˈknakvʊrst]

knaidel pl. **knaidlach** Jewish dumpling
knay-duhl, pl. **knayd**-lakh /ˈkneɪdəl/, pl. /ˈkneɪdlax/
• Standard -s plural is also possible.

knawel weed
naw-uhl /ˈnɔːəl/

knell sound of a bell
nel /nɛl/

Knesset Israeli parliament
kness-et /ˈknɛsɛt/

Knightley, Keira English actress
keer-uh /ˈkɪərə/

kniphofia plant
nip-**hoh**-fi-uh /nɪpˈhəʊfiə/

knish dumpling
knish /knɪʃ/

Knole kind of sofa
nohl /nəʊl/

knoll small hill or mound
nohl /nəʊl/

Knorr food company
nor /nɔː(r)/

Knossos city, Crete
knoss-oss /ˈknɒsɒs/

knout whip
nowt /naʊt/

Knox, John Scottish Protestant reformer
noks /nɒks/

Knoxville port, US
noks-vil /ˈnɒksvɪl/

knur wooden or porcelain ball
nur /nə:(r)/

Knut see **Canute**

koa tree
koh-uh /ˈkəʊə/

koala Australian marsupial
koh-**ah**-luh /kəʊˈɑːlə/

koan paradoxical anecdote
koh-ahn /ˈkəʊɑːn/

Kobe port, Japan
koh-bi /ˈkəʊbi/, [koobe]
• Established anglicization.

København see **Copenhagen**

kobo currency unit, Nigeria
koh-boh /ˈkəʊbəʊ/

kobold spirit in German folklore
koh-buhld /ˈkəʊbəld/

Koch, Robert German bacteriologist
roh-bairt **kokh** /ˌrəʊbɛː(r)t ˈkɒx/

Köchel number given to each of Mozart's compositions
koe-khuhl /ˈkœçəl/

Kodály, Zoltán Hungarian composer
zol-tahn **koh**-dy /ˌzɒltɑːn ˈkəʊdʌɪ/

Kodiak island, Alaska
koh-di-ak /ˈkəʊdiak/

koel cuckoo
koh-uhl /ˈkəʊəl/

Koehler, Horst see **Köhler, Horst**

Koestler, Arthur Hungarian-born British novelist
koest-luhr /ˈkœstlə(r)/

kofta rissole
kof-tuh /ˈkɒftə/

Kohima city, India
koh-**hee**-muh /kəʊˈhiːmə/

Koh-i-noor Indian diamond
koh i **noor** /kəʊ i ˈnʊə(r)/

Kohl, Helmut German statesman
hel-moot kohl /ˌhɛlmuːt ˈkəʊl/

Köhler, Horst (also **Koehler**) German president
horst koe-luhr /ˌhɔː(r)st ˈkəːlə(r)/

kohlrabi cabbage
kohl-**rah**-bi /kəʊlˈrɑːbi/

Koh Samui island, Thailand
koh sam-**oo**-i /ˌkəʊ saˈmuːi/

koi carp
koy /kɔɪ/

koine Greek language
koy-nee /ˈkɔɪniː/

koinonia Christian fellowship
koy-**noh**-ni-uh /kɔɪˈnəʊniə/

Koizumi, Junichiro Japanese prime minister
joo-**nee**-chirr-oh **koy**-zoo-mi /dʒuːˌniːtʃɪrəʊ ˈkɔɪzuːmi/

Koje island, Korea
koh-jay /ˈkəʊdʒeɪ/

kokanee salmon
koh-kan-i /ˈkəʊkani/

Kola Peninsula peninsula, Russia
koh-luh /ˈkəʊlə/

Kolhapur city, India
kohl-hah-**poor** /ˌkəʊlhɑːˈpʊə(r)/

Kolkata city, India; formerly known as Calcutta
kol-**kut**-uh /kɒlˈkʌtə/, Bengali [ˈkolkata]
• Established anglicization.

kolkhoz collective farm in the former USSR
kol-**koz** /kɒlˈkɒz/, [kʌlˈxɔs]

Köln see **Cologne**

Kol Nidre Aramaic prayer
kol **need**-ray /ˌkɒl ˈniːdreɪ/

kolo Slavic dance
koh-loh /ˈkəʊləʊ/

Kolyma river, Siberia
kol-im-**ah** /ˌkɒlɪˈmɑː/

komatik sledge drawn by dogs
kom-uh-tik /ˈkɒmətɪk/

kombu Japanese seaweed
kom-boo /ˈkɒmbuː/

Komi autonomous republic, Russia
koh-mi /ˈkəʊmi/

Komodo island, Indonesia
kuh-**moh**-doh /kəˈməʊdəʊ/

Komondor breed of sheepdog
kom-uhn-dor /ˈkɒmənˌdɔː(r)/

Komsomol Soviet organization for communist youth
kom-suh-**mol** /kɒmsəˈmɒl/

Komsomolsk city, Russia
kom-suh-**molsk** /ˌkɒmsəˈmɒlsk/

koneke farm or logging wagon
kon-ek-i /ˈkɒnɛki/

konfyt fruit preserve
kon-**fayt** /kɒnˈfeɪt/

Kongo African ethnic group
kong-goh /ˈkɒŋgəʊ/

kongoni kind of hartebeest
kong-**goh**-ni /kɒŋˈgəʊni/

Königsberg former name for Kaliningrad
koe-nikhss-bairk /ˈkəːnɪçsbɛː(r)k/

Konigsberg, Alan Stewart real name of Woody Allen
koh-**nigz**-burg /ˈkəʊnɪgzbə:(r)g/

Konkani Indian language
konk-uh-ni /ˈkɒŋkəni/

Konstanz see **Constance**

Kon-Tiki Thor Heyerdahl's raft; also Inca god
kon-**tee**-ki /kɒnˈtiːki/

Konya city, Turkey
kon-yuh /ˈkɒnjə/

kookaburra Australasian kingfisher
kuuk-uh-burr-uh /ˈkʊkəˌbʌrə/

Kooning, Willem de see **de Kooning, Willem**

Koopman, Ton Dutch conductor
ton **kohp**-muhn /ˌtɒn ˈkəʊpmən/

Koori Australian Aboriginal
koor-i /ˈkʊəri/

kopek currency unit, Russia
koh-pek /ˈkəʊpɛk/

Kopernik, Mikołaj see **Copernicus, Nicolaus**

kora West African musical instrument
kaw-ruh /ˈkɔːrə/

koradji Aboriginal who has skills in traditional medicine
korr-uh-ji /'kɒrədʒi/

Koran (also **Quran** or **Qur'an**) Islamic sacred book
korr-**ahn** /kɒ'rɑːn/, Arabic [qur'ʔɑːn]
• Established anglicization; see **ARABIC** panel.

Korbut, Olga Soviet gymnast
ol-guh kor-**buut** /ˌɒlgə 'kɔː(r)bʊt/

Korchnoi, Viktor Russian chess player
veek-tuhr kortch-**noy** /ˌviːktə(r) kɔː(r)tʃ'nɔɪ/

Korda, Alexander Hungarian-born British film director
kor-duh /'kɔː(r)də/

Kordofan region, Sudan
kor-doh-**fahn** /ˌkɔː(r)dəʊ'fɑːn/

Kore Greek mythological character
kaw-ray /'kɔːreɪ/

Korea region, Asia
kuh-**ree**-uh /kə'riːə/
• Established anglicization.

korfball ball game
korf-bawl /'kɔː(r)fbɔːl/

Kórinthos see **Corinth**

korma Indian curry dish
kor-muh /'kɔː(r)mə/

Korsakoff's syndrome mental illness
kor-suh-kofs /'kɔː(r)səkɒfs/

Kortrijk city, Belgium
kort-ryk /'kɔː(r)trʌɪk/
• See **DUTCH** panel.

koru motif in Maori carving
korr-oo /'kɒruː/

koruna currency unit, Czech Republic and Slovakia
korr-uun-uh /'kɒrʊnə/

Korup national park, Cameroon
korr-oop /kɒ'ruːp/

Koryak Russian ethnic group
kuhr-**yahk** /kə(r)'jɑːk/

Kos (also **Cos**) island, Greece
koss /kɒs/

Kosciusko, Mount mountain, Australia
koz-i-**usk**-oh /ˌkɒzɪ'ʌskəʊ/

kosher satisfying the requirements of Jewish law
koh-shuhr /'kəʊʃə(r)/

Košice city, Slovakia
kosh-it-suh /'kɒʃɪtsə/

Kosovo autonomous province, Serbia

koss-uh-voh /'kɒsəvəʊ/

Kossuth, Lajos Hungarian statesman and patriot
loy-osh kosh-**oot** /ˌlɔɪɒʃ 'kɒʃuːt/

Kostroma city, Russia
kost-ruh-**mah** /ˌkɒstrə'mɑː/

Koštunica, Vojislav Serbian prime minister
voy-iss-laf kosh-**too**-nit-suh /ˌvɔɪɪslaf kɒʃ'tuːnɪtsə/

Kosygin, Aleksei Soviet statesman
al-uhk-**say** kuh-**see**-gin /aləkˌseɪ kə'siːgɪn/

Kota city, India
koh-tuh /'kəʊtə/

Kota Baharu city, Malaysia
koh-tuh buh-**har**-oo /ˌkəʊtə bə'hɑːruː/

Kota Kinabalu port, Malaysia
koh-tuh kin-uh-bah-**loo** /ˌkəʊtə kɪnəˈbɑːluː/

Kotka port, Finland
kot-kuh /'kɒtkə/

koto Japanese musical instrument
koh-toh /'kəʊtəʊ/

Kotzebue, August von German dramatist
ow-guust fon **kot**-suh-boo /ˌaʊgʊst fɒn 'kɒtsəbuː/

koumiss fermented liquor
koo-miss /'kuːmɪs/

kouprey breed of ox
koo-pray /'kuːpreɪ/

Kournikova, Anna Russian tennis player
kor-nik-**oh**-vuh /kɔː(r)nɪ'kəʊvə/, [ˈkurnʲɪkəvə]
• Established anglicization.

kouros pl. **kouroi** ancient Greek statue of a young man
koo-ross, pl. **koo**-roy /'kuːrɒs/, pl. /-rɔɪ/

Kourou town, French Guiana
kuu-**roo** /kʊ'ruː/

kowari marsupial
kuh-**war**-i /kə'wɑːri/

Kowloon peninsula, China
kow-**loon** /ˌkaʊ'luːn/

kowtow act in a subservient manner
kow-**tow** /kaʊ'taʊ/

Kra, Isthmus of part of the Malay Peninsula
krah /krɑː/

kraal traditional African village of huts
krahl /krɑ:l/

Krafft-Ebing, Richard von German
physician and psychologist
rikh-art fon kraft ay-bing /ˌrɪçɑː(r)t
fɒn ˌkraft ˈeɪbɪŋ/

Kragujevac city, Serbia
krag-uu-yuh-vats /ˈkraɡʊjəˌvats/

krai administrative territory of Russia
kry /krʌɪ/

krait venomous Asian snake
kryt /krʌɪt/

Krajiček, Richard Dutch tennis player
kry-chek /ˈkrʌɪtʃɛk/
• Established anglicization.

Krakatoa volcanic island, Indonesia
/ˌkrakəˈtəʊə/

kraken mythical sea monster
krah-kuhn /ˈkrɑːkən/

Kraków see **Cracow**

Krall, Diana Canadian singer
krawl /krɔ:l/

Krapina town, Croatia
krah-pin-uh /ˈkrɑːpɪnə/

Krasnodar region, northern Caucasus
krass-nuh-dar /ˌkrasnəˈdɑː(r)/

Krasnoyarsk region, Russia
krass-nuh-yarsk /ˌkrasnəˈjɑː(r)sk/

Kraszewski, Józef Ignacy Polish
writer
yoo-zef ig-nat-si krash-ef-ski /ˈjuːzɛf
ɪɡˌnatsi kraˈʃɛfski/

Krause, Peter American actor
krow-zuh /ˈkraʊzə/

Krauss, Alison American singer
krowss /kraʊs/

Kraut derogatory term for a German
krowt /kraʊt/

Krav Maga Israeli form of self-defence
and physical training
krahv mah-guh /ˌkrɑːv ˈmɑːɡə/

Krefeld town, Germany
kray-felt /ˈkreɪfɛlt/

Kreisler, Fritz Austrian-born American
violinist and composer
frits kryss-luhr /ˌfrɪts ˈkrʌɪslə(r)/

Kremenchuk city, Ukraine
krem-uhn-chook /ˌkrɛmənˈtʃuːk/

kremlin citadel within a Russian town
krem-lin /ˈkrɛmlɪn/

kreplach noodles filled with meat or
cheese
krep-lahkh /ˈkrɛplɑːx/

Kriemhild Burgundian princess
kreem-hilt /ˈkriːmhɪlt/

Krio creole language of Sierra Leone
kree-oh /ˈkriːəʊ/

kris Malay or Indonesian dagger
kreess /kriːs/

Krishna Hindu god
krish-nuh /ˈkrɪʃnə/

Kristallnacht violence by Nazis against
Jews on the night of 9-10 November
1938
krist-al-nakht /krɪsˈtalnaxt/

Kristiansand port, Norway
krist-yan-san /krɪstjanˈsan/

Kriti see **Crete**

kromesky Polish dish
kruh-mesk-i /krəˈmɛski/

krona currency unit, Sweden
kroh-nuh /ˈkrəʊnə/, [ˈkruːna]
• Established anglicization.

krone currency unit, Denmark and
Norway
kroh-nuh /ˈkrəʊnə/, Danish [ˈkroːnə],
Norwegian [ˈkruːnə]
• Established anglicization.

Kronos see **Cronus**

Kropotkin, Prince Russian anarchist
kruh-pot-kin /krəˈpɒtkɪn/

Kroto, Harry English chemist
kroh-toh /ˈkrəʊtəʊ/

Kru West African ethnic group
kroo /kruː/

krummhorn medieval wind instrument
kruum-horn /ˈkrʊmhɔː(r)n/

Krupp, Alfred German arms
manufacturer
al-frayt kruup /ˌalfreɪt ˈkrʊp/

Krym see **Crimea**

krypton chemical element
krip-ton /ˈkrɪptɒn/

Kryvy Rih city, Ukraine
kriv-ee reekh /krɪˌviː ˈriːx/

Kshatriya Hindu caste
kshat-ri-uh /ˈkʃatrɪə/

Kuala Lumpur capital of Malaysia
kwah-luh luump-oor /ˌkwɑːlə
ˈlʊmpʊə(r)/

Kuala Trengganu city, Malaysia
kwah-luh truhng-**gan**-oo /ˌkwɑːlə trəŋˈɡanuː/

Kuantan city, Malaysia
kwahn-**tahn** /kwɑːnˈtɑːn/

Kuan Yin Buddhist goddess
kwahn yin /ˌkwɑːn ˈjɪn/

Kublai Khan Mongol emperor
koob-ly **kahn** /ˌkuːblʌɪ ˈkɑːn/

Kubrick, Stanley American film director
kyoo-brik /ˈkjuːbrɪk/

kuchen German cake
koo-khuhn /ˈkuːxən/

Kuching port, Malaysia
koo-ching /ˈkuːtʃɪŋ/

kudos praise and honour received for an achievement
kyoo-doss /ˈkjuːdɒs/

kudu African antelope
koo-doo /ˈkuːduː/

Kufic early form of the Arabic alphabet
kyoo-fik /ˈkjuːfɪk/

kugel Jewish savoury pudding
koo-guhl /ˈkuːɡəl/

Kuiper belt region of the solar system
ky-puhr /ˈkʌɪpə(r)/

Ku Klux Klan American extremist right-wing secret society
koo kluks **klan** /ˌkuː klʌks ˈklan/

kukri curved knife
kuuk-ri /ˈkʊkri/

kulak Russian peasant
koo-lak /ˈkuːlak/

kulcha Indian bread
kuul-chuh /ˈkʊltʃə/

kulfi Indian ice cream
kuul-fi /ˈkʊlfi/

kultarr marsupial mouse
kuul-tar /ˈkʊltɑː(r)/

Kultur German civilization and culture
kuul-**toor** /kʊlˈtʊə(r)/

Kum see **Qom**

Kumamoto city, Japan
koo-muh-**moh**-toh /ˌkuːməˈməʊtəʊ/

kumara sweet potato
koom-uh-ruh /ˈkuːmərə/

Kumasi city, Ghana
koo-**mass**-i /kuːˈmasi/

Kumbh Mela Hindu festival
kuumb **may**-luh /ˌkʊmb ˈmeɪlə/

Kumina Jamaican religious ceremony
kum-ee-nuh /ˈkʌmiːnə/

kumite freestyle fighting
koo-mit-ay /ˈkuːmɪteɪ/

kumkum red pigment
kuum-kuum /ˈkʊmkʊm/

kümmel liqueur
kuum-uhl /ˈkʊməl/, German [ˈkʏməl]

kumquat fruit
kum-kwot /ˈkʌmkwɒt/

Kuna American Indian ethnic group
koo-nuh /ˈkuːnə/

kuna currency unit, Croatia
koo-nuh /ˈkuːnə/

Kundera, Milan Czech novelist
mil-uhn **kuun**-derr-uh /ˌmɪlən ˈkʊndɛrə/

Kunduz city, Afghanistan
kuun-**dooz** /kʊnˈduːz/

Kung southern African ethnic group and language
kuung /kʊŋ/
• Established anglicization.

kung fu Chinese martial art
kung **foo** /ˌkʌŋ ˈfuː/

A pronunciation closer to the Chinese, kuung **foo**, is also sometimes heard.

Kunlun Shan range of mountains, China
kuun-luun **shahn** /ˌkʊnlʊn ˈʃɑːn/

Kunming city, China
kuun-**ming** /kʊnˈmɪŋ/

Kuomintang Chinese political party
kwoh-min-**tang** /ˌkwəʊmɪnˈtaŋ/

Kuopio city, Finland
koo-op-i-oh /ˈkuːɒpiəʊ/

Kurd Kurdish ethnic group
kurd /kəː(r)d/

Kurdish relating to the Kurds
kur-dish /ˈkəː(r)dɪʃ/

Kurdistan region, Middle East
kur-dist-**ahn** /ˌkəː(r)dɪˈstɑːn/

Kure city, Japan
koor-ay /ˈkʊəreɪ/

Kureishi, Hanif English writer
huh-**neef** kuu-**ray**-shi /həˌniːf kʊˈreɪʃi/

Kurgan city, Russia
koor-**gahn** /kʊə(r)ˈɡɑːn/

Kurile Islands islands, Pacific Ocean
kuu-**reel** /kʊˈriːl/

Kurosawa, Akira Japanese film director
ah-kirr-uh kuu-ruh-**sah**-wuh /ˌɑːkɪrə ˌkʊrəˈsɑːwə/

Kuroshio warm current, Pacific Ocean
kuu-ruh-**shee**-oh /ˌkʊrəˈʃiːəʊ/

Kursk city, Russia
koorsk /kʊə(r)sk/

Kurtág, György Hungarian composer
joerj koor-tahg /ˌdʒœ(r)dʒ ˈkʊə(r)tɑːg/

kuru degenerative disease of the brain
kuu-roo /ˈkʊruː/

Kuşadası town, Turkey
koosh-ah-dah-suh /ˈkuːʃɑːˌdɑːsə/

Kushan Iranian dynasty
kuush-ahn /ˈkʊʃɑːn/

Kut, al- town, Iraq
uhl kuut /əl ˈkʊt/

Kutaisi city, Georgia
koo-tuh-**ee**-si /ˌkuːtəˈiːsi/

Kutani kind of Japanese porcelain
kuut-ah-ni /kʊˈtɑːni/

Kutch, Gulf of inlet of the Arabian Sea
kutch /kʌtʃ/

Kuwait country
koo-**wayt** /kuːˈweɪt/

A more anglicized pronunciation, kyoo-**wayt**, is sometimes also heard.

Kuznets Basin region, Russia
kuuz-**nyets** /kʊzˈnjɛts/

kvass fermented drink
kvass /kvas/

Kwa African language group
kwah /kwɑː/

kwacha currency unit, Zambia and Malawi
kwah-chuh /ˈkwɑːtʃə/

kwaito South African style of popular music
kwy-toh /ˈkwʌɪtəʊ/

Kwakiutl American Indian ethnic group
kwah-ki-**oo**-tuhl /kwɑːkiˈuːtəl/

Kwangju city, South Korea
kwang-joo /kwaŋˈdʒuː/

kwanza currency unit, Angola
kwan-zuh /ˈkwanzə/

Kwanzaa African American festival
kwan-zah /ˈkwanzɑː/

kwashiorkor form of malnutrition
kwosh-i-**or**-kor /ˌkwɒʃiˈɔː(r)kɔː(r)/

kwela central and southern African style of popular music
kway-luh /ˈkweɪlə/

kyat currency unit, Burma
kee-aht /kiːˈɑːt/

kylin Chinese mythical animal
kee-lin /ˈkiːlɪn/

kylix ancient Greek cup
ky-liks /ˈkʌɪlɪks/

Kyoto city, Japan
kyoh-toh /ˈkjəʊtəʊ/

kyphosis curvature of the spine
ky-**foh**-siss /kʌɪˈfəʊsɪs/

Kyrgyz relating to Kyrgyzstan
kur-giz /ˈkə:(r)gɪz/

Sometimes also keer-giz.

Kyrgyzstan country
kur-gist-**ahn** /ˌkə:(r)gɪˈstɑːn/

Established anglicization; sometimes also keer-gist-**ahn**.

Kyrie Eleison section of the Mass
keer-i-ay el-**ay**-iss-on /ˌkɪərieɪ ɛˈleɪɪsɒn/

Kyushu island, Japan
kyoo-shoo /ˈkjuːʃuː/

Kyzyl city, Russia
kuh-**zil** /kəˈzɪl/

Kyzyl Kum desert region, central Asia
kuh-**zil** koom /kəˌzɪl ˈkuːm/

L

laager encampment
lah-guhr /'lɑːɡə(r)/

Laâyoune capital of Western Sahara
lah-**yoon** /lɑː'juːn/

Established anglicization. The Arabic name is El Aaiún, pronounced uhl y-**oon**.

Laban, Rudolf von Hungarian choreographer
roo-dolf fon **lah**-buhn /ˌruːdɒlf fɒn 'lɑːbən/

However, *labanotation* (a system of dance notation which he devised) is usually pronounced lay-buh-noh-**tay**-shuhn.

labia majora outer folds of the vulva
lay-bi-uh muh-**jaw**-ruh /ˌleɪbiə məˈdʒɔːrə/

labia minora inner folds of the vulva
lay-bi-uh min-**aw**-ruh /ˌleɪbiə mɪˈnɔːrə/

La Bohème opera by Puccini
lah boh-**em** /lɑː bəʊˈɛm/

laboratory room equipped for scientific experiments
luh-**borr**-uh-tuh-ri /ləˈbɒrəˌtəri/

Commonly also luh-**borr**-uh-tri. The AM pronunciation, and an alternative older BR pronunciation, is **lab**-ruh-tri.

Labrador breed of dog
lab-ruh-dor /'labrədɔː(r)/

The same pronunciation is used for a region of Canada of the same name.

La Brea tar pits in Los Angeles, US
luh **bray**-uh /lə ˈbreɪə/

The same pronunciation is used for a town in Trinidad of the same name.

labret lip ornament or piercing
lay-bruht /'leɪbrət/

La Bruyère, Jean de French writer
zhah(ng) duh lah brue-**yair** /ˌʒɑ̃ də ˌlɑː bryˈjɛː(r)/

Labuan island, Malaysia
luh-**boo**-uhn /ləˈbuːən/, [labuan]
• Established anglicization.

labyrinthine like a labyrinth
lab-uh-**rinth**-yn /ˌlabəˈrɪnθʌɪn/

Lacan, Jacques French psychoanalyst
zhahk lak-**ah(ng)** /ˌʒɑːk laˈkɑ̃/

Laccadive Islands islands, India
lak-uh-dyv /'lakədʌɪv/

Lacedaemon area of ancient Greece
lass-id-**ee**-mon /ˌlasɪˈdiːmɒn/

La Ceiba port, Honduras
lah **say**-buh /lɑː ˈseɪbə/

La Cenerentola opera by Rossini
lah chen-ay-**rent**-ol-uh /lɑː tʃɛneɪˈrɛntɒlə/

lacertid lizard
luh-**sur**-tid /ləˈsəː(r)tɪd/

laches unreasonable delay in asserting a claim
latch-uhz /'latʃəz/

Lachesis Greek mythological character
lak-iss-iss /'lakɪsɪs/

Lachlan river, Australia
lak-luhn /'laklən/

lachrymose weepy
lak-rim-ohss /'lakrɪməʊs/

lackadaisical lacking enthusiasm and determination
lak-uh-**day**-zik-uhl /ˌlakəˈdeɪzɪkəl/

Lac Léman French name for Lake Geneva
lak lem-**ah(ng)** /lak lɛˈmɑ̃/

La Clemenza di Tito opera by Mozart
lah klay-**ment**-suh dee **tee**-toh /lɑː kleɪˌmɛntsə diː ˈtiːtəʊ/

Laclos, Pierre Choderlos de French novelist
pyair shod-air-**loh** duh lak-**loh** /ˌpjɛː(r) ʃɒdɛː(r)ˌləʊ də laˈkləʊ/

Laconia ancient region, Greece
luh-**koh**-ni-uh /ləˈkəʊniə/

laconic using very few words
luh-**kon**-ik /ləˈkɒnɪk/

La Coruña see **Corunna**

lactose sugar present in milk
lak-tohz /'laktəʊz/

lacuna pl. **lacunae** gap
luh-**kyoo**-nuh, pl. luh-**kyoo**-nee
/lə'kjuːnə/, pl. /-niː/

Also lak-**oo**-nuh; see LATIN panel.

Ladakh region, India, Pakistan, and China
luh-**dahk** /lə'dɑːk/

Ladefoged, Peter English phonetician
lad-uh-**foh**-guhd /'ladəfəʊgəd/

Laden, Osama Bin see **Bin Laden, Osama**

Ladin Rhaeto-Romance dialect
luh-**deen** /lə'diːn/

Ladino language of some Sephardic Jews
luh-**dee**-noh /lə'diːnəʊ/

Ladoga lake, Russia
lah-duh-guh /'lɑːdəgə/

La donna è mobile aria by Verdi
lah **don**-uh ay **moh**-bee-lay /lɑː ˌdɒnə eɪ 'məʊbiːleɪ/

Lae port, Papua New Guinea
lay /leɪ/

Laennec's cirrhosis liver disease
luh-**en**-eks sirr-**oh**-siss /ləˌɛnɛks sɪ'rəʊsɪs/

Lafayette, Marquis de French soldier and statesman
mar-**kee** duh laf-y-**et** /mɑː(r)ˌkiː də ˌlafʌɪ'ɛt/

La Fontaine, Jean de French poet
zhah(ng) duh laf-o(ng)-**ten** /ˌʒɑ̃ də ˌla fɔ̃'tɛn/

La Forza del Destino opera by Verdi
lah **fort**-suh del dest-**ee**-noh /lɑː ˌfɒ(r)tsə dɛl dɛ'stiːnəʊ/

Lag b'Omer Jewish festival
lahg boh-muhr /ˌlɑːg 'bəʊmə(r)/

Lagerlöf, Selma Swedish novelist
sel-muh **lah**-guhr-loev /ˌsɛlmə 'lɑːgə(r)ləːv/

laggard person who makes slow progress
lag-uhrd /'lagə(r)d/

La Gioconda another name for **Mona Lisa**
lah jok-**on**-duh /ˌlɑː dʒɒ'kɒndə/

Lagos city, Nigeria
lay-goss /'leɪgɒs/

Lagos city, Portugal
lah-guush /'lɑːgʊʃ/

Lagos, Ricardo Chilean statesman

ree-**kar**-doh lag-**oss** /riːˌkɑː(r)dəʊ 'lagɒs/

• See SPANISH panel.

Lagrange, Comte de Italian-French mathematician
ko(ng)t duh lag-**rah(ng)zh** /ˌkɔ̃t də la'grɑ̃ʒ/

La Guardia airport, US
lah **gwar**-di-uh /lɑː 'gwɑː(r)diə/

lahar destructive mudflow
lah-har /'lɑːhɑː(r)/

Lahnda language
lahn-duh /'lɑːndə/

Lahore city, Pakistan
luh-**hor** /lə'hɔː(r)/

Lahoud, Emile Lebanese president
ay-meel lah-**hood** /ˌeɪmiːl lɑː'huːd/

Laing, R. D. Scottish psychiatrist
lang /laŋ/

Not all people with this surname pronounce it in this way; for instance, the English construction company Laing use the pronunciation layng.

laissez-faire policy of leaving things to take their own course
less-ay **fair** /ˌlɛseɪ 'fɛː(r)/

laity lay people
lay-it-i /'leɪɪti/

Laius Greek mythological character
ly-uhss /'lʌɪəs/

La Jolla resort, US
lah **hoy**-uh /lɑː 'hɔɪjə/

laksa Malaysian noodle dish
lahk-suh /'lɑːksə/

Lakshadweep islands, India
luk-shud-**weep** /ˌlʌkʃʌd'wiːp/

Lakshmi Hindu goddess
luksh-mi /'lʌkʃmi/

Lalique, René French jeweller
ruh-**nay** lal-**eek** /rəˌneɪ la'liːk/

Lallans Scottish literary form of English
lal-uhnz /'lalənz/

La Louvière city, Belgium
lah loov-**yair** /ˌla luː'vjɛː(r)/

lama Buddhist spiritual leader
lah-muh /'lɑːmə/

Lamartine, Alphonse de French poet and historian
al-**fo(ng)ss** duh lam-ar-**teen** /alˌfɔ̃s də ˌlamɑː(r)'tiːn/

Lamaze method of childbirth
luh-**mahz** /lə'mɑ:z/
• Established anglicization.

lambada dance
lam-**bah**-duh /lam'bɑ:də/

lambda letter of the Greek alphabet
lam-duh /'lamdə/

lambrequin drapery over a door
lam-bruh-kin /'lambrəkɪn/

Lambrusco wine grape
lam-**bruusk**-oh /lam'bruskəʊ/

lamé fabric with interwoven gold or silver
threads
lah-may /'lɑ:meɪ/

lamella pl. **lamellae** thin layer
luh-**mel**-uh, pl. luh-**mel**-ee /lə'mɛlə/,
pl. /-li:/

lamentable very bad
lam-uhn-tuh-buhl /'lamntəbəl/

Less commonly also luh-**men**-tuh-buhl.

lamington Australian sponge cake
lam-ing-tuhn /'lamɪŋtən/

Lammas first day of August
lam-uhss /'laməs/

lammergeier (also **lammergeyer**)
vulture
lam-uhr-gy-uhr /'lamə(r),gʌɪə(r)/

Lamont, Norman English politician
luh-**mont** /lə'mɒnt/

This surname is generally pronounced in
this way in England and Ireland, but usually
as **lam**-uhnt in Scotland.

Lampedusa, Giuseppe Tomasi de
Italian novelist
juuz-**ep**-ay tom-**ah**-zi day
lam-ped-**oo**-zuh /dʒu,zɛpeɪ tɒ,mɑ:zi deɪ
,lampɛ'du:zə/

Lampeter town, Wales
lamp-uh-tuhr /'lampətə(r)/

lamprey eel-like vertebrate
lamp-ri /'lampri/

Lamy, Pascal French European
Commissioner
pask-**al** lam-**ee** /pa,skal la'mi:/

Lanarkshire former county, Scotland
lan-uhrk-shuhr /'lanə(r)kʃə(r)/

Lancaster town, England
lank-ast-uhr /'laŋkastə(r)/

Lancelot mythological character, one of
Arthur's knights
lahn-suh-lot /'lɑ:nsəlɒt/

Land pl. **Länder** German province
lant, pl. **lend**-uhr /lant/, pl. /'lɛndə(r)/

Landau, Lev Soviet theoretical physicist
lyef lan-**dow** /,ljɛf lan'daʊ/

landau horse-drawn carriage
land-aw /'landɔ:/

ländler Austrian folk dance
lend-luhr /'lɛndlə(r)/

Landseer, Edwin English painter
land-seer /'landsɪə(r)/

Landshut city, Germany
lants-hoot /'lantshu:t/

langar communal free kitchen
lung-guhr /'lʌŋgə(r)/

Lange, Jessica American actress
lang /laŋ/

Langland, William English poet
lang-luhnd /'laŋlənd/

langlauf cross-country skiing
lang-lowf /'laŋlaʊf/

langoustine crustacean
long-guust-een /'lɒŋgʊsti:n/

Langtry, Lillie English actress
lang-tri /'laŋtri/

langue de chat thin biscuit
lo(ng)g duh **shah** /,lõg də 'ʃɑ:/, French
[lɑ̃:g də ʃa]

langue d'oc form of medieval French
spoken south of the Loire
lah(ng)g dok /,lɑ̃g 'dɒk/

langue d'oïl form of medieval French
spoken north of the Loire
lah(ng)g doyl /,lɑ̃g 'dɔɪl/

Languedoc-Roussillon region, France
lah(ng)g-dok roo-si-**yo(ng)** /lɑ̃g,dɒk
ru:si'jõ/

languor tiredness or inactivity
lang-guhr /'laŋgə(r)/

La Niña cool stream in the Pacific
lah **neen**-yuh /lɑ: 'ni:njə/

Lansing city, US
lan-sing /'lansɪŋ/

lansquenet gambling game
lan-skuh-net /'lanskə,nɛt/

lantana shrub
lan-**tah**-nuh /lan'tɑ:nə/

Lantau island, Hong Kong
lan-**tow** /lan'taʊ/

lanthanum chemical element
lan-thuh-nuhm /'lanθənəm/

lanugo fine hair on the body
luh-**nyoo**-goh /ləˈnjuːgəʊ/

lanyard rope
lan-yuhrd /ˈlanjə(r)d/

Lanzarote island, Spain
lan-zuh-**rot**-i /ˌlanzəˈrɒti/, [lanθaˈrote]
• Established anglicization.

Lanzhou city, China
lan-**joh** /ˌlanˈdʒəʊ/

Laocoön Greek mythological character
lay-**ok**-oh-on /leɪˈɒkəʊɒn/

Laodicean half-hearted or indifferent
lay-oh-**diss**-i-uhn /ˌleɪəʊdɪˈsiən/

laogai Chinese labour camps
low-**gy** /laʊˈɡʌɪ/

Laois (also **Laoighis**, **Leix**) county,
Republic of Ireland
leesh /liːʃ/

Laos country
lah-oss /ˈlɑːɒs/

Less commonly also lowss, and in AM
commonly **lay**-oss.

Laotian relating to Laos
low-**shuhn** /ˈlaʊʃən/

Commonly also laa-**oh**-shuhn, and in AM
lay-**oh**-shuhn.

Lao-tzu Chinese philosopher
low **tsoo** /laʊ ˈtsuː/

laparoscopy surgical procedure
lap-uh-**rosk**-uh-pi /ˌlapəˈrɒskəpi/

La Paz capital of Bolivia
lah **pass** /lɑː ˈpas/

Laphroaig whisky distillery, Scotland
luh-**froyg** /ləˈfrɔɪɡ/

lapidary relating to stones and gems
lap-id-uh-ri /ˈlapɪdəri/

lapis lazuli bright blue rock
lap-iss **laz**-yuul-i /ˌlapɪs ˈlazjʊli/

Laplace, Marquis de French
mathematician
mar-**kee** duh lap-**lass** /mɑː(r)ˈkiː də
laˈplas/

Lapland region, Europe
lap-land /ˈlapland/

La Plata port, Argentina
lah **plat**-uh /lɑː ˈplatə/

lapsang souchong variety of tea
lap-sang **soo**-shong /ˌlapsaŋ ˈsuːʃɒŋ/

lapsus linguae slip of the tongue
lap-suhss **ling**-gwy /ˌlapsəs ˈlɪŋɡwʌɪ/

Laptev Sea part of the Arctic Ocean
lap-tef /ˈlaptɛf/

Lara, Brian West Indian cricketer
lar-uh /ˈlɑːrə/

Laramie city, US
larr-uh-mi /ˈlarəmi/

larceny theft
lar-suh-ni /ˈlɑː(r)səni/

Laredo city, Texas
luh-**ray**-doh /ləˈreɪdəʊ/

lares Roman household gods
lah-reez /ˈlɑːriːz/

largesse generosity
lar-**zhess** /lɑː(r)ˈʒɛs/

largo musical term
lar-goh /ˈlɑː(r)ɡəʊ/

lari currency unit, Georgia
lar-ee /ˈlɑːriː/

lariat rope used as a lasso
larr-i-uht /ˈlariət/

Larissa city, Greece
luh-**riss**-uh /ləˈrɪsə/

Larnaca (also **Larnaka**) town, Cyprus
lar-nuh-kuh /ˈlɑː(r)nəkə/

La Rochefoucauld, Duc François de
French writer and moralist
duek frah(ng)-**swah** duh lah
rosh-foo-**koh** /ˌdyk frɑ̃ˌswaː də lɑː
rɒʃfuːˈkəʊ/

La Rochelle port, France
lah rosh-**el** /ˌla rɒˈʃɛl/

Larousse, Pierre French lexicographer
pyair larr-**ooss** /ˌpjɛː(r) laˈruːs/

larrup thrash or whip
larr-uhp /ˈlarəp/

Lars Porsenna legendary Etruscan
chieftain; also called **Lars Porsena**
larss por-**sen**-uh /ˌlɑː(r)s pɔː(r)ˈsɛnə/

larva pl. **larvae** immature form of an
insect
lar-vuh, pl. **lar**-vee /ˈlɑː(r)və/, pl. /-viː/

laryngeal relating to the larynx
luh-**rin**-juhl /ləˈrɪndʒəl/

laryngology branch of medicine that
deals with the larynx
larr-in-**gol**-uh-ji /ˌlarɪŋˈɡɒlədʒi/

larynx pl. **larynges** organ holding the
vocal cords
larr-inks, pl. luh-**rin**-jeez /ˈlarɪŋks/, pl.
/ləˈrɪndʒiːz/

lasagne pasta in the form of sheets
luh-**san**-yuh /lə'sanjə/

La Scala opera house, Milan
lah **skah**-luh /lɑː 'skɑːlə/

Lascaux site of a cave, France
lask-**oh** /la'skəʊ/

LASIK corrective eye surgery
lay-zik /'leɪzɪk/

Las Palmas port, Spain
lass **pal**-mass /las 'palmas/

La Spezia port, Italy
lah **spayt**-syuh /lɑː 'speɪtsjə/

Lassa fever viral disease
lass-uh /'lasə/

lassi Indian yogurt drink
lass-i /'lasi/

lasso rope with a noose at one end
luh-**soo** /lə'suː/

Lassus, Orlando de Flemish composer
or-**land**-oh duh **lass**-uhss /ɔː(r),landəʊ
də 'lasəs/

Las Vegas city, US
lass **vay**-guhss /las 'veɪgəs/

Latakia port, Syria
lat-uh-**kee**-uh /,latə'kiːə/

lateen triangular sail
lat-**een** /la'tiːn/

Lateran site in Rome
lat-uh-ruhn /'latərən/

latex milky fluid found in many plants
lay-teks /'leɪtɛks/

LaTeX computer typesetting program
lay-tek /'leɪtɛk/

The final X represents the Greek letter CHI,
hence this pronunciation.

lathe machine for shaping wood
lay*th* /leɪð/

Latino Latin American inhabitant of the
United States
lat-**ee**-noh /la'tiːnəʊ/

Female form is Latina, pronounced
lat-**ee**-nuh.

latke potato pancake
lut-kuh /'lʌtkə/

La Tour, Georges de French painter
zhorzh duh lah **toor** /,ʒɔː(r)ʒ də lɑː
'tʊə(r)/

La Traviata opera by Verdi
lah trav-i-**ah**-tuh /lɑː travi'ɑːtə/

La Trobe university, Australia

luh **trohb** /lə 'trəʊb/

latte milky coffee drink
lat-ay /'lateɪ/, Italian ['latte]

The pronunciation **lah**-tay is widespread
especially in AM, but deprecated because it
is felt to be less like the Italian
pronunciation.

Latvia country
lat-vi-uh /'latviə/

Laud, William English prelate
lawd /lɔːd/

Lauda, Niki Austrian motor-racing
driver
nik-i **low**-duh /,nɪki 'laʊdə/

laudanum narcotic painkiller
law-duh-nuhm /'lɔːdənəm/

Laudate Dominum part of the mass
low-**dah**-tay **dom**-in-uum /laʊ,dɑːteɪ
'dɒmɪnʊm/

laudatory expressing praise and
commendation
law-duh-tuh-ri /'lɔːdətəri/

Lauder, Harry Scottish music-hall
comedian
law-duhr /'lɔːdə(r)/

Laughton, Charles British-American
actor
law-tuhn /'lɔːtən/

launce sand eel
lahnss /lɑːns/

Launceston city, Tasmania
lawn-suh-stuhn /'lɔːnsəstən/

Launceston town, England
lawn-suhn /'lɔːnsən/

laureate person honoured with an award
lorr-i-uht /'lɒriət/

Laurier, Wilfrid Canadian statesman
law-ri-ay /'lɔːrieɪ/

Lauren, Ralph American fashion
designer
lorr-uhn /'lɒrən/

Lausanne town, Switzerland
loh-**zan** /ləʊ'zan/

lavage washing out of a body cavity
lav-ij /'lavɪdʒ/

Also luh-**vahzh**, especially in AM.

Laver, Rod Australian tennis player
lay-vuhr /'leɪvə(r)/

laver edible seaweed
lah-vuhr /'lɑːvə(r)/

Latin

Latin is an ancient language originally spoken in the Roman Empire. Despite being thought of as 'dead', Latin is spoken all the time in English contexts. Many Latin words and phrases are used in legal and medical language. There are also many more general words and phrases such as *ad hoc*, *curriculum vitae*, and *reductio ad absurdum*. English speakers may wish to know how to pronounce the Latin words to prayers, poems, or music, or perhaps botanical and zoological names.

Various systems are used today for the pronunciation of Latin. Rather than always insisting on one particular system, we feel that three different systems are appropriate for different contexts, and advise our broadcasters accordingly. Firstly, there is reconstructed classical Latin, the pronunciation taught to students of the language and as close as we can get to the way the ancient Romans spoke. Julius Caesar's famous phrase *veni, vidi, vici* was, according to the classical system, pronounced **way**-ni, **wee**-di, **wee**-ki, and his own name as **yoo**-li-uuss **ky**-sahr. Secondly, there is ecclesiastical Latin, as used by the Catholic Church. This is greatly influenced by Italian and is generally the pronunciation favoured, for example, by choirs singing in Latin. (There are small variations from country to country in the exact pronunciation of ecclesiastical Latin.) Thirdly, there is anglicized Latin, which might anachronistically be termed 'schoolboy Latin'. These are the traditional pronunciations no longer taught in schools but used for Latin which has become assimilated into English. This is generally the best system to use for words and phrases in common use and those which relate to the fields of medicine, botany, and the law.

However, even within specialist fields, there is a good deal of variation as to which pronunciation system is preferred, so no one pronounciation can be considered definitively correct. The treatment of the sequence CC is one example. *Occipito-* is pronounced ok-**sip**-it-oh and, according to the same system, *cocci* (as in e.g. *streptococci*) would be pronounced **kok**-sy. However, it is commonly also pronounced **kok**-y (perhaps because the singular form is *coccus*, always pronounced **kok**-uhss).

Consonants

In classical Latin C is always pronounced k, G is always g, and T is t, whichever vowel follows. S is always s. J (classically spelled I) is y as in *yes*, and V is w. H is pronounced.

In ecclesiastical Latin several consonants are as in classical Latin before A, O, and U, but change before I, E, Æ, and Œ. C becomes ch,

G becomes j, and SC (as in *ascendit* or *suscipe*) becomes sh. TI (as in *gratias*) is pronounced ts. The sequence GN (as in *agnus Dei*) is pronounced ny. S becomes z between vowels. V is pronounced v, although J is still y as in *yes*. H is silent.

In anglicized Latin G, V, and S are pronounced as in ecclesiastical Latin. C becomes s rather than ch before I, E, Æ, and Œ, although CI becomes sh in suffixes, as does TI (e.g. *Portia*). J is pronounced j. H is pronounced.

Vowels

Latin has a five-vowel system, and vowels can be either long or short. Long vowels are usually written with a macron (ā). The vowel pronunciations of classical and ecclesiastical Latin are broadly the same. A is pronounced a if short, ah if long; E is e if short, ay if long; I is i if short or ee if long, O is o if short or oh if long, and U (classically spelled V) is uu if short or oo if long. Anglicized Latin, however, pronounces the long vowels differently. Long A is ay, long E is ee, long I is y as in *cry*, long O is oh, and long U is yoo. Therefore *pater* is pronounced **pay**-tuhr not **pah**-tair, and *vagina* is vuh-**jy**-nuh not wag-**ee**-na.

In classical Latin diphthongs can be thought of as sequences of their component parts: AU is ow, EU is **ay**-oo, EI is ay, AI and Æ are y as in *cry*, and OI and Œ are oy. Ecclesiastical Latin pronounces AU, EU, and EI in the same way as classical Latin, but Æ and Œ are both pronounced ay. In anglicized Latin AU is aw, EU is yoo, and Æ and Œ are pronounced ee.

Stress

This stress rule applies whichever pronunciation system is being used. In words with two syllables, stress the first. In words with more than two syllables, examine the second-last syllable (the penult). If this syllable has a long vowel or is closed by a consonant (double consonants should be split between the syllables), then stress it. If this syllable is open and has a short vowel, stress the previous syllable (the antepenult). If you are not sure whether a vowel is long or not, consult a Latin dictionary.

Lavoisier, Antoine Laurent French scientist
ah(ng)-**twahn** lorr-**ah(ng)** lav-waz-**yay** /ɑ̃ˌtwɑːn lɒˈrɑ̃ lavwaˈzjeɪ/

Law, Andrew Bonar Canadian-Scottish statesman
bon-uhr /ˈbɒnə(r)/

lawrencium chemical element
lorr-**en**-si-uhm /lɒˈrɛnsiəm/

Layamon English poet and priest
ly-uh-muhn /ˈlʌɪəmən/

Lazio region, Italy
lats-yoh /ˈlatsjəʊ/

lazuli see **lapis lazuli**

Leahy, Terry English businessman
lee-hi /ˈliːhi/

Leamington Spa town, England
lem-ing-tuhn /ˈlɛmɪŋtən/

Leander Greek mythological character
li-**and**-uhr /liˈandə(r)/

Lear Shakespearean character
leer /lɪə(r)/

learned having acquired knowledge
through study
lur-nuhd /ˈlɜː(r)nəd/

leaven yeast
lev-uhn /ˈlɛvən/

Leavis, F. R. English literary critic
lee-viss /ˈliːvɪs/

Lebanon country
leb-uh-nuhn /ˈlɛbənən/

Lebensraum territory needed for a
state's development
lay-buhnz-rowm /ˈleɪbənz͵raʊm/,
German [ˈleːbns͵raʊm]
• Established anglicization.

Leblanc, Nicolas French chemist
nee-kol-ah luh-blah(ng) /niːkɒˌlɑː
ləˈblɑ̃/

Lebrun, Charles French painter
sharl luh-broe(ng) /ˌʃɑː(r)l ləˈbrœ̃/

Le Carré, John English novelist
luh karr-ay /lə ˈkareɪ/

lechery lustfulness
letch-uh-ri /ˈlɛtʃəri/

lecithin vitamin
less-ith-in /ˈlɛsɪθɪn/

Le Corbusier Swiss-French architect
luh kor-buez-yay /ˌlə kɔː(r)byˈzjeɪ/

lecythus pl. **lecythi** narrow-necked vase
from ancient Greece
less-ith-uhss, pl. less-ith-y /ˈlɛsɪθəs/, pl.
/-θʌɪ/

Leda Greek mythological character
lee-duh /ˈliːdə/

lederhosen German leather shorts
lay-duhr-hoh-zuhn /ˈleɪdə(r)͵həʊzən/

Lee Jong Wook Korean head of the
WHO
lee jong wuuk /ˌliː dʒɒŋ ˈwʊk/

The Korean surname Lee is generally
pronounced ee, but this is the anglicization
that Mr Lee prefers.

Leeuw, Ton de see **de Leeuw**

Leeuwenhoek, Anton van Dutch
naturalist
un-ton vun lay-oo-wuhn-hook
/ˌʌntɒn vʌn ˈleɪʊwənhuːk/
• See **DUTCH** panel.

Leeward Islands islands, Caribbean
lee-wuhrd /ˈliːwə(r)d/

Le Fanu, Joseph Sheridan Irish
novelist
lef-uh-noo /ˈlɛfənuː/

legalese formal legal language
lee-guh-leez /ˌliːɡəˈliːz/

legate member of the clergy
leg-uht /ˈlɛɡət/

legato musical term
luh-gah-toh /ləˈɡɑːtəʊ/

Léger, Fernand French painter
fair-nah(ng) lay-zhay /fɛː(r)͵nɑ̃ leɪˈʒeɪ/

legerdemain skilful use of one's hands
lej-uhr-duh-mayn /ˌlɛdʒə(r)dəˈmeɪn/

leger line short line added for notes
above or below the range of a stave
lej-uhr /ˈlɛdʒə(r)/

leghorn fine plaited straw; also a breed
of hen
leg-orn /ˈlɛɡɔː(r)n/

Leghorn, pronounced **leg-horn**, is also an
older anglicization for the Italian town of
Livorno.

Légion d'Honneur French award
lay-zho(ng) don-oer /ˌleɪ͵ʒɔ̃ dɒnˈœː(r)/

legionella pl. **legionellae** bacterium
lee-juh-nel-uh, pl. lee-juh-nel-ee
/ˌliːdʒəˈnɛlə/, pl. /-liː/

legionnaire member of a legion
lee-juh-nair /ˌliːdʒəˈnɛː(r)/

legislative having the power to make
laws
lej-iss-luh-tiv /ˈlɛdʒɪslətɪv/

legume plant of the pea family
leg-yoom /ˈlɛɡjuːm/

Less commonly also luh-**gyoom**.

leguminous relating to legumes
luh-gyoo-min-uhss /ləˈɡjuːmɪnəs/

Leh town, India
lay /leɪ/

Lehár, Franz Hungarian composer
frants lay-har /ˌfrants ˈleɪhɑː(r)/

Le Havre port, France
luh ahv-ruh /lə ˈɑːvrə/

lei garland of flowers
lay /leɪ/

Leia, Princess character in *Star Wars*
films
lay-uh /ˈleɪə/

However, the pronunciation **lee-uh** was also
used in the first film.

Leibniz, Gottfried German rationalist
philosopher
got-freet **lyp**-nits /ˌɡɒtfriːt ˈlaɪpnɪts/

Leibovitz, Annie American
photographer
leeb-uh-vits /ˈliːbəvɪts/

Leicester city, England
lest-uhr /ˈlɛstə(r)/

Leichhardt, Ludwig Australian
explorer
loot-vikh **lykh**-hart /ˌluːtvɪç
ˈlaɪçhɑː(r)t/

Leiden city, Netherlands
ly-duhn /ˈlaɪdən/
• See DUTCH panel.

Leinster province, Republic of Ireland
lenst-uhr /ˈlɛnstə(r)/

Leipzig city, Germany
lyp-sig /ˈlaɪpsɪɡ/, [ˈlaɪptsɪç]
• Established anglicization.

leishmaniasis disease
leesh-muh-**ny**-uh-siss /ˌliːʃməˈnaɪəsɪs/

leitmotif recurrent theme
lyt-moh-teef /ˈlaɪtməʊˌtiːf/

Leitrim county, Republic of Ireland
leet-rim /ˈliːtrɪm/

Leix see **Laois**

Lely, Peter Dutch-English painter
lee-li /ˈliːli/

Lemalu, Jonathan Samoan
bass-baritone
luh-**mal**-oo /ləˈmaluː/

Le Mans town, France
luh **mah(ng)** /lə ˈmɑ̃/

Le Mesurier, John English actor
luh **mezh**-uh-ruhr /lə ˈmɛʒərə(r)/

Some other people with this surname
pronounce it differently, but this was the
actor's preferred pronunciation.

lemma pl. **lemmata** intermediate
theorem in an argument or proof
lem-uh, pl. **lem**-uh-tuh /ˈlɛmə/, pl.
/-mətə/

Lemnos island, Greece
lem-noss /ˈlɛmnɒs/

Lemper, Ute German singer
oo-tuh **lemp**-uhr /ˌuːtə ˈlɛmpə(r)/

Lempicka, Tamara de see **de
Lempicka**

lempira currency unit, Honduras
lem-**peer**-uh /lɛmˈpɪərə/

lemur primate
lee-muhr /ˈliːmə(r)/

Lena river, Siberia
lay-nuh /ˈleɪnə/

Lendl, Ivan Czech-American tennis
player
ee-van **lend**-uhl /ˌiːvan ˈlɛndəl/

lenient more merciful than expected
lee-ni-uhnt /ˈliːnɪənt/

Lenin, Vladimir Ilyich Soviet
statesman
vluh-**dee**-meer **il**-yitch **len**-in
/vləˌdiːmɪə(r) ˌɪljɪtʃ ˈlɛnɪn/, [ˈlʲenʲɪn]

lenis weakly articulated
lee-niss /ˈliːnɪs/

Less commonly also **len**-iss or **lay**-niss.

lenity kindness
len-it-i /ˈlɛnɪti/

Leno, Jay American comedian
len-oh /ˈlɛnəʊ/

Le Nôtre, André French landscape
gardener
ah(ng)-**dray** luh **noh**-truh /ɑ̃ˌdreɪ lə
ˈnəʊtrə/

Lens town, France
lah(ng)ss /lɑ̃s/

lentigo pl. **lentigines** small brown
patches on the skin
len-**ty**-goh, pl. len-**tij**-in-eez
/lɛnˈtaɪɡəʊ/, pl. /-ˈtɪdʒɪniːz/

Leofric earl of Mercia, husband of Lady
Godiva
lay-uh-frik /ˈleɪəfrɪk/

León city, Spain
lay-on /leɪˈɒn/

Leonardo da Vinci Italian painter and
scientist
li-uh-**nar**-doh duh **vin**-chi
/lɪəˌnɑː(r)dəʊ də ˈvɪntʃi/
• Established anglicization.

Leonberg breed of dog
lee-uhn-burg /ˈliːənbə:(r)ɡ/

Leoncavallo, Ruggiero Italian
composer
roo-**jair**-oh lay-onk-av-**al**-oh
/ruːˌdʒeɪrəʊ ˌleɪɒŋkaˈvaləʊ/

Leone, Sergio Italian film director
sair-joh lee-**oh**-ni /ˌsɛː(r)dʒəʊ liˈəʊni/,
[leˈoːne]

Leonids meteor shower
lee-uh-nidz /ˈliːənɪdz/

leonine relating to lions
lee-uh-nyn /ˈliːənʌɪn/

Leopold I first king of Belgium
lee-uh-pohld /ˈliːəpəʊld/
• Established anglicization.

Lepanto naval battle site
luh-pan-toh /ləˈpantəʊ/

Le Pen, Jean Marie French politician
zhah(ng) marr-ee luh pen /ˌʒã maˌriː
lə ˈpɛn/

lepidopterist person who studies
butterflies and moths
lep-id-op-tuh-rist /ˌlɛpɪˈdɒptərɪst/

Lepidus, Marcus Aemilius Roman
statesman and triumvir
mar-kuhss ee-mil-i-uhss lep-id-uhss
/ˌmɑː(r)kəs iːˌmɪliəs ˈlɛpɪdəs/
• See LATIN panel.

leporine relating to hares
lep-uh-ryn /ˈlɛpərʌɪn/

leprechaun small, mischievous sprite
lep-ruh-kawn /ˈlɛprəkɔːn/

lepton subatomic particle
lep-ton /ˈlɛptɒn/

leptospirosis disease of animals
lep-toh-spy-roh-siss
/ˌlɛptəʊspʌɪˈrəʊsɪs/

Lepus small constellation
leep-uhss /ˈliːpəs/

Lérida city, Spain
lerr-ee-thuh /ˈlɛriːðə/

Lerwick capital of the Shetland Islands
lur-wik /ˈlə(r)wɪk/

Lesage, Alain-René French novelist
and dramatist
al-a(ng) ruh-nay luh-sahzh /aˌlã rəˌneɪ
ləˈsɑːʒ/

lese-majesty behaviour insulting to a
monarch
leez maj-uh-sti /liːz ˈmadʒəsti/

Also **layz mazh-uh-stay**, especially when
the French spelling 'lèse-majesté' is used.

Les Halles market, Paris
lay al /leɪ ˈal/
• See FRENCH panel.

lesion wound or ulcer
leezh-uhn /ˈliːʒən/

Leskovac city, Serbia
lesk-uh-vats /ˈlɛskəvats/

Lesmahagow town, Scotland
less-muh-hay-gow /lɛsməˈheɪɡaʊ/

Lesotho country
luh-soo-too /ləˈsuːtuː/

Lesseps, Ferdinand de French
diplomat
fair-di-nah(ng) duh less-uhps
/fɛː(r)diˌnã də ˈlɛsəps/

Les Six group of six Parisian composers
lay seess /leɪ ˈsiːs/

lethargy lack of energy
leth-uhr-ji /ˈlɛθə(r)dʒi/

Lethe Greek mythological river
lee-thi /ˈliːθi/

Leticia port, Colombia
let-eess-yuh /lɛˈtiːsjə/

Leto Greek mythological character
lee-toh /ˈliːtəʊ/

leu pl. **lei** currency unit, Romania
lay-oo, pl. **lay** /ˈleɪuː/, pl. /leɪ/

Leuchars village and RAF base, Scotland
lookh-uhrz /ˈluːxə(r)z/

leucocyte (also **leukocyte**) blood cell
loo-koh-syt /ˈluːkəʊsʌɪt/

leukaemia disease
loo-kee-mi-uh /luːˈkiːmiə/

Leuven town, Belgium
loe-vuhn /ˈløːvən/

This is the Flemish name. The French name
is Louvain, pronounced **loo-va(ng)**.

Levallois prehistoric flint-working
technique
luh-val-wah /ləˈvalwɑː/

Levant archaic term for the eastern
Mediterranean
luh-vant /ləˈvant/

Levantine relating to the Levant
luh-van-tyn /ləˈvantʌɪn/

Commonly also **lev-uhn-tin**.

levator muscle
luh-vay-tuhr /ləˈveɪtə(r)/

levee embankment
lev-i /ˈlɛvi/

lever bar resting on a pivot
lee-vuhr /ˈliːvə(r)/

AM is **lev-uhr**.

leverage exertion of force by means of a
lever
lee-vuh-rij /ˈliːvərɪdʒ/

Commonly also **lev-uh-rij**.

Leverhulme, Viscount English
industrialist and philanthropist
lee-vuhr-hyoom /ˈliːvə(r)hjuːm/

Leverkusen city, Germany
lay-vuhr-koo-zuhn /ˈleɪvə(r)ˌkuːzən/

Le Verrier, Urbain French
mathematician
uer-**ba(ng)** luh verr-i-**ay** /y(r)ˌbɛ̃ lə
vɛriˈeɪ/

Levi Hebrew patriarch
lee-vy /ˈliːvʌɪ/

Levi, Primo Italian novelist and poet
pree-moh **lay**-vi /ˌpriːməʊ ˈleɪvi/

leviathan sea monster
luh-**vy**-uh-thuhn /ləˈvʌɪəθən/

levirate custom by which a man may be
obliged to marry his brother's widow
lee-virr-uht /ˈliːvɪrət/

Lévi-Strauss, Claude French social
anthropologist
klohd lev-i **strowss** /ˌkləʊd ˌlɛvi
ˈstraʊs/

Leviticus book of the Bible
luh-**vit**-ik-uhss /ləˈvɪtɪkəs/

Levitra trademark drug used to treat
impotence
luh-**veet**-ruh /ləˈviːtrə/

levonorgestrel synthetic hormone
lee-vuh-nor-**jest**-ruhl
/ˌliːvəʊnɔː(r)ˈdʒɛstrəl/

levy impose
lev-i /ˈlɛvi/

Levy, Andrea English author
and-ri-uh **lee**-vi /ˌandriə ˈliːvi/

Lewes town, England
loo-iss /ˈluːɪs/

lexicography compiling of dictionaries
lek-sik-**og**-ruh-fi /ˌlɛksɪkˈɒɡrəfi/

Lewinsky, Monica American former
White House staff member
luh-**win**-ski /ləˈwɪnski/

ley farming method
lay /leɪ/

leylandii cypress tree
lay-**land**-i-y /leɪˈlandiʌɪ/

Leyte island, Philippines
lay-tay /ˈleɪteɪ/

Lhasa capital of Tibet
lah-suh /ˈlɑːsə/

li Chinese unit of distance
lee /liː/

liaise cooperate

li-ayz /liˈeɪz/

liana woody climbing plant
li-**ah**-nuh /lɪˈɑːnə/

Liao river, China; also a dynasty
lyow /ljaʊ/

Liaodong peninsula, China
lyow-**duung** /ˌljaʊˈdʊŋ/

Liaoning province, China
lyow-**ning** /ˌljaʊˈnɪŋ/

lias geological epoch
ly-uhss /ˈlʌɪəs/

libation drink poured out as an offering
to a deity
ly-**bay**-shuhn /lʌɪˈbeɪʃən/

libellous containing a libel
ly-buh-luhss /ˈlʌɪbələs/

Liberace American pianist and
entertainer
lib-uh-**rah**-chi /ˌlɪbəˈrɑːtʃi/

Libération French newspaper
lee-bair-ass-**yo(ng)** /liːbɛːraˈsjɔ̃/

Liberia country
ly-**beer**-i-uh /lʌɪˈbɪəriə/

Liberia city, Costa Rica
li-**bair**-i-uh /liˈbɛːriə/

Libeskind, Daniel American architect
lee-buhss-kind /ˈliːbəskɪnd/

libido sexual desire
lib-**ee**-doh /lɪˈbiːdəʊ/

LIBOR London InterBank Offered Rate
ly-bor /ˈlʌɪbɔː(r)/

libretto pl. **libretti** text of a vocal work
lib-**ret**-oh, pl. lib-**ret**-i /lɪˈbrɛtəʊ, pl.
/-ti/

Libreville capital of Gabon
leeb-ruh-veel /ˈliːbrəviːl/

Libya country
lib-i-uh /ˈlɪbiə/

lichen plant
ly-kuhn /ˈlʌɪkən/

Less commonly also **litch-uhn**.

Lichfield town, England
litch-feeld /ˈlɪtʃfiːld/

Lichtenstein, Roy American painter
lik-tuhn-styn /ˈlɪktən,stʌɪn/

licit not forbidden
liss-it /ˈlɪsɪt/

Liddell Hart, Basil British military
historian
lid-uhl **hart** /ˌlɪdəl ˈhɑː(r)t/

Lidice Czech town destroyed by the
Nazis during the Second World War
lid-it-suh /ˈlɪdɪtsə/

Lidingö island suburb, Stockholm
lee-ding-oe /ˈliːdɪŋøː/

lido public open-air swimming pool
lee-doh /ˈliːdəʊ/

Less commonly also **ly**-doh. **lee**-doh is
often argued to be the correct pronunciation
on the basis that there is also an Italian
island reef of the same name pronounced in
this way.

Lie, Trygve Norwegian statesman
trueg-vuh lee /ˌtrʏɡvə ˈliː/

Liebchen term of endearment
leeb-shuhn /ˈliːbʃən/, German
[ˈliːpçən]

Liebfraumilch white wine
leep-frow-milkh /ˈliːpfraʊˌmɪlç/

Liebig, Justus von German chemist
yuust-uuss fon lee-bikh /ˌjʊstʊs fɒn
ˈliːbɪç/

Liebknecht, Karl German
revolutionary leader
karl leep-knekht /ˌkɑː(r)l ˈliːpknɛçt/

Liechtenstein principality, Europe
likh-tuhn-shtyn /ˈlɪçtən ˌʃtʌɪn/

Sometimes anglicized to **lik**-tuhn-styn.

lied pl. **lieder** type of German song
leet, pl. **leed**-uhr /liːt, pl. ˈliːdə(r)/

lief as happily
leef /liːf/

Liège province, Belgium
li-ezh /liˈɛʒ/

This is the French name. The Flemish name
is Luik, pronounced **loeyk**.

liege feudal relationship
leej /liːdʒ/

lien right to keep property until a debt is
discharged
lee-uhn /ˈliːən/

Also **leen**.

lieu instead
loo /luː/

Commonly also **lyoo**.

lieutenant deputy acting for a superior
lef-ten-uhnt /lɛfˈtɛnənt/

AM is loo-**ten**-uhnt.

LIFFE London International Finance

and Futures Exchange
lyf /lʌɪf/

Liffey river, Ireland
lif-i /ˈlɪfi/

Ligeti, György Hungarian composer
joerj lig-et-i /ˌdʒœ(r)dʒ ˈlɪɡɛti/, [ˌˌjœrɟ
ˈliɡɛti]

lignocaine local anaesthetic
lig-nuh-kayn /ˈlɪɡnəkeɪn/

ligule strap-shaped part of a plant
lig-yool /ˈlɪɡjuːl/

Liguria region, Italy
lig-yoor-i-uh /lɪˈɡjʊəriə/

Likert scale scale used to represent
psychological attitudes
lyk-uhrt /ˈlʌɪkə(r)t/

Likud Israeli political party
lik-ood /lɪˈkuːd/

lilangeni pl. **emalangeni** currency unit,
Swaziland
lee-lang-gay-ni, pl.
em-uh-lang-gay-ni /ˌliːlaŋˈɡeɪni/, pl.
/ˌɛˌmələŋˈɡeɪni/

liliaceous relating to plants of the lily
family
lil-i-ay-shuhss /ˌlɪliˈeɪʃəs/

Lili Marlene German song, popular
during the Second World War
lil-i mar-layn /ˌlɪli mɑː(r)ˈleɪn/

Lilith Jewish mythological demon
lil-ith /ˈlɪlɪθ/

Lille city, France
leel /liːl/

Lillehammer town, Norway
lil-uh-ham-uhr /ˈlɪləhamə(r)/

Lillibullero folk song
lil-ib-uul-air-oh /ˌlɪlɪbʊˈlɛːrəʊ/

Lilliputian very small
lil-ip-yoo-shuhn /ˌlɪlɪˈpjuːʃən/

Lilongwe capital of Malawi
lil-ong-way /lɪˈlɒŋweɪ/

Lima capital of Peru
lee-muh /ˈliːmə/

Limassol port, Cyprus
lim-uh-sol /ˈlɪməsɒl/

Limbaugh, Rush American radio talk
show host
lim-baw /ˈlɪmbaʊ/

Limburg province, Belgium and
Netherlands
lim-burg /ˈlɪmbə(r)ɡ/, Dutch
[ˈlimbʏrx]

Established anglicization. The German town of the same name may be pronounced in the same way, or with a more German-sounding pronunciation, **lim-buurk**.

limen pl. **limina** psychological threshold
ly-men, pl. **ly-min-uh** /'lʌɪmɛn/, pl. /'lʌɪmɪnə/

Limerick county, Republic of Ireland
lim-uh-rik /'lɪmərɪk/

liminal relating to a transitional stage
lim-in-uhl /'lɪmɪnəl/

Limoges city, France
lim-ohzh /lɪ'məʊʒ/

Limón port, Costa Rica
lee-mon /li:'mɒn/

Limousin region, France
lee-moo-za(ng) /li:mu:'zɛ̃/

limousine large, luxurious car
lim-uh-zeen /ˌlɪmə'zi:n/

Limpopo river, Africa
lim-poh-poh /lɪm'pəʊpəʊ/

Linacre, Thomas English physician and scholar
lin-uh-kuhr /'lɪnəkə(r)/

Lincoln city, England
link-uhn /'lɪŋkən/

linctus thick liquid medicine
link-tuhss /'lɪŋktəs/

Lindbergh, Charles American aviator
lind-burg /'lɪndbə:(r)ɡ/

Lindgren, Astrid Swedish writer
ast-rid lind-grayn /ˌastrɪd 'lɪndɡreɪn/

Lindisfarne island, UK
lin-diss-farn /'lɪndɪsˌfɑ:(r)n/

lineage direct descent from an ancestor
lin-i-uhj /'lɪnɪədʒ/

lineament distinctive feature
lin-i-uh-muhnt /'lɪnɪəmənt/

Lineker, Gary English footballer
lin-uh-kuhr /'lɪnəkə(r)/

Lingala African language
ling-gah-luh /lɪŋ'ɡɑ:lə/

lingam Hindu symbol
ling-gam /'lɪŋɡam/

lingerie women's underwear
lan-zhuh-ri /'lanʒəri/, French [lɛ̃ʒri]

Commonly also **lon-zhuh-ri** or **lan-juh-ray**.

lingua franca common language
ling-gwuh frank-uh /ˌlɪŋɡwə 'fraŋkə/

linguine kind of pasta

ling-gwee-ni /lɪŋ'ɡwi:ni/

linguistics study of language
ling-gwist-iks /lɪŋ'ɡwɪstɪks/

liniment embrocation
lin-im-uhnt /'lɪnɪmənt/

Linklater, Magnus Scottish journalist
link-luh-tuhr /'lɪŋklətə(r)/

Linköping town, Sweden
leen-shoe-ping /'li:nˌʃø:pɪŋ/, ['linøø:pɪŋ]

Linnaeus, Carolus Swedish botanist
kuh-roh-luhss lin-ay-uhss /kə,rəʊləs lɪ'neɪəs/

His real name was Karl von Linné, pronounced lin-**ay**. This Latinized version of his name can also be pronounced lin-**ee**-uhss, but the pronunciation we recommend is that preferred by the Linnean Society (themselves pronounced lin-**ee**-uhn).

linoleum flooring material
lin-oh-li-uhm /lɪ'nəʊliəm/

Linux US trademark computer operating system
lin-uhks /'lɪnəks/

Less commonly also **ly-nuhks**. Our recommendation is that used by its designer, Linus Thorvalds, after whom it is named.

Linz city, Austria
lints /lɪnts/

lionize give public attention to
ly-uh-nyz /'lʌɪənʌɪz/

Lipari island, Italy
lee-parr-i /'li:pari/

Lipchitz, Jacques Lithuanian-French sculptor
zhahk lip-shits /ˌʒɑ:k 'lɪpʃɪts/

Lipetsk city, Russia
lee-pitsk /'li:pɪtsk/

Lipizzaner (also **Lippizaner**) breed of horse
lip-it-sah-nuhr /ˌlɪpɪ'tsɑ:nə(r)/

lipoma pl. **lipomata** benign tumour
lip-oh-muh, pl. **lip-oh-muh-tuh** /lɪ'pəʊmə/, pl. /-mətə/

liposuction cosmetic surgery to remove fat
lip-oh-suk-shuhn /'lɪpəʊˌsʌkʃən/

Sometimes also **ly-poh-suk-shuhn**, especially in AM.

Lippi, Fra Filippo Italian painter
frah fil-ee-poh lip-i /ˌfrɑ: fɪˌli:pəʊ 'lɪpi/

liqueur alcoholic spirit
lik-**yoor** /lɪˈkjʊə(r)/

Commonly also lik-**yur** or lik-**yor**.

liquor alcoholic drink
lik-uhr /ˈlɪkə(r)/

liquorice sweet
lik-uh-riss /ˈlɪkərɪs/

Lir Irish sea god
leer /lɪə(r)/

lira pl. **lire** former currency unit, Italy
leer-uh, pl. **leer**-uh /ˈlɪərə/, pl. /ˈlɪərə/

lis alibi pendens 'lawsuit pending elsewhere' (Latin)
liss **al**-ib-y **pen**-denz /lɪs ˌalɪbʌɪ ˈpɛndɛnz/

Lisbon capital of Portugal
liz-buhn /ˈlɪzbən/

Established anglicization. The Portuguese name is Lisboa, pronounced leezh-**boh**-uh.

Lisburn city, Northern Ireland
liss-burn /ˈlɪsbə(r)n/

Lisdoonvarna town, Republic of Ireland
liss-doon-**var**-nuh /ˌlɪsduːnˈvɑː(r)nə/

Lisieux town, France
leez-**yoe** /liːˈzjø/

lisle fine cotton thread used for stockings
lyl /lʌɪl/

Lissajous mathematical looped figure
liss-azh-oo /ˈlɪsaʒuː/

listeria bacterium
list-**eer**-i-uh /lɪˈstɪərɪə/

Listowel town, Republic of Ireland
list-**oh**-uhl /lɪsˈtəʊəl/

Liszt, Franz Hungarian composer and pianist
frants list /ˌfrants ˈlɪst/

Li T'ai Po Chinese poet
lee ty poh /ˌliː tʌɪ ˈpəʊ/

litany series of petitions for use in church services
lit-uh-ni /ˈlɪtəni/

litas currency unit, Lithuania
lee-tass /ˈliːtas/

literae humaniores honours course in classics, philosophy, and ancient history at Oxford University
lit-uh-ry hyoo-man-i-**aw**-rayz /ˌlɪtərʌɪ hjuːˌmanɪˈɔːreɪz/

Various other pronunciations may be used; see LATIN panel. The course is frequently referred to as Lit. Hum., pronounced lit **hum**, for short.

literati well-educated people who are interested in literature
lit-uh-**rah**-ti /ˌlɪtəˈrɑːti/

lithium chemical element
lith-i-uhm /ˈlɪθɪəm/

lithograph lithographic print
lith-uh-grahf /ˈlɪθəɡrɑːf/

Also **lyth**-oh, especially for the abbreviated form 'litho'.

lithosphere rigid outer part of the earth
lith-uhss-feer /ˈlɪθəsfɪə(r)/

Lithuania country
lith-oo-**ay**-ni-uh /ˌlɪθuːˈeɪnɪə/

Less commonly also lith-yoo-**ay**-ni-uh.

litigious tending to take legal action
lit-ij-uhss /lɪˈtɪdʒəs/

litmus indicator dye
lit-muhss /ˈlɪtməs/

litotes rhetorical understatement
ly-**toh**-teez /lʌɪˈtəʊtiːz/

littoral relating to the shore
lit-uh-ruhl /ˈlɪtərəl/

Littré, Émile French lexicographer
ay-**meel** lee-**tray** /eɪˌmiːl liːˈtreɪ/

liturgy form of public religious worship
lit-uhr-ji /ˈlɪtə(r)dʒi/

Liuzhou city, China
lyoo-**joh** /ˌljuːˈdʒəʊ/

livelong entire
liv-long /ˈlɪvlɒŋ/

Liverpool port, England
liv-uhr-pool /ˈlɪvə(r)puːl/

However, the Liver Building and Liver Birds associated with the city are pronounced ly-vuhr.

Liverpudlian native of Liverpool
liv-uhr-**pud**-li-uhn /ˌlɪvə(r)ˈpʌdlɪən/

liverwort plant
liv-uhr-wurt /ˈlɪvə(r)wə:(r)t/

Livonia region, Latvia and Estonia
liv-**oh**-ni-uh /lɪˈvəʊnɪə/

Livorno port, Italy
liv-**or**-noh /lɪˈvɔː(r)nəʊ/

Livy Roman historian
liv-i /ˈlɪvi/

Ljubljana capital of Slovenia
lyuub-**lyah**-nuh /ljʊˈbljɑːnə/

Ljungberg, Fredrik Swedish footballer
fray-drik **yuung**-bairg /ˌfreɪdrɪk
ˈjʊŋbɛː(r)g/, [ˌfreˈdrɪk ˈjøŋbærj]

Lladró Spanish porcelain manufacturers
lyad-**roh** /ljadˈrəʊ/, [ʎaðˈro]

llama animal
lah-muh /ˈlɑːmə/

Llandudno town, Wales
hlan-**did**-noh /ɬanˈdɪdnəʊ/
• See WELSH panel.

Llanelli town, Wales
hlan-**ehl**-i /ɬanˈɛɬi/
• See WELSH panel.

**Llanfairpwllgwyngyllgogery-
chwyrndrobwllllantysiliogogogoch**
village, Wales
hlan-vyr-poohl-**gwin**-gihl-goh-**gerr**-
uh-khwurn-**droh**-boohl-hlan-duh-
sil-i-oh-goh-goh-**gokh**
/ˌɬanvaɪ(r)puːɬˌgwɪngɪɬgəʊˌgɛrəxwəːˈ(r)n
ˌdrəʊbuɬˌɬandəˌsiliəʊgəʊgəʊˈgɒx/
• See WELSH panel. Official name is
Llanfair PG.

llano grassy plain
lah-noh /ˈlɑːnəʊ/

Lloyd, Marie English music-hall
entertainer
mar-i loyd /ˌmɑːri ˈlɔɪd/

Llywelyn ap Gruffydd medieval Welsh
prince
hloo-**el**-in ap **grif**-ith /ɬuːˈɛlɪn ap
ˈgrɪfɪð/

loath (also **loth**) reluctant
lohth /ləʊθ/

loathe feel intense dislike for
lohth /ləʊð/

Lobachevsky, Nikolai Ivanovich
Russian mathematician
nik-uh-**ly** iv-**ah**-nuh-vitch
lob-uh-**chef**-ski /nɪkəˌlʌɪ ɪˌvɑːnəvɪtʃ
ˌlɒbəˈtʃɛfski/

Lobito port, Angola
luub-**ee**-too /lʊˈbiːtuː/

locale place where something happens
loh-**kahl** /ləʊˈkɑːl/

Locarno resort, Switzerland
lok-**ar**-noh /lɒˈkɑː(r)nəʊ/

locative grammatical case
lok-uh-tiv /ˈlɒkətɪv/

loch lake (Scottish)
lokh /lɒx/

Lochaber district, Scotland
lokh-**ab**-uhr /lɒxˈabə(r)/

lochan small loch
lokh-uhn /ˈlɒxən/

lochia discharge from the uterus after
childbirth
lok-i-uh /ˈlɒkiə/

Lochnagar small lake, Scotland
lokh-nuh-**gar** /lɒxnəˈgɑː(r)/

Lockerbie town, Scotland
lok-uhr-bi /ˈlɒkə(r)bi/

Lockyer, Norman English astronomer
lok-yuhr /ˈlɒkjə(r)/

Locrian musical mode
lok-ri-uhn /ˈlɒkriən/

locum tenens pl. **locum tenentes**
professional stand-in
loh-kuhm **ten**-enz, pl. **loh**-kuhm
ten-**ent**-eez /ˌləʊkəm ˈtɛnɛnz/, pl.
/tɛˈnɛntiːz/

locus pl. **loci** particular position or place
loh-kuhss, pl. **loh**-ky /ˈləʊkəs/, pl. /-kʌɪ/
• See LATIN panel.

locution word or phrase
luh-**kyoo**-shuhn /ləˈkjuːʃən/

loden thick woollen cloth
loh-duhn /ˈləʊdən/

Łódź city, Poland
wootch /wuːtʃ/

Loeb American publishers
lohb /ləʊb/

loess deposit of sediment
loh-ess /ˈləʊɛs/

Lofoten Islands islands, Norway
luh-**foh**-tuhn /ləˈfəʊtən/, [ˈluːfutən]
• Established anglicization.

Logan, Mount mountain, Canada
loh-guhn /ˈləʊgən/

logarithm mathematical quantity
log-uh-rith-uhm /ˈlɒgərɪðəm/

Loge Wagnerian character
loh-guh /ˈləʊgə/

loggia gallery or room with one or more
open sides
loj-uh /ˈlɒdʒə/

logistics organization and
implementation of a complex operation
luh-**jist**-iks /ləˈdʒɪstɪks/

logo identifying symbol
loh-goh /ˈləʊgəʊ/

logorrhoea tendency to extreme
loquacity
log-uh-**ree**-uh /ˌlɒgəˈriːə/

Logos theological term
log-oss /ˈlɒgɒs/

Logroño town, Spain
log-**ron**-yoh /lɒˈgrɒnjəʊ/

Lohan, Lindsey American actress
loh-han /ˈləʊhan/

Lohengrin opera by Wagner
loh-uhn-grin /ˈləʊənˌgrɪn/, German
[ˈloːənˌgriːn]
• Established anglicization.

Loire river, France
lwar /lwɑː(r)/

Loki Norse god
loh-ki /ˈləʊki/

Lok Sabha lower house of the Indian
Parliament
lohk sub-**hah** /ˌləʊk sʌbˈhɑː/

Lolita sexually precocious girl
loh-**lee**-tuh /ləʊˈliːtə/

lollapalooza particularly impressive
thing or person
lol-uh-puh-**loo**-zuh /ˌlɒləpəˈluːzə/

Lollard follower of John Wyclif
lol-uhrd /ˈlɒlə(r)d/

lollo rosso lettuce
lol-oh **ross**-oh /ˌlɒləʊ ˈrɒsəʊ/

Lombardy region, Italy
lom-buhr-di /ˈlɒmbə(r)di/

Established anglicization. The Italian name
is Lombardia, pronounced
lom-buhr-**dee**-uh.

Lombok island, Indonesia
lom-bok /ˈlɒmbɒk/

Lomé capital of Togo
loh-may /ˈləʊmeɪ/

Lomond loch, Scotland
loh-muhnd /ˈləʊmənd/

Lomu, Jonah New Zealand rugby
player
joh-nuh **loh**-moo /ˌdʒəʊnə ˈləʊmuː/

Londonderry county, Northern Ireland
lund-uhn-derr-i /ˈlʌndən,deri/

longeron structural component of an
aircraft's fuselage
lon-juh-ron /ˈlɒndʒərɒn/

longevity long life
lon-**jev**-it-i /lɒnˈdʒɛvɪti/

Longfellow, Henry Wadsworth
American poet
wodz-wurth **long**-fel-oh
/ˌwɒdzwə:(r)θ ˈlɒŋfɛləʊ/

Longinus Greek scholar
lon-**jy**-nuhss /lɒnˈdʒʌɪnəs/

longitude distance of a place east or
west of the Greenwich meridian
long-git-yood /ˈlɒŋgɪtjuːd/

Less commonly also **lon**-jit-yood; this
applies also to *longitudinal* (below).
Because of the changing pronunciation of
'tu' in English (e.g. *Tuesday*), the
pronunciation **lon**-gitch-ood is also
possible.

longitudinal running lengthwise rather
than across
long-git-**yood**-in-uhl /ˌlɒŋgɪtjuːdməl/

longueur tedious passage, e.g. in a book
long-**gur** /lɒŋˈgəː(r)/

loop of Henle part of the kidney
hen-li /ˈhɛnli/

Loos, Anita American writer
looss /luːs/

Loos, Rebecca Dutch-born celebrity
lohss /ləʊs/

loperamide drug used to treat diarrhoea
loh-**perr**-uh-myd /ləʊˈpɛrəmʌɪd/

loquacious tending to talk a great deal
luh-**kway**-shuhss /ləˈkweɪʃəs/

loquat fruit
loh-kwot /ˈləʊkwɒt/

loquitur 'speaks' (stage direction)
lok-wit-uhr /ˈlɒkwɪtə(r)/

lorazepam drug of the benzodiazepine
group
law-**rayz**-uh-pam /lɔːˈreɪzəpam/

As with other drugs in this group, the
pronunciation law-**raz**-uh-pam is also
common. See note on BENZODIAZEPINE.

Lorca, Federico Garcia Spanish poet
and dramatist
fedd-air-**ee**-koh gar-**thee**-uh **lork**-uh
/fɛdɛːˌriːkəʊ gɑː(r),θiːə ˈlɔː(r)kə/

lordosis curvature of the spine
lor-**doh**-sis /lɔː(r)ˈdəʊsɪs/

L'Oréal international beauty company
lorr-ay-**al** /lɒreɪˈal/

Lorelei rock on the Rhine, held to be the
home of a siren
lorr-uh-ly /ˈlɒrəlʌɪ/

Loren, Sophia Italian actress
suh-**fee**-uh **law**-ruhn /səˌfiːə ˈlɔːrən/

Commonly also lorr-**en**. However, the pronunciation we recommend is confirmed by various sources and is used throughout a film of her life, in which she participated.

Lorenz, Konrad Austrian zoologist
kon-rat lorr-ents /ˌkɒnrat ˈlɒrɛnts/

Loreto town, Italy
luh-**ray**-toh /ləˈreɪtəʊ/

lorgnette (also **lorgnettes**) pair of glasses on a long handle
lor-**nyet** /lɔː(r)ˈnjɛt/

Lorient port, France
lorr-i-**ah(ng)** /lɒriˈɑ̃/

lorikeet bird
lorr-ik-eet /ˈlɒrɪkiːt/

loris primate
law-riss /ˈlɔːrɪs/

Lorraine region, France
lorr-**en** /lɒˈrɛn/

Lorre, Peter Hungarian-American actor
lorr-i /ˈlɒri/

lory parrot
law-ri /ˈlɔːri/

Los Alamos town, US
loss **al**-uh-moss /lɒs ˈaləmɒs/

Los Angeles city, US
loss an-juh-luhss /lɒs ˈandʒələs/

Lostwithiel town, England
loss-**with**-i-uhl /lɒsˈwɪθiəl/

Lot river, France
lot /lɒt/

loth see **loath**

Lothario man who behaves irresponsibly in his sexual relationships
luh-**thar**-i-oh /ləˈθɑːriəʊ/

Commonly also luh-**thair**-i-oh.

Lothian region, Scotland
loh-*thi*-uhn /ˈləʊðiən/

Loti, Pierre French novelist
pyair lot-ee /ˌpjɛː(r) lɒˈtiː/

loti pl. **maloti** currency unit, Lesotho
loo-ti, pl. muh-**loo**-ti /ˈluːti/, pl. /məˈluːti/

Lotto, Lorenzo Italian painter
luh-**rent**-soh lot-oh /ləˌrɛntsəʊ ˈlɒtəʊ/

louche disreputable in an appealing way
loosh /luːʃ/

lough lake (Irish)
lokh /lɒx/

Loughborough town, England

luf-buh-ruh /ˈlʌfbərə/

Louis name of eighteen kings of France
loo-i /ˈluːi/, [lwi]
• Established anglicization.

Louis, Joe American boxer
loo-iss /ˈluːɪs/

Louisiana state, US
loo-ee-zi-**an**-uh /luːˌiːziˈanə/

Louisville city, US
loo-i-vil /ˈluːivɪl/

loupe small magnifying glass
loop /luːp/

lour (also **lower**) look angry or sullen
low-uhr /ˈlaʊə(r)/

Lourdes town, France
loord /lʊə(r)d/

Louth county, Republic of Ireland
lowth /laʊθ/

Louvain see **Leuven**

Louvre museum, Paris
loo-vruh /ˈluːvrə/

louvre angled slat in a door or shutter
loo-vuhr /ˈluːvə(r)/

Louÿs, Pierre French poet
pyair lweess /ˌpjɛː(r) ˈlwiːs/

lovage plant of the parsley family
luv-ij /ˈlʌvɪdʒ/

lovat muted green colour
luv-uht /ˈlʌvət/

Lovell, Bernard English astronomer
luv-uhl /ˈlʌvəl/

Lowell, Percival American astronomer
loh-uhl /ˈləʊəl/

Löwenbräu trademark German beer
loev-uhn-broy /ˈløːvənbrɔɪ/

lower see **lour**

Lowestoft port, England
loh-stoft /ˈləʊstɒft/

Also pronounced loh-uh-stoft or, locally, loh-stuhf.

Lowry, L. S. English painter
low-ri /ˈlaʊəri/

lox smoked salmon
loks /lɒks/

Loya Jirga Afghan parliament
loy-uh jur-guh /ˌlɔɪə ˈdʒɜː(r)gə/

Lozells district of Birmingham
loh-**zelz** /ləʊˈzɛlz/

lozenge rhombus or diamond shape
loz-uhnj /ˈlɒzəndʒ/

Lualaba river, Africa
loo-uh-**lah**-buh /ˌluːəˈlɑːbə/

Luanda capital of Angola
loo-**and**-uh /luːˈandə/

Luang Prabang (also
Louangphrabang) city, Laos
loo-ung pruh-**bung** /ˌluːʌŋ prəˈbʌŋ/

luau Hawaiian party
loo-ow /ˈluːaʊ/

Lubbock city, US
lub-uhk /ˈlʌbək/

Lübeck port, Germany
lue-bek /ˈlyːbɛk/

Lublin city, Poland
loo-bleen /ˈluːbliːn/

Lubumbashi city, Democratic Republic
of Congo
loo-buum-**bash**-i /ˌluːbʊmˈbaʃi/

Lubyanka building in Moscow used as a
prison
loo-**byank**-uh /luːˈbjaŋkə/

Lucan Roman poet, born in Spain
loo-kuhn /ˈluːkən/

Lucan relating to St Luke
loo-kuhn /ˈluːkən/

Lucas van Leyden Dutch engraver
loo-kuhss vun **ly**-duhn /ˌluːkəs vʌn ˈlʌɪdən/
• See DUTCH panel.

Lucca city, Italy
loo-kuh /ˈluːkə/

luce pike (fish)
looss /luːs/

Lucerne lake and resort, Switzerland
loo-**surn** /luːˈsəː(r)n/, French /lysɛrn/

Established anglicization. The German
spelling is Luzern, pronounced loot-**sairn**.

Lucia di Lammermoor opera by
Donizetti
loo-**chee**-uh di **lam**-uhr-moor /luːˌtʃiːə
di ˈlamə(r)mʊə(r)/

lucite trademark perspex
loo-syt /ˈluːsʌɪt/

Lucknow city, India
luk-now /ˈlʌknaʊ/

lucre money
loo-kuhr /ˈluːkə(r)/

Lucretius Roman poet and philosopher
loo-**kree**-shuhss /luːˈkriːʃəs/

luculent clearly expressed
loo-kyuul-uhnt /ˈluːkjʊlənt/

Lucullan extremely luxurious
loo-**kul**-uhn /luːˈkʌlən/

Luda port, China
loo-dah /ˌluːˈdɑː/

Luddite English worker who destroyed
machinery
lud-dyt /ˈlʌdʌɪt/

Ludendorff, Erich German general
ay-rikh loo-**duhn**-dorf /ˌeɪrɪç
ˈluːdən.dɔː(r)f/

Ludhiana city, India
luud-i-**ah**-nuh /ˌlʊdiˈɑːnə/

Ludwig name of three kings of Bavaria
luud-vig /ˈlʊdvɪɡ/, German /ˈluːtvɪç/
• Established anglicization.

Ludwigshafen port, Germany
loot-vikhss-hah-fuhn /ˈluːtvɪçsˌhɑːfən/

Lufthansa German airline
luuft-han-zuh /ˈlʊfthanzə/

Luftwaffe German air force
luuft-vaf-uh /ˈlʊftvafə/

Luganda African language
loo-**gan**-duh /luːˈgandə/

Lugano lake and town, Switzerland
loo-**gah**-noh /luːˈgɑːnəʊ/

Lugdunum Roman name for **Lyons**
luug-**doo**-nuum /lʊɡˈduːnʊm/

luge light toboggan
loozh /luːʒ/

Luger US trademark type of German
automatic pistol
loo-guhr /ˈluːɡə(r)/

Lughnasa Celtic festival
loo-nuh-suh /ˈluːnəsə/

Lugosi, Bela Hungarian-American
actor
bel-uh loo-**goh**-si /ˌbɛlə luːˈɡəʊsi/

lugubrious looking or sounding sad
luug-**oo**-bri-uhss /lʊˈɡuːbriəs/

Luhansk city, Ukraine
loo-**hansk** /luːˈhansk/

Luhrmann, Baz Australian film
director
baz lur-**muhn** /ˌbaz ˈləː(r)mən/

Luik see **Liège**

Lukács, György Hungarian philosopher
and politician
joerj loo-**kahtch** /ˌdʒœ(r)dʒ ˈluːkɑːtʃ/,
[ˌjœrj ˈlukaːtʃ]

Lukashenko, Alexander (also **Lukashenka**) president of Belarus
al-uhk-**sahn**-duhr loo-ka-**sheng**-kuh
/alək'sɑːndə(r) lukaˈʃɛŋkuh/

Lula see **Da Silva, Luiz**

Lully, Jean-Baptiste French composer, born in Italy
zhah(ng) bat-**eest** lue-lee /ˌʒã baˌtiːst lyˈliː/

lumbago back pain
lum-**bay**-goh /lʌmˈbeɪɡəʊ/

lumen SI unit of luminous flux
loo-men /ˈluːmɛn/

Lumet, Sidney American film director
loo-**met** /luːˈmɛt/

Lumière, Louis French pioneer of cinema
lwee loom-**yair** /ˌlwiː luːˈmjɛː(r)/

Luminal trademark drug
loo-min-uhl /ˈluːmɪnəl/

luminary person who inspires others
loo-min-uh-ri /ˈluːmɪnəri/

lumme expression of surprise
lum-i /ˈlʌmi/

Lund city, Sweden
luund /lʊnd/

Lundy island, UK
lun-di /ˈlʌndi/

lunette arched aperture
loo-**net** /luːˈnɛt/

Lunghi, Cherie English actress
sherr-i **luung**-gi /ˌʃɛri ˈlʊŋgi/

lungi sarong-like garment
luung-gi /ˈlʊŋgi/

lunula pl. **lunulae** white area at the base of a fingernail
loo-nyuul-uh, pl. **loo**-nyuul-ee
/ˈluːnjʊlə/, pl. /-liː/

Luo African ethnic group
loo-oh /ˈluːəʊ/

Luoyang city, China
lwaw-**yang** /ˌlwɔːˈjaŋ/

Lupercalia (sing. **Lupercal**) ancient Roman festival
loo-puhr-**kay**-li-uh, sing. **loo**-puhr-kal
/ˌluːpə(r)ˈkeɪliə/, sing. /ˈluːpə(r)kal/

lupine relating to wolves
loo-pyn /ˈluːpʌɪn/

lupus erythematosus skin disease
loo-puhss err-rith-ee-muh-**toh**-suhss
/ˈluːpəs ˌɛrɪθiːməˈtəʊsəs/

lur (also **lure**) Scandinavian trumpet
loor /lʊə(r)/

lure tempt
loor /lʊə(r)/
───
Commonly also **lyoor** or **lyor**.
───

lurex trademark yarn or fabric with a glittering metallic thread
lyoor-eks /ˈljʊərɛks/

lurgy indeterminate illness
lur-gi /ˈləː(r)gi/

lurid unpleasantly colourful
loor-id /ˈlʊərɪd/
───
Commonly also **lyoor**-id or **lyaw**-rid.
───

Lurie, Alison American writer
lyoor-i /ˈljʊəri/

Lusaka capital of Zambia
loo-**sah**-kuh /luːˈsɑːkə/

Lushun port, China
loo-**shuun** /ˌluːˈʃʊn/

Lusitania ancient name for Portugal; also a ship
loo-sit-**ay**-ni-uh /ˌluːsɪˈteɪniə/

lusophone Portuguese-speaking
loo-suh-fohn /ˈluːsəfəʊn/

luteinizing hormone female hormone
loo-tuh-ny-zing /ˈluːtənʌɪzɪŋ/

lutetium (also **lutecium**) chemical element
loo-**tee**-shi-uhm /luːˈtiːʃiəm/

Luther, Martin German Protestant theologian
loo-thuhr /ˈluːθə(r)/, [ˈlʊtɐ]
• Established anglicization.

luthier maker of stringed instruments
loo-ti-uhr /ˈluːtiə(r)/

Luthuli, Albert John South African political leader
loo-**too**-li /luːˈtuːli/

Lutine Bell bell kept at Lloyd's in London and rung to communicate news to the underwriters
loo-**teen** /luːˈtiːn/

Lutosławski, Witold Polish composer
vee-tolt loo-toss-**waf**-ski /ˌviːtɒlt luːtɒˈswafski/

Lutyens, Edwin English architect
lut-yuhnz /ˈlʌtjənz/

lutz jump in skating
luuts /lʊts/

Luvale African ethnic group
luuv-**ah**-lay /lʊˈvɑːleɪ/

Luwian ancient language
loo-wi-uhn /'luːwiən/

lux SI unit of illuminance
luks /lʌks/

Luxembourg (also **Luxemburg**)
country
luk-suhm-burg /'lʌksəmbəː(r)g/,
French [lyksãbuːr], German
[lʊksəmbʊrk]
• Established anglicization.

Luxemburg, Rosa Polish-German
revolutionary leader
roh-zuh luuk-suhm-boork /ˌrəʊzə
'lʊksəmbʊə(r)k/

Luxemburgish language, a form of
German
luk-suhm-bur-gish /'lʌksəmˌbəː(r)gɪʃ/

Luxor city, Egypt
luk-sor /'lʌksɔː(r)/

Established anglicization; the Arabic name
is el-Uqsur, pronounced uhl **uk-soor**.

luxuriate enjoy something as a luxury
lug-zhoor-i-ayt /lʌg'ʒʊərieɪt/

Luzern see **Lucerne**

Luzon island, Philippines
loo-zon /luːˈzɒn/

Lviv city, Ukraine
lveev /lviːv/

The Russian transliteration is Lvov,
pronounced lvof, and the Polish spelling is
Lwów, pronounced lvoof.

lycaenid butterfly
ly-see-nid /lʌɪˈsiːnɪd/

lycanthrope werewolf
ly-kuhn-throhp /'lʌɪkənˌθrəʊp/

Commonly also ly-**kan**-throhp.

lycée state secondary school in France
lee-say /liːˈseɪ/

Lyceum garden at Athens in which
Aristotle taught
ly-see-uhm /lʌɪˈsiːəm/

lychee fruit
ly-chee /'lʌɪtʃiː/

lychgate roofed gateway to a churchyard
litch-gayt /'lɪtʃgeɪt/

Lycia ancient region of Asia Minor
liss-i-uh /'lɪsiə/

Lycidas poem by Milton
liss-id-ass /'lɪsɪdas/

lycopene red pigment present in
tomatoes
ly-koh-peen /'lʌɪkəʊpiːn/

Lycurgus Spartan lawgiver
ly-kur-guhss /lʌɪˈkəː(r)gəs/

Lydia ancient region of Asia Minor
lid-i-uh /'lɪdiə/

Lyell, Charles Scottish geologist
ly-uhl /'lʌɪəl/

Lyly, John English dramatist
lil-i /'lɪli/

Lyme disease form of arthritis
lym /lʌɪm/

lymphoma pl. **lymphomata** cancer of
the lymph nodes
lim-foh-muh, pl. lim-**foh**-muh-tuh
/lɪmˈfəʊmə/, pl. /-mətə/

lyonnaise cooked with onions
lee-uh-nayz /ˌliːəˈneɪz/

Lyons city, France
lee-o(ng) /'liːɔ̃/, [ljɔ̃]

Established anglicization; the French
spelling is Lyon. An older anglicization,
ly-uhnz, exists, but we have not
recommended it for fifty years.

Lyotard, Jean-François French
philosopher and critic
zhah(ng) frah(ng)-swah lyot-ar /ʒɑ̃
frɑ̃ˌswɑː 'ljɒtɑː(r)/

Lyra constellation
ly-ruh /'lʌɪrə/

Lysaght, Cornelius BBC sports
correspondent
ly-suht /'lʌɪsət/

Lysander Spartan general
ly-sand-uhr /lʌɪˈsandə(r)/

Lysenko, Trofim Denisovich Soviet
biologist and geneticist
**truh-feem din-eess-uh-vitch
liss-yen-kuh** /trəˌfiːm dɪˌniːˈsəvɪtʃ
lɪˈsjɛnkə/

lysergic acid compound from which the
drug LSD can be made
ly-sur-jik /lʌɪˈsəː(r)dʒɪk/

Lysippus Greek sculptor
ly-sip-uhss /lʌɪˈsɪpəs/

Lysistrata play by Aristophanes
ly-sist-ruh-tuh /lʌɪˈsɪstrətə/

Lysol trademark disinfectant
ly-sol /'lʌɪsɒl/

M

Ma, Yo Yo Chinese-American cellist
yoh yoh mah /ˌjəʊ jəʊ ˈmɑː/

Maal, Baaba Senegalese musician
bub-uh mahl /ˌbʌbə ˈmɑːl/

Maasai see Masai

Maastricht city, Netherlands
mah-strikht /mɑːˈstrɪxt/

There is no established anglicization,
although pronunciations such as **mah**-strikt
are sometimes used.

Maat ancient Egyptian goddess
maht /mɑːt/

Mabinogion collection of Welsh prose
tales
mab-in-og-i-uhn /ˌmabɪˈnɒɡiən/

Mabuse, Jan Flemish painter
yun muh-buez /ˌjʌn məˈbyːz/

macabre disturbing
muh-kah-bruh /məˈkɑːbrə/

macadam broken stone used for
surfacing roads
muh-kad-uhm /məˈkadəm/

macadamia tree with edible nuts
ma-kuh-day-mi-uh /ˌmakəˈdeɪmiə/

McAleese, Mary Irish stateswoman
mak-uh-leess /ˌmakəˈliːs/

Macanese native of Macao
mak-uh-neez /ˌmakəˈniːz/

Macao (also **Macau**) former Portuguese
dependency, China
muh-kow /məˈkaʊ/

Macapá town, Brazil
mak-uh-pah /ˌmakəˈpɑː/

macaque monkey
muh-kak /məˈkak/

macaroon light biscuit
mak-uh-roon /ˌmakəˈruːn/

Macaulay, Thomas English historian
and philanthropist
muh-kaw-li /məˈkɔːli/

McAvoy, Doug English trade unionist
mak-uh-voy /ˈmakəvɔɪ/

macaw parrot
muh-kaw /məˈkɔː/

Maccabees followers of Judas
Maccabaeus
mak-uh-beez /ˈmakəbiːz/

macchiato espresso coffee with steamed
milk
mak-i-ah-toh /ˌmakiˈɑːtəʊ/

McCoist, Ally Scottish footballer
muh-koyst /məˈkɔɪst/

MacDiarmid, Hugh Scottish poet
muhk-dur-mid /məkˈdəː(r)mɪd/

Macedonia ancient country
mass-uh-doh-ni-uh /ˌmasəˈdəʊniə/

Maceió port, Brazil
mass-ay-oh /ˌmaseɪˈəʊ/

McEnroe, John American tennis player
mak-uhn-roh /ˈmakənrəʊ/

macerate soften by soaking
mass-uh-rayt /ˈmasəreɪt/

Macgillicuddy's Reeks range of hills,
Republic of Ireland
muh-gil-ik-ud-iz reeks /məˌɡɪlɪˌkʌdiz
ˈriːks/

McGonagall, William Scottish poet
muh-gon-uh-guhl /məˈɡɒnəɡəl/

Mach, Ernst Austrian physicist
airnst makh /ˌɛː(r)nst ˈmax/

The unit of speed named after him is often
anglicized to mak or mahk.

Machado, Antonio Spanish poet
an-tohn-yoh match-ah-thoh
/anˌtəʊnjəʊ maˈtʃɑːðəʊ/

macher person who gets things done
(Yiddish)
makh-uhr /ˈmaxə(r)/

machete broad, heavy knife
muh-shet-i /məˈʃɛti/

Machiavelli, Niccolò Italian
philosopher
nik-uh-loh mak-yuh-vel-i /nɪkəˈləʊ
ˌmakjəˈvɛli/

machicolation defensive architectural
feature
muh-chik-uh-lay-shun
/məˌtʃɪkəˈleɪʃən/

machination scheme
mash-in-**ay**-shuhn /ˌmaʃɪˈneɪʃən/

machismo aggressive masculine pride
muh-**chiz**-moh /məˈtʃɪzməʊ/

macho aggressively masculine
match-oh /ˈmatʃəʊ/

Machtpolitik power politics
makht-**pol**-it-eek /ˈmaxtpɒlɪˌtiːk/

Machu Picchu Inca town, Peru
match-oo peek-choo /ˌmatʃuː
ˈpiːktʃuː/

Machynlleth town, Wales
muh-**khun**-hluhth /məˈxʌnɬəθ/

Mackay port, Australia
muh-**ky** /məˈkʌɪ/

Mackerras, Charles
Australian-American conductor
muh-**kerr**-uhss /məˈkɛrəs/

mackinaw short woollen coat
mak-in-aw /ˈmakɪnɔː/

McKinlay, John Scottish explorer
muh-**kin**-li /məˈkɪnli/

McKinley, William American
statesman
muh-**kin**-li /məˈkɪnli/

Maclean, Alistair Scottish novelist
muh-**klayn** /məˈkleɪn/

Maclean, Donald English Soviet spy
muh-**klayn** /məˈkleɪn/

Macleod, John Scottish physiologist
muh-**klowd** /məˈklaʊd/

McLuhan, Marshall Canadian writer
muh-**kloo**-uhn /məˈkluːən/

McNaghten rules criteria for judging
criminal responsibility
muhk-**naw**-tuhn /məkˈnɔːtən/

MacNeice, Louis Northern Irish poet
loo-i muhk-**neess** /ˌluːi məkˈniːs/

Mâcon town, France
mah-**ko(ng)** /mɑːˈkõ/

Macquarie university and river,
Australia
muh-**kworr**-i /məˈkwɒri/

macramé art of knotting string
muh-**krah**-may /məˈkrɑːmeɪ/

macrocosm whole of a complex
structure
mak-ruh-koz-uhm /ˈmakrəkɒzəm/

macron diacritic (ˉ)
mak-ron /ˈmakrɒn/

Sometimes also **may**-kron.

McTimoney form of chiropractic
treatment
muhk-**tim**-uh-ni /məkˈtɪməni/

macumba Brazilian religious cult
muh-**koom**-buh /məˈkuːmbə/

macushla affectionate form of address
(Irish)
muh-**kuush**-luh /məˈkʊʃlə/

Madagascar country
mad-uh-**gask**-uhr /ˌmadəˈɡaskə(r)/

Madame French title for a woman
muh-**dam** /məˈdam/

Madeira island, Portugal
muh-**deer**-uh /məˈdɪərə/

Madejski, John English businessman
muh-**day**-ski /məˈdeɪski/

Pronunciation also appropriate for his
various endowments, including the
Madejski football stadium in Reading and
the Madejski Fine Rooms at the Royal
Academy of Arts.

madeleine small rich sponge cake
mad-uh-len /ˈmadəlɛn/

Mademoiselle French title for a young
woman
mad-mwaz-**el** /ˌmadmwaˈzɛl/

Madhya Pradesh state, India
mud-yuh pruh-**daysh** /ˌmʌdjə
prəˈdeɪʃ/

Madikizela-Mandela, Winnie South
African politician
mad-ik-i-**zel**-uh man-**del**-uh
/madɪkiˌzɛlə manˈdɛlə/

Madras former name for Chennai
muh-**drahss** /məˈdrɑːs/

madrasa (also **madrassah**) Islamic
college
muh-**drass**-uh /məˈdrasə/

Madrid capital of Spain
muh-**drid** /məˈdrɪd/, [maðˈri∂]
• Established anglicization.

madrigal part-song
mad-rig-uhl /ˈmadrɪɡəl/

Madrileño native of Madrid
mad-ril-**ayn**-yoh /ˌmadrɪˈleɪnjəʊ/,
Spanish [maðriˈleɲo]

Madura island, Indonesia
muh-**door**-uh /məˈdʊərə/

Madurai city, India
mud-oor-**y** /mʌdʊəˈrʌɪ/

Maecenas, Gaius Roman statesman
gy-uhss my-**see**-nuhss /ˌgʌɪəs
mʌɪˈsiːnəs/

maedi sheep disease
may-di /ˈmeɪdi/

Mae Hen Wlad Fy Nhadau 'Land of
my Fathers', the Welsh national anthem
my **hen** uu-**lad** vuhn **hahd**-y /mʌɪ ˌhɛn
ʊˌlad vən ˈhaːdʌɪ/
• See WELSH panel.

maelstrom whirlpool
mayl-struhm /ˈmeɪlstrəm/

maenad female follower of Bacchus
mee-nad /ˈmiːnad/

Maersk Danish airline
mairsk /mɛː(r)sk/

maestoso musical term
my-**stoh**-soh /mʌɪˈstəʊsəʊ/

maestro pl. **maestri** distinguished
musician
my-**stroh**, pl. my-**stri** /ˈmʌɪstrəʊ/, pl.
/-stri/
• Standard -s plural is also possible.

Maeterlinck, Maurice Belgian poet
and dramatist
may-**tuhr**-link /ˈmeɪtə(r)lɪŋk/

Mafeking town, South Africa
maf-uh-king /ˈmafəkɪŋ/

Mafia organized body of criminals
maf-i-uh /ˈmafiə/

mafioso pl. **mafiosi** member of the Mafia
maf-i-**oh**-soh, pl. maf-i-**oh**-si
/ˌmafiˈəʊsəʊ/, pl. /-si/

Magadha ancient kingdom, India
mug-uh-duh /ˈmʌgədə/

magdalen name for St Mary Magdalene
mag-duh-luhn /ˈmagdələn/

However, Magdalen College, Oxford, and
Magdalene College, Cambridge, are both
pronounced **mawd**-lin.

Magdalena river, Colombia
mag-duh-**lay**-nuh /ˌmagdəˈleɪnə/

Magdeburg city, Germany
mag-duh-boork /ˈmagdəˌbʊə(r)k/

mage magician
mayj /meɪdʒ/

Magellan, Ferdinand Portuguese
explorer

muh-**gel**-uhn /məˈgɛlən/

Established anglicization. This
pronunciation is also appropriate for the
Magellan spacecraft and the Straits of
Magellan.

Magen David symbol of Judaism
mag-**en** da-**veed** /maˌgɛn daˈviːd/

Maggiore, Lake lake, Italy
maj-**aw**-ray /maˈdʒɔːreɪ/

Maghrib (also **Maghreb**) region of
Africa
mug-rib /ˈmʌgrɪb/

Magi biblical characters
may-jy /ˈmeɪdʒʌɪ/

Maginot Line system of fortifications,
France
mazh-in-oh /ˈmaʒɪnəʊ/

magisterial showing great authority
maj-ist-**eer**-i-uhl /ˌmadʒɪˈstɪəriəl/

magistrate civil officer who administers
the law
maj-ist-rayt /ˈmadʒɪstreɪt/

Commonly also **maj**-ist-ruht.

magna cum laude 'with great
distinction' (Latin)
mag-nuh kuum **low**-day /ˌmagnə kʊm
ˈləʊdeɪ/

Used largely with reference to university
degrees. More anglicized pronunciations
such as kum **law**-di are also heard; see
LATIN panel.

Magna Graecia ancient Greek cities of
southern Italy
mag-nuh **gree**-shuh /ˌmagnə ˈgriːʃə/
• See LATIN panel.

magnate influential businessperson
mag-nayt /ˈmagneɪt/

magnesium chemical element
mag-**nee**-zi-uhm /magˈniːziəm/

magnetometer instrument for
measuring magnetic forces
mag-nuh-**tom**-uh-tuhr
/ˌmagnəˈtɒmətə(r)/

Magnier, John Irish businessman
mag-nuhr /ˈmagnər/

Magnificat canticle
mag-**nif**-ik-at /magˈnɪfɪkat/

Magnitogorsk city, Russia
mag-nit-uh-**gorsk** /ˌmagnɪtəˈgɔː(r)sk/

magnum opus pl. **magna opera** great
work of art
  mag-nuhm **oh**-puhss, pl. **mag**-nuh
  op-uh-ruh /ˌmaɡnəm 'əʊpəs/, pl.
  /ˌmaɡnə 'ɒpərə/

Magritte, René Belgian surrealist
painter
  ruh-**nay** mag-**reet** /rə'neɪ ma'griːt/

magus pl. **magi** priest of ancient Persia
  may-guhss, pl. **may**-jy /'meɪɡəs/, pl.
  /'meɪdʒaɪ/

Magyar Hungarian ethnic group
  moj-or /'mɒdʒɔː(r)/

Commonly also anglicized to **mag**-yar.

Mahābād city, Iran
  muh-hah-**bahd** /ˌməhɑː'bɑːd/

Mahābhārata Sanskrit epic
  muh-hah-**bah**-ruh-tuh
  /məˌhɑː'bɑːrətə/

maharaja (also **maharajah**) Indian
prince
  mah-huh-**rah**-juh /ˌmɑːhə'rɑːdʒə/

Maharashtra state, India
  mah-huh-**rush**-truh /ˌmɑːhə'rʌʃtrə/

Maharishi Hindu sage
  mah-huh-**ree**-shi /ˌmɑːhə'riːʃi/

Mahathir bin Mohamad Malaysian
statesman
  muh-**hud**-eer bin moh-**ham**-uhd
  /məˌhʌdɪə(r) bɪn mə'haməd/

mahatma revered person
  muh-**hat**-muh /mə'hatmə/

Mahaweli river, Sri Lanka
  muh-**hah**-wel-i /mə'hɑːwɛli/

Mahayana tradition of Buddhism
  mah-huh-**yah**-nuh /ˌmɑːhə'jɑːnə/

mahdi spiritual leader or messiah
  mah-di /'mɑːdi/

Established anglicization. For the Al-Mahdi
Army (an Iraqi organization), we
recommend **makh**-dee, a pronunciation
closer to the Arabic.

Mahfouz, Naguib Egyptian writer
  nag-**eeb** maf-**ooz** /na'ɡiːb ma'fuːz/

Mahilyow city, Belarus
  mah-hil-**yoh** /ˌmɑːhɪ'ljəʊ/

mah-jong (also **mah-jongg**) Chinese
game
  mah-**jong** /mɑː'dʒɒŋ/

Mahler, Gustav Austrian composer
  guust-af mah-**luh**(r) /ˌɡʊstaf 'mɑːlə(r)/

Mahmood, Mazher English
investigative journalist
  maz-uhr muh-**mood** /ˌmazə(r)
  mə'muːd/

mahogany timber
  muh-**hog**-uh-ni /mə'hɒɡəni/

Mahón town, Spain
  mah-**on** /mɑː'ɒn/

Maia Greek and Roman goddess
  my-uh /'mʌɪə/

maieutic denoting the Socratic mode of
enquiry
  may-**yoo**-tik /meɪ'juːtɪk/

Maikop city, Russia
  my-**kop** /mʌɪ'kɒp/

Mailer, Norman American writer
  may-luhr /'meɪlə(r)/

maillot pair of tights
  my-**yoh** /mʌɪ'jəʊ/

Maimonides Jewish philosopher
  my-**mon**-id-eez /mʌɪ'mɒnɪdiːz/

Main river, Germany
  myn /mʌɪn/

Mainz city, Germany
  mynts /mʌɪnts/

maiolica earthenware
  my-**ol**-ik-uh /mʌɪ'ɒlɪkə/

mai tai cocktail
  my ty /'mʌɪ tʌɪ/

maître d'hôtel head waiter
  may-truh doh-**tel** /ˌmeɪtrə dəʊ'tɛl/,
  French [mɛtr dotɛl]

Often abbreviated to *maître d'*, pronounced
may-truh **dee**.

Maitreya Buddha of the future
  my-**tray**-uh /mʌɪ'treɪə/

majlis parliament in various countries
  maj-**leess** /madʒ'liːs/

majolica earthenware made in imitation
of Italian maiolica
  muh-**jol**-i-kuh /mə'dʒɒlɪkə/

Majorca island, Spain
  muh-**yor**-kuh /mə'jɔː(r)kə/[ma'ʎorka]

Established anglicization; the Spanish name
is Mallorca, pronounced mal-**yor**-kuh (IPA
above). We stopped recommending the
anglicized pronunciation muh-**jor**-kuh in
1973.

major-domo chief steward
  may-juhr **doh**-moh /ˌmeɪdʒə(r)
  'dəʊməʊ/

majuscule large lettering
maj-uh-skyool /'madʒəskjuːl/

Makarios III Greek Cypriot archbishop
and statesman
muh-**kar**-i-oss /məˈkɑːrɪɒs/

Makgadikgadi Pans salt pans in
Botswana
mag-uh-**dee**-guh-di /ˌmagəˈdiːgədi/

Makhachkala capital of Dagestan
makh-uhtch-kuh-**lah** /ˌmaxətʃkəˈlɑː/

Makkah see **Mecca**

mako shark
mah-koh /'mɑːkəʊ/

Makybe Diva Australian champion
racehorse
muh-**ky**-bi **dee**-vuh /məˌkʌɪbi 'diːvə/

Malabar Coast coast, India
mal-uh-bar /'maləbɑː(r)/

Malabo capital of Equatorial Guinea
muh-**lah**-boh /məˈlɑːbəʊ/

malacca cane
muh-**lak**-uh /məˈlakə/

Malachi book of the Bible
mal-uh-ky /'maləkʌɪ/

malachite bright green mineral
mal-uh-kyt /'maləkʌɪt/

maladroit inept
mal-uh-**droyt** /ˌmaləˈdrɔɪt/

Málaga port, Spain
mal-uh-guh /'maləgə/

Malagasy language spoken in
Madagascar
mal-uh-**gass**-i /ˌmaləˈgasi/

malagueña Spanish dance
mal-ag-**ayn**-yuh /ˌmalaˈgeɪnjə/

malaise feeling of unease
mal-**ayz** /maˈleɪz/

Malamud, Bernard American novelist
mal-uh-mud /'maləmʌd/

malamute breed of dog
mal-uh-myoot /'maləmjuːt/

malapropism mistaken use of a word in
place of a similar-sounding one
mal-uh-prop-iz-uhm /'maləprɒpˌɪzəm/

malar relating to the cheek
may-luhr /'meɪlə(r)/

Mälaren lake, Sweden
may-luh-ruhn /'meɪlərən/ [/'mɛːlarən/]

malarkey meaningless talk
muh-**lar**-ki /məˈlɑː(r)ki/

Malawi country

muh-**lah**-wi /məˈlɑːwi/

Malay people inhabiting Malaysia and
Indonesia
muh-**lay** /məˈleɪ/

Malayalam language
mal-uh-**yah**-luhm /ˌmaləˈjɑːləm/

Malaysia country
muh-**lay**-zhuh /məˈleɪʒə/

Also muh-**lay**-zi-uh.

mal de mer seasickness
mal duh **mair** /ˌmal də 'mɛː(r)/

Maldives country
mawl-deev /'mɔːldiːv/

Less commonly also other pronunciations,
such as **mol**-dyv and **mawl**-div.

Maldivian native or of the Maldives
mawl-**div**-i-uhn /mɔːlˈdɪviən/

Male capital of the Maldives
mah-lay /'mɑːleɪ/

malefactor wrongdoer
mal-uh-fakt-uhr /'maləˌfaktə(r)/

Malegaon city, India
mah-luh-gown /'mɑːləgaʊn/

Malenkov, Georgi Russian statesman
gyor-gi mal-uhn-**kof** /ˌgjɔː(r)gi
malənˈkɔf/

Malevich, Kazimir Russian painter
kaz-im-**eer** mal-**yay**-vitch /kaziˌmɪə(r)
maˈljeɪvɪtʃ/

malfeasance wrongdoing
mal-**feez**-uhnss /malˈfiːzəns/

Malherbe, François de French poet
frah(ng)-**swah** duh mal-**airb** /frãˌswaː
də maˈlɛː(r)b/

Mali country
mah-li /'mɑːli/

Malibu resort, US; also a kind of
surfboard
mal-ib-oo /'malɪbuː/

malignant evil in effect
muh-**lig**-nuhnt /məˈlɪgnənt/

Malik, Zubeida BBC journalist
zoo-**bay**-duh mal-ik /zuːˌbeɪdə 'malɪk/

malinger pretend to be ill
muh-**ling**-guhr /məˈlɪŋgə(r)/

Malin Head point, Republic of Ireland
mal-in /'malɪn/

Malinke African ethnic group
muh-**link**-ay /məˈlɪŋkeɪ/

Malinowski, Bronisław Polish anthropologist
bron-**eess**-waf mal-in-**of**-ski
/ˈbrɒˌniːswaf ˌmalɪˈnɒfski/

mall large enclosed shopping area
mal /mal/

Commonly also mawl or mol. The Mall in London is pronounced mal.

Mallarmé, Stéphane French poet
stay-**fan** mal-ar-**may** /ˈsteɪˌfan ˌmalɑː(r)ˈmeɪ/

Malle, Louis French film director
lwee mal /ˌlwiː ˈmal/

malleus pl. **mallei** bone in the middle ear
mal-i-uhss, pl. **mal**-i-y /ˈmaliəs/, pl. /ˈmaliʌɪ/

malm soft rock
mahm /mɑːm/

Malmö port, Sweden
mal-moe /ˈmalmø/

malmsey sweet wine
mahm-zi /ˈmɑːmzi/

Malory, Thomas English writer
mal-uh-ri /ˈmaləri/

Malpighi, Marcello Italian microscopist
mar-**chel**-oh mal-**pee**-gi /mɑːrˌtʃɛləʊ malˈpiːgi/

Malplaquet battle site, France
mal-pluh-kay /ˈmalpləˌkeɪ/
• Established anglicization.

Malraux, André French novelist and politician
ah(ng)-**dray** mal-**roh** /ɑ̃ˌdreɪ malˈrəʊ/

malt grain that has been steeped, germinated, and dried
mawlt /mɔːlt/

Commonly also molt.

Malta country
mawl-tuh /ˈmɔːltə/

Malthus, Thomas English economist
mal-thuhss /ˈmalθəs/

Malverns range of hills, England
mawl-vuhrnz /ˈmɔːlvə(r)nz/

Malvinas see **Islas Malvinas**

malvoisie grape variety
mal-vwaz-**ee** /malvwaˈziː/

Malvolio Shakespearean character
mal-**voh**-li-oh /malˈvəʊliəʊ/

mama (also **mamma**) one's mother
muh-**mah** /məˈmɑː/

The pronunciation **mam**-uh is also possible, especially in AM and in children's speech.

mamba snake
mam-buh /ˈmambə/

Mameluke ruling military caste in Ottoman Egypt
mam-uh-look /ˈmaməluːk/

Mamet, David American dramatist
mam-uht /ˈmamət/

Mammon wealth
mam-uhn /ˈmamən/

Mamoutzu capital of Mayotte
mam-**oot**-soo /maˈmuːtsuː/

Managua capital of Nicaragua
man-**ag**-wuh /maˈnagwə/

Manama capital of Bahrain
muh-**nah**-muh /məˈnɑːmə/

mañana 'tomorrow' (Spanish)
man-**yah**-nuh /manˈjɑːnə/, [maˈɲana]

manat currency unit, Azerbaijan and Turkmenistan
man-at /ˈmanat/

manatee sea cow
man-uh-**tee** /ˈmanəti/

Manaus city, Brazil
muh-**nowss** /məˈnaʊs/

Manche department, France
mah(ng)sh /mɑ̃ʃ/

Manchuria region, China
man-**choor**-i-uh /manˈtʃʊəriə/

Mancini, Henry American composer
man-**see**-ni /manˈsiːni/

manciple person in charge of buying provisions
man-sip-uhl /ˈmansɪpəl/

Mancunian native or inhabitant of Manchester
man-**kyoo**-ni-uhn /manˈkjuːniən/

mandala circular symbol
man-duh-luh /ˈmandələ/

Mandalay port, Burma
man-duh-**lay** /ˌmandəˈleɪ/

mandamus judicial writ
man-**day**-muhss /manˈdeɪməs/

Mandarić, Milan Serbian-American businessman; owns Portsmouth FC
mee-luhn **man**-duh-ritch /ˌmiːlən ˈmandərɪtʃ/

Mandarin form of Chinese
man-duh-rin /ˈmandərɪn/

mandatory required by law
man-duh-tuh-ri /ˈmandətəri/

Mande African ethnic group
man-day /ˈmandeɪ/

Mandela, Nelson Rolihlahla South
African statesman
roh-li-**hlah**-hluh man-**del**-uh
/rəʊliˌɬɑːɬə manˈdɛlə/

Mandelbrot, Benoit Polish-French
mathematician
buhn-**wah** man-duhl-broht /bənˌwɑː
ˈmandəlbrəʊt/

His surname may be Gallicized to
mah(ng)-duhl-broh, but this is less usual.
Mandelbrot sets are almost always
pronounced as we suggest.

Mandeville, John English nobleman
man-duh-vil /ˈmandəvɪl/

mandible jaw
man-dib-uhl /ˈmandɪbəl/

Mandinka African ethnic group and
language
man-**dink**-uh /manˈdɪŋkə/

mandir Hindu temple
man-deer /ˈmandɪə(r)/

mandola musical instrument
man-**doh**-luh /manˈdəʊlə/

mandragora mandrake used as a
narcotic
man-**drag**-uh-ruh /manˈdragərə/

However, there is a ballet of the same name
by Szymanowski, for which the Polish
pronunciation man-drag-**orr**-uh is
appropriate; see POLISH panel.

manège enclosed area in which horses
and riders are trained
man-ezh /maˈnɛʒ/

Manet, Édouard French painter
ay-**dwar** man-**ay** /eɪdˈwɑː(r) maˈneɪ/

Manetho ancient Egyptian priest
man-**eth**-oh /maˈnɛθəʊ/

manga Japanese genre of cartoons,
comic books, and animated films
mang-guh /ˈmaŋgə/

mangabey monkey
mang-guh-bay /ˈmaŋgəbeɪ/

manganese chemical element
mang-guh-neez /ˈmaŋgəniːz/

mange skin disease
maynj /meɪndʒ/

mangetout pea with an edible pod
mah(ng)zh-**too** /mãʒˈtuː/

mangonel military device for throwing
missiles
mang-guh-nuhl /ˈmaŋgənəl/

mangosteen tropical fruit
mang-guh-steen /ˈmaŋgəstiːn/

maniacal wild
muh-**ny**-uh-kuhl /məˈnʌɪəkəl/

Manicaland province, Zimbabwe
muh-**nee**-kuh-land /məˈniːkəland/

Manichaean (also **Manichean**) relating
to a dualistic religious system
man-ik-**ee**-uhn /ˌmanɪˈkiːən/

manifold many and various
man-if-old /ˈmanɪfəʊld/

Manila capital of the Philippines
muh-**nil**-uh /məˈnɪlə/

Use this pronunciation also for *manila* (or
manilla) ropes, envelopes, etc.

manioc cassava
man-i-ok /ˈmaniɒk/

Manipur state, India
mun-i-**poor** /ˌmʌnɪˈpʊə(r)/

Manitoba province, Canada
man-it-**oh**-buh /ˌmanɪˈtəʊbə/

manitou good or evil spirit
man-it-oo /ˈmanɪtuː/

Mannar island, Sri Lanka
muh-**nar** /məˈnɑː(r)/

Manneken Pis statue in Brussels
man-uh-kuhn **peess** /ˌmanəkən ˈpiːs/

mannequin dummy
man-uh-kin /ˈmanəkɪn/

Mannesmann German
telecommunications company
man-uhss-man /ˈmanəsman/

Mannheim port, Germany
man-hym /ˈmanhʌɪm/

mano-a-mano head-to-head
man-oh uh man-oh /ˌmanəʊ ə
ˈmanəʊ/

manoeuvre series of moves
muh-**noo**-vuhr /məˈnuːvə(r)/

manoir large French country house
man-war /manˈwɑː(r)/

Manon Lescaut opera by Puccini
man-o(ng) lesk-oh /maˈnõ lɛˈskəʊ/

manqué having failed to become what
one might have been
mah(ng)-kay /ˈmãkeɪ/

Mansart, François French architect
frah(ng)-**swah** mah(ng)-**sar** /frɑ̃ˌswɑːmɑ̃ˈsɑː(r)/

Mansell, Nigel English motor-racing driver
man-**suhl** /ˈmansəl/

Mantegna, Andrea Italian painter
and-**ray**-uh man-**tayn**-yuh /anˌdreɪə manˈteɪnjə/

Mantell, Gideon English geologist
man-**tel** /ˈmantɛl/

mantilla lace scarf
man-**til**-uh /manˈtɪlə/

Mantoux test test for immunity to tuberculosis
man-**too** /ˈmantuː/

Mantua town, Italy
mant-**yoo**-uh /ˈmantjuə/

Established anglicization. The Italian name is Mantova, pronounced **man-toh**-va.

Manu archetypal first man of Hindu mythology
mun-oo /ˈmʌnuː/

Manueline architectural style
man-**yuu**-uh-lin /ˈmanjʊəlɪn/

manuka New Zealand tree
mah-nuuk-uh /ˈmɑːnʊkə/

manumit release from slavery
man-yoo-**mit** /ˌmanjuˈmɪt/

manzanilla Spanish sherry
man-zuh-**nil**-luh /ˌmanzəˈnɪlə/, [manθaˈniʎa]
• Established anglicization.

Manze, Andrew English violinist
man-zi /ˈmanzi/

Manzoni, Alessandro Italian writer
al-ess-**and**-roh mant-**soh**-ni /ˌalɛˌsandrəʊ manˈtsəʊni/

Maori aboriginal people of New Zealand
mow-ri /ˈmaʊri/

A more authentic-sounding pronunciation, **mah**-uh-ri, is also used, especially in New Zealand.

Maoritanga Maori culture
mow-ri-**tang**-uh /ˌmaʊriˈtaŋə/

Mao Zedong (also **Mao Tse-tung**) Chinese statesman
mow dzuh **duung** /ˌmaʊ dzə ˈdʊŋ/

Mapanje, Jack Malawian poet
muh-**pan**-ji /məˈpandʒi/

Mappa Mundi 13th-century map of the world

map-uh **muun**-di /ˌmapə ˈmʊndi/

Maputo capital of Mozambique
muh-**poo**-too /məˈpuːtuː/

maquette sculptor's small preliminary model
mak-**et** /maˈkɛt/

maquillage make-up
mak-i-**yahzh** /ˌmakiˈjɑːʒ/

Maquis French resistance movement
mak-**ee** /maˈkiː/

maquisard member of the Maquis
mak-i-**zar** /ˌmakiˈzɑː(r)/

marabou large stork
marr-uh-**boo** /ˈmarəbuː/

marabout Muslim holy man
marr-uh-**boot** /ˈmarəbuːt/

maraca percussion instrument
muh-**rak**-uh /məˈrakə/

Maracaibo port and lake, Venezuela
marr-uh-**ky**-boh /ˌmarəˈkʌɪbəʊ/

Maradona, Diego Argentinian footballer
di-**ay**-goh marr-uh-**don**-uh /diˈeɪgəʊ ˌmarəˈdɒnə/

marae courtyard of a Maori meeting house
muh-**ry** /məˈrʌɪ/

maraging steel steel alloy
mah-ray-jing /ˈmɑːreɪdʒɪŋ/

Marais quarter of Paris
marr-**ay** /maˈreɪ/

Maramba city, Zambia
muh-**ram**-buh /məˈrambə/

Maran breed of chicken
marr-**uhn** /ˈmarən/

Maranhão state, Brazil
marr-uhn-**yow(ng)** /ˌmarəˈnjaʊ/

Marañón river, Peru
marr-uhn-**yon** /ˌmarəˈnjɒn/

maraschino liqueur made from cherries
marr-uh-**skee**-noh /ˌmarəˈskiːnəʊ/

Marat, Jean Paul French revolutionary and journalist
zhah(ng) pol marr-**ah** /ˌʒɑ̃ pɒl maˈrɑː/

Marathi language
muh-**rah**-ti /məˈrɑːti/

Marbella town, Spain
mar-**bay**-uh /mɑː(r)ˈbeɪə/, [marˈβeʎa]

Marburg city, Germany
mar-buurk /ˈmɑː(r)bʊ(r)k/

marcasite semi-precious stone
mar-kuh-syt /ˈmɑː(r)kəsʌɪt/

marcato musical term
mar-kah-toh /mɑː(r)ˈkɑːtəʊ/

Marceau, Marcel French mime artist
mar-**sel** mar-**soh** /mɑː(r)ˌsɛl
mɑː(r)ˈsəʊ/

marchesa pl. **marchese** Italian
marchioness
mar-**kay**-zuh, pl. mar-**kay**-zay
/mɑː(r)ˈkeɪzə/, pl. /mɑː(r)ˈkeɪzeɪ/

marchese pl. **marchesi** Italian marquis
mar-**kay**-zay, pl. mar-**kay**-zi
/mɑː(r)ˈkeɪzeɪ/, pl. /mɑː(r)ˈkeɪzi/

marchioness wife or widow of a
marquess
mar-shuh-**ness** /ˌmɑː(r)ʃəˈnɛs/

Marciano, Rocky Italian-American
boxer
mar-si-**ah**-noh /ˌmɑː(r)siˈɑːnəʊ/

The Italian pronunciation of this surname is
mar-**chah**-noh.

Marconi, Guglielmo Italian electrical
engineer
gool-**yel**-moh mar-**koh**-ni /guːlˌjɛlməʊ
mɑː(r)ˈkəʊni/

Marco Polo Italian traveller
mar-koh poh-loh /ˌmɑː(r)kəʊ ˈpəʊləʊ/

Marcos, Imelda Filipino political figure
im-**el**-duh mar-**koss** /ɪˌmɛldə
ˈmɑː(r)kɒs/

Mar del Plata port, Argentina
mar del **plah**-tuh /ˌmɑː(r) dɛl ˈplɑːtə/

Mardi Gras carnival held on Shrove
Tuesday
mar-di grah /ˌmɑː(r)di ˈɡrɑː/

Marduk Babylonian god
mar-duuk /ˈmɑː(r)dʊk/

mare pl. **maria** plain on the surface of the
moon
mar-ay, pl. **mar**-i-uh /ˈmɑː(r)eɪ/, pl.
/ˈmɑːriə/

Marfan's syndrome hereditary
disorder
mar-fah(ng)z /ˈmɑː(r)fãz/

margarine butter substitute
mar-juh-**reen** /ˌmɑː(r)dʒəˈriːn/

The older pronunciation mar-guh-**reen** is
almost never used today.

margarita cocktail
mar-guh-**ree**-tuh /ˌmɑː(r)ɡəˈriːtə/

marginalia notes written in the margins
of a text
mar-ji-**nay**-li-uh /ˌmɑː(r)dʒɪˈneɪliə/

Margolyes, Miriam English actress
mar-guh-leez /ˈmɑː(r)ɡəliːz/

Margrethe II queen of Denmark
mar-**gray**-tuh /mɑː(r)ˈɡreɪtə/

marguerite ox-eye daisy
mar-guh-**reet** /ˌmɑː(r)ɡəˈriːt/

Mari Russian ethnic group
mar-ee /ˈmɑːri/

mariachi Mexican folk music
marr-i-**ah**-chi /ˌmɑːriˈɑːtʃi/

mariage blanc unconsummated
marriage
marr-i-ahzh **blah(ng)** /ˌmɑːrɪɑːʒ ˈblã/

Marian relating to the Virgin Mary
marr-i-uhn /ˈmɛːriən/

Our research indicates that this
pronunciation is more common among
priests, although **mair**-i-uhn is also used.

Marianas islands and deep-sea trench in
the western Pacific
marr-i-**an**-uhz /ˌmɑːriˈanəz/

Maria Theresa former archduchess of
Austria
muh-**ree**-uh tuh-**ray**-zuh /məˌriːə
təˈreɪzə/

Maribor city, Slovenia
marr-ib-or /ˈmɑːrɪbɔː(r)/

Marie Antoinette former French
queen, wife of Louis XVI
marr-i ah(ng)-twan-**et** /ˌmɑːri
ˌɒ̃twaˈnɛt/

Marie Byrd Land region of Antarctica
mar-i burd /ˈmɑːri ˈbɜː(r)d/

Marie de Médicis former French queen
muh-**ree** duh may-di-**seess** /məˌriː də
ˌmeɪdiˈsiːs/

Mari El autonomous republic, Russia
mar-ee **el** /ˌmɑːriː ˈɛl/

marijuana (also **marihuana**) cannabis
marr-i-**wah**-nuh /ˌmɑːriˈwɑːnə/

marimba musical instrument
muh-**rim**-buh /məˈrɪmbə/

Marinetti, Filippo Italian poet and
dramatist
fil-**ee**-poh marr-i-**net**-i /fɪˌliːpəʊ
ˌmɑːriˈnɛti/

marionette string puppet
marr-i-uh-**net** /ˌmɑːriəˈnɛt/

Marischal College part of Aberdeen University
mar-**shuhl** /ˈmɑː(r)ʃəl/

Maris Piper variety of potato
marr-iss /ˈmarɪs/

Marist member of Roman Catholic order the Society of Mary
mar-ist /ˈmɑːrɪst/

This is the order's preferred pronunciation, although **mair**-ist and **marr**-ist are also heard.

Maritsa river, Europe
muh-**rit**-suh /məˈrɪtsə/

Mariupol port, Ukraine
marr-i-**oo**-pol /ˌmariˈuːpɒl/

marjoram herb
mar-juh-ruhm /ˈmɑː(r)dʒərəm/

Markaryan, Andranik Armenian statesman
and-ruh-**neek** mar-kuhr-**yahn** /ˌandrəˈniːk mɑː(r)kə(r)ˈjɑːn/

Markiewicz, Constance Irish politician; first woman elected as an MP
mar-kiv-itch /ˈmɑː(r)kɪvɪtʃ/

Established anglicization of her surname; the Polish pronunciation is mar-**kyev**-eetch.

Markova, Alicia English ballet dancer
uh-**leess**-i-uh mar-**koh**-vuh /əˌliːsiə mɑː(r)ˈkəʊvə/

Markov model statistical model
mar-kof /ˈmɑː(r)kɒf/

Marlborough, Duke of British general
mawl-buh-ruh /ˈmɔːlbərə/

However, Marlborough in New Zealand and in Zimbabwe, and the cigarette brand Marlboro, are pronounced **marl**-buh-ruh.

marline light rope
mar-lin /ˈmɑː(r)lɪn/

Marmara, Sea of sea, Turkey
mar-muh-ruh /ˈmɑː(r)mərə/

Marmite trademark savoury spread
mar-myt /ˈmɑː(r)mʌɪt/

marmite earthenware cooking container
mar-**meet** /mɑː(r)ˈmiːt/

marmoreal made of or compared to marble
mar-**maw**-ri-uhl /mɑː(r)ˈmɔːriəl/

marmoset monkey
mar-muh-zet /ˈmɑː(r)məzɛt/

marmot rodent

mar-muht /ˈmɑː(r)mət/

Marne river, France
marn /mɑː(r)n/

marque make of car
mark /mɑː(r)k/

marquee large tent
mar-**kee** /mɑː(r)ˈkiː/

Marquesas Islands islands, French Polynesia
mar-**kay**-suhss /mɑː(r)ˈkeɪsəs/

However, the Marquesas Keys in Florida are pronounced mar-**keez**-uhss.

marquess (also **marquis**) nobleman
mar-kwiss /ˈmɑː(r)kwɪs/

marquetry inlaid work
mar-kuh-tri /ˈmɑː(r)kətri/

Marquette, Jacques French missionary and explorer
zhahk mar-**ket** /ˌʒɑːk mɑː(r)ˈkɛt/

marquise wife or widow of a marquis
mar-**keez** /mɑː(r)ˈkiːz/

Marrakesh (also **Marrakech**) city, Morocco
marr-uh-**kesh** /ˌmarəˈkɛʃ/

Marryat, Frederick English novelist
marr-i-uht /ˈmariət/

Marsala dessert wine produced in Sicily
mar-**sah**-luh /mɑː(r)ˈsɑːlə/

Marsalis, Wynton American trumpeter
win-tuhn mar-**sah**-liss /ˌwɪntən mɑː(r)ˈsɑːlɪs/

Marseillaise French national anthem
mar-say-**yayz** /ˌmɑː(r)seɪˈjeɪz/

Marseilles city, France
mar-**say** /mɑː(r)ˈseɪ/

The French spelling is Marseille. An older anglicized pronunciation of the English spelling, mar-**saylz**, is rarely heard now.

Marsyas Greek mythological character
mar-si-uhss /ˈmɑː(r)siəs/

Martaban, Gulf of part of the Indian Ocean
mar-tuh-**bahn** /ˌmɑː(r)təˈbɑːn/

Martello small circular fort
mar-**tel**-oh /mɑː(r)ˈtɛləʊ/

Martenot, Maurice French pianist and inventor
morr-**eess** mar-tuh-**noh** /mɒˌriːs mɑː(r)təˈnəʊ/

This pronunciation is also correct for the musical instrument he invented, the *ondes-martenot*.

Martial Roman epigrammatist
mar-shuhl /'mɑː(r)ʃəl/

Martineau, Harriet English writer
mar-tin-oh /'mɑː(r)tɪnəʊ/

martinet person who demands complete obedience
mar-tin-et /ˌmɑː(r)tɪ'nɛt/

Martinique island, Caribbean
mar-tin-eek /ˌmɑː(r)tɪ'niːk/

Maruts Hindu mythological characters
murr-uuts /'mʌrʊts/

Marvell, Andrew English metaphysical poet
mar-vuhl /'mɑː(r)vəl/

Maryland state, US
mair-i-luhnd /'mɛːrɪlənd/

This is the usual BR pronunciation. AM is often also **merr**-i-luhnd or **marr**-i-luhnd.

Marylebone district of London
marr-uh-luh-buhn /'marələbən/

Sometimes also **marl**-uh-buhn.

Masaccio Italian painter
maz-ah-choh /ma'zɑːtʃəʊ/

Masada architectural ruins, Israel
muh-sah-duh /mə'sɑːdə/

Masai (also **Maasai**) Kenyan ethnic group
mah-sy /mɑː'sʌɪ/

masala mixture of spices
muh-sah-luh /mə'sɑːlə/

Masaryk, Tomáš Czechoslovak statesman
tom-ahsh mass-arr-ik /ˌtɒmɑːʃ 'masarɪk/

Masbate island, Philippines
mass-bah-ti /mas'bɑːti/

Mascagni, Pietro Italian composer and conductor
pyay-troh mask-ahn-yi /ˌpjeɪtrəʊ ma'skɑːnji/

Mascarenes group of islands, Indian Ocean
mask-uh-reenz /ˌmaskə'riːnz/

mascarpone cream cheese
mass-kuhr-poh-nay /ˌmaskə(r)'pəʊneɪ/

Masefield, John English poet and novelist

mayss-feeld /'meɪsfiːld/

Maseru capital of Lesotho
muh-sair-oo /mə'sɛːruː/

Mashal, Khaled (also **Meshal**) Palestinian statesman
khah-luhd muh-shal /ˌxɑːləd mə'ʃal/

Mashhad (also **Meshed**) city, Iran
mash-had /maʃ'had/

Mashona African ethnic group
muh-shon-uh /mə'ʃɒnə/

masjid mosque
muss-jid /'mʌsdʒɪd/

masquerade pretence
mask-uh-rayd /ˌmaskə'reɪd/

Massachusetts state, US
mass-uh-choo-suhts /ˌmasə'tʃuːsəts/

massage rubbing of the body with the hands
mass-ahzh /'masɑːʒ/

Commonly also muh-**sahzh**.

massasauga rattlesnake
mass-uh-saw-guh /ˌmasə'sɔːɡə/

Massawa port, Eritrea; also called **Mitsiwa**
muh-sah-wuh /mə'sɑːwə/

masseter cheek muscle
mass-ee-tuhr /ma'siːtə(r)/

masseur person who provides massage professionally
mass-ur /ma'sə:(r)/

masseuse female masseur
mass-u(r)z /ma'sə:z/

AM is mass-**ooss**.

Massif Central mountainous plateau, France
mass-eef sah(ng)-tral /ˌma,siːf sɑ̃'tral/

Massine, Léonide Russian-French choreographer
lay-on-eed mass-een /leɪɒˌniːd ma'siːn/

Massinger, Philip English dramatist
mass-in-juhr /'masɪndʒə(r)/

Masson, André French artist
ah(ng)-dray mass-o(ng) /ɑ̃,dreɪ 'masɔ̃/

mastaba ancient Egyptian tomb
mast-uh-buh /'mastəbə/

mastectomy surgical operation to remove a breast
mast-ek-tuh-mi /ma'stɛktəmi/

mastodon large extinct mammal
mast-uh-don /'mastədɒn/

Mastroianni, Marcello Italian actor
mar-**chel**-oh mast-ruh-**yan**-i
/ˌmɑː(r)ˌtʃɛləʊ mastrəˈjani/

Masuria region, Poland
muh-**zoor**-i-uh /məˈzʊəriə/

Matabele African ethnic group
mat-uh-**bee**-li /ˌmatəˈbiːli/

Mata Hari Dutch dancer and secret
agent
mat-uh hah-ri /ˌmatə ˈhɑːri/

Mataram town, Indonesia
mut-uh-**rahm** /mʌtəˈrɑːm/

Mataskelekele, Kalkot Vanuatuan
statesman
kal-**kot** mat-uh-skel-uh-**kay**-luh
/ˌkalˌkɒt ˌmatəskɛləˈkeɪlə/

maté bitter infusion
mat-ay /ˈmateɪ/

matelot sailor
mat-loh /ˈmatləʊ/

mater 'mother' (dated)
may-tuhr /ˈmeɪtə(r)/
• See LATIN panel.

mater dolorosa Virgin Mary sorrowing
for the death of Christ
mah-tuhr dol-uh-**roh**-suh /ˌmɑːtə
ˌdɒləˈrəʊsə/

materfamilias female head of a family
may-tuhr-fuh-**mil**-i-ass
/ˌmeɪtə(r)fəˈmɪlias/

materia medica body of remedial
substances used in medicine
muh-**teer**-i-uh **med**-ik-uh /məˌtɪəriə
ˈmɛdɪkə/

Mathura city, India
mut-oor-uh /ˈmʌtʊərə/

matinee afternoon performance
mat-in-ay /ˈmatɪneɪ/

Matisse, Henri French artist
ah(ng)-**ree** mat-eess /ɑ̃ˌriː maˈtiːs/

Mato Grosso region, Brazil
mat-oo **gross**-oo /ˌmatuː ˈɡrɒsuː/

matriarch female head of a family
may-tri-ark /ˈmeɪtriɑː(r)k/

matriculate be enrolled at a university
muh-**trik**-yuul-ayt /məˈtrɪkjʊleɪt/

matrimony state of being married
mat-rim-uh-ni /ˈmatrɪməni/

matronymic name derived from a
mother or female ancestor
mat-ruh-**nim**-ik /ˌmatrəˈnɪmɪk/

matryoshka pl. **matryoshki** Russian doll
muht-ri-**osh**-kuh, pl. muht-ri-**osh**-ki
/ˌmatriˈɒʃkə, pl. /-ki/

matsuri Shinto festival
mat-**soo**-ri /matˈsuːri/

Matsuyama city, Japan
mat-suu-**yah**-muh /ˌmatsʊˈjɑːmə/
• See JAPANESE panel.

Mattel American toy manufacturers
muh-**tel** /məˈtɛl/

Matterhorn mountain, Switzerland
mat-uhr-horn /ˈmatə(r)hɔː(r)n/

Matthau, Walter American actor
mat-ow /ˈmataʊ/

Matthias, St apostle
muh-**thy**-uhss /məˈθʌɪəs/

Maturin, Charles Irish novelist
mat-yoor-in /ˈmatjʊərɪn/

matutinal occurring in the morning
mat-yoo-**ty**-nuhl /ˌmatjuˈtʌɪnəl/

Also muh-**tyoo**-tin-uhl.

matzo (also **matzoh** or **matzah**)
unleavened biscuit, traditionally eaten by
Jews during Passover
mot-suh /ˈmɒtsə/

Can also be pronounced **mut**-suh or,
influenced by the spelling, **mat**-soh.

mauby West Indian drink
moh-bi /ˈməʊbi/

maudlin self-pityingly sentimental
mawd-lin /ˈmɔːdlɪn/

Maugham, Somerset British novelist
mawm /mɔːm/

Maui island, Hawaii
mow-i /ˈmaʊi/

Mau Mau African secret society
mow mow /ˈmaʊ maʊ/

Mauna Kea volcano, Hawaii
mow-nuh **kay**-uh /ˌmaʊnə ˈkeɪə/

Mauna Loa volcano, Hawaii
mow-nuh **loh**-uh /ˌmaʊnə ˈləʊə/

Maunganui mountain, New Zealand
mong-uh-**noo**-i /ˌmɒŋəˈnuːi/

Maundy Thursday Thursday before
Easter
mawn-di /ˈmɔːndi/

Maupassant, Guy de French writer
gee duh moh-pass-**ah(ng)** /ˌɡiː də
məʊpaˈsɑ̃/

Maupin, Armistead American writer
ar-mist-ed maw-pin /ˌɑː(r)mɪstɛd
ˈmɔːpɪn/

Mauresmo, Amélie French tennis
player
am-ay-lee maw-rez-moh /ˌameɪˌliː
mɔːˈrɛzˈməʊ/

Mauriac, François French novelist
frah(ng)-swah morr-i-ak /frɑ̃ˌswɑː
mɒriˈak/

Mauritania African country
morr-it-ay-ni-uh /ˌmɒrɪˈteɪnɪə/

Mauritius island country
muh-rish-uhss /məˈrɪʃəs/

Maury, Matthew American
oceanographer
maw-ri /ˈmɔːri/

Maurya ancient Indian dynasty
mow-ri-uh /ˈmaʊriə/

Mauser trademark make of firearm
mow-zuhr /ˈmaʊzə(r)/

mausoleum building housing a tomb or
tombs
maw-suh-lee-uhm /ˌmɔːsəˈliəm/

mauve pale purple colour
mohv /məʊv/

maven expert
may-vuhn /ˈmeɪvən/

Má Vlast symphonic poem by Smetana
mah vlast /ˌmɑː ˈvlast/

maxilla pl. **maxillae** jaw
mak-sil-luh, pl. **mak-sil-lee** /makˈsɪlə/,
pl. /-liː/
• See LATIN panel.

maxixe Brazilian dance
muh-shee-shuh /məˈʃiːʃə/

Maya Central American ethnic group
my-uh /ˈmʌɪə/

maya Hindu supernatural power
mah-yuh /ˈmɑːjə/

Mayakovsky, Vladimir Georgian poet
and dramatist
vluh-dee-meer my-uh-kof-ski
/ˌmʌɪəˈkɒfski/

Mayan family of Central American
languages
my-uhn /ˈmʌɪən/

Maynooth town, Republic of Ireland
may-nooth /meɪˈnuːθ/

mayoral relating to the office of mayor
mair-uhl /ˈmɛːrəl/

Mayotte island, Indian Ocean

mah-yot /mɑːˈjɒt/

Mayr, Ernst Walter German-American
zoologist
airnst val-tuhr myr /ˌɛː(r)nst ˌvaltə(r)
ˈmʌɪə(r)/

Mazar-e-Sharif city, Afghanistan
muh-zar-esh-uh-reef /məˌzɑːrɛʃəˈriːf/

Mazarin, Jules Italian-French
statesman
zhuel maz-arr-a(ng) /ˌʒyl mazaˈrɛ̃/

mazarine blue butterfly
maz-uh-reen /ˈmazəriːn/

Mazatlán port, Mexico
mass-at-lan /ˌmasatˈlan/

Mazdaism Zoroastrianism
maz-duh-iz-uhm /ˈmazdəˌɪzəm/

mazdoor Indian labourer
muz-door /mʌzˈdʊə(r)/

mazel tov 'congratulations' (Hebrew)
maz-uhl tof /ˈmazəl ˌtɒf/

mazer wooden drinking bowl
may-zuhr /ˈmeɪzə(r)/

mazurka Polish dance
muh-zur-kuh /məˈzə(r)kə/

Mazzini, Giuseppe Italian nationalist
leader
juuz-ep-ay mat-see-ni /dʒʊˌzɛpeɪ
matˈsiːni/

Mbabane capital of Swaziland
uhm-bab-ah-ni /ˌəmbaˈbɑːni/

mbaqanga South African popular music
style
uhm-bak-ang-guh /ˌəmbaˈkaŋgə/

Mbeki, Thabo South African statesman
tah-boh uhm-bek-i /ˌtɑːbəʊ əmˈbɛkɪ/

mbira thumb piano
uhm-beer-uh /əmˈbɪərə/

Mbundu African ethnic group
uhm-buun-doo /əmˈbʊnduː/

Mbuti African ethnic group
uhm-boo-ti /əmˈbuːti/

mea culpa acknowledgement of one's
error
may-uh kuul-puh /ˌmeɪə ˈkʊlpə/
• See LATIN panel.

meander follow a winding course
mi-and-uhr /miˈandə(r)/

Meath county, Republic of Ireland
meeth /miːθ/

meatus passage leading to the interior of
the body
mi-ay-tuhss /miˈeɪtəs/

mebos fruit preserve
mee-**boss** /'miːbɒs/

Mebyon Kernow Cornish nationalist
political party
meb-i-on **kur**-noh /ˌmɛbiɒn 'kəː(r)nəʊ/

Mecca (also **Makkah**) city, Saudi Arabia
mek-uh /'mɛkə/

Established anglicization. Sometimes also
mak-uh, a more Arabic-sounding
pronunciation.

Meccano trademark construction toy
muh-**kah**-noh /məˈkɑːnəʊ/

Mechelen city, Belgium
mekh-uh-luhn /'mɛxələn/

Mechlin type of lace
mek-lin /'mɛklɪn/

Mecklenburg former state, Germany
mek-luhn-burg /'mɛklənbəː(r)g/,
['mɛklənbʊrk]
• Established anglicization.

meconium faeces of a newborn infant
mi-**koh**-ni-uhm /mɪˈkəʊniəm/

meconopsis poppy
mek-uh-**nop**-siss /ˌmɛkəˈnɒpsɪs/

médaillon round cut of meat or fish
may-dy-**yo(ng)** /ˌmeɪdʌɪˈjɔ̃/

Medan city, Indonesia
may-dun /'meɪdʌn/

Medau rhythmical exercise
may-dow /'meɪdaʊ/

Medawar, Peter English immunologist
med-uh-wuhr /'mɛdəwə(r)/

Medb Irish mythological queen
mayv /meɪv/

Medea Greek mythological figure
muh-**dee**-uh /məˈdiːə/

Médecins sans Frontières
international charity
med-sa(ng) sah(ng) fro(ng)t-**yair**
/ˌmɛdsɛ̃ sɑ̃ frɔ̃ˈtjɛː(r)/

Medellin city, Colombia
med-el-**yeen** /ˌmɛdɛlˈjiːn/, [mɛðeˈʎin]

Media ancient region of Asia
mee-di-uh /'miːdiə/

medicament substance used for medical
treatment
muh-**dik**-uh-muhnt /məˈdɪkəmənt/

Medicean relating to the Medici family
med-i-**chee**-uhn /ˌmɛdɪˈtʃiːən/

Medici powerful Italian family
med-itch-i /'mɛdɪtʃi/, ['meːditʃi]

Established anglicization. Another
anglicization, med-**ee**-chi, is seen as less
correct.

medieval (also **mediaeval**) relating to
the Middle Ages
med-i-**eev**-uhl /ˌmɛdiˈiːvəl/

Medina city, Saudi Arabia; also the name
for the old walled part of a North African
town
med-**ee**-nuh /mɛˈdiːnə/

mediocre of average quality
mee-di-**ohk**-uhr /ˌmiːdiˈəʊkə(r)/

meditative relating to meditation
med-it-uh-tiv /'mɛdɪˌtətɪv/

Mediterranean sea, Europe
med-it-uh-**ray**-ni-uhn
/ˌmɛdɪtəˈreɪniən/

Médoc red wine
may-**dok** /meɪˈdɒk/

medulla oblongata part of the
brainstem
muh-**dul**-uh ob-long-**gah**-tuh
/məˌdʌlə ˌɒblɒŋˈɡɑːtə/

Medusa Greek mythological character
muh-**dyoo**-zuh /məˈdjuːzə/

Other pronunciations such as muh-**doo**-suh
are also used.

meerkat mongoose
meer-kat /'mɪə(r)kat/

meerschaum white clay-like material
meer-showm /'mɪə(r)ʃaʊm/

Meerut city, India
meer-uht /'mɪərət/

mefloquine antimalarial drug
mef-luh-kween /'mɛfləkwiːn/

megalopolis very large city
meg-uh-**lop**-uh-liss /ˌmɛɡəˈlɒpəlɪs/

megalosaurus dinosaur
meg-uh-loh-**saw**-ruhss
/ˌmɛɡələʊˈsɔːrəs/

Meghalaya state, India
may-**gah**-luh-yuh /meɪˈɡɑːləjə/

Megiddo ancient city, Palestine
muh-**gid**-oh /məˈɡɪdəʊ/

Megillah book of Hebrew scriptures
muh-**gil**-uh /məˈɡɪlə/

megilp mixture added to oil paints
muh-**gilp** /məˈɡɪlp/

megrim fish
mee-grim /'miːɡrɪm/

Meiji Tenno former emperor of Japan
may-ji **ten**-oh /ˌmeɪdʒi ˈtɛnəʊ/

meiosis type of cell division
my-**oh**-siss, pl. my-**oh**-seez /mʌɪˈəʊsɪs, pl. -siːz/

Meir, Golda Israeli stateswoman
gol-duh may-**eer** /ˌgɒldə meɪˈɪə(r)/

Meirelles, Fernando Brazilian film director
fair-**nan**-doo may-**rel**-ish /fɛː(r)ˌnandu: meɪˈrɛlɪʃ/

Meirionnydd district, Wales
mair-i-**on**-uh*th* /mɛːˈrɪˈɒnəð/

Meissen city, Germany; also a type of porcelain
my-suhn /ˈmʌɪsən/

Meissner effect magnetic flux
myss-nuhr /ˈmʌɪsnə(r)/

Meistersinger member of a guild of German lyric poets
my-**stuhr**-zing-uhr /ˈmʌɪstə(r)zɪŋə(r)/

Meitner, Lise Austrian-Swedish physicist
lee-zuh **myt**-nuhr /ˌliːzə ˈmʌɪtnə(r)/

meitnerium chemical element
myt-**neer**-i-uhm /mʌɪtˈnɪəriəm/

Meiwes, Armin German cannibal
ar-meen **my**-vuhss /ˌɑː(r)miːn ˈmʌɪvəs/

Mekele city, Ethiopia
muh-**kay**-li /məˈkeɪli/

Meknès city, Morocco
mek-ness /ˈmɛkˈnɛs/

Mekong river, Asia
mee-kong /miːˈkɒŋ/

mela Hindu fair or festival
may-luh /ˈmeɪlə/

Melaka state, Malaysia
muh-**lak**-uh /məˈlakə/

melamine compound used in making plastics
mel-uh-meen /ˈmɛləmiːn/

melancholia sadness
mel-uhn-**koh**-li-uh /ˌmɛlənˈkəʊliə/

Melanchthon, Philipp German Protestant reformer
fil-ip mel-**ank**-thon /ˌfɪlɪp mɛˈlaŋkθɒn/

Melanesia region of the western Pacific
mel-uh-**nee**-zhuh /ˌmɛləˈniːʒə/

melange varied mixture
may-lo(ng)zh /meɪˈlɒ̃ʒ/

melanin pigment

mel-uh-nin /ˈmɛlənɪn/

melanoma tumour
mel-uh-**noh**-muh /ˌmɛləˈnəʊmə/

melatonin hormone
mel-uh-**toh**-nin /ˌmɛləˈtəʊnɪn/

Melbourne city, Australia
mel-buhrn /ˈmɛlbə(r)n/

Melchior traditional name of one of the Magi
mel-ki-or /ˈmɛlkiɔː(r)/

Melchizedek biblical character
mel-**kiz**-uh-dek /mɛlˈkɪzədɛk/

Meleager Greek poet
mel-i-**ay**-guhr /ˌmɛliˈeɪgə(r)/

melee confused fight
mel-ay /ˈmɛleɪ/

Melilla Spanish enclave in Morocco
mel-**ee**-yuh /mɛˈliːjə/

melisma pl. **melismata** group of notes sung to one syllable of text
muh-**liz**-muh, pl. muh-**liz**-muh-tuh /məˈlɪzmə, pl. -mətə/

Melkite Orthodox Christian
mel-kyt /ˈmɛlkʌɪt/

mellifluous pleasingly smooth and musical to hear
mel-**if**-loo-uhss /mɛˈlɪfluəs/

Mellon, Andrew American financier and philanthropist
mel-uhn /ˈmɛlən/

Melos see **Milos**

Melpomene Greek mythological character
mel-**pom**-uh-ni /mɛlˈpɒməni/

meltemi Mediterranean wind
mel-**tem**-i /mɛlˈtɛmi/

Melua, Katie Georgian-born singer
mel-oo-uh /ˈmɛluə/

membrum virile man's penis
memb-ruhm **virr**-ee-li /ˌmɛmbrəm vɪˈriːli/

meme element of a culture passed from one individual to another
meem /miːm/

memento mori reminder of the inevitability of death
mem-**en**-toh **maw**-ri /mɛˌmɛntəʊ ˈmɔːri/

Memphis ancient city, Egypt; also city, US
mem-fiss /ˈmɛmfɪs/

memsahib Indian term of address for a married white woman
mem-sahb /'mɛmsɑːb/

Sometimes also **mem-sah-hib**.

ménage à trois arrangement in which three people live together
may-**nahzh** ah **trwah** /meɪˌnɑːʒ ɑː 'trwɑː/

menagerie collection of wild animals
muh-**naj**-uh-ri /mə'nadʒəri/

Menai Strait sea channel, Wales
men-y /'mɛnʌɪ/

Menander Greek dramatist
muh-**nan**-duhr /mə'nandə(r)/

Menapian relating to a glaciation in northern Europe
muh-**nap**-i-uhn /mə'napiən/

menaquinone one of the K vitamins
men-uh-**kwin**-ohn /ˌmɛnə'kwɪnəʊn/

menarche onset of menstruation
men-**ark**-i /mɛ'nɑː(r)ki/

Mencius Chinese philosopher; also called **Meng-tzu**
men-si-uhss /'mɛnsiəs/

Mencken, H. L. American journalist
menk-uhn /'mɛŋkən/

Mendel, Gregor Moravian monk, the father of genetics
greg-or men-**duhl** /ˌgrɛgɔː(r) 'mɛndəl/

The term Mendelian, referring to his theory, is usually pronounced men-**deel**-i-uhn.

Mendeleev, Dmitri Russian chemist
duh-**meet**-ri men-duhl-**yay**-uhf /dəˌmiːtri ˌmɛndə'ljeɪəf/

mendelevium chemical element
men-duh-**lee**-vi-uhm /ˌmɛndə'liːviəm/

Mendelssohn, Felix German composer and pianist
fay-liks men-duhl-suhn /ˌfeɪliks 'mɛndəlsən/, ['mɛndəlszoːn]
• Established anglicization.

Menderes river, Turkey
men-duh-**ress** /ˌmɛndə'rɛs/

Mendes, Sam English film director
men-dez /'mɛndɛz/

Mendoza city, Argentina
men-**doh**-zuh /mɛn'dəʊzə/, Spanish [men'dosa]
• Established anglicization.

Mendoza, Antonio de Spanish colonial administrator

an-**tohn**-yoh day men-**doh**-thuh /anˌtəʊnjəʊ deɪ mɛn'dəʊθə/

Menelaus Greek mythological character
men-uh-**lay**-uhss /ˌmɛnə'leɪəs/

Menelik (also **Menelek**) Ethiopian king
men-uh-**lek** /ˌmɛnə'lɛk/

Menes Egyptian pharaoh
mee-neez /'miːniːz/

Menezes, Jean Charles de see **de Menezes**

Mengele, Josef German Nazi war criminal
yoh-zuhf meng-uh-luh /ˌjəʊzəf 'mɛŋələ/

Meng-tzu Chinese philosopher; also called **Mencius**
mung-**tsoo** /mʌŋ'tsuː/

menhaden fish
men-**hay**-duhn /mɛn'heɪdən/

menhir upright stone
men-heer /'mɛnhɪə(r)/

menial not requiring much skill
mee-ni-uhl /'miːniəl/

Ménière's disease medical condition
men-**yairz** /mɛn'jɛː(r)z/

meninges sing. **meninx** membranes lining the skull
muh-**nin**-jeez, sing. **mee**-ninks /mə'nɪndʒiːz/, sing. /'miːnɪŋks/

meningitis disease in which there is inflammation of the meninges
men-in-**jy**-tiss /ˌmɛnɪn'dʒʌɪtɪs/

meningococcus pl. **meningococci** bacterium involved in some forms of meningitis
muh-ning-goh-**kok**-uhlss, pl. muh-ning-goh-**kok**-y /məˌnɪŋgəʊ'kɒkəs/, pl. /-'kɒkʌɪ/

The plural form -*cocci* is sometimes also -**kok**-sy; see LATIN panel.

meniscus pl. **menisci** curved upper surface of a liquid in a tube
muh-**nisk**-uhss, pl. muh-**niss**-y /mə'nɪskəs/, pl. /-sʌɪ/

Menkes, Suzy Australian newspaper editor
menk-uhss /'mɛŋkəs/

Mennonite member of a Protestant sect
men-uh-nyt /'mɛnənʌɪt/

menologion calendar of the Greek Orthodox Church
men-oh-**log**-i-on /ˌmɛnəʊˈlɒɡiɒn/

meno mosso musical term
men-oh **moss**-oh /ˌmɛnəʊ ˈmɒsəʊ/

menorah Jewish candelabrum
muh-**naw**-ruh /məˈnɔːrə/

menorrhagia abnormally heavy bleeding at menstruation
men-uh-**ray**-ji-uh /ˌmɛnəˈreɪdʒiə/

menorrhoea flow of blood at menstruation
men-uh-**ree**-uh /ˌmɛnəˈriːə/

menses discharge from the uterus at menstruation
men-**seez** /ˈmɛnsiːz/

Menshevik member of the moderate non-Leninist wing of the Russian Social Democratic Workers' Party
men-shuh-vik /ˈmɛnʃəvɪk/

mens rea knowledge of wrongdoing that constitutes part of a crime
menz ree-uh /ˌmɛnz ˈriːə/
• See LATIN panel.

mensural involving measuring
men-shuh-ruhl /ˈmɛnʃərəl/

Menuhin, Yehudi American-British violinist
yuh-**hoo**-di men-**yuu**-in /jəˈhuːdi ˈmɛnjʊɪn/

Menzies, Robert Gordon Australian statesman
men-ziz /ˈmɛnzɪz/

This name can be pronounced either as above or as **ming**-iss. The latter pronunciation is traditional in most parts of Scotland; see JOHN MENZIES and CAMPBELL, MENZIES.

Meo Asian ethnic group; also called **Miao** or **Hmong**
mi-**oh** /miˈəʊ/

Mephistopheles mythological demon
mef-ist-**of**-uh-leez /ˌmɛfɪsˈtɒfəliːz/

Mephistophelian (also **Mephistophelean**) wicked
mef-ist-uh-**fee**-li-uhn /ˌmɛfɪstəˈfiːliən/

Less commonly also muh-**fist**-uh-**fee**-li-uhn or **mef**-ist-of-uh-**lee**-uhn.

Mercalli scale scale for expressing the local intensity of an earthquake
muhr-**kal**-i /məˈ(r)kali/

mercantile relating to trade
mur-kuhn-tyl /ˈməː(r)kəntʌɪl/

Mercator, Gerardus Flemish cartographer
juh-**rard**-uhss mur-**kay**-tuhr /dʒəˌrɑː(r)dəs məˈ(r)keɪtə(r)/

Merced city, US
muhr-**sed** /məˈ(r)sɛd/

Mercedes Benz trademark German car manufacturers
muhr-**say**-deez **benz** /məˈ(r)ˌseɪdiːz ˈbɛnz/, [ˌmɛrˌtseːdɛs ˈbɛnts]
• Established anglicization.

Merchant, Ismail Indian film producer
iss-**myl** mur-chuhnt /ɪsˌmʌɪl ˈməː(r)tʃənt/

Mercia former kingdom of central England
mur-si-uh /ˈməː(r)siə/

Merckx, Eddy Belgian cyclist
ed-i mairks /ˌɛdi ˈmɛː(r)ks/

Mercosur customs union between Argentina, Brazil, Paraguay, and Uruguay
mair-koh-soor /ˈmɛː(r)kəʊsʊə(r)/

Mercouri, Melina Greek actress and politician
muh-**lee**-nuh muhr-**koor**-i /məˌliːnə məˈ(r)kʊəri/

mercurial subject to unpredictable changes of mood
mur-**kyoor**-i-uhl /məˈ(r)kjʊəriəl/

merde 'shit' (French)
maird /mɛˈ(r)d/

mere Maori war club
merr-i /ˈmɛri/

Meredith, George English novelist and poet
merr-uh-dith /ˈmɛrədɪθ/

However, the usual Welsh pronunciation of this surname is muh-**red**-ith.

merengue style of dance music
merr-**eng**-gay /mɛˈrɛŋɡeɪ/

mereology philosophical study
merr-i-**ol**-uh-ji /ˌmɛrɪˈɒlədʒi/

meretricious attractive but having no real value
merr-uh-**trish**-uhss /ˌmɛrəˈtrɪʃəs/

merganser diving duck
mur-**gan**-suhr /məˈ(r)ˈɡansə(r)/

merguez spicy beef and lamb sausage
mur-gez /məˈ(r)ˈɡɛz/

Mérida city, Spain
mair-id-uh /'mɛːrɪdə/, ['meriða]
• Established anglicization.

meridian circle of constant longitude
muh-**rid**-i-uhn /mə'rɪdiən/

meridional in the south
muh-**rid**-i-uh-nuhl /mə'rɪdiənəl/

meringue baked sugar and egg whites
muh-**rang** /mə'raŋ/

merino breed of sheep
muh-**ree**-noh /mə'riːnəʊ/

meritocracy government by people
selected according to merit
merr-it-**ok**-ruh-si /ˌmɛrɪ'tɒkrəsi/

meritorious deserving reward or praise
merr-it-**aw**-ri-uhss /ˌmɛrɪ'tɔːriəs/

Merkel, Angela German stateswoman
ang-gel-uh **mair**-kuhl /ˌaŋgɛlə
'mɛː(r)kəl/

merlon solid part of a crenellated
parapet
mur-luhn /'məː(r)lən/

Merlot wine grape
mur-**loh** /məː(r)'ləʊ/

Meroe ancient city, Sudan
merr-oh-i /'mɛrəʊi/

Merope Greek mythological character
merr-uh-pi /'mɛrəpi/

Merovingian Frankish dynasty of
medieval Europe
merr-uh-**vin**-ji-uhn /ˌmɛrə'vɪndʒiən/

Mersa Matruh town, Egypt
mur-suh muh-**troo** /ˌməː(r)sə mə'truː/

Mersey river, England
mur-zi /'məː(r)zi/

Mersin port, Turkey
mair-**sin** /mɛː(r)'sɪn/

Merthyr Tydfil town, Wales
mur-thuhr **tid**-vil /ˌməː(r)θə(r) 'tɪdvɪl/

mesa flat-topped hill
may-suh /'meɪsə/

mésalliance unsuitable marriage
mez-**al**-i-uhnss /mɛ'zaliəns/

mescalin (also **mescaline**)
hallucinogenic compound
mesk-uh-lin /'mɛskəlɪn/

Less commonly also **mesk**-uh-leen with the
latter spelling.

mesclun green salad
mesk-**loon** /mɛs'kluːn/

Mesdames plural form of Madame

may-**dam** /meɪ'dam/

mesembryanthemum plant
muh-zem-bri-**anth**-uh-muhm
/məˌzɛmbri'anθəməm/

Meshal, Khaled see **Mashal, Khaled**

Meshed see **Mashhad**

meshuga (also **meshugga**) crazy
(Yiddish)
muh-**shuug**-uh /mə'ʃʊgə/

meshuggener crazy person (Yiddish)
muh-**shuug**-uh-nuhr /mə'ʃʊgənə(r)/

Mesić, Stjepan Croatian president
styep-an **mess**-itch /ˌstjɛpan 'mɛsɪtʃ/

Mesmer, Franz Anton Austrian
physician
frants an-ton **mez**-muhr /ˌfrants
ˌantɒn 'mɛzmə(r)/

mesmeric causing a person to become
transfixed
mez-**merr**-ik /mɛz'mɛrɪk/

Mesnes region near Wigan, England
maynz /meɪnz/

meson subatomic particle
mee-zon /'miːzɒn/

Mesopotamia ancient region, Asia
mess-uh-puh-**tay**-mi-uh
/ˌmɛsəpə'teɪmiə/

mesothelioma cancer
mez-oh-thee-li-**oh**-muh
/ˌmɛzəʊˌθiːli'əʊmə/

Mesozoic geological era
mess-uh-**zoh**-ik /ˌmɛsə'zəʊɪk/

mesquite tree
mesk-**eet** /mɛ'skiːt/

Messalina (also **Messallina**) Roman
empress
mess-uh-**lee**-nuh /ˌmɛsə'liːnə/

Messerschmidt, Willy German
aircraft designer
vil-i **mess**-uhr-shmit /ˌvɪli
'mɛsə(r)ˌʃmɪt/

Messiaen, Olivier French composer
ol-eev-**yay** mess-**yah(ng)** /ɒliːˌvjeɪ
mɛ'sjɑ̃/

messiah promised deliverer of the
Jewish nation
muh-**sy**-uh /mə'sʌɪə/

messianic relating to the Messiah
mess-i-**an**-ik /ˌmɛsi'anɪk/

Messier, Charles French astronomer
sharl mess-**yay** /ˌʃɑː(r)l mɛ'sjeɪ/

Messina city, Sicily
mess-**ee**-nuh /mɛ'siːnə/

Messines First World War battle site, France
mess-**een** /mɛ'siːn/

mestizo person of mixed race
mest-**ee**-zoh /mɛ'stiːzəʊ/, Spanish [mes'tiso]

metabolism chemical processes that occur within a living organism
muh-**tab**-uh-liz-uhm /mə'tabəlɪzəm/

metallurgy branch of science concerned with metals
met-uh-**lur**-ji /'mɛtələː(r)dʒi/

This pronunciation was preferred by metallurgists whom we consulted, but the pronunciation met-**al**-uhr-ji is also possible.

metamorphose undergo metamorphosis
met-uh-**mor**-fohz /ˌmɛtə'mɔː(r)fəʊz/

metamorphosis pl. **metamorphoses** transformation
met-uh-**mor**-fuh-siss, pl.
met-uh-**mor**-fuh-seez
/ˌmɛtə'mɔː(r)fəsɪs/, pl. /-siːz/

A differently stressed pronunciation, met-uh-mor-**foh**-siss, is also possible.

metastasis pl. **metastases** development of secondary cancers
met-**ast**-uh-siss, pl. met-**ast**-uh-seez
/mɛ'tastəsɪs/, pl. /-siːz/

Metazoa division of the animal kingdom
met-uh-**zoh**-uh /ˌmɛtə'zəʊə/

mete dispense or allot justice
meet /miːt/

meteorology branch of science concerned with the atmosphere
mee-ti-uh-**rol**-uh-ji /ˌmiːtiə'rɒlədʒi/

methadone heroin substitute drug
meth-uh-dohn /'mɛθədəʊn/

methane flammable gas
mee-thayn /'miːθeɪn/

The alternative pronunciation **meth**-ayn is increasingly rare.

methanol flammable liquid alcohol
meth-uh-nol /'mɛθanɒl/

Methodius, St brother of St Cyril
muh-**thoh**-di-uhss /mə'θəʊdiəs/

Methuselah biblical character
muh-**thyoo**-zuh-luh /mə'θjuːzələ/

methyl chemical derived from methane
mee-thyl /'miːθʌɪl/

Less commonly also **meth**-il, **meth**-yl, or **mee**-thil.

metical currency unit, Mozambique
met-ik-**al** /ˌmɛtɪ'kal/

métier profession or occupation
may-tyay /'meɪtjeɪ/

metonymy substitution of the name of an attribute or adjunct for that of the thing meant
met-**on**-im-i /mɛ'tɒnɪmi/

Metro-Goldwyn-Mayer American film corporation
met-roh **gohld**-win **may**-uhr /ˌmɛtrəʊ ˌgəʊldwɪn 'meɪə(r)/

metronome device that marks time
met-ruh-nohm /'mɛtrənəʊm/

Mette-Marit Norwegian crown princess
met-uh **mar**-it /ˌmɛtə 'maːrɪt/

Metternich, Prince Austrian statesman
met-uhr-nikh /'mɛtə(r)nɪç/

Metz city, France
mets /mɛts/

Meucci, Antonio Italian engineer
an-**tohn**-yoh may-**oo**-chi /anˌtəʊnjəʊ meɪ'uːtʃi/

meunière culinary term
moen-**yair** /mœn'jɛː(r)/

Meursault burgundy wine
moer-**soh** /mœ(r)'səʊ/

Meuse river, France
moez /møːz/

Mevrouw Dutch title for a married woman
muh-**vrow** /mə'vraʊ/

Mexicali city, Mexico
mek-si-**kah**-li /ˌmɛksi'kaːli/

Meyerbeer, Giacomo German composer
jah-kuh-moh **my**-uhr-beer /ˌdʒaːkəməʊ 'mʌɪə(r)ˌbɪə(r)/, ['maɪɐbeːɐ]

Meyerhof, Otto German-American biochemist
my-uhr-hof /'mʌɪə(r)hɒf/

meze selection of dishes
mez-ay /'mɛzeɪ/

mezuzah pl. **mezuzoth** parchment attached in a case to the doorpost of a Jewish house
mez-**oo**-zuh, pl. mez-**oo**-zoht /mɛ'zuːzə/, /-zəʊt/

Sometimes also **mez-uuz-ah**, a pronunciation closer to the Hebrew.

mezzaluna semi-circular blade for chopping herbs
met-suh-loo-nuh /ˌmɛtsəˈluːnə/

mezzanine storey between two others in a building
met-suh-neen /ˈmɛtsəniːn/

Commonly also **mez-uh-neen**.

mezzo female singer
met-soh /ˈmɛtsəʊ/

Mezzogiorno region, Italy
med-zoh-jor-noh /ˌmɛdzəʊˈdʒɔː(r)nəʊ/

Mhairi Gaelic girl's name
var-i /ˈvɑːri/

Miami city, US
my-am-i /mʌɪˈami/

Miao Asian ethnic group; also called
Meo or **Hmong**
mi-ow /ˈmiˈaʊ/

miasma unhealthy vapour
mi-az-muh /mɪˈazmə/

mica shiny mineral
my-kuh /ˈmʌɪkə/

Micah Hebrew minor prophet
my-kuh /ˈmʌɪkə/

Micawber, Mr Dickensian character
mik-aw-buhr /mɪˈkɔːbə(r)/

Michaelmas feast of St Michael
mik-uhl-muhss /ˈmɪkəlməs/

Michelangelo Italian artist
my-kuhl-an-juh-loh
/ˌmʌɪkəlˈandʒələʊ/
• Established anglicization.

Michelin tyre manufacturers
mitch-uh-lin /ˈmɪtʃəlɪn/

Established anglicization. This pronunciation is appropriate for the company and its products. The French pronunciation **meesh-la(ng)** [miʃlɛ̃] is appropriate for the names of the company's French founders.

Michelob American beer brand
mik-uh-lohb /ˈmɪkələʊb/

Michelozzo Italian architect and sculptor
mik-el-ot-soh /ˌmɪkɛˈlɒtsəʊ/

Michigan lake and state, US
mish-ig-uhn /ˈmɪʃɪɡən/

Michoacán state, Mexico
mee-choh-ak-an /ˌmiːtʃəʊaˈkan/

Mickiewicz, Adam Polish poet
ad-am meets-kyev-eetch /ˌadam
miːtsˈkjɛviːtʃ/

microcosm encapsulation in miniature
my-kroh-koz-uhm /ˈmʌɪkrəʊkɒzəm/

microfiche film containing microphotographs of the pages of a document
my-kroh-feesh /ˈmʌɪkrəʊfiːʃ/

micrometer gauge which measures small distances
my-krom-uh-tuhr /mʌɪˈkrɒmətə(r)/

micrometre unit of measurement
my-kroh-mee-tuhr
/ˈmʌɪkrəʊˌmiːtə(r)/

micron unit of measurement
my-kron /ˈmʌɪkrɒn/

Micronesia region, Pacific
my-kroh-nee-zhuh /ˌmʌɪkrəʊˈniːʒə/

micturate urinate
mik-tyoor-ayt /ˈmɪktjʊreɪt/

Midas Greek mythological character
my-duhss /ˈmʌɪdəs/

Midler, Bette American entertainer
bet mid-luhr /ˌbɛt ˈmɪdlə(r)/

Midlothian area, Scotland
mid-loh-thi-uhn /mɪdˈləʊðiən/

Mido Egyptian footballer
mee-doh /ˈmiːdəʊ/

Midrash ancient commentary on part of the Hebrew scriptures
mid-rash /ˈmɪdraʃ/

Miele German appliance manufacturers
mee-luh /ˈmiːlə/

mien person's appearance or manner
meen /miːn/

Mies van der Rohe, Ludwig German-American architect and designer
loot-vikh meess van dair roh-uh
/ˌluːtvɪç ˌmiːs van dɛː(r) ˈrəʊə/

mifepristone drug given to induce abortion
mif-ep-rist-ohn /ˌmɪfɛˈprɪstəʊn/

migraine throbbing headache
mee-grayn /ˈmiːɡreɪn/

Commonly also **my-grayn**.

Mihailović, Draža Yugoslav general
drazh-uh mi-**hy**-luh-vitch /ˌdraʒə
miˈhʌɪləvɪtʃ/

mihrab niche in the wall of a mosque at
the point nearest to Mecca
mee-rahb /ˈmiːrɑːb/

mikado title given to the emperor of
Japan
mik-**ah**-doh /mɪˈkɑːdəʊ/

mikva Jewish ritual bath
mik-vuh /ˈmɪkvə/

Milan city, Italy
mil-**an** /mɪˈlan/

Established anglicization. The Italian name
is Milano, pronounced mil-**ah**-noh.

milch cow kept for milk
miltch /mɪltʃ/

miles gloriosus pl. **milites gloriosi**
boastful soldier
mee-layz glaw-ri-**oh**-suhss, pl.
mil-it-ayz glaw-ri-**oh**-see /ˌmiːleɪz
ˌɡlɔːrɪˈəʊsəs/, pl. /ˌmɪlɪteɪz ˌɡlɔːrɪˈəʊsiː/

Milesian inhabitant of ancient Miletus
my-**leesh**-uhn /mʌɪˈliːʃən/

Miletus ancient city, Asia Minor
my-**lee**-tuhss /mʌɪˈliːtəs/

Milhaud, Darius French composer
darr-i-**uess** mee-**yoh** /dariˌʏs miːˈjəʊ/

milieu pl. **milieux** social environment
mil-**yoe**, pl. mil-**yoe** /mɪˈljø/, pl.
/mɪˈljø/

Millais, John Everett English painter
mil-ay /ˈmɪleɪ/

millefeuille pastry cake
meel-**foey** /miːlˈfœɪ/

millefiori ornamental glass
mil-i-**fyaw**-ri /ˌmɪlɪˈfjɔːri/

millenary period of a thousand years
mil-**en**-uh-ri /mɪˈlɛnəri/

Millet, Jean French painter
zhah(ng) mee-**yay** /ˌʒɑ̃ miːˈjeɪ/

Millett, Kate American feminist
mil-uht /ˈmɪlət/

Milngavie town, Scotland
mul-**gy** /mʌlˈɡʌɪ/

milometer instrument for measuring
the number of miles travelled
my-**lom**-uh-tuhr /mʌɪˈlɒmətə(r)/

Milos island, Greece
mee-loss /ˈmiːlɒs/

The former name, Melos, is pronounced in
the same way, although there are a number
of musical ensembles named Melos who
generally use the more classical
pronunciation **may**-loss.

Milošević, Slobodan Serbian
statesman
slob-**od**-an mil-**osh**-uh-vitch
/slɒˌbɒdan mɪˈlɒʃəvɪtʃ/

Milquetoast timid person
milk-tohst /ˈmɪlktəʊst/

Miltiades Greek general
mil-**ty**-uh-deez /mɪlˈtʌɪədiːz/

Milton Keynes town, England
keenz /kiːnz/

Milupa baby food manufacturers
mil-**oo**-puh /mɪlˈuːpə/

Milwaukee port, US
mil-**waw**-ki /mɪlˈwɔːki/

Mimas moon of Saturn
my-mass /ˈmʌɪmas/

Mime Wagnerian character
mee-muh /ˈmiːmə/

mimesis imitation
mim-**ee**-siss /mɪˈmiːsɪs/

mimosa Australian tree
mim-**oh**-suh /mɪˈməʊsə/

Mina site of pilgrimage near Mecca
mee-nuh /ˈmiːnə/

Minangkabau Indonesian language
mee-nank-uh-**bow** /ˌmiːnaŋkəˈbaʊ/

minaret part of a mosque
min-uh-ret /ˈmɪnərɛt/

Minas Gerais state, Brazil
mee-nuhzh zhuh-**ryss** /ˌmiːnəʒ
ʒəˈrʌɪs/

Minas Morgul fictional place in *The
Lord of the Rings*
min-ass mor-gool /ˌmɪnas ˈmɔː(r)ɡuːl/

Minas Tirith fictional place in *The Lord
of the Rings*
min-ass tirr-ith /ˌmɪnas ˈtɪrɪθ/

minatory expressing a threat
min-uh-tuh-ri /ˈmɪnətəri/

minaudière small handbag
min-ohd-**yair** /ˌmɪnəʊˈdjɛː(r)/

Mindanao island, Philippines
min-duh-**now** /ˌmɪndəˈnaʊ/

Mindoro island, Philippines
min-**daw**-roh /mɪnˈdɔːrəʊ/

Minerva Roman goddess
min-**ur**-vuh /mɪˈnɜː(r)və/

Minervois French wine
min-air-**vwah** /ˌmɪnɛ:(r)'vwɑ:/

minestrone thick soup
min-uh-**stroh**-ni /ˌmɪnə'strəʊni/

Minghella, Anthony English film
director
ming-**gel**-uh /mɪŋ'gɛlə/

minging foul-smelling
ming-ing /'mɪŋɪŋ/

Mingus, Charlie American jazz
musician
ming-**guhss** /'mɪŋgəs/

mingy mean
min-ji /'mɪndʒi/

Minho river, Portugal; also called **Miño**
in Spain
meen-yoo /'mi:nju:/

Minicoy Islands islands, Indian Ocean
min-ik-oy /'mɪnɪkɔɪ/

miniver fur used for lining or trimming
clothes
min-iv-uhr /'mɪnɪvə(r)/

minke whale
mink-i /'mɪŋki/

Minkowski, Hermann
Russian-German mathematician
hair-man min-**kof**-ski /ˌhɛ:(r)man
mɪŋ'kɒfski/

Minneapolis city, US
min-i-**ap**-uh-liss /ˌmɪni'apəlɪs/

Minnelli, Liza American singer
ly-zuh min-**el**-i /ˌlaɪzə mɪ'nɛli/

minneola citrus fruit
min-i-**oh**-luh /ˌmɪni'əʊlə/

Minnesinger German lyric poet
min-uh-zing-uhr /'mɪnəzɪŋə(r)/

Minnesota state, US
min-uh-**soh**-tuh /ˌmɪnə'səʊtə/

Miño river, Spain; also called **Minho** in
Portugal
meen-yoh /'mi:njəʊ/

Minoan relating to a Bronze Age
civilization centred on Crete
min-**oh**-uhn /mɪ'nəʊən/

Minorca Balearic island
min-**or**-kuh /mɪ'nɔ:(r)kə/

Minogue, Kylie Australian singer
ky-li min-**ohg** /ˌkaɪli mɪ'nəʊg/

Minos Greek mythological character
my-noss /'maɪnɒs/

Minotaur Greek mythological creature

my-nuh-tor /'maɪnətɔ:(r)/

Minquiers islands, Jersey, UK
mink-iz /'mɪŋkɪz/

Minsk capital of Belarus
minsk /mɪnsk/

minuscule extremely small
min-**uhss**-kyool /'mɪnəskju:l/

minutiae precise details of something
my-**nyoo**-shi-ee /maɪ'nju:ʃii:/

Commonly also min-**yoo**-shi-y.

minyan pl. **minyanim** quorum of ten
men required for traditional Jewish
public worship
min-yuhn, pl. **min**-yuhn-im /'mɪnjən/,
pl. /'mɪnjənɪm/

Miocene geological epoch
my-oh-seen /'maɪəʊsi:n/

miosis excessive constriction of the pupil
of the eye
my-**oh**-siss /maɪ'əʊsɪs/

Miquelon islands, Atlantic
mee-kuh-lon /mi:'kələn/, French
[miklɔ̃]
● Established anglicization.

Mir Soviet space station
meer /mɪə(r)/

Mira star
my-ruh /'maɪrə/

Mirabeau, Comte de French
revolutionary politician
ko(ng)t duh mirr-uh-**boh** /ˌkɔ̃t də
mɪrə'bəʊ/

mirabelle plum-like fruit
mirr-uh-bel /'mɪrəbɛl/

mirabile dictu wonderful to relate
mirr-**ah**-bil-ay dik-**too** /mɪˌrɑ:bɪleɪ
'dɪktu:/

mirage optical illusion
mirr-**ahzh** /mɪr'ɑ:ʒ/

Mirchandani, Rajesh BBC journalist
rah-jesh mur-chuhn-**dah**-ni /ˌrɑ:dʒɛʃ
mə:(r)tʃən'dɑ:ni/

mirepoix mixture of sautéed chopped
vegetables used in sauces
meer-**pwah** /ˌmɪə(r)'pwɑ:/

mirin rice wine
mirr-in /'mɪrɪn/

Miró, Joan Spanish painter
zhoo-**an** mee-**roh** /ʒu:ˌan mi:'rəʊ/

misandry hatred of men
miss-**an**-dri /mɪ'sandri/

Top ten mispronunciations

The following list gives examples of ten words and names that are commonly mispronounced. Look up each individual entry for the Pronunciation Unit recommendation!

Beijing
Mohamed ElBaradei
genealogy
Medici
Melbourne

Slobodan Milošević
nuclear
Vladimir Putin
restaurateur
J. K. Rowling

---

misanthrope person who dislikes humankind
miss-uhn-throhp /ˈmɪsənθrəʊp/

miscegenation interbreeding
miss-ej-uh-**nay**-shuhn /ˌmɪsɛdʒəˈneɪʃən/

miscellany collection of different items
miss-**el**-luh-ni /mɪˈsɛləni/

mischievous causing trouble
miss-chuh-vuhss /ˈmɪstʃɪvəs/

The mispronunciation mis-**cheev**-i-uhss, probably founded on a misspelling, is sometimes heard but should be avoided.

miscreant wrongdoer
misk-ri-uhnt /ˈmɪskriənt/

mise en scène arrangement of scenery in a play
meez ah(ng) **sen** /ˌmiːz ã ˈsɛn/

miserere psalm
miz-uh-**rair**-uh /mɪzəˈrɛːrə/
• See LATIN panel.

misericord ledge projecting from the underside of a hinged seat
miz-**air**-i-kord /mɪˈzɛːrɪkɔː(r)d/

Mishcon de Reya British law firm
mish-kon duh **ray**-uh /ˌmɪʃkɒn də ˈreɪə/

Mishima, Yukio Japanese writer
yoo-ki-oh **mee**-shim-uh /ˌjuːkiəʊ ˈmiːʃɪmə/

Misirlou Greek folk song
miz-eer-**loo** /mɪzɪəˈ(r)ˈluː/

Miskolc city, Hungary
mish-kolts /ˈmɪʃkɒlts/

miso paste made from fermented soya beans
mee-soh /ˈmiːsəʊ/

misogyny hatred of women
miss-**oj**-uh-ni /mɪˈsɒdʒəni/

missa brevis short mass
miss-uh **bray**-viss /ˌmɪsə ˈbreɪvɪs/

missal book containing the texts used in the Catholic Mass
miss-uhl /ˈmɪsəl/

Mississauga town, Canada
miss-iss-**aw**-guh /ˌmɪsɪˈsɔːgə/

Mississippi river, US
miss-iss-**ip**-i /ˌmɪsɪˈsɪpi/

Missolonghi city, Greece
miss-uh-**long**-gi /ˌmɪsəˈlɒŋgi/

Missoula town, US
miz-**ool**-uh /mɪˈzuːlə/

Missouri river, US
miz-**oor**-i /mɪˈzʊəri/

mistral strong French wind
mist-**rahl** /mɪˈstrɑːl/

Mitchell, Joni Canadian singer
joh-ni /ˈdʒəʊni/

mithai Indian sweets
mit-y /mɪˈtʌɪ/

mither make a fuss
my-*th*uhr /'mʌɪðə(r)/

Mithraeum temple of the god Mithras
mith-**ree**-uhm /mɪˈθriːəm/

Mithras god, probably of Persian origin
mith-rass /'mɪθras/

Mithridates ancient king of Pontus
mith-rid-**ay**-teez /ˌmɪθrɪˈdeɪtiːz/

Mitla ancient city, Mexico
meet-luh /'miːtlə/

mitochondrion pl. **mitochondria**
organelle found in most cells
my-tuh-**kon**-dri-uhn, pl.
my-tuh-**kon**-dri-uh /ˌmʌɪtəˈkɒndriən/,
pl. /-riə/

mitosis type of cell division
my-**toh**-siss /mʌɪˈtəʊsɪs/

Mitsiwa port, Eritrea; also called
Massawa
mit-**see**-wuh /mɪˈtsiːwə/

Mittal, Lakshmi Indian businessman
luk-shmi **mit**-uhl /ˌlʌkʃmi 'mɪtəl/

Mittelland canal, Germany
mit-uhl-lant /'mɪtəlˌlant/

Mitterrand, François French
statesman
frah(ng)-**swah** meet-uhr-**ah(ng)**
/frɑ̃ˌswɑ miːtəˈrɑ̃/

mitzvah pl. **mitzvoth** Jewish precept or
commandment
mits-vuh, pl. **mits**-voht /'mɪtsvə/, pl.
/-vəʊt/

Mixolydian musical mode
mik-suh-**lid**-i-uhn /ˌmɪksəˈlɪdiən/

Miyagi prefecture, Japan
mi-**yah**-gi /mɪˈjɑːgi/

Miyake, Issey Japanese fashion
designer
iss-i mi-**yak**-i /ˌɪsi miˈjaki/, [ɪsi
mijake]
• Established anglicization.

Mizoram state, India
miz-aw-ram /'mɪzɔːram/

Mizrahi, Isaac American fashion
designer
miz-**rah**-hi /mɪzˈrɑːhi/

mizuna salad leaves
miz-**oo**-nuh /mɪˈzuːnə/

Mmabatho city, South Africa
mab-**ah**-toh /maˈbɑːtəʊ/

mnemonic device which assists in
remembering something
ni-**mon**-ik /nɪˈmɒnɪk/

Mnemosyne Greek mythological
character
nim-**oz**-in-i /nɪˈmɒzɪni/

Moab ancient kingdom, Dead Sea
moh-ab /'məʊab/

Moabite biblical people
moh-uh-byt /'məʊəbʌɪt/

moai Easter Island statues
moh-y /'məʊʌɪ/

Mobile city, Alabama
moh-**beel** /məʊˈbiːl/

Möbius strip surface with one
continuous side
moe-bi-uhss /'məːbiəs/

Mobutu Sese Seko African statesman
muh-**boo**-too **sess**-ay **sek**-oh
/məˈbuːtuː ˌsɛseɪ ˌsɛkəʊ/

mocha type of coffee
mok-uh /'mɒkə/

modal relating to form as opposed to
substance
moh-duhl /'məʊdəl/

modem device for modulation and
demodulation
moh-dem /'məʊdɛm/

Modena city, Italy
mod-in-uh /'mɒdɪnə/[ˈmoːdena]

Established anglicization. Less commonly
also mod-**ee**-nuh, an anglicization which we
do not recommend.

moderne artistic style
muh-**dairn** /məˈdɛː(r)n/

modicum small quantity
mod-ik-uhm /'mɒdɪkəm/

Modigliani, Amedeo Italian painter
and sculptor
am-uh-**day**-oh mod-il-**yah**-ni
/aməˈdeɪəʊ ˌmɒdɪˈljɑːni/

modus operandi pl. **modi operandi**
particular way of doing something
moh-duhss op-uh-**ran**-di, pl. **moh**-di
/ˌməʊdəs ɒpəˈrandi/, pl. /ˌməʊdi/

Moesia ancient country, Europe
meesh-uh /'miːʃə/

Moët et Chandon brand of champagne
moh-uht ay **shah(ng)**-do(ng) /ˌməʊət
eɪ 'ʃɑ̃dɔ̃/

The company's preferred anglicization, influenced by the Dutch origins of the first name. However, the pronunciation **moh-ay** is also often heard.

Mogadishu capital of Somalia
mog-uh-**dish**-oo /ˌmɒɡəˈdɪʃuː/

Mogadon trademark drug
mog-uh-don /ˈmɒɡədɒn/

Mogae, Festus president of Botswana
fest-uhss **muukh**-y /ˌfɛstəs ˈmʊxʌɪ/

Mogul (also **Moghul**) Muslim dynasty of Mongol origin
moh-**guhl** /ˈməʊɡəl/

This pronunciation is also appropriate for other meanings of the word: an important person or a bump on a ski slope. The etymologically related word MUGHAL is pronounced differently.

Mohács port, Hungary
moh-hahtch /ˈməʊhɑːtʃ/

Mohammed see **Muhammad**

Mohave see **Mojave**

Mohegan (also **Mohican**) American Indian ethnic group
moh-**hee**-guhn /məʊˈhiːɡən/

mohel Jew who performs the rite of circumcision
moh-**huhl** /ˈməʊhəl/

Mohenjo-Daro ancient city, Pakistan
moh-**hen**-joh **dah**-roh /məʊˌhɛndʒəʊ ˈdɑːrəʊ/

Moholy-Nagy, László Hungarian-American artist
lah-sloh **moh**-hoy noj /ˌlɑːsləʊ ˌməʊhɔɪ ˈnɒdʒ/

Mohorovičić discontinuity surface between the earth's crust and the mantle
moh-huh-**rov**-itch-itch /ˌməʊhəˈrɒvɪtʃɪtʃ/

Often shortened by geologists to 'Moho', pronounced **moh**-hoh.

Mohs' scale scale of hardness of minerals
mohz /məʊz/

Moi, Daniel Arap Kenyan statesman
arr-uhp **moy** /ˌarəp ˈmɔɪ/

moiety each of two parts into which a thing is divided
moy-uh-ti /ˈmɔɪəti/

Moirai Greek mythological characters
moy-ry /ˈmɔɪrʌɪ/

moiré silk fabric
mwar-ay /ˈmwɑːreɪ/

Moissan, Ferdinand French chemist
fair-di-**nah(ng)** mwass-ah(ng) /fɛː(r)diˈnɑ̃ mwaˈsɑ̃/

Mojave (also **Mohave**) desert, US
moh-**hah**-vi /məʊˈhɑːvi/

mojito cocktail
moh-**hee**-toh /məʊˈhiːtəʊ/

mojo magic charm
moh-joh /ˈməʊdʒəʊ/

moko traditional Maori tattoo
moh-koh /ˈməʊkəʊ/

Mold town, Wales
mohld /məʊld/

Moldavia former principality, Europe
mol-**day**-vi-uh /mɒlˈdeɪvɪə/

Moldova country
mol-**doh**-vuh /mɒlˈdəʊvə/

mole (also **mol**) SI unit of amount of substance
mohl /məʊl/

mole Mexican sauce
moh-lay /ˈməʊleɪ/

Molière French dramatist
mol-i-**air** /ˈmɒliɛː(r), [mɒljɛr]

Molinaro, Simone Italian composer
sim-**oh**-nay mol-in-**ar**-oh /sɪˌməʊneɪ mɒlɪˈnɑːrəʊ/

Molise region, Italy
mol-**ee**-zay /mɒˈliːzeɪ/

Mollweide map projection
mol-vy-duh /ˈmɒlvʌɪdə/

Molnár, Ferenc Hungarian writer
ferr-ents mol-nar /ˌfɛrɛnts ˈmɒlnɑː(r)/

Moloch Canaanite idol to whom children were sacrificed
moh-lok /ˈməʊlɒk/

Molokai island, Hawaii
moh-luh-**ky** /məʊləˈkʌɪ/

Molotov, Vyacheslav Soviet statesman
vyatch-uh-**slaf** mol-uh-tuhf /vjatʃəˌslaf ˈmɒlətəf/

Molsheim town, France
mol-**zem** /mɒlˈzɛm/

As is common in Alsace-Lorraine, this town has a German name which is given a French pronunciation as standard. The German pronunciation is **mohlz**-hym.

molto musical term
mol-toh /ˈmɒltəʊ/

Molucca island group, Indonesia
muh-**luk**-uh /məˈlʌkə/

molybdenum chemical element
muh-**lib**-duh-nuhm /məˈlɪbdənəm/

Molyneaux, James Northern Irish politician
mol-in-oh /ˈmɒlɪnəʊ/

Mombasa port, Kenya
mom-**bass**-uh /mɒmˈbasə/

Mommsen, Theodor German historian
tay-uh-dor **mom**-zuhn /ˌteɪədɔː(r) ˈmɒmzən/

Mompou, Federico Spanish composer
fed-err-**ee**-koh muum-**poh**-oo /ˌfɛdɛˌriːkəʊ mʊmˈpəʊuː/, Catalan [mʊmˈpou]

Monaco principality, Europe
mon-uh-koh /ˈmɒnəkəʊ/

monad single unit
mon-ad /ˈmɒnad/

Monadhliath mountains, Scotland
mon-uh-**lee**-uh /mɒnəˈliːə/

monadnock isolated hill or ridge
muh-**nad**-nok /məˈnadnɒk/

Monaghan county, Republic of Ireland
mon-uh-huhn /ˈmɒnəhən/

Mona Lisa painting by Leonardo da Vinci
moh-nuh **lee**-zuh /ˌməʊnə ˈliːzə/

Monash university, Australia
mon-ash /ˈmɒnaʃ/

Monbazillac sweet white wine
mo(ng)-**baz**-i-**yak** /ˌmɔ̃baziˈjak/

Monbiot, George English writer and activist
mon-bi-oh /ˈmɒnbiəʊ/

Mönchengladbach city, Germany
moen-khuhn-**glat**-bakh /ˌmœnçənˈɡlatbax/

Monck, George English general
munk /mʌŋk/

mondaine belonging to fashionable society
mo(ng)-**den** /mɔ̃ˈdɛn/

Mondeo model of Ford car
mon-**day**-oh /mɒnˈdeɪəʊ/

mondial relating to the whole world
mon-di-uhl /ˈmɒndɪəl/

Mondrian, Piet Dutch painter
peet mon-dri-ahn /ˌpiːt ˈmɒndrɪɑːn/

Monégasque native of Monaco

mon-eg-ask /ˌmɒnɛˈɡask/

Monel trademark alloy metal
moh-nuhl /ˈməʊnəl/

Monet, Claude French painter
klohd mon-**ay** /ˌkləʊd mɒˈneɪ/

Mongol native of Mongolia
mong-guhl /ˈmɒŋɡəl/

Mongolia country
mon-**goh**-li-uh /mɒŋˈɡəʊlɪə/

Monmouth town, Wales
mon-muhth /ˈmɒnməθ/

Monoceros constellation
muh-**noss**-uh-ruhss /məˈnɒsərəs/

Monod, Jacques French biochemist
zhahk mon-**oh** /ˌʒɑːk mɒˈnəʊ/

monodactyly malformation of the hands or feet
mon-uh-**dak**-til-i /ˌmɒnəˈdaktɪli/

monody Greek ode
mon-uh-di /ˈmɒnədi/

monomer molecule that forms a polymer
mon-uh-muhr /ˈmɒnəmə(r)/

monophthong vowel that has a single perceived auditory quality
mon-uhf-thong /ˈmɒnəfθɒŋ/

Sometimes also **mon**-uhp-thong or, especially in AM, muh-**nop**-thong.

Monostatos character in Mozart opera
mon-**ost**-uh-toss /mɒˈnɒstatɒs/

monotheism belief that there is only one God
mon-uh-thee-iz-uhm /ˈmɒnəˌθiːɪzəm/

Monroe, James American statesman
muhn-**roh** /mənˈrəʊ/

The same pronunciation is used for Marilyn and others of the name, and for the US city.

Monrovia capital of Liberia
muhn-**roh**-vi-uh /mənˈrəʊvɪə/

Mons town, Belgium
monz /mɒnz/

Monsanto American agrichemical company
mon-**san**-toh /mɒnˈsantəʊ/

Monsarrat, Nicholas English writer
mon-suh-rat /ˈmɒnsərat/

Monseigneur pl. **Messeigneurs** title of a French-speaking prince, cardinal, or bishop
mo(ng)-sen-**yoer**, pl. mess-en-**yoer** /ˌmɔ̃sɛˈnjœː(r)/, pl. /ˌmɛsɛˈnjœː(r)/

Monsieur pl. **Messieurs** title of a
French-speaking man
muh-**syoe**, pl. mess-**yoe** /mə'sjø/, pl.
/mɛ'sjø/

Monsignor title of various senior
Roman Catholic posts
mon-**seen**-yor /mɒn'siːnjɔː(r)/

monstera plant
mon-**steer**-uh /mɒn'stɪərə/

Montagnard Vietnamese Christian
ethnic group
mont-uhn-**yard** /ˌmɒntə'njɑː(r)d/

Montaigne, Michel de French essayist
mee-**shel** duh mon-**tayn** /miːˌʃɛl də
mɒn'teɪn/, [miʃɛl də mɔ̃tɛɲ]
• Established anglicization.

Montana state, US
mon-**tan**-uh /mɒn'tanə/

Mont Blanc peak in the Alps
mo(ng) blah(ng) /mɔ̃ 'blɑ̃/

Montcalm, Louis French general
lwee mo(ng)-**kalm** /ˌlwiː mɔ̃'kalm/

This pronunciation also correct for the place
in Quebec of the same name.

Monte Albán ancient city, Mexico
mon-tay al-**ban** /ˌmɒnteɪ al'ban/

Monte Carlo resort, Monaco
mon-ti kar-**loh** /ˌmɒnti 'kɑː(r)ləʊ/
• Established anglicization.

Monte Cassino hill, Italy
mon-tay kass-**ee**-noh /ˌmɒnteɪ
ka'siːnəʊ/

Monte Cervino Italian name for
Matterhorn
mon-tay chair-**vee**-noh /ˌmɒnteɪ
tʃɛː(r)'viːnəʊ/

Montego Bay port, Jamaica
mon-**tee**-goh /mɒn'tiːgəʊ/

Montenegro autonomous republic,
Europe
mon-ti-**neeg**-roh /ˌmɒntɪ'niːgrəʊ/

Established anglicization. The native name
is Crna Gora, pronounced **tsur**-nuh gorr-uh
[ˈtsrːna ˌgɒra].

Montepulciano red wine
mon-tay-puul-**chah**-noh
/ˌmɒnteɪpʊl'tʃɑːnəʊ/

Monterey city, US
mon-tuh-**ray** /ˌmɒntə'reɪ/

Monterrey city, Mexico
mon-terr-**ay** /ˌmɒntɛ'reɪ/

Montesquieu, Baron French political
philosopher
mo(ng)-tesk-**yoe** /mɔ̃tɛ'skjø/

Montessori system of education for
young children
mon-tiss-**aw**-ri /ˌmɒntɪ'sɔːri/

Monteverdi, Claudio Italian composer
klow-di-oh mon-tiv-**air**-di /ˌklaʊdiəʊ
ˌmɒntɪ'vɛː(r)di/

Montevideo capital of Uruguay
mon-tiv-id-**ay**-oh /ˌmɒntɪvɪ'deɪəʊ/,
Spanish /monteβi'ðeo/
• Established anglicization.

Montez, Lola Irish dancer
mon-tez /'mɒntez/

Montezuma Aztec emperor
mont-uh-**zoo**-muh /ˌmɒntə'zuːmə/

Montfort, Simon de English soldier
mont-fort /'mɒntfɔː(r)t/

Montgolfier brothers French hot-air
balloon pioneers
mo(ng)-golf-**yay** /mɔ̃gɒl'fjeɪ/

Montgomery capital of Alabama, US
muhnt-**gum**-uh-ri /mənt'gʌməri/

Montgomery, Field Marshal English
soldier
muhnt-**gum**-uh-ri /mənt'gʌməri/

Montmartre district, Paris
mo(ng)-**mar**-truh /mɔ̃'mɑː(r)trə/

Montonero member of a left-wing
guerrilla organization in Argentina
mont-on-**air**-oh /ˌmɒntɒ'nɛːrəʊ/

Montparnasse district, Paris
mo(ng)-par-**nass** /mɔ̃pɑː(r)'nas/

Montpelier capital of Vermont
mont-**peel**-yuhr /mɒnt'piːljə(r)/

Montpellier city, France
mo(ng)-pel-**yay** /mɔ̃pɛl'jeɪ/

Montreal port, Canada
mon-tri-**awl** /ˌmɒntri'ɔːl/

Established anglicization. Sometimes also
mo(ng)-ray-al, a pronunciation closer to the
French version.

Montreux town, Switzerland
mo(ng)-**troe** /mɔ̃'trø/

Mont St Michel rocky islet, France
mo(ng) sa(ng) mee-**shel** /ˌmɔ̃ sɛ̃
miː'ʃɛl/

Montserrat island, Caribbean
mont-suh-**rat** /ˌmɒntsə'rat/

Moodyson, Lukas Swedish film
director
loo-kuhss **mod**-iss-on /ˌluːkəs
ˈmɒdɪsɒn/

Moog electronic music synthesizer
mohg /məʊg/

Invented by Robert Moog, who advised that
his name should rhyme with 'vogue'.
Nevertheless, commonly pronounced moog.

moolah money
moo-luh /ˈmuːlə/

Moor north African ethnic group
moor /mʊə(r)/

Also mawr. This difference in pronunciation
depends on regional accent. The same is
true, and the same two pronunciations
possible, for other meanings of the word
moor and for the surname Moore.

Moore, Demi American actress
duh-**mee mawr** /dəˌmi: ˈmɔː(r)/

Mopti city, Mali
mop-ti /ˈmɒpti/

moquette thick pile fabric used for
carpets
mok-**et** /mɒˈkɛt/

Moradabad city, India
maw-rah-duh-**bad** /ˌmɔːrɑːdəˈbad/

moraine rocks deposited by a glacier
muh-**rayn** /məˈreɪn/

Morales, Cristobal de see de Morales,
Cristobal

Morales, Evo president of Bolivia
ay-voh morr-**ah**-less /ˌeɪvəʊ mɒˈrɑːlɛs/

Moran, Dylan Irish comedian
maw-ruhn /ˈmɔːrən/

Morar, Loch loch, Scotland
maw-ruhr /ˈmɔːrə(r)/

morass area of boggy ground
muh-**rass** /məˈras/

Moravia region of the Czech Republic
muh-**ray**-vi-uh /məˈreɪviə/
• Established anglicization.

Moray area and firth, Scotland
murr-i /ˈmʌri/

moray eel-like fish
morr-ay /ˈmɒreɪ/

morbilli measles
mor-**bil**-y /mɔː(r)ˈbɪlʌɪ/

morceau short literary or musical
composition
mor-**soh** /mɔː(r)ˈsəʊ/

Mordor fictional place in *The Lord of the
Rings*
mor-dor /ˈmɔː(r)dɔː(r)/

Mordred Arthurian character
mor-druhd /ˈmɔː(r)drəd/

Mordvinia autonomous republic, Russia
mord-**vin**-i-uh /mɔː(r)ˈdvɪniə/

Moreau, Jeanne French actress
zhan morr-**oh** /ˌʒan mɒˈrəʊ/

morel edible fungus
muh-**rel** /məˈrɛl/

Morelia city, Mexico
morr-**ay**-li-uh /mɒˈreɪliə/

morello cherry
muh-**rel**-oh /məˈrɛləʊ/

Morelos state, Mexico
morr-**ay**-loss /mɒˈreɪlɒs/

mores customs and conventions of a
society
maw-rayz /ˈmɔːreɪz/

morganatic denoting a marriage in
which one spouse has no claim to the
other's possessions
mor-guh-**nat**-ik /ˌmɔː(r)gəˈnatɪk/

Morgan le Fay legendary enchantress
mor-guhn luh **fay** /ˌmɔː(r)gən lə ˈfeɪ/

MORI Market and Opinion Research
International
morr-i /ˈmɒri/

moribund at the point of death
morr-i-bund /ˈmɒrɪbʌnd/

Mörike, Eduard German poet
ayd-wart **moe**-rik-uh /ˌeɪdwɑː(r)t
ˈməːrɪkə/

Morisco Spanish Moor
muh-**risk**-oh /məˈrɪskəʊ/

Morisot, Berthe French painter
bairt morr-iz-**oh** /ˌbɛː(r)t mɒrɪˈzəʊ/

Mormon member of the Church of Jesus
Christ of Latter-Day Saints
mor-muhn /ˈmɔː(r)mən/

mornay served in a cheese-flavoured
white sauce
mor-nay /ˈmɔː(r)neɪ/

Morocco country
muh-**rok**-oh /məˈrɒkəʊ/

Moroni capital of Comoros
muh-**roh**-ni /məˈrəʊni/

Morpeth town, England
mor-puhth /ˈmɔː(r)pəθ/

Top ten most frequently asked questions

The following list gives examples of the words and names we are asked about the most, both by BBC programme makers and by members of the audience.

Look up each individual entry for the Pronunciation Unit recommendation!

Basle/Basel

Boudicca

cervical

Niger

al-Qaeda

Roosevelt

scone

Shrewsbury

Van Gogh

Uranus

Morpheus Roman mythological character
morf-yooss /ˈmɔː(r)fjuːs/

Commonly also **mor**-fi-uhss.

morphine drug
mor-feen /ˈmɔː(r)fiːn/

Morpurgo, Michael English children's writer
mor-**pur**-goh /mɔː(r)ˈpəː(r)gəʊ/

Morricone, Ennio Italian composer
en-yoh morr-i-**koh**-nay /ˌɛnjəʊ mɒriˈkəʊnei/

mortadella Italian sausage
mor-tuh-**del**-uh /ˌmɔː(r)təˈdɛlə/

mortgage loan
mor-gij /ˈmɔː(r)gɪdʒ/

mosaic picture produced by arranging tiles
moh-**zay**-ik /məʊˈzeɪɪk/

moscato Italian dessert wine
mosk-**ah**-toh /mɒˈskɑːtəʊ/

Moschino Italian fashion label
mosk-**ee**-noh /mɒˈskiːnəʊ/

Moscow capital of Russia

mosk-oh /ˈmɒskəʊ/

Established anglicization; AM commonly **mosk**-ow. The Russian name is Moskva, pronounced muhsk-**vah**.

Mosel river, Europe
moh-zuhl /ˈməʊzəl/

This is the German pronunciation; the river also runs through France, where the spelling is Moselle and the pronunciation is moz-**el**. Wine of the same name is produced in both countries.

moshav cooperative association of Israeli smallholders
moh-**shahv** /məʊˈʃɑːv/

Moslem see Muslim

Mosley, Oswald English fascist leader
mohz-li /ˈməʊzli/

Mossad Israeli secret intelligence service
moss-**ad** /mɒˈsad/

Mössbauer effect chemical nuclear effect
moess-bow-uhr /ˈmœsbaʊə(r)/

Mostar city, Bosnia-Herzegovina
most-ar /ˈmɒstɑː(r)/

Mosul city, Iraq
moo-suhl /'muːsəl/

Commonly also **moh**-suhl, which is becoming an established anglicization. Our recommendation is based on the advice of Iraqi Arabic speakers.

motet short piece of sacred choral music
moh-**tet** /məʊ'tɛt/

motif decorative image
moh-**teef** /məʊ'tiːf/

mot juste appropriate word
moh **zhuest** /,məʊ 'ʒyst/

Moto, Severo Equatorial Guinean statesman
sev-**air**-oh **mot**-oh /sɛ,vɛːrəʊ 'mɒtəʊ/

motorcade procession of motor vehicles
moh-**tuhr**-kayd /'məʊtə(r)keɪd/

Motown trademark type of music
moh-town /'məʊtaʊn/

motte mound forming the site of a castle
mot /mɒt/

moue pouting expression
moo /muː/

moules marinière mussels cooked in a wine and onion sauce
mool marr-in-**yair** /,muːl marɪn'jɛː(r)/

Mouli trademark kitchen utensil
moo-li /'muːli/

Moulin Rouge cabaret in Montmartre, Paris
moo-la(ng) **roozh** /,muːlɛ̃ 'ruːʒ/

mountebank person who deceives others
mown-tuh-bank /'maʊntəbaŋk/

Mount Isa town, Australia
y-zuh /'ʌɪzə/

Mourne Mountains range of hills, Northern Ireland
morn /mɔː(r)n/

moussaka (also **mousaka**) Greek dish
moo-**sah**-kuh /muː'sɑːkə/

mousseline fine fabric
mooss-leen /'muːsliːn/

mousseux sparkling
moo-**soe** /muː'sø/

Mowgli character in *The Jungle Book*
mow-gli /'maʊgli/

Various sources indicate that this is the pronunciation Kipling would have used, although the name was pronounced **moh**-gli in the Disney film.

Moygashel trademark type of Irish linen
moy-**gash**-uhl /mɔɪ'gaʃəl/

Mozambique country
moh-zam-**beek** /,məʊzam'biːk/

Mozart, Wolfgang Amadeus Austrian composer
volf-gang am-uh-**day**-uuss **moht**-sart /,vɒlfgaŋ amə,deɪʊs 'məʊtsɑː(r)t/

mozzarella cheese
mot-suh-**rel**-uh /,mɒtsə'rɛlə/

MPEG international standard for encoding and compressing video images
em-peg /'ɛmpɛg/

Mpumalanga province, South Africa
uhm-poo-muh-**lang**-guh /əm,puːmə'laŋgə/

mridangam drum
uhm-rid-**ung**-guhm /əmrɪ'dʌŋgəm/

Ms woman's title
muhz /məz/

MSS manuscripts
em-**ess**-iz /ɛm'ɛsɪz/

Mswati Swazi king
uhm-**swat**-i /əm'swati/

mu letter of the Greek alphabet
myoo /mjuː/

Mubarak, Hosni Egyptian statesman
huuss-ni moo-**bar**-uhk /,hʊsni muː'bɑːrək/

Mucha, Alphonse Czech painter and designer
al-fonss **muukh**-uh /,alfɒns 'mʊxə/

muchacha 'young woman' (Spanish)
moo-**chatch**-uh /muː'tʃatʃə/

muchacho 'young man' (Spanish)
moo-**chatch**-oh /muː'tʃatʃəʊ/

Muchinga Mountains mountain range, Zambia
moo-**ching**-guh /muː'tʃɪŋgə/

mucho 'much' or 'many' (Spanish)
muutch-oh /'mʊtʃəʊ/

mucosa pl. **mucosae** mucous membrane
myoo-**koh**-suh, pl. myoo-**koh**-see /mjuː'kəʊsə, pl. /-siː/

Mudejar pl. **Mudejares** Gothic-Islamic architectural style
moo-day-**khar**, pl. moo-day-**khar**-ayss /muːdeɪ'xɑː(r)/, pl. /-reɪs/

mudra symbolic hand gesture used in Indian dance
mud-ruh /'mʌdrə/

muesli cereal mixture
mooz-li /ˈmuːzli/

Sometimes also **myooz**-li; both are anglicizations of the German word *müsli*, pronounced **muess**-li [ˈmyːsli].

muezzin man who calls Muslims to prayer
moo-**ez**-in /muːˈɛzɪn/

mufti plain clothes
/ˈmʌfti/

Mugabe, Robert Zimbabwean statesman
muug-**ah**-bi /mʊˈgɑːbi/

Mughal Muslim dynasty of Mongol origin
moog-uhl /ˈmuːgəl/

Muhajiroun, al- extremist Islamic group
uhl muu-haj-irr-**oon**
/əl mʊˌhadʒɪrˈruːn/

Muhammad (also **Mohammed**) Arab prophet and founder of Islam
moh-**ham**-uhd /məʊˈhaməd/

Muhammad Ali see **Ali, Muhammad**

Muharram Islamic month
muh-**hurr**-uhm /məˈhʌrəm/

Muir, Jean English fashion designer
myoor /mjʊə(r)/

mujahidin (also **mujahedin, mujaheddin,** or **mujahideen**) guerrilla fighters in Islamic countries
moo-jah-huh-**deen** /ˌmuːdʒɑːhəˈdiːn/

Mujibur Rahman Bangladeshi statesman
muuj-**ee**-boor rakh-**mahn**
/mʊˌdʒiːbʊə(r) raxˈmɑːn/

Mukalla port, Yemen
muuk-**al**-uh /mʊˈkalə/

mukhtar Arab head of local government
muukh-tar /ˈmʊxtɑː(r)/

mukluk high, soft boot
muk-luk /ˈmʌklʌk/

muktuk whale blubber
muk-tuk /ˈmʌktʌk/

Muldoon, Robert New Zealand statesman
mul-**doon** /mʌlˈduːn/

mulefa creature in Philip Pullman's *His Dark Materials*
muul-**ef**-uh /mʊˈlɛfə/

Mulhacén mountain, Spain
moo-lath-**en** /ˌmuːlaˈθɛn/

Mülheim city, Germany
muel-hym /ˈmyːlhʌɪm/

Mulhouse city, France
muel-**ooz** /myˈluːz/

The German name of this city in Alsace-Lorraine is Mühlhausen, pronounced **muel**-how-zuhn [ˈmyːlhauzən].

mullah Muslim learned in Islamic theology
muul-luh /ˈmʊlə/

mullein plant
mul-in /ˈmʌlɪn/

Muller, Hermann Joseph American geneticist
mul-uhr /ˈmʌlə(r)/

Müller, Johannes German anatomist and zoologist
yoh-**han**-uhss **muel**-uhr /jəʊˌhanəs ˈmyːlə(r)/

muller grinding stone
mul-uhr /ˈmʌlə(r)/

Müller-Thurgau white wine grape
muel-uhr **toor**-gow /ˌmyːlə(r) ˈtʊə(r)gaʊ/

mulligatawny spicy soup
mul-ig-uh-**taw**-ni /ˌmʌlɪgəˈtɔːni/

Mullingar town, Republic of Ireland
mul-ing-**gar** /ˌmʌlɪŋˈgɑː(r)/

Mulroney, Brian Canadian statesman
mul-**roo**-ni /mʌlˈruːni/

Multan city, Pakistan
muul-**tahn** /mʊlˈtɑːn/

multiparous having borne more than one child
mul-**tip**-uh-ruhss /mʌlˈtɪpərəs/

multiply in several different ways
mul-tip-li /ˈmʌltɪpli/

multivalent having many applications
mul-ti-**vay**-luhnt /ˌmʌltiˈveɪlənt/

multum in parvo a great deal in a small space
muul-tuhm in **par**-voh /ˌmʊltəm ɪn ˈpɑː(r)vəʊ/

Mumbai city, India; also called **Bombay**
muum-**by** /mʊmˈbʌɪ/

mumpsimus traditional custom or idea adhered to although shown to be unreasonable
mump-sim-uhss /ˈmʌmpsɪməs/

Munch, Edvard Norwegian painter
ed-vard **muunk** /ˌɛdvɑː(r)d ˈmʊŋk/

Munchausen syndrome mental disorder in which a person feigns illness
muuntch-ow-zuhn /'mʊntʃ,aʊzən/

Established anglicization. The German pronunciation of the original Baron Münchhausen's name (note the difference in spelling) is **muenkh**-how-zuhn ['mʏnçhaʊzən].

Munich city, Germany
myoo-nik /'mjuːnɪk/

Established anglicization. The German name is München, pronounced **muen**-khuhn ['mʏnçən].

Munro high mountain in Scotland
mun-**roh** /mʌn'rəʊ/

Munsell system of classifying colours
mun-suhl /'mʌnsəl/

Munster province, Republic of Ireland
mun-stuhr /'mʌnstə(r)/

Münster city, Germany
muen-stuhr /'mʏnstə(r)/

Müntefering, Franz German politician
frants muen-tuh-fay-ring /,frants 'mʏntəfeɪrɪŋ/

muntjac small deer
munt-jak /'mʌntdʒak/

muon subatomic particle
myoo-on /'mjuːɒn/

Murano glass decorative glassware, associated with the island of Murano, near Venice
myuu-**rah**-noh /mjʊ'rɑːnəʊ/

Established anglicization; the island itself is pronounced moor-**ah**-noh.

Murat, Joachim French general and former king of Naples
zhoh-ash-a**(ng)** mue-**rah** /ʒəʊa'sɛ̃ my'rɑː/

Murcia region, Spain
moor-thi-uh /'mʊə(r)θiə/

murex pl. **murices** mollusc
myoor-eks, pl. **myoor**-iss-eez /'mjʊəreks/, pl. /-rɪsiːz/

murgh chicken (Indian)
moorg /mʊə(r)g/

Murillo, Bartolomé Spanish painter
bar-tol-uh-**may** moor-**eel**-yoh /ba:(r)tɒlə,meɪ mʊə'riːljəʊ/
• See SPANISH panel.

murine relating to rodents
myoor-yn /'mjʊərʌɪn/

Murmansk port, Russia
moor-**mansk** /mʊə(r)'mansk/

Murnau, Friedrich (F.W.) German film director
freed-rikh **moor**-now /,fri:drɪç 'mʊə(r)naʊ/

murrain disease affecting cattle
murr-in /'mʌrɪn/

Murrumbidgee river, Australia
murr-uhm-**bij**-ee /,mʌrəm'bɪdʒiː/

Mururoa atoll, French Polynesia
moor-oo-**roh**-uh /,mʊərʊ'rəʊə/

Musala mountain, Bulgaria
moo-sal-**ah** /muːsa'lɑː/

Muscadet white wine
musk-uh-day /'mʌskədeɪ/

Muscat capital of Oman
musk-at /'mʌskat/

muscat grape variety
musk-at /'mʌskat/

muscatel muscat grape
musk-uh-**tel** /,mʌskə'tɛl/

muscovado unrefined sugar
muss-kuh-**vah**-doh /,mʌskə'vɑːdəʊ/

Muscovite native or citizen of Moscow
musk-uh-vyt /'mʌskəvʌɪt/

Muscovy medieval principality, Russia
muss-kuh-vi /'mʌskəvi/

musculature arrangement of muscles
musk-yuul-uh-chuhr /'mʌskjʊlətʃə(r)/

Musée d'Orsay museum, Paris
mue-**zay** dor-**say** /my,zeɪ dɔ:(r)'seɪ/

musette small bagpipe
myoo-**zet** /mju:'zɛt/

Museveni, Yoweri Ugandan statesman
yoh-**werr**-i moo-**sev**-en-i /jʊ,wɛri mu:'sɛvɛni/

mush person's mouth or face
muush /mʊʃ/

Musharraf, Pervez Pakistani president
pair-**vayz** muush-**arr**-uhf /pɛ:(r),veɪz mʊ'ʃarəf/

Musil, Robert Austrian novelist
mooss-eel /'mu:si:l/

In standard German the name is pronounced **moo**-zeel; our recommendation reflects the author's own Austrian pronunciation.

muskellunge pike fish
musk-uh-lunj /'mʌskə,lʌndʒ/

Muskogee American Indian ethnic group
musk-**oh**-gi /mʌ'skəʊgi/

Muslim (also **Moslem**) follower of the religion of Islam
muuss-lim /'mʊslɪm/

Our research indicates that pronunciations with z such as **muuz**-lim or **muz**-lim, although common, can cause offence among Arabic speakers.

---

muso musician, especially one over-concerned with technique
myoo-zoh /'mju:zəʊ/

musquash muskrat
musk-wosh /'mʌskwɒʃ/

Mussolini, Benito Italian Fascist statesman
ben-**ee**-toh muuss-uh-**lee**-ni /bɛ,ni:təʊ ,mʊsə'li:ni/

Mussorgsky, Modest Russian composer
mod-**est** muuss-**org**-ski /mɒ,dɛst mʊ'sɔ:(r)gski/

mustang American feral horse
must-ang /'mʌstaŋ/

mustelid weasel
must-uh-lid /'mʌstəlɪd/

Mustique island, Caribbean
must-**eek** /mʌ'sti:k/

Mut Egyptian goddess
muut /mʊt/

mutagen agent which causes mutation
myoo-tuh-juhn /'mju:tədʒən/

Mutare town, Zimbabwe
moo-**tar**-i /mu:'tɑ:ri/

mutatis mutandis making necessary alterations while not affecting the main point at issue
moo-**tah**-tiss moo-**tan**-diss /mu:,tɑ:tɪs mu:'tandɪs/

Mutharika, Bingu wa Malawian president
bing-goo wuh muut-**arr**-ee-kuh /,bɪŋgu: wə mʊ'tari:kə/

muti African medicine or magical charms
moo-ti /'mu:ti/

muumuu loose, brightly coloured dress
moo-moo /'mu:mu:/

Muzaffarabad town, Pakistan
muuz-**uf**-uh-ruh-bad /mʊ'zʌfərə,bad/

muzak trademark light background music
myoo-zak /'mju:zak/

muzhik Russian peasant
moo-**zhik** /mu:'ʒɪk/

Muztag mountain, China
moo-**stahg** /mu:s'tɑ:g/

myalgia pain in a muscle
my-al-juh /mʌɪ'aldʒə/

myalism Jamaican folk religion
my-uh-liz-uhm /'mʌɪəlɪzəm/

Myanmar alternative name for Burma
myan-**mar** /,mjan'mɑ:(r)/

Mycenae ancient city, Greece
my-**see**-ni /mʌɪ'si:ni/

Mycenaean (also **Mycenean**) late Bronze Age civilization in Greece
my-sin-ee-uhn /,mʌɪsɪ'ni:ən/

mycology scientific study of fungi
my-**kol**-uh-ji /mʌɪ'kɒlədʒi/

myelitis inflammation of the spinal cord
my-uh-**ly**-tiss /,mʌɪə'lʌɪtɪs/

myeloma pl. **myelomata** malignant tumour of the bone marrow
my-uh-**loh**-muh, pl. my-uh-**loh**-muh-tuh /,mʌɪə'ləʊmə/, pl. /-mətə/

Mykolayiv city, Ukraine
mik-uh-**lah**-yif /,mɪkə'lɑ:jɪf/

Mykonos island, Greece
mik-uh-noss /'mɪkənɒs/

My Lai site of a massacre, Vietnam
mee ly /,mi: 'lʌɪ/

Mymensingh port, Bangladesh
my-men-**sing** /,mʌɪmɛn'sɪŋ/

mynah bird
my-nuh /'mʌɪnə/

myocarditis inflammation of the heart muscle
my-oh-kar-**dy**-tiss /,mʌɪəʊkɑ:(r)'dʌɪtɪs/

myopathy disease of muscle tissue
my-**op**-uh-thi /mʌɪ'ɒpəθi/

myopia short-sightedness
my-oh-pi-uh /mʌɪ'əʊpiə/

myrmidon follower of a powerful person
mur-mid-uhn /'mə:(r)mɪdən/

Myron Greek sculptor
my-ruhn /'mʌɪrən/

myrrh fragrant gum resin
mur /mə:(r)/

Mysia ancient region, Asia Minor
miss-i-uh /'mɪsiə/

Mysore city, India
my-**sawr** /mʌɪˈsɔː(r)/

mythopoeia myth-making
mith-oh-**pee**-uh /ˌmɪθəʊˈpiːə/

mythos pl. **mythoi** myth or mythology
mith-oss, pl. **mith**-oy /ˈmɪθɒs/, pl. /-θɔɪ/

Mytileni town, Greece
mit-il-**ee**-ni /ˌmɪtɪˈliːni/

myxomatosis disease of rabbits
mik-suh-muh-**toh**-siss
/ˌmɪksəməˈtəʊsɪs/

mzungu white person
uhm-**zuung**-goo /əmˈzʊngu/

N

NAAFI Navy, Army, and Air Force
Institutes
naf-i /ˈnafi/

Naas town, Republic of Ireland
nayss /neɪs/

Nabeul town, Tunisia
nab-**oel** /naˈbœl/

Nablus town, West Bank
nah-bluhss /ˈnɑːbləs/

nabob Mogul official
nay-bob /ˈneɪbɒb/

Nabokov, Vladimir Russian-born
American novelist
vluh-**dee**-meer nuh-**boh**-kof
/vləˌdiːmɪə(r) nəˈbəʊkɒf/

Although the author's surname is often
pronounced **nab**-uh-kof, he told the BBC
that this was his preferred English
pronunciation, with the middle syllable
stressed, and rhyming with 'smoke'.

Nabucco opera by Verdi
nuh-**boo**-koh /nəˈbuːkəʊ/

nacelle aircraft engine casing
nuh-**sel** /nəˈsɛl/

naches (also **nachas**) parental pride
nukh-uhss /ˈnʌxəs/

nacho Spanish food
natch-oh /ˈnatʃəʊ/

Nachtigal, Gustav German explorer
guust-af **nakh**-tig-al /ˌɡʊstaf
ˈnaxtɪɡal/

nacre mother-of-pearl
nay-kuhr /ˈneɪkə(r)/

nada 'nothing' (Spanish)
nah-duh /ˈnɑːdə/, [ˈnaða]
• Established anglicization.

Na-Dene North American Indian
language group
nah **den**-ay /nɑː ˈdɛneɪ/

Nader, Ralph American politician
nay-duhr /ˈneɪdə(r)/

nadir lowest point
nay-deer /ˈneɪdɪə(r)/

Commonly also **nad**-eer.

Nadolig Llawen 'Happy Christmas'
(Welsh)
nuh-**dol**-ig hlah-wen /nəˌdɒlɪɡ ˈɬaːwɛn/
• See WELSH panel.

naevus birthmark
nee-vuhss /ˈniːvəs/

Nagaland state, India
nah-guh-land /ˈnɑːɡəland/

Nagasaki city, Japan
nag-uh-**sah**-ki /naɡəˈsɑːki/
• See JAPANESE panel.

Nagorno-Karabakh region, Azerbaijan
nuh-**gor**-noh karr-uh-**bakh**
/nəˌɡɔː(r)nəʊ karəˈbax/

Nagoya city, Japan
nuh-**goy**-uh /nəˈɡɔɪə/

Nagpur city, India
nag-**poor** /naɡˈpʊə(r)/

Nagra, Parminder British actress
par-**min**-duhr **nah**-gruh
/pɑː(r)ˌmɪndə(r) ˈnɑːɡrə/

Nagy, Imre Hungarian politician
im-ruh **noj** /ˌɪmrə ˈnɒdʒ/, [ˈnɒɟ]
• Established anglicization for surname.

Naha port, Japan
nah-huh /ˈnɑːhə/

Na h-Eileanan an Iar 'Western Isles'
(Scottish Gaelic)
nuh **hil**-uh-nuhn uhn **yeer** /nə
ˈhɪlənən ənˈjɪə(r)/

Nahuatl Central American ethnic group
and language
nah-wah-tuhl /ˈnɑːwɑːtəl/

Nahum Hebrew prophet
nay-huhm /ˈneɪhəm/

naiad pl. **naiades** water nymph
ny-ad, pl. **ny**-uh-deez /ˈnʌɪad/, pl.
/ˈnʌɪədiːz/

naif (also **naïf**) ingenuous person
ny-**eef** /nʌɪˈiːf/

Naipaul, V. S. Trinidadian writer
ny-pawl /ˈnʌɪpɔːl/

naira currency unit, Nigeria
ny-ruh /ˈnʌɪrə/

Nairobi capital of Kenya
ny-**roh**-bi /nʌɪˈrəʊbi/

Naisi (also **Naoise**) Irish boy's name
nee-shuh /ˈniːʃə/

naissant heraldic term
nay-suhnt /ˈneɪsənt/

Najaf (also **an-Najaf**) city, Iraq
naj-af, uh-**naj**-af /ˈnadʒaf/, /əˈnadʒaf/
• See ARABIC panel.

nakfa currency unit, Eritrea
nak-fuh /ˈnakfə/

Nakhichevan see **Naxçivan**

Nakuru city, Kenya
nak-**oo**-roo /naˈkuːruː/

Nalbandian, David Argentinian tennis
player
dav-**eeth** nal-ban-**dyan** /daˌvið
nalbanˈdjan/

Commonly also anglicized to **day**-vid
nal-**band**-i-uhn.

Nalchik capital of Kabardino-Balkarian
republic, Russia
nal-chik /ˈnaltʃɪk/

Namangan city, Uzbekistan
nam-uhn-**gahn** /namənˈɡaːn/

Namaqualand region, Africa
nuh-**mah**-kwuh-land
/nəˈmɑːkwəland/

namaskar South Asian greeting
num-uh-**skar** /nʌməsˈkɑː(r)/

namaste South Asian greeting
num-uh-stay /ˈnʌməsteɪ/

namaz Islamic prayers
nuh-**mahz** /nəˈmɑːz/

Namib desert, Africa
nah-mib /ˈnɑːmɪb/

Namibia country
nuh-**mib**-i-uh /nəˈmɪbiə/

Namoi river, Australia
nam-oy /ˈnamɔɪ/

Namur town, Belgium
nam-**oor** /naˈmʊə(r)/, French [namyːr]
• Established anglicization.

nan bread (Indian)
nahn /nɑːn/

Nanaimo port, Canada
nan-**y**-moh /naˈnʌɪməʊ/

Nanak Sikh guru

nah-nuk /ˈnɑːnʌk/

Nanchang city, China
nan-**chang** /ˌnanˈtʃaŋ/

Nancy city, France
nah(ng)-**see** /ˈnãˈsi/
• See FRENCH panel.

nandrolone steroid
nan-druh-lohn /ˈnandrələʊn/

nan Gaidheal Radio nan Gaidheal is the
BBC's Gaelic language radio in Scotland
nuhn **gayl** /nən ˈɡeɪl/

Nanga Parbat mountain, Pakistan
nung-guh **par**-but /ˌnʌŋɡə ˈpɑː(r)bʌt/

Nanjing city, China
nan-**jing** /ˌnanˈdʒɪŋ/

Historically also called Nanking,
pronounced nan-**king**.

Nanning capital of Guangxi, China
nan-**ning** /ˌnanˈnɪŋ/

nanometre unit of measurement
nan-oh-mee-tuhr /ˈnanəʊˌmiːtə(r)/

Nansen, Fridtjof Norwegian explorer
freet-yof **nan**-suhn /ˈfriːtjɒf ˈnansən/

Nanterre city, France
nah(ng)-**tair** /ˈnãˈtɛ(r)/

Nantes city, France
nah(ng)t /nãt/

Nantucket island, USA
nan-**tuk**-it /nanˈtʌkɪt/

Naoise see **Naisi**

napalm weapon
nay-pahm /ˈneɪpɑːm/

napery household linen
nay-puh-ri /ˈneɪpəri/

Naphtali Hebrew patriarch
naf-tuh-ly /ˈnaftəlʌɪ/

naphtha flammable oil
naf-thuh /ˈnafθə/

Napier port, New Zealand
nayp-yuhr /ˈneɪpjə(r)/

Napier, John Scottish mathematician
nayp-yuhr /ˈneɪpjə(r)/

Naples city, Italy
nay-puhlz /ˈneɪpəlz/

Established anglicization; the Italian name
is Napoli, pronounced **nah**-pol-i [ˈnaːpoli]
but often anglicized to **nap**-uh-li where it
appears e.g. in the name of sports teams.

Napoleon French emperor
nuh-**poh**-li-uhn /nə'pəʊliən/,
[napɔleɔ̃]
• Established anglicization.

Napoleonic relating to Napoleon
nuh-poh-li-**on**-ik /nəpəʊli'ɒnɪk/

Nara city, Japan
nah-ruh /'nɑːrə/

Narayan, R. K. Indian writer
nuh-**rah**-yuhn /nə'rɑːjən/

Narayanan, K. R. Indian statesman
nuh-**rah**-yuh-nuhn /nə'rɑːjənən/

Narayanganj port, Bangladesh
nuh-**rah**-yuhn-gunj /nə'rɑːjən,gʌndʒ/

Narbonne city, France
nar-**bon** /nɑː(r)'bɒn/

narcissism vanity
nar-siss-iz-uhm /'nɑː(r)sɪsɪzəm/

Narcissus Greek mythological character
nar-**siss**-uhss /nɑː(r)'sɪsəs/

narcolepsy medical condition
nar-kuh-lep-si /'nɑː(r)kəlɛpsi/

Nares, James British composer
nairz /nɛː(r)z/

nares sing. **naris** nostrils
nair-eez, sing. **nair**-iss /'nɛːriːz/, sing.
/'nɛːrɪs/

narghile hookah
nar-gil-ay /'nɑː(r)ɡɪleɪ/

Narita airport, Japan
narr-ee-tuh /'narɪtə/
• See JAPANESE panel.

Narmada river, India
nar-mud-uh /'nɑː(r)mʌdə/

Narragansett North American Indian
ethnic group
narr-uh-**gan**-suht /narə'gansət/

Narvik port, Norway
nar-vik /'nɑː(r)vɪk/

narwhal Arctic whale
nar-wuhl /'nɑː(r)wəl/

nary not
nair-i /'nɛːri/

NASA National Aeronautics and Space
Administration
nass-uh /'nasə/

Nasca see **Nazca**

nascent coming into existence
nass-uhnt /'nasənt/

Also **nay**-suhnt.

Naseby English civil war battle site
nayz-bi /'neɪzbi/

nasi goreng Indonesian rice dish
nah-si guh-**reng** /,nɑːsi ɡə'rɛŋ/

Nasik city, India
nah-sik /'nɑːsɪk/

Nasiriyah, al- city, Iraq
uh-**nass**-i-**ree**-yuh /ə,nasi'riːjə/
• See ARABIC panel.

Nasmyth, James Scottish engineer
nay-smith /'neɪsmɪθ/

Nassau capital of Bahamas
nass-aw /'nasɔː/

Nassau former duchy, Germany
nass-ow /'nasaʊ/

Nastase, Ilie Romanian tennis player
il-**ee**-uh nuh-**stah**-say /ɪ'liːə nə'stɑːseɪ/

Natal former province, South Africa
nuh-**tal** /nə'tal/

NATO North Atlantic Treaty
Organization
nay-toh /'neɪtəʊ/

Natron lake, Tanzania
nay-truhn /'neɪtrən/

naturopathy alternative medicine
nay-chuh-**rop**-uh-thi /,neɪtʃə'rɒpəθi/

Naugahyde US trademark artificial leather
naw-guh-hyd /'nɔːɡəhʌɪd/

Naughtie, James Scottish broadcaster
nokh-ti /'nɒxti/

Nauru island, Pacific
now-**roo** /naʊ'ruː/

nausea sickness
naw-zi-uh /'nɔːziə/

nauseous affected by nausea
naw-zi-uhss /'nɔːziəs/

AM is **naw**-zhuhss or naw-**shuhss**.

Nausicaa Greek mythological name
naw-**sik**-ay-uh /nɔː'sɪkeɪə/

Navajo (also **Navaho**) North American
Indian ethnic group and language
nav-uh-hoh /'navəhəʊ/

Navan town, Republic of Ireland
nav-uhn /'navən/

Navanagar former state, India
nuv-uh-**nug**-uhr /,nʌvə'nʌɡə(r)/

Navaratri Hindu festival
nuv-uh-**rut**-ri /,nʌvə'rʌtri/

navarin French casserole
nav-uh-rin /'navərɪn/, [navarɛ̃]

Navarino naval battle
nav-uh-**ree**-noh /navə'riːnəʊ/

Navarone, The Guns of film title
nav-uh-**rohn** /navə'rəʊn/

Navarre region, Spain
nuh-**var** /nə'vɑː(r)/

Navratilova, Martina Czech-born
American tennis player
mar-**tee**-nuh nav-rat-il-**oh**-vuh
/mɑː(r),tiːnə navratɪ'ləʊvə/

This is her preferred anglicization. The
Czech pronunciation would be **mar-tee-na
nav-ruh-til-ov-ah.**

nawab Indian mogul governor
nuh-**wahb** /nə'wɑːb/

Naworth town, England
nah-wuhrth /'nɑːwə(r)θ/

However, Naworth Castle is pronounced
narth.

Naxçivan (also **Nakhichevan**) republic,
Azerbaijan
nakh-chiv-**ahn** /naxtʃɪ'vɑːn/

Naxos island, Greece
nak-soss /'naksɒs/

Nazarene native of Nazareth
naz-uh-reen /'nazəriːn/

Nazareth town, Israel
naz-uh-ruhth /'nazərəθ/

Nazca (also **Nasca**) ancient culture, Peru
nass-kuh /'naskə/

Nazi German fascist
naht-si /'nɑːtsi/

Nazran capital of Ingushetia, Russia
naz-rahn /'nazrɑːn/

Ncube, Welshman Zimbabwean
politician
noo-bay /'nuːbeɪ/

Established anglicization. When not
anglicized, the surname contains a dental
click sound; the BBC was told by Mr Ncube
that he preferred the sound to be omitted
altogether in English, rather than another
consonant being substituted. See CLICKS
panel.

Ndebele African ethnic group and
language
uhn-duh-**bay**-li /əndə'beɪli/

N'Djamena capital of Chad
uhn-ja-**may**-nuh /əndʒa'meɪnə/

Ndola city, Zambia
uhn-**doh**-luh /ən'dəʊlə/

N'Dour, Youssou Senegalese singer
yoo-soo uhn-**door** /,juːsuː ən'dʊə(r)/

Neagh, Lough lake, Northern Ireland
lokh **nay** /,lɒx 'neɪ/

Neanderthal early human
ni-**an**-duhr-tahl /ni'andə(r)tɑːl/

Neapolitan relating to Naples
nee-uh-**pol**-i-tuhn /,niːə'pɒlɪtən/

Nearchus Macedonian general
ni-**ar**-kuhss /ni'ɑː(r)kəs/

Neath town, Wales
neeth /niːθ/

Neatishead RAF base, England
neets-hed /'niːtshɛd/

Nebbiolo grape variety
neb-**yoh**-loh /nɛb'jəʊləʊ/

Nebo, Mount mountain, Jordan
nee-boh /'niːbəʊ/

Nebraska state, US
nuh-**brass**-kuh /nə'braskə/

Nebuchadnezzar Babylonian king; also
a large wine bottle
neb-yuu-kuhd-**nez**-uhr
/,nɛbjʊkəd'nɛzə(r)/

nebula gas cloud
neb-yuu-luh /'nɛbjʊlə/

Necaxa river, Mexico
nek-**akh**-uh /nɛ'kaxə/

necessarily inevitably
ness-uh-**sair**-uh-li /,nɛsə'sɛːrəli/

An alternative pronunciation with the stress
on the first syllable, **ness-uh-suh-ruh-li,** is
also possible, but is becoming less common.

Nechells suburb of Birmingham,
England
nee-chuhlz /'niːtʃəlz/

Neckar river, Germany
nek-ar /'nɛkɑː(r)/

necrosis death of tissue
nek-**roh**-siss /nɛ'krəʊsɪs/

necrotizing fasciitis flesh-eating
disease
nek-ruh-ty-zing fash-i-**y**-tiss
/'nɛkrətʌɪzɪŋ ,faʃi'ʌɪtɪs/

née (also **né**) originally called
nay /neɪ/

Nefertiti Egyptian queen
nef-uhr-**tee**-tee /,nɛfə(r)'tiːtiː/

Negev region, Israel
neg-ev /'nɛgɛv/

négligée garment
neg-li-zhay /'nɛglɪʒeɪ/

Negombo port, Sri Lanka
nuh-**gom**-boh /nə'gɒmbəʊ/

Negri Sembilan state, Malaysia
neg-ree sem-bee-luhn /,nɛgri:
sɛm'bi:lən/

negroni cocktail
nuh-**groh**-ni /nə'grəʊni/

Negroponte, John American politician
neg-roh-**pon**-tay /,nɛgrəʊ'pɒnteɪ/

Negros island, Philippines
neg-ross /'nɛgrɒs/

Nehemiah book of the Bible
nee-huh-**my**-uh /ni:hə'mʌɪə/

Nehru, Jawaharlal Indian statesman
juh-**wah**-huhr-lahl nair-oo
/dʒə'wɑ:hə(r)lɑ:l 'nɛ:ru:/

Neisse river, Europe
ny-suh /'nʌɪsə/

neither not one nor the other
ny-thuhr /'nʌɪðə(r)/

Equally commonly **nee**-thuhr. Traditionally,
BR is **ny**-thuhr and AM is **nee**-thuhr.

Nejd region, Saudi Arabia
nejd /nɛdʒd/

Nellore city, India
nel-or /nɛ'lɔ:(r)/

Nelspruit town, South Africa
nel-sproeyt /'nɛlsprœɪt/

Nemean lion Greek mythological
animal
nuh-**mee**-uhn /nə'mi:ən/

nemesis agent of downfall
nem-uh-siss /'nɛməsɪs/

nemo dat legal term
nee-moh dat /,ni:məʊ 'dat/
• See LATIN panel.

nemo me impune lacessit 'no-one
provokes me with impunity' (Latin),
motto of the kings of Scotland
nay-moh may im-**poo**-nay lak-**ess**-it
/,neɪməʊ meɪ ɪm,pu:neɪ la'kɛsɪt/
• See LATIN panel.

Nene river, England
nenn, neen /nɛn, ni:n/

Pronounced differently in different
locations. Usually nenn in
Northamptonshire; neen in
Cambridgeshire.

Nennius Welsh chronicler
nen-i-uhss /'nɛnɪəs/

Neogaea zoogeographical area
nee-oh-jee-uh /,ni:əʊ'dʒi:ə/

neonatal newborn
nee-oh-**nay**-tuhl /,ni:əʊ'neɪtəl/

Neot, St English monk
nee-uht /'ni:ət/

Nepal country
nuh-**pawl** /nə'pɔ:l/

Nepalese relating to Nepal
nep-uh-**leez** /nɛpə'li:z/

ne plus ultra perfect example
nay pluuss **uul**-trah /,neɪ plʊs 'ʊltrɑ:/

nepotism favouring of relatives
nep-uh-tiz-uhm /'nɛpətɪzəm/

nereid Greek nymph
neer-i-id /'nɪəriɪd/

Nernst, Walther Hermann German
chemist
val-tuhr hair-mann nairnst /,valtə(r)
hɛ:(r)man 'nɛ:(r)nst/

Nero Roman emperor
neer-oh /'nɪərəʊ/

Neruda, Pablo Chilean poet
pab-loh nerr-oo-thuh /,pabləʊ
nɛ'ru:ðə/

nescient lacking knowledge
ness-i-uhnt /'nɛsɪənt/

Nesperennub Egyptian mummy
nes-puh-**ren**-uub /,nɛspə'rɛnʊb/

Nestlé food company
ness-lay /'nɛsleɪ/

The company used to be known as
ness-uhlz in the UK, but has been using
this pronunciation for at least the last
twenty years.

Nestor Greek mythological character
ness-tuhr /'nɛstə(r)/

Netanyahu, Binyamin Israeli
politician
bin-yuh-**meen** net-uhn-**yah**-hoo
/bɪnjə'mi:n nɛtən'jɑ:hu:/

netsuke Japanese ornament
net-skay /'nɛtskeɪ/
• See JAPANESE panel.

Neuberger, Julia English rabbi
noy-bur-guhr /'nɔɪbə:(r)gə(r)/

Neuchâtel canton and lake, Switzerland
noe-shat-el /nøʃa'tɛl/

Neue Sachlichkeit arts movement
noy-uh **zakh**-likh-kyt /ˌnɔɪə ˈzaxlɪçkʌɪt/

Neumann, John von
Hungarian-American mathematician
noy-man /ˈnɔɪman/

neuralgia nerve pain
nyoor-**al**-juh /ˌnjʊəˈraldʒə/

neurosis pl. **neuroses** mental condition
nyoor-**oh**-siss, pl. nyoor-**oh**-seez /ˌnjʊəˈrəʊsɪs/, pl. /-siːz/

Neusiedler See lake, Austria
noy-zeed-luhr **zay** /ˈnɔɪziːdlə(r) ˌzeɪ/

Neva river, Russia
nee-vuh /ˈniːvə/, [nʲ ˈva]
• Established anglicization.

Nevada state, US
nuh-**vah**-duh /nəˈvɑːdə/

Nevers city, France
nuh-**vair** /nəˈvɛː(r)/

Nevis island, Caribbean
nee-viss /ˈniːvɪs/

Newark city, US and UK
nyoo-uhrk /ˈnjuːə(r)k/

Newcastle city, England
nyoo-kah-suhl /ˈnjuːkɑːsəl/

This is a standardized version of the place name; locally, the pronunciation is nyoo-**kass**-uhl.

Newfoundland island, Canada
nyoo-fuhnd-**land** /ˌnjuːfəndˈland/

The stress can fall on all three syllables but this is the pronunciation preferred by Newfoundlanders. However, the breed of dog is usually nyoo-**fownd**-luhnd.

Ne Win Burmese politician
nay **win** /ˌneɪ ˈwɪn/

New Orleans city, US
nyoo **or**-li-uhnz /njuː ˈɔː(r)liənz/

Other pronunciations are also heard; this stress placement is the most common in both BR and AM.

Newry city, Northern Ireland
nyoor-i /ˈnjʊəri/

Nez Percé North American ethnic group
nez **pair**-say /ˌnɛz ˈpɛː(r)seɪ/

Ng Cantonese family name
ng /ŋ/

ngaio New Zealand tree
ny-oh /ˈnʌɪəʊ/

Ngaliema mountain, central Africa
ng-gah-li-**ay**-muh /ŋˌɡɑːliˈeɪmə/

Ngbandi language, Democratic Republic of Congo
ng-**ban**-di /ŋˈbandi/

Ngoni Malawian ethnic group
ng-**goh**-ni /ŋˈɡəʊni/

Ngorongoro volcanic crater, Tanzania
ng-gorr-ong-**gorr**-oh /ŋˌɡɒrɒŋˈɡɒrəʊ/

ngultrum currency unit, Bhutan
ng-**guul**-truhm /ŋˈɡʊltrəm/

Nguyen Vietnamese family name
nue-**en** /nyˈɛn/

Nhulunbuy town, Australia
nuul-uhn-boy /ˈnʊlənbɔɪ/

Ní 'daughter of' in Irish surnames
nee /niː/

niacin vitamin
ny-uh-sin /ˈnʌɪəsɪn/

Niagara Falls city and waterfalls, Canada/US
ny-**ag**-ruh /nʌɪˈaɡrə/

Niamey capital of Niger
nyah-**may** /njɑːˈmeɪ/

Niamh Irish girl's name
neev /niːv/

Nibelung mythological dwarf
nee-buh-luung /ˈniːbəlʊŋ/

Nibelungenlied German poem
nee-buh-luung-uhn-leet /ˈniːbəlʊŋənˌliːt/

Nicaea ancient city, Asia Minor
ny-**see**-uh /nʌɪˈsiːə/

Nicam digital sound format
ny-kam /ˈnʌɪkam/

Nicaragua country
nik-uh-**rag**-yuu-uh /ˌnɪkəˈraɡjʊə,/
Spanish [nikaˈraɣwa]

Established anglicization. A pronunciation closer to the Spanish, nik-uh-**rag**-wuh, is also common, and nik-uh-**rah**-gwuh is typical of AM.

NICE National Institute for Clinical Excellence
nyss /nʌɪs/

Nice city, France
neess /niːs/

Nicene Creed Christian text
ny-seen /ˈnʌɪsiːn/

niche recess
neesh /niːʃ/

AM is nitch.

Nichiren Buddhist sect
nish-uh-ruhn /'nɪʃərən/

Nicklaus, Jack American golfer
nik-luhss /'nɪkləs/

Nicobar island group, India
nik-uh-bar /'nɪkəbɑː(r)/

niçoise salad
nee-swahz /niːˈswɑːz/

Nicosia capital of Cyprus
nik-uh-see-uh /ˌnɪkəˈsiːə/

Niemöller, Martin German pastor
mar-teen nee-moel-uhr /ˌmɑː(r)tiːn
'niːmœlə(r)/

Niépce, Joseph Nicéphore French
inventor
zhoh-zef nee-say-for nyeps /ʒəʊˈzef
niːseɪˌfɔː(r) 'njeps/

Niersteiner white wine
neer-shty-nuhr /'nɪə(r)ˌʃtʌɪnə(r)/

Nietzsche, Friedrich German
philosopher
freed-rikh neet-shuh /ˌfriːdrɪç 'niːtʃə/

Niflheim Nordic mythological
underworld
niv-uhl-haym /'nɪvəlheɪm/

Established anglicization. The Icelandic
version of the name, Niflheimr, is
pronounced **nee**-buhl-hay-muhr.

Niger country
nee-zhair /niːˈʒɛː(r)/

An older, more anglicized pronunciation
ny-juhr is also heard, but we no longer
recommend this.

Niger river, Africa
ny-juhr /'nʌɪdʒə(r)/

Nigeria country
ny-jeer-i-uh /nʌɪˈdʒɪəriə/

nihilism philosophy
ny-il-iz-uhm /'nʌɪɪlɪzəm/

Niigata port, Japan
nee-gat-uh /'niːgatə/

Nijinsky, Vaslav Russian dancer
vass-luhf nizh-in-ski /ˌvasləf nɪˈʒɪnski/

Sometimes anglicized to nij-**in**-ski.

Nijmegen town, Netherlands
ny-may-guhn /'nʌɪmeɪgən/,
[ˈnɛimeːɣə(n)]

Nike Greek goddess, also a sportswear
company
ny-ki /'nʌɪki/

Nikkei stock market index
nik-ay /'nɪkeɪ/

nil desperandum 'don't give up' (Latin)
nil desp-uh-ran-duhm /'nɪl
ˌdespəˈrandəm/

nimbostratus cloud
nim-boh-strah-tuhss
/ˌnɪmbəʊˈstrɑːtəs/

NIMBY Not In My Back Yard
nim-bi /'nɪmbi/

Nîmes city, France
neem /niːm/

Nin, Anaïs French writer
an-uh-eess neen /anəˌiːs 'niːn/

Nineveh ancient city, Assyria
nin-uh-vuh /'nɪnəvə/

Ningxia autonomous region, China
ning-shyah /ˌnɪŋˈʃjɑː/

Ninian, St Scottish bishop
nin-i-uhn /'nɪniən/

Niobe Greek mythological name
ny-uh-bi /'nʌɪəbi/

niobium chemical element
ny-oh-bi-uhm /nʌɪˈəʊbiəm/

Nipissing district, Canada
nip-iss-ing /'nɪpɪsɪŋ/

NIREX Nuclear Industry Radioactive
Waste Executive
ny-reks /'nʌɪrɛks/

nirvana transcendent state
neer-vah-nuh /nɪə(r)'vɑːnə/

Niš (also **Nish**) city, Serbia
neesh /niːʃ/

nisi legal term
ny-sy /'nʌɪsʌɪ/

Niterói port, Brazil
nee-tuh-roy /ˌniːtəˈrɔɪ/

nitrogen chemical element
ny-truh-juhn /'nʌɪtrədʒən/

Niue island, New Zealand
ni-oo-ay /niˈuːeɪ/

Nizhniy Novgorod port, Russia
nizh-ni nov-guh-rod /ˌnɪʒnɪ
'nɒvgərɒd/, [ˌnʲiʒnɪ 'nɒvgərət]
• Established anglicization.

Njál Icelandic mythological character
nyowl /njaʊl/

Nkrumah, Kwame Ghanaian politician
kwam-i ng-**kroo**-muh /ˌkwami
ŋ'kruːmə/

Nobel, Alfred Swedish chemist
al-fred noh-**bel** /ˌalfrɛd nəʊˈbɛl/

Stress sometimes shifts to the first syllable
in the phrase 'Nobel Prize': **noh**-bel **pryz**.

nobelium chemical element
noh-**bee**-li-uhm /nəʊˈbiːlɪəm/

noblesse oblige aristocratic duty
noh-**bless** uh-**bleezh** /nəʊˌblɛs əˈbliːʒ/

Noh (also **No**) Japanese theatre
noh /nəʊ/

noisette piece of meat
nwaz-**et** /nwaˈzɛt/

noisome smelly
noy-suhm /ˈnɔɪsəm/

Nokia telecommunications company
nok-i-uh /ˈnɒkɪə/

noli me tangere 'don't touch me'
(Latin)
noh-li may **tang**-guh-ray /ˌnəʊlɪ meɪ
ˈtaŋgəreɪ/

Other pronunciations are possible; see LATIN
panel.

nolle prosequi legal term
nol-i **pross**-uh-kwy /ˌnɒlɪ ˈprɒsəkwʌɪ/

Nolte, Nick American actor
nohl-ti /ˈnəʊlti/

nom de guerre assumed name
nom duh **gair** /ˌnɒm də ˈɡɛː(r)/

nom de plume pen name
nom duh **ploom** /ˌnɒm də ˈpluːm/

Nome city, US
nohm /nəʊm/

nomenclature naming
nuh-**men**-kluh-chuhr
/nəˈmɛnklətʃə(r)/

AM is **noh**-muhn-klay-chuhr.

nonagon nine-sided shape
non-uh-guhn /ˈnɒnəɡən/

nonchalant relaxed
non-shuh-luhnt /ˈnɒnʃələnt/

nonpareil matchless
non-puh-**rayl** /ˌnɒnpəˈreɪl/

non sequitur illogical statement
non **sek**-wi-tuhr /nɒn ˈsɛkwɪtə(r)/

Nootka Canadian ethnic group
nuut-kuh /ˈnʊtkə/

nori edible seaweed

naw-ri /ˈnɔːri/

Noriega, Manuel Panamanian
statesman
man-**wel** norr-i-**ay**-guh /manˌwɛl
ˌnɒrɪˈeɪɡə/

Norrköping city, Sweden
nor-shoe-ping /ˈnɔː(r)ˌʃøːpɪŋ/

Northampton town, England
nor-**thamp**-tuhn /nɔː(r)ˈθamptən/

Northumberland county, England
nor-**thum**-buhr-luhnd
/nɔː(r)ˈθʌmbə(r)lənd/

Norway country
nor-way /ˈnɔː(r)weɪ/

Established anglicization. The Norwegian
name is Norge, pronounced **nor**-guh.

Norwalk virus virus causing
gastroenteritis
nor-wawk /ˈnɔː(r)wɔːk/

Norwich city, England
norr-ij /ˈnɒrɪdʒ/

Nosferatu vampire
noss-fuh-**rah**-too /ˌnɒsfəˈraːtuː/

Nostradamus French astrologer
noss-truh-**dah**-muhss /ˌnɒstrəˈdɑːməs/

Nostratic hypothetical language group
noss-**trat**-ik /nɒˈstratɪk/

nota bene 'observe carefully' (Latin)
noh-tuh ben-ay /ˌnəʊtə ˈbɛneɪ/

Notogaea zoogeographical area
noh-tuh-**jee**-uh /ˌnəʊtəˈdʒiːə/

Notre-Dame cathedral in Paris
not-ruh-**dahm** /ˌnɒtrəˈdɑːm/

However, the US university of the same
name is pronounced **noh**-tuhr **daym**.

Nottingham city, England
not-ing-uhm /ˈnɒtɪŋəm/

Nouadhibou port, Mauritania
nwad-i-**boo** /ˌnwadɪˈbuː/

Nouakchott capital of Mauritania
nwak-**shot** /nwakˈʃɒt/

nougat sweet
noo-gah /ˈnuːɡɑː/

Less commonly also **nug**-uht. AM is
noo-guht.

Nouméa capital of New Caledonia
noo-**may**-uh /nuːˈmeɪə/

nous common sense
nowss /naʊs/

nouveau riche recently wealthy people
noo-voh reesh /ˌnuːvəʊ ˈriːʃ/

nouvelle cuisine modern cookery
noo-vel kwi-zeen /nuːˌvɛl kwɪˈziːn/

Nova Scotia peninsula, Canada
noh-vuh skoh-shuh /ˌnəʊvə ˈskəʊʃə/

Novaya Zemlya islands, Arctic Ocean
nov-uh-yuh zuhm-lyah /ˌnɒvəjə zəmˈljɑː/

Novello, Ivor Welsh songwriter
nuh-vel-oh /nəˈvɛləʊ/

Novgorod city, Russia
nov-guh-rod /ˈnɒvɡərɒd, [ˈnɒvɡərət]
• Established anglicization.

Novosibirsk city, Russia
nov-uh-sib-eersk /ˌnɒvəsɪˈbɪə(r)sk/

Novotný, Antonin Czechoslovakian statesman
an-ton-een nov-ot-nee /ˌantɒniːn ˈnɒvɒtˌniː/

Noye's Fludde opera by Britten
noh-uhz flud /ˌnəʊəz ˈflʌd/

NSAID Non-Steroidal Anti-Inflammatory Drug
en-sed /ˈɛnsɛd/

nu letter of the Greek alphabet
nyoo /njuː/

Nuala Irish girl's name
noo-luh /ˈnuːlə/

nuance subtle difference
nyoo-ahnss /ˈnjuːɑːns/

Nubia ancient region of Africa
nyoo-bi-uh /ˈnjuːbiə/

Nubuck leather
nyoo-buk /ˈnjuːbʌk/

nuchal relating to the nape of the neck
nyoo-kuhl /ˈnjuːkəl/

nuclear relating to the nucleus of an atom
nyoo-kli-uhr /ˈnjuːkliə(r)/

An incorrect pronunciation, **nyoo-kyuul-uhr**, is sometimes heard.

nugatory unimportant
nyoo-guh-tri /ˈnjuːɡətri/

Nuku'alofa capital of Tonga
noo-koo-uh-loh-fuh /ˌnuːkuːəˈləʊfə/

Nullarbor Plain arid zone in Australia
nul-uhr-bor /ˈnʌlə(r)bɔː(r)/

numismatics study of coins
nyoo-miz-mat-iks /ˌnjuːmɪzˈmatɪks/

Nunavut territory, Canada
noo-nuh-vuut /ˈnuːnəvʊt/

Nunc Dimittis Christian canticle
nuunk di-mit-tiss /ˌnʊŋk dɪˈmɪtɪs/

nunchaku Japanese weapon
nun-chak-oo /nʌnˈtʃaku:/

nuncio papal envoy
nun-si-oh /ˈnʌnsiəʊ/

nuoc mam Vietnamese fish sauce
nwok mahm /nwɒk ˈmɑːm/

nuptial marital
nup-shuhl /ˈnʌpʃəl/

Nürburgring motor-race track, Germany
nuer-boork-ring /ˈnyː(r)bʊə(r)krɪŋ/

Nuremberg city, Germany
nyoor-uhm-burg /ˈnjʊərəmbə:(r)ɡ/

Established anglicization. The German name is Nürnberg, pronounced **nuern-bairk**.

Nureyev, Rudolf Russian ballet dancer
roo-dolf noo-ray-uhf /ˌruːdɒlf nuːˈreɪəf/

Nut Egyptian goddess
nuut /nʊt/

Nuuk capital of Greenland
nook /nuːk/

Nyala city, Sudan
nyah-luh /ˈnjɑːlə/

Nyerere, Julius Tanzanian statesman
joo-li-uhss nyerr-air-i /ˌdʒuːliəs njɛˈrɛːri/

nyckelharpa musical instrument
nuek-el-har-puh /ˈnʏkɛlˌhɑ:(r)pə/

Nyman, Michael English composer
ny-muhn /ˈnʌɪmən/

Nynorsk literary form of Norwegian
nue-norshk /ˈnyːnɔː(r)ʃk/

Sometimes anglicized to **nee-norsk**.

Nyquist criterion electronics term
ny-kwist /ˈnʌɪkwɪst/

Nyström, Gösta Swedish composer
yoess-tuh nue-stroem /ˌjøstə ˈnyːstrøm/

Nyx Greek goddess
niks /nɪks/

O

Oahu island, Hawaii
oh-**ah**-hoo /əʊˈɑːhuː/

Oaxaca city and state, Mexico
wuh-**hah**-kuh /wəˈhɑːkə/, Spanish
[waˈxaka]
• Established anglicization.

Obadiah Hebrew prophet
oh-buh-**dy**-uh /ˌəʊbəˈdʌɪə/

Oban port, Scotland
oh-buhn /ˈəʊbən/

Obasanjo, Olusegun Nigerian
president
ol-**oo**-sheg-oon ob-**ass**-an-joh
/ɒˈluːʃɛɡuːn ɒˈbasandʒəʊ/

obbligato instrumental part
ob-lig-**ah**-toh /ˌɒblɪˈɡɑːtəʊ/

obdurate stubborn
ob-dyuu-ruht /ˈɒbdjʊrət/

obeah sorcery
oh-bi-uh /ˈəʊbɪə/

obeisance respect
oh-**bay**-suhnss /əʊˈbeɪsəns/

obelisk tapering stone pillar
ob-uh-lisk /ˈɒbəlɪsk/

Oberammergau village, Germany
oh-buhr-**am**-uhr-gow
/ˌəʊbərˈaməʳɡaʊ/

Oberhausen city, Germany
oh-buhr-how-zuhn /ˈəʊbə(r)ˌhaʊzən/

Oberon Shakespearean character, also
one of Uranus's moons
oh-buh-ron /ˈəʊbərɒn/

obfuscate make unclear
ob-fuss-kayt /ˈɒbfʌskeɪt/

obi kimono sash
oh-bi /ˈəʊbi/

obiter dictum judge's opinion, not
legally binding
ob-it-uhr **dik**-tuhm /ˌɒbɪtə(r) ˈdɪktəm/

obituary death notice
uh-**bich**-oo-uhr-i /əˈbɪtʃʊəri/

object thing
ob-jekt /ˈɒbdʒɛkt/

object disagree

uhb-**jekt** /əbˈdʒɛkt/

objet d'art decorative item
ob-zhay **dar** /ˌɒbʒeɪ ˈdɑː(r)/

objet trouvé found object, displayed as a
work of art
ob-zhay **troo**-vay /ˌɒbʒeɪ ˈtruːveɪ/

oblast administrative region in Russia
ob-last /ˈɒblast/

obligatory required by rule
uh-**blig**-uh-tuh-ri /əˈblɪɡətəri/

Oblomov play by Goncharov
uh-**blom**-uhf /əˈblɒməf/

obloquy public condemnation
ob-luh-kwi /ˈɒbləkwi/

oboe d'amore musical instrument
oh-boh dam-**aw**-ray /ˌəʊbəʊ
daˈmɔːreɪ/

Obote, Milton Ugandan statesman
uh-**boh**-tay /əˈbəʊteɪ/

obscurantism deliberate hiding of
information
ob-skyuu-**rant**-iz-uhm
/ˌɒbskjʊˈrantɪzəm/

obsequies funeral rites
ob-suh-kwiz /ˈɒbsəkwɪz/

obsequious attentive to an excessive
degree
uhb-**see**-kwi-uhss /əbˈsiːkwiəs/

obsidian volcanic rock
uhb-**sid**-i-uhn /əbˈsɪdiən/

obstetrician doctor specializing in
obstetrics
ob-stuh-**trish**-uhn /ˌɒbstəˈtrɪʃən/

obstetrics medicine concerned with
childbirth
uhb-**stet**-riks /əbˈstɛtrɪks/

obstreperous difficult to control
uhb-**strep**-uh-ruhss /əbˈstrɛpərəs/

obstruent speech sound
ob-stroo-uhnt /ˈɒbstruənt/

ocarina wind instrument
ok-uh-**ree**-nuh /ˌɒkəˈriːnə/

O'Cathain, Detta Irish-born British
politician
det-uh oh-kuh-**hoyn** /ˌdɛtə əʊkəˈhɔɪn/

Occam's razor reductionist principle
ok-uhmz /'ɒkəmz/

Occident countries of the West
ok-sid-uhnt /'ɒksɪdənt/

occipital bone bone in the skull
ok-**sip**-it-uhl /ɒk'sɪpɪtəl/

Occitan language of southern France
ok-si-tuhn /'ɒksɪtən/

occult supernatural
ok-ult /'ɒkʌlt/

Less commonly also ok-**ult**.

Oceania islands of the Pacific Ocean
oh-si-**ah**-ni-uh /ˌəʊsi'ɑ:niə/

Commonly also oh-shi-**ah**-ni-uh; this
variation in pronunciation is also possible
with all the *ocean-* words below.

oceanic relating to the ocean
oh-si-**an**-ik /ˌəʊsi'anɪk/

Oceanid pl. **Oceanides** sea nymph
oh-**see**-uh-nid, pl. oh-si-**an**-id-eez
/əʊ'si:ənɪd/, pl. /ˌəʊsɪ'anɪdi:z/
• Standard -s plural is also possible.

Oceanus Greek god
oh-**see**-uh-nuhss /əʊ'si:ənəs/

ocelot wild cat
oss-uh-lot /'ɒsəlɒt/

och Scottish interjection
okh /ɒx/

oche line behind which darts players
stand
ok-i /'ɒki/

ochre pigment
oh-kuhr /'əʊkə(r)/

Ockeghem, Johannes Flemish
composer
yoh-**han**-uhss ok-uh-khuhm
/jəʊ,hanəs 'ɒkəxəm/

Ocracoke island, US
oh-kruh-kohk /'əʊkrəkəʊk/

octahedron three-dimensional shape
ok-tuh-**hee**-druhn /ˌɒktə'hi:drən/

octameter line of verse consisting of
eight metrical feet
ok-**tam**-uh-tuhr /ɒk'tamətə(r)/

octave series of eight notes
ok-tuhv /'ɒktəv/

Octavian Roman emperor Augustus
ok-**tay**-vi-uhn /ɒk'teɪvɪən/

octavo page size
ok-**tah**-voh /ɒk'tɑ:vəʊ/

Less commonly also ok-**tay**-voh.

octet group of eight people or things
ok-**tet** /ɒk'tɛt/

octopus pl. **octopodes**, **octopi** sea
creature
ok-tuh-puhss, pl. ok-tuh-**poh**-deez,
ok-tuh-py /'ɒktəpəs/, pl. /ɒktə'pəʊdi:z/,
/'ɒktəpAɪ/
• Standard -es plural is also possible.

octuple consisting of eight parts
ok-**tyoo**-puhl /ɒk'tju:pəl/

Less commonly also ok-tyuup-uhl; see
STRESS panel.

ocular connected with the eyes or vision
ok-yuul-uhr /'ɒkjʊlə(r)/

odalisque female slave
oh-duh-lisk /'əʊdəlɪsk/

Odense port, Denmark
oh-duhn-suh /'əʊdənsə/

Odent, Michel French obstetrician
mee-**shel** oh-**dah(ng)** /mi:'ʃɛl əʊ'dã/

Oder river, central Europe
oh-duhr /'əʊdə(r)/

Odessa port, Ukraine
oh-**dess**-uh /əʊ'dɛsə/

Odets, Clifford American dramatist
oh-**dets** /əʊ'dɛts/

Odin Norse god; also called **Wodin** or
Wotan
oh-din /'əʊdɪn/

odium hatred or unpopularity
oh-di-uhm /'əʊdɪəm/

odometer instrument for measuring
distance
oh-**dom**-uh-tuhr /əʊ'dɒmətə(r)/

Odone, Christina British journalist
kriss-**tee**-nuh oh-**doh**-nay /krɪs'ti:nə
əʊ'dəʊneɪ/

odontology scientific study of teeth
od-on-**tol**-uh-ji /ˌɒdɒn'tɒlədʒi/

odoriferous giving off a smell
oh-duh-**rif**-uh-ruhss /ˌəʊdə'rɪfərəs/

Odysseus Greek mythological character
uh-**diss**-yooss /ə'dɪsju:s/

Commonly also uh-**diss**-i-uhss.

Odyssey Greek epic poem; also any long
journey
od-iss-i /'ɒdɪsi/

oedema medical condition
ee-dee-muh /i:'di:mə/

Oedipus Greek mythological character
ee-dip-**uhss** /'iːdɪpəs/

AM also ed-ip-uhss.

OEIC Open-Ended Investment Company
oyk /ɔɪk/

oenology study of wines
ee-nol-uh-ji /iːˈnɒlədʒi/

Oenone Greek mythological character
ee-**noh**-ni /iːˈnəʊni/

oenophile connoisseur of wines
ee-nuh-fyl /'iːnəfʌɪl/

Oersted, Hans Christian Danish
physicist
hanss **krist**-yuhn oer-ste*th* /ˌhans
ˌkrɪstjən 'œ(r)stɛð/

oesophagus pl. **oesophagi** part of the
alimentary canal
uh-**sof**-uh-guhss, pl. uh-**sof**-uh-jy
/əˈsɒfəgəs/, pl. /-fədʒʌɪ/

Commonly also ee-sof-uh-guhss. Standard
-es plural is also possible.

oestrogen female hormone
ee-struh-juhn /'iːstrədʒən/

AM is est-ruh-juhn.

oestrus period of fertility
ee-struhss /'iːstrəs/

AM is est-ruhss.

oeuvre artist's body of work
ur-vruh /'əːvrə/

Offa historical king of Mercia
of-uh /'ɒfə/

Offaly county, Republic of Ireland
of-uh-li /'ɒfəli/

Offenbach, Jacques German composer
zhahk of-uhn-bakh /ˌʒɑːk 'ɒfənbax/

officiate act in charge
uh-**fish**-i-ayt /əˈfɪʃɪeɪt/

Ofgem OFfice of Gas and Electricity
Markets
of-jem /'ɒfdʒɛm/

Ofili, Chris English artist
kriss uh-**fee**-li /ˌkrɪs əˈfiːli/

often frequently
of-uhn /'ɒfən/

Commonly also oft-uhn.

Ofwat OFfice of WATer Services
of-wot /'ɒfwɒt/

Ogaden desert, Ethiopia
og-uh-**den** /ˌɒɡəˈdɛn/

Ogbomosho city, Nigeria
og-buh-**moh**-shoh /ˌɒɡbəˈməʊʃəʊ/

ogdoad group of eight
og-doh-ad /'ɒɡdəʊad/

Ogen melon variety
oh-gen /'əʊɡɛn/

ogham ancient British and Irish alphabet
og-uhm /'ɒɡəm/

ogonek diacritic symbol
og-**on**-ek /ɒˈɡɒnɛk/

Ohio state, US
oh-**hy**-oh /əʊˈhʌɪəʊ/

Ohm, Georg Simon German physicist
gay-ork zee-mon ohm /ˌɡeɪɔː(r)k
ziːmɒn 'əʊm/

ohm unit of resistance
ohm /əʊm/

Ohrid lake between Macedonia and
Albania
okh-rid /'ɒxrɪd/

Oireachtas legislature of the Irish
Republic
err-**uhk**-tuhss /'ɛrəktəs/, Irish
/'ɛrʲəxtəs/

Oisin mythical Irish bard; also called
Ossian
oh-**sheen** /əʊˈʃiːn/

okapi large mammal
oh-**kah**-pi /əʊˈkɑːpi/

Okara city, Pakistan
oh-**kah**-ruh /əʊˈkɑːrə/

Okayama city, Japan
oh-kuh-**yah**-muh /ˌəʊkəˈjɑːmə/

Okeechobee, Lake lake, US
oh-kuh-**choh**-bee /ˌəʊkəˈtʃəʊbiː/

O'Keeffe, Georgia American painter
jor-juh oh-keef /ˌdʒɔː(r)dʒə əʊˈkiːf/

Okefenokee swamp, US
oh-kuh-fuh-**noh**-kee /ˌəʊkəfəˈnəʊkiː/

Okhotsk sea and town, Russia
uh-**khotsk** /əˈxɒtsk/

Okinawa region, Japan
oh-kin-**ah**-wuh /ˌəʊkɪˈnɑːwə/

Oklahoma state, US
oh-kluh-**hoh**-muh /ˌəʊkləˈhəʊmə/

okra edible plant
oh-kruh /'əʊkrə/

Okri, Ben Nigerian writer
ben oh-kri /bɛn 'əʊkri/

Olaf name of five kings of Norway
oh-lav /'əʊlav/, [uːlaf]

• Established anglicization.

Öland island, Sweden
oe-land /'øːland/

olde worlde quaint
ohl-di wurl-di /ˌəʊldi 'wəː(r)ldi/

A pseudo-archaic pronunciation, often used to suggest inauthenticity.

Oldenburg, Claes Swedish-American artist
klahss ohl-duhn-burg /ˌklɑːs 'əʊldənbəː(r)g/

Oldham town, England
ohl-duhm /'əʊldəm/

Oldowan early Lower Palaeolithic culture of Africa
ol-doh-wuhn /'ɒldəʊwən/

Olduvai gorge, Tanzania
ol-duuv-y /'ɒldʊvʌɪ/

olé 'bravo' (Spanish)
oh-lay /əʊ'leɪ/

oleaginous oily
oh-li-aj-in-uhss /ˌəʊlɪ'adʒɪnəs/

oleander poisonous shrub
oh-li-an-duhr /ˌəʊlɪ'andə(r)/

Oleanna play by David Mamet
ol-i-an-uh /ˌɒlɪ'anə/

Olestra trademark synthetic fat substitute
ol-est-ruh /ɒ'lɛstrə/

olfactory relating to smell
ol-fak-tuh-ri /ɒl'faktəri/

oligarch ruler
ol-ig-ark /'ɒlɪgɑː(r)k/

Oligocene geological epoch
ol-ig-uh-seen /'ɒlɪgəsiːn/

olingo nocturnal mammal
ol-ing-goh /ɒ'lɪŋgəʊ/

olio spiced stew
oh-li-oh /'əʊlɪəʊ/

Olivier, Laurence English actor
lorr-uhnss uh-liv-i-ay /ˌlɒrəns ə'lɪvieɪ/

Olmec ancient Meso-American civilization
ol-mek /'ɒlmɛk/

Olomouc city, Czech Republic
ol-uh-mohts /'ɒləməʊts/

oloroso dark sherry
ol-uh-roh-soh /ˌɒlə'rəʊsəʊ/

Olsztyn city, Poland
ol-shtin /'ɒlʃtɪn/

Olympiad occasion when Olympic Games are held

uh-lim-pi-ad /ə'lɪmpiad/

Olympus home of the Greek gods
uh-lim-puhss /ə'lɪmpəs/

om Hindu mystic mantra
ohm /əʊm/

Omaar, Rageh Somali BBC reporter
rag-i oh-mar /ˌragi 'əʊmɑː(r)/

Omaha city, US
oh-muh-hah /'əʊməhɑː/

Oman country
oh-mahn /əʊ'mɑːn/

Omar Khayyám Persian poet and mathematician
oh-mar ky-ahm /ˌəʊmɑː(r) kʌɪ'ɑːm/

ombudsman official who investigates complaints
om-buudz-muhn /'ɒmbʊdzmən/

Omdurman city, Sudan
om-duhr-mahn /ˌɒmdə(r)'mɑːn/

omega letter of the Greek alphabet
oh-mig-uh /'əʊmɪgə/

omertà code of silence
oh-mair-tah /ˌəʊmɛː(r)'tɑː/

omicron letter of the Greek alphabet
oh-my-kron /əʊ'mʌɪkrɒn/

Commonly also **om-i-kron**.

omnipotent having unlimited power
om-nip-uh-tuhnt /ɒm'nɪpətənt/

omniscient knowing everything
om-niss-i-uhnt /ɒm'nɪsiənt/

omnivorous eating food of both plant and animal origin
om-niv-uh-ruhss /ɒm'nɪvərəs/

omphalos pl. **omphaloi** centre or hub
om-fuh-loss, pl. **om-fuh-loy** /'ɒmfələs/, pl. /-lɔɪ/

Omsk city, Russia
omsk /ɒmsk/

onanism masturbation
oh-nuh-niz-uhm /'əʊnənɪzəm/

Onassis, Aristotle Greek businessman
arr-ist-ot-uhl oh-nass-iss /ˌarɪstɒtəl əʊ'nasɪs/

onchocerciasis river blindness
on-koh-sur-ky-uh-siss /ˌɒŋkəʊsəː(r)'kʌɪəsɪs/

oncology study and treatment of tumours
ong-kol-uh-ji /ɒŋ'kɒlədʒi/

Ondaatje, Michael Sri
Lankan-Canadian writer
my-kuhl on-**dah**-tyuh /ˌmʌɪkəl
ɒnˈdɑːtjə/

ondes martenot electronic musical
instrument
o(ng)d **mar**-tuh-noh /ɒ̃d ˈmɑː(r)tənəʊ/

on dit piece of gossip
o(ng) **dee** /ɒ̃ ˈdiː/

Onega port and lake, Russia
uh-**nyeg**-uh /əˈnjɛgə/

Onegin, Eugene see **Eugene Onegin**

Oneida American Indian ethnic group
oh-**ny**-duh /əʊˈnʌɪdə/

oneiromancy interpretation of dreams
uh-**ny**-ruh-man-si /əˈnʌɪrəˌmansi/

onerous difficult
oh-nuh-ruhss /ˈəʊnərəs/

Commonly also **on**-uh-ruhss.

Ono, Yoko Japanese-American musician
yoh-koh **oh**-noh /ˌjəʊkəʊ ˈəʊnəʊ/

onomastic relating to the study of
proper names
on-uh-**mass**-tik /ɒnəˈmastɪk/

onomatopoeia formation of a word
from an associated sound
on-uh-mat-uh-**pee**-uh /ˌɒnəmatəˈpiːə/

Ontario province, Canada
on-**tair**-i-oh /ɒnˈtɛːrɪəʊ/

ontology branch of metaphysics
on-**tol**-uh-ji /ɒnˈtɒlədʒi/

onus responsibility
oh-nuhss /ˈəʊnəs/

onyx semi-precious variety of agate
on-iks /ˈɒnɪks/

oocyte cell in an ovary
oh-uh-syt /ˈəʊəsʌɪt/

oogenesis production or development of
an ovum
oh-uh-**jen**-uh-siss /əʊəˈdʒɛnɪsɪs/

oology collecting of birds' eggs
oh-**ol**-uh-ji /əʊˈɒlədʒi/

oolong dark-coloured China tea
oo-long /ˈuːlɒŋ/

Oort, Jan Hendrik Dutch astronomer
yun **hend**-rik ort /jʌn ˌhɛndrɪk ˈɔː(r)t/

opacity opposite of transparency
uh-**pass**-it-i /əˈpasɪti/

opaque not able to be seen through
oh-**payk** /əʊˈpeɪk/

OPEC Organization of Petroleum

Exporting Countries
oh-pek /ˈəʊpɛk/

Opel, Wilhelm von German motor
manufacturer
vil-helm fon **oh**-puhl /ˌvɪlhɛlm fɒn
ˈəʊpəl/

opéra bouffe French comic opera
op-air-uh **boof** /ˌɒpɛːrə ˈbuːf/

opera buffa Italian comic opera
op-air-uh **boo**-fuh /ˌɒpɛːrə ˈbuːfə/

Ophelia Shakespearean character
uh-**fee**-li-uh /əˈfiːliə/

ophicleide organ stop
of-ik-lyd /ˈɒfɪklʌɪd/

Ophiuchus constellation
oh-**fyoo**-kuhss /əʊˈfjuːkəs/

ophthalmology branch of medicine
concerned with the eye
of-thal-**mol**-uh-ji /ˌɒfθalˈmɒlədʒi/

Commonly also op-thal-**mol**-uh-ji.

Oporto see **Porto**

opossum mammal
uh-**poss**-uhm /əˈpɒsəm/

oppidum ancient Celtic fortified town
op-id-uhm /ˈɒpɪdəm/

opportune especially convenient
op-puhr-tyoon /ˈɒpə(r)tjuːn/

opprobrium harsh criticism
uh-**proh**-bri-uhm /əˈprəʊbriəm/

oppugn question the truth of
uh-**pyoon** /əˈpjuːn/

opsimath person who begins to study
late in life
op-sim-ath /ˈɒpsɪmaθ/

optative grammatical mood
op-tuh-tiv /ˈɒptətɪv/

Less commonly also op-**tay**-tiv.

opus pl. **opera** musical composition
oh-puhss, pl. **op**-uh-ruh /ˈəʊpəs/, pl.
/ˈɒpərə/
• Standard -es plural is also possible.

Opus Dei Catholic organization; 'God's
work' (Latin)
oh-puhss **day**-ee /ˌəʊpəs ˈdeɪiː/

oracy ability to speak fluently
aw-ruh-si /ˈɔːrəsi/

Oradea city, Romania
aw-**rah**-di-uh /ɔːˈrɑːdiə/

Oran port, Algeria
aw-**rahn** /ɔːˈrɑːn/

orang-utan ape
uh-**rang**-oo-tan /əˈraŋuːˌtan/

If spelt *orang-utang*, pronounced
uh-**rang**-oo-tang.

Oranienburg town, Germany; site of a
Second World War concentration camp
orr-**ah**-ni-uhn-buurk /ɒˈrɑːniənbʊ(r)k/

Oranjestad capital of Aruba
aw-**ran**-yuh-staht /ɔːˈranjəˌstɑːt/

oratorio large-scale musical work
o-ruh-**tor**-i-oh /ˌɒrəˈtɔːriəʊ/

oratory small chapel
orr-uh-tuh-ri /ˈɒrətəri/

Orbison, Roy American singer
roy **or**-biss-uhn /ˌrɔɪ ˈɔː(r)bɪsən/

orca whale
or-kuh /ˈɔː(r)kə/

Orcadian relating to the Orkney Islands
or-**kay**-di-uhn /ɔː(r)ˈkeɪdiən/

Orcagna, Andrea Italian painter and
architect
an-**dray**-uh or-**kah**-nyuh /anˈdreɪə
ɔː(r)ˈkɑːnjə/

orchitis inflammation of the testicles
or-**ky**-tiss /ɔː(r)ˈkaɪtɪs/

Orczy, Emmuska Hungarian-British
novelist
em-uush-kuh **ort**-si /ˌɛmʊʃkə ˈɔː(r)tsi/

ordinand trainee priest
or-di-nand /ˈɔː(r)dɪnand/

ordinarily usually
or-duh-nuh-**ril**-i /ˌɔː(r)dənərɪli/

Commonly also or-di-**nair**-il-i.

ordinary usual
or-duh-nuh-ri /ˈɔː(r)dənəri/

Reduced pronunciations such as **ord**-nuh-ri
or **ord**-uhn-ri are common, and **or**-din-err-i
is also possible.

ordinate mathematical line
or-di-nuht /ˈɔː(r)dɪnət/

Ordnance Survey organization which
produces maps
ord-nuhnss **sur**-vay /ˌɔː(r)dnəns
ˈsəː(r)veɪ/

Ordovician geological period
or-duh-**vish**-i-uhn /ˌɔː(r)dəˈvɪʃiən/

ordure excrement
or-dyuur /ˈɔː(r)djʊə(r)/

Örebro city, Sweden
oe-ruh-**broo** /ˌœːrəˈbruː/

orecchiette small pieces of ear-shaped
pasta
orr-ek-**kyet**-ay /ˌɒrɛˈkjɛteɪ/

oregano culinary herb
o-ruh-**gah**-noh /ˌɒrəˈɡɑːnəʊ/

AM is uh-**reg**-uh-noh.

Oregon state, US
orr-uh-guhn /ˈɒrəɡən/

Orel city, Russia
uh-**rel** /əˈrɛl/

Orenburg city, Russia
orr-uhn-burg /ˈɒrənbəː(r)ɡ/

Oreo trademark American chocolate
biscuit
aw-ri-oh /ˈɔːriəʊ/

Oresteia play trilogy by Aeschylus
orr-**est**-y-uh /ˌɒrɛsˈtʌɪə/

Orestes Greek mythological character
orr-**est**-eez /ɒˈrɛstiːz/

Øresund (also **Öresund**) strait between
Sweden and Denmark
oe-ruh-**suund** /ˌœːrəˈsʊnd/

orfe fish
orf /ɔː(r)f/

Orfeo ed Euridice opera by Gluck
or-**fay**-oh ed ay-oo-rid-**ee**-chay
/ɔː(r)ˈfeɪəʊ ed eɪuːrɪˈdiːtʃeɪ/

Orff, Carl German composer
karl orf /ˌkɑː(r)l ˈɔː(r)f/

organdie cotton fabric
or-guhn-di /ˈɔː(r)ɡəndi/

organum type of polyphonic music
or-guh-nuhm /ˈɔː(r)ɡənəm/

organza dress fabric
or-**gan**-zuh /ɔː(r)ˈɡanzə/

orgone excess life force
or-gohn /ˈɔː(r)ɡəʊn/

oriel large upper-storey bay with a
window
aw-ri-uhl /ˈɔːriəl/

orifice opening
orr-if-iss /ˈɒrɪfɪs/

origami Japanese art of folding paper
orr-ig-**ah**-mi /ˌɒrɪˈɡɑːmi/

Origen Christian scholar and theologian
orr-ij-uhn /ˈɒrɪdʒən/

Orinoco river, South America
orr-in-**oh**-koh /ˌɒrɪˈnəʊkəʊ/

oriole bird
aw-ri-ohl /ˈɔːriəʊl/

Orion constellation
uh-**ry**-uhn /əˈrʌɪən/

orison prayer
orr-**iz**-uhn /ˈɒrɪzən/

Orissa state, India
uh-**riss**-uh /əˈrɪsə/

Orkneys islands, Scotland
ork-**neez** /ˈɔː(r)kniːz/

Orlando city, US
or-**lan**-doh /ɔː(r)ˈlandəʊ/

Orleans city, France
or-lay-**ah(ng)** /ɔː(r)leɪˈɑ̃/

Less commonly anglicized to or-**lee**-uhnz, which is the pronunciation used for the place of the same name in Quebec. See also NEW ORLEANS.

Ormazd Zoroastrian god
or-**muhzd** /ˈɔː(r)məzd/

ormolu metal alloy
or-muh-**loo** /ˈɔː(r)məluː/

ornery bad-tempered
or-**nuh**-ri /ˈɔː(r)nəri/

ornithology study of birds
or-nith-**ol**-uh-ji /ˌɔː(r)nɪˈθɒlədʒi/

orography branch of geography dealing with mountains
orr-**og**-ruh-fi /ɒˈrɒgrəfi/

Oromo member of an East African ethnic group
orr-uh-**moh** /ˈɒrəməʊ/

Orontes river, Asia
uh-**ron**-teez /əˈrɒntiːz/

oropharynx part of the throat
aw-roh-**farr**-inks /ˌɔːrəʊˈfarɪŋks/

orotund imposing
orr-oh-**tund** /ˈɒrəʊtʌnd/

orpharion stringed instrument
or-**farr**-i-uhn /ɔː(r)ˈfariən/

Orpheus Greek mythological character
or-**fyooss** /ˈɔː(r)fjuːs/

Commonly also or-**fi**-uhss.

orrery model of the solar system
orr-uh-ri /ˈɒrəri/

ortanique citrus fruit
or-tuh-**neek** /ˌɔː(r)təˈniːk/

Ortega, Daniel Nicaraguan statesman
dan-**yel** or-**tay**-guh /dan,jɛl ɔː(r)ˈteɪgə/

orthodontics treatment of dental irregularities
or-thuh-**don**-tiks /ˌɔː(r)θəˈdɒntɪks/

orthoepy correct or accepted pronunciation of words
or-**thoh**-uh-pi /ɔː(r)ˈθəʊəpi/

Less commonly also or-thoh-**ep**-i or or-thoh-**ee**-pi. We find it ironic that the pronunciation of this word is so variable.

orthognathous having a jaw which does not project forwards
or-**thog**-nuh-thuhss /ɔː(r)ˈθɒgnəθəs/

orthogonal involving right angles
or-**thog**-uh-nuhl /ɔː(r)ˈθɒgənəl/

orthography spelling system
or-**thog**-ruh-fi /ɔː(r)ˈθɒgrəfi/

orthopaedics branch of medicine dealing with bones or muscle deformity
or-thuh-**pee**-diks /ˌɔː(r)θəˈpiːdɪks/

orthosis pl. **orthoses** splint or brace
or-**thoh**-siss, pl. or-**thoh**-seez /ɔː(r)ˈθəʊsɪs/, pl. /-siːz/

ortolan bird
or-tuh-**luhn** /ˈɔː(r)tələn/

Oruro city, Bolivia
uh-**roo**-roh /əˈruːrəʊ/

Orvieto town, Italy
or-**vyay**-toh /ɔː(r)ˈvjeɪtəʊ/

oryx antelope
orr-iks /ˈɒrɪks/

orzo small pieces of pasta
ort-soh /ˈɔː(r)tsəʊ/

Osaka port, Japan
oh-**sah**-kuh /əʊˈsɑːkə/
• See **Japanese** panel.

oscillate move in a regular rhythm
oss-il-ayt /ˈɒsɪleɪt/

oscular relating to kissing
osk-yuul-uhr /ˈɒskjʊlə(r)/

Osh city, Kyrgyzstan
osh /ɒʃ/

Oshawa city, Canada
osh-uh-wuh /ˈɒʃəwə/

osier willow
oh-zi-uhr /ˈəʊziə(r)/

Osijek city, Croatia
oss-i-yek /ˈɒsɪjɛk/

Osiris Egyptian god
oh-**sy**-riss /əʊˈsʌɪrɪs/

Oslo capital of Norway
oz-loh /ˈɒzləʊ/, [ˈuslu]
• Established anglicization.

Osman I Turkish founder of the Ottoman empire
oz-muhn /ˈɒzmən/

osmium chemical element
oz-mi-uhm /ˈɒzmiəm/

osmosis process of diffusion
oz-**moh**-siss /ˈɒzˈməʊsɪs/

Osnabrück city, Germany
oz-nuh-bruuk /ˈɒznəbrʊk/,
[ˌɔsnaˈbrʏk]

osnaburg coarse linen
oz-nuh-burg /ˈɒznəbəː(r)g/

osprey bird of prey
osp-ri /ˈɒsprɪ/

Less commonly also **osp**-ray.

Ossetia region, Caucasus
oss-et-i-uh /ɒsˈɛtɪə/

An older anglicized pronunciation,
uh-**see**-shuh, is given in various reference
works. Our research has indicated that the
pronunciation we recommend, which is
closer to the Russian, is more acceptable.

Ossi citizen of the former German
Democratic Republic
oss-i /ˈɒsi/

Ossian legendary Irish bard; also called
Oisin
oss-i-uhn /ˈɒsɪən/

ossify turn into bone
oss-i-fy /ˈɒsɪfʌɪ/

osso buco Italian dish made of shin of
veal
oss-oh **boo**-koh /ˌɒsəʊ ˈbuːkəʊ/

ossuary receptacle for bones
oss-yoo-uh-ri /ˈɒsjuərɪ/

Ostade, Adriaen van Dutch painter
and engraver
ah-dri-ahn vun ost-**ah**-duh /ˈɑːdriɑːn
vʌn ɒˈstɑːdə/

Ostend port, Belgium
ost-**end** /ɒˈstɛnd/

ostensible appearing to be true, but not
necessarily so
ost-**en**-sib-uhl /ɒˈstɛnsɪbəl/

ostentatious showy
ost-en-**tay**-shuhss /ˌɒstɛnˈteɪʃəs/

osteomyelitis inflammation of bone and
bone marrow
ost-i-oh-my-uh-**ly**-tiss
/ˌɒstɪəʊmʌɪəˈlʌɪtɪs/

osteopathy branch of complementary
medicine
ost-i-**op**-uh-thi /ˌɒstiˈɒpəθi/

osteoporosis medical condition
ost-i-oh-puh-**roh**-siss
/ˌɒstiəʊpəˈrəʊsɪs/

Ostia ancient city, Italy
ost-i-uh /ˈɒstɪə/

ostinato pl. **ostinati** repeated musical
phrase
ost-in-**ah**-toh, pl. ost-in-**ah**-ti
/ˌɒstɪˈnɑːtəʊ, pl. -/-ˈnɑːti/
• Standard -s plural is also possible.

ostler person employed to look after
guests' horses
oss-luhr /ˈɒslə(r)/

Ostpolitik foreign policy of détente with
the former communist bloc
ost-pol-it-eek /ˈɒstpɒlɪˌtiːk/

ostracize exclude
ost-ruh-syz /ˈɒstrəsʌɪz/

Ostrava city, Czech Republic
ost-ruh-vuh /ˈɒstrəvə/

Ostrogoth member of an ancient people
ost-ruh-goth /ˈɒstrəgɒθ/

Ostwald, Friedrich German physical
chemist
freed-rikh **ost**-valt /ˌfriːdrɪç ˈɒstvalt/

Oświęcim town, Poland; site of
Auschwitz concentration camp
osh-**vyen**-cheem /ɒʃˈvjɛntʃiːm/

Otago region, New Zealand
ot-**ah**-goh /ɒˈtɑːgəʊ/

otaku young people highly skilled in
computer technology
oh-**tah**-koo /əʊˈtɑːkuː/

otiose serving no practical purpose
oh-ti-ohss /ˈəʊtɪəʊs/

otology study of the ear
oh-**tol**-uh-ji /əʊˈtɒlədʒi/

Otomanguean family of American
Indian languages
oh-tuh-**mang**-gi-uhn /ˌəʊtəˈmaŋgiən/

otorhinolaryngology study of diseases
of the ear, nose, and throat
oh-toh-ry-noh-larr-in-**gol**-uh-ji
/ˌəʊtəʊˌrʌɪnəʊˌlarɪŋˈgɒlədʒi/

Otranto strait between Italy and Albania
oh-tran-toh /ˈəʊtrantəʊ/

Ottawa city, Canada
ot-uh-wuh /ˈɒtəwə/

ottocento relating to the 19th century in
Italy
ot-oh-**chen**-toh /ˌɒtəʊˈtʃɛntəʊ/

Ötzi mummified Stone Age man,
discovered in Austria
oet-si /ˈœtsi/

Ottoman Turkish dynasty
ot-uh-muhn /ˈɒtəmən/

Ouagadougou capital of Burkina
wag-uh-**doo**-goo /ˌwagəˈduːguː/

oubliette secret dungeon
oo-bli-**et** /ˌuːbliˈɛt/

oud musical instrument
ood /uːd/

Oudenarde town and battle site,
Belgium
oo-duh-nard /ˈuːdənɑː(r)d/, Flemish
[ˈɔudənɑːrdə]

Oudh region, India
owd /aʊd/

ouguiya (also **ougiya**) currency unit,
Mauritania
oo-**gee**-yuh /uːˈgiːjə/

Ouida English novelist
wee-duh /ˈwiːdə/

Ouija board board with letters,
numbers, and symbols around its edge
wee-juh /ˈwiːdʒə/

Oulu city, Finland
oh-loo /ˈəʊluː/

Ouse river, England
ooz /uːz/

oust drive out
owst /aʊst/

outage period without power supply
ow-tuhj /ˈaʊtədʒ/

outjie child (South African)
oh-ki /ˈəʊki/

outré unusual or shocking
oo-**tray** /ˈuːtreɪ/

Outremer medieval French crusader
states
oo-truh-mair /ˈuːtrəmɛː(r)/

ouzo Greek aniseed-flavoured spirit
oo-zoh /ˈuːzəʊ/

ovarian relating to the ovaries
oh-**vair**-i-uhn /əʊˈvɛːriən/

Overijssel province, Netherlands
oh-**vuhr**-y-suhl /ˌəʊvərˈʌɪsəl/

overt done openly
oh-**vurt** /əʊˈvəː(r)t/

Ovid Roman poet

ov-id /ˈɒvɪd/

Oviedo city, Spain
ov-**yay**-*th*oh /ˌɒvˈjeɪðəʊ/

ovine relating to sheep
oh-vyn /ˈəʊvʌɪn/

ovulate discharge ova from the ovary
ov-yuul-ayt /ˈɒvjʊleɪt/

ovum pl. **ova** female reproductive cell
oh-vuhm, pl. **oh**-vuh /ˈəʊvəm/, pl.
/ˈəʊvə/

owt anything (dialect)
owt /aʊt/

oxalis plant
ok-suh-liss /ˈɒksəlɪs/

Less commonly also ok-**sah**-liss.

oxbow loop in a river
oks-boh /ˈɒksbəʊ/

Oxonian relating to Oxford or Oxford
University
ok-**soh**-ni-uhn /ɒkˈsəʊniən/

OxyContin trademark analgesic drug
ok-si-**kon**-tin /ˌɒksiˈkɒntɪn/

oxygenate supply with oxygen
ok-sij-uh-nayt /ˈɒksɪdʒəneɪt/

oxymoron contradictory figure of speech
ok-si-**maw**-ron /ˌɒksiˈmɔːrɒn/

oxytocin female hormone
ok-si-**toh**-sin /ˌɒksiˈtəʊsɪn/

Oyeyemi, Helen Nigerian writer
oy-**ay**-uh-mi /ɔɪˈeɪəmi/

oyez call given to command attention
before an announcement
oh-**yay** /əʊˈjeɪ/

Less commonly also oh-**yez**.

oy vey (also **oy veh**) Yiddish interjection
of dismay
oy **vay** /ɔɪ ˈveɪ/

Ozarks mountains, US
oh-zarks /ˈəʊzɑː(r)ks/

ozonosphere ozone layer
oh-**zohn**-uh-sfeer /əʊˈzəʊnəsfɪə(r)/

Ozymandias poem by Shelley
oz-i-**man**-di-ass /ˌɒzɪˈmandias/

P

pa'anga currency unit, Tonga
pah-**ahng**-guh /pɑːˈɑːŋɡə/

pace with due respect to
pay-si /ˈpeɪsi/

Sometimes also pah-chay; see LATIN panel.

Pachelbel, Johann German composer
yoh-han pakh-uhl-bel /ˌjəʊhan ˈpaxəlbɛl/

pachinko Japanese form of pinball
puh-**chink**-oh /pəˈtʃɪŋkəʊ/

pachisi Indian board game
puh-**chee**-zi /pəˈtʃiːzi/

Marketed in the US as *parcheesi*,
pronounced par-**chee**-zi.

Pachuca de Soto city, Mexico
patch-**oo**-kuh day **soh**-toh /pɑˌtʃuːkə
deɪ ˈsəʊtəʊ/

pachyderm thick-skinned mammal
pak-id-urm /ˈpakɪdə(r)m/

Pacino, Al American actor
puh-**chee**-noh /pəˈtʃiːnəʊ/

Padang port, Indonesia
pud-ung /ˈpʌdʌŋ/

Less commonly puh-**dang**.

pademelon (also **paddymelon**) wallaby
pad-i-mel-uhn /ˈpadiˌmɛlən/

Paderewski, Ignacy Jan Polish
composer and statesman
eeg-**nat**-si yan pad-uh-**ref**-ski
/iːɡˌnatsi jan ˌpadəˈrɛfski/

Padma river, Bangladesh
pud-muh /ˈpʌdmə/

Padraig Irish boy's name
paw-rig /ˈpɔːrɪɡ/

padre chaplain
pah-dray /ˈpɑːdreɪ/

padrona female boss
pad-**roh**-nuh /paˈdrəʊnə/

pad thai Thai noodle dish
pad ty /pad ˈtʌɪ/

Padua city, Italy
pad-yoo-uh /ˈpadjuə/

Established anglicization. The Italian name
is Padova, pronounced **pah**-dov-uh.

paean song of praise
pee-uhn /ˈpiːən/

paediatrics medicine dealing with
children
pee-di-**at**-riks /ˌpiːdiˈatrɪks/

paedophilia sexual interest in children
pee-duh-**fil**-i-uh /piːdəˈfɪliə/

paella Spanish rice dish
py-**el**-uh /pʌɪˈɛlə/

Sometimes also py-**ay**-yuh, a more
Spanish-sounding pronunciation.

Pagan town, Burma
puh-**gahn** /pəˈɡɑːn/

Paganini, Niccolò Italian violinist and
composer
nee-kol-**oh** pag-uh-**nee**-ni /niːkəˌləʊ
ˌpaɡəˈniːni/

Paget's disease medical condition
paj-uhts /ˈpadʒəts/

Paglia, Camille American critic
kuh-**meel** pahl-yuh /kəˌmiːl ˈpɑːljə/

Pagnol, Marcel French dramatist
mar-**sel** pan-yol /mɑː(r)ˌsɛl paˈnjɒl/

pagoda temple
puh-**goh**-duh /pəˈɡəʊdə/

Pahang state, Malaysia
puh-**hung** /pəˈhʌŋ/

pahoehoe smooth lava
puh-**hoh**-i-hoh-i /pəˈhəʊihəʊi/

paideia system of cultural education
py-**dy**-uh /pʌɪˈdʌɪə/

pain au chocolat pastry
pan oh **shok**-uh-lah /ˌpan əʊ ˈʃɒkəlɑː/

Paine Towers granite peaks, Chile
py-nay /ˈpʌɪneɪ/

paisan fellow countryman
py-**zahn** /pʌɪˈzɑːn/

pak choi Chinese cabbage
pak choy /pak ˈtʃɔɪ/

Pakeha non-Maori New Zealander
pah-kuh-hah /ˈpɑːkəhɑː/

Pakenham village, England
pay-kuhn-uhm /ˈpeɪkənəm/

However, the family name is usually
pronounced **pak**-uhn-uhm.

Pakistan country
pah-kist-**ahn** /pɑːkɪsˈtɑːn/

Commonly also pak-ist-**an**.

pakora Indian snack
puh-**kaw**-ruh /pəˈkɔːrə/

Palaeocene geological epoch
pal-i-oh-seen /ˈpaliəʊsiːn/

Commonly also **pay**-li-oh-, especially in
AM. The same variation occurs in
Palaeolithic and *palaeontology* (below).

palaeography study of writing systems
pay-li-**og**-ruh-fi /ˌpeɪliˈɒgrəfi/

Palaeolithic early phase of the Stone
Age
pal-i-oh-**lith**-ik /ˌpaliəʊˈlɪθɪk/

palaeontology science concerned with
fossils
pal-i-on-**tol**-uh-ji /ˌpaliɒnˈtɒlədʒi/

palaestra wrestling school
puh-**lee**-struh /pəˈliːstrə/

palais dance hall
pal-ay /ˈpaleɪ/

palanquin covered litter
pal-uhn-**keen** /ˌpalənˈkiːn/

palantir object from *The Lord of the
Rings*
pal-**an**-teer /palˈantɪə(r)/

palatal relating to the palate
pal-uh-tuhl /ˈpalətəl/

palatinate territory
puh-**lat**-i-nuht /pəˈlatɪnət/

Palau islands, Pacific
puh-**low** /pəˈlaʊ/

palaver fuss
puh-**lah**-vuhr /pəˈlɑːvə(r)/

Palawan island, Philippines
puh-**lah**-wuhn /pəˈlɑːwən/

palazzo pl. **palazzi** palatial building
puh-**lat**-soh, pl. puh-**lat**-si /pəˈlatsəʊ/,
pl. /-tsi/

Palembang city, Indonesia
pul-**em**-bung /pʌˈlɛmbʌŋ/

Palenque former Mayan city, Mexico
pal-**eng**-ky /paˈlɛŋkeɪ/

Palermo port, Italy
pal-**air**-moh /paˈlɛː(r)məʊ/

Palestine territory, Middle East
pal-uh-styn /ˈpaləstʌɪn/

Palestrina, Giovanni Pierluigi da
Italian composer
juh-**vah**-ni pyair-**lwee**-ji dah
pal-uh-**stree**-nuh /dʒəˌvɑːni
pjɛː(r)ˌlwiːdʒi dɑː ˌpaləˈstriːnə/

palette thin board
pal-uht /ˈpalət/

palfrey docile horse
pawl-fri /ˈpɔːlfri/

Palgrave, Francis Turner English
critic and poet
pal-grayv /ˈpalgreɪv/

Pali Indian language
pah-li /ˈpɑːli/

palimony compensation after separation
pal-im-uh-ni /ˈpalɪməni/

palimpsest manuscript on which later
writing has been superimposed
pal-imp-sest /ˈpalɪmpsɛst/

palindrome sequence that reads the
same backwards as forwards
pal-in-drohm /ˈpalɪndrəʊm/

palisade fence
pal-iss-**ayd** /ˌpalɪˈseɪd/

Palissy, Bernard French potter
bair-**nar** pal-iss-**i** /bɛː(r)ˌnɑː(r) palɪˈsi/

Palk Strait inlet of the Bay of Bengal
pawlk /pɔːlk/

Palladian relating to the architecture of
Andrea Palladio
puh-**lay**-di-uhn /pəˈleɪdiən/

Palladio, Andrea Italian architect
and-**ray**-uh pal-**ah**-di-oh /anˌdreɪə
pəˈlɑːdiəʊ/

palladium chemical element
puh-**lay**-di-uhm /pəˈleɪdiəm/

palliasse straw mattress
pal-i-ass /ˈpalias/

palliative relieving pain
pal-i-uh-tiv /ˈpaliətɪv/

Palma port, Majorca
pal-muh /ˈpalmə/

Palmas town, Brazil
pal-mass /ˈpalmas/

palmate botanical term
pal-mayt /ˈpalmeɪt/

Palme, Olof Swedish statesman
oo-lof **pal**-muh /ˌuːlɒf ˈpalmə/

Palmerston, Lord English statesman
pah-muhr-stuhn /ˈpɑːmə(r)stən/

Palmyra city, Syria; also called **Tadmur**
pal-**my**-ruh /palˈmʌɪrə/

Palo Alto city, US
pal-oh **al**-toh /ˌpaləʊ ˈaltəʊ/

Palomar, Mount mountain, US
pal-uh-mar /ˈpaləmɑː(r)/

palomino horse
pal-uh-**mee**-noh /ˌpaləˈmiːnəʊ/

palsy paralysis
pawl-zi /ˈpɔːlzi/

Paltrow, Gwyneth American actress
pal-troh /ˈpaltrəʊ/

paly heraldic term
pay-li /ˈpeɪli/

Pamir Mountains mountain system,
central Asia
puh-**meer** /pəˈmɪə(r)/

pampas treeless plains
pam-puhss /ˈpampəs/

Pamphylia ancient region, Asia Minor
pam-**fil**-i-uh /pamˈfɪliə/

Pamplona city, Spain
pam-**ploh**-nuh /pamˈpləʊnə/

panacea cure-all
pan-uh-**see**-uh /ˌpanəˈsiːə/

panache flamboyance
puh-**nash** /pəˈnaʃ/

Panaji city, India
pun-uj-i /ˈpʌnʌdʒi/

Panama country
pan-uh-mah /ˈpanəmɑː/,
Spanish [panaˈma]

Panay island, Philippines
pan-**y** /paˈnʌɪ/

pancetta pork
pan-**chet**-uh /panˈtʃɛtə/

panchayat Indian village council
pun-**chy**-uht /pʌnˈtʃʌɪət/

pancreas gland
pank-ri-uhss /ˈpaŋkriəs/

Pandarus Greek mythological character
pan-duh-ruhss /ˈpandərəs/

pandemic prevalent over a whole area
pan-**dem**-ik /panˈdɛmɪk/

pandemonium wild disorder
pan-duh-**moh**-ni-uhm
/ˌpandəˈməʊniəm/

Pandit, Vijaya Lakshmi Indian
politician
vij-uh-yuh **luk**-shmi **pun**-dit /ˌvɪdʒəjə
ˌlʌkʃmi ˈpʌndɪt/

paneer curd cheese
pan-**eer** /paˈnɪə(r)/

panegyric praiseful speech
pan-uh-**jirr**-ik /ˌpanəˈdʒɪrɪk/

panettone rich Italian bread
pan-et-**oh**-nay /ˌpanɛˈtəʊneɪ/

panga machete
pang-guh /ˈpaŋgə/

Pangaea prehistoric supercontinent
pan-**jee**-uh /panˈdʒiːə/

Pangloss optimistic person
pan-gloss /ˈpanglɒs/

pangolin ant-eater
pang-guh-**lin** /ˌpaŋgəˈlɪn/

Panini Indian grammarian
pah-nin-i /ˈpɑːnɪni/

panino pl. **panini** sandwich
pan-**ee**-noh, pl. pan-**ee**-ni /paˈniːnəʊ/,
pl. /-ni/

Panjabi see **Punjabi**

panjandrum influential person
pan-**jan**-druhm /panˈdʒandrəm/

Pankhurst family of English suffragettes
pank-hurst /ˈpaŋkhəː(r)st/

panoply extensive collection
pan-uh-pli /ˈpanəpli/

Pantagruel Rabelaisian giant
pan-tuh-**groo**-el /ˌpantəɡruˈɛl/, French
[pɑ̃taɡryɛl]

The absence of syllable stress in French
gives rise to other anglicized pronunciations
such as pan-**tag**-roo-el.

Pantagruelian enormous
pan-tuh-groo-**el**-i-uhn
/ˌpantəɡruˈɛliən/

Pantalaimon fictional creature in Philip
Pullman's *His Dark Materials*
pan-tuh-**ly**-muhn /ˌpantəˈlʌɪmən/

Pantanal swampland, Brazil
pan-tuh-**now** /ˌpantəˈnaʊ/

Pantelleria island, Italy
pant-el-uh-**ree**-uh /ˌpantɛləˈriːə/

pantheism religion
pan-thee-iz-uhm /ˈpanθiːɪzəm/

pantheon gods
pan-thi-uhn /ˈpanθiən/

Pantocrator title of Christ
pan-**tok**-ruh-tuhr /panˈtɒkrətə(r)/

panzer German armoured unit
pan-zuhr /ˈpanzə(r)/, [ˈpantsɐ]
• Established anglicization.

Paolozzi, Eduardo Scottish sculptor
ed-**war**-doh pow-**lot**-si /ɛdˈwɑ:(r)dəʊ
paʊˈlɒtsi/

papa one's father
puh-**pah** /pəˈpɑ:/

The pronunciation **pap**-uh is also possible, especially in children's speech.

papabile eligible to be pope
pap-**ah**-bil-ay /paˈpɑːbɪleɪ/

papacy office of the Pope
pay-puh-si /ˈpeɪpəsi/

Papageno character in Mozart opera
pap-uh-**gay**-noh /papəˈɡeɪnəʊ/

paparazzo pl. **paparazzi** freelance
photographer
pap-uh-**rat**-soh, pl. pap-uh-**rat**-si
/ˌpapəˈratsəʊ/, pl. /-tsi/

papaya tropical fruit
puh-**py**-uh /pəˈpʌɪə/

Papeete capital of French Polynesia
pah-pi-**ay**-tay /ˌpɑːpiˈeɪteɪ/

Papiementu Creole language
pap-i-uh-**men**-too /ˌpapiəˈmɛntuː/

papier mâché mixture of paper and
glue
pap-yay **mash**-ay /ˌpapjeɪ ˈmaʃeɪ/

papilla pl. **papillae** protuberance
puh-**pil**-uh, pl. puh-**pil**-ee /pəˈpɪlə/, pl.
/-liː/

papilloma pl. **papillomata** wart-like
growth
pap-il-**oh**-muh, pl. pap-il-**oh**-muh-tuh
/ˌpapɪˈləʊmə/, pl. /-mətə/

papillon breed of dog
pap-il-on /ˈpapɪlɒn/

Sometimes also pap-ee-**yo(ng)**, a more
French-sounding pronunciation.

pappardelle kind of pasta
pap-ar-**del**-ay /ˌpapɑ:(r)ˈdɛleɪ/

paprika spice
pap-rik-uh /ˈpaprɪkə/

Also puh-**pree**-kuh, especially in AM.

Papua New Guinea country
pap-wuh nyoo **gin**-i /ˈpapwə njuː
ˈɡɪni/

papyrus material
puh-**py**-ruhss /pəˈpʌɪrəs/

Pará state, Brazil
parr-**ah** /pəˈrɑː/

parabola pl. **parabolae** curve
puh-**rab**-uh-luh, pl. puh-**rab**-uh-lee
/pəˈrabələ/, pl. /-liː/

Paracel Islands islands, South China
Sea
parr-uh-**sel** /ˌparəˈsɛl/

Paracelsus Swiss physician
parr-uh-**sel**-suhss /ˌparəˈsɛlsəs/

paracetamol drug
parr-uh-**see**-tuh-mol /ˌparəˈsiːtəmɒl/

Commonly also parr-uh-**set**-uh-mol.

Paraclete Holy Spirit
parr-uh-kleet /ˈparəkliːt/

paradiddle drumming pattern
parr-uh-did-uhl /ˈparəˌdɪdəl/

paradigm typical example
parr-uh-dym /ˈparədʌɪm/

paradigmatic relating to a paradigm
parr-uh-dig-**mat**-ik /ˌparədɪɡˈmatɪk/

parador pl. **paradores** government hotel
in Spain
parr-uh-**dor**, pl. parr-uh-**daw**-rayss
/ˌparəˈdɔ:(r)/, pl. /-ˈdɔːreɪs/

Paraguay country
parr-uh-gwy /ˈparəɡwʌɪ/, [para'ɣwaj]
• Established anglicization.

Paraiba state, Brazil
parr-uh-**ee**-buh /ˌparəˈiːbə/

parallax visual effect
parr-uh-laks /ˈparəlaks/

Paramaribo capital of Suriname
parr-uh-**marr**-i-boh /ˌparəˈmaribəʊ/

paramecium single-celled animal
parr-uh-**mee**-si-uhm /ˌparəˈmiːsiəm/

parameter factor
puh-**ram**-uh-tuhr /pəˈramətə(r)/

Paraná river, South America
parr-uh-**nah** /ˌparəˈnɑː/

paraphernalia miscellaneous articles
parr-uh-fuhr-**nay**-li-uh
/ˌparəfə(r)ˈneɪliə/

paraplegia paralysis of the lower body
parr-uh-**plee**-juh /ˌparəˈpliːdʒə/

paraquat herbicide
parr-uh-kwot /ˈparəkwɒt/

paratha flat bread
puh-**rah**-tuh /pəˈrɑːtə/

par avion by airmail
par av-**yo(ng)** /pɑːr aˈvjɔ̃/

Parcae Roman mythological characters
par-ky /ˈpɑː(r)kʌɪ/

parens patriae legal term
parr-enz **pat**-ri-ee /ˌparɛnz ˈpatriiː/

parenthesis pl. **parentheses** bracket
puh-**ren**-thuh-siss, pl.
puh-**ren**-thuh-seez /pə'rɛnθəsɪs/, pl.
/-siːz/

pareve kosher food
pah-ruh-vuh /'pɑːrəvə/

par excellence better than others
par ek-suh-**lah(ng)ss** /ˌpɑːr ɛksə'lãns/

parfait cold dessert
par-**fay** /pɑː(r)'feɪ/

parget cover with plaster
par-**juht** /'pɑː(r)dʒət/

pariah outcast
puh-**ry**-uh /pə'rʌɪə/

Paribas French bank
parr-i-**bah** /'paribɑː/

Paris capital of France
parr-iss /'parɪs/, [pari]

Established anglicization. Occasionally also
referred to jocularly in English as parr-**ee**.

Parisian relating to Paris
puh-**riz**-i-uhn /pə'rɪzɪən/

AM is usally puh-**ree**-zhuhn.

parlance particular way of speaking
par-**luhnss** /'pɑː(r)ləns/

parlando musical term
par-**land**-oh /pɑː(r)'landəʊ/

parley conference
par-li /'pɑː(r)li/

parliament legislature
par-luh-muhnt /'pɑː(r)ləmənt/

The alternative pronunciation
parl-yuh-muhnt is increasingly rare.

Parma city, Italy
par-muh /'pɑː(r)mə/

Parmenides Greek philosopher
par-**men**-id-eez /pɑː(r)'mɛnɪdiːz/

Parmesan hard cheese
par-muh-**zan** /pɑː(r)mə'zan/

Parmigiana cooked with Parmesan
cheese
par-mi-**jah**-nuh /ˌpɑː(r)mi'dʒɑːnə/

Parmigianino Italian painter
par-mi-jan-**ee**-noh
/ˌpɑː(r)midʒa'niːnəʊ/

Parnassus, Mount mountain, Greece
par-**nass**-uhss /pɑː(r)'nasəs/

Parnell, Charles Stewart Irish
nationalist leader
par-**nuhl** /'pɑː(r)nəl/

parochial relating to a parish
puh-**roh**-ki-uhl /pə'rəʊkɪəl/

Paros island, Greece
parr-oss /'parɒs/

paroxysm sudden attack
parr-uhk-siz-uhm /'parəksɪzəm/

parquet wooden flooring
par-kay /'pɑː(r)keɪ/

parramatta fabric
parr-uh-**mat**-uh /ˌparə'matə/

parse resolve into component parts
parz /pɑː(r)z/

AM is parss.

parsec unit of astronomical distance
par-sek /'pɑː(r)sɛk/

Parsifal opera by Wagner
par-sif-al /'pɑː(r)sɪfal/

parsimonious frugal
par-sim-**oh**-ni-uhss /ˌpɑː(r)sɪ'məʊnɪəs/

Pärt, Arvo Estonian composer
ar-voh pairt /ˌɑː(r)vəʊ pɛː(r)t/, [ˌarvo
'pært]

Partenope opera by Handel
par-**ten**-oh-pay /pɑː(r)'tɛnəʊpeɪ/

parthenogenesis reproduction without
fertilization
par-thuh-noh-**jen**-uh-siss
/ˌpɑː(r)θənəʊ'dʒɛnəsɪs/

Parthenon temple, Greece
par-thuh-nuhn /'pɑː(r)θənən/

participle word formed from a verb
par-tiss-ip-uhl /'pɑː(r)tɪsɪpəl/

parti pris preconceived view
par-ti **pree** /ˌpɑː(r)ti 'priː/

partisan supporter of a cause
par-tiz-an /'pɑː(r)tɪzan/

partita pl. **partite** musical suite
par-**tee**-tuh, pl. par-**tee**-tay
/pɑː(r)'tiːtə, pl. -teɪ/

Parvati Hindu goddess
par-vuh-ti /'pɑː(r)vəti/

parvenu person of humble origin who
has gained wealth
par-vuh-noo /'pɑː(r)vənuː/

Pasadena city, California
pass-uh-**dee**-nuh /ˌpasə'diːnə/

Pascal, Blaise French physicist
blayz pask-al /ˌbleɪz pas'kal/

Pascal computer programming language
pask-al /pas'kal/

pascal SI unit of pressure
pask-al /pas'kal/

Sometimes also **pask**-uhl.

paschal relating to Easter
pask-uhl /ˈpaskəl/

pas de bourrée ballet step
pah duh boor-**ay** /ˌpɑː də bʊəˈreɪ/

pas de chat ballet jump
pah duh **shah** /ˌpɑː də ˈʃɑː/

pas de deux dance for two
pah duh **doe** /ˌpɑː də ˈdə/

paseo leisurely walk
pass-**ay**-oh /paˈseɪəʊ/

pasha Turkish officer
pash-uh /ˈpaʃə/

pashmina shawl
pash-**mee**-nuh /paʃˈmiːnə/

Pashto language
push-toh /ˈpʌʃtəʊ/

Pašić, Nikola Serbian statesman
nee-kol-uh **pash**-itch /ˌniːkɒlə ˈpaʃɪtʃ/

Pasiphaë Greek mythological character
puh-**sif**-uh-ee /pəˈsɪfəiː/

paso doble ballroom dance
pass-oh **doh**-blay /ˌpasəʊ ˈdəʊbleɪ/

Pasolini, Pier Italian film director
pyair pass-uh-**lee**-ni /ˌpjɛː(r) ˌpasəˈliːni/

passacaglia musical composition
pass-uh-**kahl**-yuh /ˌpasəˈkɑːljə/

passant heraldic term
pass-uhnt /ˈpasənt/

passata tomato paste
puh-**sah**-tuh /pəˈsɑːtə/

Passau city, Germany
pass-ow /ˈpasaʊ/

Passchendaele, Battle of First World
War battle
pash-uhn-dayl /ˈpaʃəndeɪl/

The Belgian village is now called Passendale,
pronounced puss-uhn-**dah**-luh.

passé no longer fashionable
pass-**ay** /paˈseɪ/

passeggiata leisurely walk
pass-ej-**ah**-tuh /ˌpasɛˈdʒɑːtə/

passepartout mounted picture
pasp-ar-**too** /ˌpaspɑː(r)ˈtuː/

Pasternak, Boris Russian writer
borr-iss **past**-uhr-nak /ˈbɒrɪs ˈpastə(r)nak/
● Established anglicization.

Pasteur, Louis French bacteriologist

lwee past-**oer** /ˌlwiː paˈstœː(r)/

pastiche imitative artistic work
past-**eesh** /paˈstiːʃ/

pastille sweet
past-uhl /ˈpastəl/

pastis aperitif
past-**eess** /paˈstiːs/

pastoral relating to care
pah-stuh-ruhl /ˈpɑːstərəl/

Commonly also **past**-uh-ruhl.

pastorale instrumental composition
past-uh-**rahl** /ˌpastəˈrɑːl/

pasty filled pastry
past-i /ˈpasti/

pasty unhealthily pale
pay-sti /ˈpeɪsti/

pataca currency unit, Macao
puh-**tah**-kuh /pəˈtɑːkə/

Patagonia region, South America
pat-uh-**goh**-ni-uh /ˌpatəˈgəʊniə/

patas monkey primate
puh-**tah** /pəˈtɑː/

Patau's syndrome congenital disorder
pat-owz /ˈpataʊz/

patchouli aromatic oil
puh-**choo**-li /pəˈtʃuːli/

pâté de foie gras goose liver paste
pat-ay duh fwah **grah** /ˌpateɪ də fwɑː ˈɡrɑː/

Patel surname of Indian origin
puh-**tel** /pəˈtɛl/

patella pl. **patellae** kneecap
puh-**tel**-uh, pl. puh-**tel**-ee /pəˈtɛlə/, pl. /-liː/

paten metal plate
pat-uhn /ˈpatən/

patent government licence
pay-tuhnt /ˈpeɪtənt/

Sometimes also **pat**-uhnt, particularly with
reference to the Patent Office or letters
patent. Patent leather is usually **pay**-tuhnt.

Pater, Walter English essayist
pay-tuhr /ˈpeɪtə(r)/

pater father (dated)
pay-tuhr /ˈpeɪtə(r)/
● See LATIN panel.

paterfamilias pl. **patresfamilias** male
head of a family
pay-tuhr-fuh-**mil**-i-ass,
pl. **pay**-treez-fuh-**mil**-i-ass
/ˌpeɪtə(r)fəˈmɪlias/, pl. /ˌpeɪtriːz-/

Also **pat-uhr-**; see LATIN panel.

paternoster the Lord's Prayer
pat-uhr-nost-uhr /ˌpatə(r)'nɒstə(r)/

Pathé, Charles French film pioneer
sharl path-ay /ˌʃɑː(r)l pa'θeɪ/

pathogen micro-organism
path-uh-juhn /'paθədʒən/

pathos quality that evokes sadness
pay-thoss /'peɪθɒs/

patina film on metal
pat-in-uh /'patɪnə/

patisserie cake shop
puh-tee-suh-ri /pə'tiːsəri/

Patmos island, Greece
pat-moss /'patmɒs/

Patna city, India
pat-nuh /'patnə/
• Established anglicization.

patois dialect
pat-wah /'patwɑː/

Paton, Alan South African writer
pay-tuhn /'peɪtən/

Patras port, Greece
puh-trass /pə'tras/

patria native country
pat-ri-uh /'patriə/

Sometimes also **pay-tri-uh**.

patriarch male head
pay-tri-ark /'peɪtriɑː(r)k/

patrician nobleman
puh-trish-uhn /pə'trɪʃən/

patriot person who supports their
country
pay-tri-uht /'peɪtriət/

Commonly also **pat-ri-uht**.

Patroclus Greek mythological character
puh-trok-luhss /pə'trɒkləs/

patronymic name derived from a father
pat-ruh-nim-ik /ˌpatrə'nɪmɪk/

Pattaya resort, Thailand
pat-ay-ah /'pateɪɑː/

Patum Peperium trademark anchovy
relish
pat-uhm pep-air-i-uhm /ˌpatəm
pɛ'pɛːriəm/

paua abalone
pow-uh /'paʊə/

paucity insufficiency
paw-sit-i /'pɔːsɪti/

Pauli, Wolfgang Austrian-born

American physicist
volf-gang pow-li /ˌvɒlfgaŋ 'paʊli/

Pauline relating to St Paul
paw-lyn /'pɔːlʌɪn/

Pauling, Linus American chemist
ly-nuhss paw-ling /ˌlʌɪnəs 'pɔːlɪŋ/

Pausanias Greek geographer and
historian
paw-say-ni-uhss /pɔː'seɪniəs/

pavane dance
puh-van /pə'van/

Pavarotti, Luciano Italian operatic
tenor
loo-chah-noh pav-uh-rot-i /luːˌtʃɑːnəʊ
ˌpavə'rɒti/

Pavese, Cesare Italian writer
chay-zuh-ray pav-ay-zay /ˌtʃeɪzəreɪ
pa'veɪzeɪ/

Pavlov, Ivan Russian physiologist
ee-vahn pav-luhf /iːˌvɑːn 'pavləf/

Pavlova, Anna Russian dancer
an-uh pav-luh-vuh /ˌanə 'pavləvə/

The anglicized pronunciation pav-**loh**-vuh
is used for the dessert named after her. Our
research indicates that the Russian
pronunciation given above is the one heard
and preferred in ballet circles.

Pavlovian relating to conditioning
pav-loh-vi-uhn /pav'ləʊviən/

Pavord, Anna English writer
pay-vord /'peɪvɔː(r)d/

pawpaw tropical fruit
paw-paw /'pɔːpɔː/

Pax Romana peace within the Roman
Empire
paks roh-mah-nuh /ˌpaks rəʊ'mɑːnə/

paysage landscape
pay-zahzh /peɪ'zɑːʒ/

Pays Basque Basque Country
pay bask /ˌpeɪ 'bask/

Paz, Octavio Mexican poet
ok-tahv-yoh pass /ɒk'tɑːvjəʊ 'pas/

Peano, Giuseppe Italian
mathematician
juuz-ep-ay pay-ah-noh /dʒʊ'zɛpeɪ
peɪ'ɑːnəʊ/

Pearce, Padraig Irish nationalist
paw-rig peerss /ˌpɔːrɪk 'pɪə(r)s/

Pears, Peter English operatic tenor
peerz /pɪə(r)z/

peau-de-soie fabric
poh duh swah /ˌpəʊ də 'swɑː/

pecan nut
pee-kan /'piːkan/

Sometimes also pi-**kan** or pi-**kahn**, especially in AM.

peccadillo minor sin
pek-uh-**dil**-oh /ˌpɛkə'dɪləʊ/

peccavi expression of guilt
pek-**ah**-vi /pɛ'kɑːvi/

Pechenga region, Russia
petch-uhng-guh /'pɛtʃəŋgə/

Pechora river, Russia
puh-**chaw**-ruh /pə'tʃɔːrə/

Peckinpah, Sam American film director
pek-in-pah /'pɛkɪnpɑː/

pecorino Italian cheese
pek-uh-**ree**-noh /ˌpɛkə'riːnəʊ/

Pécs city, Hungary
paytch /peɪtʃ/

pectoral relating to the chest
pek-tuh-ruhl /'pɛktərəl/

pedagogue teacher
ped-uh-gog /'pɛdəgɒg/

pedagogy practice of teaching
ped-uh-goj-i /'pɛdəgɒdʒi/

Also **ped**-uh-gog-i.

pedalo pleasure boat
ped-uh-loh /'pɛdələʊ/

pederasty paedophilia
ped-uh-rast-i /'pɛdərasti/

Pedersen, Mogens Danish composer
moh-uhnss **pay**-*th*uhr-suhn /ˌməʊəns 'peɪðə(r)sən/

pedometer step-counter
ped-**om**-uh-tuhr /pɛ'dɒmətə(r)/

peely-wally sickly in appearance (Scottish)
pee-li wal-i /ˌpiːlɪ'wali/

Peenemünde village, Germany
pay-nuh-**muen**-duh /ˌpeɪnə'mʏndə/

Peer Gynt opera by Grieg
peer gint /ˌpɪə(r) 'gɪnt/

Pegu city, Burma
peg-**oo** /pɛ'guː/

Pei, I. M. Chinese-American architect
pay /peɪ/

peignoir nightwear
payn-**war** /peɪn'wɑː(r)/

Pejačević, Dora Croatian composer
daw-ruh-pay-**ah**-chuh-vitch /ˌdɔːrə

pecan | **pemmican**

peɪ'ɑːtʃəvɪtʃ/

pejorative expressing disapproval
puh-**jorr**-uh-tiv /pə'dʒɒrətɪv/

Pekinese lapdog
pee-kin-**eez** /ˌpiːkɪ'niːz/

Peking former name for **Beijing**
pee-**king** /piː'kɪŋ/

pekoe tea
pee-koh /'piːkəʊ/

pelagic relating to the open sea
puh-**laj**-ik /pə'ladʒɪk/

Pelagius British or Irish monk
puh-**lay**-ji-uhss /pə'leɪdʒiəs/

pelau spicy West Indian dish
puh-**low** /pə'laʊ/

Pelé Brazilian footballer
pel-ay /'pɛleɪ/

Pelée, Mount volcano, Caribbean
puh-**lay** /pə'leɪ/

Peleus Greek mythological character
peel-i-uhss /'piːliəs/

pelike pl. **pelikai** amphora
pel-ik-i, pl. **pel**-ik-y /'pɛlɪki/, pl. /'pɛlɪkʌɪ/

Pelion mountain, Greece
pee-li-uhn /'piːliən/

pelisse cloak
puh-**leess** /pə'liːs/

pellagra disease
pel-**ag**-ruh /pɛ'lagrə/

Pelléas et Mélisande opera by Debussy
pel-ay-**ass** ay may-liz-**ah(ng)d** /ˌpɛleɪˌas eɪ meɪlɪ'zãd/

Pelmanism memory training
pel-muh-niz-uhm /'pɛlmənɪzəm/

Peloponnese peninsula, Greece
pel-uh-puh-**neez** /ˌpɛləpə'niːz/

Pelops Greek mythological character
pee-lops /'piːlɒps/

pelorus sighting device
puh-**law**-ruhss /pə'lɔːrəs/

pelota ball game
pel-**oh**-tuh /pɛ'ləʊtə/

Pemba port, Mozambique
pem-buh /'pɛmbə/

Pembroke port, Wales
pem-bruuk /'pɛmbrʊk/

There are also Oxford and Cambridge colleges of the same name, pronounced in the same way.

pemmican dried meat cake
pem-ik-uhn /'pɛmɪkən/

pemphigus skin disease
pem-fig-**uhss** /ˈpɛmfɪɡəs/

Peña, Paco Spanish guitarist
pak-oh **payn**-yuh /ˌpakəʊ ˈpeɪnjə/

Penang island, Malaysia
puh-**nang** /pəˈnaŋ/

penates Roman household gods
puh-**nah**-teez /pəˈnɑːtiːz/

penchant fondness for something
po(ng)-sho(ng) /ˈpɒ̃ʃɒ̃/

Commonly also **pen**-shuhnt, a more
anglicized pronunciation.

Pencoed town, Wales
pen-**koyd** /pɛnˈkɔɪd/

Penderecki, Krzysztof Polish
composer
kshish-tof pen-duh-**ret**-ski /ˌkʃɪʃtɒf
pɛndəˈrɛtski/

Pendolino trademark tilting train
pen-duh-**lee**-noh /pɛndəˈliːnəʊ/

Pendragon ancient British title
pen-**drag**-uhn /pɛnˈdragən/

Penelope Greek mythological character
puh-**nel**-uh-pi /pəˈnɛləpi/

Penge district of London
penj /pɛndʒ/

penillion improvised Welsh singing
pen-**ihl**-i-on /pɛˈnɪlɪɒn/

penistone woollen cloth
pen-is-tuhn /ˈpɛnɪstən/

penne kind of pasta
pen-ay /ˈpɛneɪ/

Pennine Hills hills, England
pen-yn /ˈpɛnʌɪn/

penn'orth pennyworth
pen-uhrth /ˈpɛnə(r)θ/

Pennsylvania state, US
pen-sil-**vay**-ni-uh /ˌpɛnsɪlˈveɪnɪə/

Penobscot American Indian ethnic
group
pen-**ob**-skot /pɛˈnɒbskɒt/

Pensacola resort, US
pen-suh-**koh**-luh /ˌpɛnsəˈkəʊlə/

pensée reflection
pah(ng)-**say** /pɑ̃ˈseɪ/

pension small hotel, especially in France
po(ng)-syo(ng) /ˈpɒ̃sjɒ̃/

pensione pl. **pensioni** small hotel in Italy
pen-**syoh**-nay, pl. pen-**syoh**-ni
/ˌpɛnˈsjəʊneɪ/, pl. /-ni/

pentameter line of verse

Pentateuch first five books of the Old
Testament
pen-tuh-tyook /ˈpɛntətjuːk/

pentatonic five-note scale
pen-tuh-**ton**-ik /ˌpɛntəˈtɒnɪk/

Pentecost Christian festival
pen-tuh-kost /ˈpɛntəkɒst/

Penthesilea Greek mythological
character
pen-thess-il-**ee**-uh /ˌpɛnθɛsɪˈliːə/

Pentothal trademark drug
pen-tuh-thal /ˈpɛntəθal/

penult penultimate syllable
pen-ult /ˈpɛnʌlt/

penumbra pl. **penumbrae** shadow
region
pen-**um**-bruh, pl. pen-**um**-bree
/pɛˈnʌmbrə/, pl. /-briː/

penury state of being very poor
pen-yuh-ri /ˈpɛnjəri/

Penza city, Russia
pyen-zuh /ˈpjɛnzə/

Penzance town, England
pen-**zanss** /pɛnˈzans/

peony plant
pee-uh-ni /ˈpiːəni/

Peoria city, US
pi-**aw**-ri-uh /piˈɔːriə/

pepino plant
pep-**ee**-noh /pɛˈpiːnəʊ/

Pepys, Samuel English diarist
peeps /piːps/

Péquiste supporter of the Canadian Parti
Québecois
pay-**keest** /peɪˈkiːst/

Pequot American Indian ethnic group
pee-kwot /ˈpiːkwɒt/

Perak state, Malaysia
peer-uh /ˈprərə/

percale cotton fabric
puhr-**kayl** /pə(r)ˈkeɪl/

per capita for each person
pur **kap**-it-uh /pə(r) ˈkapɪtə/

Perceval legendary figure
pur-suh-vuhl /ˈpə(r)səvəl/

percheron draught horse
pur-shuh-ron /ˈpə(r)ʃərɒn/

perchloroethylene dry-cleaning fluid
puhr-klaw-roh-**eth**-il-een
/pə(r)ˌklɔːrəʊˈɛθɪliːn/

per curiam legal term
pur **kyoor**-i-am /ˌpə:(r) ˈkjʊəriam/

percuss tap gently
puhr-**kuss** /pə(r)ˈkʌs/

per diem for each day
pur **dee**-em /pə:(r) ˈdi:ɛm/

perdition eternal punishment
puhr-**dish**-uhn /pə(r)ˈdɪʃən/

père father
pair /pɛ:(r)/

peregrine falcon
perr-uh-grin /ˈpɛrəgrɪn/

Perelman, S. J. American writer
perr-uhl-muhn /ˈpɛrəlmən/

Peres, Shimon Israeli statesman
shi-**mon perr**-ess /ˈʃi,mɒn ˈpɛrɛs/

perestroika policy of reform
perr-uh-**stroy**-kuh /ˌpɛrəˈstrɔɪkə/

Pérez de Cuéllar, Javier Peruvian
diplomat
khav-**yair perr**-ess day **kwel**-yar
/xav,jɛ:(r) ˌpɛrɛs deɪ ˈkwɛljɑ:(r)/

perfidy deceitfulness
pur-fid-i /ˈpə:(r)fɪdi/

Pergamum city, ancient Asia Minor
pur-guh-muhm /ˈpə:(r)gəməm/

Pergau dam, Malaysia
puhr-**gow** /pə(r)ˈgaʊ/

pergola arched structure
pur-guh-luh /ˈpə:(r)gələ/

Pergolesi, Giovanni Battista Italian
composer
juh-**vah**-ni bat-ee-stuh pair-gol-**ay**-zi
/dʒə,vɑːni baˈtiːstə pɛ:(r)gɒˈleɪzi/

Peri, Jacopo Italian composer
yah-kuh-poh **pair**-i /ˈjɑːkəpəʊ ˈpɛːri/

peri mythical superhuman being
peer-i /ˈpɪəri/

pericardium membrane enclosing the
heart
perr-i-**kar**-di-uhm /ˌpɛrɪˈkɑː(r)diəm/

Pericles Greek statesman
perr-ik-leez /ˈpɛrɪkliːz/

pericope extract from a text
puh-**rik**-uh-pi /pəˈrɪkəpi/

peridot semi-precious stone
perr-id-ot /ˈpɛrɪdɒt/

Périgord area, France
perr-ig-awr /ˈpɛrɪɡɔː(r)/

perihelion astronomical term
perr-i-**hee**-li-uhn /ˌpɛrɪˈhiːliən/

periodicity quality of occurring at
regular intervals
peer-i-uh-**diss**-it-i /ˌpɪərɪəˈdɪsɪti/

peripatetic roving
perr-ip-uh-**tet**-ik /ˌpɛrɪpəˈtɛtɪk/

peripeteia reversal of fortune
perr-ip-uh-**tee**-uh /ˌpɛrɪpəˈtiːə/

periphery edge
puh-**rif**-uh-ri /pəˈrɪfəri/

periphrasis pl. **periphrases** indirect
speech
puh-**rif**-ruh-siss, pl. puh-**rif**-ruh-seez
/pəˈrɪfrəsɪs/, pl. /-siːz/

perique tobacco
perr-**eek** /pɛˈriːk/

peritoneum abdominal lining
perr-it-uh-**nee**-uhm /ˌpɛrɪtəˈniːəm/

peritus theological adviser
puh-**ry**-tuhss /pəˈrʌɪtəs/

perjury lying under oath
pur-juh-ri /ˈpə:(r)dʒəri/

Perlis state, Malaysia
pur-liss /ˈpə:(r)lɪs/

Perm city, Russia
pyairm /pjɛ:(r)m/

A semi-established anglicization, purm, is
also heard.

permeable able to be passed through
pur-mi-uh-buhl /ˈpə:(r)miəbəl/

Permian geological era
pur-mi-uhn /ˈpə:(r)miən/

Pernambuco state, Brazil
pair-nam-**boo**-koo /ˌpɛ:(r)namˈbuːkuː/

Pernod trademark aperitif
pur-noh /ˈpə:(r)nəʊ/

Perón, Eva Argentinian politician
ay-vuh perr-**on** /ˌeɪvə pɛˈrɒn/

Perón, Juan Argentinian statesman
khwan perr-**on** /ˌxwan pɛˈrɒn/

perorate speak at length
perr-uh-rayt /ˈpɛrəreɪt/

Perot, Ross American businessman
puhr-**oh** /pəˈrəʊ/

Pérotin early French composer
pay-rot-**a(ng)** /peɪrɒˈtɛ̃/

perpetuum mobile perpetual motion
pur-**pet**-yoo-uhm **moh**-bil-ay
/pə:(r)ˌpɛtjuəm ˈməʊbɪleɪ/

Perpignan city, France
pair-peen-**yah(ng)** /pɛ:(r)piːˈnjɑ̃/

perquisite benefit
pur-kwiz-it /'pə:(r)kwɪzɪt/

Perrault, Charles French writer
sharl perr-oh /,ʃɑ:(r)l pɛ'rəʊ/

Perrier trademark mineral water
perr-i-ay /'pɛrɪeɪ/

Persaud, Raj English psychiatrist
rahj puhr-sawd /,rɑ:dʒ pə(r)'sɔ:d/

per se in itself
pur say /,pə:(r) 'seɪ/

Perseids meteor shower
puhr-see-idz /pə(r)'si:ɪdz/

Persephone Greek goddess
puhr-sef-uh-ni /pə(r)'sɛfəni/

Persepolis ancient city, Persia
puhr-sep-uh-liss /pə(r)'sɛpəlɪs/

Perseus Greek mythological character
purss-yooss /'pə:(r)sju:s/

Commonly also **pur-si-uhss**.

perseverate prolong
puhr-sev-uh-rayt /pə(r)'sɛvəreɪt/

Persia former name for Iran
pur-zhuh /'pə:(r)ʒə/

persiflage mockery
pur-sif-lahzh /'pə:(r)sɪflɑ:ʒ/

persimmon fruit
puhr-sim-uhn /pə(r)'sɪmən/

persona non grata pl. **personae non
grata** unwelcome person
**puhr-soh-nuh non grah-tuh,
pl. puhr-soh-nee non grah-tee**
/pə(r),səʊnə nɒn 'grɑ:tə/, pl. /-ni:/, /-ti:/
• See LATIN panel.

Persson, Göran Swedish prime
minister
yoe-ran pair-shon /,jœ:ran 'pɛ:(r)ʃɒn/

pertussis whooping cough
puhr-tuss-iss /pə(r)'tʌsɪs/

Peru country
puh-roo /pə'ru:/

Perugia city, Italy
puh-roo-juh /pə'rʊ:dʒə/

peruke wig
puh-rook /pə'ru:k/

peruse read thoroughly
puh-rooz /pə'ru:z/

Pesach Jewish Passover festival
pay-sahkh /'peɪsɑ:x/

Peshawar city, Pakistan
puh-show-uhr /pə'ʃaʊə(r)/

peshmerga Kurdish nationalist

pesh-mur-guh /pɛʃ'mə:(r)gə/

peso currency unit, various Latin
American countries
pay-soh /'peɪsəʊ/

pessary medicine administered vaginally
pess-uh-ri /'pɛsəri/

Pestalozzi, Johann Heinrich Swiss
educational reformer
yoh-han hyn-rikh pest-uh-lots-i
/,jəʊhan ,hʌɪnrɪç ,pɛstə'lɒtsi/

pestle grinding tool
pess-uhl /'pɛsəl/

Pétain, Philippe French statesman
fil-eep pay-ta(ng) /fɪ'li:p peɪ'tɛ̃/

pétanque game
puh-tah(ng)k /pə'tɑ̃k/

petard small bomb
puh-tard /pə'tɑ:(r)d/

petechia pl. **petechiae** spot on the skin
pit-ee-ki-uh, pl. pit-ee-ki-ee /pɪ'ti:kiə/,
pl. /-ki:/

pethidine painkilling drug
peth-id-een /'pɛθɪdi:n/

pétillant sparkling
pet-i-yo(ng) /'pɛtɪjɒ̃/

petiole leaf stalk
pet-i-ohl /'pɛtɪəʊl/

Petipa, Marius French choreographer
marr-i-uhss pet-ip-ah /,mariəs
pɛtɪ'pɑ:/

petit four small cake
puh-ti for /,pəti 'fɔ:(r)/

petit mal seizure
puh-ti mal /,pəti 'mal/

petit point embroidery
puh-ti pwa(ng) /,pəti 'pwɛ̃/

Also anglicized to **puh-ti poynt**.

petits pois young peas
puh-ti pwah /,pəti 'pwɑ:/

Pető, András Hungarian educationalist
ond-rahsh pet-oe /,ɒndrɑ:ʃ 'pɛtø:/

Petra ancient city, Jordan
pet-ruh /'pɛtrə/

Petrarch Italian poet
pet-rark /'pɛtrɑ:(r)k/

Petri dish shallow, transparent dish
pet-ri /'pɛtri/

Petrie, Flinders English archaeologist
flin-duhrz peet-ri /,flɪndə(r)z 'pi:tri/

Petrine relating to St Peter
peet-ryn /'pi:trʌɪn/

petroglyph rock carving
pet-ruh-glif /'pɛtrəglɪf/

Petronas Towers building in Kuala
Lumpur
pet-ruh-nass /'pɛtrənas/

Petronius, Gaius Roman writer
gy-uhss pet-**roh**-ni-uhss /ˌgaɪəs
pɛ'trəʊniəs/

Petropavlovsk port, Russia
pet-ruh-**pav**-luhfsk /ˌpɛtrə'pavləfsk/

petrosal part of the skull
puh-**troh**-suhl /pə'trəʊsəl/

Petrozavodsk city, Russia
pet-ruh-zuh-**votsk** /ˌpɛtrəzə'vɒtsk/

Petrushka ballet by Stravinsky
puh-**troosh**-kuh /puh'truːʃkə/

pe tsai Chinese salad leaf
pay **tsy** /peɪ 'tsʌɪ/

Peugeot car manufacturers
poe-zhoh /'pəʒəʊ/

Pevsner, Nikolaus British art historian
pevz-nuhr /'pɛvznə(r)/

peyote cactus
pay-**oh**-ti /peɪ'əʊti/

Peyronie's disease medical condition
perr-uh-neez /'pɛrəniːz/

Pforzheim city, Germany
pforts-hym /'pfɔː(r)tshʌɪm/

phacelia plant
fuh-**see**-li-uh /fə'siːliə/

Phaeacians ancient people
fee-**ay**-shuhnz /fiː'eɪʃənz/

Phaedra Greek mythological character
feed-ruh /'fiːdrə/

Sometimes also **fyd**-ruh or **fay**-druh; see
GREEK panel.

Phaëthon Greek mythological character
fay-uh-thuhn /'feɪəθən/

phaeton carriage
fay-tuhn /'feɪtən/

phagocyte cell
fag-uh-syt /'fagəsʌɪt/

Phaidon British publishing company
fy-duhn /'fʌɪdən/

phalanx pl. **phalanges** troops in close
formation
fal-anks, pl. fuh-**lan**-jeez /'falaŋks/, pl.
/fə'landʒiːz/

phalarope bird
fal-uh-rohp /'falərəʊp/

phallus pl. **phalli** penis

fal-uhss, pl. **fal**-y /'faləs/, pl. /-lʌɪ/

Phanerozoic geological aeon
fan-uh-roh-**zoh**-ik /ˌfanərəʊ'zəʊɪk/

phantasm ghost
fan-taz-uhm /'fantazəm/

phantasmagoria sequence of real or
imaginary images
fan-taz-muh-**gorr**-i-uh
/ˌfantazmə'gɒriə/

pharaoh ruler in ancient Egypt
fair-oh /'fɛːrəʊ/

Pharisee member of an ancient Jewish
sect
farr-iss-ee /'farɪsiː/

Phar Lap Australian racehorse
far **lap** /ˌfɑː(r) 'lap/

pharmacopoeia list of medicinal drugs
far-muh-kuh-**pee**-uh /ˌfɑː(r)məkə'piːə/

Pharos lighthouse, Egypt
fair-oss /'fɛːrɒs/

pharyngitis inflammation of the
pharynx
farr-in-**jy**-tiss /ˌfarɪn'dʒʌɪtɪs/

pharynx pl. **pharynges** throat
farr-inks, pl. fuh-**rin**-jeez /'farɪŋks/, pl.
/fə'rɪndʒiːz/

phascogale marsupial
fask-**og**-uh-li /fa'skɒgəli/

phatic used for social interaction
fat-ik /'fatɪk/

Pheidippides ancient Greek messenger
fy-**dip**-id-eez /fʌɪ'dɪpɪdiːz/

phenobarbitone drug
fee-noh-**bar**-bit-ohn
/ˌfiːnəʊ'bɑː(r)bɪtəʊn/

phenolphthalein pH indicator
fee-nolf-**thal**-een /ˌfiːnɒl'fθaliːn/

phenotype set of biological
characteristics
fee-noh-typ /'fiːnəʊtʌɪp/

phenylketonuria inherited condition
fee-nyl-keet-uh-**nyoor**-i-uh
/ˌfiːnʌɪl,kiːtə'njʊəriə/

pheromone chemical substance
ferr-uh-mohn /'fɛrəməʊn/

phi letter of the Greek alphabet
fy /fʌɪ/

phial small bottle
fy-uhl /'fʌɪəl/

Phidias Greek sculptor
fid-i-ass /'fɪdias/

Philadelphia city, US
fil-uh-**delf**-i-uh /ˌfɪləˈdɛlfiə/

philanthrope philanthropist
fil-uhn-throhp /ˈfɪlənˌθrəʊp/

philanthropic seeking to promote the welfare of others
fil-uhn-**throp**-ik /ˌfɪlənˈθrɒpɪk/

philately collection of postage stamps
fil-**at**-uh-li /fɪˈlatəli/

Phileas Fogg fictional character
fil-i-uhss fog /ˌfɪliəs ˈfɒg/

Philemon Greek mythological character
fil-**ee**-muhn /fɪˈliːmən/

Philippi ancient city, Macedonia
fil-**ip**-y /ˈfɪlɪpʌɪ/

Philippians epistle of St Paul
fil-**ip**-i-uhnz /fɪˈlɪpiənz/

Philippines country
fil-ip-eenz /ˈfɪlɪpiːnz/

Philistine ancient Palestinian people
fil-ist-yn /ˈfɪlɪstʌɪn/

philodendron climbing plant
fil-uh-**den**-druhn /ˌfɪləˈdɛndrən/

Philo Judaeus Alexandrian Jewish philosopher
fy-loh joo-**dee**-uhss /ˌfʌɪləʊ dʒuːˈdiːəs/

Philomel Greek mythological character
fil-uh-mel /ˈfɪləmɛl/

Philomela Greek mythological character
fil-uh-**mee**-luh /ˌfɪləˈmiːlə/

philtre love potion
fil-tuhr /ˈfɪltə(r)/

Phintias Greek mythological character
fin-ti-ass /ˈfɪntɪas/

Phi Phi island, Thailand
pee pee /ˌpiː ˈpiː/

Phiz English illustrator
fiz /fɪz/

phlebotomy taking blood
fluh-**bot**-uh-mi /fləˈbɒtəmi/

Phlegethon Greek mythological river
fleg-uh-thon /ˈflɛgəθɒn/

phlegm substance
flem /flɛm/

phlegmatic calm
fleg-**mat**-ik /flɛgˈmatɪk/

phloem vascular tissue in plants
floh-em /ˈfləʊɛm/

Phnom Penh capital of Cambodia
pnom pen /ˌpnɒm ˈpɛn/

A more anglicized pronunciation, nom **pen**, is also used.

Phobos moon of Mars
foh-boss /ˈfəʊbɒs/

phocomelia congenital deformity
foh-kuh-**mee**-li-uh /ˌfəʊkəˈmiːliə/

Phoebe Greek mythological character
fee-bi /ˈfiːbi/

Phoebus Greek god
fee-buhss /ˈfiːbəs/

Phoenicia ancient country
fuh-**nee**-shuh /fəˈniːʃə/

Phoenix city, US
fee-niks /ˈfiːnɪks/

However, Phoenix in Mauritius is pronounced **fay**-neeks.

Phoenix, Joaquin American actor
wah-**keen fee**-niks /wɑːˌkiːn ˈfiːnɪks/

pholcodine drug
fol-kuh-**deen** /ˈfɒlkədiːn/

phonation production of speech sounds
foh-**nay**-shuhn /fəʊˈneɪʃən/

phoneme sound unit
foh-neem /ˈfəʊniːm/

phonetic relating to speech sounds
fuh-**net**-ik /fəˈnɛtɪk/

phonic relating to speech sounds
fon-ik /ˈfɒnɪk/

phoresy association between organisms
fuh-**ree**-si /fəˈriːsi/

phosphoresce emit light
foss-fuh-**ress** /ˌfɒsfəˈrɛs/

phosphorus chemical element
foss-fuh-ruhss /ˈfɒsfərəs/

phot unit of illumination
foht /fəʊt/

Photius Byzantine scholar
foh-ti-uhss /ˈfəʊtɪəs/

photogenic looking attractive in photographs
foh-tuh-**jen**-ik /ˌfəʊtəˈdʒɛnɪk/

Sometimes also foh-tuh-**jeen**-ik.

photometer instrument for measuring light intensity
foh-**tom**-uh-tuhr /fəʊˈtɒmətə(r)/

photon particle
foh-ton /ˈfəʊtɒn/

phragmites reed
frag-**my**-teez /fragˈmʌɪtiːz/

phratry kinship group
fray-tri /ˈfreɪtri/

phreatic relating to underground water
fri-at-ik /ˈfriːatɪk/

phrenic relating to the diaphragm
fren-ik /ˈfrɛnɪk/

Phrygia ancient region, Asia Minor
frij-i-uh /ˈfrɪdʒɪə/

phthalate chemical substance
fthal-ayt /ˈfθaleɪt/

phthisis wasting disease
fthy-siss /ˈfθʌɪsɪs/

Phuket island, Thailand
poo-ket /puːˈkɛt/

phulkari ornamental shawl
puul-kah-ri /pʊlˈkɑːri/

phycology botany concerned with algae
fy-kol-uh-ji /fʌɪˈkɒlədʒi/

phylactery box containing Hebrew texts
fil-ak-tuh-ri /frˈlaktəri/

phyllo see **filo**

phyllotaxis arrangement of leaves on a stem
fil-oh-tak-siss /ˌfɪləʊˈtaksɪs/

phylum pl. **phyla** taxonomic category
fy-luhm, pl. **fy-luh** /ˈfʌɪləm/, pl. -lə/

physalis Chinese lantern plant
fy-say-liss /fʌɪˈseɪlɪs/

Also fiss-uh-liss or fy-suh-liss; see LATIN panel.

physiognomy facial features
fiz-i-on-uh-mi /ˌfɪziˈɒnəmi/

Less commonly also fiz-i-og-nuh-mi.

physique body form
fiz-eek /fɪˈziːk/

pi letter of the Greek alphabet
py /pʌɪ/

pia mater brain membrane
pee-uh mah-tuhr /ˌpiːə ˈmɑːtə(r)/

Piaf, Edith French singer
ee-dith pyaf /ˌiːdɪθ ˈpjaf/

First name customarily anglicized; French pronunciation is ay-deet.

Piaget, Jean Swiss psychologist
zhah(ng) pyah-zhay /ˌʒɑ̃ pjaˈʒeɪ/

pianissimo very softly
pyuh-niss-im-oh /ˌpjaˈnɪsɪməʊ/

piano musical instrument
pi-an-oh /piˈanəʊ/

piano softly
pyah-noh /ˈpjɑːnəʊ/

pianoforte musical instrument
pi-an-oh-for-tay /piˌanəʊˈfɔː(r)teɪ/

pianola trademark automatic piano
pi-uh-noh-luh /ˌpiəˈnəʊlə/

piapiac crow
pee-uh-pee-uhk /ˈpiːəpiːak/

Piatigorsky, Gregor Russian-American cellist
greg-or pyat-ig-or-ski /ˌɡrɛɡɔː(r) pjatɪˈɡɔː(r)ski/

Piaui state, Brazil
pyow-ee /pjaʊˈiː/

piazza public square
pi-at-suh /piˈatsə/

Piazzolla, Astor Argentine composer
ast-or pyass-oh-luh /ˌastɔː(r) pjaˈsəʊlə/

pibroch bagpipe music
pee-brokh /ˈpiːbrɒx/

pica craving to eat unusual substances
py-kuh /ˈpʌɪkə/

picador horseback bullfighter
pik-uh-dor /ˈpɪkədɔː(r)/

picante spicy
pik-an-tay /pɪˈkanteɪ/

Picardy region, France
pik-uhr-di /ˈpɪkə(r)di/
• Established anglicization.

picaresque style of fiction
pik-uh-resk /ˌpɪkəˈrɛsk/

picaro rogue
pik-uh-roh /ˈpɪkərəʊ/

Picasso, Pablo Spanish artist
pab-loh pik-ass-oh /ˌpabləʊ pɪˈkasəʊ/

picayune of little value
pik-uh-yoon /ˌpɪkəˈjuːn/

pickelhaube spiked helmet
pik-uhl-how-buh /ˈpɪkəlˌhaʊbə/

Pico da Neblina mountain, Brazil
pee-koo dah neb-lee-nuh /ˌpiːkuː dɑː nɛˈbliːnə/

Pico della Mirandola Italian philosopher
pee-koh del-uh mirr-and-uh-luh /ˌpiːkəʊ ˌdɛlə mɪˈrandələ/

Pico de Orizaba mountain, Mexico
pee-koh day orr-ee-sab-uh /ˌpiːkəʊ deɪ ɒriˈsabə/

picot loop
pee-koh /ˈpiːkəʊ/

pièce de résistance most important feature
pyess duh ruh-**ziss**-to(ng)ss /ˌpjɛs də rəˈzɪstõs/

Also pyess duh rez-ist-**ah(ng)ss**, especially in AM.

Pieck, Wilhelm German statesman
vil-helm **peek** /ˌvɪlhɛlm ˈpiːk/

pied having two or more different colours
pyd /paɪd/

pied-à-terre small home for occasional use
pyed-ah-**tair** /ˌpjɛdɑːˈtɛː(r)/

Piedmont region, Italy
peed-mont /ˈpiːdmɒnt/

Established anglicization. The Italian is Piemonte, pronounced pyay-**mon**-tay.

pierid butterfly
py-uh-rid /ˈpaɪərɪd/

Piero della Francesca Italian painter
pyair-oh **del**-uh fran-**chesk**-uh /ˌpjɛːrəʊ ˌdɛlə franˈtʃɛskə/

pierogi dumplings
peer-**oh**-gi /pɪəˈrəʊgi/

Pierre French boy's name
pyair /pjɛː(r)/

Pierre city, US
peer /pɪə(r)/

Pierrot clown character
peer-oh /ˈpɪərəʊ/

Also pyerr-oh.

Piesporter white wine
peez-port-uhr /ˈpiːzˌpɔː(r)tə(r)/

pietà picture of the Virgin Mary
pyay-**tah** /pjeɪˈtɑː/

Pietermaritzburg city, South Africa
pee-tuhr-**marr**-its-burg /ˌpiːtə(r)ˈmarɪtsbə(r)g/

pietism pious sentiment
py-uh-**tiz**-uhm /ˈpaɪətɪzəm/

piet-my-vrou South African cuckoo
pit may froh /ˈpɪt meɪ ˌfrəʊ/

pietra dura mosaic work
pyet-ruh **doo**-ruh /ˌpjɛtrə ˈduːrə/

piety religiosity
py-uh-ti /ˈpaɪəti/

piezoelectricity electric polarization in a substance
py-**ee**-zoh-el-ek-**triss**-it-i /paɪˌiːzəʊɛlɛkˈtrɪsɪti/

pika rabbit-like mammal
py-kuh /ˈpaɪkə/

Pik Pobedy mountain, Kyrgyzstan
peek puh-**byed**-uh /ˌpiːk pəˈbjɛdə/

pilaf rice dish
pee-laf /ˈpɪlaf/

pilaster rectangular column
pil-**ast**-uhr /pɪˈlastə(r)/

Pilate, Pontius Roman procurator of Judaea
pon-shuhss py-luht /ˌpɒnʃəs ˈpaɪlət/

Pilates system of exercises
pil-**ah**-teez /pɪˈlɑːtiːz/

pilau rice dish
pee-low /ˈpiːlaʊ/

pileus pl. **pilei** mushroom cap
py-li-uhss, pl. **py**-li-y /ˈpaɪliəs/, pl. /-liaɪ/

Pillai, Nisha BBC journalist
nee-shuh **pil**-ay /ˌniːʃə ˈpɪleɪ/

Pilsen city, Czech Republic
pil-zuhn /ˈpɪlzən/

Pilsner lager beer
pilz-nuhr /ˈpɪlznə(r)/

pilule a small pill
pil-yool /ˈpɪljuːl/

pimento red sweet pepper; also pimiento
pim-**en**-toh /pɪˈmɛntəʊ/

pimiento red sweet pepper; also pimento
pim-**yen**-toh /pɪˈmjɛntəʊ/

pimpernel plant
pim-puhr-nel /ˈpɪmpə(r)nɛl/

pina colada cocktail
pee-nuh kuh-**lah**-duh /ˌpiːnə kəˈlɑːdə/

piñata sweet-filled container
peen-yah-tuh /piːˈnjɑːtə/

pince-nez eyeglasses with a nose clip
pa(ng)ss-nay /pɛ̃sˈneɪ/

Pindar Greek lyric poet
pin-duhr /ˈpɪndə(r)/

Pindus mountain range, Greece
pin-duhss /ˈpɪndəs/

pineal gland
pin-i-uhl /ˈpɪnɪəl/

Pinero, Arthur Wing English dramatist
pin-**eer**-oh /pɪˈnɪərəʊ/

pinguid plump
ping-gwid /ˈpɪŋgwɪd/

pinguin prickly plant
ping-gwin /ˈpɪŋgwɪn/

pinion cogwheel
pin-yuhn /ˈpɪnjən/

pinnace boat
pin-uhss /ˈpɪnəs/

Pinochet, Augusto Chilean statesman
ow-goo-stoh pee-noh-shay
/aʊˌguːstəʊ piːnəʊˈʃeɪ/

A hispanized pronunciation, pee-notch-et, is also common in Chile (see BACHELET, MICHELLE). For this particular name, however, our research indicates that the French-sounding pronunciation we recommend is best.

pinochle card game
pee-nok-uhl /ˈpiːnɒkəl/

piñon pine tree
pin-yon /ˈpɪnjɒn/

Pinot wine grape
pee-noh /ˈpiːnəʊ/

pinotage red wine grape
pin-uh-tahzh /ˈpɪnətɑːʒ/

Pinter, Harold English dramatist
pin-tuhr /ˈpɪntə(r)/

pinto piebald
pin-toh /ˈpɪntəʊ/

Pinyin romanized spelling for Chinese
pin-yin /pɪnˈjɪn/

piolet ice pick
pyoh-lay /pjəʊˈleɪ/

pion particle
py-on /ˈpʌɪɒn/

pipa Chinese musical instrument
pee-puh /ˈpiːpə/

pipette dropper
pip-et /pɪˈpɛt/

pipistrelle bat
pip-ist-rel /ˌpɪpɪˈstrɛl/

piquant appetizing
pee-kont /ˈpiːkɒnt/

pique irritation
peek /piːk/

piqué fabric
pee-kay /ˈpiːkeɪ/

piquet card game
pik-et /pɪˈkɛt/

Piraeus port, Greece
py-ree-uhss /pʌɪˈriːəs/
• Established anglicization.

piragua canoe

pirr-ag-wuh /pɪˈragwə/

Pirandello, Luigi Italian dramatist
lwee-ji pirr-uhn-del-oh /ˌlwiːdʒi ˌpɪrənˈdɛləʊ/

Piranesi, Giovanni Battista Italian engraver
juh-vah-ni bat-ee-stuh pirr-uh-nay-zi /dʒəˌvɑːni baˌtiːstə ˌpɪrəˈneɪzi/

piranha fish
pirr-ah-nuh /pɪˈrɑːnə/

Less commonly also pirr-ah-nyuh, a more Portuguese-sounding pronunciation.

piri-piri chilli sauce
pirr-i pirr-i /ˈpɪri ˌpɪri/

pirog Russian pie
pirr-og /pɪˈrɒg/

pirogue canoe
pirr-ohg /pɪˈrəʊg/

piroshki Russian savoury pastries
peer-uhsh-kee /pɪərəˈʃkiː/

pirouette spin
pirr-oo-et /ˌpɪrʊˈɛt/

Pisa city
pee-zuh /ˈpiːzə/, [ˈpiːsa]
• Established anglicization.

Pisano family of Italian sculptors
pee-sah-noh /piːˈsɑːnəʊ/

piscatorial concerning fishing
pisk-uh-taw-ri-uhl /ˌpɪskəˈtɔːriəl/

Pisces constellation
py-seez /ˈpʌɪsiːz/

piscine concerning fish
piss-yn /ˈpɪsʌɪn/

pishogue superstitious belief
pish-ohg /pɪˈʃəʊg/

Pisidia region, ancient Asia Minor
py-sid-i-uh /pʌɪˈsɪdiə/

Pisistratus tyrant of Athens
py-sist-ruh-tuhss /pʌɪˈsɪstrətəs/

pissaladière open tart
piss-al-ad-yair /ˌpɪsalaˈdjɛː(r)/

pissant insignificant person or thing
piss-ant /ˈpɪsant/

Pissarro, Camille French painter
kam-ee pee-sarr-oh /kaˌmi: piːsaˈrəʊ/

Sometimes also piss-ah-roh, a somewhat established anglicization.

pistachio nut
pist-ash-i-oh /pɪˈstaʃiəʊ/

piste ski run
peest /piːst/

pistil female parts of a flower
pist-il /'pɪstɪl/

pistole gold coin
pist-ohl /pɪ'stəʊl/

pistolero gunman
pist-uh-lair-oh /ˌpɪstə'lɛːrəʊ/

pitahaya cactus
pit-uh-hy-uh /ˌpɪtə'hʌɪə/

Pitcairn Islands islands, South Pacific
pit-kairn /'pɪtkɛː(r)n/

pithivier tart
pit-iv-yay /ˌpɪtɪ'vjeɪ/

piton spike
pee-ton /'piːtɒn/

Pitti Florence art gallery
pit-i /'piːti/

Pittsburgh city, US
pits-burg /'pɪtsbə:(r)g/

pituitary gland
pit-yoo-it-uh-ri /pɪ'tjuːɪtəri/

più mosso musical term
pyoo moss-oh /pju: 'mɒsəʊ/

Pius name of several popes
py-uhss /'pʌɪəs/

Pizarro, Francisco Spanish
conquistador
fran-thee-skoh pee-tharr-oh
/franˌθiːskəʊ piː'θarəʊ/

pizza Italian dish
peet-suh /'piːtsə/

pizzeria pizza restaurant
peet-suh-ree-uh /ˌpiːtsə'riːə/

pizzicato plucking an instrument's
strings
pit-sik-ah-toh /ˌpɪtsɪ'kɑːtəʊ/

placate mollify
pluh-kayt /plə'keɪt/

placebo sugar pill
pluh-see-boh /plə'siːbəʊ/

placenta pl. **placentae** organ in the
uterus
pluh-sen-tuh, pl. pluh-sen-tee
/plə'sɛntə, pl. -tiː/

Placentia port, Canada
pluh-sen-shuh /plə'sɛnʃə/

placet affirmative vote
play-set /'pleɪsɛt/

plagal musical term
play-guhl /'pleɪgəl/

Plagge, Karl German army officer
karl plag-uh /ˌkɑː(r)l 'plagə/

plagiarize copy
play-juh-ryz /'pleɪdʒərʌɪz/

plaid chequered cloth
plad /plad/

Plaid Cymru Welsh Nationalist party
plyd kum-ri /ˌplʌɪd 'kʌmri/

Plaistow various locations, England
plah-stoh /'plɑːstəʊ/

This is correct for the Plaistows in London
and West Sussex. However, the one in Kent
is sometimes also pronounced **play**-stoh,
and those in Derbyshire and Herefordshire
always are.

planchette small board on castors
plahn-shet /plɑːn'ʃɛt/

plangent resonant
plan-juhnt /'plandʒənt/

Plano city, US
play-noh /'pleɪnəʊ/

Plantagenet English royal dynasty
plan-taj-uh-nuht /plan'tadʒənət/

plantain banana
plan-tayn /'planteɪn/

plantar relating to the sole of the foot
plan-tuhr /'plantə(r)/

plaque ornamental tablet
plak /plak/

Plataea, Battle of battle of the Persian
Wars
pluh-tee-uh /plə'tiːə/

plat du jour dish of the day
plah doo zhoor /ˌplɑː duː 'ʒʊə(r)/,
French [pla dy ʒur]

Plate, River estuary, South America
playt /pleɪt/

Spanish name is Río de la Plata,
pronounced **ree**-oh day la **plat**-uh.

Platée ballet by Rameau
plat-ay /pla'teɪ/

Plater, Alan English playwright
play-tuhr /'pleɪtə(r)/

plateau area of level high ground
plat-oh /'platəʊ/

platen plate in a printing press
plat-uhn /'platən/

Plath, Sylvia American poet
plath /plaθ/

platinum chemical element
plat-in-uhm /'platɪnəm/

Plato Greek philosopher
play-toh /'pleɪtəʊ/

Platonic associated with Plato
pluh-ton-ik /pləˈtɒnɪk/

Plattdeutsch German dialect
plat-doytch /ˈplatdɔɪtʃ/

platypus egg-laying mammal
plat-ip-uhss /ˈplatɪpəs/

platysma pl. **platysmata** neck muscles
pluh-tiz-muh, pl. **pluh-tiz-muh-tuh**
/pləˈtɪzmə/, pl. /-mətə/

plaudit praise
plaw-dit /ˈplɔːdɪt/

Plautus, Titus Roman comic dramatist
ty-tuhss **plaw**-tuhss /ˌtʌɪtəs ˈplɔːtəs/

Also classical pronunciation **plow**-tuuss;
see LATIN panel.

playa area of land
ply-uh /ˈplʌɪə/

plebeian commoner
pluh-bee-uhn /pləˈbiːən/

plebiscite direct vote
pleb-iss-it /ˈplɛbɪsɪt/

Sometimes also **pleb-iss**-yt.

Pleiades constellation
ply-uh-deez /ˈplʌɪədiːz/

plein-air outdoors
plen air /plɛn ˈɛː(r)/

Pleistocene geological epoch
ply-stuh-seen /ˈplʌɪstəsiːn/

plenary general meeting
plee-nuh-ri /ˈpliːnəri/

plenipotentiary diplomat
plen-ip-uh-**ten**-shuh-ri
/ˌplɛnɪpəˈtɛnʃəri/

plenum assembly
plee-nuhm /ˈpliːnəm/

pleonasm use of more words than are
necessary to convey meaning
plee-uh-naz-uhm /ˈpliːəˌnazəm/

pleroma spiritual universe
pluh-roh-muh /pləˈrəʊmə/

plesiosaur dinosaur
plee-si-uh-sawr /ˈpliːsiəsɔː(r)/

plethora excess
pleth-uh-ruh /ˈplɛθərə/

pleura pl. **pleurae** membrane enveloping
the lungs
ploor-uh, pl. **ploor-ee** /ˈplʊərə/, pl.
/-riː/

pleurisy inflammation of the pleurae
ploor-iss-i /ˈplʊərɪsi/

Pleven town, Bulgaria
plev-en /ˈplɛvɛn/

plié knee-bend in ballet
plee-ay /ˈpliːeɪ/

Pliny name of two Roman statesmen
plin-i /ˈplɪni/

Pliocene geological epoch
ply-uh-seen /ˈplʌɪəsiːn/

Ploieşti city, Romania
ploh-yesht /pləʊˈjɛʃt/

plongeur dish-washer
plo(ng)-**zhoer** /plɔ̃ˈʒœː(r)/

Plotinus Roman philosopher
pluh-ty-nuhss /pləˈtʌɪnəs/

Plovdiv city, Bulgaria
plov-dif /ˈplɒvdɪf/

plover wading bird
pluv-uhr /ˈplʌvə(r)/

plumage bird's feathers
ploo-mij /ˈpluːmɪdʒ/

plus ça change expression
acknowledging the fundamental
immutability of human nature
plue sah **shah(ng)zh** /ˌply sa ˈʃɑ̃ʒ/

Plutarch Greek biographer
ploo-tark /ˈpluːtɑː(r)k/

Plutino planet-like body
ploo-tee-noh /pluːˈtiːnəʊ/

plutocracy government by the wealthy
ploo-tok-ruh-si /pluːˈtɒkrəsi/

Plymouth port, England
plim-uhth /ˈplɪməθ/

pneuma vital spirit
nyoo-muh /ˈnjuːmə/

pneumoconiosis miners' lung disease
nyoo-muh-koh-ni-**oh**-siss
/ˌnjuːməkəʊnɪˈəʊsɪs/

Pnyx place of assembly in ancient Athens
pniks /pnɪks/

Poblacht na hEireann Republic of
Ireland
pob-lakht nuh **hair**-uhn /ˌpɒblaxt nə
ˈhɛːrən/

poblano green chilli pepper
pob-lah-noh /pɒˈblɑːnəʊ/

Pocahontas American Indian princess
pok-uh-**hont**-uhss /ˌpɒkəˈhɒntəs/

pochard duck
poh-chuhrd /ˈpəʊtʃə(r)d/

pochette small handbag
posh-et /pɒˈʃɛt/

poco musical term
poh-koh /ˈpəʊkəʊ/

Podgorica capital of Montenegro
pod-gorr-it-suh /ˈpɒdɡɒrɪtsə/

podiatry chiropody
puh-**dy**-uh-tri /pəˈdʌɪətri/

Podolsk city, Russia
puh-**dolsk** /pəˈdɒlsk/

Podunk hypothetical dull small
American town
poh-dunk /ˈpəʊdʌŋk/

poesy poetry
poh-uh-zi /ˈpəʊəzi/

poetaster bad poet
poh-uh-**tast**-uhr /ˌpəʊəˈtastə(r)/

poète maudit unappreciated poet
poh-**et** moh-**dee** /pəʊˌɛt məʊˈdi/

pogrom organized massacre
pog-rom /ˈpɒɡrɒm/

Pohamba, Hifikepunye Namibian
statesman
hif-ee-kuh-**poon**-yuh poh-**ham**-buh
/hɪfiːkəˌpuːnjə pəʊˈhambə/

Pohnpei (also **Ponape**) island,
Micronesia
pon-uh-pay /ˈpɒnəpeɪ/

pohutukawa tree
puh-hoo-tuh-**kah**-wuh
/pəˌhuːtəˈkɑːwə/

poi Hawaiian dish
poy /pɔɪ/

poignant evoking a sense of regret
poyn-yuhnt /ˈpɔɪnjənt/

poilu French infantry soldier
pwal-**ue** /pwaˈly/

Poincaré, Jules-Henri French
mathematician
zhuel ah(ng)-**ree** pwa(ng)-karr-**ay**
/ˌʒyl ɑ̃ˌriː pwækaˈreɪ/

Poindexter boringly studious person
poyn-dek-stuhr /ˈpɔɪndɛkstə(r)/

poinsettia plant
poyn-**set**-i-uh /ˌpɔɪnˈsɛtiə/

pointe tips of the toes
pwa(ng)t /pwɛ̃t/

Pointe-à-Pitre port, Guadeloupe
pwa(ng)t-ap-**eet**-ruh /ˌpwɛ̃taˈpiːtrə/

pointelle lacy knitted fabric
poyn-**tel** /ˌpɔɪnˈtɛl/

Pointe-Noire port, Congo
pwa(ng)t **nwar** /pwɛ̃t ˈnwɑː(r)/

pointillism painting technique
pwant-il-iz-uhm /ˈpwantɪlɪzəm/

Poitier, Sidney American actor
pwah-ti-ay /ˈpwɑːtieɪ/

Poitiers city, France
pwat-yay /ˈpwatjeɪ/

Poitou-Charentes region, France
pwat-oo sharr-**o(ng)t** /pwatuː ʃaˈrɔ̃t/

Pokémon Japanese game character
poh-kay-mon /ˈpəʊkeɪmɒn/

Less commonly also **pok**-em-on. This
pronunciation seems etymologically more
accurate, since the name is derived from the
English words 'pocket monster'. However,
the pronunciation we recommend is that
used in the theme tune of the television
cartoon.

Polanski, Roman French film director
roh-muhn puh-**lan**-ski /ˌrəʊmən
pəˈlanski/

Polaris star
puh-**lar**-iss /pəˈlɑːrɪs/

polder low-lying reclaimed land
pohl-duhr /ˈpəʊldə(r)/

polemic verbal attack
puh-**lem**-ik /pəˈlɛmɪk/

polenta maize flour
puh-**lent**-uh /pəˈlɛntə/

Poliakoff, Stephen English playwright
pol-yuh-kof /ˈpɒljəkɒf/

policier crime film
pol-iss-**yay** /ˌpɒlɪˈsjeɪ/

poliomyelitis disease
poh-li-oh-my-uh-**ly**-tiss
/ˌpəʊliəʊmʌɪəˈlʌɪtɪs/

polis 'police' (Scottish and Irish)
poh-liss /ˈpəʊlɪs/

polis city state in ancient Greece
pol-iss /ˈpɒlɪs/

politburo policy-making committee
pol-it-byoor-oh /ˈpɒlɪtˌbjʊərəʊ/

Polites Greek mythological character
puh-**ly**-teez /pəˈlʌɪtiːz/

politesse etiquette
pol-i-**tess** /ˌpɒliˈtɛs/

polity form of government
pol-it-i /ˈpɒlɪti/

Polk, James Knox American statesman
pohk /pəʊk/

polka dance
pol-kuh /ˈpɒlkə/

Polish

Polish is a Slavic language, written in the Roman alphabet. It is spoken by about 40 million people, mainly in Poland, but also in neighbouring countries of the former Soviet Union, and in Polish communities around the world.

Polish pronunciation is fairly predictable from the spelling. This is far from straightforward, however, due to the many diacritical marks that can be placed on letters to change the pronunciation. The correct Polish spelling must therefore be established before the pronunciation can be worked out, and the result may be unexpected! The city of *Łódź*, for example, is pronounced wootch.

The Polish given here is, as always, somewhat anglicized in line with BBC policy and the constraints of the phonetic respelling.

Stress

Polish stress always falls on the second to last syllable.

Vowels

A is always pronounced a. *Jan* is yan. In anglicized Polish, A followed by R and another consonant is given as ar, and sometimes as schwa (uh) in unstressed positions.

Ą is pronounced o(ng) word-finally and before the sounds f, v, s, z, sh, and zh. It is pronounced on before t, d, ch, j, ts, and dz, om before p and b, ong before k and g, and o before l and w.

E is always pronounced e. *Ewa* is **ev**-uh. In anglicized Polish, E followed by R and another consonant is given as air, E followed by a vowel as ay, and sometimes as schwa (uh) in unstressed positions.

Ę is pronounced a(ng) word-finally and before f, v, s, z, sh, and zh. It is pronounced en before t, d, ch, j, ts, and dz, em before p and b, and eng before k and g.

I is usually represented as ee, although it is not as long as the ee in *sleep*. It is pronounced y as in *yes* before vowels. *Marcin* is **mar**-cheen and *Gierek* is **gyerr**-ek.

O is always pronounced o. *Antoni* is an-**ton**-i. In anglicized Polish, O followed by R and another consonant is given as or, and O at the end of a word is given as oh.

Ó is pronounced oo. *Józef* is **yoo**-zef.

U is pronounced oo. *Janusz* is **yan**-oosh.

Y is pronounced close to i. *Krystyna* is krist-**in**-uh.

Consonants

Polish has some consonant sounds that do not occur in English, which are difficult to represent in the respelling. There are also some rather tricky consonant combinations, which can be real tongue-twisters for English speakers. Former president *Aleksander Kwaśniewski*, for example, is pronounced kfash-**nyef**-ski.

B, D, F, G, K, L, M, N, P, T, V, and Z are pronounced as in English. However, B, D, G, V, and Z are devoiced to p, t, k, f, and s respectively in word-final position, and next to other voiceless consonants (i.e. pronounced without vibration of the vocal cords). See also D and Z in combination with other letters below.

C is pronounced ts.

Ć and CI are pronounced close to ch, and CZ is pronounced ch.

CH is pronounced kh (as in Scottish *loch*).

DZI and DŹ are pronounced close to j, and close to ch in word-final position. DŻ is pronounced j.

H is pronounced h initially, and kh (as in Scottish *loch*) before consonants.

J is pronounced y.

Ł is pronounced w.

Ń is pronounced i(ng), but ny as in *onion* finally. *Gdańsk* is g(uh)-**dy(ng)sk** (although often anglicized to guh-**dansk**) and *Wleń* is **vlen**-y(uh).

RZ is pronounced zh, but sh finally and next to other voiceless consonants.

S is always pronounced s.

SI and Ś are pronounced close to sh, and SZ is pronounced sh.

W is pronounced v, but f finally and next to other voiceless consonants.

ZI and Ź are pronounced close to zh, and Ż is pronounced zh, but sh in word-final position.

Pollaiuolo, Antonio Italian sculptor
   an-**toh**-nyoh pol-y-**woh**-loh
   /anˌtəʊnjəʊ ˌpɒlʌɪˈwəʊləʊ/
Pollux Greek mythological character
   pol-uhks /ˈpɒləks/
Polokwane town, South Africa
   pol-oh-**kwah**-ni /ˌpɒləʊˈkwɑːni/
polonaise dance
   pol-uh-**nayz** /ˌpɒləˈneɪz/
polonium chemical element
   puh-**loh**-ni-uhm /pəˈləʊniəm/
Polonius fictional character
   puh-**loh**-ni-uhss /pəˈləʊniəs/
Polonnaruwa Sri Lanka

polony bologna ham
   pol-on-uh-**roo**-wuh /pɒˌlɒnəˈruːwə/
polony bologna ham
   puh-**loh**-ni /pəˈləʊni/
Pol Pot Cambodian leader
   pol **pot** /ˌpɒl ˈpɒt/
Poltava city, Ukraine
   pol-**tah**-vuh /pɒlˈtɑːvə/
poltergeist ghost
   pol-tuhr-gyst /ˈpɒltə(r)gʌɪst/
polyamide synthetic polymer
   pol-i-**ay**-myd /ˌpɒliˈeɪmʌɪd/
polyamory having multiple sexual
   partners
   pol-i-**am**-uh-ri /ˌpɒliˈaməri/

polyanthus plant
pol-i-**an**-thuhss /ˌpɒliˈanθəs/

Polybius Greek historian
puh-**lib**-i-uhss /pəˈlɪbiəs/

Polyclitus Greek sculptor
pol-i-**kly**-tuhss /ˌpɒliˈklʌɪtəs/

Polydeuces Greek mythological
character
pol-i-**dyoo**-seez /ˌpɒliˈdjuːsiːz/

Polyeucte play by Corneille
pol-**yoekt** /pɒˈljøːkt/

polygyny polygamy in which a man has
more than one wife
puh-**lij**-in-i /pəˈlɪdʒɪni/

polyhedron pl. **polyhedra** solid figure
with many plane faces
pol-i-**hee**-druhn, pl. pol-i-**hee**-druh
/ˌpɒlɪˈhiːdrən/, pl. /-drə/

Commonly also pol-i-**hed**-ruhn.

Polyhymnia Greek mythological
character
pol-i-**him**-ni-uh /ˌpɒliˈhɪmniə/

Polynesia region of the Pacific
pol-i-**nee**-zhuh /ˌpɒliˈniːʒə/

polynomial consisting of several terms
pol-i-**noh**-mi-uhl /ˌpɒliˈnəʊmiəl/

Polyphemus Greek mythological
character
pol-if-**ee**-muhss /ˌpɒlɪˈfiːməs/

polyphony musical style
puh-**lif**-uh-ni /pəˈlɪfəni/

polysemy coexistence of possible
meanings
puh-**liss**-uh-mi /pəˈlɪsəmi/

polytheism belief in more than one god
pol-i-**thee**-iz-uhm /ˈpɒliˌθiːɪzəm/

polyurethane synthetic resin
pol-i-**yoor**-uh-thayn /ˌpɒlijʊərəθeɪn/

Polzeath town, England
pol-**zeth** /pɒlˈzɛθ/

pomace fruit pulp
pum-iss /ˈpʌmɪs/

pomade hair oil
puh-**mayd** /pəˈmeɪd/

pomander aromatic ball
puh-**man**-duhr /pəˈmandə(r)/

pombe fermented drink
pom-bay /ˈpɒmbeɪ/

pomelo citrus fruit
pom-uh-loh /ˈpɒmələʊ/

Pomerania region, Europe

pom-uh-ray-ni-uh /ˌpɒməˈreɪniə/

pommes frites potato chips
pom **freet** /ˌpɒm ˈfriːt/

Pomona city, US
puh-**moh**-nuh /pəˈməʊnə/

pompadour woman's hairstyle
pom-puh-door /ˈpɒmpədʊə(r)/

pompano fish
pom-puh-noh /ˈpɒmpənəʊ/

Pompeii ancient city, Italy
pom-**pay**-i /pɒmˈpeɪi/

Pompey Roman statesman
pom-pi /ˈpɒmpi/

Pompidou, Georges French statesman
zhorzh pom-pid-**oo** /ˌʒɔː(r)ʒ
pɒmpɪˈduː/

Ponape see Pohnpei

Ponce de León, Juan Spanish explorer
khwan **pon**-thay day lay-**on** /ˌxwan
ˌpɒnθeɪ deɪ leɪˈɒn/

ponderosa pine tree
pon-duh-**roh**-suh /ˌpɒndəˈrəʊsə/

Pondicherry territory, India
pon-ditch-**err**-i /ˌpɒndɪˈtʃɛri/

pone maize bread
pohn /pəʊn/

ponga see punga

pongal Tamil New Year festival
pong-guhl /ˈpɒŋɡəl/

pongee fabric
pon-**jee** /pɒnˈdʒiː/

pons Varolii part of the brainstem
ponz vuh-**roh**-li-y /ˌpɒnz vəˈrəʊlɪʌɪ/

Pontchartrain lake, US
pon-chuhr-trayn /ˈpɒntʃərtreɪn/

Pontefract cake liquorice sweet
pon-tuh-frakt /ˈpɒntəfrakt/

Pontiac fever disease
pont-i-ak /ˈpɒntiak/

Pontianak port, Indonesia
pont-i-**ah**-nak /ˌpɒntiˈɑːnak/

pontifex pl. **pontifices** member of the
principal college of priests
pon-tif-eks, pl. pon-**tif**-iss-eez
/ˈpɒntɪfɛks/, pl. /pɒnˈtɪfɪsiːz/

pontificate express one's opinions in a
pompous way
pon-**tif**-ik-ayt /pɒnˈtɪfɪkeɪt/

pontificate office of a pope or bishop
pon-**tif**-ik-uht /pɒnˈtɪfɪkət/

Pontine Marshes marshland, Italy
pon-tyn /ˈpɒntʌɪn/

Pont l'Évêque soft cheese
po(ng) luh-vek /ˌpɔ̃ ləˈvɛk/

Pontormo, Jacopo da Italian painter
yah-kuh-poh dah pon-tor-moh
/ˌjɑːkəpəʊ dɑː pɒnˈtɔː(r)məʊ/

Pontypridd town, Wales
pont-uh-**preeth** /ˌpɒntəˈpriːð/

pooka hobgoblin
poo-kuh /ˈpuːkə/

Poona see Pune

popinjay vain person
pop-in-jay /ˈpɒpɪndʒeɪ/

Popocatépetl volcano, Mexico
pop-uh-**kat**-uh-pet-uhl
/ˌpɒpəˈkatəˌpɛtəl/

poppadom (also **popadom**) Indian fried
bread
pop-uh-duhm /ˈpɒpədəm/

Poppaea Sabina Roman empress, wife
of Nero
pop-ee-uh suh-by-nuh /pɒˌpiːə
səˈbaɪnə/
• See LATIN panel.

porcelain ceramic
por-suh-lin /ˈpɔː(r)səlɪn/

porcine relating to pigs
por-syn /ˈpɔː(r)sʌɪn/

porcini wild mushrooms
por-chee-ni /pɔː(r)ˈtʃiːni/

Porgy and Bess opera by Gershwin
por-gi /ˈpɔː(r)gi/

Pori port, Finland
porr-i /ˈpɒri/

porphyria hereditary disease
por-firr-i-uh /pɔː(r)ˈfɪriə/

porphyry rock
por-firr-i /ˈpɔː(r)fɪri/

porpoise small whale
por-puhss /ˈpɔː(r)pəs/

porringer bowl
porr-in-juhr /ˈpɒrɪndʒə(r)/

Porsche Austrian car manufacturer
porsh-uh /ˈpɔː(r)ʃə/

Commonly also porsh, an anglicized
pronunciation. Our recommendation is the
pronunciation preferred by the company in
the UK.

portamento musical slide between notes
por-tuh-men-toh /ˌpɔː(r)təˈmɛntəʊ/

Port-au-Prince capital of Haiti
port-oh-prinss /ˌpɔː(r)təʊˈprɪns/

Established anglicization, also common in
Haiti. A French pronunciation,
por-oh-pra(ng)ss, and a French Creole
pronunciation, port-oh-pra(ng)ss, are also
both in current use.

Port-Gentil port, Gabon
por zhah(ng)-tee /ˌpɔː(r) ʒɑ̃ˈtiː/

Portia Shakespearean character
porsh-uh /ˈpɔː(r)ʃə/

portico roofed structure
por-tik-oh /ˈpɔː(r)tɪkəʊ/

Portimão city, Portugal
poor-tim-ow(ng) /puə(r)tɪˈmãʊ/

Portishead town, England
por-tiss-hed /ˈpɔː(r)tɪshɛd/

Portlaoise (also **Portlaoighise**) town,
Republic of Ireland
port-leesh /pɔː(r)tˈliːʃ/

Port Louis capital of Mauritius
port loo-ee /ˌpɔː(r)t ˈluːi/

portmanteau travelling bag
port-man-toh /pɔː(r)tˈmantəʊ/

Port Moresby capital of Papua New
Guinea
port morz-bi /ˌpɔː(r)t ˈmɔː(r)zbi/

Porto port, Portugal
por-toh /ˈpɔː(r)təʊ/

Established anglicization. The Portuguese
name is Oporto, pronounced oo-**por**-too.

Pôrto Alegre city, Brazil
port-oo uh-leg-ri /ˌpɔː(r)tu əˈlɛgri/

Porto Novo capital of Benin
port-oh noh-voh /ˌpɔː(r)təʊ ˈnəʊvəʊ/

Pôrto Velho town, Brazil
port-oo vel-yoo /ˌpɔː(r)tu ˈvɛlju/

Port Pirie port, Australia
pirr-i /ˈpɪri/

Port Said port, Egypt
syd /sʌɪd/
• Established anglicization.

Port Salut mild cheese
por sal-oo /ˌpɔː(r) saˈluː/

Portugal country
port-yuu-guhl /ˈpɔː(r)tjʊgəl/,
[portuˈgal]
• Established anglicization.

posada hotel in Spain
poss-ah-thuh /pɒˈsɑːðə/

Poseidon Greek god
puh-sy-duhn /pəˈsʌɪdən/

Portuguese

Portuguese is a Romance language spoken in Brazil, in various parts of Africa, particularly Angola and Mozambique, and of course in Portugal. Some English speakers, who perhaps know a little Spanish, may imagine that the pronunciation of Portuguese is much more similar to Spanish than it actually is, and attempt to pronounce Portuguese in a Spanish manner. It is a common mistake, for example, to mispronounce Portuguese *José* as Spanish khoh-**zay**, rather than Portuguese zhuuz-**ay**. This can be particularly offensive to Portuguese speakers, who understandably do not wish to be lumped in with their Spanish-speaking neighbours. In fact, although the language is lexically and structurally similar to Spanish, the pronunciation is markedly different.

Portuguese pronunciation is complicated. Although generalizations are usually made about European Portuguese compared to Brazilian Portuguese, there is also considerable variation within these and other lusophone countries. As with all the brief panels in this book, this is a rough and by no means exhaustive guide, and gives details of how we advise on the pronunciation of Portuguese, subject to the constraints of our anglicization policy and the respelling system.

Stress

Portuguese stress falls on the second-last syllable of the word if the word ends in A, E, O, M, or S; otherwise it falls on the last syllable. Exceptions to this rule are indicated in the spelling by an accent over the vowel of the syllable to be stressed, for example *inglês*, *débil*.

Vowels

In our recommendations we advise that A, I, and U are pronounced as a (if short) or ah (if long), ee, and oo. É is e, and Ê is ay; Ó is o, Ô is oh. Vowels which appear with no accent may be pronounced in either way; a dictionary or a native speaker must be consulted to be certain. O is pronounced uu when it is unstressed, and oo at the end of a word. Other vowels in unstressed syllables are reduced to uh. Vowels can be nasalized, which may be indicated with a tilde (Ã). There is also a large set of diphthongs in Portuguese, which are pronounced more or less as sequences of their component parts.

Consonants

C is pronounced k before A, O, and U and s before E and I. Ç is pronounced s, and CH is pronounced sh.

D is pronounced d unless it appears between vowels or at the end of words, in which case it is *th* as in *this*. In Brazilian Portuguese D before I is pronounced j.

G is pronounced g, except for before E and I, where it is zh.

H is always silent. J is pronounced zh.

L sometimes becomes w after vowels, and LH is pronounced ly as in *million*.

NH is pronounced ny as in *onion*.

S is pronounced as s, z between vowels, and sh or zh before consonants. At the end of a word it is sh in Portugal and parts of Brazil, s in other parts of Brazil.

T before I or E is pronounced ch in Brazilian Portuguese; in European Portuguese it is always t.

X is pronounced sh, ks or s.

Z is usually z, but at the end of a word it is sh in Portugal, and zh in Brazil.

---

positron subatomic particle
  poz-it-ron /ˈpɒzɪtrɒn/

posse body of men
  poss-i /ˈpɒsi/

posset milk drink
  poss-uht /ˈpɒsət/

POSSLQ Person of the Opposite Sex Sharing Living Quarters
  poss-uhl-kyoo /ˈpɒsəl‚kjuː/

poste restante mail kept in a post office
  pohst **rest**-uhnt /pəʊst ˈrɛstənt/

postern back entrance
  post-uhrn /ˈpɒstə(r)n/

posthumous after death
  post-yuum-uhss /ˈpɒstjʊməs/

potable safe to drink
  poh-tuh-buhl /ˈpəʊtəbəl/

potage thick soup
  pot-**ahzh** /pɒˈtɑːʒ/

potager kitchen garden
  pot-uh-juhr /ˈpɒtədʒə(r)/

potassium chemical element
  puh-**tass**-i-uhm /pəˈtasiəm/

pot-au-feu meat soup
  pot-oh-**foe** /‚pɒtəʊˈfəː/

Potawatomi American Indian ethnic group
  pot-uh-**wot**-uh-mi /‚pɒtəˈwɒtəmi/

Potëmkin Russian battleship
  puh-**tyom**-kin /pəˈtjɒmkɪn/

Sometimes anglicized to puh-**tem**-kin, especially in figurative use.

Potenza town, Italy
  puh-**tent**-suh /pəˈtɛntsə/

Potiphar biblical character
  pot-if-uhr /ˈpɒtɪfə(r)/

potjie cast-iron pot (South Africa)
  poy-ki /ˈpɔɪki/

Potomac river, US
  puh-**toh**-muhk /pəˈtəʊmək/

Potosi city, Bolivia
  pot-oh-**see** /‚pɒtəʊˈsiː/

potpourri perfumed dried petals
  poh-puh-**ree** /pəʊpəˈriː/

Potsdam city, Germany
  pots-dam /ˈpɒtsdam/

potsherd broken piece of ceramic material
  pot-shurd /ˈpɒtʃəː(r)d/

POTUS President Of The United States
  poh-tuhss /ˈpəʊtəs/

pouchong kind of tea
  poo-**chong** /puːˈtʃɒŋ/

pouffe footstool
  poof /puːf/

Poughkeepsie town, US
  puh-**kip**-si /pəˈkɪpsi/

Pouilly-Fumé white wine
  poo-yi-**foo**-may /‚puːjiˈfuːmeɪ/

Poulenc, Francis French composer
frah(ng)-**seess** poo-**la(ng)k** /frɑ̃ˌsiːs puːˈlɛ̃k/
• See FRENCH panel.

poult young fowl
pohlt /pəʊlt/

poult corded fabric
poolt /puːlt/

poultice moist mass of material
pohl-tiss /ˈpəʊltɪs/

poundal unit of force
pownd-uhl /ˈpaʊndəl/

pourboire gratuity
poor-**bwar** /pʊə(r)ˈbwɑː(r)/

Poussin, Nicolas French painter
nee-koh-**lah** poo-**sa(ng)** /niːkəʊˌlɑː puːˈsɛ̃/

poussin chicken
poo-san /ˈpuːsan/

Powell, Anthony English novelist
poh-uhl /ˈpəʊəl/

Powell, Colin American statesman
koh-lin **pow**-uhl /ˌkəʊlɪn ˈpaʊəl/

The unusual pronunciation for the first name is his own.

Powell, Enoch British politician
ee-nok **pow**-uhl /ˌiːnɒk ˈpaʊəl/

Powhatan American Indian ethnic group
pow-uh-tan /ˈpaʊətan/

Powys county, Wales
pow-iss /ˈpaʊɪs/

Pozidriv trademark type of cross-head screwdriver
poz-i-dryv /ˈpɒzɪdrʌɪv/

Poznań city, Poland
poz-nan /ˈpɒznan/, [ˈpoznaɲ]
• Established anglicization.

Prader–Willi syndrome congenital disorder
prah-duhr vil-i /ˌprɑːdə(r) ˈvɪli/

Prado Spanish art gallery
prah-doh /ˈprɑːdəʊ/

praecipe legal order requesting a document
pree-sip-i /ˈpriːsɪpi/

praepostor prefect or monitor
pri-**post**-uhr /prɪˈpɒstə(r)/

Praesepe cluster of stars in the constellation Cancer
pry-**see**-pi /prʌɪˈsiːpi/

Prague capital of the Czech Republic
prahg /prɑːɡ/

Established anglicization. The Czech name is Praha, pronounced **prah**-huh [ˈpraha].

Praia capital of the Cape Verde Islands
pry-uh /ˈprʌɪə/

Prakrit ancient dialects of India
prah-krit /ˈprɑːkrɪt/

praline sweet nut paste
prah-leen /ˈprɑːliːn/

pralltriller musical ornament
pral-tril-uhr /ˈpralˌtrɪlə(r)/

pranam respectful greeting
prun-**ahm** /prʌˈnɑːm/

pranayama regulation of the breath
prun-uh-**yah**-muh /ˌprʌnəˈjɑːmə/

prandial relating to dinner or lunch
pran-di-uhl /ˈprandɪəl/

Prandtl, Ludwig German physicist
luut-vikh **prant**-uhl /ˌlʊtvɪç ˈprantəl/

prasad devotional offering
pruss-**ahd** /prʌˈsɑːd/

praseodymium chemical element
pray-zi-oh-**dim**-i-uhm /ˌpreɪzɪəʊˈdɪmɪəm/

pratique permission granted to a ship
prat-ik /ˈpratɪk/

Prato city, Italy
prah-toh /ˈprɑːtəʊ/

Pravda Russian daily newspaper
prahv-duh /ˈprɑːvdə/

praxis practice
prak-siss /ˈpraksɪs/

Praxiteles Greek sculptor
prak-**sit**-uh-leez /prakˈsɪtəliːz/

Prayer of Manasses book of the Apocrypha
muh-**nass**-eez /məˈnasiːz/

preamble preparatory statement
pree-am-buhl /priːˈambəl/

prebendary honorary canon
preb-uhn-duh-ri /ˈprɛbəndəri/

Precambrian geological aeon
pree-kam-bri-uhn /priːˈkambrɪən/

precatory relating to a wish
prek-uh-tuh-ri /ˈprɛkətəri/

precis pl. **precis** summary
pray-si, pl. **pray**-seez /ˈpreɪsi/, pl. /-siːz/

predilection special liking for something
pree-dil-**ek**-shuhn /ˌpriːdɪˈlɛkʃən/

prednisolone steroid
pred-**niss**-uh-lohn /prɛdˈnɪsələʊn/

preface introduction to a book
pref-uhss /ˈprɛfəs/

prelapsarian characteristic of the time before the Fall of Man
pree-lap-**sair**-i-uhn /ˌpriːlapˈsɛːriən/

prelate bishop
prel-uht /ˈprɛlət/

prelude introduction
prel-yood /ˈprɛljuːd/

premier first in importance
prem-i-uhr /ˈprɛmɪə(r)/

AM usually pruh-**meer**.

premier cru wine of a superior grade
prem-yay **kroo** /ˌprɛmjeɪ ˈkruː/

premiere first performance or showing
prem-i-air /ˈprɛmɪɛː(r)/

Preminger, Otto Austrian-American film director
ot-oh **prem**-in-juhr /ˌɒtəʊ ˈprɛmɪndʒə(r)/

This is his own preferred anglicization; the usual German pronunciation is **prem**-ing-uhr.

premise previous proposition
prem-iss /ˈprɛmɪs/

premonition strong feeling that something is about to happen
prem-uh-**nish**-uhn /ˌprɛməˈnɪʃən/

Premonstratensian member of an order of canons founded at Prémontré in France
pree-mon-struh-**tensh**-uhn /ˌpriːmɒnstrəˈtɛnʃən/

prepuce foreskin
pree-pyooss /ˈpriːpjuːs/

Pre-Raphaelite member of a group of artists
pree-**raf**-uh-lyt /priːˈrafəlʌɪt/

prerogative exclusive right
pruh-**rog**-uh-tiv /prəˈrɒɡətɪv/

presage be a sign of
press-uhj /ˈprɛsədʒ/

presbyopia long-sightedness
prez-bi-**oh**-pi-uh /ˌprɛzbɪˈəʊpiə/

Presbyterian Christian denomination
prez-bit-**eer**-i-uhn /ˌprɛzbɪˈtɪəriən/

prescient having knowledge of events
press-i-uhnt /ˈprɛsiənt/

presentiment intuitive feeling
pruh-**zen**-ti-muhnt /prəˈzɛntɪmənt/

presidio fortified military settlement
press-**id**-i-oh /prɛˈsɪdiəʊ/

Presocratic relating to philosophers
pree-suh-**krat**-ik /ˌpriːsəˈkratɪk/

pressé juice drink
press-ay /ˈprɛseɪ/

prestidigitation conjuring tricks
prest-id-ij-it-**ay**-shuhn /ˌprɛstɪˌdɪdʒɪˈteɪʃən/

prestissimo musical term
prest-**iss**-im-oh /prɛˈstɪsɪməʊ/

Prestonpans battle site near Edinburgh
prest-uhn-**panz** /ˌprɛstənˈpanz/

prêt-à-porter ready-to-wear designer clothes
pret-uh-**por**-tay /ˌprɛtəˈpɔː(r)teɪ/

preterite grammatical term
pret-uh-rit /ˈprɛtərɪt/

preternatural beyond what is normal
pree-tuhr-**natch**-uh-ruhl /ˌpriːtə(r)ˈnatʃərəl/

Pretoria capital of South Africa
pruh-**taw**-ri-uh /prɪˈtɔːriə/

prevalent widespread
prev-uh-luhnt /ˈprɛvələnt/

Previn, André German-American musician
ah(ng)-dray **prev**-in /ˌɑːdreɪ ˈprɛvɪn/

Prévost d'Exiles, Antoine-François French novelist
ah(ng)-**twahn** frah(ng)-**swah** pray-**voh** deg-**zeel** /ɑ̃ˈtwɑːn frɑ̃ˌswɑː preɪˌvəʊ dɛɡˈziːl/

Priam Greek mythological character
pry-am /ˈprʌɪam/

priapic relating to a phallus
pry-**ap**-ik /prʌɪˈapɪk/

Priapus Greek god of fertility
pry-**ay**-puhss /prʌɪˈeɪpəs/

Pribilof Islands islands, US
prib-il-of /ˈprɪbɪlɒf/

prie-dieu piece of furniture
pree **dyoe** /priː ˈdjə/

primacy importance
pry-muh-si /ˈprʌɪməsi/

prima donna chief female opera singer
pree-muh **don**-uh /ˌpriːmə ˈdɒnə/

prima facie based on the first impression
pry-muh fay-shi /ˌprʌɪmə ˈfeɪʃi/

Other pronunciations, such as **fay-si-ee**, are used; see LATIN panel.

primarily for the most part
pry-merr-il-i /prʌɪˈmɛrɪli/

Also **pry-mair-il-i** or **pry-muh-ril-i**. This second pronunciation is traditional BR but is increasingly less common.

primate chief bishop
pry-muht /ˈprʌɪmət/

Sometimes also **pry-mayt**.

primate mammal
pry-mayt /ˈprʌɪmeɪt/

Primavera painting by Botticelli
pree-muh-vair-uh /ˌpriːməˈvɛːrə/

primeval of the earliest time in history
pry-mee-vuhl /prʌɪˈmiːvəl/

Primo de Rivera, Miguel Spanish statesman
mee-gel pree-moh day riv-air-uh /miːˌɡɛl ˌpriːməʊ deɪ rɪˈvɛːrə/
● See SPANISH panel.

primogenitor ancestor
pry-muh-jen-it-uhr /ˌprʌɪməˈdʒɛnɪtə(r)/

primordial existing at the beginning of time
pry-mor-di-uhl /prʌɪˈmɔː(r)dɪəl/

Primorsky territory, Russia
pree-mor-ski /priːˈmɔː(r)ski/

primo uomo principal male opera singer
pree-moh woh-moh /ˌpriːməʊ ˈwəʊməʊ/

Primus trademark portable cooking stove
pry-muhss /ˈprʌɪməs/

primus inter pares 'first among equals'
pree-muhss in-tuhr pah-rayz /ˌpriːməs ˌɪntə(r) ˈpɑːreɪz/
● See LATIN panel.

Princeton American university
prin-stuhn /ˈprɪnstən/

Príncipe island in the Gulf of Guinea
pree(ng)-sip-uh /ˈprĩːsɪpə/

principe pl. **principi** prince
prin-chip-ay, pl. **prin-chip-ee** /ˈprɪntʃɪpeɪ/, pl. /-pi/

principessa pl. **principesse** princess
prin-chip-ess-uh, pl. **prin-chip-ess-ay**

/ˌprɪntʃɪˈpɛsə/, pl. /-ˈpɛseɪ/

prion protein particle
pree-on /ˈpriːɒn/

Pripyat river, Ukraine and Belarus
preep-yuht /ˈpriːpjət/

Priscian Byzantine grammarian
prish-i-uhn /ˈprɪʃiən/

Priscoan geological aeon
prisk-oh-uhn /prɪˈskəʊən/

Priština city, Serbia
preesh-tin-uh /ˈpriːʃtɪnə/

pristine in original condition
prist-een /ˈprɪstiːn/

prithee 'please'
prith-ee /ˈprɪðiː/

Prius trademark model of car which uses hybrid fuel
pry-uhss /ˈprʌɪəs/

We were firmly advised of this pronunciation by Toyota UK. The pronunciation **pree-uhss** is common in AM.

privacy state in which one is not disturbed by others
priv-uh-si /ˈprɪvəsi/

Also **pry-vuh-si**, especially in AM.

privation state of lacking essentials
pry-vay-shuhn /prʌɪˈveɪʃən/

Prix de Rome French artistic award
pree duh rom /ˌpriː də ˈrɒm/

prix fixe fixed price meal
pree feeks /ˌpriː ˈfiːks/

Prix Goncourt French literary award
pree go(ng)-koor /ˌpriː ɡɔ̃ˈkʊə(r)/

probity morality
proh-bit-i /ˈprəʊbɪti/

pro bono publico legal term; 'for the public good'
proh boh-noh puub-lik-oh /prəʊ ˌbəʊnəʊ ˈpʊblɪkəʊ/

proboscis pl. **probosces, proboscides** mammal's nose
pruh-boss-iss, pl. **pruh-boss-eez, pruh-boss-id-eez** /prəˈbɒsɪs/, pl. /-siːz/, /-sɪdiːz/

Commonly also **pruh-bosk-iss**; see LATIN panel.

procès-verbal pl. **procès-verbaux**
written report of proceedings
pross-ay-vair-**bal**, pl.
pross-ay-vair-**boh** /prɒˌseɪvɛː(r)'bal/,
pl. /-'bəʊ/

proclivity fondness
pruh-**kliv**-it-i /prə'klɪvɪti/

Procne Greek mythological character
prok-ni /'prɒkni/

proconsul ancient Roman governor
proh-**kon**-suhl /prəʊ'kɒnsəl/

Procopius Byzantine historian
pruh-**koh**-pi-uhss /prə'kəʊpiəs/

Procrustean enforcing uniformity
proh-**krust**-i-uhn /prəʊ'krʌstiən/

Procrustes Greek mythological
character
proh-**krust**-eez /prəʊ'krʌstiːz/

Procyon star
proh-si-uhn /'prəʊsiən/

prodigious remarkably great in size
pruh-**dij**-uhss /prə'dɪdʒəs/

prodrome early symptom
proh-drohm /'prəʊdrəʊm/

profanity obscene language
pruh-**fan**-it-i /prə'fanɪti/

profiterole cream-filled pastry
pruh-**fit**-uh-rohl /prə'fɪtərəʊl/

Profumo, John English politician
pruh-**fyoo**-moh /prə'fjuːməʊ/

progenitor production of offspring
proh-**jen**-itch-uhr /prəʊ'dʒenɪtʃə(r)/

progeny descendant
proj-uh-ni /'prɒdʒəni/

progesterone female hormone
pruh-**jest**-uh-rohn /prə'dʒestərəʊn/

progestogen natural or synthetic
hormone
pruh-**jest**-uh-juhn /prə'dʒestədʒən/

prognathous having a projecting lower
jaw
prog-**nay**-thuhss /prɒg'neɪθəs/

prognosis pl. **prognoses** likely course of
a medical condition
prog-**noh**-siss, pl. prog-**noh**-seez
/prɒg'nəʊsɪs/, pl. /-siːz/

prohibition action of forbidding
proh-ib-**ish**-uhn /ˌprəʊɪ'bɪʃən/

Also proh-hib-**ish**-uhn.

prokaryote single-celled organism
proh-**karr**-i-oht /prəʊ'kariəʊt/

Prokofiev, Sergei Russian composer
suhr-**gay** pruh-**kof**-i-ef /sə(r)ˌgeɪ
prə'kɒfiɛf/

Prokopyevsk city, Russia
pruh-**kop**-yuhfsk /prə'kɒpjəfsk/

prolactin female hormone
proh-**lak**-tin /prəʊ'laktɪn/

prolegomenon introduction to a book
proh-luh-**gom**-uh-nuhn
/ˌprəʊlə'ɡɒmənən/

proletariat working class
proh-luh-**tair**-i-at /ˌprəʊlə'tɛːriat/

proliferate increase rapidly in number
pruh-**lif**-uh-rayt /prə'lɪfəreɪt/

prolix verbose
proh-liks /'prəʊlɪks/

Prolog computer programming language
proh-log /'prəʊlɒɡ/

promenade paved public walk
prom-uh-**nahd** /ˌprɒmə'nɑːd/

AM also prom-uh-**nayd**.

Prometheus Greek mythological
character
pruh-**mee**-thi-uhss /prə'miːθiəs/

promethium chemical element
pruh-**mee**-thi-uhm /prə'miːθiəm/

promissory conveying a promise
prom-iss-uh-ri /'prɒmɪsəri/

promontory point of high land
prom-uhn-tuh-ri /'prɒməntəri/

pronaos pl. **pronaoi** vestibule at the
front of a classical temple
proh-**nay**-oss, pl. proh-**nay**-oy
/prəʊ'neɪɒs/, pl. /-'neɪɔɪ/

propane flammable gas
proh-payn /'prəʊpeɪn/

Propertius, Sextus Roman poet
sek-**stuhss** pruh-**pur**-shuhss /ˌsɛkstəs
prə'pəː(r)ʃəs/

prophesy make a prophecy
prof-uh-sy /'prɒfəsʌɪ/

prophylactic intended to prevent
disease
prof-il-**ak**-tik /ˌprɒfɪ'laktɪk/

propinquity closeness
pruh-**pink**-wit-i /prə'pɪŋkwɪti/

propitiate win favour
pruh-**pish**-i-ayt /prə'pɪʃieɪt/

proprioceptive relating to stimuli
proh-pri-uh-**sep**-tiv /ˌprəʊpriə'septɪv/

propylaeum pl. **propylaea** entrance to a temple
prop-il-**ee**-uhm, pl. prop-il-**ee**-uh
/ˌprɒprˈliːəm/, pl. /-ˈliːə/

pro rata proportional
proh **rah**-tuh /ˌprəʊ ˈrɑːtə/

prorogue discontinue a session
pruh-**rohg** /prəˈrəʊg/

prosaic unpoetic
proh-**zay**-ik /prəʊˈzeɪɪk/

proscenium part of a theatre stage
pruh-**see**-ni-uhm /prəˈsiːniəm/

prosciutto raw cured Italian ham
pruh-**shoo**-toh /prəˈʃuːtəʊ/

proselytize attempt to convert
pross-uh-lit-yz /ˈprɒsəlɪtaɪz/

Proserpina Roman mythological character
pruh-**sur**-pin-uh /prəˈsəː(r)pɪnə/

She is also a character in various Italian operas, for which the pronunciation is proz-**air**-pin-uh. An anglicized version of her name, Proserpine, is pronounced **pross**-uhr-pyn.

prosit 'cheers' (German)
proh-zit /ˈprəʊzɪt/

prosody patterns of rhythm and sound in poetry or speech
pross-uh-di /ˈprɒsədi/

prosopography description of people
pross-uh-**pog**-ruh-fi /ˌprɒsəˈpɒgrəfi/

Prospero Shakespearean character
pross-puh-roh /ˈprɒspərəʊ/

Prost, Alain French motor-racing driver
al-**a(ng)** prost /aˌlɛ̃ ˈprɒst/

prostaglandin compound with hormone-like effects
prost-uh-**glan**-din /ˌprɒstəˈglandɪn/

prosthesis pl. **prostheses** artificial body part
pross-**thee**-siss, pl. pross-**thee**-seez
/prɒsˈθiːsɪs/, pl. /-siːz/

Sometimes also **pross**-thuh-siss, pl. -seez.

protactinium chemical element
proh-tak-**tin**-i-uhm /ˌprəʊtakˈtɪniəm/

protean changeable
proh-ti-uhn /ˈprəʊtiən/

protease enzyme
proh-ti-ayz /ˈprəʊtieɪz/

protégé person guided by an older and more experienced person

prot-ezh-ay /ˈprɒtɛʒeɪ/

Also **proh-tuh-zhay**, especially in AM.

Proterozoic geological aeon
proh-tuh-ruh-**zoh**-ik /ˌprəʊtərəˈzəʊɪk/

protestation emphatic declaration
prot-uh-**stay**-shuhn /ˌprɒtɪˈsteɪʃən/

Proteus Greek god
proh-ti-uhss /ˈprəʊtiəs/

Protista biological kingdom; also called **Protoctista**
proh-**tist**-uh /prəʊˈtɪstə/

Protoctista biological kingdom; also called **Protista**
proh-tok-**tist**-uh /ˌprəʊtɒkˈtɪstə/

Protozoa zoological phylum
proh-tuh-**zoh**-uh /ˌprəʊtəˈzəʊə/

Proudhon, Pierre French social philosopher
pyair proo-**do(ng)** /ˌpjɛː(r) pruːˈdɔ̃/

Proust, Marcel French writer
mar-**sel** proost /maː(r)ˌsɛl ˈpruːst/

Prout, William English chemist
prowt /praʊt/

proven demonstrated
proov-uhn /ˈpruːvən/

Sometimes also **proh**-vuhn. The Scottish legal verdict 'not proven' is usually pronounced in this way.

Provençal relating to Provence in France
prov-**ah(ng)**-**sahl** /ˌprɒvãˈsɑːl/

The culinary term *provençale* is pronounced in the same way.

Provence former province, France
prov-**ah(ng)ss** /prɒˈvãs/

provender animal fodder
prov-uhn-duhr /ˈprɒvəndə(r)/

proviso condition
pruh-**vy**-zoh /prəˈvaɪzəʊ/

provolone Italian soft smoked cheese
prov-uh-**loh**-nay /ˌprɒvəˈləʊneɪ/

provost the head of certain university colleges
prov-uhst /ˈprɒvəst/

However, the word is pronounced pruh-**voh** in military contexts.

Proxima Centauri star
prok-sim-uh sen-**taw**-ry /ˌprɒksɪmə sɛnˈtɔːrʌɪ/

• See LATIN panel.

proxime accessit runner-up
prok-sim-ay ak-**sess**-it /ˌprɒksɪmeɪ ak'sesɪt/
• See LATIN panel.

Prozac trademark antidepressant drug
proh-zak /'prəʊzak/

Prudhoe Bay inlet in Alaska, US
proo-doh /'pruːdəʊ/

However, Prudhoe in north-east England is pronounced **prud**-oh or **prud**-uh.

pruritus itching of the skin
pruu-**ry**-tuhss /prʊ'rʌɪtəs/

prusik climbing method
pruss-ik /'prʌsɪk/

Prut (also **Pruth**) river, Europe
proot /pruːt/

Przewalski's horse wild Mongolian horse
przhuh-**val**-ski /ˌprʒə'valski/

psalm sacred song
sahm /sɑːm/

psalmody singing of psalms
sah-muh-di /'sɑːmədi/

psalter Book of Psalms
sawl-tuhr /'sɔːltə(r)/

Psammead fictional character in E. Nesbit's *Five Children and It*
sam-i-ad /'samiad/

psephology statistical study of voting
see-**fol**-uh-ji /siː'fɒlədʒi/

Commonly also **sef**-ol-uh-ji; the pronunciation we recommend was preferred by the psephologist we consulted.

pseudonym fictitious name
syoo-duh-nim /'sjuːdənɪm/

This and other related words are commonly also pronounced sood-.

psi letter of the Greek alphabet
psy /psʌɪ/

psilocybin hallucinogenic compound
sy-loh-**sy**-bin /ˌsʌɪləʊ'sʌɪbɪn/

psittacosis contagious disease of birds
sit-uh-**koh**-siss /ˌsɪtə'kəʊsɪs/

Psmith fictional Wodehouse character
smith /smɪθ/

psoas large muscle
soh-ass /'səʊas/

psoriasis skin disease
suh-**ry**-uh-siss /sə'rʌɪəsɪs/

psyche human soul

sy-ki /'sʌɪki/

psychopathy mental illness
sy-**kop**-uh-thi /sʌɪ'kɒpəθi/

psychosis pl. **psychoses** severe mental disorder
sy-**koh**-siss, pl. sy-**koh**-seez /sʌɪ'kəʊsɪs, pl. /-siːz/

psychosomatic caused by a mental factor
sy-koh-suh-**mat**-ik /ˌsʌɪkəʊsə'matɪk/

psychotropic relating to drugs that affect mental state
sy-koh-**troh**-pik /ˌsʌɪkəʊ'trəʊpɪk/

Also sy-koh-**trop**-ik.

psy-ops manipulative tactics
sy-ops /'sʌɪɒps/

Ptah ancient Egyptian god
tah /tɑː/

ptarmigan grouse
tar-mig-uhn /'tɑː(r)mɪgən/

pteranodon dinosaur
terr-**an**-uh-don /tɛ'ranədɒn/

pterodactyl dinosaur
terr-uh-**dak**-til /ˌterə'daktɪl/

Ptolemaic relating to Ptolemy
tol-uh-**may**-ik /ˌtɒlə'meɪɪk/

Ptolemy Greek astronomer and geographer; also the name of all the Macedonian rulers of Egypt
tol-uh-mi /'tɒləmi/

pubis pl. **pubes** bone forming the side of the pelvis
pyoo-biss, pl. **pyoo**-beez /'pjuːbɪs, pl. /-biːz/

Puccini, Giacomo Italian composer
jah-kuh-moh poo-**chee**-ni /'dʒɑːkəʊ puː'tʃiːni/

pudendum pl. **pudenda** genitals
pyuu-**den**-duhm, pl. pyuu-**den**-duh /pjʊ'dɛndəm, pl. /-də/

pudeur sense of shame
pyoo-**dur** /pjuː'dəː(r)/, French /pydœr/

Pudong airport, China
poo-**duung** /puː'dʊŋ/

Puebla state, Mexico
pway-bluh /'pweɪblə/

Puente, Tito American bandleader
tee-toh **pwen**-tay /ˌtiːtəʊ 'pwɛnteɪ/

puerile childish
pyoor-yl /'pjʊərʌɪl/

puerperal relating to childbirth
pyoo-**ur**-puh-ruhl /ˌpjuː'əː(r)pərəl/

Puerto Cortés port, Honduras
　pwair-toh kor-**tayss** /ˌpwɛː(r)təʊ kɔː(r)ˈteɪs/

Puerto Rico island, Caribbean
　pwair-toh **ree**-koh /ˌpwɛː(r)təʊ ˈriːkəʊ/

Puget Sound inlet, US
　pyoo-juht /ˈpjuːdʒət/

Pugin, Augustus English architect
　pyoo-jin /ˈpjuːdʒɪn/

Puglia see **Apulia**

pugnacious quick to argue
　pug-**nay**-shuhss /pʌɡˈneɪʃəs/

puirt-a-beul Gaelic mouth music
　poorsht uh bayl /ˌpʊə(r)ʃt ə ˈbeɪl/

puissant influential
　pwee-suhnt /ˈpwiːsənt/

pukka genuine
　puk-uh /ˈpʌkə/

pula currency unit, Botswana
　puul-uh /ˈpʊlə/

pulchritude beauty
　pul-krit-yood /ˈpʌlkrɪtjuːd/

Pulitzer prize journalism award
　puul-it-suhr /ˈpʊlɪtsə(r)/

Pullein-Thompson, Josephine
English author
　puul-in /ˈpʊlɪn/

pullulate spread rapidly
　pul-yoo-layt /ˈpʌljuleɪt/

pulmonary relating to the lungs
　pul-muh-nuh-ri /ˈpʌlmənəri/

pulsar celestial object
　pul-sar /ˈpʌlsɑː(r)/

pumice light volcanic rock
　pum-iss /ˈpʌmɪs/

pumpernickel German rye bread
　puum-puhr-nik-uhl /ˈpʊmpə(r)ˌnɪkəl/

punani female genitals
　poo-**nah**-ni /puˈnɑːni/

Pune (also **Poona**) city, India
　poo-nuh /ˈpuːnə/

punga (also **ponga**) tree fern
　pung-uh /ˈpʌŋə/

Punic relating to ancient Carthage
　pyoo-nik /ˈpjuːnɪk/

Punjab region of India and Pakistan
　pun-**jahb** /pʌnˈdʒɑːb/

Punjabi (also **Panjabi**) native or
inhabitant of Punjab
　pun-**jah**-bi /pʌnˈdʒɑːbi/

punt flat-bottomed boat
　punt /pʌnt/

punt former currency unit, Republic of
Ireland
　puunt /pʊnt/

Punta Arenas port, Chile
　poon-tuh arr-**ay**-nass /ˌpuːntə aˈreɪnas/

Punxsutawney town, US
　punk-suh-**taw**-ni /pʌŋksəˈtɔːni/

pupa pl. **pupae** insect in immature form
　pyoo-puh, pl. **pyoo**-pee /ˈpjuːpə/, pl. /-piː/

purblind having impaired vision
　pur-blynd /ˈpəː(r)blʌɪnd/

Purcell, Henry English composer
　pur-suhl /ˈpəː(r)səl/

> We were advised of this pronunciation by a
> descendant of the composer. It is also
> somewhat supported by evidence from the
> ode written on his death by his
> contemporary Dryden, which includes the
> lines 'So ceas'd the rival Crew when Purcell
> came' and 'The Gods are pleas'd alone with
> Purcell's Lays', both of which must be
> stressed on the first syllable to conform to
> the metre.

purdah practice of screening women
from men
　pur-duh /ˈpəː(r)də/

purée liquidize
　pyoor-ay /ˈpjʊəreɪ/

purgatory place of suffering
　pur-guh-tuh-ri /ˈpəː(r)ɡətəri/

puri unleavened bread
　poor-i /ˈpuːri/

Purim Jewish festival
　poor-im /ˈpʊərɪm/

> Sometimes also puu-**reem**, a pronunciation
> closer to the Hebrew.

purlieu area surrounding a place
　pur-lyoo /ˈpəː(r)ljuː/

purslane plant
　purss-luhn /ˈpəː(r)slən/

pursuant in accordance with
　puhr-**syoo**-uhnt /pə(r)ˈsjuːənt/

pursuivant heraldic officer
　pur-siv-uhnt /ˈpəː(r)sɪvənt/

purulent containing pus
　pyoor-uul-uhnt /ˈpjʊərʊlənt/

Pusan city, South Korea
　poo-**san** /ˌpuːˈsan/

Pusey, Edward Bouverie English theologian
boo-vuh-ri **pyoo**-zi /ˌbuːvəri ˈpjuːzi/

Pushkin, Aleksandr Russian writer
al-uhk-**sahn**-duhr **puush**-kin
/aləkˌsɑːndə(r) ˈpʊʃkɪn/

pusillanimous showing a lack of courage
pyoo-si-**lan**-im-uhss /ˌpjuːsɪˈlanɪməs/

Puskás, Ferenc Hungarian footballer
ferr-ents **puush**-kahsh /ˌfɛrɛnts ˈpʊʃkɑːʃ/

Putin, Vladimir Russian president
vluh-**dee**-meer **poo**-tin /vləˌdiːmɪə(r) ˈpuːtɪn/

putlog horizontal pole projecting from a wall
put-log /ˈpʌtlɒg/

putonghua standard spoken form of modern Chinese
poo-**tuung**-hwah /puːˈtʊŋhwɑː/

Putrajaya federal territory, Malaysia
puut-ruh-**jy**-uh /ˈpʊtrəˈdʒʌɪə/

putrescent decaying
pyoo-**tress**-uhnt /pjuːˈtrɛsənt/

putsch violent attempt to overthrow a government
puutch /pʊtʃ/

puttanesca pasta sauce
puut-uh-**nesk**-uh /pʊtəˈnɛskə/

putto pl. **putti** representation of a naked child
puut-oh, pl. **puut**-i /ˈpʊtəʊ/, pl. /ˈpʊti/

Putumayo region and river, Colombia
poo-tuum-**y**-oh /puːtʊˈmʌɪəʊ/

putz stupid person
puts /pʌts/

puy variety of green lentil
pwee /pwiː/

Pwllheli town, Wales
poohl-**hel**-i /puːɬˈhɛli/

pyaemia blood poisoning
py-**ee**-mi-uh /pʌɪˈiːmiə/

Pyatigorsk city, Russia

pyat-ig-**orsk** /pjatɪˈgɔː(r)sk/

pygidium segment of an invertebrate's body
py-**jid**-i-uhm /pʌɪˈdʒɪdiəm/

Also py-**gid**-i-uhm; see Latin panel.

Pygmalion Greek mythological character; play by Shaw
pig-**may**-li-uhn /pɪgˈmeɪliən/

Also a ballet by Rameau, which has the French pronunciation peeg-mal-**yo(ng)**.

Pynchon, Thomas American novelist
pintch-uhn /ˈpɪntʃən/

Pyongyang capital of North Korea
pyong-**yang** /ˌpjɒŋˈjaŋ/

pyracantha shrub
py-ruh-**kan**-thuh /ˌpʌɪrəˈkanθə/

pyramidal resembling a pyramid in shape
pirr-**am**-id-uhl /pɪˈramɪdəl/

Pyramus Roman mythological character
pirr-uh-muhss /ˈpɪrəməs/

Pyrenees mountain range, France and Spain
pirr-uh-**neez** /ˌpɪrəˈniːz/, French [pirene]

pyretic feverish or inducing fever
py-**ret**-ik /pʌɪˈrɛtɪk/

pyrites shiny yellow mineral
py-**ry**-teez /pʌɪˈrʌɪtiːz/

pyrope deep red garnet
py-**rohp** /ˈpʌɪrəʊp/

pyrrhic won at too great a cost
pirr-ik /ˈpɪrɪk/

Pyrrhus ancient king of Epirus
pirr-uhss /ˈpɪrəs/

Pythagoras Greek philosopher
py-**thag**-uh-ruhss /pʌɪˈθagərəs/

Pythia priestess of Apollo in ancient Greece
pith-i-uh /ˈpɪθiə/

pyx container for consecrated bread
piks /pɪks/

Q

Qabis see **Gabès**

Qaeda, al- (also **Qaida, al-**) terrorist group
uhl kah-**id**-uh /əl kɑːˈɪdə/, [əl ˈqaːʕɪda]

> The name means 'the Base' in Arabic, and our recommendation is as close as possible to the Arabic pronunciation. Other anglicized pronunciations such as uhl **ky**-duh or uhl kah-**ee**-duh are often heard.

Qaddafi, Muammar see **Gaddafi**

Qahira, al- see **Cairo**

Qalqilya city, West Bank
kal-**keel**-yuh /kalˈkiːljə/

qanat water channel
kuh-**naht** /kəˈnɑːt/

QANTAS Australian airline
kwon-tuhss /ˈkwɒntəs/

qanun zither
kah-**noon** /kɑːˈnuːn/

Qaradawi, Yusif al- Egyptian cleric
yoo-suuf uhl karr-uh-**dah**-wi /juːsʊf əl karəˈdɑːwi/
• See ARABIC panel.

Qaraghandy city, Kazakhstan
karr-uh-**gan**-di /ˈkarəˌɡandi/

> The Russian name is Karaganda, pronounced karr-uh-guhn-**dah**.

qat narcotic
kaht /kɑːt/

Qatar sheikhdom, Persian Gulf
kut-uhr /ˈkʌtə(r)/
• Established anglicization.

qawwali Muslim devotional music
kuh-**wah**-li /kəˈwɑːli/

qi life force in Chinese medicine
chee /tʃiː/

qibla direction of Mecca
kib-luh /ˈkɪblə/

qigong Chinese system of physical exercises
chee-**guung** /tʃiːˈɡʊŋ/

Qinetiq trademark defence technology company
kin-**et**-ik /kɪˈnɛtɪk/

Qingdao port, China
ching-**dow** /ˌtʃɪŋˈdaʊ/

Qinghai province, China
ching-**hy** /ˌtʃɪŋˈhʌɪ/

Qiqihar port, China
chich-i-**har** /ˌtʃɪtʃiˈhɑː(r)/

Qom (also **Qum** or **Kum**) city, Iran
kuum /kʊm/

qua in the capacity of
kwah /kwɑː/

Quaalude US trademark sedative drug
kway-lood /ˈkweɪluːd/

Quadragesima first Sunday in Lent
kwod-ruh-**jess**-im-uh /ˌkwɒdrəˈdʒɛsɪmə/

quadriceps thigh muscle
kwod-riss-eps /ˈkwɒdrɪsɛps/

quadrille dance
kwod-**ril** /kwɒˈdrɪl/

quadriplegia paralysis of all four limbs
kwod-rip-**lee**-juh /ˌkwɒdrɪˈpliːdʒə/

quadruped four-footed animal
kwod-ruup-ed /ˈkwɒdrʊpɛd/

quadruplet each of four children born at one birth
kwod-**roop**-luht /kwɒˈdruːplət/

> Sometimes also **kwod**-ruup-luht.

quaestor Roman official
kwee-stuhr /ˈkwiːstə(r)/

quagga extinct type of zebra
kwag-uh /ˈkwaɡə/

quagmire bog
kwog-my-uhr /ˈkwɒɡmʌɪə(r)/

> Less commonly also **kwag**-my-uhr.

quahog edible clam
kwaw-hog /ˈkwɔːhɒɡ/

quaich shallow cup (Scottish)
kwaykh /kweɪx/

Quai d'Orsay street in Paris
kay dor-**say** /ˌkeɪ dɔː(r)ˈseɪ/

quale pl. **qualia** perceived quality or property
kway-li, pl. **kway**-li-uh /ˈkweɪli/, pl. /ˈkweɪliə/

qualitative relating to quality
kwol-it-uh-tiv /ˈkwɒlɪtətɪv/

qualm uneasy feeling
kwahm /kwɑːm/

quango semi-public administrative body
kwang-goh /ˈkwaŋɡəʊ/

Quant, Mary English fashion designer
kwont /kwɒnt/

quantitative relating to quantity
kwon-tit-uh-tiv /ˈkwɒntɪtətɪv/

quark subatomic particle
kwork /kwɔː(r)k/

Commonly also kwark. Our recommendation is the pronunciation used by the physicist who coined the term.

quark curd cheese
kwark /kwɑː(r)k/

Sometimes also kvark, a pronunciation closer to the original German.

quartier district of a French city
kart-yay /ˈkɑː(r)tjeɪ/

quasar remote celestial object
kway-zar /ˈkweɪzɑː(r)/

Quasimodo fictional hunchback
kwoz-i-**moh**-doh /ˌkwɒziˈməʊdəʊ/

Quatermass Experiment, The cult television series
kway-tuhr-mass /kweɪˈtə(r)mas/

quaternary fourth
kwuh-**tur**-nuh-ri /kwəˈtəː(r)nəri/

quatrain stanza of four lines
kwot-rayn /ˈkwɒtreɪn/

quatrefoil design of four leaves
kat-ruh-foyl /ˈkatrəfɔɪl/

quattrocento 15th century
kwat-ruh-**chen**-toh /ˌkwatrəˈtʃɛntəʊ/

Quds, al- Arabic-language newspaper
uhl **kuudz** /əl ˈkuudz/

Quebec province, Canada
kwuh-**bek** /kwəˈbɛk/

Québécois relating to Quebec
kay-bek-**wah** /keɪbɛkˈwɑː/

Quechua ethnic group and language, South America
ketch-wuh /ˈkɛtʃwə/

quenelle meatball
kuh-**nel** /kəˈnɛl/

Querétaro state, Mexico
kerr-**ay**-tarr-oh /kɛˈreɪtarəʊ/

querulous complaining
kwerr-uul-uhss /ˈkwɛrʊləs/

quesadilla cheese tortilla
kay-suh-**dee**-yuh /ˌkeɪsəˈdiːjə/

questionnaire set of questions
kwess-chuh-**nair** /ˌkwɛstʃəˈnɛː(r)/

The older pronunciation kess-chuh-**nair** is now very rarely heard.

Quetta city, Pakistan
kwet-uh /ˈkwɛtə/

quetzal bird
ket-suhl /ˈkɛtsəl/

Quetzalcóatl Aztec god
ket-suhl-koh-**at**-uhl /ˌkɛtsəlkəʊˈatəl/

Quezon city, Philippines
kay-zon /ˈkeɪzɒn/

Qufu town, China
choo-**foo** /ˌtʃuːˈfuː/

Quiché Guatemalan ethnic group
kee-**chay** /kiːˈtʃeɪ/

quiche flan
keesh /kiːʃ/

quiddity essence
kwid-it-i /ˈkwɪdɪti/

quid pro quo favour granted in return
kwid proh **kwoh** /ˌkwɪd prəʊ ˈkwəʊ/

quiescent dormant
kwi-**ess**-uhnt /kwiˈɛsənt/

quietus death
kwy-**ee**-tuhss /kwʌɪˈiːtəs/

quila fort
kil-uh /ˈkɪlə/

Quiller-Couch, Arthur English author
kwil-uhr **kootch** /ˌkwɪlə(r) ˈkuːtʃ/

Quimper city, France
ka(ng)-**pair** /kɛ̃ˈpɛː(r)/

quinine compound
kwin-een /ˈkwɪniːn/

quinoa grain
kee-noh-uh /ˈkiːnəʊə/

Quinquagesima Sunday before Lent
kwing-kwuh-**jess**-im-uh /ˌkwɪŋkwəˈdʒɛsɪmə/

quinquereme Roman or Greek galley
kwing-kwuh-reem /ˈkwɪŋkwəˌriːm/

Quintana Roo state, Mexico
keen-**tah**-nuh **roh** /kiːnˌtɑːnə ˈrəʊ/

Quintilian Roman rhetorician
 kwin-**til**-i-uhn /kwɪnˈtɪlɪən/

quintuplet each of five children born at
 one birth
 kwin-**tyoop**-luht /kwɪnˈtjuːplət/

Sometimes also kwin-**tup**-luht or
 kwin-tyuup-luht.

Quirinal one of the seven hills of Rome
 kwirr-in-uhl /ˈkwɪrɪnəl/

Quirinale Palace offical residence of
 the Italian prime minister
 kwee-rin-**ah**-lay /kwiːrɪˈnɑːleɪ/

quisling collaborator
 kwiz-ling /ˈkwɪzlɪŋ/

Quito capital of Ecuador
 kee-toh /ˈkiːtəʊ/

qui vive on the alert
 kee **veev** /ˌkiː ˈviːv/

qui tollis peccata mundi 'who takes
 away the sins of the world' (Latin)
 kwee **tol**-iss pek-**ah**-tuh **muun**-di
 /kwi ˌtɒlɪs pɛˌkɑːtə ˈmʊndi/

Quixote, Don see **Don Quixote**

quixotic idealistic
 kwik-**sot**-ik /kwɪkˈsɒtɪk/

Qum see **Qom**

Qumran region, Jordan
 kuum-**rahn** /kʊmˈrɑːn/

quodlibet musical term
 kwod-lib-et /ˈkwɒdlɪbɛt/

quod erat demonstrandum used to
 convey that a situation demonstrates the
 truth of one's theory
 kwod **err**-at dem-uhn-**strand**-uum
 /kwɒd ˌɛrat dɛmənˈstrandʊm/

quoit ring
 koyt /kɔɪt/

quokka wallaby
 kwok-uh /ˈkwɒkə/

quondam that once was
 kwon-dam /ˈkwɒndam/

Quorn trademark vegetable protein
 kworn /kwɔː(r)n/

quorum minimum number
 kwaw-ruhm /ˈkwɔːrəm/

quoth said
 kwohth /kwəʊθ/

quotidian daily
 kwoh-**tid**-i-uhn /kwəʊˈtɪdɪən/

quotient a result obtained by dividing
 one quantity by another
 kwoh-shuhnt /ˈkwəʊʃənt/

Qur'an (also **Quran**) see **Koran**

Qurei, Ahmed (also **Qureia**)
 Palestinian prime minister
 akh-muhd kuu-**ray**-uh /ˌaxməd
 kʊˈreɪə/

qwerty standard layout on
 English-language keyboards
 kwur-ti /ˈkwəː(r)ti/

R

Raban, Jonathan English writer
ray-buhn /ˈreɪbən/

Rabat capital of Morocco
ruh-**bat** /rəˈbat/

Rabaul port, Papua New Guinea
ruh-**bowl** /rəˈbaʊl/

rabbi Jewish scholar or teacher
rab-y /ˈrabʌɪ/

rabbinic relating to rabbis or to Jewish teachings
ruh-**bin**-ik /rəˈbɪnɪk/

Rabelais, François French satirist
frah(ng)-**swah** rab-lay /frãˈswɑː
rabˈleɪ/

rabid fanatical
rab-id /ˈrabɪd/

Less commonly also **ray-bid**.

rabies contagious disease of mammals
ray-beez /ˈreɪbiːz/

Rabin, Yitzhak Israeli statesman
yits-**hahk** rab-een /jɪtsˌhɑːk raˈbiːn/

rachis (also **rhachis**) pl. **rachides** stem of a plant
ray-kiss, pl. ray-kid-eez /ˈreɪkɪs/, pl.
/-kɪdiːz/

Rachmaninov, Sergei Russian composer and pianist
suhr-**gay** rakh-**man**-in-of /sə(r)ˌgeɪ
raxˈmanɪnɒf/

Rachmanism exploitation of tenants by landlords
rak-muh-niz-uhm /ˈrakmənɪzəm/

Racine, Jean French dramatist
zhah(ng) rass-een /ˌʒã raˈsiːn/

Rackham, Arthur English illustrator
rak-uhm /ˈrakəm/

raclette Swiss cheese dish
rak-**let** /raˈklɛt/

raconteur amusing story-teller
rak-on-**tur** /ˌrakɒnˈtə:(r)/

RADA Royal Academy of Dramatic Art
rah-duh /ˈrɑːdə/

Radhakrishnan, Sarvepalli Indian statesman
sur-vuh-pul-i rah-duh-**krish**-nuhn
/ˌsə:(r)vəpʌli ˌrɑːdəˈkrɪʃnən/

radian unit of measurement of angles
ray-di-uhn /ˈreɪdiən/

radicchio chicory
rad-**ee**-ki-oh /raˈdiːkiəʊ/

Radice, William English translator
rad-ee-chay /raˈdiːtʃeɪ/

radiometer instrument for measuring radiation
ray-di-**om**-uh-tuhr /ˌreɪdɪˈɒmɪtə(r)/

radioscopy examination by X-rays
ray-di-**osk**-uh-pi /ˌreɪdɪˈɒskəpi/

Radió Telifís Éireann Irish broadcaster
rah-di-oh **tel**-uh-feesh **air**-uhn
/ˌrɑːdiəʊ ˌtɛləfiːʃ ˈɛːrən/

radium chemical element
ray-di-uhm /ˈreɪdiəm/

radius pl. **radii** straight line from the centre to the circumference of a circle
ray-di-uhss, pl. ray-di-y /ˈreɪdiəs/, pl.
/-dɪʌɪ/
• Standard -es plural is also possible.

radix pl. **radices** base of a numeration system
ray-diks, pl. ray-diss-eez /ˈreɪdɪks/, pl.
/-dɪsiːz/

Radnorshire former county, Wales
rad-nuhr-shuhr /ˈradnə(r)ʃə(r)/

Radom city, Poland
rad-om /ˈradɒm/

radon chemical element
ray-don /ˈreɪdɒn/

Raeburn, Henry Scottish portrait painter
ray-burn /ˈreɪbə:(r)n/

Raëlian movement atheistic cult
ry-ee-li-uhn /rʌɪˈiːliən/

Rafah town, Palestine
raf-uh /ˈrafə/

Raffarin, Jean-Pierre French statesman
zhah(ng) **pyair** raf-uh-**ra(ng)** /ʒã
pjɛː(r) rafəˈrɛ̃/

Rafsanjani, Ali Akbar Hashemi
Iranian statesman
al-ee ak-**bar** hah-shem-**ee**
raf-san-jah-**nee** /a‚li: ak‚bɑː(r)
hɑːʃɛ‚mi: ‚rafsandʒɑːˈni/

raga (also **rag**) musical mode
rahg /ˈrɑːg/

ragga style of dance music
rag-uh /ˈragə/

ragged torn
rag-id /ˈragɪd/

Ragnarök Norse mythological battle
rag-nuh-rok /ˈragnərɒk/
• Established anglicization.

ragout meat stew
rag-**oo** /raˈguː/

raguly heraldic term
rag-yuul-i /ˈragjʊli/

Ragusa city, Italy
rag-**oo**-zuh /raˈguːzə/

ragwort plant
rag-wurt /ˈragwəː(r)t/

rai style of music
ry /rʌɪ/

raillery good-humoured teasing
rayl-uh-ri /ˈreɪləri/

Raimi, Sam American film director
ray-mi /ˈreɪmi/

Rainier, Mount mountain, US
ruh-**neer** /rəˈnɪə(r)/

Rainier, Prince former ruler of Monaco
rayn-yay /ˈreɪnjeɪ/

Raipur city, India
ry-**poor** /rʌɪˈpʊə(r)/

raison d'être reason for existence
rez-o(ng) **det**-ruh /ˌrezɔ̃ ˈdetrə/

raita Indian yogurt dish
ry-tuh /ˈrʌɪtə/

Raj British sovereignty in India
rahj /rɑːdʒ/

raja (also **rajah**) Indian king or prince
rah-juh /ˈrɑːdʒə/

Rajapakse, Manhinda president of Sri
Lanka
muh-**hin**-duh ruj-uh-**puk**-shuh
/məˌhɪndə rʌdʒəˈpʌkʃə/

Rajasthan state, India
rah-juh-**stahn** /ˌrɑːdʒəˈstɑːn/

Rajkot city, India
rahj-**koht** /rɑːdʒˈkəʊt/

Rajneesh, Bhagwan Shree Indian
guru
buhg-**wahn shree** ruhj-**neesh**
/bəˌgwɑːn ˌʃri: rʌdʒˈni:ʃ/

Rajputana ancient region, India
rahj-puut-**ah**-nuh /ˌrɑːdʒpʊˈtɑːnə/

Rajshahi port, Bangladesh
rahj-**shah**-hi /rɑːdʒˈʃɑːhi/

Rajya Sabha upper house of the Indian
parliament
rahj-yuh sub-ah /ˌrɑːdʒjə sʌˈbɑː/

raki alcoholic spirit
ruh-**kee** /rəˈkiː/

Rákóczy March composition by Berlioz
rah-**koht**-si /ˈrɑːkəʊtsi/

Rákosi, Mátyás Hungarian statesman
maht-yahsh rah-**kosh**-i /ˌmɑːtjɑːʃ
ˈrɑːkɒʃi/

Raksha Bandhan Hindu festival
ruk-shah **bund**-uhn /ˌrʌkʃɑː ˈbʌndən/

Rakvere town, Estonia
rak-vuh-ruh /ˈrakvərə/

rale rattling sound made by unhealthy
lungs
rahl /rɑːl/

Raleigh city, US
raw-li /ˈrɔːli/

Raleigh cycle manufacturers
ral-i /ˈrali/

Raleigh, Walter (also **Ralegh**) English
explorer
raw-li /ˈrɔːli/

Our research indicates that this is the
correct pronunciation, although **rah**-li and
ral-i are also used.

rallentando pl. **rallentandi** musical
term
ral-uhn-**tan**-doh, pl. ral-uhn-**tan**-di
/ˌralənˈtandəʊ/, pl. /-di/
• Standard -s plural is also possible.

Rama Hindu god
rah-muh /ˈrɑːmə/

Ramadan Muslim month
ram-uh-**dahn** /ˌraməˈdɑːn/

Commonly also **ram**-uh-dan and, outside
Arab countries, ram-uh-**zahn**.

Ramadi, al- town, Iraq
uh-ruh-**mah**-di /ərəˈmɑːdi/
• See ARABIC panel.

Ramallah town, Palestine
rah-**mal**-uh /rɑːˈmalə/

Raman, Chandrasekhara Indian
physicist
chund-ruh-say-kuh-ruh rah-muhn
/ˌtʃʌndrəˌseɪkərə ˈrɑːmən/

Ramanujan, Srinivasa Indian
mathematician
srin-i-vahss rah-mah-nuuj-uhn
/ˌsrɪnivɑːs rɑːˈmɑːnʊdʒən/

Ramapithecus fossil ape
rah-muh-**pith**-ik-uhss /ˌrɑːməˈpɪθɪkəs/

Rāmāyana Sanskrit epic
rah-mah-yun-uh /rɑːˈmɑːjʌnə/

Rambert, Marie Polish-born English
ballet dancer and director
rah(ng)-bair /ˈrãbɛː(r)/

Rambouillet breed of sheep
ram-buh-lay /ˈrambəleɪ/

rambutan tropical fruit
ram-**boo**-tuhn /ramˈbuːtən/

Rameau, Jean-Philippe French
composer
zhah(ng) fee-**leep** ram-**oh** /ʒã fiːˌliːp
raˈməʊ/

ramekin small dish
ram-uh-kin /ˈraməkɪn/

ramen noodles
rah-men /ˈrɑːmɛn/

Rameses Egyptian pharaoh
ram-uh-seez /ˈraməsiːz/

Ramillies, Battle of battle in the War
of the Spanish Succession
ram-il-iz /ˈramɪlɪz/, French [ramiji]
• Established anglicization.

Ramón y Cajal, Santiago Spanish
physician
sant-**yah**-goh ram-**on** ee kakh-**al**
/sanˈtjɑːgəʊ raˌmɒn iː kaˈxal/

Ramsay, William Scottish chemist
ram-zi /ˈramzi/

ranchera Mexican country music
ran-**chair**-uh /ranˈtʃɛːrə/

ranchero person who works on a ranch
ran-**chair**-oh /ranˈtʃɛːrəʊ/

Ranchi city, India
run-chi /ˈrʌntʃi/

Rand, Ayn Russian-born American
writer
yn rand /ˌaɪn ˈrand/

rand currency unit, South Africa
rand /rand/, Afrikaans [rɑnt]
• Established anglicization.

Randers port, Denmark

ran-uhrss /ˈranə(r)s/

Randstad region, Netherlands
runt-stuht /ˈrʌntstət/

Ranelagh Gardens park in London
ran-uh-luh /ˈranələ/

rangatira Maori chief
rang-uh-**teer**-uh /ˌraŋəˈtɪərə/

rangé orderly
rah(ng)-zhay /ˈrãʒeɪ/

Rangoon capital of Burma
rang-**goon** /raŋˈguːn/

rangy tall and slim
rayn-ji /ˈreɪndʒi/

ranitidine antihistamine drug
ruh-**nit**-id-een /rəˈnɪtɪdiːn/

Ranjit Singh Indian statesman
run-jit sing /ˌrʌndʒɪt ˈsɪŋ/

ranunculus pl. **ranunculi** plant
ruh-**nunk**-yuul-uhss,
pl. ruh-**nunk**-yuul-y /rəˈnʌŋkjʊləs/, pl.
/-lʌɪ/
• Standard -es plural is also possible.

Rao, P. V. Narasimha Indian
statesman
narr-uh-**sim**-huh row /narəˌsɪmhə
ˈraʊ/

Raoult's law law of physics
rowlt /raʊlt/

rapacious aggressively greedy or
grasping
ruh-**pay**-shuhss /rəˈpeɪʃəs/

Rapa Nui Easter Islands
rap-uh **noo**-ee /ˌrapə ˈnuːiː/

Raphael Italian painter and architect
raf-ay-uhl /ˈrafeɪəl/

Raphael British surname
ray-fuhl /ˈreɪfəl/

raphe pl. **raphae** groove or ridge in body
tissue
ray-fi, pl. ray-fee /ˈreɪfi/, pl. /ˈreɪfiː/

rappel abseil
rap-el /raˈpɛl/

rapport understanding relationship
rap-**or** /raˈpɔː(r)/

rapprochement resumption of
harmonious relations
rap-**rosh**-mah(ng) /raˈprɒʃmã/

rarefy (also **rarify**) make less dense or
solid
rair-if-y /ˈrɛːrɪfʌɪ/

Rarotonga island, South Pacific
rarr-uh-**tong**-guh /ˌrarəˈtɒŋgə/

Ras al Khaimah member state, United Arab Emirates
rahss uhl **khy**-muh /ˌrɑːs əl ˈxʌɪmə/

rasam Indian soup
russ-uhm /ˈrʌsəm/

rascasse fish used in bouillabaisse
rask-**ass** /rasˈkas/

ras malai Indian sweet dish
russ mul-**y** /ˌrʌs mʌˈlʌɪ/

Rasmussen, Anders Fogh prime minister of Denmark
an-uhrss **foh rass**-muuss-uhn /ˌanə(r)s ˌfəʊ ˈrasmʊsən/

Rasputin, Grigori Russian monk
grig-**aw**-ri rasp-**yoo**-tin /ˌɡrɪˌɡɔːri raˈspjuːtɪn/

Rastafarian follower of a Jamaican religious movement
rast-uh-**fair**-i-uhn /ˌrastəˈfɛːriən/

Sometimes also rast-uh-**far**-i-uhn.

ratafia almond liqueur
rat-uh-**fee**-uh /ˌratəˈfiːə/

ratamacue basic drumming pattern
rat-uh-muh-kyoo /ˈratəməˌkjuː/

Ratana Maori church
rah-tuh-nuh /ˈrɑːtənə/

rataplan drumming or beating sound
rat-uh-**plan** /ˌratəˈplan/

ratatouille vegetable dish
rat-uh-**too**-i /ˌratəˈtuːi/, [ratatuj]

Rathaus pl. **Rathäuser** German town hall
raht-howss, pl. **raht**-hoy-zuhr /ˈrɑːthaʊs, pl. /ˈrɑːthɔɪzə(r)/

Rather, Dan American news broadcaster
rath-uhr /ˈraðə(r)/

rathskeller beer hall in a basement
rahts-kel-uhr /ˈrɑːts,kɛlə(r)/

rath yatra Hindu ceremonial procession
rut yut-ruh /ˈrʌt ˌjʌtrə/

ratiocinate form judgements
rat-i-**oss**-in-ayt /ˌratiˈɒsɪneɪt/

rationale logical basis
rash-uh-**nahl** /ˌraʃəˈnɑːl/

Ratisbon see **Regensburg**

rattan palm stems
ruh-**tan** /rəˈtan/

Rattigan, Terence English dramatist
rat-ig-uhn /ˈratɪɡən/

Ratzinger, Joseph Alois Pope Benedict XVI
yoh-zuhf **ah**-loyss **rat**-sing-uhr /ˌjəʊzəf ˌɑːlɔɪs ˈratsɪŋə(r)/

raucous making a harsh noise
raw-kuhss /ˈrɔːkəs/

Rauschenberg, Robert American artist
row-shuhn-burg /ˈraʊʃənbəː(r)ɡ/

rauwolfia shrub
row-**wol**-fi-uh /raʊˈwɒlfiə/

rav rabbi
rov /rɒv/

Ravel, Maurice French composer
morr-**eess** rav-el /mɒˈriːs raˈvɛl/

raven hunt for prey
rav-uhn /ˈravən/

Ravenna city, Italy
rav-**en**-uh /raˈvɛnə/

Ravensbrück Nazi concentration camp
rah-vuhnss-bruek /ˈrɑːvənsbrʏk/

ravigote (also **ravigotte**) mixture of chopped herbs and shallots
rav-ig-ot /ˈravɪɡɒt/

ravioli stuffed pasta envelopes
rav-i-**oh**-li /ˌraviˈəʊli/

Rawalpindi city, Pakistan
rah-wuhl-**pin**-di /ˌrɑːwəlˈpɪndi/

Raworth, Sophie BBC journalist
ray-wuhrth /ˈreɪwə(r)θ/

Ray, Man American photographer
man **ray** /ˌman ˈreɪ/

Ray, Satyajit Indian film director
sut-yuh-jit **ry** /ˌsʌtjədʒɪt ˈrʌɪ/

Rayleigh, John English physicist
ray-li /ˈreɪli/

Raynaud's disease medical condition
ray-nohz /ˈreɪnəʊz/

rayonnant French style of Gothic architecture
ray-on-**ah(ng)** /ˌreɪjɒˈnã/

Razzall, Tim English politician
raz-uhl /ˈrazəl/

razzia hostile raid
raz-i-uh /ˈraziə/

re in the matter of
ray /reɪ/

Commonly also ree; see LATIN panel.

Rea, Chris English singer
ree-uh /ˈriːə/

This British surname can also be pronounced ray or ree, depending on individual preference.

Reading town, England
red-ing /ˈrɛdɪŋ/

Reagan, Ronald American statesman
ray-guhn /ˈreɪgən/

reagent substance for use in chemical reactions
ri-**ay**-juhnt /rɪˈeɪdʒənt/

real currency unit, Brazil
ray-al /ˈreɪˈal/

Real Madrid Spanish football team
ray-al muh-**drid** /ˌreɪˌal məˈdrɪd/
• Established anglicization; see MADRID.

realpolitik system of politics based on practical considerations
ray-al-**pol**-it-eek /ˈreɪˌalpɒlɪˌtiːk/

realtor estate agent
ree-uhl-tuhr /ˈriːəltə(r)/

Réaumur scale obsolete temperature scale
ray-oh-myoor /ˈreɪəʊˌmjʊə(r)/

rebab musical instrument
ruh-**bahb** /rəˈbɑːb/

rebbetzin (also **rebbitzin**) wife of a rabbi
reb-it-sin /ˈrɛbɪtsɪn/

rebec (also **rebeck**) medieval musical instrument
ree-bek /ˈriːbɛk/

Less commonly also **reb**-ek.

reblochon soft French cheese
ruh-blosh-**o(ng)** /ˈrəblɒˈʃɔ̃/

rebozo Mexican shawl
reb-**oh**-soh /rɛˈbəʊsəʊ/

rebus puzzle
ree-buhss /ˈriːbəs/

recce reconnaissance mission
rek-i /ˈrɛki/

Rechabite biblical family
rek-uh-byt /ˈrɛkəbʌɪt/

réchauffé dish of warmed-up food
ray-shoh-**fay** /reɪʃəʊˈfeɪ/

recherché rare or exotic
ruh-**shair**-shay /rəˈʃɛː(r)ʃeɪ/

recidivist convicted criminal who reoffends
ruh-**sid**-iv-ist /rɪˈsɪdɪvɪst/

Recife port, Brazil
ruh-**see**-fi /rəˈsiːfi/

reciprocity exchanging things with others for mutual benefit
ress-ip-**ross**-it-i /ˌrɛsɪˈprɒsɪti/

recitative musical declamation
ress-it-uh-**teev** /ˌrɛsɪtəˈtiːv/

Recklinghausen city, Germany
rek-ling-**how**-zuhn /ˌrɛklɪŋˈhaʊzən/

recluse solitary person
ruh-**klooss** /rəˈkluːs/

recognizant (also **recognisant**) conscious of something
ruh-**kog**-niz-uhnt /rəˈkɒgnɪzənt/

recollect remember
rek-uh-**lekt** /ˌrɛkəˈlɛkt/

recondite little known
rek-uhn-dyt /ˈrɛkəndʌɪt/

Commonly also ruh-**kon**-dyt.

reconnaissance military observation
ruh-**kon**-iss-uhnss /rəˈkɒnɪsəns/

reconnoitre make a military observation
rek-uh-**noy**-tuhr /ˌrɛkəˈnɔɪtə(r)/

rectrices sing. **rectrix** feathers in a bird's tail
rek-triss-eez, sing. **rek**-triks /ˈrɛktrɪsiːz/, sing. /-trɪks/

recusant person who refuses to submit to authority
rek-yuuz-uhnt /ˈrɛkjʊzənt/

redan embankment forming part of a fortification
ruh-**dan** /rəˈdan/

redingote woman's long coat
red-ing-goht /ˈrɛdɪŋgəʊt/

redolent reminiscent of
red-uh-luhnt /ˈrɛdələnt/

Redon, Odilon French artist
od-il-**o(ng)** ruh-**do(ng)** /ɒdɪˈlɔ̃ rəˈdɔ̃/

reductio ad absurdum method of proving the falsity of a premise
ruh-**duk**-ti-oh ad ab-**sur**-duhm /rɪˌdʌktɪəʊ ad abˈsəː(r)dəm/

redux brought back
ree-duks /ˈriːdʌks/

reebok see **rhebok**

Reeves, Keanu American actor
ki-**ah**-noo /kiˈɑːnuː/

reflet lustre or iridescence
ruh-**flay** /rəˈfleɪ/

refulgent shining very brightly
ruh-**ful**-juhnt /rəˈfʌldʒənt/

refusenik Jew refused permission to emigrate to Israel
ruhf-**yooz**-nik /rəˈfjuːznɪk/

regalia emblems of royalty
ruh-**gay**-li-uh /rəˈgeɪlɪə/

Regensburg city, Germany
ray-guhnz-burg /ˈreɪgənzbəː(r)g/, [ˈreːgənsbʊrk]

Established anglicization. An older name for the city is Ratisbon, pronounced **rat**-iz-bon.

Reger, Janet English lingerie designer
ray-guhr /ˈreɪgə(r)/

reggae musical style
reg-ay /ˈrɛgeɪ/

Reggio di Calabria port, Italy
rej-oh di kal-**ab**-ri-uh /ˌrɛdʒəʊ di kəˈlabriə/

regime government
ray-**zheem** /reɪˈʒiːm/

regimen prescribed course of treatment
rej-im-uhn /ˈrɛdʒɪmən/

Regina city, Canada; also reigning queen
ruh-**jy**-nuh /rəˈdʒʌɪnə/

Regiomontanus, Johannes German astronomer and mathematician
yoh-**han**-uhss
reg-yoh-mon-**tah**-nuuss /jəʊˌhanəs ˌrɛgjəʊmɒnˈtaːnʊs/

regisseur theatrical producer
rezh-iss-**oer** /ˌrɛʒɪˈsœː(r)/

Regius professor holder of a university chair
ree-juhss /ˈriːdʒəs/

regnal of a reign or monarch
reg-nuhl /ˈrɛgnəl/

Rego, Paula Portuguese painter
pow-luh **ray**-goo /ˌpaʊlə ˈreɪguː/

Regulus star
reg-yuul-uhss /ˈrɛgjʊləs/

Rehnquist, William American judge
renk-wist /ˈrɛŋkwɪst/

Rehoboam king of ancient Israel
ree-uh-**boh**-uhm /ˌriːəˈbəʊəm/

Reich former German state
rykh /rʌɪç/

Reichstag German parliament
rykhss-tahk /ˈrʌɪçsˌtɑːk/

reify make something more real
ree-if-y /ˈriːɪfʌɪ/

Commonly also **ray**-if-y.

reiki healing technique
ray-ki /ˈreɪki/

Reims (also **Rheims**) city, France
reemz /riːmz/, [rɛ̃s]
• Established anglicization.

Reinhardt, Django Belgian jazz guitarist
jang-goh **ryn**-hart /ˌdʒaŋgəʊ ˈrʌɪnhɑː(r)t/

reishi mushroom
ray-**ee**-shi /ˈreɪɪʃi/

Reiter's syndrome medical condition
ryt-uhr /ˈrʌɪtə(r)/

reive plunder
reev /riːv/

rejuvenescence renewal of youth
ruh-joo-vuh-**ness**-uhnss /rəˌdʒuːvəˈnɛsəns/

relativism philosophical doctrine
rel-uh-tiv-iz-uhm /ˈrɛlətɪvɪzəm/

relevé ballet movement
ruh-luh-**vay** /ˌrələˈveɪ/

reliquary container for holy relics
rel-ik-wuh-ri /ˈrɛlɪkwəri/

Remagen city, Germany
ray-mah-guhn /ˈreɪmɑːgən/

Remarque, Erich Maria German-born American novelist
ay-rikh muh-**ree**-uh ruh-**mark** /ˌeɪrɪç məˌriːə rəˈmɑː(r)k/

Rembrandt Dutch painter
rem-brant /ˈrɛmbrant/

REME Royal Electrical and Mechanical Engineers
ree-mi /ˈriːmi/

Remi, Georges Belgian cartoonist
zhorzh ray-**mee** /ˌʒɔː(r)ʒ reɪˈmiː/

remiges sing. **remex** flight feathers
rem-ij-eez, sing. **ree**-meks /ˈrɛmɪdʒiːz, sing. ˈriːmɛks/

remit area of activity
ree-mit /ˈriːmɪt/

Remonstrant brotherhood Dutch religious society
ruh-**mon**-struhnt /rəˈmɒnstrənt/

remonstrate make protest
rem-uhn-strayt /ˈrɛmənstreɪt/

remora fish
rem-uh-ruh /ˈrɛmərə/

remoulade egg dressing
rem-oo-lahd /ˈrɛmʊlɑːd/

remuda herd of horses
ruh-**moo**-duh /rəˈmuːdə/

remunerate pay
ruhm-**yoo**-nuh-rayt /rə'mju:nəreɪt/

Remus Roman mythological character
ree-muhss /'ri:məs/

Remy Martin trademark brand of cognac
rem-i mar-**ta(ng)** /,rɛmi mɑ:(r)'tɛ̃/

Renaissance European art revival
ruh-**nay**-suhnss /rə'neɪsəns/

Less commonly also ruh-**ness**-ah(ng)ss or,
in AM, ren-uh-**sahnss**.

renal relating to the kidneys
ree-nuhl /'ri:nəl/

Renan, Ernest French historian and
philosopher
air-**nest** ruh-**nah(ng)** /ɛ:(r),nɛst rə'nɑ̃/

Renault French car manufacturers
ren-oh /'rɛnəʊ/

Rendell, Ruth English writer
ren-duhl /'rɛndəl/

rendezvous pl. **rendezvouses** meeting
ron-day-voo, pl. **ron**-day-vooz
/'rɒndeɪvu:/, pl. /'rɒndeɪvu:z/

rendzina fertile soil
rend-**zee**-nuh /rɛnd'zi:nə/

renege go back on a promise
ruh-**nayg** /rə'neɪg/

RENFE Spanish railway system
ren-fay /'rɛnfeɪ/

Renfrewshire county, Scotland
ren-froo-shuhr /'rɛnfru:ʃə(r)/

renga Japanese poem
reng-guh /'rɛŋgə/

Rennes city, France
ren /rɛn/

rennet used in making cheese
ren-it /'rɛnɪt/

Reno city, US
ree-noh /'ri:nəʊ/

Renoir, Jean French film director
zhah(ng) ruhn-**war** /,ʒɑ̃ rə'nwɑ:(r)/

Renoir, Auguste French painter
oh-**guest** ruhn-**war** /əʊ,gyst
rə'nwɑ:(r)/

renosterbos shrub
ren-**ost**-uhr-boss /rɛ'nɒstə(r)bɒs/

rentier person living on income from
property
ro(ng)-ti-ay /'rɒ̃tieɪ/

Renwick, David English comedy writer
ren-wick /'rɛnwɪk/

This British surname can also be
pronounced **ren**-ik, according to individual
preference.

reparable possible to rectify
rep-uh-ruh-buhl /'rɛpərəbəl/

repartee witty conversation
rep-ar-**tee** /,rɛpɑ:(r)'ti:/

Commonly also rep-ar-**tay**.

repêchage contest for runners-up
rep-esh-**ahzh** /rɛpɛ'ʃɑːʒ/

repertoire stock of performances
rep-uhr-twar /'rɛpə(r)twɑː(r)/

repertory performance of various plays
by a company
rep-uhr-tuh-ri /'rɛpə(r)təri/

répétiteur ballet or music tutor
rep-et-it-**ur** /rɛ,petɪtə:(r)/

reportage reporting of news
rep-or-**tahzh** /,rɛpɔ:(r)'tɑːʒ/

reposado aged tequila
rep-oss-**ah**-doh /,rɛpɒ'sɑːdəʊ/

repoussé hammered into relief
ruh-**poo**-say /rə'pu:seɪ/

reprise repeated passage in music
ruh-**preez** /rə'pri:z/

reprobate unprincipled person
rep-ruh-bayt /'rɛprəbeɪt/

requiem Mass for the dead
rek-wi-em /'rɛkwiem/

requiescat prayer for the repose of a
dead person
rek-wi-**esk**-at /,rɛkwi'ɛskat/

requinto small guitar
rek-**in**-toh /rɛ'kɪntəʊ/

reredos ornamental screen behind an
altar
reer-doss /'rɪə(r)dɒs/

research investigation
ruh-**surtch** /rə'sə:(r)tʃ/

Commonly also **ree**-surtch, especially in
AM.

réseau network or grid
ray-zoh /'reɪzəʊ/

res gestae events which relate to a
particular case
rayz **gest**-y /reɪz 'gɛstʌɪ/

Resnais, Alain French film director
al-**a(ng)** ruh-**nay** /a,lɛ̃ rə'neɪ/

resolute admirably purposeful
rez-uh-loot /'rɛzəlu:t/

resource stock of assets
ruh-**zorss** /rəˈzɔː(r)s/

Commonly also **ree-sorss**, especially in AM.

Respighi, Ottorino Italian composer
ot-uh-**ree**-noh resp-**ee**-gi /ɒtəˌriːnəʊ
rɛˈspiːgi/

respiratory relating to respiration
ruh-**spirr**-uh-tuh-ri /rəˈspɪrətəri/

Less commonly also **resp-uh-ruh-tri**.

respite rest from something difficult
resp-yt /ˈrɛspʌɪt/

Less commonly also **resp-it**.

res publica state or republic
rayz **puub**-lik-uh /ˌreɪz ˈpʊblɪkə/

restaurant eating-house
rest-uh-ront /ˈrɛstərɒnt/

Commonly also **rest-ruhnt** or
rest-uh-ro(ng).

restaurateur person who owns a
restaurant
rest-uh-ruh-**tur** /ˌrɛstərəˈtəː(r)/

Restormel castle, England
ruh-**stor**-muhl /rəˈstɔː(r)məl/

résumé summary
rez-yuum-ay /ˈrɛzjʊmeɪ/

retable decorated panels above and
behind an altar
ruh-**tay**-buhl /rəˈteɪbəl/

Less commonly also **ree-tay-buhl**.

rete pl. **retia** network of blood vessels or
nerve cells
ree-ti, pl. **ree**-ti-uh /ˈriːti/, pl. /-tiə/

Rethymnon port, Crete
reth-im-non /ˈrɛθɪmnɒn/

Reti chess gambit
ray-ti /ˈreɪti/

retiarius pl. **retiarii** Roman gladiator
who used a net
ret-i-**ar**-i-uhss, pl. ret-i-**ar**-i-y
/ˌrɛtiˈɑːriəs/, pl. /-riʌɪ/
• See LATIN panel.

reticule small handbag
ret-ik-yool /ˈrɛtɪkjuːl/

reticuloendothelial physiological
system
ruh-**tik**-yuul-oh-end-oh-**thee**-li-uhl
/rəˌtɪkjʊləʊɛndəʊˈθiːliəl/

reticulum pl. **reticula** fine network
ruh-**tik**-yuul-uhm, pl. ruh-**tik**-yuul-uh
/rəˈtɪkjʊləm/, pl. /-lə/

retina pl. **retinae** part of the eye
ret-in-uh, pl. **ret**-in-ee /ˈrɛtɪnə/, pl.
/-niː/
• Standard -s plural is also possible.

retinitis pigmentosa eye disease
ret-in-**y**-tiss pig-men-**toh**-suh
/rɛtɪˌnʌɪtɪs ˌpɪgmɛnˈtəʊsə/

retinue group of advisers
ret-in-yoo /ˈrɛtɪnjuː/

retiré ballet step
ruh-**teer**-ay /rəˈtɪəreɪ/

retrochoir area of a cathedral behind
the altar
ret-roh-kwy-uhr /ˈrɛtrəʊˌkwʌɪə(r)/

retroussé turned-up (nose)
ruh-**troo**-say /rəˈtruːseɪ/

retsina Greek wine flavoured with resin
ret-**see**-nuh /rɛtˈsiːnə/

Reuben biblical character
roo-buhn /ˈruːbən/

Réunion island, Indian Ocean
ree-**yoon**-yuhn /riːˈjuːnjən/, French
[reynjõ]
• Established anglicization.

Reuters international news agency
roy-tuhrz /ˈrɔɪtə(r)z/

reveille signal sounded to wake soldiers
ruh-**val**-i /rəˈvali/

AM is **rev-uh-li**.

revelatory revealing something hitherto
unknown
rev-uh-**lay**-tuh-ri /ˌrɛvəˈleɪtəri/

Less commonly also **rev-uh-luh-tuh-ri**.

Revere, Paul American patriot
ruh-**veer** /rəˈvɪə(r)/

reverie dream
rev-uh-ri /ˈrɛvəri/

revers turned-back edge of a garment
ruh-**veer** /rəˈvɪə(r)/

revetment retaining wall
ruh-**vet**-muhnt /rəˈvɛtmənt/

revue light theatrical entertainment
ruh-**vyoo** /rəˈvjuː/

rewarewa New Zealand tree
ray-wuh-ray-wuh /ˈreɪwəˌreɪwə/

Reye's syndrome metabolic disorder
ryz /ˈrʌɪz/

Sometimes also **rayz**.

Reykjavik capital of Iceland
rayk-yuh-veek /ˈreɪkjəviːk/

Reynard name for a fox
ren-ard /ˈrɛnɑː(r)d/

Reynolds, Albert Irish statesman
ren-uhldz /ˈrɛnəldz/

Reynolds, Joshua English painter
ren-uhldz /ˈrɛnəldz/

rhabdomancy dowsing with a rod
rab-duh-man-si /ˈrabdə‚mansi/

rhachis see **rachis**

Rhadamanthus Greek mythological
character
rad-uh-**man**-thuhss /‚radəˈmanθəs/

Rhaeto-Romanic Romance dialects
ree-toh roh-**man**-ik /‚riːtəʊ
rəʊˈmanɪk/

rhapsodic ecstatic
rap-**sod**-ik /rapˈsɒdɪk/

rhatany astringent substance
rat-uh-ni /ˈratəni/

Rhea Greek mythological character
ree-uh /ˈriːə/

rhea flightless bird
ree-uh /ˈriːə/

rhebok (also **reebok**) antelope
ree-bok /ˈriːbɒk/

Rheims see **Reims**

Rhein see **Rhine**

Rheinland-Pfalz see
Rhineland-Palatinate

Rhenish of the Rhine
ren-ish /ˈrɛnɪʃ/

rhenium chemical element
ree-ni-uhm /ˈriːnɪəm/

rheostat electrical instrument
ree-uh-stat /ˈriːəstat/

rhesus baby infant suffering from
haemolytic disease
ree-suhss /ˈriːsəs/

rhetoric art of effective speaking
ret-uh-rik /ˈrɛtərɪk/

rheum watery fluid
room /ruːm/

rheumatoid relating to rheumatism
roo-muh-toyd /ˈruːmətɔɪd/

Rhiannon Welsh girl's name
ri-**an**-uhn /rɪˈanən/

Rhine river, Europe
ryn /rʌɪn/

The German name Rhein is also
pronounced ryn, and the French name Rhin
is pronounced ra(ng).

Rhineland-Palatinate state, Germany
ryn-land puh-**lat**-in-uht /‚rʌɪnland
pəˈlatɪnət/

The German name is Rheinland-Pfalz,
pronounced **ryn**-lant **pfalts**.

rhinitis inflammation of the nose
ry-**ny**-tiss /rʌɪˈnʌɪtɪs/

rhinoplasty plastic surgery on the nose
ry-noh-plast-i /ˈrʌɪnəʊ‚plasti/

rhizome horizontal underground stem
ry-zohm /ˈrʌɪzəʊm/

rho letter of the Greek alphabet
roh /rəʊ/

Rhodes island, Greece
rohdz /rəʊdz/

The Greek name is Ródhos, pronounced
roh-*th*oss.

Rhodesia former country, Africa
roh-**dee**-zi-uh /rəʊˈdiːzɪə/

rhodium chemical element
roh-di-uhm /ˈrəʊdɪəm/

rhododendron shrub
roh-duh-**den**-druhn /‚rəʊdəˈdɛndrən/

Rhodope Mountains mountain
system, Europe
rod-uh-pi /ˈrɒdəpi/

Rhodri Welsh boy's name
rod-ri /ˈrɒdri/

rhomboideus pl. **rhomboidei** back
muscle
rom-**boy**-di-uhss, pl. rom-**boy**-di-y
/rɒmˈbɔɪdɪəs/, pl. /-dʌɪ/

rhombus pl. **rhombi** quadrilateral
rom-buhss, pl. **rom**-by /ˈrɒmbəs/, pl.
/-bʌɪ/
• Standard -es plural is also possible.

Rhondda district, Wales
ron-*th*uh /ˈrɒnðə/

Rhône river, Europe
rohn /rəʊn/

rhotic denoting a variety of English in
which *r* is pronounced after vowels
roh-tik /ˈrəʊtɪk/

Rhuddlan town and castle, Wales
rith-lan /ˈrɪðlan/

Rhum (also **Rum**) island, Scotland
/rʌm/

rhumba see **rumba**

Rhymney town, Wales
rum-ni /ˈrʌmni/

Rhys, Jean Dominican-born British writer
reess /riːs/

rhythm repeated pattern
ri*th*-uhm /ˈrɪðəm/

rial (also **riyal**) currency unit, Iran and Oman
ree-ahl /ˈriːɑːl/

Rialto island in Venice
ri-al-toh /rɪˈaltəʊ/

ribald rude or irreverent
rib-uhld /ˈrɪbəld/

Ribbentrop, Joachim von German Nazi politician
yoh-uh-khim fon rib-uhn-trop
/ˌjəʊəxɪm fɒn ˈrɪbəntrɒp/

Ribera, José de Spanish painter
khoss-ay day rib-air-uh /xɒˌseɪ deɪ rɪˈbɛːrə/

riboflavin vitamin
ry-boh-flay-vin /ˌrʌɪbəʊˈfleɪvɪn/

ribonucleic acid chemical substance
ry-boh-nyoo-klay-ik
/ˌrʌɪbəʊnjuːˈkleɪɪk/

Ricardian relating to Richard I, II, or III
rik-ar-di-uhn /rɪˈkɑː(r)diən/

Ricci tensor set of components in physics
ree-chi /ˈriːtʃi/

Rice, Condoleeza American stateswoman
kon-duh-lee-zuh /kɒndəˈliːzə/

ricercar (also **ricercare**) musical composition
ree-chuhr-kar, ree-chuhr-kar-ay
/ˌriːtʃə(r)ˈkɑː(r), ˌriːtʃə(r)ˈkɑːreɪ/

Richelieu, Cardinal French statesman
reesh-uh-lyoe /riːʃəˈljø/

Richler, Mordecai Canadian writer
mor-duh-ky ritch-luhr /ˌmɔː(r)dəkʌɪ ˈrɪtʃlə(r)/

Richter, Karl German conductor and organist
karl rikh-tuhr /ˌkɑː(r)l ˈrɪçtə(r)/

Richter scale scale for measuring earthquakes
rik-tuhr /ˈrɪktə(r)/

Richthofen, Manfred von German fighter pilot
man-frayt fon rikht-hoh-fuhn
/ˌmanfreɪt fɒn ˈrɪçtˌhəʊfən/

ricin toxic substance

ry-sin /ˈrʌɪsɪn/

ricochet rebound off a surface
rik-uh-shay /ˈrɪkəʃeɪ/

Less commonly also **rik-uh-shet**.

Ricoh office equipment manufacturer
ree-koh /ˈriːkəʊ/

ricotta soft white cheese
rik-ot-uh /rɪˈkɒtə/

Riddell British surname
rid-uhl, rid-el /ˈrɪdəl/, /rɪˈdɛl/

Rie, Lucie Austrian-born British potter
loo-si ree /ˌluːsi ˈriː/

Riefenstahl, Leni German film-maker
lay-ni ree-fuhn-shtahl /ˌleɪni ˈriːfənˌʃtɑːl/

Riel, Louis Canadian political leader
lwee ri-el /ˌlwiː riˈɛl/

riel currency unit, Cambodia
ri-el /ˈriːɛl/

Riemann, Bernhard German mathematician
bairn-hart ree-man /ˌbɛː(r)nhɑː(r)t ˈriːman/

Riesling wine grape
reess-ling /ˈriːslɪŋ/

Rievaulx village and abbey, England
ree-voh /ˈriːvəʊ/

An older anglicized pronunciation, **riv-uhrz**, is also possible, but increasingly less common.

rifampicin antibiotic
rif-amp-iss-in /rɪˈfampɪsɪn/

Riga port, Latvia
ree-guh /ˈriːgə/

rigatoni pasta
rig-uh-toh-ni /ˌrɪgəˈtəʊni/

Rigel star
ry-guhl /ˈrʌɪgəl/

righteous morally justifiable
ry-chuhss /ˈrʌɪtʃəs/

rigmarole lengthy and complicated procedure
rig-muh-rohl /ˈrɪgmərəʊl/

Rigoletto opera by Verdi
rig-uh-let-oh /rɪgəˈlɛtəʊ/

rigor mortis stiffening of the body after death
rig-uhr mor-tiss /ˌrɪgə(r) ˈmɔː(r)tɪs/

Rig Veda Hindu text
rig vay-duh /ˌrɪg ˈveɪdə/

Rijeka port, Croatia
ree-**yek**-uh /riːˈjɛkə/

The Italian name is Fiume, pronounced
fyoo-may.

Rijksmuseum art gallery, Amsterdam
ryks-mue-zay-uhm /ˈrʌɪksmyˌzeɪəm/

rijsttafel rice meal
ryst-tah-fuhl /ˈrʌɪstˌtɑːfəl/

Rikers Island jail, New York
ry-kuhrz /ˈrʌɪkə(r)z/

rikishi sumo wrestler
rik-ish-i /ˈrɪkɪʃi/

Rila Mountains mountains, Bulgaria
ree-luh /ˈriːlə/

Rilke, Rainer Maria Austrian poet
ry-nuhr muh-**ree**-uh **ril**-kuh /ˌrʌɪnə(r)
məˌriːə ˈrɪlkə/

rillettes pâté
ree-yet /ˈriːjɛt/

Rimbaud, Arthur French poet
ar-**tuer** ra(ng)-**boh** /ɑː(r)ˌtyː(r) rɛ̃ˈbəʊ/

Rimet, Jules former president of FIFA
zhuel ree-**may** /ˌʒyl riˈmeɪ/

Rimini port, Italy
rim-in-i /ˈrɪmɪni/

rimonabant weight-loss drug
rim-**on**-uh-bant /rɪˈmɒnəbant/

Rimsky-Korsakov, Nikolai Russian
composer
nik-uh-**ly rim**-ski **kor**-suh-kof /ˌnɪkəˌlʌɪ
ˌrɪmski ˈkɔː(r)səkɒf/

rimy covered with frost
ry-mi /ˈrʌɪmi/

Rincewind fictional character in Terry
Pratchett's *Discworld*
rinss-wind /ˈrɪnswɪnd/

rinderpest disease of ruminants
rin-duhr-pest /ˈrɪndə(r)pɛst/

ringgit currency unit, Malaysia
ring-git /ˈrɪŋɡɪt/

rinkhals (also **ringhals**) cobra
rink-halss /ˈrɪŋkhals/

Rinpoche Buddhist religious teacher
rin-poh-chay /ˈrɪnpəʊtʃeɪ/

Rio Branco city, Brazil
ree-oo **brank**-oo /ˌriːuː ˈbraŋkuː/

Rio de Janeiro port and state, Brazil
ree-oh duh juh-**neer**-oh /ˌriːəʊ də
dʒəˈnɪərəʊ/, Portuguese [ˌriːu dʒi
ʒaˈneiru]
• Established anglicization.

Río de la Plata see Plate, River

Río de Oro region, Africa
ree-oh day **aw**-roh /ˌriːəʊ deɪ ˈɔːrəʊ/

Rio Grande river, US and Mexico
ree-oh **grand** /ˌriːəʊ ˈɡrand/, Spanish
[ˌrio ˈɡrande]

Rio Grande do Norte state, Brazil
ree-oo **grand**-i doo **nor**-ti /ˌriːuː
ˌɡrandi duː ˈnɔː(r)ti/

Rio Grande do Sul state, Brazil
ree-oo **grand**-i doo **sool** /ˌriːuː ˌɡrandi
duː ˈsuːl/

Rioja Spanish wine
ri-**okh**-uh /riˈɒxə/

Rio Muni region, Equatorial Guinea
ree-oh **moo**-ni /ˌriːəʊ ˈmuːni/

Rio Negro river, South America
ree-oh **nay**-groh /ˌriːəʊ ˈneɪɡrəʊ/

ripieno pl. **ripieni** musical term
rip-i-**ay**-noh, pl. rip-i-**ay**-ni
/ˌrɪpiˈeɪnəʊ/, pl. /-ni/
• Standard -s plural is also possible.

Ripon town, England
rip-uhn /ˈrɪpən/

rishi Hindu sage
rish-i /ˈrɪʃi/

risible provoking laughter
riz-ib-uhl /ˈrɪzɪbəl/

Risley prison, England
riz-li /ˈrɪzli/

Risør city, Norway
ree-soer /ˈriːsœ(r)/

Risorgimento Italian unification
movement
riss-or-jim-**en**-toh /rɪˌsɔː(r)dʒɪˈmɛntəʊ/

risotto Italian rice dish
riz-**ot**-oh /rɪˈzɒtəʊ/

risqué slightly indecent
risk-**ay** /rɪˈskeɪ/

ristorante pl. **ristoranti** Italian
restaurant
rist-orr-**an**-tay, pl. rist-orr-**an**-ti
/ˌrɪstɒˈranteɪ/, pl. /-ti/

Ritalin trademark drug
rit-uh-lin /ˈrɪtəlɪn/

ritardando pl. **ritardandi** musical term
rit-ar-**dan**-doh, pl. rit-ar-**dan**-di
/ˌrɪtɑː(r)ˈdandəʊ/, pl. /-di/
• Standard -s plural is also possible.

ritenuto pl. **ritenuti** musical term
rit-en-**oo**-toh, pl. rit-en-**oo**-ti
/ˌrɪtɛˈnuːtəʊ/, pl. /-ti/

• Standard -s plural is also possible.

Rivera, Diego Mexican painter
dyay-goh riv-**air**-uh /ˌdjeɪɡəʊ rɪ'veːrə/

riviera coastal region
riv-i-**air**-uh /ˌrɪvi'ɛːrə/

rivière necklace of gems
riv-i-**air** /ˌrɪvi'ɛː(r)/

Rivne city, Ukraine
riv-nuh /'rɪvnə/

Riyadh capital of Saudi Arabia
ree-**yahd** /riː'jɑːd/

riyal see **rial**

Roaccutane trademark hair-loss drug
roh-**ak**-yuut-ayn /rəʊ'akjʊteɪn/

Roanoke town, US
roh-uh-nohk /'rəʊənəʊk/

robata charcoal grill
rob-**ah**-tuh /rɒ'bɑːtə/

Robbe-Grillet, Alain French novelist
al-**a(ng)** rob gree-**yay** /aˌlɛ̃ rɒb
gri:'jeɪ/

Robben Island island, South Africa
rob-uhn /'rɒbən/

Robert, Paul French lexicographer
pol rob-**air** /ˌpɒl rɒ'bɛː(r)/

Robeson, Paul American singer
rohb-suhn /'rəʊbsən/

Robespierre, Maximilien de French
revolutionary
mak-sim-il-**ya(ng)** duh **rohbz**-pyair
/maksɪmɪ'ljɛ̃ də 'rəʊbzpjɛː(r)/

Robinson Crusoe novel by Daniel
Defoe
kroo-soh /'kruːsəʊ/

rocaille ornamental style
roh-**ky** /rəʊ'kʌɪ/

Rocamadour village, France
rok-am-ad-**oor** /rɒkamaˈdʊə(r)/

Rocha, John English fashion designer
rosh-uh /'rɒʃə/

Roche Swiss pharmaceutical firm
rosh /rɒʃ/

Roche, Barbara English politician
rohtch /rəʊtʃ/

Roche limit astronomical term
rohsh /rəʊʃ/

roche moutonnée rock shaped by
glacial erosion
rosh moo-**ton**-ay /ˌrɒʃ muːˈtɒneɪ/

Rochefort name of several places in
France and Belgium

rosh-**for** /rɒʃ'fɔː(r)/

Rochester town, England
rotch-uh-stuhr /'rɒtʃəstə(r)/

Rochester, Earl of English poet
rotch-uh-stuhr /'rɒtʃəstə(r)/

rochet surplice
rotch-uht /'rɒtʃət/

Rockefeller, John D. American
industrialist
rok-uh-fel-uhr /'rɒkəfɛlə(r)/

rococo ornamental style
ruh-**koh**-koh /rə'kəʊkəʊ/

Roddenberry, Gene American
television producer
rod-uhn-berr-i /'rɒdən,bɛri/

Roden, Claudia Egyptian-born cookery
writer
klaw-di-uh roh-**duhn** /ˌklɔːdiə
'rəʊdən/

rodeo cowboy exhibition
roh-di-oh /'rəʊdiəʊ/

Less commonly also roh-**day**-oh. This latter
pronunciation is also appropriate for the
ballet by Copland, and for Rodeo Drive in
Beverley Hills.

Ródhos see **Rhodes**

Rodin, Auguste French sculptor
oh-**guest** roh-**da(ng)** /əʊˌɡyst rəʊ'dɛ̃/

Rød-Larsen, Terje Norwegian
diplomat
tair-yuh **roed** lar-shuhn /ˌtɛː(r)jə ˌrøːd
'lɑː(r)ʃən/, [ˌtærjə ˌrøːd 'lɑːʃən]

rodomontade boastful talk
rod-oh-mon-**tayd** /ˌrɒdəʊmɒn'teɪd/

Rodrigo, Joaquin Spanish composer
khoh-ak-**een** rod-**ree**-goh /xəʊaˌkiːn
rɒ'driːɡəʊ/, [xoaˌkin ro'ðriɣo]

Rodriguez Zapatero, José Luis see
Zapatero, José Luis Rodriguez

Roeg, Nicolas English film director
rohg /rəʊɡ/

roentgen unit of ionizing radiation
ront-guhn /'rɒntɡən/

Commonly also **runt**-juhn; both are
established anglicizations. See RÖNTGEN,
WILHELM, after whom the unit is named, for
the German pronunciation.

Roeselare town, Belgium
roo-suh-lar-uh /'ruːsələːrə/, Flemish
['ruːsəlaːrə]

Established anglicization. The French name
is Roulers, pronounced roo-**lair**.

rogan josh Indian dish
roh-**guhn johsh** /ˌrəʊgən ˈdʒəʊʃ/

Roget, Peter Mark English scholar
rozh-ay /ˈrɒʒeɪ/

Rogge, Jacques Belgian president of
the International Olympic Committee
zhahk **rokh**-uh /ˌʒɑːk ˈrɒxə/

This is his own pronunciation of this
Flemish surname. French speakers tend to
pronounce this name rog.

Rohan fictional place in *The Lord of the
Rings*
roh-han /ˈrəʊhan/

Rohmer, Eric French film director
err-**eek** rom-**air** /ˌɛˌriːk rɒˈmɛː(r)/

Roh Moo-hyun president of South
Korea
noh moo hyun /ˌnəʊmuːˈhjʌn/

Rohypnol trademark sedative drug
roh-**hip**-nol /rəʊˈhɪpnɒl/

Róisín Irish girl's name
rosh-**een** /rɒˈʃiːn/

Roissy airport in Paris
rwah-**see** /rwɑːˈsi/

Roland Garros see **Garros, Roland**

Rolland, Romain French novelist
rom-**a(ng)** rol-**ah(ng)** /rɒˌmɛ̃ rɒˈlɑ̃/

Rolodex trademark card index
roh-luh-deks /ˈrəʊlədɛks/

romaine cos lettuce
roh-**mayn** /rəʊˈmeɪn/

romaji spelling system used to
transliterate Japanese
roh-muh-ji /ˈrəʊmədʒi/

roman-à-clef coded novel
roh-**mah(ng)** ah klay /rəʊˌmɑ̃ ɑː ˈkleɪ/

Roman de la rose French medieval
poem
roh-**mah(ng)** duh lah rohz /rəʊˌmɑ̃ də
lɑː ˈrəʊz/

Romanesque architectural style
roh-muh-**nesk** /ˌrəʊməˈnɛsk/

Romania (also **Rumania**) country
roo-may-ni-uh /ruːˈmeɪnɪə/

Romanize bring under Roman influence
roh-muh-nyz /ˈrəʊmənʌɪz/

Romano hard cheese
roh-**mah**-noh /rəʊˈmɑːnəʊ/

Romanov Russian dynasty

ruh-**mah**-nuhf /rəˈmɑːnəf/

Romansh language spoken in
Switzerland
roh-**mansh** /rəʊˈmanʃ/

Romany gypsy language
rom-uh-ni /ˈrɒməni/

Commonly also **roh**-muh-ni.

Romberg, Sigmund Hungarian-born
American composer
sig-muhnd **rom**-burg /ˌsɪgmənd
ˈrɒmbəː(r)g/

Romeo Shakespearean character
roh-mi-oh /ˈrəʊmɪəʊ/

However, the Italian pronunciation (suitable
for use with reference to the Bellini opera) is
roh-**may**-oh.

Rommel, Erwin German field marshal
air-veen **rom**-uhl /ˌɛː(r)viːn ˈrɒməl/

Romney, George English portrait
painter
rum-ni /ˈrʌmni/

Romney Marsh region of Kent,
England; also a breed of sheep
rom-ni /ˈrɒmni/

Romulus Roman mythological character
rom-yuul-uhss /ˈrɒmjʊləs/

Ronaldinho Brazilian footballer
ron-al-**jeen**-yoo /rɒnalˈdʒiːnjuː/

Ronaldo Brazilian footballer
ron-al-**doo** /rɒˈnalduː/

The names Ronaldinho and Ronaldo are
commonly also anglicized to ron-al-**dee**-noh
and ron-**al**-doh.

Roncesvalles, Battle of battle in the
Pyrenees
ron-suh-val /ˈrɒnsəval/, Spanish
[ˈronθesˈvaʎes]

Established anglicization. The French form
of the name is Roncevaux, pronounced
ro(ng)ss-**voh**.

rondavel circular African hut
ron-**dah**-vuhl /rɒnˈdɑːvəl/

rond de jambe ballet step
ro(ng) duh zhah(ng)b /ˌrɔ̃ də ˈʒɑ̃b/

ronde dance
rond /rɒnd/

rondeau pl. **rondeaux** poem
ron-doh, pl **ron**-dohz /ˈrɒndəʊ/, pl.
/-əʊz/

Rondônia state, Brazil
ron-**dohn**-yuh /rɒn'dəʊnjə/

rongo-rongo ancient script
rong-goh-**rong**-goh /ˌrɒŋɡəʊ'rɒŋɡəʊ/

ronin wandering samurai
roh-nin /'rəʊnɪn/

ronquil fish
ron-kil /'rɒŋkɪl/

Röntgen, Wilhelm German physicist
vil-helm **roent**-guhn /ˌvɪlhɛlm 'rœntɡən/
• See also **ROENTGEN**.

rooibos South African shrub
roy-boss /'rɔɪbɒs/

Roosevelt, Franklin D. American
statesman
roh-zuh-velt /'rəʊzəvɛlt/

The same pronunciation is used for Eleanor
and Theodore Roosevelt.

Roquefort trademark soft blue cheese
rok-for /'rɒkfɔː(r)/

roquette salad leaves
rok-**et** /rɒ'kɛt/

Roraima mountain, South America
roh-**ry**-muh /rəʊ'rʌɪmə/

rorqual whale
ror-kwuhl /'rɔː(r)kwəl/

Rorschach test psychoanalytic test
ror-shakh /'rɔː(r)ʃax/

Named after Swiss psychiatrist Hermann
Rorschach. Sometimes also anglicized to
ror-shahk.

rosacea facial skin condition
roh-**zay**-shuh /rəʊ'zeɪʃə/

rosaceous relating to rose plants
roh-**zay**-shuhss /rəʊ'zeɪʃəs/

Rosario port, Argentina
roh-**sar**-i-oh /rəʊ'sɑːriəʊ/

rosarium rose garden
roh-**zair**-i-uhm /rəʊ'zɛːriəm/

rosary repetition of prayers
roh-zuh-ri /'rəʊzəri/

Roscoff port, France
rosk-**of** /rɒs'kɒf/

Roscommon county, Republic of
Ireland
rosk-**om**-uhn /rɒs'kɒmən/

rosé light pink wine
roh-zay /'rəʊzeɪ/

roseate rose-coloured
roh-zi-uht /'rəʊzɪət/

Roseau capital of Dominica
roh-**zoh** /rəʊ'zəʊ/

Rosebery, Earl English statesman
rohz-buh-ri /'rəʊzbəri/

rosella parakeet
roh-**zel**-uh /rəʊ'zɛlə/

rosemaling art of painting flower motifs
roh-suh-mah-ling /'rəʊsəˌmɑːlɪŋ/

Rosenthal, Jack English playwright
roh-zuhn-thawl /'rəʊzənθɔːl/

This was his own pronunciation. This
surname can also be pronounced
roh-zuhn-tal, **roh**-zuhn-tahl, or
roh-zuhn-thal, according to individual
preference.

roseola skin rash
roh-**zee**-uh-luh /rəʊ'ziːələ/

Rosetta Stone inscribed stone
roh-**zet**-uh /rəʊ'zɛtə/

Rosh Hashana (also **Rosh Hashanah**)
Jewish festival
rosh huh-**shah**-nuh /ˌrɒʃ hə'ʃɑːnə/

Roshi Buddhist leader of monks
roh-shi /'rəʊʃi/

Rosicrucian member of a secret society
roh-zik-**roo**-shuhn /ˌrəʊzɪ'kruːʃən/

rosin resin
roz-in /'rɒzɪn/

Roskilde port, Denmark
rosk-il-uh /'rɒskɪlə/

rosolio sweet cordial
roh-**zoh**-li-oh /rəʊ'zəʊliəʊ/

Rossellini, Roberto Italian film
director
rob-**air**-toh ross-uh-**lee**-ni /rɒˌbɛː(r)təʊ ˌrɒsə'liːni/

Rossetti, Dante Gabriel English
painter and poet
dan-ti **gay**-bri-uhl ruh-**zet**-i /ˌdanti ˌɡeɪbriəl rə'zɛti/

The same pronunciation is used for
Christina Rossetti.

Rossignol French ski equipment
manufacturers
ross-in-**yol** /rɒsɪ'njɒl/

Rossini, Gioacchino Italian composer
joh-uh-**kee**-noh ross-**ee**-ni /dʒəʊəˌkiːnəʊ rɒ'siːni/

Rosslare port, Republic of Ireland
ross-lair /rɒsˈlɛː(r)/

Rostand, Edmond French dramatist
ed-mo(ng) ross-tah(ng) /ˌɛdˌmɔ̃ rɒˈstɑ̃/

roster list
rost-uhr /ˈrɒstə(r)/

rösti Swiss potato dish
roesh-ti /ˈrøːʃti/

Rostock port, Germany
rost-ok /ˈrɒstɒk/

Rostov port, Russia
rost-of /ˈrɒstɒf/, [rəˈstɔf]
• Established anglicization.

Roswell town, US
roz-wel /ˈrɒzwɛl/

Roth, Philip American writer
roth /rɒθ/

Rotherham town, England
roth-uhr-uhm /ˈrɒðərəm/

Rothko, Mark American painter
roth-koh /ˈrɒθkəʊ/

Rothschild, Meyer Amschel German
financier
my-uhr am-shuhl roht-shilt /ˌmaɪə(r)
ˌamʃəl ˈrəʊtʃɪlt/

Many other people with this surname
pronounce it **rothss-chyld**, an anglicized
pronunciation.

roti Indian flat bread
roh-ti /ˈrəʊti/

rotisserie restaurant
roh-tiss-uh-ri /rəˈtɪsəri/

Rotorua city, New Zealand
roh-tuh-roo-uh /ˌrəʊtəˈruːə/

Rotterdam city, Netherlands
rot-uhr-dam /ˈrɒtə(r)dam/

Rottweiler breed of dog
rot-vy-luhr /ˈrɒtvaɪlə(r)/

Rouault, Georges French painter and
engraver
zhorzh roo-oh /ˌʒɔː(r)ʒ ruːˈəʊ/

Roubaix city, France
roo-bay /ruːˈbeɪ/

rouble currency unit, Russia
roob-uhl /ˈruːbəl/

roucou orange-red dye, annatto
roo-koo /ruːˈkuː/

roué debauched man
roo-ay /ˈruːeɪ/

Rouen port, France
roo-ah(ng) /ruːˈɑ̃/

Sometimes also **roo-on**, an older
anglicization.

rouge cosmetic
roozh /ruːʒ/

rouille Provençal sauce
roo-i /ˈruːi/

roulade dish in the form of a roll
roo-lahd /ruːˈlɑːd/

roulement movement of troops or
equipment
rool-mo(ng) /ˈruːlmɔ̃/

Roulers see **Roeselare**

Roumania see **Romania**

roundelay simple song
rown-duh-lay /ˈraʊndəleɪ/

roup auction
rowp /raʊp/

roup disease of poultry
roop /ruːp/

Rous form of tumour
rowss /raʊs/

Rousse (also **Ruse**) city, Bulgaria
roo-suh /ˈruːsə/

Rousseau, Henri French painter
ah(ng)-ree roo-soh /ˌɑ̃ˌriː ruːˈsəʊ/

The same pronunciation is used for
Jean-Jacques and Théodore Rousseau.

Roussel, Athina Greek heiress
ath-ee-nuh roo-sel /aθˌiːnə ruːˈsɛl/

Roussillon former province, France
roo-see-yo(ng) /ruːsiːˈjɔ̃/

roustabout casual labourer
rowst-uh-bowt /ˈraʊstəbaʊt/

rout disorderly retreat
rowt /raʊt/

router cutting tool
row-tuhr /ˈraʊtə(r)/

router computer device
roo-tuhr /ˈruːtə(r)/

routier French medieval mercenary
roo-ti-ay /ˈruːtieɪ/

Routledge English publishers
rowt-luhj /ˈraʊtlədʒ/

Rovaniemi town, Finland
rov-uhn-yem-i /ˈrɒvəˌnjɛmi/

rowan tree
roh-uhn /ˈrəʊən/

Less commonly also **row-uhn**.

Rowlandson, Thomas English painter
roh-luhnd-suhn /ˈrəʊləndsən/

Rowling, J. K. English novelist
roh-ling /ˈrəʊlɪŋ/

rowlock fitting on a boat
rol-uhk /ˈrɒlək/

Rowntree, Joseph English
philanthropist
rown-tree /ˈraʊntriː/

Roxburghshire former county, Scotland
roks-buh-ruh-shuhr /ˈrɒksbərəʃə(r)/

Roy, Arundhati Indian writer
uh-**roon**-dut-i **roy** /əˌruːndʌti ˈrɔɪ/

Ruaridh Scottish boy's name
raw-ri /ˈrɔːri/

Rubaiyat of Omar Khayyam
collection of poems
roo-by-**yaht** oh-mar ky-**ahm**
/ruːbʌɪˈjaːt ˌəʊmɑː(r) kʌɪˈɑːm/

Rub' al Khali desert, Arabian peninsula
roob uhl **khah**-li /ˌruːb əl ˈxɑːli/

rubato pl. **rubati** musical term
ruub-**ah**-toh, pl. ruub-**ah**-ti /rʊˈbɑːtəʊ,
pl. /-ti/
• Standard -s plural is also possible.

Rubbra, Edmund English composer
rub-ruh /ˈrʌbrə/

rubella German measles
roo-**bel**-uh /rʊˈbɛlə/

Rubens, Peter Paul Flemish painter
roo-buhnz /ˈruːbənz/, [ˈryːbəns]
• Established anglicization.

rubeola measles
ruub-**ee**-uh-luh /rʊˈbiːələ/

rubescent reddening
ruub-**ess**-uhnt /rʊˈbɛsənt/

Rubicon stream, Italy
roo-bik-uhn /ˈruːbɪkən/

rubidium chemical element
ruub-**id**-i-uhm /rʊˈbɪdiəm/

Rubik's cube trademark puzzle
roo-biks /ˈruːbɪks/

Rubinstein, Anton Russian composer
uhn-**ton** ruub-in-**shtayn** /ənˌtɒn
ˌrʊbɪnˈʃteɪn/

Rubinstein, Artur Polish-born
American pianist
ar-toor **roo**-bin-styn /ˌɑː(r)tʊə(r)
ˈruːbɪnstʌɪn/

rubric heading on a document
roo-brik /ˈruːbrɪk/

ruche frill or pleat

roosh /ruːʃ/

rucksack bag with shoulder straps
ruk-sak /ˈrʌksak/

Less commonly also **ruuk**-sak.

rucola rocket (plant)
roo-kuh-luh /ˈruːkələ/

Rudaki Persian poet
roo-**dak**-ee /rʊˈdaːkiː/

rudbeckia plant
rood-**bek**-i-uh /ruːdˈbɛkiə/

Rudra minor Hindu god
ruud-ruh /ˈrʊdrə/

ruffe fish
ruf /rʌf/

rufiyaa currency unit, Maldives
roo-**fee**-yah /ˈruːfiːjaː/

rufous reddish brown
roo-fuhss /ˈruːfəs/

Rügen island, Germany
rue-guhn /ˈryːgən/

rugose wrinkled
roo-gohss /ˈruːgəʊs/

Commonly also **ruug**-ohss.

Ruhr region, Germany
roor /rʊə(r)/

Ruisdael, Jacob van (also **Ruysdael**)
Dutch painter
yah-kop vun **roeyss**-dahl /ˌjɑkɒp vʌn
ˈrœɪsdɑːl/
• See DUTCH panel.

Ruislip suburb of London
ryss-lip /ˈrʌɪslɪp/

Ruiz de Alarcón y Mendoza, Juan
Mexican dramatist
khwan ruu-**eess** day al-ar-**kon** ee
men-**doh**-suh /ˌxwan rʊˌiːs deɪ
ˌalɑː(r)ˈkɒn iː mɛnˌdəʊsə/

Rukh Ukrainian nationalist movement
rookh /ruːx/

rukh mythical bird
rook /ruːk/

Rum see Rhum

Rumania see Romania

rumba (also **rhumba**) dance
rum-buh /ˈrʌmbə/

Rumelia former Ottoman territories
roo-**mee**-li-uh /ruːˈmiːliə/

rumen pl. **rumina** first stomach of a ruminant
roo-men, pl. **roo**-min-uh /ˈruːmɛn/, pl. /-mɪnə/
• Standard -s plural is also possible.

Rumi, Jalal al-Din Sufi poet
juh-**lahl** uh-**deen** roo-**mee** /dʒə,lɑːl ə,diːn ruːˈmiː/

Rumsfeld, Donald American politician
rumz-felt /ˈrʌmzfɛlt/

rune letter of an ancient alphabet
roon /ruːn/

Runnymede meadow near Windsor, England
run-im-eed /ˈrʌnɪmiːd/

rupee currency unit, India and several other countries
roo-**pee** /ruːˈpiː/

rupiah currency unit, Indonesia
roo-**pee**-uh /ruːˈpiːə/

Ruritania imaginary kingdom
roor-it-**ay**-ni-uh /ˌrʊərɪˈteɪnɪə/

Rusedski, Greg Canadian-born British tennis player
roo-**zet**-ski /ruːˈzɛtski/

Ruse see **Rousse**

ruse trick
rooz /ruːz/

Rushdie, Salman Indian-born British novelist
sal-**mahn ruush**-di /sal,mɑːn ˈrʊʃdi/

Rusholme suburb of Manchester
rush-hohm /ˈrʌʃhəʊm/

rus in urbe countryside within a city
rooss in **oor**-bay /ˌruːs ɪn ˈʊə(r)beɪ/

Russify make Russian
russ-if-y /ˈrʌsɪfaɪ/

Russo, Rene American actress
ruh-**nay** roo-**soh** /rə,neɪ ˈruːsəʊ/

russula toadstool
russ-uh-luh /ˈrʌsələ/

rutabaga swede
roo-tuh-**bay**-guh /ˌruːtəˈbeɪɡə/

Rutgers American university
rut-guhrz /ˈrʌtɡə(r)z/

Ruthenia region, Europe
roo-**thee**-ni-uh /ruːˈθiːnɪə/

ruthenium chemical element
ruuth-**ee**-ni-uhm /ruːˈθiːnɪəm/

Rutherford, Ernest New Zealand physicist
ruth-uhr-fuhrd /ˈrʌðə(r)fə(r)d/

rutherfordium chemical element
ru**th**-uhr-**for**-di-uhm /ˌrʌðə(r)ˈfɔː(r)dɪəm/

Ruthven Scottish family name
riv-uhn /ˈrɪvən/

However, Ruthven Barracks and Ruthven village in the Scottish Highlands are pronounced **ruth**-vuhn.

rutilant glittering with red or golden light
root-il-uhnt /ˈruːtɪlənt/

Ruwenzori mountain range, Africa
roo-wuhn-**zaw**-ri /ˌruːwənˈzɔːri/

Ruy Blas overture by Mendelssohn
rwee **blass** /ˌrwiː ˈblas/

Ruysdael, Jacob van see **Ruisdael, Jacob van**

Rwanda country
roo-**and**-uh /ruˈandə/

Ryazan city, Russia
ryuh-**zahn** /ˌrjəˈzɑːn/

Rybinsk city, Russia
rib-insk /ˈrɪbɪnsk/

Rydberg, Johannes Swedish physicist
yoo-**han**-uhss **rued**-bairg /juː,hanəs ˈryːdbɛː(r)ɡ/, [juː,hannɛs ˈryːdbærj]

Rydberg atoms and the Rydberg constant are anglicized to **rid**-burg.

Ryder, Sue English philanthropist
ry-duhr /ˈraɪdə(r)/

Ryle, Martin English astronomer
ryl /ˈraɪl/

ryokan Japanese inn
ryoh-kan /ˈrjəʊkan/

Rysy peak, Tatra Mountains
riss-i /ˈrɪsi/

ryu Japanese style of art
ryoo /rjuː/

Ryukyu Islands islands, western Pacific
ryoo-kyoo /ˈrjuːkjuː/

S

Saadi see **Sādi**

saag spinach (Indian)
sahg /sɑːɡ/

Saakashvili, Mikheil Georgian president
mee-khayl **sah**-kuhsh-vil-i /ˌmiːxeɪl ˈsɑːʃəʃvɪli/

Saale river, Germany
zah-luh /ˈzɑːlə/

Saanen breed of goat
sah-nuhn /ˈsɑːnən/

Saarbrücken city, Germany
zar-**bruek**-uhn /zɑː(r)ˈbrʏkən/

Commonly also anglicized to
sar-**bruuk**-uhn.

Saarland state, Germany
zar-lant /ˈzɑː(r)lant/

Saas Fee resort, Switzerland
zahss **fay** /ˌzɑːs ˈfeɪ/

Saatchi, Charles English gallery owner
sah-chi /ˈsɑːtʃi/

Saba island, Caribbean
sah-buh /ˈsɑːbə/

Sabaean ancient Semitic people
sab-**ee**-uhn /saˈbiːən/

Sabah state, Malaysia
sub-uh /ˈsʌbə/

Sabaoth hosts of heaven
sab-**ay**-ot /saˈbeɪɒt/

Sometimes also **sab**-ay-ot, especially when
sung in hymns etc.

Sabellian ancient Italian people
suh-**bel**-i-uhn /səˈbeliən/

Sabhal mor Ostaig Scottish Gaelic college
soh-uhl mor **ost**-ayk /ˌsəʊəl mɔː(r) ˈɒsteɪk/
• See GAELIC panel.

Sabine ancient Italian ethnic group
sab-yn /ˈsabʌɪn/

Sabine river, US
suh-**been** /səˈbiːn/

Sabin vaccine

say-bin /ˈseɪbɪn/

sabot clog shoe
sab-**oh** /saˈbəʊ/

sabotage deliberately destroy
sab-uh-tahzh /ˈsabɑːʒ/

saboteur person who engages in sabotage
sab-uh-**tur** /ˌsabəˈtəː(r)/

sabra Jew born in Israel
sab-ruh /ˈsabrə/

sabreur cavalryman using a sabre
sab-**rur** /saˈbrəː(r)/

sabzi vegetables (Indian)
sub-zi /ˈsʌbzi/

Sacajawea American Indian woman explorer
sak-uh-juh-**wee**-uh /ˌsakədʒəˈwiːə/

The spelling and translation of her name are
disputed; the less common spelling
Sacagawea is pronounced either as above or
as sak-ag-uh-**wee**-uh.

saccade rapid movement of the eye
sak-**ahd** /saˈkɑːd/

saccharin (also **saccharine**) sugar substitute
sak-uh-rin /ˈsakərɪn/

sacerdotal relating to priests
sass-uhr-**doh**-tuhl /ˌsasə(r)ˈdəʊtəl/

Sometimes also sak-uhr-**doh**-tuhl or
satch-uhr-**doh**-tuhl.

sachem chief
say-chuhm /ˈseɪtʃəm/

Sachertorte chocolate gateau
zakh-uhr-tor-tuh /ˈzaxə(r)ˌtɔː(r)tə/

Sachs, Hans German poet and dramatist
hanss **zaks** /ˌhans ˈzaks/

Sachsen see **Saxony**

Sachsen-Anhalt see **Saxony-Anhalt**

sackbut early musical instrument
sak-but /ˈsakbʌt/

sacrament ceremony
sak-ruh-muhnt /ˈsakrəmənt/

Sacramento river, US
sak-ruh-**men**-toh /ˌsakrəˈmɛntəʊ/

Sacranie, Iqbal Malawi-born British
Muslim campaigner
ik-bahl suh-**krah**-ni /ˌɪkbɑːl səˈkrɑːni/

sacré bleu French expression of surprise
sak-ray **bloe** /ˌsakreɪ ˈblø/

sacrilege violation of something sacred
sak-ril-ij /ˈsakrɪlɪdʒ/

sacristy room in a church
sak-rist-i /ˈsakrɪsti/

sacroiliac relating to the sacrum and the
ilium
say-kroh-**il**-i-ak /ˌseɪkrəʊˈɪliak/

sacrosanct too important to be
interfered with
sak-ruh-sankt /ˈsakrəsaŋkt/

sacrum bone in the lower back
say-kruhm /ˈseɪkrəm/

Sadat, Anwar al- (also **es-Sadat**)
Egyptian statesman
un-wuhr uh-suh-**dat** /ˌʌnwə(r)
əsəˈdat/
• See ARABIC panel.

Saddam Hussein see **Hussein,**
Saddam

Sadducee member of a Jewish sect
sad-yuuss-ee /ˈsadjʊsiː/

Sade, Comte de French writer
ko(ng)t duh **sahd** /kɔ̃t də ˈsɑːd/

Sade Nigerian-born British singer
shah-day /ˈʃɑːdeɪ/

sadhu Indian holy man
sah-doo /ˈsɑːduː/

Sādi (also **Saadi**) Persian poet
sah-**dee** /sɑːˈdiː/

sadomasochism sexual practice
say-doh-**mass**-uh-kiz-uhm
/ˌseɪdəʊˈmasəkɪzəm/

Sadr City city, Iraq
sad-uhr /ˈsadə(r)/

Sadr, Moqtada al- Iraqi Shia leader
mook-**tad**-uh uh-**sad**-uhr /muːkˌtadə
əˈsadə(r)/

Safavid Persian dynasty
saf-uh-vid /ˈsafəvɪd/

Saffron Walden town, England
saf-ruhn **wawl**-duhn /ˌsafrən
ˈwɔːldən/

saga long story
sah-guh /ˈsɑːɡə/

sagacious having good judgement

suh-**gay**-shuhss /səˈɡeɪʃəs/

sagacity wisdom
suh-**gass**-it-i /səˈɡasɪti/

Sagan, Carl American astronomer
say-guhn /ˈseɪɡən/

Sagan, Françoise French writer
frah(ng)-**swahz** sag-ah(ng) /frɑ̃ˌswɑːz
saˈɡɑ̃/

Sagitta small constellation
suh-**jit**-uh /səˈdʒɪtə/

Sagittarius large constellation
saj-it-**air**-i-uhss /ˌsadʒɪˈtɛːriəs/

sago edible starch
say-goh /ˈseɪɡəʊ/

saguaro giant cactus
suh-**gwah**-roh /səˈɡwɑːrəʊ/

Saguia el Hamra intermittent river,
Western Sahara
suh-**gee**-uh el **ham**-ruh /səˌɡiːə ɛl
ˈhamrə/

Saha, Meghnad Indian physicist
mayg-nud suh-**hah** /ˌmeɪɡnʌd səˈhɑː/

Sahara desert, North Africa
suh-**har**-uh /səˈhɑːrə/

Sahel region, North Africa
suh-**hel** /səˈhɛl/

sahib Indian form of address for a man
sahb /sɑːb/

Sometimes also **sah-hib**.

Sahiwal breed of cattle
sah-hiv-ahl /ˈsɑːhɪvɑːl/

sai Japanese dagger
sy /sʌɪ/

Said, Edward Palestinian-American
critic
sah-**eed** /sɑːˈiːd/

Saigon city, Vietnam
sy-**gon** /sʌɪˈɡɒn/

saint person acknowledged as holy
saynt /seɪnt/

When 'saint' (or 'St') appears before a name,
it is usually pronounced suhnt.

St Albans city, England
suhnt **awl**-buhnz /sənt ˈɔːlbənz/

St Asaph city, Wales
suhnt **ass**-uhf /sənt ˈasəf/

St Briavels village, England
suhnt **brev**-uhlz /sənt ˈbrɛvəlz/

St Croix island, Caribbean
suhnt **kroy** /sənt ˈkrɔɪ/

Saint-Denis suburb, Paris
sa(ng) duh-**nee** /ˌsɛ̃ dəˈniː/

Sainte-Beuve, Charles French critic
and writer
sharl sa(ng)t **boev** /ˌʃɑː(r)l sɛt ˈbœv/

St-Émilion town, France
sa(ng)t ay-mil-**yo(ng)** /ˌsɛt eɪmɪlˈjɔ̃/

St-Étienne an industrial city in SE
central France, south-west of Lyons
sa(ng)t ay-**tyen** /ˌsɛt eɪˈtjɛn/

Saint-Exupéry, Antoine de French
writer and aviator
ah(ng)-**twahn** duh sa(ng)t
eg-zue-pay-**ree** /ˌɑ̃ˌtwɑːn də sɛt
ɛgzupeɪˈriː/

St Gotthard Pass mountain pass in the
Alps
suhnt **got**-uhrd /sənt ˈɡɒtə(r)d/,
German [zankt ˈɡɔthart]
• Established anglicization.

St Helena island, South Atlantic
suhnt huh-**lee**-nuh /sənt həˈliːnə/
• See also **Helena, St**.

St Helier capital of Jersey
suhnt **hel**-i-uhr /sənt ˈhɛliə(r)/

St Kilda island group, Scotland
suhnt **kil**-duh /sənt ˈkɪldə/

Saint Laurent, Yves French couturier
eev sa(ng) lorr-**ah(ng)** /ˌiːv ˌsɛ̃ lɒˈrɑ̃/

St Leger horse race
suhnt **lej**-uhr /sənt ˈlɛdʒə(r)/

St Lucia country, Caribbean
suhnt **loosh**-uh /sənt ˈluːʃə/

St-Malo port, France
sa(ng) mah-**loh** /sɛ̃ mɑːˈləʊ/

St Martin island, Caribbean
sa(ng) mar-**ta(ng)** /sɛ̃ mɑː(r)ˈtɛ̃/

St Moritz resort, Switzerland
sa(ng) morr-**its** /sɛ̃ mɒˈrɪts/

St-Nazaire port, France
sa(ng) naz-**air** /sɛ̃ naˈzɛː(r)/

St Petersburg city, Russia
suhnt **peet**-uhrz-burg
/sənt ˈpiːtə(r)zbə(r)ɡ/, [saŋkt
pʲɪtʲɪrˈburk]
• Established anglicization.

St Pölten city, Austria
zankt **poel**-tuhn /zankt ˈpœltən/

Saint-Saëns, Camille French
composer
kam-ee sa(ng) **sah(ng)ss** /kaˌmiː
sɛ̃ ˈsɑ̃s/

• See **FRENCH** panel.

Saint-Simon, Comte de French social
reformer
ko(ng)t duh sa(ng) see-**mo(ng)** /ˌkɔ̃t
də ˌsɛ̃ siːˈmɔ̃/

St Sophia Byzantine monument
suhnt soh-**fee**-uh /sənt səʊˈfiːə/

St-Tropez resort, France
sa(ng) troh-**pay** /ˌsɛ̃ trəʊˈpeɪ/

St Vincent island, Caribbean
suhnt **vin**-suhnt /sənt ˈvɪnsənt/

Saipan islands, Pacific
sy-**pan** /sʌɪˈpan/

saith says (archaic third person singular)
seth /sɛθ/

saithe fish
sayth /seɪθ/

Saiva branch of modern Hinduism
sy-vuh /ˈsʌɪvə/

Sakai city, Japan
sah-ky /ˈsɑːkʌɪ/

Sakamoto, Ryuichi Japanese composer
ryoo-itch-i sak-uh-**moh**-toh /ˌrjuːɪtʃi
sakəˈməʊtəʊ/

sake Japanese alcoholic drink
sak-ay /ˈsakeɪ/

saker large Eurasian falcon
say-kuhr /ˈseɪkə(r)/

Sakha, Republic of official name for
Yakutia
sah-kuh /ˈsɑːkə/

Sakhalin island, Russia
sak-uh-**leen** /ˌsakəˈliːn/

Sakharov, Andrei Russian physicist
and civil rights campaigner
and-**ray sakh**-uh-ruhf /anˌdreɪ
ˈsaxərəf/

Saki British short-story writer
sah-ki /ˈsɑːki/

salaam aleikum greeting in many
Arabic-speaking and Muslim countries
suh-**lahm** uh-**lay**-kuum /səˌlɑːm
əˈleɪkʊm/

salacious unduly interested in sex
suh-**lay**-shuhss /səˈleɪʃəs/

Saladin sultan of Egypt and Syria
sal-uh-din /ˈsalədɪn/

Established anglicization of Salah al-Din, an
Arabic honorific title for which an
acceptable anglicized pronunciation would
be sal-**ah**-uh-din.

Salafi member of an orthodox Muslim
sect
suh-**lah**-fi /sə'lɑːfi/

salal heather plant
suh-**lal** /sə'lal/

Salam, Abdus Pakistani physicist
ab-duuss suh-**lahm** /ˌabdʊs sə'lɑːm/

Salamanca city, Spain
sal-am-**ank**-uh /ˌsalə'maŋkə/

salamander newt-like amphibian
sal-uh-man-duhr /'saləˌmandə(r)/

Salamis island, Greece
sal-uh-miss /'saləmɪs/

salat ritual prayer of Muslims
sal-**aht** /sə'lɑːt/

Salazar, António de Oliveira
Portuguese statesman
an-**tohn**-yoo di ol-iv-**ay**-ruh
suh-luh-**zar** /anˌtɒnju di ɒlɪ'veɪrə
sələ'zɑː(r)/

salbutamol synthetic compound related
to aspirin
sal-**byoo**-tuh-mol /sal'bjuːtəmɒl/

salchow jump in figure skating
sal-koh /'salkəʊ/

Salem city, US
say-luhm /'seɪləm/

Salerno port, Italy
sal-**air**-no /sə'lɛː(r)nəʊ/

Salesian relating to St Francis de Sales
suh-**lee**-zi-uhn /sə'liːziən/

Salford city, England
sawl-fuhrd /'sɔːlfə(r)d/

salicional organ stop
suh-**lish**-uh-nuhl /sə'lɪʃənəl/

salicylic acid bitter compound
sal-**iss**-il-ik /ˌsalɪ'sɪlɪk/

salient most noticeable or important
say-li-uhnt /'seɪliənt/

Salieri, Antonio Italian composer
an-**tohn**-yoh sal-**yair**-i /anˌtəʊnjəʊ
sal'jɛːri/

salina salt lake or marsh
suh-**ly**-nuh /sə'lʌɪnə/

saline containing salt
say-lyn /'seɪlʌɪn/

There are several places worldwide called
Saline. The place in Scotland is pronounced
sal-in, in Italy sal-**ee**-nay, and in the US
suh-**leen**.

Salinger, J. D. American writer

Salisbury city, England
sawlz-buh-ri /'sɔːlzbəri/

Salish American Indian ethnic group
say-lish /'seɪlɪʃ/

Salk, Jonas American microbiologist
joh-nuhss **sawlk** /ˌdʒəʊnəs 'sɔːlk/

Sallust Roman historian and politician
sal-uhst /'saləst/

salmanazar large wine bottle
sal-muh-**nay**-zuhr /ˌsalmə'neɪzə(r)/

Salmond, Alex Scottish politician
sam-uhnd /'saimənd/

salmonella pl. **salmonellae** bacterium
sal-muh-**nel**-uh, pl. sal-muh-**nel**-ee
/ˌsalmə'nɛlə/, pl. /-liː/

Salome biblical character
suh-**loh**-may /sə'ləʊmeɪ/

Oscar Wilde's play *Salomé* is usually
pronounced **sal**-oh-may, and the Strauss
opera based on it is given the German
pronunciation **zah**-loh-may.

Salonen, Esa-Pekka Finnish conductor
ess-uh **pek**-uh **sal**-on-uhn /ˌɛsə ˌpɛkə
'salɒnən/

Salonica former name of Thessaloniki
suh-**lon**-ik-uh /sə'lɒnɪkə/

Salop former name of Shropshire
sal-uhp /'saləp/

salopettes trousers with shoulder straps
sal-uh-**pets** /ˌsalə'pɛts/

salpingectomy surgical removal of the
Fallopian tubes
sal-pin-**jek**-tuh-mi /ˌsalpɪn'dʒɛktəmi/

salpingostomy surgical unblocking of a
Fallopian tube
sal-ping-**gost**-uh-mi /ˌsalpɪŋ'ɡɒstəmi/

salsa Latin American dance music
sal-suh /'salsə/

salsify edible plant
sal-sif-i /'salsɪfi/

salt white crystalline substance
sawlt /sɔːlt/

Commonly also solt. This variation in
pronunciation applies to a wide range of
words spelled with *al* (e.g. Salisbury,
Walter).

saltarello energetic dance
sal-tuh-**rel**-oh /ˌsaltə'rɛləʊ/

Saltillo city, Mexico
sal-**tee**-yoh /sal'tiːjəʊ/

saltimbocca Italian dish
sal-tim-**bok**-uh /ˌsaltɪm'bɒkə/

saltine savoury biscuit
sawl-**teen** /sɔːl'tiːn/

saltire diagonal cross
sawl-ty-uhr /'sɔːltʌɪə(r)/

saltpetre potassium nitrate
sawlt-**peet**-uhr /sɔːlt'piːtə(r)/

salubrious health-giving
suh-**loo**-bri-uhss /sə'luːbrɪəs/

salud 'cheers' (Spanish)
sal-**ooth** /sa'luːð/

saluki breed of dog
suh-**loo**-ki /sə'luːki/

salut 'cheers', 'hi' (French)
sal-**ue** /sa'ly/

salutary producing good effects
sal-yuut-uh-ri /'saljʊtəri/

Salvador port, Brazil
sal-vad-**or** /salva'dɔː(r)/

Salvadorean relating to El Salvador
sal-vuh-**dor**-i-uhn /ˌsalvə'dɔːriən/

Salve Regina Roman Catholic hymn
sal-vay ruh-**jee**-nuh /ˌsalveɪ rə'dʒiːnə/

sal volatile scented solution of
ammonium carbonate in alcohol
sal vuh-**lat**-il-i /ˌsal və'latɪli/

salwar loose, pleated trousers; also called
shalwar
sul-**war** /sʌl'wɑː(r)/

Salyut Soviet manned space station
suhl-**yoot** /sə'ljuːt/

Salzburg city, Austria
salts-burg /'saltsbəː(r)g/, German
/'zaltsbʊrk/
• Established anglicization.

Salzgitter city, Germany
zalts-git-uhr /'zalts,gɪtə(r)/

Salzkammergut resort area, Austria
zalts-kam-uhr-goot
/'zaltskamə(r),guːt/

samadhi state of concentration achieved
through meditation
sum-**ah**-di /sʌ'mɑːdi/

Samar island, Philippines
sam-ar /'sɑːmɑː(r)/

Samara city, Russia
suh-**mar**-uh /sə'mɑːrə/

Samaranch, Juan Antonio Spanish
former president of the International
Olympic Committee

khwan an-**tohn**-yoh sam-arr-**ang**
/xwan an,təʊnjəʊ sama'raŋ/

Samaria ancient city, Palestine
suh-**mair**-i-uh /sə'mɛːriə/

Samarinda city, Indonesia
sam-uh-**rind**-uh /ˌsamə'rɪndə/

samarium chemical element
suh-**mair**-i-uhm /sə'mɛːriəm/

Samarkand (also **Samarqand**) city,
Uzbekistan
sam-ar-**kand** /ˌsamɑː(r)'kand/

Samarra city, Iraq
suh-**mar**-uh /sə'mɑːrə/

Sama Veda Hindu text
sah-muh vay-duh /'sɑːmə ,veɪdə/

sambal spicy relish
sam-bal /'sambal/

sambhar spicy lentil dish
sahm-bar /'sɑːmbɑː(r)/

sambuca aniseed-flavoured liqueur
sam-**boo**-kuh /sam'buːkə/

samfu Chinese trouser suit
sam-foo /'samfuː/

Samhain Celtic winter festival
sah-win /'sɑːwɪn/

Sami Scandinavian ethnic group
sah-mi /'sɑːmi/

samisen (also **shamisen**) Japanese lute
sam-i-sen /'samisɛn/

samite rich silk fabric
sam-yt /'samʌɪt/

samizdat clandestine copying and
distribution of banned literature
sam-iz-dat /'samɪzdat/

Samoa islands, Polynesia
suh-**moh**-uh /sə'məʊə/

Samos island, Greece
say-moss /'seɪmɒs/, ['sɑːmɒs]
• Established anglicization.

samosa triangular savoury pastry
suh-**moh**-suh /sə'məʊsə/

samovar tea urn
sam-uh-**var** /ˌsamə'vɑː(r)/

Samoyed Siberian ethnic group
sam-**oy**-ed /sam'ɔɪɛd/

Sampdoria Italian football club
samp-**daw**-ri-uh /samp'dɔːriə/

samphire plant
sam-fy-uhr /'samfʌɪə(r)/

samsara material world
sum-**sah**-ruh /sʌm'sɑːrə/

samskara Hindu purification rite
sum-**skah**-ruh /sʌmˈskɑːrə/

Samson Agonistes poem by Milton
sam-suhn ag-uh-**nist**-eez /ˌsamsən
agəˈnɪstiːz/

Samsung Korean electronics company
sam-sung /ˈsamsʌŋ/

samurai member of a Japanese military
caste
sam-uu-ry /ˈsamʊrʌɪ/

Sana'a (also **Sanaa**) capital of Yemen
san-ah /ˈsanɑː/

San Andreas fault fault line, California
san and-**ray**-uhss /ˌsan anˈdreɪəs/

Sancerre white wine
sah(ng)-**sair** /sɑ̃ˈsɛː(r)/

Sanchi archaeological site, India
sun-chi /ˈsʌntʃi/

Sancho Panza fictional character in
Don Quixote
san-choh **pan**-zuh /ˌsantʃəʊ ˈpanzə/
• Established anglicization.

Sanctus part of the Mass
sank-tuuss /ˈsaŋktʊs/

Sand, George French novelist
zhorzh **sah(ng)** /ˌʒɔ(r)ʒ ˈsɑ̃/

sandhi phonological process
sun-di /ˈsʌndi/

San Diego city, US
san di-**ay**-goh /ˌsan diˈeɪɡəʊ/

Sandinista member of a Nicaraguan
political organization
sand-i-**neest**-uh /ˌsandiˈniːstə/

sandiver scum on molten glass
san-div-uhr /ˈsandɪvə(r)/

Sandringham House British royal
residence
sand-ring-uhm /ˈsandrɪŋəm/

San Francisco city, US
san fran-**sisk**-oh /ˌsan franˈsɪskəʊ/

Sangatte immigration centre, France
sah(ng)-**gat** /sɑ̃ˈgat/

sang-de-boeuf deep red colour
sah(ng) duh **boef** /ˌsɑ̃ də ˈbœf/

sangfroid composure
sah(ng)-**frwah** /sɑ̃ˈfrwɑː/

San Gimignano town, Italy
san jim-in-**yah**-noh
/ˌsandʒɪmɪˈnjɑːnəʊ/

Sangiovese wine grape
san-joh-**vay**-zay /ˌsandʒəʊˈveɪzeɪ/

sangrail (also **sangreal**) holy grail
sang-**grayl** /saŋˈgreɪl/

sangria red wine drink
sang-**gree**-uh /saŋˈgriːə/

sanguine cheerfully optimistic
sang-gwin /ˈsaŋgwɪn/

Sanhedrin supreme council in ancient
Jerusalem
san-**heed**-rin /sanˈhiːdrɪn/

Sometimes also san-uh-drin.

San Jacinto town, US
san juh-**sint**-oh /ˌsan dʒəˈsɪntəʊ/

San Jose city, US
san hoh-**zay** /ˌsan həʊˈzeɪ/

San José capital of Costa Rica
san khoss-**ay** /ˌsan xɒˈseɪ/

San Juan capital of Puerto Rico
san hwahn /ˌsan ˈhwɑːn/

Established anglicization. Other places of
this name in Latin America are pronounced
san khwan.

San Luis Potosí state, Mexico
san loo-**eess** pot-oss-ee /ˌsan luːˌiːs
ˌpɒtɒˈsiː/

San Marino republic enclave in Italy
san muh-**ree**-noh /ˌsan məˈriːnəʊ/

San Martín, José de Argentinian
soldier and statesman
khoss-**ay** day san mar-**teen** /xɒˌseɪ deɪ
san mɑː(r)ˈtiːn/

sannyasi (also **sanyasi**) Hindu
mendicant
sun-**yah**-si /sʌnˈjɑːsi/

San Pedro Sula city, Honduras
san **ped**-roh **soo**-luh /ˌsan ˌpɛdrəʊ
ˈsuːlə/

San Remo resort, Italy
san **ray**-moh /ˌsan ˈreɪməʊ/

sans without
sanz /sanz/

This is the literary English pronunciation.
A French pronunciation, sah(ng), is also
common.

San Salvador capital of El Salvador
san **sal**-vad-or /ˌsan ˈsalvadɔː(r)/,
Spanish [ˌsan salβaˈðor]

San Sebastián port, Spain
san suh-**bast**-i-uhn /ˌsan səˈbastiən/,
[san seβasˈtjan]
• Established anglicization.

Sanskrit ancient language
san-skrit /'sanskrɪt/

Sansovino, Jacopo Italian sculptor
yah-kop-oh san-suh-**vee**-noh
/ˌjɑːkɒpəʊ ˌsansəˈviːnəʊ/

sans serif (also **sanserif**) style of type
san **serr**-if /ˌsan ˈsɛrɪf/

Sans Souci château, Germany
sah(ng) soo-**see** /ˌsɑ̃ suːˈsiː/

Santa Ana city, El Salvador
san-tuh an-uh /ˌsantə ˈanə/

Santa Cruz city, Bolivia
sant-uh **krooss** /ˌsantə ˈkrus/

Santa Fe city, US
san-tuh fay /ˌsantə ˈfeɪ/

Santana, Carlos Mexican guitarist
kar-loss san-**tah**-nuh /ˌkɑː(r)lɒs
sanˈtɑːnə/

Santander port, Spain
san-tan-**dair** /ˌsantanˈdɛː(r)/

Santayana, George Spanish
philosopher
san-tuh-**yah**-nuh /ˌsantəˈjɑːnə/

santeria Afro-Cuban religious cult
san-terr-**ee**-uh /ˌsantɛˈriːə/

Santiago capital of Chile
san-ti-**ah**-goh /ˌsantiˈɑːgəʊ/

Santiago de Compostela city, Spain
san-ti-**ah**-goh day kom-post-**ay**-luh
/ˌsantiˌɑːgəʊ deɪ kɒmpɒˈsteɪlə/

Santo Domingo capital of the
Dominican Republic
san-toh duh-**ming**-goh /ˌsantəʊ
dəˈmɪŋgəʊ/

santoor Indian musical instrument
sun-**toor** /sʌnˈtʊə(r)/

Santorum, Rick American politician
san-**taw**-ruhm /sanˈtɔːrəm/

Santos port, Brazil
san-tuuss /'santʊs/

sanyasi see **sannyasi**

San Ysidro town, US
san ee-**seed**-roh /ˌsan iːˈsiːdrəʊ/

Saoirse Irish girl's name
seer-shuh /'sɪə(r)ʃə/

São Luis port, Brazil
sow(ng) loo-**eess** /ˌsɑ̃ luːˈiːs/
• See **PORTUGUESE** panel.

Saône river, France
sohn /səʊn/

São Paulo state, Brazil

sow(ng) **pow**-loo /ˌsɑ̃ ˈpaʊluː/

São Tomé e Príncipe island country
sow(ng) tuh-**may** uh pree(ng)-sip-uh
/ˌsɑ̃ təˌmeɪ ə ˈpriːsɪpə/

sapele timber
suh-**pee**-li /səˈpiːli/

sapient wise
say-pi-uhnt /'seɪpiənt/

Sapir–Whorf linguistic hypothesis
suh-peer **worf** /səˌpɪə(r) ˈwɔː(r)f/

saponaceous like or containing soap
sap-uh-**nay**-shuhss /ˌsapəˈneɪʃəs/

sapphic relating to lesbianism
saf-ik /'safɪk/

sapphire precious stone
saf-y-uhr /'safʌɪə(r)/

Sappho Greek lyric poet
saf-oh /'safəʊ/
• See **GREEK** panel.

Sapporo city, Japan
sap-aw-roh /'sapɔːrəʊ/
• See **JAPANESE** panel.

Saqlawiya town, Iraq
sak-luh-**wee**-yuh /sakləˈwiːjə/

Saqqara necropolis in Memphis, Egypt
suh-**kar**-uh /səˈkɑːrə/, /ˌsʌkˈqɑːrə/
• Established anglicization.

saraband (also **sarabande**) slow dance
sarr-uh-band /'sarəband/

Saracen an Arab or Muslim, especially at
the time of the Crusades
sarr-uh-suhn /'sarəsən/

Saragossa see **Zaragoza**

Sarajevo capital of Bosnia-Herzegovina
sarr-uh-**yay**-voh /ˌsarəˈjeɪvəʊ/,
['sarajɛvɒ]
• Established anglicization.

Sarandon, Susan American actress
suh-**ran**-duhn /səˈrandən/

Saran Wrap US trademark cling film
suh-**ran** /səˈran/

sarangi Indian musical instrument
sah-rung-gi /'sɑːrʌŋgi/

Saransk city, Russia
suh-**ransk** /səˈransk/

sarape see **serape**

Saraswati Hindu goddess
surr-**uss**-vut-i /sʌˈrʌsvʌti/

Saratoga, Battle of battle of the War of
American Independence
sarr-uh-**toh**-guh /ˌsarəˈtəʊgə/

Saratov city, Russia
suh-**rah**-tuhf /sə'rɑːtəf/

Sarawak state, Malaysia
suh-**rah**-wuhk /sə'rɑːwək/

sarcoma pl. **sarcomata** tumour
sar-**koh**-muh, pl. sar-**koh**-muh-tuh
/sɑː(r)'kəʊmə/, pl. /-tə/
• Standard -s plural is also possible.

sarcophagus pl. **sarcophagi** stone coffin
sar-**kof**-uh-guhss, pl. sar-**kof**-uh-jy
/sɑː(r)'kɒfəgəs/, pl. /-dʒʌɪ/

Plural commonly also sar-**kof**-uh-gy; see
LATIN panel.

sardar (also **sirdar**) Persian leader
suhr-**dar** /sə(r)'dɑː(r)/

Sardinia island, Italy
sar-**din**-i-uh /sɑː(r)'dɪnɪə/

Established anglicization. The Italian name
is Sardegna, pronounced sar-**dayn**-yuh.

sargasso seaweed
sar-**gass**-oh /sɑː(r)'gasəʊ/

Sargodha city, Pakistan
suhr-**goh**-duh /sə(r)'gəʊdə/

sari (also **saree**) Indian garment
sar-i /'sɑːri/

sarin nerve gas
sar-in /'sɑːrɪn/

Sarkozy, Nicolas French politician
nee-kol-**ah** sar-koh-**zee** /niːkɒˌlɑː
sɑː(r)kəʊ'ziː/

sarod Indian lute
suh-**rohd** /sə'rəʊd/

sarong garment
suh-**rong** /sə'rɒŋ/

saros period between eclipses
sair-oss /'sɛːrɒs/

Saro-Wiwa, Ken Nigerian author
sar-oh **wee**-wuh /sɑːrəʊ 'wiːwə/

sarsaparilla preparation made from
plants
sar-suh-puh-**ril**-uh /ˌsɑː(r)səpə'rɪlə/

Sarto, Andrea del Italian painter
and-**ray**-uh del sar-**toh** /anˌdreɪə dɛl
'sɑː(r)təʊ/

Sartre, Jean-Paul French philosopher
zhah(ng) pol sar-**truh** /ˌʒɑ̃ pɒl
'sɑː(r)trə/

Sarum old name for **Salisbury**
sair-uhm /'sɛːrəm/

Saruman fictional character in *The Lord*
of the Rings
sarr-oo-man /'saruːman/

sashimi Japanese raw fish
sash-ee-mi /'saʃiːmi/

Commonly also sash-**ee**-mi; see JAPANESE
panel.

Saskatchewan province, Canada
suh-**skatch**-uh-wuhn /sə'skatʃəwən/

Saskatoon city, Canada
sask-uh-**toon** /ˌsaskə'tuːn/

sassafras tree
sass-uh-frass /'sasəfras/

Sassari town, Italy
sass-uh-ri /'sasari/

Sassenach English person
sass-uh-nakh /'sasənax/

Sassoon, Siegfried English poet
seeg-freed suh-**soon** /ˌsiːgfriːd
sə'suːn/

Sassoon, Vidal English hairdresser
vid-**al** suh-**soon** /vɪdˌal sə'suːn/

sastrugi ridges on the surface of snow
sast-**roo**-gi /sa'struːgi/

satay (also **saté**) Indonesian dish
sat-ay /'sateɪ/

satiate sate
say-shi-ayt /'seɪʃɪeɪt/

Satie, Erik French composer
err-**reek** sat-**ee** /ɛˌriːk sa'tiː/

satiety feeling of being sated
suh-**ty**-uh-ti /sə'tʌɪəti/

satori Buddhist enlightenment
suh-**taw**-ri /sə'tɔːri/

satsuma citrus fruit
sat-**soo**-muh /sat'suːmə/

Saturnalia Roman festival
sat-uhr-**nay**-li-uh /ˌsatə(r)'neɪlɪə/

saturniid silk moth
suh-**tur**-ni-id /sə'tə(r)niɪd/

saturnine gloomy
sat-uhr-nyn /'satə(r)nʌɪn/

satyr Greek mythological creature
sat-uhr /'satə(r)/

satyriasis uncontrollable sexual desire
sat-uh-**ry**-uh-siss /ˌsatə'rʌɪəsɪs/

Sauchiehall St street, Glasgow
sokh-i-**hawl** /ˌsɒxi'hɔːl/

saucisson French sausage
soss-ee-**so(ng)** /sɒsiː'sɔ̃/

Saucony American sportswear manufacturers
sok-uh-**nee** /ˌsɒkəˈniː/

saudade feeling of nostalgia
sow-**dah**-duh /saʊˈdɑːdə/

Saudi Arabia country
sow-di uh-**ray**-bi-uh /ˌsaʊdi əˈreɪbiə/

sauerkraut German cabbage dish
sow-uhr-krowt /ˈsaʊə(r)kraʊt/,
[ˈzaʊəkraʊt]

sauger fish
saw-guhr /ˈsɔːɡə(r)/

Sault Sainte Marie port, US
soo saynt muh-**ree** /ˌsuː seɪnt məˈriː/

sauna hot-air room
saw-nuh /ˈsɔːnə/

Less commonly also **sow**-nuh, a pronunciation closer to the original Finnish.

Sauron fictional character in *The Lord of the Rings*
sow-ron /ˈsaʊrɒn/

sauropod dinosaur
saw-ruh-pod /ˈsɔːrəpɒd/

Saussure, Ferdinand de Swiss linguistics scholar
fair-din-**ah(ng)** duh soh-**suer**
/fɛː(r)diˌnɑ̃ də səʊˈsy(r)/

sauté fried quickly
soh-tay /ˈsəʊteɪ/

Sauternes white wine
soh-**tairn** /səʊˈtɛː(r)n/

Sauvignon white wine grape
soh-vin-**yo(ng)** /ˈsəʊvɪnjɔ̃/

Sauze d'Oulx resort, Italy
sohz **doo** /ˌsəʊz ˈduː/

Savai'i (also **Savaii**) island, Samoa
sah-**vy**-i /saːˈvʌii/

Savalas, Telly Greek actor
tel-i suh-**val**-uhss /ˌtɛli səˈvaləs/

Savannah port, Georgia
suh-**van**-uh /səˈvanə/

Savannakhet (also **Savannaket**) town, Laos
suv-un-uh-**ket** /ˌsʌvʌnəˈkɛt/

savant learned person
sav-uhnt /ˈsavənt/

saveloy pork sausage
sav-uh-loy /ˈsavəlɔɪ/

Savery, Thomas English engineer
say-vuh-ri /ˈseɪvəri/

Savoie department, France
sav-**wah** /savˈwɑː/

savoir faire ability to act appropriately
sav-war **fair** /ˌsavwɑː(r) ˈfɛː(r)/

Savonarola, Girolamo Italian religious reformer
jirr-**ol**-uh-moh sav-on-uh-**roh**-luh
/dʒɪˌrɒləməʊ ˌsavɒnəˈrəʊlə/

Savonlinna town, Finland
sav-on-lin-uh /ˈsavɒnlɪnə/

Savoy region, France
suh-**voy** /səˈvɔɪ/

Established anglicization. The French name is Savoie, pronounced sav-**wah**.

Sawalha, Julia English actress
suh-**wahl**-huh /səˈwɑːlhə/

Sawhney, Nitin English composer
nit-in **saw**-ni /ˌnɪtɪn ˈsɔːni/

Saxe-Coburg-Gotha British royal house
saks **koh**-burg **goh**-thuh /ˌsaks ˌkəʊbəː(r)g ˈɡəʊθə/

saxifrage plant
saks-if-rayj /ˈsaksɪfreɪdʒ/

Saxony region, Germany
sak-suh-ni /ˈsaksəni/

Established anglicization. The German name is Sachsen, pronounced **zakh**-suhn.

Saxony-Anhalt state, Germany
sak-suh-ni **an-halt** /ˌsaksəni ˈanhalt/

Established anglicization. The German name is Sachsen-Anhalt, pronounced **zakh**-suhn an-halt.

sayonara 'goodbye' (Japanese)
sy-uh-**nar**-uh /ˌsʌɪəˈnɑːrə/

sayyid Muslim claiming descent from Muhammad
say-yid /ˈseɪjɪd/

scabies skin disease
skay-beez /ˈskeɪbiːz/

Scacchi, Greta Italian-English actress
gret-uh **skak**-i /ˌɡrɛtə ˈskaki/

Scafell Pike mountain, England
skaw-**fel** /ˌskɔːˈfɛl/

scagliola imitation marble
skal-**yoh**-luh /skalˈjəʊlə/

scald see **skald**

scalene having sides unequal in length
skay-leen /ˈskeɪliːn/

scalenus pl. **scaleni** neck muscle
skuh-**lee**-nuhss, pl. skuh-**lee**-ny
/skə'li:nəs/, pl. /-nʌɪ/

scallop edible mollusc
skol-uhp /'skɒləp/

Commonly also **skal**-uhp.

Scania international vehicle
manufacturers
skan-yuh /'skanjə/

scandium chemical element
skan-di-uhm /'skandɪəm/

Scapa Flow strait, Scotland
skah-puh **floh** /ˌskɑːpə 'fləʊ/

scapula pl. **scapulae** shoulder blade
skap-yuul-uh, pl. **skap**-yuul-ee
/'skapjʊlə/, pl. /-liː/
• Standard -s plural is also possible.

scarab beetle
skarr-uhb /'skarəb/

scaramouch boastful but cowardly
person
skarr-uh-**mootch** /skarə'muːtʃ/

Scarborough port, England
skar-buh-ruh /'skɑː(r)bərə/

scarify cut and remove debris from a
lawn
skarr-if-y /'skarɪfʌɪ/

Scarlatti, Alessandro Italian composer
al-ess-**and**-roh skar-**lat**-i /alɛˌsandrəʊ
skɑː(r)'lati/

scatological preoccupied with
excrement
skat-uh-**loj**-ik-uhl /skatə'lɒdʒɪkəl/

scaup diving duck
skawp /skɔːp/

scavenge collect from waste
skav-uhnj /'skavəndʒ/

scenario outline of a film
suh-**nar**-i-oh /sə'nɑːriəʊ/

Schadenfreude pleasure derived from
another's misfortune
shah-duhn-froy-duh /'ʃɑːdənˌfrɔɪdə/

Schama, Simon English historian
shah-muh /'ʃɑːmə/

schedule plan
shed-yool /'ʃɛdjuːl/

AM is **sked**-yool, also increasingly common
in BR.

Scheele, Carl Wilhelm Swedish
chemist

karl vil-helm **shay**-luh /ˌkɑː(r)l
ˌvɪlhɛlm 'ʃeɪlə/

Scheherazade fictional narrator of the
Arabian Nights
shuh-herr-uh-**zahd** /ʃəˌhɛrə'zɑːd/

Scheldt river, Europe
skelt /skɛlt/

Established anglicization. The
Dutch/Flemish name is Schelde,
pronounced **skhel**-duh, and the French
name is Escaut, pronounced esk-**oh**.

schema pl. **schemata** representation of a
plan
skee-muh, pl. **skee**-muh-tuh /'skiːmə/,
pl. /-mətə/
• Standard -s plural is also possible.

Schenectady town, US
skuh-**nek**-tuh-di /skə'nɛktədi/

Schengen agreement European
agreement on border controls
sheng-uhn /'ʃɛŋən/

Schering pharmaceutical company
sheer-ing /'ʃɪərɪŋ/

scherzo musical composition
skair-tsoh /'skɛː(r)tsəʊ/

Schiaparelli, Elsa Italian-born French
fashion designer
el-suh skyap-uh-**rel**-i /ˌɛlsə skjapə'rɛli/

Schiavo, Terry brain-damaged
American woman in right-to-die case
shy-voh /'ʃʌɪvəʊ/

Schiele, Egon Austrian painter
ay-gon **shee**-luh /ˌeɪgɒn 'ʃiːlə/

Schiller, Friedrich von German
dramatist
freed-rikh **shil**-uhr /ˌfriːdrɪç 'ʃɪlə(r)/

Schindler, Oskar German industrialist
osk-uhr **shind**-luhr /ˌɒskə(r) 'ʃɪndlə(r)/

Schiphol airport, Netherlands
skhip-hol /'sxɪphɒl/

Commonly also anglicized to **skip**-ol.

schipperke breed of dog
skip-uhr-kuh /'skɪpə(r)kə/

schism split or division
skiz-uhm /'skɪzəm/

Less commonly also **siz**-uhm.

schist metamorphic rock
shist /ʃɪst/

schizandra Chinese herb
skit-**sand**-ruh /skɪt'sandrə/

schizophrenia mental disorder
skit-suh-**free**-ni-uh /ˌskɪtsəˈfriːnɪə/

schizophrenic relating to schizophrenia
skit-suh-**fren**-ik /ˌskɪtsəˈfrɛnɪk/

Schlegel, August Wilhelm von
German poet
ow-guust **vil**-helm fon **shlay**-guhl
/ˌaʊɡʊst ˌvɪlhɛlm fɒn ˈʃleɪɡəl/

schlemiel stupid or unlucky person
shluh-**meel** /ʃləˈmiːl/

schlep haul
shlep /ʃlɛp/

Schleswig-Holstein state, Germany
shless-vig **hol**-styn /ˌʃlɛzvɪɡ ˈhɒlstʌɪn/,
[ˌʃleːsvɪç ˈhɔlʃtaɪn]
• Established anglicization.

Schlick, Moritz German philosopher
morr-its **shlik** /ˌmɒrɪts ˈʃlɪk/

Schliemann, Heinrich German
archaeologist
hyn-rikh **shlee**-man /ˌhʌɪnrɪç
ˈʃliːman/

schlimazel unlucky person
shluh-**moz**-uhl /ʃləˈmɒzəl/

schlock inferior goods or material
shlok /ʃlɒk/

Schmalkaldic League historical
alliance
shmal-**kal**-dik /ʃmalˈkaldɪk/

schmaltz excessive sentimentality
shmawlts /ʃmɔːlts/

Schmeichel, Peter Danish footballer
pay-duhr **shmy**-kuhl /ˌpeɪdə(r)
ˈʃmʌɪkəl/

Schmidt-Cassegrain type of telescope
shmit **kass**-uh-grayn /ˌʃmɪt
ˈkasəɡreɪn/

schmooze talk cosily
shmooz /ʃmuːz/

schmuck contemptible person
shmuk /ʃmʌk/

Schnabel, Artur German composer
ar-toor **shnah**-buhl /ˌɑː(r)tʊə(r)
ˈʃnɑːbəl/

schnapps alcoholic drink
shnaps /ʃnaps/

schnauzer breed of dog
shnow-zuhr /ˈʃnaʊzə(r)/

Less commonly also **shnowt**-suhr, a more
German-sounding pronunciation.

schnitzel thin slice of veal

shnit-suhl /ˈʃnɪtsəl/

Schoenberg, Arnold Austrian-born
American composer
shoen-bairg /ˈʃøːnbɛ(r)ɡ/

scholasticism system of theology and
philosophy
skuh-**last**-iss-iz-uhm /skəˈlastɪˌsɪzəm/

Scholl, Andreas German singer
and-**ray**-ass **shol** /anˌdreɪas ˈʃɒl/

Schönbrunn palace in Vienna
shoen-bruun /ˈʃøːnbrʊn/

schooner sailing ship
skoo-nuhr /ˈskuːnə(r)/

Schopenhauer, Arthur German
philosopher
ar-toor **shoh**-puhn-how-uhr
/ˌɑː(r)tʊə(r) ˈʃəʊpənˌhaʊə(r)/

schottische slow polka
shot-**eesh** /ʃɒˈtiːʃ/

Schreiner, Olive South African novelist
shry-nuhr /ˈʃrʌɪnə(r)/

Schröder, Gerhard German statesman
gair-hart **shroe**-duhr /ˌɡɛː(r)hɑː(r)t
ˈʃrøːdə(r)/

Schrödinger, Erwin Austrian
theoretical physicist
air-veen **shroe**-ding-uhr /ˌɛː(r)viːn
ˈʃrøːdɪŋə(r)/

schtum see **shtum**

schtup see **shtup**

Schubert, Franz Austrian composer
frants **shoo**-buhrt /ˌfrants ˈʃuːbə(r)t/

Schulz, Charles American cartoonist
shuults /ʃʊlts/

Schumacher, Michael German racing
driver
shoo-mak-uhr /ˈʃuːmakə(r)/, [ˌmɪçaɛl
ˈʃuːmaxɐ]
• Established anglicization.

Schumann, Robert German composer
rob-airt **shoo**-man /ˌrɒbɛː(r)t ˈʃuːman/

schuss downhill run on skis
shuuss /ʃʊs/

Schütz, Heinrich German composer
hyn-rikh **shuets** /ˌhʌɪnrɪç ˈʃʏts/

schwa unstressed central vowel
shwah /ʃwɑː/

Schwaben see **Swabia**

Schwäbisch Gmünd city, Germany
shvay-bish **gmuent** /ˌʃveɪbɪʃ ˈɡmʏnt/

Schwann, Theodor German
physiologist
tay-uh-dor **shvan** /ˌteɪədɔː(r) ˈʃvan/

Schwarzenegger, Arnold
Austrian-born American actor
shworts-uh-neg-uhr
/ˈʃwɔː(r)tsəˌnɛɡə(r)/, [ˈʃvartsənɛɡɐ]
• Established anglicization.

Schwarzkopf, Elisabeth German
soprano
ay-**leez**-uh-bet **shvarts**-kopf
/eɪˌliːzəbɛt ˈʃvɑː(r)tskɒpf/

Schwarzschild type of black hole
shvarts-shilt /ˈʃvɑː(r)ts,ʃɪlt/

Schwarzwald forest, Germany
shvarts-valt /ˈʃvɑː(r)tsvalt/

Schweinfurt city, Germany
shvyn-fuurt /ˈʃvaɪnfʊə(r)t/

Schweitzer, Albert German theologian
al-bairt **shvyt**-suhr /ˌalbɛ(r)t
ˈʃvaɪtsə(r)/

Schweiz see **Switzerland**

Schweppes soft drinks manufacturers
shweps /ˈʃwɛps/

Schwerin city, Germany
shverr-**een** /ʃvɛˈriːn/

Schwyz city, Switzerland
shveets /ˈʃviːts/

sciatic relating to the hip
sy-**at**-ik /saɪˈatɪk/

Scilly Isles islands, UK
sil-i /ˈsɪli/

scimitar curved sword
sim-it-uhr /ˈsɪmɪtə(r)/

scintilla tiny trace
sin-**til**-uh /sɪnˈtɪlə/

scintillate emit flashes of light
sin-til-ayt /ˈsɪntɪleɪt/

scion young shoot or twig of a plant
sy-uhn /ˈsaɪən/

Scipio Aemilianus Roman general
skip-i-oh ee-mil-i-**ah**-nuhss /ˌskɪpiəʊ
iːˌmɪliˈɑːnəs/
• See LATIN panel.

scirocco (also **sirocco**) wind
sirr-**ok**-oh /sɪˈrɒkəʊ/

scission action of cutting or being cut
sish-uhn /ˈsɪʃən/

sclera white outer layer of the eyeball
skleer-uh /ˈsklɪərə/

sclerosis hardening of body tissue

sclerous hardened or bony
skleer-uhss /ˈsklɪərəs/

scoliosis curvature of the spine
skoh-li-**oh**-siss /ˌskəʊlɪˈəʊsɪs/

Scone settlement, Scotland
skoon /skuːn/

scone small cake
skon /skɒn/

Equally commonly also **skohn**.

scops owl small owl
skops /skɒps/

scordatura altering the normal tuning
of a stringed instrument
skor-duht-**yoor**-uh /ˌskɔː(r)dəˈtjʊərə/

Scorsese, Martin American film
director
skor-**say**-zi /skɔː(r)ˈseɪzi/

scorzonera edible plant
skor-zoh-**neer**-uh /ˌskɔː(r)zəʊˈnɪərə/

scoter diving duck
skoh-tuhr /ˈskəʊtə(r)/

Scouse Liverpudlian dialect
skowss /skaʊs/

scramasax Anglo-Saxon knife
skram-uh-saks /ˈskraməsaks/

Scriabin, Aleksandr (also **Skryabin**)
Russian composer
al-uhk-**sahn**-duhr skri-**ab**-in
/alək,sɑːndə(r) skriˈabɪn/

scrivener clerk or scribe
skriv-uh-nuhr /ˈskrɪvənə(r)/

scrofula disease
skrof-yuul-uh /ˈskrɒfjʊlə/

scuba aqualung
skoo-buh /ˈskuːbə/

scullery small kitchen
skul-uh-ri /ˈskʌləri/

Scunthorpe town, England
skun-thorp /ˈskʌnθɔː(r)p/

scurrilous making scandalous claims
skurr-il-uhss /ˈskʌrɪləs/

scutage money paid in lieu of military
service
skyoo-tuhj /ˈskjuːtədʒ/

Scutari former name for **Üsküdar**
skoo-**tar**-i /skuːˈtɑːri/

Scutum constellation
skyoot-uhm /ˈskjuːtəm/

Scylla Greek mythological monster
sil-uh /ˈsɪlə/

Scythia ancient region of Europe
sith-i-uh /ˈsɪðɪə/

seaborgium chemical element
see-**borg**-i-uhm /siːˈbɔː(r)ɡiəm/

Seagal, Steven American actor
see-**gahl** /siːˈɡɑːl/

Sealyham breed of terrier
see-li-uhm /ˈsiːliəm/

Seanad upper House of Parliament in
the Republic of Ireland
shan-ad /ˈʃanad/, Irish [ˈsʲanəd]

seance meeting at which people attempt
to contact the dead
say-onss /ˈseɪɒns/

Searle, Ronald English cartoonist
surl /səː(r)l/

Seat car manufacturers
say-at /ˈseɪat/

Seattle city, US
si-**at**-uhl /siˈatəl/

sebaceous relating to oil or fat
suh-**bay**-shuhss /səˈbeɪʃəs/

Sebastopol port, Ukraine; also called
Sevastopol
suh-**bast**-uh-puhl /səˈbastəpəl/
• Established anglicization.

seborrhoea excessive discharge of
sebum
seb-uh-**ree**-uh /ˌsɛbəˈriːə/

sebum oily secretion
see-buhm /ˈsiːbəm/

SECAM television broadcasting system
see-kam /ˈsiːkam/

secant mathematical ratio
see-kuhnt /ˈsiːkənt/

secateurs pruning clippers
sek-uh-**turz** /ˌsɛkəˈtəː(r)z/

Secombe, Harry English actor
see-kuhm /ˈsiːkəm/

Seconal trademark barbiturate drug
sek-uh-nal /ˈsɛkənal/

second transfer temporarily to another
position
suh-**kond** /səˈkɒnd/

secretaire small writing desk
sek-ruh-**tair** /ˌsɛkrəˈtɛː(r)/

secretariat permanent administrative
office
sek-ruh-**tair**-i-uht /ˌsɛkrəˈtɛːriət/

secrete produce and discharge a
substance

suh-**kreet** /səˈkriːt/

secular not religious
sek-yuul-uhr /ˈsɛkjʊlə(r)/

Securitate Romanian internal security
force
suhk-yoor-it-**ah**-tay /səˌkjʊərɪˈtɑːteɪ/

Sedaka, Neil American singer
suh-**dah**-kuh /səˈdɑːkə/

sedan enclosed carrying chair
suh-**dan** /səˈdan/

sedentary tending to spend much time
seated
sed-uhn-tuh-ri /ˈsɛdəntəri/

Sedaris, David American writer
suh-**dair**-iss /səˈdɛːrɪs/

Seder Jewish ceremonial dinner
say-duhr /ˈseɪdə(r)/

Sedna Inuit goddess
sed-nuh /ˈsɛdnə/

sedulous showing dedication
sed-yuul-uhss /ˈsɛdjʊləs/

Sefer Hebrew religious texts
say-fuhr /ˈseɪfə(r)/

Segovia city, Spain
seg-**oh**-vi-uh /sɛˈɡəʊvɪə/, [seˈɣoβja]

Segovia, Andrés Spanish guitarist and
composer
and-**rayss** seg-**oh**-vi-uh /anˈdreɪs
sɛˈɡəʊvɪə/, [seˈɣoβja]

segue move from one thing to another
seg-way /ˈsɛɡweɪ/

Segundo, Compay Cuban guitarist
kom-**py** seg-**uun**-doh /kɒmˌpʌɪ
sɛˈɡʊndəʊ/

Seguridad Spanish security service
seg-oor-id-**ad** /sɛˌɡʊərɪˈdad/,
[seˌɣuriˈðað]

Sehnsucht yearning
zayn-zuukht /ˈzeɪnzʊxt/

seicento 17th century
say-**chen**-toh /seɪˈtʃɛntəʊ/

Seierstad, Äsne Norwegian writer
awss-nuh **say**-uhr-stah /ˌɔːsnə
ˈseɪə(r)stɑː/

seigneur feudal lord
say-**nyur** /seɪˈnjəː(r)/

Seikan underwater tunnel, Japan
say-kan /ˈseɪkan/

Seiko watch manufacturers
say-koh /ˈseɪkəʊ/

Seine river, France
sen /sen/

Seinfeld, Jerry American comedian
syn-feld /'sʌɪnfɛld/

seisin (also **seizin**) possession of land by
freehold
see-zin /'siːzɪn/

Sei Shonagon Japanese writer
say shoh-**nag**-on /ˌseɪ ʃəʊ'nagɒn/

seismic relating to earthquakes
syz-mik /'sʌɪzmɪk/

sei whale
say /seɪ/

sejant heraldic term
see-juhnt /'siːdʒənt/

Sekhmet Egyptian goddess
sek-met /'sɛkmɛt/

Sekt German sparkling white wine
zekt /zɛkt/

Selangor state, Malaysia
suh-lang-uhr /sə'laŋə(r)/

Selassie, Haile Ethiopian emperor
hy-li suh-**lass**-i /ˌhʌɪli sə'lasi/

Selene Greek goddess
suh-lee-ni /sə'liːni/

selenium chemical element
suh-lee-ni-uhm /sə'liːniəm/

selenology scientific study of the moon
sel-in-ol-uh-ji /ˌsɛlɪ'nɒlədʒi/

Seleš, Monika Yugoslav-born American
tennis player
mon-ik-uh **sel**-ez /ˌmɒnɪkə 'sɛlɛz/
• This is her own preferred anglicization.

Seleucid ancient Syrian dynasty
sil-oo-sid /sɪ'luːsɪd/

self-aggrandizement process of
promoting oneself
self uh-**grand**-iz-muhnt /sɛlf
ə'grandɪzmənt/

Seljuk ancient Turkish dynasty
sel-jook /'sɛldʒuːk/

Selkirk, Alexander Scottish sailor
sel-kurk /'sɛlkə(r)k/

Selous, Frederick English explorer
suh-loo /sə'luː/

seltzer soda water
selt-suhr /'sɛltsə(r)/

selvedge edge produced on woven fabric
sel-vuhj /'sɛlvədʒ/

Selye, Hans Austrian-born Canadian
physician
hanss **sel**-yay /ˌhans 'sɛljeɪ/

Selznick, David O. American film
producer
selz-nik /'sɛlznɪk/

Semarang port, Indonesia
suh-mah-rang /sə'mɑːraŋ/

Semei (also **Semey**) city, Kazakhstan
suh-may /sə'meɪ/

Semele Greek goddess
sem-uh-li /'sɛməli/

semibreve musical note
sem-i-breev /'sɛmibriːv/

Sémillon white wine grape
sem-ee-yo(ng) /'sɛmijɔ̃/

seminary training college for priests or
rabbis
sem-in-uh-ri /'sɛmɪnəri/

Seminole American Indian ethnic group
sem-in-ohl /'sɛmɪnəʊl/

semiotics study of signs and symbols
sem-i-ot-iks /ˌsɛmi'ɒtɪks/

Less commonly also see-mi-**ot**-iks.

Semiramis Greek mythological
character
suh-mirr-uh-miss /sə'mɪrəmɪs/

Semitic family of languages
suh-mit-ik /sə'mɪtɪk/

Semmelweis, Ignaz Hungarian
obstetrician
ig-nats **zem-uhl**-vyss /ˌɪgnats
'zɛməlvʌɪs/

semper fidelis 'always faithful' (Latin)
sem-puhr fid-**ay**-liss /ˌsɛmpə(r)
fɪ'deɪlɪs/

sempiternal eternal and unchanging
sem-pi-tur-nuhl /ˌsɛmpɪ'təː(r)nəl/

semplice musical term
sem-plee-chay /'sɛmpliːtʃeɪ/

sempre musical term
sem-pray /'sɛmpreɪ/

Sen, Amartya Indian economist
uh-**mart**-yuh sen /əˌmɑː(r)tjə 'sɛn/

Senanayake, Don Stephen Sinhalese
statesman
sen-uh-ny-uh-kuh /ˌsɛnə'nʌɪəkə/

Sendai city, Japan
sen-dy /'sɛndʌɪ/

Seneca Roman statesman
sen-ek-uh /'sɛnɛkə/

Senedd Welsh parliament
sen-eth /'sɛnɛð/

Senegal country
sen-uh-**gawl** /ˌsɛnəˈɡɔːl/

senescence deterioration with age
suh-**ness**-uhnss /səˈnɛsəns/

seneschal steward of a medieval great
house
sen-uh-shuhl /ˈsɛnəʃəl/

senhor pl. **senhores** Portuguese title for a
man
sen-**yor**, pl. sen-**yor**-uush /sɛnˈjɔː(r)/,
pl. /-rʊʃ/

senhora Portuguese title for a woman
sen-**yaw**-ruh /sɛnˈjɔːrə/

senhorita Portuguese title for a young
woman
sen-yuh-**ree**-tuh /ˌsɛnjəˈriːtə/

Senkaku islands, East China sea
sen-kak-oo /ˈsɛnkakuː/

Senna, Ayrton Brazilian racing driver
ah-**eer**-tuhn **sen**-uh /ɑːˌɪə(r)tən ˈsɛnə/

señor pl. **señores** Spanish title for a man
sen-**yor**, pl. sen-**yor**-ayss /sɛˈnjɔː(r)/, pl.
/-reɪs/

señora Spanish title for a woman
sen-**yaw**-ruh /sɛˈnjɔːrə/

señorita Spanish title for a young
woman
sen-yuh-**ree**-tuh /ˌsɛnjəˈriːtə/

sensei 'teacher' (Japanese)
sen-**say** /sɛnˈseɪ/

sentient able to perceive things
sen-ti-uhnt /ˈsɛntiənt/

Sometimes also **sen**-shuhnt.

Sentamu, John English archbishop
sent-uh-moo /ˈsɛntəmuː/

Seoul capital of South Korea
sohl /səʊl/
• Established anglicization.

sepal part of a flower
sep-uhl /ˈsɛpəl/

Sephardi pl. **Sephardim** Jew of Spanish
or Portuguese descent
sef-**ar**-di, pl. sef-**ar**-dim /sɛˈfɑː(r)di/, pl.
/-dɪm/

sephira pl. **sephiroth** attribute in
Hebrew mythology
sef-irr-ah, pl. **sef**-irr-oht /ˈsɛfɪrɑː/, pl.
/ˈsɛfɪrəʊt/

sepia brown colour
see-pi-uh /ˈsiːpiə/

seppuku ritual suicide
sep-uh-koo /ˈsɛpəkuː/
• See JAPANESE panel.

septcentenary 700th anniversary
sept-sen-**tee**-nuh-ri /ˌsɛptsɛnˈtiːnəri/

Commonly also sept-sen-**ten**-uh-ri.

septicaemia blood poisoning
sep-tiss-**ee**-mi-uh /ˌsɛptɪˈsiːmiə/

Septuagesima Sunday before
Sexagesima
sept-yoo-uh-**jess**-im-uh
/ˌsɛptjuəˈdʒɛsɪmə/

sepulchral relating to a tomb
suh-**pul**-kruhl /səˈpʌlkrəl/

sepulchre stone monument
sep-uhl-kuhr /ˈsɛpəlkə(r)/

sequential forming or following in a
logical order or sequence
suh-**kwen**-shuhl /səˈkwɛnʃəl/

sequester isolate or hide away
suh-**kwest**-uhr /səˈkwɛstə(r)/

sequestrate take legal possession of
see-kwuh-strayt /ˈsiːkwəstreɪt/

sequoia redwood tree
suh-**kwoy**-uh /səˈkwɔɪə/

Serafinowicz, Peter English comedian
serr-uh-**fin**-uh-wits /ˌsɛrəˈfɪnəwɪts/

seraglio women's apartments in a
Muslim palace
serr-**ah**-li-oh /sɛˈrɑːliəʊ/

Seraing town, Belgium
suh-**ra(ng)** /səˈrɛ̃/

serape (also **sarape**) shawl
suh-**rah**-pay /səˈrɑːpeɪ/

seraph pl. **seraphim** angelic being
serr-uhf, pl. serr-uhf-im /ˈsɛrəf/, pl.
/-fɪm/
• Standard -s plural is also possible.

seraphic angelic
suh-**raf**-ik /səˈrafɪk/

Serapis Egyptian god
suh-**rap**-iss /səˈrapɪs/

Seremban city, Malaysia
suh-**rem**-buhn /səˈrɛmbən/

serendipity happy chance
serr-uhn-**dip**-it-i /ˌsɛrənˈdɪpɪti/

Serengeti plain in Tanzania
serr-en-**get**-i /ˌsɛrɛnˈɡɛti/

Sereny, Gitta English sociologist
gee-tuh suh-**ree**-ni /ˌɡiːtə səˈriːni/

sergeant army rank
sar-juhnt /ˈsɑː(r)dʒənt/

Sergipe state, Brazil
sair-**zhee**-pi /sɛ:(r)ˈʒiːpi/

serif projection finishing off a stroke of a letter
serr-if /ˈsɛrɪf/

Serota, Nicholas English curator
suh-**roh**-tuh /səˈrəʊtə/

serotine bat
serr-uh-teen /ˈsɛrətiːn/

serotonin chemical compound
serr-uh-**toh**-nin /ˌsɛrəˈtəʊnɪn/

Seroxat trademark antidepressant drug
suh-**rok**-sat /səˈrɒksat/

Serpens constellation
sur-puhnz /ˈsəː(r)pənz/

serpentine like a snake
sur-puhn-tyn /ˈsəː(r)pəntʌɪn/

SERPS State Earnings-Related Pension Scheme
surps /səː(r)ps/

Serraillier, Ian English author
suh-**ral**-i-ay /səˈralɪeɪ/

Serse see Xerxes

serum pl. **sera** liquid in blood
seer-uhm, pl. seer-uh /ˈsɪərəm/, pl. /-rə/
• Standard -s plural is also possible.

serval African wild cat
sur-vuhl /ˈsəː(r)vəl/

sesame edible seed
sess-uh-mi /ˈsɛsəmi/

Sesotho language of Lesotho
sess-oo-too /sɛˈsuːtuː/

sesquialtera denoting a ratio of 3:2
sesk-wi-**alt**-uh-ruh /ˌsɛskwiˈaltərə/

sesquicentenary 150th anniversary
sesk-wi-sen-**tee**-nuh-ri /ˌsɛskwisɛnˈtiːnəri/

Commonly also sesk-wi-sen-**ten**-uh-ri.

sesterce pl. **sesterces** ancient Roman coin
sest-urss, pl. sest-**ur**-seez /ˈsɛstəː(r)s/, pl. /sɛˈstəː(r)siːz/

sestertius pl. **sestertii** ancient Roman coin (Latin name)
sest-**ur**-shuhss, pl. sest-**ur**-shi-y /sɛˈstəː(r)ʃəs/, pl. /-ˈstəː(r)ʃiaɪ/

sestina poetic form
sest-ee-nuh /sɛˈstiːnə/

Sestriere resort, Italy
sest-ri-**air**-ay /sɛstriˈɛːreɪ/

The French name is Sestrières, pronounced sest-ri-**air**.

Seth, Vikram Indian novelist and poet
vik-ruhm **sayt** /ˌvɪkrəm ˈseɪt/

Seth Egyptian god
seth /sɛθ/

Setswana language, Africa
set-**swah**-nuh /sɛˈtswɑːnə/

Setúbal port, Portugal
suh-**too**-buhl /səˈtuːbəl/

Seurat, Georges Pierre French painter
zhorzh soe-**rah** /ˌʒɔː(r)ʒ səˈrɑː/

Sevastopol port, Ukraine; also called Sebastopol
suh-**vast**-uh-puhl /səˈvastəpəl/, [sʲɪvaˈstopəlʲ]
• Established anglicization.

Severnaya Zemlya islands, Arctic Ocean
syay-vuhr-nuh-yuh zuhm-**lyah** /ˌsjeɪvə(r)nəjə zəmˈljɑː/

Severodvinsk port, Russia
syay-vuh-ruh-**dvinsk** /ˌsjeɪvərəˈdvɪnsk/

Seville city, Spain
suh-**vil** /səˈvɪl/

Established anglicization. The Spanish name is Sevilla, pronounced say-**veel**-yuh [seˈβiʎa].

Sèvres type of fine porcelain
sev-ruh /ˈsɛvrə/

sevruga sturgeon fished for its caviar
sev-**roo**-guh /sɛvˈruːɡə/

sewage waste water and excrement
soo-ij /ˈsuːɪdʒ/

Less commonly **syoo**-ij.

Seward, Anna English poet
see-wuhrd /ˈsiːwə(r)d/

sewer underground conduit
soo-uhr /ˈsuːə(r)/

Less commonly **syoo**-uhr.

sewin (also **sewen**) sea trout
syoo-in /ˈsjuːɪn/

Sexagesima Sunday before Quinquagesima
sek-suh-**jess**-im-uh /ˌsɛksəˈdʒɛsɪmə/

sexcentenary 600th anniversary
sek-sen-**tee**-nuh-ri /ˌsɛksɛnˈtiːnəri/

Commonly also sek-sen-**ten**-uh-ri.

Sextans constellation
sek-stuhnz /ˈsɛkstənz/

sextant instrument
seks-tuhnt /ˈsɛkstənt/

sextuplet each of six children born at one birth
seks-**tyoop**-luht /sɛksˈtjuːplət/

Commonly also seks-**tup**-luht or seks-**tyuup**-luht.

Seychelles country
say-**shelz** /seɪˈʃɛlz/

Seychellois native of the Seychelles
say-shel-**wah** /seɪʃɛlˈwɑː/

Seyfert type of galaxy
say-fuhrt /ˈseɪfəːrt/

Seymour, Jane third wife of Henry VIII
see-mor /ˈsiːmɔːr/

Sezession avant-garde art movement
zayt-sess-**yohn** /ˌzeɪtsɛsˈjəʊn/

Sfax port, Tunisia
sfaks /sfaks/

sforzando musical term
sfor-**tsan**-doh /sfɔːrˈtsandəʊ/

sgraffito pl. **sgraffiti** decoration made by scratching
sgraf-**ee**-toh, pl. sgraf-**ee**-ti /sgraˈfiːtəʊ/, pl. /-ti/

Shaanxi province, China
shahn-**shee** /ʃɑːnˈʃiː/

Shabaka Egyptian pharaoh
shab-uh-kuh /ˈʃabəkə/

shabbaba musical instrument
shuh-**bab**-uh /ʃəˈbabə/

Shabbat Sabbath (Hebrew)
shab-**at** /ʃaˈbat/

Shabbos (also **Shabbes**) Sabbath (Yiddish)
shab-uhss /ˈʃabəs/

shabu-shabu Japanese beef dish
shab-oo **shab**-oo /ˌʃabuːˈʃabuː/

shadchan (also **shadkhan**) pl. **shadchanim** Jewish marriage broker
shad-**khuhn**, pl. **shad**-khuhn-im /ˈʃadxən/, pl. /ˈʃadxənɪm/

Shadjareh, Massood Iranian chairman of Islamic Human Rights Commission
muh-**sood** shah-juh-ruh /məˌsuːd ˈʃɑːdʒərə/

shadoof pole with a bucket used for raising water
shuh-**doof** /ʃəˈduːf/

Shaffer, Peter and Anthony English playwrights
shaf-uhr /ˈʃafə(r)/

Shaftesbury, Earl of English philanthropist
shahfts-buh-ri /ˈʃɑːftsbəri/

shagreen sharkskin
shag-**reen** /ʃaˈɡriːn/

shah title of the former monarch of Iran
shah /ʃɑː/

shahada (also **shahadah**) Muslim profession of faith
shuh-**hah**-duh /ʃəˈhɑːdə/

Shah Alam city, Malaysia
shah **ah**-luhm /ˌʃɑː ˈɑːləm/

shahid (also **shaheed**) Muslim martyr
shuh-**heed** /ʃəˈhiːd/

Shaik, Schabir South African businessman
shab-**eer** shayk /ʃəˌbɪə(r) ˈʃeɪk/

Shaitan (also **Shaytan**) the Devil in Islam
shay-**tahn** /ʃeɪˈtɑːn/

Shaka (also **Chaka**) Zulu chief
shak-uh /ˈʃakə/

Shakhty city, Russia
shakh-ti /ˈʃɑːxti/

Shakti Hindu feminine expression of the divine
shuk-tee /ˈʃʌkti/

shakuhachi bamboo flute
shak-uu-**hatch**-i /ˌʃakʊˈhatʃi/

Shakur, Tupac American rap artist
too-pak shak-**oor** /ˌtuːpak ʃaˈkʊə(r)/

shallot onion-like vegetable
shuh-**lot** /ʃəˈlɒt/

Shalmaneser ancient king of Assyria
shal-muh-**nee**-zuhr /ˌʃalməˈniːzə(r)/

shalom 'peace' (Hebrew)
shuh-**lom** /ʃəˈlɒm/

shalwar loose, pleated trousers; also called **salwar**
shul-**war** /ʃʌlˈwɑː(r)/

shaman person regarded as having access to the spirit world
sham-uhn /ˈʃamən/

Commonly also **shay**-muhn.

Shamir, Yitzhak Israeli statesman
yits-**hahk** sham-**eer** /ˌjɪts,hɑːk
ʃaˈmɪə(r)/

shamisen see **samisen**

Shan Chinese and Burmese ethnic group
shahn /ʃɑːn/

Shandong province, China
shan-**duung** /ˌʃanˈdʊŋ/

Shanghai city, China
shang-**hy** /ˌʃaŋˈhʌɪ/

Shango religious cult
shang-goh /ˈʃaŋgəʊ/

Shangri-La Tibetan utopia
shang-gri-**lah** /ˌʃaŋgriˈlɑː/

Shankar, Ravi Indian sitar player
ruv-i shunk-uhr /ˌrʌvi ˈʃʌŋkə(r)/

Shantou port, China
shan-**toh** /ʃanˈtəʊ/

shantung silk fabric
shan-**tung** /ʃanˈtʌŋ/

Shanxi province, China
shan-**shee** /ˌʃanˈʃiː/

shapka Russian fur hat
shap-kuh /ˈʃapkə/

sharara loose pleated trousers
shuh-**rar**-uh /ʃəˈrɑːrə/

sharia (also **shariah**) Islamic canonical
law
shuh-**ree**-uh /ʃəˈriːə/

Sharif, Nawaz Pakistani statesman
nuh-**wahz** shuh-**reef** /nəˌwɑːz ʃəˈriːf/

Sharif, Omar Egyptian actor
oh-mar shuh-**reef** /ˌəʊmɑː(r) ʃəˈriːf/

Sharjah state, United Arab Emirates
shar-juh /ˈʃɑː(r)dʒə/

Sharma, Shankar Dayal Indian
statesman
shunk-uhr dy-**ul** shar-muh /ˌʃʌkə(r)
dʌɪˌʌl ˈʃɑː(r)mə/

Sharm el-Sheikh resort, Egypt
sharm uhl shayk /ˌʃɑː(r)m əl ˈʃeɪk/

Sharon plain, Israel
shair-uhn /ˈʃɛːrən/

Sharon, Ariel Israeli statesman
arr-i-el shuh-ron /ariˌɛl ʃəˈrɒn/

sharon fruit persimmon
shair-uhn /ˈʃɛːrən/

Shar Pei breed of dog
shar **pay** /ˌʃɑː(r) ˈpeɪ/

shashlik mutton kebab
shash-lik /ˈʃaʃlɪk/

Shatt al-Arab river, Asia
shut uhl **arr**-uhb /ˌʃʌt əl ˈarəb/

Shavian relating to George Bernard
Shaw
shay-vi-uhn /ˈʃeɪvɪən/

Shavuoth (also **Shavuot**) Jewish festival
shah-voo-**ot** /ʃɑːvuˈɒt/

Commonly also shuh-**voo**-uhss, a Yiddish
pronunciation.

Shaytan see **Shaitan**

Shea stadium in New York
shay /ʃeɪ/

shea nut-bearing tree
shee-uh /ˈʃiːə/

sheading administrative division of the
Isle of Man
shee-ding /ˈʃiːdɪŋ/

Sheaffer American pen manufacturers
shay-fuhr /ˈʃeɪfə(r)/

Sheba biblical place name
shee-buh /ˈʃiːbə/

shebang matter or set of circumstances
shuh-**bang** /ʃəˈbaŋ/

shebeen unlicensed establishment
selling alcohol
shuh-**been** /ʃəˈbiːn/

Sheela-na-gig medieval stone female
figure
shee-luh nuh gig /ˌʃiːlə nə ˈgɪg/

sheikh (also **sheik**) Arab leader
shayk /ʃeɪk/

Established anglicization. The more
Arabic-sounding pronunciation shaykh is
also sometimes used. Less commonly also
sheek.

sheitel wig worn by a Jewish woman
shay-tuhl /ˈʃeɪtəl/

shekel currency unit, Israel
shek-uhl /ˈʃɛkəl/

Shekinah (also **Shekhinah**) Jewish
symbol
shuh-**ky**-nuh /ʃɪˈkʌɪnə/

shellac resin melted into thin flakes
shuh-lak /ʃəˈlak/

Shelley, Percy Bysshe English poet
bish shel-i /ˌbɪʃ ˈʃɛli/

Shelob spider in *The Lord of the Rings*
shee-lob /ˈʃiːlɒb/

Shenandoah river, US
shen-uhn-**doh**-uh /ˌʃɛnənˈdəʊə/

shenanigans secret activity
shuh-**nan**-ig-uhnz /ʃɪˈnanɪɡənz/

sheng Chinese musical instrument
shung /ʃʌŋ/

Shenyang city, China
shuhn-**yahng** /ˌʃənˈjɑːŋ/

Shenzhen city, China
shuhn-**juhn** /ˌʃənˈdʒən/

Shenzhou Chinese spacecraft
shuhn-**joh** /ˌʃənˈdʒəʊ/

Sheol Jewish underworld
shee-**ohl** /ˈʃiːəʊl/

Sher, Anthony English actor
shur /ˈʃəː(r)/

Sheraton, Thomas English
furniture-maker
sherr-uh-tuhn /ˈʃɛrətən/

's-Hertogenbosch city, Netherlands
sair-toh-khuhn-**boss**
/ˌsɛː(r)təʊxən'bɒs/

sherwani knee-length man's coat
shur-**wah**-ni /ʃəː(r)ˈwɑːni/

Shevardnadze, Eduard Soviet
statesman
ed-wuhrd shuh-vuhrd-**nahd**-zuh
/ˌɛdwə(r)d ˌʃəvə(r)dˈnɑːdzə/

Shia (also **Shi'a**) branch of Islam
shee-uh /ˈʃiːə/

shiatsu Japanese massage therapy
shi-**at**-soo /ʃiˈatsuː/

shibboleth distinctive custom
shib-uh-leth /ˈʃɪbələθ/

Shibuya district of Tokyo
shib-**oo**-yuh /ʃɪˈbuːjə/

shidduch Jewish arranged marriage
shid-uhkh /ˈʃɪdəx/

shih-tzu breed of dog
shit-**soo** /ʃiˈtsuː/

shiitake mushroom
shit-**ah**-kay /ʃɪˈtɑːkeɪ/
• See JAPANESE panel.

Shiite (also **Shi'ite**) adherent of the Shia
branch of Islam
shee-**yt** /ˈʃiːʌɪt/

Shijiazhuang city, China
shuh-ji-ah-**jwahng** /ʃədʒiɑːˈdʒwɑːŋ/

shikhara (also **shikara**) spire on a
Hindu temple
shik-**ar**-uh /ʃɪˈkɑːrə/

Shikoku island, Japan
shik-**oh**-koo /ʃɪˈkəʊkuː/

shiksa non-Jewish woman
shik-suh /ˈʃɪksə/

shillelagh thick stick
shil-**ay**-li /ʃɪˈleɪli/

Shillong city, India
shil-**ong** /ʃɪˈlɒŋ/

Shilluk African ethnic group
shil-**uuk** /ʃɪˈlʊk/

Shiloh, Battle of American civil war
battle
shy-loh /ˈʃʌɪləʊ/

Shimano bicycle component
manufacturers
shim-**ah**-noh /ʃɪˈmɑːnəʊ/

Shin Bet (also **Shin Beth**) security
service of Israel
shin **bet** /ʃɪn ˈbɛt/

Shinkansen Japanese high speed
railway
shin-kan-sen /ˈʃɪnkanˌsɛn/

Shinola US trademark brand of boot polish
shy-**noh**-luh /ʃʌɪˈnəʊlə/

Shinto Japanese religion
shin-toh /ˈʃɪntəʊ/

Shiraz city, Iran
sheer-**az** /ʃɪəˈraz/

Shiraz black wine grape
shirr-**az** /ʃɪˈraz/

shire county
shy-uhr /ˈʃʌɪə(r)/

This is the pronunciation for the word in
isolation or in phrases such as 'shire horse'.
As a suffix, e.g. in Lancashire or Cheshire,
the pronunciation is much reduced to
-shuhr or, less commonly, -sheer.

Shiva (also **Siva**) Hindu god
shee-**vuh** /ˈʃiːvə/

shiva (also **shivah**) Jewish period of
mourning
shiv-uh /ˈʃɪvə/

Shiv Sena Hindu nationalist
organization
shiv **say**-nuh /ˌʃɪv ˈseɪnə/

Shizuoka city, Japan
shiz-oo-**oh**-kuh /ˌʃɪzuːˈəʊkə/

Shkodër city, Albania
shkoh-**duhr** /ˈʃkəʊdə(r)/

Shoah Holocaust
shoh-uh /ˈʃəʊə/

Shoemaker-Levy comet
shoo-may-kuhr **lee**-vi /ˌʃuːmeɪkə(r)
'liːvi/

shofar ram's-horn trumpet used in
Jewish ceremonies
shoh-fuhr /'ʃəʊfə(r)/

shogun hereditary commander-in-chief
in feudal Japan
shoh-guun /'ʃəʊgʊn/

shoji sliding screen door
shoh-ji /'ʃəʊdʒi/

Sholapur city, India
shoh-luh-**poor** /ˌʃəʊlə'pʊə(r)/

Shona African ethnic group
shoh-nuh /'ʃəʊnə/

shoogly unsteady (Scottish)
shuug-li /'ʃʊgli/

Shorinji Kempo martial art
shuh-**rin**-ji **kem**-poh /ʃəˌrɪmdʒi
'kɛmpəʊ/

Shoshone American Indian ethnic group
shuh-**shoh**-ni /ʃə'ʃəʊni/

Shostakovich, Dmitri Russian
composer
duh-**meet**-ri shost-uh-**koh**-vitch
/dəˌmiːtri ˌʃɒstə'kəʊvɪtʃ/

Shotokan style of karate
shoh-toh-kan /'ʃəʊtəʊkan/

Showalter, Elaine American writer
shoh-wawl-tuhr /'ʃəʊwɔːltə(r)/

shoyu Japanese soy sauce
shoh-yoo /'ʃəʊjuː/

Shreveport city, US
shreev-port /'ʃriːvpɔː(r)t/

Shrewsbury town, England
shrohz-buh-ri /'ʃrəʊzbəri/

Equally commonly **shrooz**-buh-ri. Both
pronunciations are used in the town.

Shri (also **Sri**) Indian title of respect
shree /ʃriː/

shrimati Indian title of respect for a
woman
shree-mut-i /'ʃriːmʌti/

Shriner member of a US charitable
society
shry-nuhr /'ʃrʌɪnə(r)/

shtetl pl. **shtetlach** small Jewish town in
eastern Europe
shtet-uhl, pl. **shtet**-lakh /'ʃtɛtəl/, pl.
/'ʃtɛtlax/

• Standard -s plural is also possible.

shtum (also **schtum**) silent
shtuum /ʃtʊm/

shtup (also **schtup**) have sexual
intercourse with
shtuup /ʃtʊp/

shubunkin goldfish
shuub-**unk**-in /ʃʊ'bʌŋkɪn/

shufti look or reconnoitre
shuuf-ti /'ʃʊfti/

Shugiin Japanese parliament
shoo-**gee**-in /'ʃuːgiːɪn/

shul synagogue
shool /ʃuːl/

Shumen city, Bulgaria
shoo-**muhn** /'ʃuːmən/

shura Islamic council
shoor-uh /'ʃʊərə/

shuriken weapon in the form of a star
shoor-ik-en /'ʃʊərɪkɛn/

Siachen Glacier glacier, India
see-uh-chen /'siːətʃɛn/

Sialkot city, Pakistan
si-**ahl**-koht /si'ɑːlkəʊt/

Siam former name for Thailand
sy-**am** /sʌɪ'am/

Sibelius, Jean Finnish composer
zhah(ng) sib-**ay**-li-uhss /ˌʒɑ̃ sɪ'beɪliəs/

Šibenik city, Croatia
shee-buh-nik /'ʃiːbənɪk/

Sibiu city, Romania
sib-**yoo** /sɪ'bjuː/

sibyl woman prophet
sib-il /'sɪbɪl/

Sibneft Russian oil company
sib-**nyeft** /sɪb'njɛft/

sic 'thus' (Latin)
sik /sɪk/

Sichuan province, China
suh-**chwan** /sə'tʃwan/
• See also Szechuan.

Sickert, Walter English painter
sik-uhrt /'sɪkə(r)t/

Siddhartha Gautama founder of
Buddhism; also called **Siddhartha
Gotama**
sid-**ar**-tuh **gow**-tuh-muh /sɪˌdɑː(r)tə
'gaʊtəmə/

Siddhartha Gotama founder of
Buddhism; also called **Siddhartha
Gautama**
sid-**ar**-tuh **goh**-tuh-muh /sɪˌdɑː(r)tə
'gəʊtəmə/

siddhi complete understanding
sid-i /'sɪdi/

sidereal of the distant stars
sy-**deer**-i-uhl /sʌɪ'dɪəriəl/

Sidhe Irish mythological fairy people
shee /ʃiː/

Sidi bel Abbès town, Algeria
sid-i bel uh-**bess** /ˌsɪdi bɛl ə'bɛs/

Sidi bou Said town, Tunisia
sid-i boo suh-**eed** /ˌsɪdi bu: sə'iːd/

Sidon city, Lebanon
sy-duhn /'sʌɪdən/

Sidra inlet, Libya; also called **Sirte**
sid-ruh /'sɪdrə/

Siebengebirge range of hills, Germany
zee-buhn-guh-beer-guh
/'ziːbənɡəˌbɪə(r)ɡə/

Siegessäule column, Berlin
zee-guhss-zoy-luh /'ziːɡəszɔɪlə/

Siegfried Wagnerian character and hero
of the *Nibelungenlied*
seeg-freed /'siːɡfriːd/, German
[ˈziːkfriːt]
• Established anglicization.

Sieg Heil Nazi victory salute
zeek **hyl** /ˌziːk 'hʌɪl/

Sieglinde Wagnerian character
zeek-**lin**-duh /ziːk'lɪndə/

Siegmund Wagnerian character
zeek-muunt /'ziːkmʊnt/

Siemens German family of scientists
zee-muhnss /'ziːməns/

The name of the company founded by the
family is usually anglicized to **see**-muhnz.

siemens SI unit of conductance
see-muhnz /'siːmənz/

Siem Reap city, Cambodia
syem **ryahp** /sjɛm 'rjɑːp/

Siena city, Italy
si-**en**-uh /si'ɛnə/

sierra jagged mountain chain
si-**air**-uh /si'ɛːrə/

Commonly also si-**err**-uh.

Sierra Leone country
si-**err**-uh li-**ohn** /siˌɛrə li'əʊn/

Sierra Madre mountain range, Mexico
si-**err**-uh **mah**-dray /siˌɛrə 'mɑːdreɪ/,
Spanish [ˌsjera 'maðre]
• Established anglicization.

Sierra Nevada mountain range, Spain

si-**err**-uh nuh-**vah**-duh /siˌɛrə
nə'vɑːdə/, [ˌsjera ne'βaða]
• Established anglicization.

siesta afternoon nap
si-**est**-uh /si'ɛstə/

sievert SI unit of dose equivalent
see-vuhrt /'siːvə(r)t/

sigil magical symbol
sij-il /'sɪdʒɪl/

Sigişoara town, Romania
sig-ish-**war**-uh /sɪɡɪʃ'wɑːrə/

sigma letter of the Greek alphabet
sig-muh /'sɪɡmə/

sigmoidoscopy examination of the
colon
sig-moy-**dosk**-uh-pi /ˌsɪɡmɔɪ'dɒskəpi/

Signac, Paul French painter
pol seen-**yak** /ˌpɒl siː'njak/

signatory party that has signed an
agreement
sig-nuh-tuh-ri /'sɪɡnətəri/

signor pl. **signori** Italian title for a man
seen-**yor**, pl. seen-**yor**-i /'siːnjɔː(r)/, pl.
/-'njɔːri/

signora Italian title for a woman
seen-**yor**-uh /siː'njɔːrə/

signorina Italian title for a young
woman
seen-yuh-**ree**-nuh /ˌsiːnjə'riːnə/

Sigur Rós Icelandic rock band
see-guhr **rohss** /ˌsiːɡə(r) 'rəʊs/

Sihanouk, Norodom Cambodian
statesman
norr-uh-**dom** see-uh-**nuuk** /ˌnɒrəˌdɒm
siːə'nʊk/

Sikhism religion
seek-iz-uhm /'siːkɪzəm/

Sikkim state, India
sik-im /'sɪkɪm/

Sikorsky, Igor Russian-American
aircraft designer
ee-gor sik-**or**-ski /ˌiːɡɔː(r) sɪ'kɔː(r)ski/

silage compacted fodder
sy-lij /'sʌɪlɪdʒ/

Sildenafil trademark drug
sil-**den**-uh-fil /sɪl'dɛnəfɪl/

Silenus Greek god
sy-**lee**-nuhss /sʌɪ'liːnəs/

Silesia region, Europe
sy-**lee**-zi-uh /sʌɪ'liːziə/

This region is mostly in Poland. The Polish name is Śląsk, pronounced shlo(ng)sk.

silhouette dark shape
sil-oo-**et** /ˌsɪlʊˈɛt/

silicon chemical element
sil-ik-uhn /ˈsɪlɪkən/

silicone synthetic material
sil-ik-ohn /ˈsɪlɪkəʊn/

silo tower used to store grain
sy-loh /ˈsaɪləʊ/

Siloam biblical pool near Jerusalem
sy-**loh**-uhm /saɪˈləʊəm/

Silurian geological era
sy-**lyoor**-i-uhn /saɪˈljʊəriən/

Silvanus Roman god
sil-**vah**-nuhss /sɪlˈvɑːnəs/

Silverstein, Shel American cartoonist
shel sil-vuhr-steen /ˌʃɛl ˈsɪlvə(r)stiːn/

Simbirsk city, Russia
sim-**beersk** /sɪmˈbɪə(r)sk/

Simenon, Georges Belgian novelist
zhorzh see-muh-**no(ng)** /ˌʒɔː(r)ʒ siːməˈnɔ̃/

Simeon Hebrew patriarch
sim-i-uhn /ˈsɪmiən/

Simeon Stylites, St Syrian monk
sty-**ly**-teez /staɪˈlaɪtiːz/

Simferopol city, Ukraine
seem-fuh-**rop**-uhl /ˌsiːmfəˈrɒpəl/

simian relating to apes or monkeys
sim-i-uhn /ˈsɪmiən/

simile figure of speech
sim-il-i /ˈsɪmɪli/

Simla city, India
sim-luh /ˈsɪmlə/

simnel cake fruit cake eaten at Easter
sim-nuhl /ˈsɪmnəl/

Simon Boccanegra opera by Verdi
see-**mon** bok-uh-**nay**-gruh /siːˌmɒn bɒkəˈneɪɡrə/

Simonides Greek lyric poet
sy-**mon**-id-eez /saɪˈmɒnɪdiːz/

simony buying or selling of ecclesiastical privileges
sy-muh-ni /ˈsaɪməni/

simpatico likeable
sim-**pat**-ik-oh /sɪmˈpatɪkəʊ/

Simplon pass, Switzerland
simp-lon /ˈsɪmplɒn/

simulacrum pl. **simulacra** representation of something

sim-yuul-**ay**-kruhm, pl.
sim-yuul-**ay**-kruh /ˌsɪmjʊˈleɪkrəm/, pl. /-krə/
• Standard -s plural is also possible.

simurg mythical bird
sim-**urg** /sɪˈmə:(r)ɡ/

simvastatin drug
sim-vuh-**stat**-in /sɪmvəˈstatɪn/

Sinai peninsula, Egypt
sy-ny /ˈsaɪnaɪ/

Sinaloa state, Mexico
see-nuh-**loh**-uh /ˌsiːnəˈləʊə/

Sinatra, Frank American singer
sin-**ah**-truh /sɪˈnɑːtrə/

Sinclair, Clive English engineer
sink-lair /ˈsɪŋklɛ:(r)/

sine trigonometric function
syn /saɪn/

sinecure position requiring little work
sin-uh-kyoor /ˈsɪnəkjʊə(r)/

Less commonly also **syn**-uh-kyoor.

sine die with no appointed date for resumption (Latin)
see-nay dee-ay /ˌsaɪneɪ ˈdiːeɪ/

sine qua non essential condition (Latin)
sin-ay kwah **non** /ˌsɪneɪ kwɑː ˈnɒn/

Commonly also other pronunciations such as **sin**-i kwah **nohn**; see LATIN panel.

sinfonia symphony; also the name of a London-based orchestra
sin-**foh**-ni-uh /sɪnˈfəʊniə/

Established anglicization. The Italian pronunciation, however, is sin-foh-**nee**-uh, which is less commonly also used.

sinfonietta short symphony
sin-foh-ni-**et**-uh /ˌsɪnfəʊniˈɛtə/

Singapore country
sing-uh-**por** /ˌsɪŋəˈpɔː(r)/

Singh, Manmohan Indian prime minister
mun-**moh**-hun sing /mʌnˌməʊhʌnˈsɪŋ/

The first name is commonly also pronounced **mun**-moh-hun by Hindi speakers.

Singspiel pl. **Singspiele** form of German light opera
zing-shpeel, pl. **zing**-shpeel-uh /ˈzɪŋʃpiːl/, pl. /-lə/

Sinhala (also **Singhala**) ethnic group and language, Sri Lanka; also called **Sinhalese**
sing-huh-luh /ˈsɪŋhələ/

Sinhalese (also **Singhalese**) ethnic group and language, Sri Lanka; also called **Sinhala**
sing-huh-**leez** /ˌsɪŋhəˈliːz/

sinistral of the left side
sin-ist-ruhl /ˈsɪnɪstrəl/

Sinn Féin Irish political party
shin fayn /ˌʃɪn ˈfeɪn/

sinology study of China
sy-**nol**-uh-ji /saɪˈnɒlədʒi/

sinsemilla variety of cannabis
sin-suh-**mil**-uh /ˌsɪnsəˈmɪlə/

Sint-Niklaas town, Belgium
sint nik-lahss /ˌsɪnt ˈnɪklɑːs/

Sintra (also **Cintra**) town, Portugal
sint-ruh /ˈsɪntrə/

Sinuiju city, North Korea
sin-wee-joo /ˌsɪnwiːˈdʒuː/

sinuous curvy
sin-yoo-uhss /ˈsɪnjuəs/

sinus cavity within a bone
sy-nuhss /ˈsaɪnəs/

Siobhan Irish girl's name
shiv-awn /ʃɪˈvɔːn/

Sion see **Zion**

Sioux North American ethnic group
soo /suː/

siphon tube
sy-fuhn /ˈsaɪfən/

Sirdar see **Sardar**

Sirius star
sirr-i-uhss /ˈsɪriəs/

Sirleaf Johnson, Ellen Liberian president
sur-leef /ˈsəː(r)liːf/

sirocco see **scirocco**

sirrah term of address for a man
sirr-uh /ˈsɪrə/

Sirte inlet, Libya; also called **Sidra**
seer-tay /ˈsɪə(r)teɪ/

sisal fibrous plant
sy-suhl /ˈsaɪsəl/

Sisley, Alfred French painter
al-fruhd siz-li /ˌalfrəd ˈsɪzli/

Sistani, Ayatollah Ali al- Iraqi senior Shia cleric
y-uh-**tol**-ah al-ee uh-sist-**ah**-ni /ʌɪə,tɒlɑː aˌli: əsɪsˈtɑːni/

Sistine Chapel chapel in the Vatican
sist-een /ˈsɪstiːn/

Sisyphean denoting a task that can never be completed
siss-if-**ee**-uhn /ˌsɪsɪˈfiːən/

Sisyphus Greek mythological character
siss-if-uhss /ˈsɪsɪfəs/

Sita wife of Rama
see-tuh /ˈsiːtə/

sitar musical instrument
sit-ar /sɪˈtɑː(r)/

Sitges resort, Spain
see-chuhss /ˈsiːtʃəs/

sitka spruce tree
sit-kuh /ˈsɪtkə/

situs inversus medical condition
sy-tuhss in-**vur**-suhss /ˌsaɪtəs ɪnˈvəː(r)səs/

sitzfleisch buttocks
zits-flysh /ˈzɪtsflaɪʃ/

Siva see **Shiva**

Sivan Jewish month
see-vahn /ˈsiːvɑːn/

Siwalik Hills foothills in the Himalayas
si-**wah**-lik /sɪˈwɑːlɪk/

sjambok whip
sham-bok /ˈʃambɒk/

Sjögren's syndrome autoimmune condition
shoe-graynz /ˈʃøːɡreɪmz/

This pronunciation is closest to the Swedish pronunciation of Sjögren's name. Anglicizations **shoh**-gruhn and **shur**-gruhn are also common.

ska style of music
skah /skɑː/

Skagen town, Denmark
skag-uhn /ˈskaɡən/, [ˈsɡɛɣən]
• Established anglicization.

Skagerrak strait between Norway and Denmark
skag-uh-rak /ˈskaɡərak/

skål 'cheers' (Swedish, Norwegian, and Danish)
skawl /skɔːl/
• See also **skol**.

skald (also **scald**) Norse bard
skald /skald/

Skanda Hindu god
skan-duh /ˈskandə/

skean-dhu dagger
skee-uhn **doo** /ˌskiːən ˈduː/

skedaddle depart quickly or hurriedly
skuh-**dad**-uhl /skəˈdadəl/

skein length of yarn
skayn /skeɪn/

skeletal relating to a skeleton
skel-uh-tuhl /ˈskɛlətəl/

Less commonly also skuh-**lee**-tuhl.

skene part of the set in Greek theatre
skee-ni /ˈskiːni/

ski device for travelling over snow
skee /skiː/

Eighty years ago our BBC predecessors recommended the pronunciation shee, which is how the word is pronounced in Norwegian. However, the anglicization skee quickly took hold.

Skiathos island, Greece
ski-**ath**-oss /skiˈaθɒs/

Skibo castle, Scotland
skee-boh /ˈskiːbəʊ/

Skidoo trademark motorized toboggan
skid-**oo** /skɪˈduː/

skijoring being pulled on skis by a horse or dog
skee-jaw-ring /ˈskiːdʒɔːrɪŋ/

Skłodowska, Maria see **Curie, Marie**

skol 'cheers'
skol /skɒl/

Less commonly also skohl, sometimes with the spelling *skoal*. Cognate with modern Scandinavian SKÅL.

Skopje capital, Macedonia
skop-yuh /ˈskɒpjə/

Skraeling indigenous inhabitant of Greenland
skray-ling /ˈskreɪlɪŋ/

Skryabin see **Scriabin**

skua seabird
skyoo-uh /ˈskjuːə/

skulduggery (also **skullduggery**) dishonest behaviour
skul-**dug**-uh-ri /skʌlˈdʌgəri/

sláinte 'cheers' (Gaelic)
slahn-chuh /ˈslɑːntʃə/

slalom downhill ski race
slah-luhm /ˈslɑːləm/

Slav ethnic group
slahv /slɑːv/

slaver saliva running from the mouth
slav-uhr /ˈslavə(r)/

Slavic language family
slah-vik /ˈslɑːvɪk/

Commonly also **slav**-ik.

Slavonic Slavic
sluh-**von**-ik /sləˈvɒnɪk/

sleight use of dexterity or cunning
slyt /slʌɪt/

Sligo county, Republic of Ireland
sly-goh /ˈslʌɪgəʊ/

Sliven city, Bulgaria
slee-vuhn /ˈsliːvən/

slivovitz plum brandy
sliv-uh-vits /ˈslɪvəvɪts/

sloth reluctance to work
slohth /sləʊθ/

Slough town, England
slow /slaʊ/

slough swamp
slow /slaʊ/

slough shed dead skin
sluf /slʌf/

Slovak native of Slovakia
sloh-vak /ˈsləʊvak/

Slovakia country
sluh-**vak**-i-uh /sləˈvakiə/

Slovene native of Slovenia
sloh-veen /ˈsləʊviːn/

Slovenia country
sluh-**vee**-ni-uh /sləˈviːniə/

Slovo, Joe South African activist
sloh-voh /ˈsləʊvəʊ/

Smaug dragon in *The Hobbit*
smowg /smaʊg/

Sméagol fictional character in *The Lord of the Rings*
smee-gol /ˈsmiːgɒl/

smetana sour cream
smuh-**tah**-nuh /sməˈtɑːnə/

Smetana, Bedřich Czech composer
bej-ikh **smet**-uh-nuh /ˈbɛdʒɪx ˈsmɛtənə/

Smethwick town, England
smeth-ik /ˈsmɛðɪk/

smilodon prehistoric sabre-toothed cat
smil-uh-don /ˈsmɪlədɒn/

smithereens small pieces
smith-uh-**reenz** /ˌsmɪðəˈriːnz/

Smirnoff brand of vodka
smur-nof /ˈsmə(r)nɒf/

Established anglicization. Originally produced by Piotr Smirnov: this common Russian surname is pronounced smeer-**nof** [smʲɪrˈnɔf].

Smith–Magenis syndrome chromosome disorder
muh-**gen**-iss /məˈɡɛnɪs/

Smithsonian Institution US foundation in Washington DC
smith-**soh**-ni-uhn /smɪθˈsəʊnɪən/

smithy blacksmith's workshop
smith-i /ˈsmɪði/

Smolensk city, Russia
smuhl-**yensk** /sməˈljɛnsk/

Smollett, Tobias Scottish novelist
tuh-**by**-uhss smol-it /təˌbʌɪəs ˈsmɒlɪt/

smorgasbord buffet
smor-guhz-bord /ˈsmɔː(r)ɡəsbɔː(r)d/

smorzando musical term
smor-**tsan**-doh /smɔː(r)ˈtsandəʊ/

Smuts, Jan South African statesman
yan smuts /ˌjan ˈsmʌts/

Smyrna ancient city, Asia Minor
smur-nuh /ˈsmɜː(r)nə/

Smyth, Ethel English composer
smyth /ˈsmʌɪð/

This British surname is variously pronounced smyth, smyth, and smith, depending on individual preference.

Smythson English firm of stationers
smyth-suhn /ˈsmʌɪðsən/

snafu chaotic state
snaf-oo /snaˈfuː/

snood ornamental hairnet
snood /snuːd/

Snorri Sturluson Icelandic poet
snorr-i stur-luh-son /ˌsnɒrɪ ˈstɜː(r)ləsɒn/
• Established anglicization.

Snowdonia national park, Wales
snoh-**doh**-ni-uh /snəʊˈdəʊnɪə/

Soave white wine
swah-vay /ˈswɑːveɪ/

Soay breed of sheep
soh-ay /ˈsəʊeɪ/

soba buckwheat noodles
soh-buh /ˈsəʊbə/

Sobel, Dava American writer
dah-vuh soh-bel /ˌdaːvə səʊˈbɛl/

Sobibór site of a Nazi extermination camp, Poland

sob-**ee**-boor /sɒˈbibʊə(r)/

sobriety state of being sober
suh-**bry**-uh-ti /səˈbrʌɪəti/

sobriquet affectionate nickname; also **soubriquet**
soh-brik-ay /ˈsəʊbrɪkeɪ/

soca calypso music
soh-kuh /ˈsəʊkə/

SOCA Serious and Organized Crime Agency
sok-uh /ˈsɒkə/

Sochi port, Russia
sotch-i /ˈsɒtʃi/

sockdolager forceful blow
sok-**dol**-uh-juhr /sɒkˈdɒlədʒə(r)/

socle plinth
soh-kuhl /ˈsəʊkəl/

Socotra island, Arabian Sea
suh-**koh**-truh /səˈkəʊtrə/

Socrates Greek philosopher
sok-ruh-teez /ˈsɒkrətiːz/

Socratic relating to Socrates
suh-**krat**-ik /səˈkratɪk/

sodality confraternity
soh-**dal**-it-i /səʊˈdalɪti/

Soderbergh, Steven American film director
soh-duhr-burg /ˈsəʊdə(r)bɜː(r)ɡ/

Söderblom, Nathan Swedish theologian
nah-tan soe-duhr-bluum /ˌnɑːtan ˈsøːdə(r)blʊm/

Södertälje city, Sweden
soe-duhr-**tel**-yuh /ˌsøːdə(r)ˈtɛljə/

Sodom town in ancient Palestine
sod-uhm /ˈsɒdəm/

Soe Win Burmese prime minister
soh win /səʊ ˈwɪn/

Sofia capital of Bulgaria
soh-fi-uh /ˈsəʊfiə/

Sofia Spanish queen
suh-**fee**-uh /ˈsəfiːə/

Sogne Fjord fjord, Norway
song-nuh /ˈsɒŋnə/

sogo shosha large company (Japanese)
soh-goh shoh-shuh /ˌsəʊɡəʊ ˈʃəʊʃə/

Soham village, Cambridgeshire
soh-uhm /ˈsəʊəm/

soi-disant self-styled
swah dee-**zo(ng)** /ˌswɑː diːˈzɔ̃/

soigné dressed elegantly
swahn-**yay** /swɑːˈnjeɪ/

soirée an evening party or gathering
swah-**ray** /swɑːˈreɪ/

soixante-neuf sexual activity
swass-o(ng)t **noef** /ˌswasɔ̃t ˈnœf/

sojourn temporary stay
soj-uhrn /ˈsɒdʒə(r)n/

Less commonly also **soj**-urn. AM commonly **soh**-jurn.

Sokol Czechoslovakian athletics movement
sok-ol /ˈsɒkɒl/

Sol Roman sun god
sol /sɒl/

solace consolation
sol-uhss /ˈsɒləs/

Solana, Javier Spanish politician
khav-**yair** sol-**ah**-nuh /xaˌvjɛː(r) sɒˈlɑːnə/

solanaceous relating to plants of the nightshade family
sol-uh-**nay**-shuhss /ˌsɒləˈneɪʃəs/

solander box in the form of a book
suh-**land**-uhr /səˈlandə(r)/

solarium room equipped with sunlamps
suh-**lair**-i-uhm /səˈlɛːriəm/

solder low-melting alloy
sohl-duhr /ˈsəʊldə(r)/

solecism grammatical mistake
sol-uh-siz-uhm /ˈsɒləsɪzəm/

solemnity seriousness
suh-**lem**-nit-i /səˈlɛmnɪti/

solenoid electromagnet
sol-uh-noyd /ˈsɒlənɔɪd/

Solent channel, England
soh-luhnt /ˈsəʊlənt/

soleus calf muscle
soh-**lee**-uhss /səʊˈliːəs/

solfeggio pl. **solfeggi** singing exercise
sol-**fej**-oh, pl. sol-**fej**-i /sɒlˈfɛdʒəʊ/, pl. /-dʒi/

Solidarność Polish trade union
sol-ee-**dar**-noshch /sɒliːˈdɑː(r)nɒʃʧ/

solidus pl. **solidi** slash (/)
sol-id-uhss, pl. **sol**-id-y /ˈsɒlɪdəs/, pl. /-dʌɪ/

Solihull town, England
soh-li-**hul** /ˌsəʊlɪˈhʌl/

This is the pronunciation most commonly used locally. Commonly also **sol**-i-hul.

soliloquy speaking one's thoughts aloud

suh-**lil**-uh-kwi /səˈlɪləkwi/

solipsism view that the self is all that can be known to exist
sol-ip-siz-uhm /ˈsɒlɪpsɪzəm/

solitaire game for one player
sol-i-tair /ˈsɒlɪtɛː(r)/

Sóller town, Majorca
sol-yair /ˈsɒljɛː(r)/

Solnhofen village, Germany
zohln-hoh-fuhn /ˈzəʊlnˌhəʊfən/

Solomon king of ancient Israel
sol-uh-muhn /ˈsɒləmən/

Solon ancient Athenian statesman
soh-lon /ˈsəʊlɒn/

solstice longest or shortest day
sol-stiss /ˈsɒlstɪs/

Solti, Georg Hungarian-born British conductor
jorj **shol**-ti /ˌdʒɔː(r)dʒ ˈʃɒlti/

Solutrean archaeological culture
suh-**loot**-ri-uhn /səˈluːtriən/

Solveig character in *Peer Gynt*
sool-vay /ˈsuːlveɪ/

Solzhenitsyn, Alexander Russian novelist
al-uhk-**sahn**-duhr sol-zhuh-**neet**-sin /aləkˌsɑːndə(r) ˌsɒlʒəˈniːtsɪn/

som currency unit, Kyrgyzstan and Uzbekistan
sohm /səʊm/

Somalia country
suh-**mah**-li-uh /səˈmɑːliə/

somatization manifestation of psychological distress by the presentation of bodily symptoms
soh-muh-ty-**zay**-shuhn /ˌsəʊmətʌɪˈzeɪʃən/

sombrero broad-brimmed hat
som-**brair**-oh /sɒmˈbrɛːrəʊ/

Somerset county, England
sum-uhr-set /ˈsʌmə(r)sɛt/

Somme river, France
som /sɒm/

sommelier wine waiter
som-**el**-i-ay /sɒˈmɛlieɪ/

somnambulism sleepwalking
som-**nam**-byuul-iz-uhm /sɒmˈnambjʊlɪzəm/

somoni currency unit, Tajikistan
som-**oh**-ni /sɒˈməʊni/

sonar detection system
soh-nar /ˈsəʊnɑː(r)/

sonata musical composition
suh-**nah**-tuh /sə'nɑːtə/

sonatina short sonata
son-uh-**tee**-nuh /ˌsɒnə'tiːnə/

Sondheim, Stephen American composer
sond-hym /'sɒndhʌɪm/

son et lumière entertainment
son ay loom-**yair** /ˌsɒn eɪ luː'mjɛː(r)/

Songhai African ethnic group
song-**gy** /sɒŋ'ɡʌɪ/

Song Hong river, Vietnam
song hong /ˌsɒŋ 'hɒŋ/

Songhua river, China
suung-**khwah** /ˌsʊŋ'xwɑː/

sonography analysis of sound
suh-**nog**-ruh-fi /sə'nɒɡrəfi/

Sonora state, Mexico
suh-**naw**-ruh /sə'nɔːrə/

sonorant speech sound
son-uh-ruhnt /'sɒnərənt/

sonorous imposingly deep and full
son-uh-ruhss /'sɒnərəs/

Less commonly also suh-**naw**-ruhss.

Sontag, Susan American writer
son-tag /'sɒntaɡ/

Sony electronics company
soh-ni /'səʊni/

sooth truth
sooth /suːθ/

sopaipilla deep-fried pastry
sop-y-**peel**-juh /ˌsɒpʌɪ'piːljə/

sophistry use of clever but false arguments
sof-ist-ri /'sɒfɪstri/

Sophocles Greek dramatist
sof-uh-kleez /'sɒfəkliːz/

sophomore second-year student
sof-uh-mor /'sɒfəmɔː(r)/

sophomoric immature
sof-uh-**morr**-ik /ˌsɒfə'mɒrɪk/

soporific tending to induce drowsiness
sop-uh-**rif**-ik /ˌsɒpə'rɪfɪk/

soprano singing voice
suh-**prah**-noh /sə'prɑːnəʊ/

sorbet water ice
sor-bay /'sɔː(r)beɪ/

AM is **sor**-buht. This pronunciation is also possible, but much less common, in BR.

Sorbonne part of the University of Paris

sor-**bon** /sɔː(r)'bɒn/

sordino pl. **sordini** mute for a musical instrument
sor-**dee**-noh, pl. sor-**dee**-ni /sɔː(r)'diːnəʊ, pl. /-ni/

sorghum cereal
sor-guhm /'sɔː(r)ɡəm/

Soroca city, Moldova
suh-**rok**-uh /sə'rɒkə/

Soroptimist member of an international women's association
suh-**rop**-ti-mist /sə'rɒptɪmɪst/

sorority university club for female students
suh-**rorr**-it-i /sə'rɒrɪti/

sorrel plant
sorr-uhl /'sɒrəl/

Sorrento town, Italy
suh-**ren**-toh /sə'rɛntəʊ/

Sosnowiec town, Poland
soss-**nov**-yets /sɒs'nɒvjɛts/

sostenuto musical term
sost-uh-**noo**-toh /ˌsɒstə'nuːtəʊ/

Sotheby's English auctioneers
suth-uh-beez /'sʌðəbiːz/

Sotho African ethnic group
soo-too /'suːtuː/

sotto voce in a quiet voice
sot-oh **voh**-chay /ˌsɒtəʊ 'vəʊtʃeɪ/

sou old French coin
soo /suː/

soubise onion sauce
soo-**beez** /suː'biːz/

soubresaut ballet jump
soob-ruh-soh /'suːbrəsəʊ/

soubrette minor female role in a comedy
soo-**bret** /suː'brɛt/

soubriquet affectionate nickname; also **sobriquet**
soob-rik-ay /'suːbrɪkeɪ/

Souch, John English painter
soosh /suːʃ/

soucouyant malignant witch
soo-koo-**yah(ng)** /ˌsuːkuː'jã/

souffle blowing sound heard through a stethoscope
soo-fuhl /'suːfəl/

soufflé egg dish
soof-**lay** /suː'fleɪ/

Soufrière name of various volcanoes in the Caribbean
soof-**reer** /suː'frɪə(r)/

This is the common pronunciation in St Vincent and Montserrat, although in St Lucia the pronunciation is suuf-**rair**.

sough whistling or rushing sound
sow /saʊ/

Commonly also suf.

souk (also **suk** or **sukh**) Arab marketplace
sook /suːk/

Soumak rug or carpet
soo-mak /'suːmak/

Souness, Graham English footballer
soo-nuhss /'suːnəs/

soupçon very small quantity of something
soop-son /'suːpsɒn/

Sousa, John Philip American composer
soo-zuh /'suːzə/

sousaphone musical instrument
soo-zuh-fohn /'suːzəfəʊn/

Sousse port, Tunisia
sooss /suːs/

soutane priest's cassock
soo-tahn /suːˈtɑːn/

souterrain underground chamber
soo-tuh-rayn /'suːtəreɪn/

Southampton city, England
sowth-**hamp**-tuhn /saʊθˈhamptən/

Commonly also sowth-**amp**-tuhn.

Southey, Robert English poet
sow-*th*i /'saʊði/

Southwark borough of London
suth-uhrk /'sʌðə(r)k/

Southwell town, Nottingham
sowth-wuhl /'saʊθwəl/

Commonly also **suth**-uhl. This latter pronunciation is also appropriate for Southwell Minster and Viscount Southwell.

Soutine, Chaïm French painter
kuh-**eem** soo-**teen** /kəˌiːm suːˈtiːn/

souvlaki pl. **souvlakia** Greek meat dish
soov-**lak**-i, pl. soov-**lak**-i-uh /suːˈvlaki/, pl. /-kiə/

sou'wester waterproof hat
sow-**est**-uhr /saʊˈwɛstə(r)/

soviet elected council in the USSR
soh-vi-uht /'səʊviət/

Commonly also **sov**-yuht.

Sowerby town, England
sor-bi /'sɔ(r)bi:/

Soweto urban area, South Africa
suh-**wet**-oh /sə'wɛtəʊ/

Soyinka, Wole Nigerian dramatist
wol-i shoy-**ink**-uh /ˌwɒli ʃɔɪ'ɪŋkə/

Soyuz Soviet spacecraft
suh-**yooz** /sə'juːz/

Spacek, Sissy American actress
spay-sek /'speɪsɛk/

spaetzle dumplings
shpets-luh /'ʃpɛtslə/

Spago restaurant in Los Angeles
spah-goh /'spɑːɡəʊ/

Spallanzani, Lazzaro Italian physiologist
lat-suh-roh spal-ant-**sah**-ni /ˌlatsərəʊ spalan'tsɑːni/

spalpeen rascal
spal-**peen** /spal'piːn/

spanakopita spinach and feta cheese pie
span-uh-**kop**-it-uh /ˌspanə'kɒpitə/

Spandau prison in Berlin
span-dow /'spandaʊ/

sparable headless nail
sparr-uh-buhl /'sparəbəl/

Sparta city, Greece
spar-tuh /'spɑː(r)tə/

Spartacus Thracian slave and gladiator
spar-tuh-kuhss /'spɑː(r)təkəs/

spatial relating to space
spay-shuhl /'speɪʃəl/

Spätlese white wine
shpayt-lay-zuh /'ʃpeɪtˌleɪzə/

speciality particular area of knowledge
spesh-i-**al**-it-i /ˌspɛʃɪ'alɪti/

AM is *specialty*, pronounced **spesh**-uhl-ti.

specie money in the form of coins
spee-shi /'spiːʃi/

species group of living organisms
spee-sheez /'spiːʃiːz/

Less commonly also **spee**-seez.

spectrometer apparatus used for measuring spectra
spek-**trom**-uh-tuhr /spɛk'trɒmətə(r)/

spectroscopy branch of science concerned with spectra
spek-**trosk**-uh-pi /spɛk'trɒskəpi/

Spanish

Spanish is spoken by more than 350 million people worldwide. It is a Romance language quite similar to Italian and even more closely related to Catalan and Galician (minority languages of Spain). Spanish pronunciation is relatively straightforward, and—bearing in mind some salient differences between Latin American and European Spanish—is entirely predictable from the spelling.

When we make recommendations on the pronunciation of Spanish we can usually come quite close to a native pronunciation, subject as always to a degree of anglicization. The details given below are not an exhaustive list of the features of Spanish, as some are too subtle to be described using our respelling. In particular, the pronunciation of B, G, and V are distinctively different from English. These sounds are anglicized in our recommendations.

Stress

Spanish stress falls on the second-last syllable of the word, unless the last letter of the word is a consonant other than N or S, in which case stress falls on the last syllable. Exceptions to this rule are indicated in the spelling by an accent over the vowel of the syllable to be stressed, for example *inglés, Córdoba*.

Vowels

The five vowels A, E, I, O, and U are monophthongs and are pronounced approximately a, ay, ee, oh, and oo. In some anglicizations A is pronounced ah, e.g. *macho*. Diphthongs such as AI and EU are pronounced as sequences of their component parts, **a**-ee (or y as in *cry*) and **ay**-oo.

Consonants

C is pronounced k before A, O, and U. Before E and I it is pronounced th as in *thin* in European Spanish and s in Latin American Spanish.

CH is pronounced ch.

D is pronounced th as in *this*, or d at the beginning of a word or after L or N. In our recommendations we sometimes anglicize the sound to d in all positions.

G is pronounced kh (as in *loch*) or kh with added voicing (i.e. pronounced with vibration of the vocal cords), but is sometimes anglicized to g. GUA is pronounced gwa, GUE is gay, and GUI is gee; however, GÜE is gway and GÜI is gwee.

H is always silent.

J is pronounced kh (as in *loch*). *José* is khoss-**ay**.

LL is pronounced ly as in *million* in formal Spanish, but many Spanish speakers just pronounce it y as in *yes*. We generally give ly, as that is the pronunciation that still appears in dictionaries, although in individual cases we sometimes judge that y would be better.

Ñ is pronounced ny as in *onion*.

Z is pronounced th as in *thin* in European Spanish and s in Latin American Spanish.

speculum pl. **specula** medical instrument
spek-yuul-uhm, pl. **spek**-yuul-uh
/'spɛkjʊləm/, pl. /-lə/

speedometer instrument for measuring a vehicle's speed
spee-**dom**-uh-tuhr /spiːˈdɒmətə(r)/

Speenhamland system historical system of poor relief
speen-uhm-land /'spiːnəmland/

Speer, Albert German architect and Nazi official
al-**bairt shpair** /ˌalbɛː(r)t ˈʃpɛː(r)/,
[ˈʃpeːɐ]

Speke, John Hanning English explorer
speek /spiːk/

speleology study or exploration of caves
spee-li-**ol**-uh-ji /ˌspiːliˈɒlədʒi/

spelunking exploration of caves
spuh-**lunk**-ing /spəˈlʌŋkɪŋ/

Spencerian style of handwriting
spen-**seer**-i-uhn /spɛnˈsɪəriən/

Spengler, Oswald German philosopher
oss-valt **speng**-luhr /ˌɒsvalt ˈspɛŋlə(r)/

spermaceti waxy substance produced by the sperm whale
spur-muh-**see**-ti /ˌspəː(r)məˈsiːti/

Commonly also spur-muh-**set**-i.

spermatozoon pl. **spermatozoa** male sex cell
spur-muh-toh-**zoh**-on,
pl. spur-muh-toh-**zoh**-uh
/ˌspəː(r)mətəʊˈzəʊɒn/, pl. /-ˈzəʊə/

Spetsnaz Russian military unit
spets-**nass** /spɛtsˈnas/

Spey river, Scotland
spay /speɪ/

sphagnum moss plant
sfag-nuhm /'sfagnəm/

sphenoid bone in the skull
sfee-noyd /'sfiːnɔɪd/

spheroid sphere-like body
sfeer-oyd /'sfɪərɔɪd/

spherical sphere-shaped
sferr-ik-uhl /'sfɛrɪkəl/

sphincter ring of muscle
sfink-tuhr /'sfɪŋktə(r)/

sphygmomanometer instrument for measuring blood pressure
sfig-moh-muh-**nom**-uh-tuhr
/ˌsfɪɡməʊməˈnɒmətə(r)/

Spica star
spee-kuh /'spiːkə/

spiccato style of playing on stringed instruments
spik-**ah**-toh /spɪˈkɑːtəʊ/

Spiegl, Fritz Austrian-born British musician and broadcaster
frits **shpee**-guhl /ˌfrɪts ˈʃpiːɡəl/

spiel elaborate or glib speech
shpeel /ʃpiːl/

Spielberg, Steven American film director and producer
speel-burg /'spiːlbəː(r)ɡ/

Spiers, Bob British television director
speerz /'spɪə(r)z/

spigot small peg or plug
spig-uht /'spɪɡət/

Spillane, Mickey American writer
spil-**ayn** /spɪˈleɪn/

spina bifida congenital defect
spy-nuh **bif**-id-uh /ˌspʌɪnə ˈbɪfɪdə/

spinach vegetable
spin-itch /'spɪnɪtʃ/

Commonly also **spin**-ij.

Spin Boldak town, Afghanistan
speen bawl-dak /ˌspiːn ˈbɔːldak/

spinet small harpsichord
spin-**et** /spɪˈnɛt/

Commonly also **spin-uht**.

spinnaker three-cornered sail
spin-nuh-kuhr /ˈspɪnəkə(r)/

Spinoza, Baruch Dutch philosopher
buh-**rook** spin-**oh**-zuh /bə.ruːk
spɪˈnəʊzə/
• Established anglicization.

spiraea shrub
spy-**ree**-uh /spʌɪˈriːə/

spirochaete bacterium
spy-roh-keet /ˈspʌɪrəʊkiːt/

spirogyra alga
spy-roh-**jy**-ruh /ˌspʌɪrəʊˈdʒʌɪrə/

spirometer instrument for measuring
lung capacity
spy-**rom**-uh-tuhr /spʌɪˈrɒmətə(r)/

spirulina protein-rich bacteria
spy-**ruul**-**y**-nuh /ˌspʌɪrʊˈlʌɪnə/

Less commonly also spirr-uul-**ee**-nuh; see
LATIN panel.

Spitsbergen island, Norway
spits-bur-guhn /ˈspɪts.bəː(r)gən/
• Established anglicization.

splenectomy surgical removal of the
spleen
spluh-**nek**-tuh-mi /spləˈnɛktəmi/

splenetic bad-tempered
spluh-**net**-ik /spləˈnɛtɪk/

splenius pl. **splenii** neck muscle
splee-ni-uhss, pl. **splee**-ni-y
/ˈspliːnɪəs, pl. /-nɪʌɪ/

Split port, Croatia
split /splɪt/

Spokane city and river, US
spoh-**kan** /spəʊˈkan/

Spoleto town, Italy
spuh-**lay**-toh /spəˈleɪtəʊ/

spoliation action of ruining something
spoh-li-**ay**-shuhn /ˌspəʊliˈeɪʃən/

spondaic concerning spondees
spon-**day**-ik /spɒnˈdeɪɪk/

spondee metrical foot
spon-dee /ˈspɒndiː/

spondulicks money
spon-**dyoo**-liks /spɒnˈdjuːlɪks/

spondylosis condition of the spine
spon-dil-**oh**-siss /ˌspɒndɪˈləʊsɪs/

Sporades islands, Greece
sporr-uh-deez /ˈspɒrədiːz/

sporadic occurring at irregular intervals

spuh-**rad**-ik /spəˈradɪk/

sporran pouch worn around the waist
sporr-uhn /ˈspɒrən/

sportif interested in athletic sports
spor-**teef** /spɔː(r)ˈtiːf/

Sprachgefühl intuitive feeling for a
language
shprahkh-guh-fuel /ˈʃprɑːxgəˌfyːl/

sprauncy smart in appearance
sprawn-si /ˈsprɔːnsi/

Sprechgesang style of dramatic
vocalization
sprekh-guh-zang /ˈʃprɛçgəˌzaŋ/

Sprechstimme another term for
Sprechgesang
sprekh-**shtim**-uh /ˈʃprɛçˌʃtɪmə/

sprezzatura studied carelessness
spret-suh-**toor**-uh /ˌsprɛtsəˈtʊərə/

springbok gazelle
spring-bok /ˈsprɪŋbɒk/

spritsail extended sail
sprit-suhl /ˈsprɪtsəl/

spruit small stream
sprayt /spreɪt/

spumante sparkling white wine
spoo-**man**-tay /spuːˈmanteɪ/

spume froth or foam
spyoom /spjuːm/

spurious not being what it purports
to be
spyoor-i-uhss /ˈspjʊəriəs/

sputnik Soviet satellite
spuut-nik /ˈspʊtnɪk/

Spyri, Johanna Swiss author
yoh-**han**-uh **shpeer**-i /jəʊˌhanə ˈʃpɪəri/

squall sudden violent gust of wind
skwawl /skwɔːl/

squalor dirtiness
skwol-uhr /ˈskwɒlə(r)/

squamous covered with scales
skway-muhss /ˈskweɪməs/

squeegee scraping implement
skwee-jee /ˈskwiːdʒiː/

squirearchy landowners collectively
skwy-uhr-ar-ki /ˈskwʌɪəˌrɑː(r)ki/

squireen minor landowner
skwy-uh-**reen** /ˌskwʌɪəˈriːn/

Srebrenica town, Bosnia-Herzegovina
sreb-ren-it-suh /ˈsrɛbrɛˌnɪtsə/

Sri see **Shri**

Sri Lanka country
sri **lank**-uh /srɪ ˈlaŋkə/

Srinagar city, India
srin-**ug**-uhr /srɪˈnʌgə(r)/

St see **Saint**

Stabat Mater medieval Latin hymn
stah-bat **mah**-tuhr /ˌstɑːbat ˈmɑːtə(r)/

stabile free-standing abstract sculpture
or structure
stay-byl /ˈsteɪbʌɪl/

staccato musical term
stuh-**kah**-toh /stəˈkɑːtəʊ/

staffage accessory items in a painting
stuh-**fahzh** /stəˈfɑːʒ/

Stafford town, England
staf-uhrd /ˈstafə(r)d/

staithe landing stage
stay*th* /steɪð/

Stakhanovite productive worker in the
former USSR
stuh-**khahn**-uh-vyt /stəˈxɑːnəvʌɪt/

stalactite structure hanging from the
roof of a cave
stal-uhk-tyt /ˈstaləktʌɪt/

Stalag German prison camp
shtal-ag /ˈʃtalag/

stalagmite structure rising from the
floor of a cave
stal-uhg-myt /ˈstaləgmʌɪt/

Stalin, Joseph Soviet statesman
joh-zuhf **stah**-lin /ˌdʒəʊzəf ˈstɑːlɪn/,
Russian [ˌjosʲɪf ˈstalʲɪn]
• Established anglicization.

Stallone, Sylvester American actor
stuh-**lohn** /stəˈləʊn/

stalwart loyal and hard-working
stawl-wuhrt /ˈstɔːlwə(r)t/

Less commonly also **stal**-wuhrt.

Stalybridge town, England
stay-li-brij /ˈsteɪlibrɪdʒ/

Stambolić, Ivan Serbian statesman
ee-van **stam**-buh-litch /ˌiːvan
ˈstambəlɪtʃ/

stamen male organ of a flower
stay-muhn /ˈsteɪmən/

stanchion upright bar or frame
stan-shuhn /ˈstanʃən/

Stanford, Charles Villiers Irish-born
composer
vil-uhrz **stan**-fuhrd /ˌvɪlərz
ˈstanfə(r)d/

Stanhope, Hester English traveller
stan-uhp /ˈstanəp/

Stanier, William English railway
engineer
stan-i-uhr /ˈstaniə(r)/

Stanislaus, St patron saint of Poland
stan-iss-lowss /ˈstanɪslaʊs/

Established anglicization. The Polish name
is Stanisław, pronounced stan-**eess**-waf.

Stanislavsky, Konstantin Russian
theatre director
kon-stuhn-**teen** stan-iss-**laf**-ski
/ˌkɒnstəntiːn ˌstanɪsˈlafski/

Stansted airport, England
stan-sted /ˈstansted/

stanza group of lines in a poem
stan-zuh /ˈstanzə/

stapes bone in the middle ear
stay-peez /ˈsteɪpiːz/

staphylococcus pl. **staphylococci**
bacterium
staf-il-oh-**kok**-uhss,
pl. staf-il-oh-**kok**-y /ˌstafɪləʊˈkɒkəs/, pl.
/-ˈkɒkʌɪ/

Plural is sometimes also -**kok**-sy; see LATIN
panel.

Stara Zagora city, Bulgaria
star-uh zuh-**gorr**-uh /ˌstɑːrə zəˈgɒrə/

starboard one side of a ship
star-buhrd /ˈstɑː(r)bə(r)d/

Sometimes also **star**-bord.

Starck, Philippe French interior
designer
fee-**leep** stark /fiːˌliːp ˈstɑː(r)k/

stargazy pie Cornish fish pie
star-gay-zi /ˈstɑː(r)geɪzi/

starveling undernourished person
starv-ling /ˈstɑː(r)vlɪŋ/

Stasi internal security force of the former
German Democratic Republic
shtah-zi /ˈʃtɑːzi/

stasis period of inactivity
stay-sis /ˈsteɪsɪs/

statant heraldic term
stay-tuhnt /ˈsteɪtənt/

Staten Island borough of New York City
stat-uhn /ˈstatən/

statice sea lavender
stat-iss-i /ˈstatɪsi/

statin cholesterol-lowering drug
stat-in /ˈstatɪn/

status quo existing state of affairs
stay-tuhss kwoh /ˌsteɪtəs ˈkwəʊ/

statutory required or permitted by statute
statch-oo-tuh-ri /ˈstatʃʊtəri/

Stauffenberg, Claus von German aristocrat; attempted to assassinate Hitler
klowss fon shtow-fuhn-bairk /ˌklaʊs fɒn ˈʃtaʊfənbɛː(r)k/

Stavanger port, Norway
stuh-vang-uhr /stəˈvaŋə(r)/

Stavropol territory, Russia
stav-ruh-puhl /ˈstavrəpəl/

steak au poivre peppered steak
oh pwahv-ruh /əʊ ˈpwɑːvrə/

steatopygia accumulation of fat on the buttocks
stee-uh-toh-pij-i-uh /ˌstiːətəʊˈpɪdʒiə/

Steaua Bucharest Romanian football club
styah-wuh boo-kuh-rest /ˌstjɑːwə buːkəˈrest/

Stedelijk museum in Amsterdam
stay-duh-lik /ˈsteɪdəlɪk/

Steen, Jan Dutch painter
yun stayn /ˌjʌn ˈsteɪn/

stegosaurus dinosaur
steg-uh-sawr-uhss /ˌstɛɡəˈsɔːrəs/

Steiff German toy manufacturers
shtyf /ʃtʌɪf/

Stein, Gertrude American writer
styn /stʌɪn/

stein earthenware beer mug
styn /stʌɪn/

Steinbeck, John American novelist
styn-bek /ˈstʌɪnbɛk/

steinbock ibex
styn-bok /ˈstʌɪnbɒk/

Steinem, Gloria American feminist
sty-nuhm /ˈstʌɪnəm/

Steiner, Rudolf Austrian philosopher
roo-dolf shty-nuhr /ˌruːdɒlf ˈʃtʌɪnə(r)/

stela pl. **stelae** upright stone slab
stee-luh, pl. **stee-lee** /ˈstiːlə/, pl. /-liː/

stele stem and root of a plant
steel /stiːl/

Stella Maris 'star of the sea' (Latin)
stel-uh marr-iss /ˌstɛlə ˈmarɪs/

Stellenbosch town, South Africa
stel-uhn-boss /ˈstɛlənbɒs/

Stena English ferry company
sten-uh /ˈstɛnə/

Stendhal French novelist
sta(ng)-dal /stɛ̃ˈdal/

Stenhammar, Wilhelm Swedish composer
vil-helm stayn-ham-uhr /ˌvɪlhɛlm ˈsteɪnhamə(r)/

stenography writing in shorthand
sten-og-ruh-fi /stɛˈnɒɡrəfi/

stentorian loud and powerful
sten-taw-ri-uhn /stɛnˈtɔːriən/

stephanotis climbing plant
stef-uh-noh-tiss /ˌstɛfəˈnəʊtɪs/

steppe area of flat land in Europe or Siberia
step /stɛp/

Steppenwolf novel by Herman Hesse
shtep-uhn-volf /ˈʃtɛpənvɒlf/

steradian SI unit of solid angle
stuh-ray-di-uhn /stəˈreɪdiən/

stercoraceous consisting of dung
stur-kuh-ray-shuhss /ˌstəː(r)kəˈreɪʃəs/

stereophonic using two or more channels of transmission
sterr-i-oh-fon-ik /ˌstɛriəʊˈfɒnɪk/

Less commonly also **steer-i-oh-fon-ik**; the same variation is possible for most other words with *stereo-*.

stereotype widely held but oversimplified image
sterr-i-oh-typ /ˈstɛriəʊˌtʌɪp/

Sterne, Laurence Irish novelist
sturn /stəː(r)n/

sternocleidomastoid neck muscle
stur-noh-kly-doh-mast-oyd /ˌstəː(r)nəʊˌklʌɪdəʊˈmastɔɪd/

steroid class of organic compounds
sterr-oyd /ˈstɛrɔɪd/

Less commonly also **steer-oyd**.

stertorous noisy and laboured
ster-tuh-ruhss /ˈstəː(r)tərəs/

stevedore dock employee
stee-vuh-dor /ˈstiːvədɔː(r)/

Stevenage town, England
stee-vuh-nij /ˈstiːvənɪdʒ/

Stevenson, Adlai American politician
ad-ly /ˈadlʌɪ/

Stevenson, Robert Louis Scottish
writer
loo-iss /ˈluːɪs/
• This is the family's own pronunciation.

Steyn, Mark Canadian journalist
styn /stʌɪn/

Stieglitz, Alfred American
photographer
steeg-lits /ˈstiːɡlɪts/

stifado Greek meat dish
stif-**ah**-doh /stɪˈfɑːdəʊ/

Stiffkey village, Norfolk
stif-ki /ˈstɪfki/

Rarely also **styoo**-ki, a local pronunciation
which is becoming increasingly uncommon.

stigma pl **stigmata** mark of disgrace
stig-muh, pl. **stig**-muh-tuh /ˈstɪɡmə/,
pl. /-mətə/

Unusually for plurals formed in this way, the
pronunciation stig-**mah**-tuh is also
common.

stimulus pl. **stimuli** thing that evokes a
reaction
stim-yuul-uhss, pl. **stim**-yuul-ee
/ˈstɪmjʊləs/, pl. /-liː/

Plural also **stim**-yuul-y; see LATIN panel.

stingy mean
stin-ji /ˈstɪndʒi/

stipend regular sum paid as a salary
sty-pend /ˈstʌɪpɛnd/

stipendiary receiving a stipend
sty-**pen**-juh-ri /stʌɪˈpɛndʒəri/

stochastic having a random probability
distribution
stuh-**kast**-ik /stəˈkastɪk/

Stockhausen, Karlheinz German
composer
karl-hynts **shtok**-how-zuhn
/ˌkɑː(r)lhʌɪnts ˈʃtɒkˌhaʊzən/

Stockholm capital of Sweden
stok-hohm /ˈstɒkhəʊm/, [ˈstɔkhɔlm]
• Established anglicization.

stoep veranda
stoop /stuːp/

stogy (also **stogie**) cigar
stoh-gi /ˈstəʊɡi/

stoicism endurance of pain without
complaint
stoh-iss-iz-uhm /ˈstəʊɪsɪzəm/

Stokowski, Leopold British-born

American conductor
stok-**of**-ski /stɒˈkɒfski/

stollen German loaf
shtol-uhn /ˈʃtɒlən/

stoma pl. **stomata** pore in a leaf
stoh-muh, pl. **stoh**-muh-tuh /ˈstəʊmə/,
pl. /-mətə/
• Standard -s plural is also possible.

Stopes, Marie Scottish birth-control
campaigner
marr-i **stohps** /ˌmari ˈstəʊps/

Stoppard, Tom Czech-born British
dramatist
stop-ard /ˈstɒpɑː(r)d/

Stormont Castle castle in Belfast
stor-muhnt /ˈstɔː(r)mənt/

Stornoway port, Scotland
stor-nuh-way /ˈstɔː(r)nəweɪ/

Storting Norwegian parliament
stor-ting /ˈstɔː(r)tɪŋ/, [ˈstuːrtɪŋ]
• Established anglicization.

stoup basin for holy water
stoop /stuːp/

Stour various rivers, England
stow-uhr, stoor, **stoh**-uhr /ˈstaʊə(r)/,
/stʊə(r)/, /ˈstəʊə(r)/

Pronounced differently in different
locations, and with some variation even
when used in reference to the same river.
The Stour in Suffolk/Essex is stoor, the one
in Kent is stoor or **stow**-uhr, and those in
Oxfordshire and Worcestershire/West
Midlands (as in Stourbridge) are **stow**-uhr
or **stoh**-uhr.

stovies potato dish
stoh-veez /ˈstəʊviːz/

Strabo Greek historian and geographer
stray-boh /ˈstreɪbəʊ/

stracciatella Italian soup
stratch-uh-**tel**-uh /ˌstratʃəˈtɛlə/

Strachan Scottish family name
strawn, **strakh**-uhn /strɔːn/, /ˈstraxən/

This surname can be pronounced in either
way, depending on individual preference.

Strachey, Lytton English biographer
lit-uhn **stray**-chi /ˌlɪtən ˈstreɪtʃi/

Stradivari, Antonio Italian
violin-maker
an-**toh**-ni-oh strad-iv-**ar**-i /anˌtəʊniəʊ
ˌstradɪˈvɑːri/

Violins made by him or his followers are
called Stradivarius, usually pronounced
strad-iv-**air**-i-uhss.

strafe attack repeatedly with low-flying
aircraft
strahf /strɑːf/

Commonly also strayf.

Stralsund town, Germany
shtrahl-zuunt /ˈʃtrɑːlzʊnt/

stramash uproar (Scottish)
struh-**mash** /strəˈmaʃ/

strangury bladder condition
strang-gyuu-ri /ˈstraŋɡjʊri/

Stranraer port, Scotland
stran-**rar** /stranˈrɑː(r)/

strappado form of punishment or
torture
strap-**ah**-doh /straˈpɑːdəʊ/

Strasberg, Lee American actor and
drama teacher
straz-burg /ˈstrazbə(r)ɡ/

Strasbourg city, France
straz-burg /ˈstrazbə(r)ɡ/, [strazbuːr]
• Established anglicization.

stratagem plan or scheme
strat-uh-juhm /ˈstratədʒəm/

Strathclyde region, Scotland
strath-**klyd** /straθˈklʌɪd/

strathspey slow Scottish dance
strath-**spay** /straθˈspeɪ/

stratosphere layer of the earth's
atmosphere
strat-uh-sfeer /ˈstratəˌsfɪə(r)/

stratum pl. **strata** layer
strah-tuhm, pl. **strah**-tuh /ˈstrɑːtəm/,
pl. /-tə/

Less commonly also stray-tuhm.

stratus type of cloud
strah-tuhss /ˈstrɑːtəs/

Strauss, Richard German composer
ritch-uhrd **strowss** /ˌrɪtʃə(r)d ˈstraʊs/
• Established anglicization.

stravaig roam (Scottish)
struh-**vayg** /strəˈveɪɡ/

Stravinsky, Igor Russian-born
composer
ee-gor struh-**vin**-ski /ˌiːɡɔː(r)
strəˈvɪnski/

Streatfeild, Noel English author
stret-feeld /ˈstrɛtfiːld/

Streatham district of London

stret-uhm /ˈstrɛtəm/

Strega trademark liqueur
stray-guh /ˈstreɪɡə/

Streisand, Barbra American singer
stry-sand /ˈstrʌɪsand/

streptococcus pl. **streptococci**
bacterium
strep-toh-**kok**-uhss, pl.
strep-toh-**kok**-y /ˌstrɛptəʊˈkɒkəs/, pl.
/-ˈkɒkʌɪ/

Plural is sometimes also -kok-sy; see LATIN
panel.

streptomycin antibiotic drug
strep-toh-**my**-sin /ˌstrɛptəʊˈmʌɪsɪn/

streusel crumbly topping
stroy-zuhl /ˈstrɔɪzəl/

stria pl. **striae** linear ridge or groove on a
surface
stry-uh, pl. **stry**-ee /ˈstrʌɪə/, pl. /-ʌiː/

strigil scraping instrument
strij-il /ˈstrɪdʒɪl/

Strindberg, August Swedish dramatist
ow-guust **strind**-bairg /ˌaʊɡʊst
ˈstrɪndbɛ(r)ɡ/

Strine English language as spoken by
Australians
stryn /strʌɪn/

stringendo musical term
strin-**jen**-doh /strɪnˈdʒɛndəʊ/

stringent strict and exacting
strin-juhnt /ˈstrɪndʒənt/

strobilus pl. **strobili** tree cone
stroh-**bil**-uhss pl. **stroh**-bil-y
/ˈstrəʊbɪləs/, pl. /-lʌɪ/

stroganoff stew
strog-uh-nof /ˈstrɒɡənɒf/

Stromboli volcanic island, Italy
strom-buh-li /ˈstrɒmbəli/

strongyloidiasis intestinal infestation
with threadworms
stron-jil-oy-**dy**-uh-siss
/ˌstrɒndʒɪlɔɪˈdʌɪəsɪs/

strontium chemical element
stron-ti-uhm /ˈstrɒntiəm/

strophe section of an ancient Greek
choral ode
stroh-fi /ˈstrəʊfi/

Stroud town, England
strowd /straʊd/

strudel pastry dessert
shtroo-duhl /ˈʃtruːdəl/

Struve, Otto Russian-born American
astronomer
stroo-vuh /ˈstruːvə/

Struwwelpeter fictional character in
German fairytale
stroo-vuhl-**pay**-tuhr
/ˈstruːvəlˌpeɪtə(r)/

strychnine poison
strik-neen /ˈstrɪkniːn/

stucco fine plaster
stuk-oh /ˈstʌkəʊ/

Stuckism contemporary art movement
stuk-iz-uhm /ˈstʌkɪzəm/

studdingsail additional sail
stun-suhl /ˈstʌnsəl/

Stuka German military aircraft
shtook-uh /ˈʃtuːkə/

stupa dome-shaped building erected as a
Buddhist shrine
stoo-puh /ˈstuːpə/

Sturmer variety of apple
stur-muhr /ˈstə(r)mə(r)/

Sturm und Drang artistic movement
shtoorm uunt **drang** /ˌʃtʊə(r)m ʊnt
ˈdraŋ/

Stuttgart city, Germany
shtuut-gart /ˈʃtʊtɡɑː(r)t/

Stuyvesant, Peter Dutch-born
American statesman
sty-vuh-suhnt /ˈstaɪvəsənt/

Stygian relating to the River Styx
stij-i-uhn /ˈstɪdʒiən/

stymie prevent progress
sty-mi /ˈstaɪmi/

styptic capable of causing bleeding to
stop
stip-tik /ˈstɪptɪk/

Styria state, Austria
stirr-i-uh /ˈstɪriə/

Established anglicization. The German
name is Steiermark, pronounced
shty-uhr-mark.

Styx Greek mythological river
stiks /stɪks/

suave charming and elegant
swahv /swɑːv/

subaltern officer in the British army
sub-uhl-tuhrn /ˈsʌbəltə(r)n/

Subaru Japanese car manufacturers
soo-bar-oo /ˈsuːbɑːruː/

Subbuteo trademark tabletop soccer

sub-**yoo**-ti-oh /sʌˈbjuːtiəʊ/

sub judice under judicial consideration
sub **joo**-diss-i /sʌb ˈdʒuːdɪsi/

Less commonly also suub **yoo**-dik-ay; see
LATIN panel.

subjugate bring under control
sub-juug-ayt /ˈsʌbdʒʊɡeɪt/

suborn bribe
suh-**born** /səˈbɔː(r)n/

Subotica city, Serbia
soo-buh-tit-suh /ˈsuːbətɪtsə/

subpoena writ ordering a person to
attend a court
suh-**pee**-nuh /səˈpiːnə/

sub rosa happening in secret
sub **roh**-zuh /ˌsʌb ˈrəʊzə/

subsequence state of following
something
sub-sik-wuhnss /ˈsʌbsɪkwəns/

subsequence sequence contained in
another sequence
sub-seek-wuhnss /ˈsʌbˌsiːkwəns/

subsidence gradual caving in of an area
of land
suhb-**sy**-duhnss /səbˈsʌɪdəns/

Less commonly also **sub**-sid-uhnss.

subsidiarity political principle
suhb-sid-i-**arr**-it-i /ˌsəbˌsɪdiˈarɪti/

substantive having a firm basis in reality
sub-stuhn-tiv /ˈsʌbstəntɪv/

Sometimes also suhb-**stan**-tiv.

subsume absorb
suhb-**syoom** /səbˈsjuːm/

subterfuge deceit
sub-tuhr-fyooj /ˈsʌbtə(r)fjuːdʒ/

subtle delicate or precise
sut-uhl /ˈsʌtəl/

Subud mystical movement
suub-**ood** /sʊˈbuːd/

succah (also **sukkah**) booth in which a
practising Jew spends part of Succoth
suuk-uh /ˈsʊkə/

succedaneum pl. **succedanea** substitute,
especially for a medicine
suk-suh-**day**-ni-uhm,
pl. suk-suh-**day**-ni-uh /ˌsʌksəˈdeɪniəm/,
pl. /-niə/

succès de scandale success due to notoriety
suek-**say** duh skah(ng)-**dal** /syk,seɪ də skã'dal/

succinct briefly expressed
suhk-**sinkt** /sək'sɪŋkt/

succotash maize and bean dish
suk-uh-tash /'sʌkətaʃ/

Succoth (also **Sukkot**) Jewish festival
suuk-**oht** /sʊ'kəʊt/

This is the Hebrew pronunciation; **suk-uht** and **suuk-uhss** are also possible.

succour assistance and support
suk-uhr /'sʌkə(r)/

succubus pl. **succubi** female demon
suk-yuub-uhss, pl. suk-yuub-y /'sʌkjʊbəs/, pl. /-bʌɪ/

Suchard Swiss confectionery manufacturers
soo-shard /'suːʃɑː(r)d/

Suchet, David English actor
soo-shay /'suːʃeɪ/

Sucre legal capital of Bolivia
sook-ray /'suːkreɪ/

sucre currency unit, Ecuador
sook-ray /'suːkreɪ/

sucrose chemical compound
soo-krohz /'suːkrəʊz/

Less commonly also **syoo**-krohss.

Sudan country
soo-**dan** /suː'dan/

Commonly also soo-**dahn**; both pronunciations are widely used.

Süddeutsche Zeitung German newspaper
zuet-doy-chuh **tsy**-tuung /,zy:tdɔɪtʃə 'tsʌɪtʊŋ/

Sudetenland region, Czech Republic
zoo-**day**-tuhn-land /zu:'deɪtən,land/

Sudjic, Deyan English architecture critic
day-an soo-jitch /,deɪan 'suːdʒɪtʃ/

sudoku Japanese number puzzle
soo-**doh**-koo /su:'dəʊku:/

The puzzle has only recently become popular in the UK, and various anglicized pronunciations are in use. Less commonly also soo-**dok**-oo or soo-dok-oo. This last pronunciation was the one preferred by native speakers of Japanese whom we consulted.

Sudra Hindu caste
sood-ruh /'suːdrə/

suerte action performed by a bullfighter
swair-tay /'swɛː(r)teɪ/

Suetonius Roman biographer
soo-uh-**toh**-ni-uhss /suə'təʊniəs/

Suez isthmus between the Mediterranean and the Red Sea
soo-iz /'suːɪz/

suffice be enough
suh-**fyss** /sə'fʌɪs/

Suffolk county, England
suf-uhk /'sʌfək/

suffragan assistant bishop
suf-ruh-guhn /'sʌfrəgən/

suffrage right to vote
suf-rij /'sʌfrɪdʒ/

Sufi Muslim ascetic and mystic
soo-fi /'suːfi/

Suharto, Mohamed Indonesian statesman
moh-**ham**-uhd soo-**har**-toh /məʊ,haməd su:'hɑː(r)təʊ/

Sui Chinese dynasty
sway /sweɪ/

sui generis unique
soo-i **jen**-uh-riss /,su:i 'dʒɛnərɪs/

Suisse see **Switzerland**

suk (also **sukh**) see **souk**

Sukarno, Achmad Indonesian statesman
akh-mad suuk-**ar**-noh /,axmad sʊ'kɑː(r)nəʊ/

Sukarnoputri, Megawati Indonesian stateswoman
meg-uh-**wah**-ti suuk-ar-noh-**poot**-ri /mɛgəwɑːti sʊ,kɑː(r)nəʊ'pu:tri/

Sukhoi Russian military aircraft
suukh-**oy** /sʊ'xɔɪ/

Sukhotai (also **Sukhothai**) town, Thailand
suuk-uh-**ty** /,sʊkə'tʌɪ/

sukiyaki Japanese meat dish
suuk-i-**yak**-i /,sʊkɪ'jaki/
• See JAPANESE panel.

sukkah see **succah**

Sukkot see **Succoth**

Sukkur city, Pakistan
suk-uhr /'sʌkə(r)/

Sulawesi island, Indonesia
soo-luh-**way**-si /,su:lə'weɪsi/

Sulaymaniyah, al- (also **as-Sulaimaniya**) town, Iraq
uh-soo-lay-mah-**nee**-yuh
/ə‚suːleimaˈniːjə/
• See **ARABIC** panel.

sulcus pl. **sulci** groove or furrow
sul-kuhss, pl. **sul**-sy /ˈsʌlkəs/, pl. /-sʌɪ/
• See **LATIN** panel.

Suleiman (also **Sulayman**) name of
several Muslim rulers, after an Islamic
prophet
soo-lay-**mahn** /‚suːleiˈmɑːn/

Sulla Roman general
sul-uh /ˈsʌlə/

Sullom Voe inlet on Shetland, Scotland
suul-uhm **voh** /‚sʊləm ˈvəʊ/

sulphuric containing sulphur or
sulphuric acid
sulf-**yoor**-ik /sʌlˈfjʊərɪk/

Sulpician secular Roman Catholic priest
sul-**pish**-uhn /sʌlˈpɪʃən/

Sulu Sea sea, Malay Archipelago
soo-loo /ˈsuːluː/

sumac (also **sumach**) shrub
soo-mak /ˈsuːmak/

Sumatra island, Indonesia
soo-**mah**-truh /suːˈmɑːtrə/

Sumbawa island, Indonesia
suum-**bah**-wuh /sʊmˈbɑːwə/

Sumer ancient region, Iraq
soo-muhr /ˈsuːmə(r)/

Sumerian relating to Sumer
suum-**eer**-i-uhn /sʊˈmɪəriən/

Sumer is icumen in early piece of
English music
sum-uhr iz uh-**kum**-in in /‚sʌmə(r) ɪz
əˈkʌmɪn ‚ɪn/

summa cum laude 'with highest
distinction' (Latin)
suum-uh kuum **low**-day /‚sʊmə kʊm
ˈlaʊdeɪ/

Used largely with reference to university
degrees. More anglicized pronunciations
such as **sum**-uh kum **law**-di are also heard;
see **LATIN** panel.

summat 'something' (dialect)
sum-uht /ˈsʌmət/

sumo Japanese heavyweight wrestling
soo-moh /ˈsuːməʊ/

Sumqayit city, Azerbaijan
suum-kah-**yeet** /‚sʊmkɑːˈjiːt/

Sumy city, Ukraine
soo-mi /ˈsuːmi/

Sunda Islands islands, Malay
Archipelago
suun-duh /ˈsʊndə/

Sundarbans region, India and
Bangladesh
suun-duhr-bunz /ˈsʊndə(r)bʌnz/

Sunna Muslim law based on
Muhammad's words or acts
suun-uh /ˈsʊnə/

Sunni orthodox branch of Islam
suun-i /ˈsʊni/

sunyata Buddhist doctrine
shoon-yuh-tah /ˈʃuːnjətɑː/

Sun Yat-sen Chinese statesman
suun yat **sen** /‚sʊn jat ˈsɛn/

Suomi see Finland

Suor Angelica opera by Puccini
swor an-jel-ik-uh /‚swɔː(r) anˈdʒɛlikə/

superciliary relating to the eyebrow
soo-puhr-**sil**-i-uh-ri /‚suːpə(r)ˈsɪliəri/

This and other words with *super-* are less
commonly also pronounced **syoo**-puhr.

superfluity unnecessarily large amount
soo-puhr-**floo**-it-i /‚suːpə(r)ˈfluːɪti/

superlative of the highest quality
soo-**pur**-luh-tiv /suːˈpəː(r)lətɪv/

supernal relating to the sky or the
heavens
soo-**pur**-nuhl /suːˈpəː(r)nəl/

supersede take the place of
soo-puhr-**seed** /‚suːpə(r)ˈsiːd/

suppurate form pus
sup-yuh-rayt /ˈsʌpjʊreɪt/

supraventricular tachycardia
irregular heartbeat
soop-ruh-vent-**rik**-yuul-uhr
tak-i-**kar**-di-uh /suːprəvɛn‚trɪkjʊlə(r)
taki'kɑː(r)diə/

supremacy superiority
soop-**rem**-uh-si /suːˈprɛməsi/

sura (also **surah**) chapter of the Koran
soor-uh /ˈsʊərə/

Surabaya port, Indonesia
soor-uh-**by**-uh /‚sʊərəˈbʌɪə/

Surat city, India
soor-uht /ˈsʊərət/

surcingle strap for a horse
sur-sing-guhl /ˈsəː(r)sɪŋɡəl/

Sûreté French police department
suer-tay /syr'teɪ/

surety person who takes responsibility
for another
shoor-uh-ti /'ʃʊərəti/

surfactant chemical substance
suhr-fak-tuhnt /sə(r)'faktənt/

surimi minced fish
soo-ree-mi /suː'riːmi/

Suriname (also **Surinam**) country
soor-in-am /ˌsʊərɪ'nam/, Dutch
[syri'na:mə]
• Established anglicization.

surmise suppose that something is true
suhr-myz /sə(r)'mʌɪz/

surplice white vestment
sur-pliss /'sə:(r)plɪs/

surrogate substitute
surr-uh-guht /'sʌrəgət/

Surtees, Robert Smith English
journalist and novelist
sur-teez /'sə:(r)tiːz/

Surtsey island, Iceland
surt-si /'sə:(r)tsi/

surveillance close observation
suhr-vay-luhnss /sə(r)'veɪləns/

Surya Hindu god
soor-yuh /'sʊə(r)jə/

sushi Japanese rice dish
soo-shi /'suːʃi/

Susquehanna river, US
susk-wuh-han-uh /ˌsʌskwə'hanə/

Sustrans environmental charity
suss-tranz /'sʌstranz/

Süssmayr, Franz Xaver Austrian
composer
frants ksah-vuhr zuess-my-uhr
/ˌfrants ˌksaːvə(r) 'zʏsmʌɪə(r)/

Susu West African ethnic group
soo-soo /'suːsuː/

susurration whispering or rustling
soo-suh-ray-shuhn /ˌsuːsə'reɪʃən/

Sutherland, Joan Australian operatic
soprano
suth-uhr-luhnd /'sʌðə(r)lənd/

Sutlej river, India and Pakistan
sut-lej /'sʌtlɛdʒ/

sutra rule or aphorism in Sanskrit
literature
soot-ruh /'suːtrə/

suture stitch holding together a wound

soo-chuhr /'suːtʃə(r)/

Suva capital of Fiji
soo-vuh /'suːvə/

Suwannee (also **Swanee**) river, US
suu-won-i /sʊ'wɒni/

suzerain sovereign having some control
over another state
soo-zuh-rayn /'suːzəreɪn/

Suzhou city, China
soo-joh /ˌsuː'dʒəʊ/

Suzman, Helen South African
politician
suuz-muhn /'sʊzmən/

Suzuki Japanese motorcycle
manufacturers
suuz-oo-ki /sʊ'zuːki/

Svalbard islands, Arctic Ocean
svahl-bar /'svɑːlbɑː(r)/

Svedberg unit of time equal to 10⁻¹³
seconds
sved-burg /'svɛdbə:(r)g/

Svengali person who exercises a
controlling influence on another
sven-gah-li /svɛn'gɑːli/

Svenska Dagbladet Swedish
newspaper
sven-skuh dahg-blah-duht /ˌsvɛnskə
'dɑːɡblɑːdət/

Sverige see **Sweden**

Svetambara sect of Jainism
swet-ahm-buh-ruh /swɛ'tɑːmbərə/

Svizzera see **Switzerland**

Svoboda, Lutvik Czechoslovakian
statesman
luud-veek svob-od-uh /ˌlʊdviːk
'svɒbɒdə/

Swabia former duchy, Germany
sway-bi-uh /'sweɪbiə/

Established anglicization. The German
name is Schwaben, pronounced
shvah-buhn.

swadeshi made in India
swad-esh-i /swa'dɛʃi/

Swaffham town, England
swof-uhm /'swɒfəm/

Swahili language
swuh-hee-li /swə'hiːli/

swami Hindu male religious teacher
swah-mi /'swɑːmi/

Swammerdam, Jan Dutch naturalist and microscopist
yun swum-uhr-**dum** /ˌjʌn swʌmə(r)ˈdʌm/

Swanee see **Suwannee**

SWAPO South West Africa People's Organization
swah-poh /ˈswɑːpəʊ/

sward expanse of short grass
sword /swɔː(r)d/

Swarofski cut-crystal manufacturers
swuh-rof-ski /swəˈrɒfski/

swathe wrap in layers of fabric
swayth /sweɪð/

SWAT team group of police marksmen
swot /swɒt/

Swaziland country, Africa
swah-zi-land /ˈswɑːziland/

Sweden country
sweed-uhn /ˈswiːdən/

Established anglicization. The Swedish name is Sverige, pronounced **svair-yuh** [ˈsvɛrjə].

Swedenborg, Emanuel Swedish scientist and mystic
sweed-uhn-borg /ˈswiːdənbɔː(r)g/, [eˈmɑːnəel ˈsveːdənbɔrj]
• Established anglicization.

Sweelinck, Jan Pieterzoon Dutch composer
yun pee-tuhr-sohn sway-link /ˌjʌn ˌpiːtə(r)səʊn ˈsweːlɪŋk/

swingeing severe or extreme
swin-jing /ˈswɪndʒɪŋ/

swingometer device used to demonstrate a political swing
swing-om-uh-tuhr /swɪŋˈɒmətə(r)/

Swiss Re building London landmark, better known as the Gherkin
swiss ree /ˌswɪs ˈriː/

Switzerland country
swit-suhr-luhnd /ˈswɪtsə(r)lənd/

Established anglicization. The French name is Suisse, pronounced **sweess**, the German name is Schweiz, pronounced **shvyts**, and the Italian name is Svizzera, pronounced **zvit-serr-uh**.

Syal, Meera English comedian
meer-uh sy-uhl /ˌmɪərə ˈsʌɪəl/

sybaritic fond of sensuous pleasure
sib-uh-**rit**-ik /ˌsɪbəˈrɪtɪk/

sycophant person who acts obsequiously in order to gain advantage
sik-uh-fant /ˈsɪkəfant/

Sycorax Shakespearean witch
sik-uh-raks /ˈsɪkəraks/

Sydenham, Thomas English physician
sid-uh-nuhm /ˈsɪdənəm/

Sydow, Max von Swedish actor
fon **sue-dov** /fɒn ˈsyːdʊv/

Syktyvkar city, Russia
sik-tif-**kar** /ˌsɪktɪfˈkɑː(r)/

Sylhet region, Bangladesh
sil-het /ˈsɪlˈhɛt/

syllabary set of written characters representing syllables
sil-uh-buh-ri /ˈsɪləbəri/

syllabification division of words into syllables
sil-ab-if-ik-**ay**-shuhn /sɪˌlabɪfɪˈkeɪʃən/

syllable unit of pronunciation having one vowel sound
sil-uh-buhl /ˈsɪləbəl/

syllabub whipped cream dessert
sil-uh-bub /ˈsɪləbʌb/

syllabus pl. **syllabi** subjects in a course of study
sil-uh-buhss, pl. **sil-uh-by** /ˈsɪləbəs/, pl. /-bʌɪ/
• Standard -es plural is also possible.

syllepsis pl. **syllepses** figure of speech
sil-**ep**-siss, pl. sil-**ep**-seez /sɪˈlɛpsɪs/, pl. /-siːz/

syllogism form of reasoning
sil-uh-jiz-uhm /ˈsɪləˌdʒɪzəm/

sylph mythological spirit
silf /sɪlf/

Sylvaner variety of wine grape
sil-**vah**-nuhr /sɪlˈvɑːnə(r)/

symbiosis pl. **symbioses** interaction between two different organisms
sim-by-**oh**-siss, pl. sim-by-**oh**-seez /ˌsɪmbʌɪˈəʊsɪs/, pl. /-siːz/

Symonds Yat village, England
sim-uhnz yat /ˌsɪmənz ˈjat/

Symons, Arthur English poet
sim-uhnz /ˈsɪmənz/

Symons, Julian English writer
sy-muhnz /ˈsʌɪmənz/

Swedish

Swedish (*svenska* in Swedish, pronounced **sven**-skuh) is a North Germanic language. It is spoken by about 8 million people in Sweden, and as mother tongue by about 300,000 people in Finland. This makes Swedish the most widely spoken of the Scandinavian languages. Swedish, Danish, and Norwegian are closely related, although Danish pronunciation differs in many aspects, and a Swede will find it much easier to understand Norwegian than (spoken) Danish. Many of the points discussed below will be true for Norwegian as well.

This is not intended to be a full account of Swedish phonology, and the pronunciations given here are, as always, somewhat anglicized in line with BBC policy and the constraints of the phonetic respelling.

Tone

One distinguishing feature of Swedish, famously caricatured by the Swedish chef in *The Muppet Show*, is the 'sing-song' quality. Swedish is a tone language, and there are around 300 word pairs that differ only in the use of tonal accent. Swedish has two tones, sometimes referred to as acute and grave accent. Acute accent, or single tone, makes the word *anden* mean *the duck*. Grave accent, or double tone, makes the same word mean *the spirit*. This is not a feature we can retain in anglicized Swedish. For more on tone please refer to the Tone panel.

Stress

Stress (whether it is acute or grave accent) often falls on the first syllable of a word, but this is variable and it is advisable to check each individual case by consulting a Swedish dictionary.

Vowels

There are nine vowels, which can all be long or short. Vowels are usually long before a single consonant and short before a double consonant. *Rata* is **rah**-tuh and *ratta* is **rat**-uh.

A is pronounced ah when long and a when short.

E is pronounced close to ay (although not diphthongal in Swedish) when long and e when short. Unstressed E is commonly schwa (uh).

I is pronounced ee when long and i when short.

O is pronounced oo when long and either uu or o when short. *Mor* is moor, *moster* is **muust**-uhr, but *monster* is **mon**-stuhr.

U is pronounced close to oo when long and uu when short.

Y is pronounced ue (as in French *vu*) when short and ue (as in German *fünf* when short).

Å is pronounced close to oh (but not diphthongal in Swedish) when long, and o when short. We often also use aw to reflect long Å.

Ä is pronounced air, without the -r, when long and e when short. When no R is present in the orthography we have to respell long Ä as ay or ah.

Ö is pronounced oe (as in French *peu*) when long and oe (as in French *coeur*) when short.

Ä and Ö are written Æ and Ø respectively in Norwegian and Danish.

Consonants

Most Swedish consonants are straightforward, although certain consonant combinations, such as TJ and SJ, can be difficult for English speakers, and often get inconsistently anglicized in different ways.

Double consonants, like the BB in *Abba*, are, as in Italian, pronounced as such, but since this does not occur in English, it is not something we can reflect when giving recommendations for Swedish.

B, D, F, H, L, M, N, P, T, and V are pronounced as in English, but see D, T, and L in combination with other letters below.

C is usually pronounced k before A, O, U, and Å, and s before E, I, Y, Ä, and Ö.

CH is usually pronounced close to sh, but CHR is kr.

DJ, GJ, and LJ are pronounced y (as in *yes*). *Fredrik 'Freddie' Ljungberg* is **yuung**-bairg, not **lung**-bairg!

G is pronounced g before A, O, U, and Å, and usually y before E, I, Y, Ä, and Ö. The G in *Borg* and *Berg* is always y, although in this position we usually anglicize to g—as in *Ljungberg* above.

J is pronounced y.

K is pronounced k before A, O, U, and Å, and usually close to sh before E, I, Y, Ä, and Ö.

KJ is pronounced close to sh.

S is always pronounced s.

R plus another consonant makes that consonant retroflex (i.e. pronounced with the tongue curled back, sounds which are common in Hindi and other Indian languages). The R itself is silent.

SJ is pronounced as sh and kh (as in Scottish *loch*) simultaneously. There is some variation in the Swedish pronunciation, and it is usually anglicized to sh.

SK is pronounced in the same way as SJ, but only before E, I, Y, Ä, and Ö. Otherwise it is pronounced sk.

TJ is pronounced close to sh.

W only exists in old-fashioned spellings, and is pronounced v.

Z exists mostly in loanwords and is pronounced s. *Zoo* is soo.

symposium pl. **symposia** conference or meeting to discuss a particular subject
sim-**poh**-zi-uhm, pl. sim-**poh**-zi-uh
/sɪm'pəʊziəm/, pl. /-ziə/
• Standard -s plural is also possible.

synagogue building where a Jewish congregation meets
sin-uh-gog /'sɪnəgɒg/

synapse junction between two nerve cells
sy-naps /'sʌɪnaps/

Commonly also **sin-aps**.

synchronicity simultaneous occurrence of events
sink-ruh-**niss**-it-i /ˌsɪŋkrə'nɪsɪti/

syncopate displacing musical beats
sink-uh-payt /'sɪŋkəpeɪt/

syncope fainting spell
sink-uh-pi /'sɪŋkəpi/

syncretism amalgamation of different religions or cultures
sink-ruh-tiz-uhm /'sɪŋkrətɪzəm/

syndactyly webbed fingers or toes
sin-**dak**-til-i /sɪn'daktɪli/

syne ago
syn /sʌɪn/

synecdoche figure of speech
sin-**ek**-duh-ki /sɪ'nɛkdəki/

Synge, J. M. Irish dramatist
sing /sɪŋ/

synod church assembly
sin-uhd /'sɪnəd/

synonymous having the same meaning
sin-**on**-im-uhss /sɪ'nɒnɪməs/

synopsis pl. **synopses** brief summary
sin-**op**-siss, pl. sin-**op**-seez /sɪ'nɒpsɪs/, pl. /-siːz/

synovial physiological joint surrounded by fluid
sy-**noh**-vi-uhl /sʌɪ'nəʊviəl/

syntagmatic grammatical
sin-tag-**mat**-ik /ˌsɪntag'matɪk/

syntax grammar
sin-taks /'sɪntaks/

synthesis pl. **syntheses** combination of elements to form a whole
sin-thuh-siss, pl. sin-thuh-seez /'sɪnθɪsɪs/, pl. /-siːz/

Syracuse town, Sicily
sy-ruh-kyooz /'sʌɪrəkjuːz/

Established anglicization. Italian name is Siracusa, pronounced **see-rak-oo-zuh**.

Syracuse city, US
sirr-uh-kyooz /'sɪrəkjuːz/

Syrah black wine grape
seer-uh /'sɪərə/

Syria country
sirr-i-uh /'sɪriə/

syringe tube for sucking in and ejecting liquid
sirr-**inj** /sɪ'rɪndʒ/

syrinx pan pipes
sirr-inks /'sɪrɪŋks/

syrtaki Greek folk dance
seer-**tak**-i /sɪə(r)'taki/

systemic relating to a system
sist-**em**-ik /sɪ'stɛmɪk/

Less commonly also sist-**ee**-mik.

systole phase of the heartbeat
sist-uh-li /'sɪstəli/

syzygy conjunction or opposition
siz-uh-ji /'sɪzədʒi/

Szczecin city, Poland
shchetch-een /'ʃtʃɛtʃiːn/

Szechuan type of Chinese cuisine
setch-**wahn** /sɛ'tʃwɑːn/

Established anglicization. This is also an alternative transliteration of the Chinese province SICHUAN.

Szeged city, Hungary
seg-ed /'sɛgɛd/

Szigeti, Joseph Hungarian-American violinist
sig-et-i /sɪ'gɛti/

Established anglicization. The Hungarian pronunciation for this surname is **sig-et-i**.

Szilard, Leo Hungarian-American physicist
zil-ard /'zɪlɑː(r)d/

Szirtes, George Hungarian-British poet
sur-teez /'səː(r)tiːz/

Szpilman, Władysław Polish pianist
vvad-**iss**-waf **shpeel**-man /vwaˌdɪswaf 'ʃpiːlman/

Szymanowski, Karol Polish composer
karr-ol shim-an-**of**-ski /ˌkarɒl ʃɪma'nɒfski/

T

tabard sleeveless garment
tab-ard /'tabɑ:(r)d/

Tabasco state, Mexico
tuh-**bask**-oh /tə'baskəʊ/

tabbouleh Middle Eastern salad
tuh-**boo**-lay /tə'bu:leɪ/

tabernacle dwelling
tab-uhr-nak-uhl /'tabə(r),nakəl/

tabes emaciation
tay-beez /'teɪbi:z/

tabi Japanese sock
tah-bi /'tɑ:bi/

tabla drum
tub-luh /'tʌblə/

tablature musical notation
tab-luh-chuh(r) /'tablətʃə(r)/

tableau vivant group of people arranged
to represent a scene
tab-loh **vee**-vo(ng) /,tabləʊ 'vi:vɒ̃/

table d'hôte fixed price restaurant meal
tah-bluh doht /,tɑ:blə 'dəʊt/

tabor drum
tay-buhr /'teɪbə(r)/

Tabriz city, Iran
tab-**reez** /ta'bri:z/

tabula rasa pl. **tabulae rasae** blank slate
tab-yuul-uh **rah**-zuh, pl. **tab**-yoo-lee
rah-zee /,tabjʊlə 'rɑ:zə/, pl. /,tabjʊli:
'rɑ:zi:/

tacamahac poplar tree
tak-uh-muh-hak /'takəmə,hak/

tacet musical term
tass-uht /'tasət/

tachi samurai sword
tatch-i /'tatʃi/

tachism French art movement
tash-iz-uhm /'taʃɪzəm/

tachometer speedometer
tak-**om**-uh-tuhr /ta'kɒmətə(r)/

tachycardia abnormally rapid heart rate
tak-i-**kar**-di-uh /,taki'kɑ:(r)diə/

tachyon hypothetical particle
tak-i-on /'takiɒn/

tacit understood without being stated

tass-it /'tasɪt/

taciturn uncommunicative
tass-it-urn /'tasɪtə:(r)n/

Tacitus Roman historian
tass-it-uhss /'tasɪtəs/

taco Mexican dish
tak-oh /'takəʊ/

Tadhg Irish boy's name
tyg /tʌɪg/

Tadmur city, Syria; also called **Palmyra**
tad-moor /'tadmʊə(r)/

tae-bo trademark exercise system
ty-boh /'tʌɪbəʊ/

taedium vitae state of ennui
tee-di-uhm vee-ty /,ti:diəm 'vi:tʌɪ/
• See LATIN panel.

Taegu see **Daegu**

Taejon city, South Korea
tej-on /'tɛdʒɒn/

tae kwon do Korean martial art
ty kwon doh /,tʌɪ kwɒn 'dəʊ/

tael weight used in China
tayl /teɪl/

Taff river, Wales
taf /taf/, [tɑv]
• Established anglicization.

taenia pl. **taeniae** flat physiological
structure
tee-ni-uh, pl. tee-ni-ee /'ti:niə/, pl.
/-ni:/
• Standard -s plural is also possible.

taffeta silk fabric
taf-uh-tuh /'tafətə/

Tagalog Philippine language and people
tuh-**gah**-log /tə'gɑ:lɒg/

Taganrog port, Russia
tag-uhn-**rog** /,tagən'rɒg/

tagetes daisy plant
tuh-**jeet**-eez /tə'dʒi:ti:z/

tagine (also **tajine**) North African stew
tuh-**zheen** /tə'ʒi:n/

Less commonly also tuh-**jeen**; see ARABIC
panel.

tagliatelle kind of pasta
tal-yuh-**tel**-ay /,taljə'tɛleɪ/

Commonly also tag-li-uh-**tel**-i, a more anglicized pronunciation.

Tagore, Rabindranath Indian writer
ruh-**bin**-drun-ut tuh-**gor** /rə‚bɪndrʌnʌt
təˈgɔː(r)/

Tagus river, Spain and Portugal
tay-guhss /ˈteɪgəs/

Established anglicization. The Portuguese name is Tejo, pronounced **tezh**-oo [ˈtɛʒu], and the Spanish name is Tajo, pronounced **takh**-oh [ˈtaxo].

tahini sesame seed paste
tuh-**hee**-ni /təˈhiːni/

Tahiti island, South Pacific
tuh-**hee**-ti /təˈhiːti/

Tahitian native of Tahiti
tuh-**hee**-shuhn /təˈhiːʃən/

Tahoe lake, US
tah-hoh /ˈtɑːhəʊ/

Tai'an city, China
ty-**an** /‚tʌɪˈan/

t'ai chi ch'uan Chinese system of callisthenics
ty chee **chwan** /‚tʌɪ tʃiː ˈtʃwan/

Taichung city, Taiwan
ty-**juung** /‚tʌɪˈdʒʊŋ/

Ta'if, al- city, Saudi Arabia
uh-**tah**-if /əˈtɑːɪf/
• See ARABIC panel.

Taig insulting name for a Catholic
tayg /teɪg/

taiga swampy forest
ty-guh /ˈtʌɪgə/

taiko Japanese drum
ty-koh /ˈtʌɪkəʊ/

Tailleferre, Germaine French composer and pianist
zhair-**men** ty-**fair** /ʒɛː(r)‚mɛn tʌɪˈfɛː(r)/

Taimyr peninsula, Russia
ty-**meer** /tʌɪˈmɪə(r)/

Táin Bó Cúailnge Irish tale
tawn boh **kool**-nyuh /‚tɔːn bəʊ ˈkuːlnjə/

taipan snake
ty-pan /ˈtʌɪpan/

Taipei capital of Taiwan
ty-**pay** /‚tʌɪˈpeɪ/

Taittinger brand of champagne
tay-ta(ng)-**zhay** /teɪtɛ̃ˈʒeɪ/

Taiwan country
ty-**wahn** /tʌɪˈwɑːn/

Commonly also ty-**won** or ty-**wan**.

Taiyuan city, China
ty-yue-**an** /‚tʌɪjyˈan/

Ta'iz city, Yemen
tah-**iz** /tɑːˈɪz/

Taizé Christian community
tez-**ay** /tɛˈzeɪ/

Tajik Asian ethnic group
taj-**ik** /ˈtadʒɪk/

Tajikistan independent republic
tuh-jik-ist-**ahn** /tə‚dʒɪkɪˈstɑːn/

tajine see **tagine**

Taj Mahal mausoleum, India
tahj muh-**hahl** /‚tɑːdʒ məˈhɑːl/

Tajo see **Tagus**

taka currency unit, Bangladesh
tah-kuh /ˈtɑːkə/

takahe flightless bird
tah-kuh-hi /ˈtɑːkəhi/

takin animal
tah-kin /ˈtɑːkɪn/

Taklimakan (also **Takla Makan**) desert, China
tah-kluh-muh-**kahn** /‚tɑːkləməˈkɑːn/

Takoradi port, Ghana
tak-uh-**rah**-di /‚takəˈrɑːdi/

tala currency unit, Samoa
tah-luh /ˈtɑːlə/

Talafar town, Iraq
tal-ah-**fuhr** /taˈlɑːfə(r)/

talapoin Buddhist monk or priest
tal-uh-**poyn** /ˈtaləpɔɪn/

talaq Islamic divorce
tal-**ahk** /taˈlɑːk/

talaria winged sandals
tuh-**lair**-i-uh /təˈlɛːriə/

Talbot, Fox English pioneer of photography
tawl-buht /ˈtɔːlbət/

This British surname is variously pronounced **tal**-buht or **tawl**-buht, depending on individual preference.

taleggio soft Italian cheese
tal-**ej**-oh /taˈlɛdʒəʊ/

tales writ for summoning jurors
tay-leez /ˈteɪliːz/

Taliban (also **Taleban**) fundamentalist Muslim movement
tal-ib-an /ˈtalɪban/

Taliesin Welsh bard
tal-**yay**-sin /‚talˈjeɪsɪn/

talipes club foot
tal-ip-eez /'talɪpiːz/

talisman lucky object
tal-iz-muhn /'talɪzmən/

tallage medieval taxation system
tal-uhj /'taladʒ/

Tallaght town, Republic of Ireland
tal-uh /'talə/

Tallahassee city, US
tal-uh-hass-i /,talə'hasi/

Talleyrand French statesman
tal-i-rand /'talirand/, [talɛrɑ̃]
• Established anglicization.

Tallinn capital of Estonia
tal-in /'talɪn/

Tallis, Thomas English composer
tal-iss /'talɪs/

tallith Jewish prayer shawl
tal-ith /'talɪθ/

Talmud body of Jewish law
tal-muud /'talmʊd/

talus pl. **tali** ankle bone
tay-luhss, pl. **tay-ly** /'teɪləs/, pl. /'teɪlʌɪ/

talwar Indian sword
tul-war /tʌl'wɑː(r)/

tamagotchi trademark electronic toy
tam-uh-gotch-i /,tamə'gɒtʃi/

tamale Mexican dish
tuh-mah-lay /tə'mɑːleɪ/

tamanduá anteater
tam-and-wah /taman'dwɑː/

Tamar river, England
tay-mar /'teɪmɑː(r)/

tamari Japanese soy sauce
tuh-mar-i /tə'mɑːri/

tamarind ingredient in Indian cookery
tam-uh-rind /'tamərɪnd/

tamarisk tree
tam-uh-risk /'tamərɪsk/

Tamaulipas state, Mexico
tam-ow-lee-pass /,tamaʊ'liːpas/

Tambo, Oliver South African politician
tam-boh /'tambəʊ/

tambotie African tree
tam-boo-ti /tam'buːti/

tambour small drum
tam-boor /'tambʊə(r)/

tamboura (also **tambura**) lute-like
musical instrument
tam-boor-uh /tam'bʊərə/

tambourine percussion instrument

tam-buh-reen /,tambə'riːn/

Tambov city, Russia
tam-bof /tam'bɒf/

Tamburlaine play by Marlowe
tam-buhr-layn /'tambə(r)leɪn/

Tamerlane Mongol ruler of Samarkand
tam-uhr-layn /'tamə(r)leɪn/

Tamil Indian language and ethnic group
tam-il /'tamɪl/
• Established anglicization.

Tamil Nadu state, India
tum-il nah-doo /,tamɪl 'nɑːduː/

Tammany organization within the US
Democratic Party
tam-uh-ni /'taməni/

Tammuz Mesopotamian god
tam-uuz /'tamʊz/

tam-o'-shanter woollen cap
tam-uh-shan-tuhr /,tamə'ʃantə(r)/

tamoxifen breast cancer drug
tuh-mok-sif-en /tə'mɒksɪfɛn/

Tampa port, US
tam-puh /'tampə/

Tampere city, Finland
tam-perr-uh /'tampɛrə/

Tampico port, Mexico
tam-pee-koh /tam'piːkəʊ/

Tamworth town, England
tam-wuhrth /'tamwə(r)θ/

Tana lake, Ethiopia
tah-nuh /'tɑːnə/

Tanagra ancient Greek city
tan-uh-gruh /'tanəgrə/

Tánaiste deputy Prime Minister of the
Republic of Ireland
taw-nish-tyuh /'tɔːnɪʃtjə/

Tancredi opera by Rossini
tank-ray-di /taŋ'kreɪdi/

tandoori style of Indian cooking
tan-door-i /tan'dʊəri/

Tang Chinese dynasty
tang /taŋ/

Tanga port, Tanzania
tang-guh /'taŋgə/

tangata whenua Maori people
tang-at-uh fen-oo-uh /,taŋatə 'fɛnʊə/

Tange, Kenzo Japanese architect
ken-zoh tang-gay /,kɛnzəʊ 'taŋgeɪ/

tangent straight line
tan-juhnt /'tandʒənt/

tangi Maori funeral
tang-i /'taŋi/

Tangier seaport, Morocco
tan-**jeer** /tanˈdʒɪə(r)/

Tangshan city, China
tang-**shan** /taŋˈʃan/

tanh hyperbolic tangent
tan-**aytch** /tanˈeɪtʃ/

Sometimes the *h* is incorporated into the
pronunciation in other ways, as tansh or
than.

taniwha Maori legendary monster
tan-if-ah /ˈtanɪfɑ/

Tannhäuser German poet
tan-hoy-zuhr /ˈtanhɔɪzə(r)/

tanpura Indian musical instrument
tun-**poo**-ruh /tʌnˈpuːrə/

Tantallon castle, Scotland
tan-**tal**-uhn /tanˈtalən/

tantalum chemical element
tan-tuh-luhm /ˈtantələm/

Tantalus Greek mythological character
tant-uh-luhss /ˈtantələs/

tant mieux 'so much the better' (French)
tah(ng) **myoe** /ˌtã ˈmjə/

tant pis 'so much the worse' (French)
tah(ng) **pee** /ˌtã ˈpiː/

Tanzania country
tan-zuh-**nee**-uh /ˌtanzəˈniːə/

Tao Chinese principle
tow /taʊ/

Taoiseach Prime Minister of the Irish
Republic
tee-shok /ˈtiːʃɒk/

Taoism Chinese philosophy
tow-iz-uhm /ˈtaʊɪzəm/

Taormina town, Sicily
towr-**mee**-nuh /taʊrˈmiːnə/

Tao-te-Ching Taoist text
tow tuh **ching** /ˌtaʊ tə ˈtʃɪŋ/

tapas small Spanish savoury dishes
tap-ass /ˈtapas/

tapenade olive paste
tap-uh-**nahd** /ˈtapənɑːd/

Tapiola tone poem by Sibelius
tap-i-ol-uh /ˈtapɪɒlə/

tapis tapestry
tap-ee /ˈtaˈpiː/

tapotement massage technique
tuh-**poht**-muhnt /təˈpəʊtmənt/

taqueria taco restaurant
tak-uh-**ree**-uh /ˌtakəˈriːə/

Tara ancient residence of Irish kings

tar-uh /ˈtɑːrə/

taramasalata fish roe paste
tarr-uh-muh-suh-**lah**-tuh
/ˌtarəməsəˈlɑːtə/

Taranaki mountain, New Zealand
tarr-uh-**nak**-i /ˌtarəˈnaki/

tarantella dance
tarr-uhn-**tel**-uh /ˌtarənˈtɛlə/

Tarantino, Quentin American film
director
tarr-uhn-**tee**-noh /ˌtarənˈtiːnəʊ/

Taranto port, Italy
tarr-**an**-toh /taˈrantəʊ/

tarantula spider
tuh-**ran**-chuul-uh /təˈrantʃʊlə/

Tarawa atoll, South Pacific
tarr-uh-wuh /ˈtarəwə/

tarboosh man's cap
tar-**boosh** /taːˈ(r)ˈbuːʃ/

Tardis time machine
tar-diss /ˈtaː(r)dɪs/

tare weight allowance
tair /tɛː(r)/

Tarim river, China
tar-**eem** /ˌtaːˈriːm/

tariqa Sufi doctrine
tarr-**ee**-kuh /taˈriːkə/

Tarkovsky, Andrei Russian film
director
and-**ray** tar-**kof**-ski /anˌdreɪ
taː(r)ˈkɒfski/

tarlatan thin fabric
tar-luh-tuhn /ˈtaː(r)lətən/

Tarleton, Banastre English soldier
ban-uh-stuhr **tar**-luh-tuhn
/ˌbanəstə(r) ˈtaː(r)lətən/

Tarlev, Vasile Moldovan prime minister
vuh-**see**-li **tar**-luhv /vəˌsiːli ˈtaː(r)ləv/

tarmacadam tarmac
tar-muh-**kad**-uhm /ˌtaː(r)məˈkadəm/

Tarn-et-Garonne department, France
tarn ay garr-**on** /ˌtaː(r)n eɪ gaˈrɒn/

Tarnów Poland
tar-noof /ˈtaː(r)nuːf/

tarot divination cards
tarr-oh /ˈtarəʊ/

tarpaulin waterproof cloth
tar-**paw**-lin /taːˈ(r)ˈpɔːlɪn/

Tarpeian Rock cliff in ancient Rome
tar-**pee**-uhn /taːˈ(r)ˈpiːən/

Tarquinius semi-legendary Etruscan king
tar-**kwin**-i-uhss /tɑː(r)ˈkwɪniəs/

tarragon herb
tarr-uh-guhn /ˈtarəgən/

Tarragona region, Spain
tarr-uh-**goh**-nuh /ˌtarəˈɡəʊnə/

tarsus pl. **tarsi** ankle bones
tar-suhss, pl. **tar**-sy /ˈtɑː(r)səs, pl. /-sʌɪ/

Tartar central Asian ethnic group
tar-tuhr /ˈtɑː(r)tə(r)/

tartar deposit on the teeth
tar-tuhr /ˈtɑː(r)tə(r)/

tartare served raw
tar-**tar** /tɑː(r)ˈtɑː(r)/

Tartarus Greek god
tar-tuh-ruhss /ˈtɑː(r)tərəs/

Tartary historical region of Asia
tar-tuh-ri /ˈtɑː(r)təri/

tarte Tatin upside-down apple tart
tart tat-**a(ng)** /ˌtɑː(r)t taˈtɛ̃/

tartrazine yellow dye
tar-truh-zeen /ˈtɑː(r)trəziːn/

Tartu city, Estonia
tar-too /ˈtɑː(r)tuː/

Tartuffe religious hypocrite
tar-**toof** /tɑː(r)ˈtuːf/

Established anglicization; this epithet is a reference to a play by Molière of the same name. The French pronunciation is tar-**tuef** [tartyf].

---

tartufo edible fungus
tar-**too**-foh /tɑː(r)ˈtuːfəʊ/

taser trademark weapon causing temporary paralysis
tay-zuhr /ˈteɪzə(r)/

Tashkent capital of Uzbekistan
tash-**kent** /taʃˈkɛnt/

Tasman, Abel Dutch navigator
ay-buhl **taz**-muhn /ˌeɪbəl ˈtazmən/, [ˌaːbəl ˈtɑsmən]
• Established anglicization.

Tasmania state, Australia
taz-**may**-ni-uh /tazˈmeɪniə/

Tasso, Torquato Italian poet
tor-**kwah**-toh **tass**-oh /tɔː(r)ˌkwɑːtəʊ ˈtasəʊ/

tastevin cup for tasting wine
tast-uh-va(ng) /ˈtastəvɛ̃/

tatami straw mat

tuh-**tah**-mi /təˈtɑːmi/

Tatarstan autonomous republic, Russia
tah-tuhr-**stahn** /ˌtɑːtə(r)ˈstɑːn/

Tate, Nahum English librettist
nay-huhm tayt /ˌneɪhəm ˈteɪt/

Tathagata honorific title of a Buddha
tuh-**tah**-guh-tuh /təˈtɑːɡətə/

tathata Buddhist concept
tat-uh-**tah** /ˌtatəˈtɑː/

Tati, Jacques French film director
zhahk tat-**ee** /ˌʒɑːk taˈtiː/

Tatra Mountains mountain range, Europe
tat-ruh /ˈtatrə/

tatterdemalion dilapidated
tat-uhr-duh-**may**-li-uhn /ˌtatə(r)dəˈmeɪliən/

tattersall woollen fabric
tat-uhr-suhl /ˈtatə(r)səl/

Tattersalls English firm of horse auctioneers
tat-uhr-sawlz /ˈtatə(r)sɔːlz/

Tatum, Art American jazz pianist
tay-tuhm /ˈteɪtəm/

tau letter of the Greek alphabet
tow /taʊ/

Commonly also taw.

Taunton town, England
tawn-tuhn /ˈtɔːntən/

taupe grey-brown
tohp /təʊp/

Taupo, Lake lake, New Zealand
tow-poh /ˈtaʊpəʊ/

Tauranga port, New Zealand
tow-**rang**-uh /taʊˈraŋə/

taurine like a bull
taw-ryn /ˈtɔːrʌɪn/

tauromachy bullfighting
taw-**rom**-uh-ki /tɔːˈrɒməki/

Taurus constellation
taw-ruhss /ˈtɔːrəs/

tautology saying the same thing twice
taw-**tol**-uh-ji /tɔːˈtɒlədʒi/

Tautou, Audrey French actress
oh-**dray** toh-**too** /əʊˌdreɪ təʊˈtuː/

Tavel French rosé wine
tav-**el** /taˈvɛl/

taverna small restaurant
tuh-**vur**-nuh /təˈvɜː(r)nə/

Tawhid and Jihad Iraqi militant group
tow-hid ji-had /ˌtaʊhɪd dʒiˈhad/

taxidermy stuffing animals
tak-sid-**ur**-mi /ˈtaksɪˌdəː(r)mi/

taxis pl. **taxes** restoration of displaced
bones or organs by manual pressure
tak-siss, pl. **tak**-seez /ˈtaksɪs, pl.
/ˈtaksiːz/

taxon pl. **taxa** classification group
tak-son, pl. **tak**-suh /ˈtaksɒn, pl.
/ˈtaksə/

taxonomy classification
taks-**on**-uh-mi /takˈsɒnəmi/

Taxotere trademark breast cancer drug
tak-suh-teer /ˈtaksətɪə(r)/

tayra animal
ty-ruh /ˈtʌɪrə/

Tay–Sachs disease metabolic disorder
tay saks /teɪ ˈsaks/

Tbilisi capital of Georgia
tib-**lee**-si /ˌtɪbˈliːsi/, [tblisi]

Established anglicization. Sometimes still
called by its former name of Tiflis,
pronounced **tif**-liss.

Tchaikovsky, Pyotr Russian composer
pyot-uhr chy-**kof**-ski /ˌpjʊtə(r)
ˌtʃʌɪˈkɒfski/

tchotchke small decorative object
chotch-kuh /ˈtʃɒtʃkə/

Teachta Dála member of the Dáil
tyukh-tuh **daw**-luh /ˌtjʌxtə ˈdɔːlə,
Irish /ˌtʲaxtə ˈdɑːlə/

technetium chemical element
tek-**nee**-shuhm /tɛkˈniːʃəm/

tectonic relating to the earth's crust
tek-**ton**-ik /tɛkˈtɒnɪk/

tectrices sing. **tectrix** tailfeathers
tek-triss-eez, sing. **tek**-triks
/ˈtɛktrɪsiːz/, sing. /-trɪks/

Tecumseh American Indian leader
tuh-**kum**-si /təˈkʌmsi/

Te Deum hymn
tay **day**-uum /teɪ ˈdeɪʊm/

Less commonly also tee **dee**-uhm; see
LATIN panel.

Tees river, England
teez /tiːz/

teetotal abstaining from alcohol
tee-**toh**-tuhl /tiːˈtəʊtəl/

tefillin Jewish phylacteries
tuh-**fil**-een /təˈfɪliːn/

TEFL Teaching of English as a Foreign
Language
tef-uhl /ˈtɛfəl/

Tegel airport, Berlin
tay-guhl /ˈteɪɡəl/

tegmentum region of the brain
teg-**men**-tuhm /tɛɡˈmɛntəm/

tegu lizard
teg-oo /ˈtɛɡuː/

Tegucigalpa capital of Honduras
teg-oo-si-**gal**-puh /tɛˌɡuːsiˈɡalpə/

tegula pl. **tegulae** part of an insect's wing
teg-yuul-uh, pl. **teg**-yuul-ee /ˈtɛɡjʊlə/,
/-liː/
• Standard -s plural is also possible.

Tehachapi mountains, US
tuh-**hatch**-uh-pi /təˈhatʃəpi/

Tehran (also **Teheran**) capital of Iran
tair-**ahn** /tɛːˈrɑːn/, Farsi [tehˈrɑːn]
• Established anglicization.

Teignmouth town, England
tin-muhth /ˈtɪnməθ/

Teilhard de Chardin, Pierre French
philosopher and palaeontologist
pyair tay-**ar** duh shar-**da(ng)** /ˌpjɛː(r)
teɪˌɑː(r) də ʃɑː(r)ˈdɛ̃/

tej Ethiopian drink
tej /tɛdʒ/

Tejano Mexican-American Texan
tekh-**ah**-noh /tɛˈxɑːnəʊ/

Tejo see Tagus

Te Kanawa, Kiri New Zealand soprano
keer-i tuh **kah**-nuh-wuh /ˌkɪə(r)i tə
ˈkɑːnəwə/

tekke monastery of dervishes
tek-ay /ˈtɛkeɪ/

telamon pl. **telamones** male figure used
as a pillar
tel-uh-mon, pl. tel-uh-**moh**-neez
/ˈtɛləmɒn, pl. /tɛləˈməʊniːz/

telangiectasia spider veins
tel-**an**-ji-ek-**tay**-zi-uh
/tɛˌlandʒiɛkˈteɪziə/

Tel Aviv city, Israel
tel uh-**veev** /ˌtɛl əˈviːv/

teledu badger
tel-uh-doo /ˈtɛləduː/

Telefónica Spanish telecommunications
company
tel-uh-**fon**-ik-uh /tɛləˈfɒnɪkə/

Telegu see Telugu

telekinesis ability to move objects by
mental power
tel-uh-**kin**-**ee**-siss /ˌtɛlɪkɪ'niːsɪs/

Less commonly also tel-uh-ky-**nee**-siss.

Telemachus Greek mythological
character
tuh-**lem**-uh-kuhss /tə'lɛməkəs/

Telemann, Georg Philipp German
composer
gay-ork **fee**-lip **tay**-luh-man
/ˌgeɪɔː(r)k ˌfiːlɪp 'teɪləman/

Telemark region, Norway
tel-uh-mark /'tɛləmɑː(r)k/,
['teːləmark]
• Established anglicization.

teleology explanation of phenomena by
the purpose they serve
tel-i-**ol**-uh-ji /ˌtɛli'ɒlədʒi/

The prefix *tel-* on this and words such as
telic and *telos* can also be pronounced teel-.

téléphérique cableway
tel-ef-err-**eek** /ˌtɛlɛfɛ'riːk/

telephony working or use of telephones
tuh-**lef**-uh-ni /tə'lɛfəni/

telic directed to a definite end
tel-ik /'tɛlɪk/

Tell el-Amarna ruins, Egypt
tel uhl uh-**mar**-nuh /ˌtɛl əl ə'mɑː(r)nə/

tellurian of or inhabiting the earth
tel-**yoor**-i-uhn /tɛ'ljʊəriən/

Telluride resort, US
tel-yoor-yd /'tɛljʊərʌɪd/

tellurium chemical element
tel-**yoor**-i-uhm /tɛ'ljʊəriəm/

telos pl. **teloi** ultimate aim
tel-oss, pl. **tel**-oy /'tɛlɒs, pl. /-lɔɪ/

Telugu (also **Telegu**) Indian ethnic group
tel-uh-goo /'tɛləguː/

Temaru, Oscar president of French
Polynesia
tuh-**mar**-oo /tə'mɑːruː/

temazepam drug
tuh-**mayz**-uh-pam /tə'meɪzəpam/

As with other drugs in this group, the
pronunciation -**az**-uh-pam is also common.

temenos pl. **temenoi** piece of ground
surrounding a temple
tem-uh-noss, pl. **tem**-uh-noy
/'tɛmənɒs, pl. /-nɔɪ/

Temeraire British naval ship

tem-uh-**rair** /temə'rɛː(r)/

temerity excessive confidence
tuh-**merr**-it-i /tə'mɛrɪti/

tempeh soya bean dish
tem-pay /'tɛmpeɪ/

Tempelhof airport, Berlin
tem-puhl-hohf /'tɛmpəlhəʊf/

tempera method of painting
tem-puh-ruh /'tɛmpərə/

tempestuous turbulent
tem-**pest**-yoo-uhss /tɛm'pɛstjuəs/

Templar order of knights
temp-luhr /'tɛmplə(r)/

temporal relating to worldly affairs
tem-puh-ruhl /'tɛmpərəl/

temporalis jaw muscle
tem-puh-**ray**-liss /ˌtɛmpə'reɪlɪs/

temporomandibular joint jaw hinge
tem-puh-roh-man-**dib**-yuul-uhr
/ˌtɛmpərəʊman'dɪbjʊlə(r)/

Tempranillo Spanish wine grape
temp-ran-**eel**-yoh /ˌtɛmprə'niːljəʊ/

temps levé ballet movement
tah(ng) luh-**vay** /ˌtɑ̃ lə'veɪ/

tempura Japanese dish
tem-puu-ruh /'tɛmpʊrə/
• See JAPANESE panel.

tenacious keeping a firm hold
tuh-**nay**-shuhss /tə'neɪʃəs/

tendresse feeling of fondness or love
to(ng)-**dress** /tɔ̃'drɛs/

tendu ballet term
tah(ng)-due /tɑ̃'dy/

Tendulkar, Sachin Indian cricketer
satch-in **ten**-duul-kuhr /ˌsatʃɪn
'tɛndʊlkə(r)/

Tenebrae matins and lauds during Holy
Week
ten-uh-bray /'tɛnəbreɪ/

tenebrism style of painting
ten-uh-briz-uhm /'tɛnəbrɪzəm/

tenement set of rooms
ten-uh-muhnt /'tɛnəmənt/

Tenerife island, Canaries
ten-uh-**reef** /ˌtɛnə'riːf/, Spanish
/tene'rife/
• Established anglicization.

tenesmus bowel disorder
tuh-**nez**-muhss /tə'nɛzməs/

tenet principle or belief
ten-uht /'tɛnət/

tenge currency unit, Kazakhstan
teng-gay /ˈtɛŋgeɪ/

Tennessee river, US
ten-uh-**see** /ˌtɛnəˈsiː/

Tenniel, John English illustrator
ten-i-uhl /ˈtɛnɪəl/

Tenno emperor of Japan
ten-oh /ˈtɛnəʊ/

Tennyson, Alfred English poet
ten-iss-uhn /ˈtɛnɪsən/

Tennysonian relating to Tennyson
ten-iss-**oh**-ni-uhn /ˌtɛnɪˈsəʊnɪən/

Tenochtitlán ancient Aztec capital
ten-otch-tit-**lahn** /tɛˌnɒtʃtɪˈtlɑːn/

tensile relating to tension
ten-syl /ˈtɛnsaɪl/

tensor mathematical object
ten-sor /ˈtɛnsɔː(r)/

tenuto musical term
tuh-**noo**-toh /təˈnuːtəʊ/

Tenzing Norgay Sherpa mountaineer
ten-zing **nor**-gay /ˌtɛnzɪŋ ˈnɔː(r)geɪ/

teocalli Aztec temple
tay-ok-**al**-i /ˌteɪɒˈkali/

Teotihuacán ancient city, Mexico
tay-ot-i-wak-**an** /ˌteɪɒtiwaˈkan/

tepache Mexican drink
tep-**atch**-ay /tɛˈpatʃeɪ/

tepal part of a flower
tep-uhl /ˈtɛpəl/

tepee conical tent
tee-pee /ˈtiːpiː/

Tepic city, Mexico
tep-eek /tɛˈpiːk/

tepidarium warm room in a Roman
bath
tep-id-**air**-i-uhm /ˌtɛpɪˈdɛːrɪəm/

teppanyaki Japanese dish
tep-an-**yak**-i /ˌtɛpanˈjaki/

tequila Mexican alcoholic spirit
tek-**ee**-luh /tɛˈkiːlə/

teratoma pl. **teratomata** type of tumour
terr-uh-**toh**-muh,
pl. terr-uh-**toh**-muh-tuh /ˌtɛrəˈtəʊmə/,
pl. /-mətə/
● Standard -s plural is also possible.

terbium chemical element
tur-bi-uhm /ˈtɜː(r)bɪəm/

terce church service
turss /tɜː(r)s/

tercel male hawk

tur-suhl /ˈtɜː(r)səl/

Terengganu state, Malaysia
terr-eng-**gah**-noo /ˌtɛrɛŋˈgɑːnuː/

Te Reo Maori language
tay **ray**-oh /teɪ ˈreɪəʊ/

teres shoulder muscle
terr-eez /ˈtɛriːz/

Teresa, Mother Roman Catholic nun
tuh-**ree**-zuh /təˈriːzə/

Teresa of Ávila, St Spanish mystic
terr-**ay**-zuh **av**-il-uh /tɛˌreɪzə ˈavɪlə/

Tereshkova, Valentina Russian
cosmonaut
val-uhn-**tee**-nuh terr-uhsh-**kov**-uh
/ˌvalənˌtiːnə ˌtɛrəʃˈkɒvə/

Teresina city, Brazil
terr-ez-**ee**-nuh /ˌtɛrɛˈziːnə/

Terezin see **Theresienstadt**

Terfel, Bryn Welsh operatic bass
brin tair-vel /ˌbrɪn ˈtɛː(r)vɛl/

tergiversate make conflicting
statements
tur-jiv-uhr-sayt /ˈtɜː(r)dʒɪvə(r)ˌseɪt/

teriyaki Japanese dish
terr-i-**yak**-i /ˌtɛriˈjaki/

termagant harsh-tempered woman
tur-muh-guhnt /ˈtɜː(r)məgənt/

Termini town, Sicily
tair-mee-ni /ˈtɛː(r)miːni/

Terpsichore Greek mythological
character
turp-**sik**-uh-ri /tɜː(r)pˈsɪkəri/

terpsichorean relating to dancing
turp-sik-uh-**ree**-uhn
/ˌtɜː(r)psɪkəˈriːən/

terrain stretch of land
terr-**ayn** /tɛˈreɪn/

terraqueous consisting of land and
water
terr-**ay**-kwi-uhss /tɛˈreɪkwɪəs/

Terrassa town, Spain
tuh-**rass**-uh /təˈrasə/

terrasse paved area outside a cafe
terr-**ass** /tɛˈras/

terrazzo flooring material
terr-**at**-soh /tɛˈratsəʊ/

Terre Haute city, US
terr-uh **hoht** /ˌtɛrə ˈhəʊt/

terribilità emotional intensity in a work
of art
terr-ib-il-it-**ah** /ˌtɛrɪbɪlɪˈtɑː/

tertiary third in order or level
tur-**shuh**-ri /ˈtəː(r)ʃəri/

Tertullian early Christian theologian
tur-**tul**-i-uhn /təː(r)ˈtʌliən/

terza rima poetry style
tairt-suh **ree**-muh /ˌtɛː(r)tsə ˈriːmə/

terzetto pl. **terzetti** musical trio
tairt-**set**-oh, pl. tairt-**set**-i
/tɛː(r)tˈsɛtəʊ/, pl. /-ti/
• Standard -s plural is also possible.

Tesla, Nikola American inventor
nik-uh-luh **tess**-luh /ˌnɪkələ ˈtɛslə/

tesla SI unit of magnetic flux density
tess-luh /ˈtɛslə/

TESOL Teaching of English to Speakers
of Other Languages
tee-sol /ˈtiːsɒl/

tessera pl. **tesserae** small mosaic block
tess-uh-ruh, pl. **tess**-uh-ree /ˈtɛsərə/,
pl. /-riː/

Tessin see **Ticino**

tessitura vocal range
tess-it-**yoor**-uh /ˌtɛsɪˈtjʊərə/

testate having made a will
test-ayt /ˈtɛsteɪt/

testis pl. **testes** male reproductive organ
test-iss, pl. **test**-eez /ˈtɛstɪs/, pl. /-tiːz/

testosterone male hormone
test-**ost**-uh-rohn /tɛˈstɒstərəʊn/

tête-à-tête private conversation between
two people
tet uh **tet** /ˌtɛt ə ˈtɛt/

Sometimes also tayt ah **tayt**.

tête de cuvée wine from the first grape
pressing
tet duh kue-**vay** /ˌtɛt də kyˈveɪ/

Tethys Greek goddess
teth-iss /ˈtɛθɪs/

Teton mountains, US
tee-tuhn /ˈtiːtən/

Tétouan city, Morocco
tay-**twahn** /teɪˈtwɑːn/

tetracycline antibiotic
tet-ruh-**syk**-leen /ˌtɛtrəˈsʌɪkliːn/

Tetragrammaton name of God
transliterated in four letters
tet-ruh-**gram**-uh-ton
/ˌtɛtrəˈgramətɒn/

tetrahydrocannabinol compound in
cannabis
tet-ruh-hyd-ruh-**kan**-uh-bin-ol
/ˌtɛtrəˌhʌɪdrəˈkanəbɪnɒl/

Teuton ancient ethnic group
tyoo-tuhn /ˈtjuːtən/

Tevere see **Tiber**

Teviot river, Scotland
tee-vi-uht /ˈtiːviət/

Tewa American Indian ethnic group
tay-wuh /ˈteɪwə/

TeX computer typesetting program
tek /tɛk/

The final X represents the Greek letter CHI,
hence this pronunciation.

Texarkana city, US
tek-sar-**kan**-uh /ˌtɛksɑː(r)ˈkanə/

Thackeray, William Makepeace
British novelist
thak-uh-ri /ˈθakəri/

Thaddaeus apostle
thad-i-uhss /ˈθadiəs/

Commonly also thuh-**dee**-uhss.

Thaïs opera by Massenet
tah-**eess** /tɑːˈiːs/

thalamus pl. **thalami** part of the brain
thal-uh-muhss, pl. **thal**-uh-my
/ˈθaləməs/, pl. /-mʌɪ/

thalassaemia blood disease
thal-uh-**see**-mi-uh /ˌθaləˈsiːmiə/

thaler German silver coin
tah-luhr /ˈtɑːlə(r)/

Thales Greek philosopher
thay-leez /ˈθeɪliːz/

thali set meal at an Indian restaurant
tah-li /ˈtɑːli/

Thalia Greek mythological character
thuh-**ly**-uh /θəˈlʌɪə/

Commonly also thay-li-uh or thal-i-uh.

thalidomide drug
thuh-**lid**-uh-myd /θəˈlɪdəmʌɪd/

thallium chemical element
thal-i-uhm /ˈθaliəm/

thalweg line connecting the lowest
points along a valley
tahl-veg /ˈtɑːlvɛg/

Thames river, England
temz /tɛmz/

There is also a river of this name in the US,
which is pronounced thaymz.

Thammuz Jewish month
tam-uuz /ˈtamʊz/

Thanatos death instinct
than-uh-toss /'θanətɒs/

Thar desert, India and Pakistan
tar /tɑː(r)/

thaumaturge performer of miracles
thaw-muh-turj /'θɔːmətə(r)dʒ/

the for names containing 'the', see under headword: e.g. **Hague, The**

Thebes ancient cities, Greece and Egypt
theebz /θiːbz/

thegn historical nobleman
thayn /θeɪn/

theism belief in a god or gods
thee-iz-uhm /'θiːɪzəm/

Themis Greek goddess
them-iss /'θɛmɪs/

Themistocles Athenian statesman
thuh-**mist**-uh-kleez /θə'mɪstə,kliːz/

Theocritus Greek poet
thi-**ok**-rit-uhss /θi'ɒkrɪtəs/

theodolite surveying instrument
thi-**od**-uh-lyt /θi'ɒdəlʌɪt/

Theodorakis, Mikis Greek composer and politician
mee-kiss thee-uh-duh-**rak**-iss /,miːkɪs ,θiədə'rakɪs/

Theodoric king of the Ostrogoths
thi-**od**-uh-rik /θi'ɒdərɪk/

Theophrastus Greek philosopher and scientist
thi-uh-**frast**-uhss /θiə'frastəs/

theorbo large lute
thi-**or**-boh /θi'ɔː(r)bəʊ/

theorem general proposition
theer-uhm /'θɪərəm/

therapeutic healing
therr-uh-**pyoo**-tik /,θɛrə'pjuːtɪk/

Theravada tradition of Buddhism
therr-uh-**vah**-duh /,θɛrə'vɑːdə/

thereanent concerning that matter
*th*air-uh-**nent** /,ðɛːrə'nɛnt/

theremin electronic musical instrument
therr-uh-min /'θɛrəmɪn/

Theresienstadt Nazi concentration camp, Czech Republic
tuh-**ray**-zi-uhn-shtat /tə'reɪzɪənʃtat/

The Czech name for the town is Terezin, pronounced **terr**-ez-een.

thermion ion emitted by a substance at high temperature
thurm-i-on /'θəː(r)mɪɒn/

thermogenesis production of heat
thur-moh-**jen**-uh-siss /,θəː(r)məʊ'dʒɛnəsɪs/

Thermopylae mountain pass, Greece
thurm-**op**-il-ee /θəː(r)'mɒpɪliː/

Theron, Charlize South African actress
shar-**leez** therr-uhn /ʃɑː(r),liːz 'θɛrən/

Theroux, Paul American travel writer
thuh-**roo** /θə'ruː/

thesaurus pl. **thesauri** book of synonyms
thuh-**saw**-ruhss, pl. thuh-**saw**-ry /θə'sɔːrəs/, pl. /-rʌɪ/

Theseus Greek mythological character
theess-yooss /'θiːsjuːs/

Sometimes also **thee**-si-uhss, as with ODYSSEUS and PERSEUS; see GREEK panel.

Thesiger, Wilfred English explorer
thess-ij-uhr /'θɛsɪdʒə(r)/

thesis pl. **theses** theory
thee-siss, pl. **thee**-seez /'θiːsɪs/, pl. /-siːz/

Thespis Greek dramatic poet
thesp-iss /'θɛspɪs/

Thessalonians book of the Bible
thess-uh-**loh**-ni-uhnz /,θɛsə'ləʊnɪənz/

Thessaloniki port, Greece
thess-uh-lon-**ee**-ki /,θɛsəlɒ'niːki/

Thessaly region, Greece
thess-uh-li /'θɛsəli/

theta letter of the Greek alphabet
thee-tuh /'θiːtə/

Thetis Greek mythological character
thet-iss /'θɛtɪs/

However, the girl's name and the island in Canada are commonly also pronounced **thee**-tiss.

thiamine vitamin
thy-uh-meen /'θʌɪəmiːn/

Thimphu capital of Bhutan
tim-poo /'tɪmpuː/

Thisbe Roman mythological character
thiz-bi /'θɪzbi/

Thomas, Dylan Welsh poet
dil-uhn /'dɪlən/

The Welsh pronunciation of this first name is more like **dul**-an, but the poet preferred this anglicization for English-language broadcasts.

Thomas à Kempis German theologian
tom-uhss uh **kem**-piss /,tɒməs ə 'kɛmpɪs/

Thomism theology of Thomas Aquinas
toh-miz-uhm /ˈtəʊmɪzəm/

Thor Norse god
thor /θɔː(r)/

thoracic relating to the thorax
thaw-**rass**-ik /θɔːˈrasɪk/

thoracolumbar relating to the thoracic
and lumbar regions of the spine
thaw-ruh-koh-**lum**-buhr
/ˌθɔːrəkəʊˈlʌmbə(r)/

thorax pl. **thoraces** chest
thaw-raks, pl. **thaw**-ruh-seez
/ˈθɔːraks/, pl. /ˈθɔːrəsiːz/
• Standard -es plural is also possible.

Thorazine trademark drug
thaw-ruh-zeen /ˈθɔːrəziːn/

Thoreau, Henry David American
essayist and poet
thaw-roh /ˈθɔːrəʊ/

thorium chemical element
thaw-ri-uhm /ˈθɔːriəm/

Thorvaldsen, Bertel Danish sculptor
bair-tuhl **tor**-val-suhn /ˌbɛː(r)təl
ˈtɔː(r)valsən/

Thoth Egyptian god
thohth /θəʊθ/

Sometimes also thoth or toht.

Thrace ancient country
thrayss /θreɪs/

thrall being in someone's power
thrawl /θrɔːl/

threepence sum of three pence
thrup-uhnss /ˈθrʌpəns/

threepenny worth three pence
thrup-uh-ni /ˈθrʌpəni/

threnody lament
thren-uh-di /ˈθrɛnədi/

thrombosis pl. **thromboses** blood clot
throm-**boh**-siss, pl. throm-**boh**-seez
/θrɒmˈbəʊsɪs/, pl. /-siːz/

Thucydides Greek historian
thyoo-**sid**-id-eez /θjuːˈsɪdɪdiːz/

thulium chemical element
thoo-li-uhm /ˈθuːliəm/

Commonly also **thyoo**-li-uhm.

thurible censer
thyoor-ib-uhl /ˈθjʊərɪbəl/

Thuringia state, Germany
thoor-**ing**-gi-uh /ˌθʊəˈrɪŋɡiə/

Established anglicization. An older
anglicized pronunciation, thyoor-**in**-ji-uh, is
also common. The German name is
Thüringen, pronounced **tuer**-ing-uhn.

Thurman, Uma American actress
oo-muh **thur**-muhn /ˌuːmə ˈθəː(r)mən/

Thurso port, Scotland
thur-soh /ˈθəː(r)səʊ/

Thyestes Greek mythological character
thy-**est**-eez /θaɪˈɛstiːz/
• See GREEK panel.

thyme herb
tym /tʌɪm/

thymus gland
thy-muhss /ˈθʌɪməs/

thyroid gland
thy-royd /ˈθʌɪrɔɪd/

Thyssen German family of industrialists
tue-suhn /ˈtʏsən/

Tiamat Babylonian mythological dragon
tee-uh-mat /ˈtiːəmat/

tian vegetable dish
tyah(ng) /tjɑ̃/

Tiananmen Square square, Beijing
tyen-uhn-muhn /ˈtjɛnənmən/

Tianjin port, China
tyen-**jin** /ˌtjɛnˈdʒɪn/

Tian Shan see Tien Shan

Tiber river, Italy
ty-buhr /ˈtʌɪbə(r)/

Established anglicization. The Italian name
is Tevere, pronounced **tev**-err-ay.

Tiberius Roman emperor
ty-**beer**-i-uhss /tʌɪˈbɪəriəs/

Tibesti Mountains mountain range,
Africa
tib-**est**-i /tɪˈbɛsti/

Tibet country
tib-**et** /tɪˈbɛt/

tibia leg bone
tib-i-uh /ˈtɪbiə/

Tibullus, Albius Roman poet
al-bi-uhss tib-**ul**-uhss /ˌalbiəs tɪˈbʌləs/

Ticino canton, Switzerland
titch-**ee**-noh /tɪˈtʃiːnəʊ/

This is the Italian name. The German and
French name is Tessin, pronounced **tess**-een
in German and tess-**a(ng)** in French.

Ticonderoga town, US
ty-kon-duh-**roh**-guh /tʌɪkɒndəˈrəʊgə/

tienda general store
tyen-duh /ˈtjɛndə/

Tien Shan (also **Tian Shan**) mountain range, China
tyen **shan** /ˌtjɛn ˈʃan/

Tiepolo, Giovanni Battista Italian painter
juh-**vah**-ni bat-**eest**-uh **tyep**-ol-oh /dʒə va:ni ba'ti:stə 'tjɛpɒləʊ/

Tiergarten suburb of Berlin
teer-gar-tuhn /ˈtɪə(r)gɑ:(r)tən/

Tierra del Fuego island, South America
tyerr-uh del **fway**-goh /ˌtjɛ:rə dɛl ˈfweɪgəʊ/

Tiflis see **Tbilisi**

Tigray (also **Tigre**) province, Ethiopia
teeg-ray /ˈtiːgreɪ/

Tigris river, Asia
ty-griss /ˈtʌɪgrɪs/

Established anglicization. The Arabic name is Dijla, pronounced **dij**-luh.

Tijuana town, Mexico
ti-**wah**-nuh /tɪˈwaː nə/, Spanish [tiˈxwana]
• Established anglicization.

Tikal ancient Mayan city, Guatemala
ti-**kahl** /tɪˈkaːl/

Tikrit town, Iraq
tik-**reet** /tɪˈkriːt/

The Iraqi surname al-Tikriti is pronounced uh-tik-**ree**-ti.

tilak mark worn by a Hindu on the forehead
til-uk /ˈtɪlʌk/

tilapia fish
til-**ay**-pi-uh /tɪˈleɪpiə/

Commonly also til-**ap**-i-uh.

Tilburg city, Netherlands
til-burg /ˈtɪlbə:(r)g/, [ˈtɪlbʏrx]
• Established anglicization.

tilde diacritic (˜)
til-duh /ˈtɪldə/

tilleul lime tree
tee-**yoel** /tiːˈjœːl/

Till Eulenspiegel German literary character
til oy-luhn-shpee-guhl /ˌtɪl ˈɔɪlən ˌʃpiːgəl/

Tillich, Paul German-born American theologian

til-ik /ˈtɪlɪk/

Timaru port, New Zealand
tim-uh-roo /ˈtɪməruː/

timbale dish
tam-**bahl** /tamˈbɑːl/

timbre quality of a musical sound or voice
tam-buhr /ˈtambə(r)/

Timbuktu (also **Timbuctoo**) town, Mali
tim-buk-**too** /ˌtɪmbʌkˈtuː/

timeous in good time
ty-muhss /ˈtʌɪməs/

Timişoara city, Romania
tim-ish-**war**-uh /ˌtɪmɪˈʃwɑːrə/

Timor island and sea, Pacific
tee-mor /ˈtiːmɔː(r)/

timpani kettledrums
tim-puh-ni /ˈtɪmpəni/

tinea ringworm
tin-i-uh /ˈtɪniə/

tinnitus ringing or buzzing in the ears
tin-**y**-tuhss /tɪˈnʌɪtəs/

Commonly also **tin**-it-uhss, although the pronunciation recommended in medical dictionaries is tin-**y**-tuhss.

Tintagel village and castle, England
tin-**taj**-uhl /tɪnˈtadʒəl/

Tintoretto Italian painter
tin-torr-**et**-oh /ˌtɪntɒˈrɛtəʊ/

Tipperary county, Republic of Ireland
tip-uh-**rair**-i /ˌtɪpəˈrɛːri/

tirade long, angry speech
ty-**ayd** /tʌɪˈreɪd/

Commonly also tirr-**ayd**.

tiramisú Italian dessert
tirr-uh-miss-**oo** /ˌtɪrəmɪˈsuː/

Tirana (also **Tiranë**) capital of Albania
tirr-**ah**-nuh /tɪˈrɑːnə/

Tiree island, Scotland
ty-**ree** /tʌɪˈriː/

Tiresias Greek mythological character
ty-**ree**-si-uhss /tʌɪˈriːsiəs/

Tîrgu Mureş city, Romania
teer-goo **moor**-esh /ˌtɪə(r)guː ˈmʊəreʃ/

Tír-na-nÓg Irish mythological place
teer nuh **nohg** /ˌtɪə(r) nə ˈnəʊg/

Tirol see **Tyrol**

Tiruchirapalli city, India
tirr-uutch-irr-**ah**-puh-li /ˌtɪrʊtʃɪˈrɑːpəli/

tisane herb tea
tiz-**an** /tɪˈzan/

Tiscali internet service company
tisk-uh-li /ˈtɪskəli/

Tisiphone Greek mythological character
tiss-**if**-uh-ni /tɪˈsɪfəni/

tissue type of material
tish-oo /ˈtɪʃuː/

Sometimes also **tiss**-yoo, a pronunciation
which is increasingly uncommon.

Tisza river, Europe
tiss-uh /ˈtɪsə/

Titan Greek god
ty-tuhn /ˈtʌɪtən/

Titania moon of Uranus
tit-**ah**-ni-uh /tɪˈtɑːnɪə/

Less commonly also tit-**ay**-ni-uh.

titanium chemical element
tit-**ay**-ni-uhm /tɪˈteɪnɪəm/

tithe tax
ty*th* /tʌɪð/

Tithonus Greek mythological character
tith-**oh**-nuhss /tɪˈθəʊnəs/

Titian Italian painter
tish-uhn /ˈtɪʃən/

Established anglicization. The Italian
version of the name is Tiziano, pronounced
tit-**syah**-noh.

Titicaca lake, Peru and Bolivia
tit-ik-**ah**-kuh /ˌtɪtɪˈkɑːkə/

titivate make minor enhancements to
tit-iv-ayt /ˈtɪtɪveɪt/

Tito, Josip Yugoslav statesman
yoss-ip **tee**-toh /ˌjɒsɪp ˈtiːtəʊ/

titrate measurement
ty-**trayt** /tʌɪˈtreɪt/

titular holding a purely formal position
tit-yuul-uhr /ˈtɪtjʊlə(r)/

Titus Roman emperor
ty-tuhss /ˈtʌɪtəs/

Tivoli city, Italy
tee-vol-i /ˈtiːvɒli/

Tlaxcala state, Mexico
tlask-**ah**-luh /tlasˈkɑːlə/

Tlemcen city, Algeria
tlem-**sen** /tlɛmˈsɛn/

Tlingit American Indian ethnic group
tling-git /ˈtlɪŋgɪt/

tmesis pl. **tmeses** separation of parts of a
compound word by an intervening word

tmee-siss, pl. **tmee**-seez /ˈtmiːsɪs/, pl.
/-siːz/

Tobago see **Trinidad and Tobago**

Tobermory town, Scotland
toh-buhr-maw-ri /ˈtəʊbə(r)mɔːri/

Tobruk (also **Tubruq**) port, Libya
tuh-**bruuk** /təˈbrʊk/

Tocantins river, South America
toh-kuhn-**teenss** /ˌtəʊkənˈtiːns/

toccata musical composition
tuh-**kah**-tuh /təˈkɑːtə/

Tocharian ancient language
tuh-**kair**-i-uhn /təˈkɛːrɪən/

Less commonly also tuh-**kar**-i-uhn.

tochus person's buttocks
tokh-uhss /ˈtɒxəs/

tocopherol substance found in food
tok-**of**-uh-rol /tɒˈkɒfərɒl/

Tocqueville, Alexis de French writer
al-ek-**see** duh tok-**veel** /aˌlɛkˌsiː də
tɒkˈviːl/

tofu soya protein
toh-foo /ˈtəʊfuː/

Togliatti (also **Tolyatti**) city, Russia
tol-**yat**-i /tɒˈljati/

Togo country
toh-goh /ˈtəʊgəʊ/

Tohoku region, Japan
toh-**hoh**-koo /təʊˈhəʊkuː/
● See **JAPANESE** panel.

Tóibín, Colm Irish writer
kol-uhm toh-**been** /ˌkɒləm təʊˈbiːn/

toile version of a garment made in cheap
material
twahl /twɑːl/

toile de Jouy printed calico
twahl duh **zhwee** /ˌtwɑːl də ˈʒwiː/

Tojo, Hideki Japanese statesman
hee-dek-i **toh**-joh /ˌhiːdɛki ˈtəʊdʒəʊ/

Tokaji Hungarian wine
tok-oy /ˈtɒkɔɪ/

The name, also spelt Tokay or Tocai, is also
used with reference to wines produced
elsewhere. An anglicized pronunciation
toh-**kay** is sometimes used, particularly of
non-Hungarian wines.

Tokelau three islands, Pacific
tok-uh-low /ˈtɒkəˌlaʊ/

Tok Pisin Creole language
tok **piss**-in /ˌtɒk ˈpɪsɪn/

Tokugawa shogunate in Japan
tok-oo-**gah**-wuh /ˌtɒkuːˈgɑːwə/

Tokyo capital of Japan
toh-kyoh /ˈtəʊkjəʊ/

tolar currency unit, Slovenia
tol-uhr /ˈtɒlə(r)/

tolbutamide diabetes drug
tol-**byoo**-tuh-myd /tɒlˈbjuːtəmʌɪd/

Toledo city, Spain
tol-**ay**-doh /tɒˈleɪdəʊ/, [tɒˈleðo]

Established anglicization. Toledo in the US
is pronounced tuh-**lee**-doh.

Tolkien, J. R. R. (Reuel) English
scholar and author
roo-uhl **tol**-keen /ˌruːəl ˈtɒlkiːn/

Tollemache British surname
tol-mash /ˈtɒlmaʃ/

Tollund Man well-preserved corpse of
an Iron Age man
tol-uhnd /ˈtɒlənd/

Tolstoy, Leo (Lev) Russian writer
lee-oh **tol**-stoy /ˈliːəʊ ˈtɒlstɔɪ/, [ˌljɛf
təlˈstɔj]
• Established anglicization.

toluene solvent
tol-yoo-een /ˈtɒljuiːn/

Tolyatti see **Togliatti**

tomahawk light axe
tom-**uh**-hawk /ˈtɒməhɔːk/

tomalley part of a lobster
tom-uh-li /ˈtɒməli/

Sometimes also tuh-**mah**-li.

tomatillo fruit
tom-uh-**teel**-yoh /tɒməˈtiːljəʊ/

Tomatin village and whisky distillery,
Scotland
tuh-**mat**-in /təˈmatɪn/

Tombaugh, Clyde William American
astronomer
tom-baw /ˈtɒmbɔː/

tomography imaging technique
tuh-**mog**-ruh-fi /təˈmɒɡrəfi/

ton unit of weight
tun /tʌn/

ton fashionable style
to(ng) /tɒ̃/

Tonga country
tong-uh /ˈtɒŋə/

Tongariro mountain, New Zealand
tong-uh-**reer**-oh /ˌtɒŋəˈrɪərəʊ/

Tonge, Jenny English politician
tong /tɒŋ/

This British surname is variously
pronounced tong or tung, depending on
individual preference.

Tonkin region, Vietnam
tonk-in /ˈtɒŋˈkɪn/

Tonlé Sap lake, Cambodia
ton-**lay sahp** /tɒnˌleɪ ˈsɑːp/

tonne metric ton
tun /tʌn/

tonsorial relating to hairdressing
ton-**saw**-ri-uhl /tɒnˈsɔːrɪəl/

Tonton Macoute Haitian militia
to(ng)-to(ng) mak-**oot** /ˌtɔ̃tɔ̃ maˈkuːt/

Toowoomba town, Australia
tuh-**wuum**-buh /təˈwʊmbə/

Topeka city, US
tuh-**pee**-kuh /təˈpiːkə/

topgallantsail type of sail
tuh-**gan**-suhl /təˈɡansəl/

topiary art of clipping shrubs
toh-pi-uh-ri /ˈtəʊpiəri/

Topkapi Palace museum, Istanbul
top-kap-i /ˈtɒpkapi/

toponym place name
top-uh-nim /ˈtɒpənɪm/

topos pl. **topoi** traditional theme in
literature
top-oss, pl. **top**-oy /ˈtɒpɒs, pl. /ˈtɒpɔɪ/

toque woman's small hat
tohk /təʊk/

Tora Bora village, Afghanistan
toor-uh **boor**-uh /ˌtʊərə ˈbʊərə/

Torah Hebrew scriptures
taw-ruh /ˈtɔːrə/, [tɔˈrɑː]
• Established anglicization.

torchère ornamental stand
tor-**shair** /tɔː(r)ˈʃɛː(r)/

torchon type of bobbin lace
tor-shuhn /ˈtɔː(r)ʃən/

toreador bullfighter
torr-i-uh-dor /ˈtɒriədɔː(r)/

torii gateway of a Shinto shrine
taw-ree /ˈtɔːriː/
• See JAPANESE panel.

Torino see **Turin**

Tornio river, Sweden
tor-ni-oh /ˈtɔː(r)niəʊ/

torpor state of inactivity
tor-puhr /ˈtɔː(r)pə(r)/

torque twisting force
tork /tɔː(r)k/

Tone

Pitch is used in all languages to indicate differences in meaning, but there are two basic ways in which this is achieved. In a language like English, pitch operates at sentence level, so that different intonation in the utterance *Ben loves cycling* can make it a statement or a question. In so-called tone languages, on the other hand, pitch operates at word level to change the meaning of words. Even when *yes* is said with a falling or rising intonation in English, to make it either a statement or question respectively, it is still the whole utterance that has changed, not the meaning of the word itself.

Chinese is a tone language with four basic tones. The word *ma* has four different meanings, depending on which tone is used. Pronounced with a high level tone it means *mother*, with a high rising tone *hemp*, with a low falling rising tone *horse*, and finally with a high falling tone it means *scold*.

We do not expect BBC announcers to be able to make these tonal distinctions, and we cannot retain them when giving Chinese recommendations in our phonetic respelling, even though this may on occasion result in some pronunciations that are rather bewildering to Chinese ears!

Many languages of western and southern Africa, such as Ewe, Yoruba, and Lingala, are tone languages. The only European tone languages are Swedish and Norwegian, where tone is used to a lesser extent than in Chinese. In Swedish there are around 300 word pairs that differ only in the use of tonal accent. There are two tones, sometimes referred to as acute and grave accent. Acute accent, or single tone, makes the word *anden* mean *the duck*. Grave accent, or double tone, makes the same word mean *the spirit*.

Torquemada, Tomás de Spanish Grand Inquisitor
tom-**ass** day tor-kem-**ah**-*th*uh /tʊˈmas deɪ ˌtɔː(r)kɛˈmɑːðə/

Torres Strait channel north of Australia
torr-uhz /ˈtɒrəz/

Torricelli, Evangelista Italian mathematician and physicist
ev-an-juh-**lee**-stuh torr-i-**chel**-i /ˌɛvandʒəˈliːstə ˌtɒriˈtʃɛli/

Tórshavn capital of the Faroe Islands
torss-hown /ˈtɔː(r)shaʊn/

torte pl. **torten** cake or tart

tor-tuh, pl. **tor**-tuhn /ˈtɔː(r)tə/, pl. /ˈtɔː(r)tən/

Tortelier, Paul French cellist
tor-**tel**-i-ay /tɔː(r)ˈtɛlieɪ/, [tɔrtəlje]
• Established anglicization.

tortilla Spanish pancake
tor-**tee**-yuh /tɔː(r)ˈtiːjə/

tortoise reptile
tor-tuhss /ˈtɔː(r)təs/

Commonly also **tor**-toyz.

Tortola island, Caribbean
tor-**toh**-luh /tɔː(r)ˈtəʊlə/

Toruń city, Poland
torr-oon /'tɒruːn/, ['toruɳ]
• Established anglicization.

tosa breed of dog
toh-suh /'təʊsə/

Toscana see **Tuscany**

Toscanini, Arturo Italian conductor
ar-**toor**-oh tosk-uh-**nee**-ni
/ɑː(r),tʊərəʊ ,tɒskə'niːni/

tostada Mexican pancake
tost-**ah**-duh /tɒ'stɑːdə/

totara New Zealand tree
toh-tuh-ruh /'təʊtərə/

Totnes town, England
tot-nuhss /'tɒtnəs/

toucan tropical bird
too-kuhn /'tuːkən/

touché acknowledgement of a hit
too-**shay** /tuː'ʃeɪ/

Toulon port, France
too-**lo(ng)** /tuː'lõ/

Toulouse city, France
too-**looz** /tuː'luːz/

Toulouse-Lautrec, Henri French
painter and lithographer
ah(ng)-**ree** too-**looz** loh-**trek** /ã,riː
tuː:,luːz ləʊ'trek/

toupee artificial hairpiece
too-pay /'tuːpeɪ/

tour de force skilful performance
toor duh **forss** /,tʊə(r) də 'fɔː(r)s/

Tourette's syndrome neurological
disorder
tuu-**rets** /tʊ'rɛts/

tourmaline mineral
toor-muh-leen /'tʊə(r)məliːn/

Tournai town, Belgium
toor-**nay** /tʊə(r)'neɪ/

This is the French name. The Flemish name
is Doornik, pronounced **dor**-nik.

tournedos small cut of beef
toor-nuh-doh /'tʊə(r)nədəʊ/

tourney medieval tournament
toor-ni /'tʊə(r)ni/

Sometimes also **tor**-ni.

tourniquet device for stopping the flow
of blood
toor-nik-ay /'tʊə(r)nɪkeɪ/

Commonly also **tor**-nik-ay.

Tours city, France

toor /tʊə(r)/

tout attempt to sell
towt /taʊt/

Toutatis Celtic god
too-**tah**-tiss /tuː'tɑːtɪs/

tout court with no addition
too **koor** /,tuː 'kʊə(r)/

tout de suite immediately
too duh **sweet** /,tuː də 'swiːt/

tovarish (also **tovarich**) comrade
tov-**ar**-ish /tɒ'vɑːrɪʃ/

toxaemia blood poisoning
tok-**see**-mi-uh /tɒk'siːmiə/

toxocariasis larval infection
tok-soh-kuh-**ry**-uh-siss
/,tɒksəʊkə'rʌɪəsɪs/

toxophilite lover of archery
tok-**sof**-il-yt /tɒk'sɒfɪlʌɪt/

Toynbee, Arnold English economist
toyn-bi /'tɔɪnbi/

trabeation use of beams in architectural
construction
tray-bi-**ay**-shuhn /,treɪbi'eɪʃən/

Trâblous see **Tripoli**

Trabzon port, Turkey
trab-zuhn /'trabzən/

An older name for the port, Trebizond, is
pronounced **treb**-iz-ond.

trachea pl. **tracheae** windpipe
truh-**kee**-uh, pl. truh-**kee**-ee /trə'kiːə/
pl. /-'kiːiː/

Commonly also **tray**-ki-uh. Standard -s
plural is also possible.

tracheotomy incision in the windpipe
trak-i-**ot**-uh-mi /,traki'ɒtəmi/

trachoma eye infection
truh-**koh**-muh /trə'kəʊmə/

Tradescant, John English botanist
truh-**desk**-ant /trə'dɛskant/

Trafalgar, Battle of naval battle
truh-**fal**-guhr /trə'falgə(r)/

tragedian tragic actor
truh-**jee**-di-uhn /trə'dʒiːdiən/

traghetto pl. **traghetti** jetty for gondolas
trag-**et**-oh, pl. trag-**et**-i /tra'gɛtəʊ/, pl.
/-'gɛti/

tragus part of the external ear
tray-guhss /'treɪgəs/

Traherne, Thomas English religious
writer
truh-**hurn** /trə'həː(r)n/

trahison des clercs betrayal of standards by artists or writers
trah-iz-o**(ng)** day **klair** /ˌtrɑːizɔ̃ deɪ ˈklɛː(r)/

trait distinguishing quality
trayt /treɪt/

Commonly also **tray**.

Trajan Roman emperor
tray-juhn /ˈtreɪdʒən/

trajectory path of a flying object
truh-**jek**-tuh-ri /trəˈdʒɛktəri/

Trakehner breed of horse
trak-**ay**-nuhr /traˈkeɪnə(r)/

Tralee town, Republic of Ireland
truh-**lee** /trəˈliː/

Traminer white wine grape
truh-**mee**-nuhr /trəˈmiːnə(r)/

tramontana cold north wind
tram-on-**tah**-nuh /ˌtramɒnˈtɑːnə/

tranche portion of something
trahnsh /trɑːnʃ/

transept part of a church
tran-sept /ˈtransɛpt/

transferable able to be transferred
transs-**fur**-uh-buhl /transˈfəːrəbəl/

Commonly also **trahnss**- or **trans-fuh-ruh-buhl**.

Transkei region, South Africa
tran-**sky** /tranˈskʌɪ/

transparent allowing light to pass through
tran-**sparr**-uhnt /tranˈsparənt/

Less commonly also **trahn**- or **tran-spair-uhnt**.

transubstantiate convert into the body and blood of Christ
tran-suhb-**stan**-shi-ayt /ˌtransəbˈstanʃieɪt/

Transvaal former province, South Africa
tranz-**vahl** /tranzˈvɑːl/

Transylvania region, Romania
tran-sil-**vay**-ni-uh /ˌtransɪlˈveɪnɪə/

Trapani town, Italy
trah-puh-ni /ˈtrɑːpəni/

trapezium pl. **trapezia** quadrilateral
truh-**pee**-zi-uhm, pl. truh-**pee**-zi-uh /trəˈpiːziəm, pl. /-ziə/
• Standard -s plural is also possible.

trapezoid quadrilateral
trap-uh-zoyd /ˈtrapəzɔɪd/

Trapido, Barbara South African-born novelist
truh-**pee**-doh /trəˈpiːdəʊ/

Trás-os-Montes region, Portugal
traz oozh **mont**-uhsh /ˌtraz uːʒ ˈmɒntəʃ/

trattoria Italian restaurant
trat-uh-**ree**-uh /ˌtratəˈriːə/

trauma distressing experience
traw-muh /ˈtrɔːmə/

Less commonly also **trow**-muh.

travois sledge
truh-**voy** /trəˈvɔɪ/

Treacy, Phillip English milliner
tray-si /ˈtreɪsi/

treadle foot lever
tred-uhl /ˈtrɛdəl/

treatise written work on a particular subject
tree-tiss /ˈtriːtɪs/

Trebbiano variety of wine grape
treb-**yah**-noh /ˌtrɛbˈjɑːnəʊ/

Trebizond see **Trabzon**

Treblinka Nazi concentration camp, Poland
treb-**link**-uh /trɛˈblɪŋkə/

trebuchet large catapult
treb-yuush-ay /ˈtrɛbjʊʃeɪ/

Less commonly also **treb**-yuush-et.

trecento 14th century
tray-**chen**-toh /treɪˈtʃɛntəʊ/

trefa against Jewish law
tray-fuh /ˈtreɪfə/

trefoil clover-like plant
tref-oyl /ˈtrɛfɔɪl/

trenchant vigorous or incisive
tren-chuhnt /ˈtrɛntʃənt/

Trenchard, Hugh British air marshal
trensh-uhrd /ˈtrɛnʃə(r)d/

Trentino-Alto Adige region, Italy
tren-**tee**-noh **al**-toh **ad**-ij-ay /trɛnˌtiːnəʊ ˌaltəʊ ˈadɪdʒeɪ/

trepan saw used to perforate the skull
truh-**pan** /trəˈpan/

trephine surgical saw
truh-**fyn** /trəˈfʌɪn/

Tretyakov art gallery in Moscow
truht-**yuh**-kof /ˈtrɒtjəkɒf/

Trèves see **Trier**

Trevino, Lee American golfer
truh-**vee**-noh /trə'viːnəʊ/

Trevelyan, George Macaulay English
historian
truh-**vil**-yuhn /trə'vɪljən/

This British surname is variously
pronounced truh-**vel**-yuhn or
truh-**vil**-yuhn, depending on individual
preference.

Trevithick, Richard English engineer
trev-ith-ik /'trɛvɪθɪk/

triad group of three
try-ad /'trʌɪad/

triage preliminary assessment
tree-ahzh /'triːɑːʒ/

Triassic geological period
try-**ass**-ik /trʌɪ'asɪk/

tribadism lesbian sexual practice
trib-uh-diz-uhm /'trɪbədɪzəm/

Tribeca area of New York City
try-**bek**-uh /trʌɪ'bɛkə/

tribunal body established to settle
dispute
try-**byoo**-nuhl /trʌɪ'bjuːnəl/

triceps arm muscle
try-seps /'trʌɪsɛps/

triceratops dinosaur
try-**serr**-uh-tops /trʌɪ'sɛrətɒps/

Trichet, Jean-Claude French
president of the European Central Bank
zhah(ng) **klohd** tree-**shay** /ʒɑ̃ ˌkləʊd
triː'ʃeɪ/

trichology study of the hair and scalp
trik-**ol**-uh-ji /trɪ'kɒlədʒi/

trichomoniasis infection
trik-oh-muh-**ny**-uh-siss
/ˌtrɪkəʊmə'nʌɪəsɪs/

triclinium dining table with couches
along three sides
try-**klin**-i-uhm /trʌɪ'klɪniəm/

This and many other words with *tri-* can be
pronounced either tri- or try-; see LATIN
panel.

tricolour three-coloured flag
trik-uh-luhr /'trɪkələ(r)/

tricot fine knitted fabric
tree-koh /'triːkəʊ/

tricoteuse woman who knits
tree-kot-**oez** /ˌtriːkɒ'tœːz/

Tridentine Catholic catechism
trid-**en**-tyn /trɪ'dɛntʌɪn/

triduum period of three days' observance
trid-yoo-uhm /'trɪdjuəm/

Trier city, Germany
treer /trɪə(r)/

The same pronunciation is an appropriate
anglicization for Danish film director Lars
von Trier's name. The city is near the border
with Luxembourg. The French name is
Trèves, pronounced trev.

Trieste city, Italy
tri-**est** /tri'ɛst/

trigeminal nerve
try-**jem**-in-uhl /trʌɪ'dʒɛmɪnəl/

trigonometry branch of mathematics
tri-guh-**nom**-uh-tri /ˌtrɪɡə'nɒmətri/

trilobite fossil
try-loh-byt /'trʌɪləʊbʌɪt/

trimaran yacht with three hulls
try-muh-ran /'trʌɪməran/

trimester period of three months
try-**mest**-uhr /trʌɪ'mɛstə(r)/

trimeter line of verse
trim-uh-tuhr /'trɪmɪtə(r)/

Trimurti Hindu trinity
trim-**oor**-ti /trɪ'mʊə(r)ti/

Trincomalee port, Sri Lanka
trink-uh-muh-**lee** /ˌtrɪŋkəmə'liː/

Trinidad and Tobago country,
Caribbean
trin-id-ad tuh-**bay**-goh /'trɪnɪdad
tə'beɪɡəʊ/

Trinitarian relating to the Trinity
tri-nit-**air**-i-uhn /ˌtrɪnɪ'tɛːrɪən/

trinitrotoluene explosive
try-ny-troh-**tol**-yoo-een
/trʌɪˌnʌɪtrəʊ'tɒljuiːn/

triphthong three vowels combined in
one syllable
trif-thong /'trɪfθɒŋ/

Commonly also **trip**-thong.

Tripitaka sacred Buddhist canon
trip-it-uh-kuh /trɪ'pɪtəkə/

triplex trademark safety glass
trip-leks /'trɪplɛks/

Tripoli capital of Libya
trip-uh-li /'trɪpəli/

The Arabic name is Trâblous, pronounced
trah-**blooss**.

tripos examination at Cambridge
University
try-poss /'trʌɪpɒs/

triptych picture on three panels
trip-tik /'trɪptɪk/

Tripura state, India
trip-oor-uh /'trɪpʊərə/

trireme ancient war galley
try-reem /'trʌɪriːm/

triskaidekaphobia superstition
regarding the number thirteen
trisk-y-dek-uh-**foh**-bi-uh
/ˌtrɪskʌɪdɛkə'fəʊbɪə/

triskelion Celtic symbol
trisk-**el**-i-uhn /trɪ'skɛlɪən/

trisomy chromosome abnormality
triss-uh-mi /'trɪsəmi/

Tristan da Cunha island, South
Atlantic
trist-uhn duh **koon**-yuh /ˌtrɪstən də
'kuːnjə/

tristesse melancholia
treest-**ess** /triː'stɛs/

Tristan legendary knight, lover of Isolde;
also called **Tristram**
trist-uhn /'trɪstən/

Tristram legendary knight, lover of
Iseult; also called **Tristan**
trist-ruhm /'trɪstrəm/

triticale cereal crop
trit-ik-**ay**-li /ˌtrɪtɪ'keɪli/

Triton Greek god
try-tuhn /'trʌɪtən/

triumvir pl. **triumviri** Roman officer
try-**um**-vuhr, pl. **try**-**um**-vuh-ry
/trʌɪ'ʌmvə(r)/, pl. /-rʌɪ/

triumvirate three men holding power
try-**um**-virr-uht /trʌɪ'ʌmvɪrət/

triune consisting of three in one
try-yoon /'trʌɪjuːn/

Trivandrum port, India
triv-**and**-ruhm /trɪ'vandrəm/

Troad ancient region, Asia Minor
troh-ad /'trəʊad/

Trobriand Islands islands, Pacific
troh-bri-uhnd /'trəʊbriand/

trocar surgical instrument
troh-kar /'trəʊkɑː(r)/

trochaic consisting of trochees
truh-**kay**-ik /trə'keɪɪk/

trochee metrical foot
troh-kee /'trəʊkiː/

Trockenbeerenauslese sweet German
white wine

trok-uhn-bair-uhn-**owss**-lay-zuh
/'trɒkən,bɛːrən,aʊsleɪzə/

troglodyte cave-dweller
trog-luh-dyt /'trɒglədʌɪt/

troika Russian vehicle
troy-kuh /'trɔɪkə/

troilism sexual activity involving three
participants
troy-liz-uhm /'trɔɪlɪzəm/

Troilus and Criseyde poem by
Chaucer
troy-luhss kriss-**ay**-duh /'trɔɪləs
krɪ'seɪdə/

Trollope, Anthony English novelist
trol-uhp /'trɒləp/

trompe l'œil visual illusion
tromp **loy** /ˌtrɒmp 'lɔɪ/, French /trɔ̃p
lœi/
• Established anglicization.

Tromsø city, Norway
truum-soe /'trʊmsøː/

Trondheim town, Norway
trond-hym /'trɒndhʌɪm/, ['trɔnhɛjm]
• Established anglicization.

troposphere region of the atmosphere
trop-oh-sfeer /'trɒpəʊsfɪə(r)/

Trossachs valley, Scotland
tross-uhks /'trɒsəks/

troth faith or loyalty
trohth /trəʊθ/

Trotsky, Leon Russian revolutionary
li-**on** trot-ski /ˌliːɒn 'trɒtski/

Trottiscliffe village, England
troz-li /'trɒzli/

troubadour French medieval lyric poet
troo-buh-dor /'truːbədɔː(r)/

Troughton, Patrick English actor
trow-tuhn /'traʊtən/

trousseau pl. **trousseaux** items collected
by a bride for her marriage
troo-soh, pl. **troo**-sohz /'truːsəʊ/, pl.
/-səʊz/

trouvaille lucky find
troo-**vy** /truː'vʌɪ/

trow think or believe
troh /trəʊ/

Trowbridge town, England
troh-brij /'trəʊbrɪdʒ/

Troyes town, France
trwah /trwɑː/

truculent quick to argue
truk-yuul-uhnt /'trʌkjʊlənt/

Trudeau, Pierre Canadian statesman
pyair **troo**-doh /ˌpjɛː(r) ˈtruːdəʊ/

Trudgill, Peter English linguist
trud-gil /ˈtrʌdɡɪl/

Truffaut, François French film director
frah(ng)-swah true-foh /frãˌswaː
tryˈfəʊ/

Trujillo city, Peru
troo-**kheel**-yoh /truːˈxiːljəʊ/

Truk Islands islands, Micronesia
truk /trʌk/

Truro town, England
troor-oh /ˈtrʊərəʊ/

trypanosomiasis tropical disease
trip-uh-noh-suh-**my**-uh-siss
/ˌtrɪpənəʊsəˈmʌɪəsɪs/

tryptophan amino acid
trip-tuh-fan /ˈtrɪptəfan/

Tsang, Donald chief executive of Hong
Kong
jung /dʒʌŋ/

tsar (also **czar** or **tzar**) emperor of Russia
tsar /tsɑː(r)/

tsarevich (also **czarevich** or **tzarevich**)
son of a tsar
tsar-uh-vitch /ˈtsɑːrəvɪtʃ/

tsarina (also **czarina** or **tzarina**) wife of
a tsar
tsar-**ee**-nuh /tsɑːˈriːnə/

Tsavo national park, Kenya
tsah-voh /ˈtsɑːvəʊ/

tsessebi antelope
tsess-**ay**-bi /tsɛˈseɪbi/

tsetse bloodsucking fly
tset-si /ˈtsɛtsi/

Tshwane another name for Pretoria
chwah-nay /ˈtʃwaːneɪ/

tsimmes (also **tzimmes** or **tzimmis**)
Jewish stew
tsim-uhss /ˈtsɪməs/

Tsing Tao Chinese brewery
ching **dow** /ˌtʃɪŋ ˈdaʊ/

Tsiolkovsky, Konstantin Russian
aeronautical engineer
kon-stuhn-**teen** tsi-uhl-**kof**-ski
/kɒnstənˈtiːn ˌtsiəlˈkɒfski/

Tskhinvali capital of South Ossetia
tskhin-**vah**-li /tsxɪnˈvɑːli/

Tsotsi young criminal (South African)
tsot-si /ˈtsɒtsi/

tsukemono Japanese pickled vegetable
dish

tsoo-**kem**-oh-noh /tsuːˈkɛməʊnəʊ/
• See JAPANESE panel.

tsunami tidal wave
tsoo-**nah**-mi /tsuːˈnɑːmi/

tsuris problems or difficulties
tsoor-iss /ˈtsʊərɪs/

Tsushima island, Japan
tsoo-shee-muh /ˈtsuːʃiːmə/

Tsvangirai, Morgan Zimbabwean
politician
chang-girr-**y** /tʃaŋɡɪrˈʌɪ/

Tswana African ethnic group
tswah-nuh /ˈtswɑːnə/

Tuamotu Archipelago island group,
Polynesia
too-uh-**moh**-too /ˌtuːəˈməʊtuː/

Tuareg African nomadic ethnic group
twar-eg /ˈtwɑːrɛɡ/

Tuatha Dé Danann Irish mythological
race
too-uh-huh dair **dan**-uhn /ˌtʊəhə
dɛː(r) ˈdanən/
• See GAELIC panel.

tuber cinereum part of the
hypothalamus
tyoo-buhr sin-**eer**-i-uhm /ˌtjuːbə(r)
sɪˈnɪərɪəm/

tuberculosis infectious disease
tyuub-ur-kyuul-**oh**-siss
/tjʊˌbəː(r)kjʊˈləʊsɪs/

tuberose plant
tyoo-buh-rohz /ˈtjuːbərəʊz/

Tübingen city, Germany
tue-bing-uhn /ˈtyːbɪŋən/

Tubruq see Tobruk

Tubuai islands, Polynesia
toob-**wy** /tuːbˈwaɪ/

Tucana constellation
tuuk-**ah**-nuh /tʊˈkɑːnə/

Tucson city, US
too-son /ˈtuːsɒn/

tucuxi small dolphin
tuuk-**oo**-hi /tʊˈkuːhi/

tufa porous rock
tyoo-fuh /ˈtjuːfə/

tugrik currency unit, Mongolia
too-greek /ˈtuːɡriːk/

Tuileries gardens in Paris
twee-luh-ri /ˈtwiːləri/

tuk-tuk three-wheeled vehicle
tuuk-tuuk /ˈtʊktʊk/

Tula city, Russia
too-luh /'tu:lə/

Tulcea city, Romania
tuul-chuh /'tʊltʃə/

Tull, Jethro English agriculturalist
jeth-roh tul /,dʒɛθrəʊ 'tʌl/

Tullamore town, Republic of Ireland
tul-uh-**mor** /,tʌlə'mɔ:(r)/

tulle fine material
tyool /tju:l/

Tulsa port, US
tul-suh /'tʌlsə/

Tulsidas Indian poet
tuul-sid-ahss /'tʊlsɪdɑ:s/

tumescent becoming swollen
tyuum-**ess**-uhnt /tjʊ'mɛsənt/

tumulus pl. **tumuli** ancient burial mound
tyoo-myuu-luhss, pl. **tyoo**-myuu-lee
/'tju:mjʊləs/, pl. /-li:/

tundra Arctic region
tun-druh /'tʌndrə/

tungsten chemical element
tung-stuhn /'tʌŋstən/

Tunguska river, Russia
tuung-**goo**-skuh /tʊŋ'gu:skə/

tunica pl. **tunicae** membranous sheath
enveloping an organ
tyoo-nik-uh, pl. **tyoo**-nik-ee
/'tju:nɪkə/, pl. /-ki:/

Tunis capital of Tunisia
tyoo-niss /'tju:nɪs/

Tunisia country
tyoo-**niz**-i-uh /tju:'nɪzɪə/
• Established anglicization.

Tupelo city, US
too-puh-loh /'tu:pələʊ/

Tupolev, Andrei Russian aeronautical
engineer
and-**ray too**-puh-luhf /an,dreɪ
'tu:pələf/

tupuna Maori ancestor
too-puun-uh /'tu:pʊnə/

tuque knitted cap
took /tu:k/

tur wild goat
toor /tʊə(r)/

turaco bird
toor-uh-koh /'tʊərəkəʊ/

Turandot opera by Puccini
toor-an-dot /'tʊərandɒt/

turbinal part of the nasal cavity

tur-bin-uhl /'tə:(r)bɪnəl/

tureen soup serving dish
tyoor-**een** /tjʊə'ri:n/

Turgenev, Ivan Russian writer
ee-**vahn** toor-**gay**-nyef /i:,vɑ:n
tʊə(r)'geɪnjɛf/

turgid tedious
tur-jid /'tə:(r)dʒɪd/

Turin city, Italy
tyoor-**in** /tjʊə'rɪn/

Established anglicization. The Italian name
is Torino, pronounced torr-**ee**-noh.

Turing, Alan English mathematician
tyoor-ing /'tjʊərɪŋ/

Turkana African ethnic group
tur-**kah**-nuh /tə:(r)'kɑ:nə/

Turkestan (also **Turkistan**) region,
central Asia
turk-ist-**ahn** /,tə:(r)kɪ'stɑ:n/

Turkmenistan republic
turk-**men**-ist-ahn /tə:(r)k,mɛnɪ'stɑ:n/

Turks and Caicos islands, Caribbean
kay-koss /'keɪkɒs/

Turku port, Finland
toor-koo /'tʊə(r)ku:/

This is the Finnish name. The Swedish
name is Åbo, pronounced **aw**-boo.

turmeric spice
tur-muh-rik /'tə:(r)mərɪk/

turpitude depraved or wicked behaviour
turp-it-yood /'tə:(r)pɪtju:d/

turquoise semi-precious stone
tur-kwoyz /'tə:(r)kwɔɪz/

turron Spanish nougat
toor-**on** /tʊə'rɒn/

Tuscaloosa city, US
tusk-uh-**loo**-suh /tʌskə'lu:sə/

Tuscany region, Italy
tusk-uh-ni /'tʌskəni/

Established anglicization. The Italian name
is Toscana, pronounced tosk-**ah**-nuh.

tush person's buttocks
tuush /tʊʃ/

Tussaud, Madame French founder of
waxworks in London
tuh-**sawd** /tə'sɔ:d/, [tyso]
• Established anglicization.

tussive relating to coughing
tuss-iv /'tʌsɪv/

Tutankhamen (also **Tutankhamun**)
Egyptian pharaoh
too-tuhn-**kah**-muhn /ˌtuːtənˈkɑːmən/

Less commonly also too-tuhn-kah-**moon**.

tutelage protection or supervision
tyoo-tuh-lij /ˈtjuːtəlɪdʒ/

Tuthmosis Egyptian pharaoh
tuth-**moh**-siss /tʌθˈməʊsɪs/

Tutsi African ethnic group
tuut-si /ˈtʊtsi/

tutti musical term
tuut-i /ˈtʊti/

Tutu, Desmond South African
clergyman
too-too /ˈtuːtuː/

Tuvalu country, Pacific
too-**vah**-loo /tuːˈvɑːluː/

tuxedo man's dinner jacket
tuk-**see**-doh /tʌkˈsiːdəʊ/

Tuxtla Gutiérrez city, Mexico
toost-luh goot-**yerr**-ess /ˌtuːstlə ˌguːˈtjɛːres/

Tuzla town, Bosnia
tooz-luh /ˈtuːzlə/

Tver port, Russia
tvair /tvɛː(r)/

twopence sum of two pence
tup-uhnss /ˈtʌpəns/

twopenn'orth amount of something
that costs twopence
too-**pen**-uhrth /tuːˈpɛnə(r)θ/

twopenny worth two pence
tup-uh-ni /ˈtʌpəni/

Tybalt Shakespearean character
tib-uhlt /ˈtɪbəlt/

Tyburn place in London
ty-burn /ˈtʌɪbə(r)n/

tychism philosophical doctrine
tyk-iz-uhm /ˈtʌɪkɪzəm/

Tyddewi Welsh name for St David's,
Wales
ti*th*-**ew**-i /tɪˈðewi/

Tylenol trademark paracetamol
ty-luh-nol /ˈtʌɪlənɒl/

Tymoshenko, Yuliya Ukrainian
politician
yoo-li-uh tim-uh-**shenk**-uh /ˌjuːliə

tımə'ʃɛŋkə/

tympanum eardrum
tim-puh-nuhm /ˈtɪmpənəm/

Tynan, Kenneth English writer
ty-nuhn /ˈtʌɪnən/

Tyndale, William English translator
and martyr
tin-duhl /ˈtɪndəl/

Tyndall, John Irish physicist
tin-duhl /ˈtɪndəl/

Tynwald parliament of the Isle of Man
tin-wuhld /ˈtɪnwəld/

Tyr Norse god
teer /tɪə(r)/

tyrannical exercising power in a cruel
way
tirr-**an**-ik-uhl /tɪˈranɪkəl/

Less commonly also ty-**ran**-ik-uhl.

tyrannosaurus dinosaur
tirr-an-uh-**sawr**-uhss /tɪˌranəˈsɔːrəs/

Tyre port, Lebanon
ty-uhr /ˈtʌɪə(r)/

tyro beginner or novice
ty-roh /ˈtʌɪrəʊ/

Tyrol state, Austria
tirr-**ohl** /tɪˈrəʊl/

Spelled Tirol in German; the pronunciation
is more or less the same.

Tyrone county, Northern Ireland
tirr-**ohn** /tɪˈrəʊn/

Tyrrhenian sea
tirr-**ee**-ni-uhn /tɪˈriːnɪən/

Tyumen city, Russia
tyuum-**yen** /tjʊˈmjɛn/

tzar see tsar

Tzara, Tristan Romanian-born French
poet
treest-**ah(ng) zar**-uh /triːstã ˈzɑːrə/

tzatziki Greek yogurt dish
tsat-**see**-ki /tsatˈsiːki/

tzedakah charitable giving
tsed-**ok**-ah /tsɛˈdɒkɑː/

tzigane Hungarian Gypsy
tsig-**ahn** /tsɪˈɡɑːn/

tzimmes see tsimmes

U

U characteristic of upper social classes
oo **yoo** /juː/

U Burmese man's title
oo /uː/

U-Bahn underground train system
oo-**bahn** /ˈuːbɑːn/

Übermensch superman
ue-**buhr-mensh** /ˈyːbə(r)ˌmɛnʃ/

The German prefix *über-* is sometimes
anglicized to **oob**-uhr, here and in other
words.

ubique motto of the Royal Engineers and
the Royal Artillery; 'everywhere' (Latin)
yuu-**by-kway** /jʊˈbaɪkweɪ/

Our research indicates that this heavily
anglicized pronunciation was used by the
majority of RE and RA officers. The classical
Latin pronunciation is **oo**-bik-way.

ubiquitous found everywhere
yoo-**bi**-kwi-tuhss /juːˈbɪkwɪtəs/

UCAS Universities and Colleges
Admissions Service
yoo-kass /ˈjuːkas/

Uccello, Paolo Italian painter
pow-loh oo-**chel**-oh /ˌpaʊləʊ uːˈtʃɛləʊ/

Udall, Nicholas English dramatist
nik-uh-luhss **yoo**-duhl /ˌnɪkələs
ˈjuːdəl/

Udine province, Italy
oo-**din**-ay /ˈuːdɪneɪ/

Udmurtia autonomous republic, Russia
uud-**moor**-ti-uh /ʊdˈmʊə(r)tiə/

udon thick Japanese noodles
oo-don /ˈuːdɒn/

UEFA Union of European Football
Associations
yoo-**ay**-fuh /juːˈeɪfə/

Various pronunciations have been used for
this body since its inception, including
yoo-fuh and yoo-ee-fuh; our
recommendation is the one used by UEFA
and FIFA officials.

Ueno park, Tokyo
oo-**ay**-noh /uːˈeɪnəʊ/

Ufa capital of Bashkiria
oo-**fah** /uːˈfɑː/

UFAW Universities Federation for
Animal Welfare
yoo-faw /ˈjuːfɔː/

Uffizi art gallery, Florence
uu-**feet**-si /ʊˈfiːtsi/
• See ITALIAN panel.

ufology study of UFOs
yoo-**fol**-uh-ji /juːˈfɒlədʒi/

ugali maize porridge
oo-**gah**-li /uːˈɡɑːli/

Uganda country
yoo-**gan**-duh /juːˈɡandə/

Ugli trademark citrus fruit
ug-li /ˈʌɡli/

Ugric language family
yoo-grik /ˈjuːɡrɪk/

Uighur (also **Uigur**) member of a Turkic
people of China
wee-guhr /ˈwiːɡə(r)/

uillean pipes Irish musical instrument
il-uhn /ˈɪlən/

Uist two islands, Scotland
yoo-ist /ˈjuːɪst/

Ujjain city, India
oo-**jyn** /uːˈdʒʌɪn/

Ujung Pandang port, Indonesia
oo-**juung** pan-**dang** /uːˌdʒʊŋ panˈdaŋ/

UKIP UK Independence Party
yoo-kip /ˈjuːkɪp/

ukiyo-e school of Japanese art
oo-kee-yoh-**ay** /uːˌkiːjəʊˈeɪ/

Ukraine country
yoo-**krayn** /juːˈkreɪn/
• Established anglicization.

ukulele musical instrument
yoo-kuh-**lay**-li /ˌjuːkəˈleɪli/

Ulan Bator (also **Ulaanbaatar**) capital
of Mongolia
oo-lahn bah-**tuhr** /ˌuːlɑːn ˈbɑːtə(r)/

Ulanova, Galina Russian ballet dancer
guh-**lee**-nuh oo-**lah**-nuh-vuh /ɡəˈliːnə
uːˈlɑːnəvə/

Ulan-Ude capital of Buryatia
oo-**lahn** oo-**day** /uːˌlɑːn uːˈdeɪ/

ulema (also **ulama**) body of Muslim scholars
uu-lam-ah /ˈʊlamɑː/

Ulfilas Gothic bishop and Bible translator; also called **Wulfila**
uul-fil-ass /ˈʊlfɪlas/

Ulhasnagar city, India
ool-huhss-**nug**-uhr /ˌuːlhəsˈnʌɡə(r)/

ullage amount by which a container falls short of being full
ul-ij /ˈʌlɪdʒ/

Ulm city, Germany
uulm /ʊlm/

ulna pl. **ulnae** bone in the forearm
ul-nuh, pl. **ul**-nee /ˈʌlnə/, pl. /-niː/
• Standard -s plural is also possible.

Ulpian Roman jurist
ulp-i-uhn /ˈʌlpiən/

Ulsan port, Korea
ool-**sahn** /uːlˈsɑːn/

ultimo 'of last month' (Latin)
ul-tim-oh /ˈʌltɪməʊ/

ultramundane existing outside the known world
ult-ruh-**mun**-dayn /ˌʌltrəˈmʌndeɪn/

ultra vires beyond one's authority
ult-ruh **vy**-reez /ˌʌltrə ˈvʌɪriːz/

As is typical with legal Latin, this is an anglicized pronunciation. A more classical-sounding pronunciation, ult-ruh **veer**-ayz, is also used; see LATIN panel.

ululate howl or wail
ul-yuh-layt /ˈʌljəleɪt/

Less commonly also **yoo**-lyoo-layt.

Ulundi town, South Africa
oo-**luun**-di /uːˈlʊndi/

Uluru sacred mountain, Australia
oo-luu-**roo** /uːlʊˈruː/

Ulysses Roman name for Odysseus
yoo-**liss**-eez /juːˈlɪsiːz/

Sometimes also **yoo**-liss-eez.

umami category of taste in food
oo-**mah**-mi /uːˈmɑːmi/

Umayyad Arab dynasty
uum-y-ad /ʊˈmʌɪad/

Umbanda Brazilian folk religion
uum-**band**-uh /ʊmˈbandə/

umbellifer plant of the parsley family

um-**bel**-if-uhr /ʌmˈbɛlɪfə(r)/

umber yellow-brown pigment
um-buhr /ˈʌmbə(r)/

umbo pl. **umbones** central boss of a shield
um-boh, pl. um-**boh**-neez /ˈʌmbəʊ/, pl. /ʌmˈbəʊniːz/
• Standard -s plural is also possible.

umbra pl. **umbrae** inner region
um-bruh, pl. **um**-bree /ˈʌmbrə/, pl. /-briː/
• Standard -s plural is also possible.

umbrage offence
um-brij /ˈʌmbrɪdʒ/

Umbria region, Italy
um-bri-uh /ˈʌmbriə/
• Established anglicization.

Umbriel moon of Uranus
um-bri-uhl /ˈʌmbriəl/

Umeå city, Sweden
oo-muh-aw /ˈuːmə.ɔː/

umiak Eskimo boat
oo-mi-ak /ˈuːmiak/

umlaut diacritic mark (¨)
uum-lowt /ˈʊmlaʊt/

umma (also **ummah**) community of Muslims
uum-uh /ˈʊmə/

Umm al Qaiwain state, United Arab Emirates
uum uhl ky-wyn /ˌʊm al kʌɪˈwʌɪn/

Umm Qasr port, Iraq
uum kass-uhr /ʊm ˈkasər/

umrah lesser pilgrimage to Mecca
uum-rah /ˈʊmrɑː/

Umwelt world
uum-velt /ˈʊmvɛlt/

una corda musical term
oo-nuh kor-duh /ˌuːnə ˈkɔː(r)də/

unanimous in agreement
yoo-**nan**-im-uhss /juːˈnanɪməs/

uncial script
un-si-uhl /ˈʌnsiəl/

UNCTAD United Nations Conference on Trade and Development
unk-tad /ˈʌŋktad/

unction religious rite
unk-shuhn /ˈʌŋkʃən/

unctuous ingratiating
unk-tyoo-uhss /ˈʌŋktjuəs/

undine water nymph
un-deen /ˈʌndiːn/

undulate move with a wave-like motion
un-dyuh-**layt** /ˈʌndjəleɪt/

UNESCO United Nations agency
yoo-**nesk**-oh /juːˈnɛskəʊ/

ungainsayable undeniable
un-gayn-**say**-uh-buhl
/ˌʌngeɪnˈseɪəbəl/

ungual relating to a nail, hoof, or claw
ung-gwuhl /ˈʌŋgwəl/

unguent ointment
ung-gwuhnt /ˈʌŋgwənt/

ungulate hoofed mammal
ung-gyuul-uht /ˈʌŋgjʊlət/

unheimlich uncanny
uun-**hym**-likh /ʊnˈhʌɪmlɪç/

unicameral having a single legislative chamber
yoo-ni-**kam**-uh-ruhl /ˌjuːnɪˈkamərəl/

UNICEF United Nations agency
yoo-niss-ef /ˈjuːnɪsɛf/

UNIDO United Nations International Development Organization
yoo-**nee**-doh /juːˈniːdəʊ/

unify make whole
yoo-ni-fy /ˈjuːnɪfʌɪ/

uniparous producing a single offspring
yoo-**nip**-uh-ruhss /juːˈnɪpərəs/

uniped having only one foot or leg
yoo-nip-ed /ˈjuːnɪpɛd/

UNITA Angolan nationalist movement
yoo-**nee**-tuh /juːˈniːtə/

UNITAR United Nations Institute for Training and Research
yoo-**nee**-tar /juːˈniːtɑː(r)/

unitard one-piece garment
yoo-nit-ard /ˈjuːnɪtɑː(r)d/

Unix trademark computer operating system
yoo-niks /ˈjuːnɪks/

unkempt dishevelled
un-**kempt** /ʌnˈkɛmpt/

Untermensch pl. **Untermenschen** person considered inferior
uun-tuhr-**mensh**,
pl. **uun**-tuhr-mensh-uhn
/ˈʊntə(r)mɛnʃ/, pl. /-mɛnʃən/

unwonted unaccustomed
un-**wohn**-tuhd /ʌnˈwəʊntəd/

Upanishad Hindu sacred treatise
oo-**pan**-ish-ad /uːˈpanɪʃad/

Updike, John American writer

up-dyk /ˈʌpdʌɪk/

Up-Helly-Aa annual festival held in the Shetland Islands
uup hel-i **ah** /ˌʊp hɛli ˈɑː/

upholster cover furniture
up-**hohl**-stuhr /ʌpˈhəʊlstə(r)/

Uppsala city, Sweden
uup-sah-luh /ˈʊpsɑːlə/

upsilon letter of the Greek alphabet
yoop-**sy**-luhn /juːpˈsʌɪlən/

Commonly also **up**-sil-on.

Uqsur, el- see Luxor

Ur ancient Sumerian city
ur /əː(r)/

Uralic family of languages
yuu-**ral**-ik /jʊˈralɪk/

Urals mountain range, Russia
yoor-uhlz /ˈjʊərəlz/

Urania Greek mythological character
yuh-**ray**-ni-uh /jəˈreɪnɪə/

uranium chemical element
yuh-**ray**-ni-uhm /jəˈreɪnɪəm/

Uranus planet
yoor-uh-nuhss /ˈjʊərənəs/

Commonly also yuh-**ray**-nuhss. Our recommendation is based on the preferred usage of astronomers.

urbane refined in manner
ur-**bayn** /əː(r)ˈbeɪn/

Urdu language
oor-doo /ˈʊə(r)duː/

Commonly also **ur**-doo.

urea chemical compound in urine
yuh-**ree**-uh /jəˈriːə/

ureter duct from the kidney
yuh-**ree**-tuhr /jəˈriːtə(r)/

urethra duct from the bladder
yuh-**reeth**-ruh /jəˈriːθrə/

Urey, Harold American chemist
yoor-i /ˈjʊəri/

Uriah biblical character
yuh-**ry**-uh /jəˈrʌɪə/

urinal receptacle for urine
yuh-**ry**-nuhl /jəˈrʌɪnəl/

urine waste fluid
yoor-in /ˈjʊərɪn/

urology branch of medicine concerned with the urinary system
yuh-**rol**-uh-ji /jəˈrɒlədʒi/

uropygium rump of a bird
yoor-oh-**pij**-i-uhm /ˌjʊərəʊˈpɪdʒɪəm/

Ursa Major constellation
ur-suh **may**-juhr /ˌəː(r)sə ˈmeɪdʒə(r)/
Ursa Minor constellation
ur-suh **my**-nuhr /ˌəː(r)sə ˈmaɪnə(r)/
Ursula saint and martyr
ur-syuul-uh /ˈəː(r)sjʊlə/
Ursuline order of nuns
ur-syuul-yn /ˈəː(r)sjʊlʌɪn/
urtext pl. **urtexte** earliest version of a text
oor-tekst, pl. **oor**-teks-tuh
/ˈʊə(r)tɛkst/, pl. /-tɛkstə/
• Standard -s plural is also possible.
urticaria skin rash
ur-tik-**air**-i-uh /ˌəː(r)tɪˈkɛːriə/
Uruguay country
yoor-uh-gwy /ˈjʊərəgwʌɪ/, Spanish
[uruˈɣwaj]
• Established anglicization.
Uruk ancient city, Mesopotamia
uu-ruuk /ˈʊrʊk/
Uruk-Hai fictional creatures in *The Lord
of the Rings*
oo-ruuk hy /ˌuːrʊk ˈhʌɪ/
Urumqi (also **Urumchi**) city, China
uu-**ruum**-chee /ˌʊrʊmˈtʃi/
Usdaw Union of Shop, Distributive and
Allied Workers
uz-daw /ˈʌzdɔː/
Ushuaia port, Argentina
oo-**swy**-uh /uːˈswʌɪə/
Uspallata pass, South America
oo-**spuhl**-**yat**-uh /ˌuːspəlˈjatə/,
[uspaˈʎata]
Ustinov, Peter British actor of Russian
descent
yoo-stin-of /ˈjuːstɪnɒf/
usurer moneylender
yoo-zhuh-ruhr /ˈjuːʒərə(r)/
usurp take a position of power
yoo-**zurp** /juːˈzəː(r)p/
usury lending money
yoo-zhuh-ri /ˈjuːʒəri/
Utah state, US
yoo-tah /ˈjuːtɑː/

AM is **yoo**-taw.

Utamaro, Kitagawa Japanese artist
kee-tag-ah-wuh uu-tam-**ah**-roh
/kiːˈtaɡaːwə ˌʊtəˈmaːrəʊ/
• See **JAPANESE** panel.

Ute American Indian ethnic group
yoot /juːt/
uterine relating to the womb
yoo-tuh-ryn /ˈjuːtərʌɪn/
Uther Pendragon legendary figure;
father of Arthur
oo-thuhr pen-**drag**-uhn /ˌuːθə(r)
pɛnˈdragən/
Utica town, US
yoo-tik-uh /ˈjuːtɪkə/
Utopia imagined perfect place
yoo-**toh**-pi-uh /juːˈtəʊpiə/
Utrecht city, Netherlands
yoo-trekht /ˈjuːtrɛxt/, [ˈytrɛxt]
• Established anglicization.
Utrillo, Maurice French painter
morr-iss yoo-**tril**-oh /ˈmɒrɪs juːˈtrɪləʊ/,
[moris ytrijo]
• Established anglicization.
Utsire island, Norway; also shipping
areas
uut-seer-uh /ʊtˈsɪərə/
Uttaranchal state, India
uut-uh-**run**-chuhl /ˌʊtəˈrʌntʃəl/
Uttar Pradesh state, India
uut-uhr pruh-**daysh** /ˌʊtə(r) prəˈdeɪʃ/
Uttoxeter town, England
yoo-**tok**-suh-tuhr /juːˈtɒksətə(r)/

There are other local pronunciations of this
place name, including ut-**ok**-suh-tuhr and
uk-sit-uhr.

Utzon, Jörn Danish architect
yoern uut-son /ˌjœ(r)n ˈʊtsɒn/
uvea part of the eye
yoo-vi-uh /ˈjuːviə/
uvula pl. **uvulae** fleshy extension at the
back of the soft palate
yoo-vyuul-uh, pl. **yoo**-vyuul-ee
/ˈjuːvjʊlə/, pl. /-liː/
• Standard -s plural is also possible.
uxorious fond of one's wife
uk-**saw**-ri-uhss /ʌkˈsɔːriəs/
Uzbek member of a Turkic people living
mainly in Uzbekistan
uuz-bek /ˈʊzbɛk/
Uzbekistan independent republic
uuz-bek-ist-**ahn** /ʊzˌbɛkɪˈstɑːn/
Uzi sub-machine gun
oo-zi /ˈuːzi/

V

Vaal river, South Africa
vahl /vɑːl/

Vaasa port, Finland
vah-suh /'vɑːsə/

vaccine inoculation
vak-seen /'vaksiːn/

Vacherin soft cheese
vash-uh-ra(ng) /'vaʃərɛ̃/

vacillate waver
vass-il-ayt /'vasɪleɪt/

vacuum space devoid of matter
vak-yoom /'vakjuːm/

Less commonly also **vak-yuu-uhm**, a more
careful pronunciation.

vade mecum handbook
vah-di may-kuhm /,vɑːdi 'meɪkəm/
• See LATIN panel.

Vadodara city, India
vuh-doh-duh-ruh /və'dəʊdərə/

Vaduz capital of Liechtenstein
fad-uuts /fa'dʊts/

vagary unexpected change
vay-guh-ri /'veɪgəri/

vaginoplasty surgery to create a vagina
vuh-jy-noh-plast-i /və'dʒʌɪnəʊplasti/

vagrant person without a settled home
vay-gruhnt /'veɪgrənt/

vagus pl. **vagi** cranial nerve
vay-guhss, pl. **vay-jy** /'veɪgəs/, pl.
/-dʒʌɪ/

Väinämöinen central character in the
Kalevala
vay-nuh-moey-nuhn /'veɪnəmœɪnən/,
Finnish ['væinæmøjnɛn]

Vaishnava member of a branch of
modern Hinduism
vysh-nuv-uh /'vʌɪʃnʌvə/

Vajpayee, Atal Bihari Indian
statesman
ut-uhl bi-hah-ri **vahj-pay** /,ʌtəl bɪ,hɑːri
'vɑːdʒpeɪ/

The pronunciation **vahj-py** is sometimes
heard. However, our recommendation is
based on the advice of several Hindi
speakers and the High Commission of India.

vajra thunderbolt or mythical weapon
vuj-ruh /'vʌdʒrə/

vakil lawyer
vuh-**keel** /və'kiːl/

Val d'Isère resort, France
val dee-zair /,val diː'zɛː(r)/

vale valley
vayl /veɪl/

vale farewell
vah-lay /'vɑːleɪ/

valedictory serving as a farewell
val-uh-**dik**-tuh-ri /,valə'dɪktəri/

Valencia city, Spain
vuh-**len**-si-uh /və'lɛnsiə/, [βa'lenθja]
• Established anglicization.

Valenciennes bobbin lace
val-ah(ng)-**syen** /,valã'sjɛn/

valency combining power of an element
vay-luhn-si /'veɪlənsi/

Valentia island and coastal station,
Republic of Ireland
vuh-**len**-shi-uh /və'lɛnʃiə/

Valentino, Rudolph Italian-born
American actor
val-uhn-**tee**-noh /,valən'tiːnəʊ/

Valerian Roman emperor
vuh-**leer**-i-uhn /və'lɪəriən/

Commonly also vuh-**lair**-i-uhn; see LATIN
panel.

valerian plant
vuh-**leer**-i-uhn /və'lɪəriən/

As with many botanical names, more than
one pronunciation is possible. Commonly
also vuh-**lair**-i-uhn.

Valéry, Paul French poet
pol val-air-**ee** /,pɒl ,valɛ'riː/

valet man's personal male attendant
val-uht /'valət/

This is the traditional BR pronunciation;
val-ay is also used.

valeta see **veleta**

valetudinarian hypochondriac
val-uh-tyoo-din-**air**-i-uhn
/,valətjuː'dɪ'nɛːriən/

valgus limb deformity
val-guhss /'valgəs/

Valhalla Norse mythological palace
val-**hal**-uh /val'halə/

valise small suitcase
vuh-**leez** /vəˈliːz/

Valium trademark tranquillizing drug
val-i-uhm /'valiəm/

Valkyrie Norse mythological characters
val-kuh-ri /'valkəri/

Less commonly also val-**keer**-i. See also DIE
WALKÜRE.

Valladolid city, Spain
val-uh-doh-**leed** /ˌvalədəʊˈliːd/,
[βaʎaðoˈlið]

Established anglicization. Sometimes also
val-yuh-dol-**eeth**, a less anglicized
pronunciation.

vallecula pl. **valleculae** furrow
val-**ek**-yuu-luh, pl. val-**ek**-yuu-lee
/vaˈlɛkjʊlə/, pl. /-liː/
• Standard -es plural is also possible.

Valle d'Aosta region, Italy
val-ay dah-**ost**-uh /ˌvaleɪ dɑːˈɒstə/

Valletta capital, Malta
vuh-**let**-uh /vəˈlɛtə/

vallum defensive wall
val-uhm /'valəm/

Valois medieval duchy, France
val-**wah** /val'wɑː/

valonia tree
val-**oh**-ni-uh /vaˈləʊniə/

Valparaiso port, Chile
val-puh-**ry**-zoh /ˌvalpəˈraɪzəʊ/, Spanish
[βalparaˈiso]
• Established anglicization.

Valpolicella red wine
val-pol-i-**chel**-uh /ˌvalpɒliˈtʃɛlə/

valse waltz
valss /vals/

valuta exchange value of currency
vuh-**lyoo**-tuh /vəˈljuːtə/

vambrace armour
vam-brayss /'vambreɪs/

vamoose depart hurriedly
vuh-**mooss** /vəˈmuːs/

vanadium chemical element
vuh-**nay**-di-uhm /vəˈneɪdiəm/

vanaspati thick vegetable oil
vuh-**nuss**-puh-tee /vəˈnʌspəˌtiː/

Vanbrugh, John English architect and
dramatist
van-bruh /'vanbrə/

Van Buren, Martin former American
president
van **byoor**-uhn /van ˈbjʊərən/

Van Cleef & Arpels American jewellers
van **kleef** ar-**pelz** /van ˈkliːf ɑː(r)ˈpɛlz/

vancomycin bacterial antibiotic
vank-uh-**my**-sin /ˌvaŋkəˈmʌɪsɪn/

Vancouver city, Canada
van-**koo**-vuhr /vanˈkuːvə(r)/

van de Graaff generator machine
which generates static charge
van duh **grahf** /ˌvan də ˈɡrɑːf/

Vanderbijlpark city, South Africa
fund-uhr-bayl-**park**
/ˈfʌndə(r)beɪlˌpɑː(r)k/

Vanderbilt, Cornelius American
philanthropist
kor-**nee**-li-uhss **van**-duhr-bilt
/kɔː(r)ˌniːliəs ˈvandə(r)bɪlt/

Van der Post, Laurens South African
explorer and writer
lorr-uhnss **van** duhr **post** /ˈlɒrəns ˌvan
də(r) ˈpɒst/

van de Velde family of Dutch painters
vun duh **vel**-duh /ˌvʌn də ˈvɛldə/

Van Diemen's Land former name for
Tasmania
van **deem**-uhnz /van ˈdiːmənz/

Van Dyck, Anthony (also **Vandyke**)
Flemish painter
van **dyk** /van ˈdʌɪk/ [van ˈdɛik]
• Established anglicization.

Vänern lake, Sweden
vay-nuhrn /'veɪnə(r)n/, [ˈvɛːŋɛn]

vanessid butterfly
vuh-**ness**-id /vəˈnɛsɪd/

Van Eyck, Jan Flemish painter
yun vun **yk** /ˌjʌn vʌn ˈʌɪk/

Vangelis Greek composer
van-**gel**-iss /vanˈɡɛlɪs/

Van Gogh, Vincent Dutch painter
van **gokh** /van ˈɡɒx/, [vɪnˌsɛnt van
ˈɣɒx]

Established anglicization. Another
anglicization, van **goh**, is used especially in
AM.

Vanir Norse gods
vah-neer /'vɑːnɪə(r)/

vanitas painting containing symbols of death
van-it-ahss /ˈvanɪtɑːs/

vanquish defeat thoroughly
vank-wish /ˈvaŋkwɪʃ/

Vantaa city, Finland
van-tah /ˈvantɑː/

Vanuatu country
van-oo-uh-**too** /vanuəˈtuː/

Commonly also van-**wah**-too, an anglicized form.

vaporetto pl. **vaporetti** canal boat
vap-uh-**ret**-oh, pl. vap-uh-**ret**-i /ˌvapəˈrɛtəʊ/, pl. /-ti/

vaquero cowboy
vuh-**kair**-oh /vəˈkɛːrəʊ/

Varah, Chad English founder of the Samaritans
chad var-uh /ˌtʃad ˈvɑːrə/

Varanasi city, India
vuh-**rah**-nuh-si /vəˈrɑːnəsi/

vardo Gypsy caravan
var-doh /ˈvɑː(r)dəʊ/

varec seaweed
varr-ek /ˈvarɛk/

Varese town, Italy
vuh-**ray**-say /vəˈreɪseɪ/

Varèse, Edgard French-American composer
ed-**gar** varr-ez /ˌɛdˌɡɑː(r) vaˈrɛz/

Vargas Llosa, Mario Peruvian writer
mah-ri-oh var-gass **lyoh**-suh /ˌmɑːriəʊ ˌvɑː(r)gas ˈljəʊsə/

varicella chickenpox
varr-i-**sel**-luh /ˌvariˈsɛlə/

varicose swollen or twisted (veins)
varr-i-kohss /ˈvarɪkəʊs/

variegated exhibiting different colours
vair-i-uh-gay-tid /ˈvɛːriəgeɪtɪd/

varietal made from a single specified variety of grape
vuh-**ry**-uh-tuhl /vəˈrʌɪətəl/

varifocal lens that allows different focusing distances
vair-i-**fohk**-uhl /ˌvɛːriˈfəʊkəl/

variola smallpox
vuh-**ry**-uh-luh /vəˈrʌɪələ/

varix pl. **varices** varicose vein
vair-iks, pl. **varr**-iss-eez /ˈvɛːrɪks/, pl. /ˈvarɪsiːz/

varlet boy servant

var-luht /ˈvɑː(r)lət/

varmint wild animal
var-mint /ˈvɑː(r)mɪnt/

Varna port, Bulgaria
var-nuh /ˈvɑː(r)nə/

varna each of the four Hindu castes
var-nuh /ˈvɑː(r)nə/

Varro, Marcus Terentius Roman satirist
mark-uhss tuh-**rensh**-uhss **varr**-oh /ˌmɑː(r)kəs təˌrɛnʃəs ˈvarəʊ/
• See LATIN panel.

varroa microscopic mite
varr-oh-uh /ˈvarəʊə/

Varuna Hindu god
vurr-uun-uh /ˈvʌrʊnə/

varus limb deformity
vair-uhss /ˈvɛːrəs/

vas pl. **vasa** vessel or duct
vass, pl. **vay**-suh /vas/, pl. /ˈveɪsə/

Vasari, Giorgio Italian painter
jor-joh vuh-**sah**-ri /ˌdʒɔ(r)dʒəʊ vəˈsɑːri/

vas deferens sperm duct
vass **def**-uh-renz /ˌvas ˈdɛfərɛnz/

vasectomy sterilization
vuh-**sek**-tuh-mi /vəˈsɛktəmi/

vaseline trademark petroleum jelly
vass-uh-leen /ˈvasəliːn/

vasopressin hormone
vay-zoh-**press**-in /ˌveɪzəʊˈprɛsɪn/

vassal tenant landholder
vass-uhl /ˈvasəl/

vastation purification
vast-**ay**-shuhn /vaˈsteɪʃən/

Västerås port, Sweden
vest-uhr-**awss** /ˌvɛstəˈrɔːs/

vaticinate foretell the future
vat-**iss**-in-ayt /vaˈtɪsɪneɪt/

Vättern lake, Sweden
vet-uhrn /ˈvɛtə(r)n/

vatu currency unit, Vanuatu
vat-oo /ˈvatuː/

Vaud canton, Switzerland
voh /vəʊ/

vaudeville entertainment
vaw-duh-vil /ˈvɔːdəvɪl/

Vaudois relating to Vaud
voh-**dwah** /vəʊˈdwɑː/

Vaughan, Sarah American jazz singer
vawn /vɔːn/

Vaughan Williams, Ralph English composer
rayf vawn /'reɪf ˌvɔːn/

vault leap
vawlt /vɔːlt/

Commonly also volt.

Vauxhall district of London
voks-awl /'vɒksɔːl/

vavasour vassal
vav-uh-soor /'vavəsʊə(r)/

Vavilov, Nikolai Soviet plant geneticist
nik-uh-ly vuh-vee-luhf /nɪkəˌlʌɪ vəˈviːləf/

Veblen, Thorstein American economist
thor-styn veb-luhn /ˌθɔː(r)stʌɪn 'vɛblən/

Veda Indian scripture
vay-duh /'veɪdə/

vedalia beetle ladybird
vuh-day-li-uh /vəˈdeɪliə/

Vedanta Hindu philosophy
ved-ahn-tuh /vɛˈdɑːntə/

vedette mounted sentry
ved-et /vɛˈdɛt/

Vedic relating to the Vedas
vay-dik /'veɪdɪk/

Vega, Lope de Spanish dramatist
loh-pay day vay-guh /ˌləʊpeɪ deɪ 'veɪɡə/

Vega star
vee-guh /'viːɡə/

vega grassy plain
vay-guh /'veɪɡə/

vegan person who avoids eating animal products
vee-guhn /'viːɡən/

Vegemite trademark savoury spread
vej-uh-myt /'vɛdʒəmʌɪt/

vegetal relating to plants
vej-uh-tuhl /'vɛdʒətəl/

vehement showing strong feeling
vee-uh-muhnt /'viːəmənt/

veitchberry hybrid plant
veetch-buh-ri /'viːtʃbəri/

Vela constellation
vee-luh /'viːlə/

velar relating to a veil or velum
vee-luhr /'viːlə(r)/

Velázquez, Diego Rodriguez de Silva y Spanish painter
dyay-goh rod-ree-gess day seel-vuh ee vel-ass-kwuhss /ˌdjeɪɡəʊ rɒdˌriːɡes deɪ ˌsiːlvə i: veˈlaskwəs/, [βeˈlaskeθ]
• Established anglicization.

Velázquez de Cuéllar, Diego Spanish conquistador
dyay-goh vel-ath-kweth day kwel-yar /ˌdjeɪɡəʊ vɛˈlaθkwɛθ deɪ ˈkweɪljɑː(r)/

veld (also **veldt**) open grassland
velt /vɛlt/

veleta (also **valeta**) ballroom dance
vuh-lee-tuh /vəˈliːtə/

velleity inclination
vel-ee-it-i /vɛˈliːɪti/

Velleius Paterculus Roman historian and soldier
vel-ay-uhss puh-tair-kyuul-uhss /vɛˌleɪəs pəˈtɛː(r)kjʊləs/

vellum parchment
vel-uhm /'vɛləm/

velocimeter instrument for measuring velocity
vel-uh-sim-uh-tuhr /ˌvɛləˈsɪmətə(r)/

velociraptor small dinosaur
vuh-loss-i-rap-tuhr /vəˌlɒsɪˈraptə(r)/

velocity speed
vuh-loss-it-i /vəˈlɒsɪti/

velodrome cycle-racing track
vel-uh-drohm /'vɛlədrəʊm/

velour plush woven fabric
vuh-loor /vəˈlʊə(r)/

velouté white sauce
vuh-loo-tay /vəˈluːteɪ/

velum pl. **vela** membrane
vee-luhm, pl. vee-luh /'viːləm/, pl. /-lə/

Velux trademark roof window
vee-luks /'viːlʌks/

vena cava pl. **venae cavae** cardiac vein
vee-nuh kay-vuh, pl. vee-nee kay-vee /ˌviːnə 'keɪvə/, pl. /ˌviːniː 'keɪviː/

venal susceptibile to bribery
vee-nuhl /'viːnəl/

vendace fish
ven-diss /'vɛndɪs/

vendange grape harvest
vah(ng)-dah(ng)zh /vãˈdãʒ/

Vendée river, France
vah(ng)-day /vãˈdeɪ/

vendetta blood feud
ven-det-uh /vɛnˈdɛtə/

vendeuse saleswoman
vah(ng)-doez /vãˈdøz/

vendue public auction
ven-**dyoo** /ˈvɛnˈdjuː/

venereal relating to sex
vuh-**neer**-i-uhl /vəˈnɪəriəl/

venery sexual indulgence
ven-uh-ri /ˈvɛnəri/

Venetia region, Italy
ven-**ee**-shuh /vɛˈniːʃə/

Established anglicization. The Italian name is Veneto, pronounced **vay**-net-oh.

Venezuela country
ven-uh-**zway**-luh /ˌvɛnəˈzweɪlə/,
Spanish [βeneˈswela]
• Established anglicization.

venial relating to a lesser sin
vee-ni-uhl /ˈviːniəl/

Venice city, Italy
ven-iss /ˈvɛnɪs/

venison meat from a deer
ven-iss-uhn /ˈvɛnɪsən/

Venite canticle
vuh-**ny**-ti /vəˈnʌɪti/

This is a particularly anglicized pronunciation used with reference to Psalm 93 when sung at matins services. Other pronunciations such as ven-**ee**-tay are also used; see LATIN panel.

veni, vidi, vici 'I came, I saw, I conquered' (Latin)
way-ni **wee**-di **wee**-ki /ˌweɪni ˌwiːdi ˈwiːki/

This is the classical Latin pronunciation for this well-known quotation of Julius Caesar. More anglicized pronunciations such as **vay**-ni **vee**-di **vee**-chi are often used; see LATIN panel.

venomous secreting venom
ven-uh-muhss /ˈvɛnəməs/

venous relating to veins
vee-nuhss /ˈviːnəs/

Ventnor town, Isle of Wight
vent-nuhr /ˈvɛntnə(r)/

Ventolin trademark drug used to treat asthma
ven-tuh-lin /ˈvɛntəlɪn/

ventouse cup-shaped suction device
ven-tooss /ˈvɛntuːs/

Venturi, Robert American architect
ven-**tyoor**-i /vɛnˈtjʊəri/

Venus de Milo classical sculpture
vee-nuhss duh **my**-loh /ˌviːnəs də ˈmʌɪləʊ/

Also commonly **mee**-loh.

veracity truth
vuh-**rass**-it-i /vəˈrasɪti/

Veracruz state, Mexico
vair-uh-**krooss** /ˌvɛrəˈkruːs/

verbatim in exactly the same words
vur-**bay**-tim /vəˈ(r)ˈbeɪtɪm/

verbena herbaceous plant
vur-**bee**-nuh /vəˈ(r)ˈbiːnə/

verbiage speech
vur-bi-uhj /ˈvəˈ(r)bɪədʒ/

verboten forbidden
fuhr-**boh**-tuhn /fəˈ(r)ˈbəʊtən/

Vercingetorix chieftain of Gaul
vur-sin-**jet**-uh-riks /ˌvəˈ(r)sɪnˈdʒɛtərɪks/

Established anglicization. Sometimes also vair-**sa**(ng)-**zhet**-uh-reeks, a more French-sounding pronunciation.

verdant green with grass
vur-duhnt /ˈvəˈ(r)dənt/

Verdelho white grape
vuhr-**del**-yoo /vəˈ(r)ˈdɛljuː/

Verdi, Giuseppe Italian composer
juuz-**ep**-ay **vair**-di /dʒʊˌzɛpeɪ ˈvɛːˈ(r)di/

Verdicchio white wine grape
vair-**deek**-yoh /vɛːˈ(r)ˈdiːkjəʊ/

verdigris copper patina
vur-dig-ree /ˈvəˈ(r)dɪgriː/

Verdun First World War battle site, France
vur-**dun** /vəˈ(r)ˈdʌn/, [vɛrdœ̃]
• Established anglicization.

verdure vegetation
vur-dyuhr /ˈvəˈ(r)djə(r)/

Vereeniging city, South Africa
fuh-**ree**-nikh-ing /fəˈriːnɪxɪŋ/

Vergil see Virgil

veridical truthful
vuh-**rid**-ik-uhl /vəˈrɪdɪkəl/

verisimilitude appearance of being real
verr-i-sim-**il**-it-yood /ˌvɛrɪsɪˈmɪlɪtjuːd/

verismo realism
verr-**iz**-moh /vɛˈrɪzməʊ/

vérité naturalistic genre
verr-it-ay /ˈvɛrɪteɪ/

verjuice sour fruit juice
vur-jooss /ˈvəˈ(r)dʒuːs/

verlag publishing house (German)
fair-**lahk** /fɛː(r)'lɑːk/

Verlaine, Paul French poet
pol vair-**lenn** /ˌpɒl vɛː(r)'lɛn/

Vermeer, Jan Dutch painter
yun vur-**meer** /ˌjʌn və:(r)'mɪə(r)/
• Established anglicization.

vermeil gilded silver or bronze
vur-mayl /'və:(r)meɪl/

vermicelli pasta threads
vair-mi-**chel**-i /ˌvɛː(r)mi'tʃɛli/

vermilion red pigment
vuhr-**mil**-yuhn /və(r)'mɪljən/

vermis part of the brain
vur-miss /'və:(r)mɪs/

Vermont state, US
vur-**mont** /və(r)'mɒnt/

vermouth flavoured wine
vuhr-**mooth** /və(r)'muːθ/

Less commonly also **vur**-muhth.

Vernaccia wine grape
vuhr-**natch**-uh /və(r)'natʃə/

vernacular language variety
vur-**nak**-yuul-uhr /və(r)'nakjʊlə(r)/

Verne, Jules French novelist
joolz vurn /ˌdʒuːlz 'vɛː(r)n/, [ʒyl vɛrn]
• Established anglicization.

Verner's Law linguistic principle
vair-nuhrz /'vɛː(r)nə(r)z/

vernissage private view of paintings
vair-niss-**ahzh** /ˌvɛː(r)nɪ'sɑːʒ/

vernix deposit covering baby's skin at
birth
vur-niks /'və:(r)nɪks/

Vero board trademark used to make
electronic circuits
verr-oh /'vɛrəʊ/

Verona city, Italy
vuh-**roh**-nuh /və'rəʊnə/

veronal barbiturate drug
verr-uh-nuhl /'vɛrənəl/

Veronese, Paolo Italian painter
pow-loh verr-uh-**nay**-zay /ˌpaʊləʊ ˌvɛrə'neɪzeɪ/

veronique dish garnished with grapes
verr-uh-**neek** /ˌvɛrə'niːk/

Verrazano-Narrows Bridge bridge
between Brooklyn and Staten Island, US
verr-uh-**zah**-noh /ˌvɛrə'zɑːnəʊ/

verre églomisé glass decorated on the
back

vair ay-gloh-mee-**zay** /ˌvɛː(r) ˌeɪɡlɒmiː'zeɪ/

verruca wart on the foot
vuh-**roo**-kuh /və'ruːkə/

Versace, Gianni Italian fashion
designer
jah-ni vair-**sah**-chay /ˌdʒɑːni vɛː(r)'sɑːtʃeɪ/

The pronunciation of his fashion label is
commonly also anglicized to vur-**satch**-i.

Versailles palace, France
vair-**sy** /vɛː(r)'sʌɪ/

vers libre free verse
vair **leeb**-ruh /vɛː(r) 'liːbrə/

Verstehen empathic understanding
fair-**shtay**-uhn /fɛː(r)'ʃteɪən/

vertebra pl. **vertebrae** small bones
forming the backbone
vur-tuh-bruh, pl. **vur**-tuh-bree
/'və:(r)təbrə/, pl. /-briː/

vertebrate animal with a backbone
vur-tuh-bruht /'və:(r)təbrət/

vertex pl. **vertices** highest point
vur-teks, pl. **vur**-tiss-eez /'və:(r)tɛks/,
pl. /-tɪsiːz/
• Standard -es plural is also possible.

verticillium fungus
vur-**tiss**-il-i-uhm /ˌvə:(r)tɪ'sɪliəm/

vertiginous extremely high or steep
vur-**tij**-in-uhss /və:(r)'tɪdʒɪnəs/

vertigo loss of balance
vur-tig-oh /'və:(r)tɪɡəʊ/

Verulamium Roman name for St Albans
verr-uh-**lay**-mi-uhm /ˌvɛrə'leɪmiəm/

Verviers town, Belgium
vairv-**yay** /vɛː(r)'vjeɪ/

Verwoerd, Hendrik South African
statesman
hend-rik fuhr-**voort** /ˌhɛndrɪk fə(r)'vʊə(r)t/

Very light flare fired into the air
verr-i /'vɛri/

Vesak Buddhist festival; also called
Wesak
vess-ak /'vɛsak/

Vesalius, Andreas Flemish anatomist
and-**ray**-uhss vuh-**say**-li-uhss
/andˌreɪəs və'seɪliəs/

vesical relating to the bladder
vess-ik-uhl /'vɛsɪkəl/

vesicle sac or cyst
vess-ik-uhl /'vɛsɪkəl/

Vespasian Roman emperor
vess-**pay**-zhuhn /vɛˈspeɪʒən/

vespertine relating to the evening
vesp-uhr-tyn /ˈvɛspə(r)tʌɪn/

Vespucci, Amerigo Italian explorer
am-uh-**ree**-goh vesp-**oo**-chi
/əməˈriːɡəʊ vɛˈspuːtʃi/

Vesterålen islands, Norway
vest-uhr-aw-luhn /ˈvɛstəˌrɔːlən/

vestibule antechamber
vest-ib-yool /ˈvɛstɪbjuːl/

vestige trace
vest-ij /ˈvɛstɪdʒ/

vestigial forming a remnant
vest-**ij**-uhl /vɛˈstɪdʒəl/

Vesuvius volcano, Italy
vuh-**soo**-vi-uhss /vəˈsuːvɪəs/

veterinary relating to the treatment of
animals
vet-uh-rin-uh-ri /ˈvɛtərɪnəri/

Commonly also **vet**-nuh-ri or **vet**-in-ri,
reduced pronunciations.

Veuve Cliquot brand of champagne
voev klee-**koh** /ˌvœːv kliːˈkəʊ/

vexillology study of flags
vek-sil-**ol**-uh-ji /ˌvɛksɪˈlɒlədʒi/

via by way of
vy-uh /ˈvʌɪə/

Commonly also **vee**-uh, especially in
phrases.

viable capable of working successfully
vy-uh-buhl /ˈvʌɪəbəl/

Via Crucis way of the Cross
vee-uh **kroo**-chiss /ˌviːə ˈkruːtʃɪs/

via dolorosa route believed to have been
taken by Christ to Calvary
vee-uh dol-uh-**roh**-zuh /ˌviːə
ˌdɒləˈrəʊzə/

Viagra trademark drug used to enhance
male potency
vy-**ag**-ruh /vʌɪˈaɡrə/

vial small container
vy-uhl /ˈvʌɪəl/

viand item of food
vy-uhnd /ˈvʌɪənd/

viaticum part of the last rites
vy-**at**-ik-uhm /vʌɪˈatɪkəm/

vibrato rapid, slight variation in pitch
vib-**rah**-toh /vɪˈbrɑːtəʊ/

vibrissae whiskers

vy-**briss**-ee /vʌɪˈbrɪsi/
• See LATIN panel.

viburnum shrub
vy-**bur**-nuhm /vʌɪˈbəː(r)nəm/

vicarious experienced through others
vik-**air**-i-uhss /vɪˈkɛːrɪəs/

vice as a substitute for
vy-si /ˈvʌɪsi/

vice anglais vice considered
characteristic of the English
veess ah(ng)-**glay** /ˌviːs ãɡˈleɪ/

vicegerent person exercising delegated
power on behalf of a ruler
vyss-**jerr**-uhnt /vʌɪsˈdʒɛrənt/

Less commonly also vyss-**jeer**-uhnt.

Vicente, Gil Portuguese dramatist
zheel vi-**sent**-uh /ˌʒiːl vɪˈsɛntə/

Vicenza city, Italy
vitch-**ent**-suh /vɪˈtʃɛntsə/

vicereine wife of a viceroy
vyss-rayn /ˈvʌɪsreɪn/

viceroy deputy ruler
vyss-roy /ˈvʌɪsrɔɪ/

vice versa other way round
vyss **vur**-suh /ˌvʌɪs ˈvəː(r)sə/

Vichy town, France
vee-shi /ˈviːʃi/

Established anglicization. The town is
known for its mineral water, sometimes
called Vichy water, for which the same
pronunciation is appropriate.

vichyssoise leek soup
vee-shee-**swahz** /ˌviːʃiːˈswɑːz/

vicissitude change of fortune
viss-**iss**-it-yood /vɪˈsɪsɪtjuːd/

Vico, Giambattista Italian philosopher
jam-bat-**eest**-uh **vee**-koh
/dʒambaˈtiːstə ˈviːkəʊ/

vicomte French nobleman
vee-ko(ng)t /ˈviːkɔ̃t/

vicomtesse French noblewoman
vee-ko(ng)-**tess** /ˌviːkɔ̃ˈtɛs/

Victoria, Tomás Luis de Spanish
composer
tom-**ass** luu-**eess** day vik-**tawr**-ya
/tɒˌmas lʊˌiːs deɪ vɪkˈtɔːrjə/

victor ludorum overall champion
vik-tuhr loo-**dawr**-uhm /ˌvɪktə(r)
luːˈdɔːrəm/

victrix pl. **victrices** female champion
vik-triks, pl. **vik**-triss-eez /'vɪktrɪks/, pl. /-'trɪsiːz/

Victrola trademark gramophone
vik-troh-luh /vɪk'trəʊlə/

victual food or provisions
vit-uhl /'vɪtəl/

victualler person licensed to sell alcohol
vit-luhr /'vɪtlə(r)/

vicuña llama
vik-oon-yuh /vɪ'kuːnjə/

Vidal, Gore American writer
gor vi-**dahl** /ˌɡɔː(r) vɪ'dɑːl/

vide see
vee-day /'viːdeɪ/

videshi not Indian
vid-esh-i /vɪ'dɛʃi/

vielle hurdy-gurdy
vyel /vjɛl/

Vienna capital of Austria
vi-**en**-uh /vɪ'ɛnə/

Established anglicization. The German name is Wien, pronounced veen.

Vientiane capital of Laos
vyent-**yahn** /ˌvjɛn'tjɑːn/

Vierwaldstättersee lake, Switzerland
feer-**valt**-shtet-uhr-zay
/ˌfɪə(r)'valt,ʃtɛtə(r),zeɪ/

Vietcong guerrilla movement
vyet-**kong** /vjɛt'kɒŋ/

Vietnam country
vyet-**nam** /vjɛt'nam/

vieux jeu old-fashioned
vyoe zhoe /vjə 'ʒə/

viga roof timber
vee-guh /'viːɡə/

Vigée-Lebrun, Élisabeth French painter
ay-**leez**-uh-**bet** vee-**zhay**
luh-**broe(ng)** /eɪliːzə,bɛt ,viːʒeɪ lə'brœ̃/

vigesimal relating to the number twenty
vij-**ess**-im-uhl /vɪ'dʒɛsɪməl/

vigilante unofficial law enforcer
vij-il-**an**-ti /ˌvɪdʒɪ'lanti/

vigneron person who cultivates grapes
veen-yuh-**ro(ng)** /ˌviːnjə'rɒ̃/

vignette brief description
veen-**yet** /viː'njɛt/

Vignola, Giacomo da Italian architect
jah-kuh-moh dah vin-**yoh**-luh
/ˌdʒɑːkəməʊ dɑː vɪ'njəʊlə/

Vigny, Comte de French writer
ko(ng)t duh veen-**yi** /ˌko(ng)t də viː'nji/

Vigo port, Spain
vee-goh /'viːɡəʊ/

Vigo, Jean French film director
zhah(ng) vee-goh /ˌʒɑ̃ viː'ɡəʊ/

vigoro Australian team ball game
vig-uh-roh /'vɪɡərəʊ/

vihara Buddhist temple or monastery
vi-**har**-uh /vɪ'hɑːrə/

vihuela stringed musical instrument
vi-**way**-luh /vɪ'weɪlə/

Vijayawada city, India
vij-y-uh-**wah**-duh /ˌvɪdʒʌɪə'wɑːdə/

Vila capital of Vanuatu
vee-luh /'viːlə/

Villa, Pancho Mexican revolutionary
pan-choh **veel**-yuh /ˌpantʃəʊ 'viːljə/
• See **SPANISH** panel.

Villahermosa city, Mexico
veel-yuh-**air**-**moh**-suh
/ˌviːljæː(r)'məʊsə/

Villa-Lobos, Heitor Brazilian composer
ay-tor vil-uh **loh**-boss /ˌeɪtɔː(r) ,vɪlə 'ləʊbɒs/

villancico song
veel-yan-**see**-koh /ˌviːljan'siːkəʊ/

villanella pl. **villanelle** Italian part-song
vil-uh-**nel**-uh, pl. vil-uh-**nel**-ay
/ˌvɪlə'nɛlə/, pl. /-'nɛleɪ/

villanelle lyrical poem
vil-uh-**nel** /ˌvɪlə'nɛl/

villein feudal tenant
vil-uhn /'vɪlən/

Sometimes also **vil**-ayn, particularly to distinguish it from the word *villain*.

Villon, François French poet
frah(ng)-**swah** vee-**yo(ng)** /frɑ̃,swɑː viː'jɔ̃/

villus pl. **villi** minute elongated projections
vil-uhss, pl. **vil**-y /'vɪləs/, pl. /-lʌɪ/

Vilnius capital of Lithuania
vil-ni-uhss /'vɪlniəs/, ['vⁱilʲnⁱus]
• Established anglicization.

Vimy Ridge First World War battle
vee-mi /'viːmi/

vinaigrette salad dressing
vin-uh-**gret** /ˌvɪnə'ɡrɛt/

vindaloo spicy curry
vin-duh-**loo** /ˌvɪndəˈluː/

vin de paille dessert wine
va(ng) duh **py** /ˌvɛ̃ də ˈpʌɪ/

vin de pays French wine produced in a
particular area
va(ng) duh **pay** /ˌvɛ̃ də peɪ/

vin de table French table wine
va(ng) duh **tahb**-luh /ˌvɛ̃ də ˈtɑːblə/

vingt-et-un card game
va(ng) tay **oe(ng)** /ˌvɛ̃teɪ ˈœ̃/

vinho verde young Portuguese wine
veen-yoh **vair**-di /ˌviːnjəʊ ˈvɛː(r)di/

Vinnytsya city, Ukraine
vee-nits-yuh /ˈviːnɪtsjə/

vino Spanish or Italian wine
vee-noh /ˈviːnəʊ/

vino da tavola Italian table wine
vee-noh duh **tah**-vol-uh /ˌviːnəʊ də
ˈtɑːvɒlə/

vin ordinaire cheap everyday wine
va(ng) or-din-**air** /ˌvɛ̃ ˌɔː(r)dɪˈnɛː(r)/

Vinson Massif mountain range,
Antarctica
vin-suhn **mass-eef** /ˌvɪnsən maˈsiːf/

vintner wine merchant
vint-nuhr /ˈvɪntnə(r)/

vinyl synthetic resin
vy-nuhl /ˈvʌɪnəl/

Viognier white wine grape
vee-on-yay /viːˈɒnjeɪ/

viol musical instrument
vy-uhl /ˈvʌɪəl/

viola stringed instrument
vi-**oh**-luh /viˈəʊlə/

viola plant
vy-uh-luh /ˈvʌɪələ/

This is also the pronunciation normally used
for the girl's name Viola, e.g. the
Shakespearean character.

viola da braccio early musical
instrument
vi-**oh**-luh duh **bratch**-oh /viˌəʊlə də
ˈbratʃəʊ/

viola da gamba bass viol
vi-**oh**-luh duh **gam**-buh /viˌəʊlə də
ˈgambə/

viola d'amore musical instrument
vi-**oh**-luh dam-**aw**-ray /viˌəʊlə
daˈmɔːreɪ/

violoncello musical instrument

vy-uh-luhn-**chel**-oh /ˌvʌɪələnˈtʃɛləʊ/

violone early musical instrument
vi-uh-**loh**-nay /vɪəˈləʊneɪ/

vipassana meditation
vip-**ass**-uh-nuh /vɪˈpasənə/

virago domineering woman
virr-**ah**-goh /vɪˈrɑːgəʊ/

Virchow, Rudolf German pathologist
roo-dolf **feer**-khoh /ˌruːdɒlf ˈfɪə(r)çəʊ/

virelay short lyric poem
virr-uh-lay /ˈvɪrəleɪ/

virement accounting term
vy-uhr-muhnt /ˈvʌɪə(r)mənt/

Commonly also **veer**-mo(ng), a more
French-sounding pronunciation.

vireo songbird
virr-i-oh /ˈvɪriəʊ/

Virgil (also **Vergil**) Roman poet
vur-jil /ˈvəː(r)dʒɪl/

Virgo constellation
vur-goh /ˈvəː(r)gəʊ/

virgo intacta woman who has never had
sexual intercourse
vur-goh in-**tak**-tuh /ˌvəː(r)gəʊ
ɪnˈtaktə/

virgule slash
vur-gyool /ˈvəː(r)gjuːl/

virilization development of male
physical characteristics
virr-il-y-**zay**-shuhn /ˌvɪrɪlʌɪˈzeɪʃən/

virino hypothetical infectious particle
virr-**ee**-noh /vɪˈriːnəʊ/

virion form of a virus outside a host cell
virr-i-on /ˈvɪriɒn/

virology study of viruses
vy-**rol**-uh-ji /vʌɪˈrɒlədʒi/

virtuoso pl. **virtuosi** highly skilled person
vur-tyoo-**oh**-soh, pl. vur-tyoo-**oh**-si
/ˌvəː(r)tjʊˈəʊsəʊ, pl. -si/
• Standard -s plural is also possible.

virulent severe
virr-yuul-uhnt /ˈvɪrjʊlənt/

visage face
viz-uhj /ˈvɪzədʒ/

Visakhapatnam port, India
viss-ah-kuh-**put**-nuhm
/vɪˌsɑːkəˈpʌtnəm/

vis-à-vis in relation to
veez-uh-**vee** /ˌviːzəˈviː/

Visby port, Sweden
veess-bue /ˈviːsbyː/

viscacha rodent
visk-**atch**-uh /vɪˈskatʃə/

viscera (sing. **viscus**) internal organs
viss-uh-ruh, sing. visk-**uhss** /ˈvɪsərə/,
sing. /ˈvɪskəs/

viscid glutinous
viss-id /ˈvɪsɪd/

Visconti, Luchino Italian director
luuk-**ee**-noh visk-**on**-ti /luˈkiːnəʊ
vɪsˈkɒnti/

viscose polymer fibre
visk-ohz /ˈvɪskəʊz/

viscosity stickiness
visk-**oss**-it-i /vɪˈskɒsɪti/

viscount British nobleman
vy-kownt /ˈvʌɪkaʊnt/

viscous sticky
viss-kuhss /ˈvɪskəs/

Vishnu Hindu god
vish-noo /ˈvɪʃnuː/

Visigoth ethnic group
viz-i-goth /ˈvɪzɪɡɒθ/

Visking trademark seamless cellulose
tubing
visk-ing /ˈvɪskɪŋ/

vis medicatrix naturae the body's
natural ability to heal itself
viss med-ik-**ay**-triks **natch**-uh-ry /ˌvɪs
mɛdɪˌkeɪtrɪks ˈnatʃərʌɪ/

visna disease of sheep
viz-nuh /ˈvɪznə/

visor part of a helmet
vy-zuhr /ˈvʌɪzə(r)/

Vistula river, Poland
vist-yuul-uh /ˈvɪstjʊlə/

vita curriculum vitae
vee-tuh /ˈviːtə/

vitamin substance required by the body
vit-uh-min /ˈvɪtəmɪn/

AM is usually **vy**-tuh-min.

Vitellius, Aulus Roman emperor
aw-luhss vit-**el**-i-uhss /ˌɔːləs vɪˈtɛliəs/

Classical Latin pronunciation would be
ow-luuss wit-**el**-i-uhss; see LATIN panel.

---

vitellus yolk
vit-**el**-uhss /vɪˈtɛləs/

viticulture cultivation of grapevines
vit-i-kul-chuhr /ˈvɪtɪˌkʌltʃə(r)/

Viti Levu island, Fiji
vee-ti **lay**-voo /ˌviːti ˈleɪvuː/

vitiligo skin condition
vit-il-**y**-goh /ˌvɪtɪˈlʌɪɡəʊ/

Vitoria city, Spain
vit-**awr**-yuh /vɪˈtɔːrjə/

Vitória port, Brazil
vit-**aw**-ri-uh /vɪˈtɔːriə/

vitreous like glass
vit-ri-uhss /ˈvɪtriəs/

vitrine glass display case
vit-reen /ˈvɪtriːn/

vitriol bitter malice
vit-ri-uhl /ˈvɪtriəl/

Vitruvius Roman architect and engineer
vit-**roo**-vi-uhss /vɪˈtruːviəs/

Vitsebsk city, Belarus
veet-sebsk /ˈviːtsɛbsk/

vituperative bitter
vi-**choo**-puh-ruh-tiv /vɪˈtʃuːpərətɪv/

Vitus, St Christian martyr
vy-tuhss /ˈvʌɪtəs/

viva oral examination
vy-vuh /ˈvʌɪvə/

viva 'long live' (Italian and Spanish)
vee-vuh /ˈviːvə/

vivace lively
viv-**ah**-chay /vɪˈvɑːtʃeɪ/

Vivaldi, Antonio Italian composer and
violinist
an-**tohn**-yoh viv-**al**-di /anˌtəʊnjəʊ
vɪˈvaldi/

vivarium enclosure for keeping animals
viv-**air**-i-uhm /vɪˈvɛːriəm/

viva voce oral rather than written
vy-vuh **voh**-chay /ˌvʌɪvə ˈvəʊtʃeɪ/

Vivekananda, Swami Indian spiritual
leader
swah-mi viv-ay-kun-**un**-duh /ˌswɑːmi
ˌvɪveɪkʌˈnʌndə/

vivers food
vy-vuhrz /ˈvʌɪvə(r)z/

viviparous bringing forth live young
viv-**ip**-uh-ruhss /vɪˈvɪpərəs/

Viyella trademark fabric
vy-**el**-uh /vʌɪˈɛlə/

vizard disguise
viz-uhrd /ˈvɪzə(r)d/

Vizetelly, Henry English publisher
viz-uh-**tel**-i /ˌvɪzəˈtɛli/

vizier high official
viz-**eer** /vɪˈzɪə(r)/

vizsla breed of dog
vizh-luh /ˈvɪʒlə/

Vlaanderen see **Flanders**

Vlach central European ethnic group
vlakh /vlax/

Vladikavkaz capital of North Ossetia
vluh-dik-uhf-kass /ˌvlædɪkəfˈkas/

Vladimir city, Russia
vluh-dee-meer /vləˈdiːmɪə(r)/

This pronunciation is also more accurate for
the Russian boy's name than the common
anglicization **vlad-im-eer**.

Vladivostok city, Russia
vlad-iv-ost-ok /ˌvlædɪˈvɒstɒk/,
[vlədʲɪvɐˈstɔk]
• Established anglicization.

Vlaminck, Maurice de French painter
and writer
morr-eess duh vlam-**a(ng)k** /mɒˌriːs
də vlaˈmɛ̃k/

vlast pl. **vlasti** political power
vlast, pl. **vlast-i** /vlast/, pl. /-ti/

vlei natural pool of water
flay /fleɪ/

Vlissingen see **Flushing**

Vlorë port, Albania
vlaw-ruh /ˈvlɔːrə/

Vltava river, Czech Republic
vuhl-tuh-vuh /ˈvəltəvə/

vobla dried smoked roach
vob-luh /ˈvɒblə/

vocalic relating to vowels
voh-kal-ik /vəʊˈkalɪk/

vocative grammatical term
vok-uh-tiv /ˈvɒkətɪv/

vocoder synthesizer
voh-koh-duhr /vəʊˈkəʊdə(r)/

voe creek
voh /vəʊ/

voetsak 'go away' (Afrikaans)
fuut-sak /ˈfʊtsak/

voilà 'there it is' (French)
vwa-lah /vwaˈlɑː/

voile thin fabric
voyl /vɔɪl/

Commonly also vwahl, a more
French-sounding pronunciation.

Vojvodina province, Serbia
voy-vod-ee-nuh /ˈvɔɪvɒdiːnə/

Volans constellation

voh-luhnss /ˈvəʊləns/

volant able to fly
voh-luhnt /ˈvəʊlənt/

Volapük artificial language
vol-uh-pook /ˈvɒləˌpuːk/

vol-au-vent pastry canapé
vol oh vo(ng) /ˈvɒl əʊ vɒ̃/

Voldemort, Lord fictional character in
the *Harry Potter* books
vol-duh-mort /ˈvɒldəmɔː(r)t/

volet panel of a triptych
vol-ay /ˈvɒleɪ/

Volga river, Russia
vol-guh /ˈvɒlgə/

Volgograd city, Russia
vol-guh-grad /ˈvɒlgəgrad/

volk people
folk /fɒlk/

Völkerwanderung migration of
peoples
foel-kair-van-duh-ruung
/ˈfœlkɛː(r)ˌvandərʊŋ/

völkisch populist
foel-kish /ˈfœlkɪʃ/

Volkov, Ilan Russian conductor
il-**an** volk-uhf /ɪˌlan ˈvɒlkəf/

Volodymyr Ukrainian archbishop
vol-uh-dim-eer /vɒləˈdɪmɪə(r)/

Vologda city, Russia
vol-uhg-duh /ˈvɒləgdə/

Volos port, Greece
vol-oss /ˈvɒlɒs/

Volpone play by Ben Jonson
vol-poh-nay /vɒlˈpəʊneɪ/

Volscian ancient ethnic group
volsh-uhn /ˈvɒlʃən/

volt unit of electromotive force
vohlt /vəʊlt/

The pronunciation volt is also common.

Volta, Alessandro Italian physicist
al-ess-**and**-roh vol-tuh /alɛˈsandrəʊ
ˈvɒltə/

voltaic relating to electricity in a battery
vol-**tay**-ik /vɒlˈteɪɪk/

Voltaire French writer
vol-**tair** /vɒlˈtɛː(r)/

volte-face act of turning round
volt fass /vɒlt ˈfas/

volumetric relating to the measurement
of volume
vol-yuum-et-rik /ˌvɒljʊˈmɛtrɪk/

voluminous very loose
vuh-**lyoo**-min-uhss /vəˈljuːmɪnəs/

voluptuary person devoted to luxury
vuh-**lup**-choo-uh-ri /vəˈlʌptʃuəri/

volute spiral scroll
vuh-**lyoot** /vəˈljuːt/

volvulus pl. **volvuli** bowel twist
vol-vyuul-uhss, pl. **vol**-vyoo-ly
/ˈvɒlvjʊləs/, pl. /-lʌɪ/

Volzhsky city, Russia
volzh-ski /ˈvɒlʒski/

vomer small bone separating the nasal
cavities
voh-muhr /ˈvəʊmə(r)/

Vonnegut, Kurt American writer
von-uh-guht /ˈvɒnəɡət/

von Recklinghausen's disease
hereditary illness
fon **rek**-ling-how-zuhnz /fɒn
ˈrɛklɪŋˌhaʊzənz/

Voortrekker an Afrikaner who migrated
north
foor-trek-uhr /ˈfʊə(r)ˌtrɛkə(r)/

Vorarlberg state, Austria
fawr-arl-bairk /ˈfɔːrˌɑː(r)lbɛː(r)k/

Voronezh city, Russia
vuh-**ron**-yuhzh /vəˈrɒnjɛʒ/

Vorstellung pl. **Vorstellungen** mental
image
for-shtel-uung,
pl. **for**-shtel-uung-uhn /ˈfɔː(r)ˌʃtɛlʊŋ/,
pl. /-lʊŋən/

vortex pl. **vortices** whirling mass
vor-teks, pl. **vor**-tiss-eez /ˈvɔː(r)tɛks/,
pl. /-tɪsiːz/
• Standard -es plural is also possible.

Vosges mountain system, France

vohzh /vəʊʒ/

Vostok Soviet spacecraft
vost-ok /ˈvɒstɒk/

votary monk or nun
voh-tuh-ri /ˈvəʊtəri/

voussoir stone used to construct an arch
voo-swar /ˈvuːswɑː(r)/

Vouvray white wine
voov-ray /ˈvuːvreɪ/

vox humana organ stop
voks hyoo-**mah**-nuh /ˌvɒks
hjuːˈmɑːnə/

vox populi opinions of the majority
voks pop-yoo-lee /ˌvɒks ˈpɒpjuliː/

voyeur watcher
vwy-**ur** /vwʌɪˈə:(r)/

Vuillard, Édouard French painter
ayd-war vwee-yar /ˌeɪdwɑː(r)
vwiːˈjɑː(r)/

Vuitton, Louis French fashion designer
lwee vwee-**to(ng)** /ˌlwiː vwiːˈtɔ̃/

Various anglicizations may be heard with
reference to his fashion label.

Vukovar battle site, Croatia
voo-kuh-var /ˈvuːkəvɑː(r)/

Vulgate Latin version of the Bible
vul-gayt /ˈvʌlgeɪt/

Vulpecula constellation
vul-**pek**-yuul-uh /vʌlˈpɛkjʊlə/

vulpine relating to foxes
vul-pyn /ˈvʌlpʌɪn/

Vyatka town and river, Russia
vyaht-kuh /ˈvjɑːtkə/

vygie flower
fay-khi /ˈfeɪxi/

W

Waal river, Netherlands
vahl /ˈvɑːl/

wabbit exhausted (Scottish)
wab-it /ˈwabɪt/

wadi valley
wod-i /ˈwɒdi/

Wadi Halfa town, Sudan
wod-i hal-fuh /ˌwɒdi ˈhalfə/
• Established anglicization.

Waffen SS combat units in Nazi
Germany
vaf-uhn /ˈvafən/

Wagga Wagga town, Australia
wog-uh wog-uh /ˌwɒgə ˈwɒgə/

Wagner, Richard German composer
rikh-art vahg-nuhr /ˌrɪçɑː(r)t
ˈvɑːgnə(r)/

wagon-lit railway sleeping car
vag-o(ng) lee /ˌvagō ˈliː/

Wahhabi (also **Wahabi**) Sunni
Muslim sect
wuh-hah-bi /wəˈhɑːbi/

waiata Maori song
wy-uh-tuh /ˈwaɪətə/

Waikato river, New Zealand
wy-kah-toh /waɪˈkɑːtəʊ/

Waikiki beach, Hawaii
wy-kik-ee /ˈwaɪkɪˌkiː/

wainscot wooden panelling on walls
wayn-skuht /ˈweɪnskət/

Waitangi, Treaty of founding
document of New Zealand
wy-tang-i /waɪˈtaŋi/

Wajda, Andrzej Polish film director
an-jay vy-duh /ˌandʒeɪ ˈvaɪdə/

wakame Japanese edible seaweed
wak-am-ay /ˈwakameɪ/

Wakhan salient corridor of land,
Afghanistan
wuh-kahn /wəˈkɑːn/

wakizashi short Japanese sword
wak-i-zash-i /ˌwakiˈzaʃi/

Waldenses puritan religious sect
wol-den-seez /wɒlˈdɛnsiːz/

Waldheim, Kurt Austrian statesman
kuurt valt-hym /ˌkʊ(r)t ˈvalthʌɪm/

waldo remote-controlled device
wawl-doh /ˈwɔːldəʊ/

Waldorf type of salad
wawl-dorf /ˈwɔːldɔː(r)f/

Waldsterben death of forest trees
valt-shtair-buhn /ˈvaltˌʃtɛː(r)bən/

Waler breed of horse
way-luhr /ˈweɪlə(r)/

Wałęsa, Lech Polish statesman
lekh va-wa(ng)-suh /ˌlex vaˈwɛ̃sə/

wali governor
wah-li /ˈwɑːliː/

Wallacea zoogeographical area
wol-ay-si-uh /wɒˈleɪsiə/

wallaroo kangaroo
wol-uh-roo /ˌwɒləˈruː/

Wallasey town, England
wol-uh-si /ˈwɒləsi/

Wallenberg, Raoul Swedish diplomat
rowl val-uhn-bairg /ˌraʊl
ˈvalənbɛː(r)g/

Waller, Fats American jazz musician
fats wol-uhr /ˌfats ˈwɒlə(r)/

Wallis and Futuna Islands islands,
South Pacific
wol-iss foo-too-nuh /ˈwɒlɪs fuːˈtuːnə/

Walloon French-speaking Belgian
wol-oon /wɒˈluːn/

Walpole, Robert English statesman
wawl-pohl /ˈwɔːlpəʊl/

Walpurgisnacht May Day's eve
val-puur-giss-nakht
/valˈpʊə(r)gɪsnaxt/

Walras' law economic law
val-rahss /ˈvalrɑːs/

Walsall town, England
wawl-sawl /ˈwɔːlsɔːl/

Walsingham, Francis English
politician
wawl-sing-uhm /ˈwɔːlsɪŋəm/

Walther, Johann Gotfried German composer
yoh-han **got**-freet **val**-tuhr /ˌjəʊhan ˌɡɒtfriːt ˈvaltə(r)/

Walvis Bay port, Namibia
wawl-viss /ˈwɔːlvɪs/

Wampanoag member of a confederacy of American Indian peoples
wahm-puh-**noh**-uhg /ˌwɑːmpəˈnəʊəɡ/

wampum beads used as money
wom-puhm /ˈwɒmpəm/

wan pale
won /wɒn/

Wanamaker, Sam American actor and director
won-uh-may-kuhr /ˈwɒnəmeɪkə(r)/

This pronunciation is also correct for his actress daughter, Zoë.

Wanderjahr pl. **Wanderjahre** year spent travelling abroad
van-duhr-yar, pl. **van**-duhr-yar-uh /ˈvandə(r)jɑː(r)/, pl. /-rə/

wanderlust desire to travel
won-duhr-lust /ˈwɒndə(r)lʌst/

Sometimes also **van**-duhr-luust, a more German-sounding pronunciation.

Wanganui port, New Zealand
wong-uh-**noo**-i /ˌwɒŋəˈnuːi/

Wankel engine rotary internal-combustion engine
wank-uhl /ˈwaŋkəl/

Established anglicization. The surname of the engine's German inventor is pronounced **vank**-uhl.

Wannsee lake resort and location of a Nazi conference, Germany
van-zay /ˈvanzeɪ/

wapentake county subdivision
wop-uhn-tayk /ˈwɒpənteɪk/

wapiti red deer
wop-it-i /ˈwɒpɪti/

waqf charitable endowment made by a Muslim
wokf /wɒkf/

waratah Australian shrub
worr-uh-**tah** /ˌwɒrəˈtɑː/

Warbeck, Perkin Flemish claimant to the English throne
pur-kin **wor**-bek /ˌpəː(r)kɪn ˈwɔː(r)bɛk/

Warburg, Otto German biochemist

ot-oh **var**-buurk /ˌɒtəʊ ˈvaː(r)bʊrk/

Wardour Street used to allude to the British film industry
wor-duhr /ˈwɔː(r)də(r)/

warfarin rat poison and drug
wor-fuh-rin /ˈwɔː(r)fərɪn/

Warhol, Andy American artist
wor-hohl /ˈwɔː(r)həʊl/

Warlpiri Australian Aboriginal language
worl-puh-ri /ˈwɔː(r)lpəri/

warmonger advocate of warfare
wor-mung-guhr /ˈwɔː(r)ˌmʌŋɡə(r)/

warrigal dingo dog
worr-ig-uhl /ˈwɒrɪɡəl/

Warrington town, England
worr-ing-tuhn /ˈwɒrɪŋtən/

Warsaw capital of Poland
wor-saw /ˈwɔː(r)sɔː/

Established anglicization. The Polish name is Warszawa, pronounced var-**shav**-uh.

Warwick town, England
worr-ik /ˈwɒrɪk/

Warwick, Dionne American singer
dee-on **wor**-wik /ˌdiɒn ˈwɔː(r)wɪk/

wasabi Japanese paste
wuh-**sah**-bi /wəˈsɑːbi/

wassail spiced ale or mulled wine
woss-ayl /ˈwɒseɪl/

wat Buddhist monastery or temple
wat /wat/

Waterloo battle site, Belgium
waw-tuhr-**loo** /ˌwɔːtə(r)ˈluː/

Established anglicization. The French pronunciation is vat-air-**loh** [vatɛrlo], and the Flemish is **wah**-tuhr-loh [ˈwaːtərlo].

Watteau, Jean Antoine French painter
zhah(ng) ah(ng)-**twahn wot**-oh /ˌʒɑ̃ ɑ̃ˌtwɑːn ˈwɒtəʊ/, [vato]
• Established anglicization of surname.

wattle building material
wot-uhl /ˈwɒtəl/

Waugh, Auberon English writer
aw-buh-ruhn **waw** /ˌɔːbərən ˈwɔː/

Waugh, Evelyn English novelist
eev-lin **waw** /ˌiːvlɪn ˈwɔː/

wavicle entity having properties of both waves and particles
way-vik-uhl /ˈweɪvɪkəl/

wayang Javanese theatrical performance
wah-yang /'wɑːjaŋ/

Wayland the Smith legendary character
way-luhnd /'weɪlənd/

wazir vizier
wuh-zeer /wə'zɪə(r)/

Weald district in south England
weeld /wiːld/

Weaver, Sigourney American actress
sig-oor-ni /sɪ'gʊə(r)ni/

Weber, Carl Maria von German composer
karl muh-ree-uh fon vay-buhr /ˌkɑː(r)l mə,riːə fon 'veɪbə(r)/

Weber, Wilhelm German physicist
vil-helm vay-buhr /ˌvɪlhɛlm 'veɪbə(r)/

The SI unit of magnetic flux is named after this scientist, and pronounced in the same way.

Webern, Anton von Austrian composer
an-ton fon vay-buhrn /ˌantɒn fon 'veɪbə(r)n/

Weddell Sea arm of the Atlantic Ocean
wed-uhl /'wɛdəl/

Wedekind, Frank German dramatist
frank vay-duh-kint /ˌfraŋk 'veɪdəkɪnt/

Wedgwood trademark English pottery
wej-wuud /'wɛdʒwʊd/

Weejee pseudonym of American photographer Arthur Felig
wee-jee /'wiːjiː/

Weelkes, Thomas English composer
wilks /wɪlks/

Wegener, Alfred German meteorologist
al-frayt vay-guh-nuhr /ˌalfreɪt 'veɪgənə(r)/

Wehrmacht German armed forces
vair-makht /'vɛː(r)maxt/

Wei Chinese dynasty
way /weɪ/

wei ch'i Chinese board game
way chee /weɪ 'tʃiː/

Weidenfeld, George English publisher
vy-duhn-felt /'vaɪdənfɛlt/

Weifang city, China
way-fang /ˌweɪ'faŋ/

Weil, Simone French essayist
see-mon vay /siːˌmɒn 'veɪ/

Weill, Kurt German composer
koort vyl /ˌkʊ(r)t 'vaɪl/

Weil's disease leptospirosis
vylz /vaɪlz/

Weimar city, Germany
vy-mar /'vaɪmɑː(r)/

Weimaraner breed of dog
vy-muh-rah-nuhr /vaɪmə,rɑː:nə(r)/

Weinberg, Steven American physicist
wyn-burg /'waɪnbə(r)g/

Weinstein, Harvey American film producer
wyn-steen /'waɪnstiːn/

Weinstube pl. **Weinstuben** small German tavern
vyn-shtoob-uh, pl. **vyn-shtoob-uhn** /'vaɪnˌʃtuːbə/, pl. /-ˌʃtuːbən/

Weismann, August German biologist
ow-guust vyss-man /ˌaʊgʊst 'vaɪsman/

Weissmuller, Johnny American swimmer and actor
wyss-muul-uhr /'waɪsˌmʊlə(r)/

Weisswurst German veal sausage
vyss-voorst /'vaɪsvʊə(r)st/

Weizmann, Chaim Russian-born Israeli statesman
khym vyts-muhn /ˌxaɪm 'vaɪtsmən/

welch fail to pay debts
weltch /wɛltʃ/

welkin sky
wel-kin /'wɛlkɪn/

Welkom town, South Africa
vel-kuhm /'vɛlkəm/

Welles, Orson American film director
or-suhn welz /ˌɔː(r)sən 'wɛlz/

wellingtonia giant redwood tree
wel-ing-toh-ni-uh /ˌwɛlɪŋ'təʊniə/

wels fish
velss /vɛls/

Weltanschauung pl. **Weltanschauungen** view of life
velt-an-show-uung, pl. **velt-an-show-uung-uhn** /'vɛltˌanʃaʊʊŋ/, pl. /-ʊŋən/

Weltschmerz world-weariness
velt-shmairts /'vɛltˌʃmɛː(r)ts/

Welty, Eudora American writer
yoo-daw-ruh wel-ti /'wɛlti/

Wenceslas king of Bohemia; also called **Wenceslaus**
wen-suhss-lass /'wɛnsəslas/

Welsh

Welsh is one of the native languages of the UK, a Celtic language spoken mostly in Wales. The BBC broadcasts extensively in Welsh (see http://www.bbc.co.uk/cymru), and we usually consult native speakers working within the BBC to verify our recommendations. The pronunciation of Welsh is complicated by several factors, including the influence of English on some spellings and pronunciations and the considerable variation in pronunciation between different parts of Wales. Some broad guidelines are given here, but in practice we always check Welsh pronunciations with native speakers for acceptability.

Stress

Stress in Welsh generally falls on the penultimate syllable. If the final syllable is stressed, this is marked with an acute accent.

Consonants

Most consonants are pronounced as in English.

CH is pronounced kh as in Scottish *loch*.

DD is pronounced *th* as in there; *Dafydd* is pronounced **dav**-*ith*.

F is usually pronounced v, and FF is pronounced f.

LL is pronounced hl. To make this sound, position your tongue as if you are about to say an English L, then blow air around the sides.

Vowels

A circumflex indicates that a vowel is long, and a grave indicates that a vowel is short. However, these accents do not always appear.

In our recommendations A is pronounced a if short, and ah if long.

E is pronounced e, air, or ay.

I is pronounced i or ee, or y as in yes when followed by a vowel, unless the I has a diaeresis (Ï), in which case it is i or ee despite the following vowel.

O is pronounced o if short, oh if long, and U is pronounced i if short, ee if long.

W, which is a vowel in Welsh, is pronounced uu or oo; *Clwyd* is pronounced **kloo**-id.

Y, which is a vowel in Welsh, is pronounced u as in *bun*, i, or ee. This varies with regional accent as well as vowel length. When it appears on its own it is the Welsh word for *the*, and has an unstressed pronunciation uh.

Diphthongs are usually sequences of their component parts.

Wenceslaus king of Bohemia; also called **Wenceslas**
wen-suhss-**lowss** /'wɛnsəslaʊs/

Wenger, Arsène French football manager
ar-**sen veng**-uhr /ɑ:(r),sɛn 'vɛŋə(r)/

Established anglicization for his surname. The French pronunciation is va(ng)-**gair** [vɛ̃gɛr].

Wensleydale cheese
wenz-li-dayl /'wɛnzlɪdeɪl/

Wenzhou city, China
wen-**joh** /wɛn'dʒəʊ/

werewolf person who changes into a wolf
wair-wuulf /'wɛ:(r)wʊlf/

Werner, Abraham German geologist
ah-bruh-ham **vair**-nuhr /,ɑ:brəham 'vɛ:(r)nə(r)/

Werner, Alfred French-born Swiss chemist
al-fruhd vair-**nair** /,alfrəd vɛ:(r)'nɛ:(r)/

Wernicke's area region of the brain
wur-nik-uhz /'wə:(r)nɪkəz/

Established anglicization. Discovered by German scientist Carl Wernicke, pronounced **vair**-nik-uh.

Wertenbaker, Timberlake Basque-born playwright
tim-buhr-layk **wurt**-uhn-bayk-uhr /,tɪmbə(r)leɪk wə:(r)tənbeɪkə(r)/

Wesak Buddhist festival; also called **Vesak**
wess-ak /'wɛsak/

Weser river, Germany
vay-zuhr /'veɪzə(r)/

Wesker, Arnold English dramatist
wesk-uhr /'wɛskə(r)/

Wesley, John English preacher
wez-li /'wɛzli/

West Bromwich town, England
west **brom**-itch /,wɛst 'brɒmɪtʃ/

West, KanYe American rap singer
kahn-yay west /,kɑ:njeɪ 'wɛst/

Westmann Islands islands, Iceland
vest-muhn /'vɛstmən/

Westmeath county, Republic of Ireland
west-**meeth** /wɛst'mi:θ/

Westmorland former county, England
west-muhr-luhnd /'wɛstmə(r)lənd/

Weston-super-Mare town, England

west-uhn **soo**-puhr **mair** /,wɛstən ,su:pə(r) 'mɛ:(r)/

Westphalia former province, Germany
west-**fay**-li-uh /wɛst'feɪliə/

Established anglicization. The German name is Westfalen, pronounced **vest**-fah-luhn.

weta grasshopper-like insect
wet-uh /'wɛtə/

Also the name of a New Zealand film effects company, particularly noted for their work on the *Lord of the Rings* trilogy.

Weyden, Rogier van der Flemish painter
rokh-**eer** vun duhr **vy**-duhn /rɒ,xɪə(r) vʌn də(r) 'vʌɪdən/, Dutch [ro,ɣi:r vɑn dər 'vɛidən]
• See DUTCH panel.

Weymouth port, England
way-muhth /'weɪməθ/

whanau Maori extended family or community
fah-now /'fɑ:naʊ/

Whangarei port, New Zealand
fong-uh-ray /'fɒŋəreɪ/

wharfinger keeper of a wharf
wor-fin-juhr /'wɔ:(r)fɪndʒə(r)/

Wharton, Edith American writer
wor-tuhn /'wɔ:(r)tən/

whaup curlew
wawp /wɔ:p/

Wheatstone, Charles English physicist
weet-stuhn /'wi:tstən/

wheesht interjection used to demand silence (Scottish)
weesht /wi:ʃt/

whinchat songbird
win-chat /'wɪntʃat/

whippoorwill nightjar
wip-puhr-wil /'wɪpə(r)wɪl/

Whitlam, Gough Australian statesman
gof wit-**luhm** /,gɒf 'wɪtləm/

Whitsuntide part of the church calendar
wit-suhn-tyd /'wɪtsəntʌɪd/

whoa command to a horse to make it stop or slow down
woh /wəʊ/

wholly entirely
hohl-li /'həʊli/

Commonly pronounced in this way, with a long or double *l*, to avoid confusion with *holy*.

whooping cough disease
hoo-ping /ˈhuːpɪŋ/

whoreson unpleasant or disliked person
hor-suhn /ˈhɔː(r)sən/

whorl turn in the shell of a gastropod or mollusc
worl /wɔːl/

Whyalla town, Australia
wy-**al**-uh /waɪˈalə/

whydah weaver bird
wid-uh /ˈwɪdə/

Whymper, Edward English mountaineer
wimp-uhr /ˈwɪmpə(r)/

Wicca religious cult of modern witchcraft
wik-uh /ˈwɪkə/

Wichita city, US
witch-it-aw /ˈwɪtʃɪtɔː/

wickiup American Indian hut
wik-i-up /ˈwɪkiʌp/

Wicklow county, Republic of Ireland
wik-loh /ˈwɪkləʊ/

Wickremesinghe, Ranil Sri Lankan prime minister
run-il wik-ruh-muh-**sing**-huh /ˌrʌnɪl ˌwɪkrəməˈsɪŋhə/

widdershins anticlockwise
wid-uhr-shinz /ˈwɪdə(r)ʃɪnz/

widget small device
wij-uht /ˈwɪdʒət/

Widnes town, England
wid-nuhss /ˈwɪdnəs/

Wien see Vienna

wiener sausage
wee-nuhr /ˈwiːnə(r)/

Wiener means 'Viennese' in German; a less anglicized pronunciation **veen**-uhr is usual in phrases such as 'Wiener schnitzel' and 'Wiener waltz'.

Wiesbaden city, Germany
veess-bah-duhn /ˈviːsbɑːdən/

Wiesel, Elie Romanian-born American human rights campaigner
el-i vee-**sel** /ˌɛli viːˈsɛl/

Wiesenthal, Simon Austrian Jewish investigator of Nazi war crimes
zee-mon **vee**-zuhn-tahl /ˌziːmɒn ˈviːzəntɑːl/

The Simon Wiesenthal centres in the US usually anglicize the first name to **sy**-muhn.

Wigan town, England
wig-uhn /ˈwɪgən/

Wilberforce, William English politician
wil-buhr-forss /ˈwɪlbə(r)fɔː(r)s/

wildebeest mammal
wil-duh-beest /ˈwɪldəbiːst/

Wilder, Billy Austrian-born American film director
wyl-duhr /ˈwaɪldə(r)/

Wilder, Thornton American writer
wyl-duhr /ˈwaɪldə(r)/

Wilhelm former emperor of Germany
vil-helm /ˈvɪlhɛlm/

Wilhelmina former queen of the Netherlands
wil-hel-**mee**-nuh /ˌwɪlhɛlˈmiːnə/

Wilhelmshaven port, Germany
vil-helmz-hah-vuhn /ˈvɪlhɛlmzˌhɑːvən/

Wilkes Land region of Antarctica
wilks /wɪlks/

Willemstad capital of the Netherlands Antilles
wil-uhm-staht /ˈwɪləmstɑːt/

William of Occam see Occam

wily skilled at gaining an advantage
wy-li /ˈwaɪli/

Wimereux town, France
vee-muh-roe /ˈviːmərœ/

winceyette fabric
win-si-**et** /ˌwɪnsiˈɛt/

Winchester city, England
win-chuh-stuhr /ˈwɪntʃəstə(r)/

Winckelmann, Johann German archaeologist
yoh-han **vink**-uhl-man /ˌjəʊhan ˈvɪŋkəlman/

Windermere lake, England
wind-uhr-meer /ˈwɪndə(r)mɪə(r)/

Windhoek capital of Namibia
vint-huuk /ˈvɪnthʊk/

windigo cannibalistic giant
wind-ig-oh /ˈwɪndɪgəʊ/

wing chun simplified form of kung fu
wing **chuun** /wɪŋ ˈtʃʊn/

Winnebago American Indian ethnic group
win-uh-**bay**-goh /ˌwɪnəˈbeɪgəʊ/

ˈviːzəntɑːl/

Winnipeg city, Canada
win-ip-eg /ˈwɪnɪpeg/

Winterhalter, Franz German painter
frants vint-uhr-halt-uhr /ˌfrants
ˈvɪntə(r)ˌhaltə(r)/

Winterthur town, Switzerland
vint-uhr-toor /ˈvɪntə(r)ˌtʊə(r)/

Wirral peninsula, England
wirr-uhl /ˈwɪrəl/

Wirtschaftswunder economic miracle
veert-shafts-vuund-uhr
/ˈvɪə(r)tʃafts,vʊndə(r)/

Wirtshaus pl. **Wirtshäuser** inn in a
German-speaking country
veerts-howss, pl. **veerts**-hoyz-uhr
/ˈvɪə(r)tshaʊs/, pl. /-hɔɪzə(r)/

Wisbech town, England
wiz-beech /ˈwɪzbiːtʃ/

Wisconsin state, US
wiss-**kon**-sin /wɪsˈkɒnsɪn/

Wisden, John English cricketer
wiz-duhn /ˈwɪzdən/

wiseacre person with an affectation of
knowledge
wyz-ayk-uhr /ˈwʌɪzeɪkə(r)/

wisent bison
wee-zuhnt /ˈwiːzənt/

Wissenschaft pursuit of knowledge
viss-uhn-shaft /ˈvɪsənʃaft/

wisteria climbing shrub
wist-**eer**-i-uh /wɪˈstɪərɪə/

witchetty large beetle larva
witch-uh-ti /ˈwɪtʃəti/

witenagemot Anglo-Saxon council
wit-uhn-uh-guh-moht
/ˈwɪtənəgəˌməʊt/

withal in addition
with-**awl** /wɪˈðɔːl/

withy willow branch
with-i /ˈwɪði/

Wittenberg town, Germany
vit-uhn-bairk /ˈvɪtənbɛː(r)k/

Wittgenstein, Ludwig
Austrian-British philosopher
loot-vikh **vit**-guhn-shtyn /ˌluːtviç
ˈvɪtɡənʃtʌɪn/

Witwatersrand region, South Africa
vit-**vah**-tuhrz-rant /vɪtˈvɑːtə(r)zˌrant/

Less commonly also wit-**waw**-tuhrz-rand.

wizened shrivelled with age
wiz-uhnd /ˈwɪzənd/

Władysław former king of Poland
vwad-**iss**-waf /vwadˈɪswaf/

wobbegong carpet shark
wob-uh-gong /ˈwɒbəgɒŋ/

Wodehouse, P. G. English writer
wuud-howss /ˈwʊdhaʊs/

Woden Norse god; also called **Odin** or
Wotan
woh-duhn /ˈwəʊdən/

woebegone sad in appearance
woh-buh-gon /ˈwəʊbəgɒn/

Wöhler, Friedrich German chemist
freet-rikh **voe**-luhr /ˌfriːtrɪç ˈvəːlə(r)/

Woking town, England
woh-king /ˈwəʊkɪŋ/

wold piece of high uncultivated land
wohld /wəʊld/

Wolf, Hugo Austrian composer
hoo-goh volf /ˌhuːgəʊ ˈvɒlf/

Wolfenden Report landmark study in
gay rights
wuulf-uhn-duhn /ˈwʊlfəndən/

wolfram tungsten
wuul-fruhm /ˈwʊlfrəm/

Wolfsburg city, Germany
volfs-buurk /ˈvɒlfsbʊ(r)k/

Wolfson, Isaac Scottish philanthropist
wuulf-suhn /ˈwʊlfsən/

Wollaston, William English chemist
wuul-uh-stuhn /ˈwʊləstən/

Wollongong city, Australia
wuul-uhn-gong /ˈwʊləŋgɒŋ/

Wollstonecraft, Mary English writer
wuul-stuhn-krahft /ˈwʊlstənˌkrɑːft/

Wolsey, Thomas English churchman
wuul-zi /ˈwʊlzi/

Wolverhampton city, England
wuul-vuhr-**hamp**-tuhn
/ˌwʊlvə(r)ˈhamptən/

wolverine carnivorous mammal
wuul-vuh-reen /ˈwʊlvəriːn/

woma python
woh-muh /ˈwəʊmə/

women plural of woman
wim-in /ˈwɪmɪn/

The spelling *womyn*, favoured by some
feminists, is pronounced in the same way.

won currency unit, Korea
won /wɒn/

wonga money
wong-guh /ˈwɒŋgə/

wont customary behaviour
wohnt /wəʊnt/

wonton Chinese dumpling
won-ton /wɒnˈtɒn/

Woolf, Virginia English writer
wuulf /wʊlf/

Woomera town, Australia
woo-muh-ruh /ˈwuːmərə/

woonerf pl. **woonerven** road in which
devices for slowing traffic have been
installed
voo-nurf, pl. **voo-nurv-uhn**
/ˈvuːnɜː(r)f/, pl. /-ɜː(r)vən/

Woop Woop humorous name for a
hypothetical remote Australian town
wuup wuup /ˈwʊp wʊp/

Worcester city, England
wuust-uhr /ˈwʊstə(r)/

Worms town, Germany
vormss /vɔ(r)ms/

Sometimes also anglicized to wurmz,
especially in historical reference to Luther's
Diet.

worsted yarn
wuust-id /ˈwʊstɪd/

wort herb
wurt /wə(r)t/

Wotan Norse god; also called **Woden** or
Odin
woh-tahn /ˈwəʊtɑːn/

wraith ghost
rayth /reɪθ/

Wrangel island, Russia
rang-guhl /ˈraŋɡəl/

wrasse fish
rass /ras/

wrath fury
roth /rɒθ/

Wrath, Cape headland, Scotland
kayp rahth /keɪp ˈrɑːθ/

Although *Wrath* can also be pronounced
roth (see above), we recommend this
Scottish pronunciation for the place name.

Wrexham town, Wales
reks-uhm /ˈrɛksəm/

writhe squirm
ryth /rʌɪð/

Wrocław city, Poland
vrot-swaf /ˈvrɒtswaf/

Wuhan port, China
woo-khan /ˌwuːˈxan/

Wulfila Gothic bishop and Bible
translator; also called **Ulfilas**
wuul-fil-uh /ˈwʊlfɪlə/

wunderkind person who achieves great
success when relatively young
vuun-duhr-kint /ˈvʊndə(r)kɪnt/

Wundt, Wilhelm German psychologist
vil-helm vuunt /ˌvɪlhɛlm ˈvʊnt/

Wuppertal city, Germany
vuup-uhr-tahl /ˈvʊpə(r)tɑːl/

Wurlitzer trademark musical instrument
wur-lit-suhr /ˈwə(r)lɪtsə(r)/

wurst German sausage
voorst /vʊə(r)st/

Commonly also anglicized to vurst or wurst.

Würzburg city, Germany
vuerts-boork /ˈvʏ(r)tsbʊə(r)k/

wushu Chinese martial arts
woo-shoo /wuːˈʃuː/

wuss weak person
wuuss /wʊs/

Wuxi city, China
woo-shee /ˌwuːˈʃiː/

wuxia Chinese martial arts film genre
woo shi-ah /ˌwuːˈʃiˈɑː/

Wyatt, Thomas English poet
wy-uht /ˈwʌɪət/

Wycherley, William English dramatist
witch-uhr-li /ˈwɪtʃə(r)li/

Wyclif, John (also **Wycliffe**) English
religious reformer
wik-lif /ˈwɪklɪf/

Wykehamist member of Winchester
College
wik-uh-mist /ˈwɪkəmɪst/

wynd narrow street
wynd /wʌɪnd/

Wyndham, John English writer
wind-uhm /ˈwɪndəm/

Wynette, Tammy American singer
win-et /wɪˈnɛt/

Wyoming state, US
wy-oh-ming /wʌɪˈəʊmɪŋ/

WYSIWYG What You See Is What You
Get
wiz-i-wig /ˈwɪziwɪɡ/

wyvern heraldic dragon
wy-vuhrn /ˈwʌɪvə(r)n/

X

Xai-Xai port, Mozambique
shy-shy /ˈʃʌɪˌʃʌɪ/

Xanadu idealized place
zan-uh-doo /ˈzanədu:/

Xanax trademark drug
zan-aks /ˈzanaks/

Xankändi capital of Nagorno-Karabakh
khahn-kuhn-dee /ˌxɑːnkənˈdiː/

Xanten town, Germany
ksan-tuhn /ˈksantən/

Xanthe girl's name
zan-thi /ˈzanθi/

Xanthippe Socrates' wife
zan-tip-i /zanˈtɪpi/

Xanthus ancient city, Asia Minor
zan-thuhss /ˈzanθəs/

Xavier, St Francis Spanish Catholic missionary
zayv-yuhr /ˈzeɪvjə(r)/, [xaˈβjer]

This is also the usual pronunciation for the British boy's name.

xebec (also **zebec**) three-masted ship
zee-bek /ˈziːbɛk/

Xenakis, Iannis Greek-French composer and architect
yan-iss ksen-ak-iss /ˌjanɪs ksɛˈnakɪs/

Xenia city, US
zeen-yuh /ˈziːnjə/

xenon chemical element
zee-non /ˈziːnɒn/

Xenophanes Greek philosopher
zen-of-uh-neez /zɛˈnɒfəniːz/

xenophobia hatred of strangers
zen-uh-foh-bi-uh /ˌzɛnəˈfəʊbiə/

Xenophon Greek historian
zen-uh-fuhn /ˈzɛnəfən/

Xenopus kind of toad, formerly used in pregnancy testing
zen-uh-puhss /ˈzɛnəpəs/

Xenova trademark biotech company
zuh-noh-vuh /zəˈnəʊvə/

xeroderma dryness of the skin
zeer-oh-dur-muh /ˌzɪərəʊˈdəː(r)mə/

Xerox trademark photocopy
zeer-oks /ˈzɪərɒks/

Xerxes Persian king
zurk-seez /ˈzəː(r)ksiːz/

There is an opera by Handel of the same name, which is spelled and pronounced either in this way or in Italian as Serse, pronounced **sair-say**.

Xhosa South African ethnic group and language
kaw-suh /ˈkɔːsə/
• Established anglicization. See CLICKS panel.

xi letter of the Greek alphabet
ksy /ksʌɪ/

Xiamen port, China
shyah-muhn /ˌʃjaːˈmən/

Xian (also **Xi'an**) city, China
shee-an /ˌʃiˈan/

xiao musical instrument
shyow /ʃjaʊ/

Xingtai city, China
shing-ty /ˌʃɪŋˈtʌɪ/

Xingú river, South America
shin-goo /ʃɪŋˈguː/

Xinhua Chinese press agency
shin-khwah /ˌʃɪnˈxwɑː/

Xining city, China
shee-ning /ˌʃiːˈnɪŋ/

Xinjiang autonomous region, China
shin-ji-ang /ˌʃɪnʒiˈaŋ/

xiphoid sword-shaped
zif-oyd /ˈzɪfɔɪd/

Xmas Christmas
kriss-muhss /ˈkrɪsməs/

Less commonly also **eks-muhss**.

Xochimilco lake, Mexico
sotch-i-meel-koh /ˌsɒtʃiˈmiːlkəʊ/

Xochipilli Aztec god
sotch-i-pee-li /ˌsɒtʃiˈpiːli/

xöömij type of Mongolian singing
khoe-mee /ˈxøːmiː/

Xsara trademark model of Citroën car
zah-ruh /ˈzɑːrə/

Xuzhou city, China
shoo-joh /ˈʃuːdʒəʊ/

xylem plant tissue
zy-luhm /ˈzʌɪləm/

Y

yacht sailing boat
yot /jɒt/

Yad Vashem holocaust memorial
yad vash-**em** /ˌjad vaˈʃɛm/

Yahweh god
yah-way /ˈjɑːweɪ/

Yajur Veda Hindu text
yuj-oor **vay**-duh /ˌjʌdʒʊə(r) ˈveɪdə/

yakitori Japanese dish
yak-i-**taw**-ri /ˌjakiˈtɔːri/

Yakutia autonomous republic, Russia
yak-**oo**-ti-uh /jaˈkuːtiə/

Yakutsk capital of Yakutia
yak-**ootsk** /jaˈkuːtsk/

yakuza Japanese criminal organization
yuh-**koo**-zuh /jəˈkuːzə/

y'all 'you all'
yawl /jɔːl/

Yalta port, Ukraine
yal-tuh /ˈjaltə/

Yalu river, Asia
yah-loo /ˈjɑːluː/

Yama Hindu god
yum-uh /ˈjʌmə/

Yamamoto, Yohji Japanese fashion
designer
yoh-ji yam-uh-**moh**-toh /ˈjəʊdʒi
ˌjaməˈməʊtəʊ/

Yamoussoukro capital of Côte d'Ivoire
yam-oo-**sook**-roh /ˌjamuːˈsuːkrəʊ/

yangqin musical instrument
yang-**chin** /jaŋˈtʃɪn/

Yangtze (also **Yangtse**) river, China
yang-tsi /ˈjaŋˌtsi/

Established anglicization. The Chinese
name is Chang Jiang, pronounced
approximately **chang** ji-**ang**.

Yanomami American Indian ethnic
group
yan-uh-mah-mi /ˈjanəˌmɑːmi/

Yantai port, China
yan-**ty** /ˌjanˈtʌɪ/

Yao Chinese ethnic group
yow /jaʊ/

Yaoundé capital of Cameroon
yah-**uun**-day /jɑːˈʊndeɪ/

Yaqui American Indian ethnic group
yak-i /ˈjaki/

yarmulke (also **yarmulka**) skullcap
yar-muul-kuh /ˈjɑː(r)mʊlkə/

Yarmouth town, England
yar-muhth /ˈjɑː(r)məθ/

Yaroslavl port, Russia
yah-ruh-slah-vuhl /ˈjɑːrəsˌlɑːvəl/

Yashere, Gina British comedian
yash-**eer** /jaˈʃɪər/

yashmak veil
yash-mak /ˈjaʃmak/

Yawar, Ghazi al- Iraqi politician
gah-zi uhl **yah**-wuhr /ˌɡɑːzi əl
ˈjɑːwə(r)/
• See ARABIC panel.

yclept by the name of
ik-**lept** /ɪˈklɛpt/

Yeager, Chuck American pilot
yay-guhr /ˈjeɪɡə(r)/

Yeats, W. B. Irish poet
yayts /jeɪts/

Yekaterinburg see Ekaterinburg

Yeltsin, Boris Russian statesman
borr-iss **yelt**-sin /ˌbɒrɪs ˈjɛltsɪn/
• Established anglicization.

Yemen country
yem-uhn /ˈjɛmən/

Yenisei (also **Enisey**) river, Asia
yen-iss-**ay** /ˌjɛnɪˈseɪ/

yeoman freeholder
yoh-muhn /ˈjəʊmən/

yerba buena herb
yair-buh **bway**-nuh /ˌjɛː(r)bə ˈbweɪnə/

Yerevan (also **Erevan**) capital of
Armenia
yerr-iv-**an** /ˌjɛrɪˈvan/

yeshiva Jewish college
yuh-**shee**-vuh /jəˈʃiːvə/

yeti legendary creature
yet-i /ˈjɛti/

Yevtushenko, Yevgeni Russian poet
yuhv-**gay**-ni yef-tuush-**enk**-oh
/jəvˈgeɪni ˌjɛftuˈʃɛŋkəʊ/

Yggdrasil Nordic mythological tree
ig-druh-sil /ˈɪgdrəsɪl/

Yichun city, China
yee-**chuun** /jiːˈtʃʊn/

Yinchuan capital of Ningxia
yin-**chwan** /jɪnˈtʃwan/

Yizkor Jewish memorial service
yiz-kuhr /ˈjɪzkə(r)/

ylang-ylang perfume
ee-lang ee-lang /ˌiːlaŋ ˈiːlaŋ/

ylem primordial matter
ee-lem /ˈiːlɛm/

Ymir (also **Ymer**) mythological giant
ee-muhr /ˈiːmə(r)/

yngling small sailing boat
ing-ling /ˈɪŋlɪŋ/

Based on the Norwegian word for
'youngster', which is pronounced **ueng**-ling.

Ynys Môn Welsh name for Anglesey
un-iss mawn /ˌʌnɪs ˈmɔːn/

yodel form of singing
yoh-duhl /ˈjəʊdəl/

yogh Middle English letter
yog /jɒg/

yogurt (also **yoghurt**) dairy food
yog-uhrt /ˈjɒgə(r)t/

AM is usually **yoh**-guhrt.

Yogyakarta (also **Jogjakarta**) city,
Indonesia
yog-yuh-**kar**-tuh /jɒgjəˈkɑː(r)tə/

Yokohama port, Japan
yoh-koh-**hah**-muh /ˌjəʊkəʊˈhɑːmə/

Yom Kippur Jewish festival
yom kip-**oor** /ˌjɒm kɪˈpʊə(r)/

Yomiuri Japanese newspaper
yom-i-**oor**-i /ˌjɒmiˈʊəri/

Yonge Street longest street in the world,
Toronto
yung /jʌŋ/

yoni vulva
yoh-ni /ˈjəʊni/

Yoruba Nigerian ethnic group and
language
yorr-uub-uh /ˈjɒrʊbə/

Yorvik see **Jorvik**

Yosemite national park, US
yoh-**sem**-it-i /jəʊˈsɛmɪti/

Yoshkar-Ola capital of Mari El, Russia
yosh-kar uh-**lah** /jɒʃˌkɑːr əˈlɑː/

Youghal town, Republic of Ireland
yawl /jɔːl/

Yourcenar, Marguerite French writer
mar-guh-**reet** yoor-suh-**nar**
/mɑː(r)gəˌriːt jʊə(r)səˈnɑː(r)/

youse (also **yous**) 'you', usually plural
yooz /juːz/

Ypres town, Belgium
eep-ruh /ˈiːprə/, French /ipr/

A jocular pronunciation **wy**-puhrz was also
used during the First World War.

Yr Wyddfa Welsh name for Mount
Snowdon
uhr **with**-vuh /ər ˈwɪðvə/

Yseult see **Iseult**

Ystad city, Sweden
ue-stahd /ˈyːstɑːd/

ytterbium chemical element
it-**ur**-bi-uhm /ɪˈtɜː(r)biəm/

yttrium chemical element
it-ri-uhm /ˈɪtriəm/

yuan currency unit, China
yuu-**an** /juˈan/

Yucatán state, Mexico
yuuk-uh-**tahn** /jʊkəˈtɑːn/

yucca plant
yuk-uh /ˈjʌkə/

Yudhoyono, Susilo Bambang
Indonesian president
soo-**see**-loh bam-bang
yoo-doh-**yoh**-noh /suːˌsiːləʊ ˌbambaŋ
juːdəʊˈjəʊnəʊ/

yukata cotton kimono
yuuk-at-uh /ˈjʊkatə/
• See **JAPANESE** panel.

Yukon river, US
yoo-kon /ˈjuːkɒn/

Yunnan province, China
yoo-**nan** /juːˈnan/, [ˌjynˈnan]
• Established anglicization.

yurt circular tent
yurt /jɜː(r)t/

Yushchenko, Viktor Ukrainian
president
veek-tor **yoosh**-chen-koh /ˌviːktɔː(r)
ˈjuːʃtʃɛnkəʊ/

Commonly also **yoo**-shen-koh, because of
variable treatment of -*shch*- in Ukrainian
and Russian.

Yvelines department, France
eev-leen /iːvˈliːn/

Z

Z letter of the alphabet
zed /zɛd/

AM is zee.

zabaglione Italian dessert
zab-al-**yoh**-ni /ˌzabaˈljəʊni/

Zabrze city, Poland
zab-zhuh /ˈzabʒə/

Zacapa town, Guatemala
sak-ap-uh /saˈkapə/

Zacatecas state, Mexico
sak-at-**ay**-kass /ˌsakaˈteɪkas/

Zadig novel by Voltaire
zad-**eeg** /zaˈdiːg/

Zadok the Priest anthem by Handel
zay-dok /ˈzeɪdɒk/

zaftig curvaceous
zaf-tig /ˈzaftɪg/

Zagazig city, Egypt
zag-uh-zig /ˈzagəzɪg/

Zagreb capital of Croatia
zah-greb /ˈzɑːgrɛb/, [ˈzagrɛb]
• Established anglicization.

Zagros mountains, Iran
zag-ross /ˈzagrɒs/

Zaire (also **Zaïre**) former country, now
called Democratic Republic of Congo
zy-**eer** /zʌɪˈɪə(r)/

zakat Islamic payment
zuh-**kaht** /zəˈkɑːt/

Zakayev, Akhmed Chechen statesman
ahkh-**med** zak-**y**-uhf /ɑːxˌmɛd
zakˈʌɪəf/

Zakinthos (also **Zakynthos**) island,
Greece
zak-in-thoss /ˈzakɪnθɒs/

Zakopane town, Poland
zak-op-**an**-ay /ˌzakɒˈpaneɪ/

Zambezi river, Africa
zam-**bee**-zi /zamˈbiːzi/

Zambia country, Africa
zam-bi-uh /ˈzambɪə/

Zamboanga port, Philippines
zam-boh-**ang**-guh /ˌzambəʊˈaŋgə/

Zamość city, Poland

zam-oshch /ˈzamɒʃtʃ/

Zante island, Greece
zan-ti /ˈzanti/

Zanu-PF Zimbabwean political party
zah-noo pee ef /ˈzɑːnuː piː ˌɛf/

Zanzibar island, Africa
zan-zib-ar /ˈzanzɪˌbɑː(r)/

Zaozhuang city, China
zow-**jwang** /ˌzaʊˈdʒwaŋ/

Zapata, Emiliano Mexican
revolutionary
em-eel-**yan**-oh sap-**at**-uh /ɛmiːlˌjanəʊ
saˈpatə/

A Zapatista, pronounced sap-at-**eess**-tuh, is
a supporter of Zapata or his ideas.

Zapatero, José Luis Rodrigues
Spanish prime minister
khoss-**ay** lweess roth-**ree**-gess
thap-at-**air**-oh /xɒˌseɪ lwiːs rɒðˌriːgɛs
θapaˈtɛːrəʊ/

Zaporizhzhya city, Ukraine
zap-orr-**izh**-yuh /ˌzapɒˈrɪʒjə/

Zapruder film footage of John F.
Kennedy's assassination
zuh-**proo**-duhr /zəˈpruːdə(r)/

Zaragoza city, Spain
tharr-ag-**oh**-thuh /ˌθaraˈgəʊθə/

Saragossa, pronounced sarr-uh-**goss**-uh, is
a former established anglicization, but is
now dated.

Zarathustra Persian prophet; also called
Zoroaster
zarr-uh-**thoost**-ruh /ˌzarəˈθuːstrə/

Zaria city, Nigeria
zar-i-uh /ˈzɑːriə/

Zarqa city, Jordan
zar-kuh /ˈzɑː(r)kə/

Zarqawi, Abu Musab al- Jordanian
terrorist
ab-oo muuss-**ab** uh-zuhr-**kah**-wi
/ˌabuː mʊˌsab əzə(r)ˈkɑːwi/

The al- assimilates to the consonant which
follows; see **ARABIC** panel.

zarzuela Spanish musical comedy
thar-**thway**-luh /θɑː(r)ˈθweɪlə/

Zátopek, Emil Czech runner
em-il **zah**-top-ek /ˌɛmɪl ˈzɑːtɒpɛk/

Zawahiri, Ayman al- Egyptian terrorist
y-muhn uh-zuh-**wah**-hirr-i /ˌʌɪmən əzəˈwɑːhɪri/

Zealand island, Denmark
zee-luhnd /ˈziːlənd/

zealot fanatic
zel-uht /ˈzɛlət/

zealous fanatical
zel-uhss /ˈzɛləs/

zebec see **xebec**

zebra striped animal
zeb-ruh /ˈzɛbrə/

The AM pronunciation **zebra** **zee**-bruh also used to be the preferred BR pronunciation.

Zebulun (also **Zebulon**) Hebrew patriarch
zeb-yuul-uhn /ˈzɛbjʊlən/

Zechariah Hebrew prophet
zek-uh-**ry**-uh /ˌzɛkəˈrʌɪə/

Zedekiah biblical character
zed-uh-**ky**-uh /ˌzɛdəˈkʌɪə/

Zeebrugge port, Belgium
zay-**bruug**-uh /zeɪˈbrʊgə/, Flemish [ˈzeːˌbrʏxə]
• Established anglicization.

Zeeland province, Netherlands
zay-luhnt /ˈzeɪlənt/

Zeffirelli, Franco Italian film director
fran-koh dzef-irr-**el**-i /ˌfraŋkəʊ ˌdzɛfɪˈrɛli/

Zehetmair, Thomas Austrian violinist
toh-mass **tsay**-uht-myr /ˌtəʊmas ˈtseɪətmʌɪr/

zeitgeist spirit of the times
tsyt-gyst /ˈtsʌɪtgʌɪst/

Commonly also **zyt**-gyst.

Zell am See town, Austria
tsel am **zay** /ˈtsɛl am ˈzeɪ/

Zellweger, Renée American actress
ruh-**nay** **zel**-weg-uhr /rəˈneɪ ˈzɛlwɛgə(r)/

Zemeckis, Robert American film director
zuh-**mek**-iss /zəˈmɛkɪs/

Zener cards cards used in parapsychology experiments

zee-nuhr /ˈziːnə(r)/

zenith highest point
zen-ith /ˈzɛnɪθ/

Zeno Greek philosopher
zee-noh /ˈziːnəʊ/

Zenobia ancient queen of Palmyra
zen-**oh**-bi-uh /zɛˈnəʊbiə/

Zephaniah Hebrew prophet
zef-uh-**ny**-uh /ˌzɛfəˈnʌɪə/

zephyr gentle breeze
zef-uhr /ˈzɛfə(r)/

Zeppelin German airship
zep-lin /ˈzɛplɪn/, [ˈtsɛpəliːn]

Zermatt town, Switzerland
zur-mat /ˈzəː(r)mat/, German [tsɛɛˈmat]
• Established anglicization.

zeta letter of the Greek alphabet
zee-tuh /ˈziːtə/

Zetec trademark model of Ford car
zee-tek /ˈziːtɛk/

zetetic proceeding by inquiry
zuh-**tet**-ik /zəˈtɛtɪk/

zeugma figure of speech
zyoog-muh /ˈzjuːgmə/

Zeus Greek god
zyooss /zjuːs/

Zhejiang province, China
juh-ji-**ang** /ˌdʒədʒiˈaŋ/

Zhengzhou city, China
jung-**joh** /dʒʌŋˈdʒəʊ/

Zhivago, Dr see **Doctor Zhivago**

zho see **dzo**

Zhongshan city, China
jong-**shan** /dʒɒŋˈʃan/

Zhou Enlai Chinese statesman
joh uhn-**ly** /ˌdʒəʊ ənˈlʌɪ/

Zhvania, Zurab Georgian politician
zoo-rab **zhvan**-i-uh /ˈzuːrab ˈʒvaniə/

Zhytomyr city, Ukraine
zhit-**om**-eer /ʒɪˈtɒmɪə(r)/

Zia ul-Haq, Muhammad Pakistani statesman
moh-**ham**-uhd **zee**-uh uul **huk** /məʊˌhaməd ˌziːə ʊl ˈhʌk/

Zidane, Zinédine French footballer
zee-nay-**deen** zee-**dan** /ziːneɪˌdiːn ziːˈdan/

Ziegfeld, Florenz American theatre manager
florr-uhnz **zeeg**-feld /ˌflɒrənz ˈziːɡfɛld/

Zielona Góra city, Poland
zhel-**on**-uh **goo**-ruh /ˌʒɛˌlɒnə ˈɡuːrə/

ziggurat a rectangular stepped tower
zig-uh-rat /ˈzɪɡərat/

Zildjian cymbal and percussion company
zil-juhn /ˈzɪldʒən/

Zimbabwe country
zim-**bahb**-wi /zɪmˈbɑːbwi/

Established anglicization; less commonly also zim-**bahb**-way.

Zimbabwean relating to Zimbabwe
zim-**bahb**-wi-uhn /zɪmˈbɑːbwiən/

Zimmer trademark walking frame
zim-uhr /ˈzɪmə(r)/

Zinfandel wine grape variety
zin-fuhn-del /ˈzɪnfəndɛl/

zinnia daisy
zin-i-uh /ˈzɪniə/

Zion (also **Sion**) hill of Jerusalem
zy-uhn /ˈzʌɪən/

Zionism pro-Israeli movement
zy-uh-niz-uhm /ˈzʌɪənɪzəm/

zirconium chemical element
zur-**koh**-ni-uhm /zəˈ(r)kəʊniəm/

zither musical instrument
zith-uhr /ˈzɪðə(r)/

Ziua Romanian newspaper
zee-wuh /ˈziːwə/

zloty currency unit, Poland
zlot-i /ˈzlɒti/

zodiac astrological system
zoh-di-ak /ˈzəʊdɪak/

zoetrope optical toy
zoh-it-rohp /ˈzəʊɪtrəʊp/

Zoffany, Johann Anglo-German painter
yoh-han **zof**-uh-ni /ˌjəʊhan ˈzɒfəni/

Zog ruler, Albania
zog /zɒɡ/

Zohar text of the Jewish Kabbalah
zoh-har /ˈzəʊhɑː(r)/

Zola, Émile French novelist
ay-**meel zoh**-luh /eɪˌmiːl ˈzəʊlə/, [emil zɔla]
• Established anglicization.

Zollverein 19th-century German

customs union
tsol-fuh-ryn /ˈtsɒlfəˌrʌɪn/

zoology study of animals
zoo-**ol**-uh-ji /zuːˈɒlədʒi/

Less commonly also zoh-**ol**-uh-ji.

zoomorphic in animal form
zoh-oh-**mor**-fik /ˌzəʊəˈmɔː(r)fɪk/

The *zoo-* prefix can also be pronounced **zoh**-uh-, **zoo**-oh-, **zoo**-uh-, or **zoo**-.

zori Japanese flip-flop shoe
zaw-ri /ˈzɔːri/

Zoroaster Persian prophet; also called **Zarathustra**
zorr-oh-**ast**-uhr /ˌzɒrəʊˈastə(r)/

Zoroastrianism religion founded by Zoroaster
zorr-oh-**ast**-ri-uh-niz-uhm /ˌzɒrəʊˈastriənɪzəm/

zounds archaic interjection
zoondz /zuːndz/

A contraction of '(by) God's wounds'. Sometimes also pronounced zowndz.

Zovirax trademark drug
zoh-**vy**-raks /zəʊˈvʌɪraks/

Zsigmondy, Richard Austrian-German chemist
rikh-art **zhig**-mon-di /ˌriçɑː(r)t ˈʒɪɡmɒndi/

zucchetto priest's skullcap
tsuuk-**et**-oh /tsʊˈkɛtəʊ/

zucchini courgette
zuuk-**ee**-ni /zʊˈkiːni/

Zug canton, Switzerland
tsook /tsuːk/

Zugspitze mountain, Germany
tsook-shpit-suh /ˈtsuːkʃpɪtsə/

zugzwang forced move in chess
zoog-zwang /ˈzuːɡzwaŋ/, German [ˈtsuːktsvaŋ]

Zuider Zee former inlet of the North Sea, Netherlands
zy-duhr zee /ˌzʌɪdə(r) ˈziː/, [ˌzœɪdərˈzeː]
• Established anglicization.

Zulu South African ethnic group
zoo-loo /ˈzuːluː/

zum Beispiel 'for example' (German)
tsuum **by**-shpeel /tsʊm ˈbʌɪʃpiːl/

Zuni American Indian ethnic group and language
zoo-ni /'zu:ni/

If spelled Zuñi, the pronunciation is **zoon**-yi.

Zurbarán, Francisco de Spanish painter
fran-**thiss**-koh day thoor-barr-**an** /fran'θiskəʊ deɪ ˌθʊə(r)ba'ran/

Zürich city and lake, Switzerland
zyoor-ik /'zjʊərɪk/, German ['tsy:rɪç]
• Established anglicization.

Zwickau city, Germany
tsvik-ow /'tsvɪkaʊ/

zwieback rusk
zwee-bak /'zwi:bak/

The original, German pronunciation, **tsvee**-bak, is sometimes also heard.

Zwingli, Ulrich Swiss Protestant reformer
uul-rikh **tsving**-li /ˌʊlrɪç 'tsvɪŋli/

Zwolle town, Netherlands
zwol-uh /'zwɒlə/

zydeco music
zy-duh-koh /'zʌɪdəkəʊ/

zygote diploid cell
zy-goht /'zʌɪgəʊt/

Zyklon B poison gas
zyk-lon **bee** /ˌzʌɪklɒn 'bi:/

zymurgy fermentation
zy-mur-ji /'zʌɪmə:(r)dʒi/